Development Studies

An Introduction Through Selected Readings

edited by

RON AYRES

PRINCIPAL LECTURER IN ECONOMICS
UNIVERSITY OF GREENWICH

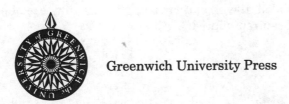
Greenwich University Press

910.
1330
1724
DEV

First published in 1995 by
Greenwich University Press
Unit 42
Dartford Trade Park
Hawley Road
Dartford
Kent DA1 1PF
United Kingdom

11212616

Learning Resources
Centre

British Library Cataloguing in Publication Data.
A CIP catalogue record for this book is available from the British Library.

ISBN 1 874529 32 9

Designed and produced for Greenwich University Press by
Angela Allwright and Kirsten Brown.

Printed in Great Britain by The Bath Press, Avon.

Publisher's note

The contents of the readings in this anthology have been reproduced as they appear in the publications from which they are taken. In the majority of cases footnotes and bibliographic material are included, the exceptions being where they are of excessive length. Photographs have not been reproduced.

7·2·97

Contents

Introduction: A Review of Development Studies

This book of readings in development studies provides students of economics with an introduction to some of the main areas of debate within the subject. Students from other disciplines within the social sciences will also find the book useful. Its major aim is to introduce the reader to different theoretical approaches to economic and social change and further to provide an understanding of some of the major difficulties faced by Third World countries. This is not meant to be a comprehensive survey of development studies; indeed given the breadth of the subject and the size of the book there are inevitably some omissions. The interested student may wish to compare this selection with recent surveys of the subject by Gemmell (1987), Chenery and Srinivasan (1988; 1989) and Stern (1989). There have also been a number of assessments of development economics, most recently by Bhagwati (1988) and Chakravarty (1987). Students are also advised to consult the most recent editions of the World Bank's *World Development Report* and the IMF's *World Economic Outlook* in order to get the latest data on developing countries.

The study of developing countries raises issues which have concerned human beings since the dawn of civilisation. Yet in the early post-war period the main input to an understanding of development, i.e. learning about the problems of development and the process of growth, drafting policy and formulating strategies, was made by economists. Economics was regarded as the most respectable of the social sciences and economists were often asked to advise governments and planners on how growth and development could be achieved. Nevertheless, the results turned out to be disappointing and the gap in per capita incomes between rich and poor countries widened. It was partly the failure of these early attempts to achieve growth (and development) that stimulated a number of alternative theoretical approaches to the problem but this self-examination also raised the issue of what constitutes development.

For Seers (1), development is inevitably a normative concept but it is important to be precise about its dimensions if meaningful targets or indicators are to be devised and appropriate policies prepared. Increases in national income are at best seen as necessary but certainly not sufficient for solving social and political problems. Development is taken to mean 'creating the conditions for the realisation of human personality' and implies a reduction in poverty, unemployment and inequality. Seers also makes it clear that development is about change in social, political and economic structures and with 'relations between countries as well as within countries'.

GNP per capita may be an adequate measure of economic performance but it has weaknesses as a measure of development. This led to several attempts to revise the system of national accounts, including measures based on purchasing power parities, but none of the modifications have been entirely satisfactory in relating GNP to meaningful international welfare levels. Few economists have gone as far as Kuznets (1953) who suggested that a broader concept of welfare was required which depended less on "the appraisals of the market system". There have, however, been several attempts to measure social performance or human development directly and recent research within the UN Development Programme has resulted in a Human Development Report (2). The first Report in 1990 produced a Human Development Index (HDI) based on per capita income, literacy and life expectancy. There have been some modifications to the index since 1990, but although it is a better measure than per capita income it is still conceptually weak and does not adequately allow for gender or distribution.

Terminology has been an issue. The term 'Third World' originally referred to a third path for humanity as an alternative to capitalism and communism. The concept of north-south was later coined as an attempt to get away from the ideological roots of the Third World and to emphasise the mutual interests between North and South. Nevertheless, the term 'Third World' no longer symbolises a third political alternative but merely represents an arbitrary definition of a group of countries which are also described as less developed. The World Bank arbitrarily subdivides the less developed world into 'low-income' countries, with a per capita income below $650 in 1991, and 'middle-income' countries (upper and lower), with a per capita income between $650 and $7820 in 1991.

Toye (3), in considering whether the Third World is still there, draws our attention to the diversity that exists in the less developed world. While the newly industrialising countries (NICs) have made considerable economic progress and become major exporters of manufactured goods and oil producing less developed countries (LDCs) were able to gain a bigger slice of world output, much of the remainder of the Third World still faces problems of poverty, famine and international debt. There may be common international roots to Third World problems (colonialism) but it is important to differentiate between the contemporary obstacles facing Africa, Asia and Latin America which require different national strategies for development.

Poverty remains one of the urgent problems of the 1990s and its reduction is a major objective. The World Development Report 1990 (4) surveys the problem of poverty, its definition and measurement, and points to two important determinants: access to income-earning opportunities and the capacity to respond. This suggests that creating job opportunities and providing individuals with education and health facilities are central to the elimination of poverty. Sen (5) relates the problem of hunger (in the midst of plenty) to entitlements. If individuals, families or large groups are hungry then it is because they lack the means to acquire food. The solution is partly to provide people with jobs and training but also to provide support for those most vulnerable to economic instability.

Thirlwall (6) reports on the failure of economic growth to improve the standard of living of the poorest individuals. In the early stages of economic transformation income inequality increased in many countries and it is only when per capita incomes are at about $1500 at 1992 prices that disparities of income and wealth appear to diminish. Yet there is evidence that a number of the fast growing LDCs have a relatively equal income distribution indicating that income inequality is not necessary for fast growth.

Social scientists and historians have long been concerned with trying to explain development and the process of economic and social change. The paper by Ayres (7) provides an outline of the main schools of thought in development. The orthodox analysis (neo-classical, vicious circle, Harrod-Domar, dual sector, historical stages and modernisation theories) assumes an 'ideal type' economic and social system and emphasises the importance of trade and free markets. In contrast, the radical theories (structuralist, post-Keynesian, Marxist/dependency and regulation schools) locate the problems of the Third World in the prevailing international division of labour and emphasise the need for government intervention to achieve development.

Roxborough (1982) and Webster (8) locate the starting point for the major approaches to development in the theories that were developed by Marx, Weber and Durkheim to explain the original transition of today's advanced industrialised countries from pre-capitalist society to contemporary capitalism. The LDCs were regarded as traditional societies and the problem was to reproduce the culture and institutions found in the developed world, i.e. to modernise. John Toye (3) has touched on modernisation theory and the article by Webster elaborates on the 'tradition versus modernity' debate. The contributions of Parsons, McClelland and Lerner are considered in relation to the notion of modern values and attitudes and the implications of this for policy issues. Webster also provides a critique of modernisation theory and points to its failure to address the impact of colonialism and imperialism on the less developed world.

The reading by Gillis et al. (9) provides a useful summary and critique of the major orthodox economic theories of growth and development. The one-sector growth model of Harrod-Domar is reviewed and linked to Solow's work on the sources of growth. The relationship between growth and the pattern of development, as reflected in the studies of Chenery et al. (1979;1988) is also considered. Chenery et al. use time-series and cross-section data to analyse the relationship between changes in economic structure and GNP per capita. The authors concede that structural change is not sufficient for explaining growth, nevertheless, there are common elements in the process to enable us to reduce them to a set of stylised facts. Country size, trade (manufacturing) orientation and the degree of openness of the economy appear to have a significant impact on the patterns of structural change.

Gillis et al. also analyse the theoretical underpinnings of the neo-classical two-sector growth model and its policy implications. In the later sections of this reading the authors outline a number of theoretical debates and policy issues: balanced versus unbalanced growth; the notion of a big push; and backward and forward linkages.

The Lewis two-sector model and its variants was touched on in Gillis et al. but is analysed further in the reading from Basu (10). For Lewis the modern (industrial) sector, which is assumed to have unlimited supplies of labour drawn from the traditional sector, is the main driving force in the thrust for development. Modern sector capitalists are assumed to save and invest in a relentless cycle of surplus until the wage levels in the two sectors reach parity. Despite generating considerable interest the Lewis model has been subjected to a number of criticisms relating to both its assumptions and the empirical evidence. Harris and Todaro (1970) provide an alternative analysis of the migration of labour based on expected earnings which has important implications for public policy and the functioning of labour markets.

There are a number of variants of the historical stages approach to theorising about development and these are reviewed by Meier (11). Rostow's (1960) attempt to map out the "sweep of modern economic history "is considered in some depth and Meier provides a critique of the methodology and assesses the empirical evidence. Despite the criticisms, Rostow's concept of 'take-off' has had a great impact and has stimulated considerable debate about how to raise the rate of investment.

Radical theories of development are concerned with explaining why the orthodox theory of international economic relations does not eliminate poverty. For the structuralist the solution lay in pursuing inward-looking development based on state protected and directed import substituting industrialisation. The Marxist/neo-Marxist analysis, on the other hand, emphasises the need to overthrow both the internal social structure and international economic relations. The reading by Palma (12) traces the main developments in Marxist theories from their origins in the fragmentary writings of Marx, via Lenin, and the theory of Imperialism, to Baran and Dependency.

The readings by Frank (13), Browett (14), Brenner (15), Smith (16) and Corbridge (17) provide a clear understanding of the main tenets of the dependency paradigm and the concept of underdevelopment. While there is a common element in the work of Frank, Amin and Emmanuel which locates underdevelopment in the way that pre-capitalist societies were inserted into the world economy there are theoretical differences between them relating to the specific form of the metropolis-satellite contradiction. The readings assess the usefulness of the dependency paradigm and discuss the major theoretical criticisms of the theories of Frank and Amin. The debate about capitalism as a progressive force (Warren, 1980) is discussed and assessed in the light of recent empirical evidence.

Section III looks in more detail at the theoretical and empirical debates relating to the major forms of international interaction: trade; aid; investment and debt. The reading by Thirlwall (18) outlines the orthodox analysis of trade and contrasts this with the new theories of the structuralists. Part of the debate centres on the relation between technical progress and the terms of trade, the income elasticity of demand for primary products and the structure of tariffs. The implications for trade policies and trade preferences are also discussed. Singer and Alizadeh (19) review the import substituting industrialisation (ISI) vs export oriented industrialisation (EOI) debate and conclude that a synthesis is necessary. Rather than ISI and EOI being in conflict they argue that there is a "natural sequential development in the progress to industrialisation". The article by Bello (20) provides some support for the Singer/Alizadeh thesis. Bello argues that Third World industrialisation is costly in ecological terms and, moreover, that the newly industrialising countries (NICs) are finding it increasingly difficult to establish new export markets in the First World because of the growth of protectionism. The extent to which the NICs have remained technologically dependent and the implications for an interventionist strategy are also considered. The issue of the welfare gains and losses from trade as a result of the GATT Uruguay Round is reported on in the UNCTAD (21) reading. The liberalisation of trade in agriculture may open up markets for the export of tropical goods, but these gains to LDCs could be much smaller than the losses incurred through higher import prices for other agricultural products. The implication is that accompanying measures to compensate LDCs for the effects of the Uruguay Round are necessary.

The benefits, costs and effectiveness of concessional grants and loans from the viewpoint of the recipient has dominated much of the debate surrounding foreign aid. Because flows from the rich to the poor come in various forms, are often tied and may be overvalued, it is not always clear whether they should be described as aid. Hayter (22) has argued that aid is not an effective way of helping the poor, and in many instances it is politically motivated and used by donors as a form of leverage to secure markets. Such aid not only allows the companies of the imperialist powers to continue their exploitation of newly independent states but has a more general role in the preservation of the capitalist system. From the right, Bauer (1971; 1984) and others have attacked aid for interfering with market forces, perpetuating inefficient policies, leading to corruption and promoting a culture of dependency. Nevertheless, there may be a case for aid assuming it is beneficial. The Pearson Report (1969) put the case for more aid and so did the Brandt Commission (23), which also argued for a new international order within the context of the mutual interest of the North and South.

Following the controversy surrounding the giving of aid there have been numerous studies concerned with assessing its effectiveness. This raises questions about aims, the time perspective, the criteria to be used to judge effectiveness and the methods to be employed. The reading by White (24) emphasises that there are considerable empirical difficulties in assessing the macroeconomic impact of aid. The studies on the relationship between aid and growth and aid's impact on savings are flawed by inadequate theoretical specification and poor econometric methodology. White suggests that country-level case studies employing more detailed macroeconomic models are required. The reading by Lele and Nabi (25) supports the White view but also provides a useful review of the effects of: project and programme aid; food aid; and aid for poverty alleviation. This reading also draws together the results of country experiences with aid to suggest some important lessons for recipients, donors (developed countries and international organisations) and for international private lenders and investors.

Private investment from abroad has become an important alternative source of finance for many LDCs. Portfolio investment was discouraged for many years but the recent promotion of privatisation in the Third World has led to a significant increase in this form of foreign private investment. Nevertheless, as Hogendorn (26) points out, flows of private direct investment have been larger and, because they involve the activities of the multinationals, also subject to more critical analysis and investigation. The orthodox analysis suggests that foreign direct investment benefits both parties but several critical studies of multinational firm behaviour have cast doubt on the generality of this benign assumption. The main controversies relate to profit repatriation, monopolistic behaviour, the control of patents and technical knowledge, and the appropriateness of goods and technology. Recent debate has centred on what optimum regulation strategy to employ towards foreign capital.

The international debt crisis, which moved to centre stage in the 1980s, is reviewed in the readings by Lever and Huhne (27), Pastor (28) and Jaywardena (29). The size and growth of Third World debt reached such levels that it threatened the international financial system. LDC debts were rescheduled and new loans made available on condition that IMF negotiated structural adjustment programmes (SAPs) were implemented. The theoretical economic assumptions underlying the SAPs have been questioned and the required austerity measures, which prioritise the external balance, widely criticised because of their welfare effects within LDCs. The SAPS have also been challenged because the responsibility for adjustment lies exclusively with debtor countries. Recent debate has focused on proposals for debt reduction and debt forgiveness linked to debt buy-backs and debt-equity swaps, but there have also been calls for reform of the IMF and the World Bank.

The final section of readings is more heterogeneous and highlights some of the policy issues and social questions that have concerned developing countries over the years. Much of the discussion on population has been concerned either with the consequences (both positive and negative) of rapid growth or strategies for reducing it. Furthermore, as the readings by Birdsall (30) and Kelley (31) make clear, population, by virtue of its size and composition, is likely to have a major impact on many other problems confronting LDCs. But population is only one element in the problems LDCs face and population control programmes may have disappointing results if other causes of problems are ignored.

For Simon (1981) population is the ultimate resource and while this may be disputed few would disagree with Schultz (32) that education and investment in human capital can be important for economic and social progress. Nevertheless, as Psacharopoulos (33 and 34) points out, the methods employed to measure the rate of return to education are controversial and the results have to be interpreted with care. Moreover, the reading by Dore (35) suggests that in many developing (and developed) countries education has become an industry producing formal qualifications or diplomas and that the original purposes of education have been neglected.

In recent years there has been a growing concern with the differential impact of development in the Third World on men and women. The reading by Sen (5) drew attention to entitlements and gender bias giving rise to intrahousehold disparities in ownership rights, inheritance and the distribution of food. The reading by Pearson (36) considers whether tradition or backwardness keeps women in a secondary position and the extent to which unequal relations between men and women are at the root of the problem. In so far as planners and policy makers discriminate against women it may be necessary to completely rethink the objectives and strategies of development.

More than half of the labour force in a typical LDC is employed in agriculture. While the proportion of output originating in agriculture is much less, due to low productivity levels, the importance of the industry for overall economic growth, the external balance and social welfare is widely recognised. Much of the debate about agriculture has focused on the need to raise productivity through land reform and technological change. Lipton and Longhurst (37) emphasise that the Green Revolution with its modern varieties (MV) of seeds adversely affects many poor people and is biased towards imported machinery, inputs and techniques. They conclude that new poverty-reducing MV research is important given the continuing role of agriculture in the livelihoods of so many people in Asia and Africa.

The readings by Lofchie (38) and Storey (39) focus on Africa's agricultural crisis. Africa houses some of the poorest people in the world and in the 1980s it became one of the world's major debtor regions. An increasing number of African countries have been unable to feed themselves and responsibility for this is either assigned to the international economic system or internal economic policies. Lofchie argues that part of the blame lies with the advice of international donor agencies which led to the promotion of cash crop production at the expense of worsening economic conditions elsewhere in the countryside. Storey's investigation suggests that export (cash) crop and food crop production are not necessarily in conflict but this conclusion depends on appropriate policies being implemented.

The reading by Singer and Alizadeh (20) argued that the ISI debate needs to be reinterpreted. There is a considerable body of evidence based on the achievements of Europe, the USA and Japan that points to the central role of industrialisation in economic development. Moreover, this view is supported by the experience of a few east Asian economies whose economic progress was based on a process of successful export oriented industrialisation. Yet the reading by Bagchi (40) questions whether the EOI model is easily diffusible. Part of the problem relates to the slow-down in the world economy but there is also the growth of protectionism within the industrialised world to consider. The alternative for many Third World countries is to rely on building industries for domestic markets or the growth of south-south trade. The potential role of privatisation in this strategy is considered in the reading by Ayres (41). Privatisation is often seen primarily as the way of raising economic efficiency but it can also contribute to improved public finances. Profitability may be difficult to achieve in the context of global recession and internal macroeconomic stabilisation measures. Moreover, the efficiency objective may be dependent on effective regulation of anti-competitive practices and new forms of competition augmenting regulation and deregulation. It is also important for LDCs to appreciate the positive role that government can play in supporting domestic enterprises operating in an open economy.

Ron Ayres
1994

References

Bauer, P.T., (1971) *Dissent on Development: Studies and Debates in Development Economics*, Weidenfeld and Nicolson, London.

Bauer, P.T., (1984) *Reality and Rhetoric*, Weidenfeld, London.

Bhagwati, J., (1988) 'Poverty and public policy', *World Development*, Vol 16 (5).

Chakravarty, S., (1987) 'The state of development economics', *The Manchester School of Economic and Social Studies*, Vol 66 (2).

Chenery, H.B., (1979) *Structural Change and Development Policy*, OUP, London.

Chenery, H.B. and Srinivasan, T.N. (eds), (1988; 1989) *Handbook of Development Economics*, Vols I and II, Elsevier Science Publishers, North Holland.

Gemmell, N., (1987) *Surveys in Development Economics*, Basil Blackwell, Oxford.

Harris, J. R. and Todaro, M. P., (1970) 'Migration, unemployment and development: A two-sector analysis', *American Economic Review,* 60.

Kuznets, S., (1953) *Economic Change*, Norton, New York, p. 178.

Pearson, L. B., (Chairman) (1969) *Partners in Development*, Report of the Commission on International Development, Praeger, New York.

Rostow, W. W., (1960) *The Stages of Economic Growth*, Cambridge University Press.

Roxborough, I., (1982) *Theories of Underdevelopment,* Macmillan.

Simon, J.L., (1981) *The Ultimate Resource*, Princeton University Press, Princeton.

Stern, N., (1989) 'The Economics of Development: A Survey', *The Economic Journal*, 99.

Syrquin, M. and Chenery, H.B., (1988) 'Patterns of Development, 1950-1983 ', *World Bank Discussion Papers*, No. 41.

Warren, B., (1980) *Imperialism: Pioneer of Capitalism,* Verso, London.

CONCEPTUALISING DEVELOPMENT

1. What are we Trying to Measure?
Dudley Seers

Summary

Development means creating the conditions for the realization of human personality. Its evaluation must therefore take into account three linked economic criteria: whether there has been a reduction in (i) poverty; (ii) unemployment; (iii) inequality. G.N.P. can grow rapidly without any improvement on these criteria; so development must be measured more directly. The conceptual and practical problems of a number of indicators are discussed and also the implications for planning, both national and international.

Why do we confuse development with economic growth? Surely one could hardly say that the situation depicted by a set of projections was preferable to that shown by another set simply because the former implied higher *per capita* income. After all, in what sense is South Africa more developed than Ghana, or Kuwait than the U.A.R., or the United States than Sweden?

One explanation is that the national income is a very convenient indicator. Politicians find a single comprehensive measure useful, especially one that is at least a year out of date. Economists are provided with a variable which can be quantified and movements in which can be analysed into changes in sectoral output, factor shares or categories of expenditure, making model-building feasible.

We can, of course, fall back on the supposition that increases in national income, if they are sufficiently fast, sooner or later lead to the solution of social and political problems. But the experience of the past decade makes this belief look rather naive. Social crises and political upheavals have emerged in countries at all stages of development. Moreover, we can see that these afflict countries with rapidly rising *per capita* incomes, as well as those with stagnant economies. In fact it looks as if economic growth not merely may fail to solve social and political difficulties; certain types of growth can actually cause them.

Now that the complexity of development problems is becoming increasingly obvious, this continued addiction to the use of a single aggregative indicator, in the face of the evidence, takes on a rather different appearance. It begins to look like a preference for avoiding the real problems of development.

The definition of development

In discussing the challenges we now face, we have to dispel the fog around the word 'development' and decide more precisely what we mean by it. Only then will we be able to devise meaningful targets or indicators, and thus to help improve policy, national or international.

Dudley Seers: 'What are we Trying to Measure?' *JOURNAL OF DEVELOPMENT STUDIES* (1972), Vol. 8, No. 3, pp. 21-36. Reproduced by permission of Frank Cass & Co. Ltd.

The starting-point is that we cannot avoid what the positivists disparagingly refer to as 'value judgements'. 'Development' is inevitably a normative concept, almost a synonym for improvement. To pretend otherwise is just to hide one's value judgements.

But from where are these judgements to come? The conventional answer, which Tingerben accepts for his system of economic planning, is to draw our values from governments. But governments have necessarily a rather short-term view, in some cases discounting the future at a very high rate. More seriously, some governments are themselves the main obstacles to development, on any plausible definition, and once this is conceded, where is one to obtain the yardsticks by which government objectives are to be judged? Even supposing that governments represented faithfully, in some sense, popular attitudes, these are endogenous to the development process and therefore cannot provide a means of assessing it.

Another approach is to copy the development paths of other countries, which implicitly means aiming at their present state as the goal. This is what model-builders, for example, are really doing when coefficients are taken from an international cross-section analysis, or from functions that fit the experience of an industrial country. Yet few if any of the rich countries now appear to the outside world as really desirable models. Some aspects, such as their consumption levels, seem enviable, but these are associated, perhaps inseparably, with evils such as urban sprawl, advertising pressures, air pollution and chronic tension. Besides it is by no means obvious or even likely that the rest of the world could trace the history of the industrial countries even if they wanted to.

If values are not to be found in politics or history, does this mean that we are each left to adopt our own personal set of values? This is fortunately not necessary. Surely the values we need are staring us in the face, as soon as we ask ourselves: what are the necessary conditions for a universally acceptable aim, the realization of the potential of human personality?

If we ask what is an *absolute* necessity for this, one answer is obvious — enough food. Below certain levels of nutrition, a man lacks not merely bodily energy and good health but even interest in much besides food. He cannot rise significantly above an animal existence. If anyone has any doubt on the primacy of food, they should reflect on the implications of recent research (Scrimshaw and Gordon, 1968) showing that if young children are not properly nourished the result may well be lasting impairment not merely of the body, but also of the mind.

Since foodstuffs have prices, in any country the criterion can be expressed in terms of income levels. This enables it to take account also of certain other minimum requirements. People never spend all their money (or energy) on food, however poor they are. To be enough to feed a man, his income has also to cover basic needs of clothing, footwear and shelter.

But I am not talking about consumption needs in general; I am talking about the capacity to buy physical necessities.

Peter Townsend and others who support a 'relative' concept of poverty describe those in any society as poor if they are unable to 'participate in the activities and have the living conditions and amenities which are customary in that society. These activities and customs have to be described empirically. In addition to food and clothing customs, they include, for example, in the United Kingdom, such things as birthday parties for children, summer holidays and evenings out' (Townsend, 1970, p. 42). This concept of poverty as social deprivation implies that the poverty standard would rise as living conditions improve, and indeed that poverty could *never* be eliminated, except perhaps by making the distribution of income very equal. But to see one's child doomed by malnutrition to lifelong physical and mental inferiority or to be unable to buy a blood transfusion to save one's wife's life is surely a different sort of poverty from being unable to afford the cakes for a children's party or to take one's wife out to the pictures.

What I am asserting is that below the level at which a man can in some sense provide 'enough' food for his family, the marginal utility of income is much greater than it is above that level. This is of course an old-fashioned view, and it raises many problems of concepts and measurement to which I return later. But wherever there is serious poverty, a normative approach to development, which I have argued to be inevitable, implies a utility function of this general shape.

Another basic necessity, in the sense of something without which personality cannot develop, is *a job*. This does not necessarily mean paid employment: it can include studying, working on a family farm or keeping house. But to play none of these accepted roles, i.e. to be chronically dependent on another person's productive capacity, even for food, is incompatible with self-respect for a non-senile adult, especially somebody who has been spending years at school, perhaps at university, preparing for an economically active life.

It is true, of course, that both poverty and unemployment are associated in various ways with income. But even a fast increase in *per capita* income is in itself far from enough, as the experience of many economies shows, to reduce either poverty or unemployment. In fact, certain processes of growth can easily be accompanied by, and in a sense cause, growing unemployment.[1]

The direct link between *per capita* income and the numbers living in poverty is *income distribution*. It is a truism that poverty will be eliminated much more rapidly if any given rate of economic growth is accompanied by a declining concentration of incomes. Equality should, however, in my belief, be considered an objective in its own right, the third element in development. Inequalities to be found today, especially in the Third World where there is massive poverty, are objectionable by any religious or ethical standards. The social barriers and inhibitions of an unequal society distort the personalities of those with high incomes no less than of those who are poor. Trivial differences of accent, language, dress, customs, etc., acquire an absurd importance and contempt is engendered for those who lack social graces, especially country dwellers. Since race is usually highly correlated with income, economic inequality lies at the heart of racial tensions. More seriously, inequality of income is associated with other inequalities, especially in education and political power, which reinforce it.

The questions to ask about a country's development are therefore: What has been happening to poverty? What has been happening to unemployment? What has been happening to inequality? If all three of these have become less severe, then beyond doubt this has been a period of development for the country concerned. If one or two of these central problems have been growing worse, especially if all three have, it would be strange to call the result 'development', even if *per capita* income had soared. This applies, of course, to the future too. A 'plan' which conveys no targets for reducing poverty, unemployment and inequality can hardly be considered a 'development plan'.[2]

Of course, the true fulfilment of human potential requires much that cannot be specified in these terms. I cannot spell out all the other requirements, but this paper would be very unbalanced if I did not mention them at all. They include adequate educational levels (especially literacy), participation in government and belonging to a nation that is truly independent, both economically and politically, in the sense that the views of other governments do not largely predetermine one's own government's decisions.[3]

As undernourishment, unemployment and inequality dwindle, these educational and political aims become increasingly important objectives of development. Later still, freedom from repressive sexual codes, from noise and pollution, become major aims.[4] But these would not override the basic economic priorities, at least for really poor countries, with large numbers of undernourished children. A government could hardly claim to be 'developing' a country *just because* its educational system was being expanded or political order was being established, or limits set on engine noise, if hunger, unemployment and inequality were significant and growing, or even if they were not diminishing. Indeed, one would doubt the viability of political order in these circumstances, if one didn't consider the claim *prima facie* somewhat suspect; on the other hand, certain political patterns may well be incompatible with development.

Before leaving this issue I must make it clear that the national income is not totally meaningless, just because it is an inappropriate indicator of development. It has some significance as a measure of development *potential*. Suppose that two countries start a decade with the same *per capita* income and one grows faster than the other over ten years, but that the increase in income in the former goes entirely to the rich, and that, because growth has been due to highly capital-intensive techniques, unemployment rates remain unchanged, while in the latter growth has been slower but has meant lower unemployment and thus benefited the poorest class. Then, although the country with faster growth has, on my criteria, developed least — in fact not developed at all — it has achieved greater potential for developing later .

In the first place, the fiscal system could bring about development more rapidly the greater the income available for transfer to the poor. Moreover, a fast growth rate implies a greater savings capacity, which could more easily mean true development in the future. Indeed the faster-growing country may well already have a higher level of investment *per capita;* if this investment is in agricultural projects which will raise food production and provide more rural employment, or in rural schools, genuine development could already be foreshadowed for the future.[5]

From a long-term view point, economic growth is for a poor country a necessary condition of reducing poverty. But it is not a sufficient condition. To release the development potential of a high rate of economic growth depends on policy. A country where economic growth is slow or negligible may be busy reshaping its political institutions so that, when growth comes, it will mean development; such a country could develop faster in the long run than one at present enjoying fast growth but with political power remaining very firmly in the hands of a rich minority. It will be interesting to compare, for example, what happens in Cuba and Brazil in the remainder of this century.

Priorities in the social sciences

It may help us to withstand the strong intellectual attraction of the national income as a yardstick of development if we look back a little.

By about 1950 the great economic problems had been brought largely under control in the industrial countries. Unemployment had been reduced to historically very low levels; absolute poverty in the sense I use the word had been largely eliminated; taxation and educational advances had reduced economic inequalities, and, though a good deal of what remained was associated with race, this was not a source of great political [concern] at that time, and it was largely overlooked by the social scientists, especially the economists.

We could say that these countries had managed in various ways to meet, in some degree at least, the challenges they had faced in the 19th century. One reason, of course, was that they benefited from world economic leadership and political power — to this I'll return later. But another was that social scientists such as Booth, Rowntree, Boyd-Orr, the Webbs, Keynes, Beveridge and Tawney focused attention sharply on poverty, unemployment and inequality in the first half of this century. (I hope I am not being excessively nationalistic in choosing British examples: the names *are* rather significant.) Most economists, even Pigou, took greater equality as an obviously desirable objective.

With the easing of the big problems, however, economists turned their attention to innovations in professional techniques. In as far as they retained interest in current affairs, it was mainly in the progress of the nation conceived as a whole. The national income seemed ideal for comparing growth rates of a country during different periods, or for constructing an international league table. Moreover, it has maintained its role as a predictor of the level of employment — if the economy is diversified and the labour force is mobile, big short term changes in the national income are closely associated with changes in employment.[4]

We now see that even in the industrial countries basic economic problems had not really been cured. Their social scientists, notably in the United States, have been rediscovering their own poverty. Moreover, unemployment has recently grown, and inequality may well have done so too.

But the fundamental problems have never even started to disappear from sight in the Third World. In Africa, Asia or Latin America, development had been very limited on any of the three economic criteria until 1950. Since then, there has certainly been some reduction in the proportion, even if not in absolute numbers, living in poverty. But it has recently been estimated by Francis Keppel that seven out of every ten children in the entire world are 'affected by the apathy typical of chronic protein deficiency, an apathy which translates into diminished learning potential' (Scrimshaw and Gordon, 1969); the fraction among many countries of the Third World, such as India, must of course be higher. Unemployment seems to have grown, judging from the countries for which data are available. It is probable, though data are extremely poor, that in most countries inequality has not been reduced; in many, it may well have increased. A paper by A. J. Jaffe (1969) on five Latin American countries for which comparable studies over time are available concludes that all showed increasing inequalities, with the possible exception of Mexico. It is even possible that, were the data available, we would find economic growth to be directly associated with growing unemployment and increasing inequality. If that has indeed been the case, there has been a negative correlation between growth and development. Even if that were not so, it is clear that the connection between them is not at all as straightforward as was once believed.

Conceptual and measurement problems

One defence of the *national income* is that it is an objective, value-free indicator. Yet it is in fact heavily value-loaded: every type of product and service is assigned its own particular weight (many being zero). This weight is mainly determined by market forces, which reflect the country's income distribution. A familiar question in economics — how adequately income measures demand when its distribution is unequal — gets additional point when the distribution is as highly concentrated as it is in the countries of the Third World. Another question — how objective demand is when it is partially determined by salesmanship — appears even more cogent when tastes are to some extent imported from abroad. But, in addition, official policies, e.g. fostering import substitution by controls, often increase the prices of luxuries much more than of necessities. There are often egalitarian reasons for such policies, but the outcome is paradoxically that increases in production of luxuries count very much more highly in the estimation of rates of economic growth than they do in industrial countries.[7] While prices of staple foods and clothing may be comparable between poor countries and rich, perhaps lower in the former, prices of cars, refrigerators, etc., are several times as high. The absurd consequence may be that in a country where there is serious poverty, a car counts for more than ten tons of rice.

To estimate or use the national income also implies a set of judgements about what activities it should cover — what are the 'final' products, as against 'intermediate' products which are not considered intrinsically valuable and only produced because they make possible the production of other, more desirable, products. This raises the basic question: what activities are we trying to maximize? — a question once posed by Kuznets and now revived by Sametz (1968).[8] The issue of distribution can be raised in these terms too — are the luxuries of the professional classes a 'necessary cost' of raising the incomes of the poor, the real maximand?

It has also been argued on behalf of national income as a development indicator that it could at least be quantified. But what are all the voluminous tables of national income accounts really worth? So far as the Third World is concerned, much of what they ought to cover is virtually outside the scope of official statistics. This applies above all to output of domestic foodstuffs, even the staples, let alone subsidiary crops which come under the general heading of 'market gardening' (American 'truck farming'), not to speak of fish, forest products, etc. Extremely rough methods of estimation are often used, much of the output being assumed to rise in proportion to the increase in rural population, an increase which is in turn assumed to be some constant arbitrary rate in the absence of registration of births and deaths, or data on migration.[9] Secondly, we know very little about construction in the countryside by the farming community itself; this apparently amounts to a good deal if one takes account not only of building houses, but also clearing land, digging wells and ditches, constructing fences and hedges, etc. Thirdly, there are practically no basic data on domestic service and other personal services, even those which are remunerated.

We should ask national income estimators conceptual questions such as: which of the activities a farm family does for itself without payment, such as haircutting for example, have you included in the national income? And why? And practical questions such as: how many fishes were caught in Province A in the years concerned? How many huts were constructed in Province B? How many barbers worked in Province C? And how do you know?

We should also ask those who quote the national income, for example in a planning office or a university, how much time they have spent with the estimators? It is unsafe and therefore unprofessional to use national income data until one has personally satisfied oneself on how such questions have been handled.

I have examined the worksheets in about twenty countries; the blunt truth of the matter is that when one takes into account the difficulties of allowing for inventory changes and depreciation, and of deflating current-price data, the published national income series for a large number of countries have very little relevance to economic reality.[10] In many countries, any reasonably competent statistician could produce from the meagre basic data series showing the real *per capita* income either rising or falling. Decimal places are fantasy. Some series are in fact in a way more misleading than sets of random numbers would be, because they *appear* to have a significance. It would, of course, be very convenient if the national income data published in such quantities had objective meaning, but unfortunately this does not make them meaningful.

It might be argued that some numbers called national income series are at least available, whereas data on poverty, unemployment and inequality are very scrappy. This is, however, the result not so much of basic differences in estimation possibilities as of attitudes to development. The type of data collected reflects priorities. What work is done by a statistical office depends in practice partly on what its own government demands, partly on the advice it receives from various U.N. agencies, especially the U.N. Statistical Office. As a realization of the importance of social problems spreads, statistical offices will put less weight on national income estimation, more on preparing appropriate social indicators.[11]

I do not deny that there are conceptual problems with development indicators too. The difficulties in assessing *poverty* standards, or even minimum nutritional standards, are well known.[12] For a household these should reflect the ages and also the physical activities of its members.[13] Moreover, many households which can afford to exceed the nutritional minimum expenditure will not in fact do so, because they spend their money in a sense unwisely (whether because of conventional expenditures on non-essentials, lack of information or personal taste).[14] The recognition of this is indeed implicit in the official U.S. poverty line which allows $750 a head, of which about $250 is for food.

But we need not give up. When as in India, an official poverty line has been established, the resultant estimates of the proportion with incomes below a specified poverty line are not without meaning.[15] However rough, they have some significance as a yardstick for measuring development over time — certainly such comparisons convey more than changes in the *per capita* national income.

There are other well-known measures of poverty which I can only mention briefly here. One is the infant mortality rate (though this reflects in particular the effectiveness of health services, as well as diet, housing, etc.). Data on protein consumption and the incidence of diseases of undernourishment, such as rickets, are further clues on development, as are the height and weight of children.[16] However, they are only clues, and may well be misleading if used to compare nations of very different genetic stock, dietary habits, etc.

Unemployment is, of course, notoriously difficult to define in non-industrial societies. An urban unemployed person can be roughly identified by the usual test questions designed to reveal the last occasion when work was sought (though this means excluding from the unemployed those who would only look for a job if they thought there was any chance of finding it, and on the other hand including those who would in fact only accept particular types of work). In addition there is involuntary short time working, and people are more or less idle, at least for most of the day, in jobs which are more or less fictional (from superfluous posts in government to shining shoes). The volume of this is hard to measure; so is disguised rural under-employment because of seasonal variations in activity. One needs much more detail by sector, by region, by sex, by age, by educational qualification, to throw light on the nature of unemployment and underemployment in any country and on the attitudes of people to work.[17]

Inequality can be measured in many ways — by size, race, region, or by factor shares. All have their uses for different purposes, and they are of course all interconnected. They are also all limited in one important respect, namely that there are other sources of inequality than income. One's standard of living may be affected by access to free cars, for example. (An ambassador may well have a higher level of living than somebody with ten times his salary.) It also depends on access to public services such as health (especially important in urban-rural comparisons). More fundamentally, political power may greatly influence the inequality of people in terms of their ability to develop their personality, even to speak their minds.

Even concentration of income by size can be measured in many ways. If one wants a single measure, the Gini coefficient, derived from the Lorenz curve (showing cumulative proportions of income received by cumulative proportions of recipients), is probably still the most useful, for either income or wealth. But, if we are mainly concerned with inequality as a cause of poverty, a more meaningful measure may be to express (say) the lowest decile as a fraction of the median (following the general approach in a recent study by Harold Lydall (1968).[18] We are after all not greatly interested in changes *within* the top half of the income ladder.

Of course, all these measures of distribution raise the same conceptual problems as national income measurement — for example, where to draw the boundary between activities which are marketed and those which are not. In addition, such measures take no account of the price structure, which may well affect the concentration of *real* income — an important point in, e.g., countries where the burden of protection is borne mainly by the rich.

All in all, however, the conceptual problems of these indicators do not seem to be more formidable than those of the national income — we have just grown accustomed to ignoring the latter. And many of the practical problems are the same as those that face the national income estimators. But indicators of any of the elements of development I have mentioned also require supplementary information. Thus to measure the proportion of the population above a poverty line one needs to know how many people share each household income (and whether they are males or females, adults or children). To measure unemployment meaningfully, one needs to know what jobs people would be prepared to take (and at what income), and what hours they work. To measure distribution in any of its dimensions, one needs to know more than the national estimator about who receives various types of income.

But again we must not be diverted by such technical problems from attempting the assessment which really matters. There is one possible source for all of these measures, surveys of households designed to provide them; these can yield the necessary cross-classifications by region, race, income, etc. The systematic development of the information required to study trends in poverty, unemployment and income distribution in any country requires pilot surveys in depth to clarify the conceptual issues in their local context and guide the construction of indicators. This is best achieved if a permanent sampling organization, such as India has in its National Sample Survey, is established to collect the necessary information professionally, systematically and regularly.

I can only mention briefly indicators for the educational and political dimensions of development. In as far as education is provided by the formal educational system (which is very much open to argument) the main source is, of course, inputs and outputs of various levels of education. A technique for combining these in a diagram showing trends over time has been developed by Richard Jolly (1969).

Measurement of the extent to which the political aims have been achieved is of course much more difficult; possible clues include the number of prisoners held for political or quasi-political reasons, and the social and racial composition of parliaments, business boards, senior public administrative grades, etc., and also of those enjoying secondary and university education.

More general indicators of welfare, reflecting political and other influences, include the rates per million people of crimes of violence, suicide, alcoholism and other types of drug addiction. Here the main problem is to cope with the consequences of different standards of reporting, stemming from differences in definition (what is an alcoholic?) and in coverage (e.g. comprehensiveness of police records, death registers, etc.). Interpretation raises further problems. Thus is rural violence to be treated as a reflection of intolerable living conditions or of envy — or is it to be considered a necessary cost of a desirable social change?

Clues on the degree of national independence include the proportion of capital inflows in exchange receipts, the proportion of the supply of capital goods (or intermediates) which is imported, the proportion of assets, especially subsoil assets, owned by foreigners, and the extent to which one trading partner dominates the patterns of aid and trade. But there are also qualitative indicators such as the existence of foreign military bases and overflying rights, and the extent to which the country follows the lead of one of the great powers in the United Nations.

The compatibility of indicators

This section raises the problem of weighing and comparing different indicators, a major indicator problem. It is, of course, impossible to explore all its aspects here, but it may be useful to indicate some major possibilities of inconsistency and how serious these seem to be.

On the face of it, there is a strong causal interrelation between the three leading indicators. Development on any of them implies, or helps bring about, or may even be a necessary condition for, development on one or more of the others. To reduce unemployment is to remove one of the main causes of poverty and inequality. A reduction in inequality will of course reduce poverty, *ceteris paribus*.

But are other things equal? Does lowering the concentration of income imply a slower rate of economic growth — and growth is, as we have seen, in the long run a necessary condition for eliminating poverty. And would slower growth impair employment prospects? There is a well-known, indeed classical, argument that inequality generates savings and incentives and thus promotes economic growth and employment.

I find the argument that the need for savings justifies inequality unconvincing in the Third World today. Savings propensities are after all very low precisely in countries with highly unequal distributions; the industrial countries with less concentration of income have, by contrast, much higher savings propensities. Savings are, of course, also affected by the absolute level of incomes, but the explanation of this paradox must in part lie in the high consumption standards of an unequal society.

Moreover, the rich in most countries tend to have extremely high propensities, not merely to spend, but to spend on goods and services with a high foreign exchange content, and, for countries suffering from an acute foreign exchange bottleneck, this is a major obstacle to development.[19] It is true that import demand can be held in check by administrative controls, but this leads to the elaboration of a bureaucratic apparatus which is expensive, especially in terms of valuable organizing ability, and which in some countries becomes riddled with corruption. In fact, the result of import control is often to create a protected and highly profitable local industry, which itself depends heavily on imports of intermediate products and capital goods, and remits abroad a large flow of money in profits, interest, royalties, licence fees and service charges of various sorts.[20] In any case, in a highly unequal society, personal savings often flow abroad or go into luxury housing and other investment projects of low or zero priority for development, or even for growth.

The argument that only inequality can provide the incentives that are necessary is also obviously of limited validity in a country where there are barriers of race or class or caste to advancement. Still, we cannot dismiss it out of hand. The needs for private entrepreneurial talent vary according to the circumstances of different economies, but there are very few where this need is small. Countries relying on growing exports of manufactures, as many do, depend heavily on the emergence of businessmen with the drive to penetrate foreign markets. All countries depend in some degree on the appearance of progressive farmers. Will these emerge without financial rewards on a scale that will make nonsense of an egalitarian policy? Are rising profits of companies, especially foreign companies, an inevitable feature of growth in many countries? Or are we exaggerating the importance of financial incentives? Can other non-financial rewards partially take their place?[21] Can social incentives be developed to a point where people will take on such tasks with little or no individual reward (as the governments of China and Cuba are trying to procure)?

The compatibility of growing equality and rising output and employment has recently become doubtful for an additional set of reasons. Can the people who are professionally necessary be kept in the country if they earn only a small fraction of which they could earn elsewhere? How much unemployment will their departure involve, because their labour is complementary to that of the rest of the labour force? Yet what are the costs in terms of human welfare and even efficiency if they are prevented from leaving?[22]

On the other hand, there are also very serious reasons for questioning the compatibility of *in*equality and the growth of income and employment. One is implied by the discussion of the composition of consumption above. Can a manufacturing industry be created to correspond to the structure of demand that arises in a highly inequitable society (leaving aside the question of whether it *should* be created)? Will production rise rapidly if the proportion of the labour force which is too badly nourished for full manual and mental work is only sinking slowly? Can the government obtain the co-operation of the population in wage restraint, and in many other ways that are necessary for development, if there is visible evidence of great wealth which is being transmitted from generation to generation, so that the wage earner sees his children and his children's children doomed indefinitely to subordinate positions? Or if there is little prospect of reducing unemployment? Can political leaders under such circumstances mobilize the energies of the population and break down social customs which obstruct development, especially in rural areas?

I do not pretend to know the answers to this complex of questions, which point to a set of 'internal contradictions' in the development processes more severe than those to which Marx drew attention. Any answer must in any case be specific to the country concerned. All I would say is that such questions have usually been ignored in the past, leading to a failure to appreciate the damaging consequences of inequality.

Yet another set of questions arises out of the potential inconsistency between employment in the short-run and employment in the longer term — which is often formulated as a conflict between employment and growth. There has recently been much discussion of this (Stewart and Streeten, 1971). All I would say is that here too the conflict has been exaggerated. It would after all be surprising if the mobilization of all the above labour in a typical economy caused anything but a big rise in output.

My original paper, to which I referred in the first footnote, went on to discuss the consistency between these economic objectives and those mentioned above, in the political and social planes — political order and liberty, independence and education. I will not go over this ground here — it would take us rather far from the subject of development indicators (the interested reader can turn to the references given in that paper — though this is not to deny that political and economic dimensions of development are connected, certain political systems are incompatible with progress towards equality, because of the relationship between the distribution of income and political power.

Implications for planning

The most important use of development indicators is to provide the targets for planning. The realization that the national income is in itself an inadequate yardstick of development implies a recognition that national income targets are not very relevant. We need instead targets for poverty, employment and income distribution, specifying some of the dimensions of the structure of society at which we are aiming.

The difference in approach is more profound than it seems. Formerly the basic technique consisted in extrapolating past trends and choosing investment patterns that would produce an acceptable increase in national income in a five-year period, tacitly assuming many constraints as given — thus consumption patterns were projected in a way that assumed little or no change in income distribution or in tastes or attitudes. Now we must try to envisage what might be a satisfactory pattern at some time in the future, in terms not only of production and employment structures, but of the patterns of income distribution, consumer demand and jobs, and then work backwards, to see if there is any plausible path for getting there.

The econometrician searches for planning models with multiple objectives, in response to this challenge. But perhaps the task is much simpler: to lift every family above a poverty line, based on food requirements, bare minimum though it may be. To achieve this must imply the elimination of poverty and unemployment and (especially if the time span is short) a reduction in inequality. It implies setting target incomes for various sizes of families and working out what measures would be needed to achieve these (the measures may include not only employment creation, but also welfare schemes such as special food programmes for children, pensions, etc.). The final step is to estimate what measures need to be taken in policy areas such as taxation and incomes.

This approach raises statistical problems. In the first place, sufficiently detailed income and expenditure studies are rarely available; even if they were, there would be problems of relating poverty lines to household composition, referred to above. Further, it would be hard to incorporate complicated indicators in development models and one might have to settle for something as crude as a minimum household income. Converting targets into policies raises further problems because of the many different influences on the income of the poor and because typically there is no machinery for straightforward fiscal redistribution. But the approach is nevertheless worth pursuing — its difficulties are no excuse for persisting with inappropriate, even dangerously misleading, planning models designed to maximize economic growth.

To concentrate on the elimination of poverty implies that increased income for the rest of the population is irrelevant so long as there is under nourishment, especially of children. So be it. We must however, recognize the risk that some redistributive strategies *may* in some circumstances hamper economic growth and thus the more fundamental long-term solution of the problem of poverty.

International development

The criteria suggested above can in principle be applied to any unit — a village, a province, a nation, a continent or the world. Let me in closing refer briefly to indicators of world development. Basically the same concepts of poverty and employment apply, but in the case of inequality we are now primarily concerned with comparisons between incomes of different nations, as a guide to the policy tasks which face the rich countries if they are to contribute to the development of the poor.

There has been progress, especially since the 1930s, on the poverty criterion; the proportion of the whole human population living below any subsistence line must have fallen. But total overt world unemployment must have grown, since the emergence of unemployment in the Third World must numerically outweigh the decline of unemployment in the industrial countries. In recent years, in any case, unemployment has risen in the latter too, so there can be no doubt of the world trend (though it is not very meaningful to add together national statistics for something like unemployment which takes so many forms). Moreover, since the middle of the last century enormous gaps have opened between rich countries and poor: inequality on the present scale is an entirely new phenomenon, as papers by Simon Kuznets (1971, pp. 27ff.; 1966, pp. 390-400) and Surendra Patel (1964) have brought out.

Economic inequality between nations, like inequality within them means differences in status and power, poisoning the attitudes of men towards each other. This, again as on the national level, means growing tensions between races, broadly in this case (as also inside many countries) between the whites and the remainder. Moreover, the incompatibility of inequality with the elimination of poverty is clearer for development on the international than on the national plane. The seepage, through many channels, of the consumption habits of rich countries has contributed to unemployment in poorer countries (see above), and probably also meant slower economic growth. The transfer of technologies designed for rich countries has had similar effects; available technologies are becoming increasingly inappropriate for the world's needs. The growing difference in *per capita* incomes also stimulates the 'brain drain' and exerts an upward pull on professional salaries in poor countries. Thus national and international inequality are linked.[23]

When we consider the world scene, it is wrong to talk about 'development', on the criteria suggested above. One cannot really say that there has been development for the world as a whole, when the benefits of technical progress have accrued to minorities which were already relatively rich. To me, this word is particularly misleading for the period since the war, especially the 'development decade' when the growth of economic inequality and unemployment may have actually accelerated. (The prospect of a 'second development decade' is daunting: a repetition of the 1960s with unemployment and inequality rising still further, would be socially, economically and politically disastrous whatever the pace of economic growth!)

The measurement of international inequality raises its own set of conceptual problems. Egalitarians like myself face a theoretical paradox. If we argue that the national income is an inappropriate measure of a nation's development, we weaken the significance of a growing *per capita* income 'gap' between rich nations and poor. However, there is really no alternative — a world income distribution by size, showing the magnitude of absolute poverty, would be immensely difficult to construct.

There are, moreover, special conceptual difficulties about international comparisons of income. Comparisons of incomes have limited significance when life styles are so different (affecting among other things the proportion of activity covered by cash transactions and thus included in 'income'), and when there are differences in climate.

A familiar measurement problem is the inapplicability of exchange rates as means of converting incomes in different currencies to a standard of comparison (such as the U.S. dollar). Attempts have been made to prepare exchange rates more appropriate for measuring the true purchasing power of different currencies, but these run up against well-known problems of weighting.[24]

Still, we must not fall into the familiar trap of criticizing statistics to the point where we deny them any meaning. Despite all its limitations (including the additional one of defining a 'rich' country) the statement that during the first 'development decade' the ratio between the average income of rich countries and poor has increased from about 12:1 to about 15:1 is not entirely lacking in content, either morally or analytically. It illustrates the widespread impact on poor countries of increasingly inappropriate salaries, consumption patterns and technologies, aggravating their own intractable problems of inequality and unemployment.

One thing this critique suggests [is] the need for the continued worldwide development of subsidiary indicators mentioned above, such as infant mortality rates, calorie and protein consumption, and the incidence of diseases of poverty and under-nourishment.

There are of course political dimensions to international as to national development. A big step was taken in the first post-war decade with the creation of a whole system — the United Nations and its agencies. But since then progress has been very gradual, due basically to the unwillingness of the rich countries to limit their sovereignty and accept the authority of international organizations. The continued eruption of wars is an eloquent indicator of a lack of political progress which goes far to explain the negative development of the world as a whole.

The first third of this paper is derived from 'The meaning of development' published in the *International Development Review* (Vol. 11, No. 4, 1969), and republished in I.D.S. Communications Series, No. 44; *Revista Brasilelra de Economia*, (Vol. 24, No. 3); *Internationale Spectator*, (Vol. XXIV, No. 21); *Ekistics*, 1970; *Sociological Abstracts*, U.S.A., 1970; *The Political Economy of Development* (ed. Ilchman and Uphoff) 1971; and *INSIGHT*, July 1971. I am grateful for comments from Hans Singer on a draft of this part, which was also discussed at seminars at the Universities of Boston and Toronto, and formed the basis of a lunch talk at the 11th World Conference of the Society for International Development (New Delhi, November 1969).

Notes

1. Thus in Trinidad the growth in *per capita* income averaged more than 5 per cent a year during the whole period 1953-68, while overt unemployment showed a steady increase to more than 10 per cent of the labour force.

2. Suppose, for example, that a perspective plan specified that *per capita* income of Brazil doubled in the next thirty years, but assumed no change in distribution or in the proportion unemployed. Then at the turn of the century, a big landowner in the Matto Grosso could run four cars, instead of two, and a peasant in the North-East could eat two kilogrammes of meat a year instead of one. His son might well be still out of work. Could we really call that 'development'?

3. These dimensions are discussed in Mrs Baster's introduction.

4. Even for countries at a high level of development in any sense, the use of national income as an indicator is being widely challenged, e.g. by Mishan (1967), on the grounds that the environmental costs are ignored.

5. In an interesting paper Divatia and Bhatt (1969) put forward a different index of development potential, based on fundamental factor inputs such as capital and skills (though it is misleadingly described as a measure of the 'pace of development'). Movements in such an index could foreshadow what the future pace of economic growth could be. The Index for India, for example, is encouraging because it shows a rate of increase twice as fast as the real national income. But, of course, it does not follow that growth potential *will* be released, let alone that development will take place.

6. This use of the national income had been developed by Colin Clark (1937). In fact the great spurt forward in national income statistics in the 1930s and 1940s was due largely to the unemployment problem, although also to the need to quantify alternative wartime policies.

7. In addition, indirect taxes of various kinds on luxuries are relatively heavy, so such biases are particularly severe when market prices are used as weights.

8. For example, is a journey to work really an end product, as national estimators assume (especially a journey on a metropolitan underground railway!)? Additional issues are now being posed in industrial countries by the failure of national income to allow for the costs of environmental destruction, i.e. to be a sufficiently 'net' concept in that sense.

9. Every so often a researcher tries to draw conclusions about trends in *per capita* food consumption, which of course simply means revealing the implications of assumptions made by official statisticians.

10. There is an upward bias as well. The share of output covered by official statistics, and included in the national income, tends to rise, partly because a growing proportion of output passes through the hands of organized business, which is more adequately covered by official statistics, but also partly because of the general improvement in data collection.

11. The U.N. Statistical Office's 'A Complementary system of Statistics of the Distribution of Income, Expenditure and Wealth' is a useful starting-point.

12. Various poverty lines in India, where there has been much work on this question, are discussed by Fonseca (1970).

13. See papers by Abel-Smith, Bagley, Rein and Townsend in Townsend (1970).

14. This problem was first recognized by Rowntree (1901) in his classic enquiry in York, leading him to distinguish between 'primary' and 'secondary' poverty — the latter referring to the poverty of those who could afford the nutritional minimum but do not in fact attain it.

15. See, however, an interesting pair of articles by Minhas (1970) and Bardhan (1970), which show that even using the same criterion of poverty (one proposed in 1962 by a distinguished group of economists to the Planning Mission) very different conclusions can be reached on trends in the proportions lying below the poverty line through using different sources of consumption data, different allowances for price changes and different interpolation procedures.

16. Several indicators can be combined to give us an indicative profile of the prevalence of poverty in a nation, such as the U.N. Research Institute for Social Development has been experimenting with in Geneva. In fact they have taken a step further and produced a tentative 'development indicator', a weighted average of various series. The Institute's investigations of multiple associations are interesting and worth while, but we should not fall into the trap (as we could, although the Institute's Director warns us against it) of treating this indicator as 'normative'. It simply measures the extent to which a country has advanced along a path indicated by data from countries at different states of progress; see UNRISD (1969).

17. See I.L.O. (1970). The point is made there that the measurement of unemployment depends very much on the dimension of the problem that concerns one — unemployment as a cause of personal frustration, low income or loss of output.

18. The Pareto coefficient, on the other hand, which long had its advocates, is expressly limited to measuring distribution among higher incomes.

19. To draw the conclusion that the income distributions should be changed, one has to assume that Engel curves are non-linear, but this seems not to need specifying. Consumption of such luxuries is zero over a considerable income range.

20. See I.L.O. (1970) for a discussion of the compatibility of a high concentration of income with full employment. Unfortunately most theoretical texts concentrate on the relation between income distribution, savings and growth, ignoring the more important effects via the composition of consumption.

21. Though, of course, these imply inequalities of other types, even if only of social prestige.

22. I have dealt with these issues elsewhere (Seers, 1971).

23. See Seers (1971) and Jolly and Seers (1970).

24. Although this problem takes the form of finding the right expenditure weights for a price deflator, what we are actually doing is obtaining price weights for quantity comparisons,

and this is extremely hard when price structures vary so much (see above). Analogous difficulties arise whenever comparisons are made between regions of a country (due to geographical variations in prices and consumption patterns) but much less severely.

References

Bardhan, Pranab K., (1970) 'On the Minimum Level of Living and the Rural Poor', *Indian Economic Review*, Vol. 5, April.

Clark, Colin, (1937) *National Income and Outlay*, London: Macmillan

Divatia, V. V., and Bhatt, V. V., (1969) 'On Measuring the Pace of Development', *Quarterly Review*, Banco Nazionale del Lavoro, No. 89, June.

Fonseca, A. J., (1970) 'The need-based Wage in India: A Computerized Estimate', reprinted from *Wage Policy and Wage Distribution in India*, Bombay: University of Bombay.

I.L.O., (1970) *Towards Full Employment, Geneva: International Labour Office.*

Jaffe, A.J., (1969) 'Notes on Family Income Distribution in Developing Countries in Relation to Population and Economic Changes'; paper given at meeting of International Association for Research in Income and Wealth, August; to be published in *Estadistica,* Inter-American Statistical Institute, No. 104.

Jolly, Richard, (1969) *Planning Education for African Development*, Nariobi: East Africa Publishing house.

Jolly, Richard, and Seers, Dudley, (1970) 'The Brain Drain and the Development Process', proceedings of the International Economic Association Conference to be published in E.A.G. Robinson (ed.), *The Gap Between the Rich and the Poor Countries*, London: Macmillan.

Kuznets, Simon, (1966) *Modern Economic Growth*, Studies in Comparative Economics No. 7, New Haven: Yale University Press.

Kuznets, Simon, (1971) *Economic Growth of Nations: Total Output and Production Structure*, Cambridge, Mass.: Belknap.

Lydall, Harold, (1968) *The Structure of Earnings*, Oxford: Clarendon Press.

Minhas, B.S., (1970) 'Rural Poverty, Land Redistribution and Development', *Indian Economic Review,* Vol. 5, April.

Mishan, E. J., (1967) *The Costs of Economic Growth*, London: Staples Press.

Patel, Surrendra, (1964) 'The Economic Distance Between Nations', *Economic Journal,* Vol. 74, March.

Rowntree, B. Seebohm, (1901) *Poverty: A Study of Town Life*, London: Macmillan.

Sametz, A. W., (1968) 'Production of Goods and Services: The Measurement of Economic Growth, in E. Sheldon and W. B. Moore (eds), *Indicators of Social Change: Concepts and Measurements*, New York: Russell Sage Foundation.

Scrimshaw, N. S., and Gordon, J. E. (ed.), (1968) *Malnutrition, Learning and Behaviour,* Cambridge, Mass.: M. I. T. Press.

Seers, Dudley, (1971) 'The Transmission of Inequality' in Robert K. A. Gardiner (ed.), *Africa and the World*, London: Oxford University Press.

Stewart, Frances, and Streeten, Paul, (1971) 'Conflicts between Output and Employment Objectives' in Ronald Robinson and Peter Johnston (eds), *Prospects for Employment*

Opportunities in the Nineteen Seventies, London: Her Majesty's Stationery Office.

Townsend, Peter (ed.), (1970) *The Concept of Poverty*, London: Heinemann.

UNRISD, (1969) *Research Notes No. 2,* July, Geneva: United Nations Research Institute for Social Development.

2. Defining and Measuring Human Development

UN Development Programme

People are the real wealth of a nation. The basic objective of development is to create an enabling environment for people to enjoy long, healthy and creative lives. This may appear to be a simple truth. But it is often forgotten in the immediate concern with the accumulation of commodities and financial wealth.

Technical considerations of the means to achieve human development — and the use of statistical aggregates to measure national income and its growth — have at times obscured the fact that the primary objective of development is to benefit people. There are two reasons for this. First, national income figures, useful though they are for many purposes, do not reveal the composition of income or the real beneficiaries. Second, people often value achievements that do not show up at all, or not immediately, in higher measured income or growth figures: better nutrition and health services, greater access to knowledge, more secure livelihoods, better working conditions, security against crime and physical violence, satisfying leisure hours, and a sense of participating in the economic, cultural and political activities of their communities. Of course, people also want higher incomes as one of their options. But income is not the sum total of human life.

This way of looking at human development is not really new. The idea that social arrangements must be judged by the extent to which they promote "human good" goes back at least to Aristotle. He also warned against judging societies merely by such things as income and wealth that are sought not for themselves but desired as means to other objectives. "Wealth is evidently not the good we are seeking, for it is merely useful and for the sake of something else."

Aristotle argued for seeing "the difference between a good political arrangement and a bad one" in terms of its successes and failures in facilitating people's ability to lead "flourishing lives". Human beings as the real end of all activities was a recurring theme in the writings of most of the early philosophers. Emmanuel Kant observed: "So act as to treat humanity, whether in their own person or in that of any other, in every case as an end withal, never as means only."

The same motivating concern can be found in the writings of the early leaders of quantification in economics — William Petty, Gregory King, François Quesnay, Antoine Lavoisier and Joseph Lagrange, the grandparents of GNP and GDP. It is also clear in the writings of the leading political economists — Adam Smith, David Ricardo, Robert Malthus, Karl Marx and John Stuart Mill.

But excessive preoccupation with GNP growth and national income accounts has obscured that powerful perspective, supplanting a focus on ends by an obsession with merely the means.

Recent development experience has once again underlined the need for paying close attention to the link between economic growth and human development — for a variety of reasons.

Table 1.1   GNP per capita and selected social indicators

Country	GNP per capita (US$)	Life expectancy (years)	Adult literacy (%)	Infant mortality (per 1,000 live births)
Modest GNP per capita with high human development				
Sri Lanka	400	71	87	32
Jamaica	940	74	82	18
Costa Rica	1, 610	75	93	18
High GNP per capita with modest human development				
Brazil	2, 020	65	78	62
Oman	5, 810	57	30	40
Saudi Arabia	6, 200	64	55	70

- Many fast-growing developing countries are discovering that their high GNP growth rates have failed to reduce the socioeconomic deprivation of substantial sections of their population.

- Even industrial nations are realizing that high income is no protection against the rapid spread of such problems as drugs, alcoholism, AIDS, homelessness, violence and the breakdown of family relations.

- At the same time, some low-income countries have demonstrated that it is possible to achieve high levels of human development if they skilfully use the available means to expand basic human capabilities.

- Human development efforts in many developing countries have been severely squeezed by the economic crisis of the 1980s and the ensuing adjustment programmes.

Recent development experience is thus a powerful reminder that the expansion of output and wealth is only a means. The end of development must be human well-being. How to relate the means to the ultimate end should once again become the central focus of development analysis and planning.

How can economic growth be managed in the interest of the people? What alternative policies and strategies need to be pursued if people, not commodities, are the principal focus of national attention? This Report addresses these issues.

Defining human development

Human development is a process of enlarging people's choices. The most critical ones are to lead a long and healthy life, to be educated and to enjoy a decent standard of living. Additional choices include political freedom, guaranteed human rights and self-respect — what Adam Smith called the ability to mix with others without being "ashamed to appear in publick" (box 1.1).

BOX 1.1

Human development defined

Human development is a process of enlarging people's choices. In principle, these choices can be infinite and change over time. But at all levels of development, the three essential ones are for people to lead a long and healthy life, to acquire knowledge and to have access to resources needed for a decent standard of living. If these essential choices are not available, many other opportunities remain inaccessible.

But human development does not end there. Additional choices, highly valued by many people, range from political, economic and social freedom to opportunities for being creative and productive, and enjoying personal self-respect and guaranteed human rights.

Human development has two sides: the formation of human capabilities — such as improved health, knowledge and skills — and the use people make of their acquired capabilities — for leisure, productive purposes or being active in cultural, social and political affairs. If the scales of human development do not finely balance the two sides, considerable human frustration may result.

According to this concept of human development, income is clearly only one option that people would like to have, albeit an important one. But it is not the sum total of their lives. Development must, therefore, be more than just the expansion of income and wealth. Its focus must be people.

It is sometimes suggested that income is a good proxy for all other human choices since access to income permits exercise of every other option. This is only partly true for a variety of reasons:

- Income is a means, not an end. It may be used for essential medicines or narcotic drugs. Well-being of a society depends on the uses to which income is put, not on the level of income itself.

- Country experience demonstrates several cases of high levels of human development at modest income levels and poor levels of human development at fairly high income levels.

- Present income of a country may offer little guidance to its future growth prospects. If it has already invested in its people, its potential income may be much higher than what its current income level shows, and vice versa.

- Multiplying human problems in many industrial, rich nations show that high income levels, by themselves, are no guarantee for human progress.

The simple truth is that there is no automatic link between income growth and human progress. The main preoccupation of development analysis should be how such a link can be created and reinforced.

The term *human development* here denotes both the *process* of widening people's choices and the *level* of their achieved well-being. It also helps to distinguish clearly between two sides of human development. One is the formation of human capabilities, such as improved health or knowledge. The other is the use that people make of their acquired capabilities, for work or leisure.

This way of looking at development differs from the conventional approaches to economic growth, human capital formation, human resource development, human welfare or basic human needs. It is necessary to delineate these differences clearly to avoid any confusion:

- GNP growth is treated here as being necessary but not sufficient for human development. Human progress may be lacking in some societies despite rapid GNP growth or high per capita income levels unless some additional steps are taken.

- Theories of human capital formation and human resource development view human beings primarily as means rather than as ends. They are concerned only with the supply side — with human beings as instruments for furthering commodity production. True, there is a connection, for human beings *are* the active agents of all production. But human beings are more than capital goods for commodity production. They are also the ultimate ends and beneficiaries of this process. Thus, the concept of human capital formation (or human resource development) captures only one side of human development, not its whole.

- Human welfare approaches look at human beings more as the beneficiaries of the development process than as participants in it. They emphasise distributive policies rather than production structures.

- The basic needs approach usually concentrates on the bundle of goods and services that deprived population groups need: food, shelter, clothing, health care and water. It focuses on the provision of these goods and services rather than on the issue of human choices.

Human development, by contrast, brings together the production and distribution of commodities and the expansion and use of human capabilities. It also focuses on choices — on what people should have, be and do to be able to ensure their own livelihood. Human development is, moreover, concerned not only with basic needs satisfaction but also with human development as a participatory and dynamic process. It applies equally to less developed and highly developed countries.

Human development as defined in this Report thus embraces many of the earlier approaches to human development. This broad definition makes it possible to capture better the complexity of human life — the many concerns people have and the many cultural, economic, social and political differences in people's lives throughout the world.

The broad definition also raises some questions: Does human development lend itself to measurement and quantification? Is it operational? Can it be planned and monitored?

Measuring human development

In any system for measuring and monitoring human development, the ideal would be to include many variables, to obtain as comprehensive a picture as possible. But the current lack of relevant comparable statistics precludes that. Nor is such comprehensiveness entirely desirable. Too many indicators could produce a perplexing picture — perhaps distracting policymakers from the main overall trends. The crucial issue therefore is of emphasis.

The key indicators

This Report suggests that the measurement of human development should for the time being focus on the three essential elements of human life — longevity, knowledge and decent living standards.

For the first component — longevity — life expectancy at birth is the indicator. The importance of life expectancy lies in the common belief that a long life is valuable in itself and in the fact that various indirect benefits (such as adequate nutrition and good health) are closely associated with higher life expectancy. This association makes life expectancy an important indicator of human development, especially in view of the present lack of comprehensive information about people's health and nutritional status (box 1.2).

For the second key component — knowledge — literacy figures are only a crude reflection of access to education, particularly to the good quality education so necessary for productive life in modern society. But literacy is a person's first step in learning and knowledge-building, so literacy figures are essential in any measurement of human development. In a more varied set of indicators, importance would also have to be attached to the outputs of higher levels of education. But for basic human development, literacy deserves the clearest emphasis.

The third key component of human development — command over resources needed for a decent living — is perhaps the most difficult to measure simply. It requires data on access to land, credit, income and other resources. But given the scarce data on many of these variables, we must for the time being make the best use of an income indicator. The most readily available income indicator — per capita income — has wide national coverage. But the presence of nontradable goods and services and the distortions from exchange rate anomalies, tariffs and taxes make per capita income data in nominal prices not very useful for international comparisons. Such data can, however, be improved by using purchasing-power-adjusted real GDP per capita figures, which

BOX 1.2

What price human life?

The use of life expectancy as one of the principal indicators of human development rests on three considerations: the intrinsic value of longevity, its value in helping people pursue various goals and its association with other characteristics, such as good health and nutrition.

The importance of life expectancy relates primarily to the value people attach to living long and well. That value is easy for theorists to underestimate in countries where longevity is already high. Indeed, when life expectancy is very high, the challenge of making the lives of the old and infirm happy and worthwhile may be regarded by some as an exciting task. For the less fortunate people of the world, however, life is battered by distress, deprivation and the fear of premature death. They certainly attach a higher value to longer life expectancy.

Longevity also helps in the pursuit of some of life's other most valued goals. Living long may not be people's only objective, but their other plans and ambitions clearly depend on having a reasonable life span to develop their abilities, use their talents and carry out their plans.

A long life correlates closely with adequate nutrition, good health and education and other valued achievements. Life expectancy is thus a proxy measure for several other important variables in human development.

provide better approximations of the relative power to buy commodities and to gain command over resources for a decent living standard.

A further consideration is that the indicator should reflect the diminishing returns to transforming income into human capabilities. In other words, people do not need excessive financial resources to ensure a decent living. This aspect was taken into account by using the logarithm of real GDP per capita for the income indicator.

All three measures of human development suffer from a common failing: they are averages that conceal wide disparities in the overall population. Different social groups have different life expectancies. There often are wide disparities in male and female literacy. And income is distributed unevenly.

The case is thus strong for making distributional corrections in one form or another (box 1.3). Such corrections are especially important for income, which can grow to enormous heights. The inequality possible in respect of life expectancy and literacy is much more limited: a person can be literate only once, and human life is finite.

Reliable and comparable estimates of inequality of income are hard to come by, however. Even the Gini coefficient, probably the most widely used measure of income inequality, is currently available for fewer than a quarter of the 130 countries in the Human Development Indicators at the end of this Report — and many of those estimates are far from dependable. Distributional data for life expectancy and literacy by income

BOX 1.3

What national averages conceal

Averages of per capita income often conceal widespread human deprivation. Look at Panama, Brazil, Malaysia and Costa Rica in the table below. That is the order of their ranking by GNP per capita.

If the GNP figures are corrected for variations in purchasing power in different countries, the ranking shifts somewhat — to Brazil, Panama, Malaysia and Costa Rica.

But if distributional adjustments are made using each country's Gini coefficient, the original ranking reverses to Costa Rica, Malaysia, Brazil, Panama.

The average value of literacy, life expectancy and other indicators can be similarly adjusted. There is a great deal of technical literature on the subject, but the basic approach is simple. If inequality is seen as reducing the value of average achievement as given by an unweighted mean, that average value can be adjusted by the use of inequality measures. Such distributional corrections can make a significant different to evaluations of country performance.

Country	GNP per capita (US$) 1987	Real GDP per capita (PPP$) 1987	Gini coefficient of inequality	Distribution-adjusted GDP per capita (PPP$)
Panama	2, 240	4, 010	.57	1, 724
Brazil	2, 020	4, 310	.57	1, 852
Malaysia	1, 810	3, 850	.48	2, 001
Costa Rica	1, 610	3, 760	.42	2, 180

group are not being collected and those available on rural-urban and male-female disparities are still too scant for international comparisons.

The conceptual and methodological problems of quantifying and measuring human development become even more complex for political freedom, personal security, interpersonal relations and the physical environment. But even if these aspects largely escape measurement now, analyses of human development must not ignore them. The correct interpretation of the data on quantifiable variables depends on also keeping in mind the more qualitative dimensions of human life. Special effort must go into developing a simple quantitative measure to capture the many aspects of human freedom.

Attainments and shortfalls

Progress in human development has two perspectives. One is attainment: what has been achieved, with greater achievements meaning better progress. The second is the continuing shortfall from a desired value or target.

In many ways the two perspectives are equivalent — the greater the attainments, the smaller the shortfalls. But they also have some substantive differences. Disappointment and dismay at low performance often originate in the belief that things could be much better, an appraisal that makes the concept of a shortfall from some acceptable level quite central. Indeed, human deprivation and poverty inevitably invoke shortfalls from some designated value, representing adequacy, acceptability or achievability.

The difference between assessing attainments and shortfalls shows up more clearly in a numerical example. Performances often are compared in percentage changes: a 10-year rise in life expectancy from 60 years to 70 years is a 17% increase, but a 10-year rise in life expectancy from 40 years to 50 years is a 25% increase. The less the attainment already achieved, the higher the percentage value of the same absolute increase in life expectancy.

Raising a person's life expectancy from 40 years to 50 years would thus appear to be a larger achievement than going from 60 years to 70 years. In fact, raising life expectancy from the terribly low level of 40 years to 50 years is achievable through such relatively easy measures as epidemic control. But improving life expectancy from 60 years to 70 years may often be a much more difficult and more creditable accomplishment. The shortfall measure of human progress captures this better than the attainment measure does.

Taking once again the example of life expectancy, if 80 years is the target for calculating shortfalls, a rise of life expectancy from 60 years to 70 years is a 50% reduction in shortfall — halving it from 20 years to 10 years. That is seen as a bigger achievement than the 25% reduction in shortfall (from 40 years to 30 years) when raising life expectancy from 40 years to 50 years.

The shortfall thus has two advantages over the attainment in assessing human progress. It brings out more clearly the difficulty of the tasks accomplished, and it emphasises the magnitude of the tasks that still lie ahead.

The human development index

People do not isolate the different aspects of their lives. Instead, they have an overall sense of well-being. There thus is merit in trying to construct a composite index of human development.

Past efforts to devise such an index have not come up with a fully satisfactory measure. They have focussed either on income or on social indicators, without bringing them together in a composite index. Since human beings are both the means and the end of development, a composite index must capture both these aspects. This Report carries forward the search for a more appropriate index by suggesting an index that captures the three essential components of human life — longevity, knowledge and basic income for a decent living standard. Longevity and knowledge refer to the formation of human capabilities, and income is a proxy measure for the choices people have in putting their capabilities to use.

BOX 1.4

Constructing a human development index

Human deprivation and development have many facets, so any index of human progress should incorporate a range of indicators to capture this complexity. But having too many indicators in the index would blur its focus and make it difficult to interpret and use. Hence the need for compromise — to balance the virtues of broad scope with those of retaining sensitivity to critical aspects of deprivation.

This Report has chosen three types of deprivation as the focus of attention: people's deprivation in life expectancy, literacy and income for a decent living standard. Each measure could have been further refined (especially by making distributional adjustments) if there had been adequate comparable data. But in the absence of such data, the focus here represents a move in the right direction — away from the narrow and misleading attention to only one dimension of human life, whether economic or social.

The first two indicators — life expectancy and adult literacy — are commonly used concepts. But the third — the purchasing power to buy commodities for satisfying basic needs — is not as well understood. The GNP figures typically used for international comparisons do not adequately account for national differences in purchasing power or the distorting effect of official exchange rates. To overcome these inadequacies, we use here the purchasing-power-adjusted GDP estimates developed in the International Price Comparison Project, a collaborative effort of the UN Statistical Office, the World Bank, EUROSTAT, OECD, ECE and ESCAP, now being expanded by USAID. And since there are diminishing returns in the conversion of income into the fulfilment of human needs, the adjusted GDP per capita figures have been transformed into their logarithms.

To construct a composite index, a *minimum* value (the maximum deprivation set equal to one) and a *desirable* or *adequate* value (no deprivation set equal to zero) had to be specified for each of the three indicators.

The minimum values were chosen by taking the lowest 1987 national value for each indicator. For life expectancy at birth, the minimum value was 42 years, in Afghanistan, Ethiopia and Sierra Leone. For adult literacy, it was 12%, in Somalia. For the purchasing-power-adjusted GDP per capita, the value was $220 (log value 2.34), in Zaire.

The construction of the human development index (HDI) starts with a deprivation measure (box 1.4). For life expectancy, the target is 78 years, the highest average life expectancy attained by any country. The literacy target is 100%. The income target is the logarithm of the average poverty line income of the richer countries, expressed in purchasing-power-adjusted international dollars. Human development indexes for 130 countries with more than a million people are presented in the Human Development indicators, table 1. Those for another 32 countries with fewer than a million people are

BOX 1.4 cont/d

The values of desirable or adequate achievement were Japan's 1987 life expectancy at birth of 78 years, an adult literacy rate of 100%, and the average official "poverty line" income in nine industrial countries, adjusted by purchasing power parities, of $4,861. The nine countries are Australia, Canada, the Federal Republic of Germany, the Netherlands, Norway, Sweden, Switzerland, the United Kingdom and the United States.

The minimum and desirable or adequate values are the end-points of a scale indexed from one to zero for each measure of deprivation. Placing a country at the appropriate point on each scale and averaging the three scales gives its average human deprivation index, which when subtracted from 1 gives the human development index (HDI). [A mathematical formulation of the HDI is given in technical note 3.]

in the Human Development Indicators, [table 25].

Country ranking by HDI and GNP

The human development index ranks countries very differently from the way GNP per capita ranks them. The reason is that GNP per capita is only one of life's many dimensions, while the human development index captures other dimensions as well.

Sri Lanka, Chile, Costa Rica, Jamaica, Tanzania and Thailand, among others, do far better on their human development ranking than on their income ranking, showing that they have directed their economic resources more towards some aspects of human progress. But Oman, Gabon, Saudi Arabia, Algeria, Mauritania, Senegal and Cameroon, among others, do considerably worse on their human development ranking than on their income ranking, showing that they have yet to translate their income into corresponding levels of human development.

To stress again an earlier point, the human development index captures a few of people's choices and leaves out many that people may value highly — economic, social and political freedom (box 1.5), and protection against violence, insecurity and discrimination, to name but a few. The HDI thus has limitations. But the virtue of broader coverage must be weighed against the inconvenience of complicating the basic picture it allows policymakers to draw. These tradeoffs pose a difficult issue that future editions of the *Human Development Report* will continue to discuss.

Figure 1.1 GNP per capita and the HDI

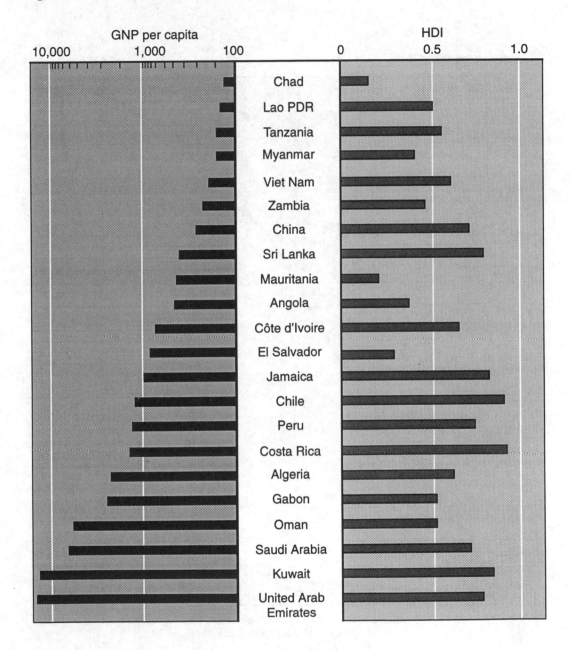

Figure 1.2   Ranking of countries' GNP per capita and HDI

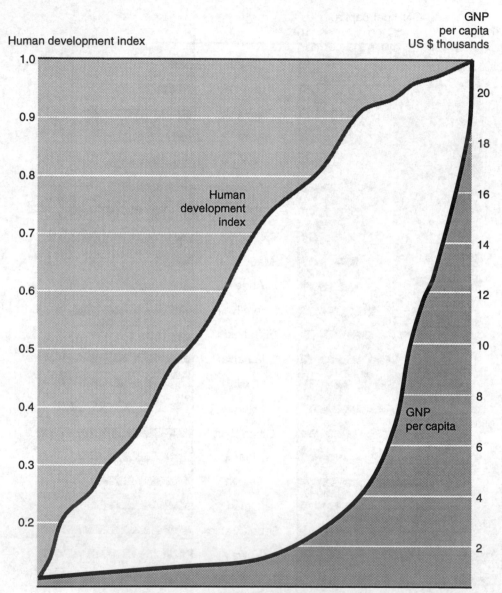

Human development index

GNP
per capita
US $ thousands

130 countries ranked by human development index (grey line)
and by GNP per capita (black line)

The chart shows two separate distributions of countries. The upper curve represents their
ranking according to the human development index while the lower curve shows their
ranking according to GNP per capita. The two curves reveal that the disparity among
countries is much greater in income than in human development. There is no automatic link
between the level of per capita income in a country and the level of its human development.

BOX 1.5

Freedom and human development

Human development is incomplete without human freedom. Throughout history, people have been willing to sacrifice their lives to gain national and personal liberty. We have witnessed only recently an irresistible wave of human freedom sweep across Eastern Europe, South Africa and many other parts of the world. Any index of human development should therefore give adequate weight to a society's human freedom in pursuit of material and social goals. The valuation we put on similar human development achievements in different countries will be quite different depending on whether they were accomplished in a democratic or an authoritarian framework.

While the need for qualitative judgement is clear, there is no simple quantitative measure available yet to capture the many aspects of human freedom — free elections, multiparty political systems, uncensored press, adherence to the rule of law, guarantees of free speech and so on. To some extent, however, the human development index (HDI) captures some aspects of human freedom. For example, if the suppression of people suppresses their creativity and productivity, that would show up in income estimates or literacy levels. In addition, the human development concept, adopted in this Report, focusses on people's capabilities or, in other words, people's strength to manage their affairs — which, after all, is the essence of freedom.

For illustrative purposes, the table (in box 1.5a) shows a selection of countries (within each region) that have achieved a high level of human development (relative to other countries in the region) within a reasonably democratic political and social framework. And a cursory glance at the ranking of countries in table 1 of the Human Development Indicators, given at the end of this report, shows that countries ranking high in their HDI also have a more democratic framework — and vice versa — with some notable exceptions.

What is needed is considerable empirical work to quantify various indicators of human freedom and to explore further the link between human freedom and human development.

BOX 1.5a

Top 15 countries in democratic human development

Country	HDI	Country	HDI
Latin American and the Caribbean		*Middle East and North Africa*	
Costa Rica	0.916	Turkey	0.751
Uruguay	0.916	Tunisia	0.657
Trinidad and Tobago	0.885		
Mexico	0.876	*Sub-Saharan Africa*	
Venezuela	0.861	Mauritius	0.788
Jamaica	0.824	Botswana	0.646
Colombia	0.801	Zimbabwe	0.576
Asia			
Malaysia	0.800		
Sri Lanka	0.789		
Thailand	0.783		

3.   Is the Third World Still There?
John Toye

Diverse reports from distant places

One summer when there was nothing more amusing for them to do, the subeditors working on *The Times* held a competition to see which of them could insert the most boring headline into their famous newspaper. The most boring headline to appear in print was unanimously agreed to be: 'Small Earthquake in Chile: Not Many Hurt'. A routine disaster a long way away — is there anything with less power to attract our attention than that? But sometimes the scale of the disaster is so great that the news of it manages to sneak behind our mental defences. When hundreds of thousands, or even millions of people are involved, curiosity may get the better of long-established habit. When there are also colour photographs of the suffering, or television footage, curiosity may turn briefly to sympathy, or even indignation that too little is being done to help. Indignation may then be followed by a definite resolve to do something helpful for the distant victims, or at least to try and find out more about the causes of their plight.

The most dramatic recent distant disaster has been the terrible famine in Somalia, which occurred almost unnoticed, obscured by the civil wars in the Balkans. Terrible though the loss of human life has been, not to mention the suffering and the disruption experienced by those who have survived, these events will not have been entirely without mitigation if, as seems likely, they have created greater concern for the human misery endured by many in remote regions of the world.

The first lesson which great disasters like the Somalian famine should have taught is that, although disaster relief is the top priority in the short term, the long-term avoidance of vulnerability to disaster requires a successful development policy. Those who would transform their concern into more permanently constructive action will thus necessarily have to try to come to grips with development issues and the many debates which surround the question of devising a successful development policy. For a start, they will have a go back to their newspapers, weekly magazines and television programmes and discipline themselves to read and watch those boring bits. These should indeed become very much less boring, if one wrestles to make sense of them and fit them into an overall pattern. Not everything is going to fit in at the first, or even the second or third attempt. But many things do become clearer as one struggles to put different pieces of the development jigsaw together.

Widespread famine represents the most visible and most shocking distant disaster. But it is also a complex event, for which simple and obvious explanations will not always suffice. Famines can occur in the midst of plenty, when particular groups of people lose their accustomed means of access to the available food supply. Famine among

John Toye: 'Is the Third World Still There?' from *DILEMMAS OF DEVELOPMENT* (Basil Blackwell Ltd., 2nd ed., 1993), pp. 21-37.

pastoralists often occurs in a deteriorating natural environment. But it is difficult to sort out whether the deterioration has autonomous physical causes, or whether it results from population growth, or simple abuse of the habitat based on ignorance. And what role does politics play in causing famine? Cultivators who are moved on to new land for military reasons may be being put at risk, and governments may give or withhold relief supplies as a weapon in a political game.

A country will not suffer from famine just because its inhabitants are poor. India's per capita income lies in between those of Ethiopia and Sudan, but India has managed to avoid famines for all of the forty-odd years since she became independent.[1] There are many other poor countries which can make the same claim. Although at present famine and the threat of famine seem to haunt Africa, particularly sub-Saharan Africa, the contrast between Africa and Asia is not absolute. China experienced severe famine in the early 1960s, as did Bangladesh in the early 1970s. Clearly, the cause and the incidence of famine are not easy to unravel.

The reports from faraway places do not tell only of famine. Finance as well as food is currently a major issue of development policy. When the oil price rose by leaps and bounds in 1973 and again in 1979, its effect was to withdraw substantial amounts of purchasing power from oil-consuming economies, and to transfer these amounts in the first instance to oil producers who were unable all at once to spend their great increases in income. This was evidently a depressing influence on world economic activity and, in an attempt to lessen the impact of the depression, oil revenues (or petro-dollars) were 'recycled' by the private banking system. A large part of this recycling was done by lending petro-dollars to governments of poor countries, in the belief that this kind of lending ('sovereign debt') carried minimal risk of default. From 1973 to 1982, the governments of many countries took on more loans than they could possibly repay, given their ability to generate foreign exchange earnings. Their poor foreign exchange earning ability at the end of the borrowing spree indicated that many had borrowed more than they could invest in hard-currency-earning enterprises.

In the last few years, the media have carried many reports on this debt crisis, which was allowed to reach the point where the stability of some large private US banks began to be questioned, as well as where numerous governments of poor countries were pleading to have their debts re-scheduled. Bail-out plan has followed bail-out plan, bankers' revolts and debtors' revolts have come and gone, austerity packages have been devised, imposed, evaded and re-imposed. The crisis is far from over and its management shifts from tactic to tactic, trying to learn something along the way.[2]

Just as famine is said to be Africa's problem, so the debt crisis is said to be Latin America's. This is because it was Mexico and Brazil in 1982 who first indicated that their debt burden had become unsustainable. But no continent has exclusive proprietorship of particular development problems. Although ten of the fifteen countries which the IMF defines as heavily indebted are Latin American, three are African (Nigeria, Morocco and the Ivory Coast), one is Asian (Philippines) and one is European (the former Yugoslavia).

The examples of Mexico and Nigeria indicate that having indigenous supplies of oil was no guarantee of being able to avoid the debt crisis. Borrowing undertaken when the oil price was high quickly became unsustainable when the oil price softened and collapsed. The crux of the matter was never just the possession or non-possession of domestic oil supplies. It was the ability to manage resources well in the face of great turbulence in a key commodity price. India, though on balance hurt economically by the oil price rise, did not begin heavy commercial borrowing until the mid-1980s. The debt crisis did not reach India until the early 1990s.

In oil-exporting countries, the rapid growth of the 1970s has been followed by stagnation in the 1980s as the oil price has fallen. In addition to Mexico and Nigeria, it is the countries of the Middle East which have been the most seriously affected. In the 1980s, countries that relied on primary product exports had somewhat faster growth than the Middle East, benefiting from the slight acceleration in economic activity in industrialized countries after the trough of the recession in 1982. But the only group of poor countries to have grown consistently fast in the 1970s and 1980s are those that export manufactures. These include the newly industrializing countries (NICs) whose growth performance has been held up as a model for the development of countries still caught up in the toils of famine or debt.

It is important not to confuse economic growth, the expansion of the measured output of goods and services, with development. One can imagine some forms of economic growth that would not seem much like development. For example, output can be produced by the severe exploitation of labour — the payment of mere subsistence wages, bad health and safety conditions and the unfair treatment of workers — with the resulting profits being channelled to private bank accounts in foreign tax havens. This would be the kind of development that few people would vote for, if they were allowed to vote. So would growth that was accompanied by environmental pollution and gross overcrowding. The process of very rapid industrialization, new or old, can create widespread social distress and conflict, as well as previously undreamt-of levels of material wealth and technical advance.

These ambivalences of rapid industrialization are characteristic of what have become known to journalists as 'the four Asian tigers' — the two city-states of Hong Kong and Singapore, and the two larger political entities of South Korea and Taiwan. But these are not the only NICs. There is another important group in Eastern Europe (Romania, Hungary and Yugoslavia before its break-up), plus the big, heavily populated, countries which have pursued industrialization by import-substitution, India and Brazil.

Trying to make sense of the information which reaches us about poor countries a long way away seems, then, to lead to the identification of a set of contemporary problems — famine and the related problems of the production and distribution of food; the financing of development through the private banking system and the related problems of debt, the oil price, inflation and the choice of productive investments; and the social costs of rapid industrialization.

Although at first glance, it might appear that these problems were to be found in different continents — famine in Africa, the debt crisis in Latin America and the agony and the ecstasy of rapid industrialization in Asia — a closer look showed that this was not entirely so. Although each problem was concentrated to a noticeable degree in one continent more than the others, a sharp geographical demarcation of problem locations was not warranted. Similar phenomena appeared to a lesser degree elsewhere.

The continents of Africa, Asia and Latin America are diverse, both geographically and historically. This diversity accounts for the tendency of particular development problems to concentrate in particular continents. Asia has much greater pressure of population on cultivable land than Latin America or Africa, but Africa has a much more unfavourable ratio of food availability from domestic supply and imports to its food requirements than does Latin America, or (to a lesser extent) Asia. Land is but one term in the agricultural equation and other historical and geographical factors have put Africa at a special disadvantage.[3]

Latin America (apart from Colombia and Venezuela) is much more diversified economically than Africa, where even the discovery of oil has hardly altered the pattern of relying on one or two sectors to generate most export revenue. But Latin America has also drawn much more heavily than either Africa or Asia on foreign sources for its direct investment. So its economies are much more influenced by decisions taken by multinational corporations (particularly US multinationals) than are those of Asia or Africa (notably excepting Liberia). Politically, Latin America and Africa have been more prone to military *coups d'état*, while Asia has found greater political stability, although often by authoritarian means. Given these contrasts, it is explicable why Latin America has had less sustained rapid industrialization than parts of Asia and greater entanglement in the problems of international debt.

The basis of the Third World: politics and psychology

These continental contrasts, combined with the evident differences between the most pressing problems of development in different places, naturally lead people to ask whether there really is 'a Third World'. Does it make sense to lump the problems and circumstances of Latin America, Africa and Asia together as those of 'the Third World', and talk of that world in a way which inevitably emphasizes similarities rather than differences? Might it not be better to confine discussion of development policy to a regional rather than a global perspective?

In the flood of comment on the dilemmas of development policy, an abrasive new approach came strongly to the fore in the 1980s. This new approach has been called a counter-revolution in the theory and practice of development. The later chapters of this book look quite closely at the teaching of the apostles of this counter-revolution, to examine what they have to say and the evidence they produce for their views. But before going on to do that in a systematic way, it may be instructive to pick out first one particular opinion which is highly relevant to the question posed in the previous paragraph — does the Third World really exist?

The answer of the development counter-revolution is that the Third World exists only because it has been created. Further, the creative force was not history or geography, or economics. It was psychology and politics, namely 'Western guilt' and the politics of foreign aid, which between them conjured up 'the Third World'.

> The Third World and its antecedents and synonyms, such as the under-developed world, the less developed world and the developing world (all still used) and now also the South, are for all practical purposes the collection of countries whose governments, with the odd exception, demand and receive official aid from the West ... The Third World is the creation of foreign aid: without foreign aid there is no Third World.

(Bauer 1981: 87)

In turn, 'insistence on foreign aid is a major theme of the recent literature of Western guilt', which holds that the West is responsible for the poverty of most of Asia, Africa and Latin America. If there is no truth in this suggestion of 'responsibility' and no virtue in the policy of aid, as some development counter-revolutionaries believe, the Third World itself exists only as a kind of collective psychological delusion.

In responding to assertions of the kind just quoted, it is necessary to begin by examining the psychological and political aspects of the concept of a Third World. What truth is there in the suggestion that it denotes an association of countries dedicated to the moral blackmail of a guilt-afflicted West? Once the psychological and political influences on the identity of the Third World have been clarified, the further question of whether they share a common type of economy will be addressed.

In would be misleading to argue that being a Third World country is simply a matter of experiencing certain economic conditions and problems. There are also, and possibly even predominantly, psychological and political elements in 'Third Worldliness'. But they are of a distinctly different character than that alleged by the development counter-revolutionaries.

What then is the political significance of a Third World? The term has been traced to several different origins. In Europe in the 1920s, there was some talk in political circles of finding a 'third way', meaning a political programme that was neither explicitly capitalist nor explicitly socialist in orientation. The details of the programmes, clerical, fascist and business variants of social corporatism, are less important than the enduring idea that some third alternative was possible, and that the struggle between capitalism and socialism did not have to be all-engulfing. An alternative origin with a related connotation lies in the French term 'the third estate'. Just as, in the approach to the French Revolution, the third estate found its political opportunity in the quarrel between nobility and clergy, so at the end of the Second World War, the US-USSR conflict provided the political opportunity for independence in the less developed countries. The analogy here is with benefiting from the struggle between two superior forces, not merely surviving it.

This is not the political interpretation which the development counter-revolutionaries gave to the idea of the Third World. They ignored the struggle between two superpowers with opposing ideologies and, therefore, Third Worldism was seen by them as a form of hostility to the West which was inspired by a positive (if covert) preference for socialism. Hence their constant criticism of developing countries for socialistic behaviour, or what is read as such. Third World countries as a group were blamed for over-extended public sectors — which are actually smaller proportionally than that of the US is to the size of its total economy — and excessive reliance on government controls, even when those controls are known to be easily circumvented by private enterprise firms, which are nowhere near to being centrally planned in Soviet style.

If the political thrust of Third Worldism were merely anti-Western, it should have found some favour with those committed to socialism. But this presumption is wrong. On the contrary, 'radicals ... are usually reluctant to posit a third world, for they see most, perhaps all, of these countries as under-developed capitalist ones, tied in subordinately to the first world. Thus, the main radical view is that there are only two worlds, one of capitalism and one on Marxian socialism' (Griffin and Gurley, 1985: 1090). The orthodox socialist position is thus that the Third World does not exist, because it is really subordinated to the first, capitalist world. This is uncannily similar to the position of the counter-revolution itself, that the Third World only exists to the extent that it is able, by exploiting Western guilt feelings, to be insubordinate and anti-Western. The second world (socialism) did not recognize the third, on the pretext that it was really part of the first. But the first did not do so either, on the pretext that the third was indistinguishable from the second.

The political interpretation which the development counter-revolution gives to the concept of the Third World is one which derives from its continuing political engagement with the struggle against socialism. By the same token, the orthodox socialist position on the Third World derives, although much more self-consciously and with much more open public acknowledgement, from the struggle against capitalism. Both are declaring, in effect, that there cannot be independents or non-combatants in their ideological confrontations. It is precisely this kind of doctrinaire exclusiveness which fuelled, until the collapse of the USSR, the search for a 'third way'.

Moving on from political ideas to political practice, the origin of the Third World as an active group of cooperating countries was a desire to establish a strong group of neutrals during the US-USSR 'cold war'. Their aims were to avoid any entanglement with superpower rivalries and to safeguard their national sovereignty as (mainly) countries which had recently become independent of European colonial powers. In fact, the actual political coherence of the Third World nations as a group has been greater in relation to the politics of decolonization than in relation to the politics of US-USSR superpower rivalry. Ironically, the posture of non-alignment adopted by many Third World countries since 1961 was adhered to less strictly than the posture of opposition to colonialism and imperialism (Willetts 1978). It is the latter, rather than the now-defunct competition between capitalism and socialism as social systems and as power blocs, which holds the key to the politics of the Third World.

The advocates of a counter-revolution in development thinking place the emphasis the other way round from this. They stress the anti-West attitudes of Third Worldism, the West's irrational guilt that supposedly encourages these attitudes and the alleged crypto-socialist policies of Third World governments. For them, Third World politics is nothing if not a by-product of the cold war. That Third World politics is centrally about decolonization and the future security and prosperity of former colonial countries is thus denied and treated as an irrelevant distraction.

The basis for dismissing decolonization as the central Third World issue is the fact that some countries which are now generally recognized to be part of the Third World have been continuously independent of formal control by a foreign power at least since 1815. Paraguay, Saudi Arabia, Turkey and Nepal fall into this category (Crow and Thomas 1983: 11). There are a few other countries where either the period of colonization was relatively brief or relatively informal, such as Thailand, Iran and Ethiopia. The fact that colonial expansion was to this degree less than worldwide in its reach is taken as an argument against the political definition of the Third World in terms of the politics of decolonization. It is difficult to follow the logic of this. Some very inhospitable parts of the world are both relatively unattractive to foreign imperialists and relatively inaccessible for military conquest. But countries located there still share with their neighbours who have experienced colonization a common interest in avoiding it. There is no country so remote, so inaccessible and so well entrenched in its history of independence that it cannot become a battleground for foreign troops. The history of Afghanistan in the 1980s should illustrate that proposition vividly. And the real experience of colonization has been overwhelmingly more commonplace than the untutored fear of it.

Decolonization

'Decolonization', like 'Third World' itself, is a modern term of mid-twentieth-century vintage. The modern politics of decolonization have not directly affected Latin America very much, with the exception of Guyana and Surinam and the 1982 conflict over the Falklands/Malvinas. Most Central and South American countries had freed themselves from Spanish and Portuguese colonialism in the nineteenth century, only to find themselves, from the Monroe Doctrine of 1842 onwards, coming under the growing hemispheric overlordship of a rapidly industrializing United States. Thus by the end of the Second World War, and the arrival of the modern episode of decolonization, any declaration of non-alignment by the Latin American states would have been construed by the United States as a hostile act. Latin America, therefore, occupied a special position within the Third World. It was the first continent to liberate itself from colonialism and, yet, it was not able to participate fully in the political construction of the Third World.

The psychology of Third Worldism is the psychology of decolonization. If decolonization wrongly implies that the initiative for independence was always taken by the colonial powers, the psychology of Third Worldism can also be described as the psychology of national liberation (Chamberlain 1985: 1). The classic account of the psychology of national liberation was that of Fanon. According to Fanon, the social relationships of colonial societies denied the native populations a true human identity. True identity could only be achieved by a violent struggle against the colonialists who created and imposed a sub-human personality on the native. In turn, this historical necessity for redeeming violence created a dilemma for the supporters of decolonization in the colonial countries. Their support derived from a Western cultural humanism. But Western culture has to be rejected because it condemns violence and also because it is shot through with a radically biased hypocrisy. Its claim to universal values is said to be contradicted by the racism practised in the colonial situation.

41

Sartre paraphrased Fanon's essential message as follows: 'The rival blocks take opposite sides and hold each other in check; let us [i.e. the Third World] take advantage of this paralysis, let us burst into history, forcing it by our invasion into universality for the first time. Let us start fighting; and if we have no other arms, the waiting knife's enough' (Fanon 1967: 11). It was this message that led Sartre to conclude that 'the Third World finds itself and speaks to *itself* through [Fanon's] voice' (p. 9).

There is much to quarrel with in *The Wretched of the Earth*. The notion of redeeming violence is inexcusably romantic; the understanding of Western humanism is superficial: the politics of a national peasant revolution are wildly utopian. So one could go on. What it provides is neither an accurate description of colonialism, nor a useful prescription for how to overcome it. What it provides instead is an excellent intuitive account of the psycho-pathology caused by colonial wars and the deformations of values and vision caused by the acutely stressful conflicts of decolonization. How else than like Fanon could people feel, at the end of a long war of atrocity and counter-atrocity, such as that of Algerian liberation between 1954 and 1962?

Fanon usefully reminds Anglo-Saxon readers that decolonization has not just been a matter of the peaceful transfer of power by metropolitan countries benignly seeking the future welfare of colonial populations. Although in India the worst bloodshed was caused by communal violence within the newly independent country, Britain itself had conducted fierce military campaigns against 'terrorists' in countries soon to become independent, for example, in Palestine (1946-8), Kenya (1952-5), Malaya (1957-63), Cyprus (1956-60) and Aden in the 1960s. The war in Algeria, however, dwarfed all of these, with France committing an army of half a million men there by 1962. When decolonization intersected with superpower rivalry, as it did in Vietnam between 1965 and 1973, the scale of conflict was even larger. There the US committed over two million ground troops, of whom 55,000 were killed, while half a million Vietnamese were slaughtered in both ground and aerial bombing attacks.

The voices of the development counter-revolution speak of 'Western guilt' as the psychological force which gives coherence to the Third World. Western guilt is presented as an abstract neurosis, a subjective feeling detached from the objective circumstances of contemporary history. But objectively, colonial conflicts create intense brutalization and trauma on both sides. The effects do not cease when the conflict ceases. The intensification of racism and drug abuse in ex-colonial countries is directly connected to the brutalization of some participants and the trauma of others in the course of recent colonial wars. Anxiety about these self-inflicted social evils combines with the self-doubt of Western humanism described by Fanon to create a psychological unease which is well grounded in fact and history.

The ex-colonies themselves do not escape unscarred. The counter-revolution in development thinking is quick to condemn the many instances of illiberalism to be found in countries of the Third World. But is does not pause to consider the social forces which make oppression and persecution so relatively simple to organize. One important force is the great power of the army, often with foreign training and technology, when political independence comes at the end of a long armed struggle, as in Mozambique and

Zimbabwe. It takes immense political skill to keep the armed forces under civilian control in such circumstances. Too often that political skill is lacking.

The full trauma of the process of decolonization is not yet over. South Africa still has to find its way out from white settler colonialism, despite the fact that, since 1991, the apartheid legislation has begun to be dismantled. The pressure towards violence; the unwillingness of liberals to support wholeheartedly the national liberation struggle; the dragon's teeth, to use the phrase of Kiernan (1982: 227) about armies, sown in the course of conflict and bringing forth their harvest once the political victory has been won — all of these could be replayed one more time and perhaps more fiercely than ever before, in the years ahead.

The Third World is not, despite all that the development counter-revolution says, yet able to be dismissed from our minds. It is not a figment of our imagination ready to vanish when we blink. It is a result of our collective lack of imagination, our inability in our present difficult circumstances yet to see ourselves as belonging to one world, and not several.

The basis of the Third World: economics

The term 'Third World' when applied to a country is often taken to be synonomous with descriptions like underdeveloped, less developed and developing. But these latter terms have a different point of reference, the degree of economic and social backwardness. 'Underdeveloped' and 'less developed' imply relative backwardness, while 'developing' implies movement away from backwardness. That is, perhaps, clear enough. But what is 'backwardness'? Evidently, being at some remove from 'forwardness'. So what is 'forwardness'? Well, there can be more than one opinion about that, surely?

It is important to realize that an apparently neutral and scientific word like 'development' is no such thing. Definitions of the goals of development and of the process by which these goals should be striven for, unavoidably depend on the values of the person doing the defining, as well as on facts that are in principle falsifiable. Further, people's values are not identical, nor are they completely at variance, fortunately. Although all theories are to some extent contestable because of differences in values rather than problems of logic or observation, theories of development are particularly subject to disagreements arising out of value differences.

Modernization theory

The original theory of socioeconomic development that accompanied the post-1945 decolonization of Asia and Africa rested on the idea of modern society as the goal of development. Modern society supposedly had typical social patterns of demography, urbanization and literacy; typical economic patterns of production and consumption, investment, trade and government finance; and typical psychological attributes of rationality, ascriptive identity and achievement motivation. The process of development consisted, on this theory, of moving from traditional society, which was taken as the polar opposite of the modern type, through a series of stages of development — derived essentially from the history of Europe, North America and Japan — to modernity, that is, approximately the United States of the 1950s.

It was the idea of countries that were less developed (LDCs) according to the above modernization paradigm of development which was most closely linked in practice to the giving of foreign aid. Within this paradigm, Western experts have an extremely prominent and powerful position as guides and advisers in poor countries. Not only are their values being imported wholesale, usually without much awareness on anyone's part that this is what is happening, but Western technology is assumed to be appropriate and the embodied technology of Western machines and equipment is assumed to be transferrable with only modest difficulty. All of these assumptions are convenient to support large-scale capital aid programmes.

This theory and practice of development was bound to come into question before long. Leaving aside the social and psychological side of modernization theory and concentrating on the economic side, it had a conception of a typical less developed economy. This was predominantly agricultural, with small cultivators growing crops primarily for household subsistence needs. It had low rates of investment, low stocks of capital employed per worker and low rates of economic growth. The foreign trade sector was small, and so was the share of national resources passing through the government budget. Infrastructure was poor as a result of low government investment. The typical less developed economy admittedly showed some variation from place to place, but the variations were essentially natural. Some were islands, some were landlocked; some were big and some were small; some were arid, some were flood-prone; some were mountainous and some were on the plain. But all were typical less developed economies.[4]

Criticism gradually focused on the part of this story that concerned trade. Two main reasons for this focus stand out. The idea of development as the passage through a series of predetermined stages assumes that *timing* of the development process, in relation to the development of other countries, is of no major consequence. Countries can embark on their journey and reach their desired destination without regard for the timetables that others have followed, or are about to follow. In other words, development is independent, national development and there are no 'late developers' whose prospects are damaged by their very lateness. Trade forms part of the network of international interdependence. It is, therefore, one of the key linkages that binds the national development processes together — for better or worse.

The second reason why criticism of the idea of the typical LDC focused on trade was that the link did not appear, on inspection, to be of the negligible kind posited by modernization theory. Most LDCs seemed to have developed one or more major export sectors: specialized agricultural commodities like cocoa, bananas, sugar or tea; raw materials like rubber or jute; or minerals particularly copper, tin or bauxite. Moreover, 'underdeveloped countries generally trade with advanced countries and not with each other. This pattern is clearly quite unlike that of an "untouched" pre-capitalist economy ...' (Brewer 1980: 9). This raised the possibility not allowed for in modernization accounts of development that the typical LDC economy had already been shaped by its trade contacts with other countries into a distorted form, from which a 'normal' development process, through the usual stages of modernization, would not be possible.

This possibility was seized on as a certainty by some writers in the 1960s who believed that modernization theory was a way of denying the adverse economic effects of colonial rule and legitimizing foreign aid as an instrument to maintain former, colonial patterns of international relations. The nexus of international exchange, often referred to loosely as 'the capitalist system', was credited with the major role in creating the specific form of backwardness found in the Third World. This specific form was called 'underdevelopment': it was not a pristine condition of low productivity and poverty but an historical condition of blocked, distorted and dependent development.

It is this conception of underdevelopment created by the capitalist system which the counter-revolution in development rejects most vehemently. Rightly so, because it is an extreme position, the logical and empirical supports for which were never properly worked out by its own advocates. In adopting this position for the decade between 1965 and 1975, its partisans were allowing values, in this case strident anti-imperialism, to dominate almost completely their choice of theory.

The theory of underdevelopment implied a continuous polarization in income and welfare between developed and underdeveloped countries. However, the normal indicators of income and welfare did not show that such a polarization was taking place. The average rate of growth of income per head in both groups of countries was, between 1950 and 1975, just over 3 per cent a year. If anything (though recalling that these kinds of statistics are subject to large margins of error), the under-developed group grew more quickly, indicating a slight movement towards closing the relative income gap (Morawetz 1977: 26). A rate of growth of just over 3 per cent a year was also faster than that of today's developed countries during the second half of the nineteenth century.

Physical indicators told a story that was consistent with that of the group growth rates. Between 1950 and 1979, life expectancy rose on average in all developing countries from 43 to 58 years, while literacy rose from 33 to 56 persons in every hundred and the mortality rate in children between 1 and 4 years old fell from 28 to 12 per thousand. Again, these rates of improvement are faster than those experienced by today's developed countries during their period of fastest development. At the same time, there is still massive scope for further improvement before developing countries reach the levels of health and education currently enjoyed by today's developed countries (Killick 1986).

If the facts rule against the idea of a long-period process of polarization between rich countries and poor, there is no need to spend time discussing the causes of such a process. However, that does not mean that one must deny that colonialism produced negative economic effects. Certain pre-colonial forms of economic activity were destroyed, certain colonial investments were inappropriate except within the context of colonialism itself and liberation conflicts have often burdened countries after independence with costly and turbulent military establishments. Economies have been distorted by colonialism in a way which hampers their future action for development. But these negative effects are not insuperable; they can be struggled against successfully. In the end, whatever the extent of the economic damage of colonialism, countries which do nothing but persuade themselves that they are the victims of history will let slip such opportunities for development as they do have now.

The evident absence of a long-period process of polarization should lead us neither to deny the negative economic impacts of colonialism nor to deny short-period setbacks which developing countries have experienced as a group. Certainly, since about 1980, economic recession has badly affected all countries, developed and developing, by greatly slowing their growth of income per head. It has also affected the developing countries as a group more seriously than the developed countries. Any past tendency for the relative income gap to narrow has thus, since 1980, been put into reverse. The main causes of the present severe slackening in developing countries' growth have been falling commodity prices, rising real interest rates and the reduction in concessional and other financial flows (Singh 1986).

What at present appears to be a short-period interruption to a long period of buoyant growth may, unless wise policy action is taken, stretch out some considerable way into the future. The prospects for quick remedies to the specific problems of debt, food availability and falling export prices do not at present (early 1993) seem bright, although one always hopes that such statements will be disproved.

Growing diversity in the Third World

But looking at the economic performance of developing countries only as a group would conceal something that is highly relevant to the question of whether, from an economic perspective, the Third World is still with us. For within the average results for the whole Third World group, an increasing differentiation between regions and types of countries has been taking place. The growth that has been achieved has not been uniform and across the board. It has affected some countries and some regions very much more than others. As a result, the Third World in the last twenty years has increasingly departed from economic homogeneity.

The relative position of Africa has worsened steadily during the last twenty years, with the continent as a whole seeing little growth in the 1970s and falls in output in the 1980s. Some African countries were not affected by stagnation (for example, Cameroon and Tunisia), but the general picture has been very bleak. More recently, economic retrogression has extended itself, via the debt crisis and falling oil prices, to Central and Latin America and the OPEC countries. Economies least affected by the recession of the 1980s were those already growing very fast. Important in this group were the East Asian economies achieving their growth through investment in industries that could produce manufactured exports, plus India and China, who were following an inward-looking strategy of industrialization.

The differentiation within the Third World economies has resulted in two very different responses, one at each end of the economic spectrum. At the top, a debate has been begun on the issue of 'graduation', that is, the formal recognition that a developing country has developed sufficiently for it no longer to be regarded as a developing country. Rather little has been achieved except verbal sparring on the graduation issue. Whatever its degree of economic progress, a developing country is reluctant to graduate, because it thereby loses its access to certain privileged financial facilities, like concessional World Bank loans. There is also reluctance on the part of international organizations concerned with developing country interests to lose the participation of their more successful and powerful members. These institutional pressures obscure the degree of differentiation that has taken place at the top of the group.

At the bottom of the group, however, the inhibitions to recognition have been less powerful. Although UNCTAD was initially unhappy about doing so, a separate lower-end sub-group has been identified since 1979 among the members of the 'Group of 77' (which confusingly contains over 100 Third World countries). This sub-group is composed of 31 'least developed countries', also known as LLDCs. The LLDCs are defined as countries with an average income of less than $100 per head, an adult literacy rate of less than 20 per cent and a manufacturing sector which provides less than 10 per cent of gross domestic product. The Third World average for literacy was 56 per cent and for share of industry in output was about 20 per cent in 1980.

The emergence of the LLDCs is a reflection of the particular development problem faced by small, underpopulated and often landlocked African states like Chad, Mali, Niger, Burkina Faso, Uganda, Malawi, Rwanda and Burundi. In all, Africa has two-thirds of all LLDCs. With a few exceptions like Nepal, Ethiopia and Afghanistan, the great majority of LLDCs are former European colonies.

What has happened then over the last forty years has been neither the uncomplicated succession of economic take-offs which modernization theory predicted, nor the continuously growing gap in income and welfare between the rich countries and the poor countries prophesied by underdevelopment theorists. Instead, there has been a combination of some take-offs, mainly in East Asia, and some severe cases of economic retrogression, mainly in Africa. Thus the polarization that has taken place has done so *within* the Third World, but not between the Third World taken as a group and the developed economies of the non-socialist world.

Does this intra-Third World economic differentiation matter? The answer to this depends on one's values and viewpoint. Politically, it makes the cohesion of the Third World more difficult, as conflicts between different sub-groups increase. In the 1970s, such a conflict was always threatening between the oil exporters and the oil importers in the Third World. In the 1980s, with new commercial lending almost non-existent, the main conflict was over the division of the remaining concessional finance between the least developed countries — whose need is greater — and the rest — whose ability to use the finance productively is probably greater. So to all who see the building up of the political unity of the Third World as the major task, economic differentiation does matter because it makes that task more difficult.

Economically, what most people would say mattered ultimately is the ending of large-scale poverty. It is the sickness, ignorance and premature death, not to mention the violence, ugliness and despair of daily life, which accompany poverty and underemployment, that revolt most people. Those things can be found in any Third World country on a scale that would never be tolerated elsewhere and they must be eliminated as quickly as humanly possible. Thus increasing inequality between countries is, in itself, a matter of indifference. What matters is whether mass poverty is expanding or contracting and whether the means are at hand for doing something effective to reduce it. Economic development should have as its fundamental objective the reduction of poverty (cf. World Bank 1990: 24).

If that is how one sees things, then it could be argued further that inequality within Third World countries is of concern to the extent that it prevents the reduction of mass poverty. How much scope does the existing degree of inequality provide for redistributing resources towards the desperately poor? What incentives are necessary to encourage and sustain economic growth and increase the resources available for redistribution? How much of the existing inequalities arise from oppression and exploitation which cause and perpetuate poverty, as well as being intrinsically unjust? Although judgements are hard to make in particular cases, these at least are the relevant questions about inequality. They suggest that the reduction of inequality should be seen as a secondary rather than a primary goal of development policy. Inequality appears to have no systematic link with poverty in the Third World, or indeed with the type of economic system — capitalist or socialist — which is in operation. Income distribution is only slightly less unequal in Nepal than in Brazil, and among the more equal distributions, there is nothing to choose between that of Tanzania and that of Thailand. Simple guidelines are not forthcoming from the bald statistics.

Backwardness, and specifically the interaction between poverty and inequality, can thus take many varied forms. As Griffin and Gurley remarked 'heterogeneity is the name of the game in the Third World' (1985: 1090). The development counter-revolutionaries are right when they criticize envisaging 'the Third World as an undifferentiated, passive entity, helplessly at the mercy of its environment and of the powerful West' (Bauer 1981: 84). Economically, it is certainly not undifferentiated, one of the differences being precisely in the extent to which particular countries are exposed to hazards either of their natural environment, or of their international economic environment.[5]

Politically, too, the Third World is not passive, although it certainly is relatively weak. This weakness has always been recognised as stemming in part from lack of unity and the absence of solidarity. As long ago as 1961, Sartre wrote of the Third World:

> We know that it is not a homogeneous world; we know too that enslaved peoples are still to be found there; together with some who have achieved a simulacrum of phoney independence, others who are still fighting to attain sovereignty and others again who have obtained complete freedom, but who live under the constant menace of imperialist aggression ... Thus the unity of the Third World is not yet achieved. It is a work in progress ...

(Fanon 1967: 9-10)

From the 1950s onwards, much has been done to strengthen the collective organization of Third World states, both as a global grouping and at the level of regional co-operation. Most recently, as the recession has undermined their economic prospects, certain developed countries have come out in open opposition to the Third World's political pretensions, particularly in the United Nations organizations where the one vote per country system of decision-making operates. However one cares to evaluate these trends, the Third World cannot correctly be described as either passive or homogeneous. It has been actively seeking a political unity it does not yet fully possess.

Notes

1. See the dicussion of India's experience with famine, in contrast with that of China, in Sen (1983: 757-60).

2. The origins and current state of the debt crisis are discussed in more detail in chapter 8.

3. The varying characteristics of soils in tropical areas can be found in brief in Kamarck (1976: 22-9).

4. The failure of development economists to take some of these natural variations more seriously as discriminators of radically different modes of rural economy has been attacked by economic anthropologists, notably Polly Hill (see Grillo and Rew 1985: 117-30).

5. Mention of the hazards of developing countries' natural environments serves to remind us of one unifying characteristic of the Third World which has been insufficiently stressed in the foregoing discussion. Many Third World countries share, by virtue of their geographical location, a special set of hazards which the now developed countries did not have to negotiate successfully — namely poor soils for agriculture, abundant pests and plagues of predators and the tropical diseases of trypanosomiasis, bilharzia, malaria, river blindness and hookworm disease (Kamarck 1976: passim). The degree of exposure to these tropical hazards does differ between individual Third World countries, however, as does the ability to adopt policies that will reduce the degree of exposure. In the context of the development counter-revolution's account of the Third World, it is interesting to note that the references to climatic influences on development prospects which are to be found in Bauer (1972) disappear in his subsequent books (1981, 1984).

4.   What Do We Know About The Poor?
The World Bank

Reducing poverty is the fundamental objective of economic development. It is estimated that in 1985 more than one billion people in the developing world lived in absolute poverty. Clearly, economic development has a long way to go. Knowledge about the poor is essential if governments are to adopt sound development strategies and more effective policies for attacking poverty. How many poor are there? Where do they live? What are their precise economic circumstances? Answering these questions is the first step toward understanding the impact of economic policies on the poor. This chapter draws on a number of detailed household surveys done over the past ten years or so, including some conducted by the World Bank, to estimate the number of poor people and to establish what is known about them.

Three poor families

We begin by focusing on the people this Report is intended to help — by telling the stories of three poor families living in three different countries. These families have much in common. For them, the difference between a tolerable quality of life and mere survival depends on their capacity to work and on their opportunities to work. Lack of education, landlessness, and acute vulnerability to illness and seasonal hard times affect all of them to varying degrees. Problems such as these are at the core of poverty.

A poor subsistence farmer's household in Ghana

In Ghana's Savannah region a typical family of seven lives in three one-room huts made from mud bricks, with earthen floors. They have little furniture and no toilet, electricity, or running water. Water is obtained from a stream a fifteen minute walk away. The family has few possessions, apart from three acres of unirrigated land and one cow, and virtually no savings.

The family raises sorghum, vegetables, and groundnuts on its land. The work is seasonal and physically demanding. At peak periods of tilling, sowing, and harvesting, all family members are involved, including the husband's parents, who are sixty and seventy years old. The soil is very low in quality, but the family lacks access to fertilizer and other modern inputs. Moreover, the region is susceptible to drought; the rains fail two years out of every five. In addition to her farm work, the wife has to fetch water, collect firewood, and feed the family. The market town where the husband sells their meager cash crops and buys essentials is five miles away and is reached by dirt tracks and an unsealed road that is washed away every time the rains come.

None of the older family members ever attended school, but the eight-year-old son is now in the first grade. The family hopes that he will be able to stay in school, although there is pressure to keep him at home to help with the farm in the busy periods. He and his two younger sisters have never had any vaccinations and have never seen a doctor.

A poor urban household in Peru

In a shantytown on the outskirts of Lima a shack made of scraps of wood, iron, and cardboard houses a family of six. Inside there is a bed, a table, a radio, and two benches. The kitchen consists of a small kerosene stove and some tins in one corner. There is no toilet or electricity. The shantytown is provided with some public services, but these tend to be intermittent. Garbage is collected twice a week. Water is delivered to those who have a cement tank, but this family has been unable to save enough for the cement. In the meantime, the mother and eldest daughter fill buckets at the public standpipe 500 yards away.

Husband and wife are Indians from the same mountain village in the Sierra. Neither completed primary school. They came to Lima with two children almost four years ago, hoping to find work and schools. Although they have jobs, the economic recession of the past few years has hit them hard. Better-off neighbors who arrived in Lima three to six years before they did say that it was easier to get ahead then. Still, husband and wife are hopeful that they will soon be able to rebuild their house with bricks and cement and, in time, install electricity, running water, and a toilet like their neighbors. They now have four children, after losing one infant, and the two oldest attend the local community school, recently built with funds and assistance from a nongovernmental organization (NGO). All the children were given polio and diphtheria-pertussis-tetanus (DPT) inoculations when a mobile clinic came to the shantytown. Community solidarity is strong, and a community center is active in the shantytown.

The father works in construction as a casual laborer. The work is uncertain, and there are periods when he must take any odd job he can find. When he is hired on a construction site, however, it is frequently for a month or so. His wife worries that he will be injured on the job like some of his fellow workers, who can no longer work and yet receive no compensation. She earns some income doing laundry at a wealthy person's house twice a week. To get there she must take a long bus ride, but the job does enable her to look after her one- and three-year-old children. She is also in charge of all domestic chores at home. When she is away from the house for long periods, the two oldest children take morning and afternoon turns at school so as not to leave the house unattended. There have been many burglaries in the neighborhood recently, and although the family has few possessions, radios and kerosene stoves are much in demand. The family lives on rice, bread, and vegetable oil (all subsidized by the government), supplemented with vegetables and, occasionally, some fish.

A poor landless laborer's household in Bangladesh

In a rural community in a drought-prone region of Bangladesh a landless laborer and his family attempt to get through another lean season.

Their house consists of a packed mud floor and a straw roof held up by bamboo poles from which dry palm leaves are tied to serve as walls. Inside there is straw to sleep on and burlap bags for warmth. The laborer and his wife, three children, and niece do not own the land on which the shack is built. They are lucky, however, to have a kindly neighbor who has indefinitely lent them the plot and a little extra on which they are able to grow turmeric and ginger and have planted a jackfruit tree.

The father is an agricultural day laborer and tends to be underemployed most of the year. During slow agricultural periods in the past he could sometimes find nonagricultural wage labor — for example, in construction in a nearby town — but he lost the strength to do much strenuous work after a bout of paratyphoid. He therefore engages in petty services around the village for very low pay.

The wife typically spends her day cooking, caring for the children, husking rice, and fetching water from the well. She is helped in these tasks by her thirteen-year-old niece, whose parents died in a cholera epidemic some years ago. The woman and her niece are always on the lookout for ways to earn a little extra. Such work as husking rice, weeding fields, and chopping wood is sometimes available from better-off neighbors. The nine-year-old son attends school a few mornings a week in a town an hour's walk away. The rest of the day he and his seven-year-old sister gather fuel and edible roots and weeds. The sister also looks after the baby when her mother or cousin cannot.

The household spends about 85 percent of its meager income on food — predominantly rice. Family members are used to having only two meals a day. They hope to struggle through to the rice harvest without having to cut down and sell their jackfruit tree or the bamboo poles supporting their roof.

Measuring poverty

These are the people behind the statistics. Lifting them out of poverty will depend to a large extent on a better understanding of how many poor there are, where they live, and, above all, why they are poor. None of these questions turns out to be straightforward. To begin with, it is necessary to be more precise about what "poverty" really means.

Poverty is not the same as inequality. The distinction needs to be stressed. Whereas poverty is concerned with the absolute standard of living of a part of society — the poor — inequality refers to relative living standards across the whole society. At maximum inequality one person has everything and, clearly, poverty is high. But minimum inequality (where all are equal) is possible with zero poverty (where no one is poor) as well as with maximum poverty (where all are poor).

This Report defines poverty as the inability to attain a minimal standard of living. To make this definition useful, three questions must be answered. How do we measure the standard of living? What do we mean by a minimal standard of living? And, having thus identified the poor, how do we express the overall severity of poverty in a single measure or index?

Measuring the standard of living

Household incomes and expenditures per capita are adequate yardsticks for the standard of living as long as they include own production, which is very important for most of the world's poor (Box 2.1). Neither measure, however, captures such dimensions of welfare as health, life expectancy, literacy, and access to public goods or common-property resources. Being able to get clean drinking water, for example, matters to one's standard of living, but it is not reflected in consumption or income as usually measured. Households with access to free public services are better off than those without, even though their incomes and expenditures may be the same. Because of these drawbacks, this Report supplements a consumption-based poverty measure with others, such as nutrition, life expectancy, under 5 mortality, and school enrollment rates.

Box 2.1 How should we measure living standards?

Current consumption (including consumption from own production) reflects households' ability to buffer their standard of living through saving and borrowing, despite income fluctuations. To that extent, consumption is a better measure of well-being than income. A study of Sri Lanka, however, found that both consumption and income indicators identified the same people, by and large, as poor. Furthermore, current consumption may not be a good measure of a household's typical standard of living (although it is probably better than current income). In another study, which looked at a set of Indian households over nine years, 54 percent of households, on average, were deemed poor on the basis of current-year consumption. Slightly fewer, 50 percent, were deemed poor on the basis of their nine-year mean consumption.

Another problem is that different households may face different prices. In developing countries prices often vary between urban and rural areas. A study of Sri Lanka that allowed for this difference found that price variability made little difference to estimates of poverty. In bigger countries, however, rural-urban differences are a more significant problem. In Indonesia, for example, regional price differentials are large and affect regional comparisons of poverty.

Household size and composition are also relevant. Researchers estimate "equivalent adult scales" based on the consumption needs of individuals according to age, sex, and activity. Allowing for household composition in the Sri Lanka estimates, however, yielded a poverty estimate similar to that based on the per capita measures; the overlap in classifying people as poor was 90 percent.

Such corrections typically assume that the distribution of consumption within the household is equal. What if this is not the case? A recent study of data for the Philippines concluded that allowing for inequality in distribution might change the figures for the overall incidence of poverty but not the pattern across socio-economic groups.

The poverty line

All the measures described above are judged in relation to some norm. For example, we deem life expectancies in some countries to be low in relation to those attained by other countries at a given date. The choice of the norm is particularly important in the case of the consumption-based measures of poverty.

A consumption-based poverty line can be thought of as comprising two elements: the expenditure necessary to buy a minimum standard of nutrition and other basic necessities and a further amount that varies from country to country, reflecting the cost of participating in the everyday life of society. The first part is relatively straightforward. The cost of minimum adequate caloric intakes and other necessities can be calculated by looking at the prices of the foods that make up the diets of the poor. The second part is far more subjective; in some countries indoor plumbing is a luxury, but in others it is a "necessity".

The perception of poverty has evolved historically and varies tremendously from culture to culture. Criteria for distinguishing poor from nonpoor tend to reflect specific national priorities and normative concepts of welfare and rights. In general, as countries become wealthier, their perception of the acceptable minimum level of consumption — the poverty line — changes. Figure 2.1 plots country-specific poverty lines against per capita consumption (both in 1985 purchasing power parity — PPP — dollars) for thirty-four developing and industrial countries. The poverty threshold rises slowly at low levels of average consumption but more sharply at higher levels.

Figure 2.1   Poverty and average standards of living, developed and developing countries *(1985 PPP dollars per capita a year)*

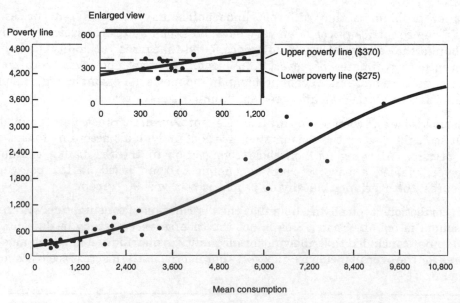

Note: PPP, purchasing power parity

When discussing poverty within countries, this Report uses country-specific poverty lines. In this chapter and in Chapter 9, however, a universal poverty line is needed to permit cross-country comparison and aggregation. This global poverty line is inevitably somewhat arbitrary. Rather than settle for a single number, this chapter employs two: $275 and $370 per person a year. (The amounts are in constant 1985 PPP prices.) This range was chosen to span the poverty lines estimated in recent studies for a number of countries with low average incomes — Bangladesh, the Arab Republic of Egypt, India, Indonesia, Kenya, Morocco, and Tanzania (see the inset in Figure 2.1). The lower limit of the range coincides with a poverty line commonly used for India.

How much poverty is there?

Once the poor have been distinguished from the nonpoor, the simplest way to measure poverty is to express the number of poor as a proportion of the population. This *headcount index* is a useful measure, although it is often criticized because it ignores the extent to which the poor fall below the poverty line. The income shortfall, or *poverty gap*, avoids this drawback. It measures the transfer that would bring the income of every poor person exactly up to the poverty line, thereby eliminating poverty. This Report relies on both the headcount index and the poverty gap. Box 2.2 discusses some other measures.

The use of the upper poverty line — $370 — gives an estimate of 1,115 million people in the developing countries in poverty in 1985. That is roughly one-third of the total population of the developing world. Of these, 630 million — 18 percent of the total population of the developing world — were extremely poor: their annual consumption was less than $275, the lower poverty line. Despite these massive numbers, the aggregate poverty gap — the transfer needed to lift everybody above the poverty line — was only 3 percent of developing countries' total consumption. The transfer needed to lift everybody out of extreme poverty was, of course, even smaller — just 1 percent of developing countries' consumption. Mortality for children under 5 averaged 121 per thousand for all developing countries, aggregate life expectancy was 62 years, and the overall net primary school enrollment rate was 83 percent. These figures hide considerable variation within and among countries. Table 2.1 sets out a detailed regional breakdown of these estimates.

Although care has been taken to make the table as precise as possible, the margins of error are inevitably wide, and the figures, it must be stressed, are only estimates. The quality of the underlying data varies. Reputable household income and expenditure surveys have been used where available. These surveys encompass 2.5 billion people, or almost 75 percent of the total. For other countries, including most of the Sub-Saharan Africa, extrapolations have been made on the basis of indicators that are strongly correlated with the measures of poverty derived from the household surveys. The notes to Table 2.1 give calculations of the potential imprecision of the estimates as a result of inadequacies in the data.

Box 2.2 Does how we measure poverty really matter?

The poverty gap and the headcount index are insensitive to the extent of inequality among the poor. If income is transferred from a poor person to someone who is poorer, neither measure changes. Distributionally sensitive measures are designed to capture such effects.

Suppose we want to know how an increase in the price of basic food staples affects poverty. A recent study examined this question for Java, Indonesia, using data for 1981. Households close to the poverty line were found to be, on average, net producers of rice, the main food staple. Thus, the headcount index of poverty will fall when the price of rice increases — assuming that this price change is passed on to producers. But the study found that the poorest of the poor — many of them landless agricultural laborers or farmers with little land but with some other source of income — are net consumers of rice. They are worse off, at least in the short run, when the price of rice increases. The study showed that measures that take the severity of poverty into account tend to show an increase in poverty when the price of rice goes up — exactly the opposite of the message conveyed by the headcount index.

Consider next the design of a scheme for transferring income to the poor. If success is judged solely by the headcount index, it is plain that the money should go first to the least poor because a given transfer will push more of them over the poverty line. Small transfers to the poorest of the poor will have absolutely no effect on the headcount measure of poverty. A similar issue arises in designing public employment schemes. For a given budget, a scheme can aim for wide coverage at low wages, leaving many participants still in poverty (albeit better off), or it can ration participation at a wage rate sufficient to allow more people to rise above the threshold.

So, although simple poverty measures often give a good indication of what has happened to poverty over time, for many other purposes — including evaluations of the effects of policy on poverty — it is necessary to look carefully at the distribution of income below the poverty line.

Nearly half of the developing world's poor, and nearly half of those in extreme poverty, live in South Asia. Sub-Saharan Africa has about one-third as many poor, although in relation to the region's overall population, its poverty is roughly as high. Table 2.1 also shows that both South Asia and Sub-Saharan Africa have low scores on several other social indicators; in Sub-Saharan Africa, in particular, life expectancy and primary school enrollment rates are alarmingly low, and under 5 mortality rates are alarmingly high. The Middle Eastern and Northern African countries have the next highest poverty, according to all the indicators. They are followed by Latin America and the Caribbean and by East Asia. China's overall performance is impressive, although the size of its population means that a relatively low headcount index still translates into large numbers of poor.

Table 2.1 How much poverty is there in the developing countries? The situation in 1985

Region	Extremely poor			Poor (including extremely poor)			Social indicators		
	Number (millions)	Headcount index (percent)	Poverty gap	Number (millions)	Headcount index (percent)	Poverty gap	Under 5 mortality (per thousand)	Life expectancy (years)	Net primary enrollment rate (percent)
Sub-Saharan Africa	120	30	4	180	47	11	196	50	56
East Asia	120	9	0.4	280	20	1	96	67	96
China	80	8	1	210	20	3	58	69	93
South Asia	300	29	3	520	51	10	172	56	74
India	250	33	4	420	55	12	199	57	81
Eastern Europe	3	4	0.2	6	8	0.5	23	71	90
Middle East and North Africa	40	21	1	60	31	2	148	61	75
Latin America and the Caribbean	50	12	1	70	19	1	75	66	92
All developing countries	633	18	1	1,116	33	3	121	62	83

Note: The poverty line in 1985 PPP dollars is $275 per capita a year for the extremely poor and $370 per capita a year for the poor.
The headcount index is defined as the percentage of the population below the poverty line. The 95 percent confidence intervals around the point estimates for the headcount indices are Sub-Saharan Africa, 19, 76; East Asia, 21, 22; South Asia, 50, 53; Eastern Europe, 7, 10; Middle East and North Africa, 13, 51; Latin America and the Caribbean, 14, 30; and all developing countries, 28, 39.
The poverty gap is defined as the aggregate income shortfall of the poor as a percentage of aggregate consumption. Under 5 mortality rates are for 1980-85, except for China and South Asia, where the period is 1975-80.
Source: Hill and Pebley 1988, Ravallion and others (background paper), and United Nations and World Bank data 1989.

The characteristics of the poor

If governments are to reduce poverty or to judge how their economic policies affect poverty, they need to know a lot about the poor. For example, information on how the poor derive and spend their incomes can help policymakers assess how changes in relative prices will affect real income. Policies targeted directly to the poor can hardly succeed unless governments know who the poor are and how they respond to policies and to their environment. Unfortunately, gathering this sort of information is not always easy. The poor are heterogeneous, and data about their characteristics are patchy. The following discussion looks at where the poor live, the size and composition of their households, what they do for a living, what they own and purchase, what risks they face, and how they fit into the society around them.

Rural and urban poverty

In many countries poverty has a significant regional dimension. In general, it is more common in areas with low average incomes, but the link is sometimes surprisingly weak. Figure 2.2 plots the headcount index of poverty (in the upper panel) and the infant mortality rate (in the lower panel) against average monthly consumption per capita for urban and rural areas in India. At any given level of consumption, the headcount index and (especially) the infant mortality rate can vary widely. This underlines the need to look beyond average incomes to the distribution of income and the provision of social services.

Figure 2.2 Poverty and infant mortality rates, India, 1983, by urban and rural areas of states

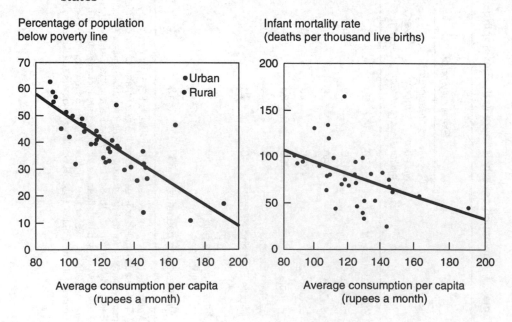

Source: Datt and Ravallion 1990 (upper panel); India 1987 (lower panel)

Poverty as measured by low income tends to be at its worst in rural areas, even allowing for the often substantial differences in cost of living between town and countryside. The problems of malnutrition, lack of education, low life expectancy, and substandard housing are also, as a rule, more severe in rural areas. This is still true in Latin America, despite high urbanization rates. The importance of rural poverty is not always understood, partly because the urban poor are more visible and more vocal than their rural counterparts. In 1980 El Salvador's infant mortality rate was 81 per thousand live births in rural areas and 48 in the towns; the incidence of malnutrition was five times higher in Peru's Sierra than in Lima. Table 2.2 confirms that in many countries rural poverty is a critical factor in the overall incidence and depth of poverty.

Table 2.2   Rural and urban poverty in the 1980s

Region and country	Rural population as percentage of total	Rural poor as percentage of total	Infant mortality (per thousand live births)		Access to safe water (percentage of population)	
			Rural	Urban	Rural	Urban
Sub-Saharan Africa						
Côte d' Ivoire	57	86	121	70	10	30
Ghana	65	80	87	67	39	93
Kenya	80	96	59	57	21	61
Asia						
India	77	79	105	57	50	76
Indonesia	73	91	74	57	36	43
Malaysia	62	80	..	..	76	96
Philippines	60	67	55	42	54	49
Thailand	70	80	43	28	66	56
Latin America						
Guatemala	59	66	85	65	26	89
Mexico	31	37	79	29	51	79
Panama	50	59	28	22	63	100
Peru	44	52	101	54	17	73
Venezuela	15	20	..	..	80	80

The extent of poverty can vary greatly among rural areas within the same country. The acute deprivation in Brazil's Northeast Region, which has more than 50 percent of the country's poor but only 27 percent of its total population, is well known. Regional disparities are equally stark in many other countries. Thailand's Northeast Region, Cote d'Ivoire's Savannah, Indonesia's Nusa Tenggara, the Andean highlands of Bolivia, Ecuador, Guatemala, and Peru, rural Gansu Province in China, parts of the central Asian region of the U.S.S.R., and Appalachia in the United States are all areas of concentrated poverty.

Many of the poor are located in regions where arable land is scarce, agricultural productivity is low, and drought, floods, and environmental degradation are common. In Latin America, for example, the worst poverty occurs predominantly in arid zones or in steep hill-slope areas that are ecologically vulnerable. Such areas are often isolated in every sense. Opportunities for nonfarm employment are few, and the demand for labor tends to be highly seasonal. Others among the poor live in regions that have a more promising endowment of natural resources but lack access to social services (education and health) and infrastructure (irrigation, information and technical assistance, transport, and market centers).

Although urban incomes are generally higher and urban services and facilities more accessible, poor town-dwellers may suffer more than rural households from certain aspects of poverty. The urban poor, typically housed in slums or squatter settlements, often have to contend with appalling overcrowding, bad sanitation, and contaminated water. The sites are often illegal and dangerous. Forcible eviction, floods and landslides, and chemical pollution are constant threats. Some of these people are migrants from the countryside who are seeking better-paid work. For many, particularly in Latin America, migration is permanent. For others, as in East Africa and parts of Southeast Asia, it may be temporary, reflecting (for example) seasonality in agriculture. The effect that migration to the towns has on poverty depends crucially on whether urban employment opportunities are better or worse than in rural areas. The evidence suggests that urban areas do offer more opportunities for higher-paid work, and this implies that, on balance, urbanization helps to reduce poverty.

What are the demographic characteristics of the poor?

Households with the lowest income per person tend to be large, with many children or other economically dependent members. In Pakistan in 1984 the poorest 10 percent of households had an average of 7.7 members, of whom 3.3 were children under age 9. The corresponding national averages were 6.1 and 2.0. Lack of a fit male adult can be crucial, especially if women have small children to care for or are culturally discouraged from taking paid employment.

Does family size determine living standards, or is it the other way around? The decision to have many children can be a sensible response to poverty. Mortality is high for children in destitute families, but it is essential to ensure that some children survive to support the household in the parents' old age, if not sooner. Even before they can earn income, children can free adults from various domestic tasks. Still, many poor parents report that they want no more children and that their last-born child had been unwanted. These couples often lack access to modern family planning services.

In the rural areas of many developing countries the aged often rely on the extended family — a structure that tends to be stable over time. In urban areas multigenerational households are more likely to break up, and the elderly are becoming more vulnerable. Moreover, traditions such as kinship in Africa and the duty of sons in India and Bangladesh to care for widowed mothers may be in decline. In India widows without an adult son are already a particularly underprivileged group.

Poverty and hunger among children is of particular concern. The very young are highly susceptible to disease, and malnutrition and poverty-related illnesses can cause permanent harm. Child poverty is strongly self-perpetuating. Child labor is common; many households depend on it, and much of the work has the social purpose of engaging the child in family activities. But work is often at the expense of schooling. For many poor people the opportunity costs of sending children to school outweigh the future benefits — especially for girls, whose economic value is often reckoned to be lower in various parts of the world. Some of the work that children do is highly exploitative; cases of debt bondage and of long hours worked in unhealthy conditions for low wages are widely documented.

Are women poorer than men? The data on incomes are too weak to give a clear answer. But the available figures on health, nutrition, education, and labor force participation show that women are often severely disadvantaged. For example, data for 1980 indicate that the literacy rate for women was only 61 percent of that for men in Africa; the figures were 52 percent in South Asia, 57 percent in the Middle East, 82 percent in Southeast Asia and 94 percent in Latin America. Women face all manner of cultural, social, legal, and economic obstacles that men — even poor men — do not. They typically work longer hours and, when they are paid at all, for lower wages. A study in Nepal found that, on average, poor women worked eleven hours a day, men seven-and-a-half. In many developed countries the poorest include large numbers of single-mother households. Poor female-headed households are also increasingly common in southern Africa and Latin America. In Brazil female-headed households account for 10 percent of all households but for 15 percent of the poor.

Assets

The poor usually lack assets as well as income. In local economies in which wealth and status come from the land, disadvantaged households are typically land poor or landless. Poverty is highly correlated with landlessness in South Asia, southern Africa, and much of Latin America. (See the data in Table 2.3 for Bangladesh.) When the poor do own land, it is often unproductive and frequently lies outside irrigated areas. The poor are usually unable to improve such plots, since they lack income and access to credit.

Many of the poor have access to land without having ownership rights. Tenancy is common — although the poorest are often locked out of these arrangements because they lack the other resources needed for farming. Tenancy does not provide collateral or a secure hedge against risk, and access to the land from one year to the next is often uncertain.

In other cases the poor have access to land that is owned by the community or is common property. Such arrangements are increasingly jeopardized by population pressure, privatization, overexploitation of resources, and deterioration of the environment. Studies of Rajasthani villages in India over twenty years found that the income earned from common-property resources has declined for all these reasons. In the Sahel region of Africa common ownership of the (generally unproductive) land is considered a principal cause of overgrazing and deforestation. Environmental degradation of common-property resources can badly hurt the assetless poor. Improving their access to income-earning opportunities while protecting the environment is an important policy issue.

Table 2.3   Poverty and landholding in Bangladesh, 1978-79.

Landholding class (acres of land owned)	Percentage of total households in class	Mean income (taka a month)	Mean landholdings (acres)	Headcount index (percentage of population)
Landless	7.1	508	0	93
0-0.5	36.1	560	0.1	93
0.5-1.0	10.5	711	0.7	84
1.0-1.5	8.9	783	1.2	78
1.5-2.5	12.1	912	2.0	68
2.5-5.0	13.8	1,163	3.5	45
5.0-7.5	5.7	1,516	6.0	23
7.5+	5.8	2,155	14.0	10
Total	100.0	865	2.1	70

Source: Ravallion 1989b.

The poor are also lacking in human capital. Everywhere, they have a lower level of educational achievement than the population at large. (Figure 2.3 illustrates this with data from India.) Poor women often have too many children, spaced too close together, to the detriment of their health. The poor frequently suffer from hunger and malnutrition and from related illnesses. This undermines their capacity for labor — often their main or only asset.

Figure 2.3   Poverty and illiteracy in India, 1981.

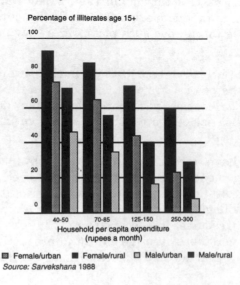

Percentage of illiterates age 15+

Household per capita expenditure (rupees a month)

▨ Female/urban   ■ Female/rural   ▨ Male/urban   ■ Male/rural

Source: Sarvekshana 1988

62

The ownership of assets directly affects income opportunities (Box 2.3). Without assets such as land, the poor must hire out their labor. Without adequate human capital, they are limited to unskilled work. The elderly and the incapacitated may not even be able to offer their labor and may be forced to rely on charity. The importance of assets, broadly defined, suggests that policies should seek to increase the assets owned by the poor — especially skills, health, and other aspects of human capital and, in agricultural economies, land.

Box 2.3 Village-level perspectives on asset poverty

Much has been learned about asset poverty from village studies. In Palanpur, a well-studied village in India's Uttar Pradesh State, the most disadvantaged groups were invariably landless casual laborers for whom work was not available on a regular basis and households without an able-bodied male. In 1983-84 all households with both these characteristics were found to be poor. They had very few opportunities for raising their incomes. Self-employment was either restricted to certain castes or required skills and physical capital that poor households lacked. As entry to regular wage employment was also limited, poor men had no choice but to take occasional agricultural work. Local tradition denied even this option to most women.

In Kenya, where population pressure on the land has been rising, landholding was found to be an important determinant of welfare. Another study, however, suggests that among smallholders education is more important; it enables family members to bring in urban wages that can then be invested in farm innovation and higher productivity.

A study of rural Tanzanian households in 1980 found that the poorest in the twenty sampled villages did not possess significantly less land or labor resources than others. Differences in living standards were largely attributable to differences in human capital and in ownership of nonlabor resources such as livestock. The poorer households were less likely to participate in market transactions than the nonpoor, since they lacked the resources to grow cash crops and could not take the chance of a bad harvest that would leave them dependent on the market for their food needs. The poor also had much lower rates of return on work away from the family farm. Weak skills restricted them to marginal pursuits such as handicrafts, while the better-off captured more lucrative wage employment.

Sources of income

Besides having lower incomes and fewer assets than the nonpoor, the poor often have distinctive sources of livelihood. Most of the destitute mix many different earning activities. It is common for the poor to work as cultivators, hunters and gatherers, small artisans, petty traders, and wage laborers at various times of the year. The poor are rarely self-sufficient. They need cash to buy small household items such as soap, clothes, salt, and cooking oil, and they have to pay taxes and medical and school costs. So they need to sell at least some of their produce or obtain some paid work.

Agriculture is still the main source of income for the world's poor. We have seen that the greatest numbers of the poor, including the very poorest, are found overwhelmingly in rural areas. Their livelihoods are linked to farming, whether or not they earn their incomes directly from it. The demand for nonfarm goods and services often depends on the health of the farm economy. To help the rural poor, policies should strive to raise agricultural productivity — through investment in infrastructure and through appropriate pricing, for example.

Within agriculture, there are two groups of poor: the self-employed and wage laborers. The distinction is often imprecise. Many casual farm laborers also own tiny plots of land. These plots are not sufficient to ensure family survival, but if they are productive, they can provide extra income and some collateral against risk. Most of the poor in Botswana, Côte d'Ivoire, Ghana, Kenya, Nigeria, and Tanzania are small-scale agriculturalists or pastoralists. In 1981-82 the poorest tenth of Kenya's population earned two-thirds of its income from farming. In Côte d'Ivoire in 1985 most poor households were headed by self-employed cultivators. (This group also had the lowest literacy rate and the largest poverty gap.) In these African countries agricultural wage earners are still relatively unimportant among the poor. The situation is somewhat different in southern Africa; there many households hire out their labor, although not necessarily in farming.

Agricultural self-employment is also important in Southeast Asia. In Thailand a study of 1981 data found that 75 percent of poor rural households were self-employed in agriculture; for nonpoor rural households the figure was 64 percent. Seventeen percent of all households, poor and nonpoor, depended primarily on agricultural wage labor. Recent data for Indonesia indicate that in 1987 households that were self-employed in farming (as tabulated by the principal activity of the head of household) accounted for 58 percent of the poor and 41 percent of the total population. Farm wage laborers, in contrast, accounted for only 14 percent of the poor and 9 percent of the population.

The picture is more varied in South Asia. In India households self-employed in agriculture accounted for 35 percent of poor rural households in 1977-78 and for 46 percent of all rural households. Households engaged in agricultural labor accounted for a further 44 percent of poor rural households but for only 30 percent of all rural households. Figures for Pakistan suggest that among the poor there are fewer farm laborers than own-account cultivators; the opposite is true for Bangladesh.

In Latin America most of the poor are small-scale farmers, but few derive adequate subsistence from their plots. In the plantation economies of Central America, especially in Costa Rica, wage labor in agriculture is important. Peru's poor are mainly small farmers and herders. In a survey conducted in 1985-86, 78 percent of the heads of poor households said they were self-employed and 71 percent said they worked in farming; the corresponding figures for all Peruvians were 60 and 40 percent. In the Sierra, Peru's poorest region, the numbers are even higher. In Mexico, too, poverty is concentrated among cultivator families.

Rural nonfarm employment mainly consists of cottage industries, services, and commerce. In Asia, Sub-Saharan Africa, and Latin America rural nonfarm work tends to be highly seasonal or part-time. In Asia wages in these jobs are generally lower than wages in agriculture. The poor are concentrated in traditional industries with low skill and capital requirements and very low labor productivity. Their products are normally intended for home consumption or for the local market. Demand is an important constraint on nonfarm economic activities, which depend heavily on the primary farm sector. In areas in which agricultural incomes have grown, nonfarm employment has flourished and wages have risen. Nonfarm employment is particularly important in providing work in slack seasons for landless laborers and women from poor households.

In some of the poorest villages in Thailand, for example, woven bamboo baskets and other forest by-products provide extra income for rice farmers. Forest protection laws make this a risky and unprofitable business — another illustration of how the loss of common-property resources harms the poor in the short term. Studies have found that virtually all poor farmers in western Guatemala and the northernmost region of the Peruvian Sierra supplement their farming income with artisanal production and petty trade. In the poorest households much of this additional work is done by women.

Informal sector jobs of one sort or another — generally the jobs that pay least — are the main source of livelihood for the urban poor. In Brazil in 1985 an estimated 75 percent of heads of poor families worked in the informal sector, compared with 35 percent of the population as a whole. Disadvantaged urban groups are largely self-employed. They sell services and engage in trade or work on a casual basis in construction, manufacturing, and transport. Some are full-time beggars, garbage sifters, prostitutes, or pickpockets. Incomes are low and insecure. In Bombay poverty was found to be more common among casual workers than among regular employees, and there was little mobility between the two forms of employment. About half the urban poor in Pakistan are self-employed, mostly in trade and manufacturing. They are generally less skilled than people who work for wages.

Transfers can be an important source of income for some of the poor. In most developing countries transfers are made by relatives and friends or through village support systems rather than by the government. Transfers accounted for 9 percent of the incomes of poor Kenyan smallholders in 1974-75. In rural Java transfers are targeted toward the sick and elderly; in urban areas the unemployed receive assistance. For the most disadvantaged households, transfers can be crucial.

How does income variability affect the poor?

Because incomes fluctuate, a static picture of poverty can be deceptive. Evidence indicates that some people move in and out of poverty, whereas others never cross the poverty threshold (Box 2.4).

Box 2.4 Moving in and out of poverty in rural India

How much of the poverty that we observe at any one date is persistent and how much is transient, reflecting variability in individual incomes over time? Data collected by the International Crops Research Institute for the Semi-Arid Tropics (ICRISAT), based in Hyderabad, India, track the incomes and consumption of 211 agricultural households in central India between 1975 and 1983. Drought conditions are common in this region.

In Box figure 2.4a the percentage of households deemed to be poor fluctuates over time around a generally downward trend, from 64 percent at the beginning of the period to a low of 41 percent in 1982; the average proportion of poor was 50 percent. For each year the poor are divided into those who were poor in the previous period and those who were not, and the same is done for the nonpoor. On average, 84 percent of the poor at each date had been poor in the previous period, and 16 percent were newcomers to poverty. Of the nonpoor, 75 percent had been nonpoor in the previous period, and 25 percent had moved out of poverty. The income fluctuations are large: more than half the households that moved into poverty did so with incomes of less than 80 percent of the poverty line, and more than half of those who moved above the poverty line moved at least 20 percent above it.

Box figure 2.4b shows the number of years (not necessarily consecutive) that were spent in poverty. Only about 12 percent of households were never poor during the nine years. At the other extreme, 44 percent were poor for six or more years, and 19 percent were poor in every year. Thus, most households in these villages do experience poverty at one time or another. Whereas 50 percent are poor in a typical year, nearly 90 percent of the households are poor for at least one of the nine years. The transient component is large. Yet it is also clear that there is a substantial core of persistent, chronic poverty in these villages — poverty experienced by the same households year after year.

Box figure 2.4a Dynamics of rural poverty, sample villages, India

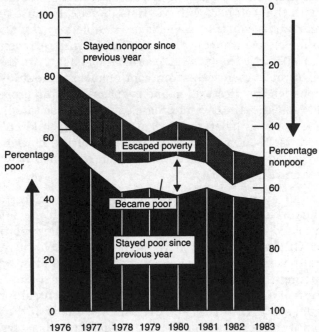

Box figure 2.4b Number of years in poverty, sample villages, India

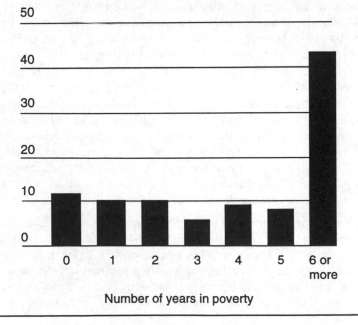

Households deliberately diversify their sources of income to reduce the risk that adverse circumstances will cause a sharp drop in income. But living standards still fluctuate considerably — with the weather, with the time of year, because of the death of the family breadwinner, and so on. If households are unable to cushion a fall (through, for example, borrowing or insurance), an unfavorable turn of events, especially an unexpected one, can be catastrophic. The poorest households are the most vulnerable and the least able to protect themselves from contingencies. One study tells how a young household in Guinea fell into destitution and eventually disintegrated after the father contracted river blindness. As he became progressively incapacitated, the mother's work load multiplied and her health deteriorated, along with the children's. Soon the family was unable to feed itself. In time, various members of the household succumbed to illness or left the village. After fifteen years what remained of the household was entirely dependent on village charity.

Often, unanticipated events affect the poor not merely in certain localities but nationwide. For instance, a sudden decline in the terms of trade, followed perhaps by policy changes intended to cope with that decline, may change relative prices in ways that hurt the poor. Others may gain from the same events. Real currency devaluations, for example, usually benefit farmers who are net suppliers of internationally traded produce while hurting the urban poor, who are typically net consumers of tradable goods. In some parts of the world — such as Afghanistan, Central America, Indochina, Iran, Iraq, Lebanon, southern Africa, and Sri Lanka — many of the poor are uprooted people fleeing from wars, persecution, famine, and natural disasters. Previously, they may not have been poor. In Angola and Mozambique about 8.5 million people have become war refugees. Poverty in these countries reflects a massive destruction of rural infrastructure and productive assets.

Incomes in rural households vary substantially according to the season. For example, wage work is readily available only at certain times of the crop year, and it often depends on the weather. In many African countries the dry season puts an extra burden on women, who may have to walk miles to find water. In some busy seasons heavy agricultural work coincides with depleted food stocks and higher prices. Undernutrition and illnesses are more common at certain times of the year. The rains typically increase water contamination and the incidence of waterborne diseases. Acute weight loss during the "hungry season" has been documented among farmers in The Gambia; adult weight fluctuated as much as 4.5 kilograms within one year. In northeast Ghana losses of 6 percent of body weight were recorded. Among women farmers in Lesotho the figure was 7 percent, and for pastoralists in Niger it was 5 percent. For vulnerable groups such as children, the aged, and others whose biological defenses are already weakened, seasonal weight change can be extremely damaging.

Most of the rural poor, however, can cope reasonably well with normal seasonality. Saving and dissaving help to smooth consumption over the ups and downs. Figure 2.4 shows consumption and income over the course of a year for 178 poor households in Bangladesh. Consumption is clearly smoother than income, which varies markedly with the crop cycle. For these households, earnings from labor are less than consumption in most periods, and the remaining sources of income — transfers, asset sales, and borrowing — small as they are, can be crucial to survival. Widespread indebtedness to local moneylenders and shop-keepers has been reported for various countries. Friends and family are often a preferable source of small amounts of credit, but they are likely to have little to spare. (One study of the Philippines described extensive short-term borrowing and lending among poor families as a form of shared poverty.) Borrowing may often be the only way to maintain a minimum level of consumption.

Figure 2.4 Seasonality in rural Bangladesh: poor households in six villages, July 1984 to June 1985

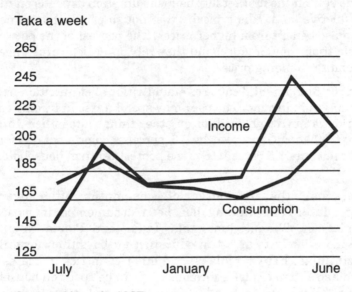

Source: Hossain 1987

Credit is rarely available for accumulating productive assets. Savings and borrowings often have to be held in unproductive forms such as cash or grain to hedge against future calamities. The poor have few opportunities to obtain insurance, and they are not able to use credit and savings to bolster their capacity for bearing risk or to become entrepreneurs. Those on the edge of survival can not afford to gamble.

Another way of coping with risk is to diversify income sources. A study of rural Java found that the poorest landless households coordinate their members' activities much more carefully than do asset-owning households. The main purpose of this coordination is to establish a steady stream of income. The household may adjust its overall supply of labor, either through hours worked or through changes in labor force participation. Members of the household may migrate in search of work. Farmers are known to intercrop and to choose crops that are quick to mature or are more resilient, even though they may have lower yields and be less valuable.

How do the poor spend their incomes?

Over a typical year the poor spend nearly all their incomes on consumption of one sort or another, and at least half of this consumption is likely to be in the form of food. Data for both Côte d'Ivoire and Peru in 1985 indicate that about 70 percent of the expenditure of poor households goes for food; the corresponding figure for all households is about 50 percent. A high proportion of the food budget — 60 percent in the case of the Indonesian poor, for instance — is devoted to the local food staple.

The relative prices of food staples can be crucial to the welfare of the poor. The number of rural poor who rely on the market for their consumption depends on the distribution of access to productive land. It is typically the "not so poor" who are net suppliers of farm produce and so benefit from higher prices. The poorest of the poor consume more of the food staple than they produce, and they rely on agricultural wages, which may be slow to respond to changing prices.

Poverty is often the fundamental cause of malnutrition. Yet nutrition need not be very responsive to changes in income. The poor may spend a rise in income on "better" food (rather than on more nutritious food) or on other things altogether. In Indonesia one study found that when income rose by 10 percent, calorie intake for the average household increased only 1.5 percent. For the poorest tenth of households the increase was 4 percent.

Within the household the distribution of consumption often favors males and income-earning adults. This finding has been documented in various countries, including Bangladesh, Ghana, Guatemala, India, and Papua New Guinea. Poor households are more likely to invest in education for boys than for girls. A series of studies in Brazil, India, Kenya, Malawi, and other countries indicates that a larger proportion of women's than of men's incomes tends to be spent on household nutrition and basic welfare. Of the studies conducted in India, one covering twenty villages in the south found that 80 to 100 percent of women's wage income was devoted to family maintenance, whereas men committed between 40 and 90 percent of their earnings. This suggests that raising women's incomes directly is a good way to reach children as well as to strengthen women's status and bargaining power within the household.

What is the position of the poor in the society around them?

In general, the poor have less access to publicly provided goods and infrastructure than do other groups. On the whole, governments fail to reach the rural poor. Even in urban areas poor neighborhoods are less well supplied with services than well-to-do ones. Data for Latin America show that the pattern of social expenditures is regressive in most countries. In Brazil, according to some estimates, it is only slightly more equal than the distribution of income, which is known to be among the most unequal in the world. The primary school enrollment rate for the wealthiest 20 percent in Côte d'Ivoire is twice that of the poorest 20 percent. In both India and Nepal enrollment rates for the top 10 percent of families are 50 to 100 percent higher than for the poor. Morbidity and mortality figures tell a similar story. Access is not the only issue; use of services by the poor can also be low. But the fact remains that fewer social services are available to the poor.

There are exceptions. In Eastern Europe and in a few low-income and lower-middle-income countries — including Chile, China, Costa Rica, Cuba, Mauritius, and Sri Lanka as well as India's Kerala State — governments have tried hard to provide basic services widely and have largely succeeded. For example, in Sri Lanka 93 percent of the population has access to health services. Chile's social services are carefully targeted toward the neediest. Through its commune organization China was able to meet certain basic needs such as health care, education, and family planning services for most of its people.

The poor are often set apart by cultural and educational barriers. Illiterate people may be intimidated by officials or may simply lack information about programs. Sometimes the design of the services unintentionally adds to the problem. Agricultural extension programs, for example, are usually geared toward men even where — as is often the case — many, if not most, cultivators are women. The requirement that birth certificates be produced for admission to school in urban areas of India prevents poor migrant women from enrolling children and taking needed work. The poor play little part in politics and are often, in effect, disenfranchised.

In many countries poverty is correlated with race and ethnic background. Indigenous peoples in Bolivia, Ecuador, Guatemala, Mexico, and Peru are disproportionately represented among the poor. Scheduled castes and tribal peoples are among those most at risk of poverty in India and Bangladesh. In Australia the aborigines are prominent among the poor. In the United States 45 percent of all black children were poor in 1984, compared with 17 percent of white children. In South Africa the mortality rate for white infants averaged 12 per thousand live births between 1981 and 1985; for black Africans it was estimated to fall between 94 and 124. The risk of contracting tuberculosis — a disease closely associated with poverty — was twenty-two times greater for blacks than for whites in South Africa, excluding the homelands, and fifty-five times greater in Transkei.

From diagnosis to treatment

This chapter's survey of what we know about the poor points to two overwhelmingly important determinants of poverty: access to income-earning opportunities and the capacity to respond. When households have secure opportunities to use their labor to good purpose and household members are skilled, educated, and healthy, minimal standards of living are ensured and poverty is eliminated. When such opportunities are lacking and access to social services is limited, living standards are unacceptably low. The living standards of many in the developing world are also highly vulnerable to a variety of misfortunes, ranging from illness to drought. Inability to cope with shocks can render relatively well-off households poor and lead to starvation and death for those already impoverished.

5. Hunger and Entitlements: Research for Action

Amartya Sen

1. Hunger in the modern world

Hunger is not a recent phenomenon. Nor is famine. Life has been short and hard in much of the world, most of the time. Both chronic undernourishment and recurrent famines have been among the casual antecedents of the brutishness and brevity of human life in history.

Hunger in the modern world is more intolerable than past hunger not because it is typically more intense, but because it is now so unnecessary. The enormous expansion of productive power that has taken place over the last few centuries has made it possible, for the first time in history, to guarantee adequate food for all. It is in this context that the persistence of chronic hunger and the recurrence of virulent famines must be seen as being morally outrageous and politically unacceptable. If politics is "the art of the possible", then conquering world hunger has become a political issue in a way it could not have been in the past.

This is the main background to the research on hunger and poverty that is being undertaken at WIDER. The research is policy-oriented in the sense that diagnostic analysis and critical assessment are ultimately geared to the choice of action. The action in question is not necessarily confined to the sort that can be undertaken by governments alone. The effective removal of hunger in the modern world calls for combative action not only from governments, but also from many other institutions and groups of individuals. For example, the news media may have a major role to play in acting as an early warning system against threatening famines, and also in forcing the hands of those in authority to act quickly and adequately. More generally, public understanding and participation in the battle to end hunger can alter institutions and behavioural modes, and can be a decisive influence on the success or failure of that objective.

The research undertaken at WIDER on the subject of hunger and poverty is, thus, geared not merely to advising governments and those in public office, but also to raising the general understanding of the different problems involved. Informed action coming from different sections of society, from different groups of persons, and from national and international institutions can be crucial for winning the battle against hunger and famine.

The various research projects in operation at WIDER in this field are described briefly in the Appendix.[1] This text is devoted to outlining some of the main issues that are being addressed in these research projects. The intention is to provide a general introduction to some of the major research themes pursued at WIDER connected with the elimination of famines and the removal of endemic hunger across the world.

One of the extraordinary aspects of the observed reaction to world hunger is the coexistence of continued inaction, on the one hand, and frequent invocation of alarming statistics, on the other. One important and widely-quoted study puts the number of people suffering from nutritional deprivation (in the form of having inadequate calories to prevent stunted growth and serious health risk) at 340 million, which represents about 16% of the population of the developing countries as a whole. For the low income countries the ratio of the deprived population rises to 23%. The same study suggests that 730 million people in the developing world suffer from undernourishment in terms of having "not enough calories for an active working life". This amounts to 34% of the population of those countries as a whole, including 51% of the population of low-income countries.[2]

Many methodological doubts can be raised about estimating the number of the hungry and the undernourished by comparing calorie intake figures with "requirement" norms.[3] There are, it has been argued, considerable interpersonal as well as intrapersonal variations in the relationship between calorie intakes and nutritional states of persons. This question has some relevance to policy choice, on which more presently (section 4.2), but what is really remarkable is not so much the level of accuracy of the estimates, but the coexistence of such dramatic statistics — figures that would remain alarming even if they were cut by a half or two-thirds — with smugness about the inaction that characterises the world reaction to extensive hunger. The recognition of the disastrous nature of the nutritional situation in the world seems to co-survive with an unrebellious acceptance of passivity in encountering these disasters. While public reaction can be raised to a temporary height by harrowing stories of suffering, or by unbearable television pictures, and a fair amount of public participation may be obtained for a short period in activities such as Band Aid, Live Aid, Sports Aid, etc., the general reaction is one of resilient apathy.

Part of the explanation lies undoubtedly in the fact that most people find it hard to believe that they can do anything substantial to change the situation in a significant way. The donations that they can make seem trivial in comparison with the enormous magnitude of the task. There is also much skepticism as to what the governments of the respective developing countries can and will do with the assistance that they may receive from elsewhere. All this contributes to a sense of comforting impotence — comforting because nothing need to be done to deal with what is acknowledged to be a terrible problem since nothing "useful" can be done.

Research alone cannot, of course, change this situation, but there is much scope for a better understanding of what can be achieved by sensible economic policy, and by political and social activities. We have to know more about what feasible opportunities exist. That is the task of research for action. Even the courage and determination to confront the problem of hunger and famine in the modern world may be influenced by a better understanding of what can be achieved by public action.

2. Entitlements and vulnerability

2.1. Entitlement failures

When millions of people suddenly die in a famine, it is hard to avoid the thought that there must have been a major decline in the output and availability of food in the economy. But while that is sometimes the case, there have frequently been famines in which food output and availability have remained high and undiminished. Indeed some famines have occurred in periods of peak food availability for the economy as a whole (e.g., the Bangladesh famine of 1974).

The real issue is not primarily the over-all availability of food, but its acquirement by individuals and families. If a person lacks the means to acquire food, the presence of food in the market is not much consolation. To understand hunger, we have to look at people's entitlements, i.e., what commodity bundles (including food) they can make their own. The entitlement approach to hunger concentrates on the determination of command over commodities, including food. Famines are seen as the result of entitlement failures of large groups, often belonging to some specific occupations (e.g., landless rural labourers, pastoralists).[4]

The entitlement of a person stands for the set of different alternative commodity bundles that the person can acquire through the use of the various legal channels of acquirement open to someone in his position. In a private ownership market economy, the entitlement set of a person is determined by his original bundle of ownership (what is called his "endowment") and the various alternative bundles he can acquire starting from each initial endowment, through the use of trade and production (what is called his "exchange entitlement mapping"). A person has to starve if his entitlement set does not include any commodity bundle with adequate amounts of food. A person is reduced to starvation if some change either in his endowment (e.g., alienation of land, or loss of labour power due to ill health), or in his exchange entitlement mapping (e.g., fall in wages, rise in food prices, loss of employment, drop in the price of the good he produces and sells), makes it no longer possible for him to acquire any commodity bundle with enough food.

The approach of analyzing famines in terms of declines of entitlements of particular occupation groups has been used in recent years to study many famines, e.g., the Bengal famine in 1943, the Sahel famines in the 1970s, the Bangladesh famine of 1974, the Ethiopian famines of 1973-85, the Malawi (in fact, Nyasaland) famine of 1949-50, and also various historical famines.[5]

For the bulk of humanity, about the only substantial asset that a person owns is his or her ability to work, i.e., labour power. If a person fails to secure employment, then that means of acquiring food (through getting a job, earning an income and buying food with that income) fails. If, in addition to that, the laws of the land do not provide any social security arrangements, e.g., unemployment insurance, the person will fail to secure the means of subsistence. And that can be the end of the tale — at least for that erst while person.

This elementary analysis points immediately to two aspects of the action needed to combat hunger and famine. There is, on the one hand, the need for a better functioning economic system, to provide people with regular means of income and survival. There is, on the other hand, need for security in providing economic support to vulnerable individuals (or families) when they fail to get that support from the regular economic system itself. Importance has to be attached to functioning economic mechanisms that provide means and entitlements to the population. And at the same time, attention also has to be paid to public security measures that can be used to guarantee entitlements to those who happen to remain vulnerable to fluctuation and instability in earning an income and acquiring economic power (e.g., landless labourers falling victim to employment decline or a fall in real wages).

2.2. Output, availability and entitlements

Seeing hunger as entitlement failure points to possible remedies immediately, since we are induced to understand and address the forces that generate deprivation and help sustain it. Food problems have often been discussed in terms of the output and availability of food without going into the question of entitlement — this is a tradition that received much encouragement from Malthus's famous "Essay on Population" (1798).[6] It is particularly important to understand the relevance of seeing famines and intensification of hunger as entitlement failures which can occur even when food availability is not reduced, and even when the ratio of food to population — on which Malthus concentrated — may have gone up sharply. The relentless persistence of famines and the enormous reach of world hunger, despite a steady and substantial increase in food availability, makes it imperative for us to reorient our approach away from food availability and towards the ability to command food. The dissonance between the casual analysis of famines in terms of availability and that in terms of entitlements does not lie in any belief that availability and entitlements are unrelated to each other. In fact, they are linked in many different ways and the connections are indeed worth emphasizing. First, for some people, the output grown by themselves is also their basic entitlement to food (e.g., for peasants growing food crops). Second, one of the major influences on the ability of anyone to purchase food is clearly the price of food, and that price is, of course, influenced *inter alia* by the production and availability of food in the economy. Third, food production can also be a major source of employment, and a reduction in food production (due to, say, a drought or a flood) may reduce employment and wage income by the same process that may lead eventually to a decline in the output and availability of food. Fourth, if and when a famine develops, having a stock of food available in the public distribution system is clearly of great strategic relevance for combatting starvation. This can be done either by distributing food directly (in cooked or uncooked form), or by adding to the food supply in the market, thereby exerting downward pressure on possibly rocketing prices.

The conflict between the availability view and the entitlement view of food deprivation has to be seized only after these (and other) basic connections have been recognised. The dissonance arises from the fact that the links do not establish a tie-up between availability and entitlement in such a tight way that the food commands of different sections of the population move up and down in proportion with the total availability of food in the economy. If food were to be distributed over the population on some egalitarian principles operated by some central authority, that assumption might indeed be sensible. However, the actual command over food that different sections of the population can exercise depends on a set of legal and economic factors, including those governing ownership, transfer, production and exchange. It is, thus, quite possible for some groups e.g., a particular occupation group such as landless rural labourers, to have a sharply reduced food entitlement, even when the overall availability of food in the economy is unaffected or enhanced. Most famines hit some particular occupation groups, and there is no paradox in the fact that a famine can occur, e.g., in Bengal in 1943, in Ethiopia in 1973, or in Bangladesh in 1974, without any significant decline in food output and availability, with members of particular occupation groups losing the means of acquiring food and succumbing to starvation and death.[7]

2.3. Occupations and economic policy

One basic difference between the availability approach and that of entitlement lies in the fact that the entitlement approach is necessarily disaggregative and thus contrasts sharply with the aggregative perspective presented by the concentration on total food availability in the economy. Indeed, the logic of entitlement relations entails that the focus of this analysis for a given region has to be primarily on occupation groups, supplemented by other parameters such as gender and age. This contrast applies even when we shift our attention from the disastrous phenomenon of famines to the more regular characteristics of endemic hunger and undernourishment. In each case we have to look at the ability of particular groups to command adequate amounts of food for unimpaired nutritional functioning. The concentration on food entitlements provides a different view of the role of policy making and the characteristics of the actions needed.

This is the case even when the continuation and intensification of hunger happens to be associated and correlated with a decline in food output and availability. This is, for example, the case in Africa, which is the only substantial area in the world in which food output per head has fallen significantly over the last decade or two. In fact, for all developing economies put together, between 1974-76 and 1984-86 there has been an increase of 13% in food output per head, which is a sharper rise than that for the developed economies on average (up 9%). But while per-capita food output has gone up in this period by about 12% in Latin America and by nearly 20% in Asia, it has fallen by about 12% in Africa (comparing the average of 1984-86 with that of 1974-76). But food production is not only a source of food supply, it is also the source of income and livelihood for vast sections of the African population. As a result, falls in food output per head also tend to be temporally associated with reduction in overall income of many occupation groups in Africa. However, even if food output per head had gone down in Africa by as much as it did, there need not have been a collapse of food entitlements if that food output decline had been compensated by an expansion of income from other sources and by other means of establishing command over food (including, if necessary, by importing from abroad).

This contrast can be illustrated by comparing the experiences of many of the sub-Saharan economies, which have experienced declines in food output per head and have also experienced food entitlement problems, with those of economies elsewhere which have experienced declines in food output per head without having either famines or hunger in the way Africa has experienced them. Compared with an African decline of food output of 12% between 1974-76 and 1984-86, the output of food per head over the same period has gone down by 12% in Israel, 14% in Venuzuela, 15% in Portugal, 17% in Costa Rica, 19% in Singapore, 36% in Hong Kong, and 40% in Trinidad and Tobago. These latter economies have not experienced famines and widespread hunger both because food production is a less important source of income and entitlement in these economies, and also because there has tended to be a more than compensating expansion of other production and related to it, of incomes and entitlements. What may superficially appear to be a problem of African food supply has to be seen in the more general terms of entitlement problems in Africa.

In seeking policy remedies for problems of hunger in Africa, policy should concentrate on the enhancement of entitlements, and this may be brought about by an expansion of income from other sources, and not merely through an increase in the output of food. It is, of course, true that having to establish command over food through exchange adds a further source of vulnerability in that the market conditions may undergo fast — indeed, sometimes violent — shifts. But that is not an argument for concentrating exclusively on food production despite the fact that this may add to risks of other kinds, e.g., those arising from the variability of weather conditions. Of course, that variability itself can be eventually dealt with through irrigation, and also through planned changes in the environment by means of afforestation and other nature-oriented policies. However, these are long-run remedies, and the problem of vulnerability in the short run remains. The entitlement approach would suggest a move in the direction of diversification of production and of sources of income in African conditions, rather than concentrating exclusively on the expansion of food output (irrespective of costs and risks).[8]

2.4. Intrahousehold disparities and sex bias

The legal associations of the term entitlement also happen to have some directional and suggestive value. Inter-household divisions, ownership rights and the rights of transaction and bequeathing are, obviously, relevant to the determination of entitlements of families. The perceived legitimacy of these legal or semi-legal rights has a powerful influence on the nature of personal and public action related to the distributional problem. While the lines are not so sharply drawn in the case of intra-household divisions, there are important issues of perceived legitimacy in that context as well. This can become a particularly difficult problem, yielding unequal distributions of food within the family, when perceptions have a bias in the direction of acknowledging more desert, or identifying magnified needs, of some members of the family against others (e.g., biasing towards boys vis-a-vis girls in rural north India).[9]

There are important issues of "extended entitlements" influencing intra-household divisions, and these issues too have to be addressed in a policy context. Once again, the policy in question is not confined to what the government may be able to do. Actions can come also from political as well as educational and social movements. Issues or perceived legitimacy and entitlement can be deeply influenced by a re-examination of the social and political aspects of intra-family inequality and disparity. In the research undertaken at WIDER on hunger and poverty, these and other diverse aspects of entitlement relations are being extensively explored, with a view to providing a basis for informed and enlightened public action in the broadest sense.[10]

3. Preventing famines

3.1. Anticipation and action

Anti-famine policy calls for several distinct operations, including anticipation, relief and prevention. The history of anti-famine policy in the world provides a rich mixture of success as well as failures in these different respects.

As far as anticipation is concerned, a recurrent source of failure has been the reliance — often implicit — on a theory of famine that concentrates on food output and availability only. Sometimes famines have not been anticipated precisely because the ratio of food to population has remained high, despite the failure on the part of substantial sections of the population (usually belonging to a few vulnerable occupation groups) to retain the means of commanding enough food. It is easy to cite examples from South Asia as well as sub-Saharan Africa to illustrate such failures of anticipation.

This is not the only source of problem in anticipating famine threats. Food output per head is frequently a fluctuating variable in any case, so that it is easy to be in a state of alert whenever the ratio of food output to population falls, since that occurs so often. There is need for discrimination between one situation and another, based on occupation-specific economic analysis, even though the situation may look rather similar in terms of food availability or output per head.

The problem of anticipation can be dealt with by making better use of economic analysis that focuses on entitlement failures of particular occupation groups rather than on output fluctuations in the economy as a whole.[11] But in addition, other sources of information can be used in order to provide an adequately sensitive system of early warning and prediction. Widespread starvation does not hit an economy simultaneously in all sectors and in all regions. By making discriminating use of available information, it is possible to see early signs of a growing famine threat. This is a field in which active journalism can fruitfully supplement the work of economic analysis, by reporting early signs of distress with predictive significance.[12]

Another complication concerning famine anticipation relates to the question of agency. Precisely who is to anticipate famines? In so far as the object of the exercise is counteracting action, the answer clearly must be: those who would provide relief and also take other steps for curing famine threats. This role, naturally enough, falls primarily on the government of the country in question.

But how soon, how urgently and how actively the government will act will also depend on the nature of the politics of the country, and the forces that operate on the government to act without delay. Depending on the nature of the political structure, it is often possible for an inactive or uncaring government to get away with implicit manslaughter, if not murder. Many governments have been extraordinarily sluggish and insensitive to information coming in about threatening famines. Here again the extent of public knowledge of and involvement in social issues can be crucial. Effective famine anticipation and counteracting policies are not merely matters of economic analysis, they are also significantly dependent on the nature of political agitprop and active journalism, which operate on the government, influencing its concerns and forcing its hand.[13]

Even though the primary onus of taking anti-famine action lies with the government, there are other organizations, institutions and groups which can play an effective part in providing relief to famine victims. The role of such organizations as OXFAM, War on Want, Save the Children, etc., is obvious enough and recently other voluntary organizations and movements have emerged. There is a certain amount of public skepticism as to what institutions of this kind can in fact do, and in view of the scales of starvation and mortality involved in many famines, perhaps this is not surprising. On the other hand, providing famine relief is not just an "all or nothing" matter. Any help that is provided in reducing starvation and suffering and in recreating the economic means of subsistence has obvious benefits even when the proportion of the victim population covered by these activities may not be very large.

In recent years, substantial amounts of famine relief and entitlement support have been provided, especially in Africa, by inter-governmental and international agencies, e.g., UNICEF, and various *ad hoc* institutions. The problem of early warning and famine anticipation is extremely important, and here again a discriminating economic analysis, concentrating on the economics of entitlements and the politics of public action, can have a significant informative and activist role.

3.2. Famine relief: forms and strategies

A second problem concerns the provision of relief to famine victims. Once again, it is possible to be misled by over-simple theorizing about the causation of famine. If famines are seen exclusively in terms of a decline in food availability, the challenge of effective and efficient provision of relief may suffer from various misdirections related to an unduly narrow concentration. Once again, the superficial plausibility of the food-availability view can act as a barrier.

If famines are caused by failures of entitlements of particular occupation groups, the remedy has to lie in recreating those entitlements. This can be done in a variety of ways, and it would be a mistake to concentrate only on a programme of directly feeding the population. A recent USAID report on the famines in Ethiopia captures a commonly shared belief about the nature of famine relief adequately when it pronounces: "The number one priority was supplying food and getting it to the people who needed it".[14] But taking the food to the people may not always be the easiest, quickest or the most effective way of providing relief.

The historical experience of famine relief in different parts of the world bears testimony to a rather impressive variety of approaches to the protection of food entitlements: direct feeding of cooked food; distribution of uncooked food; food for work programmes; cash wages for public works; cash doles; tax relief; price control and rationing; support of livestock prices; insurance of crops; and many others. Indeed, in many contexts, bureaucratic arrangements for the transportation and movement of food and its distribution to destitutes herded together in relief camps provide a method of relief that is neither fast, not efficient, nor cost-effective, not humane.

The possibility of providing cash relief to regenerate lost entitlements, perhaps in the form of cash wages paid for public works, remains an important one to consider in many contexts. This has been a crucial part of famine relief policy in India, even though it has been relatively little tried in Africa. Severe famine threats in India, e.g., in Bihar in 1967 or in Maharashtra in 1973, with declines in food output and availability considerably larger than in most sub-Saharan African famines, have been dealt with effectively by providing speedy relief through employment projects and wage payments, regenerating lost entitlements and giving the potential victims an ability to command food in the market. The process has, undoubtedly, been helped by the availability of some food in the public distribution system. But there have remained exceptionally large shortfalls in the affected regions even after taking note of the use of these public food stocks and the movement of foodgrains across the state boundaries within India. The areas threatened by famine have managed to get by despite much-reduced overall availability of food by making the distribution of the available food significantly more equal through the redistribution of purchasing power.[15]

The failure of a person to command food in a market economy can arise from one of two different dysfunctions. There can be a "pull failure" if the person loses his or her ability to demand food in the market, e.g., through loss of employment, loss of output, or reduction in real wages. On the other hand, if there is no such change but the person's ability to command food suffers because of supply not responding to the market demand, then there is a case of "response failure". This can occur as a result of market disequilibria, or monopolistic imperfections, e.g., the cornering of the market by some manipulative traders.

The rationale of cash relief rests on the assumption that "pull failure" is the main problem to deal with, and that the problem of "response failure" will not provide a barrier to curing the entitlement problem through regenerating purchasing power. This need not always work, and the possibility of using this type of relief must depend to a great extent on the nature of the markets as well as the limits of bureaucratic management. On the one hand, the more imperfect the markets, the less reliance can be placed on the ability of the market to "respond" to the newly provided "pull". On the other hand, the less efficient the bureaucracy, the more difficult it is to arrange for food movements and distributions to be effectively performed by bureaucratic means without involving the market in any way. It is, of course, largely a matter of choosing pragmatically the appropriate balance of policy instruments, and it would be a mistake to advocate one general method of famine relief for all countries and all circumstances. The important point is not to rule out certain alternatives as a result of defective understanding of famines arising from overconcentration on the physical aspects of food supply, and from ignoring the economic processes involved in the establishment of food entitlement.

These policy issues, along with other matters of strategic choice and logistic planning, have received attention in a number of WIDER studies on anti-famine policy.[16]

3.3. *Famine prevention and removal of vulnerability*

The third aspect of anti-famine policy is the important one of the long-run elimination of vulnerability to famine conditions. Here again, important clues are provided by the economic analysis of the fragility and fluctuation of entitlements of different occupation groups. One of the basic problems does, of course, arise from the fact that most people have no substantial assets other than their ability to work, i.e., their labour power. Thus, the problem of vulnerability can be ultimately resolved only if employment can be guaranteed to all at a living wage, or if social security provisions can provide compensatory entitlements when employment rewards are inadequate or absent.

This is a problem that applies even to the richer developed economies. Indeed, with the high levels of unemployment that have been experienced in Western Europe and North America in recent years, famines could well have occurred, but for the entitlement guarantees provided by unemployment benefits and other means of social insurance. The basic vulnerability of human beings as social animals, surviving on the basis of exchanging their labour or products for food, is a common problem that unites rather than divides different parts of the world. The basic contrasts come, instead, from the social provisioning against entitlement failures that are taken for granted in the richer economies but are very rare in the poorer ones. The need to think about social security provisions even for the poorer countries is undoubtedly strong, and this is a subject with which WIDER's ongoing research is much concerned.[17]

Two different features of the long-run eradication of famine vulnerability have to be distinguished. The first concerns the normal operation of the economy, without social security backing. Variability of entitlements arising from employment fluctuations, output declines, collapse of exchange and prices of particular commodities, etc., can be substantially reduced by adequate diversification and by macroeconomic stabilization policies.[18] Economic stability is undoubtedly important in preventing disastrous losses of entitlements of particular occupation groups.

The other aspect of the elimination of famine vulnerability relates to the provision of public support in recreating entitlements lost due to unavoided — possibly unavoidable — failures in the functioning of the market mechanism. As mentioned earlier, even in the richer countries of Europe and America, slumps do occur and millions of people do lose their jobs, and their survival depends crucially on social insurance and public support. These two aspects of famine prevention have to be considered together, since one is essentially a supplement to the other. The direction of WIDER's research efforts in this important but difficult field has been largely guided by the recognition of this interdependence.[19]

4. Removing endemic hunger

4.1. *Economic pressures and public action*

While famines are related to disastrous declines of entitlements, endemic hunger and regular undernourishment are associated with inadequate entitlements on a sustained basis. Some economies of the world have not experienced famines in any real sense in recent years, but have nevertheless suffered from chronic hunger on a regular but non-acute basis. Examples can be found in South Asia, including India, Pakistan and Bangladesh, as well as in Latin America, in addition to parts of Africa. In a sense, combatting endemic hunger is a harder problem than conquering famines, since the extreme deprivation involved in famine situations can be speedily remedied, in a way that a sustained eradication of entitlement inadequacies for all sections of the population cannot be easily achieved.

The two components of the long-run elimination of famines identified in the last section, viz, maintenance of economic stability and provision of social security, have corresponding counterparts in the battle against endemic hunger as well. The nature of the economy and its functioning are obviously important in making it possible to earn — without social security support — enough income and means of command over food and other necessities to avoid endemic deprivation. However, no matter how efficient the economic system might be, inadequacy of entitlements on a regular basis (with possibly a pattern of seasonality) is particularly hard to avoid in the poorer developing countries. This is where social security, in a different role, becomes relevant again. Supplementary public support as a means of providing regular nourishment (and command over other necessities), to counter endemic hunger and deprivation, is needed in most developing countries. This is no less crucial a challenge for social security planning than the task of entitlement guarantees to eliminate famines, discussed earlier.

The elimination of endemic hunger in some economies has been dependent largely on economic expansion in general. The experience of South Korea is a case in point. On the other hand, some economies that are very much poorer than South Korea, e.g., Sri Lanka and China, have been able to deal effectively with endemic hunger without having to wait for their general opulence to reach levels comparable with the more successful newly industrializing countries. This group of activist but poorer countries has tended to depend to a great extent on public provisioning of food and other necessities. Part of WIDER's research activities in this area has been concerned with learning from the experiences of public intervention in eliminating endemic hunger in these and other countries.[20]

The readings of the experiences of these countries have been the subject of considerable controversy in recent years. There is a need for discriminating analysis in assessing these lessons, and in investigating the possibility of their use in other countries and other regions. It is important also to examine cases of moderate success, without spectacular achievements, in providing entitlement support through a variety of means. There are lessons to be learnt also from the continued undernourishment of sections of the population even in rapidly growing, relatively affluent economies. For example, the persistence of hunger in Brazil despite spectacular economic growth, and the persistence of poverty and malnutrition in other parts of Latin America, deserve attention. The reach and affectiveness of economic growth seem to leave gaps that can be costly in human terms and which have to be studied with a view to reorienting economic policy and public action.[21]

Just as fast economic growth has not always achieved the results that might have been expected, interventionist activism has also sometimes been less than spectacularly successful. For example, one of the Indian states, West Bengal, has now had for over a decade a "Left Front" government, the dedication of which to economic and social reform has been widely admired. It has also brought about by far the greatest extent of land redistribution in India (judged both in absolute and in relative terms), and has used various programmes of entitlement support, including food-for-work projects, on a regular basis to deal with endemic hunger, especially in the lean seasons. The results of these activities have not been, at least so far, dazzlingly clear. While some commentators have seen in this reasons for doubting the wisdom of such policies, others have suggested that the impact of these policies tends to be much slower and that some early signs can already be seen in the field. This is a subject of very considerable confusion, and to sort out the lessons to be learnt — both positive and negative — WIDER has just initiated a probing research project, including collection of field-survey primary data, in West Bengal.[22]

Similarly, the various experiences of intervention and entitlement support in different parts of sub-Saharan Africa, both through production expansion and public provision of entitlement support, have been the subject of critical scrutiny in ongoing research at WIDER.[23] One important lesson is that these two strategies should be seen not as alternatives, but as complementary parts of an integrated programme of action that the African situation demands.[24]

4.2. Undernourishment: measurement and policy

The various well-known estimates of the size of the population suffering from calorie deficiency and undernourishment, to which reference was made earlier, have tended to be based on the use of simple calorie norms. Questions have been raised in recent years about the reliability of these norms, given the observed fact of: (i) interpersonal variations of nutritional requirements: (ii) the possibility of intertemporal variations of intakes for a given person (without affecting the "homeostasis" of nutritional equilibrium); and (iii) the possibility of adjustment and perhaps even adaptation to a long-run decline of nutritional intake. The nutritional literature on this subject has been scrutinized and reassessed from a policy point of view in a part of the ongoing research at WIDER.[25]

It is clear that any mechanical and uncritical use of norms of "calorie requirements" and of other intake figures in identifying the undernourished can be misleading. If these norms are to be used, this has to be done by taking note of possible interpersonal variations, so that a probabilistic formulation of norms would almost certainly have to be chosen. Furthermore, nutritional information has to be supplemented by social and economic data, in order to integrate the nature of nutritional variations, e.g., whether caused by a lower "requirement"or by economic deprivation. This is one field among many in which the fruitfulness of collaborative work between nutritionists and medical experts, on the one hand, and social scientists, on the other, has strongly emerged from WIDER's policy-oriented research efforts.[26]

The measurement problems, as such, should not, however, be made to look more important than they are since — as was discussed earlier — not a lot may depend on the precise estimate of the number of people who are poor or undernourished. But there is an implicit policy aspect of these measurement issues. Limitation of resources forces certain choices as to whether nutritional intervention should be targeted at a relatively small group of severely deprived population, or more broadly spread over a larger category of generally undernourished people. For these choices, the nutritional implications of deprivation have to be better understood, and this is the main rationale for the involvement of WIDER in this particular subject. The importance of these measurement problems lies ultimately in their implications for policy and action.

In directing attention to different aspects of policy requirements for removing endemic hunger, attention has to be paid to diagnostic issues (related to the nature and consequences of undernourishment), general economic questions (related to economic growth and development and the poverty of particular sections of the populations), public intervention issues (the role, results and incentive problems of entitlement support through social security provisions), and problems of politics, journalism and public participation (including the role of the media in providing information and forcing response). These different but interrelated problems have all been the subject of research activities at WIDER to provide an informed and enlightened basis of public action in combatting world hunger.

* For helpful comments I am most grateful to Sudhir Anand, Max Bond, Sukhamoy Chakravarty, Jean Drèze, Eric Hobsbawm, Lal Jayawardena, Martha Nussbaum, Siddiq Osmani, Robert Pringle and V. K. Ramachandran.

References

1. Prepared by S. R. Osmani.

2. World Bank, *Poverty and Hunger* (Washington, D. C.: The World Bank, 1986).

3. See particularly P. Payne, "Undernutrition: Measurement and Implications", and T. N. Srinivasan, "Undernutrition: Concepts, Measurement and Policy Implications", both WIDER conference papers, 1987. A more defensive position can be found in C. Gopalan, "Undernutrition: Concepts, Measurement and Implications", WIDER conference paper, 1987. These papers and also two others by Kakwani and Osmani on related subjects will be published in S. Osmani (ed), *Nutrition and Poverty*, forthcoming.

4. On this general approach, see Amartya Sen, *Poverty and Famines: An Essay on Entitlement and Deprivation*. (Oxford: Clarendon Press, 1981).

5. Amartya Sen, *Poverty and Famines* (1981): L. Oughton, "The Maharashtra Droughts of 1970-73: An Analysis of Scarcity", *Oxford Bulletin of Economics and Statistics*, 44(1982): Q. M. Khan, "A Model of Endowment-Constrained Demand for Food in an Agricultural Economy with Empirical Applications to Bangladesh", *World Development 13 (1985)*: P. Snowdon, "The Political Economy of Ethiopian Famine", *National Westminster Bank Quarterly Review*, November 1985; L. A. Tilly, "Food Entitlement, Famine and Conflict", in R. I. Rotberg and T. K. Rabb, eds., *Hunger and History* (Cambridge: C. U. P., 1985): S. Devereux and R. Hay, *The Origins of Famine*, (Queen Elizabeth House, Oxford); M. Ravallion, *Markets and Famines* (Oxford: Clarendon Press, 1987); M. Vaughan, *The Story of an African Famine* (Cambridge: C. U. P., 1987). See also B. G. Kumar, "Ethiopian Famines 1973-85: A Case Study", WIDER conference paper, 1986, and S. Osmani, "The Food Problems

of Bangladesh", WIDER conference paper, 1986, both to be published in *Hunger: Economics and Policy*, edited by Jean Drèze and Amartya Sen, to be published by Clarendon Press, Oxford.

6. However, in a paper published two years later ("An Investigation of the Cause of the Present High Price of Provisions", 1800), Malthus makes implicit but extensive use of entitlement-centred reasoning to discuss the pattern of hunger in a class-divided society. Even though he evidently saw no ethical objection whatsoever to such inequalities (and viewed the prospect of everyone starving "together" as a "tragic" possibility), his analysis is deeply illuminating on the cause-effect relationships between inequalities of ownership and hunger. On Malthus' modelling of famines, see Sen, *Poverty and Famines* (1981), Appendix B. The relevance of ownership, employment, wages and prices to the acquirement of food and in the causation of hunger was also discussed with clarity by Adam Smith, David Ricardo and Karl Marx, pointing *inter alia* to the possibility of famines without any decline in food availability (on these see Amartya Sen, "Food, Economics and Entitlements", Elmhirst Lecture at the Triennial Meeting of the International Association of Agricultural Economists at Malaga, 1985; WIDER Working Paper No. 1, 1986; published in Lloyds Bank Review, 160, 1986).

7. In the case of the Bangladesh famine of 1974, food output per head was in fact at a peak, on which — and on several other important aspects of that famine, and famines in general — see M. Alamgir, *Famine in South Asia — Political Economy of Mass Starvation in Bangladesh* (Boston: Oelgeschlager, 1980). See also Ravallion's penetrating analysis in *Markets and Famines* (1987), cited earlier.

8. These policy issues are discussed, along with other issues, in the forthcoming 4-volume WIDER publication entitled *Hunger: Economics and Policy*. Other contrasts between the implications of the entitlement approach and that of concentrating on food availability only are also discussed in this document and in other recent publications of WIDER in this area.

9. These issues are discussed by Barbara Harriss and Ann Whitehead in their paper for the forthcoming WIDER study *Hunger: Economics and Policy*, edited by Drèze and Sen. See also Jere Behrman, "Intra-house-hold Allocation of Nutrients and Gender Effects", WIDER conference paper, to be published in S. Osmani, ed., *Nutrition and Poverty*, forthcoming: N. Kakwani, "Is Sex Bias Significant?" WIDER Working Paper, 1986; Amartya Sen, "Gender and Cooperative Conflicts", and "Africa and India: What Do We Have to Learn from Each Other?", both WIDER Working Papers, 1987.

10. See Drèze and Sen, *Hunger: Economics and Policy*, Vols. 1 and 2.

11. On this see J. Drèze, "Famine Prevention in India", WIDER conference papers, and M. J. Desai, "Modelling an Early Warning System for Famines", WIDER conference paper, both included in Drèze and Sen, *Hunger: Economics and Policy*.

12. On this see N. Ram, "An Independent Press and Anti-Hunger Strategies", WIDER conference paper, to be published in Drèze and Sen, *Hunger: Economics and Policy*.

13. These and many other political aspects of anti-famine policies are a part of the WIDER research programme dealing with famines and hunger on a broad basis. See particularly Rehman Sobhan, "Politics of Hunger and Entitlements", WIDER conference paper, to be published in Drèze and Sen, *Huger: Economics and Policy*. The issue receives attention also in volume 1 of the 4-volume book, viz., *Combatting World Hunger*, written by Drèze and Sen. See also the paper by Ram, "An Independent Press and Anti-hunger Strategies", cited earlier. On the relation between politics and policies in the rich, developed countries, on the

one hand, and the fate of the hungry in the poor, developing economies, see Kirit Parikh, "Chronic Hunger in the World: Impact of International Policies," WIDER conference paper, to be published in Drèze and Sen, *Hunger: Economics and Policy*.

14. Office of Foreign Disasters Assistance, U.S., *Annual Report 1985*, p. 27. It is important to emphasize that it is not the intention here to blame USAID in particular for mis-specifying a problem. This type of oversimplification can be found in the pronouncements of other action-oriented agencies and institutions dealing with famine relief in Africa and elsewhere. Also, to be fair it is right to note that summary statements are often difficult to make, without losing the nuances of policy that may be dealt with adequately when it comes to translating the aphorisms into action. But unfortunately there is considerable evidence in the nature of institutional interventions, especially in Africa, that indicate an overconcentration on food supply as such, neglecting other features of the failure of food entitlements.

15. For a major study of food relief in India, and the lessons that there might be in this for anti-famine policy elsewhere, see Jean Drèze, "Famine Prevention in India", WIDER conference paper, to be published in Drèze and Sen, *Hunger: Economics and Policy*. See also Amartya Sen "Food Economics and Entitlements", text of the Elmhirst Lecture at the triennial meeting of the International Association of Agricultural Economists in 1985 (WIDER Working Paper, 1985), to be published in Drèze and Sen. There have been some successful uses of cash payments to regenerate entitlements in Africa also, e.g., in Botswana and Cape Verde. This and other aspects of these experiences have also been studied. See Drèze and Sen, *Combatting World Hunger*, volume 1 of *Hunger: Economics and Policy*.

16. In addition to the works already cited, see also B. G. Kumar, "Ethiopian Famines 1973-85: A Case Study", WIDER conference paper; S. Osmani, "The Food Problems of Bangladesh", WIDER conference paper; M. Ravallion, "Market Responses to Anti-Hunger Policies: Effects of Wages, Prices and Unemployment", WIDER conference paper; all to be published in Drèze and Sen, *Hunger: Economics and Policy*. Related issues have also been examined by Peter Svedberg in a WIDER study on sub-Saharan Africa to be published as a separate monograph.

17. This is one aspect of the general investigation of possible social security arrangements in developing countries currently being undertaken by Jean Drèze and Amartya Sen, which is expected to be completed by 1989. A conference is also being jointly organized by WIDER and STICERD at the London School of Economics, to be held in London in July 1988. Other organizers of the conference are John Hills and Ehtisham Ahmad, of the London School of Economics (see Appendix, page 35).

18. One of the research studies undertaken by WIDER has taken the form of studying the impact of global recession on the standards of living of six developing countries, in particular Chile, Mexico, Nigeria, The Philippines, Sri Lanka, and Tanzania. The studies indicate *inter alia* that entitlement declines have often resulted not merely from the fact of the global recession itself, but also from the nature of the policy response that many of the countries have pursued. The latter has tended to include adjusting in the direction of greater reliance on market forces, often at the cost of providing public support for the more vulnerable sections of the population. Sometimes, these policy packages have been required by international organizations (e.g., the IMF and the World Bank) providing support for economic stabilization programmes of these countries. While these countries have not been particularly prone to famine, there have often been substantial enhancements of mild to acute hunger for vulnerable parts of the population.

19. On this see Drèze and Sen, *Combatting World Hunger*, Part II.

20. See particularly C. Riskin, "Feeding China: The Experience since 1949", WIDER conference paper; S. Anand and R. Kanbur, "Public Policy and Basic Needs Provision: Intervention and Achievement in Sri Lanka", WIDER conference paper; K. Basu, "Combatting Chronic Poverty and Hunger in South Asia: Some Policy Options", WIDER conference paper, all to be published in Drèze and Sen, *Hunger: Economics and Policy*.

21. On this see I. Sachs, "Growth and Poverty: Lessons from Brazil", WIDER conference paper, and R. Kanbur, "Malnutrition and Poverty in Latin America", WIDER conference paper; both to be published in Drèze and Sen, *Hunger: Economics and Policy*.

22. The project is directed by Sunil Sengupta, and is located at Santiniketan, in West Bengal, India. The work will continue for two years, in the first instance, and possibly for another couple of years, depending on the early findings.

23. Peter Svedberg in particular has been concerned with critically evaluating the plurality of experiences of sub-Saharan Africa, the results of which will be reported in the monograph referred to earlier. See also P. Svedberg, "Undernutrition in sub-Saharan Africa: A Survey of Evidence", WIDER conference paper: J-P. Platteau, "The African Food Crisis: A Comparative Structural Analysis", WIDER conference paper; F. Idachaba, "Policy Options for African Agriculture", WIDER conference paper; J. Heyer, "Hunger and Poverty in Kenya's Smallholder Agricultural Areas: Some Regional Comparisons", WIDER conference paper; S. Wangwe, "The Contribution of Industry to Solving the Food Problem in Africa", WIDER conference paper; A Whitehead, "Women in Rural Food Production in sub-Saharan Africa: Some Implications for Food Strategies", WIDER conference paper; all to be published in Drèze and Sen, *Hunger: Economics and Policy*. The issues addressed include production problems (incorporating questions of incentives and rewards as well as distribution of benefits), intersectoral interdependence (including industry-agriculture relations), public distribution (including provisions for food security), and other related matters (e.g., intrahousehold divisions).

24. See Drèze and Sen, *Combatting World Hunger*.

25. Partha Dasgupta and Debraj Ray present a critical analysis of the possibility of costless "adaptation" in their paper "Adapting to Undernourishment: The Biological Evidence and its Implications", WIDER conference paper, to be published in Drèze and Sen, *Hunger: Economics and Policy*. This issue is taken up from different points of view in a series of papers presented at a conference on "Nutrition and Poverty" held at WIDER in July 1987, with papers presented on this subject by C. Gopalan, S. Osmani, P. Payne, and T. N. Srinivasan. Other papers in the conference discuss related themes (by Floud, Fogel, Anand, Harris, Kanbur, Behrman, Kakwani, Jorgenson and Slesnick). A selection of these papers will be published in a volume, referred to earlier, provisionally entitled *Nutrition and Poverty*, to be edited by S. Osmani, which will also include a paper on this subject by N. Kakwani, "On Measuring Undernutrition", WIDER Working Paper, 1986. See also S. Osmani "Nutrition and the Economics of Food: Implications of Some Recent Controversies", included in Drèze and Sen, *Hunger: Economics and Policy*.

26. The connections between living standards, food expenditure, and nutritional levels are investigated in an innovative approach by Sudhir Anand and Christopher Harris, "Food and the Standard of Living: An Analysis Based on Sri Lankan Data", WIDER conference paper, to be published in Drèze and Sen, *Hunger: Economics and Policy*, and "Food, Nutrition and the Standard of Living in Sri Lanka", WIDER conference paper, to be published in Osmani, *Nutrition and Poverty*. Anand and Harris are also producing a more extensive study on this and related subjects for publication as a WIDER monograph.

6.   The Distribution of Income
and
Growth and Distribution
Anthony P. Thirlwall

The average level of *per capita* income in the developing countries has increased fairly substantially over the last two decades, (see Thirlwall, 1994; table 1.2: pp. 15-18), yet the evidence suggests that growth and development in many countries has left the vast mass of people untouched. The growth that has taken place has served largely to benefit the few — the richest 20 per cent of the population. Rural and urban poverty are still widespread, and if anything the degree of income inequality within the developing countries has increased. It should not come as a surprise, however, that the transformation of economies from a primitive subsistence state into industrial societies, within a basically capitalist framework, should be accompanied in the early stages by widening disparities in the personal distribution of income. Some people are more industrious than others, and more adept at acccumulating wealth than others. Opportunities cannot, in the very nature of things, be equal for all. In the absence of strong redistributive taxation, income inequality will inevitably accompany industrialisation because of the inequality of skills and wealth that differences in individual ability and initiative, and industrialisation, produce.

The evidence for individual countries suggests, however, that income inequality ceases to increase at quite low levels of *per capita* income — at about $300 per annum at 1965 prices, or at about $1500 at 1992 prices. Beyond this level, income inequality tends to decrease as industrialisation proceeds. Kuznet's work (1955, 1963) shows that in many of the present developed countries, the extent of inequality decreased in the later stages of industrialisation, and certainly the degree of inequality in the developing countries is greater than in the present developed countries, largely as a result of the heavy concentration of income among the top 5 to 10 per cent of income recipients. The work of Kravis (1960) also shows that the degree of inequality first increases within countries and then declines.

The most comprehensive data assembled to date are those by Adelman and Morris (1971), and extended by Paukert (1973), which show the size distribution for fifty-six countries, developed and developing (see Table 1.5). The table also shows two measures of income concentration calculated from these figures — the Gini coefficient and the maximum equalisation percentage, which indicates what percentage of total income would have to be shifted between the quintiles of income recipients in order to achieve an equal distribution of income. The data show fairly conclusively that inequality increases up to a certain stage of development and then declines, tracing out an inverted U-shape similar to the pioneer work of Kuznets for the now developed countries. The

Anthony P. Thirlwall: 'The Distribution of Income' and 'Growth and Distribution' from *GROWTH AND DEVELOPMENT* (Macmillan Press Limited, 5th ed., 1994), pp. 31-35 © Author 1972, 1978, 1983, 1989, 1994.

average Gini coefficient for forty-three developing countries is 0.467 compared with 0.392 for thirteen developed countries. The maximum equalisation percentage is 35.8 for the developing countries compared with 28.4 for the developed countries. The greater degree of income inequality in the developing countries appears largely due to the higher share of income received by the richest 5 per cent of income recipients. In developing countries this share is 28.7 per cent, compared with 19.9 per cent in developed countries. The share going to the poorest 20 per cent in developing countries is slightly higher than in the developed countries, but there can be no comfort in this fact. The focus must be on absolute, as well as relative, poverty; and the poorest in countries with average *per capita* incomes less than $1000 per annum must be very poor indeed. On average, the *per capita* income of the poorest 20 per cent of the population in the typical developing country is about 30 per cent of the national average. There are about 600 million people living on *per capita* incomes of less than $275 per annum at 1985 prices: 50 million in Latin America; 450 million in Asia, and 100 million in Africa.

Several formidable barriers exist to raising the living standards of the poorest, and to narrowing the income distribution overall. There is the dualistic nature of many economies, perpetuated by feudal land-tenure systems and urban bias in the allocation of investment resources. There is inequality in the distribution of education facilities to contend with, particularly the lack of facilities in rural areas where the poorest are concentrated. Third, there is disguised unemployment on the land and underemployment and open unemployment in urban areas created by rural-urban migration, a shortage of investment resources, and inappropriate technological choices. Until development policy comes to grips with these problems, there will continue to be large pockets of absolute poverty and a marked degree of inequality in income distribution. In deciding on the allocation of investment resources and the choice of projects, a high weight needs to be given to projects which raise the income of the poorest in the income distribution. Fortunately, evidence from the World Bank does not suggest that growth and equity necessarily conflict. If anything, countries with a greater degree of equality have grown fastest. This is shown in Figure 1.2 where the growth of income per head is measured on the vertical axis, and income inequality is measured on the horizontal axis, and it can be seen than many of the fastest growing countries have a comparatively equal income distribution while many of the slowest growing countries have a high degree of income inequality. It appears that income inequality is not necessary for high levels of saving and investment or other factors that contribute to fast growth.

Table 1.5   Size Distribution of Personal Income Before Tax in Fifity-Six Countries: Income Shares Received by Quintiles of Recipients in the Neighbourhood of 1965.

Country and level of GDP per head	Percentiles of recipients						Gini coefficient	Maximum equalisation percentage	GDP per head in 1965 ($US)
	Below 20	21-40	41-60	61-80	81-95	95-100			
Under $100									
Chad (1958)	8.0	11.6	15.4	22.0	20.0	23.0	0.35	25.0	68
Dahomey (1959)	8.0	10.0	12.0	20.0	18.0	32.0	0.42	30.0	73
Niger (1960)	7.8	11.6	15.6	23.0	19.0	23.0	0.34	25.0	81
Nigeria (1969)	7.0	7.0	9.0	16.1	22.5	38.4	0.51	40.9	74
Sudan (1969)	5.6	9.4	14.3	22.6	31.0	17.1	0.40	30.7	97
Tanzania (1964)	4.8	7.8	11.0	15.4	18.1	42.9	0.54	41.0	61
Burma (1958)	10.0	13.0	13.0	15.5	20.3	28.2	0.35	28.5	64
India (1956-7)	8.0	12.0	16.0	22.0	22.0	20.0	0.33	24.0	95
Madagascar (1960)	3.9	7.8	11.3	18.0	22.0	37.0	0.53	39.0	92
Group average	*7.0*	*10.0*	*13.1*	*19.4*	*21.4*	*29.1*	*0.419*	*31.6*	*78.3*
$101-200									
Morocco (1965)	7.1	7.4	7.7	12.4	44.5	20.6	0.50	45.4	180
Senegal (1960)	3.0	7.0	10.0	16.0	28.0	36.0	0.56	44.0	192
Sierra Leone (1968)	3.8	6.3	9.1	16.7	30.3	33.8	0.56	44.1	142
Tunisia (1971)	5.0	5.7	10.0	14.4	42.6	22.4	0.53	44.9	187
Bolivia (1968)	3.5	8.0	12.0	15.5	25.3	35.7	0.53	41.0	132
Ceylon (Sri Lanka) (1963)	4.5	9.2	13.8	20.2	33.9	18.4	0.44	32.5	140
Pakistan (1963-4)	6.5	11.0	15.5	22.0	25.0	20.0	0.37	27.0	101
South Korea (1966)	9.0	14.0	18.0	23.0	23.5	12.5	0.26	19.0	107
Group average	*5.3*	*8.6*	*12.0*	*17.5*	*31.6*	*24.9*	*0.468*	*37.2*	*147.6*
$201-300									
Malaya (1957-8)	6.5	11.2	15.7	22.6	26.2	17.8	0.36	26.6	278
Fiji (1968)	4.0	8.0	13.3	22.4	30.9	21.4	0.46	34.7	295
Ivory Coast (1959)	8.0	10.0	12.0	15.0	26.0	29.0	0.43	35.0	213
Zambia (1959)	6.3	9.6	11.1	15.9	19.6	37.5	0.48	37.1	207
Brazil (1960)	3.5	9.0	10.2	15.8	23.1	38.4	0.54	41.5	207
Ecuador (1968)	6.3	10.1	16.1	23.2	19.6	24.6	0.38	27.5	202
El Salvador (1965)	5.5	6.5	8.8	17.8	28.4	33.0	0.53	41.4	249
Peru (1961)	4.0	4.3	8.3	15.2	19.3	48.3	0.61	48.2	237
Iraq (1956)	2.0	6.0	8.0	16.0	34.0	34.0	0.60	48.0	285
Philippines (1961)	4.3	8.4	12.0	19.5	28.3	27.5	0.48	35.8	240
Colombia (1964)	2.2	4.7	9.0	16.1	27.7	40.4	0.62	48.0	275
Group average	*4.8*	*8.0*	*11.3*	*18.1*	*25.7*	*32.0*	*0.499*	*38.5*	*244.4*
$301-500									
Gabon (1960)	2.0	6.0	7.0	14.0	24.0	47.0	0.64	51.0	368
Costa Rica (1969)	5.5	8.1	11.2	15.2	25.0	35.0	0.50	40.0	360
Jamaica (1958)	2.2	6.0	10.8	19.5	31.3	30.2	0.56	41.5	465
Surinam (1962)	10.7	11.6	14.7	20.6	27.0	15.4	0.30	23.0	424
Lebanon (1955-60)	3.0	4.2	15.8	16.0	27.0	34.0	0.55	41.0	440
Barbados (1951-2)	3.6	9.3	14.2	21.3	29.3	22.3	0.45	32.9	368
Chile (1968)	5.4	9.6	12.0	20.7	29.7	22.6	0.44	33.0	486
Mexico (1963)	3.5	6.6	11.1	19.3	30.7	28.8	0.53	39.5	441
Panama (1969)	4.9	9.4	13.8	15.2	22.2	34.5	0.48	36.7	490
Group average	*4.5*	*7.9*	*12.3*	*18.0*	*27.4*	*30.0*	*0.494*	*37.6*	*426.9*

90

Table 1.5 (continued)   **Size Distribution of Personal Income Before Tax in Fifity-Six Countries: Income Shares Received by Quintiles of Recipients in the Neighbourhood of 1965.**

Country and level of GDP per head	Percentiles of recipients						Gini coefficient	Maximum equalisation percentage	GDP per head in 1965 ($US)
	Below 20	21-40	41-60	61-80	81-95	95-100			
$501-1000									
Republic of South Africa (1965)	1.9	4.2	10.2	18.0	26.4	39.4	0.58	43.7	521
Argentina	7.0	10.4	13.2	17.9	22.2	29.3	0.42	31.5	782
Trinidad and Tobago (1957-8)	3.4	9.1	14.6	24.3	26.1	22.5	0.44	32.9	704
Venezuela (1962)	4.4	9.0	16.0	22.9	23.9	23.2	0.42	30.6	904
Greece (1957)	9.0	10.3	13.3	17.9	26.5	23.0	0.38	29.5	591
Japan (1962)	4.7	10.6	15.8	22.9	31.5	14.8	0.39	28.9	838
Group average	*5.1*	*8.9*	*13.9*	*22.1*	*24.7*	*25.4*	*0.438*	*32.9*	*723.3*
$1001-2000									
Israel (1957)	6.8	13.4	18.6	21.8	28.2	11.2	0.30	21.2	1243
United Kingdom (1964)	5.1	10.2	16.6	23.9	25.0	19.0	0.38	28.1	1590
Netherlands (1962)	4.0	10.0	16.0	21.6	24.8	23.6	0.42	30.0	1400
Federal Republic of Germany (1964)	5.3	10.1	13.7	18.0	19.2	33.7	0.45	32.9	1667
France (1962)	1.9	7.6	14.0	22.8	28.7	25.0	0.50	36.5	1732
Finland (1962)	2.4	8.7	15.4	24.2	28.3	21.0	0.46	33.5	1568
Italy (1948)	6.1	10.5	14.6	20.4	24.3	24.1	0.40	28.8	1011
Puerto Rico (1963)	4.5	9.2	14.2	21.5	28.6	22.0	0.44	32.1	1101
Norway (1963)	4.5	12.1	18.5	24.4	25.1	15.4	0.35	24.9	1717
Australia (1966-7)	6.6	13.4	17.8	23.4	24.4	14.4	2.30	22.2	1823
Group average	*4.7*	*10.5*	*15.9*	*22.2*	*25.7*	*20.9*	*0.401*	*29.0*	*1485.2*
$2001 and above									
Denmark (1963)	5.0	10.8	18.8	24.2	26.3	16.9	0.37	25.4	2078
Sweden (1963)	4.4	9.6	17.4	24.6	26.4	17.6	0.39	28.6	2406
United States (1969)	5.6	12.3	17.6	23.4	26.3	14.8	0.34	24.5	3233
Group average	*5.0*	*10.9*	*17.9*	*24.1*	*26.3*	*16.4*	*0.365*	*26.5*	*2572.3*

Source: F. Paukert, 'Income distribution at different levels of development: A survey of evidence', in *International Labour Review*, Volume 108, Nos. 2-3 (August-September 1973), table 6.

Growth and distribution

Progress towards achieving the twin objectives of faster growth and a more equal distribution of income can be examined simultaneously by constructing **poverty-weighted indices of growth.**

GNP growth as conventionally measured is a weighted average of the growth of income of different groups of people, where the relevant weights are each group's share of total income. The measured growth rate pays no regard to the distribution of income. A high growth rate may be recorded, which has benefited only the rich. For example, suppose *Source: World Development Report* 1991.

Figure 1.2 **Income inequality and economic growth**
Source: World Development Report 1991.

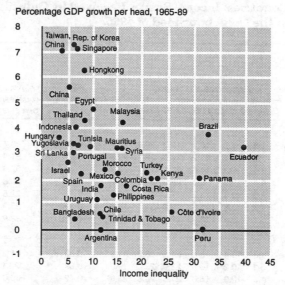

Percentage GDP growth per head, 1965-89

The multiple of the income of the richest 20% to the income of the poorest 20%

the bottom one-third of the population receive 10 per cent of income; the middle one-third receive 30 per cent of income, and the top one-third receive 60 percent of income. GNP growth would be measured as:

% growth of GNP = r_1 (0.1) + r_2 (0.3) + r_3 (0.6)

where r_1, r_2 and r_3 are the respective rates of growth of income of the three groups. Suppose r_1 = 1 per cent; r_2 = 2 per cent and r_3 = 10 per cent. A growth rate of GNP of 6.4 per cent would then be recorded which looks very respectable but the position of the poorest would hardly have changed.

The idea of constructing poverty weighted indices of growth is to give at least equal weight to all income groups in society, if not a greater weight to the poor, in order to obtain a better measure of the growth of overall welfare combining the growth of income with its distribution. In the above example, for instance, if each group is given an equal weight of one-third, the measured growth of welfare becomes:

% growth of 'welfare' = 1(0.33) + 1(0.33) + 10(0.33) = 4%

which is much less than the rate of growth shown by the conventional measure of GNP growth when distributional considerations are taken into account.

A society could go further and say it places no value or weight on income growth for the richest third of the population, and places all the weight on the lower income groups with, say, a 60 per cent weight to the bottom third and a 40 per cent weight to the middle third. The growth of 'welfare' would then look derisory:

% growth of 'welfare' = 1(0.6) + 1(0.4) + 10(0) = 1%

This approach has been experimented with by economists from the World Bank (see Ahluwalia, Carter and Chenery (1979)) to compare countries, giving a 60 per cent weight to the lowest 40 per cent of the population; a 40 per cent weight to the middle 40 per cent and no weight to the top 20 per cent. In countries where the distribution of income deteriorated, the poverty-weighted measure of the growth of welfare shows less improvement than GNP growth, and where the distribution of income improved, the poverty-weighted growth rate shows more improvement than GNP growth.

THEORIES OF DEVELOPMENT

7. Schools of Development Thought

Ron Ayres

Development economics has its roots in Classical Political Economy (Smith, Ricardo and Mill) and the writings of Marx but did not emerge in its modern forms until after the Second World War. In the post-war period there was a renewed concern to understand and theorise the process of transformation and growth taking place in a reconstructed world. Moreover, the rapid and widespread break-up of colonial empires in Asia and Africa left many former colonies in a state of low productivity and economic backwardness while at the same time the emergence of new national states changed the balance of world forces and precipitated a motivation and push for development in the periphery.

From its earliest post-war origins the most important themes that have dominated development economics are: (1) the role of the state as planner and economically active agent, (2) the scarcity of capital and the need for accumulation, (3) the economic case for industrialisation, (4) unemployment and the associated issue of human resource utilisation, (5) poverty, inequality, growth, and distribution, and (6) international interaction through trade, aid and capital flows.

Much of the theorising about development has been concerned to explain the economic, political and social forces that produce, maintain or change international inequalities. The first part of this paper outlines the 'orthodox' approaches to development.

Orthodox theories of development

The *neo-classical approach* to development, a minority view until the 1970s, puts emphasis on economic growth, capital accumulation, free trade policies, open markets and individual decision-making. The neo-classicals argue that the choice between agricultural and industrial commodities should be based on comparative advantage. The rigidities and bottlenecks that LDC economies appear to face and which are used to justify public intervention are according to the neo-classicals the outcome of previous state directed development. Governments have an important role in creating the right kind of institutional arrangements which will allow economic decisions to be based on market prices derived from competitive markets. It is when governments intervene to set prices or direct activity that inefficiency and distorted development occurs. Governments should roll back the frontiers of the state, liberalise all markets and pursue privatisation in order to increase incentives and achieve gains in economic efficiency.

A major strand in orthodox thought explained 'backwardness' in terms of *vicious circle theories*. The root of the problem and the solution to the endlessly repeating circle is to be found in the level of productive capital. The *Harrod-Domar model* ($g = s/v$) also

© Ron Ayres 1994. Some parts of this paper also appear in the author's article 'Development', in Arestis, P. and Sawyer, M.C. (eds), *THE ELGAR COMPANION TO RADICAL POLITICAL ECONOMY* (Edward Elgar Publishing Ltd, 1994).

emphasises the importance of investment and in this case the rate of savings in the economy becomes the critical variable determining the rate of economic growth.

W. Arthur Lewis's model emphasises the *'dual sector'* nature of LDC economies. The traditional sector has low levels of productivity, particularly at the margin, and employs labour intensive techniques but has unlimited supplies of labour. Over time the traditional sector declines in importance but the modern sector which employs capitalist intensive techniques is dynamic and as it grows it absorbs increasing amounts of labour. Within orthodox thought the dual sector model provides a rationale for fully-fledged capitalism.

A number of writers have employed an *'historical stages' approach* to development. One of the most influential variants of this approach is found in Rostow (1969). Rostow attempts to map the history of all societies, past and present, on a linear path through a uniform development process. His work has been criticised for assuming that all societies progress along the same path as the USA and it is only a matter of time before they become a copy of it. Nevertheless, Rostow's concept of the 'take-off' stage generated considerable interest and the required rate of investment (10% or 15%) to raise real output per capita is still debated.

The closely related *modernisation theories* developed by sociologists and psychologists in the 1950s and 1960s emphasised the ideal social structures and institutions for sustained development. Drawing on the work of Durkheim and Weber, modern society with its complex economic arrangements was assumed to depend crucially on changes in the values, attitudes and norms of people. Modernisation theory stresses the importance of individual motivation and capital accumulation and also justifies the flow of foreign aid, trade, investment and technical assistance for development.

Radical theories of development

In the early years most contributions to the development debate were based on the assumption that the state had a central role to play in the transformation of both advanced and backward economies. The case for state intervention was partly founded on the contrasting experiences of the Soviet Union and the developed and developing countries during the capitalist crisis of the 1930s, but it was also justified on clear theoretical grounds; namely, that the conditions necessary for competitive efficiency were not met. State intervention was regarded as necessary to achieve externalities, realise economies of scale, particularly in infrastructural investment, to overcome imperfections and segmentation in markets, including the market for mobilising financial resources, and to take on the role of the entrepreneur. Moreover, developing countries were confronted with two additional problems. Firstly, they were late starters in a world that was dominated by powerful advanced capitalist states. Secondly, they were primarily producing and exporting a narrow range of agricultural commodities and were faced with the need to industrialise.

Radical development economics which rejected the orthodox theory of free trade and the prevailing international division of labour can be split into four broad, albeit arbitrary and overlapping, theoretical approaches:

the Structuralist/Institutionalist School, which emphasizes the existence of rigidities, bottlenecks and lags in the economic structure requiring government intervention and specific economic and other policies,

The Post-Keynesian School, which is concerned with problems of growth and distribution,

The Marxist/neo-Marxist/Dependency Schools, which analysé development and 'underdevelopment' in terms of the historical process through which capitalism was exported and inserted into the less developed countries,

and

The Regulation School, which analyses capitalist change in terms of 'modes of development' that are characterized by a distinct 'mode of regulation' and 'regime of accumulation'.

This categorisation is inevitably somewhat arbitrary. The structuralist and post-Keynesian approaches are by no means self-contained and there is an overlap both of views and the use of theoretical constructs. A common distinguishing characteristic was a rejection of the orthodox theory of 'free trade' and the prevailing international division of labour which left LDCs specialising in the production and export of primary products in exchange for manufactured goods.

The Structuralist School

The 1950s was a rich period for structuralist analysis which explained many of the economic problems facing the LDCs in terms of the failure of the price system. In Latin America Raul Prebisch theorised the long-run deterioration in the terms of trade for primary producers as a function of technical economic factors and/or the monopolization of factor and commodity markets in centre countries, and used this to argue for inward-looking development based on state protected and directed import substituting industrialization (ISI).

Subsequent disillusionment with ISI led Prebisch (1950) and others to explain its failures in terms of social obstacles and inequalities in land and income distribution which limited the market for mass consumption goods. Singer and Alizadeh (1988) have also argued that the problems with ISI were not inherent in the strategy itself but due to the way it was implemented. In the 1940s and 1950s ISI was the only realistic way for LDCs to industrialise. ISI can be seen as a necessary stage in creating an industrial base which later leads to exports of manufacturers. This appears to conform with the experience of the NICs which pursued a flexible mix of ISI and EOI using a combination of market forces and state intervention. For the future the structuralists believe not all LDCs can become NICs and they will need to develop South-South trade if the growth of manufacturing exports is to be sustained.

More recently, with the rise in oil prices in the late 1970s and the growth of international debt in the 1980s, many structuralists have become concerned with analysing short-run adjustment problems in the context of long-run structural change.

The Post-Keynesian School

The Post-Keynesian School has its roots in the work of Ricardo and Marx and more recently Keynes and Kalecki. Keynesian theory and policies were recognised as being inadequate for the type of unemployment to be found in LDCs, but the post-Keynesian analysis of growth, capital accumulation and distribution was relevant to both backward and developed economies.

The development of two-gap models, which linked external transactions with domestic savings, represented an important extension to the Harrod-Domar equation but Kalecki (1976) and other post-Keynesians emphasized that investment and growth had to be analysed together with employment and income distribution. Moreover, the orthodox assumption that the benefits of growth would trickle down or be redistributed to the poor proved to be unduly optimistic in the less developed world.

Kalecki's pioneering work emphasized that there are fundamental differences between developed and less developed countries. Firstly, there is the importance of investment for the supply side, that is as a means of increasing the capacity to produce in addition to creating effective demand. Secondly, that sufficient private investment may not be forthcoming or that resource constraints might limit the scope for producing investment goods. Thirdly, that even if other constraints could be overcome there are structural rigidities which result in an inelastic supply of wage-goods which become more pronounced as employment expands and consumer demand increases.

The notion of balanced (as opposed to unbalanced) growth, which is central to the models of Nurkse (1953) and Rosenstein-Rodan (1943), takes on a wider meaning in the work of Kalecki. He stresses the need for rises and changes in the pattern of demand to be matched by the expansion of output. But Kalecki, unlike dual sector theorists and many of the structuralists who emphasise ISI, gives special attention to the problems of expanding agricultural production. It is not just a technical economic problem but one also requiring institutional and land reform to change the pattern of land ownership, the structure of property rights and tenancy arrangements in order to provide the necessary security and incentives for agricultural production to increase. For Kalecki the notion of a 'big push' takes on a more complex meaning which includes institutional change.

With the assumption of an inelastic supply of wage-goods Kalecki's model explains how a rise in output in the capital goods sector will cause a rise in the price of consumer goods. By further assuming a fixed real wage and monopoly elements in production with fixed mark-ups or profit margins the model shows how the rise in prices becomes generalized. Workers force up wages to restore real wage levels which in turn leads to further price rises in a continuous inflationary spiral.

The structuralists have also been concerned with inflation and reach similar conclusions to Kalecki, but early theorizations, as exemplified in the work of V. Rao (1952), took the relevant structural rigidity to be in the supply of capital goods. Furthermore, whereas Rao predicted that inflation would peter out (MPC<1), for Kalecki there is no such inevitability. Later structuralist analysis of inflation incorporates a propagation mechanism which is heavily influenced by Kalecki.

The link between growth and distribution continues to be central to the post-Keynesian analysis. The basic model assumes different propensities to save out of profits and wages and implies conflict between growth and distributional equality. However, recent developments have been concerned to explore how the Kaldor-Pasinetti-Kalecki model can be extended with different kinds of government intervention (planning and economic policy with respect to incremental production and the pattern of government expenditure) so as to avoid the trade-off.

Dependency Schools

The Marxist, neo-Marxist and Dependency schools analyse development and underdevelopment in the context of the international capitalist system. There are only scattered writings by Marx and Engels on dependency which appear to indicate that they believed that all backward countries would eventually become autonomous capitalist states. As Marx put it in the Preface to *Capital* volume 1, "the country that is more developed industrially only shows, to the less developed, the image of its own future".

Lenin's theory of imperialism, as the highest stage of capitalism, highlights the export of capital and the territorial division of the world as the prime features of the system but the nature of the exploitative relationship is not clearly specified. In other writings Lenin followed Marx and Engels in arguing that backward nations (Russia) would eventually become full capitalist states but there is an implicit recognition that future development would be fraught with difficulties because of:

    (a) the weakness of the peripheral bourgeoisie,
    (b) the effects of competition from the centre, and
    (c) the survival of traditional structures.

Paul Baran (1957) provided the first major analysis of the effects of imperialism from the point of view of the less developed countries. Baran explains underdevelopment not as 'an original state of affairs' but as the result of a particular historical process. In this process developed countries became so by exploiting and colonizing the LDCs and independent industrialization is blocked by an alliance between local (comprador) elites and the metropolitan states. The analysis of A.G. Frank (1967) led to the 'impossibility thesis' and further that underdevelopment was part of the process of development itself. There were several other versions of neo-colonialism (e.g. Admin, Arrighi, Wallerstein) but the common logic was that capitalism was the impediment and de-linking or de-coupling was necessary. The central political message was the need for revolutionary national liberation.

In the 1970s criticism of both the structuralist and dependency approaches and evidence of growth and industrialization in the less developed world was used against protectionism and inward directed development. The success of the NICs and other LDCs was used to justify the benefits to be reaped from outward directed development. Marxist writers such as Warren (1980) used empirical evidence to argue that Marx was right to stress the progressive nature of capitalism and, moreover, that imperialism was in decline as capitalism was growing. Frank and others were criticised for using the concepts of 'capitalism' and 'dependency' in ways which were not Marxist. Moreover, such dependency analysis demonstrated what was empirically false.

Such criticisms led to fragmentation among Marxists. Some disputed the evidence as surface phenomena or explained the success of the NICs in terms of special factors and state involvement, while others emphasised the notion of distorted development and pointed to the growth of inequality, unemployment and impoverishment in the midst of growing wealth. Others, including some structuralists, partly as a response to criticism of dependency theory, attempted to redefine dependency relations in terms of multinational corporations, technology, finance, aid and Third World debt. While another group of Marxists, including some feminists, turned their attention to gender issues and the subordination of women in the context of the spread of world market factories.

The Regulation School

The Regulation school has its roots in the debates of the late 1960s and 1970s between a number of French economists dissatisfied with existing theories of development. There are links with the Marxist approach to development but the school introduces new concepts to analyse the laws of capital accumulation. Thus in the work of Michael Aglietta (1979) the concept of the 'mode of development' is used to distinguish four phases of capitalist development, each defined according to the 'regime of accumulation' and 'mode of regulation'. Phases one and two were regulated by competitive markets with the former characterised by extensive accumulation and the latter by intensive accumulation. According to Aglietta the third phase emerged out of the crisis of the 1930s and was characterized by an 'intensive regime of accumulation' in the new capital embodying technical advance, and a monopoly 'mode of regulation' which provided for a rise in mass consumption. This regime of Fordism employing Taylorist modes of work organisation resulted in a considerable rise in productivity and per capita incomes. Yet by the late 1960s Fordism was also in crisis, the nature of which was theorized by the Regulationists either in terms of unbalanced accumulation or the insufficiency of labour-productivity growth with a consequent fall in the rate of profit.

The response of capital was to introduce a more flexible and fragmented system of work organisation and to relocate primitive-Taylorist and Fordist labour activities in the periphery to exploit lower wage rates elsewhere and weaken the power of trade unions. In the 1960s the relocation took place in the less industrialized countries of the Mediterranean, Eastern Europe, Latin America and South East Asia. Unlike the dependency theorists, however, the Regulationists stress that a new pattern of autonomous local capital was being established in the periphery. This 'Peripheral Fordism' allows for industrialization and growth in the periphery and is defined in terms of a regime of accumulation and a mode of regulation which are conditioned by the globalization of capital.

From the end of the 1970s peripheral Fordism was also entering a period of crisis which the Regulationists attempted to explain in terms of the consequences of central monetarism, the general recession and the resulting financial/debt crisis.

The Regulation approach has been criticised both in terms of its empirical validity and its theoretical adequacy. Nevertheless, it spawned attempts to understand the nature of post-Fordist society and through the internationalization of capital the links with the developing world and this remains an important area of research.

References

Aglietta, M. (1979) *A Theory of Capitalist Regulation*, London: New Left Books.

Baran, P. (1957) *The Political Economy of Growth*, New York: Monthly Review Press.

Frank, A.G. (1967) *Capitalism and Underdevelopment in Latin America*, New York: Monthly Review Press.

Kalecki, M. (1976) *Essays on Developing Economies*, Hassocks: Harvester Press.

Nurkse, R. (1953) *Problems of Capital Formation in Underdeveloped Countries*, Oxford: Basil Blackwell.

Prebisch, R. (1950) *The Economic development of Latin America and its Principal Problems*, New York: U.N. Dept. of Economic Affairs.

Rao, V.K.R.V. (1952) 'Investment, Income and the Multiplier in and Underdeveloped Economy', *Indian Economic Review*, 1.

Rosenstein-Rodan, P. (1943) 'Problems of Industrialisation in Eastern and South-Eastern Europe', *Economic Journal*, 53.

Rostow, W.W. (1969) The Stages of Economic Growth.

Singer, H.W. & Alizadeh, P. (1988) "Import Substitution Revisited in a Darkening External Environment", in Dell, S. (ed), *Policies for Development: Essays in Honour of Gameni Corea*, Macmillan.

Warren, B. (1980) *Imperialism: the Pioneer of Capitalism*, London: New Left Books.

8. Modernisation Theory
Andrew Webster

1. Introduction

We have seen in Chapter 2 [of *Introduction to the Sociology of Development*] that there is considerable inequality and poverty in the world today. However, we have also seen that the nature of this disadvantage depends on the perceptions one has of social and material 'needs' and thereby how a society should 'develop' to make good these 'deficiencies'. The various policies of planned social change which are implemented today to alleviate such problems are rooted in general conceptions of socio-economic change and development that can be traced back to the nineteenth century.

The widespread interest in socio-economic change among European scholars in the nineteenth century was in part a direct reflection of the circumstances of their time. Among other processes, the period saw rapid expansion of industrial manufacturing, a growth in population and urban centres, and the increasing national importance of the political and bureaucratic activity of the State. These processes were not, of course, initiated during the nineteenth century but much earlier, in the British case, for example, as early as the 1600s. Moreover, all European countries did not experience such developments to the same extent. Indeed many, for example Spain, Portugal and the Scandanavian countries, remained relatively untouched by the dynamics of industrialisation. But within certain countries, particularly Britain, France and Germany, the pace and extent of change were comparatively massive. Polanyi (1944, p. 73) speaks of this period as the 'great transformation' and writes of the 'acute social dislocation' created by the 'ravages of [the] satanic mill'. The demands of businesses for cheap materials and low labour costs have always existed, but in the nineteenth century such demands were given new meaning principally because of the development of new systems of production entailing large scale factory manufacturing. In addition, labour productivity and new sources of power (for example the replacement of water by steam-power), along with the growth of national markets, made nineteenth century capitalists much more effective and ambitious than any of their forebears: hence the so-called 'Industrial Revolution'.

The changes this brought about were, according to Dobb (1963, p. 256), 'entirely abnormal, judged by the standards of previous centuries'. He suggests that the period saw a major change from 'the more or less static conception of a world ... where departure from tradition was contrary to nature, into a conception of progress as a law of life and of continued improvement as the normal state of a healthy society'. As Dobb remarks, given such a change in consciousness, 'it is evident ... that interpretation of the nineteenth century economy would most essentially be an interpretation of its change and movement'. And indeed there were many in the universities, academies,

Andrew Webster: 'Modernisation Theory' from *INTRODUCTION TO THE SOCIOLOGY OF DEVELOPMENT* (Macmillan Press Limited, 2nd ed., 1990; reprinted 1993), pp. 41-64.© Andrew Webster 1984, 1990.

philosophical societies and political clubs who regarded an analysis of such changes as their most important task.

The interpretation of these processes of social change varied considerably among those whose work is now regarded as constituting 'classical sociology', in particular that of Marx (1818-83), Durkheim (1858-1917) and Weber (1864-1920). They produced very different theories about the origins, character and future path of industrial society. They also had divergent views about the positive and negative effects of this transition. While their specific ideas on deviance, religion, education, politics etc. have been a source of much interest, it is their general theories of social change that have commanded most attention and which inspired in the twentieth century the emergence of the 'sociology of development'. As we shall see later on, however, the more information that is obtained about past and present day societies of the Third World the more evidently limited are these classical, European-centred analyses.

Despite their considerable differences, Marx, Durkheim and Weber shared the intellectual concern of their time in trying to identify the basic features of societies that promote or inhibit their development. They all, more or less, shared in the spirit of Darwinian thought that came to dominate the philosophical, scientific, economic and political spheres of debate. Darwin's theory of the evolution of nature challenged the established notion of an unchanging, predetermined, God-given order to the world. The idea that one could not only identify but also explain the origin of things and how they develop gripped the imagination of the early social scientists. They were especially interested in Darwin's use of the *comparative* method. He compared different animal forms and organisms in distinct kinds of environments suggesting which were, as biological structures, more functionally adapted for survival.

Darwin's ideas raised the possibility that social change could similarly be charted according to some principle of social evolution: do societies develop through certain 'stages', what have these been in the past and what will they be? Could such questions be answered by comparing aspects of different societies, such as their economic patterns, kinship systems, religions and so on, in order to find out how far they had 'developed'? These were the issues in which the classical sociologists, especially Marx and Durkheim, immersed themselves. Weber was not so obviously tied to the evolutionist approach though he too has elements of it within his work.

The twentieth century has seen the critique, refinement and even attempted synthesis of the ideas of these men. Two main schools of thought now dominate the literature on development and change. The first, which came to prominence in the 1950s and 1960s, is called *'modernisation'* theory. This offers an account of the common features of the process of development drawing on the analyses of Durkheim and Weber. The second, which came to occupy a central place in the development debate in the 1970s, is called *'underdevelopment'* theory and draws its ideas from the analysis of the economic system of capitalism developed by Marx. We shall look at this second school of thought in Chapter 4. In this chapter we shall examine the origins and development of the first approach to social change, that being modernisation theory.

2. The theoretical origins of modernisation theory

As noted above, modernisation theory has its roots in the ideas of Durkheim and Weber which we can now examine more closely.

Emile Durkheim

To appreciate Durkheim's theory of the development of complex modern society from a simple 'primitive' past we must understand his theory of social order and stability. For Durkheim, the crucial question was how do people combine in stable groups to form cohesive societies and what is the nature of their relationship to one another as society grows and becomes more complex?

Durkheim tried to answer this question in his doctoral thesis, which subsequently became his first major book, *The Division of Labour in Society*, published in 1893. In this he proposes that there are two basic types of society, the 'traditional' and the 'modern' which have very different forms of social cohesion between their members. The people of a traditional society perform the limited tasks of a simple agrarian community based on groups of families or clans in village settlements. One village is like any other in what people do, think and believe. In these circumstances, social cohesion is based on the simple common lifestyle and beliefs that prevail within and between settlements. Durkheim calls this form of cohesion 'mechanical solidarity', 'mechanical' in the sense that the separate groups are very similar to one another, conforming to a rigid pattern of traditional norms and beliefs.

The similarity of groups within traditional society does *not* mean that they are heavily dependent on each other: quite the contrary. Each group, though similar to all others, is relatively self-contained, its members performing all the required roles of farming, childrearing, social control, defence, and so on. In other words, the 'division of labour' is restricted and within the capabilities of all in the group. Each group is then a sort of 'segment' — a discrete unit — in a larger society: hence Durkheim also called this a 'segmental society'.

The traditional or segmental society is contrasted with the modern society. How does the latter develop? The basic mechanism that undermines the traditional way of life is the ever increasing number and density of the population. This leads to more people competing for relatively scarce resources. Adopting his evolutionist position, Durkheim believed that in these circumstances, when competition was most fierce, a social resolution to this problem had to emerge: society had in some way to adapt to the circumstances or go under. The problem was resolved by a gradual increase in the social division of labour. New resources could be generated by people taking on the role of producers (as cultivators, livestock farmers, etc.) on a full-time basis while others became similarly specialised in other areas of life outside of material production. Thus, the division of labour became more complex and created an increasing *interdependency* among people. Just as the cells in a growing body differentiate to form specialised organs for particular functions, so social differentiation occurred as specialised institutions were formed by people to deal with particular needs of society (religious, economic, political, educational, and so on). And so, in this way modern society is created. It is more complex and integrated and has a cohesion Durkheim called 'organic solidarity': each part, like a natural organism, is specialised in function and reliant on others.

The modern system creates a new pattern of morality and a system of norms; these social rules are much less rigid than those of a traditional society since they have to act as guides for much more complex and diverse social activities. This means that the 'modern' individual has a much greater freedom of action within a general set of moral constraints. Durkheim believed, however, that this carries potential dangers to society if the individual's desires and ambitions get out of step with the general moral code. When individual desires go beyond the moral order then people become dissatisfied with life and social cohesion begins to break down. Thus, Durkheim believed, being the conservative moralist he was, that the individual must be encouraged to conform to the collective morals of society and to do so for his or her own good.

Some key features of Durkheim's argument can be isolated. First, one should note the stress on the system of morality and norms as the foundation stone of social integration, whether 'mechanical' or 'organic' in form. Secondly, although Durkheim regarded the coming of modernity as progress inasmuch as modern society was more cultured, less rigid, and allowed more scope for individual expression, it is also clear that this flexibility could potentially be a source of individual frustration and unhappiness. At a more theoretical level two comments are worth making. Primarily, it is clear that Durkheim give us little *explanation* for the passage to modernity other than population growth and density. His arguments about increasing social differentiation are not explanations but *descriptions* of the modernising process. His theory is then, relatively limited in its explanatory power. Secondly, we ought to be cautious about his claims for the good reason that they are speculative with little regard for historical evidence.

We shall see shortly how Durkheim's ideas have influenced the development of modernisation theory. The other major sociologist whose work has had at last as great an impact was Weber whose theory of the development of capitalism we can now consider.

Max Weber

Like Durkheim, Weber sought to explain the emergence of industrialisation, though he focused his attention on answering why capitalist manufacturing became dominant only in the economies of Western Europe. In his work, most of which appeared in the first decade of this century, he argued that the basic explanation for this occurrence was the existence of a cultural process peculiar to Western society, namely, 'rationalisation'. Weber proposed that a crucial element in the expansion of capitalist manufacturing was the rational organisation of business enterprise to establish steady profitability and the accumulation of capital. This involved a number of tasks, including an assessment of the most efficient use of capital, expansion through cost reduction and diligent investment, a continual effort to better one's competitors, and an attempt to meet consumers' demands. Weber (1971, p.7) characterised the transition from the 'traditional', 'leisurely' pre-capitalist culture to the diligent hard working ethos of 'modern' capitalism in the following manner:

> What happened was often no more than this: some young man from one of the putting-out families went out into the country, carefully chose weavers for his employ, greatly increased the rigour of his supervision of their work, and thus turned them from peasants into labourers. On the other hand, he would begin to change his marketing methods by so far as possible going directly to the final consumer ... and above all would adapt the quality of the product directly to their needs and wishes. At the same time he began to introduce the principle of low prices and large turnover. There was repeated what everywhere and always is the result of such a process of rationalisation: those who would not follow suit had to go out of business ... [T]he new spirit, the spirit of modern capitalism, had set to work.

While this rational economic activity would no doubt bring good profits, making money was not, argued Weber, the principal factor behind it. Such a motive had always existed throughout the world in business transactions. The particularly significant additional force at work which brought about the transition from just money-making to large-scale capitalist enterprise was that to which he alludes at the end of the above quote: the rational ethos of the 'spirit of capitalism'. Unlike other societies, especially in the East, when the profits of business were 'wasted' on the purchase of exotic or luxurious items for immediate consumption, Western Europeans were typically committed to hard work and the steady accumulation of capital through careful investment. Weber suggested this was not an easy nor natural form of behaviour. One of the important factors that promoted this work ethic was, according to Weber, not economic but *religious*.

In his now famous text, *The Protestant Ethic and the Spirit of Capitalism*, Weber argued that the distinctive care, calculation and hard work of Western business was encouraged by the development of the protestant ethic which came to pre-eminence in the sixteenth century and which was promoted most forcefully by the doctrines of Calvinism. John Calvin (1509-64) was a major Christian reformer. His central doctrine was that of *predestination*. This is the belief that God has already decided on the saved and the damned. The 'sting in the tail' is that according to an additional doctrine no one can know whether he or she is one of this chosen few. Moreover, salvation cannot be earned through good works or declarations of faith. These beliefs must have aroused considerable anxiety among followers of Calvin: Weber suggested that believers must have experienced 'salvation panic'. The only way to bring about a degree of calm, claimed Weber, would be to think that, like the good tree that cannot bear evil fruit, people could not be successful in this world without God's blessing. Thus, the doctrine of unknowable predestination was made less awesome by believing that success was a *sign* (though never a proof) of election.

For this reasoning to work, however, believers had to ensure that they glorified God through all that they did: any weakness, self-indulgence or failure would be an immediate sign of damnation. This would be true in whatever one did, including work. Diligence, discipline, moderation and success was as crucial in business as anywhere else. Thus, according to Weber, these *religious* concerns shared by Protestants throughout Western Europe helped fashion a work ethic which was in tune with the spirit of capitalism, a combination that led to the development of modern capitalist society throughout the west.

Unlike Durkheim's primarily speculative analysis, Weber actually supported his propositions with historical evidence. As suggested earlier, supporting evidence is always a matter of selection and thus there have been those who have challenged Weber's particular selection of data and interpretation of the history of capitalism. We shall not go into the details of this debate which have been carefully discussed by Marshall (1982). Perhaps the central theme in Weber's entire body of work is his belief that as Western Society has developed, more and more of its members act in ways that are guided by the *principles of rationality* and less by the *customs of tradition*. Like Durkheim, Weber thus draws a distinction between traditional and modern society and again like Durkheim sees much of this distinction in terms of a fundamental contrast of ideas and values. Both see the coming of the 'modern' era as the social birth of the 'individual' as a relatively free agent not bound by rigid and unquestioning conformity to past tradition.

In their different ways Durkheim and Weber have provided many of the basic themes of present day modernisation theory in particular their contrast between traditional and modern societies. Each conceives of this contrast in different terms yet this has not discouraged today's social scientists from attempting to combine Durkheim's and Weber's notions into a grand theory of development that incorporates an analysis of changing normative systems, differentiation, rationalisation, business motivation and individual ambition. Such a synthesis on occasions does an injustice to some of the original ideas on which it relies. (As we shall see, this is particularly true of the use of some of Weber's ideas). Nevertheless, drawing on these ideas, modernisation theorists identified the basic features of 'development' and believed that they could construct a useful model which could be used as a yardstick to measure the stage of development of *any* society today: much of the deprivation of the world could then be seen in terms of the continued stranglehold of backward looking traditionalism. We can now consider these ideas more closely.

3. Modernisation theory

In the 1950s and early 1960s modernisation theory was developed by a number of social scientists, particularly a group of American scholars the most prominent of whom was Talcott Parsons. As noted in chapter 1 [of *Introduction to the Sociology of Development*], much of this interest in modernisation was prompted by the decline of the old colonial empires. The Third World became a focus of attention by politicians who were keen to show countries pushing for independence that sustained development was possible under the western wing (rather than that of the Soviet Union). Academics reflected this interest by examining the socio-economic conditions conducive to modernisation.

Tradition versus modernity

In constructing their accounts of development, theorists drew on the tradition-modernity distinction of classical sociologists. Like Durkheim and Weber, these theorists placed most emphasis on the values and norms that operate in these two types of society and their economic systems. Like Durkheim, most argued that the transition from the limited economic relationships of traditional society to the innovative, complex economic associations of modernity depended on a prior change in the values, attitudes and norms of people. Bauer (1976, p 41), for example, argues that:

> Economic achievement and progress depend largely on human aptitudes and attitudes, on social and political institutions and arrangements which derive from these, on historical experience, and to a lesser extent on external contacts, market opportunities and on natural resources.

Development then depends on 'traditional', 'primitive' values being displaced by modern ones.

In a 'traditional' society, three crucial features are noted:

(a) The value of traditionalism itself is dominant: that is, people are oriented to the past and they lack the cultural ability to adjust to new circumstances;

(b) The kinship system is the decisive reference point for all social practices, being the primary means through which economic, political and legal relationships are controlled. One's position in the kinship system and hence in the society is ascribed, not achieved — that is, is a reflection of the status or standing of the family, clan or tribe into which one is born; one's position only changes as one moves up the family hierarchy. Status is then, not earned or achieved, but conferred by virtue of kin relationships;

(c) Members of the traditional society have an emotional, superstitious and fatalistic approach to the world: 'what will be will be'; 'things have always been this way'.

In contrast, 'modern' society is made up of completely opposite characteristics:

(a) People may still have traditions but they are not slaves to them and will challenge any that seem unnecessary or get in the way of continued cultural progress (that is they do not suffer from 'traditionalism');

(b) Kinship has a very much less important role in all areas of society (even within the family) because of the need for geographical and social mobility which weakens family ties; moreover, one's position in the economy, polity etc., is earned through hard work and high achievement — motivation and not determined by kinship;

(c) Members of the modern society are not fatalistic but forward-looking and innovative, ready to overcome the obstacles they find in their way, particularly in business affairs, reflecting a strong entrepreneurial spirit and rational, scientific approach to the world.

It is evident that various ideas from classical sociology are incorporated in these profiles of the two types of society. For example, the description of the modern society includes reference to the splitting off or 'differentiation' of kinship from the economy, stresses individual freedom from constraint especially in business and points to the rational, calculating character of innovative entrepreneurs. Parsons (1951) develops this model in considerable detail elaborating on the choice of actions or behavioural orientations that tend to typify the two types of society. For example, he argues that in modern society an achievement orientation is the likely choice of action for people particularly within the economic sphere since it is a much more rational criterion for deciding who should be given what sort of jobs with what level of reward, than are ascriptive criteria. In the achievement oriented society jobs are allocated and rewarded on the basis of achieved skills and hard work: it is what one can do, not who one is that gets rewarded.

The necessity of developing an 'achievement' orientation in the values system has not merely been regarded as part of a wider process of development. For some theorists of social change the desire to achieve has been seen as the crucial or determinant factor of development. For example, McClelland (1961) and Hagen (1962) claim that the level of achievement in a society is expressed in terms of the level of innovation and entrepreneurship. In traditional cultures both are at an exceptionally low level. Economic constraints or limitations can be overcome given a sufficiently high motivation to do well by the individual entrepreneur. As McClelland (1961, p. 105) argues,

> Men with high achievement will find a way to economic achievement given fairly wide variations in opportunity and social structure ... These results serve to direct our attention as social scientists away from an exclusive concern with the external events in history to the internal psychological concerns that in the long run determine what happen in history.

The stress on ideas and psychological factors in shaping history and the rate of development is clearly evident.

Lerner (1964) adopts a similarly socio-psychological approach to explain the transition from traditional to modern society. There is in fact, he believes, a 'transitional' society, a society which has, through the process of cultural diffusion from more advanced sectors of the world, been exposed to modernity. For Lerner, the 'transitional society' is the 'empathetic society'. The society is defined by what it *wants* to become: the transitional man 'wants really to see the things he has hitherto "seen" only in his mind's eye, really to live in the world he has "lived" only vicariously'. (p. 72). Empathy involves the ability to 'rearrange the self-esteem on short notice', the capacity to 'incorporate new roles', and to have a publicly minded orientation that encourages participation. Lerner's description of traditional society is similar to that offered by Durkheim's notion of mechanical solidarity: Lerner (1964, p. 50) says that,

> Traditional society is non-participant — it deploys people by kinship into communities isolated from each other and from a center ... [it lacks] the bands of interdependence, people's horizons are limited by locale.

In general, then, for Lerner, the more a society exhibits empathy the more it will be engaged in the process of modernisation and the more likely is it to be modern. Like McClelland's measurement of achievement orientation in society, Lerner's empathetic criterion of modernity has quantifiable dimensions:

The latent statistical assertion involved here is this: In modern society *more* individuals exhibit *higher* empathetic capacity than in any previous society (1964, p. 51).

Lerner's account of modernisation is somewhat different from the simple model of two societies, traditional and modern, seen so far, since he tries to identify an *intervening* stage, the 'transitional society'. A more elaborate 'stage' model has been provided by the development economist W.W. Rostow. In his *Stages of Economic Growth: A Non-Communist Manifesto* (1960, p. 4) he claims that,

> It is possible to identify all societies, in their economic dimensions, as lying within one of five categories; the traditional society, the preconditions for take-off, take off, the drive to maturity, and the age of high mass-consumption.

These five stages are derived from an analysis of the British industrial revolution, and take-off he defined as the 'great watershed in the life of modern societies' when obstacles to economic growth are removed, particularly by the onset of an adequate rate of capital investment so that growth becomes a normal condition.

It seems clear that entrepreneurial ambition combined with sustained capital accumulation and investment are seen by most modernisation theorists as two of the principal forces of development. As Roxborough (1979, p. 16) says,

> This emphasis on entrepreneurship and capital accumulation is the single most pervasive theme in the literature on economic growth. It always appears as *the* lesson to be learnt from Western experience and to be mechanically applied to the rest of the world so that they can repeat the transition.

Let us briefly summarise some of the basic themes of modernisation theory and draw out their implications particularly for development policy in the Third World.

4. Summary of modernisation theory and its implications

By way of summary the following points seem most important:

(a) there is a clear mixture of sociological, psychological and economic features to modernisation theory including, for example, reference to value systems, individual motivations, and capital accumulation;

(b) most accounts give greatest priority to the role played by the values, norms and beliefs of people in determining the sort of society — traditional or modern — that they create, and thus value changes are the most important conditions for social change;

(c) the history of the development of industrialisation in the West is no longer regarded as something unique as Weber thought, but as the blueprint for development throughout the world. As one of the contributors to modernisation theory, Eisenstadt (1966, p. 1) claimed: 'Historically, modernisation is the process of change towards those types of social, economic and political systems that have developed in Western Europe and North America from the seventeenth to the nineteenth centuries.'

(d) the evolution of societies occurs as traditional behaviour patterns give way under the pressures of modernisation. While these pressures built up gradually *within* Western societies, the 'developing' countries of the Third World can be *exposed* to them from outside. That is, they can be helped along the road to modernity with the assistance of the developed countries whose ideas and technologies can be introduced and diffused throughout these poorer countries;

(e) this process of 'modernisation by diffusion' should encourage the development of a number of features in the Third World, including urbanisation based on nuclear family households, educational growth for literacy and training, the development of mass media to disseminate ideas and encourage increased awareness about society, heightened political awareness and participation in a democratic system, increased business opportunities through providing capital for investment, the replacement of patterns of authority based on traditional loyalties (for example monarchies, local chiefdoms) with a rational system of law coupled with representative national government;

(f) different societies are at different stages of development because they have been more or less successful in introducing the features of modernity highlighted above in (e).

These, then, are the major tenets of modernisation theory. What theoretical impations do they have for an understanding of development?

1) Lack of development is seen as a condition prior to development: that is, that present day Third World societies are underdeveloped countries gradually moving towards modernity. This may seem self-evident: however, as we shall see this lack of development may *not* reflect obstacles apparent from the internal history of these countries but be instead a result of the relationship they have had over the past few centuries with outside countries.

2) Lack of development is the 'fault' of Third World countries' socio-economic systems that create obstacles to modernisation and encourage little ambition or incentive among individuals, particularly in their work: they tend to have little interest in commercial production and rationally planned long-term enterprise being content to work only as long as they need to satisfy their immediate (limited) demands.

3) Development is presented as a relatively straightforward process of efficient social adaptation to periods of strain (for example one brought about by increasing population); there is little debate about the possibility of fundamental *conflict* between social groups.

4) Development occurs not only along Western lines for Third World societies but also for those countries which are now socialist states (for example the Soviet Union, China), whose future paths will, because of the forces of industrialisation, converge with the road beaten out by the pioneering West.

5) The Western economies will continue to grow and develop so that, in Rostow's (1960) terms, they enjoy the prosperity of the period of 'high mass consumption'. There is no sign given of the possible collapse or steady decline in the fortunes of these economies.

The social scientists who developed these arguments in their professional capacity as academics were co-opted to work with the development agencies, particularly of the United States and the UN. Given that their diffusionist thesis expitly argued that the developed countries could have nothing other than a benign influence in the 'developing' countries their ideas were a great source of justification for the activities of the development agencies. A whole range of policies were fostered by modernisation theory. They have included the injection of capital to aid both industrial 'take-off' and the commercialisation of agriculture, the training of an entrepreneurial elite in the values and motivations most likely to promote free enterprise, the expansion of educational programmes, and only assisting 'democratic' (or notionally democratic) countries.

This policy role for modernisation theory and its evident support of the economic strategies of the development agencies gave it a virtually impregnable position in academic circles, particularly in the United States. Parsons' work came to be regarded as having a significance of classical proportions and his fellow contributors provided further credibility for the whole theoretical edifice. It remained intact for almost twenty years, but, by the late 1960s and early 1970s a number of criticisms began to appear that developed into an out and out attack on its central assumptions and propositions. The main and most devastating attack came from those working within radical, Marxian sociology, till then very much on the margins of academic social science. Their specific criticisms we consider in Chapter 4 [of *Introduction to the Sociology of Development*]. Here we can examine a range of general criticisms made by sociologists, anthropologists and economists that initiated the attack on the foundations of modernisation theory.

5. The critique of modernisation theory

Modernisation theory claims to identify those factors crucial for economic development such as achievement motivation and a decline in the significance of extended family relationships. While it may be the case that substantial economic growth cannot occur without changes in, say, technology, the level of capital investment and market demand, it need *not* be the case that such growth requires major alterations to value systems and social institutions as modernisation theory claims. Indeed, there is a good deal of evidence to the contrary. The following section illustrates this through presenting a number of important empirical and theoretical criticisms that have appeared in the literature since the late 1960s.

First, many critics have pointed out that the principal terms of the theory — the 'traditional' and the 'modern' — are much too vague to be of much use as classifications of distinct societies. The two terms do not give any indication of the great variety of societies that have and do exist; instead, the 'traditional' label is offered as a blanket term to cover a range of pre-industrial societies that have exceedingly different socio-economic and political structures such as feudal, tribal and bureautic empires. A much more careful historical analysis is required of these distinct pre-industrial forms in order to have any hope of understanding the subsequent processes of social change they undergo. Eisenstadt, one of the more historically sensitive of the modernisation school, recognised the force of this criticism, and in a later contribution (1970, p. 25) wrote:

> The process of modernisation may take off from tribal groups, from caste societies, from different types of peasant societies, and from societies with different degrees and types of prior orientation. These groups may vary greatly in the extent to which they have the resources, and abilities, necessary for modernisation.

Secondly, although the theory is supposed to be about the way society develops there is little explanation offered for this process. This is a serious weakness. Apart from reference to the need for forward looking attitudes and healthy economic motivation we have no idea which mechanism it is that brings about the process of social differentiation of which so much is made.

Thirdly, even if, for the sake of the discussion, one were to accept the use of the terms 'traditional' and 'modern' societies is it the case that they are so mutually exclusive as the theory states? Remember, the claim is that, as societies develop, the 'traditional' world gets squeezed out by the force of modern values and attitudes. Yet there is a wealth of evidence to indicate that economic growth and the advent of modernity does *not* necessarily mean the abandonment of so-called 'traditional' patterns of action, values or beliefs. For example, Gusfield (1973) points out that the 'traditional' religion of Islam has been *reinforced* by the diffusion of modern technology, particularly transport, that makes the visit to the shrine of Mecca a much more practicable proposition for many more people than had been true in the past. At the same time, as Mair (1984) argues, the trip to Mecca may be very expensive for Muslims living a great distance from the shrine, so much so that in order to meet the costs of the journey great care had to be taken with household revenues: 'In Java the organisation of retail trade on a capitalist basis was the work of a reformist Muslim movement which not only valued austerity but insisted on the duty of making the pilgrimage to Mecca. It was that duty, a costly one, that drove the members of this sect to practise thrift' (p. 25). In this case then, *in order to sustain traditional religious practices*, the Muslims had to engage in activities typically associated with capitalist investment and economic growth, similar in character to those identified by Weber in his study of Protestantism.

There is also evidence to show that in 'modern' industrial society 'traditional' values not only persist but actually play an important role in keeping it going. Frank (1969, p. 26) shows how the norm of ascription (judging people according to their family background, age or sex for example) plays an important role in allocating reward in Japanese industry, a paragon of 'modernity' if ever there was one. Frank shows that, although recruitment to Japanese companies is based on achievement criteria — the skills and qualifications applicants have — once they are employed their level of pay and promotion prospects depend very much on the age, background and family responsibilities of the workers, highly ascriptive considerations. Frank in fact offers considerable evidence of the persistence of so-called 'traditional' values in many modern including Japan, Britain and the United States. At the same time, we can find evidence that modern industrial society does not necessarily encourage achievement by motivation among all its members, but in fact the very opposite, a lack of ambition: thus, gender relations in modern capitalist society whether expressed in the family, schools, the mass media or in employment discourage equal levels of achievement between the sexes resulting typically in male dominance and female subordination; or again, there have been many sociological studies of the educational system in advanced economies and some suggest that for many working class youths the experience of schooling is to dampen down their ambitions, being socialised into *low* achievement motivation (for example, Willis, 1977), rather than high, as McClelland would assume.

Fourthly, one should question the proposition that as industrialisation and its attendant urbanisation develop the wider kinship system is weakened as people become primarily concerned with their own nuclear family. As Long (1977, p. 37) says,

> Several studies have concluded that certain extended family systems not only survive in a modern economic context but that they often function positively to enable individuals to mobilise capital and other resources essential for modern capitalist enterprises.

Moreover, for urban poor as well as the middle class, and for those who move to towns in search of work, extended family kin are an important source of support as British studies by Anderson (1971), Penn (1986) and Willmott and Young (1971) have shown. While it would be foolish to suggest that urbanisation does not change kinship relationships it would be wrong to claim that it completely undermines the value of extended family ties; rather, these are modified or sustained in a manner different from that which prevailed prior to urbanisation. Yet again, the essential weakness of the tradition-modernity thesis is revealed here, namely, its persistent recourse to generalisations that such and such will happen without inspection of the historical or current evidence.

Fifthly, much use is made of Weber's ideas by McClelland in his analysis of 'achievement motivation' which he believes lies at the heart of economic growth. But Weber's thesis is distorted by McClelland's theoretical handiwork. As we saw at the beginning of this chapter, Weber saw the activity that derived from the concern for salvation among Protestants as an important contributory factor in the rise of rational capitalism. McClelland effectively ignores the importance Weber gives to this religious anxiety by reducing it to a latent psychological drive for success which can be found not only in post sixteenth-century Western Europe but also in a wide range of societies that experienced economic growth later. This does an injustice to Weber not only in terms of an abuse of his particular thesis about Protestantism but also in term of its failure to respect Weber's general approach which was much more sensitive to the sociologically distinct patterns of change that have occurred in history.

Sixthly, as already hinted at above in our fourth criticism, it seems that people may be able to use their 'traditional' roles and expectations (such as those associated with kinship) as *resources* that can be drawn on to serve their social and material needs. A good example of this is provided by Ortiz (1970) who examined the impact of a Mexican government development scheme on a northern community, Tzintzuntzan, whose villagers produced pottery. The government wanted the potters to develop higher quality items for sale on a wider market but, after the failure of initial attempts to do this through the installation of more sophisticated kilns, the project was abandoned. Subsequently, however, pottery production and sales increased dramatically. Ortiz argues that this was due to the growth of the local urban market for domestic cooking pots and the construction of a much better road for the potters to take their wares to town. What is of interest here is that this expanded business enterprise relied on the *traditional personal ties* of friends, kinship and immediate family, so, rather than being an obstacle to commercial growth, these ties were harnessed in such a way as to promote entrepreneurial productivity and success. Commenting on this survey, Long (1977, p. 50), in an excellent summary of many similar case studies, writes:

> It is difficult in the light of this example to accept the view that peasant culture is a major brake on change. On the contrary, once a viable set of opportunities presented themselves the peasants showed every willingness to increase production and become more involved in the market economy.

The notion, therefore, that 'traditional' peasant culture is necessarily contrary to the development of economic growth must be subject to serious question. But surely, one *does* find evidence for peasant conservatism and fatalism? After all, studies of rural development programmes in Africa have suggested that many problems were associated with the lack of peasant motivation: as DeWilde (1967, pp. 176-7) argued, 'the conservatism of the peasants, unless closely supervised, is a major problem'. However, while such conservatism may exist it is more likely that it reflects the insecurity of the rural producer, who is more vulnerable than the higher social classes to disease, death, adverse weather, fluctuating income from produce, and last but not least, exploitation by the political and social system that ultimately makes the peasants' land holding so uncertain. In many ways, then, peasants are *more* likely to be exposed to socio-economic change than other social groups. Conservatism may represent the attempt to establish some continuity and order in these precarious circumstances. When opportunities are more favourable, however, many case studies show that the peasantry will respond in an innovative and commercial manner. As Moore (1969, p. 387) says,

> They will not change simply because someone has told them to do so. That has been going on for some time. It is necessary to change the situation confronting the people on the land if they are going to alter their behaviour. And if this has not yet happened, as by and large it has not, there are likely to be good political reasons.

The final and in many ways most forceful criticism of modernisation theory, is that it entirely ignores the impact of colonialism and imperialism on Third World countries. This is a staggering omission. It is also a failure to acknowledge that economic growth is as much if not more about the *power* to control resources as it is about the 'ambition' to do so. With this in mind, Hoogvelt's (1976, p. 18) sarcasm is deadly:

> In Parson's approach one gets the impression that the history of mankind has been one happy, relaxed and peaceful exchange of ideas, stimulating

Religious fatalism?

While many sociologists have shown that peasant conservatism is a rational response to insecure circumstances, what of those societies where religious dogma appears to demand that its adherents adopt a fatalistic attitude towards life? Many modernisation theorists would claim here strong evidence for the inhibiting effect of traditional beliefs on development. But matters are perhaps sometimes more complex, as Mair (1984, p. 25) suggests:

> In some religions, the idea of an individual fate that one cannot escape may lead people to take little interest in plans to improve their fortunes. Hinduism and Islam both include such an idea, but it is very important to be aware how much or how little in a given case people's attitudes towards the practical problems of their own lives are affected by it. It is too easy to ascribe resistance or indifference to development projects to 'fatalism'. The belief may be temporarily forgotten; or there may be a way of getting round it, as there is with the Yoruba in Nigeria. They believe that everyone is endowed with a destiny at the moment of birth; it may be good or bad. But there are ways of getting the better of a 'bad destiny', and even a good one may come to nothing if its holder does not bestir himself to make the most of it. Certainly the Yoruba have not been behindhand in economic activity. We need to learn more about the real effect of such beliefs on the everyday decisions of those who hold them.

progress here, there and everywhere where contact between societies was made. Cultural diffusion appears as a friendly merchant traveller, a timeless Marco Polo, innocently roaming the world, gently picking up a few ideas in one place and harmlessly depositing them in another. Incredulously, the 'domination', 'exploitation', 'imperialism', and 'colonialism' are *not* discussed in any of Parsons' works on evolution.

This is perhaps not as surprising as it might first appear, since, in basing much of his analysis of Durkheimian evolutionary theory Parsons was merely repeating the omissions of Durkheim's original work. The latter too had little to offer by way of an analysis of power in general and nothing about the specific impact of the imperialism at work in the Third World at the very time Durkheim published his first text on the division of labour. His thesis on the division of labour itself lacks an adequate conception of power. It implies that the differentiation of roles and institutions occurs as a process of harmonious adaptation in which people choose roles appropriate to the needs of modernisation. Clearly the division of labour in the economy *has* occurred but it might be the case that certain groups in society, elites or upper classes, have the power to *impose* this division on subordinates, determining the reward for and control over the work task. As we said in the previous chapter, choice relies on an exercise of power that is unlikely to be equally shared by all people.

work task. As we said in the previous chapter, choice relies on an exercise of power that is unlikely to be equally shared by all people.

Chapter 4 of *Introduction to the Sociology of Development* discusses an alternative way of conceptualising development and the lack of it that relies very heavily on an analysis of conflict and inequalities of economic power: this is 'underdevelopment' theory.

6. Conclusion

In conclusion, two general remarks can be made. First, modernisation theory is clearly an oversimplified model of development that lacks two essential ingredients: an adequate historical input and a structural perspective. Historically, it ignores a wealth of evidence, some of which has been presented above, which indicates that the process of economic growth cannot be encapsulated in simplistic notions about the displacement of 'traditional' values systems and institutions by 'modern' ones. Structurally, the theory is insensitive to the specific ways in which factors for economic growth such as the introduction of new technology or markets may be interpreted, or modified or accommodated within *existing* social relationships. In addition, the inequalities of power and social class that structure these relationships are virtually ignored.

Secondly, despite the weakness of its thesis, modernisation theory is right to focus our attention on the role of values and attitudes in affecting people's behaviour and thereby their response to and fashioning of social change. It may be the case that economic opportunities existed for many entrepreneurs in Western European modernisation who could thereby give full rein to their innovative, calculative spirit. Yet it may well be the case that such opportunities do not exist in the Third World (nor for that matter in some of today's advanced states) for reasons we shall see in the next chapter. Thus, the values and attitudes that people in the Third World draw on do not necessarily express the ambitions of an 'achievement' drive since this would be unrealistic where economic opportunities are typically very limited.

The problem faced by the Third World peasantry is its increasing insecurity: agricultural production in the world economy is now dominated by rich industrial countries, such as the United States. This vulnerability is nothing new: as Worsley (1984) says, 'The world has never been a place where the peasants have held power, even when they constituted nine out of ten of the population. They will have even less political influence in the future' (p. 166). Perhaps in order to maintain the little influence they have, peasants may draw on 'traditional' values as repositories of some security, and be prepared to support political parties that champion nationalism, popular socialism and 'self-reliance'.

The relationship between values and the economic context is, therefore a complex and dynamic process inadequately conceived by the traditional values/traditional economy — modern values/modern economy dualism of modernisation theory.

'Modernisation' in practice: the case of a French colony

Niger is one of the poorer countries of West Africa and until the exploitation of uranium reserves in the late 1960s was one of the poorest countries in the world. It has relied on groundnut oil as its primary source of export revenue for decades. It was once a French colony (1922-60). When the French first established control over the territory there appeared little prospect, at least in their eyes, of development — which meant the extraction of raw materials and the sale of French goods: the land was poor, the population small so that, as Roberts (1981) says, 'French colonial officers found little justification for their presence, either military or economic.' The indigenous Hausa people were accused of being idle and lacking any real commercial spirit: what is particularly interesting is why the French thought this the case. Any observer would have noted that the Hausa were in fact exceptionally successful farmers producing considerable quantities of grain from poor, rain-fed fields. For example, using only one hectolitre of seed, on marginal land Hausa farmers could with fairly limited effort produce 300-400 hectolitres of grain, whereas farmers in France could produce only 30-40 hectolitres 'after *incessant* labour *and* the use of manure and fertilisers'. Rather than applauding the Hausa's efficiency, the French declared them idle for not developing their productive capacities further in the service of the colony. Such 'natural improvidence' could only be overcome through 'civilising' the Hausa.

But as Roberts writes, ' "Civilisation" had not much chance to prove itself since the improved methods of cultivation, including ploughs brought over from France, had produced disastrous results. By the end of the 1920s, government promotion of agricultural development in Niger was limited, consisting mainly of crop trials and model sheep and ostrich farms. Any peasant resistance to these marvels of Gallic civilisation simply confirmed the French in their view that the Hausa were backward, rather than an understandable reaction to inappropriate 'development'. For example, the authorities required the Hausa to stock cereal in case of drought; the Hausa resisted doing this because their custom was to trade surplus cereal for livestock from local pastoralists. In times of shortage the cattle were traded for grain from cereal farmers based in the more fertile regions to the south. Roberts comments, this north-south trade was not to the advantage of the French colonialists whose subsequent imposition of 'compulsory grain reserves hindered the development of regional trade and certainly contributed, like forced labour and conscription, to driving some of the population into Nigeria' (p. 199).

9.   Growth and Structural Change
Malcolm Gillis, Dwight H. Perkins, Michael Roemer and Donald R. Snodgrass

One-sector growth models

In Chapters 7 through 14 we shall analyze how the quality and quantity of labor and of savings and investment are mobilized and used to promote economic development. The theory explaining the relationship between these inputs and the growth in national product is based on the **production function.** At the individual firm or microeconomic level, the production function tells how much the output of a firm or factory, such as a textile mill, will increase if the number of workers or the number of spindles and looms rises by a given amount. These are mathematical expressions, often derived from engineering specifications, that relate given amounts of physical inputs to the amount of physical output that can be produced with those inputs. Often, for convenience, microeconomic production functions are expressed in money values rather than in physical quantities.

At the national or economy-wide level, production functions describe the relationship of the size of a nation's labor force and its stock of capital with the level of that nation's gross national product. These economy-wide relationships are called **aggregate production functions.** They measure increases in the value of output or national product, given the value of increases in such inputs as the stock of capital and the labor force. Because both inputs and outputs are measured in aggregate terms (national capital stock, GNP), index-number and other measurement problems of the kind just described do introduce some ambiguity into the interpretation of economy-wide production functions. Still, it is the one tool we have for relating inputs and output at the national level within a consistent framework. For that reason, it is useful to see what this aggregate production function can tell us about how inputs contribute to growth before turning in later chapters to how those inputs can be mobilized.

The Harrod-Domar model

The simplest and best known production function used in the analysis of economic development was developed independently during the 1940s by economists Roy Harrod of England and Evsey Domar of MIT, primarily to explain the relationship between growth and unemployment in advanced capitalist societies.[1] But the Harrod-Domar model has been used extensively in developing countries as a simple way of looking at the relationship between growth and capital requirements.

The underlying assumption of the model is that the output of any economic unit, whether a firm, an industry, or the whole economy, depends upon the amount of capital invested in that unit. Thus if we call output Y and the stock of capital K, then output can be related to capital stock by

$$Y = K/k, \tag{1}$$

where k is a constant, called the capital-output ratio. To convert this into a statement about the growth of output, we use the notation Δ to represent increases in output and capital, and write

$$\Delta Y = \Delta K / k. \tag{2}$$

The growth rate of output, g, is simply the increment in output divided by the total amount of output, $\Delta Y / Y$. If we divide both sides of Equation 2 by Y, then

$$g = \Delta Y / Y = \Delta K / Y . 1/k. \tag{3}$$

For the whole economy, ΔK is the same as investment, I, which must equal savings, S. Hence, $\Delta K / Y$ becomes I/Y, and this is equal to S/Y, which can be designated by the savings rate, s, a percentage of national product. Equation 3 can then he converted to

$$g = s/k, \tag{4}$$

which is the basic Harrod-Domar relationship for an economy.

Underlying this equation is the view that capital created by investment in plant and equipment is the main determinant of growth and that it is savings by people and corporations that make the investment possible. The **capital-output ratio** is simply a measure of the productivity of capital or investment. If an investment of $3,000 in a new plant and new equipment makes it possible for an enterprise to raise its output by $1,000 a year for many years into the future, then the capital-output ratio for that particular investment is 3:1. Economists often use the term **incremental capital-output ratio,** abbreviated ICOR, because in studying growth one is mainly interested in the impact on output of additional or incremental capital. The incremental capital-output ratio measures the productivity of additional capital while the (average) capital-output ratio refers to the relationship between a nation's total stock of capital and its total national product.

For economic planners, given this simple equation, the task is straightforward. The first step is to try to come up with an estimate of the incremental capital-output ratio (k in Equation 3) for the nation whose plan is being drawn up. There are two alternatives for the next step. Either planners can decide on the rate of economic growth (g) they wish to achieve, in which case the equation will tell them the level of savings and investment necessary to achieve that growth. Or planners can decide on the rate of savings and investment that is feasible or desirable, in which case the equation will tell planners the rate of growth in national product that can be achieved.

This procedure can be applied to the economy as a whole, or it can be applied to each sector or each industry. Incremental capital-output ratios, for example, can be calculated separately for agriculture and industry. Once planners decide how much investment will be allocated to each sector, the Harrod-Domar equations determine the growth rates to be expected in each of the two sectors.

Production functions

At the heart of this kind of analysis is the explicit or implicit assumption that the incremental capital-output ratio is a single fixed number. This assumption is consistent with a production function that employs fixed proportions of capital and labor and constant returns to scale, like that depicted in Figure 1. Output in this figure is represented by **isoquants,** which are combinations of inputs (labor and capital in this case), that produce equal amounts of output. Only two isoquants are shown in this diagram. The L-shape of the isoquants indicates production processes that use fixed proportions of capital and labor. For example, it takes capital (plant and equipment) of $10 million and 100 workers to produce 100,000 tons of cement. If more workers are added without investing in more capital, output will not rise above 10,000 tons per year. Because the diagram is also drawn with **constant returns to scale,** if capital in the cement industry is doubled to $20 million and labor is doubled to 200 workers, output also doubles to 200,000 tons per year.

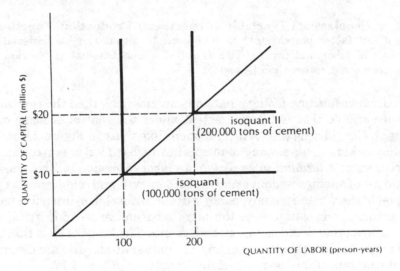

Figure 1   Production Function with Fixed Coefficients. With constant returns to scale, the isoquants will be L-shaped and the production function will be the straight line through their minimum-combination points.

Most economists, however, believe that the production function for many industries, and for the economy as a whole, looks more like that depicted in Figure 2. In this figure, if one starts with output of 100,000 tons at point *a*, using $10 million of capital and 100 workers (not shown in the figure), the industry could be expanded in any of three ways. If industry planners decide to expand at constant factor proportions and move to point *b* on isoquant II, the situation would be identical to the fixed proportions case of Figure 1. But production of 200,000 tons could be achieved by using more labor and less capital, a more *labor intensive* method, at a point like *c* on isoquant II. In that case the incremental capital-output ratio falls to 1.4:1, if the price of cement is $50 a ton. Or if

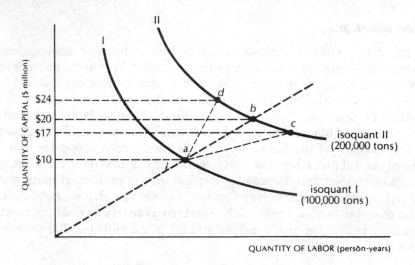

QUANTITY OF LABOR (person-years)

Figure 2   Neoclassical (Variable Proportions) Production Function. Instead of requiring fixed factor proportions, as in Figure 1, output can be achieved with varying combinations of labor and capital. This is called a **neoclassical** production function. The isoquants are curved, rather than L-shaped.

If the production function facing a nation is neoclassical, then the capital-output ratio becomes a variable that is to some extent under the control of policymakers in the government. Considering production functions like those in Figure 2 from the industry level, policymakers in developing countries in which capital is scarce can try to induce manufacturers and farmers to employ more labor-intensive technologies. Then, for a given amount of savings and investment, both growth and employment can be higher. At the level of the whole economy, policy will encourage labor-intensive technologies as well as encourage investment in the more labor-intensive industries, reducing the demand for investment and saving on both counts. The kinds of tools that policymakers may use to accomplish this reduction in the capital-output ratio are discussed in depth in several chapters of this text, especially Chapters 8, 13, and 17.

The appropriate incremental capital-output ratio will vary among countries and, for a single country, over time. Poor countries, with low savings rates and surplus (unemployed and underemployed) labor, can achieve higher growth rates by economizing on capital and utilizing as much labor as possible. As economies grow and per-capita income rises, savings rates tend to increase and the labor surplus diminishes. Thus the ICOR shifts upwards.

Table 1   **Selected Incremental Capital-Output Ratios**

Country	Incremental capital-output ratio (1970-1981)[a]
United States	6.6
Norway	6.7
Japan	7.4
South Korea	3.3
Indonesia	2.6
India	6.0
Argentina	13.3
Brazil	2.8
Venezuela	6.8
Ivory Coast	4.2
Kenya	4.0
Tanzania	5.2

Source: World Bank, World Tables, Vol. 4 3d ed., Economic Data (Baltimore: Johns Hopkins University Press, 1983) pp. 9, 23, 39, 85, 95, 101, 103, 123, 175, 239, 247, and 257.

[a] These ratios were derived by dividing the average share of gross domestic investment in gross domestic product by the rate of growth in gross domestic product, both figures being for the years 1970-1981.

In the more advanced countries it can be higher than in the developing countries without sacrificing growth. And resource-rich developing countries, such as those exporting petroleum, can afford more capital-intensive development than other LDCs. These shifts in the ICORs can come about through market mechanisms as prices of labor and capital change in response to changes in supplies. As growth takes place, savings become relatively more abundant and hence the price of capital falls while employment and wages rise. Thus all producers increasingly economize on labor and use more capital. Alternatively, in Soviet-type and other planned economies, the planners can allocate investment in ways that move the economy towards an appropriate ICOR. Finally, technological change and "learning by doing" can play important roles. Both can contribute to increased productivity of all factors of production, which reduces the ICOR. In Figures 1 and 9, increased factor productivity can be represented by a shifting inward of each isoquant toward the origin.

Data on incremental capital-output ratios for a few selected countries are presented in Table 1. These ratios vary from under 3:1 to 7:1 and even higher. Some of these differences can be explained by the point made earlier that richer nations such as the United States, Norway, and Japan tend to have higher ratios because capital is less expensive relative to labor than in poorer countries in the early stages of development. Other differences, however, such as those between Korea and India, have little to do with differences in the relative scarcity of capital. These differences are more likely to other inputs are managed.

Sources of growth

The simple Harrod-Domar production function, therefore, obscures some of the basic differences in growth performance between nations. One wants to know much more about why the capital-output ratio varies so much. To that end, economists such as Robert Solow and Edward Denison have attempted to explain the sources of growth with a different form of the production function, one that allows the analyst to separate out the various causes of growth rather than subsume all of these other causes in the capital-output ratio.

The production function used in this analysis is neoclassical like that depicted in Figure 2. However, more factors of production are included. The function relates increases in output to increases in inputs of capital, skilled and unskilled labor, and other variables. This method also attempts to separate out the contribution made by rises in the efficiency with which inputs are used. The production function takes the following form:

$$Y = f(K, L, T, A), \qquad [5]$$

where

Y = output or national product
K = the stock of capital
L = the size of the labor force
T = the stock of arable land and natural resources

and A = increases in the productivity or efficiency with which inputs are used.

The next step is to convert this production function into a form that makes measuring the contribution of each input possible. The derivation of this new form of the equation involves calculus and so is presented in the appendix to this chapter. The resulting equation is

$$g_N = a + W_K \bullet g_K + W_L \bullet g_L + W_T \bullet g_T \qquad [6]$$

where

g = the growth rate of any variable
W = the share in income of any input, (e.g., the share of wages)
N = national product
K = the capital stock
L = labor
T = arable land and natural resources

and a = the variable measuring the shift in the production function resulting from greater efficiency in the use of inputs.

Data for each of these variables can be found in the statistical handbooks of many nations and the contribution of each of these variables to growth can thus be measured and identified.

A simple numerical example illustrates the way in which this equation is used. Assume

A simple numerical example illustrates the way in which this equation is used. Assume the following values for the variables in the equation:

g_N = .06 (a GNP growth rate of 6 percent a year)

g_K = .07 (capital stock rises at 7 percent a year)

g_L = .02 (the labor force increases at 2 percent a year)

g_T = .01 (arable land is rising by one percent a year).

The share of labor in national income is 60 percent (W_L = 0.6), the share of capital is 30 percent (W_K = 0.3), and the share of land is ten percent

(W_T = 0.1). By substituting these figures into Equation 6 we get:

$$0.06 = a + 0.3 \bullet 0.07 + 0.6 \bullet 0.02 + 0.1 \bullet 0.01$$

Solving for a, we get a = 0.026.

What these figures tell us is that productivity growth is 2.6 percent a year and thus accounts for just under half of the total growth of GNP of 6 percent a year.

Growth accounting or **sources of growth analysis,** as this method has been called, has been carried out for many nations. Because of variations in the way different economists carry out growth accounting, it is not possible to summarize the results of these calculations in a simple table. Two conclusions that have arisen from this empirical work, however, provide an important basis for much of the analysis in subsequent chapters.

First, most efforts to measure the sources of growth have indicated that increases in productivity or efficiency (a in Equation 6) account for a much higher proportion of growth than was believed to be the case before these calculations were made. Increases in the capital stock frequently account for much less than half of the increase in output, particularly in rapidly growing countries. Second, while capital does not contribute as much to growth as assumed in early growth models, capital does tend to play a larger role in growth in today's developing countries than it did in those nations that had already achieved high levels of per-capita national product by the 1980s. Furthermore, some of the increases in efficiency or productivity involve advances in technology that are embodied in capital equipment. Thus mobilization of capital remains a major concern of policymakers in developing countries and is the subject of four chapters in this text (Chapters 11-14), but mobilization of labor and improvements in the quality of that labor are also important (Chapters 9-10). And of equal or even greater importance is the productivity of these inputs or the efficiency with which they are used. The sources of differences in productivity and efficiency are not the subject of a single chapter but are a recurring theme throughout this book.

make up the output side of the production function equation. These shifts in the structure of output or national product are the subject of the remainder of this chapter. In this chapter we are mainly concerned with the relationship between these sectors as growth takes place. In later chapters (notably Chapters 18-20) we shall look at development within each of these sectors individually.

One clear pattern of changing economic structure in the course of economic development is that, as per-capita income rises, the share of industry in gross national product rises also. While it is possible to conceive of a situation in which a nation moves from a condition of poverty to one of wealth while concentrating on agriculture, this kind of growth has yet to occur. Every country that has achieved a high per-capita income has also experienced a population shift — where the majority moves from rural areas and farming to cities and industrial jobs. All have also experienced an increase in industrial value-added in gross national product.

There are two principal reasons for this. The first is **Engel's law.** In the nineteenth century Ernst Engel discovered that as incomes of families rose, the proportion of their budget spent on food declined. Since the main function of the agricultural sector is to produce food, it follows that demand for agricultural output would not grow as rapidly as demand for industrial products and services, and hence the share of agriculture in national product would decline. This relationship holds for all countries that have experienced sustained development.

A second reason has reinforced the impact of the first: productivity in the agricultural sector has risen as growth has progressed. People require food to survive, and if a household had to devote all of its energies to producing enough of its own food, it would have no surplus time to make industrial products or to grow surplus food that could be traded for industrial products. In the course of development, however, increased use of machinery and other new methods of raising crops have made it possible for an individual farmer in the United States, for example, to produce enough food to feed and feed very well, another seventy to eighty people. As a result only 3 percent of the work force of the United States is in farming, while the others have been freed to produce elsewhere.

The rising share of industry also helps to explain why, as incomes rise, an increasing percentage of every country's population lives in cities rather than in the countryside. There are **economies of scale** in the manufacture of many industrial products. The existence of economies of scale implies that output per unit of input rises as the firm size increases: that is, a large industrial enterprise in an industry such as steel will produce more steel per dollar cost (made up from the cost of coal, iron ore, limestone, labor, plant machinery and electricity) than will a smaller enterprise. Furthermore it makes sense for many different kinds of industrial enterprises to locate in the same place so that common support facilities, such as electric power stations, transport, and wholesalers, can also operate at an efficient level. The result is that industry leads to the growth of cities, and the growth of cities itself tends to increase the share of manufacturing and some services in gross national product. In the rural economies of most poor countries, for example, food processing is done in the home and is not usually included in gross national product calculations at all. In urbanized nations, in contrast, food processing is often done in large factories, and the value-added produced by these factories is included in the share of the manufacturing sector.

Even though the rising share of manufacturing in gross national product and the declining share of agriculture is a pattern common to all nations, it does not follow that the rates of change are the same in each country. In fact planners around the world have been plagued by the question of how much to emphasize agriculture versus industry during the course of development. The Chinese in the 1950s, for instance, tried to follow, the Soviet example of putting most of their investment into industry, hoping that agriculture would somehow take care of itself. Disastrous harvests in 1959 through 1961 forced the government to put more resources, notably chemical fertilizer, into agriculture, but machinery, steel, and related industries continued to receive the lion's share of investment. Food production grew, but only just fast enough to hold per-capita consumption constant since population grew at 2 percent a year. When wages and farm incomes began to rise in the late 1970s, however, constant per-capita output was perceived as being insufficient, and the government once again greatly increased the share of investment going to agriculture. In the 1980s they took the even more radical step of abandoning collectivized agriculture in what proved to be a successful move to raise agricultural production at an accelerated rate.

For a decade and more after independence some African nations also felt that agriculture required little help. Increased food requirements could be met by the simple expedient of expanding the amount of land under cultivation. But population continued to growth, at rates over 3 percent a year in many countries, and the supply of readily available arable land became exhausted. On the edge of the Sahel desert the overuse of fragile land has contributed to severe ecological damage that, together with a change in weather patterns, has brought about widespread famine in the region.

In fact, virtually every government in the developing world has struggled with the question of the proper relationship between agricultural and industrial development. Would a greater awareness of the historical relationship between agriculture and industry in countries undergoing development improve performance in these countries? If planners knew that the share of agriculture in national product always remained above 40 percent until per-capita income rose above $500, those planners would have a target to aim at. Investment in agriculture could be kept at a level to ensure that the share did not fall below 40 percent. But what if there were no consistent patterns among countries at comparable levels of development?

Hollis Chenery and his co-authors, for example, found that there was no single pattern for the changes in shares and that to talk meaningfully about consistent patterns at all, the nations of the world had to be divided into three subgroups: large countries, meaning countries with a population over 15 million in 1960; small countries that emphasize primary (agriculture plus mining) exports; and small countries that emphasize industrial exports.[2] Even within these subgroups there was enormous variation. Figure 3, for example, compares Chenery's large-country pattern, estimated in this case from a sample of nineteen countries, with the actual historical performance of several European countries plus Japan. As is apparent from this figure, the average performance of these nine industrialized nations is similar to the trend estimated by

Chenery and Taylor, but no single country was on the trend line.

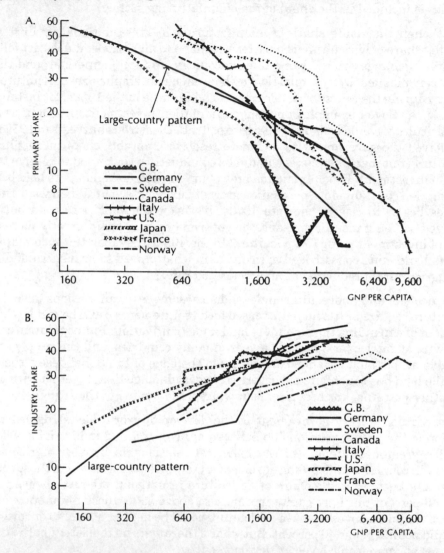

Figure 3   Development Patterns. Chenery's large-country patterns are compared here to the actual, historical performance of nine countries. Panel A depicts the primary share, and Panel B the industry share. *Source*: H. Chenery and L.J. Taylor, "Development Patterns" *Review of Economics and Statistics* (November 1968), p. 401. Per-capita GNP has been converted from 1964 to 1983 prices using a conversion ratio of 3.2:1.

Chenery and his coauthors often speak of the trends they have estimated as being the **normal pattern** of development for large (or small) countries. The term has contributed to a good deal of misunderstanding and misuse of the results. Planners have compared these estimated trends with the actual performance of their country, and if their own industrial share has grown more rapidly than the trend, they have

Chenery and his coauthors often speak of the trends they have estimated as being the **normal pattern** of development for large (or small) countries. The term has contributed to a good deal of misunderstanding and misuse of the results. Planners have compared these estimated trends with the actual performance of their country, and if their own industrial share has grown more rapidly than the trend, they have congratulated themselves for a good performance. Or if the share has grown at a rate below the general trend line they have concluded that something had to be done to correct a poor performance. In either case a deviation from the trend was seen as a cause for concern. But these patterns are nothing more than the average results obtained from comparing many diverse patterns. They are not a guide to what a country ought to do. Perhaps someday we shall be in a position to say that one trend makes more efficient use of a nation's resources than another trend or leads to a faster overall growth rate. Today all we have are data and estimates that give us a general idea of the trends to expect as economic development occurs. Under the circumstances it is better to drop the term *normal pattern* from the vocabulary and speak of **average pattern.** On the average the primary share (agriculture plus mining) of GNP in large countries falls from 32 percent at $600 per capita (in 1983 prices) to 19 percent at $1,600 per capita, but the variation around that trend is so great that these patterns provide only the crudest of guides to planners.

Two-sector models

Long before the concept of GNP was invented or economists had many statistics of any kind to work with, they recognized the fundamental importance of the relationship between industry and agriculture. To better understand the nature of that relationship, they began to design simple models to explain the key connections between the two sectors. The best known of the earlier models appeared in David Ricardo's *The Principles of Political Economy and Taxation,* published in 1817. In his model Ricardo included two basic assumptions that have played an important role in two sector models ever since. First, he assumed that the agricultural sector was subject to **diminishing returns:** given increases in inputs lead to continually smaller increases in output. The reason is that crops require land and land is limited. To increase production, Ricardo felt, farmers would have to move onto poorer and poorer land, thus making it more and more costly to produce a ton of grain. Second, Ricardo put forward the concept that today is called **labor surplus.** Britain in the early nineteenth century still had a large agricultural work force, and Ricardo felt that the industrial sector could draw away the surplus labor in the rural sector without causing a rise in wages in either the urban or rural areas.

The concept of labor surplus is closely related to concepts such as rural unemployment and underemployment or disguised unemployment. **Rural unemployment** is formally much the same as urban unemployment. When there are people who desire work, are actively looking for work, and cannot find work, they are said to be **unemployed.** Very few people in rural areas of developing countries are unemployed in this sense. While most rural people have jobs, those jobs are not very productive. In many cases there is not enough work to employ the entire rural work force full time. Instead members of farm families all work part time, sharing what work there is. Economists call this

underemployment or **disguised unemployment,** because some members of the rural work force could be removed entirely without a fall in production. Some remaining workers would simply change from part-time to full-time effort.

Underemployment and other features of developing-country labor markets will be discussed at greater length in Chapter 8. Here we are mainly interested in how an agricultural sector with diminishing returns and surplus or underemployed labor affects the development of the industrial sector. Put differently, if the industrial sector grows at a certain rate, how fast must the agricultural sector grow in order to avoid a drag on industry and on overall economic development? And will accelerated population growth help or make matters worse? To answer these and related questions we shall develop a **simple two-sector model.**

The modern version of the two-sector labor-surplus model was first developed by W. Arthur Lewis.[3] Lewis, like Ricardo before him, pays particular attention to the implications of surplus labor for the distribution of income, and hence it is the Lewis version of that labor-surplus model that is most relevant to the discussion in Chapter 4. The concern in this chapter, however, is with the relationship between industry and agriculture, and that relationship is more completely worked out in a version of the labor-surplus model developed by John Fei and Gustav Ranis.[4] Therefore it is the Fei-Ranis version of the model that is used in the discussion in this chapter.

The production function

Our starting point is the agricultural sector and the **agricultural production function.** A production function, as indicated earlier, tells us how much output we can get for a given amount of input. In our simple agricultural production function we assume two inputs, labor and land, produce and output, such as grain. The production function of Figure 4 differs from that of Figure 2, because instead of showing two inputs, labor and capital, on the axes, it shows output and one input, labor. Because increases in labor must be combined with either a fixed amount of land or with land of decreasing quality, the production function indicates diminishing returns. Put differently, the **marginal product of labor** is falling, which means that each additional unit of labor produces less and less output.

The next step in constructing our model is to show how rural wages are determined. The standard assumption in all labor surplus models from Ricardo to the present time is that rural wages will not fall below a minimum level. Thus in its more general form the concept of labor surplus includes not only situations where the marginal product of labor is zero, but also situations where the marginal product of labor is above zero but less than the minimum below which rural wages will not fall. In the Fei-Ranis model and in other labor-surplus theories the usual assumption is that rural wages do not fall below the **average product** of farm labor in households with a labor surplus. The logic behind this view is that a laborer in a farm household will not look for work outside the household unless he or she can earn at least as much as he would receive by staying at home. These concepts in diagrammatic form are presented in Figure 5.

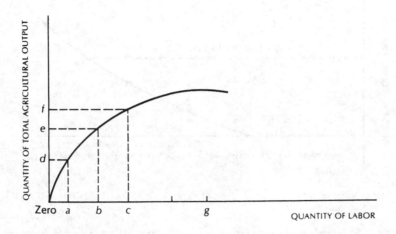

Figure 4   The Production Function. In this figure, a rise in the labor force from *a* to *b* leads to an increase in output of *de*, while an equal increase in labor from b to c leads to a smaller rise in output. At point *g* further increases in the amount of labor used do not lead to any rise in output al all. Beyond point *g* the marginal product of labor is zero or negative, so additional labor causes no increase or a reduction in output.

Figure 5 can be derived directly from Figure 4. The *total* product per unit of labor in Figure 4 is converted into the *marginal product* per unit of labor of Figure 5. The concept of a minimum wage (represented by the dotted line *hi)* was then added to the diagram. This minimum wage is also sometimes called an **institutionally fixed wage** to contrast it with wages determined by market forces. In a perfectly competitive market, wages will equal the marginal product of labor for reasons that will be discussed at greater length in Chapter 8. Thus once labor is withdrawn from agriculture to a point where the marginal product rises above the minimum wage (point *h* in Figure 5), wages in agriculture will follow the marginal product curve.

To hire away from the farm, factories in the city will have to pay at least as much as the workers are earning on the farm. Thus the line *hij* in Figure 5 can be thought of as the **supply curve of labor** facing the industrial sector. Actually the usual assumption is that the supply curve of labor in industry is a bit above the line *hij* because factories must pay farmers a bit more than they are receiving in agriculture to get them to move.

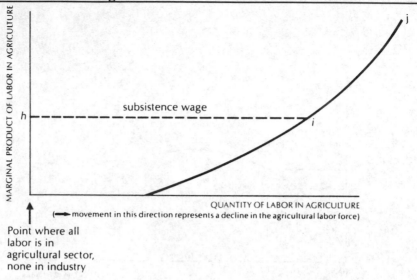

Point where all
labor is in
agricultural sector,
none in industry

Figure 5   Marginal Product of Labor in Agriculture. As the quantity of agricultural labor decreases, the marginal product increases.

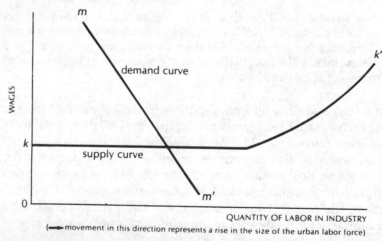

Figure 6   The Supply and Demand for Industrial Labor. The supply curve, *kk'*, is drawn directly from Figure 5. Demand, *mm'*, is derived from the industrial production function.

The key feature of this supply curve of labor is that unlike more common supply curves, it does not rise steadily as one moves from left to right but has a substantial horizontal portion. Formally this means that the supply curve of labor up to point *i* is **perfectly elastic. Elasticity**[5] is a concept used to refer to the percentage change occurring in one variable (in this case, the supply of labor) arising from a given percentage change in another variable (in this case, wages). Perfect elasticity occurs when the ratio of these two percentages equals infinity. From the point of view of the industrial sector this means that sector can hire as many workers as it wants without having to raise wages until the amount of labor is increased beyond point *i*.

The final steps are to add a demand curve for labor in the industrial sector (Figure 6) and then to combine the three figures into a single model. As we see in Figure 6, it can be derived from the industrial production function. To simplify our model, this step is ignored and we have simply drawn in the demand curve mm'. The supply curve in Figure 6 is derived from Figure 5. $0k$ in Figure 6 is assumed to be slightly higher than the subsistence wage in Figure 5. The supply curve of labor to industry turns up when withdrawal of labor from agriculture can no longer be accomplished without a decline in agricultural output (when the marginal product of labor rises above zero) because at that point the relative price of agricultural produce will rise, necessitating a commensurate rise in urban wages. The demand curve for labor in industry is determined by the marginal product of labor in industry, and hence the demand curve can be derived from the industrial production function.[6]

To combine Figures 4, 5, and 6, one additional piece of information is needed, the size of the nation's labor force. Many models use total population rather than the labor force, and this switch has little effect if the labor force is closely correlated with total population. The size of the labor force in Figure 7 is represented by the line zero to p, as labeled in Panel A. In order to combine the three figures, Figure 4's relation to the others is made clearer if it is flipped so that an increase in labor is represented by moving from right to left rather than the reverse. Handled this way, a movement from left to right represents both a decline in the agricultural labor force and a rise in the industrial labor force, that is, a transfer of labor from agriculture to industry.

If an economy starts with its entire population in agriculture, it can remove a large part of that population (pg) to industry or other employment without any reduction in farm output. Industry will have to pay that labor a wage a bit above subsistence (the difference between $p''k$ and $p'h$) to get it to move, but as long as there is some way of moving the food consumed by this labor from the rural to the urban areas, industrialization can proceed without putting any demands on agriculture. Even if agriculture is completely stagnant, industry can grow. As industry continues to grow, however, it will eventually exhaust the supply of surplus labor. Further removals of labor from agriculture will lead to a reduction in farm output. A shift in industrial demand to mm will force industry to pay more for the food of its workers; that is, the *terms of trade* between industry and agriculture will turn against industry and in favor of agriculture. It is this shift in terms of trade that accounts for the rise in the supply curve of labor between g'' and i''. Industry must pay more to get the same amount of food to feed its workers.

The Fei-Ranis model can be used to explore the implications of population growth and a rise in agricultural productivity, among other things. To simplify, if one assumes that there is a close relationship between population and the labor force, then an increase in population from, say, p to t will not increase output at all. The elastic portion of both the urban and rural labor supply curves will be extended by $p't'$ and $p''t''$ respectively, thus postponing the day when industrialization will cause wages to rise.[7] This point where wages begin to rise is sometimes referred to as the **turning point.** Most important, if population rises without any increase in food output, the average amount of food available per capita will fall. From the standpoint of everyone but a few employers who want to keep wages low and profits high population growth is an unqualified disaster. Wages may actually fall in the urban areas, and the welfare of the great mass of farmers will certainly fall. It is a model such as this, even if only imperfectly understood, that people often have in mind when they speak of population growth in wholly negative terms.

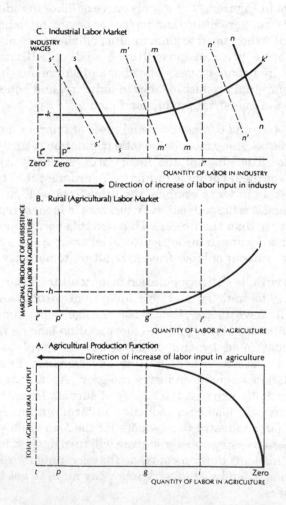

Figure 7 The Two-Sector Labor Surplus Model. The limit imposed by the country's population (zero to p in Panel A), coupled with the agricultural production function, allows us to analyze the effects of industry wages on the mix between agricultural and industrial labor.

How fast agricultural production must grow depends on what happens to a number of different variables. If industry's demand for labor is growing very rapidly, for example, agricultural productivity must grow rapidly enough to keep the terms of trade from turning sharply against industry, thereby cutting into industrial profits and slowing or halting industrial growth.[8] On the other hand, as long as there is a surplus of labor and no population growth, it is possible to ignore agricultural productivity growth and concentrate one's resources on industry.

David Ricardo, using similar although not identical reasoning, was concerned with keeping population growth down to avoid using poorer and poorer land in order to get a sufficient food supply. He also feared the impact of increasing wages, which he saw as leading to a two-fold disaster. Following Thomas Malthus, he argued that would lead to workers having more children. Further, higher wages would cut into the profits that initially provided the funds for investment in capital and that had allowed the rural surplus labor to move to cities and be employed in industry. Modern labor-surplus theorists would not agree with Ricardo's harsh policy prescriptions, but they would see the problems facing today's developing countries in a similar light.

The Neoclassical model

By changing many of the assumptions in the labor-surplus model, many of its implications can be explored. Here we take up the implications of one assumption, the labor-surplus assumption. Many economists simply do not agree that a surplus of labor exists in today's developing nations, even in India or China. These economists have developed an alternative two-sector model that is sometimes referred to as a **neoclassical model.**

The framework developed in Figure 7 can also be used to explore the implications of the neoclassical assumptions. A simple neoclassical model is presented in Figure 8.

The implications of population or labor force growth in the neoclassical model are quite different from what they were in the labor surplus model. An increase in population and labor in agriculture will raise farm output (see dotted line *t* in Figure 8A), and any removal of labor from agriculture will cause farm output to fall. Thus in a neoclassical model population growth is not such a wholly negative phenomenon. The increase in labor is much less of a drain on the food supply since that labor is able to produce much or all of its own requirements, and there is no surplus of labor that can be transferred without a consequent reduction in agricultural output.

If industry is to develop successfully, simultaneous efforts must be made to ensure that agriculture grows fast enough to feed workers in both the rural and urban sectors at ever-higher levels of consumption and to prevent the terms of trade from turning against industry. A stagnant agricultural sector, that is one with little new investment or technological progress, will cause wages of urban workers to rise rapidly,thereby cutting into profits and the funds available for industrial development. Where in the labor-surplus model planners can ignore agriculture until the surplus of labor is exhausted, in the neoclassical model there must be a balance between industry and agriculture from the beginning.

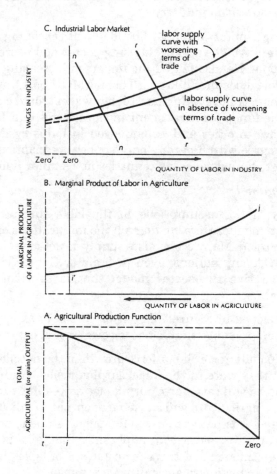

Figure 8 **A "Neoclassical" Two-Sector Model**. The key difference between Figures 7 and 8 is the agricultural production function (Figure 8A). Limited land resources do lead to slightly diminishing returns in the agricultural sector, but the curve never flattens out; that is, the marginal product of labor never falls to a minimum subsistence level so there is no minimum subsistence or **institutionally fixed** wage in Figure 8B. Wages instead are always determined by the marginal product of labor in agriculture. Finally, the supply curve of labor to industry no longer has a horizontal section. Since removal of labor from agriculture increases the marginal product of labor remaining in agriculture, industry must pay an amount equal to that marginal product plus a premium to get labor to migrate to the cities. The supply curve of labor to industry rises for another reason as well. As labor is removed from agriculture, farm output falls; and in order to extract enough food from the agricultural sector to pay its workers, industry must pay higher and higher prices for food. Only if industry is in a position to import food from abroad will it be able to avoid these worsening terms of trade. If imports are not available, rising agricultural prices will lead to a higher marginal revenue product, and hence higher wages, for workers in agriculture. As in the labor surplus case, industry will have to pay correspondingly higher wages to attract a labor force.

Two-sector models of both the labor-surplus and neoclassical type can become very elaborate, with dozens or even hundreds of equations used to describe different features of the economy. These additional equations and assumptions will also have an influence on the kinds of policy recommendations an economist will derive from the model. But at the core of these more elaborate models are the labor-surplus and neoclassical assumptions about the nature of the agricultural production function.

These same points can be made in a less abstract way by turning to Chinese and African examples of the relationship between industry and agriculture during economic development.

Labor surplus in China

In China by the 1950s most arable land was already under cultivation, and further increases in population and the labor force contributed little to increases in agricultural output. Urban wages rose in the early 1950s, but then leveled off and remained unchanged for twenty years between 1957 and 1977. If allowed to do so, tens of millions of farm laborers would have happily migrated to the cities despite urban wage stagnation. Only legal restrictions on rural-urban migration, backed up by more than a little force, held this migration to levels well below what would have been required to absorb the surplus. Population growth that averaged 2 percent a year up until the mid-1970s continued to swell the ranks of those interested in leaving the countryside. In short, China over the past three decades was a labor-surplus country.

As pointed out earlier, China did invest in agriculture, but only enough to maintain, not to raise, per-capita food production. The rural-urban migration that did occur was not fast enough to eliminate the rural labor surplus, but it was enough to require farmers to sell more of their production to the cities. Thus the prices paid to farmers for their produce were gradually raised, while the prices paid by farmers for urban products remained constant or fell — that is, the rural-urban *terms of trade* shifted slowly but markedly in favor of agriculture.

To get out of this labor-surplus situation, Chinese planners in the late 1970s had both to accelerate the transfer of workers from rural to urban employment and to take steps to keep the rural pool of surplus labor from constantly replenishing itself. Accelerating the growth of urban employment was accomplished by encouraging labor-intensive consumer goods (textiles, electronics, etc.) and service industries (restaurants, taxis, etc.). To feed this increase in urban population, the government both increased food imports, shifted more investment funds to agriculture, and allowed a further improvement in the rural-urban terms of trade.

To keep the rural pool of surplus labor from replenishing itself, planners slowed those kinds of farm mechanization that had the effect of reducing the rural demand for labor. Most important, planners attacked the surplus at its source by a massive effort to bring down the birth rate. By 1980 the population growth rate in China had slowed from 2 to 1.2 percent a year. By the early 1980s China was still a labor-surplus country, but the pursuit of similar policies under similar conditions had removed South Korea's labor surplus by the mid-1960s, and much the same thing occurred in Japan at an even earlier date.

Labor surplus in Africa

Africa, as already pointed out, had low population densities relative to the availability of arable land. In nations such as Kenya, increases in population could be readily accommodated in the 1950s and 1960s by opening up new land or by converting land to more intensive uses (for example, from pasture to crops). Therefore, increased population was more or less matched by rises in agricultural production. Food output, at least in the richer nations such as Kenya, kept up with the needs of both the expanding rural population and with the even more rapidly growing urban sector. Planners felt little pressure either to improve the rural-urban terms of trade or to increase state investment in agriculture. In short, until recently Kenya fits reasonably well the assumptions of the neoclassical model.

Because Kenya's land resources were not unlimited and because population growth continued at the extraordinarily high rate of close to 4 percent per annum, by the late 1970s Kenya was beginning to acquire some of the characteristics of a labor-surplus economy; and planners were having to adjust to the policy implications (more investment and better prices for agriculture, a greater effort to reduce population growth) of these new conditions.

This discussion of the relations between the agricultural and industrial sectors during the process of economic development has gone as far as we can productively go at this stage. Analysis of the patterns of development using data on shares of the two sectors in GNP provided an insight into the patterns that have occurred in the past and might be expected to recur in the future. Two-sector models have made it possible to go a step further and to acquire an understanding of some of the reasons why different patterns of industrial and agricultural development might occur. In later chapters the validity of the labor-surplus versus neoclassical assumptions for today's developing world will be explored at greater length. There will also be extended discussions of the nature and problems of industrial and agricultural development that will include further consideration of the nature of relations between the two sectors.

Industrial patterns of growth

To know precisely which industries would develop at each stage in a nation's growth would be a very valuable piece of information for economists. Plans could be drawn up that could concentrate a nation's energies on particular industries at particular stages. If all industrial development began with textiles, for example, then planners could focus their attention on getting a textile industry started and worry about other sectors later. Similarly, if only nations with high per-capita incomes could support the efficient production of automobiles, planners in countries beginning development would know that they should avoid investing resources in the automobile industry until a later stage.

Empirical approaches

Chenery and Taylor[9] have used the terms **early industries, middle industries,** and **late industries. Early industries** are those that supply goods essential to the populations of poor countries and are produced with simple technologies so that their manufacture can take place within the poor country. In statistical terms the share of these industries in GNP rises at low levels of per-capita income, but that share stops rising when income is still fairly low and stagnates or falls thereafter. Typically included in this group are food processing and textiles. **Late industries** are those whose share in GNP continues to rise even at high levels of per-capita income. This group includes many consumer durables (refrigerators, cars) as well as other metal products. **Middle industries** are those that fall in between the other two categories.

Unfortunately, it is frequently difficult to decide in which category a particular industry belongs. For many industries the nineteenth-century experience of European nations or of the United States is a poor guide because many industries that are important today did not even exist then. The nuclear power industry, for example, did not exist prior to World War II, and even the chemical-fertilizer sector as we think of it today did not really begin until well into the twentieth century.

Cross-section data get rid of this particular problem but introduce many others. In several Arab states petroleum accounts for a large share of GNP because these nations have unusually rich underground resources. In Malaysia soil and climate have been favorable to the rise of rubber, palm oil, and timber. Singapore and Hong Kong, which have no natural resources to speak of, have taken advantage of their vast experience in foreign trade to develop textiles, electronics, and other manufactures for export. In short, the share of particular industries in the GNP of individual countries is determined by endowments of natural resources, historical heritages of experience with commerce and trade, and many other factors. There is no single pattern of industrial development, or even two or three patterns, that all nations must follow as they progress out of poverty. Some industries where the techniques used are easier to master, such as textiles, are more likely to get started in the early stages of development than others, such as the manufacture of commercial aircraft. And there is some regularity in the patterns of what people consume as they move from lower to higher incomes. Engel's law has already been mentioned as a part of the explanation for the declining share of agriculture in GNP. The same law has much to do with why the share of food processing within industry falls as per-capita income rises. But before planners can decide which industries to push in one country, they must know the particular conditions facing that country as well as these more general patterns.

Theoretical approaches

Economists' debates on balanced and unbalanced growth predate much of the quantitative work on patterns of development. **Balanced growth** advocates such as Ragnar Nurkse or Paul Rosenstein-Rodan[10] argued that countries have to develop a wide range of industries simultaneously if they are ever to succeed in achieving sustained growth. What would happen in the absence of balanced growth has often been illustrated with a story of a hypothetical country that attempted to begin development by building a shoe factory. The factory is built, workers are hired and trained, and the factory begins to turn out shoes. Everything goes well until the factory tries to sell the shoes it is producing. The factory workers themselves use their increased income to buy new factory-made shoes; but of course they are able to produce far more shoes than they need for themselves or their families. The rest of the population is mainly poor farmers whose income has not risen, and hence they cannot afford to buy factory-made shoes. They continue to wear cheap homemade sandals. The factory in turn, unable to sell its product, goes bankrupt and the effort to start development comes to an end.

The proposed solution to this problem is to build a number of factories simultaneously. If a textile mill, a flour mill, a bicycle plant, and many other enterprises could be started at the same time, the shoe factory could sell its shoes to the workers in these factories as well. In turn, shoe-factory workers would use their new income to buy bicycles, clothing, and flour, thus keeping the other new plants solvent. This kind of development is sometimes referred to as **balanced growth on the demand side** because the industries developed are determined by the demand or expenditure patterns of consumers (and investors). **Balanced growth on the supply side** refers to the need to build a number of industries simultaneously to prevent supply bottlenecks from occurring. Thus, in building a steel mill, planners need to make sure that iron and coal mines and coking facilities are also developed, unless imports of these inputs are readily available. At a more aggregated level, it is also necessary to maintain a balance between the development of industry and agriculture. Otherwise, as pointed out earlier, the terms of trade might turn sharply against industry, thereby bringing growth to a stop.

One problem with the balanced-growth argument is that in its pure form it is a counsel of despair. A poor country with little or no industry is told that it must either start up a wide range of industries simultaneously or resign itself to continued stagnation. This across-the-board program has sometimes been referred to as a **big push** or a **critical minimum effort.** By whatever name, it is discouraging advice for a poor nation that is taxing its managerial and financial resources to the limit just to get a few factories started.

In the discussion of patterns of industrial development, however, we pointed out that there is little evidence that all nations have to follow a set pattern. Some nations have emphasized one set of industries while other nations concentrated on different ones. Proponents of **unbalanced growth,** especially Albert Hirschman, recognize these differences and use them to suggest a very different pattern of industrial development.[11] Nations, they say, could and did concentrate their energies on a few sectors during the early stages of development. In most cases there was little danger of producing more shoes than could be sold.

Certain industrial products have ready markets, even among the rural poor and even in the absence of a big push towards development. A worker in a nineteenth-century factory, for example, could produce forty times as much cotton yarn per day as a peasant with a spinning wheel in a dark rural cottage. From the peasants' point of view, therefore, it made sense to buy factory yarn and to concentrate his effort on a more productive activity, such as weaving that yarn into cloth. Initially much of this yarn was imported into places like India and China from factories in Britain, but it was not long before entrepreneurs in China and India discovered that cotton yarn could be produced more cheaply at home than purchased as an import. Thus they substituted domestic production for imports. **Import substitution,** as this process is called, is one way a nation can find a ready market for one of its own industries. The market is already there, and all a country's planners have to do is ensure that the domestic industry can compete effectively with the imported product. How this can be done is a subject to which we shall return in Chapter 16. Here the main point is that import substitution is one way of beginning industrialization on a limited and selective basis rather than with a balanced "big push." Another way is to rely on exports, as England did during the Industrial Revolution. If it is impossible to sell all of a factory's product at home, it is often possible to sell the product abroad, assuming that product could be produced at a cost that is competitive.

Backward and forward linkages

Unbalanced growth advocates such as Hirschman, however, did not content themselves with simply pointing out an escape from the dilemma posed by balanced growth proponents. Hirschman developed the unbalanced growth idea into a general interpretation of how development ought to proceed. The central concept in Hirschman's theory is that of **linkages.** Industries are linked to other industries in ways that can be taken into account in deciding on a development strategy. Industries with **backward linkages** make use of inputs from other industries. Automobile manufacturing, for example, uses the products of machinery and metal-processing plants, which in turn make use of large amounts of steel. The building of an automobile manufacturing plant, therefore, will create a demand for machinery and steel. Initially this demand may be supplied by imports, but eventually local entrepreneurs will see that they have a ready market for domestically made machinery and steel, and this demand stimulates them to set up such plants. Planners interested in accelerating growth, therefore, will emphasize industries with strong backward linkages because it is these industries that will stimulate production in the greatest number of additional sectors.

Forward linkages occur in industries that produce goods that then become inputs into other industries. Rather than start with automobiles, planners might prefer to start at the other end by setting up a steel mill. Seeing that they had a ready domestic supply of steel, entrepreneurs might then be stimulated to set up factories that would make use of this steel. In a similar way successful drilling for oil will encourage a nation to set up its own refineries and petrochemical complexes rather than ship its crude oil to other nations for processing.

Both forward and backward linkages set up pressures that lead to the creation of new industries, which in turn create additional pressures, and so on. These pressures can take the form of new profit opportunities for private entrepreneurs, or pressures can build through the political process and force governments to act. Private investors, for example, might decide to build factories in a given location without at the same time providing adequate housing facilities for the inflow of new workers or roads with which to supply the factories and transport their output. In such cases government planners might be forced to construct public housing and roads.

While on the surface the balanced and unbalanced growth arguments appear to be fundamentally inconsistent with each other, when stated in less extreme forms they can be seen as opposite sides of the same coin. Almost everyone would agree that there is no single pattern of industrialization that all nations must follow. On the other hand, quantitative analysis suggests that there are patterns that are broadly similar among large groups of nations. While nations with large amounts of foreign trade can follow an unbalanced strategy for some time, a nation cannot pick any industry or group of industries it desires and then concentrate exclusively on those industries throughout the nation's development, following in effect an extreme form of an unbalanced growth strategy. The very concept of linkages suggests that extreme imbalances of this sort will set up pressures that will force a nation back toward a more balanced path. Thus the ultimate objective is a degree of balance in the development program. But planners have a choice between attempting to maintain balance throughout the development process or first creating imbalances with the knowledge that linkage pressures will eventually force them back toward the balance. In terms of Figure 9, the issue is whether to follow the steady balanced path represented by a solid line or the unbalanced path represented by a dashed line. The solid line is shorter, but under certain conditions a nation might get to any given point faster by following the dashed line.

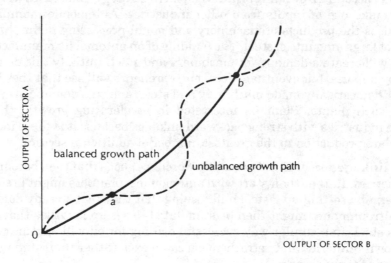

Figure 9 **Balanced and Unbalanced Growth Paths**. The solid line between points a and b is shorter than the dotted line, but because of the impact of linkages, a country travelling along the dotted line may get from point a to b in less time than a country travelling along the solid line or balanced growth path.

Notes

1. Roy F. Harrod, "An Essay in Dynamic Theory." *Economic Journal* (1939): 14-33; and Evsey Domar, "Capital Expansion, Rate of Growth, and Employment," *Econometrica* (1946): 137-47 and "Expansion and Employment," *American Economic Review* 37 (1947): 34-55.

2. H.B. Chenery and M. Syrquin, *Patterns of Development, 1950-1970* (London: Oxford University Press, 1975); and H.B. Chenery and L.J. Taylor, "Development Patterns: Among Countries and over Time," *Review of Economics and Statistics* (November 1968): 391-416.

3. W. Arthur Lewis, *The Theory of Economic Growth* (Homewood, Ill.: Richard Irwin, 1955).

4. Gustav Ranis and John C.H. Fei, *Development of the Labor Surplus Economy* (Homewood, Ill.: Richard Irwin, 1964).

5. The term **elasticity** refers to the percentage change in one variable that results from a percentage change in another variable and is presented as a ratio. In the case discussed here, the elasticity is the ratio of the percentage change in the supply of labor ($\Delta L / L$) to the percentage change in the wage rate ($\Delta W / W$). Algebraically,

$$\text{elasticity} = \frac{\Delta L / L}{\Delta W / W} = \frac{\Delta L}{\Delta W} \cdot \frac{W}{L}$$

In the case of perfect elasticity, this ratio approaches infinity.

6. A factory owner under competitive conditions is willing to pay up to but no more than what a laborer contributes to increase the volume of output of the factory. The increase in output value contributed by the last laborer hired is by definition the marginal revenue product of that laborer.

7. In the industrial labor supply and demand part of Figure 7, panel C, it is also necessary to move the labor demand curves to the left since the zero point on the horizontal axis has been moved to the left. These new demand curves, $s's'$, $m'm'$, and $n'n'$, therefore. are really the same as ss, mm, and nn. That is, the quantity of labor demanded at any given price is the same for $s's'$ as ss and so on.

8. Agricultural productivity in the model presented here refers to a shift in the agricultural production function causing a given amount of labor input in agriculture to produce a larger amount of agricultural output.

9. Chenery and Taylor, "Development Patterns."

10. Ragnar Nurkse, *Problems of Capital Formation in Underdeveloped Countries* (New York: Oxford University Press, 1953); and Paul N. Rosenstein-Rodan, "Problems of Industriallization of Eastern and Southeastern Europe", *Economic Journal* (June-September 1943), reprinted in *The Economics of Underdevelopment,* A.N. Agarwala and S.P. Singh, eds. (New York: Oxford University Press, 1963).

11. Albert O. Hirschman, *The Strategy of Economic Development* (New Haven: Yale University Press, 1958).

10.   The Lewis Model

Kaushik Basu

Consider a closed economy consisting of two sectors: the industrial sector and the rural sector ('capitalist' and 'subsistence' sectors were the expression used by Lewis). Lewis describes his model as a 'classical' one, meaning thereby that in the rural sector there is, for all practical purposes, an unlimited labour supply at the subsistence wage. More precisely, this means that at the subsistence wage there is an excess supply of labour and the excess supply is sufficiently large so that no employer — incumbent or prospective — has to worry, when considering employment expansion, about having to bid up wages or about getting rationed in the labour market.

If the capitalist sector wishes to draw on this unlimited supply of labour, it cannot, however, do so at the subsistence wage. It typically has to pay a higher wage, w, which is a mark-up on the rural subsistence wage, m. Lewis adduces reasons for the existence of this wag gap. Note first that a part of the wage gap is only apparent because the cost-of-living in the urban sector is almost invariably greater than that in the rural sector. But it is generally empirically true that even in real terms urban wages are above rural wages. This according to Lewis, could be 'because of the psychological cost of transferring from the easy going way of life of the subsistence sector to the more regimented or urbanised environment' or 'it may be a recognition of the fact that even the unskilled worker is of more use to the capitalist sector after he has been there for some time than the raw recruit from the country'. While these explanations are not to be dismissed, they are clearly not completely convincing. For the time being, therefore, we shall do what has been the standard practice in the literature that followed Lewis (1954): that is, treat the rural urban wage gap as exogenously given. The issue of how the wage gap actually emerges and is sustained is taken up in the next chapter.

To avoid as many loose ends as possible I make some more strong assumptions — no doubt deviating somewhat from Lewis' original formulation. Let L be the total amount of labour in the economy (thereby shelving the important issue of increasing populations aside). Let the rural marginal product curve of labour be horizontal over a considerable stretch with the marginal product being more or less around subsistence level. This is shown in figure 1 in which O_R is the origin of the rural sector and O_M of the modern sector. The wage in the urban sector, w, is considerably above the subsistence level, and we assume it is rigid downwards for *exogenous* reasons. Assume, for the moment, that both sectors produce the same good. In the initial period the marginal product curve of labour in the urban sector is A_1B_1. Though I write as though there is only one employer in the urban sector this is not the case and that is obvious from our assumption that the urban employer is a wage-taker. Clearly, in order to maximise profit he employs O_ML_1 units of labour. The remaining labour $L - O_ML_1 = O_RL_1$ remains in the rural sector, with the marginal worker earning m.

Kaushik Basu: 'The Lewis Model' from *THE LESS DEVELOPED ECONOMY; A CRITIQUE OF CONTEMPORARY THEORY* (Basil Blackwell Ltd, 1984), pp. 61-67.

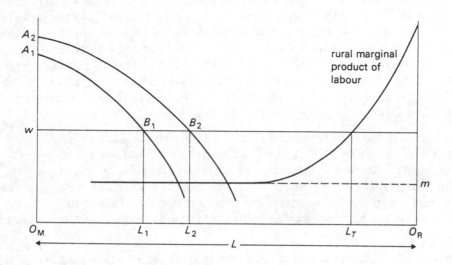

Figure 1

This may be referred to as a *snapshot view* of the Lewis economy and this has been, in many ways, the starting point for much of the literature on dual-economy analysis. As far as Lewis was concerned, the central theme was the dynamics of the system. For this, it was assumed that workers do not save because they are too poor. Rural landlords do not save because they prefer the joys of conspicuous consumption. Only the modern sector capitalists save and invest and for simplicity it was supposed that they save their entire profit. Saving in this 'classical' model is not distinguished from investment. So the capital stock with the urban employer in period 2 gets augmented by the profit in period 1, which is equal to A_1B_1w in figure 1 (assuming for simplicity that depreciation is zero). In accordance with standard theory it is supposed that the marginal product of labour rises as the capital stock increases. Hence the marginal product curve of labour in period 2 lies above A_1B_1. Let the marginal product curve in period 2 be A_2B_2. Then urban employment rises to O_ML_2 and rural employment is O_RL_2. The profit in the urban sector is given by A_2B_2w. As before this is invested causing a further shift in the urban marginal product curve of labour. This relentless cycle of surplus, reinvestment and growth continues and steadily the industrial sector absorbs the rural one.

The process continues with the urban wage remaining constant, up to the point where O_ML_T labour is employed in the urban sector. At that point the character of the economy changes in an important way. From here onwards the wages in the two sectors begin to move upwards and they maintain parity. Also at this point the rural marginal product ceases to be below the urban wage. This is the famous 'turning point' and from here onwards the economy begins to look very much like a developed economy and the classical assumption of unlimited labour ceases to hold.

While what is known as the Lewis model ends at this point, Lewis' own canvas was much larger and he used this model to bear upon a wide range of political and economic issues. Thus it may be argued that capitalists recognise the potential of the subsistence sector as a source of cheap labour and therefore have a vested interest in keeping rural wages low. To quote Lewis (1954, p. 149): 'Thus, the owners of plantations have no interest in seeing knowledge of new techniques or new seeds conveyed to the peasants, and if they are influential in the government, they will not be found using their influence to expand the facilities for agricultural extension'.[1]

The basic model can also be extended to the international sphere. At the end of the process described above, it is natural that employers would begin to look for cheap labour beyond the borders of their country. They then face two options: they could bring in cheap immigrant labour or base their factories in poor countries where labour is plentiful and cheap. Both these developments have of course taken place with profound impact on the world economy and both these matters are subjects of much research and analysis.

The Lewis model generated a lot of interest among development economists and in the sixties there were many attempts to restate it more formally (among the more interesting being Ranis and Fei, 1961, and Jorgenson, 1967). The main concern of this literature is to examine the turning points in the long-run process described by Lewis. It is clear, in retrospect, that this direction turned out to be a *cul de sac*.

A more fruitful and exciting direction of research was the one which focused on the short-run aspects of the dual-economy model of Lewis. And it is to these that we turn in the next two chapters. In a sense, what we do and what much of the literature in the seventies has been implicitly doing is to take a slice of time out of the entire process and examine it with care. Do things work out the way Lewis envisaged?

Critiques

The Lewis model has been subjected to criticism from various perspectives. This section critically examines the decision-making of the capitalists and workers.[2] It is argued that if capitalists are granted a limited rationality then the Lewis process might begin to stagnate before running its full course.

Before that, let us get a possible methodological objection out of the way. It may be claimed that my mode of examining the Lewis model violates the very spirit of Lewis' enquiry which is classical in nature. Whosoever agrees with this claim, my suspicion is that Lewis would not, because his model is not classical in this sense. In fact, it is quite evident from his paper that he was greatly concerned about the motivations of individual agents. In this respect, therefore, he was neoclassically inclined.

Regarding capitalists, Lewis assumes — what at first sight appears quite straightforward — that they maximise profit. But while the objective of profit-maximisation is well defined in a static context, it can be quite ambiguous in a dynamic model such as this. On reflection, it becomes clear, that by this assumption what he means is that in *each* time period the capitalist maximises profit. It follows that in each period the capitalist chooses his labour input such that the marginal product of labour is equal to the wage. Clearly this assumption cannot tell us how much the landlord invests because that is an intertemporal decision. So Lewis' assumption that capitalists invest their entire profit is a separate and distinct assumption.

Hence instead of assuming a single grand objective function for the capitalist and deriving various behavioural postulates, Lewis *begins* by assuming two behavioural rules. This in itself is not objectionable,[3] but it is important to check the implications of such behaviour. Are we denying the capitalist even a limited rationality?

The trouble arises when we relax the assumption of a single good. Let us assume, as does Lewis, that the industrial sector produces a good which is distinct from the product of the agricultural sector. With this, the question of terms of trade between agriculture and industry comes into play. This places serious obstacles in the path of development described above. Lewis was aware of some of the difficulties that arose from the question of terms of trade but he dealt with these rather cursorily. Others have discussed the matter at greater length (see for example, Chakravarty, 1977).

Here I take up an interesting and pointed issue. Suppose there are many producers in the industrial sector and they are all price-takers (the argument is strengthened if we assume a monopoly). Let the price of the industrial good in terms of the agricultural good be p. A representative producer's output, X, is a function of capital, K, and labour, L. Within each period, K is fixed. Given that w is expressed in terms of agricultural goods, the amount of labour employed is given by

$$pX_L(L,K) = w.$$

This is depicted in figure 2. The curve, a_1b_1 shows the *value* of marginal product curve (i.e. $pX_L(L,K)$ as a function of L). L_1 is the equilibrium employment.

In reality p is formed as the outcome of a complex general equilibrium and a definitive analysis would have to be quite detailed. For simplicity, it is reasonable to assume that p falls as the total urban output increases relatively to the rural one.

If in period 1, each firm invests its profit, a_1b_1w, then the marginal product curve will shift to the right, true. But the value of marginal product curve need not shift similarly, because with the higher industrial output, the price p will be lower. In fact it is quite possible that the value of marginal product curve (at the new equilibrium price) will lie to the left of a_1b_1.

This highlights two important difficulties. First, there arises a question of capitalists' rationality. If investment in the first period diminishes profits in the second period, would it not be more reasonable for the capitalists to consume more (instead of investing) in period 1 *and* to earn more profits in period 2? Lewis is not unaware of this difficulty, and he discusses it, somewhat tangentially, in terms of some ideas of Malthus, Ricardo and Marx. While his discussion is interesting, he dismisses this criticism for reasons which are not too convincing. There is, however, a good argument which neutralises the above criticism. If the urban sector is composed of a sufficiently large number of capitalists then the fact that the *total* urban investment causes a deterioration in terms of trade in the next period would not enter into any individual capitalist's calculations. Thus investment would not be held back for *this reason*.

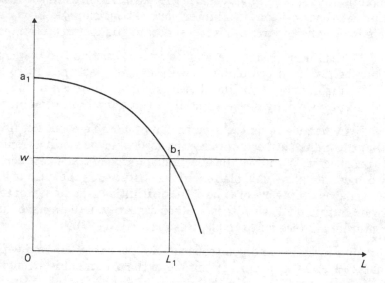

Figure 2

While this is true, this criticism nevertheless draws our attention to the question of investment criterion. Surely a capitalist would pay some attention to the rate of return that his investment will fetch him. If it drops too low, he might be tempted to consume more instead of putting away all surplus as investment. It is therefore important to recognise that the proportion of profit that is ploughed into investment is a *variable* controlled by the capitalist and is liable to change depending on the rate of profit and other signals in the economy. And it is possible that an adverse movement in these signals may lead to a short-circuit in the Lewis process because of the capitalist's refusal to invest adequately.

In order to focus on the second difficulty let us assume away the above problem by supposing that capitalists mechanically invest all their profits. But as we have already seen, this will cause a deterioration in the terms of trade. And this may be so sharp as to cause an inward shift in the value of marginal product curve for labour.

This implies the interesting possibility that even if capitalists behave exactly as postulated by Lewis and invest all their profit, urban employment may fail to grow.[4] The general upshot of this analysis and some of the literature on this seems to be that beginning from a primitive dual economy the forces which Lewis wrote about are likely to be present and are going to move the economy in the direction suggested. But the process is not an inexorable one leading an economy to the turning point and into a 'developed' state. Instead it is likely that the process itself generates forces which leads to stagnancy well before such a happy state emerges. The experience of underdeveloped countries does not seem to controvert this position.[5]

Finally, let us consider one slice of time in the whole process described above, for instance, period 1 as depicted in figure 1: $O_M L_1$ workers are employed in the urban sector at a wage w and $O_R L_1$ workers are employed in the rural sector at a considerably lower wage, m. But then, this should attract more workers from the rural sector into the urban one. It is true that they would not find jobs in this period but certainly some workers would like to be present in the urban sector in the hope of finding a job. This means that at each point of time there would exist some urban unemployment. This is precisely the starting point of the well-known Harris-Todaro model. What Harris and Todaro (1970) do is to assume a dual economy not dissimilar to the Lewis one but in their analysis the labourers' decision to locate themselves in the urban or the rural sector is based explicitly on expected earnings maximisation. The model they construct, therefore, could be thought of as an elaboration of a short-run segment in the Lewis process. Their model throws interesting light on the functioning of labour markets, migration and the consequences of urban employment policies — matters which go unnoticed as too microscopic in Lewis' ample canvas.

1. This is borne out well by recent experience in India. The 'food for work' programme, which was started by the Government of India in 1977 as a small step to alleviate abject rural poverty, has been vigorously lobbied against by landlords under various pretexts. The actual reason, however, is that the programme was having a certain measure of success in preventing wages in some regions from declining to abysmal levels.

2. Some of these same issues are examined by Enke (1962) though from a different point of view.

3. In a different context I have argued that there are situations where it is better to begin from direct behavioural postulates rather than from a utility function (Basu, 1981).

4. Lewis discusses the possibility of employment declining with mechanisation. But his reasons are different. It should be emphasised that the present argument is different from the standard one — that automation displaces labour.

5. There are many other aspects which have been discussed by economists but which I have chosen not to dwell upon here. A relatively important omission is the analysis of the distributional impact of growth. For this, the interested reader may be referred to Taylor (1979, pp. 149-60).

11.   Historical Perspectives
Gerald A. Meier

Sequence of stages — note

It has always been tempting to search for regularities in history, and many writers have adopted a unidirectional view of development in terms of some pattern of stages. As summarized by Simon Kuznets,

> a stage theory of long-term economic change implies: (1) distinct time segments, characterized by different sources and patterns of economic changes; (2) a specific succession of these segments, so that *b* cannot occur before *a*, or *c* before *b*; and (3) a common matrix, in that the successive segments are stages in one broad process — usually one of development and growth rather than of devolution and shrinkage. Stage theory is most closely associated with a uni-directional rather than cyclic view of history. In the cyclic view the stages are recurrent; in a uni-directional view, a stage materializes, runs its course, and never recurs. Even in the process of devolution and decline, the return to a level experienced previously is not viewed as a recurrence of the earlier stage.[1]

The central question raised by Kuznets is: How can such a simple design be a summary description or an analytic classification of a vast and diverse field of historical change sufficiently plausible to warrant the formulation and persistence of many variants?

At one extreme, Adam Smith referred to the sequence of hunting, pastoral, agricultural, commercial, and manufacturing stages. At the other, Karl Marx related Hegel's thesis, antithesis, and synthesis to the Marxian stages of feudalism, capitalism, and socialism. Most recently, Walt Rostow attempted to generalize "the sweep of modern economic history" in a set of stages of growth, designated as follows: the traditional society, the preconditions for take-off, the take-off, the drive to maturity, and the age of high mass-consumption.[2]

Basic to Rostow's original analysis, in *The Stages of Economic Growth*, was his sketch of a dynamic theory of production that emphasized the composition of investment and the growth of particular sectors in the economy. This theory of production allowed Rostow to identify certain "leading sectors", the growth of which is thought to be instrumental in propelling the economy forward. Rostow also indicated that a sequence of optimum patterns of investment can be postulated from a set of optimum sectoral paths determined by the level of income and population, by technology, by the quality of entrepreneurship, and by the empirical fact that deceleration is the normal optimum path of each sector. The actual course of investment, however, generally differs from these optima inasmuch as they are influenced not only by private choices, but also by

Gerald A. Meier: 'Historical Perspectives' from *LEADING ISSUES IN ECONOMIC DEVELOPMENT* (New York: Oxford University Press, 1989, 5th edition), pp. 69-75.

the politics of governments and the impact of wars. Nonetheless, Rostow believes that, at any period of time, leading sectors can be identified, and the changing sequence of leading sectors plays an important role in Rostow's stages of growth. The sequence of stages suggests, in turn, that a succession of strategic choices is open to societies, and that political and social decisions about the allocation of resources are made in terms beyond the usual market processes. Of Rostow's five stages of growth, the most relevant for poor countries at present are the first three: the traditional society, the emergence of the preconditions for take-off, and the take-off.

The "take-off" is meant to be the central notion in Rostow's schema, and it has received the most critical attention. The take-off is interpreted as "a decisive transition in a society's history" — a period "when the scale of productive economic activity reaches a critical level and produces changes which lead to a massive and progressive structural transformation in economies and the societies of which they are a part, better viewed as changes in kind than merely in degree." The take-off is defined "as requiring all three of the following related conditions":

1. a rise in the rate of productive investment from, say 5% or less to over 10% of national income (or net national product);

2. the development of one or more substantial manufacturing sectors, with a high rate of growth; and

3. the existence or quick emergence of a political, social, and institutional framework that exploits the impulses to expansion in the modern sector and the potential external economy effects of the take-off and gives to growth an ongoing character.[3]

Of the earlier proponents of stages, only Marx commands Rostow's explicit attention. Indeed, Rostow presents his analysis as an alternative to Marx's theory of modern history. Describing his system as "A Non-Communist Manifesto," Rostow poses his five stages of growth against Marx's stages of feudalism, bourgeois capitalism, socialism, and communism.

We can recognize some broad similarities between Rostow's analysis and Marx's sequence. Both are audacious attempts to interpret the evolution of whole societies, primarily from an economic perspective: both are "explorations of the problems and consequences for whole societies of building compound interest into their habits and institutions";[4] and both recognize that economic change has social, political, and cultural consequences.

From other viewpoints, however, there are fundamental differences. The basic Marxian problems of class conflict, exploitation, and inherent stresses within the capitalist process find no place in Rostow's analysis. Nor does Rostow reduce the complexities of man to a single economic dimension. Rostow recognizes that in terms of human motivation, many of the most profound economic changes must be viewed as the consequence of noneconomic human motives and aspirations. Instead of limiting human behavior to simply an act of maximization, Rostow interprets net human behavior "as an act of balancing alternative and often conflicting human objectives in the face of the range of choices men perceive to be open to them."[5] Rostow allows for the different facets of human beings, and interprets the total performance of societies as an act of balance in the patterns of choice made by individuals within the framework permitted by the changing setting of society. Rostow insists that although his "stages-of-growth are an economic way of looking at whole societies, they in no sense imply that the worlds of politics, social organization, and of culture are a mere superstructure built upon and derived uniquely from the economy."[6] On the contrary, what most concerns Rostow is how societies go about making their choices and balances: "the central phenomenon of the world of post-traditional societies is not the economy — and whether it is capitalist or not — it is the total procedure by which choices are made."[7] Marx's assumption that a society's decisions are merely a function of who owns property is therefore rejected as inaccurate; instead, it is maintained that "one must look directly at the full mechanism of choice among alternative policies, including the political process — and indeed, the social and religious processes — as independent arenas for making decisions and choices."[8]

The implications of this broader view of human motivation become especially significant when Rostow's interpretation of post-traditional societies is contrasted with Marx's account of the postfeudal phase. Thus, Rostow concludes that his account of the break-up of traditional societies is

> based on the convergence of motives of private profit in the modern sectors with a new sense of affronted nationhood. And other forces play their part as well, for example the simple perception that children need not die so young or live their lives in illiteracy: a sense of enlarged human horizons, independent of both profit and national dignity. And when independence or modern nationhood is at last attained, there is no simple, automatic switch to a dominance of the profit motive and economic and social progress. On the contrary there is a searching choice and problem of balance among the three directions policy might go: external assertion; the further concentration of power in the centre as opposed to the regions; and economic growth.[9]

This approach may have more immediate relevance for the problems now confronting many underdeveloped countries than Marx's narrower view that political behavior is dependent on economic advantage, and that the decisions of capitalist societies are made simply in terms of the free-market mechanism and private advantage.

Moreover, as Rostow observes, the Marxian sequence suffers by basing its categories on only one historical case: the British take-off and drive to maturity. Rostow reminds us that Marx presented his whole system before any society other than Britain experienced the take-off, and instead of revising his categories so as to be more applicable to other cases, Marx merely generalized and projected his interpretation of the British case. A concentration on the British case, however, misses the variety of experience in the evolution of different societies, and makes the Marxian analysis of the "march of history" unduly rigid and artificial. If for no other reason than that it draws on a far wider range of historical knowledge, and is thereby more comprehensive and less doctrinaire. Rostow's analysis can claim to be a superior alternative to the Marxian sequence.

Nonetheless, if Rostow's thesis is to assert with a high degree of generality that it is able to trace a structure of history in the form of a sequence of stages, then it must also answer a number of criticisms that have commonly been levied against stage-theorists. "Stage-making" approaches are misleading when they succumb to a linear conception of history and imply that all economies tend to pass through the same series of stages. Although a particular sequence may correspond broadly to the historical experience of some economies, no single sequence fits the history of all countries. To maintain that every economy always follows the same course of development with a common past and the same future is to overschematize the complex forces of development, and to give the sequence of stages a generality that is unwarranted. A country may attain a later stage of development without first having passed through an earlier stage, as stages may be skipped, and different types of economies do not have to succeed or evolve from one another. The sequence is also blurred inasmuch as frequently the stages are not mutually exclusive, and characteristics of earlier stages often become mixed with characteristics of later stages. Anyone who attempts to impose on economic history a one-way course of economic evolution is bound to be challenged, since it is difficult to accept one unique schema as the only real framework in which the facts truly lie; the same facts can be arranged in many patterns and seen from many perspectives.[10] What matters, therefore, is how suggestive and useful Rostow's pattern is in providing answers to our questions as we attempt to make sense out of the past and make the future more predictable. This comes down to the question of the adequacy of Rostow's pattern in helping us isolate the strategic factors that make for change, especially those factors that constitute the necessary and sufficient conditions for determining the transition of an economy from a preceding stage to a succeeding stage.

In this respect, Rostow's efforts are more substantial than those by other proponents of stages. Recognizing the importance of the search for strategic facts, Rostow adopts an approach that is more analytic and related to a wider range of issues than any of the approaches of his predecessors. His argument abounds with terms such as "forces," "process," "net result," "inner logic" — all indicative of his desire to present an analytic, not merely a descriptive, set of stages. According to Rostow, the "analytic backbone" of his argument is "rooted in a dynamic theory of production," and he believes that his set of stages reveals a "succession of strategic choices" that confronts a country as it moves forward through the development process. On this basis, perhaps the most illumination can be gained from Rostow's analysis by interpreting each stage as posing a particular type of problem, so that the sequence of stages is equivalent to a series of problems that confronts a country in the course of its development.

Comment: The "Take-Off"

Rostow has extended his analysis in *How It All Began* (1975) and *Why the Poor Get Richer and the Rich Slow Down: Essays in the Marshallian Long Period* (1970).

For a more detailed exposition of Rostow's general thesis, and criticisms levied against it, see the papers presented at the International Economic Association's conference, published in W. W. Rostow et al., *The Economics of Take-Off into Sustained Growth* (1963), and the review article by Albert Fishlow, "Empty Economic Stages?" *Economic Journal* (March 1965).

Several other critiques deserve special mention: K. Berrill, "Historical Experience: The Problem of Economic 'Take-Off,'" in *Economic Development with Special Reference to East Asia*, ed. K. Berrill (1964); Henrý Rosovsky, "The Take-Off into Sustained Controversy," *Journal of Economic History* (June 1965); P. Baran and E. Hobsbawm, "The Stages of Economic Growth," *Kyklos* 14, no. 2 (1961); P. T. Bauer and Charles Wilson, "The Stages of Growth," *Economica* (May 1962); S. G. Checkland, "Theories of Economic and Social Evolution: The Rostow Challenge," *Scottish Journal of Political Economy* (November 1960); E. E. Hagen, *On the Theory of Social Change* (1962), app. 2; D. C. North, "A Note on Professor Rostow's 'Take-Off' into Self-sustained Economic Growth," *The Manchester School* (January 1958); Goran Ohlin, "Reflections on the Rostow Doctrine," *Economic Development and Cultural Change* (July 1961); and G. L. S. Shackle, "The Stages of Economic Growth," *Political Studies* (February 1962). But see Rostow's second edition of *The Stages of Economic Growth* (1971) and *Politics and the Stages of Growth* (1971).

Of special interest is the Festschrift in honor of Rostow: C. P. Kindleberger and Guido di Tella, eds., *Economics in the Long View* (1982).

Economic backwardness in historical perspective*

The map of Europe in the nineteenth century showed a motley picture of countries varying with regard to the degree of their economic backwardness. At the same time, processes of rapid industrialization started in several of those countries from very different levels of economic backwardness. Those differences in points — or planes — of departure were of crucial significance for the nature of the subsequent development. Depending on a given country's degree of economic backwardness on the eve of its industrialization, the course and character of the latter tended to vary in a number of important respects. Those variations can be readily compressed into the shorthand of six propositions.

1. The more backward a country's economy, the more likely was its industrialization to start discontinuously as a sudden great spurt proceeding at a relatively high rate of growth of manufacturing output.[1]

2. The more backward a country's economy, the more pronounced was the stress in its industrialization on bigness of both plant and enterprise.

3. The more backward a country's economy, the greater was the stress upon producers' goods as against consumers' goods.

4. The more backward a country's economy, the heavier was the pressure upon the levels of consumption of the population.

5. The more backward a country's economy, the greater was the part played by special institutional factors designed to increase supply of capital to the nascent industries and, in addition, to provide them with less decentralized and better informed

* Alexander Gerschenkron: 'Economic Backwardness in Historical Perspective', *JOURNAL OF ECONOMIC HISTORY* (1955). Reprinted by permission of Cambridge University Press.

entrepreneurial guidance; the more backward the country, the more pronounced was the coerciveness and comprehensiveness of those factors.

6. The more backward a country, the less likely was its agriculture to play any active role by offering to the growing industries the advantages of an expanding industrial market based in turn on the rising productivity of agricultural labor.

... [T]he differences in the level of economic advance among the individual European countries or groups of countries in the last century were sufficiently large to make it possible to array those countries, or groups of countries, along a scale of increasing degrees of backwardness and thus to render the latter an operationally usable concept. Cutting two notches into that scale yields three groups of countries which may be roughly described as advanced, moderately backward, and very backward. To the extent that certain of the variations in our six propositions can also be conceived as discrete rather than continuous, the pattern assumes the form of a series of stage constructs. Understandably enough, this result obtains most naturally with regard to factors referred to in proposition 5, where quantitative differences are associated with qualitative, that is, institutional, variations....

Such an attempt to view the course of industrialization as a schematic stagelike process differs essentially from the various efforts in "stage making," the common feature of which was the assumption that all economies were supposed regularly to pass through the same individual stages as they moved along the road of economic progress. The regularity may have been frankly presented as an inescapable "law" of economic development.[2] Alternatively, the element of necessity may have been somewhat disguised by well-meant, even though fairly meaningless, remarks about the choices that were open to society.[3] But all those schemes were dominated by the idea of uniformity. Thus, Rostow was at pains to assert that the process of industrialization repeated itself from country to country lumbering through his pentametric rhythm....

The point, however, is not simply that these were important occurrences which have just claims on the historian's attention. What matters in the present connection is that observing the individual methods of financing industrial growth helps us to understand the crucial problem of prerequisites for industrial development.

The common opinion on the subject has been well stated by Rostow. There is said to be a number of certain general preconditions or prerequisites for industrial growth, without which it could not begin. Abolition of an archaic framework in agricultural organization or an increase in the productivity of agriculture; creation of an influential modern elite which is materially or ideally interested in economic change, provision of what is called social-overhead capital in physical form — all these are viewed as "necessary preconditions," except that some reference to the multifarious forms in which the prerequisites are fulfilled in the individual areas are designed to take care of the "unique" factors in development. Similarly, the existence of a value system favoring economic progress and the availability of effective entrepreneurial groups basking in the sun of social approval have been regarded as essential preconditions of industrial growth.

These positions are part and parcel of an undifferentiated approach to industrial history. But their conceptual and empirical deficiencies are very considerable, even though it is by no means easy to bid farewell to this highly simplified way of viewing the processes of industrialization. It took the present writer several years before he succeeded in reformulating the concept of prerequisites so that it could be fit into a general approach premised upon the notion of relative backwardness....

There should be a fine on the use of words such as "necessary" or "necessity" in historical writings. As one takes a closer look at the concept of necessity as it is appended to prerequisites of industrial development, it becomes clear that, whenever the concept is not entirely destitute of meaning, it is likely to be purely definitional: industrialization is defined in terms of certain conditions which then, by an imperceptible shift of the writer's wrist, are metamorphosed into historical preconditions.[4]

The recourse of tautologies and dexterous manipulations has been produced by, or at any rate served to disguise, very real empirical difficulties. After having satisfied oneself that in England certain factors could be reasonably regarded as having preconditioned the industrialization of the country, the tendency was, and still is, to elevate them to the rank of ubiquitous prerequisites of all European industrializations. Unfortunately, the attempt was inconsistent with two empirical observations: (1) some of the factors that had served as prerequisites in England either were not present in less advanced countries or at best were present to a very small extent: (2) the big spurt of industrial development occurred in those countries despite the lack of such prerequisites.

If these observations are not ignored or shrugged away, as is usually done, they quite naturally direct research toward a new question: in what way and through the use of what devices did backward countries *substitute* for the missing prerequisites? ... It appears, on the one hand, that some of the alleged prerequisites were not needed in industrializations proceeding under different conditions. On the other hand, once the question has been asked, whole series of various substitutions become visible which could be readily organized in a meaningful pattern according to the degree of economic backwardness ... [I]t is easy to conceive of the capital supplied to the early factories in an advanced country as stemming from previously accumulated wealth or from gradually plowed-back profits: at the same time, actions by banks and governments in less advanced countries are regarded as successful attempts to create *in the course* of industrialization conditions which had not been created in the "preindustrial" periods precisely because of the economic backwardness of the areas concerned ....

[T]he area of capital supply is only one instance of substitutions for missing prerequisites. As one looks at the various patterns of substitution in the individual countries, taking proper account of the effects of gradually diminishing backwardness, one is tempted to formulate still another general proposition. The more backward was a country on the eve of its great spurt of industrial development, the more likely were the processes of its industrialization to present a rich and complex picture — thus providing a curious contrast with its own preindustrial history that most often was found to have been relatively barren. In an advanced country, on the other hand, the very richness of its economic history in the preindustrial periods rendered possible a relatively simple and straightforward course in its modern industrial history.

Thus, the concept of prerequisites must be regarded as an integral part of this writer's general approach to the industrial history of Europe. At the same time, it is important to keep in mind the heuristic nature of the concept. There is no intention to suggest that backward countries necessarily engaged in deliberate acts of "substitution" for something that had been in evidence in more advanced countries. Men in a less developed country may have simply groped for and found solutions that were consonant with the existing conditions of backwardness. In fact, one could conceivably start the study of European industrializations in the east rather than in the west of the Continent and view some elements in English industrial history as substitutions for the German or the Russian way of doing things. This would not be a very good way to proceed. It would make mockery of chronology and would be glaringly artificial. True, some artificiality also inheres in the opposite approach. It is arbitrary to select England as the seat of prerequisites. Yet this is the arbitrariness of the process of cognition and should be judged by its fruits.

The main advantage of viewing European history as patterns of substitutions governed by the prevailing — and changing — degree of backwardness lies, perhaps paradoxically, in its offering a set of predictabilities while at the same time placing limitations upon our ability to predict. To predict is not to prophesy. Prediction in historical research means addressing intelligent, that is, sufficiently specific, questions as new materials are approached.

Comment: Historical Studies

No attempt can be made to do justice to the innumerable historical studies of development. Only a few survey studies can be singled out: R. M. Hartwell, "The Causes of Industrial Revolution: An Essay in Methodology," *Economic History Review* 18, no. 1 (1965); Richard A. Easterlin. "Is There a Need for Historical Research on Underdevelopment?" *American Economic Review* (May 1965); Barry E. Supple, "Economic History and Economic Underdevelopment," *Canadian Journal of Economics and Political Science* (November 1961); John C. H. Fei and Gustav Ranis, "Economic Development in Historical Perspective," *American Economic Review* (May 1969); J. Hughes, *Industrialization and Economic History* (1970), pt. II; and J. R. Hicks, *A Theory of Economic History* (1969).

An interesting collection of "successful and promising beginnings" of development is contained in Malcolm E. Falkus, ed., *Reading in the History of Economic Growth* (1968), and Barry E. Supple, ed., *The Experience of Economic Growth* (1963).

References

Sequence of stages — note

1. Simon Kuznets, "Notes on Stage of Economic Growth as a System Determinant," in *Comparison of Economic Systems*, ed. Alexander Eckstein (1971), p. 243.

2. W. W. Rostow, "The Stages of Economic Growth," *Economic History Review* (August 1959) and *The Stages of Economic Growth* (1960); W. W. Rostow et al., *The Economics of Take-Off into Sustained Growth* (1963).

3. Rostow, *Stages of Economic Growth*, pp. 36-40.

4. Ibid., p. 148.

5. Ibid., p. 149.

6. Ibid., p. 2.

7. Ibid., p. 150.

8. Ibid.

9. Ibid., p. 152.

10. Although Rostow gives little attention to the problem, his analysis raises many questions related to basic social theory. In this connection, it is illuminating to consult Isaiah Berlin, *Historical Inevitability* (1954), especially sections 2, 8.

Economic backwardness in historical perspective

1. The "great spurt" is closely related to W. W. Rostow's "take-off" (*The Stages of Economic Growth*, Cambridge University Press, 1960, Chap. 4). Both concepts stress the element of specific discontinuity in economic development; great spurts, however, are confined to the area of manufacturing and mining, whereas take-offs refer to national output. Unfortunately, in the present state of our statistical information on long-term growth of national income, there is hardly any way of establishing, let alone testing, the take-off hypotheses.

2. See, for example, Bruno Hildebrand, *Die Nationalökonomie, der Gegenwart und Zukunft und andere gesammelte Schriften*, 1, Jena, 1922, p. 357.

3. See Rostow, *The Stages of Economic Growth*, pp. 118ff.

4. It is not surprising, therefore, to see Rostow at one point (p. 49) mix conditions and preconditions of industrial development very freely.

12.   Underdevelopment and Marxism: From Marx to the Theories of Imperialism and Dependency[1]

Gabriel Palma

Introduction

When embarking on a study of the Marxist contribution to the analysis of underdevelopment, the question immediately presents itself: may one talk of a single Marxist theory of underdevelopment? Or, do we find today under this label theories of such a diverse nature that it would be rather more appropriate to speak of 'Marxist inspired' theories of underdevelopment?

Marxism is a highly complex subject, and its contribution to the analysis of capitalist development in backward nations is no less so. At the same time, it is precisely in this area of Marxist thought that we find the widest divergencies between the writings of Marx and Engels and those of many contemporary Marxists. Without doubt, the attitude of some Marxist writers today that capitalist industrialization in the periphery is no longer feasible goes against the spirit and the letter of Marx's writings. Nevertheless, as a general rule, we do not find in them an effort to explain these divergencies; but on the contrary, their writings give the impression that Marxist interest in the problems of capitalist development in peripheral countries and areas of the world only began in 1957, with the publication of Baran's *The Political Economy of Growth*.

In this context, what is important, as Sutcliffe has argued, is to ask whether the differences are attributable to changes in 'circumstance or diagnosis' (1972 a, p.180). That is to say whether capitalism has been transformed in such a way that the industrialization of the periphery cannot take place within the capitalist system, or whether it is that Marx's analysis is itself over-optimistic regarding the possibilities of industrialization in the backward areas of the world.

I distinguish three principal phases in the development of Marxist thought concerning the problems of capitalist development in backward countries and areas of the world. The first, essentially that of Marx and Engels, analyses capitalism as an historically progressive system, which will be transmitted from the advanced countries (through colonialism, free trade, etc.) and which will spread through the backward nations by a continual process of destruction and replacement of pre-capitalist structures. As a result of this process a series of new capitalist societies would arise, whose development would be similar, in the post-colonial period, to that of the advanced countries themselves; this, then, would be followed by the development of the series of contradictions proper to the capitalist system, which would tend to lead them to a higher stage of development.

Gabriel Palma: 'Underdevelopment and Marxism: From Marx to the Theories of Imperialism and Dependency' *THAMES PAPERS IN POLITICAL ECONOMY* (Summer 1978). Reproduced by permission of the author.

The second approach to the development of capitalism in backward nations, found primarily in the writings of the so-called 'classics of imperialism', concerns itself, first, with the peculiarities of the development of Russian capitalism, and afterwards with that of other backward areas of the world in the 'monopolistic' phase of the world capitalist system. As regards the development of Russian capitalism, its historically progressive character is stressed, but this development is no longer analysed simply as a process of destruction and replacement of its pre-capitalist structures, but as a far more complex process of interplay between internal and external structures. These analyses stress the difficulties resulting from 'late' industrialization, the ambiguous role of foreign capital (from Western Europe), and the great capacity for survival of pre-capitalist structures. As regards capitalist development in other backward areas of the world, we may distinguish two major historical stages in the analyses of the 'classics of imperialism'. The first is characterised by its analysis (following Marx) of capitalist development in the colonies as historically progressive, but (qualifying Marx's analysis) limited by the new imperatives of the advanced economies in their monopoly phase. Faced with these imperatives the advanced nations were, in the view of these writers, succeeding in restricting modern industrialization in the colonies. Nevertheless, they stress that once the colonial bonds are broken modern industrialization could eventually take place. Thus the capitalist development of backward nations would take on a similar character to that of the advanced nations. At the same time they insisted that this process of post-colonial industrialization would in no way be free from political and economic difficulties and contradictions; on the contrary, the emerging national bourgeoisie would face the difficult, but by no means impossible, task of developing their own bourgeois revolutions, and the no less difficult but equally possible task of 'late' industrialization.

It was only in the twenties that a second approach began to emerge as emphasis was placed on a different set of difficulties (particularly of a political nature) hindering the process of post-colonial industrialization.

The third approach was first developed at the end of the fifties, and 'took off' with the publication of the already mentioned work of Baran; it is characterised by the acceptance, almost as an axiomatic truth, of the argument that no third world country can now expect to break out of a state of economic dependency and advance to an economic position beside the major capitalist industrial powers. This is a very important proposition since it not only establishes the extent to which capitalism remains historically progressive in the modern world, but also thereby defines the economic background to political action. Yet, too often, the question is ill-defined; it is not self-evident; its intellectual origins are obscure; and its actual foundations are in need of a fuller analysis.

It is in this third phase that the analyses of the Dependency School emerge. Although there are other contributions beside those of this school of thought, my analysis will concentrate primarily on them, for being the most influential one. It would, moreover, be literally impossible to review in an article like this the overwhelming mass of writings related either in a supportive or in a critical fashion to this third phase of Marxist thought or simply to reflect its sudden ascendency in academic and institutional circles hitherto relatively closed to radical critiques of current orthodoxy.

1. Marx and Engels on the development of capitalism in backward nations

It is not easy to analyse Marx's and Engels' approach to the development of capitalism in the backward regions of the world, as their remarks on the subject are scattered throughout their respective works. In Marx's case, although the analysis of the capitalist mode of production in *Capital* is a work of profound and systematic brilliance, his specific references to the concrete forms in which this mode of production is developed in backward regions are not found there, but in various of his other works. Of relevance among his political writings is the *Communist Manifesto* (1848); among his theoretical writings, the preface *A Contribution to the Critique of Political Economy* (1859); among his correspondence, that with his contacts among the Russian left; and among his articles to newspapers, those in the *New York Daily Tribune* between 1853 and 1859. Unfortunately, his concrete references are almost all concerned with India and China, with only superficial references made to Latin America. This is unfortunate not only because we are ourselves interested in Latin America, but more significantly because the subcontinent would have provided Marx with a backward region already developing in a way which would be typical of post-colonial societies in later years, with the exception of those of European settlement. While formally free, the countries of Latin America were economically backward and dependent.

In a letter written in the closing years of his life, Marx stressed that in *Capital* he had studied only the genesis of capitalism in Western Europe (Marx, 1877, p.253). Nevertheless, it is from that same work that we can deduce with clarity his analysis of the tendencies which would guide the expansion of the capitalist economies towards the backward regions of the world. The most relevant chapters are those concerning primary accumulation (1867, Ch.XXIV) and foreign trade (1894, Ch. XIV).

The central element behind the need of the advanced capitalist economies to expand is the need to develop an effective means of countering the tendency for the rate of profit to fall; such expansion makes it possible to expand the scale of production, to lower the costs of raw materials and of the products needed to maintain and reproduce the labour force at home (making it possible to keep wages low), and thus to increase the surplus by helping to preserve the low organic composition of capital. Furthermore, for a period of time the capitalist in an advanced country can gain a higher rate of profits by selling

> in competition with commodity producers in other countries with lesser facilities for production . . . in the same way that a manufacturer exploits a new invention before it has become general (1894, Section 5).[2]

Nevertheless Marx did not confine himself to the analysis of the driving forces which lead to the expansion of capitalism. In his analysis of the effect of this upon the backward regions, following the Hegelian tradition, *he distinguishes between the subjective motivations for this expansion and its objective historical results*. On the one hand he condemns this expansion as the most brutalizing and dehumanizing that history has ever known, but on the other he argues that it is necessary if the backward societies are to develop. Only capitalism, he argues, can provide the necessary economic and technological infrastructure which will enable society to allow for the free development of every member according to his capacity; and capitalism can only develop in them through its penetration and imposition from abroad. Only on the basis of this dialectical understanding of capitalism can we understand the famous affirmation in the preface to the first edition of *Capital* that

> the backward country suffers not only from the development of capitalist production, but also from the incompleteness of that development (1867, p.xiv).

In general terms we may say that *it is analytically convenient* to distinguish two intimately connected levels in Marx's analysis of the development of capitalism in backward nations. One relates to the necessity (both political and economic) of capitalism as an essential step towards higher forms of development of productive forces, the other to the *possibility and viability* (both political and economic) of its development. These two levels of analysis are present in the Marxist tradition with differing degrees of emphasis. In Marx's writings on the subject the central concern is with the necessity for capitalist development, with its feasibility taken completely for granted. In the present day however the emphasis is placed more on the second level of analysis, that of the feasibility of capitalist development in the periphery.[3]

As regards the first aspect, the necessity of capitalist development, Marx states very clearly, at least until the important change which comes towards the end of his life, that socialism can only be attained through capitalist development, and that this will not be produced in the backward regions of the world by the development of their own productive forces, as was the case in Western Europe, but by the impact upon them of the capitalism of Western Europe itself.

Marx is overtly hostile to the modes of production in existence in non-European societies, chiefly on the grounds of their unchanging nature, which he saw as a drag on the process of history, and thus a serious threat to socialism. This led him, while condemning the brutality and hypocrisy of colonialism, to regard it as historically necessary.

Initially, in the *Communist Manifesto* Marx and Engels appear to refer to the backward nations *en masse* as 'barbarians', 'semi-barbarians', 'nations of peasants', and 'the East', in a manner which contrasts strikingly with their meticulous study of European society and history, and is particularly unsatisfactory in a work which makes the strongest possible claim to be based upon a universally applicable scientific interpretation of history. However, 11 years later, in the preface to *A Contribution to the Critique of Political Economy*, Marx made a more serious attempt to relate the socio-economic conditions of the non-European world to his general theory of history, but he did so elliptically, and in a way that has bedeviled Marxism ever since. Discussing the stages of economic development, he strongly brings out the dialectical tensions inherent in every period, saying, in a passage that has become classic:

> No social order ever disappears before all the productive forces for which there is room in it have been developed; and new, higher relations of

production never appear before the material conditions of their existence have matured in the womb of the old society (1859, p.21).

Proceeding to analyse the four modes of production, Asiatic, Ancient, Feudal and Capitalist, he leaves the Asiatic mode in a form which is difficult to understand. There is a clear perception of a kind of continuity (its movement produced by the development of contradictions) between the Ancient, Feudal, Capitalist and Socialist modes of production, but the Asiatic mode is left disconnected, as if it had neither past nor future.[4]

If Marx never directly discusses this problem in his work he does so indirectly, stressing time and again that it should not be forgotten that the horizon of his work on the discussion of historical development is essentially European. In a letter written to a Russian Socialist journal in 1877, and already mentioned on page 166, he warns his readers not to

> metamorphose [his] historical sketch of the genesis of capital in Western Europe into a historical-philosophical theory of the general path every people is fated to tread, whatever the historical circumstances in which it finds itself,

and goes on to criticize any approach which seeks to understand history

> by using as one's master-key a general historical-philosophical theory, the supreme virtue of which consists in being supra-historical.

The problem of the Asiatic mode of production is not merely the academic one of establishing how far Marx's theory of history is consistent and universal; it is that as it does not possess a dialectic of internal development *it can only evolve through the penetration of European capitalism*. For this reason Marx analyses European expansion in India as brutal, but 'a necessary step towards Socialism' (1853). Such an expansion would have a destabilizing and disintegrating effect on the Asiatic mode of production, re-stabilizing and re-integrating such societies in a capitalist mode of development which would bring with it the development of productive forces and generate an internal dynamic which would lead such societies towards higher stages of development.

It is essential to note here that Marx makes no distinction between endogenous capitalist development (such as occurred in Western Europe) and that which is introduced from outside. Irrespective of its origins, capitalism once implanted in a society will develop in a certain way. If one of its central characteristics is to develop both objective wealth and poverty, this would exist within each society, rather than between societies.

Only fleetingly in the case of China and with much greater clarity, towards the end of his life, in the case of Russia, does Marx recognize the possibility that different traditional structures could be capable of serving as a starting-point for movement towards more advanced stages of development; in the first case he speaks ironically of the possibility of a bourgeois revolution, in the second of a socialist revolution.

In February 1850 there was a wave of agrarian unrest in China, and Marx wrote:

> when our European reactionaries, on their next flight through Asia will have finally reached the Chinese Wall, the gates that lead to the seat of primeval reaction and conservatism-who knows, perhaps they will read the following inscription on the Wall: République Chinoise-Liberté, Egalite, Fraternité! (quoted in Averini, 1976, p.251).

Regarding the Russian case, in reply to a letter from the Russian Marxist, Vera Sassoulitch, in February 1881 (to which we shall return later) Marx stresses the possibility that the particular traditional agrarian structures of Russia could serve as a starting-point for socialist development. He reaffirms this point of view together with Engels, in the preface to a new Russian edition of the *Communist Manifesto* in 1882.[5]

Passing now to the analysis of Marx's attitude regarding the possibility of capitalist development in the non-European world, it must be stated that Marx leaves no room for misinterpretation; the dynamism and capacity for expansion of the youthful capitalism of his period would be reproduced in any society which it penetrated; furthermore, he seemed to expect a proliferation of autonomous capitalist societies, fundamentally similar to those in Western Europe. There are three particular excerpts which have become obligatory points of reference, and to which we need refer only briefly. In the *Communist Manifesto* Marx and Engels argue that the development of capitalism in Western Europe will

> compel all nations, on pain of extinction, to adopt the bourgeois mode of production.

and 5 years later, in his article on the *Future Results of British Rule in India* (1853), Marx argues that English imperialism will not be able to avoid the industrialization of India:

> when you have once introduced machinery into the locomotion of a country which possesses iron and coals *you are unable* to withhold it from its fabrications (the emphasis is mine).

Finally, 14 years later, in the preface to the first edition of *Capital* we find this famous statement:

> the country that is more developed industrially only shows, to the less developed, the image of its own future.

We may then conclude, with Kierman, that

> So far as can be seen, what he [Marx] had in mind was not a further spread of Western imperialism, but a proliferation of autonomous capitalism, such as he expected in India and did witness in North America (1967, p.183).

As was stated in the introduction, there is no question that the attitude of some Marxist writers today that capitalist industrialization in the periphery is no longer feasible goes against the spirit and the letter of Marx's writings. Throughout the analysis I shall attempt to establish whether the divergencies are attributable to changes in circumstance or diagnosis.

2. From Marx and Engels to the 'Classics of Imperialism'

If Hilferding (1910) had already provided an important Marxist study of imperialism, it is in Luxemburg (1913), Bukharin (1915) and Lenin (1916) that we find the most important contributions from the period in which capitalism was moving through its monopoly phase. I shall refer only briefly to the works of Luxemburg and Bukharin; as regards Lenin's work, I shall concentrate on those aspects which are most relevant to the issues under discussion.

Rosa Luxemburg's *The Accumulation of Capital* (1913) was the first Marxist analysis of the world capitalist economy in the light of the three concerns outlined earlier in this paper, and remains among the most complete; it is certainly the only one of the classic writings on imperialism which sets out to provide a systematic analysis of the effect which imperialism would have on the backward countries. Unfortunately, the rigour, profundity and creativity of the analysis are limited by the fact that, following the Marxist tradition of the period, she underestimates both the increase in real wages which takes place as capitalism develops in the advanced countries, and the internal inducement to invest provided by technological progress. Consequently she overplays and misunderstands the role of the periphery in the process of accumulation of capital in the developed countries, for these two factors have played a vital role in rescuing capitalism from the difficulties and contradictions which it creates for itself. Thus the periphery has played a role both qualitatively different and quantitatively less important than that which her analysis depicts.[6]

Nikolai Ivanovitch Bukharin contributed to the analysis of imperialism principally in his works of 1915 and 1926. In the first he analyses the two most important tendencies in the world economy of the time, tendencies which were made manifest jointly and in contradiction to each other. These were the rapid process of internationalization of economic life (the integration of the different national economies into a world economy) and the process of 'nationalization' of capital (the withdrawing of the interests of the national bourgeoisies within their respective frontiers). The most interesting feature of the second work is its polemic against Luxemburg's *The Accumulation of Capital*. From the point of view of our interest, it is unfortunate that although Bukharin stresses continually throughout the course of his work that imperialism is a phenomenon which connects the advanced and the backward economies, and criticises Luxemburg's view on the subject, in no part of his work does he analyse in concrete terms the effect of imperialism upon the backward countries.[7]

When one is analysing Lenin's work it is particularly important to bear in mind (as with the work of any political leader who is not writing for purely academic reasons, but with specific and concrete political ends in view), the political context in which the works were written. In fact it is necessary not only to consider the usual problems concerning the separation of 'history' and 'concept', 'theory' and 'practice', and the 'role' of ideology, but also to be aware that the relative emphases in these works are frequently functions of tactical moves related to factional disputes.[8] Furthermore in the case of Lenin's *Imperialism, The Highest Stage of Capitalism* (1916) he himself was careful to point out that he wrote it

> with an eye to the Tsarist censorship . . . with extreme caution, by hints,
> in an allegorical language (1916, p.1).

The political situation within which and as a contribution to which Lenin wrote his analysis of imperialism was characterized by the outbreak of the First World War and the subsequent collapse of the Second International.

Within a week of Austria's declaration of war on Serbia on 28 July 1914, the whole of Europe was at war. Lenin himself arrived in Switzerland on 5 September after a long odyssey, and set himself up in Berne. He was faced with a difficult double task: firstly, to explain to the international socialist movement the nature of the forces which had unleashed the war, and secondly, to account for the position adopted by the working class parties of the advanced capitalist countries (which had led to the collapse of the Second International). If for the first of these tasks he could avail himself of the analysis provided by Marx of the tendencies of capitalist development, and the later contributions of Marxists such as Hilferding, for the second he could draw on no previous analyses. Traditional Marxist analysis could not be applied simply and directly to explain why the proletariat of the advanced capitalist countries in general, and the social-democratic parties of the left in particular, had placed themselves alongside their respective bourgeoisies and against one another when the war broke out.[9]

It was no easy task to explain the capacity, unforeseen by Marx, of capitalism to extend to important sectors of the working classes some of the benefits of its development; nor was it simple to derive the relevant political conclusions. This would in fact be the most important contribution of *Imperialism, The Highest Stage of Capitalism*, and would make it Lenin's most important theoretical work, just as the *Development of Capitalism in Russia* (1899) is his most important study of the development of capitalism in a backward nation, and is in my view the pioneering classic of dependency studies.

To prepare himself for his difficult task Lenin re-read Marx and Hegel with great care, and produced his *Philosophical Notebook* (1915) as a result. In it he stresses the necessity to understand Hegel's logic (and to give due importance to the subjective element of the dialectic) in order to understand the development of capitalism in advanced countries. After this, now settled in Zurich, he wrote, between January and July 1916, his own study of imperialism, emphasizing in the 1917 preface to the Russian edition and the 1920 prefaces to the French and German editions the dual political purpose I have mentioned above. He thus makes it clear that his purpose in writing the work is different from that of Bukharin or Luxemburg.[10]

For analytical purposes we may distinguish three major themes in Lenin's work.[11] The first is the description of the most important political and economic changes in the advanced countries of the capitalist system, the second, the analysis of the changes in international relations which had resulted, and particularly the role played by international capital, and the third, the discussion of the future tendencies of the capitalist system in its monopoly or imperialist phase, and above all the effect these would have on its historical progressiveness. There is no systematic analysis of the effect that this phase of the development of capitalism will have on the backward regions of the world (the third concern to which I referred earlier). However, as we shall see later, it is possible to deduce from the analysis of the development of capitalism in the advanced countries in the system an implicit account of the effects it will tend to have in those backward regions. Nevertheless, in order to understand this implicit account it is necessary to go back 17 years to the *Development of Capitalism in Russia*, which is intimately connected with the analysis in the later work.[12]

3. Lenin's 'Development of Capitalism in Russia'

Within the Marxist tradition it is in Lenin's work that we find the first systematic attempt to provide a concrete analysis of the development of capitalism in a backward nation. In his analysis he

> formulated with simplicity what would be the core of the dependency analyses: the forms of articulation between the two parts of a single mode of production, and the subordination of one mode of production to another (Cardoso. 1974a, p.325).

In this work then, we find a detailed and profound study of the forms in which developing capitalism in Russia is articulated both to the economies of Western Europe and to the other existing modes of production in Russia itself. That is to say, the way in which Russia — its classes, state and economy — is articulated to the corresponding elements in the countries of Western Europe. The essay was written as part of a profound controversy in Russia itself regarding the necessity and the feasibility of capitalist development there. Discussion of this controversy is particularly relevant, as it was in the context of an identical controversy in Latin America in the 1950s and 1960s that the contribution to dependency studies was made.

Given that Russia was the first backward country in which Marxism developed, it is not surprising that it should have been the setting for the first Marxist debates regarding the feasibility of capitalist development, and as I have stated, Lenin's *Development of Capitalism in Russia* was part of this debate and of his constant polemic with the Narodniks.[13]

The central argument of the Narodniks was that capitalist development was not necessary for the attainment of socialism in Russia, and that from an economic point of view it was by no means clear that capitalism was a viable system for a backward country such as Russia. They laid great stress upon the problems created by 'late' entry into the process of capitalist industrialization.

Regarding the necessity for capitalist development in Russia, the Narodniks were convinced that the Russian peasant commune[14] with its system of communal ownership was essentially socialist, and capable of forming the basis of a future socialist order; hence Russia might indeed lead the rest of Europe on the road to socialism.

From what Marx and Engels had written before they became interested in the Russian case it is possible to deduce *a priori* their disagreement with Narodniks. It was a central point of their analysis that the peasantry, fundamentally on account of its feudal origins, was a backward element in European society, in relation to the capitalist bourgeoisie and, *a fortiori*, in relation to the proletariat. Wherever capitalism was advanced, the peasantry was a decadent class.[15] On this account it is placed in the *Communist Manifesto* alongside a number of petty bourgeois groups, as Marx and Engels speak of

> the small manufacturers, the shopkeepers, the artisan and the peasant ...

Only when the bourgeoisie and the proletariat, together or apart, are incapable of carrying out the bourgeois revolution and the overthrow of feudalism would it be permissible to support the peasantry and its political organizations, let alone to fight for its interest in individual ownership of the land.

At the end of the 1860s, attracted by the development of the left in Russia, Marx and Engels learnt Russian and threw themselves into the current debates there. In 1875 Engels was stressing the necessity for capitalist development, though less as a necessity of an absolute nature than as a result of the fact that the Russian system of communal property was already decadent. For this reason it was impossible to 'leap over' the capitalist stage through the transformation of the communal institutions of the feudal past into the fundamental bases of the socialist future. On the other hand, he argued, the triumph of the socialist revolution in the advanced capitalist countries would help Russia itself to advance rapidly towards socialism (see Carr, Vol.2, 1966, p.385).

Two years later Marx entered the debate with the letter I have already discussed (p.163). In it he expresses a position similar to that of Engels, arguing that the possibility that a different transition to socialism might take place in Russia no longer appeared to exist:

> If Russia continues on the path which she has been following since 1861 [the emancipation of the serfs] she will be deprived of the finest chance ever offered by history to a nation of avoiding all the ups and downs of the capitalist order.

In the following year a group of young Narodniks led by Plekhanov broke with the rest and headed for Switzerland; their differences were both political and theoretical, in that they opposed the use of terrorism and embraced the spirit and letter of the *Communist Manifesto*. Nevertheless, they came to adopt positions 'more Marxist than those of Marx himself', and in 1881 Vera Sassoulitch wrote to Marx seeking a clarification of his views regarding the peasant commune. After composing three long drafts, which are among his papers, he contented himself with a brief response. His analysis of *Capital*, he stated, was based upon conditions in Western Europe, where communal property had long since disappeared; this analysis was by no means mechanically applicable to Russia, where such forms of property still survived in peasant communes. Nevertheless, for these to serve as a starting-point for a 'socialist regeneration of Russia' they would require a series of conditions which allowed them to develop freely. Nowhere in his reply does Marx express any doubt that capitalist development is possible in Russia; his argument is that perhaps given the specificity of the Russian situation the price of capitalist development in human terms would be too high for it to be counted as a progressive development.[16]

Regarding the other facet of the controversy with the Narodniks, that of the possibility of capitalist development in Russia, it is in the writings of the Narodniks that it is first suggested that capitalism may not be viable in a backward nation. Thus the Narodnik writer Vorontsov argued that

> the more belated is the process of industrialization, the more difficult it is to carry it on along the capitalist lines (quoted in Walicki, 1969, p.121).

For the Narodniks, furthermore,

> backwardness provided an advantage in that the technological benefits of modern capitalism could be used, while its structure is rejected (Sutcliffe, 1974a, p.182).

For these reasons then, for the Narodniks it was not only possible but economically imperative to escape from the capitalist stage and move directly towards socialism. This same position will be found, as we shall see, in the 1960s in Latin America in the writings of one group of dependency writers.

In the last decade of the 19th century, along with the first industrial strikes in Russia, there appeared a number of Marxist groups, while the Narodniks, caught in the blind alley of terrorism, were beginning to lose influence. One of these was the 'League of Struggle for the Liberation of the Working Class', which appeared in Petrograd in 1895; among its members was a disciple of Plekhanov, who wrote successively under the pseudonyms of 'Petrov', 'Frei' and 'Lenin', the latter after 1902. The young Lenin entered vigorously into the debate with the Narodniks, writing his major contribution towards it, the *Development of Capitalism in Russia*, between 1896 and 1899.

Lenin agreed with the Narodniks only in one respect — that capitalism was a brutalizing and degrading economic system. Nevertheless, like Marx, he distinguished clearly between this aspect of capitalism and the historical role which it played in Russia:

> Recognition of the progressiveness of capitalism is quite compatible . . . with the full recognition of its negative and dark sides. . . with the full recognition of the profound and all around social contradictions which are inevitably inherent in capitalism, and which reveal the historically transient nature of this economic regime. *It is the Narodniks who exert every effort to show than an admission of the historically progressive nature of capitalism means an apology for capitalism.* . . The progressive historical role of capitalism may be summed up in two brief propositions: increase in the productive forces of social labour, and the socialization of that labour (1899, pp.602-603). (The emphasis is mine.)

Their differences were not only at a theoretical level however; for Lenin the Narodniks were in error over basic matters of fact. Lenin shows, after a long and detailed study of the labour market in Russia, that capitalism was already developing rapidly, and that it should already be considered as essentially a capitalist country, although

> very backward as compared with other capitalist countries in her economic development (1899, p.507).

Furthermore, regarding the 'obstacles' to the development of capitalism in Russia identified by the Narodniks, such as unemployment and underemployment, he states that these are the *characteristics* of capitalist development, and that the Narodniks are guilty of transforming

> the basic conditions for the development of capitalism into proof that capitalism is impossible (1899, pp.589-590).

For Lenin what was indispensable was the profound study of why the development of capitalism in Russia, while rapid in relation to development in the pre-capitalist period, was slow in comparison to the development of other capitalist nations. It is in his approach to this question that, in my opinion, we find his most important contribution to the study of the development of capitalism in backward nations.

His analysis of the slowness of capitalist development in Russia (which some dependency writers would still insist on describing as 'the development of Russian underdevelopment') has three inter-related themes:

> (i) the weakness of the Russian bourgeoisie as an agent for the furthering of capitalist development;
> (ii) the effect of competition from Western Europe in slowing the growth of modern industry in Russia; and
> (iii) the great and unexpected capacity for survival of the traditional structures of Russian society.

Regarding the weakness of the Russian bourgeoisie, Lenin was taking up a theme already discussed by the Russian left.[17] The interesting feature of his analysis is that he relates this weakness to the ambiguous role played by foreign capital (from Western Europe) in the development of Russian capitalism. On the one hand it accelerates the process of industrialization, while on the other it lies behind the weak and dependent nature of the small Russian bourgeoisie.

In what he says in relation to the second factor which explains the slower pace of Russian capitalist development, Lenin stresses that as Russia was industrializing 'late' the development of its modern industry had to compete not only with the production of traditional industry (as the first countries to industrialize had had to do) but also with the far more efficient industrial production of advanced countries within the capitalist system.

Finally, Lenin places great emphasis and explanatory value upon the great capacity for survival of traditional structures in Russia:

> In no single capitalist country has there been such an abundant survival of ancient institutions that are incompatible with capitalism, producers who [quoting Marx] 'suffer not only from the development of capitalist production, but also from the incompleteness of that development' (1899, p.607).

An important aspect of Lenin's analysis of the survival of traditional structures (and one that is particularly relevant to the present situation in backward nations) is his treatment of the interconnections which develop between the different modes of production which existed in Russia:

> the facts utterly refute the view widespread here in Russia that 'factory' and 'handicraft' industry are isolated from one another. On the contrary, such a division is purely artificial (1899, p.547).

Lenin's view of capitalist development in Russia can be summarized as follows:

> (i) in conformity with the central tradition of classical Marxist analysis he sees it as politically necessary and economically feasible;
> (ii) through a concrete analysis he shows that its development is fully underway;
> (iii) the development of capitalism in backward nations is seen for the first time not simply as a process of destruction and replacement of pre-capitalist structures, but as a more complex process of interplay between internal and external structures; in this interplay, the traditional structures play an important role, and their replacement will be slower and more difficult than previously supposed; and
> (iv) despite the complexity of Russian capitalist development, both it and the bourgeois revolution which would accompany it would eventually develop and become relatively similar to that of Western Europe. (The development of capitalism in Russia would therefore be a kind of 'slow-motion replay' of the same development in Western Europe.)

I shall now go on to examine the relationship between this analysis of Russian capitalism and Lenin's theory of imperialism.

4. The later development of Lenin's thought regarding the development of capitalism in backward nations

The two historical events which had a profound influence upon the future development of Lenin's thought in all its aspects were the revolution of 1905 and the collapse of the Second International. If the second of these showed that it was by no means clear that the development of capitalism led necessarily and 'inevitably' to socialism, the first had shown the concrete possibility of interrupting capitalist development, avoiding its potential risks, and transferring to the proletariat the task of completing the democratic- bourgeois revolution.

The collapse of the Second International showed that as it developed, capitalism also created an unforeseen capacity to assimilate important sectors of the proletariat, and that therefore the development of its internal contradictions would take a more complex path than had hitherto been realized.

Marx had emphasized that capitalist development was condemned by its own nature to resolve its difficulties and contradictions through transformations which would necessarily lead to the creation of others even greater. Nevertheless, there seemed to be one aspect of capitalist development which at least in the medium term was acting in the opposite direction: rising real wages. These, essentially a result of the organization and struggle of the working class, played a crucial role in the development of capitalism, both from the point of view of its political stability, and of the increase in effective demand, so essential for the realization of surplus value.

In explaining both this capacity of capitalism to increase real wages much more than had been foreseen, and the political effect which it had upon the working class in the advanced capitalist countries, Lenin placed great emphasis upon the 'superprofits of imperialist exploitation' (1916, p.9). Not long afterwards, Henry Ford, following the analysis already proposed by Hobson (1902, 1911), stated:

> If we can distribute high wages, then that money is going to be spent and it will serve to make storekeepers and distributors and manufacturers in other lines more prosperous and this prosperity will be reflected in our sales. Country-wide high wages spell country-wide prosperity (1922, p. 124).

Kalecki (1933, 1934, 1935) and Keynes (1936) would later incorporate this insight into a new theoretical conceptualization of the development of capitalism; two years later, Harold Macmillan would refer as follows to the enormous political importance of extending to the working class some of the material benefits of capitalist development:

> Democracy can live only so long as it is able to cope satisfactorily with the problems of social life. While it is able to deal with these problems, and secure for its people the satisfaction of their reasonable demands, it will retain the vigorous support sufficient for its defence (1938, p.375; quoted in Kay, 1975, p.174).

In this context it is important to recall that although Marx's expectations regarding the standard of living of the working-class under capitalism are not entirely clear, it seems evident that he did not expect an increase of the magnitude which eventually occurred. It emerged later that capitalism was going to provide rising real wages at a rate relatively similar to the rhythm of its development but only after a considerable 'time-lag' (See Hicks, 1969, pp.148-159). In 1923, in what would be his last article, Lenin wrote:

> but the Western European countries are not completing this development [towards socialism] as we previously expected they would. They are completing it not through a steady 'maturing' of socialism, but through the exploitation of some states by others (quoted in Foster-Carter, 1974, p.67).

The train of history was not going to drop its passengers off at the station of their choice, socialism, unless they took charge of it at an earlier stage. The contribution of the events of 1905 in Russia was precisely that it showed that it was possible, though by no means necessarily economically feasible.

From 1905 onwards, first in Trotsky and Parvus and later in Lenin, there began a change of position regarding the necessity of continuing with capitalist development. As we saw earlier, Marx had stated that no social order would disappear before having developed all the productive forces it could contain, and that higher relationships of production would not appear until the old order had run its full course. The events of 1905 showed both the limitations of the development of capitalism in Russia and the concrete possibility of interrupting it, transferring to the proletariat the task of completing the democratic-bourgeois revolution. Nevertheless, Engels had argued (see p. 170) that for this to happen there would have to be a revolution in Western Europe. Russia could play the role of the weakest link in the capitalist chain, and with the help of more developed socialist societies could follow the path towards socialism more rapidly. Therefore the socialist revolution could begin in a country such as Russia, but it could not be completed there.[18]

However, the events of 1905 did not only show Lenin and the Bolsheviks the path to follow; they also showed Nicolas II and his brilliant Minister, Stolypin, the need to embark upon a rapid process of social, economic and political restructuring if revolution was to be avoided. Of the transformations which they initiated Lenin said:

> our reactionaries are distinguished by the extreme clarity of their class consciousness. They know very well what they want, where they are going, and on what forces they can count (quoted in Conquest, 1972, p.61).

By this time Lenin's attitude towards the necessity for capitalist development was different than it had been in 1899. Should the policies of Stolypin succeed, and Russia enter definitively onto the capitalist path, the revolution would have to be postponed for a long time. As early as 1908 Lenin saw the dangers of Stolypin's policies:

> The Stolypin constitution and the Stolypin agrarian policy mark a new phase in the breakdown of the old semi-patriarchal and semi-feudal system of Tsarism, a new movement towards its transformation into a middle-class monarchy. . . It would be empty and stupid democratic (sic) phrase-mongering to say that the success of such a policy is 'impossible' in Russia. It is possible! If Stolypin's policy continues, Russia's agrarian structure will become completely bourgeois (quoted in Laclau, 1972, p.69, my translation) .

The events of the subsequent period, which ended with the assumption of power by the Bolsheviks in October 1917, are the subject of one of the great controversies of modern history. On the one hand the policies initiated by Stolypin showed clearly that Lenin's analysis of the potential of capitalist development was correct; during that period Russia enjoyed a considerable industrial boom; and by 1917 the peasants were owners of more than threequarters of Russian farmland. Perhaps it was factors such as these which led Lenin to conclude a lecture given in Zurich on 9 January 1917, only months before he was to come to power, with the words

> we of the old generation will perhaps not live to see the decisive battles of our own revolution (1917, p.158, my translation).[19]

But on the other hand it was precisely that industrial boom which strengthened the left in general and the Bolsheviks in particular. As the Mensheviks exercised political control over the older proletariat, the Bolsheviks needed a new proletariat to strengthen them — the industrial boom supplied them with it.

This already lengthy analysis can be pursued no further here. I have tried to extract from it its most important contributions to the debate which would later develop concerning the development of capitalism in other backward nations.

Russia then had a series of characteristics in common with countries which would later attempt capitalist development, such as those related to 'late' industrialization, and to the leading role played by foreign capitalism and technology, and those linked to the emergence of a social class structure somewhat different from that resulting from capitalist development in Western Europe, and more complex in its composition, with a relatively weak and dependent bourgeoisie, a small but strong proletariat, and a relatively large 'sub-proletariat' which is its potential ally.[20]

Equally however, there are also significant differences: Russia was never the colony of a Western European power; late industrialization is not always the same if it occurs at different stages of development of the world capitalist system; and as Lenin demonstrates brilliantly for the Russian case, the particular features of the development of capitalism in any backward region will depend significantly on the characteristics of the pre-capitalist mode of production. In the case of Latin America for example, if there were countries (such as Brazil, Mexico, Chile and Argentina) which were attempting to industrialize in the same period as industrialization was taking place in Russia, the social formations of those countries, inherited from Portuguese and Spanish colonization, were very different from those of Russia itself. In any case, it is clear that the analyses of Lenin and his contemporaries cannot be applied mechanically to the development of capitalism in other periods and in other backward regions of the world, it remains true that in Lenin's analysis especially we find the essential road to follow; this is the study of the concrete forms of articulation between the capitalist sectors of the backward nations and the advanced nations in the system, and of the concrete forms taken by the subordination of precapitalist forms of production to the former, and to the rest of the system. It is essentially the study of the dynamic of the backward nations as a synthesis of the general determinants of the capitalist system (external factors) and the specific determinants of each (internal factors).

But if neither Lenin, Bukharin nor Luxemburg studied the concrete development of capitalism in other backward regions of the world, it is possible to derive from their analyses of imperialism the 'general determinants of the capitalist system' or the 'external factors' as they are generally labelled, which those regions will confront in their attempts to pursue capitalist development. These are essentially the driving forces which impelled the advanced capitalist countries towards the domination and control of the backward regions of the world: the specific determinants, or 'internal factors' as they are generally called, will depend upon the characteristics of the particular backward societies.

The driving forces behind the economic expansion of the advanced capitalist countries are identified, with differences of emphasis in each analysis, in the financial and in the productive spheres. The two are intimately connected, and are the result of a single process of transformation in the advanced capitalist countries. The financial driving forces are related to the need to find new opportunities for investment, due to the fact that their own economies are incapable of generating them at the same rate as they generate capital; those of the productive sphere are related to the necessity of ensuring a supply of raw materials, and continued markets for manufactured products. Thus it is that Bukharin and Preobrazhensky define imperialism as:

> the policy of conquest which financial capital pursues in the struggle for markets, for the sources of raw material, and for places in which capital can be invested (1919, p.155).

The result of this would be a tendency towards a greater integration of the world economy, a considerable degree of capital movement, and an international division of labour which would restrict the growth of backward economies to the production of mineral and agricultural primary products. For these primary products to be supplied cheaply, the labour force in the backward countries would have to be kept at subsistence level.

As a result of the effects of the expansion of the advanced capitalist economies as they enter the monopoly phase of their development, the economies of the backward countries will tend to be characterized by increasing indebtedness and by a productive structure which leads them to consume what they do not produce, and to produce what they do not consume. The fundamental characteristics of the development of such economies will obviously depend upon the particular characteristics of the export sectors they develop, and the terms on which they exchange products and obtain capital.

If these relationships were shaped within a colonial context, they would clearly be unequal, and therefore for the colonial nation the possibilities of development would be very restricted. If they were shaped within a post-colonial context, the possibilities of development would depend upon the capacity of the national bourgeoisies and other dominant groups to establish a more favourable relationship with the advanced countries in the system, or upon their capacity to transform the economic structure of their respective countries, in an effort to develop through a different type of integration into the world economy.

We may summarise the classical writers' conception of what capitalist development in the backward regions of the world would tend to be as follows: imperialism would tend to hinder industrial development, but once the colonial bonds had been broken the backward countries would be able to develop their economies in a different way, and eventually to industrialize. This industrialization, given its 'late' start and probably with the presence of foreign capital and technology, would face problems and contradictions, but as in the Russian case, these would not be insuperable. In the words of Rosa Luxemburg:

> the imperialist phase of capital accumulation . . . comprises the industrialisation, and capitalist emancipation of the hinterland . . . [bourgeois] revolution is an essential for the process of capitalist emancipation. The backward communities must shed their obsolete political organisations, and create a modern State machinery adapted to the purpose of capitalist production (quoted in O'Brien, 1975, p.16).

This description of the role of capitalism in the colonies clearly differs from that of Marx and Engels, as it refers to different stages of capitalist development in the advanced countries. Discussing their writings, I showed how for them the Asiatic mode of production was characterized by its lack of internal tensions, which bestowed upon it an unchanging nature. The penetration of capitalism from abroad would therefore perform the task of 'awakening' them. It follows directly that the concrete forms which the process would adopt would necessarily depend upon the type of capitalism involved.

Marx expected that the process which began with the development of railways in India would necessarily end with the placing of that country on the path towards industrialization. For the classical writers on imperialism on the other hand, while capitalism continued to be progressive in the backward nations of the world, it was precisely its progressiveness which would create contradictions with the needs of monopoly capitalism in the advanced countries; within a colonial context the imperialist countries can and will hinder the industrialization of the colonies. Once the colonial bonds are broken the incipient national bourgeoisies can proceed with the development which was hindered by the colonial bonds, completing the bourgeois revolution and attempting to industrialize. These writers did not of course mean to suggest in any way that such attempts at post-colonial industrialization would be free of problems and contradictions: they felt that as in the Russian case such countries would be able to overcome such problems and industrialize. Should that prove to be the case, there would appear in the post-colonial period new capitalist societies relatively similar to those in Western Europe (as in the United States and her regions of European settlement).

Nevertheless, the political independence of the backward nations has not been followed by development, contrary to the expectations of the authors I have been discussing. Even more, *in the case of Latin America it is precisely in the post-colonial period* that the development of individual nations (with the due economic and political variations) has taken upon itself the articulation with the advanced capitalist countries which the classical writers on imperialism noted in the colonies — the growth of their productive sectors concentrated on primary products, whether mineral or agricultural; the limited degree of industrialization; and financial dependence.

5. From Imperialism to Dependency

Only around 1920 did a new vision of capitalist development in the backward nations begin to be developed within Marxist thought (see Lenin, 1920). It would be formulated explicitly at the Sixth Congress of the Communist International (the Comintern) in 1928. This approach differs from that which preceded it in that in its analysis it gives more importance to the role played by the traditional dominant classes of the backward countries (generally termed oligarchies). The power of these elites was seen to be in contradiction with the transformations of internal structures which would necessarily be brought about by capitalist development in general and industrialization in particular (the 'bourgeois revolution'). There would therefore exist objective conditions for alliances between these groups and imperialism, destined to avoid such transformations.

In the 1928 Congress then, Kusinen introduced new 'Theses on the Revolutionary Movement in Colonial and Semicolonial Countries' (Degras, 1960, pp.526-548). In them he argues that

> the progressive consequences of capitalism, on the contrary, are not to be seen there [despite the increase in foreign investment] . When the dominant imperialist power needs social support in the colonies it makes an alliance first and foremost with the dominant classes of the old pre-capitalist system, the feudal-type commercial and moneylending bourgeoisie (sic), against the majority of the people.

In my opinion this Congress may be considered the turning point in the Marxist approach to the concrete possibilities of the historical progressiveness of capitalism in backward countries. From this point onwards, the emphasis will be placed not only on the obstacles which imperialism can and does impose on the process of industrialization during the colonial period (obstacles which could be overcome once the colonial bonds had been broken), nor simply on the obstacles to any process of industrialization which starts late (the technological gap, the ambiguous role of foreign capital, and so on), which could be overcome, as had been demonstrated during the Stolypin period in Russia; now the historical progressiveness of capitalism in the backward regions of the world — in the colonial *and* post-colonial periods — is analysed as being limited by the previously mentioned alliance between imperialism and traditional elites, the so-called 'feudal — imperialist alliance'.

As the process of industrialization in the backward countries was seen in contradiction not only with imperialism, but also with some internally dominant groups, the ability of the incipient national bourgeoisies to develop it in the post-colonial phase would depend upon their political capacity to assert themselves over that alliance, and to impede the adoption of such policies as, for example, those of free trade which it sought to impose.

This double contradiction in capitalist development in Latin America (particularly in the process of industrialization) which would tend to be transformed into a single contradiction through the alliance of the groups in question, figures prominently in the political and economic analysis of large sectors of the Latin American left (including the Communist parties of the sub-continent), right into the 1960s.[22] Furthermore, it seems to have had an influence (albeit naturally an unacknowledged one) upon the ECLA analysis of the obstacles facing Latin American development, as we shall see later; the attempt to go beyond the terms of this analysis would be the common starting-point of the different approaches that I shall distinguish within the dependency school.

On this analysis then, the major enemy was identified as imperialism (in one way or another the omnipresent explanation of every social and ideological process that occurred), and the principal target in the struggle was unmistakable: North American imperialism. The allied camp, on the same analysis, was also clear: everyone, minus those internal groups allied with that imperialism (and in particular those groups linked to the traditional export sector). Thus the anti-imperialist struggle was at the same time the struggle for industrialization. The local state and national bourgeoisie appears as the potential agent for the development of the capitalist economy, which in turn was looked upon as a necessary stage. The popular fronts would draw on this analysis both of the historical role which capitalism should play in Latin America, and of the obstacles which it would find in its path.

This simple analysis of Latin American capitalist development would be maintained by the majority of Latin American left-wing groups until the time of the Cuban Revolution (1959). The discrepancies which originally existed between the guerrilla movement and the old Cuban Communist Party (the Partido Socialista Popular) regarding the character which that revolution should assume are well known, with the former arguing for an immediate transition to socialism,[23] the latter for the process previously analysed, which was traditionally sought in Latin America.

The Second Declaration of Havana (1962) and the declarations and resolutions of the first conference of OLAS (the Latin American Solidarity Organization) of 1967 left no doubt regarding the path which was chosen: the democratic and anti-imperialist revolution which the continent required could only take a socialist form:

> The so called Latin American bourgeoisie, because of its origins and because of its economic connections and even kinship-links with landowners, forms a part of the oligarchies which rule our America and is in consequence incapable of acting independently .... It would be absurd to suppose that . . . the so-called Latin American bourgeoisie is capable of developing a political line independent . . . of imperialism, in defence of the interest and aspiration of the nation. The contradiction within which it is objectively trapped is, by its nature, inescapable (quoted in Booth, 1975, pp.65-66).

It is precisely within this framework, and with the explicit motive of developing theoretically and documenting empirically this new form of analysis of the Latin American revolution that Frank enters the scene, initially with his article in the *Monthly Review* (1966) and later in a more elaborated form in his well-known study of the development (or underdevelopment) of Chile and Brazil (1967).

In this way Frank was to initiate one of the most important lines of analysis within the dependency school. At the same time, both within and outside ECLA, there began the development of the other two major approaches which I shall distinguish in this type of analysis of Latin American development.

6. The Dependency Analyses

The general field of study of the dependency analyses is the development of peripheral capitalism. Its most important characteristic is its attempt to analyse it from the point of view of the interplay between internal and external structures. Nevertheless, we find this interplay analysed in different ways.

The majority of the survey articles which have been written regarding these analyses tend to distinguish between three major approaches within them. The first is that of those who do not accept the possibility of capitalist development in the periphery, but only of the 'development of underdevelopment'; the second, of those who concentrate upon the obstacles which confront capitalist development in those countries (particularly market constrictions); and the third, of those who accept the possibility of capitalist development in the periphery, placing the emphasis upon the subservient forms which it adopts with respect to capitalism of the centre.

While I accept that this classification is adequate from a certain perspective, I feel that on a more profound analysis it is less than satisfactory. In my opinion, the differences which divide dependency analyses go further than discrepancies regarding simply the possibility of development within a capitalist context in the backward areas of the world.

For my part (and with the necessary degree of simplification which every classification of intellectual tendencies entails) I shall distinguish three major approaches — not mutually exclusive from the point of view of intellectual history — in dependency analyses. The first is that begun by Frank and continued by the 'CESO School' (CESO being the Centre de Estudios Sociales of the Universidad de Chile), and in particular by dos Santos, Marini, Caputo and Pizarro, with contributions by Hinkelammert, of CEREN — (Centro de Estudios de la Realidad Nacional of the Universidad Catolica de Chile). Its essential characteristic is that it attempts to construct a 'theory of underdevelopment' in which the dependent character of the peripheral economies is the hub on which the whole analysis of underdevelopment turns: the dependent character of these economies would trace certain processes causally linked to its underdevelopment. The second approach, found principally in Sunkel and Furtado, is that which is characterized by the attempt to reformulate the ECLA analyses of development from the perspective of a critique of the obstacles to 'national development'. This attempt at reformulation is not a simple process of adding new elements (both political and social) which were lacking in the ECLA analysis, but a thorough-going attempt to proceed beyond that analysis, adopting an increasingly different perspective. Finally, I distinguish that approach which deliberately attempts not to develop a mechanico-formal theory of dependency, by concentrating its analysis on what have been called 'concrete situations of dependency'. In the words of Cardoso:

> The question which we should ask ourselves is why, it being obvious that the capitalist economy tends towards a growing internationalization, that societies are divided into antagonistic classes, and that the particular is to a certain extent conditioned by the general, with these premises we have not gone beyond the partial-and therefore abstract in the Marxist sense[25] — characterization of the Latin American situation and historical process (Cardoso, 1974, pp.326, 327).

What would be needed therefore is the study of the concrete forms in which dependent relationships develop; that is to say, the specific forms in which the economies and politics of peripheral nations are articulated with those of the advanced nations.

It is not that this approach does not recognize the need for a theory of capitalist development in the different parts of the periphery, but that (in part as a reaction to the excessive theorizing in a vacuum characteristic of other analyses of dependency) it places greater emphasis upon the analysis of concrete situations. The theoretical reasoning which can be developed at present concerning capitalist development in backward nations is strictly limited by the lack of case studies; the need at the moment is for 'analytic' rather than 'synthetic' work.

That is, without a considerable number of concrete studies any new theory which may be elaborated concerning capitalist development in the periphery will necessarily fall into the trap of the 'dialectic of thought', which consists of the working out upon itself of an abstract dialectic, starting from previously constructed concepts.

6.1 Dependency as a theory of underdevelopment

There is no doubt that the 'father' of this approach is Paul Baran. His principal contribution to the general literature on development (Baran 1957) continues the central line of Marxist thought regarding the contradictory character of the needs of imperialism and the process of industrialization and general economic development of the backward nations.[26] Thus he affirms at the outset that

> What is decisive is that economic development in underdeveloped countries is profoundly inimical to the dominant interests in the advanced capitalist countries (1957, p.28).

To avoid such development the advanced nations will form alliances with pre-capitalistic domestic elites (who will also be adversely affected by the transformations of capitalist development), intended to inhibit such transformations. In this way the advanced nations would have easy access to domestic resources and thus be able to maintain traditional modes of surplus extraction. Within this context the possibilities of economic growth in dependent countries would be extremely limited; the surplus they generated would be expropriated in large part by foreign capital, and otherwise squandered on luxury consumption by traditional elites. Furthermore, not only would resources destined for investment thereby be drastically reduced, but so would their internal multiplying effect, as capital goods would have to be purchased abroad. This process would necessarily lead to economic stagnation, and the only way out would be political.

Starting out with this analysis Frank attempts to develop the thesis that the only political solution is a revolution of an immediately socialist character; for within the context of the capitalist system there could be no alternative to underdevelopment (Frank, 1967).

For the purpose of this analysis we may distinguish three levels in Frank's 'model of underdevelopment'. The first is that in which he attempts to demonstrate that areas in the periphery have been incorporated into the world economy since the early stages of their colonial periods. The second is that in which he attempts to show that such incorporation into the world economy has transformed the countries in question immediately and necessarily into capitalist economies. Finally, there is a third level, in which Frank tries to prove that the integration of these supposedly capitalist economies into the world economy is necessarily achieved through an interminable metropolis — satellite chain, in which the surplus generated at each stage is successively drawn off towards the centre. On account of this he develops a subsidiary thesis:

If it is satellite status which generates underdevelopment, then a weaker or lesser degree of metropolis-satellite relations may generate less deep structural underdevelopment and/or allow for more possibility of local development (Frank, 1967 , p. 11) .

But as the weakening of the satellite-metropolis network can, according to Frank, *only take place* for reasons external to the satellite economies, of a necessarily transient nature, it follows that there is no real possibility of sustained development within the system.[27] According to this analysis, the only alternative becomes that of breaking completely with the metropolis-satellite network through socialist revolution or continuing to 'underdevelop' within it.

In my opinion, the value of Frank's analysis is his critique of the supposedly dual structure of peripheral societies.[28] Frank shows clearly that the different sectors of the economies in question are and have been since very early in their colonial history linked closely to the world economy. Moreover, he has correctly emphasized that this connection has not automatically brought about capitalist economic development, such as optimistic models (derived from Adam Smith) would have predicted, by means of which the development of trade and the division of labour inevitably would bring about economic development. Nevertheless Frank's error (shared by the whole tradition of which he is part, including Sweezy and Wallerstein among the better known) lies in his attempt to explain this phenomenon using the same economic determinist framework of the model he purports to transcend; in fact, he merely turns it upside-down: the development of the 'core' necessarily requires the underdevelopment of the 'periphery'. Thus he criticizes both the alternative proposed by the traditional Latin American left (the possibility of a democratic bourgeois revolution, because in this context the only political solution is a revolution of an immediately socialist character), and the policies put forward by ECLA.

Nevertheless, his critique is not directed towards the real weaknesses in the analysis made by the Latin American left — the mechanical determination of internal by external structures; on the contrary, he strengthens that mechanical determination in his attempt to construct a model to explain the mechanisms through which the expropriation of the surplus takes place. Probably still unduly influenced by his training as an economist at the University of Chicago, he constructs a mechanico-formal model which is no more than a set of equations of general equilibrium (static and unhistorical), in which the extraction of the surplus takes place through a series of satellite-metropolis relationships, through which the surplus generated at each stage is syphoned off.

It is not surprising that his method leads Frank to displace class relations from the centre of his analysis of economic development and underdevelopment. Thus he develops a circular concept of capitalism; although it is evident that capitalism is a system where production for profit via exchange predominates, the opposite is not necessarily true: the existence of production for profits in the market is not necessarily a signal of capitalist production. For Frank, this is *a sufficient* condition for the existence of capitalist relations of production. Thus for Frank, the problem of the origins of capitalism (and therefore the origins of the development of the few and the underdevelopment of the majority) comes down to the origins of the expanding world market *and not to the emergence of a system of free wage labour*.

Although Frank did not go very far in his analysis of the capitalist system as a whole, its origins and development, Immanuel Wallerstein tackled this tremendous challenge in his remarkable book, *The Modern World System: Capitalist Agriculture and the Origins of the European World-Economy in the Sixteenth Century* (1974a).

Frank has reaffirmed his ideas in a series of articles published jointly in 1969; a year later he sought to enrich his analysis with the introduction of some elements of Latin American class structure (Frank, 1970).

Frank has been criticized from all sides, and on almost every point in his analysis.[29] Prominent among his critics is Laclau (1971), who provides an excellent synthesis of Frank's theoretical model, and shows that the only way in which Frank can 'demonstrate' that all the periphery is capitalist and has been since the colonial period is by using the concept of capitalism in a sense which is erroneous from a Marxist point of view, and useless for his central proposition, that of showing that a bourgeois revolution in the periphery is impossible. As regards this point then, Laclau concludes that Frank makes no contribution, leaving the analysis exactly where it started.[30]

Robert Brenner (1977) takes Laclau's analysis of Frank (as well as Dobb's critique of Sweezy), and demonstrates how the work of Sweezy, Frank and Wallerstein — brilliantly summarized and analysed by him — is doomed to negate the model put forward first by Adam Smith in *The Wealth of Nations*, Book 1, but

> because they have failed . . . to discard the underlying individualistic-mechanist presuppositions of this model, they have ended up by erecting an alternative theory of capitalist development which is, in its central aspects, the mirror image of the 'progressist' thesis they wish to surpass. Thus, very much like those they criticize, they conceive of (changing) class relations as emerging more or less directly from the (changing) requirements for the generation of surplus and development of production, under the pressures and opportunities engendered by a growing world market. Only, whereas their opponents tend to see such market-determined processes [the development of trade and the division of labour], as setting off, automatically, a dynamic of economic development, they see them as enforcing the rise of economic backwardness. As a result, they fail to take into account either the way in which class structures, once established, will in fact determine the course of economic development or underdevelopment over an entire epoch, or the way in which these class structures themselves emerge: as the outcome of class struggles whose results are incomprehensible in terms merely of market forces (Brenner, 1977, p.27).

Thus the way in which Frank uses the concepts 'development' and 'underdevelopment' seems incorrect from a Marxist point of view; furthermore, they do not seem useful for demonstrating what Frank attempts to demonstrate. But as this critique can also be applied to other authors who adopt the same approach I shall reserve discussion on this point to page 187.

To summarize, Frank's direct contribution to our understanding of the process of Latin American development is largely limited to his critique of dualist models for Latin America.[31] Nevertheless, his indirect contribution is considerable. By this I mean that his work has inspired a significant quantity of research by others (whether to support or rebut his arguments), in their respective disciplines, particularly in the sociology of development.

The central line of Frank's thought regarding the 'development of underdevelopment' is continued, though from a critical point of view, by the Brazilian sociologist Theotonio dos Santos,[32] for whom

> the process under consideration [Latin American development] rather than being one of satellization as Frank believes, is a case of the formation of a certain type of internal structures conditioned by international relationships of dependence' (1969, p.80).

Dos Santos distinguishes different types of relations of dependency (essentially colonial, industrial — financial and industrial — technological, the latter having grown up since the Second World War), and consequently distinguishes different kinds of internal structures generated by them. Dos Santos emphasizes the differences and discontinuities between the different types of dependency and between the internal structures which result from them, while Frank himself stresses the continuity and similarity of dependency relations in a capitalist context. In other words, while Frank wishes to emphasize the similarities between economic structures in the times of Cortez, Pizarro, Clive and Rhodes, and between those and the structures typified by the activity of multinational corporations, dos Santos is more concerned with the differences and discontinuities between them.

There is within dos Santos's analysis the beginnings of an interesting attempt to break with the concept of a mechanical determination of internal by external structures which dominated the traditional analysis of the left in Latin America, and which particularly characterized Frank's work. One perceives initially in his analysis the perception not only that both structures are contradictory, but that movement is produced precisely through the dynamic of the contradictions between the two. Nevertheless, as he proceeds in the analysis he re-establishes, little by little, the priority of external over internal structures, separating almost metaphysically the two sides of the opposition — the internal and the external — and losing the notion of movement through the dynamic of the contradictions between these structures. The analysis which begins to emerge is again one typified by 'antecedent causation and inert consequences'. The culmination of this process is his well-known *formal definition of dependency, which because of its formal nature is both static and unhistorical*; it is found in his 1970 article in the *American Economic Review*:

> Dependence is a conditioning situation in which the economies of one group of countries are conditioned by the development and expansion of others. A relationship of interdependence between two or more economies or

between such economies and the world trading system becomes a dependent relationship when some countries can expand through self-impulsion while others, being in a dependent position, can only expand as a reflection of the dominant countries, which may have positive or negative effects on their immediate development (1970, pp.289-290).

A further analysis along the same lines of Frank's 'accumulation of backwardness' and the 'development of underdevelopment' is that of Rui Mauro Marini (1972b). His work, which is fundamentally an attempt to develop a far more sophisticated model than that of Frank or dos Santos, can be summarized as primarily an attempt to apply Luxemburg's schema (1913) to the Latin American situation.[33]

Finally, Caputo and Pizarro (1974) and Hinkelammert (1970 a,b,c) have made contributions to this approach to the study of dependency from this same perspective of the 'development of underdevelopment'.

This type of approach has inspired an unending stream of works, mostly theoretical,[34] the most thorough-going critiques of this type of 'theory of underdevelopment', in addition to that of Laclau and Brenner already discussed, have come from Cardoso (1974), Lall (1975) and Weisskopf (1976).

Lall (1975) offers an interesting critique of a number of dependency studies.[35] He argues that the characteristics to which underdevelopment in dependent countries is generally attributed are not exclusive to these economies, but are also found in so-called 'non-dependent' economies, and that therefore they are properly speaking characteristics of capitalist development in general and not necessarily only of dependent capitalism. He further argues that such analyses are not surprisingly unable to show causal relationships between these characteristics and underdevelopment.

Thomas Weisskopf (1976) takes Lall's analysis as a starting-point and provides empirical data to substantiate it.[36] The most systematic critique is that of Cardos, who argues that these 'theories' are based on five interconnected erroneous theses concerning capitalist development in Latin America. These are:

(i) that capitalist development in Latin America is impossible,
(ii) that dependent capitalism is based on the extensive exploitation of labour and tied to the necessity of underpaying labour,
(iii) that local bourgeoisies no longer exist as an active social force,
(iv) that penetration by multinational firms leads local states to pursue an expansionist policy that is typically 'sub-imperialist', and
(v) that the political path of the sub-continent is at the crossroads, with the only conceivable options being socialism or fascism.

After rejecting one by one these erroneous theses upon which this line of analysis of dependency is based, and showing that they have been developed in order to support one another, Cardoso argues that in the case of Brazil the writers in question have in fact identified some of the *conditions* which give capitalist development its *specificity*. He shows, in his own words that some 'pieces of the puzzle are the same, but the way they go together . . . is different' (1973, p.21).

For my part, I would argue, following Cardoso's analysis, that these theories of dependency I have been examining are mistaken not only because they do not 'fit the facts', but also — and more importantly — because *their mechanico-formal nature renders them both static and unhistorical.*

The central nucleus around which the analysis of these dependency writers is organized is that capitalism, in a context of dependency, loses its historical progressive character, and can only generate underdevelopment. In this respect, I would argue that though it is not difficult to see that the specific forms of development adopted by capitalism in dependent countries are different from those of advanced countries (this development is marked by a series of specific economic, political and social contradictions — many of which have been correctly identified by these writers and these contradictions appear to have become sharper with the passage of time), to leap from that assertion to the claim that for that reason capitalism has lost, or never even had, a historically progressive role in Latin America, is to take a leap into the dark. We need only recall Lenin's critique to the Narodniks: their contemporaries are equally 'wrong in their facts'; for example, in my own analysis of the Chilean case (which covers the period from 1910 to (1970) I have shown that Lenin's criteria for assessing the progressiveness of capitalism — increase in the productive forces of social labour and in the socialization of that labour — were both met during the period under study.

Now, if the argument is that such processes have been manifested differently than in other capitalist countries, particularly those of the centre, or in diverse ways in the different branches of the Chilean economy, or that they have generated inequality at regional levels and in the distribution of income, have been accompanied by such phenomena as underemployment and unemployment, and have benefited the elite almost exclusively, or again that they have taken on a cyclical nature, then it does no more than affirm that the development of capitalism in Latin America, as everywhere else and at all times, has been characterized by its contradictory and exploitative nature. *The specificity of capitalist development in Latin America stems precisely from the particular ways in which these contradictions have been manifested, and the different ways in which many Latin American countries have faced and temporarily overcome them, the ways in which this process has created further contradictions, and so on.* It is through this process that the *specific dynamic* of capitalist development in different Latin American countries has been generated. In this connection we should recall that the whole of Lenin's analysis of the development of capitalism in Russia was a detailed study of the specific ways in which capitalism there temporarily overcame its contradictions, and that he *criticized the Narodniks for transforming those contradictions into a proof that capitalism was impossible in Russia, and for failing to understand that the same contradictions were the very ones which were basic to capitalist development, and which took specific forms in Russia.*

In this context, I would also argue that the form in which the concepts 'capitalist development' and 'capitalist underdevelopment' are used by these dependency writers does not seem adequate. (I now take up the point discussed on page 185.)

Capitalist development is essentially a process of capital accumulation which produces as it evolves modifications in the composition of the productive forces, in resource allocation, in class relations, and in the character of the state; that is, which produces as it evolves modifications in the different structures of society. Whether the cyclical nature of capital accumulation or the modifications and contradictions which this accumulation produces are or are not 'desirable' or 'optimal' is another question entirely.

To deny, as the 'contemporary Narodniks' do, that capitalist development is taking place in some countries in Latin America and in some parts of the rest of the periphery is no less than absurd. To recognize it on the other hand, as Lenin told the Narodniks, is quite compatible with the full recognition of the negative side of capitalism, and in no way an apology for it.

If one agrees with Cardoso (1976, p.1) that the standard that one has to use to assess the analytical adequacy, the interpretative and predictive capacity and the creative strength of new explanatory schema in the social sciences *is the sensitivity with which they detect new social processes and the precision with which they are able to explain mechanisms of social reproduction and modes of social transformation*, one should agree that the dependency analyses which have attempted to construct a formal theory of underdevelopment are of relatively low standard; they have been unable to meet these requirements in their study of the economic development and political domination of the peripheral nations.[39]

6.2 Dependency as a reformulation of the ECLA analysis of Latin American development

Towards the middle of the 1960s the ECLA analyses were overtaken by a gradual decline, in which many factors intervened. The statistics relating to Latin American development in the period after the Korean War presented a gloomy picture (see Booth, 1975, pp.62-64) which was interpreted in different ways as indicating the failure of the policies ECLA had been proposing since its foundation. Furthermore, the first attempts to introduce into the traditional ECLA analysis a number of 'social aspects' (Prebisch, 1963), far from strengthening the analysis, revealed its fragility (see Cardoso, 1977, p.32).[40]

One of the results of the relative decline in the influence of ECLA's analyses was the emergence of an attempt to reformulate its thought.

When it became evident that capitalist development in Latin America was taking a path different from that expected, a number of ECLA members began a process of reformulation of the traditional thought of that institution, just at the time that an important sector of the Latin American left was breaking with the traditional Marxist view that capitalist development was both necessary and possible in Latin America, but hindered by the 'feudal-imperialist' alliance. Not only did the different processes of reformulation take place at the same time, but despite the apparently growing divergencies (particularly seen in the vocabulary adopted), they had one extremely important element in common: *pessimism* regarding the possibility of capitalist development.

But works written by both groups during this period were in each case accompanied by the same error: the failure to take duly into account the cyclical pattern characteristic of capitalist development.

The irony was that while both groups were busy writing and publishing different versions of stagnationist theories (the most sophisticated perhaps being Furtado, 1966), international trade was picking up, the terms of trade were changing in favour of Latin American exporters of agricultural and mineral products, and some countries were able to take advantage of the favourable situation and accelerate rapidly the rhythm of their economic development. Thus, as Cardoso (1977, p.33) remarks, 'history had prepared a trap for pessimists'.

Perhaps the other distinctive aspect of this line of Latin American thought was that it made a basically *ethical* distinction between 'economic growth' and 'economic development'. According to this, development did not take place when growth was accompanied by:

(i) increased inequality in the distribution of its benefits;
(ii) a failure to increase social welfare, in so far as expenditure went to unproductive areas-or even worse to military spending-or the production of unnecessarily refined luxury consumer durables;
(iii) the failure to create employment opportunities at the rate of the growth in population, let alone in urbanization; and
(iv) a growing loss of national control over economic, political, social and cultural life.

By making the distinction in these terms, their research developed along two separate lines, one concerned with the obstacles to *growth* (and in particular to industrial growth), the other concerned with the perverse character taken by *development*. The fragility of such a formulation consists in its confusing a socialist critique of capitalism with the analysis of the obstacles of capitalism in Latin America. For a review of these issues see Faria (1976, pp 37-49).[41]

But if the attempt at reformulation which followed the crisis in the ECLA school of thought did not succeed in grasping the transformations which were occurring at that moment in time in the world capitalist system,[42] it did in time produce together with the abandonment of stagnationist theories, a movement towards a more structural-historical analysis of Latin America.[43] The first substantial critique of stagnationist theories came from Tavares and Serra (1970). Pinto (1965, 1974) in his turn, less seduced throughout by those theories, discussed the concept of structural heterogeneity, and the process of 'marginalization of the periphery' (Pinto and Knakel, 1973). Vuscovich (1970) studied the 'concentrated and exclusive' character of Latin American development, and later (1973) analysed the way in which the economic policy of the Unidad Popular government had to adjust itself to the constraints, both political and economic, facing Chile at that moment in time.[44] Sunkel (1973a; Sunkel and Paz, 1970) studied the relationship between internal economic problems and the world capitalist system, in an attempt to show that development and underdevelopment were two sides of the same coin. His most significant contribution is his analysis of the process by which international integration leads to greater national disintegration in the less developed countries; this work was complemented by analyses of the effects of multinational corporations in Latin America (1972, 1973b, 1974). He later went on to write with Cariola a revealing analysis of the relationship between the expansion of nitrate exports and socio-economic transformation in Chile between 1860 and 1930 (1976), and the effects which this had on class formation in Chile (1977).

6.3 A methodology for the analysis of concrete situations of dependency

In my critique of the dependency studies reviewed so far I have already advanced the fundamental elements of what I understand to be the third of the three approaches within the dependency school. It is primarily related to the work of the Brazilian sociologist Fernando Henrique Cardoso, dating from the completion in 1967 of *Dependencia y Desarrollo en America Latina*, written with the Chilean historian Enzo Faletto.

Briefly, this third approach to the analysis of dependency can be expressed as follows:

(i) In common with the two approaches discussed already, this third approach sees the Latin American economies as an integral part of the world capitalist system, in a context of increasing internationalization of the system as a whole; it also argues that the central dynamic of that system lies outside the peripheral economies and that therefore the options which lie open to them are limited by the development of the system at the centre; in this way the particular is in some way conditioned by the general. Therefore a basic element for the understanding of these societies is given by the 'general determinants' of the world capitalist system, which is itself changing through time; *the analysis therefore requires primarily an understanding of the contemporary characteristics of the world capitalist system*. However, the theory of imperialism, which was originally developed to provide an understanding of that system, had remained practically 'frozen' where it was at the time of the death of Lenin until the end of the 1950s. During this period, capitalism underwent significant and decisive stages of development and the theory failed to keep up with them. The depression of the 1930s, the Second World War, the emergence of the United States as the undisputed hegemonic power in the capitalist world, the challenge of the growing socialist bloc, and its attendant creation of new demands on the capitalist world if its system were to be maintained, the decolonization of Africa and Asia, and the beginning of the process of the transnationalization of capitalism had all contributed to create a world very different from that which had confronted Lenin. As the theory of imperialism once again began to place itself at the centre of Marxist analysis this failure to make any theoretical advance began to make itself felt; the transformations which had occurred and which continued to occur were slowly if at all incorporated into its analysis. Contributions as important as those of Gramsci[45] and Kalecki have remained almost unintegrated until very recently.[46]

One characteristic of the third approach to dependency, and one which has been widely recognized, has been to incorporate more successfully into its analysis of Latin American development the transformations which are occurring and have occurred in the world capitalist system, and in particular the changes which became significant towards the end of the 1950s in the rhythm and the form of capital movement, and in the international division of labour. The emergence of the so-called multinational corporations progressively transformed centre-periphery relationships, and relationships between the countries of the centre. As foreign capital has increasingly been directed towards manufacturing industry in the periphery,[47] the struggle for industrialization, which was previously seen as an anti-imperialist struggle, has become increasingly the goal of foreign capital. Thus dependency and industrialization cease to be contradictory and a path of 'dependent development' becomes possible.[48]

(ii) Furthermore, the third approach not only accepts as a starting-point and improves upon the analysis of the location of the economies of Latin America in the world capitalist system, but also accepts and enriches their demonstration that Latin American societies are structured through unequal and antagonistic patterns of social organization, showing the social asymmetries and the exploitative character of social organization which arise from its socio-economic base, giving considerable importance to the effect of the diversity of natural resources, geographic location, and so on of each economy, thus extending the analysis of the 'internal determinants' of the development of the Latin American economies.

(iii) But while these improvements are important, the most significant feature of this approach is that it goes beyond these points, and insists that from the premises so far outlined *one arrives at a partial, abstract and indeterminate characterization of the Latin American historical process*, which can only be overcome by understanding how the general and specific determinants interact in particular and concrete situations. It is only by understanding the specificity of movement in these societies as a dialectical unity of both, and a synthesis of these 'internal' and 'external' factors, that one can explain the particularity of social, political and economic processes in the dependent societies. Only in this way can one explain why, for example, the single process of mercantile expansion should have produced in different Latin American societies slave labour, systems based on the exploitation of indigenous populations, and incipient forms of wage labour.

What is important is not simply to show that mercantile expansion was the basis of the transformation of the Latin American economies, and less to deduce mechanically that that process made them capitalist, but to avoid losing the specificity of history in a welter of vague abstract concepts by explaining how the mercantilist drive led to the creation of the phenomena mentioned, and to show how, throughout the history of Latin America, different sectors

> of local classes allied or clashed with foreign interests, organized different forms of state, sustained distinct ideologies or tried to implement various policies or defined alternative strategies to cope with imperialist challenges in diverse moments of history (Cardoso and Faletto, 1977, p.12).

The study of the dynamic of the dependent societies as the dialectical unity of internal and external factors implies that the conditioning effect of each in the movement of these societies can be separated only by making a static analysis. Equally, if the internal dynamic of the dependent society is a particular aspect of the general dynamic of the capitalist system, that does not imply that the latter *produces* concrete effects in the former, but finds *concrete expression in them*.

The system of 'external domination' reappears as an 'internal' phenomenon through the social practices of local groups and classes, who share its interests and values. Other internal groups and forces oppose this domination, and in the concrete development of these contradictions the specific dynamic of the society is generated. It is not a case of seeing one part of the world capitalist system as 'developing' and another as 'underdeveloping', or of seeing imperialism and dependency as two sides of the same coin, with the underdeveloped or dependent world reduced to a passive role determined by the other, but in the words of Cardoso and Faletto,

> We conceive the relationship between external and internal forces as forming a complex whole whose structural links are not based on mere external forms of exploitation and coercion, but are rooted in coincidences of interests between local dominant classes and international ones, and, on the other side, are challenged by local dominated groups and classes. In some circumstances, the networks of coincident or reconciled interests might expand to include segments of the middle class, if not even of alienated parts of working classes. In other circumstances, segments of dominant classes might seek internal alliance with middle classes, working classes, and even peasants, aiming to protect themselves from foreign penetration that contradicts its interests (1977, pp. 10, 11).

There are of course elements within the capitalist system which affect all the Latin American economies, but it is precisely the *diversity within this unity* which characterizes historical processes. *Thus the effort of analysis should be oriented towards the elaboration of concepts capable of explaining how the general trends in capitalist expansion are transformed into specific relationships between men, classes and states, how these specific relations in turn react upon the general trends of the capitalist system, how internal and external processes of political domination reflect one another, both in their compatibilities and their contradictions, how the economies and politics of Latin America are articulated with those of the centre, and how their specific dynamics are thus generated.*

Nevertheless, I do not mean to support a naïve expectation that a 'correct' approach to the analysis of dependency would be capable of explaining everything; or that if it does not yet do so, it is *necessarily* due to the fact that the method was wrongly applied, or has not yet been developed enough. I do not have any illusions that our findings could explain every detail of our past history, or should be capable of predicting the exact course of future events, because I do not have any illusions that our findings can take out from history all its ambiguities, uncertainties, contradictions and surprises. As it has done so often in the past, history will undoubtedly continue to astonish us with unexpected revelations as unexpected as those that astonished Lenin in 1917 (see page 175).

In my view, some of the most successful analyses within the dependency school have been those which analyse specific situations in concrete terms. A case in point is

Chudnovsky (1974), who after analysing the effect of multinational corporations in Colombia, goes on to relate it to the theory of imperialism. For other successful attempts at concrete analysis one should consult the already mentioned works of Laclau (1969), Pinto (1965, 1974), Cariola and Sunkel (1976, 1977), and Singer (1971).

By way of conclusion

Throughout this survey of Marxist studies of underdevelopment, I have shown that there is no such thing as a single Marxist theory of underdevelopment; under this label we find approaches so different that it may probably be more appropriate to speak of 'Marxist inspired' theories of underdevelopment, if one wishes to contain them all under one heading.

I have also shown how the metamorphosis which the Marxist view of underdevelopment has undergone is due in some cases to changes in diagnosis and in others to the circumstances under which capitalism in the backward countries is developing. Among the former, the new way of looking at the relationships between capitalist and pre-capitalist structures in the peripheral areas of the world stands out. Since the Russian experience of capitalist development, this process has ceased to be analysed by most Marxist writers as one of pure destruction and replacement of pre-capitalist structures by capitalist ones; and has begun to be analysed as a far more complex process of interplay between both structures.

As concerns the 'changes in circumstances', the form in which Marxism analyses the relationships between advanced capitalism and the peripheral areas of the world (i.e. the way in which the backward countries serve the needs of advanced capitalist countries), passes through three different phases. In the first, the one which Marx and Engels dwelt on, the analysis is concerned with the way in which capitalist countries exported their manufactures to the peripheral countries while at the same time plundering wealth and slaves.

In the second, which stands out in Lenin's writings, the analysis had to do with the export of capital, the competition for supplies of raw material and the process of monopolisation in advanced capitalist countries. In the third phase, the analysis deals with a much more complex post-colonial dependency of the peripheral countries, where foreign capital (in particular international corporations), profit repatriation, adverse changes in the terms of trade (i.e. unequal exchange) work together to hinder and distort economic development and industrialization.

In so far as we are concerned with the dependency school which has arisen since the beginning of the sixties,[49] we can conclude that its principal contribution is the attempt to analyse peripheral societies through a 'comprehensive social science', which stresses the socio-political nature of the economic relations of production; in short, the approach is one of *political economy*, and thus an attempt to revive the 19th and early 20th century tradition in this respect.

From this perspective, there is a critique of those who divide reality into dimensions analytically independent of each other and of the economic structures of a given society, as if these elements were in reality separable. Thus, the dependency school offers an important critique of such approaches as Rostow's stages of growth, 'modern-traditional' sociological typologies, dualism, functionalism, and in general all those which do not integrate into their analysis an account of the socio-political context in which development takes place (or fails to take place).

Nevertheless, as I have attempted to show, not all the approaches within the dependency school are successful in showing *how* these distinct spheres — social, economic and political — are related. While we find in the dependency analyses a methodology adequate for the analyses of concrete situations of underdevelopment, we also find writers who fail to understand the specificity of the historical process of the penetration of capitalism into the peripheral countries, and only condemn its negative aspects, complementing their analysis with a series of stagnationist theses in an attempt to build a formal theory of underdevelopment. These analyses are mistaken not only because they do not 'fit the facts', but because their mechanico-formal nature renders them both static and unhistorical. Such writers have thus developed schemas that are unable to explain the specificity of economic development and political domination in the backward countries; indeed, their models lack the sensitivity to detect the relevant social processes, and are unable to explain with precision the mechanisms of social reproduction and modes of social transformation of these societies. This leads them to use vague and imprecise concepts, as vague and imprecise as those used at the other end of the political spectrum, as for example the 'Brazilian miracle'.[50] To use their own language, by transforming their analyses into a mechanico-formal theory of peripheral underdevelopment — thus losing the richness that a dialectical analysis would provide — these writers have underdeveloped their contribution to the Dependency School.

Notes

1. An extended version of this article appeared under the title "Dependency: a formal theory of underdevelopment, or a methodology for the analysis of concrete situations of underdevelopment?" (*World Development*, Vol.6, 1978; pp.881- 924). We would like to thank the said Journal for permission to reproduce this material.

   I would also like to thank Gemma Bullent, Paul Cammack, Carlos Fortin, Anne Gordon, Sanjaya Lall, Blanca Muniz, Luis Ortega, Elizabeth Spillius, Thanos Skouras and Bob Sutcliffe for their stimulating co-operation.

2. In this respect see Lenin, 1899, pp.65-68; Dos Santos, 1968; Barrat-Brown, 1972, pp.43-47; Sutcliffe, 1972a, pp.180-185; Caputo and Pizzarro, 1974, pp. 118-123.

3. This is due in part to the experience of the transitions of socialism, and to the existence today of developed socialist economies which can provide what otherwise would have been obtained from capitalist development.

4. For further discussions of the Asiatic mode of production see Hobsbawm, 1964; Dos Santos, 1968; Averini, 1968. 1976; D'Encausse and Schram, 1969; Batra, 1971; Foster-Carter, 1974.

5. The great importance of these statements towards the end of Marx's life is that they show that he saw history not as a mechanical continuum of discrete stages through which each society must pass, but as a process in which the particularity of each historical situation had an important role to play. His position regarding the Russian case illustrates well the flexibility of his approach, which was informed by the dialectical unity of subjective and

objective factors. Stalin (1934, p.104) would later pervert this approach, stating that the Soviet form of dictatorship of the proletariat was 'suitable and obligatory for all countries without exception, including those where capitalism is developed', thus condemning all countries except the USSR to have no history of their own.

6. On Rosa Luxemburg see Sweezy, 1942, pp.124-129; Robinson, 1963; Lichtheim, 1971, pp.117-125; Barrat-Brown, 1974, pp.50-52; Caputo and Pizarro, 1974, pp.148-166; Furtado, 1974, pp.229-233; Nettl, 1975; Bradby, 1975, p.86.

7. For a further discussion, see Caputo and Pizarro, 1974, pp.135-145; O'Brien, 1975, p.21.

8. Similarly, Lukacs stresses, in his preface to the 1967 edition of *Geschichte and Klassenbowusstein* (1923), that his work should be read with an eye to the factional disputes of the time at which he wrote it.

9. Even less could it explain why it was precisely the Social Democratic groups of France, Italy, Germany and England who were the first to break the agreements taken in Congress after Congress during the Second International to oppose the war on account of its imperialist nature. The only ones to stand by those agreements were the Russians, both Bolsheviks and Mensheviks, and some minority groups in other countries, such as Luxemburg's followers in Germany. The Russian left opposed the granting of war credits in the Duma. Later the Mensheviks followed the line of Social Democrats elsewhere, as did some Bolshevik groups. Those in Paris enrolled in the French Army, and Plekhanov the 'father of Russian Marxism' and collaborator with Lenin for many years, went so far in their support according to Lenin's widow, Krupskaya, (1930, p.247) as to 'make a farewell speech in their honour'.

10. This point is emphasized by Lukacs, 1924, p.75; it is important not to seek in the essay what Lenin did not set out to provide, an 'economic theory' of imperialism; in this respect Lenin is largely content to follow Hobson, 1902, and Hilferding, 1910. The substantive element of his contribution is in the analysis of the effect which economic changes have on the world capitalist system in general, and on the class struggle in individual countries in particular. Approaches to Lenin's work from different points of view have led to some misdirected criticism; for a summary of it see Sutcliffe, 1972b, pp.370-375.

11. I am here following Rudenko, 1966.

12. For further discussions of Lenin's work and its relation to other work on imperialism see Varga and Mendelson (eds.),1939; Kruger, 1955; Kemp, 1967, 1972; L. Shapiro and P. Reddaway, 1967; Horowitz, 1969; Pailloix, 1970; Hinkelammert, 1971; Lichtheim, 1971; Barrat-Brown, 1972, 1974.

13. The Narodniks were a group of intellectuals and a series of terrorist groups who were the leading Russian revolutionaries during the last three decades of the 19th century, reaching their peak in the 1870s. From this group emerged later the 'Social Revolutionaries', a party which played an important role in the period from February to October 1917, and of which Kerensky was a member. The base of the party was fundamentally peasant, although it had some strength in the towns, dominating the first democratic municipalities, many Soviets, and some sectors of the army. The Narodniks were a complex group of 18th century Enlightenment materialists and radicals in the tradition of the French Revolution; their theoretical roots were in Marxism, their political practice was inspired by anarchism. The first translation of *Capital*, by a Narodnik, appeared as early as 1872.

14. The peasant commune, a system of common land tenure with periodical redistribution of individual allotments, prevailed under serfdom and survived its abolition in 1861.

15. They went on to explain the ambiguity of the class position of the peasant as follows: 'If by a chance they are revolutionaries, they are so only in the view of their impending transfer to the proletariat; they thus defend not their present, but their future interest; they desert their own standpoint to place themselves at that of the proletariat'.

16. A year later, and only a year before he died, Marx (with Engels) returned to the theme in a new preface to the Russian edition of the *Communist Manifesto* using similar arguments. Ten years later, Engels would affirm that if there had ever been a possibility of avoiding capitalist development in Russia there was no longer. The Russian commune was by then part of the past, and Russia could therefore not escape passage through the stage of capitalism.

17. Thus, for example, a year before (in February 1898) in the founding Congress of the 'Russian Social Democratic Workers' Party' (the first concerted attempt to create a Russian Marxist party on Russian soil, and the forerunner of the Russian Communist Party (Bolshevik), delegates stressed that the principal dilemma of the Russian revolution was the incapacity of the bourgeoisie to make its own revolution; from that they derived the consequent need to extend to the proletariat the leadership in the bourgeois democratic revolution. In this context they stated, 'The farther east one goes in Europe, the weaker, meaner and more cowardly in the political sense becomes the bourgeoisie, and the greater the cultural and political tasks which fall to the lot of the proletariat' (cited in Carr, 1966, Vol.1, p.15).

18. It was only some years later that Stalin developed his well-known thesis of 'Socialism in one country'.

19. Lenin's widow herself has testified to the great surprise with which Lenin received the news of the February revolution. See Krupskaya, 1930, p.286.

20. For a general discussion of the problems of late industrialization see Gerschenkron, 1952; for a discussion of the impact of the expansion of capitalism into backward nations, see Rey, 1971.

21. In 1824 the British Chancellor, Lord Canning, made an oft-quoted statement: 'Spanish America is free, and if we do not badly mismanage our affairs, she is English'. History would prove that his optimism was justified.

22. It is surprising that other lines of Marxist analysis were practically absent in the debate; Trotsky's work, for example, was not influenced, or at least, not acknowledged as influential, despite his important contributions, and in particular that of 1930, in which he insisted that the specific historical circumstances of individual countries would preclude their repeating the path to capitalist development traced out by the advanced nations.

23. It should be noted that this did not preclude, for example, an alliance with small rural producers. For a full account of the whole controversy mentioned briefly here see Suarez, 1967.

24. ECLA (United Nations' Commission for Latin America).

25. A characterization is abstract in the Marxist sense when it is based *on partial or indeterminate relationships*. See Luporini, 1965, and Sassoon, 1965.

26. Baran enriches the theoretical framework of this line of Marxist thought. See also Baran and Sweezy, 1966, and Mandel, 1968.

27. Hence, according to Frank, the continual failure of attempts, such as those in Latin America in the 1830s, to weaken the metropolis-satellite chain. See Frank, 1967, pp.57-66.

28. For the presentation of dualist analyses see Lewis 1954, 1958; Jorgenson, 1961, 1967, Fei and Ranis, 1964. Other critiques of dualism have come from Griffin, 1969; Laclau, 1969; Novack, 1970; Singer, 1970; Rweyemamu, 1971; Cole and Saunders, 1972; and Seligson, 1972. The thesis that Latin America had been capitalist since colonial times had previously been advanced by Bagu, 1949, and Vitale, 1966.

29. Frank himself has kept his audience up to date with the growing bibliography relating to his own work (Frank, 1972, 1974, 1977). Here we would only mention a critique commonly made of Frank, of other dependency writers, and of Marxists in general, regarding the role of ideology in their analysis (see for example Nove, 1974). Marxist analysis, as a general rule, springs simultaneously from political and intellectual praxis, and therefore only on a logical level is it possible to make a clear distinction between 'concept' and 'history' and between 'theory' and 'practice'. From this point of view it is only of formally scholastic interest to claim that a concept is generated 'impure', and 'stained' with ideology. This is how any theory emerges in the social sciences. As Cardoso (1974, p.328) states, 'Ideology reflects the real inversely and at times perversely'. To criticize Frank and other authors because their concepts are 'impregnated' with ideology is only to state the obvious; to criticize them because their ideology reflects reality perversely may be an important element of a critique of their work. For further ideas relating to this subject see Larrain, 1977.

30. Laclau (1971) points out that by restricting his analysis to the circulation of capital Frank fails to realize that integration into the world economy sometimes even strengthens pre-capitalist relations of production; it does not follow however that if such relations were not capitalist they were feudal (Cardoso, 1974b). In my judgement, the frequent use of the term 'feudal' to characterize pre-capitalist relations of production in Latin America illustrates the folly of purely theoretical analysis. It is precisely the lack of concrete analysis which leaves a vacuum, and there is a tendency to fill it with concepts developed for other situations. It is time to attempt to analyse the Latin American experience in terms of categories derived from its own history, rather than continue to squeeze her history into Western European categories. For interesting studies of pre-capitalist relations in Latin America see Cardoso, 1960, 1962; Glaucer, 1971; Barbosa-Ramirez, 1971.

31. Frank of course also criticized models of economic development such as that of Rostow, which claimed that all nations could and should follow the same path. For a discussion of Frank and Rostow, see Foster-Carter, 1976.

32. For an analysis of the work of Dos Santos see Fausto, 1971.

33. For a critique of Marini, see Laclau, 1971, pp.83-88, Cardoso, 1973, pp.7-11. See also Marini's earlier works (Marini, 1969, 1972a).

34. See (among others) Lebedinsky, 1968; Galeno, 1969; Petras, 1969,1970: Cecena Cervantes, 1970; Fernandez, 1970; De la Pena, 1971; Bagchi, 1972; Cockroft, Frank and Johnson (eds.),1972, Malave-Mata, 1972; Meeropol, 1972; Alschuler, 1973; Müller, 1973.

35. Although Lall (and later Weisskopf) appears to direct his critique at the whole dependency school, it is applicable in fact only to those whom I classify as attempting to build a mechanico-formal theory of dependent development.

36. We should note here that the figures for industrial growth of many less developed countries should be regarded with caution. They may be inflated due to monopoly pricing; the industrial sector may be so small as to make its rate of growth appear misleadingly high; the repatriation of profits carried by foreign capital may be high, and in that case the growth

rate of industrial production may overstate, in some cases significantly, the growth in national income derived from industry.

37. This error is the reverse of that committed by others, who (as we shall see later) focus upon the high point of the cycle and project it as a permanent state of affairs. Both forget that the basic permanent features which capitalism has shown are the cyclical character of capital accumulation and the spontaneous tendency towards the concentration of income and wealth, particularly when the state does not take measures to avoid this.

38. See for example the works of Regis Debray, 1970.

39. A series of empirical works related to this approach to dependency has been produced. For a critique of these refer to Palma (1978, pp.905-906).

40. Among the many analyses of the thought of ECLA the best are Hirschman, 1961, 1967, and Cardoso, 1977. ECLA itself has contributed a good synthesis in ECLA, 1969.

41. For the discussion of stagnationist theses, see pp.37-41; for that regarding 'distorted' development, pp.42-49.

42. And thus lacking what was perhaps the most important element in the creative and original aspects of the first ECLA analyses.

43. In the meantime, furthermore, ECLA as an institution continued to produce weighty reports, of which the most outstanding is that of 1965.

44. For a collection and discussion of articles concerning the different aspects of the government of the Unidad Popular, see Palma (ed.), 1973.

45. For a good collection of Gramsci's work (the most original contribution to Marxist thought since Lenin), see Gramsci, 1971.

46. For attempts to up-date the theory of imperialism, see Rhodes (ed.),1970; Owen and Sutcliffe (eds.), 1972; Barrat-Brown, 1974; and Radice (ed.),1975.

47. For empirical evidence on this point see O'Connor, 1970; Bodenheimer, 1970; Quijano, 1971; Fajnzylber, 1971; Cardoso, 1972; Barrat-Brown, 1974; and Warren, 1973.

48. This does not mean, as Warren (1973) seems to argue, that it became possible *throughout* the periphery.

49. For other surveys of dependency literature, see Chilcote, 1974 and O'Brien, 1975. For a survey of the literature relating to the Caribbean, see Girvan, 1973.

I have not attempted in this essay to integrate the growing literature related to Africa. For a recent survey article on this subject, see Shaw and Grieve, 1977; see also Harris, 1975. I would just like to mention that from the point of view of the subject covered, this literature has placed particular emphasis on the analysis of the way in which political independence has been followed by a process of strong economic and social 'dependence' (Amin, 1972; Fanon, 1967; Jorgenson, 1975; Okumu, 1971); and how these relationships of dependence have developed in an increasingly complex framework (Bretton, 1973; Rothchild and Curry, 1975; Selwyn 1975 b and c); and considerable attention has been given to the particular role that the new ruling classes have played in it (Cronje, Ling and Cronje, 1976; Green, 1970; Markovitz, 1977; Shaw, 1975; Shaw and Newbury, 1977; Wallerstein, 1973 and 1975; and Zartman, 1976).

The possibilities of a capitalist development for the African countries are analysed from all points of view (Amin, 1973; Davidson, 1974; Fanon, 1970 a and b; Nyerere, 1973; Wallerstein,

1973 and 1974b); and special emphasis has been placed on the problem involved in the elaboration of alternative development strategies (Falk, 1972; Green, 1975; Ghai, 1972 and 1973; Huntington and Nelson, 1976; Rood, 1975; Schumacher, 1975; Seidman, 1972; Selwyn, 1975a; Thomas, 1974, 1975 and 1976; Vernon, 1976; Wallerstein 1971 and 1974b). Finally, for analysis of specific African countries, see Callaway, 1975; Cliffe and Saul (eds.),1972; Godfrey and Langdon, 1976; Green, 1976; Grundy, 1976; Johns, 1971 and 1975; McHenry, 1976; Pratt, 1975; Rweyemans, 1973; Sandbrook, 1975; Saul, 1973; Seidman, 1974; and Shaw, 1976.

50. It is not surprising therefore that the most penetrating analyses of Brazilian economic development are found in dependency analyses already cited, or in those which place the post-1967 boom in its historical context. For example, Bacha (1977) shows how the aggregate Brazilian economic growth from 1968 to 1974 is not a 'miracle', but conforms rather closely to the cyclical growth pattern of the Brazilian economy in the post-war period.

References

Editions cited are those quoted in the text of the essay itself; however, given the importance of the date of writing or first publication this is placed in brackets immediately after the author's name, both in this bibliography and in the text of the essay itself.

Some of the works cited are unpublished; I would like to thank those who made them available to me and allowed me to discuss and quote them freely.

Alschuler, L. R. (1973) 'A sociological theory of Latin American underdevelopment', *Comparative Studies*, Vol.VI (April 1972), pp.41-60.

Amin, S. (1972) 'Underdevelopment and dependence in Black Africa: origins and contemporary forms', *Journal of Modern African Studies*, Vol.10, No.4 (December 1972), pp.503-525.

Amin, S. (1973) *Neocolonialism in West Africa* (Harmondsworth: Penguin, 1973).

Avineri, S. (ed.) (1968) *Karl Marx on Colonialism and Modernization: His Despatches and Other Writings on China, India, Mexico, the Middle East and North Africa* (New York: Doubleday, 1968).

Avineri, S. (1976) 'Karl Marx and colonialism and modernization', in M. C. Howard and J. E. King, *Marx* (Harmondsworth: Penguin, 1976).

Bacha, E. L. (1977) 'Issues and evidence on recent Brazilian economic growth', *World Development* Vol.5, Nos. 1 and 2 (January, February 1977), pp.47-68.

Bagchi, A. K. (1972) 'Some international foundations of capitalist growth and underdevelopment'; *Economic and Political Weekly*, Special Number (August 1972) pp.155-170.

Bagu, S. (1949) *Economias de la Sociedad Colonial* (Buenos Aires: Ateneo, 1949).

Baran, P. (1957) *La Economia Politica del Crecimiento* (Mexico: F.C.E., 1969).

Baran, P. and P. Sweezy (1966) *Monopoly Capital: An Essay on the American Economic and Social Order* (New York: Monthly Review Press, 1966).

Barbosa-Ramirez, A. R. (1971) *La Estructura Economica de la Neuva Espana* (Mexico: Siglo XXI Editores, 1971).

Barrat-Brown, M. (1974) *Economics of Imperialism* (Harmondsworth: Penguin 1974).

Bath, C. R. and D. D. James, (1976) 'Dependency analysis of Latin America: some criticisms, some suggestions', *Latin American Research Review*, Vol.XI, No.3 (1976), pp.3-54.

Batra, R. (1971) *El Modo de Produccion Asiatico* (Mexico: ERA 1971).

Beckford, G. (1972) *Persistent Poverty: Underdevelopment in Plantation Economics of the Third World* (New York: Oxford University Press, 1972).

Bettelheim, C. (1970) *Chine et URSS: Deux Modeles d'Industrialisation* (Paris: Temps Modernes, 1970).

Bodenheimer, S. (1970) 'Dependency and imperialism', *Politics and Society* (May 1970), pp.327-358.

Booth, D. (1975) 'Andre Gunder Frank: an introduction and appreciation', in I. Oxaal, T. Barnett and D. Booth, *Beyond the Sociology of Development* (London: Routledge and Kegan Paul, 1975).

Bradby, R. 'The destruction of natural economy', *Economy and Society*, Vol.4, No.2 (May 1975) pp.127-161.

Brenner, R. (1977) 'The origins of capitalist development: a critique of neo-Smithian Marxism', *New Left Review*, No.104 (July, August 1977), pp.25-93.

Bretton, H. (1973) *Power and Politics in Africa* (Chicago: Aldine, 1973).

Bukharin, N. I. (1915) *Imperialism and World Economy* (London: Martin Lawrence, 1929)

Bukharin, N. (1926) *Der Imperialismus und die Akkumulation des Kapitals* (Berlin/Vienna: 1926).

Bukharin, N. and F. Preobrazhensky (1917) *The ABC of Communism* (Harmondsworth: Penguin, 1969).

Callaway, B. (1975) 'The political economy of Nigeria', in R. Harris (ed.)(1975).

Cammack, P. (1977) 'Dependency, class structure and the state in the writings of F. H. Cardoso' (Ms. 1977).

Caputo, O. y Pizarro (1974) *Dependencia y Relaciones Internacionales* (Costa Rica: EDUCA, 1974).

Cardoso, F. H. (1960) *Cor e Mobilidade Social en Florianopolis* (Sao Paulo: Editora Nacional, 1960).

Cardoso, F. H. (1962) *Capitalismo e Escravidao no Brasil Meridional* (Sao Paulo: Difusao Europeia do Livro, 1962).

Cardoso, F. H. (1970) 'Teoria de la dependencia o analisis concretos de situaciones de dependencia?', F. H. Cardoso (1972b).

Cardoso, F. H. (1972a) 'Dependency and development in Latin America', *New Left Review*, No.74 (July-August 1972), pp.83-95.

Cardoso, F. H. (1972b) *Estado y Sociedad en America Latina* (Buenos Aires: Ediciones Nueva Vision, 1972).

Cardoso, F. H. (1973) 'The contradiction of associated development' (Ms. 1973); reprinted in 'Current theses on Latin American development and dependency: a critique' (1976a).

Cardoso, F. H. (1974a) 'Notas sobre el estado actual de los estudios sobre la dependencia', in J. Serra (ed.), *Desarrollo Latinoamericano: Ensayos Criticos* (Mexico: F.C.E.,1974).

Cardoso, F. H. (1974b) 'The paper enemy', *'Latin American Perspectives*, Vol.I, No.1 (Spring 1974), pp.66-74.

Cardoso, F. H. (1976a) 'Current theses on Latin American development and dependency: a critique' (paper presented to the III Scandinavian Research Conference on Latin America, Bergen, 17-19 June 1976).

Cardoso, F. H. (1976b) 'The consumption of dependency theory in the US' (paper presented to the III Scandinavian Research Conference on Latin America; Bergen, 17-19 June 1976); reprinted in *Latin American Research Review*, Vol.XII, No.3 (1977), pp.7-24.

Cardoso, F. H. (1977) 'The originality of the copy: ECLA and the idea of development' (Ms. 1977).

Cardoso, F. H. and E. Faletto (1967) *Dependencia y Desarrollo en America Latina* (Mexico: Siglo XXI Editores, 1969).

Cardoso, F. H. and E. Faletto (1977) *Dependency and Development in Latin America* (American ed. with new preface, forthcoming).

Cariola, C. and O. Sunkel (1976) 'Expansion salitrera y transformaciones socio-economicas en Chile 1860-1930' (Ms.1976)

Cariola, C. and O. Sunkel (1977) 'Some preliminary notes on nitrate expansion and class formation in Chile in the period 1860-1930' (Ms. 1977).

Carr, E. H. (1966) *The Bolshevik Revolution* (Harmondsworth: Penguin, 1966).

Cecna-Cervantes, J. L. (1970) *Superexploitacion, Dependencia y Desarrollo* (Mexico: Editorial Nuestro Tiempo, 1970).

Chilcote, R. H. (1974) 'Dependency: a critical synthesis of the literature', *Latin American Perspective*, Vol.1, No.1 (Spring 1974), pp.4-29.

Chudnovsky, D. (1974) *Empresas Multinacionales y Ganancias Monopolicas en una Economia Lationoamericana* (Buenos Aires: Siglo XXI Editores, 1974).

Cliffe, L. and J. S. Saul (eds.) (1972) *Socialism in Tanzania Vols. 1 and 2* (Nairobi: East African Publishing House, 1972 and 1973).

Cockcroft, J. D., A. G. Frank and D. K. Johnson. (1972) *America's Political Economy* (New York: Doubleday and Co.).

Cole, W. and R. Sanders (1972) 'A modified dualism model for Latin American economies', *Journal of Developing Areas*, Vol.VI I (January 1972), pp.185-198.

Conquest, R. (1972) *Lenin* (London: Fontana, 1972).

Cronje, S., M. Ling and G. Cronje (1976) *Lonrho: Portrait of a Multinational* (Harmonsworth: Pelican, 1976).

Davidson, B. (1974) *Can Africa Survive? Arguments against Growth without Development* (Boston: Little Brown, 1974).

Debray, R. (1970) *Strategy for Revolution: Essays on Latin America*, written between 1965 and 1969 and edited in 1970 by R. Blackburn (London: Jonathan Cape, 1970).

Degras, J. (ed.) (1960) *The Communist International, 1919-1943: Documents, Vol.2*, 1928-1938 (London: Oxford University Press, 1960).

De Kadt, E. and G. Williams (1974) *Sociology and Development* (London: Tavistock Publications, 1974); with an introduction by E. de Kadt, pp.1-19.

De la Pena, S. (1971) *El Antidesarrollo de America Latina* (Mexico: Siglo XXI Editores, 1971).

D'Encause, H. C. and S. R. Schram (1969) *Marxism in Asia* (London: Allen Lane, 1969).

Dos Santos, T. (1968) 'Colonialismo, imperialismo y monopolios en "El Capital" ', in CESO, *Imperialismo y Dependencia Externa* (Santiago: CESO, 1968).

Dos Santos, T. (1969) 'The crisis of development theory and the problems of dependence in Latin America', in H. Bernstein (ed.), *Underdevelopment and Development* (Harmondsworth: Penguin 1973).

Dos Santos, T. (1970) 'The structure of dependence', *American Economic Review*, Vol.60, No.2 (1970), pp.231-236.

ECLA (1965) *El Proceso de Industrialization de America Latina* (Santiago: ECLA, December 1965).

ECLA (1969) *El Pensamiento de la CEPAL* (Santiago: Editorial Universitaria, 1969).

Fajnzylber, F. (1971) *Sistema Industrial e Exportacao de Manufacturados: Analise da Experiencia Brasiliera* (Rio de Janeiro: IPEA/INPES, 1971).

Falk, R. A. (1972) 'Zone II as a world order construct', in J. N. Rosenau, V. Davis and M. A. East (eds.), *The Analysis of International Politics* (New York: Free Press, 1972).

Fanon, F. (1967) *The Wretched of the Earth* (Harmondsworth: Penguin, 1967).

Fanon, F. (1970a) *Black Skins: White Masks* (London: Paladin, 1970).

Fanon, F. (1970b) *Towards the African Revolution* (Harmondsworth: Pelican, 1970).

Faria, U. 61976) 'Occupational marginality, employment and poverty in urban Brazil' (unpublished Ph.D. dissertation, Harvard University, 1976).

Fausto, A. (1971) 'La nueva situacion de la dependencia y el analisis sociopolitico de Theotonia dos Santos', *Revista Latinoamericana de Ciencias Sociales*, Nos.1/2, (June-December 1971), pp.198-211.

Fei, J. C. H. and G. Ranis (1964) *Development of the Labour Surplus Economy: Theory and Policy* (New Haven: Yale University Press, 1964).

Fernandez, F. (1970) 'Patrones de dominacion externa en America Latina', *Revista Mexicana de Sociologia*, Vol.XXXII (November-December 1970), pp.1439-1459.

Fernandez, R. and J. Ocampo, (1974) 'The Latin American revolution: a theory of imperialism not dependency', *Latin American Perspective*, Vol.l, No.1 (Spring 1974), pp.30-61.

Flanders, J. (1973) 'Prebisch on protectionism: an evaluation', *Economic Journal*, Vol.74, No.6 (1973), pp.305-326.

Ford, H. (1922) *My Life and Work* (London: William Heinemann, 1922).

Foster-Carter, A. (1974) 'Neo-Marxist approaches to development and underdevelopment', in E. de Kadt and G. Williams (1974).

Foster-Carter, A. (1976) 'From Rostow to Gunder Frank: conflicting paradigms in the analysis of underdevelopment', *World Development*, Vol.4, No.3 (1976), pp.167-180.

Frank, A. G. (1966) 'The development of underdevelopment' *Monthly Review*, Vol.18, No.4 (September 1966), pp.17-31.

Frank,A. G. (1967) *Capitalism and Underdevelopment in Latin America: Historical Studies of Chile and Brasil* (New York: Monthly Review Press, 1967).

Frank, A. G. (1969) *Latin America: Underdevelopment or Revolution* (New York: Monthly Review Press, 1969).

Frank, A. G. (1970) *Lumpenhourgeoisie: Lumpen Development Dependence, Class and Politics in Latin America*, reprinted (New York: Monthly Review Press, 1972).

Frank, A. G. (1972, 1974 and 1977) 'Dependence is dead, long live dependence and the class struggle: an answer to critics', (Ms. University of Dar es Salaam,1972; *Latin American Perspectives*, Vol.1, No.1 (1974), pp.87-106; and *World Development*, Vol.5, No.4 (April 1977), pp.355-370).

Furtado, C. (1966) *Subdesarrollo V Estancamiento en America Latina* (Buenos Aires: C.E.A.L.,1966).

Galeno, E. (1969) 'The de-nationalization of Brazilian industry', *Monthly Review*, Vol.XXI, No.7 (December 1969), pp.11-30.

Gerschenkron, A. (1952) 'Economic backwardness in historical perspective', in B. Hoselitz (ed.), *The Progress of Underdeveloped Areas* (Chicago: Chicago Universitv Press,1952), reprinted in A. Gerschenkron (1962), *Economic Backwardness in Historical Perspective* (Cambridge, Mass: The Belknap Press,1962).

Ghai, D. P. (1972) 'Perspectives on future economic prospects and problems in Africa', in J. N. Bhaawati (ed.), *Economics and World Order* (New York: Macmillan, 1972) .

Ghai, D. P. (1973) 'Concepts and strategies of economic independence' *Journal of Modern African Studies*, Vol.11, No.1 (March 1973), pp.21-42.

Girvan, N. (1973) 'The development of dependency economics in the Caribbean and Latin America: review and comparison', *Social and Economic Studies*, Vol.22 (March 1977), pp.1-33.

Glaucer, K. (1971) 'Origenes del regimen de produccion vigente en Chile', in *Cuadernos de la Realidad Nacional*, No.6 (Santiago: 1971), pp.78-152.

Godfrey, M. and S. Langdon (1976) 'Partners in underdevelopment?: the transnationalisation thesis in a Kenyan context', *Journal of Commonwealth and Comparative Politics*, Vol.14, No.1 (March 1976), pp.42-63.

Gramsci, A. (1971) *Selection from his Prison Notebooks* (London: Lawrence and Wishart, 1971).

Green, R. H. (1970) 'Political independence and the national economy: an essay on the political economy of decolonisation', in C. Allen and R. W. Johnston (eds.), *African Perspectives: Papers in the History, Politics and Economics of Africa, presented to Thomas Hodgkin* (Cambridge: Cambridge University Press,1970).

Green, R. H. (1975) 'The peripheral African economy and the MNC', in C. Widstrand (ed.), *Multinational Firms in Africa* (Uppsala: Scandinavian Institute of African Studies,1975).

Green, R. H. (1976) 'Tanzanian goals, strategies, results: notes toward an interim assessment' (Ms., Seminar on Socialist Development in Tanzania since 1967, Toronto, April 1976).

Griffin, K. (1969) *Underdevelopment in Spanish America* (London: Allen and Unwin, 1969).

Grundy, K. W. (1976) 'Intermediary power and global dependency: the case of South Africa', *International Studies Quarterly*, No.20 (December 1976), pp.553-580.

Harris, R. (ed.) (1975) *The Political Economy of Africa* (Cambridge, Mass.: Schenkman, 1975).

Hilferding, R. (1910) *Finanz Kapital: eine Studie uber die junte Entwicklung des Kapitalismus* (Vienna: 1910).

Hinkelammert, F. (1970a) *El Subdesarrollo Latino-americano: Un Caso de Desarrollo Capitalista* (Santiago: Ediciones Nueva Universidad, Universidad Catolica de Chile, 1970).

Hinkelammert, F. (1970b) 'La teoria clasica del imperialismo, el subdesarrolo y la acumulacion socialista', reprinted in M. A. Garreton (ed.) *Economia Politica en la Unidad Popular* (Barcelona: Libros de Confrontacion, 1975).

Hinkelammert, F. (1970c) 'Teoria de la dialectica del desarrollo desigual', *Cuadernos de la Realidad Nacional*, No. 6 (December 1970) pp. 15-220.

Hinkelammert, F. (1971) *Dialectica del Desarrollo Desigual* (Valparaiso: Ediciones Universitarias de Valparaiso, 1970)

Hirshman, A. (1958) *The Strategy of Economic Development* (New Haven: Yale University Press, 1958).

Hirshman, A. (1961) 'Ideologies of economic development', reprinted in *A Bias for Hope* (New Haven: Yale University Press, 1971).

Hobsbawn, E. (1964) *Introduction to Karl Marx: Pre-capitalist Economic Foundations* (London: Lawrence and Wishart, 1964).

Hobson, J. A. (1902) *Imperialism-A Study* (London: Allen and Unwin, 1938).

Hobson, J. A. (1911) *The Economic Interpretation of Investment* (London: The Financial Review of Reviews, 1911).

Hodgson, J. L. (1966) 'An evaluation of the Prebisch thesis' (unpublished Ph.D. dissertation, University of Wisconsin, Madison, 1966).

Horowitz, D. (ed.) (1968) *Marx and Modern Economics* (New York: Monthly Review Press, 1968).

Horowitz, D. (1969) *Imperialism and Revolution* (Harmondsworth: Penguin,1969).

Huntington, S. P. and J. M. Nelson (1976) *No Easy Choice: Political Participation in Developing Countries* (Cambridge, Mass.: Harvard University Press, 1976).

Johns, S (1971) 'Parastatal bodies in Zambia: problems and prospects', in H. and U. E. Simonis (eds.) (1971). *Socio-Economic Development in Dual Economies: The Example of Zambia* (Munich: Weltform Verlag, for African Studies Institute, 1971).

Johns, S. (1975) *State Capitalism in Zambia: The Evolution of the Parastatal Sector* (San Francisco: African Studies Association, October 1975).

Jorgenson, D. W. (1961) 'The development of a dual economy', *Economic Journal* (June 1961), pp.309-334.

Jorgenson, D. W. (1967) 'Surplus agricultural labour and the development of a dual economy', *Oxford Economic Papers* (November 1967) pp.288-312.

Jorgenson, J. J. (1975) 'Multinational corporations in the indigenization of the Kenyan economy', in C. Widstrand led.) *Multinational Firms in Africa* (Uppsala: Scandinavian Institute of African Studies, 1975).

Kahl, J. A. (1976) *Modernization, Exploitation and Dependency in Latin America* (New Jersey: Transaction Books, 1976).

Kalecki, M. (1933, 1934 and 1935) *Selected Essays on the Dynamics of the Capitalist Economy 1930-1970*, (Cambridge: Cambridge University Press, 1971).

Kautsky, K. (1914) 'Ultra imperialism', *New Left Review* (January-February 1970).

Kay, G. (1975) *Development and Underdevelopment: a Marxist Analysis* (London: Macmillan 1975).

Kemp, T. (1967) *Theories of Imperialism* (London: Dobson Books, 1967).

Kemp, T. (1972) 'The Marxist theory of imperialism', in R. Owen and B. Sutcliffe (1972).

Keynes, J. M. (1938) *The General Theory of Employment, Interest and Money* (London: Macmillan, 1960).

Kierman, V. G. (1967) 'Marx on India', *Socialist Register 1967* (London: Merlin Press, 1967).

Kruger, D. H. (1955) 'Hobson, Lenin and Schumpeter on Imperialism', *Journal of the History of Ideas* (April 1955) pp.250-260.

Krupskaya, N. (1930) *Memories of Lenin* (London: Lawrence and Wishart, 1970).

Laclau, E. (1969) 'Modos de produccion, sistemas economicos y poblacion excedente: aproximacion historica a los casos Argentinos y Chilenos', *Revista Latinoamericama de Sociologia*, Vol2, No.2 (1969) pp.776-816.

Laclau, E. (1971) 'Feudalism and capitalism in Latin America', *New Left Review* (May-June 1971) pp.19-38.

Lall, S. (1975) 'Is dependence a useful concept in analysing underdevelopment?', *World Development*, Vol.3, No.11 (1975) pp.799-810.

Larrain, J. (1977) The concept of ideology: some theoretical and methodological questions' (unpublished Ph.D. dissertation, Sussex University, 1977).

Lebedinsky, M. (1968) *Del Subdesarrollo al Desarrollo* (Buenos Aires: Editorial Quipo, 1968).

Lenin (1899) *The Development of Capitalism in Russia* (Moscow: Progress Publishers, 1967).

Lenin (1915) *Philosophical Notebook* (Moscow: Progress Publishers, 1967).

Lenin (1916) *Imperialism, the Highest State of Capitalism* (Peking: Foreign Languages Press, 1970).

Lenin (1917) *1905-Jornadas Revolucionarias* (Santiago: B.E.P., 1970).

Lenin (1920) '1920 theses', in *La Guerra y la Humanidad* (Mexico: Ediciones Frente Cultural, 1939).

Lewis, A. (1954) 'Economic development with unlimited supplies of labour', *Manchester School of Economic and Social Studies*, Vol 22, No.2 I May 1954) pp.139-192.

Lewis, A. (1958) 'Unlimited labour: further notes', *Manchester School* (January 1958).

Lukacs, G. (1923) *History and Class Consciousness: Studies in Marxist Didactics* (London: Merlin Press, 1971).

Lukacs, G. (1924) *Lenin: A Study on the Unity of his Thought* (London: New Left Books, 1970).

Luporini, C. (1975) 'Reality and historicity: economy and dialectics in Marxism', *Economy and Society*, Vol.4, No.2 (May 1975), pp.206-321, and Vol.4, No. 3 (August 1975), pp.283-308.

Luxemburg, R. (1913) *The Accumulation of Capital* (London: Routledge and Kegan Paul Ltd., 1963).

Mandel, E. (1968) *Marxist Economic Theory* (London: Merlin Press, 1968).

Mandel, E. (1970) *La Formacion del Pensamiento Economico de Marx* (Mexico: Siglo XXI Editores, 1970).

Malave-Mata, H. (1972) 'Dialectica del subdesarrollo y dependencia', *Problemas de Desarrollo*, No. III (August-October 1972) pp.23-52.

Marini, R. M. (1969) *Subdesarrollo y Revolucion* (Mexico: Siglo XXI Editores, 1969).

Marini, R.-M. (1972a) 'Brazilian sub-imperialism', *Monthly Review*, No. 9 (February 1972) pp.14-24.

Marini, R. M. (1972b) 'Dialectica de la dependencia: la economia exportadora', *Sociedad y Desarrollo*, No.1 (January-May 1972), pp.5-31.

Markovitz, L. L. (1977) *Power and Class in Africa: An introduction to Change and Conflict in African Politics* (Englewood Cliffs: Prentice Hall, 1977).

Marx, K. (1848) 'The Communist Manifesto', in L. Feuer (ed.) *Marx and Engels: Basic Writings on Politics and Philosophy* (London: Fontana Library, 1969).

Marx, K. (1853) 'Future results of British rule in India', *New York Daily Tribune* (25 June 1853) reprinted in L. Feuer (ed.), *Marx and Engels: Basic Writings on Politics and Philosophy* (London: Fontana Library, 1969).

Marx, K. (1859) *Grundrisse Foundations of the Critique of Political Economy* (Harmondsworth: Penguin, 1973).

Marx, K. (1867) *El Capital*, Vol.1 (Mexico: F.C.E. 1946).

Marx, K. (1877) 'Russia's pattern of development', Letter to the Editorial Board of the Otechestvennige Zapiski, reprinted in L. Feuer (ed.) *Marx and Engels: Basic Writings on Politics and Philosophy* (London: Fontana Library 1969).

Marx, K. (1885) *El Capital* Vol.ll (Mexico: F.C.E. 1946).

Marx, K. (1894) *El Capital* Vol.III (Mexico: F.C.E., 1946).

McGowan, P. (1976) 'Economic dependence and economic performance in Black Africa', *The Journal of Modern African Studies*, Vol.14, No.1 (1976), pp.25-40.

McHenry, D. E. (1976) 'The underdevelopment theory: a case-study from Tanzania', *The Journal of Modern African Studies*, Vol. 14, No.1 (1976) pp.621-636.

Meeropol, M. (1972) 'Towards a political economy analysis of underdevelopment', *Review of Radical Political Economy*, Vol. lV (Spring 1972) pp.77-108.

Muller, R. (1973) 'The multinational corporation and the underdevelopment of the third world', in C. K. Wilbee (ed.) *The Political Economy of Devolopment and Underdevelopment* (New York: Random House, 1973).

Nettl, P. (1975) *Rosa Luxemburgo* (Mexico: ERA, 1975).

Novack, G. (1970) 'The permanent revolutlon in Latin America', *International Press*, Vol. lll (November 1970), pp. 978-983.

Nove, A. (1974) 'On reading Andre Gunder Frank' *Journal of Development Studies*, Vol.10, Nos. 3 and 4 (April-July 1974), pp-445-455

Nyerere, J. K. (1973) *Freedom snd Development* (Dar es Salaam: Oxford University Press, 1973)

O'Brien, P. (1975) 'A critique of Latin American theories of dependency', in I. Oxaal, T. Barnet and D. Booth (eds.) *Beyond the Sociology of Development* (London: Routledge and Kegan Paul, 1975).

O'Connor, J. (1970) 'The meaning of imperialism', in R. I. Rhodes (1970).

Okumu, J. (1971) 'The place of African states in international relations' in A. Schou and A. Brundtland (eds.), *Small States in International Relations* (Stockholm: Almqvist and Wiksell, Nobel Symposium 17, 1971).

Owen, R. and B. Sutcliffe (eds.) (1972) *Studies in the Theory of Imperialism* (London: Longman, 1972).

Palloix, C. (1970) 'La question de l'imperialisme chez V. I. Lenin et Rosa Luxemburg', *L'Homme et Societe* (January-March 1970).

Palma, G. (ed.) (1973) *La Via Chilena al Socialismo* (Mexico: Siglo XXI Editores, 1973).

Palma, G. (1978) 'Dependency: a formal theory of underdevelopment, or a methodology for the analysis of concrete situations of underdevelopment?, *World Development*, Vol.6 (July 1978), pp. 881-924.

Palma, G. (forthcoming) 'Essays on the development of the Chilean manufacturing industry: a case of capitalist associated development'.

Petras, J. (1969) *Politics and Social Forces in Chilean Development* (Berkeley: University of California Press, 1969).

Petras, J. (1970) *Politics and Social Structure in Latin America* (New York: Monthly Review Press, 1970).

Pinto, A. (1965) 'La concentracion del progreso tecnico y de sus frutos en el desarrollo', *Trimestre Economico*, No.25 (January-March 1965) pp.3-69; reprinted in A. Pinto (1973).

Pinto, A. (1973) *Inflacion: Raices Estructurales* (Mexico: F.C.E., 1973).

Pinto, A. (1974) 'Heterogencidad estructural y el metodo de desarrollo reciente' in J. Serra (ed.) *Desarrollo Latinoamericano, Ensayos Criticos* (Mexico: F.C.E., 1974).

Pinto, A. and J. Knakel (1973) 'The centre-periphery system 20 years later', *Social and Economic Studies* (March 1973) pp.34-89.

Pratt, R. C. (1975) 'Foreign policy issues and the emergence of socialism in Tanzania, 1961-68'; *International Journal*, Vol.30, No.3, (Summer 1975) pp.445-470.

Poulantzas, N. (1972) *Poder Politico y Clases Sociales en el Estado Capitalista* (Mexico: Siglo XXI Editores, 1972).

Prebisch, R. (1963) *Hacia una Dinamica del Desarrollo Economico* (Mexico: F.C.E. 1963).

Quijano, A. (1971) 'Nationalism and capitalism in Peru; a study of neo-imperialism', *Monthly Review* (July-August, 1971).

Radice, H. (ed.) (1975) *International Firms and Modern Imperialism* (Harmondsworth: Penguin 1975).

Ray, D. (1973) 'The dependency model of Latin American underdevelopment: three basic fallacies', *Journal of Interamerican Studies and World Affairs*, Vol. XV (February 1973), pp.4-20.

Rey, P. P. (1971) *Les Alliances des Classes* (Paris: Maspero, 1971).

Rhodes, R. I. (eds.) (1970) *Imperialism snd Underdevelopment: A Reader* (New York: Monthly Review Press, 1970).

Robinson, J. (1963) *'Introduction'* in *Rosa Luxemburg, Accumulation of Capital* (London: Routledge and Kegan Paul, 1963).

Rood, L. L. (1975) 'Foreign investment in African manufacturing', *Journal of Modern African Studies*, Vol.13, No.1 (March 1975), pp.19-34.

Rothchild, D. and R. L. Curry (1975) *Beyond the Nation-State: The Political Economy of Regionalism* (San Francisco: American Political Science Association, September 1975).

Rudenko, G. (1966) *La Metodologia Leninsta en la Investigacion del Imperislismo* (Havana: Publicaciones Economicas, 1966).

Rweyemamu, J. F. (1971) 'The causes of poverty in the periphery', *Journal of Modern African Studies*, Vol.IX (October 1971), pp.453-455.

Rweyernamu, J. (1973) *Underdevelopment and Industrialization in Tanzania* (Nairobi: Oxford University Press, 1973).

Salera, V. (1971) 'Prebisch's change and development', *Interamerican Economic Affairs*, Vol .24, No.4 (1971) pp.67-79.

Sandbrook, R. (1975) *Proletarians and African Capitalism: The Kenyan Case 1960-1972* (London: Cambridge University Press, 1975).

Sassoon, D., 'An introduction to Luporini', *Economy and Society*, Vol.4, No.2 (May 1975), pp.194-205.

Saul, J. S. (1973) 'Socialism in one country: Tanzania', in G. Arrighi and J. S. Saul, *Essays on the Political Economy of Africa* (New York: Monthly Review Press, 1973).

Schumacher, E. F. (1975) *Small is Beautiful: Economics as if People Mattered* (New York: Harper and Row, 1975).

Seidman, A. (1972) *Comparative Development Strategies in West Africa* (Nairobi: East African Publishing House, 1972).

Seidman, A. (1974) 'The distorted growth of import-substitution industry: the Zambian case', *Journal of Modern African Studies*, Vol.12, No.4 (December 1974), pp.601-631.

Seligson, M. (1972) 'The "dual society" thesis in Latin America: a reexamination of the Costa Rica case', *Social Froces*, Vol. LI (September 1972) pp.91-98.

Selwyn, P. (ed.) (1975a) *Development Policy in Small Countries*, (London: Croom Helm, 1975).

Selwyn, P. (1975b) *Industries of the Southern African Periphery* (London: Croom Helm, 1975).

Serra, J. (ed.) (1974) *Desarrollo Latinoamericano, Ensayos Criticos* (Mexico: F.C.E. 1974).

Shapiro, L. and P. Reddaway (1967) *Lenin: The Man, The Theorist, The Leader* (London: 1967).

Shaw, T. M. (1975) 'The political economy of African international relations', *Issue*, Vol.5, No.4 (Winter 1975) pp.29-38.

Shaw, T. M. (1976) *Dependence and Underdevelopment: The Development and Foreign Policies of Zambia* (Athens: Ohio University, Papers in International Studies, Africa Series No.28, 1976).

Shaw, T. M. and M. C. Newbury (1977) 'Dependence or interdependence? Africa in the global political economy', in M. W. Delancey (ed.), *African International Relations* (New York: Africana, 1977).

Shaw, T. M. and M. Grieve (1977) 'Dependence or development: international and internal inequalities in Africa', *Development and Change*, No.8 (1977) pp. 377-408.

Singer, H. W. (1970) 'Dualism revisited: a new approach to the problems of the dual society in developing countries', *Journal of Development Studies*, Vol.VI I (October 1970), pp.60-75.

Singer, P. (1971) *Forca de Trabalho e Emprogo, no Brazil 1920-1969* (Sao Paulo: CEBRAP Cuaderno, Numero 3, 1971).

Stalin, J. (1934) *Problems of Leninism* (Moscow: Cooperative Publishing Society of Foreign Workers in the USSR, 1934).

Stenberg, M. (1974) 'Dependency, imperialism and the relations of production', *Latin American Perspective*, Vol.1, No.1 (Spring 1974), pp.75-86.

Sunkel, O. (1972) 'Big business and dependency', *Foreign Affairs*, Vol.24, No.1 (1972), pp.517-531.

Sunkel, O. (1973a) 'The pattern of Latin American development', in V. I. Urguidi and E. R. Thorp (eds.) *Latin America in the International Economy* (London: Macmillan, 1973).

Sunkel, P. (1973b) 'Transnational capitalism and national disintegration in Latin America', *Social and Economic Studies*, Vol.22, No.1 (1973), pp.132-176.

Sunkel, O. (1974) 'A critical commentary on the United Nations Report on multinational corporations in world development', (Sussex: IDS, 1974).

Sunkel, O. and P. Paz (1970) *El Subdesarrollo Latinoamoricano y la Teoria del Desarrollo* (Mexico: Siglo XXI Editores, 1970).

Sutcliffe, B. (1972a) 'Imperialism and industrialization in the third world', in R. Owen snd B. Sutcliffe (1972).

Sutcliffe, B. (1972b) 'Conclusions', in R. Owen and B. Sutcliffe (1972).

Suarez, A. (1967) *Cuba: Castroism and Communism: 1959-1966* (Cambridge Mass.: M I T Press, 1967) .

Sweezy, P. (1942) *La Teoria del Desarrollo Capitalista* (Mexico: F .C. E. 1969).

Tavares, M. C. and J. Serra (1970) 'Mas alla del estancamiento', in J. Serra (1974).

Thomas, C. V. (1974) *Dependence and Transformation: The Economics of the Transition to Socialism* (New York: Monthly Review Press, 1974).

Thomas, C. V. (1975) 'Industrialization and the transformation of Africa: an alternative to MNC expansion', in C. Widstrand (ed.) *Multinational Firms in Africa* (Uppsala: Scandinavian Institute of African Studies, 1975).

Thomas, C. V. (1976) 'Class struggle, social development and the theory of the non-capitalist path' (Scandinavian Seminar on Non-capitalist Development in Africa, Helsinki, August 1976).

Trotsky, L. (1930) *Historia de la Revolucion Rusa* (Santiago: Quimantu, 1972).

Varga, E. and L. Mendelson (eds.) (1939) *New Data for V. I. Lenin's Imperialism, the Highest Stage of Capitalism* (London: Lawrence and Wishart, 1939).

Vernon, R. (1976) 'The distribution of power', in R. Vernon (ed.), *The Oil Crisis* (New York: W. W. Norton, 1976).

Viner, J. (1951) 'Seis conferencias', *Revista Brasileira de Economia*, Vol.2 (Rio Janeiro, 1951).

Vitale, L. (1966) 'America Latina: feudal o capitalista', *Estrategia*, No.3 (1966) .

Vuscovich, P. (1970) 'Distribucion del ingreso y opciones de desarrollo' reprinted in M. A. Garrteon. *Economia Politica de la Unidad Popular* (Barcelona: Libros de Confrontacion, 1975).

Vuscovich, P. (1973) 'La politica economica del gobierno de la Unidad Popular', in G. Palma (1973).

Walicki, A. (1969) *The Controversy over Capitalism* (London: Oxford University Press, 1969).

Wallerstein, I. (1971) 'The range of choice: constraints on the policies of governments of contemporary African independent states', in M. F. Lofchie (ed.) *The State of the Nations* (Berkeley: University of California Press, 1971).

Wallerstein, I. (1973) 'Africa in a capitalist world', *Issue*, Vol.3, No.3 (Fall 1973) pp.1-12.

Wallerstein, I. (1974a) *The Modern World System: Capitalist Agriculture and the Oripins of the European World-Economy in the Sixteenth Century* (New York: Academic Press, 1974).

Wallerstein, I. (1974b) 'Dependence in an interdependent world: the limited possibilities of a transformation within the capitalist world economy', *African Studies Review*, Vol .17, No.1 (April 1974), pp.1-26.

Wallerstein, I. (1975) 'Class and class conflict in contemporary Africa', *Monthly Review*, No.26 (February 1975) pp.34-42 (originally published in the *Canadian Journal of African Studies*, Vol.7, No.3, pp.375-380).

Warren, B. (1973) 'Imperialism and capitalist industrialization', *New Left Review* (September-October 1973), pp.3-44.

Weisskopf, T. E. (1976) 'Dependence as an explanation of underdevelopment: a critique' (Ms., University of Michigan, 1976).

Zartman, I. W. (1976) 'Europe and Africa: decolonization or dependency?', *Foreign Affairs*, Vol.54, No.2 (January 1976) pp.325-343.

13. The Thesis of Capitalist Underdevelopment

André Gunder Frank

This essay contends that underdevelopment in Chile is the necessary product of four centuries of capitalist development and of the internal contradictions of capitalism itself. These contradictions are the expropriation of economic surplus from the many and its appropriation by the few, the polarization of the capitalist system into metropolitan centre and peripheral satellites, and the continuity of the fundamental structure of the capitalist system throughout the history of its expansion and transformation, due to the persistence or re-creation of these contradictions everywhere and at all times. My thesis is that these capitalist contradictions and the historical development of the capitalist system have generated underdevelopment in the peripheral satellites whose economic surplus was expropriated, while generating economic development in the metropolitan centres which appropriate that surplus — and, further, that this process still continues.

The Spanish conquest incorporated and fully integrated Chile into the expanding mercantile capitalist system of the sixteenth century. The contradictions of capitalism have generated structural underdevelopment in Chile ever since she began to participate in the development of this world-embracing system. Contrary to widespread opinion, underdevelopment in Chile and elsewhere is not an original or traditional state of affairs; nor is it a historical stage of economic growth which was passed through by the now developed capitalist countries. On the contrary, underdevelopment in Chile and elsewhere, no less than economic development itself, became over the centuries the necessary product of the contradiction-ridden process of capitalist development. This same process continues to generate underdevelopment in Chile, and this underdevelopment cannot and will not be eliminated by still further capitalist development. Accordingly, structural underdevelopment will continue to be generated and deepened in Chile until the Chileans liberate themselves from capitalism itself.

The interpretation offered here differs not only from widely accepted interpretations of the nature and causes of underdevelopment and development in general but also from the views of important commentators on and analysts of past and present Chilean society. Thus, during the 1964 election campaign both the Christian Democrat-Liberal-Conservative presidential candidate and the Socialist-Communist candidate referred to contemporary Chilean society as containing 'feudal' elements; and in his post-election commentary, Fidel Castro also referred to 'feudal' elements in Chile. G. M. McBride, in his deservedly famous *Chile: Land and Society* written in the 1930s, maintained that all Chile suffered from 'the dominance of a small class of landed aristocracy in the old feudal order'.

The Marxist Julio César Jobet, in his *Ensayo critico del desarrollo económico-social de Chile*, suggested that the nineteenth century witnessed the formation of a bourgeoisie which rose 'over the ruins of the exclusively feudal economy of the first part of the nineteenth century' (cited in Pinto 1862:3F). Anibal Pinto, in his path-breaking *Chile: Un caso de desarrollo frustrado*, which has influenced all historical and economic work on Chile since it appeared in 1957, went somewhat further back to suggest that 'independence opened the doors'; but he nonetheless maintained that only subsequently did 'foreign trade come to be the driving force of the domestic economic system' and that to the end of the eighteenth century Chile was and remained a 'recluse economy' (Pinto 1962: 13-15). Max Nolff, elaborating on Pinto's analysis, develops his theory of Chilean industrial development on the basis of the view that during the entire colonial period Chile had a 'closed subsistence economy'. Even the Marxist Hernán Ramírez (1959), whose *Antecedentes económicos de la independencia de Chile* supplies ample proof that the foregoing views of Chile in the eighteenth and later centuries are not well based, refers to a supposed 'autarchic tendency' in the Chilean economy before that time.

According to my reading of Chilean history, and Latin American history generally, such references to an autarchic, closed, recluse, feudal, subsistence economy misrepresent the reality of Chile and Latin America since the sixteenth-century conquest. Moreover, failure to recognize and understand the nature and significance of the open, dependent, capitalist export economy which has characterized and plagued Chile and her sister countries throughout their post-conquest history bears inevitable consequences in misinterpretation and misunderstanding of the real nature of capitalism today, of the real causes not only of past and present but of the still deepening underdevelopment and of the policies necessary to eliminate that underdevelopment in the future. It is to the clarification of these matters that this essay is devoted.

More specifically, I cannot accept the supposed empirical foundations and therefore the formulations of the problem of, and policy for, development in Chile as set forth by Anibal Pinto and Max Nolff (the latter, chief economic adviser to Allende, 1964 presidential candidate on the Socialist-Communist ticket) and others associated with the principles of analysis of the United Nations Economic Commission for Latin America. These analysts, beginning with the inaccurate view that Chile had a closed, recluse, subsistence economy throughout the centuries before political independence, attribute the subsequent underdevelopment of Chile's economy to Chile's supposed error in choosing development 'towards the outside' instead of development 'towards the inside', after independence, according to them, opened the door in the nineteenth century. Had Chile only chosen capitalist development towards the inside then, it would be developed now, they suggest; and they argue similarly that Chile could still develop today if it would only hurry up and finally turn to (still capitalist) development towards the inside now.

My reading of Chilean history and my analysis of capitalism oblige me to reject both this premise and conclusion. Because of capitalism, Chile's economy was already underdeveloping throughout the three centuries before independence. And, if the innate contradictions of capitalism continue to operate in Chile today, as my analysis contends that they must and my observation that they do, then no kind of capitalist development, be it towards the outside or towards the inside, can save Chile from further underdevelopment. Indeed, if dependent and underdeveloped development towards the outside has been ingrained in the Chilean economy since the conquest itself, then the supposed option for independent national capitalist development towards the inside did not even exist in the nineteenth century; much less does it exist in reality today.

1. The contradiction of expropriation/appropriation of economic surplus

The first of the three contradictions to which I trace economic development and underdevelopment is the expropriation/appropriation of economic surplus. It was Marx's analysis of capitalism which identified and emphasized the expropriation of the surplus value created by producers and its appropriation by capitalists. A century later, Paul Baran emphasized the role of economic surplus in the generation of economic development and also of underdevelopment. What Baran called 'actual' economic surplus is that part of current production which is saved and in fact invested (and thus is merely one part of surplus value). Baran also distinguished and placed greater emphasis on 'potential' or potentially investible economic surplus which is not available to society because its monopoly structure prevents its production or (if it is produced) it is appropriated and wasted through luxury consumption. The income differential between high- and low-income recipients and much of the failure of the former to channel their income into productive investment may also be traced to monopoly. Therefore, the non-realization and unavailability for investment for 'potential' economic surplus is due essentially to the monopoly structure of capitalism. I investigate below how the monopoly structure of world capitalism resulted in the underdevelopment of Chile.

The contradiction of monopolistic expropriation/appropriation of economic surplus in the capitalist system is ubiquitous and its consequences for economic development and underdevelopment manifold. To investigate the development or underdevelopment of a particular part of the world capitalist system, such as Chile (or a part of Chile), we must locate it in the economic structure of the world system as a whole and identify its own economic structure. In this study, we will see that Chile has always been subject to a high degree of external and internal monopoly. However competitive the economic structure of the metropolis may have been in any given stage of its development, the structure of the world capitalist system as a whole, as well as that of its peripheral satellites, has been highly monopolistic throughout the history of capitalist development. Accordingly, external monopoly has always resulted in the expropriation (and consequent unavailability to Chile) of a significant part of the economic surplus produced in Chile and its appropriation by another part of the world capitalist system. Specifically, I review the findings of two students of the Chilean economy who attempt to identify the contemporary potential economic surplus appropriated by others which is not available to Chile.

The monopoly capitalist structure and the surplus expropriation/appropriation contradiction run through the entire Chilean economy, past and present. Indeed, it is this exploitation relation which in chain-like fashion extends the capitalist link between the capitalist world and national metropolizes to the regional centres (part of whose surplus they appropriate), and from these to local centres, and so on to large landowners or merchants who expropriate surplus from small peasants or tenants, and sometimes even from these latter to landless labourers exploited by them in turn. At each step along the way, the relatively few capitalists above exercise monopoly power over the many below, expropriating some or all of their economic surplus and, to the extent that they are not expropriated in turn by the still fewer above them, appropriating it for their own use. Thus as each point, the international, national, and local capitalist system generates economic development for the few and underdevelopment for the many.

2. The contradiction of metropolis — satellite polarization

The second, and for our analysis the most important, capitalist contradiction was introduced by Marx in his analysis of the imminent *centralization* of the capitalist system. This contradiction of capitalism takes the form of polarization into metropolitan centre and peripheral satellites; and it was this that Viceroy Armendaris of Peru described in 1736 when he noted that the commerce of the mercantile capitalist empire of Spain, of his own Viceroyalty of Peru within it, and of the General Captaincy of Chile within that in turn, 'is a paradox of trade and a contradiction of riches ... thriving on what ruins others and being ruined by what makes others thrive'. Paul Baran observed this same contradiction two centuries later when he noted that 'the rule of monopoly capitalism and imperialism in the advanced countries and economic and social backwardness in the underdeveloped countries are intimately related, represent merely different aspects of what is in reality a global problem' (Baran 1957).

The consequences of the metropolitan centre-peripheral satellite contradiction of capitalism for economic development and underdevelopment are summarized in the *Fundamentals of Marxism-Leninism*:

> It is characteristic of capitalism that the development of some countries takes place at the cost of suffering and disaster for the peoples of other countries. For the soaring development of the economy and culture of the so-called 'civilized world', a handful of capitalist powers of Europe and North America, the majority of the world's population, the people of Asia, Africa, Latin America, and Australia paid a terrible price. The colonization of these continents made possible the rapid development of capitalism in the West. But to the enslaved peoples, it brought ruin, poverty, and monstrous political oppression. The extremely contradictory character of progress under capitalism applies even to different regions of one and the same country. The comparatively rapid development of the towns and industrial centres is, as a rule, accompanied by lagging and decline in the agricultural districts. (Kuusinen N.D.: 247-8).

Thus the metropolis expropriates economic surplus from its satellites and appropriates it for its own economic development. The satellites remain underdeveloped for lack of access to their own surplus and as a consequence of the same polarization and exploitative contradictions which the metropolis introduces and maintains in the satellite's domestic economic structure. The combination of these contradictions, once firmly implanted, reinforces the processes of development in the increasingly dominant metropolis and underdevelopment in the ever more dependent satellites until they are resolved through the abandonment of capitalism by one or both interdependent parts.

Economic development and underdevelopment are the opposite faces of the same coin. Both are the necessary result and contemporary manifestation of internal contradictions in the world capitalist system. Economic development and underdevelopment are not just relative and quantitative, in that one represents more economic development than the other; economic development and underdevelopment are relational and qualitative, in that each is structurally different from, yet caused by its relation with, the other. Yet development and underdevelopment are the same in that they are the product of a single, but dialectically contradictory, economic structure and process of capitalism. Thus they cannot be viewed as the products of supposedly different economic structures or systems, or of supposed differences in stages of economic growth achieved within the same system. One and the same historical process of the expansion and development of capitalism throughout the world has simultaneously generated — and continues to generate — both economic development and structural underdevelopment.

However, as *Fundamentals of Marxism-Leninism* suggests, the metropolis-satellite contradiction exits not only between the world capitalist metropolis and peripheral satellite countries; it is also found within these countries among their regions and between 'rapid development of the towns and industrial centres (and) lagging and decline in the agricultural districts'. This same metropolis-satellite contradiction extends still deeper and characterizes all levels and parts of the capitalist system. This contradictory metropolitan centre-peripheral satellite relationship, like the process of surplus expropriation-appropriation, runs through the entire world capitalist system in chain-like fashion from its uppermost metropolitan world centre, through each of the various national, regional, local, and enterprise centres. An obvious consequence of the satellite economy's external relations is the loss of some of its economic surplus to the metropolis. The appropriation by the metropolis of the economic surplus from this (and other satellites) is likely to generate development in the former unless, as happened to Spain and Portugal, the metropolis is in turn converted into a satellite, its surplus being appropriated by others before it can firmly launch its own development. In either event, the metropolis tends increasingly to dominate the satellite and renders it ever more dependent.

For the generation of structural underdevelopment, more important still than the drain of economic surplus from the satellite after its incorporation as such into the world capitalist system, is the impregnation of the satellite's domestic economy with the same capitalist structure and its fundamental contradictions. That is, once a country or a people is converted into the satellite of an external capitalist metropolis, the exploitative metropolis-satellite structure quickly comes to organize and dominate the domestic economic, political and social life of that people. The contradictions of capitalism are recreated on the domestic level and come to generate tendencies towards development in the national metropolis and towards underdevelopment in its domestic satellites just as they do on the world level — but with one important difference: The development of the national metropolis necessarily suffers from limitations, stultification, or underdevelopment unknown in the world capitalist metropolis — because the national metropolis is simultaneously also a satellite itself, while the world metropolis is not. Analogously, the regional, local, or sectoral metropolises of the satellite country find the limitations on their development multiplied by a capitalist structure which renders them dependent on a whole chain of metropolises above them.

Therefore, short of liberation from this capitalist structure or the dissolution of the world capitalist systems as a whole, the capitalist satellite countries, regions, localities, and sectors are condemned to underdevelopment. This feature of capitalist development and underdevelopment, the penetration of the entire domestic economic, political and social structure by the contradictions of the world capitalist system, receives special attention in this review of the Chilean experience, because it poses the problem of analysing underdevelopment and formulating political and economic policy for development in a manner signficantly different from — and I believe more realistic than — other approaches to the problem.

The above thesis suggests a subsidiary thesis with some important implications for economic development and underdevelopment: If it is satellite status which generates underdevelopment, then a weaker or lesser degree of metropolis-satellite relations may generate less deep structural underdevelopment and/or allow for more possibility of local development. The example of Chile helps to confirm these hypotheses. Moreover, from the world-wide perspective, no country which has been firmly tied to the metropolis as a satellite through incorporation into the world capitalist system has achieved the rank of an economically developed country, except by finally abandoning the capitalist system. Some countries, notably Spain and Portugal, which were part of the world capitalist metropolis at one time, did, however, become underdeveloped through having become commercial satellites of Great Britain beginning in the seventeenth century.* It is also significant for the confirmation of our thesis that the satellites have typically managed such temporary spurts in development as they have had, during wars or depressions in the metropolis, which momentarily weakened or lessened its domination over the life of the satellites. As we shall see, Chile's greater isolation from the Spanish metropolis relative to other colonies and the lessened degree of interdependence with and dependence on the metropolis in times of war or depression, have been of material aid in increasing Chile's development efforts over the centuries.

3. The contradiction of continuity in change

The foregoing two major contradictions suggest a third contradiction in capitalist economic development and underdevelopment: The continuity and ubiquity of the structural essentials of economic development and underdevelopment throughout the expansion and development of the capitalist system at all times and places. As Engels suggested, 'there is a contradiction in a thing remaining the same and yet constantly

* The development of the British ex-colonies in North America and Oceania was rendered possible because the ties between them and the European metropolis at no time matched the dependency of the now underdeveloped countries of Latin America, Africa, and Asia. The industrilization of Japan after 1868 must be traced to the fact that it was at that time the only major country that had not yet begun to underdevelop. Similarly, the fact that Thailand is today less underdeveloped than other countries of Southeast Asia is due to the fact that it was never a colony like the others, until the recent advent of United States protection initiated underdevelopment there as well.

changing'. Though structural stability and continuity may or may not have characterized 'classical' capitalist development in Europe (the metropolis), the capitalist system, throughout its expansion and development on a world scale, as a whole maintained the essential structure and generated the same fundamental contradictions. And this continuity of the world capitalist system's structure and contradictions is the determinant factor to be identified and understood if we are to analyse and effectively combat the underdevelopment of the greater part of the world today.

For this reason, my emphasis is on the continuity of capitalist structure and its generation of underdevelopment rather than on the many undoubtedly important historical changes and transformations that Chile has undergone within this structure. My general purpose is to contribute to the building of a more adequate general theory of capitalist economic development and particularly underdevelopment rather than to undertake the detailed study of past and present Chilean reality.

My emphasis on the contradiction of continuity in change implies that this contradiction in Chile has not been resolved. This does not mean that it will not be resolved. My review of the history of capitalist development in Chile shows that a number of important contradictions have been resolved through the course of time. Though it may have been thought at the time of independence, for example, that events had led or would lead to the resolution of the fundamental contradiction determining the course of Chilean history, this turned out not to be the case. It is important, therefore, to understand the really fundamental contradictions, and not to confuse them with minor contradictions that are resolved more easily and at less cost but which change nothing essential in the end, and in the long run even render the resolution of the fundamental contradictions more costly and/or more distant. I believe that a number of contemporary policies for the 'liberation' of the underdeveloped countries and the elimination of underdevelopment, well meaning though their proponents may be, make matters worse in the long run (and often in the short run as well). Understanding the realities of capitalism and underdevelopment is of course not sufficient, but it is certainly essential; there can be no successful revolution without adequate revolutionary theory. Herein lies my purpose.

Related to continuity also is discontinuity. My review of Chilean experience suggests that there may have been times in which even certain structural changes within Chile's capitalist structure *might* have materially changed the course of the country's remaining history. When these changes were not made, or the attempts to make them were not carried out as the circumstances of the times required, these opportunities — such as investment of the economic surplus produced in Chile's nitrate mines — were lost forever. The experiences of Chile suggest that the history of the development of underdevelopment in many parts of the world probably was — and still is — punctuated by such failures to take advantage of opportunities to eliminate or shorten the suffering created by underdevelopment.

14.   The Newly Industrializing Countries and Radical Theories of Development*

John Browett

Summary.— *The failure of neo-Marxist dependency perspectives to accommodate and come to terms with the possibilities of peripheral capitalist development in the four Newly Industrializing Countries (NICs) of East and Southeast Asia should not then result in the embracing of the stages approaches espoused either by modernization theory or by Warren. Rather, consideration should be given to approaches which emphasize, within the backdrop of the changing internationalization of the self-expansion of capital, the historical specificities of capital accumulation, class struggle and the role of the state in the process of social reproduction.*

1. Introduction

Kuhn (1962), in contrast to Popper, argued that scientific progress can be regarded as revolutionary in character since it involves the abandonment of one theoretical structure (paradigm) and its replacement by another one that is incompatible with the previous one (Chalmers, 1976, p. 85). Such an epistemological interpretation has previously been used in the review of the profound changes that have taken place over the last three decades in the approaches adopted by those analyzing processes which lead to patterns of unequal development within and between nations. In brief, what can be recognized is the rise and demise of the diffusionist and dependency paradigm perspectives and the subsequent attempts at their reformulation and/or transcendence by those advocating either reformist or Marxist approaches to the analysis of unequal development (see Browett, 1982).

Within this framework, this paper examines and evaluates the various conflicting interpretations that have been advanced in the attempt to explain and understand the swift and sustained economic growth performance, over the last two decades and under the stimulus of an expansion of manufactured exports, of a group of countries which have been defined and distinguished as separate entities by virtue of their attainment of these growth characteristics — the Newly Industrializing Countries (NICs). While there is no universally accepted definition of the criteria by which a country is classified as a NIC (and hence no agreement as to which countries should be so defined), a number of authors have adopted the OECD (1979) grouping of South Korea, Taiwan, Hong Kong, Singapore, Mexico, Brazil, Portugal, Greece, Yugoslavia and Spain. In this study, the particular focus is on the four NICs of East and Southeast Asia, all of which, from the early or mid-1960s onwards, have been credited with a remarkable statistical record,

* This paper was originally presented to a seminar organized by the Centre for Development Studies at Flinders University in July 1983.

especially in terms of growth rates in income and GDP per capita and manufacturing employment, output and exports (see Cypher, 1979, pp. 36-38). Though clear and obvious differences exist between the specific growth paths and processes of the four countries (a topic to be discussed later), it is their common characteristics that have commanded the most attention. In particular, what tends to be highlighted is their rapid, but narrowly based, industrial development from the 1960s onwards which, initially at least, was founded upon the labor-intensive and export-orientated production of 'non-traditional' light consumer goods, by a highly disciplined and productive but poorly paid labor force, in the context of political stability and overt foreign domination. Moreover, their impressive economic growth performance was sustained throughout the 1970s, a decade which, in comparison with the previous one, witnessed a considerable reduction in the rate of expansion of the world capitalist economy.

There tends to be some debate as to the exact nature of the economic growth and export performance of the NICs, but what is in greater dispute, and which forms the substance of this paper, is the interpretation that is to be placed upon such growth paths (and the processes underlying them) and their significance for other dependent peripheral capitalist nations, some of which are at present actively encouraging the promotion of free production zones or export platforms in an attempt to persuade multinational companies to establish manufacturing plants within their boundaries. In brief, can industrialization based on the production and export of manufactures achieve what import-substitution could not — the creation of indigenous, self-expanding capitalist development — or will it still result in dependent industrialization and a new form of imperialist domination? (Landsberg, 1979, p. 50.)

That various interpretations of the growth performance of the NICs exist is in large part due to development studies having undergone a phase not of paradigm replacement (Kuhn envisaged paradigm change as a diachronous process), but rather of paradigm accumulation. To some extent, this co-existence of competing paradigms can be attributed to the relativism inherent in the paradigm concept itself. That is, there can be no objective grounds of verification or of falsification on which to base a decision to accept or reject a particular paradigm. Neither can the expansion of the limits of our knowledge and understanding be used as a criterion, for a new paradigm may 'unsolve' problems that were susceptible to solution under the old but not under the new paradigm. Thus, while it may be possible '. . . to determine objectively whether an explanatory framework is satisfactory and reasonable *within* a specific scientific tradition' (Holt-Jensen, 1980, p. 38), it has to be recognized that the same external reality can be viewed differently through different paradigm perspectives (Lall, 1976, p. 185).

This necessity to make a subjective choice between different paradigms poses difficulties for any comparative study such as this, for the evaluation of each paradigm's reasonableness and adequacy can only be undertaken by someone who is currently working within only one of the several competing paradigms. In this instance, my perspectives would tend to fall within those termed by others as radical political economy. From these perspectives what I wish to argue, with special reference to the four NICs of East and Southeast Asia, is that the failure of the neo-Marxist dependency paradigm approaches (Frank, Wallerstein, Amin) to accommodate and come to terms with the possibilities of peripheral capitalist development should not then result in the embracing of the stages approaches espoused either by modernization theory or by the classic Marxian approach, as recently revived by Warren. Both of the latter approaches do explicitly predict and expect the emergence of the NICs, but it is maintained that they constitute an inadequate and incomplete analysis of the processes underlying the recent economic growth performance of the NICs. Rather, it is suggested that consideration should be given to approaches that emphasize, within the backdrop of the changing internationalization of the self expansion of capital, the historical specificities of the processes of capital accumulation, the complexities of class struggles and the intervention of the state in the process of social reproduction. Doubts are, however, expressed as to the utility of this conceptual approach to do anything more than provide an understanding, *ex post facto*, of what has already happened in the NICs. By definition, its predictive and generalizing power remains low.

2. Dependency paradigm perspectives

No unified theory of dependency commands universal assent; indeed, there is not even agreement as to whether or not separate dependency theories exist or can ever exist. Nevertheless, it does tend to be acknowledged that the works of Frank, Wallerstein and Amin are so sufficiently similar that they constitute and embrace something, termed a dependency paradigm or perspective, which can be regarded as an explicit alternative both to modernization theory of the diffusionist paradigm and to the classic Marxist theories of imperialism (see Brewer, 1980). Common to all of them is the notion that, as a result of dependency and unequal exchange, capitalist development in some places (the core or the metropoles) continuously and necessarily creates underdevelopment at other places (the periphery or the satellites) in the world capitalist system. While there are many deficiencies, lacunae and conceptual inadequacies associated with this position, it is not my intention to pursue them here, for indeed many (perhaps too many) critiques and reviews have already been published (see Browett, 1981, 1982 and the references contained therein). Rather, the purpose of this study is to examine, in turn, the perspectives of Frank, Wallerstein and Amin in an attempt to derive their interpretations of, and explanations for, the emergence within the world system of the NICs.

(a) *Frank*

For Frank, the recent economic growth performance of the NICs cannot be taken as evidence either of the occurrence of development or even of its possibility in the future. This is so for three principal reasons, each of which will be discussed in turn. First, Frank argues that autarchic capitalism in dependent peripheral social formations cannot achieve generalized, autonomous and independent indigenous development. For Frank there simply is no possibility of non-dependent, auto-centric, self-generating or self-perpetuating capitalist development in the periphery; and hence underdevelopment in the periphery will only be eliminated by its liberation from capitalism. Given that the development of underdevelopment in the dominated periphery was and is an indispensable condition for capital accumulation in the dominant core, satellite development (in the NICs as elsewhere) requires an absence of capitalism and hence, by implication, the necessity for a revolutionary break, de-linking, and socialism (for critiques of this position, see Johnson, 1981). The only (partial) qualification to this is the temporary experience of satellite economic development that may occur when, due to crises in the metropoles, ties to these metropoles are momentarily weakened (Frank, 1966, p. 24). However, for this to apply to the recent growth performance of the NICs, it would have to be argued that the metropoles have been in a state of crisis from the early 1960s onwards — a position, that may be difficult to sustain and anyway one Frank does not maintain. Rather, what Frank (1981, pp. 96-111; pp. 157-187) has argued in his most recent explicit analysis of the promotion of manufacturing export-led growth in what he terms secondary client states (the four NICs of East and Southeast Asia) is that attention needs to be focused on the increase in foreign debt levels and balance of payments problems, the mythological technical improvements of the labor force and the technological development of the economy, the limited contribution to reducing unemployment (except, temporarily at least, in Hong Kong and Singapore), and the incidence of super-exploitation (hours and conditions of work; poor health and safety leading to high rates of industrial accidents and disabilities; limited provision of social welfare functions; political repression and violence).

Second, Frank tends to assume, in contrast to Marx, that capitalism will always act to accentuate existing differentials in levels of development between core and periphery. In part, this assumption is one manifestation of the mirror-image trap that Frank's work tends to fall into as a result of its origins as a critique of the diffusionist paradigm perspectives. That is, the argument is similar to Myrdal's (1958, p. 25) cumulative causation approach whereby deviation-amplifying changes move a system in the same direction as the first change but much further. More than this, though, the constant deepening of the consistently unequal and asymmetrical metropole-satellite interrelationships of dominance and dependence derives from Frank's belief in historical continuity in change so that basic structures remain intact despite apparent transformations (Frank, 1967a, pp. 30-38). Hence, with consistency and continuity in change in the reproduction of underdevelopment in satellite social formations, these latter (and thus the NICs) are condemned to remain permanently underdeveloped, distorted and deformed — the passive victims of an unchanging system of exploitation within a rigidly structured world capitalist system dating from the sixteenth century. As such, Frank's conceptualization is trapped in a static and ahistorical problematic insofar that it is not able to account for changes in the structure and nature of dependent underdevelopment (of which the emergence of the NICs is a part).

Third, for Frank development is not defined by increases in GNP per capita or any other aggregate economic indicator, but by the attainment of economic sovereignty and the meeting of culturally determined needs for all people. Thus, by way of counter-factual argument, Frank, following Baran, would compare the recent growth performance of the NICs with a hypothetical situation that would have occurred if the locally produced surplus which was extracted had been utilized rationally to meet indigenous needs (Taylor, 1974, p.7) — rather than making other possible comparisons (what was occurring previously in the NICs; what is happening elsewhere in the world; what happened in nineteenth-century England during the Industrial Revolution).

In summary, then, Frank asserts: (1) that development and underdevelopment are necessarily and causally interrelated through international exchange, and hence peripheral capitalist development is impossible in the present and in any future phases of world capitalism; (2) that the continuing integration of satellites into the world capitalist economy will create further underdevelopment there; and (3) that the growth of export-led manufacturing in the NICs and the concomitant exploitation and repression of the labor force cannot in any sense be called development. Thus, simultaneously, the growth performance of the NICs does not need to be explained by Frank, but neither can it be explained by him (either it is not development, or it is impossible). Therefore if follows from this stagnationist thesis that the recording of high rates of growth in NICs does not provide any indication either that autonomous, self-sustaining capitalist development is occurring or that a basis is being laid for its evolution in the future.

(b) *Wallerstein*

For the purposes of this study, the particular significance of Wallerstein's work on world systems is in terms of the potential interpretation to be offered by his notion of the semi-periphery (an intermediate tier in between core and periphery) to the growth performance of the NICs. None of the four NICs under consideration here is, in fact, designated by Wallerstein (1976) as a semi-periphery nation, although (North) Korea is so classified. Nevertheless, at least one author (Caporaso, 1981) has sought to investigate the reasons for the rise of the NICs in terms of their semi-peripheral status. At first glance, this notion appears useful, particularly in view of the widespread belief that the increase in the manufacturing output in the NICs has been at the expense of core nation producers. However, when viewed in greater detail, it is readily apparent that the notion of a semi-periphery, located within a world system defined by unequal relations of exchange, cannot serve as a transformation path model of development for the NICs. It is a descriptive category only, and one that does not arise as an outcome of his analysis. For Wallerstein, there is no explanation internal to his schema that explains why nations will change from one category to another. The history of the semi-periphery, and most other features, are explained by Walerstein in terms of particular sociophysical conjunctures. Because they are random in their probabilities, the conjunctures are not predictable (Aronwitz, 1981, pp. 517-518). So Wallerstein would admit that, by chance, a peripheral nation could become a semi-peripheral one, but such a change is not part of the internal dynamic of his static conceptual structure, and neither can the creation of the semi-periphery be seen to be deliberate (Brewer, 1980, p. 166).

(c) *Amin*

Amin, unlike Frank, argues that the analyses of capital accumulation and of underdevelopment can only be undertaken at a world level that comprises a center and a periphery defined in terms of the unequal specialization of production (balanced development — the production of capital goods and goods for mass consumption — in the center; and unbalanced development—the production for export and the production of luxury goods — in the periphery). Such a schema explicitly advocates the unity of the periphery and of underdevelopment (despite the diversity of appearances) and hence rejects the division of a part of the periphery into a typological classification of NICs. Such typologies are superficial (Amin, 1974, p. 167), the analysis of individual countries is misleading because of the emphasis on appearances (Smith, 1980, p. 7), and the study of the economies of individual peripheral nations pointless because they '. . . have no real conjunctural phenomena of their own, even transmitted from outside, because they are without any internal dynamism of their own' (Amin, 1976, p. 279). Thus, for Amin the need to understand the recent growth performance of the NICs is, by definition and assertion, of no consequence.

Such a perspective is reinforced by Amin's position (which is very similar to that of Frank) with regard to the possibilities for local capital accumulation and development in the periphery. Amin (1980, p. 114) asserts that from the imperialist period onwards 'the door to the establishment of new capitalist centres is henceforth closed' and that 'the development of underdevelopment necessarily results in the blocking of growth, in other words, the impossibility — whatever the level of production per capita that may be attained — of going over to autonomous and self-sustained growth, to development in the true sense' (Amin, 1974, p. 393). Such growth and development in the periphery is blocked by its internal structures of productive forces and relations (unequal specialization in production and super-exploitation) and by its external rations (the transfer out of 'super-surplus' through unequal exchange), that is, by factors internal to capitalism (Brewer, 1980, p. 268).

Addressing the NICs in particular, Amin (1976, p. 212) regards the four NICs of East and Southeast Asia (and Mexico) as exhibiting a new form of inequality, while the concentration of manufacturing activities in them '... rules out the possibility of this being a development that could be extended to *all* the countries of the Third World' (Amin, 1976, p. 213). The emergence of the NICs cannot therefore be taken as evidence of the possibility of other nations emulating their growth experience because this growth is attributed to a favourable and unique coincidence of a number of special circumstances. However, although support can be found for this position (see National Planning Association, 1981; Fajnzylber, 1981) this does not mean that the possibility of replication for some nations need be ruled out since '... the development of industry generates increased incomes, widened markets, expanded demand for manufactures, etc.' (Smith, 1980, p. 20). Indeed, empirical evidence on growth rates for manufactured exports assembled by Havrylyshyn and Alikhani (1982) indicates that the economic growth paths of the NICs may well be being followed by at least 12 New Exporting Countries (NECs). Nevertheless, even if this point is conceded, for Amin the growth experience of the NICs cannot be put forward as a development model because (a) their balance of payments remains vulnerable; (b) none has approached the stage of independent and self-maintained growth; (c) their industrial growth has engendered a 'semi-aristocracy' of labor; (d) technical advancement for the workers in their industries is ruled out; and (e) the strengthened domination of central capital forbids any formation of a bourgeoisie of national entrepreneurs (Amin, 1976, pp. 213-214).

Unfortunately for Amin, it can be demonstrated that in certain instances, especially in several of the NICs, some of the negative characteristics have not materialized. For example, as Smith (1980, p. 20) again notes, 'many "NICS" have a home-grown bourgeoisie (e.g., South Korea), considerable internal dynamism and technical progress.' Such empirical evidence, though, and any other which is at odds with his views (for example, Schiffer, 1981), is dismissed by Amin (as Smith (1982) elsewhere documents herself) as empiricist, statistical acrobatics, wrong, superficial, at the level of outward appearances rather than the inner essence (with which Amin is concerned), or put forward by people who have failed to understand Marxism.

(d) *Summary*

It seems to me, therefore, that the perspectives of Frank and Amin contribute little to an understanding of the growth performance of the NICs because they, by definition, deny both its significance and its characterization as development. In many ways this will remain an unsatisfactory position until it can be shown why the development of capitalism in the periphery must always and systematically lead to an outflow of capital rather than the initiation of a process of internal capital accumulation. As argued by non-dependency Marxists (Shaikh, 1979, 1980; Weeks and Dore, 1979) the global transfer of surplus value from backward or underdeveloped capitalist regions can be regarded merely as a phenomena of uneven development in the world economy and not its major cause. What is required from Frank and Amin, therefore, is a detailed explanation of why, how and under what conditions underdevelopment has been, and still remains, a necessary and inevitable consequence of what they define as capitalism. Failing this, they must come to terms, with less dogma than previously, with what has been happening in the NICs and directly confront the empirical evidence assembled in refutation of the overstated generalizations they and others, such as Kreye (1981, p. 90), have offered with regard to the deleterious impacts of export-led industrialization in the NICs (see Tan, 1983, pp. 9-16). At the same time, the critiques of the role assigned to 'unequal exchange' as an explanation for changes in the conditions and relations of production in the NICs must be taken into account (see Kay, 1975; Pilling, 1973).

3. Stages approaches

While the economic growth rates and structural changes recorded by the NICs can be seen as constituting a serious challenge to the neo-Marxist dependency perspectives, they are readily embraced and explained in the two major states perspectives on uneven development — those of modernization theory and the orthodox Marxist position of Warren — both of which are discussed below. However, it is suggested here that, though there may be a good fit between these theories and the 'the facts' relating to the NICs, the conceptual inadequacies and omissions within both perspectives are so great as to prejudice our understanding of the *processes* underlying the growth paths exhibited by the NICs.

(a) *Modernization Theory*

Those writing from within this perspective have claimed that the assertions of the impossibility of capitalist development and the necessary and increasing immiseration of the masses in peripheral nations since the rise of capitalism were polemical (Nove,

1974), misleading or untrue (Bauer, 1976) and an exaggerated overstatement of a doctrine whose premises are dubious, its logic questionable and its conclusions improbable (Cohen, 1974, p. 5). Rather, it was suggested that the evolution of economic systems could be conceptualized in terms of a series of stages and the process of economic development in terms of the successive achievement of these stages. Within this framework, and in the midst of overwhelming evidence to the contrary — the successful Chinese and Cuban revolutions, the revolutionary struggles in Indo-China and Africa, the 'development disasters' resulting from breakdowns in progress towards modernization that occurred in Indonesia, Pakistan, Burma, Nigeria and the Sudan (Eisenstadt, 1964) — it was the NICs that emerged as the trump card of conventional neo-classical economic development theory (Hamilton, 1983, p. 137). From this viewpoint, the evolutionary transformation path of what became the NICs is seen as a 'natural' process resulting from the implementation of sound development policies (see Stecher, 1981; Balassa, 1981).

The central argument underpinning modernization theory is that there are systemative inter-relationships between development and space such that the evolution of spatial structure proceeds from a polarized, unequal pattern to one that is more equal and spatially dispersed. From this perspective, the explanations for changes in patterns of unequal development are derived from spatial processes of interaction, integration and diffusion. Thus, it is argued that economic growth and development in the NICs have been achieved through the spread of growth impulses — capital, technology, institutions and value systems — to them from more developed areas through aid programs, financial institutions, trade and multinational corporations. This successful penetration of innovative and progressive elements of modernization into the NICs in turn is attributed to their economies and societies being organized, or being capable of being organized, along commercial, capitalist lines so that their structures are roughly isomorphic with those of the more developed areas (Friedmann and Wulff, 1976, p. 20). Hence, the onset of development in the NICs could be attributed to their increasing interaction within a changing world capitalist economy and to their particularly favorable internal conditions that allowed the spread of modern economic growth and development to occur.

From this perspective, it would seem to follow that the economic development path taken by the NICs can be replicated by other peripheral nations. What needs to be specified is a new set of conditions (export-led production in sectors with comparative cost advantages; appropriate injections of planning and aid; growth center/pole enclaves of modernization) that the rest of the peripheral nations should seek to reproduce so as to facilitate those economic growth processes which have characterized and contributed to the recent growth performance of the NICs (see Balassa, 1981). Thus, development for less developed nations will involve not so much a repetition of the Euro-American development experience (as previously envisaged), but rather the transformation path from tradition to modernity as traced by the NICs.

Such an approach has, however, been subject to considerable criticism, especially from advocates of the dependency paradigm. Modernization theory has been condemned as being empirically invalid, theoretically inadequate and ineffective in policy terms

(Frank, 1967b, p. 20) insofar as '... it does not relate to those structural conditions which prevail in today's underdeveloped nations, and that it does not leave room for the attainment of social justice' (Lefeber, 1974, p. 1). Because critiques along these lines are so well established, they are not reviewed here. However, the principal difficulty I have with this approach to the NICs is in terms of what is ignored, implicitly or explicitly — the functioning of the world capitalist economy, colonialism, imperialism, the role of the state, and class structure and struggle — all of which need to be incorporated. There is still a need to investigate, as Bernstain (1976, p. 11) remarked several years ago,

> ... changes in the capitalist system and its articulation on the world scale, the diversity of form of production it encompasses, its mechanisms of appropriation and accumulation, the class alliances engendered by the new forms and modes of operation of capital, and the class struggles against capital in its various manifestations.

To date, the modernization/diffusionist stage approaches that have been transformed through the conservative re-absorption of certain features derived from the dependency/world systems perspectives have yet to take on board and consider such issues. Indeed, they would appear to have abandoned the NIC growth model (and the associated triage and lifeboat philosophies) in favor of 'worst-first' neopopulist approaches (especially those of meeting basic needs and rural sector expansion and development). Hence, rather than expounding upon the necessary internal structural transformations required to increase the capability of less developed areas to '...receive, accept and creatively elaborate upon external injections of development, democracy and modernity' (Soja, 1976, p. 15), attention is focused on more 'appropriate' approaches — collective self-reliance, progressive land reform, intermediate technology and redistribution.

(b) *Warren*

Warren (1973) sought to demonstrate empirically that, in an era when ties to the core nations had not noticeably weakened, widespread and unprecedented increases in per capita income had benefited the great majority of the world's population and that a significant number of peripheral nations (including the NICs) had successfully promoted, by way of industrialization under the auspices of capital and technology transfer, rapid national capitalist development. Since 1945, titanic strides forward have been made, Warren (1979, p. 166) asserts, in the establishment, consolidation and growth of autonomous capitalism throughout the periphery. This has been accompanied by a corresponding and historically unprecedented advance in the material welfare of the mass of the population and in the growth of productive forces.

For Warren the interpretation of these trends is not found in the dependency paradigm approaches which, by building upon Lenin's theory of imperialism, have erased from Marxism '... the view that capitalism could be an instrument of social advance in pre-capitalist societies' (Warren, 1980, p. 8). So, along with Robinson (1964, p. 45) — 'the misery of being exploited by capitalists is nothing compared to the misery of not being exploited at all' — and Kay (1975, p. x) — '...capital created underdevelopment not because it exploited the undeveloped world, but because it did not exploit enough',

Warren explicitly rejected the dependency interpretations of exploitation and of the retrogressive character of imperialism. Instead, Warren emphasized Marx's positive assessment of the progressive role of capitalism in increasing and developing the productive forces of social labor and in the socialization of that labor — the creation of material and class forces necessary both for the reproduction of capitalism and for its eventual transcendence.

While Marx focused on the uneven nature of this capitalist development, there was no presupposition either that the uneven divisions so generated would remain fixed (static) nor did Marx state that the peripheral nations would be precluded from moving upwards through the stages of capitalist development that the advanced capitalist nations had already attained (stagnationism). Marx expected that centers of accumulation would shift across space as capital spread, driven by the force of competition, in search of cheap labor, accessible raw materials, new markets and higher profits (Brewer, 1980, p. 274). The bourgeoisie must chase over the whole surface of the globe: 'it must nestle everywhere, settle everywhere, establish connections everywhere' (Marx and Engels, 1948, p. 12) and in so doing it '... compels all nations, on pain of extinction, to adopt the bourgeois mode of production' (Marx and Engels, 1948, p. 13). Hence, it was believed that the proliferation of autonomous capitalism would eventually lead to 'them' becoming more like 'us.' In the same way that the railways were expected to lead necessarily to the industrialization of India, so 'the country that is more developed industrially only shows, to the less developed, the image of its own future' (Marx, 1954, p. 19).

Accordingly, with the internationalization of finance and then production capital, all nations are runners in the same race, and the NICs are those which are breaking ahead of the rest of the laggards at the back of the field. So, for Warren, the internationalization of capital has resulted in improvements in material welfare in the NICs and has given them a basis for generating powerful indigenous sources of independent internal economic expansion. Thus, in direct contrast to the views of Frank and Amin, the possibilities of the NICs progressing along the path towards autonomous national capitalist development were seen as excellent. Correspondingly, as the national capitalisms of the NICs gather strength, so the imperialist ties of domination and control are weakened, eventually resulting in the gradual disappearance of imperialism.

It has been this last argument, as generalized to what has been happening throughout the periphery, that has been responsible for the attacks on Warren by Emmanuel (1974) and McMichael, Petras and Rhodes (1974). However, our attention will be confined to Warren's interpretation of the growth of the NICs (rather than all of the periphery). In this regard, two substantive points need to be made. First, reservations are held against the nature of the empirical evidence put forward by Warren. It can be stated that the impressive growth rates in the NICs have been accompanied not only by political repression and violence, but also by growing unemployment, poverty and inequality (the three criteria by which Seers (1972) judges whether or not development is taking place). The suspicion remains that, while multinational corporations may be developing, the people living in the NICs are not (see Catley and McFarlane, 1979): it is not the NICs that are producing the manufactured goods for export but enterprises located within them or their Free Trade Zones. Moreover, to the dangers associated with this fetishization of space, Emmanuel (1974, p. 63) adds those of the fetishization of industrialization: that if development is made synonymous with industrialization (or even more restrictively, manufacturing), then Hong Kong is already more 'developed than the United States.

Second, considerable concern is expressed with respect to Warren's assertions regarding the independent and autonomous nature of the national capitalist development in the NICs (see Landsberg, 1979, pp. 58-60). Hoogvelt (1978, pp. 84-88), for example, cites a number of common practices by multinational firms that not only enhance their domination over peripheral economies, but also reduce the potential of these economies to achieve independent capitalist development. Evidence collected by Mouzelis (1978) from another NIC (Greece) also indicated that the industrialization underway there (dependent; disarticulated with the local economy) is not as Warren envisaged. However, it is the work of Frobel, Heinrichs and Kreye (1979) that has cast the greatest doubt on the efficacy of recent industrial growth in peripheral nations to contribute to their drive for economic independence. As summarized by Wheelwright (1980, p. 52):

> The techniques involved will keep them dependent on the technology, equipment, managerial know how and markets of the traditional industrial centres... There are few linkages towards further development, such as the training of a skilled labour force, the encouragement of local industries with a local content input... the free production zones, in particular, must be regarded more as an industrial enclave only tenuously connected to the local economy, rather than an engine of growth and development.

Similarly, with regard to the four NICs of East and Southeast Asia, it seems to me that Warren has not been able to demonstrate successfully that the industrialization there has created the conditions for the independent and continued reproduction of capitalism. Nor, I suspect, can Warren's work (or the more recent data given by Schiffer, 1981) ever do so for the analysis remains at the level of outward appearance rather than with the underlying processes responsible for the emergence of the observed patterns of growth. As noted by Hamilton (1983, p. 138), Warren '... failed to locate the appearance of industrialization of a certain form and at a certain time and place in the changing structure of class relations, and these set within the international capitalist economy.'

Thus it appears that while Warren made an outstanding contribution in pointing out, especially with regard to the NICs, the untenable nature of the impossibility position of Frank and Amin, he nevertheless has not been able to provide, from Marx, a comprehensive interpretation of the uneven progress of capitalist social relations across the world space. It is the pursuit of a suitable framework of analysis to understand and evaluate this for the NICs that constitutes the following, and concluding, section of this paper.

4. The internationalization of capital

It is to be argued, following Markusen (1979, p. 40), that the focus of attention needs to be shifted away from the outward appearance of the phenomenon of patterns of spatial unevenness in development/underdevelopment (the fetishization of space — the assignment of uneven development characteristics to places so that it is the outcome which is said to be uneven) towards the dynamics of the uneven processes of the expansion of the capitalist mode of production (the uneven progress of the reproduction of capitalist social relations of production). Such an endeavour must commence with an analysis and understanding of the nature of the transition to capitalist social-productive relations (see Brenner, 1977); but it seems to me that the most appropriate broad contextual background against which the recent economic growth performance of the NICs may be examined and evaluated is that provided by the internationalization of capital and its periodization (see Palloix, 1973; 1977 and Hymer, 1972) which is resulting, as one manifestation, in a New International Division of Labor (see Frobel, Heinrichs and Kreye, 1979).

Palloix argued that the movement of capital entails two contradictory tendencies (Dunford, 1977, p. 41); they are:

> (1) the equalization and unification of the conditions of production and exchange through the valorization of capital and the tendency towards an equalization of profit rates; and
> (2) the differentiation of the conditions of production and exchange through the process of accumulation which sets up an international division of labor and results in an unequal development of the departments of production.

Thus, in this double movement of capital the internationalization of capital is one moment (manifestation) of the tendencies towards equilization and differentiation in the levels and condition of capitalist development. The analysis of this, through time, embraces the internationalization of capital as a social relation (the socialization of the labor force through the creation of wage labor and the widening of the class struggle to a global level) and the changing internationalization of the self-expansion of social capital in its three circuits — commodity $(C'C'')$, finance $(M\text{-}M')$ and production $(P\text{-}P')$ — as shown below,

$$M\text{-}C \Big\langle {{}^{MP}_{LP}} \quad \text{-}P\text{-}C'\text{-}M'\text{-}C' \Big\langle {{}^{MP}_{LP}} \quad \text{-}P'\text{-}C''$$

With the rise of what has been termed the global sub-mode of capitalist production (Gibson *et al.,* 1984) what we have been witnessing, especially since 1945, is the increasing relative importance of the internationalization of the self-expansion of the circuit of productive capital $(P\text{-}P')$ — the worldwide reorganization of industrial production sites — and the establishment, extension and deepening of the capitalist labor process on a globally organized and coordinated basis (the internationalization of capital as a social relation). One manifestation of the dispersal of world market-oriented manufacturing industry, and its concentration in free production zones or export platforms of peripheral nations in general and in NICs in particular, has been the emergence of a New International Division of Labor and an increase in the exploitation of wage labor (the generation of absolute and relative surplus labor) in the NICs. So, to the extent that there has been (a) a shift away from the periphery being almost exclusively a dependent supplier of agricultural and mineral raw materials and (b) a rise in the internationalization of productive capital in certain peripheral nations on the basis of direct foreign investment in industrial processing and assembly activities (or the international sub-contracting of such activities), then there has been an increase in the tendency towards the internationalization of the production of surplus value (Lapple, 1982, pp. 21-22).

If such a conceptual framework is accepted, then what needs to be explained and understood is: (1) why these changes have taken place in the international capitalist economy; and (2) why the new production sites are unevenly distributed in space (that is, why the phenomenon of the NICs). With regard to the first question, attention has been directed either to the necessity for the internationalization of the circuit of productive capital or to the appearance of certain developments that have made it possible for industrial production to shift offshore to peripheral nations. Each will be discussed in turn.

For most analysts, the necessity for the internationalization of the circuit of productive capital is explained in terms of changes at production sites in advanced capitalist nations in the conditions of capital accumulation and in the production of surplus value (Lapple, 1982, p. 23). For some, the internationalization of production, as represented by the abandonment by capital of the old industrial regions of the advanced capitalist nations and its search for '. . . virgin environments (to despoil), ideological and political virgin labor forces (to exploit), and higher profits,' constitutes '. . . the spatial response to the intense development of contradiction at the centre' (Peet, 1978, p. 153). In contrast, for others, 'the main reason for the build-up of manufacturing industries in the underdeveloped countries is that in many cases production at the traditional locations in the industrialized countries is no longer as profitable as production in new sites in the Third World' (Frobel, Heinrichs and Kreye, 1978, p. 23).

It seems to me that here we have two distinct and separate issues: (1) changes in the advanced capitalist nations that are resulting in a crisis for the reproduction of social relations of production and capital accumulation; and (2) the increased relative attractiveness of the peripheral (vis-à-vis the advanced capitalist) nations for the valorization and accumulation of capital — which, because they are not always made explicit, tend to be confused. For the first issue, what needs to be explained by Peet and others is why the conditions and opportunities for the self-expansion of the circuit of productive capital in the advanced capitalist nations have deteriorated in absolute terms. This, for some, would indicate the need to investigate those mechanisms that are said to generate contradictions which capitalism must overcome and resolve. These are: (1) the cyclical imbalances arising from over-production or underconsumption (the contradictions in the capitalist mode of production of laborers as producers and consumers and the conflicts between the needs of the individual capitalist and of capital in general — see de Janvry and Garramon, 1977 — manifested in a crisis of the realization of surplus value); and (2) the tendency for the rate of profit to decline because of the rising organic composition of capital (the crisis of the generation of surplus value).

The underconsumptionists, however, must undertake much more detailed investigations of the processes underpinning the uneven progress of the reproduction of capitalist social relations and forces of production in advanced capitalist nations to explain the failure of the resolution of underconsumption through the investment of the surplus product in further means of production (i.e., in Department 1 industries). In contrast, the advocates of the tendency for a falling rate of profit need a similar investigation to explain why there has not been rapid technical progress in the production of means of production (the cheapening of the elements of constant capital, as envisaged by Marx) corresponding to, and concomitant with, the rapid technical progress in the consumer goods industries (see Brewer, 1980, p. 36).

To date there is little evidence of such explanations being provided by those examining the internationalization of capital. Nor do I believe is there much to be gained in the attempt, since the necessity viewpoint in untenable: it cannot be theoretically sustained. It is not possible to derive from the logic of capital accumulation and reproduction in general the inexorable necessity for the penetration of peripheral nations by the circuit of productive capital. Rather, it is suggested, much greater insights can be gained by analyzing the logic of capitalist competition that forces individual capitals, on pain of extinction, to search continually for cheaper labor and higher profits. This is particularly the case, as Bienefeld (1981, p. 92) points out, when competitive pressures between individual capitals in the advanced capitalist nations are intensified. Thus, as was suggested earlier in the quote by Frobel, Heinrichs and Kreye (1978, p. 23), production sites in the advanced capitalist nations, *vis-à-vis* those in peripheral nations, have proved relatively less attractive to productive capital; and it is simply the existence of this which needs to be invoked to explain the trends observed in the internationalization of capital. This is so because where such differentials exist they cannot be ignored by individual capitals; they have to be exploited because of the driving force and logic of capitalist competition. It must be emphasized, though, that the existence of these spatial differentials is not a systematic requirement nor are they necessary for the self-expansion of the circuit of productiive capital. They do, however have to be explained.

It is generally recognized that a number of changes have been particularly significant in enhancing, especially since 1945, the possibilities of accelerated accumulation and capital expansion at peripheral locations (and so to the changes in the internationalization of capital as manifest in part, in the growth performance of the NICs). At the outset, it is argued that to lay the foundations for renewed accumulation a process of restructuring according to the operation of the law of value occurs (see Kay, 1975). For certain capitals, this entails breaking the circuit of, and devalorizing, productive capital. As both cause and effect of this reorganization of the ownership of capital, there is a tendency for an increase in the centralization and concentration of capital, the joint handmaidens of the socialization of capital. That is, as both premise for, and response to, the growth in the scale of material production (Kay, 1975, p. 76-77)

231

and the growing social character of the productive forces, particularly the increasing degree of interdependence between the different sectors and branches of production (Harnecker, 1976, pp. 51-56) there has been a growing centralization of capital. By this is meant the fusion of different capitals under a common command (Dunford, 1977, p. 8), or that 'different firms collaborate with each other, set up consortiums or merge to form much larger units' (Kay, 1975, p. 76). Similarly, as both cause and effect of the growth in the scale of material production established by accumulation (and the increasing organic composition of capital and increased potentialities for production in large complex units of production — both of which reduce the possibilities of new entrants) and, more importantly, of competition that eliminates smaller and weaker firms, there has been a growing concentration of capital — a slower process that entails the growth in value in each major capitalist firm (Dunford, 1977, p. 8).

The growing concentration and centralization of capital at an international scale has facilitated the 'transnational organization of production and an internationalization of corporate-related services' (Lapple, 1982, p. 24). Particularly crucial here has been the growth of the international capital market for the mobilization of capital which, as both cause and effect, has resulted in the '... existence of enormous quantities of finance which states in question [the NICs] could borrow for a very long time at no charge, that is with interest rates below international rates of inflation' (Bienefeld, 1981, p. 92). At the same time, the increasingly high standards of production and scientific management and the concomitant increasingly socialized character of the labor process has simplified complex production processes into a variety of elementary functions that can largely be performed by briefly trained, low-paid unskilled workers at approximately the same productivity levels as those pertaining in advanced capitalist nations (Lapple, 1982, p. 24; Wheelwright, 1980, p. 49; Urry, 1981, p. 468). In combination with the emergence of a globally efficient transport and communications technology, this development has meant that deskilled and fragmented mass production and assembly work can be performed at various locations, including the global periphery (while for now at least, the skilled jobs, and the research and development, finance, technological management and control functions remain at sites in the advanced capitalist nations). These changes have made the organization of the different stages of production decreasingly dependent upon either the availability of skilled labor in the advanced capitalist nations or on geographic distance.

Such flexibility has been exploited, particularly by the larger units of capital. With the modernization (capitalization) of agriculture, the population explosion and increasing landlessness in the peripheral nations, there has emerged a huge (and potentially inexhaustible) industrial reserve army of labor. This labor is productive, less expensive and less militant than either the reserve army of labor in the advanced capitalist nations or that potentially available through the operation of a controlled overseas migrant/guest worker labor market. As a result of this, and the growing contradiction between the increasing social character of the productive forces and the private character of appropriation and ownership of means of production in the advanced capitalist nations, one dimension of the reorganization of capital has been that capital accumulation under more flexible labor supply conditions has been facilitated through the internationalization of the self-expansion of the circuit of productive capital. Indeed, such a conceptual schema is referred to by Crough and Wheelwright (1980) in their notion of the functional division of the Pacific Rim into raw material suppliers (Canada, Australia, New Zealand), manufacturing assembly (the NICs, Malaysia, Philippines) and control (United States, Japan).

It must, however, be recognized that the expected responses of capital to favorable or unfavorable spatial variations in the conditions for accumulation may not always be forthcoming. At present, certain fractions of capital are potentially more mobile than in the past. Because they may operate on a more coordinated scale they have the option to relocate their production sites if such a course ensures capital accumulation under more favorable conditions. On the other hand, they may remain in place. Apart from anything else, the historic role of stupidity and error should not be underrated (Brewer, 1980, p. 15). Hence, we can only state with any certainty that the uneven nature of the processes of the reproduction of capitalist social relations of production and of self-expansion of capital, when aggregated through a multitude of decisions and struggles, may have differential spatial outcomes.

The growth performance of the NICs must be reviewed in the context of these changes and the enhanced possibilities available to individual capitalists for generating higher levels of surplus value in the periphery (in comparison with sites in the advanced capitalist nations). Two specific questions need to be addressed. First, given that spatial concentration is not a necessary requirement or systematic consequence of the logic of capital accumulation imperatives, why did the internationalization of the circuit of productive capital result in the location of most new productive activities in only a small number of nations, that were subsequently characterized as NICs. The four NICs of East and Southeast Asia in 1972, produced almost half of the manufacture goods imported by the advanced capitalist nations from the peripheral nations (Nayyar, 1978, p. 76). Second, although the internationalization of the circuit of productive capital is not disputed, the question that remains is the extent of its relative contribution to the growth of manufacturing activity in the NICs (in comparison with other factors, such as the role of the state sector, that have promoted the expansion of indigenous industrialization). If one accepts (as I do) that the NICs are neither the deliberate creation of the world capitalist system nor its passive victims with no internal dynamic of their own, then the attempt to answer these questions appears to lead directly back to Wallerstein's conjunctures and the tyranny of the unique.

What needs to be specified, though, is the exact nature of the internal dynamics and how and why were they significant. How, and why did they emerge in the NICs, but not elsewhere? How, why, and by whom were they utilized to produce such growth and industrialization? Certainly, the internationalization of capital does not occur in the midst of undifferentiated peripheral nations (nor is there homogeneity within peripheral nations); but this trite observation is too general to be of analytic value. It is necessary to go beyond this in search of empirically based lower order theories; and the only way that I know how to do this is through detailed, and historical, empirical analyses not just of the internal structure of the NICs, but also of the internationalization of capital.

To date, the examination of this latter, even when periodized, has not been carried out at a sufficiently disaggregated level — in part because of the limited amount of consistent and comprehensive data which are available (see Nayyar, 1978). Nevertheless, explanations still need to be given as to the form of capital exports and investments and to the reasons why particular branches of production did or did not seek to shift offshore. For it is patently obvious that since 1945 not all branches of production or all components of capital within one branch have been 'internationalized' — and these differentials require explanation. The accumulation requirements of different fractions of capital are so divergent (at any one time and over time) that maintaining the analysis at the level of productive capital in general is likely to obscure more than it reveals. The responses of different components and fractions of capital to spatial unevenness in the conditions for accumulation may take a vast number of forms. In part, these forms are a function of the specific nature of the existing spatial unevenness and the requirements, at any one time, of the particular fraction of capital under consideration (Massey, 1978, p. 114). All of this needs to be understood in order to explain the growth performance of the NICs.

At the same time, the relative importance, and its change over time, of the offshore productive investment needs to be kept in mind. Evidence is already available from OECD studies (quoted in Lapple, 1982, pp. 3-4) that between 1970 and 1977 the increase in foreign direct investment by OECD members in Third World nations (from 3.7 billion US dollars to 8.8 billion) was considerably less than that of portfolio investment (from 1.2 billion US dollars to 11.3 billion). Moreover, only one-third of the total direct foreign investment takes place between advanced capitalist nations and the Third World (the remaining two-thirds takes place between the advanced capitalist nations themselves). Indeed, Nayyar (1978) has documented the relative unimportance of direct foreign investment in the volume of manufactured exports from peripheral nations vis-à-vis (1) direct foreign investment in the export of primary commodities and raw materials, (2) non-foreign owned manufacturing exports from peripheral nations, or (3) direct foreign investment in the export of manufactured goods from advanced capitalist nations. Nevertheless, Nayyar (1978) points to two factors not revealed in these comparisons, and that are particularly important for the four NICs of East and Southeast Asia; they are: (1) the significant and dominating role played by the international buying groups (retail firms and trading houses); and (2) the phenomenal growth in the international subcontracting of assembly work.

In addition, and equally important, detailed analyses of the favorable and distinctive economic and political conditions within the NICs also need to be undertaken. Again, it is patently obvious from any historically specific study that considerable differences existed in the conditions of the four NICs of East and Southeast Asia in the 1950s (for example, their different colonial experiences; the smaller labor force and agricultural sector in Hong Kong and Singapore). The nature of their subsequent economic growth paths has also been vastly different (for example, the greater domination of the export economy of Singapore by direct foreign investment; the role of indigenous capital, the growth of heavy industry and chemicals, and the greater role played by Japan in South Korea and Taiwan). Within all of this diversity it needs to be determined what were the common, yet distinctive (vis-à-vis the non-NIC peripheral nations) conditions upon which and by which the rapid growth took place (the reasons for political stability, low risk, and labor docility for example).

For me, this requires an understanding of the processes and forces underlying and maintaining the growth performance of the NICs. In particular, explanations are required as to why capital expansions in the NICs did not sow the seeds of its own downfall insofar as its presence could be expected to disrupt the favorable pre-existing social conditions that had made possible the expectations of expanded capital accumulation. It is perhaps here, in asking this question, that the task of explaining the NICs becomes clearer. If one needs to understand how conditions favorable to continued capital valorization and accumulation have been preserved, it is surely necessary to understand: (1) the articulation of those elements of the capitalist mode of production with pre-capitalist modes (where applicable); and (2) the nature of the capital-labor relation within the capitalist mode of production. This, in turn, brings into focus the consideration of the dynamics of class formation, class-consciousness and class conflict and the role of the state.

Yet again, even superficial acquaintance with the four NICs of East and Southeast Asia should be sufficient to indicate the great diversity both in the material contexts within which the state performs its functions (see Hamilton, 1983) and in the vast and intricate mosaics of internal class structures and class struggles. Hence it is suggested that the assertion of imprecise and vague abstract conceptualizations should give way to analyses that consider the specificity of the historical process in each of the NICs. Such analyses should include also an explanation of the self-expansion both of productive capital *and* of capital as a social relation so that the outcomes of capitalist development are seen as the result of the particular balance of class forces and the particular dynamics of class struggle. It must be remembered that people are not merely passive agents of the 'structure' and its reproductive requirements, but are active classes which, within certain constraints, are able to act upon, shape and transform their social world (Mouzelis, 1980, p. 371). Thus, within the context of the internationalization of capital and concrete historical experience what is required is a '. . . systematic analysis of the historical course of the process of capital accumulation, of the complex class confrontations and class struggles and of the specific intervention by the state in the process of social reproduction' (Lapple and van Hoogerstraten, 1980, pp. 131-132). The understanding of the recent economic experience of the NICs can never be derived simply by its reading off from theory, no matter how elegant or comprehensive the theory may be. Formulations such as 'the process of capital accumulation leads to the need for a perpetual increase in the productivity of social labor to maintain and increase the rate of surplus value extraction, which leads in turn to the need for increased specialization and division of labor' are far too simplistic and deterministic. The processes underlying the growth and spatial movement of capital are spontaneous and socially unplanned (Lapple and van Hoogstraten, 1980, p. 124), are extremely complex and can be mutually contradictory.

Whether or not inductively derived and supported generalization on which we can base predictions as to generation (the continuing reproduction of capitalist social relations and forces of production) or degeneration (a Frankian desolate wasteland) in the NICs will come from the analyses suggested above is open to some doubt. My own feelings are that they may not. Moreover, doubts are also raised in terms of the significance that the growth performance of the NICs has for other incipient NICs (Philippines, Malaysia, Indonesia, Thailand, Sri Lanka) and for the possible opening up there of greater potentialities for the production of surplus value (see Shinohara, 1983, pp. 66-67). Without necessarily wishing to revert to a position whereby everything is conjunctural, it does seem that we must recognize the ever-changing forces at work, both in these incipient NICs and in the world capitalist economy. On the one hand, it is the environment that capitalism encounters on its expansion path (rather than capitalism *per se*) which, in large part, renders the process of expansion uneven (Markusen, 1979, p. 42). On the other hand, reference has already been made to the rising relative importance in the 1970s of portfolio investment, while changes that may be expected in the foreseeable future (the widespread adoption of robot technology, for example) could well change again the relative attractiveness of different areas for capital accumulation and so initiate further in the location of sites utilized by productive capital (in this case back to the advanced capitalist nations).

Despite such doubts, it does seem to me that detailed study of the specific characteristics of economic, social and political change in the present-day NICs should facilitate the gaining of greater insights into the chances of other peripheral areas being able to take advantage of the current possibilities for enhanced capital accumulation. At the same time, through the analytical backdrop provided by the examination of the internationalization of capital, the possibilities for further capital accumulation in the NICs can be more fully understood and appreciated. This does not mean, however, that such a contextual approach can be regarded as definitive. An urgent need still remains for ongoing research into the theoretical conceptualization of the processes leading to transformations within the contemporary capitalist world economy and the confrontation of this with the concrete reality and lived experience of uneven development.

Note

1. For Palliox (1977, p. 1), the self-expansion of capital includes: (1) the realization of capital, '. . . which means that capital is set in motion and goes through the three circuits . . .;' and (2) 'expansion, meaning the increase in value of capital due to the action of labor upon it.'

References

Amin, S., (1974) *Accumulation on a World Scale: A Critique of the Theory of Underdevelopment* (New York: Monthly Review Press).

Amin, S. (1976) *Unequal Development: An Essay on the Social Formation of Peripheral Capitalism* (New York: Monthly Review Press).

Amin, S. (1980) *Class and Nation: Historically and in the Current Crisis* (London: Heinemann).

Aronowitz, S., (1981) 'A meta-theoretical critique of Immanuel Wallerstein's "The Modern World System,"' *Theory and Society*, Vol. 10, No. 4, pp. 503-520.

Balassa, B., (1981) *The Newly Industrializing Countries in the World Economy* (New York: Pergamon).

Bauer, P. T., (1976) 'Western guilt and Third World poverty,' *Commentary*, Vol. 61, No. 1, pp. 31-38.

Bernstein, H. (ed), (1976) *Underdevelopment and Development* (Harmondsworth: Penguin, first published in 1973).

Bienefeld, H., (1981) 'Dependency and the Newly Industrializing Countries (NICs): Towards a Reapraisal,' Chapter 2 in D. Seers (ed.), *Dependency Theory: A Critical Reassessment* (London: Francis Pinter).

Brenner, R., (1977) 'The origins of capitalist development: A critique of Neo-Smithian Marxism,' *New Left Review*, No. 104, pp. 25-92.

Brewer, A., (1980) *Marxist Theories of Imperialism: A Critical Survey* (London: Routledge & Kegan Paul).

Browett, J. G., (1981) 'Into the cul de sac of the dependency paradigm with A. G. Frank,' *Australia and New Zealand Journal of Sociology*, Vol. 17, No. 1, pp. 14-25.

Browett, J. G., (1982) 'Out of the dependency perspectives,' *Journal of Contemporary Asia*, Vol. 12, No. 2, pp. 145-157.

Caporaso, J. A., (1981) 'Industrialization in the periphery: The evolving global division of labor,' *International Studies Quarterly*, Vol. 25, No. 3, pp. 347-384.

Catley, B. and McFarlane, B., (1979) 'An Australian perspective on the "New International Economic Order,"' *Austrialian Left Review*, Vol. 71, pp. 6-17.

Chalmers, A. F., (1976) *What is This Thing Called Science?* (St. Lucia, Qld.: University of Queensland Press).

Cohen, B. J., (1974) *The Question of Imperialism* (London: Macmillan).

Crough, G. and Wheelwright, E. L., (1980) 'Australia, the Client State: A Study in Dependent Development,' mimeo. (Department of Economics, University of Sydney).

Cypher, J. M., (1979) 'The internationalization of capital and the transformation of social formations: A critique of the Monthly Review School.' *Review of Radical Political Economics*, Vol. 11, No. 4, pp. 33-49.

De Janvry, A. and Garramon, C. (1977) 'Laws of motion of capital in the center-periphery structure', *Review of Radical Political Economics*, Vol. 9, No. 2, pp. 29-38.

Dunford, M. F., (1977) 'Regional policy and restructuring of capital. '*Urban and Regional Studies Working Paper* 4 (Brighton: The University of Sussex).

Eisenstadt, S. N., (1964) 'Breakdowns of modernization,' *Economic Development and Cultural Change*, Vol. 12, pp. 345-367.

Fajnzylber, F., (1981) 'Some reflections on South-East Asian export industrialization,' *Cepal Review*, Vol. 15, pp. 111-132.

Emmanuel, A., (1974) 'Myths of development versus myths of underdevelopment,' *New Left Review*, Vol. 85, pp. 61-82.

Frank, A. G., (1966) 'The development of underdevelopment,' *Monthly Review*, Vol. 18, No. 4, pp. 17-31.

Frank. A. G., (1967a) *Capitalism and Underdevelopment in Latin America*, (New York: Monthly Review Press).

Frank A. G., (1976b) 'Sociology of underdevelopment and underdevelopment of sociology,' *Catalyst*, Vol. 3, pp. 20-73.

Frank, A. G., (1981) *Crisis: In the Third World* (London: Heinemann).

Friedmann, J. and Wulff, R., (1976) *The Urban Transition: Comparative Studies of Newly Industrializing Societies* (London: Edward Arnold).

Frobel, F., J. Heinrichs and O. Kreye., (1978) 'Export-oriented industrialization of underdeveloped countries', *Monthly Review*, Vol. 30, No. 6, pp. 22-27.

Frobel, F., J. Heinrichs and O. Kreye, (1979) *The New International Division of Labour* (Cambridge: Cambridge University Press).

Gibson, K. *et al.*, (1984) 'A theoretical approach to capital and labour restructuring,' pp. 39-64 in P. O'Keefe (ed.), *Regional Restructuring Under Advanced Capitalism* (London: Croom Helm).

Hamilton, C., (1983) 'Capitalist Industrialization in the Four Little Tigers of East Asia', Chapter 10 in P. Limequeco and B. McFarlane (eds.), *Neo-Marxist Theories of Development* (London: Croom Helm).

Harnecker, M., (1976) *The Basic Concepts of Historical Materialism* (University of Sydney, Department of Philosophy).

Havrylyshyn, O. and Alikhani, I., (1982) 'Is there a case for export optimism? An inquiry into the existence of a second generation of successful exporters,' *Weltwirtschafliches Archiv*, Vol. 118, No. 4, pp. 651-663.

Holt-Jensen, A., (1980) *Geography: Its History and Concepts* (London: Harper & Row).

Hoogevelt, A. M. M., (1978) *The Sociology of Developing Societies*, 2nd ed (London: Macmillan).

Hymer, S., (1972) 'The Multinational Corporation and the Law of Uneven Development,' pp. 113-140 in J. Bhagwati (ed.), *Economics and World Order From the 1970s to the 1990s* (London: Collier-Macmillan).

Johnson, C., (1981) 'Dependency theory and processes of capitalism and socialism,' *Latin American Perspectives*, Vol. 8, Nos. 3 and 4, pp. 55-81.

Kay, G., (1975) *Development and Underdevelopment: A Marxist Analysis* (London: Macmillan).

Kreye, O., (1981) 'Dependency in the 1980s,' Chapter 4 in C. Saunders (ed.), *The Political Economy of New and Old Industrial Countries* (London: Butterworth).

Kuhn, T. S., (1962) *The Structure of Scientific Revolutions* (Chicago: University of Chicago Press).

Lall, S., (1976) 'Conflicts of concepts: Welfare economics and developing countries,' *World Development*, Vol. 4, pp. 181-195.

Landsberg. M., (1979) 'Export-led industrialisation in the Third World: manufacturing imperialism,' *Review of Radical Political Economics*, Vol. 11, No. 4, pp. 50-63.

Lapple, D., (1982) 'Internationalization of Capital and the Regional Problems,' paper given at the 10th World Congress of Sociology, Mexico City.

Lapple, D., and P. van Hoogstraten, (1980) 'Remarks on the Spatial Structure of Capitalist Development: The Case of the Netherlands,' Chapter 6 in J. Carney, R. Hudson and J. Lewis (eds). *Regions in Crisis: New Perspectives in European Regional Theory* (London: Croom Helm).

Lefeber, L., (1974) 'On the paradigm for economic development,' *World Development*, Vol. 2, No. 1, pp. 1-8.

McMichael, P., J. Petras and R. Rhodes., (1974) 'Imperialism and the contradictions of development,' *New Left Review*, Vol 85, pp. 83-104.

Markusen, A. R., (1979) 'Regionalism and the capitalist state: The case of the United States,' *Kapitalistate*, Vol. 7, pp. 39-62.

Marx, K., (1954) *Capital*, Vol. 1 (Moscow: Progress).

Marx, K., and F. Engels, (1948) *The Communist Manifesto* (New York: International).

Massey, D., (1978) 'Regionalism: some current issues,' *Capital and Class*. Vol. 6, pp. 105-125.

Mouselis, N. P., (1978) *Modern Greece* (New York: Holmes & Meier).

Mouselis, N. P., (1980) 'Modernization, underdeveloped, uneven development: Prospects of a theory of Third World formations,' *Journal of Peasant Studies*, Vol 7, No. 3, pp. 353-374.

Mydral, G., (1958) *Economic Theory and Underdeveloped Regions* (Bombay: Vora).

National Planning Association, (1981) 'The emergence of the newly industrializing countries.' *Development Digest*, Vol. 19, No. 2, pp. 1-26.

Nayyar, D., (1978) 'Transnational corporations and manufactured exports from poor countries,' *The Economic Journal*, Vol. 88, No. 1, pp. 59-84.

Nove, A., (1974) 'On reading Andre Gunder Frank,' *Journal of Development Studies*, Vol. 10, pp. 445-455.

O.E.C.D., (1979) *The Impact of the Newly Industrializing Countries on Production and Trade in Manufactures* (Paris: OECD).

Palloix, C., (1973) *Les Firmes Multinationales et le Proces d'Internatinalisation* (Paris: Maspero), pp. 137-163, extracted and translated as 'The Internationalization of Capital and the Circuit of Social Capital,' Chapter 3 in H. Radice (ed.), *International Firms and Modern Imperialism* (Harmondsworth: Penguin, 1975).

Palloix, C., (1977) 'The self-expansion of capital on the world scale,' *Review of Radical Political Economics* Vol. 9, No. 2, pp. 1-28.

Peet, R., (1978) 'Materialism, social formation, and socio-spatial relations: An essay in Marxist geography,' *Cahiers de Geographie du Quebec*, Vol. 22, pp. 147-157.

Pilling, G., (1973) 'Imperialism, trade and "unequal exchange": The work of Aghiri Emmanuel,' *Economy and Society*, Vol. 2, No. 2, pp. 164-185.

Robinson, J., (1964) *Economic Philosophy* (Garden City, New York: Doubleday).

Shaikh, A., (1979) 'Foreign trade and the Law of Value: Part I,' *Science and Society*, Vol. 43, No. 3, pp. 281-302.

Shaikh, A., (1980) 'Foreign trade and the Law of Value: Part II,' *Science and Society*, Vol. 44, No. 1, pp. 27-57.

Schiffer, J., (1981) 'The changing post-war pattern of development: The accumulation wisdom of Samir Amin,' *World Development*, Vol. 9, No. 6, pp. 515-537.

Seers, D., (1972) 'What are we trying to measure?,' *Journal of Development Studies*, Vol. 8, pp. 21-36.

Shinohara, M., (1983) 'More NICs in time,' *Fareastern Economic Review*, 28 April, p. 66-67.

Smith, S., (1980) 'The ideas of Samir Amin: theory or tautology?,' *Journal of Development Studies*, Vol. 17, No. 1, pp. 5-21.

Smith, S., (1982) 'Class analysis versus world systems: Critique of Samir Amins's typology of underdevelopment,' *Journal of Contemporary Asia*, Vol. 12, No. 1, pp. 7-18.

Soja, E. W., (1976) 'Spatial inequality in Africa,' *Comparative Urbanization Studies Occasional Paper 17* (School of Architecture and Urban Planning, University of California at Los Angeles).

Stecher, B., (1981) 'The Pick of Economic Policies,' Chapter 1 in C. Saunders (ed.), *The Political Economy of New and Old Industrial Countries* (London: Butterworth).

Tan, G., (1983) 'The Newly Industrializing Countries of Asia,' Mimeo. (School of Social Sciences, Flinders University of South Australia).

Taylor, J., (1974) 'Neo-marxism and underdevelopment — A sociological phantasy,' *Journal of Contemporary Asia*, Vol. 4, pp. 5-23.

Urry, J., (1981) 'Localities, regions and social class,' *International Journal of Urban and Regional Research*, Vol. 5, No. 4, pp. 455-474.

Wallerstein, I., (1976) 'Semi-peripheral countries and the contemporary world crisis,' *Theory and Society*, Vol 3, No. 4, pp. 461-483.

Warren, W., (1973) 'Imperialism and capitalist industrialization,' *New Left Review*, Vol. 81, pp. 3-44.

Warren, W., (1979) 'The post-war economic experience of the Third World,' pp. 144-168 in Rothko Chapel Colloquium, *Toward a New Strategy for Development* (New York: Pergamon).

Warren, W., (1980) *Imperialism: Pioneer of Capitalism* (London: New Left Books).

Weeks, J. and E. Dore., (1979) 'International exchange and the causes of backwardness,' *Latin American Perspectives*, Vol. 6, No. 2, pp. 62-87.

Wheelwright, E. L., (1980) 'The new International Division of Labour in the age of the transnational corporation,' pp. 43-58, in J. Friedmann, T. Wheelwright and J. Connell, *Development Strategies in the Eighties*. Monograph No. 1. Development Studies Colloqueium, Department of Town and Country Planning, University of Sydney, NSW.

15. The Origins of Capitalist Development: a Critique of Neo-Smithian Marxism

Robert Brenner

The appearance of systematic barriers to economic advance in the course of capitalist expansion — the 'development of underdevelopment' — has posed difficult problems for Marxist theory. There has arisen, in response, a strong tendency sharply to revise Marx's conceptions regarding economic development. In part, this has been a healthy reaction to the Marx of the *Manifesto*, who envisioned a more or less direct and inevitable process of capitalist expansion: undermining old modes of production, replacing them with capitalist social productive relations and, on this basis, setting off a process of capital accumulation and economic development more or less following the pattern of the original homelands of capitalism. In the famous phrases of the *Communist Manifesto*: 'the bourgeoisie cannot exist without constantly revolutionizing the instruments of production and thereby the relations of production, and with them the whole relations of society. Conservation of the old modes of production in an altered form was, on the contrary, the first condition of existence for all earlier industrial classes. Constant revolutionizing of production, uninterrupted disturbance of all social conditions, everlasting uncertainty, and agitation distinguish the bourgeois epoch from all earlier ones. The bourgeoisie ... draw all, even the most barbarian nations into civilization. The cheap prices of its commodities are the heavy artillery with which it batters down all Chinese walls ... It compels all nations, on pain of extinction, to adopt the bourgeois mode of production; it compels them to introduce what it calls civilization into their midst, to become bourgeois themselves. In a word, *it creates a world after its own image.*'

Many writers have quite properly pointed out that historical developments since the mid-nineteenth century have tended to belie this 'optimistic', 'progressist' prognosis, in that the capitalist penetration of the 'third world' through trade and capital investment not only has failed to carry with it capitalist economic development, but has erected positive barriers to such development. Yet the question remains, where did Marx err? What was the theoretical basis for his incorrect expectations? As can be seen from the above quotation and many others from the same period,[1] Marx was at first quite confident that capitalist economic expansion, through trade and investment, would inevitably bring with it the transformation of pre-capitalist social-productive relations — i.e. class relations — and the establishment of capitalist social-productive relations, a *capitalist class structure*. It was clearly on the premise that capitalist expansion would lead to the establishment of capitalist social relations of production on the ruins of the old modes, that he could predict world-wide economic development in a capitalist image.

Robert Brenner: 'The Origins of Capitalist Development: a Critique of Neo-Smithian Marxism' from *NEW LEFT REVIEW* (1977), No. 104, pp. 25-33 and 90-92. Reproduced by permission of Verso/New Left Books.

But, suppose capitalist expansion through trade and investment failed to break the old modes of production (a possibility which Marx later envisaged[2]); or actually tended to strengthen the old modes, or to erect other non-capitalist systems of social relations of production in place of the old modes? In this case, Marx's prediction would fall to the ground. For whatever Marx thought about the origins of capitalist social-productive relations, he was quite clear that their establishment was indispensable for the development of the productive forces, i.e. for capitalist economic development. If expansion through trade and investment did not bring with it the transition to capitalist social-productive relations — manifested in the full emergence of labour power as a commodity — there could be no capital accumulation on an extended scale. In consequence, the analysis of capitalist economic development requires an understanding, in the first place, of the manner in which the capitalist social-productive relations underpinning the accumulation of capital on an extended scale originated. In turn, it demands a comprehension of the way in which the various processes of capitalist expansion set off by the accumulation of capital brought about, or were accompanied by, alternatively: 1. the further erection of capitalist class relations; 2. merely the interconnection of capitalist with pre-capitalist forms, and indeed the strengthening of the latter; or 3. the transformation of pre-capitalist class relations, but without their substitution by fully capitalist social-productive relations of free wage labour, in which labour power is a commodity. In every case, it is class relations which clearly become pivotal: the question of their transformation in relationship to economic development.

Introduction

I shall argue that the *method* of an entire line of writers in the Marxist tradition has led them to displace class relations from the centre of their analyses of economic development and underdevelopment. It has been their intention to negate the optimistic model of economic advance derived from Adam Smith, whereby the development of trade and the division of labour unfailingly bring about economic development. Because they have failed, however, to discard the underlying individualistic-mechanist presuppositions of this model, they have ended up by erecting an alternative theory of capitalist development which is, in its central aspects, the mirror image of the 'progressist' thesis they wish to surpass. Thus, very much like those they criticize, they conceive of (changing) class relations as emerging more or less directly from the (changing) requirements for the generation of surplus and development of production, under the pressures and opportunities engendered by a growing world market. Only, whereas their opponents tend to see such market-determined processes as setting off, automatically, a dynamic of economic development, they see them as enforcing the rise of economic backwardness. As a result, they fail to take into account either the way in which class structures, once established, will in fact determine the course of economic development or underdevelopment over an entire epoch, or the way in which these class structures themselves emerge: as the outcome of class struggles whose results are incomprehensible in terms merely of market forces. In consequence, they move too quickly from the proposition that capitalism is bound up with, and supportive of, continuing underdevelopment in large parts of the world, to the conclusion not only that the rise of underdevelopment is inherent in the extension of the world division of labour through capitalist expansion, but also that the 'development of underdevelopment' is an indispensable condition for capitalist development itself.

Frank and capitalist development

It has thus been maintained that the very same mechanisms which set off underdevelopment in the 'periphery' are prerequisite to capital accumulation in the 'core'. Capitalist development cannot take place in the core unless underdevelopment is developed in the periphery, because the very mechanisms which determine underdevelopment are required for capitalist accumulation. In the words of André Gunder Frank, 'economic development and underdevelopment are the opposite faces of the same coin'. As Frank goes on to explain: 'Both [development and underdevelopment] are the necessary result and contemporary manifestation of internal contradictions in the world capitalist system ... economic development and underdevelopment are relational and qualitative, in that each is actually different from, yet caused by its relations with, the other. Yet development and underdevelopment are the same in that they are the product of a single, but dialectically contradictory, economic structure and process of capitalism. Thus they cannot be viewed as the product of supposedly different economic structures or systems... One and the same historical process of the expansion and development of capitalism throughout the world has simultaneously generated — and continues to generate — both economic development and structural underdevelopment.'[3] Specifically: 'The metropolis expropriates economic surplus from its satellites and appropriates it for its own economic development. The satellites remain underdeveloped for lack of access to their own surplus and as a consequence of the same polarization and exploitative contradictions which the metropolis *introduces* and *maintains* in the satellite's domestic structure.'[4]

Obviously such a view of underdevelopment carries with it a view of development, the unitary process which ostensibly brought about both. Frank's primary focus has in fact been on the roots of underdevelopment, so it has not been essential for him to go into great detail concerning the origins and structure of capitalist development itself. Yet, to clarify his approach, it was necessary to lay out the mainsprings of capitalist development, as well as underdevelopment; accordingly, Frank did not neglect to do this, at least in broad outline. The roots of capitalist evolution, he said, were to be found in the rise of a world 'commercial network', developing into a 'mercantile capitalist system'. Thus 'a commercial network spread out from Italian cities such as Venice and later Iberian and Northwestern European towns to incorporate the Mediterranean world and sub-Saharan Africa and the adjacent Atlantic Islands in the fifteenth century ... until the entire face of the globe had been incorporated into a *single organic* mercantilist or mercantile capitalist, and later also industrial and financial, system, whose metropolitan centre developed in Western Europe and then in North America and whose peripheral satellites underdeveloped on all the remaining continents.'[5] With the rise of this system, there was 'created a whole series of metropolis-satellite relationships, interlinked as in the surplus appropriation chain noted above'. As the 'core' end of the chain developed, the 'peripheral' end simultaneously underdeveloped.

Frank did not go much further than this in filling out his view of capitalism as a whole, its origins and development. But he was unambiguous in locating the dynamic of capitalist expansion in the rise of a world commercial network, while specifying the roots of both growth and backwardness in the 'surplus appropriation chain' which emerged in the expansionary process:[6] surplus appropriation by the core from the periphery, and the organization of the satellite's internal mode of production to serve the needs of the metropolis. In this way, Frank set the stage for ceasing to locate the dynamic of capitalist development in a self-expanding process of capital accumulation by way of innovation in the core itself. Thus, for Frank, the accumulation of capital in the core depends, on the one hand, upon a process of original surplus creation in the periphery and surplus transfer to the core and, on the other hand, upon the imposition of a raw-material-producing, export-dependent economy upon the periphery to fit the productive and consumptive requirements of the core.

It has been left for Immanuel Wallerstein to carry to its logical conclusion the system outlined by Frank. Just as Frank and others have sought to find the sources of underdevelopment in the periphery in its relationship with the core, Wallerstein has sought to discover the roots of development in the core in its relationship with the periphery. Indeed, in his magisterial work, *The Origins of the Modern World System*,[7] Wallerstein attempts nothing less than to establish the origins of capitalist development and underdevelopment and to locate the mainsprings of their subsequent evolutions.

Wallerstein's system

Wallerstein aims to systematize the elements of the preliminary sketch put forward in Frank's work. His focus is on what he terms the 'world economy', defined negatively by contrast with the preceding universal 'world empires'. So the world empires, which ended up by dominating all economies prior to the modern one, prevented economic development through the effects of their overarching bureaucracies, which absorbed masses of economic surplus and prevented its accumulation in the form of productive investments. In this context, Wallerstein declares that the essential condition for modern economic development was the collapse of world empire, and the prevention of the emergence of any new one from the sixteenth century until the present. Wallerstein can argue in this way because of what he sees to be the immanent developmental dynamic of unfettered world trade. Left to develop on its own, that is without the suffocating impact of the world empires, developing commerce will bring with it an ever more efficient organization of production through ever increasing regional specialization — in particular, through allowing for a more effective distribution by region of what Wallerstein terms systems of 'labour control' in relation to the world's regional distribution of natural resources and population. The trade-induced world division of labour will, in turn, give rise to an international structure of unequally powerful nation states: a structure which, through maintaining and consolidating the world division of labour, determines an accelerated process of accumulation in certain regions (the core), while enforcing a cycle of backwardness in others (the periphery).[8]

Without, for the moment, further attempting to clarify Wallerstein's argument, it can be clearly seen that his master conceptions of world economy and world empire were developed to distinguish the modern economy, which can and does experience systematic economic development, from the pre-capitalist economies (called world empires), which were capable only of redistributing a relatively inflexible product, because they could expand production only within definite limits. Such a distinction is both correct and necessary. For capitalism differs from all pre-capitalist modes of production in its *systematic* tendency to unprecedented, though neither continuous nor unlimited, economic development — in particular through the expansion of what might be called (after Marx's terminology) relative as opposed to absolute surplus labour. That is, under capitalism, surplus is systematically achieved for the first time through increases of labour productivity, leading to the cheapening of goods and a greater total output from a given labour force (with a given working day, intensity of labour and real wage). This makes it possible for the capitalist class to increase its surplus, without necessarily having to resort to methods of increasing absolute surplus labour which dominated pre-capitalist modes — i.e. the extension of the working day, the intensification of work, and the decrease in the standard of living of the labour force.[9]

To be specific, a society can achieve increases in labour productivity leading to increases in relative surplus product/labour when it can produce a greater mass of use values with the same amount of labour as previously. Put another way, a given labour force achieves an increase in labour productivity when it can produce the means of production and means of subsistence which makes possible its own reproduction (continued existence) in less time than previously (working at the same intensity); or when, given the same amount of time worked as before, it produces a larger surplus above the means of production and means of subsistence necessary to reproduce itself than previously. This cannot take place without qualitative changes, innovations in the forces of production, which have historically required the accumulation of surplus, i.e. 'plough back of surplus', into production. The basis, in turn, for the operation of this mechanism, as a more or less regular means to bring about economic development was a system of production organized on the basis of capitalist social-productive or class relations. As Marx put it, relative surplus value 'presupposes that the working day is already divided into two parts, necessary labour and surplus labour. In order to prolong the surplus labour, the necessary labour is shortened by methods for producing the equivalent of the wage of labour in a shorter time. The production of absolute surplus-value turns exclusively on the length of the working day, whereas the production of relative surplus-value *completely revolutionizes the technical processes of labour* and the groupings into which society is divided. It therefore requires a specifically capitalist mode of production, a mode of production which, along with its methods, means and conditions, arises and *develops spontaneously on the basis of the formal subsumption of labour under capital*. This formal subsumption is then replaced by a real subsumption.' (emphasis added).[10]

A crucial objection

It is the fundamental difficulty in Wallerstein's argument that he can neither confront nor explain the fact of a systematic development of relative surplus labour based on growth of the productivity of labour as a regular and dominant feature of capitalism. In essence, his view of economic development is *quantitative*, revolving around: 1. the growth in size of the system itself through expansion; 2. the rearrangement of the factors of production through regional specialization to achieve greater efficiency; 3. the transfer of surplus. Thus, according to Wallerstein, the collapse of world empire made possible a worldwide system of trade and division of labour. This, in turn, determined that what for Wallerstein were the three fundamental conditions for the development of the world economy would be fulfilled: 'an expansion of the geographical size of the world in question [incorporation], the development of variegated methods of labor control for different products and different zones of the world economy [specialization] and the creation of relatively strong state machinery in what would become the core states of this capitalist world economy [to assure transfer of surplus to the core]. (MWS. p. 38.) However, as we shall show, neither the expansion of trade leading to the *incorporation* of greater human and natural material resources, nor the *transfer of surplus* leading to the build-up of wealth in the core, nor the *specialization* of labour control systems leading to more effective ruling-class surplus extraction can determine a process of economic development. This is because these cannot determine the rise of a system which 'develops itself .spontaneously'; which can and must continually 'revolutionize out and out the technical processes of labour and composition of society'.

Wallerstein does not, in the last analysis, take into account the development of the forces of production through a process of accumulation by means of innovation ('accumulation of capital on an extended scale'), in part because to do so would undermine his notion of the essential role of the underdevelopment of the periphery in contributing to the development of the core, through surplus transfer to underwrite accumulation there. More directly, Wallerstein cannot — and in fact does not — account for the systematic production of relative surplus product, because he mislocates the mechanism behind accumulation via innovation in 'production for profit on the market': 'The essential feature of a capitalist world economy ... is production for sale in a market in which the object is to realise the maximum profit. In such a system, production is constantly expanded as long as further production is profitable, and men constantly innovate new ways of producing things that expand their profit margin.' (RFD, p. 398.)

Now, there is no doubt that capitalism is a system in which production for a profit via exchange predominates. But does the opposite hold true? Does the appearance of widespread production 'for profit in the market' signal the existence of capitalism, and more particularly a system in which, as a characteristic feature, 'production is constantly expanded and men constantly innovate new ways of producing'. Certainly not, because production for exchange is perfectly compatible with a system in which it is either unnecessary or impossible, or both, to reinvest in expanded, improved production in order to 'profit'. Indeed, we shall argue that this is the norm in pre-capitalist societies. For in such societies the social relations of production in large part confine the realization of surplus labour to the methods of extending absolute labour. The increase of relative labour cannot become a *systematic feature* of such modes of production.

To state the case schematically: 'production for profit via exchange' will have the systematic effect of accumulation and the development of the productive forces only when it expresses certain specific social relations of production, namely a system of free wage labour, where labour power is a commodity. Only where labour has been separated from possession of the means of production, and where labourers have been emancipated from any direct relation of domination (such as slavery or serfdom), are both capital and labour power 'free' to make *possible* their combination at the highest possible level of technology. Only where they are free, will such combination appear *feasible* and *desirable*. Only where they are free, will such combination be *necessitated*. Only under conditions of free wage labour will the individual producing units (combining labour power and the means of production) be forced to sell in order to buy, to buy in order to survive and reproduce, and ultimately to expand and innovate in order to maintain this position in relationship to other competing productive units. Only under such a system, where both capital and labour power are thus commodities — and which was therefore called by Marx 'generalized commodity production' — is there the necessity of producing at the 'socially necessary' labour time in order to survive, and to surpass this level of productivity to ensure continued survival.

What therefore accounts for capitalist economic development is that the class (property/surplus extraction) structure of the *economy as a whole* determines that the reproduction carried out by its component 'units' is dependent upon their ability to increase their production (accumulate) and thereby develop their forces of production, in order to increase the productivity of labour and so cheapen their commodities. In contrast, pre-capitalist economies, even those in which trade is widespread, can develop only within definite limits, because the class structure of the economy as a whole determines that their component units — specifically those producing the means of subsistence and means of production, i.e. means of survival and reproduction, rather than luxuries - neither can nor must systematically increase the forces of production, the productivity of labour, in order to reproduce themselves.

If, then, the class-structured system of reproduction in which labour power is a commodity lies behind capitalist economic development, while 'production for profit in the market' cannot in itself determine the development of the productive forces, it follows that the historical problem of the origins of capitalist economic development in relation to pre-captailist modes of production becomes that of the origin of the property/surplus extraction system (class system) of free wage labour — the historical process by which labour power and the means of production become commodities. Wallerstein, like Gunder Frank, is explicit in his renunciation of this position. Consistently he argues that since 'production on the market for profit' determines capitalist economic development, the problem of the origins of capitalism comes down to the origins of the expanding world market, unfettered by world empire. He is at pains to distinguish the emergence of the capitalist world economy in the sixteenth century — the rise of the world division of labour which emerged with the great discoveries and expansion of trade routes — from the emergence of a system of free wage labour, and contends that the latter is derivative from the former.

Conclusions

Frank's original formulations aimed to destroy the suffocating orthodoxies of Marxist evolutionary stage theory upon which the Communist Parties' political strategies of 'popular front' and 'bourgeois democratic revolution' had been predicated.[11] Frank rightly stressed that the expansion of capitalism through trade and investment did not automatically bring with it the capitalist economic development that the Marx of the

Manifesto had predicted. In the course of the growth of the world market, Chinese Walls to the advance of the productive forces might be erected as well as battered down. When such 'development of underdevelopment' occurred, Frank pointed out, the 'national bourgeoisie' acquired an interest not in revolution for development, but in supporting precisely the class system of production and surplus extraction which fettered economic advance. In particular, the merchants of the periphery backed the established order, for they depended for their profits on the mining and plantation enterprises controlled by the 'reactionaries', as well as the industrial production of the imperialists in the metropolis. But even the industrial capitalists of the periphery offered no challenge to the established structure — partly as a consequence of their involvement in luxury production serving the upper classes — while they merged with the 'neo-feudalists' through family connections and state office. As Frank asserted, to expect under these circumstances that capitalist penetration would develop the country was, by and large, wishful thinking. To count on the bourgeoisie for a significant role in an anti-feudal, anti-imperialist revolution was to encourage a dangerous utopia.

Yet, the failure of Frank and the whole tradition of which he is a part — including Sweezy and Wallerstein among others — to transcend the economic determinist framework of their adversaries, rather than merely turn it upside down, opens the way in turn for the adoption of similarly ill-founded political perspectives. Where the old orthodoxy claimed that the bourgeoisie must oppose the neo-feudalists, Frank said the neo-feudalists were capitalists. Where the old orthodoxy saw development as depending on bourgeois penetration, Frank argued that capitalist development in the core depended upon the development of underdevelopment in the periphery. At every point, therefore, Frank — and his co-thinkers such as Wallerstein — followed their adversaries in locating the sources of both development and underdevelopment in an abstract process of capitalist expansion; and like them, failed to specify the particular, historically developed class structures through which these processes actually worked themselves out and through which their fundamental character was actually determined. As a result, they failed to focus centrally on the productivity of labour as the essence and key to economic development. They did not state the degree to which the latter was, in turn, centrally bound up with historically specific class structures of production and surplus extraction, themselves the product of determinations beyond the market. Hence, they did not see the degree to which patterns of development or underdevelopment for an entire epoch might hinge upon the outcome of specific processes of class formation, of class struggle. The consequence is that Frank's analysis can be used to support political conclusions he would certainly himself oppose.

Thus so long as incorporation into the world market/world division of labour is seen automatically to breed underdevelopment, the logical antidote to capitalist underdevelopment is not socialism, but autarky. So long as capitalism develops merely through squeezing dry the 'third world', the primary opponents must be core versus periphery, the cities versus the countryside — not the international proletariat, in alliance with the oppressed people of all countries, versus the bourgeoisie. In fact, the danger here is double-edged: on the one hand, a new opening to the 'national bourgeoisie'; on the other hand, a false strategy for anti-capitalist revolution.

True, bourgeois revolutions are not on the agenda. International capitalists, local capitalists and neo-feudalists alike have remained, by and large, interested in and supportive of the class structures of underdevelopment. Nevertheless, these structures have kept significant masses of use value in the form of labour power and natural resources from the field of capital accumulation. Until recently, of course, the class interests behind 'industrialization via import substitution' have not, as a rule, been strong enough to force the class structural shifts that would open the way to profitable investment in development. However, with contracting profit opportunities in the advanced industrial countries and the consequent drive for new markets and cheap labour power, potentially available in the underdeveloped world, such interests may now receive significant strength from unexpected quarters. Should a dynamic of 'development' be set in motion as a consequence — and that is far from certain — it could hardly be expected to bring much improvement to the working population of the underdeveloped areas, for its very *raison d' être* would be low wages and a politically repressed labour force. But this would in no way rule out its being accomplished under a banner of anti-dependency, national development and anti-imperialism.

Most directly, of course, the notion of the 'development of underdevelopment' opens the way to third-worldist ideology. From the conclusion that development occurred only in the absence of links with accumulating capitalism in the metropolis, it can be only a short step to the strategy of semi-autarkic socialist development. Then the utopia of socialism in one country replaces that of the bourgeois revolution — one moreover, which is buttressed by the assertion that the revolution against capitalism can come only from the periphery, since the proletariat of the core has been largely bought off as a consequence of the transfer of surplus from the periphery to the core. Such a perspective must tend to minimize the degree to which any significant national development of the productive forces depends today upon a close connection with the international division of labour (although such economic advance is not, of course, determined by such a connection). It must, consequently, tend to overlook the pressures to external political compromise and internal political degeneration bound up with that involvement in — and dependence upon — the capitalist world market which is necessary for development. Such pressures are indeed present from the start, due to the requirement to extract surpluses for development, in the absence of advanced means of production, through the methods of increasing absolute surplus labour.

On the other hand, this perspective must also minimize the extent to which capitalism's post-war success in developing the productive forces specific to the metropolis provided the material basis for (though it did not determine) the decline of radical working-class movements and consciousness in the post-war period. It must consequently minimize the *potentialities* opened up by the current economic impasse of capitalism for working-class political action in the advanced industrial countries. Most crucially, perhaps, this perspective must tend to play down the degree to which the concrete inter-relationships, however tenuous and partial, recently forged by the rising revolutionary movements of the working class and oppressed peoples in Portugal and Southern African may be taken to mark a break — to foreshadow the rebirth of international solidarity. The *necessary interdependence* between the revolutionary movements at the 'weakest link' and in the metropolitan heartlands of capitalism was a central postulate in the strategic thinking of Lenin, Trotsky and the other leading revolutionaries in the last great period of international socialist revolution. With regard to this basic proposition, nothing has changed to this day.

Notes

I wish to thank Alice Amsden, Johanna Brenner, Temma Kaplan, Barbara Laslett, Richard Smith and Jon Wiener for reading this manuscript and offering criticisms and suggestions. I am also grateful to Theda Skocpol for sending me, in advance of publication, her review essay on Immanuel Wallerstein's *The Modern World System*, which was very helpful to me, especially on problems concerning the early modern European states.

1. See, for example: 'England has to fulfil a double mission in India: one destructive, the other regenerating — the annihilation of old Asiatic society, and the laying of the material foundation of Western society in Asia.' In 'The Future Results of British Rule in India', in Karl Marx, *Surveys From Exile*, London 1973, p. 320.

2. See, for example: 'The obstacles presented by the internal solidity and organization of pre-capitalist national modes of production to the corrosive influence of commerce are strikingly illustrated in the intercourse of the English with India and China ... English commerce exerted a revolutionary influence on these communities and tore them apart, only in so far as the low prices of their goods served to destroy the spinning and weaving industries, which were an ancient integrating element of this unity of industrial and agricultural production. And even so, this work of dissolution proceeds very gradually. And still more slowly in China, where it is not reinforced by direct political power.' *Capital* in three volumes, New York 1967, III, pp. 333-4.

3. *Capitalism and Underdevelopment in Latin America*, New York 1969, p. 9.

4. Ibid.

5. Ibid. pp. 14-15.

6. It should be made clear that Frank, in more recent writings, has attempted to modify and deepen his analysis of underdevelopment through taking greater account of 'internal class structure'. However, his retention of the theoretical approach of his earlier works has prevented him from fully accomplishing his aims.

7. New York 1974 (MWS). In the following discussion, I treat this book together with a series of closely related articles by Wallerstein which further clarify and amplify his themes. These include: 'The Rise and Future Demise of the World Capitalist System: Concepts for Comparative Analysis', *Comparative Studies in Society and History*, XVI (January 1974), pp. 387-415 (RFD). 'From Feudalism to Capitalism: Transition or Transitions?,' *Social Forces*, LV (December 1976), pp. 273-81 (FFC). 'Three Paths of National Development in Sixteenth Century Europe', *Studies in Comparative International Development*, VII (Summer 1972), pp. 95-101 (TPN). 'Dependence in an Interdependent World: The Limited Possibilities of Transformation Within the Capitalist World Economy', *African Studies Review*, XVII (April 1974), pp. 1-27 (DIW). Henceforth, when quoting from Wallerstein's works, I will indicate the source through using the indicated abbreviations, with page numbers, placed in parentheses in the text.

8. *Modern World System*, pp. 16-20. See also 'Rise and Future Demise', pp. 390-92.

9. Obviously, this is not to deny that methods of absolute surplus labour are used, *indeed extensively and systematically used*, under capitalism, for of course they are.

10. *Capital*, I, Penguin/NLR edition, London 1976, p. 645.

11. See André Gunder Frank, 'Not Feudalism — Capitalism', *Monthly Review*, December 1963, pp. 468-78 and passim.

16.   The Ideas of Samir Amin:
Theory or Tautology?
Sheila Smith

This paper presents an exposition and a critique of the ideas of Samir Amin. Section I summarises Amin's views on the necessity of an analysis of underdevelopment at the world level, on the nature of peripheral economies, and on the economic relationships between centre and periphery. Section II provides a critique of these ideas, in terms of both their logical consistency and their implications for research and for economic policy. Section III draws together these criticisms. The paper concludes that Samir Amin's ideas are logically inconsistent, tautological, and imprudent in the sense that they effectively pre-empt theoretically and politically important work on specific economies, institutions and agencies.

Critiques of non-Marxist and anti-Marxist universal theories (e.g. Rostow's 'stages of growth'; vicious circle theories; theories of 'barriers to development etc.) are well-known (see, for example, (Szentes 1971); (Baran and Hobsbawm 1961), (Lehmann 1979)). Critiques of Marxist universal theories (other than anti-Marxist critiques) are less common, but there are some examples including (Brenner 1977) and (Bernstein 1979). Most Marxists accept a universalist analysis of world capitalism as a starting point. Cutler *et al* (1978) argue that, where Marxists have attempted to analyse the structure of definite national economies, it has been in the form of registering the effects of imperialism and international capitalism; this is because of the conception of the capitalist mode of production (CMP) as an entity with its basic processes and tendencies given by the concept of its structure (Cutler *et al*, 1978; Vol. II pp. 233-254).

The argument of Cutler *et al* will be discussed here in relation to the work of Samir Amin, as expounded in *Accumulation on a World Scale* (1974), *Unequal Development* (1976), and *Imperialism and Unequal Development* (1977). Amin's work is taken as an exemplar of certain kinds of theoretical work: he takes up themes such as the development of underdevelopment, dependency, unequal development, unequal exchange, and the problem of surplus utilisation in monopoly capitalism, and elaborates them in his own way. The selection of Amin's work for criticism is justified because it is a fully elaborated theoretical scheme in the Marxist tradition which claims to encompass all economic experience, and demonstrates starkly some central logical problems.

There are two main sections in this paper. Section I presents a brief exposition of Amin's theory, and Section II provides a critique in terms of the theory's logical consistency and its implications both for research and for economic policy. Finally, Section III draws together the criticisms and tentatively considers the implications of the critique for world-level theory in general.

Sheila Smith: 'The Ideas of Samir Amin: Theory or Tautology?' *JOURNAL OF DEVELOPMENT STUDIES* (October, 1980), pp. 5-21. Reproduced with permission of Frank Cass & Co. Ltd.

I. Samir Amin: an exposition

The following brief summary of Samir Amin's analysis will be organised around three major themes: first the necessity of what Amin describes as an analysis at the world level; secondly his characterisation of peripheral economies; thirdly his characterisation of economic relationships between centre and periphery.

The analysis of world capitalism is conducted in terms of two categories centre and periphery. These concepts are related to the expansionism of capitalism in general, and are not 'attenuated synonyms of imperialist countries and colonial/dependent countries'. (Amin, 1977: 107). Furthermore 'these concepts are essential for those who, from the very beginning, have a vision of capitalism which is neither western-centred nor economistic. It is not by accident that those who reject these concepts inevitably fall into the revisionist trap' (Ibid). The basic difference between centre and periphery is that capitalist relations in the centre developed on the basis of expansion of the home market, whereas capitalist relations in the periphery were introduced from the outside.[1] Thus, in the centre, Amin asserts that 'the tendency of the capitalist mode of production to become exclusive, when based on expansion and deepening of the home market is accompanied by a tendency for the social structure at the centre to come close to the pure model of *Capital* characterised by the polarisation of social classes into two basic classes bourgeoisie and proletariat', with new strata 'all situated within the framework of the essential division between bourgeoisie and proletariat'. (Amin, 1976: 293) On the other hand, at the periphery, because the capitalist mode of production is introduced from outside, it does not tend to become exclusive, only dominant; thus formations of the periphery will not tend towards this polarisation. 'The social structure of the periphery is a truncated structure that can only be understood when it is situated as an element in a world social structure' (Amin, 1976:294). The structure is truncated because it is dominated by the 'absentee' metropolitan bourgeoisie. Moreover, 'since the peripheral economy exists only as an appendage of the central economy, peripheral society is incomplete; what is missing from it is the metropolitan bourgeoisie, whose capital operates as the essential dominating force' (Amin, 1976: 345).

The centre-periphery distinction is further explained thus:

> In an autocentric economy, there is an organic relation between the two terms of the social contradiction — bourgeoisie and proletariat — that they are both *integrated* into a single *reality,* the *nation*. In an extroverted economy, this unity of opposites is not to be grasped within the national context — this unity is broken, and can only be rediscovered on the world scale... Unequal exchange means that the problem of the class struggle must necessarily be considered *on the world scale*. (Amin, 1974: 599-600).

Furthermore, typologies of underdeveloped countries are regarded by Amin as 'superficial', since typologies concentrate on appearances, which mask the underlying unity of the phenomenon of underdevelopment (Amin, 1974: 166-8); underdeveloped economies 'are a piece of a single machine, the capitalist world economy' (Amin, 1974:19). Not only are analyses of individual countries thus misleading because they would emphasise appearances, but such an endeavour is pointless anyway, for

'Actually, the economies of the system's periphery have no real conjunctural phenomena of their own, even transmitted from outside, because they are without any internal dynamism of their own.' (Amin, 1976:279). Having asserted that underdevelopment can be understood only a world level, Amin provides various accounts of the forces which propel the world system, accounts which contradict each other. Basically, the theory of underdevelopment and of development is a theory of the accumulation of capital on a world scale, i.e. between the world bourgeoisie and the world proletariat (1974 : Introduction). In *Accumulation on a World Scale*, the dynamics of the system are explained by a single tendency: 'The law of the tendency of the rate of profit to fall remains the essential, and therefore permanent, expression of the basic contradiction of the system.' (1974:123). However, in a later work, the dynamic is explained in terms of the inherent tendency of the capitalist mode of production to raise the rate of surplus value, and the search for higher profits, unrelated to any trend in the profit rate. (1977:277).

Having indicated, albeit briefly, Amin's justification for the necessity of a world-level of analysis, we can now indicate his characterisation of the nature of peripheral economies. The peripheral capitalist mode of production

> has the dual feature of a modern technology (hence high productivity) and low wages within the framework of the capitalist social organisation ... Integration [into the world capitalist system] implies that the balance between the development level of the productive forces and the value of labour power is not to be found at the level of the peripheral formation but only of the world system into which the latter is integrated. This lack of internal correspondence between the two elements in question results in the vicious circle of peripheral development: in order to reproduce its own conditions of existence, the peripheral formation must still contain pre-capitalist modes of production or else produce non-capitalist modes which, being dominated, provide the capitalist mode with its cheap labour.' (1977:218).

The approach in Amin's characterisation of peripheral capitalism is to compare peripheral capitalism with central capitalism. Differences are then labelled 'distortions'. (1976: Ch 4). The transition to peripheral capitalism was fundamentally different form the transition to central capitalism, since it was effected by means of an onslaught from without by the capitalist mode of production upon precapitalist formations, causing 'certain crucial retrogressions to take place.' Peripheral capitalism is manifested in three kinds of distortion: first, the distortion towards export activities (extraversion) and, second, the abnormal enlargement (hypertrophy) of the tertiary sector, which reflects (a) the difficulties of realising surplus value at the centre and (b) limitations of peripheral development — inadequate industrialisation and rising unemployment. This distortion is expressed in an excessive rise in administrative expenditures and a quasi-permanent crisis of government finance. Thirdly, there is distortion towards light branches of activity and the use of modern production techniques: 'This distortion is the source of special problems that dictate development policies in the periphery that are different from those on which the development of the

West was based.' (1976:201). Underdevelopment is not, however, manifested in particular levels of production per capita, but in certain characteristic structural features that 'oblige us not to confuse the UDC with the now-advanced countries as they were at an earlier stage of their development' (*Ibid*). These features are: extreme unevenness in the distribution of productivities and in the system of prices transmitted from the centre; disarticulation, because of the adjustment of the economy to the needs of the centre; and economic domination by the centre. As economic growth proceeds, features of underdevelopment are accentuated; autocentric growth is impossible, whatever output per capita is achieved.

Peripheral countries which have achieved rapid industrial growth, and which are now exporting manufactures (South Korea, Taiwan, Hong Kong, Singapore, Mexico etc.) are simply manifestations of a new form of inequality, whereby strategic activities are concentrated at the centre, and certain manufacturing activities are transferred to the periphery; in any case, 'the very fact that they (manufacturing industries) are concentrated in a few underdeveloped countries rules out the possibility of this being a development that could be extended to all countries of the Third World' (1976:213). Moreover, these countries still suffer from vulnerability in the balance of payments, none of them have achieved self-sustained growth, the development has given rise to a 'semi-aristocracy' of labour, no technical advance occurs, and the strengthened domination of central capitalism 'forbids' any formation of a national bourgeoisie. A middle class develops, but with the consumption pattern and ideology of the world system 'to which they organically belong' (1976:214).[2]

Growth in peripheral economies is 'blocked', since the periphery is 'complementary and dominated' (1976:288). The periphery is prevented from accumulating capital indigenously, since capital generated at the periphery is transmitted to the centre. Because of the domination by the centre, 'the development of underdevelopment is neither regular nor cumulative, in contrast to the development of capitalism at the centre. On the contrary, it is jerky and made up of phases of extremely rapid growth, followed by sudden blockages. These are manifested in a double crisis, of external payments and of public finances' (1976:289).[3] This double crisis is 'inevitable', and 'none of the features that define the structure of the periphery is weakened as economic growth proceeds. On the contrary, these features are accentuated' (1976:292).

This brief discussion of Amin's analysis has concentrated on the broad theoretical features of his work. In addition he presents a wealth of illustrative material which is scholarly and useful — for example the discussions of the transition to peripheral capitalism [1974: Ch2] and of contemporary social formations of the periphery (1976, Ch 5). However, despite the breadth of this concrete analysis, it is subordinated to the theoretical analysis of the world system, and introduced to demonstrate the comprehensiveness and accuracy of the theoretical analysis.

Amin's characterisation of the economic relations between central and peripheral economies is discussed in greater detail in Part IV of *Imperialism and Unequal Development*, entitled 'The End of a Debate'. The emphasis in this section is on the theory of unequal exchange, a theory generally associated with Arghiri Emmanuel. Amin has, however, many disagreements with Emmanuel, and points out the many mistakes which Emmanuel made, building on the 'correct' parts of the theory. According to Amin, two aspects of the theory are essential. One is the pre-eminence of 'world values': the world is not composed of juxtaposed national systems carrying on 'external relations'; instead the world system is a 'unity', the 'world capitalist system'. In this system, 'social labour is crystallised in goods which have an international character'. The other essential element is the universal character of capitalist commodity alienation based on the direct or indirect sale of labour power.

The 'pre-eminence of world values' is established thus: 'capital mobility shows a tendency toward equalising the profit rate throughout the world, while remuneration of labour, which is immobile, varies from one country to another according to historical conditions. Hence the transformation of international values [the only meaningful ones] into international prices [again the only meaningful ones] implies the transfer of value from some nations to others. Since all products are international commodities, the same quantity of labour used up in different parts of the world... also gives rise to a single world value... It is obvious that if the labour-hour in all countries creates the same value while the labour power in one of the countries has a lower value [i.e. the real wage is lower], the rate of surplus value is necessarily higher. Wage goods which represent the real counterparts of the value of labour power are in fact also international goods with an international value'. (1977:187).

The 'real' case of unequal exchange occurs under the following conditions: 'the rates of surplus values are different and the transfer of value takes place not as a result of different organic compositions but because of the immobility of labour, which enables real wages to vary' (1977:188).[4] At the periphery, 'the pre-eminence of world values' may be overshadowed by the appearance of non-capitalist modes of production; however in reality 'capital dominates the direct producer: petty commodity producers today are mostly proletarianised and sellers (although indirectly) of their labour power.' This 'pre-eminence of world values' constitutes 'the very essence, the core of the affirmation of the unity of the world system, the condition for this unity' (1977:190). On the other hand, if the world system were regarded merely as a juxtaposition of autonomous national systems, then international trade could not be analysed objectively by means of the law of value, only 'subjectively' by means of a Ricardian analysis.

According to Amin, Emmanuel's theory of unequal exchange contained the following errors: Emmanuel treated wages as an 'independent variable', autonomously determined in each economy, instead of analysing wages in terms of a dialectic between the laws of accumulation (objective forces) and the class struggle (subjective forces); exports from the periphery were treated as 'specific', thus separating the analysis of exchange from the analysis of production. Thus, according to Amin, 'My analysis of the transfer of value is superior to that of Emmanuel; it is the only analysis that permits a correct definition of unequal exchange; the exchange of products whose production involves wage differentials greater than those of productivity' (1977:211). Hence the lack of internal correspondence at the periphery between the level of development of the productive forces and the value of labour power, which in turn generates the vicious circle of peripheral development, in which the centre's relative price structure is transferred to the periphery, whereas the distribution of productivities is different from that which is characteristic of the centre. Amin's 'correct' formulation of the theory of unequal exchange enables him to reject two myths to which Emmanuel's analysis leads:

(1) the myth that 'development' can be achieved by an 'artificial increase of the "independent" variable', i.e. wages. Furthermore, Emmanuel's claim that multinational corporations are agents of 'development' 'is simply to revert to Rostow.' According to Amin, the analysis of unequal exchange shows that international capital certainly finds it profitable at the periphery since the rate of surplus value is higher there, but that the peripheral mode reproduces itself as such, both in economic terms (distortions) and in political terms (in terms of specific class alliances). 'To deny this evidence necessarily takes us back to Rostow' (1977:222).

(2) the myth that the proletariat at the centre benefits from unequal exchange: against this, Amin argues that the "high" wages at the centre are mainly due to the high level of development of the productive forces and not to international transfers"[5] (*Ibid*).

Unequal external exchange is accompanied, at the periphery, by unequal internal exchange: to reproduce the system, low wages must be maintained despite modern technology, thus proletarianisation must be slowed down and precapitalist modes exploited. The distortions of peripheral capitalism generate a problem of surplus absorption, solved by means of the export of capital to the centre and an increase in the proportion of surplus value spent on luxuries. This form of consumption is permitted by the importation of technology and development of protected import-substituting industries, encouraging the adoption of 'European' consumption patterns and enabling the system to be reproduced as a dependent system. 'The bourgeoisie as a whole stops being national: it cannot fulfill the historical function of primitive accumulation, i.e., radically destroy the pre-capitalist modes, 'save' the surplus value, and so on. It has to be reactionary ('protect' the precapitalist modes in order to dominate them), wasteful (consume the surplus value), and dependent. We can therefore understand that 'dependency' is not 'imposed' but necessary to generate the surplus' (1977:234).

Finally, certain implications which Amin himself derives from his work are significant:

(1) Underdeveloped countries have no freedom of manoeuvre in relation to world capitalism: 'So long as the underdeveloped country continues to be integrated in the world market, it remains helpless . . . the possibilities of local accumulation are nil' (1974:131). Furthermore, 'Analysis of the strategies of foreign monopolies in the UDC is restricted merely to the field of the 'concrete study' without any concern to develop theory. This analysis proves that, so long as the dogma of the periphery's integration into the world market is not challenged, the periphery is without economic means of action in relation to the monopolies' (1974:392 and 1976:201). There is not even any point, according to Amin, in developing forms of financial control: 'The creation of a national currency confers on the local authorities no power of effective control so long as a country's inclusion in the world market is not challenged: even control of the exchange and of transfer does

not prevent transmission to the periphery of fluctuations in the value of the dominant currencies of the centre, nor does it prevent transmission to the periphery of the centre's price structure. Money here constitutes the outward form of an essential relation of dominance but it is not responsible for this relation' (1974:483). Thus economic policy at the national level in a peripheral capitalist economy is largely ineffective.

(2) As economic growth at the periphery occurs, so underdevelopment develops: autonomous and self-sustained growth is impossible, 'whatever the level of production per capita that may be attained' (1974:393). Since no 'development' is possible, only a radical and complete break with the world capitalist system will provide the necessary conditions for genuine development.[6]

II. Critique of Samir Amin

The difficulties in criticising Samir Amin's work are severe, mainly because of certain built-in immunities which Amin himself has constructed. The first immunity is that the analysis is, according to Amin, concerned predominantly with 'essences'; these 'essences' may well be hidden, appearances may mislead us, and the underlying forces may be disguised. Thus any attempt to criticise Amin's work on the basis of actual experience in the world economy or in one particular economy will undoubtedly give rise to accusations of superficiality, of concern only with appearances and phenomena, or of empiricism. This can be illustrated by considering Amin's writing on the 'typology of under-development', (1974:166-7), in which he describes three factors which account for the diversity of peripheral economies: the structure of the precapitalist formation at the moment of its integration into the world market; the economic forms of international contact; and the political forms which accompanied the integration. Amin then states that 'The diversity of the real models of underdevelopment produced by the combined action of these three factors has led many economists to deny the unity of the phenomenon of underdevelopment, to consider that there are only underdeveloped economies, but not underdevelopment... The reality of the latter is nevertheless a fact. But the unity of the phenomenon of underdevelopment does not lie in the appearances shaped by the interaction of these different factors. It lies in the *peripheral* character that is common to all the countries of the Third World today, in relation to the development of capitalism. This is why the exercise of constructing a typology of underdevelopment, while providing some interesting descriptive elements, remains superficial.' Thus, irrespective of analyses of the significant differences between 'peripheral' social formations, Amin claims that this diversity is superficial, disguising the essential unity, that is, the 'peripheral' character of the underdeveloped countries. Since Amin's work is principally an analysis of the 'periphery' and its relations with the 'centre', it is therefore impossible to criticise his work by pointing to the diversity of experience of 'peripheral' economies. As indicated above, the analysis of national economies is pointless according to Amin, because such economies cannot be understood except at the 'world level': they are 'truncated' and have no internal dynamic of their own. Thus it is not possible to provide a critique of Amin's analysis by demonstrating that there are significant aspects of 'peripheral' social formations which are determined within those social formations, or that 'peripheral' economies do have freedom of manoeuvre in relation to world capitalism.

Amin's insistence on essential unity despite diversity, and his concentration on the analysis of that unity would be pointless without the political implications which follow from it. The political implications are, in short, that nothing can be done by peripheral economies to foster 'proper' development: that they have to break out of the world capitalist system completely. As will be argued in more detail below, these political judgements are not sustainable in relation to all 'peripheral' countries, even if they are sustainable for some; i.e. the applicability of such judgements is not a function of the 'peripheral' character of such social formations but is, instead, based on the particular conditions within such formations — conditions which include both the internal structure and the location of the formation within the world capitalist system.

The second immunity built in to the analysis is the use of 'contradictions' and 'dialectics' to reconcile seemingly antagonistic or contradictory evidence or arguments. This can be illustrated by considering Amin's criticism of Emmanuel's version of unequal exchange, in which Emmanuel emphasises the importance of autonomous factors specific to a given economy in the determination of the wage rate. Amin argues that

> some — like Emmanuel — consider only the subjective forces and, in this context, the wage becomes 'anything', an 'independent variable'. His critics have equally unilaterally affirmed the pre-eminence of the objective aspect of the dialectical relation: the 'wage-productivity' relation, badly formulated in this way, takes us right back to mechanistic economism. . . we must first understand the mechanism of this objective aspect. We shall see that this first presentation, still unilateral although it may appear to be precise, has serious limitations, which can only be overcome by re-establishing the dialectic between the objective and subjective forces. Moreover, the re-establishment of this dialectic disengages us from 'economic theory', taking us to the level of reality, that is, historical materialism (1977:195).

In this way it is possible for Amin to reconcile any level of wages with any level of development of the productive forces: these reconciliations are simply effected by means of 'the dialectic'.

These built-in immunities which Amin has constructed are associated in his work with a mode of argument that takes the form of 'assertion-plus-threat'; i.e. a statement is followed by a 'threat' which applies to those who disagree with the statement. The 'threats' are such accusations as trotskyism, anarchism or revisionism (1977:107), economism (1977:236), Ricardianism (1977:189 and 208-209) or simply a failure to understand Marxism (1977:236). The effects of this mode of argument, and of these built-in immunities are, however, that Amin's analysis is tautological, uninformative and sterile.

The analysis is tautological because the crucial categories, centre and periphery, are defined as having certain characteristics; these characteristics are asserted to be determining; then it follows that all other characteristics are secondary, or results of membership of the category. It is true that Amin's use of information both historical and current, is impressive in its scope. The analysis is nevertheless uninformative because the basis for selection of the information is given by the theory. Other information is defined from the outset as secondary. The information provided may indeed serve the function for which it was selected, i.e. to demonstrate the correctness of the theory. On the other hand, if it fails to do so, there is always the possibility of resorting to the 'appearances-essences' dichotomy, particularly the version which regards appearances of diversity as disguising the underlying unity.

In the detailed elaboration of his ideas, Amin makes use of those parts of the Marxist apparatus which lend themselves most readily to interpretation in a tautological manner. Five such themes, which are open to detailed criticism, are the following: first, 'laws of tendency' (falling rate of profit and increasing inequality); secondly, the assertion of central capitalism as a 'standard' and peripheral capitalism as a 'distortion'; thirdly, unequal exchange; fourthly, 'world values'; and finally, Amin's denial of national economies as units of analysis.

(i) Laws of tendency

Of crucial importance in Amin's analysis is an examination of the fundamental laws and tendencies of the capitalist mode of production, mapped on to actual capitalist social formations; then these social formations are said to represent possible conjunctions of the tendencies of the capitalist system.[7] One such tendency is that of the falling rate of profit: 'The law of the tendency of the rate of profit to fall remains the essential, and therefore permanent, expression of the basic contradiction of the system'. (1974:123). However, Amin's version of laws of tendency is a 'dialectical' one, in which tendencies are counteracted, that is, there is no simple realisation of the law of tendency, no simple progression towards a specified end state. Thus the role or significance of any particular event depends upon the theorisation of an underlying tendency as determining; counter-tendencies can be dismissed as secondary phenomena. The privilege accorded to tendencies, and thus to particular events, is ultimately an assertion, but it is an assertion which cannot be challenged on Amin's terms. Thus, for example, Amin argues that 'the dominant tendency in the world system is for the gulf between the centre and the periphery to get wider', (1974:606) and that 'in reality, increasing social inequality is the mode of reproduction of the conditions of externally-orientated development . . . The general law of accumulation and of impoverishment expresses the tendency inherent in the capitalist mode of production, the contradiction between productive forces and productive relations, between capital and labour. This contradiction rules out an analysis of the capitalist mode of production in terms of harmony, and leads us to understand that the quest for an ever increasing rate of surplus value in order to compensate for the downward trend in the rate of profit makes a harmonious development impossible.' (1976: 352, 364). Thus, because of the privileged status accorded by Amin to these laws of tendency, any 'counter-acting' events are secondary, however significant they may be for particular economies or particular groups and for however long they may be experienced. Much experience can thus be dismissed, irrespective of its significance, because it has been labelled 'counteracting' by reference to abstract laws. There is, therefore, an inevitability about the 'accuracy' of Amin's theory, an inevitability which is built in to the mode of analysis but which renders the theory sterile.

(ii) Peripheral capitalism = distorted capitalism

The second aspect of Amin's theory which is problematic concerns the use of central capitalism as a standard, against which other experience is measured, with differences labelled 'distortions'. (This point is also discussed in Bernstein (1979)). Thus peripheral capitalism is 'distorted' in ways which are defined by deviations from a standard, i.e. central capitalism. The problem with the distinction centre = standard, periphery = distortion is twofold. First it implicitly assumes a 'correct' type of capitalist development; thus forms of capitalist development that do not conform to this correct type are 'distortions'. The 'standard', however, is both abstract and concrete: it is concrete to the extent that it is defined by the actual course of events in the central countries, and it is abstract to the extent that central capitalism is, in Amin's view, tending toward the pure form of the capitalist mode of production as analysed in *Capital*. These two aspects of the 'standard' do not necessarily yield the same results. The equation of central capitalism as exemplified by the experience of central countries with the pure form of the capitalist mode of production has the effect of ruling out the importance of differences between national economies as significant or determining. This leads on to the second problem of the distinction centre = standard, periphery = distortion, which concerns the implicit homogeneity within the two categories. According to Amin, the essential features and mechanisms of any economy are determined by its membership of one of these categories. The apparent heterogeneity of each group merely disguises the underlying unity. This means that analyses of national economies are misleading — even misguided — since the specific aspects of that economy are not determining. This is less true for central countries, which have their own inner dynamic; for peripheral countries it is overwhelming, since they have no inner dynamic of their own. Thus, not only do peripheral economies have no internal dynamic, but also differences between peripheral economies are 'appearances', and are not significant: thus the differences between the economy of India and that of Honduras are, according to Amin, less significant than their similarities, similarities which derive from their membership of the category 'periphery'. In fact, he argues, the differences are positively misleading, since they disguise the underlying unity.

It is clear that the location of a particular national economy within the world capitalist system has important effects upon the structure of that economy; however, it is absurd to argue that this is the only determination of that economy. As will be argued in more detail below, the denial of national economies as units of analysis, the denial of differences among 'peripheral' economies as significant, and the denial of any 'freedom of manoeuvre' to 'peripheral' economies in relation to world capitalist institutions (markets, corporation, financial agencies, etc) are dangerous denials which discourage Marxists and Socialists from conducting analyses of national economies. The problems which particular economies face depend upon the structure of those economies as well as upon their location within the world capitalist system. This applies equally to 'centre' and 'periphery' — thus the problems of British capitalism are significantly different form those of US, Japanese or Swiss capitalism, and it is misleading and fruitless to assert that these differences are irrelevant.

(iii) Unequal exchange

The third criticism of Amin's analysis is concerned with the characterisation of trade between the centre and periphery as 'unequal exchange'. Amin's definition of unequal exchange is 'the exchange of products whose production involves wage differentials greater than those of productivity.' He assumes that the techniques of production which are used in those sectors of the periphery dominated by international capital are similar to those used at the centre, and since wage rates are much lower than at the centre, unequal exchange is demonstrated. The problem is that 'unequal exchange' can equally be applied to trade among central countries, by the same arguments: techniques of production and hence productivities, can be assumed to be the same, yet very wide differences can be observed in wages between Britain, the US, West Germany, France, Canada etc. Thus it is not clear that the incidence of 'unequal exchange' is necessarily more likely in trade between centre and periphery than in trade among countries of the centre or of the periphery.

Furthermore, there is a major contradiction between Amin's theoretical arguments concerning unequal exchange and his political arguments concerning the beneficiaries of unequal exchange. In the theoretical arguments, wage differentials must be greater than productivity differentials in order for unequal exchange to take place. On the other hand, Amin denies that the proletariat at the centre benefits from unequal exchange: 'the "high" wages at the centre are mainly due to the high level of development of the productive forces and not to international transfers' (1977:222). This denial is necessary to support Amin's notion of a world proletariat facing the world capitalist class, which would be undermined if the centre proletariat received 'high' wages because of unequal exchange. However if the 'high' wages at the centre are due to the high level of development of the productive forces, then productivity at the centre must be greater than at the periphery; i.e. the centre is characterised by high wages and high productivity. This contradicts the whole basis of unequal exchange, which rests on an argument that, since productivities are the same in those sectors dominated by international capital and wages are lower at the periphery, unequal exchange must be occurring. Amin's dilemma is thus solved by a contradiction.

(iv) World values

The above criticisms of Amin's version of unequal exchange arise even if his arguments are accepted on his own terms. The fourth criticism of his analysis relates to a more basic aspect of unequal exchange, that is, problems concerning the notion of 'world values'. Amin asserts that the labour-hour in all countries creates the same value, and that all commodities (both internationally traded commodities and wage goods) are 'international commodities'; thus the same quantity of labour used up in different parts of the world gives rise to a single world value. The problem is that, in order for the labour-hour in all countries to create the same value, or for all labour-hours within a given country to create the same value, definite social conditions must be specified, most importantly the condition of competitive capitalism. This condition is not met by Amin's assertion of the international mobility of capital (presumably 'perfect' mobility); the condition is contradicted by his discussion of monopolies. Conditions of capitalist competition vary enormously within economies, between different industries and branches of industry, and between economies, thus affecting the 'value' of 'the labour-hour'. Any given economy produces particular commodities, and faces particular firms: world markets for petroleum, cotton, jute, copper and bananas, for example, vary in their institutional organisation and in the conditions of capitalist competition. To assert, implicitly or explicitly, that the condition of capitalist competition is met, is to deny the effects of these variations which affect particular economies in different ways.

A further problem of Amin's assertion of 'world values' is a more general problem of analysis in terms of the value form. Amin's analysis contains a confusion: on the one hand, he equates value-and-money-forms, thus assuming that values and prices are interchangeable; on the other hand, he acknowledges that values cannot be transformed into prices. The direct equation of value-forms and money-forms is illustrated thus:

> 'An African peasant obtains. . . in return for 100 days of very hard work each year, a supply of imported manufactured goods, the value of which amounts to barely 20 days of simple labour of a European skilled worker. If this peasant produced with modern European techniques... he would work 300 days a year and obtain a product about six times as large in quantity: his productivity per hour would at best be doubled. Exchange is thus very unequal in this case: the value of these products, if the reward of labour were proportionate to its productivity, would not be of the order of $9 bn (which is what it is) but 2.5 times as much, that is, around $23 bn.' (1976:143-4).

These calculations should not be taken seriously. Even if we attempt to take them seriously, by regarding the source of the numbers as a mystery rather than an invention, they involve a direct equation of prices and values. However, Amin himself acknowledges that the transformation of prices into values is impossible: in a section of *Imperialism and Unequal Development* somewhat arrogantly entitled 'The End of a Debate', he argues that 'The importance attached by some authors to the question of 'transformation of values into prices' reflects. . . a fundamental error in the understanding of the nature of the Marxist concept of value. It is clear that it is impossible to derive the system of prices mathematically from the system of values while maintaining an equality between rates of profit and the rate of surplus value...' (1977:223).

Why the rate of profit and rate of surplus value should be equated is not clear. Perhaps the reason is that Amin himself does not understand 'the nature of the Marxist concept of value'. The basic problem is that Amin's work, in many places, uses value analysis to examine prices, and Amin himself 'transforms' values into prices. He does this without indicating the basis for this transformation, acknowledging that Marx's 'solution' was incorrect (1976, 61-62), but without providing us with a 'correct' version of the precise nature of the relationship between prices and values. If there is no systematic relationship between prices and values, then it is not clear what the purpose of value analysis is. Even if a systematic relationship between prices and values is constructed at a theoretical level, there are still vital political and economic issues which are not aided by value analysis, e.g. the terms of trade, international commodity markets, trade within multinationals (transfer prices) etc.[8] Amin himself admits that the prices at which many commodities are traded are 'arbitrary' — presumably in the sense that value-analysis will not further our understanding of such prices. Such 'arbitrary' (in Amin's sense) prices are, however, of vital importance in many UDCs, and some means of analysis of these prices, taking account of political processes, bargaining etc. is necessary. To this value analysis has nothing to contribute.

(v) *The denial of national economies as units of analysis*

The fifth criticism of Amin's analysis is concerned with his denial of the importance of national economies as units of analysis, and with implications of that denial. Amin's denial of national economies as units of analysis is based on the notion that the heterogeneity of peripheral economies disguises their underlying unity, and that, in any case, the economic and social structure of the periphery can only be comprehended at the world level, since peripheral social formations have a 'missing class', and since peripheral economics have no internal dynamism. The problem is that the level of a national economy is a level at which crucial issues are determined, which affect the conditions of operation of capitalism, and the conditions of political struggle. These conditions vary between economies, and have important effects on economic, social and political organisation. As well as denying the importance of national economies as units of analysis, Amin denies the effectiveness of national economic policies in the periphery, thus asserting that peripheral economies have no freedom of manoeuvre in relation to world capitalism and therefore denying that national economic policy is a legitimate arena of political struggle and dispute. Some examples of issues which significantly affect the conditions of operation of capitalism, and conditions of struggle, are as follows: (a) policies towards multinationals, e.g. requirements concerning localisation of personnel and training; local content requirements concerning inputs; taxation policies; disclosure requirements with respect to information; (b) policies towards wages, which can significantly affect the distribution of income, structure of demand and composition of output e.g. the distribution of income in Tanzania is significantly different from that in Brazil, South Africa or Nigeria; (c) policies towards trade unions; (d) State enterprise and the development of industry; (e) the receipt of aid from Cuba and the Soviet Union; (f) the level of long-term indebtedness and hence the relationship of a national economy to institutions such as the IMF, which significantly affects a country's 'freedom of manoeuvre' in terms of its ability to pursue independent national economic policies.

Not only does Amin deny the effectiveness of state policy, but also all other differences within the 'centre' and within the 'periphery' are regarded as secondary: thus the differences between Brazil and Tanzania, India and Chad, Spain and Japan, and the US and Italy, are dismissed as secondary. It is clear, however, that major differences between countries cannot be dismissed simply as a result of Amin's theorising. It is irresponsible to argue that a progressive government in a 'peripheral' country can do nothing to alter the conditions of operation of capitalism or the conditions of life of the population. Amin's denials dismiss vital areas of struggle, and areas of research and analysis, which can significantly alter the economic, social and political structure of 'peripheral' countries. Given that there are many 'peripheral' countries where the political forces for a socialist revolution are weak or nonexistent, these arenas cannot be dismissed without disregarding the conditions of life for the majority in such countries in the short and medium term. There are some 'peripheral' countries where the freedom of manoeuvre of a progressive government may be limited, and others where it may be less limited, but this cannot be determined in the abstract. Thus, for example, a 'peripheral' economy in debt to the IMF, forced to adopt IMF-dictated economic policies (involving 'liberalisation' of trade and capital movements, reductions in government expenditure, deflation, devaluation, etc.) has significantly less freedom of manoeuvre than a 'peripheral' economy with a strong balance of payments, less dependence on world trade, a large internal market, etc. Furthermore, the possibility of collectively increasing bargaining power *vis-à-vis* multinational corporations by developing units of economic co-operation cannot be dismissed in the abstract as irrelevant. State policies such as indigenisation, taxation, public ownership, commercial policies, wage differentials, relations with socialist countries, etc. all provide potential areas of struggle, the outcome of which has significant effects.

The basic problem with Amin's analysis is that it cannot provide an understanding of any particular economy, since it denies the necessity of doing so. Political struggle, however, is organised at national or sub-national level and is generally specific to the nation where it takes place. Therefore analysis of particular national economies is an important area of work despite Amin's denial. No information is provided by Amin which might contradict — even *prima facie* — the correctness of his analysis; thus areas of struggle which are specific to particular economics will inevitably be omitted.

III. Conclusions

In Section II it has been argued that Amin's theory is deficient in many respects. The theory is logically inconsistent, but has tried to immunise itself from important criticisms. The effect of these immunities is to render the theory tautological. In addition, the theory produces political conclusions which are irresponsible.

Amin's world-level theory contains within it an explicit rejection of other levels of analysis, such as the national or sub-national, on the grounds that his world-wide theory necessarily provides a better explanation of particular historical instances than would be generated by a study of those particular instances. In this way an analytical straightjacket is imposed on all historical experience, but since the analytical framework is ultimately derived by assertion, it requires a mighty act of faith to accept it. Since the analysis contains many errors of logic, inconsistencies, and internal contradictions, a strong case can be made for rejecting it. Even if these logical inconsistencies and contradictions could be resolved satisfactorily, a strong case can still be made for rejecting it, on the grounds that it precludes, by assertion, theoretically and politically important work at the level of national economies.

An argument which states that analyses of national economies are necessary is not a total rejection of world-level theorising. Instead it is an argument for reinstating into Marxist analysis the historical specificity of economies, institutions and agencies, whilst retaining from Marxism its emphasis on an historical approach, the setting of economic issues in their social and political context, and the analytical importance both of general forces associated with international capitalism, and of the particular forms which the development of capitalist social relations have taken in different places and at different times.[9] Such an approach would be superior to Amin's theory, since it merely provides the means of asking important questions. Amin's practical propositions indicate clearly the manner in which, in his thinking, the answers to important questions are provided in the abstract. For example, Amin's proposition that only a radical and complete break with the world capitalist system will provide the necessary conditions for genuine development, can only be described as dangerous arrogance. The tragic example of Kampuchea may be dimmissed as an 'appearance', but the attempt was clearly made in that country to break with the world capitalist system, and with disastrous consequences. It is not surprising that the theoretical purity generates the wrong answers to specific strategic questions, since specific questions require specific answers. Amin would probably regard the policies being pursued in Mozambique, Angola and Zimbabwe as disastrous, since they involve complex negotiations with various capitalist agencies. Some would think that it is fortunate that Amin's political influence has not been extended to those countries.

Notes

Shelia Smith is a Fellow of Girton College and Assistant Director of Development Studies, University of Cambridge.

I should like to thank Barry Hindess, David Lehmann, Michael Lipton, Suzy Paine and John Toye for helpful comments and constructive criticism on this paper. Any errors which remain are solely the responsibility of the author.

1. For a fuller discussion of the inadequate definition of the concepts 'centre' and 'periphery' see Disney (1977).

2. There are some curious arguments in Amin's discussion of the 'newly industrialising countries' (NICs): the concentration of manufacturing industries in a few countries hardly rules out the possibility of extending this to all countries of the Third World, since the development of industry generates increased incomes, widened markets, expanded demand for manufactures, etc. Furthermore, many 'NICs' have a home-grown bourgeoisie (e.g. South Korea), considerable internal dynamism and technical progress.

3. Progress in the centre are highly 'regular', even though the 'blockages' may have been manifested in other types of 'crisis'.

4. This definition contains within it a contradiction, which is that differences in real wages, i.e. in the value of labour power, will imply differences in organic compositions of capital for otherwise identical production processes.

5. This contradicts earlier points about labour hours having equal productivity with only wage rates varying.

6. It is not clear what a 'radical and complete break with the world capitalist system' means, even for large economies, let alone small ones.

7. The implications of Marxists' reliance on laws of tendency are discussed in detail in Cutler *et al* (1978: Vol I, Part II). Much of the criticism of Amin's use of laws of tendency is not exclusive to Amin's use of the concept.

8. Such criticisms of value theory apply to most attempts to make the labour theory of value 'operational', not just to Amin's.

9. For further discussion of these issues, see Brenner (1977), Smith and Toye (1979).

References

Amin, Samir, (1974) *Accumulation on a World Scale*, Sussex: Harvester Press.

Amin, Samir, (1976) *Unequal Development,* Sussex: Harvester Press.

Amin, Samir, (1977) *Imperialism and Unequal Development*, Sussex: Harvester Press.

Baran, P. and E. Hobsbawm, (1961) 'The Stages of Economic Growth', *Kyklos,* Vol. XIV.

Bernstein, H. (1979) 'Sociology of Underdevelopment versus Sociology of Development?', pp 77-106 in (Lehmann, D. (Ed.) 1979).

Brenner, R., (1977) 'The Origins of Capitalist Development: A Critique of Neo-Smithian Marxism', New Left Review No. 104 (July-August).

Cutler, A., B. Hindess, P. Hirst and A. Hussein, (1978) *Marx's Capital and Capitalism Today,* London: Routledge & Kegan Paul.

Disney, N., (1977) Review of Amin (1974), *The Insurgent Sociologist*, Vol. VII No. 2.

Emmanuel, A., (1972) *Unequal Exchange*, New York: Monthly Review Press.

Lehmann, D., (1979) *Development Theory: Four Critical Studies,* London: Frank Cass.

Smith, S. and J. Toye (eds.,) (1979) *Trade and Poor Economies*, London: Frank Cass.

Szentes, T. (1973) *The Political Economy of Underdevelopment*, Budapest: Akademiai Kaido.

17. Capitalism, Industrialization and Development

Stuart Corbridge

In a recent address to the Annual Conference of the Geographical Association Professor Ron Johnston argued that 'a renewal of geographical interest in the entire world and its complexity can aid the production of a more mature society' (Johnston, 1984, 443). He also insisted that if the discipline is to avoid a cloying parochialism it must recapture its roots in a 'regional geography [which] begins at the world scale' (1984, 447).

This paper shares Professor Johnston's belief. Its first premiss is that remarkable changes are afoot in the world system; changes which promise to reshape the global geography of economic and political power. Perhaps the most important of these changes is bound up with the recent industrialization of the third world. The growth of the newly industrializing countries [NICs] has encouraged development theorists to rethink those simple classifications which divide us into north and south or into the first world and the third world (see Auty, 1979; and Worsely, 1979).

The paper's second premiss is that geographers can learn much from a continuing debate on these issues within radical social theory. (See, in particular, the October 1984 Special Issue of the *Journal of Development Studies*. Neoclassical and Keynesian transition theories are not considered here. On the former see Beenstock, 1983. On the latter see Brandt, 1980. For their geographical counterparts see Chisholm, 1982 and Brookfield, 1975.) This debate has woven its way through three main phases and the structure of this paper reflects this chronology.

In Section I our focus is upon the stagnationist theories associated with Gunder Frank and others. In the mid-1960s Frank argued that capitalism was incapable of promoting the industrialization of the third world. In his judgement the continuing capitalist development of the metropolitan powers presupposed a continuing capitalist underdevelopment of the periphery. In Section II Frank's ideas are confronted with the more optimistic 'postimperial' theory developed by Bill Warren. Warren also claimed a marxist pedigree but it was his belief that capital has been set free in the postcolonial era and that it is now fulfilling a dynamic mission in the third world. In the paper's third section Warren's views are contrasted with a series of more contemporary theories of a new international division of labour [NIDL]. In some respects these theories propose a bridge between the theses of Frank and Warren. On the one hand they accept that a selective industrialization of the third world has occurred since 1950. On the other hand they resist the claim that this industrialization is 'developmental'. Most theorists of a new international division of labour prefer to speak of a new dependency and to point to a new global domination by northern transnational corporations [TNCs] paying low wages and creating few multipliers in the periphery. The paper concludes with some

Stuart Corbridge: 'Capitalism, Industrialization and Development', *PROGRESS IN HUMAN GEOGRAPHY* (1986), Vol. 10, No. 1, pp. 48-67. Reproduced by permission of Edward Arnold (Publishers) Ltd.

thoughts on the current status of this debate and on the implications it holds for geographical accounts of differential development.

I. Stagnationism

To the extent that left and right agree on anything developmental it is that industrialisation is a precondition for successful economic growth. (Obvious exceptions to this rule include Michael Lipton, 1977 and John Friedmann, 1981.) In itself this is hardly surprising. The evidence for such a view is to be found both historically, in the long-standing association between high levels and rates of growth of industrialization with high levels and rate of growth of national income, and in the positive economic effects supposedly induced by industrialization. Diversification, the spread effects of backward and forward linkages, attitudinal modernization, skill upgrading and prestige are just five of the benefits listed in a recent geographical textbook (Dickenson *et al.*, 1983, 147; see also Kemp, 1983).

When it comes to the pace and policies of and for such industrialization, however, left, right (and centre) part company and begin to chase each other's tails. Consider the case of mainstream economics first. Prior to the second world war most economists of centre and centre-right persuasions adhered to a fairly static version of comparative advantage theory wherein it was assumed that peripheral countries were naturally and eternally predisposed to the production of agricultural crops and other primary commodities; manufacturing was the preserve of the metropolitan powers. Lord Cromer, Governor of Egypt 1883-1907, underlined this most succinctly:

> The policy of the government may be summed up thus: 1) export of cotton to Europe... 2) imports of textile products manufactured abroad... nothing else enters the government's intentions, nor will it protect the Egyptian cotton industry because of the dangers and evils that arise from such measures (quoted in Hayter, 1981, 49).

By the end of the second world war this perspective was no longer in touch with global realpolitik. In an era of rising US hegemony and advancing decolonialization, a new centre-right economics emerged which quickly convinced itself that industrialization was a veritable panacea for development. All it disagreed upon was the ease of the industrial transition. In the more optimistic Rostovian analysis the take-off is all about mobilizing savings equivalent to 10-15 per cent of national income, investing it in industry, cranking the handle, and awaiting on a happy future (see Rostow, 1960). In the more distinctively *laissez-faire* formulations comparative advantage theory still retains a hold, but it is now cast in terms of the factor proportions model developed by Hecksher and Ohlin (see Todaro, 1981, Chapter 12). This holds that comparative advantages are set by the tripartite factors of capital, land and labour, thus allowing for a gradual movement towards a comparative advantage in low-level industrialization as foreign aid flows into a country and as low-cost labour moves to the cities. (A convenient theory, some would say, given the Lewis two-sector model of the 1950s and given the current concern with a new international economic order: see Lewis, 1955 and 1978.)

Meanwhile the left was changing its tack, but in the opposite direction. Prior to the second world war the left was almost alone in rejecting the tautologies of static comparative advantage theory, and in warding off the depredations prosecuted in its name. At the same time the left foresaw a world where industrialization would follow naturally enough from the political fact of decolonialization. By the mid-1960s this would be rejected as untheorized romanticism. For the development of underdevelopment school which grew up around Andre Gunder Frank the industrialization of the third world was deemed to be incompatible with capitalism. In a curious echo of prewar mainstream economics, Frank argued that capitalism never changed its spots and that the political act of decolonialization would find no economic counterpart in a world which continued to be dominated by a handful of neocolonialist capitalist powers.

The proof for this view was supposedly twofold, beginning with the postwar statistics on industrial inactivity in Latin America (and elsewhere). Writing in 1965-66, Frank argued not only that industrialization was all but absent from Latin America in 1945, but also that ECLA policies of inner-directed (import substitution) industrialization had signally failed to alter matters (Frank, 1967). Reasonably enough, Frank took this to be critical. After all, the entire strategy of the Economic Commission for Latin America was steeped in the earlier radical tradition which promised that industrialization would come quickly to any politically independent country brave enough to challenge the 'laws' of comparative advantage. (It will be recalled that Prebisch identified the oligopolistic nature of core commodity and factor markets as the determinants of a secular decline in the terms of trade of Latin America, and that he called upon state sponsored industrialization as a way out of this vicious circle. More precisely, he looked to policies of 'healthy protectionism, exchange controls, the attraction of foreign investment into Latin American industry, the stimulation and orientation of national investment, and the adoption of wage policies aimed at boosting effective demand' [Palma, 1978, 907] to secure the industrialization which would bring with it the developmental externalities absent from primary commodity based growth.) ECLA's apparent failure therefore, which manifested itself in such things as a declining balance of payments position, in mass unemployment and in massive outflows of profits (Bernstein, 1982), led Frank to the conclusion that industrialization within the capitalist world system was impossible.

This conclusion was strengthened by Frank's parallel 'discovery' that the only periods when Latin America had enjoyed some industrial growth happened to coincide with periods of weakened centre/periphery ties. Thus, if a first hypothesis of underdevelopment theory suggested that the 'development of the national and other subordinate metropoles is limited by their satellite status', a second hypothesis held that the 'the satellites experience their greatest economic development and especially their most classically capitalist industrial development if and when their ties to the metropolis are weakest' (Frank, 1969, 9-10).

These comments provided the kernel of a stagnationist account of peripheral non-industrialization. Frank's work was soon 'extended', however, by the first generation of radical geographers, who talked heatedly about the deindustrialization of Africa and Asia (see Blaut, 1973; and Buchanan, 1972), and by a group of the more prominent late-1960s new Leftists. One thinks in particular of Ernest Mandel, whose 'classic' marxist economic theory (1968, 476-79) deals at length with 'Imperialism as [an] Obstacle to the Industrialisation of Underdeveloped Countries'. One thinks also of Michael Kidron. His 1971 *New Society* article seemed to maintain that no significant progress towards industrialization is any longer possible in the third world — even after a socialist revolution in any one peripheral country — because of the growing scale of industrial and technological organization. As Sutcliffe points out: 'On this view all significant progress... is now being held up pending socialist revolution in the advanced countries; (Sutcliffe, 1972, 180) — a fair anticipation of world systems thinking.

Such stagnationist claims were not destined for a long ascendancy, however. Radical geographers continued to restate them from time to time (see Browett, 1980), but as the 1970s wore on it became clear that industrialization was occurring in selected third world countries. This point was brought home to the left, academically, by the work of Bill Warren, an English Communist and self-proclaimed marxist. In a brace of penetrating articles written for the *New Left Review* in 1971 and 1973, Warren claimed not only to destroy the main tenets of stagnationism (which was galling enough), but to demonstrate that any true marxist — as opposed to one indoctrinated in the pragmatic ways of leninist and post-leninist theories of imperialism — would actually expect, and would certainly welcome, the postwar industrialization of the third world. It is this latter claim which the left is still coming to terms with.

II. Warren

Warren's *New Left Review* articles were expanded upon in 1980 with the posthumous publication of his book 'Imperialism — pioneer of capitalism'. This text makes it clear that Warren's (in)famous statistical arrays on the facts of postwar progress are meant to be read as the culmination of a fourfold critique of neo-marxist theories of imperialism and underdevelopment.

The first stage of this critique consists of a reexamination (or for Warren a reaffirmation) of Marx's own thoughts on the historically progressive nature of both capitalism and colonialism. One can detect two strands in Warren's work here. On the one hand he is engaged in an act of critique pure and simple. Warren wants to reclaim Marx from those who would criticize capitalism on 'moral and historical' (and thus antisocialist) grounds; those who look only to capitalism's darker side and to its behavioural and institutional associates of immiseration, prostitution, uneven regional development and so on and so forth. Warren has no sympathy for such new leftism and he wastes no opportunity to remind its adherents that there is another side to the coin: that under capitalism 'the possibility of genuine moral choice . . . increases to the extent that people (and individual persons) can consciously control their own destiny' (Warren, 1980, 20); that 'equality, justice, generosity, independence of spirit and mind, the spirit of inquiry and adventure, opposition to cruelty, not to mention political democracy, are not late comers to [but] . . . are either ushered in by capitalism or achieve a relative dominance unequalled by any major earlier or contemporaneous cultures' (Warren, 1980, 21); and that 'it is the self-sustaining momentum and rapid pace of technological change under capitalism, and especially industrial capitalism, that distinguish it from *all* earlier societies' (1980, 12, his emphasis). 'Under capitalism to stand still is to perish' (1980, 14).

These reminders issued, Warren seeks to underline them with chapter and verse from Marx himself. The latter parts of Chapter 1 of 'Imperialism — pioneer of capitalism' are thus devoted to Marx's own statements on the vigour of domestic capitalism and on its imperialist mission. In this latter context pride of place is given to a series of lengthy quotations from Marx's *New York Herald* articles, the centrepiece of which is his description of England's double mission in India:

> The ruling classes of Great Britain have had, till now, but an accidental, transitory and exceptional interest in the progress of India. The aristocracy wanted to conquer it, the moneyocracy to plunder it, the millocracy to undersell it. But now the tables are turned. The millocracy has discovered that the transformation of India into a reproductive country has a vital importance to them, and that, to that end, it is necessary, above all, to gift her with the means of irrigation and of internal communication. They intend now drawing a set of railroads over India. And they will do it (Marx, 8 August 1853; quoted in Warren, 1980, 42-43).

Marx could not be clearer than this, says Warren, nor more consistent. 'Since Marx and Engels considered the role of capitalism in precapitalist societies progressive, it was entirely logical that they should have welcomed the extension of capitalism to non-European societies' (Warren, 1980, 39) — warts and all.

The question that then arises is this: if stagnationism has no roots in Marx's own writings where does it come from, and what sort of radical heritage can it claim? Warren is in no doubt as to the answer. In the second section of his critique he argues that:

> The traditional marxist view of imperialism as progressive was reversed primarily by Lenin . . . in his 'Imperialism: the highest stage of capitalism'.
> In effectively overturning Marx and Engel's view of the character of imperialist expansion, Lenin set in motion an ideological process that erased from marxism any trace of the view that capitalism could be an instrument of social progress even in precapitalist societies (Warren, 1980, 48).

The main tenets of Lenin's theory have been discussed elsewhere (Slater, 1977) so we can pass quickly over his equation of imperialism with an age of monopoly capitalism (and thus with a lack of competitive dynamic and with the need for interimperialist rivalries and capital export). Instead, we can turn to Warren's critique of Lenin, which is basically threefold. First, the details of Lenin's theory of imperialism are examined (Lenin, 1970). Warren joins a long line of critics in pointing out that it cannot be shown either that capital export was characteristic of a specific stage of capitalism, or that it was decisively connected with the scramble for territories. More specifically, he demonstrates that 'capital export, far from being a symptom of a particular (degenerate) stage of capitalism, has been a significant feature of industrial capitalism since its inception' (Warren, 1980, 61).

Warren then challenges Lenin's thesis that monopoly capitalism is necessarily parasitic and decadent. In an important and oft neglected passage, he argues that:

> The rise of oligopolistic market structures — or monopoly firms as they are popularly called — has not reduced competition but on the contrary has intensified it. The development of large monopolistic firms [has] permitted major advances in efficiency, primarily through economies of scale and the systematic application of science and new organizational methods of production (Warren, 1980, 79).

Warren also suggests that 'monopoly capitalism [has proved] far more responsive to the needs of the masses than nineteenth century capitalism ever [did]' (1980, 80), and has actually provided them with a range of consumer durables that only intellectuals are prone to sneer at.

Finally, Warren attends to Lenin's reasons for writing his pamphlet on imperialism. With some vigour he argues that Lenin was well aware of capitalism's progressive mission abroad — witness his 'The development of capitalism in Russia' (1974) — but that he chose to turn his back on Marx's theory for propagandist reasons. In essence, Lenin arrived at his theory of imperialism (and so of monopoly capitalism) as a way of explaining the 'inexplicable': the fact that at the height of the first world war (and 'Imperialism' was written in 1916) the working classes of Europe were slaughtering each other in the name of patriotism. As Warren has it: 'although his results were logically and analytically lamentable, Lenin did score marxism's glittering propaganda success of the twentieth century, for the pamphlet was really able to explain *both* the cause of the war *and* the reasons for the opportunist, nationalist proletarian support for it by one and the same phenomenon: imperialism' (Warren, 1980, 49, emphasis in the original).

This concern with propaganda is taken further in the third section of Warren's critique, where it is suggested that the inadequacies in Lenin's theory of imperialism continued to be papered over as it came to prove useful first for the Comintern (and Soviet security) and later for the nationalistic bourgeoises of the third world. Again it is difficult for me to give more than the drift of these charges. Taking them in turn, though, we find Warren dealing first with the Comintern and in particular with the Sixth Congress of the Communist International in 1928. It was at this Congress, says Warren, that 'The marxist analysis of imperialism was formally . . . sacrificed . . . to the requirements of bourgeois anti-imperialist propaganda and, indirectly, to what were thought to be the security requirements of the encircled Soviet state' (Warren, 1980, 8).

This sacrifice involved the endorsement of two theses that were at best only implicit in Lenin's original pamphlet: that imperialism actually retarded the industrialization of the colonies, and that, consequently, the Soviet Union and the industrial bourgeoises of the colonial countries were natural allies in the fight against imperialism. For Warren this is pure cant, but he recognizes it as a brilliant piece of propaganda. Here we have an ideology — imperialism — which not only served the immediate defensive interests of the Soviet Union (which could now retreat from internationalism), but which also went some way to meeting the demands of Asiatic marxists like M.N. Roy of India, who was seeking to prioritize the anti-imperialist struggle over the socialist aspirations of the western proletariats. In the longer run, however, these theses proved most critical in sustaining the 'nationalist mythologies' of postwar dependency and underdevelopment theories. The immediate roots of such theories may well lie in a critique of the alleged failures of import-substitution industralization, notes Warren, but their real genealogy, and certainly their real appeal to the political elites of the third world, can be traced back at least as far as 1928. For Warren there is a direct line of descent from Lenin and the Comintern to all that is most distinctive and most misleading in modern dependency theories: that the third world is being exploited and underdeveloped by a set of monopolistic metropolitan powers, and that the third world's bourgeoises (and workers and peasants) can be absolved of all blame for not promoting a faster industrialization of their countries than has already occurred.

Warren attempts to show just how misleading these propositions are in the fourth and final section of his book. In this section he presents a wealth of empirical material to support his contentions that imperialism has given way to interdependence in the post-colonial era, and that, as it has done so, so an already 'powerful engine of progressive social change' [imperialism] has found full fruition in the 'substantial industrialization and capitalist transformation' of the third world (Warren, 1980, 9).

Once more, the full extent of Warren's documentation defies summary here, for he deals not only with the recent industrialization of the third world, but with a series of corollary 'facts' concerning economic progress and 'the myth of marginalization'. Nevertheless, it is the statistics on industrialization which are supposed to underlie these 'facts' and it is these that have provoked the most righteous indignation. It follows that it is reasonable to deal with them at greater length. In effect Warren is seeking to do two things here: to argue that 'the underdeveloped world as a whole has made considerable progress in industrialization during the postwar period' (Warren, 1980, 241), and to ward off the more obvious assertions and arguments that might be made to the contrary.

Given these guiding lights Warren advances in three stages. He deals first with the aggregate levels and trends of postwar industrialization in the third world, pointing out (or claiming) that in the 1950s, 1960s, and 1970s third world manufacturing output grew much faster than its first world counterpart, despite record growth in the latter. In this first section too, Warren dismisses the notion that these high statistical growth rates are illusory either because they start from low base levels or because they ignore population growth rates in the less-developed world. Inspection of the figures, says Warren (see Table 1), shows that 'many underdeveloped countries are able to maintain faster rates of growth of manufacturing output than industrialized countries ... over a long period' (Warren, 1980, 242). Furthermore, 'to take the growth of per capita manufacturing output as a basis of comparison is to apply an extremely demanding criterion... from the standpoint of the distribution of world industrial power... growth rates are the central issue' (Warren, 1980, 243).

Table 1 **Annual average rates of growth of manufacturing, 1951-69 and 1965-74, for selected countries**

	1951-69	1965-74		1951-69	1965-74
Brazil	7.8	11.2	Panama	14.2	8.5
Costa Rica	9.7	—	Peru	7.5	7.8
Iran	11.2	13.3	Philippines	8.5	5.8
Iraq	6.8	7.6	Puerto Rico	6.5	—
Jamaica	5.0	—	Singapore	14.8	15.3
Jordan	15.2	—	Taiwan	16.1	—
Korea (Rep. of)	16.9	24.4	Thailand	8.7	—
Malaysia	6.4	9.6	Trinidad/Tobago	10.0	—
Mexico	7.4	7.6	Turkey	11.5	—
Nicaragua	7.6	—	Venezuela	10.5	5.0
Pakistan	15.0	—	Zambia	13.8	7.4

Source: Warren (1980)

The second stage of Warren's presentation deals with the share of manufacturing in GDP, both within selected LDCs over time and between developed and less-developed countries. His basic argument is clear enough: 'For the LDCs as a whole, manufacturing accounted for 14.5 per cent of GDP in 1950-54; the figure rose to 17.9 per cent in 1960 and 20.4 per cent in 1973. In the developed capitalist countries manufacturing contributed 28.4 per cent in 1972. *The difference is therefore becoming rather small* (Warren, 1980, 244, emphasis in the original; see also Table 2).

Finally, Warren turns his attention to the supposedly elitist pattern of manufacturing output that is said to characterize third world industrialization. Arguing that this 'is plainly incorrect for the third world countries that include the vast majority of the population of Africa and Asia, where the market for 'luxury goods' is too small to sustain profitable production' (Warren, 1980, 247), Warren concludes that such an argument is once more expressive of western intellectual snobbery. The fact is that the third world actually wants consumer durables and in Latin America at least, which tends to be more advanced than Africa and Asia, a wide market for such goods reaches 'well into the lower income urban groups' (Warren, 1980, 248; this obviously bears upon Warren's remarks on the myth of marginality).

Together, these arguments and statistics attain a powerful effect, and Warren draws on them to make three more general remarks: that stagnationism is a chimera (the more so for these developments happening in years that could not conceivably be called years of crisis, or war or depression); that 'there is nothing to gain from a refusal to recognize the existence of developing capitalist societies' in the third world; and that to the extent that 'there are obstacles to development they originate not in current relationships between imperialism and the third world, but in the internal contradictions of the third world itself' (Warren, 1980, 10) — with its policy blunders and with its neglect of agriculture.

Table 2 **Selected countries' manufacturing as a percent of gross domestic product at current factor cost (1973) and percentage of active labour force employed in manufacturing (latest estimates)**

Country	Manufacturing as % GDP[a]		% of active labour force employed in manufacturing[b]
Egypt	21.6		12.9
Taiwan	29.8		n.a.
South Korea	24.3		20.5
Argentina	38.3		19.7
Brazil	24.6		11.0
Chile	25.9		15.9
Costa Rica	21.9		11.9
Mexico	25.4		17.8
Peru	21.4		12.5
Uruguay	23.0		18.8
average =	25.6	average =	15.7
Australia	26.6		24.8
Canada	20.1		18.0
Denmark	26.6		23.1
Norway	25.4		24.4
Sweden	24.8		26.5
United States	24.7		22.4
average =	24.7	average =	23.2
Greece	20.4		17.1
Spain	26.7		25.7
Malta	26.5		27.8
Hong Kong	32.1		44.4
Singapore	26.1		25.6
average =	26.3	average =	32.1

Sources: a) World Bank, World Tables, 1976; b) ILO, International Yearbook of Labour Statistics, 1977, Geneva (1977), Table 2. (After Warren, 1980).

Reactions to Warren

It was inevitable that such views would be roundly, even abusively, criticized by the left, but what is of interest is the way in which the attack on Warren shifted its ground over the later 1970s and early 1980s.

To begin with (that is, after the publication of the *New Left Review* articles) Warren was attacked largely from within the underdevelopment paradigm. Thus various critics took issue with his statistics on the postwar industrialization of the third world and pointed out:

1) That Warren's evidence for 'substantial and sustained progress' is based on absolute figures of manufacturing output over time. A volumetric study would give a less heartening but more realistic comparison, given the low base levels of industrialization.
2) That Warren's portrait of rapid third world industrialization is sustained only by an unrepresentative choice of sample countries (compare Table 1 with Table 3).
3) That Warren's notion of industrialization is so poorly specified that it is not clear whether he is dealing with 'a. [the] simple elaboration of raw materials; b. [the] transformation of processed raw materials into parts; c. [the] assembly of parts; d. [the] creation of machinery (capital goods) to sustain the process of industrialization; e. [the] consumption of a substantial proportion of industrial output; or f. [the] research and design of products and machinery' (Petras *et al.*, 1978, 110-11; see also Emmanuel, 1974, who berates Warren for failing to distinguish between handicrafts industries employing, say, 10 people, and vast integrated iron and steel plants employing thousands with different skills).

Table 3   **Annual average rates of growth of manufacturing, 1960-70 and 1970-81, for selected countries**

	1960-70	1970-81
Burma	3.4	4.6
Senegal	6.2	2.0
Zambia	na	0.3
Argentina	5.6	0.7
Uruguay	1.5	4.3
Central African Republic	5.4	—4.3
Togo	na	—10.4
Zaire	na	—2.3

Source: World Bank — World Development Report, 1983, Table 2.

By the later 1970s, however, this sort of critique was losing its bite. Warren's statistics continued to be decried as selective and misleading — and rightly so — but the overall thrust of his argument could not be gainsaid. No matter how one massaged the figures one could not disguise the fact that a number of third world countries were industrializing apace throughout the 1970s. Global industrial geography was being reshaped.

As a consequence the critique of Warren changes tack and we begin to find him attacked less for his statistics *per se* than for the political and theoretical interpretations he put upon them. We will come to the theoretical objections soon enough. For the moment let us consider Warren's politics. For critics like Petras *et al.* and Lipietz, these are best described as 'neoliberal' (Petras *et al.*, 1978, 104) or even 'positivistic' (Lipietz, 1982, 58). Warren is said to have embraced a vulgar empiricism — that is the 'arrangement of various discrete 'facts' ' (Petras *et al.*, 1978, 107) — which renders him incapable of seeing the capitalist development of the third world for what it really is: limited, dependent, brutal and exploitative. Indeed he actually seems to welcome the darker side of capitalism (the cheap labour, the prostitution, the shanty towns), dismissing its dehumanizing effects as the necessary conditions of a future capitalist development which will in time bring the world to socialism. In a powerful attack on the 'stages theory' of politics which Warren, like Rostow, so clearly adheres to, Lipietz reminds us that for Marx capitalism always involved exploitation, and that it is not enough to talk about low wages being functional for capitalist accumulation. More woundingly, he accuses Warren of using the charge of 'moralism' to deflect the flak which should rightly descend upon his own immoral defence of the 'necessary' development of capitalism. In a brilliant concluding passage, Lipietz argues that:

> In essence [Warren] is saying: Don't fight imperialism, since it helps to spread capitalism, and capitalism itself is all right, 'functional', 'appropriate to economic growth'. Such is the thesis worn thin by so many writers from Adam Smith to Walt Rostow yet still hegemonic today, which Warren's final chapter trumpets forth in every way (Lipietz, 1982, 56).

Although I will later want to challenge some aspects of this critique of Warren I do want to endorse the thrust of Lipietz's remarks here. Warren really is so obsessed with capitalism serving as the 'bridge to socialism' (Warren, 1980, 25) that he quite abandons any moral critique of capitalism as it now exists. He also fails to consider the alternative social systems that could be constructed in its place. Having said that it seems to me that certain of Warren's prognoses on industrialization do stand or fall independently of these shortcomings. One does not have to be as impressed with recent developments as Warren is to recognize that they are taking place. It follows that a conclusive critique of Warren must also challenge the more narrowly industrial and developmental segments of his thesis. It is at this point that the concept of a new international division of labour becomes interesting.

III. Theories of the new international division of labour

Discussions of a NIDL have been circulating for some time now and it would be idle to pretend that the development of the concept owes everything to an engagement with the work of Bill Warren. Nevertheless, if one rereads the original Petras *et al,* [1974] review of Warren one finds that the bulk of his criticism is already predicted on an alternative interpretation of third world industrialization. Already the talk is of the need to theorize the 'global system . . . rather than ... distinct national economies' (Petras *et al.*, 1978, 133), and of the need to focus on the way in which selected value-added activities are being transferred to repressive third world countries as assembly operations under the control of metropolitan TNCs. For Petras and his colleagues the real failing of Warren is the way he equates 'the fragmented externally integrated, and technologically dependent industrialization of the third world with that of the western imperialist countries' (Petras *et al.,* 1978, 111).

Since the mid-1970s, however, this early concern for the possible non-independence of third world industrialization (itself an accommodation to Warren), has been superseded by a number of more formal models of a NIDL. These seek not only to describe recent changes in the world economy, but to account for them in terms of marxist economic theory. Apart form Warren's own efforts in this field, and the associated theory of postimperialism propounded by Sklar (1976) — and since taken up by Becker (1984) and Schiffer (1981) — there seem to be three main versions of this new orthodoxy: the neo-Smithian approach, the neo-Ricardian approach and the post-Palloxian approach. (The first two terms are taken from Jenkins, 1984; the last is mine). All of them extend the critique of Warren either explicitly or implicitly, and I will review them in turn before examining possible counters to each.

1. *The neo-Smithian and neo-Ricardian approaches*

It is convenient to deal with the neo-Smithian and neo-Ricardian approaches in tandem for they are both theories of the world economy, and of changes therein, which have their roots in an 'exchange-oriented' or neo-marxist perspective (Jenkins, 1984, 29: that is, their emphasis is upon circulation rather than production). The major difference between them is that the neo-Smithians look to an explanation of the NIDL in terms of the changing world market for labourpower and production sites. Thus Frobel, Heinrichs and Kreye (1980) structure their account of the NIDL in terms of: the development of a worldwide reservoir of potential labourpower; the development of the labour process in manufacturing (which has led to the decomposition of the production process into elementary units and the deskilling of the labour force); and the development of the forces of production in the fields of transport and communications which has made industry less tied to specific locations. By contrast, the neo-Ricardians trace the origins of the NIDL to a profits squeeze specific to the western industrial powers. They argue that the processes of centralization and concentration which are characteristic of the postwar accumulation of capital, plus the fact of full employment, strengthened the hand of organized labour to such an extent that profit rates in the metropolitan countries began to dip in the late 1960s. To escape this crisis the capitalists in the core either had to automate (that is, fight the working classes at home by unemployment, rationalization and the extraction of higher rates of relative surplus value), or evaporate (that is, give up), or emigrate (that is, exploit the cheap labour of the unorganized, peripheral working classes). Given that the first option was thought to be politically inexpedient, and the second unthinkable, it followed that a 'decentralization of accumulation to the periphery [made] an extremely attractive strategy for capital ... [Moreover] although industrial location is determined on the basis of all relevant cost factors, wages [in this model] are the crucial determinant' (Jenkins, 1984, 30: commenting on Frobel, 1982; Arrighi, 1978).

Aside from these different explanations of the origins of the NIDL — different from each other and from Bill Warren — the implications and pitfalls of these two perspectives are remarkably similar and tell tales of a common logic.

Consider the implications first. Both theories are united on two basic points — 1) that the NIDL was not established in response either to the changing development needs or strategies of the third world countries themselves (for Frobel *et al*, the NIDL is an 'institutional innovation of capital itself' — Frobel, 1980, 46), and 2) that the NIDL (*contra* Warren) does not alter the fundamental structures of inequality between core and periphery established in mercentilist and colonial times. Rather the reverse. For Gyorgy Adam, all that is happening now is that 'banana republics are becoming pyjama republics' (Adam, 1975, 102). This observation has since been endorsed by those critics who have sought to characterize and criticize it in terms of four more specific attributes:

1) First, it is said that the NIDL is predicated on the fact of (necessarily) cheap labour. This factor is crucial to both neo-Smithian and neo-Ricardian accounts in their different ways (the former emphasizing the role of cheap labour in extending the world market for labour power, the latter emphasizing its role in restoring profits) and no effort is spared to itemize the long hours, the short holidays, the intensity of labour, the high turnover and the high female participation rates that are the supposed counterparts of low wages.

2) Second, this superexploitation upon which the NIDL is said to be based, is itself held to be guaranteed by the actions of compliant, if not client, third world governments. The regimes in the newly industrializing countries (NICs) are not only thought to be attracting export-production capital through such means as tax incentives, subsidies and free-trade assembly zones, they are also deemed to be opposed to the democracy which Warren so blandly assumes to be the natural complement of capitalism. Instead they prefer and encourage the repressive anti-union and antilabour policies which Lipietz calls 'Bloody Taylorism' (Lipietz, 1982, 41) and of which Frank, archetypally, has claimed 'that this repressive political policy has the very clear economic purpose and function of making these economies more competitive on the world market by lowering wages and by supporting those elements of the local bourgeoisie who are tied to the internal market' (Frank, 1981, 324).

3) Third, despite the successes of selected NICs in attracting capital to the periphery, the industrialization that is occurring can in no sense be welcomed as 'real', 'developmental' or independent industrialization. There are a number of reasons for this. On the one hand it is argued that such industrialization as is occurring is creating very few jobs when compared with the size of the massive industrial reserve army now encamped in the third world. At the same time it is argued that industrial control remains firmly in the hands of the TNCs. As a result the industrialization is of an enclave nature: few linkages are forged because the manufacturing is usually of an assembly nature; production is still dependent on the vagaries of the world market; and dependency is being forged anew by the TNC's emerging monopolies over technology and marketing.

4) Finally, the NIDL is said to be detrimental to the interests of the working classes in the core countries too. In an interesting 'annexe' to their main analysis, Frobel *et al*. argue that the relocation of industry to the periphery has been a prime cause of the crisis now afflicting the major metropolitan powers, and which threatens the social harmony that has prevailed in the core. In particular it has provoked; a decline in domestic investment, which has been increasingly directed towards rationalization as opposed to the expansion of productive capacity; a rapid growth in OECD unemployment; and a fiscal crisis of the state (after Jenkins, 1984).

2. A critique of exchange-oriented theories

There can be little doubt that charges such as these have had a powerful impact on the left, where they have met with widespread approval both as a rejoinder to Warren and as a reaffirmation of dependency (if not underdevelopment) theory (see Bienefeld, 1981). This is especially true of radical development geography. Already there is a sizeable literature which concurs that 'the international economic relationships which dominated the immediate postwar period have been overturned' (Cohen, 1981, 287), and which traces through this movement from world trade to world factory in terms of the classic concerns of neo-Marxism. Today's emphasis is upon the global corporation (Susman and Schutz, 1983) and footloose capital; upon the way in which the 'potency of an industrial reserve army is [being] resuscitated' (Gibson and Horvarth, 1983, 180) as a 'global submode' of capitalism replaces monopoly capitalism; upon the way in which this new global capital uses its mobility over space to 'subvert . . . each local advance or reform' (Ross, 1983, 145), and upon the role 'of wages, the discipline of the labour force, and public policy perceived to be favourable to capital' as determinants of the decision 'to stay, leave or enter a locality' (Ross, 1983, 144; see also the table from Ross reproduced here as Table 4, and designed to show the critical role of low wages in directing a NIDL).

Table 4 **Hourly wage rates and fringe benefits in the apparel industry (in US dollars)**

Sweden	7.22
Netherlands	5.68
Belgium	5.49
* New York (legal)	4.58
USA	4.35
Puerto Rico	2.57
* New York (sweatshops)	1.75
* Singapore	1.10
Hong Kong	.96
Brazil	.86
Taiwan	.56
South Korea	.41

* = no fringe benefits

Source: reproduced from Ross, 1983, Table 3.

Whether or not such concerns are warranted, however, is another matter. Along with Jenkins (1984) and Brenner (1977) I have my doubts as to whether these neo-marxist perspectives can ever transcend the more general failings which bedevil all circulationist theories. It may be attractive to think of the growth of the world market (and thus of the role of transport and communications, capital mobility and the conquest of space: in a word, geography) as a basis of the NIDL, but it is evident that such thinking owes more to Smith and Babbage than it does to Marx. As Jenkins puts it:

> The emphasis placed by these writers on the Babbage principle as a fundamental factor underlying the fragmentation/relocation of production processes is illustrative. . . of its failure to analyse the tendency of capitalism to expand through increasing relative surplus value by raising the productivity of labour. . . Babbage's emphasis on reducing labour costs through the fragmentation of tasks in order to take advantage of workers with the minimum level of skill required for each task is characteristic of what Marx referred to as the arena of manufacture as opposed to machinofacture. It therefore highlights the tendency to neglect the role of technological change in increasing labour productivity in this approach (Jenkins, 1984, 33).

More to the point, these theoretical failings can be shown to have their empirical counterparts. In effect, the neo-marxists are ignoring four things:

1) First, that whilst wages are considerably lower in the third world than in the core capitalist countries this does not mean that unit labour costs are necessarily lower too. Tables like Table 4 (from Ross) can thus be quite misleading, if not entirely meaningless, because they fail to take into account the higher productivity of labour in the core countries. (Bettelheim, 1972, showed some years ago how this undercut Emmanuel's neo-Ricardian theory of unequal exchange. The gist of what he said then is true today. If Ford workers in the UK are paid four times as much as their Brazilian counterparts but are five times as productive, then it is the British workers that are the most exploited in terms of Marxist economic theory, all other things being equal!)

2) Second, a concern for production costs alone, as opposed to those associated with the technical development of a product, can lead to an analysis devoid of any consideration of demand conditions and factors. In practice these may be critical. Jenkins gives the example of the semiconductor industry, whose post-1960s relocation to the periphery can be traced back to a shift in demand away from military and government uses towards industrial and consumer application (Jenkins, 1984, 34).

3) Third, a neglect of points (1) and (2) must give a highly one-dimensional picture of the NIDL whereby it is associated only with the centre/periphery relocation of branch plants to cheap labour, free trade zones. This may be true of selected industries, such as textiles and semiconductors. However, it neither acknowledges the role of third world governments in promoting their own local industries nor does it admit the existence of more highly skilled and more highly paid industries such as shipbuilding, the manufacture of vehicles, metalworking and so on.

4) Fourth, just as the neo-Marxist account downplays the role of the third world state by tracing the NIDL back to the 'needs of metropolitan capital', so too does it overestimate the full extent of third world industrialization. Setting too much store both by Warren and by their own theories of metropolitan crisis, the neo-marxists fail to see that industrial relocation is only one possible response open to western capital, and that relocation to the periphery *per se* is only one possible relocation response. In fact the

export of capital is still predominantly between the countries of the core, rather than from the high-wage countries to the low-wage countries (Grahl, 1983).

Put together, these theoretical and empirical shortcomings leave our exchange-oriented theories in something of a mess. Moreover they suggest that if the left is to fashion a coherent, as opposed to merely speculative, critique of Warren, it must challenge Warren's optimism on independent industrialization and democracy from a position which is more firmly rooted in Marx's analysis of the production, distribution and exchange of commodities.

3. Palloix, Jenkins and the internationalization of capital

This is certainly Jenkins's conclusion and to this end he advances a third Marxist perspective on the industrialization of the third world (or fourth if we include Warren, of whom more later).

In effect Jenkins's work has emerged out of his critique of what he calls exchange-oriented and productionist (that is, Warrenite) theories. He argues that these are necessarily one-dimensional theories and that a 'more promising starting point is found in Marx's analysis of the circuits of capital which emphasizes the unity of production, distribution and exchange' (Jenkins, 1984, 40). This point is further elaborated via Palloix. Using the latter's distinction between the circuits of commodity capital (world trade), money capital (international capital movements) and productive capital (the operation of the TNCs), Jenkins argues that the crisis which is now upon us is in fact an attempt not just to restore profits but to restore 'harmonious relations between production, distribution and exchange' (Jenkins, 1984, 41). Less opaquely, it is Jenkins's contention that the industrialization of the third world — or the internationalization of capital as he prefers to call the NIDL — must be understood as but one moment forced upon capital by its inability to stave off a declining rate of profit either by increasing productivity, by exploiting cheaper raw materials, or by drawing on female/immigrant labour. Of equal import in this restructuring, he argues, has been the introduction of new production techniques (often via bankruptcies and/or centralization), and thus the typical (domestic) drive for increasing relative surplus value.

Three further sets of observations follow. First, in keeping with this idea of 'choice in crisis', Jenkins points out that the relocation of production to cheap labour countries has only been of limited significance. In the late 1970s ' imports of manufactures from the third world accounted for less than two per cent of total consumption of manufactured goods in North America, the EEC and Japan' (Jenkins, 1984, 43). It has also been concentrated in particular branches of industry (for instance clothing) where the further accumulation via relative surplus value was not a practical possibility. (Jenkins suggests that Warren is wrong to assume that late 1960s and early 1970s industrial growth rates in the third world will continue. This period was 'relatively short-lived' he says, and may be discontinued if new production technologies arise which can be reimported to the core countries.)

Jenkins's second point is that the conditions for what industrialization has occurred must often be traced back to developments in the circuits of commodity and money capital which are ignored in the other three theories. In particular he draws our attention to the way in which the financial sphere made available vast numbers of export credits and other loans for the 1970s industrialization of the third world. Similarly, he notes that some third world countries are invested in not so much because of their cheap labour as because of the markets they offer (pace Warren), and because the expansion of relative surplus value through technological innovation often presupposes a degree of mass production and economy of scale that must be provided globally. He also suggests that such factors as legalized shift working and state incentive policies may have been critical in inducing a limited NIDL.

Finally, Jenkins contrasts the political implications of his approach with those of Warren and the neo-marxists. Naturally he benefits from the comparison. Whilst the exchange-oriented theorists are said to make contradictory demands for the international solidarity of the working class and for core protectionism, Warren is accused of being too insensitive to the evils of industrial capitalism in the third world. He is also too convinced that an industrial labour force divided by nation, race and sex will one day unite to overthrow capitalism at the global level. By contrast the implication of Jenkins's work are less bombastic. Since his perspective points up the limited scale of the NIDL and the fact that it necessitates neither authoritarianism nor superexploitation (though this characterizes some countries and some industrial branches and accumulation processes), he can suggest that:

> . . .the implications of the NIDL for the working class in the advanced capitalist countries is not nearly as catastrophic as exchange-oriented theories imply since it is not a major factor in rising unemployment and the decline of manufacturing. . . This approach emphasizes the different forms taken by the internationalization of capital and the need for different forms of struggle in order to counter the strategies of capital. Thus a strategy for workers in the car industry might be quite different from one which would be appropriate in the clothing industry (Jenkins, 1984, 52-53).

IV. Warren reconsidered: conclusions and pointers

How right Jenkins is. The entire thrust of Jenkins's remarks here backs up a wider argument which holds that accounts of development and underdevelopment must be sensitive not only to the dynamics of a world system, but also to the relations of production and their conditions of existence that are characteristics of particular countries and development sectors. (See Corbridge, 1986 forthcoming). There are parallels too with Ron Johnston's comments on the need to theorize 'regional mosaics': Johnston, 1984, 445-47.) Moreover this disaggregating approach suggests both a middle line on the debates surrounding capitalism and the industrialization of the third world, and a number of pointers to the investigation of two more empirical debates which follow on from these: on the developmental role of the TNCs, and on the role, capacity and constitution of the state in the third world.

Let us conclude, however, with the lessons of the 'Warren debate'. Having reviewed the work of Warren and his critics at some length it would seem that the pendulum is now swinging back towards Warren. Of course there are still provisos that need to be entered. Warren does tend to eulogize the darker side of capitalism, just as he tends to overestimate the temporal and spatial significance of that third world industrialization which has occurred. Nevertheless, it is clear that stagnationism has had its day, and that it is no longer acceptable to dismiss Warren on the grounds that 'his' industrialization is of a dependent, authoritarian and superexploitative type. This may be true of some third world countries and industries but it is not true of all. In any case the whole thrust of this neo-marxist critique is based on two clear fallacies. On the one hand it denies the possibility that third world states might stand up for themselves against the all-powerful world system (which for some reason is assumed to be forever and always dead set against them alone). On the other hand it measures what is going on in the third world against a stylized and idealized model of balanced, independent industrial growth which is (wrongly) imagined to have occurred in the west. To paraphrase Henry Bernstein (1982), the world systems theorists continue to oppose capitalism and third world industrialization at a philological level. By definition, and *a priori*, they know that nothing good is happening, or could happen, in the third world. It is important that geographers resist this logic.

References

Adam, G. (1975) 'Multinational corporations and worldwide sourcing'. In Radice, H., editor, *International firms and modern imperialism*, Harmondsworth: Penguin, 89-103.

Arrighi, G. (1978) *A geometry of imperialism*. London: New Left Books.

Auty, R. (1979) 'Worlds within the third world'. *Area* 11, 232-35.

Becker, D. G. (1984) 'Development, democracy and dependency in Latin America: A post-imperialist view'. *Third World Quarterly* 6, 411-31.

Beenstock, M. (1983) *The world economy in transition*. London: George Allen and Unwin.

Bernstein, H. (1982) 'Industrialisation, development and dependence'. In Alavi, H, and Shanin, T., editors, *Introduction to the sociology of developing countries*, London, Macmillan, 218-35.

Bettelheim, C. (1972) 'Theoretical comments'. In Emmanuel, A, *Unequal exchange*, London: Monthly Review Press, 271-322.

Bienefeld, M. (1981) 'Dependency and the newly industrialising countries: Towards a reappraisal'. In Seers, D., editor, *Dependency theory: a critical reassessment*, London: Frances Pinter, 135-49.

Blaut, J. (1973) 'The theory of development'. *Antipode* 2, 64-85.

Brandt, W. Chairman, (1980) *North-south: a programme for survival*. London: Pan.

Brenner, R. (1977) 'The origins of capitalist development: a critique of neo-Smithian Marxism'. *New Left Review* 104, 25-92.

Brookfield, H. (1975) *Interdependent development*. London: Methuen.

Browett, J. (1980) 'Development, the diffusionist paradigm and geography'. *Progress in Human Geography* 4, 57-79.

Buchanan, K. (1972) *The geography of empire*. Nottingham: Spokesman.

Chisholm, M. (1982) *Modern world development — a geographical perspective*. London: Hutchinson.

Cohen, R.B. (1981) 'The new international division of labour'. In Dear, M. and Scott, A. J., editors, *Urbanization and urban planning in capitalist society,* London: Methuen, 287-315.

Corbridge, S. forthcoming: *Capitalist world development — a critique of radical development geography.* London: Macmillan.

Dickenson, J. P., Clarke, C.G., Gould, W.T.S., Prothero, R.M., Siddle, D. J., Smith, C.T. Thomas-Hope, E.M. and Hodgkiss, A.G. (1983) *A geography of the third world.* London: Methuen.

Emmanuel, A. (1974) 'Myths of development versus myths of underdevelopment', *New Left Review* 85, 61-82.

Frank, A.G. (1967) *Capitalism and underdevelopment in Latin America.* London Monthly Review Press.

— (1969) *Latin America: underdevelopment or revolution.* London: Monthly Review Press.

— (1981) *Crisis in the third world* London: Heinemann.

Friedmann, J. (1981) 'The active community: toward a political-territorial framework for rural development in Asia'. *Economic Development and Cultural Change* 29, 235-61.

Frobel, F. (1982) 'The current development of the world economy'. *Review* 5, 1-19.

Frobel, F., Heinrichs, J. and Kreye, O. 1980: *The new international division of labour.* Cambridge: Cambridge University Press.

Gibson, K.D. and Horvath, R.J. (1983) 'Global capital and the restructuring crisis in Australian manufacturing'. *Economic Geography* 59, 178-94.

Grahl, J. (1983) 'Restructuring in west European industry'. *Capital and Class* 19, 36-54.

Hayter, T. (1981) *The creation of world poverty.* London: Pluto.

Jenkins, R. (1984) 'Divisions over the international division of labour'. *Capital and Class* 22, 28-57.

Johnston, R. (1984) 'The world is our oyster'. *Transactions of the Institute of British Geographers* 9, 443-59.

Kemp, T. (1983) *Industrialisation in the non-western world.* London: Macmillan.

Kidron, M. (1971) 'Memories of development'. *New Society* 17, 360-66.

Lenin, V.I. (1970) *Imperialism — the highest stage of capitalism.* Moscow: People's Press.

— (1974) *The development of capitalism in Russia.* Moscow: People's Press.

Lewis, W.A. (1955) *The theory of economic growth.* London: George Allen and Unwin.

— (1978) *The evolution of the international economic order.* Princeton: Princeton University Press.

Lipietz, A. (1982) 'Towards global Fordism? Marx or Rostow?' *New Left Review* 132, 33-58.

Lipton, M. (1977) *Why poor people stay poor.* London: Temple Smith.

Mandel, E. (1968) *Marxist economic theory,* London: Merlin Press.

Palma, G. (1978) 'Dependency: a formal theory of underdevelopment or a methodology for the analysis of concrete situations of underdevelopment'. *World Development* 6, 881-924.

Petras, J., McMichael, P. and Rhodes, R. (1974) 'Imperialism and the contradictions of development'. *New Left Review* 85, 83-104.

— (1978) 'Industrialisation in the third world'. In Petras, J. *Critical Perspectives on imperialism and social class in the third world*, London: Monthly Review Press, 103-36.

Ross. R.J.S. (1983) 'Facing Leviathan: public policy and global capitalism'. *Economic Geography* 59, 144-60.

Rostow, W.W. (1960) *The stages of economic growth*. Cambridge: Cambridge University Press.

Schiffer, J. (1981) 'The changing post-war pattern of development'. *World development* 9, 414-27.

Skiar, R. L. (1976) 'Post-imperialism: a class analysis of multinational corporate expansion'. *Comparative Politics* 9, 75-92.

Slater, D. (1977) 'Geography and underdevelopment — II'. *Antipode* 9, 1-31.

Susman, P. and Schutz, E. (1983) 'Monopoly and competitive firm rations and regional development in global capitalism'. *Economic Geography* 59, 161-77.

Sutcliffe, B.(1972) 'Imperialism and industrialisation in the third world'. In Owen, R. and Sutcliffe, B., editors, *Studies in the theory of imperialism*, London: Longman, 171-92.

Todaro, M. (1981) *Economic development in the third world* London: Longman.

Warren, B. (1971) 'How international is capital?' *New Left Review* 68, 21-37.

— (1973) 'Imperialism and capitalist industrialisation'. *New Left Review* 81, 3-44.

— (1980) *Imperialism — pioneer of capitalism*. London: New Left Books.

Worsley, P. (1979) 'How many worlds?' *Third World Quarterly* 1, 100-108.

INTERNATIONAL INTERACTION

18.   International Trade, The Balance of Payments and Development

Anthony P. Thirlwall

The gains from trade

While it is quite legitimate to look at trade from the point of view of the balance of payments, and to regard the balance of payments as a development problem that can only be solved by new trade policies, the benefit from trade in traditional trade theory is not measured by the foreign exchange earned but by the increase in the value of output and real income from domestic resources that trade permits. Optimal trade policy, measured by the output gains from trade, must be clearly distinguished from the maximisation of foreign exchange earnings.

The gains from trade can be divided into static and dynamic gains. The **static gains** are those which accrue from international specialisation according to the doctrine of comparative advantage. The **dynamic gains** are those which result from the impact of trade on production possibilities at large. Economies of scale, international investment and the transmission of technical knowledge would be examples of dynamic gains. In addition, trade can provide a **vent for surplus** commodities, which brings otherwise unemployed resources into employment, and also enables countries to purchase goods from abroad, which can be important for two reasons. The first is that if there are no domestic substitutes, the ability to import can relieve domestic bottlenecks in production. The second is that imports may simply be more productive than domestic resources.

In this chapter we must do two things. First, we must establish the precise nature of the benefits of trade, and second we must examine critically the underlying assumptions of the comparative advantage doctrine and the classical advocacy of international specialisation and free trade. We can then go on to consider the argument that the balance-of-payments implications of international specialisation and free trade may seriously offset the allocative gains from trade, and whether this establishes a case for protection.

The static gains from trade

The static gains from trade are based on the **law of comparative advantage**. Consider the case of two countries A and B both with the capacity to produce commodities X and Y. The simple proposition of classical trade theory is that if country A has the comparative advantage in the production of commodity X, and country B has the comparative advantage in the production of commodity Y, it will be *mutually* profitable for country A to specialise in the production of X and for country B to specialise in the production of Y, and for surpluses of X and Y in excess of domestic needs to be freely

Anthony P. Thirlwall: Extracts from 'International Trade, The Balance of Payments and Development' (Ch. 15) in *GROWTH AND DEVELOPMENT* (Macmillan Press Ltd., 5th ed., 1994), pp. 360-367; 371-387. © A.P. Thirlwall 1972, 1978, 1983, 1989, 1994.

traded, provided that the international rate of exchange between the two commodities lies between the domestic rates of exchange. Comparative advantage is an opportunity-cost concept measured by the marginal rate of transformation between one commodity and another as given by the slope of the production-possibility curve. Given perfect competition, which the above analysis assumes, the domestic price ratio between two commodities will equal their marginal rate of transformation. If this were not so, it would pay producers to switch from one commodity to another to take advantage of the relatively favourable price ratio.

Now let us give a practical example of the static gains from trade. In **Figure 15.1**, the production-possibility curves for countries A and B are drawn showing the different combinations of the two goods X and Y that can be produced with each country's given factor endowments. We assume for simplicity that factors of production in both countries are sufficiently versatile as to be able to produce either commodity equally efficiently so that the production-possibility curves are linear; that is, there is a constant marginal rate of transformation. Curves I and II are indifference curves showing levels of community welfare.

Figure 15.1

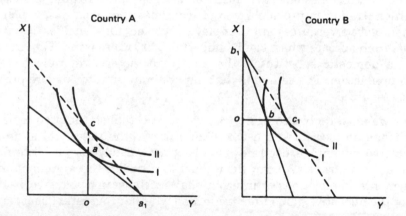

Now suppose that the marginal rate of transformation between X and Y in country A is 10/8, and in country B, 10/2. Commodity X is relatively cheaper in country B than A measured by the amount of commodity Y that must be forgone, and Y is relatively cheaper in country A. We say that country A has the comparative advantage in the production of Y, and country B in the production of X, and that it will be mutually advantageous for A to concentrate on Y, and B on X, and for A to swop Y for X and for B to swop X for Y.

Before trade each country produces combinations of goods X and Y which give a level of utility represented by indifference curve I. The two countries produce at a and b respectively. With the opening of trade there can only be one price ratio between X and Y determined by the interaction of demand and supply in both countries together, and which will lie somewhere between each country's transformation (price) ratio. Assume that the international rate of exchange settles at 10/5, shown by the broken lines in **Figure 15.1**. Country A, specialising in the production of Y, can exchange Y for more X internationally than it could domestically, and country B, specialising in the production of X, can exchange X for more Y internationally than it could domestically. For example, suppose after trade production in country A shifts to a_1 and in country B to b_1. Country A, trading oa_1 of Y, can now consume oc of X which it obtains from country B. Country B, trading ob_1 of X, can now consume oc_1 of Y which it obtains from country A. Both countries move to higher indifference curves, to higher levels of welfare on indifference curve II.

As a result of the international division of labour world production increases, and so does world welfare. Specialisation on the basis of comparative advantage enables the maximum to be produced from a given amount of factor resources. The increase in welfare that trade permits results from the opportunity to obtain foreign products more cheaply, in terms of real resources forgone, than the alternative of import substitution which means domestic production. In Hick's beautifully concise phrase, 'the gain from trade is the difference between the value of things that are got and the value of things that are given up' (Hicks (1959), p. 181). Through the international division of labour one is supposed to get more than one gives up! If comparative advantage was exactly the same in the two countries there would, of course, be no static gains and the justification for trade would be to reap economies of scale and other dynamic gains.

Whether the consumption of *both* commodities in *both* countries rises depends on the international rate of exchange. At some rates of exchange, even between the two domestic price ratios, the consumption of one of the commodities in one of the countries after trade may be less than before trade. Even so, it can still be maintained that the post-trade position is superior to the pre-trade position, if those individuals whose welfare is increased can fully compensate those who suffer and still be better off.

The static gains from trade are the same gains as from trade creation that accrue with the establishment of customs unions, when high-cost suppliers are replaced by lower-cost suppliers. It is the doctrine of comparative costs that provides the rationale for the increasing advocacy of the formation of customs unions, or trading areas, between developing countries. It should be emphasised, though, that there is nothing in the comparative cost doctrine that ensures equality in the distribution of gains from trade creation (which explains, in part, why attempts in East Africa and the West Indies to establish free-trade areas met with difficulties).

There is also the important question of whether the full employment of resources can be maintained in each country. The classical doctrine of free trade assumes that all commodities are produced under conditions of constant returns to scale and that the full employment of resources is maintained as resources are switched from one activity to another in accordance with comparative advantage. If some activities, such as primary commodities, are subject to diminishing returns, however, there is a limit to employment in these activities, and it is possible that the real income gains from specialisation will be offset by the real income losses from unemployed resources.

If industrial activities are subject to increasing returns, trade will lead to the unequal accumulation of resources between primary producing and industrial countries, and be a force perpetuating inequality.

The dynamic gains from trade

Now let us turn to the dynamic gains from trade. The major dynamic benefit of trade is that export markets widen the total market for a country's producers. If production is subject to increasing returns, the total gains from trade will exceed the static gains from a more efficient allocation of resources. With increasing returns to scale, any country may benefit from trade irrespective of the terms of trade. Hicks (1959) has argued that it is impossible to make sense of the phenomenon of internationl trade unless one lays great stress upon increasing returns owing to the close connection between increasing returns and the accumulation of capital. For a small country with no trade there is very limited scope for large-scale investment in advanced capital equipment; specialisation is limited by the extent of the market. But if the poor developing country can trade, there is some prospect of industrialisation and of dispensing with traditional methods of production. The larger the market, the easier capital accumulation becomes if there are increasing returns to scale. In this respect large countries, like India, are in a more favourable position than smaller countries, such as Sri Lanka or Jamaica. India's large population offers a promising basis for the establishment of capital-goods industries and the production of manufactured goods, since production can take place on a viable basis before trade. The smaller country, however, may need substantial protection for a commodity before it can be produced economically and compete in world markets. At least sixty countries classified as 'developing', however, have populations of less than 15 million. Other important dynamic effects of trade consist of the stimulus to competition, the acquisition of new knowledge, new ideas and the dissemination of technical knowledge, the possibility of accompanying capital flows, increased specialisation leading to more roundabout methods of production, and changes in attitudes and institutions. In terms of **Figure 15.1**, the effect of dynamic benefits is to shift outwards the production-possibility curves of both countries leading to a higer level of community welfare.

Trade as a vent for surplus

Another important potential gain from trade is the provision of an outlet for a country's surplus commodities which would otherwise go unsold and represent a waste of resources. This is the so-called 'vent for surplus' gain from trade. In **Figure 15.1** this is represented by a movement from a point inside the production-possibility frontier to a point on the frontier — which represents a higher level of welfare. For there to be a gain implies that the 'surplus' export resources have no alternative uses and could not be switched to domestic use. This may not be as unreasonable an assumption as it sounds, bearing in mind the country's resource endowments in relation to its population size and the tastes of the community. Mines and fishing grounds, for example, have no alternative uses, and the marginal utility of consuming their products would soon become zero if demand was confined to domestic consumption alone. As a theory of trade, Myint (1958) has argued that the vent for surplus theory is a much more plausible theory than the comparative cost doctrine in explaining the rapid expansion of export production in most parts of the developing world in the nineteenth century. First, had there not been unutilised resources the expansion process could not have kept going. Second, the comparative cost theory cannot explain why, when two countries are similar, one develops a major export sector while the other does not; vent for surplus (related to relative population pressures) is one possible explanation. Third, vent for surplus is a much more plausible explanation for the start of trade. It is difficult to believe that small-scale peasant farmers with no surplus would start specialising according to the law of comparative advantage in the anticipation of reaching a higher consumption-possibility curve. In response to Myint's arguments there is a distinction to be made here between the *type* of commodity traded and the *basis* for trade in the sense of what gets trade started. Vent for surplus may explain better the original basis of trade, while comparative cost theory explains the type of commodity traded. Vent for surplus has no explanatory power in this latter connection.

Finally, a fourth potential gain from trade, which merits distinguishing as a separate effect, is that exports permit imports which may be more productive than domestic resources both directly and indirectly. We saw in the discussion of dual-gap analysis in Chapter 14 that imports can be regarded as substitutes for domestic capital goods with the capacity to lower the overall capital-output ratio through their superior efficiency and impact on the economy at large, especially by relieving domestic bottlenecks. In this sense exports have supply effects as well as demand effects which it is important to take into account in considering the relation between exports and growth.

Export-led growth

Historically, David Ricardo (1772-1823) was the founder of the comparative cost, classical free-trade doctrine. Before him Adam Smith (1723-90) had stressed the importance of trade as a vent for surplus and as a means of widening the market, thereby improving the division of labour and the level of productivity. According to Smith:

> between whatever place foreign trade is carried on, they all of them derive two distinct benefits from it. It carries out the surplus part of the produce of their land and labour for which their is no demand among them, and brings back in return for it something else for which there is a demand. It gives a value to their superfluities, by exchanging them for something else, which may satisfy a part of their wants and increase their enjoyments. By means of it, the narrowness of the home market does not hinder the division of labour in any particular branch of art or manufacture from being carried to the highest perfection. By opening a more extensive market for whatever part of the produce of their labour may exceed the home consumption, it encourages them to improve its productive powers and to augment its annual produce to the utmost, and thereby to increase the real revenue of wealth and society (Smith (1776)).

In the nineteenth century Smith's productivity doctrine developed beyond a free-trade argument into an export-drive argument, particularly in the colonies. This partly explains why some critics have associated the classical theory of trade with colonialism, and why Smith has been attacked and not Ricardo, the official founder of classical free-trade theory.

J. S. Mill (1806-73) rejected Smith's vent for surplus argument on the grounds that resources are mobile. But Mill did accept the importance of the dynamic-effects of trade (what he called indirect effects) and he also stressed the favourable effect of imports on work effort (the international demonstration effect in modern parlance).

The development literature abounds with models of **export-led growth**, and it is claimed that both historically and in the contemporary world economy, trade has been the engine of growth. Chenery and Strout (1966) remark that there is almost no example of a country which has for a long period sustained a growth rate substantially higher than its growth of exports, and the Pearson Commission (1969) claimed that the growth rates of individual developing countries since 1950 correlate better with their export performance than with any other single economic indicator. We have given reasons why this might be so. In modern times countries such as Singapore, Japan, South Korea and Hong Kong have certainly achieved remarkable growth by the export of manufactures, and historically there seems to be a consensus among economic historians that in the nineteenth century trade acted as an engine of growth, not only in that it contributed to a more efficient allocation of resources within countries, but because it transmitted growth from one part of the world to another. The demand in Europe, and in Britain in particular, for raw materials brought prosperity to such countries as Canada, Argentina, South Africa, Australia and New Zealand. As the demand for their commodities increased, investment in these countries also increased. Trade was mutually profitable. Alfred Marshall wrote in the nineteenth century: 'the causes which determine the economic progress of nations belong to the study of international trade' (Marshall (1890)). One of the foremost contemporary exponents of trade as the engine of growth was Arthur Lewis, who bases his theory on what appears to be from his researches a stable relationship between economic growth in developed countries and export growth in developing countries (see, for example, Lewis (1980)).

There are two main categories of model of export-led growth. The first relates to the possibility that export growth may set up a virtuous circle of growth, such that once a country is launched on the path, it maintains its competitive position in world trade and performs continually better relative to other countries. This type of model can be used to explain geographic dualism in the world economy, and we articulated such a model in Chapter 5. The second category of model stresses that export growth relieves a country of a balance-of-payments constraint on demand, so that the faster exports grow, the faster output growth can be without running into balance-of-payments difficulties. This type of model is developed in the next chapter on the balance of payments and growth.

The statistical evidence for today's developing countries is not unequivocal, but in general it supports the hypothesis that the growth of exports plays a major part in the growth process by stimulating demand and encouraging saving and capital accumulation, and, because exports increase the supply potential of the economy, by raising the capacity to import. Some studies of the role of exports examine the export-growth relation directly, others the import-growth relation.

The export-growth studies are of two types: time-series for individual countries; and cross-section taking a sample of countries at a point in time. In a fifty-country cross-section study, Emery (1967) found a strong relation taking average values of *per capita* income growth and export growth over the period 1953-63. Syron and Walsh (1968) divided Emery's sample into 'developed' and 'less developed' countries and found the relation to be strong in both groups of countries. In a twenty-country study for the period 1961-6 Stein (1971) found a strong relation between both exports and imports and growth. The correlation between imports and growth is slightly higher than between exports and growth but both correlations are significant at the 95 per cent confidence level. Maizels (1968) has related output growth to export growth for sixteen countries over the period 1953-62, and estimates the equation $y = a + 0.55(x)$, $r^2 = 0.47$. He concludes that the relation is not particularly strong; on the other hand, he finds a stong time-series relation between exports and growth *within* countries. So, too, does the most recent work of Salvatore and Hatcher (1991) who take 26 countries over the years 1963 and 1985, and find the export growth variable significantly positive in 16 of the countries.

The South East Asian countries of Japan, South Korea, Taiwan, Singapore and Hong Kong provide classic case studies of export-led growth, as do Germany and Italy among developed countries in the 1950s and 1960s.

Studies have also been done of the direct effect of exports on savings. Exports are important for saving not only through their effects on output but also because the export sector tends to have a higher propensity to save than the rest of the economy. Exports, especially of primary commodities, tend to produce highly concentrated incomes which raises the level of saving for any given aggregate level of income. Also it should be remembered that government saving relies heavily on export taxes in many developing countries. Maizels (1968) has fitted the savings function, $S = a_0 + b(Y - X) + c_0(X)$, where Y is gross national product and X is export earnings, to data for eleven countries. In eight out of the eleven countries he finds that export earnings contributed significantly to savings. Lee (1971) has extended Maizel's analysis taking twenty-eight countries for a longer time period. Maizel's results are further supported, and Lee finds the coefficient on X substantially higher than on $Y - X$ for many countries. Chenery and Eckstein (1970) and Papanek (1973) obtain similar results for different samples and different time periods.

The disadvantages of free trade for development

Now let us consider the potential disadvantages of adherence to the comparative cost doctrine. Like most micro-welfare theory, the comparative advantage/free-trade argument is a static one based on restrictive, and very often unrealistic, assumptions. As a criterion for the international allocation of resources it suffers from the same static defects as the investment criteria of traditional micro-economic theory that were discussed in Chapter 7. There may, in short, exist a conflict between short-run allocative efficiency and long-run growth. The doctrine assumes, for example, the existence of full employment in each country (otherwise there would be no opportunity cost involved in expanding the production of commodities); it assumes that the prices of resources and goods reflect their opportunity cost (i.e. that perfect competition exists), and that factor endowments are given and unalterable. Moreover, the doctrine ignores the effect of free trade on the terms of trade (movements in which affect real income), and the dynamic feedback effects that trade itself might have on comparative advantage. As a result, it can be argued that the principles of comparative advantage and free trade are not very useful concepts to employ in the context of developing countries which are in the throes of rapid structural change and which are concerned more with long-term development than with short-term efficiency. As many economists have commented, the doctrine of comparative advantage is more useful in explaining the past pattern of trade than for providing a guide as to what the future pattern of trade should be as a stimulus to development.

The question is not whether there should be trade but whether there should be free trade, as the doctrine of comparative costs implies. Might the long-run needs of the developing countries not be better served by protection? Those who question the assumptions of the comparative cost model, and who stress the relation between development and the balance of payments, express the view that the efficiency gains from free trade are unlikely to offset the tendency in a free market for the comparative position of developing countries to deteriorate *vis-à-vis* the developed countries. Free trade is claimed to work to the disadvantage of the developing countries largely because of the nature of the products which these countries seem destined to produce and trade under such a system. The answer is said to lie in a change in the structure of production and exports of the developing countries, which can only be fostered by the protection of new industries in the early stages of their development.

The development considerations that the doctrine of free trade overlooks are numerous. First, it ignores the balance-of-payments effects of free trade and the effect of free trade on the terms of trade. If the demands for different commodities grow at different rates owing to differences in their price and income elasticity of demand, free trade will work to the benefit of some countries and to the relative detriment of others. In short, free trade cannot be discussed independently of the balance-of-payments and the terms of trade. In classical theory, Viner (1953, p. 39) quotes Torrens, J. S. Mill, Marshall, Edgeworth and Taussig as conceding that unilateral substitution by a country of free trade for protection would move the terms of trade against the country. But most 'free-traders' ignored the subject. In general, the implicit assumption was that movement from protection to free trade would not alter the commodity terms of trade, or if it did that the gains from trade would more than offset any unfavourable terms of trade effect. If the terms of trade effect does offset the gains from trade, this would appear to provide a valid argument for protection. This is one of the lines that modern protectionists take. The case for protection of manufactured goods produced by developing countries is greater: the less the demand for existing primary products is expected to grow and the lower the price elasticity; the higher the internal elasticity of demand for manufactured products from the outside world, and the less the likelihood of retaliation by other countries.

A second factor which the free-trade doctrine tends to overlook is that some activities are subject to increasing returns while others are subject to diminishing returns. The commodities most susceptible to diminishing returns are primary products, where the scope for technical progress is also probably less than in the case of manufactured goods. This being so, one might expect a rise in the ratio of primary to manufactured good prices, and diminishing returns would not matter so much if the goods were price inelastic. In practice, however, there has been a substitution of synthetic substitutes for primary products, and the terms of trade have deteriorated (see later) partly because of substitution and partly because of the fact that the demand for primary commodities in general, in relation to supply, has expanded much less than in the case of manufactured commodities. But whatever the movement in the terms of trade, it is somehow perverse to recommend a trade and development policy based on activities subject to diminishing returns, particularly in the light of the theory of cumulative causation that we discussed in Chapter 5.

A third disadvantage of adherence to the comparative advantage doctrine is that it could lead to excessive specialisation on a narrow range of products, putting the economy at the mercy of outside influences. The possibility of severe balance-of-payments instability resulting from specialisation may be damaging to development.

Fourth, comparative cost analysis glosses over the fact that comparative advantage may change over time, or that it could be changed by deliberate policies for the protection of certain activities. There is no reason why countries should be condemned to the production and export of the same commodities for ever. If comparative advantage is not given by nature, as the doctrine of free trade seems to suggest, but can be altered, the case for protection is strengthened.

It should also be remembered that the concept of comparative advantage is based on calculations of private cost. But we have seen in Chapter 8 that in developing countries social costs may diverge markedly from private costs, and that social benefit may exceed the private benefit because of externalities. If private costs exceed social costs in industry (because wage rates are artificially high, for example), and social benefits from industrial projects exceed private benefits, there is a strong argument for protecting industry in order to encourage the transfer of labour from other activities into industry to equate private and social cost and private and social benefit.

Last, it may be mentioned that the export growth of some activities has relatively little secondary impact on other activities. Primary commodities fall into this category. The evidence is abundant that the export growth of primary commodities has not had the development impact that might be expected from the expansion of industrial exports. The reasons are not hard to understand. Primary production has very few backward or forward linkages; and, historically, it has tended to be undertaken by foreign enterprise with a consequent outflow of profits. The secondary repercussions of the pattern of trade also tend to be overlooked by the free-trade doctrine.

*   *   *   *   *   *

New trade theories for developing countries: the Prebisch Doctrine[1]

Raùl Prebisch was one of the first development economists to question the mutual profitability of the international division of labour for developing countries on existing lines. Prebisch is one of those who looks at the relation between trade and development from the standpoint of the balance of payments rather than real resources. His major claim is that the unfavourable impact of unrestricted trade on the terms of trade and balance of payments of developing countries far outweighs any advantages with respect to a more efficient allocation of resources. His concern is with two distinct, but not unrelated, phenomena. One is the transference of the benefits of technical progress from the developing to the developed countries. The second is the balance-of-payments effects of differences in the income elasticity of demand for different types of products. He divides the world into industrial 'centres' and 'peripheral' countries and then conducts his analysis within the framework of the traditional two-country, two-commodity case of international trade theory — equating the developing countries with primary producers (the 'periphery') and the developed countries with secondary producers (the 'centre').

Technical progress and the terms of trade

As we said earlier, in theory the barter terms of trade might be expected to move in favour of the developing countries. For one thing, primary-product production tends to be subject to diminishing returns, and for another technical progress tends to be more rapid in manufacturing industry than in agriculture. If prices are related to costs one would expect in theory the ratio of primary-product prices to industrial-good prices to rise. According to Prebisch, however, the ratio has shown a long-run tendency to fall. He advances two explanations for this and hence why the benefits of technical progress tend to flow from the developing to developed countries and not the other way round. His first explanation concerns the relation between incomes and productivity. He suggests that whereas factor incomes tend to rise with productivity increases in developed countries, they rise more slowly than productivity in the developing countries owing to population pressure and surplus manpower. Thus there is a greater upward pressure on final goods' prices in developed than in developing countries, causing the ratio of prices to move in the opposite direction to that suggested by the pace of technical progress. The second explanation is that a ratchet effect operates with primary product prices *relative* to manufactured goods' prices falling during cyclical downturns by more than they rise *relative* to the prices of manufacturers on the upturns. Such asymmetrical cycles, illustrated in **Figure 15.4**, would produce a secular trend deterioration.[2] Furthermore, according to Prebisch, not only do the terms of trade deteriorate, but if prices must be reduced to clear the market, export earnings will fall if the demand for primary commodities is price inelastic. This is a related sense in which technical progress is 'transferred' from the developing countries to the industrial 'centres'.

Figure 15.4

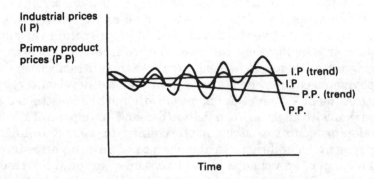

The income elasticity of demand for products and the balance of payments

The second phenomenon mentioned by Prebisch is the balance-of-payments effects of differences in the income elasticity of demand for different types of products. It is generally recognised and agreed that the income elasticity of demand for most primary commodities is lower than that for manufactured products. On average, the elasticity is probably less than unity, resulting in a decreasing proportion of income spent on those commodities (commonly known as Engel's Law). In the two-country, two-commodity case the lower-income elasticity of demand for primary commodities will mean that for a given growth of world income the balance of payments of primary-producing, developing countries will *automatically* deteriorate *vis-à-vis* the balance of payments of developed countries producing and exporting industrial goods. A simple example will illustrate the point.

Suppose that the income elasticity of demand for the exports of the developing countries is 0.8 and that the growth of world income is 3.0 per cent: exports will then grow at 2.4 per cent. Now suppose that the income elasticity of demand for the exports of developed countries is 1.3 and the growth of world income is 3.0 per cent; exports of developed countries will then grow at 3.9 per cent. Since there are only two sets of countries, the developing countries' exports are the imports of developed countries and the exports of developed countries are the imports of the developing countries. Thus developing countries' exports grow at 2.4 per cent but imports grow at 3.9 per cent; developed countries' exports grow at 3.9 per cent and imports at 2.4 per cent. Starting from equilibrium, the balance of payments of the developing countries automatically worsens while the developed countries show a surplus. This has further repercussions on the terms of trade. With imports growing faster than exports in developing countries, and the balance of payments deteriorating, the terms of trade will also deteriorate through depreciation of the currency, which may cause the balance of payments to deteriorate even more if imports and exports are price inelastic.

Moreover, this is not the end of the story if we take the *per capita* income growth between developed and developing countries. If population growth is faster in developing countries, the growth of income must also be faster than in the developed countries if *per capita* income growth rates are to remain the same. This will mean an even faster growth rate of imports into developing countries and a more serious deterioration in the balance of payments. And if the goal is to *narrow* relative or absolute differences in *per capita* income between developed and developing countries, the balance-of-payments implications will be even more severe. In the example previously given, which ignores differences in population growth, it is easily seen that the price of balance-of-payments equilibrium is slower growth for the developing countries. If their exports are growing at 2.4 per cent, import growth must be constrained to 2.4 per cent which means that with an income elasticity of demand for imports of 1.3, income growth in the developing countries must be restrained to 2.4/1.3 = 1.85 per cent for balance-of-payments equilibrium. In the absence of foreign borrowing to bridge the foreign exchange gap, or a change in the structure of exports, the result of different income elasticities of demand for primary and manufactured products is slower growth in the primary-producing countries — perpetuating the development 'gap'. In the absence of protection, the only other alternative is deliberate depreciation of the currency. This has several disadvantages. For one thing the price elasticities of exports and imports may not be right for foreign exchange earnings to be increased, and second, depreciation will encourage production in existing activities, the concentration on which has contributed to the balance-of-payments difficulties in the first place.

There are certain equilibrating mechanisms in existence which may reverse the tendencies referred to, but they are likely to be weak and fairly slow in operating. First of all, it cannot be assumed that the industrial structure of the developing countries will remain unchanged. Over time it is natural that the proportion of total resources employed in the production of manufactured goods should increase, decreasing the rate of increase of imports of manufactured goods. Second, assuming that money income and population grow at the same rate in both sets of countries, if the terms of trade are deteriorating for the developing countries, then *real per capita* income cannot be growing so rapidly in developing countries. Thus even with a high income elasticity of demand for imports in developing countries, the absolute increments in imports may eventually equal exports through a terms of trade effect. Prebisch recognises this latter equilibrating mechanism, but rejects reliance upon it because of the sacrifice of real growth that it clearly involves.

For balance-of-payments and terms-of-trade reasons (which are not unconnected), Prebisch therefore argues for the protection of certain domestically produced goods and the virtual establishment of monopolist export pricing by developing countries. Prebisch's balance-of-payments argument reinforces the classical infant-industry argument for protection to safeguard the terms of trade. Scitovsky (1942) showed long ago that in the two-country, two-commodity case a country can always gain by levying certain tariffs to improve its terms of trade which offset any losses from resource 'misallocation' as a result of the tariff — provided, of course, the other country does not retaliate. This is the notion of the 'optimum' tariff.

There are several benefits that Prebisch expects from protection. Protection would enable scarce foreign exchange to be rationed between different categories of imports, and could help to correct balance-of-payments disequilibrium resulting from a high income elasticity of demand for certain types of imports. Second, it could help to arrest the deterioration in the terms of trade by damping down the demand for imports; and third, it provides the opportunity to diversify exports and to start producing and exporting goods with a much higher income elasticity of demand in world markets. Following our earlier argument, however, protection by tariffs is only appropriate if the arguments for protection do no arise from domestic distortions.

Recent trends in the terms of trade

Whether the terms of trade have moved unfavourably against primary commodities and the developing countries is an empirical question. Prebisch originally suggested an average deterioration of the terms of trade of primary commodities between 1876 and 1938 of 0.9 per cent per annum. Work by Hans Singer at the United Nations in 1949 also suggested a trend deterioration of 0.64 per cent per annum over the same period. The **Prebisch-Singer thesis** of the declining terms of trade for primary commodities was born (see Singer (1950)). In a detailed reappraisal of Prebisch's work, Spraos (1980) confirms the historical trend deterioration, but at the lower rate of approximately 0.5 per cent, having corrected the statistics for the changing quality of goods, shipping costs and so on. Extending the data to 1970, however, Spraos concluded that there is no significant trend deterioration. Sapsford ((1985) and (1988)), however, shows that it is the wartime structural break which makes the whole series look trendless. If the series is divided into two sub-periods — pre- and post-Second World War — there is a trend deterioration in both subperiods and the estimated trend deterioration over the whole period 1900-82 is 1.2 per cent per annum, allowing for the wartime structural break. The downward trend has continued (see **Figure 15.5**).

Grilli and Yang (1988) at the World Bank reach the same conclusion as Sapsford. Over the period 1900 to 1983, they put the percentage terms of trade deterioration of all primary commodities at 0.5 per cent per annum, and 0.6 per cent per annum for non-fuel commodities (allowing for the wartime structural break). For individual commodities, the trend deterioration is estimated as: food (-0.3 per cent p.a.); cereals (-0.6 per cent p.a.); non-food agricultural commodities (-0.8 per cent p.a.), and metals (-0.8) per cent p.a.). Only tropical beverages registered an improvement (0.6 per cent p.a.)

My own work with Bergevin (Thirlwall and Bergevin (1985)) concentrated on the post-war years, distinguishing between primary commodities exported by developing countries on the one hand and by developed countries on the other, estimating separately from 1960 to 1972 (before the oil shock) and 1973 to 1982 using quarterly data. For all primary commodities from developing countries, the annual trend deterioration was 0.5 per cent from 1960 to 1972 and 0.36 per cent from 1973 to 1982 (excluding oil). For primary commodities from developed countries, the trend was not significant.

Figure 15.5 *Movements in net barter terms of trade.*

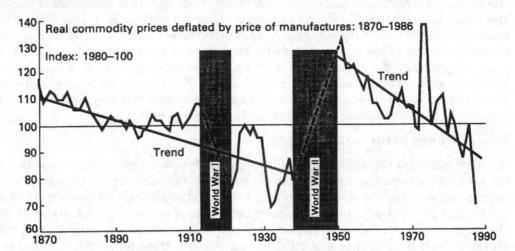

Source: South Magazine, October, 1987.

The terms of trade of primary commodities relative to manufactures is not necessarily the same as the terms of trade of developing countries relative to industrial countries, because both sets of countries export and import both types of goods (albeit in different ratios), but in practice there is likely to be a close overlap and parallel movement between the two. Sarkar (1986) has looked at the export prices of developing countries relative to developed countries, and also at the prices of exports from developing to developed countries relative to prices of imports from developed countries to developing countries (both excluding fuel). In the first case, the trend deterioration was 0.51 per cent per annum; in the second case, the relative deterioration was 0.93 per cent per annum. Overall, there can be little doubt that over the last 30 years or so both the terms of trade of primary commodities, and the terms of trade of the developing countries as a whole, have deteriorated at roughly the average rate of the deterioration in the terms of trade of primary commodities since the turn of the century.

Sarkar and Singer (1991) have also looked at the terms of trade of *manufactures* exported by developing countries relative to developed countries over the period 1970-87, and find a deterioration of approximately 1 per cent per annum. It appears, therefore, that the developing countries suffer double jeopardy. Not only do the prices of their primary products decline relative to manufactured goods, but also the prices of these manufactured exports decline relative to those of developed countries, reflecting, no doubt, the commodity composition of their exports — their lower value-added and lower income elasticity of demand in world markets.

The terms of trade for each developing country between 1985 and 1990 is shown in a previous table [Table 15.1]. It can be seen from the table that there is a wide variety of experience between countries reflecting the diverse commodity composition of their exports and imports; but taking the low-income and middle-income countries together, the evidence shows a deterioration for the developing countries as a whole of 6 per During the previous twenty years there had already been a 15 per cent deterioration in low-income countries. For the industrialised countries there was virtually no change — the rise in the price of manufactures being offset by the rise in the price of oil. A large part of the debt problem was the result of the collapse of commodity prices in the 1980s.

There is a distinction to be made between the **barter (or commodity) terms of trade** which measures the ratio of export to import prices, and the **income terms of trade**, which is the ratio of export to import prices times the quantity of exports (i.e. *(Px / Pm)* x *Qx*). The income terms of trade is thus a measure of the total purchasing power of exports over imports.

From the point of view of development, measured by *per capita* income, the income terms of trade is perhaps the more relevant concept to consider than the barter terms of trade. It may well be, for instance, that the price of exports falls relative to imports owing to increased efficiency in the exporting country, and this releases resources for further exports which subsequently expand more than proportionately to the fall in price. The barter terms of trade would have worsened, but development would be stimulated. It is also worth remembering that when a country devalues its currency it deliberately worsens its barter terms of trade in the hope that the balance of payments will improve, providing scope for a faster growth of real income through a rapidly improved income terms of trade. On the other hand, if the demand for a country's exports is inelastic, then a decline in the barter terms of trade will also mean a deterioration in the income terms of trade.

In the long run, if world trade is buoyant, every country can experience an improvement in its income terms of trade. The question is not who are the gainers and who are the losers, as in the case of the barter terms of trade, but what are the relative rates of improvement in the income terms of trade? It is fairly clear that since the barter terms of trade has deteriorated for developing countries, and the rate of export growth has been slower in developing countries than in developed countries, the income terms of trade has also grown slower for the developing countries.

Trade theory and dual-gap analysis

Another dimension to the protectionist argument has been added by Linder (1967), drawing explicitly on dual-gap analysis. The crucial question, argues Linder, is whether a developing country's economic potential can be fully utilised at the same time as equilibrium is maintained externally. Free trade may not lead to the full employment of resources for two reasons: first, because of factor immobility; and second, because certain imports may be required to achieve full utilisation of resources and these import requirements may exceed exports. In our earlier discussion of dual-gap analysis in Chapter 14, we saw that if the import-export gap is dominant and foreign exchange is scarce, domestic resources may go unutilised in the absence of development policies to equate the import-export gap and the investment-savings gap *ex ante*. Potential domestic saving will fall either through a fall in the potential level of output or through a fall in the propensity to save through a redirection of expenditure. One solution, however, is to devote more domestic resources to import substitution or export promotion.

But Linder argues that in developing countries it may not be possible to solve the problem of the domestic underutilisation of resources through trade because of an export maximum. Classical trade theory, however, does not admit this. The notion of an export maximum is related to what Linder calls the **theory of 'representative demand'**, which determines the relative price structure for goods. The theory of representative demand states that the production function for a commodity will be the more advantageous in a country the more the demand for a commodity is typical of the economic structure of a country compared with other countries. The chief determinant of demand structure is *per capita* income, so that goods in demand in advanced countries have unfavourable production functions in developing countries and vice versa. The developing countries are therefore faced with severe marketing problems if they are to develop by trade. The goods they are best at producing are not demanded in developed countries, and they are very inefficient at producing the goods that are demanded in developed countries. Productivity may not be high enough to support resources in the production of these goods, and imported inputs for export production might absorb more foreign exchange than the exports eventually yield.

In Linder's view these circumstances provide a case for protection to save foreign exchange and to enable the full utilisation of domestic resources. This contrasts with conventional theory which does not allow for protection for balance-of-payments reasons or to increase the effective demand for domestic products to eliminate underemployment. Moreover, protection in this model involves no allocation losses because if foreign exchange is required to utilise domestic resources fully, the opportunity cost of resources is zero. The only qualification Linder makes to his argument for development based on import substitution and the expansion of domestic demand is if value-added is negative; that is, if imported inputs for domestic production involve a higher foreign exchange cost than the importation of the end-products themselves. Except in these circumstances, there is no conflict between allocation and capacity considerations or allocative efficiency and import substitution as long as a foreign exchange gap exists. Import substitution frees foreign exchange for imported inputs which allow the full utilisation of domestic resources.

Trade policies

Prebisch and Linder both provide powerful critiques of neoclassical trade theory, but attack from different angles. While Linder argues the case for protection for the full utilisation of domestic resources, Prebisch argues the case for protection on the more 'orthodox' grounds of improving the terms of trade, and as a substitute for exchange depreciation to preserve simultaneous internal and external equilibrium. Moreover, while Linder argues explicitly for import substitution because of the existence of an export maximum, Prebisch seems to be more optimistic about growth through trade and against 'inward-looking' development policies. New export activities may, of course, require tariff protection or subsidisation in the early stages of their establishment, but there is a distinct difference between identifying lines of activity in which to promote exports and identifying lines of activity in which to develop import substitutes, and we must briefly examine these different strategies. In the fomer case, one is seeking out lines of comparative advantage; in the latter case, one is attempting to reverse the pattern of trade by altering comparative advantage.

If we accept the possibility of an import-export gap, because of a lack of substitutability in the short run between imports and domestic resources, Linder's argument for import substitution basically reduces to pessimism over the chances of promoting exports as an alternative means of fully utilising domestic resources. He admits that import-substitution activities will themselves require imports and presumably thinks, therefore, that, per unit of expansion of domestic output, import substitution would save more foreign exchange than could be earned by export promotion. The traditional case for export promotion is that it allows growth to proceed without foreign exchange difficulties and without suffering the allocative losses from violating comparative advantage.

What trade policy should be adopted by any particular country clearly depends on circumstances. Certainly not all developing countries fit the Linder model. Most developing countries do suffer from severe foreign exchange shortages, but one must be a little suspicious of the concept of the export maximum. It is true that the demand for developing countries' exports tends to lag behind that of the developed countries, but as our earlier figures showed [Table 15.1], the export record of developing countries as a whole over the last two decades is not unrespectable. This, in some measure, is due to the greater diversification of exports than in the past, and there must be room for considerable improvement. The great danger of import-substitution policies is that by violating comparative advantage, increasing costs, and reducing competitiveness, they may impair the long-run efficiency and export-growth prospects of a country in the future.

The more lasting solution to balance-of-payments difficulties would seem to be the promotion of manufactured-goods exports, preferably with high price and income elasticities of demand, coupled with policies to substitute domestic resources for imports. If the prices of domestic and foreign resources reflected more accurately their opportunity costs, the import content of many activities might be reduced substantially. At the same time new areas of comparative advantage must be sought. If trade is not the engine of growth, it is probably a more desirable hand-maiden than development by import substitution.

The policy recommendation of export-led growth leads on to the question of the trading relation between developed and developing countries. There are several ways in which the developed countries can contribute to a solution of the balance-of-payments problems of developing countries, especially by helping export earnings. The means of help fall into two main categories which we shall consider in turn: first, the granting of trade preferences; and second, international commodity agreements to stabilise or increase earnings from exports.

Trade preferences

The main pressure group for trade preferences for developing countries' exports is the UN Conference on Trade and Development (UNCTAD), which was first convened in

Geneva in 1964. It was in this year that the Conference was converted into a permanent organisation consisting of 132 member countries, with a fifty-five-member Directing Board and a permanent Secretariat under Prebisch (who previously headed the UN Commission for Latin America) as Secretary-General. There have been seven further meetings of UNCTAD, the latest being in Colombia in 1992. Apart from these periodic meetings, the organisation exists as a continuous pressure group with the aim of assisting developing countries through trade and aid — primarily trade. Included among its objectives are: greater access to the markets of the developed countries through the reduction of trade restrictions; more stable commodity prices; assistance from the developed countries equivalent to 1 per cent of their national income; and compensation for developing countries whose foreign exchange earnings fall below 'expectations' owing to deterioration in their terms of trade. Its main platform, however, is for a system of tariff preferences for the developing countries' exports of manufactured and semi-manufactured goods on the lines of the Commonwealth preference agreement, or in the form of quotas of duty-free imports. In this respect, there is an important difference between UNCTAD and other bodies merely concerned with non-discriminatory reductions in barriers to world trade, e.g. the General Agreement on Tariffs and Trade (GATT).

Following the 1964 UNCTAD Conference, the establishment of a preferential system of tariff rates was negotiated whereby industrial nations would lower duties on imports from developing countries while continuing import duties at the same level on goods from other countries. On paper the agreement looked attractive. In practice, however, the scheme only covered 23 per cent of the value of export flows from developing countries, one-half of which went to the United States, which did not implement the scheme. Other countries excluded some commodities for protectionist reasons. According to calculations by Murray (1973), only about one billion dollars' worth of trade was covered, or 5 per cent of total trade. The scheme also embodied restrictive ceilings (quotas) so that the preferential tariff advantages disappeared for marginal trade. Over all, the benefits of the scheme have gone mainly to the ten or so more advanced developing countries who export products covered by the scheme, and not to the smaller, poorer developing nations.

Perhaps the most significant trade agreement negotiated to date to help poorer developing nations is that signed at the **Lomé Convention** 1975 between the European Economic Community and forty-six developing countries, mainly in Africa, which provided for free access to the European market for all the developing countries' manufactured goods and also for 90 per cent of their agricultural exports. In addition agreement was reached to stabilise the foreign exchange earnings of twelve key commodities: cocoa, groundnuts, coffee, cotton, coconuts, palm, hides and skins, wood, bananas, tea, sisal and iron ore (the so-called **Stabex scheme**). The producers of these commodities are guaranteed a certain level of earnings, provided the commodity concerned represents a certain minimum proportion of total export earnings of the producer country. If so, it may request a transfer from the EEC when export earnings fall by more than 7.5 per cent below a four-year moving average. The Lomé Convention also disperses aid to the African, Caribbean and Pacific (ACP) countries through the

European Development Fund. Since 1975 the Convention has been renegotiated three times.

Effective protection

In arguing for lower tariffs and tariff preferences, a distinction needs to be made between nominal protection and effective rates of protection. It is now widely recognised, in theory and in practice, that nominal tariffs on commodities are not the appropriate basis for assessing the restrictive effect of a tariff structure on trade.[3]

The nominal rate does not measure how inefficient (or costly) a producer can be without incurring competition and losing his market. This is measured by the protection of **value added**, which is the difference between the value of output and the value of inputs. The protection of value added is the so-called **effective rate of protection**. Since value added is the difference between the value of output and inputs, not only is the tariff on output important in measuring the degree of protection, but also the tariff on inputs.

Formally, the effective rate of protection is measured as the excess of domestic value added over value-added at world prices expressed as a percentage of the latter. Thus the effective rate of protection of industry X may be defined as:

$$EP_x = \frac{V'_x - V_x}{V_x} = \frac{V'_x}{V_x} - 1$$

where V'_x is domestic value added under protection and V_x is value added under free-market conditions (at world prices). Domestic value added is equal to the sales of the industry's product minus the sum of intermediate inputs, all valued at domestic market prices, i.e. including the effect of tariffs on the finished good and on the inputs into the finished good. The free-market value added can be defined identically, but with the final product and input prices measured exclusive of tariffs on them. It is clear that the height of the effective tariff rate depends on three variables: (i) the level of nominal tariffs on output, (ii) the proportion of value added to total output, and (iii) the level of nominal tariffs on the industry's inputs. The higher the nominal tariff, the lower the tariff on imported inputs, and the higher the proportion of value added to total output, the higher the effective rate of protection. If the tariff on finished goods is very high and the tariff on inputs is low, domestic value added can be very high; world value added in turn can be very low, giving enormous rates of effective protection, sometimes in excess of 1000 per cent.

Let us now give a practical example. Suppose Indian textiles have a world price of $5, of which $3 represents raw-material costs and $2 represents value added. Now let us suppose that imports of Indian textiles into a developed country are subject to a tariff of 20 per cent while domestic producers must pay a tariff of 10 per cent on textile raw materials. To remain competitive, the domestic producer must produce the commodity for not more than $6. The value added can be $6 minus the cost of raw materials plus the tariff on raw materials, i.e. $6 — ($3 + $0.30) = $2.70. The effective rate of protection is the difference between the domestic value added and Indian value added (i.e. value added at world prices) expressed as a percentage of Indian value added, i.e. (2.70 — 2)/2

= 35 per cent. This is the effective rate of protection equal to the difference between the gross subsidy on value added provided by the tariff on the final product ($(1/2) = 50 per cent) and the implicit tax on value added as a result of the tariff on raw materials ($(0.30/2) = 15 per cent). This is the extent (35 per cent) to which production can be more costly in the developed country without losing competitive advantage, or, to put it another way, it is the degree to which Indian textile producers would have to be more productive to compete in the developed country market.

Effective rates of protection almost always exceed nominal rates. At one extreme if a country gets raw material inputs duty free (at world prices) but puts a tariff on the final good, the effective rate must be higher than the nominal rate. At the other extreme, if a country puts a tariff on inputs but no tariff on the finished good, the effective rate of protection is negative.[4]

The calculations of the effective rate of protection also depend on what exchange rate is employed. If the exchange rate of a country in the protected situation is overvalued, the price of imported inputs measured in domestic currency will be undervalued and this will affect the calculation of the domestic value added and the value added at world market prices. Without adjustment for this factor, effective rates of protection are described as 'gross'; with adjustment they are referred to as 'net'.

Our example of the effective rate of protection also assumed that all inputs are traded. Some inputs will be non-traded, however, and their price enters into both the value of total output and total inputs. If the effect of protection on the price of non-traded goods is ignored, the rates of effective protection will be overestimated. It is not in practice easy to estimate the effect of protection on the price of non-traded goods.

The theory of effective protection suggests that the same *nominal* tariff cuts mean different degrees of change in effective rates of protection, and it may thus by unwise for the developing countries to press for across-the-board tariff cuts on all commodities. Reductions in tariffs against their primary products will increase the effective rate of protection against their manufactures, which, we have argued, are more important exports as far as long-run development prospects are concerned. The average nominal level of protection in developed countries is about 12 per cent, but effective protection against the goods of developing countries may well be in the region of 30 per cent or more. Developing countries themselves may give their own producers very high rates of effective protection. Little, Scitovsky and Scott (1970) quote average rates on manufactured goods of 162 per cent in Argentina, 116 per cent in Brazil, 271 per cent in Pakistan and 313 per cent in India.[5]

The argument for reductions in tariffs against the final manufactured goods of developing countries is unexceptional, but is it doubtful whether there is much scope for preferences to contribute substantially to an increase in export earnings. Export prices would have to be less than the domestic price in the preference-giving country and must not exceed the competitor's price by more than the amount of the preference. On the assumption that the tariff rate on manufactured goods in the advanced industrial countries is between 10 and 15 per cent, and that the advanced countries were willing to give 50 per cent preference, this would mean a preference margin of only

5-8 per cent. Industries in which a preference margin of 5-8 per cent would enable developing countries to take markets away from domestic producers and developed country competitors are likely to be few and far between.

But it is not only tariffs that restrict trade. There are many non-tariff barriers to trade in manufactures between developed and developing countries, the removal of which might contribute more to increasing export earnings than a simple reduction in tariff barriers, e.g. licensing requirements, quotas, foreign exchange restrictions, procurement policies favouring domestic products, anti-dumping regulations, subsidies to export in developed countries, and so on.

Trade between developing countries

Trade between developed and developing countries is likely to involve the developing countries in continual deficit. Moreover, it is difficult for the developing countries to penetrate the developed countries' markets for manufactured goods when the cost of producing manufactured goods is frequently much higher than in the developed countries. A possible simultaneous solution to the achievement of a higher utilisation of manufacturing capacity and the avoidance of payments problems with developed countries is for the developing countries to issue their own international money, on lines originally suggested by the Stewarts (1972), which would increase the purchasing power of each developing country and encourage trade between the developing countries themselves. The Stewarts suggest that the developing countries as a group should issue their own international money, *rocnabs* (*bancor* backwards, which was the name for the new international money suggested by Keynes at Bretton Woods in 1944), which they would agree to accept in part payment for goods sold to each other. This would have the effect of increasing the purchasing power of every developing country over the goods and services of every other country in the group. Exports would expand, but the reserve position of the importing country would be unimpaired. In effect *rocnabs* would work like Special Drawing Rights work on a world scale. Because countries would accept *rocnabs* in part payment for exports there would be an incentive for countries with foreign exchange difficulties to switch imports from developed countries to other developing countries because imports would cost less in convertible currencies. Exports to other developing countries would be encouraged where countries could not sell all they could produce in hard-currency markets. One problem that might arise is some countries accumulating *rocnabs* which they had no use for, while other countries in persistent deficit run short. To make the scheme workable it might be necessary to get each country into trading balance with all other countries taken as a group (although not with any one country). Alternatively, accumulated *rocnabs* could be sold back at a discount to deficit countries and used again. The main advantage of the scheme is that it requires little cooperation for it to be workable once the initial decision to issue and accept *rocnabs* has been taken, and it does not require action by the developed countries, which is so often a major stumbling block to the implementation of measures to improve the economic condition of the developing countries.

International Commodity Agreements[6]

The developing countries in particular, and the world economy in general, suffer several problems from the uncontrolled movements of primary commodity prices. First there is the fact already mentioned of the gradual trend deterioration in the prices of primary commodities relative to industrial goods, which reduces the real income and welfare of the developing countries directly. Secondly, primary product prices are much more cyclically volatile than industrial goods' prices. Since 1960, for every 1 per cent change (up and down) in the prices of industrial goods, primary product prices have fluctuated by 2.4 per cent (see Thirlwall and Bergevin (1985)). Disaggregation by commodity group shows a cyclical elasticity of 1.25 for food; 1.3 for agricultural non-food products, and 2.9 for minerals (including petroleum). This volatility has a number of detrimental consequencs. First it leads to a great deal of instability in the foreign exchange earnings and balance of payments position of developing countries which makes investment planning and economic management much more difficult than otherwise would be the case. Secondly, because of asymmetries in the economic system, volatility imparts inflationary bias combined with tendencies to depression in the world economy at large. When primary product prices fall, the demand for industrial goods falls but their prices are sticky downwards. When primary product prices rise, industrial goods' prices are quick to follow suit and governments depress demand to control inflation. The result is stagflation. Thirdly, the volatility of primary product prices leads to volatility in the terms of trade which may not reflect movements in the equilibrium terms of trade between primary products and industrial goods in the sense that supply and demand are equated in both markets. In these circumstances world economic growth becomes either supply constrained if primary product prices are 'too high' or demand constrained if primary product prices are 'too low' (see Chapter 3, p. 101; Thirlwall 1986). On all these macroeconomic grounds there is a *prima facie* case for attempting to introduce a greater degree of stability into markets for primary commodities (including, I believe, oil).

The issue of primary product price instability is not something new. It preoccupied Keynes both before and during the Second World War. In a memorandum in 1942 on the 'International Regulation of Primary Commodities' he remarked: 'one of the greatest evils in international trade before the war was the wide and rapid fluctuations in the world price of primary commodities ... It must be the primary purpose of control to prevent these wide fluctuations' (Moggridge 1980). Keynes followed up his observations and proposals with a more detailed plan for what he called '**commod control**' — an international body representing leading producers and consumers that would stand ready to buy 'commods' (Keynes's name for typical commodities), and store them, at a price (say) 10 per cent below the fixed basic price and sell them at 10 per cent above (Moggridge (1980)). The basic price would have to be adjusted according to whether there was a gradual run-down or build-up of stocks, indicating that the price is either 'too low' or 'too high'. If production did not adjust (at least downwards), Keynes recognised that production quotas might have to be implemented. Commodities should be stored as widely as possible across producing and consuming centres. This proposal is of some contemporary relevance as a means of responding quickly to conditions of famine. There could be a system of granaries strategically placed across the world under international supervision which could store surpluses and release them at time of need. The finance for the storage and holding of 'commods' in Keynes's scheme would have been provided through his proposal for an International Clearing Union, acting like a world Central Bank, with which 'commod controls' would keep accounts.

At the present time, finance for storage and holding could be provided through the issue of Special Drawing Rights (SDRs) by the IMF. A scheme, such as 'commod control' could make a major contribution to curing the international trade cycle with all its attendant implications. Over fifty years on from Keynes's wartime proposal, primary product price fluctuations still plague the world economy. The world still lacks the requisite international mechanisms to rectify what is a major source of instability for the world economy. From 1980 to 1991, primary product prices fell on average by 40 per cent, and this has been a major cause of the international debt crisis which still lingers.

In the recent past there have been five main international commodity agreements in operation accounting for some 35 per cent of non-oil exports of the developing countries, but all have had their difficulties in achieving price objectives. The agreements which have operated with spasmodic success are the International Sugar Agreement (1977), the Sixth International Tin Agreement (1981), the International Natural Rubber Agreement (1979), the International Cocoa Agreement (1980), and the International Coffee Agreement (1963).[7] Only the Rubber and Coffee agreements still function. The basic problem with all agreements is getting suppliers to abide by quotas to restrict output in the face of declining prices. Participants must share a common purpose. The most successful 'commodity agreement' of all in the world economy is the Common Agricultural Policy of the EEC.

Small fluctuations in the export earnings of developing countries, arising from falling prices, are capable of offsetting the whole of the value of foreign assistance to developing countries in any one year. Approximately a 10 per cent fall in export earnings would be equivalent to the annual flow of offical development assistance in 1991. Stability of export earnings, it would appear, is at least as important as foreign assistance.[8] In general, the instability of export proceeds is the joint product of variations in price and quantity. Large fluctuations in earnings may be causally related to four factors: (i) excessive variability of supply and demand; (ii) the low price elasticity of supply and demand; (iii) excessive specialisation on one or two commodities; (iv) the concentration of exports in particular markets. An early study by Macbean (1966) examined these casual factors for a selection of developing countries. He found variations in supply as the major determinant of the instability of export earnings. If the source of instability does come from the side of supply, stabilising prices will not, of course, stabilise earnings. It will positively impair them in times of scarcity and boost them in periods of glut. If there is a tendency towards perpetual over-supply, and demand is price inelastic, price stabilisation will maintain earnings, but price stabilisation will further encourage supply, which may then necessitate production quotas and lead to inefficiency in production if producing countries are allocated quotas to satisfy equity rather than efficiency. This is not to argue that there is not a case for compensation, but that methods should be avoided which encourage overproduction or inefficiency. It may be better to let prices find their market level and for the producing countries to be compensated by the beneficiaries under long-term agreements, with the compensation used to encourage some producers into other activities. Alternatively, income-compensation schemes could be worked out, especially in cases where export instability resulted from variations in domestic supply. In practice, several alternative methods of price stabilisation have been tried or recommended, including buffer stock schemes, export restriction schemes, and price compensation schemes and we must briefly examine these.

Buffer stock schemes

Buffer stock schemes operate by buying up the stock of a commodity when its price is abnormally low and selling the commodity when its price is unusually high. The success of such schemes rests on the foresight of those who manage them. Purchases must be made when prices are low relative to future prices and sold when prices are high relative to future prices. Clearly, buffer stock schemes are only suitable for evening out price fluctuations. They cannot cope with persistent downward trends in price without accumulating large stocks of the commodity which must be paid for — and presumably sold in the future at still lower prices. In 1986 the buffer stock for tin ran into severe financial difficulties by trying to maintain the price of tin 'too high' for 'too long'. Storage schemes are also only appropriate for goods that can easily be stored, and for which the cost of storage is not excessive.

Restriction schemes

In contrast to buffer stock schemes, which are concerned with stabilising prices, restriction schemes are more concerned with maintaining the purchasing power of commodity prices in relation to industrial goods; that is, in preventing a deterioration in the terms of trade of primary commodities. The essence of a restriction scheme is that major producers or nations (on behalf of producers) get together and agree to restrict the production and export of a good whose price is falling, thus maintaining or increasing (if demand is inelastic) revenue from a smaller volume of output. In practice, it is very difficult to maintain and supervise a scheme of this nature, largely because it becomes extremely attractive for any one producer or nation to break away from, or refuse to join, the scheme. This is something Prebisch overlooks in his recommendation for monopoly exporting pricing. It is convenient to conduct theoretical analysis in terms of two countries and two commodities, but when it comes to practical policies the reality of the existence of many countries must be contended with. The disadvantages of restriction schemes are, first, that it is by no means certain that demand is not elastic in the long run, so that raising price by restricting supply may reduce export earnings in the long run. Restriction schemes may ultimately lead to substitution for the product, and falling sales. Second, restriction schemes can lead to substantial resource allocation inefficiencies stemming from the arbitrary allocation of export quotas between countries, and production quotas between producers within countries, unless the quotas are revised regularly to take account of changes in the efficiency of production between producers and between regions of the world. There is also a danger with any form of price-support scheme of a multilateral nature, where both developed and developing countries produce the good in question, that 'assistance' does not all go where it is most needed. In this event there is a stronger case for bilateral arrangements over commodities between developed and developing countries, rather than schemes which embrace developed countries which subsequently reap the benefit.

Price compensation agreements

Price compensation agreements lend themselves to this form of bilateral arrangement. For example, if the price of a commodity falls, two countries could agree upon a sliding scale of compensation such that the importing country pays an increasing sum of money to the exporter as the price falls below a 'normal' price specified in advance. The sliding scale of compensation could be applied to the deviations of the actual price from the 'normal' price. Since restrictions on output and quotas are no part of the scheme, arrangements of this kind have the beauty of divorcing the efficiency aspects of pricing and commodity arrangements from the distributional aspects. The commodity would be traded at world prices, and the lack of full compensation would ensure that if world prices were falling some countries would decide to shift resources so maintaining some degree of allocative efficiency.

Agreements need not only be bilateral. It would also be possible to draw up mulitlateral price compensation agreements, with the governments of all exporting and importing countries of a commodity agreeing jointly on a standard price, and on a 'normal' quantity of imports and exports of the commodity for each country concerned. There could also be a common sliding scale of compensation. For reasons mentioned earlier, however, there is perhaps a greater case for bilateral deals so that assistance can be given where it is most needed and where countries are not bound by the conventions of an international agreement.

There is no reason why price compensation schemes should not run concurrently with other types of international commodity agreements. Indeed, if there is a continually declining price of a commodity, it may be necessary to couple a restriction scheme with a price compensation scheme, otherwise importing countries will be *persistently* subsidising the exporting countries which may not be welcomed. There is also the danger in this case, and also in the case of price-support schemes, that one form of assistance will replace another. If developed countries continually have to pay higher than market prices for their primary products, and argue at the same time that the major constraint on financial assistance to developing countries is their balance of payments, they may use price compensation agreements as an excuse for cutting other forms of assistance. If so, what primary producers gain in the form of higher price or higher export earnings than if the market was free, they lose in other ways.

If fluctuations in price emanate from the supply side, and not from changes in demand, price compensation will operate perversely on the stabilisation of export earnings. This is illustrated in **Figure 15.6**. Price in the market is determined by the intersection of the supply and demand curves, D_1D_1 and S_1S_1, giving equilibrium price, P_1. Now suppose that there is a decrease in demand to D_2D_2, causing price to fall to P_2. Earnings before the price fall were OP_1XS_1; after the price fall, $OP_2X_1S_1$. Assume P_1 to be the 'normal' price agreed under the price compensation scheme, and the P_2C represents the appropriate amount of price compensation in relation to the deviation from 'normal' price following the decrease in demand. Total revenue under the price compensation scheme will be OCC_1S_1, which is not far short of total revenue before the price fall. Consider, however, an equivalent fall in price from P_1 to P_2 as a result of an increase in supply from S_1S_1 to S_2S_2. Under the same price compensation scheme total revenue is now OCC_2S_2, which is greatly in excess of the original total revenue, before the price fall, of OP_1XS_1. Conversely, if the supply falls, and the price rises above the 'normal' price, revenue will be less than before the price rise since the exporting country would presumably be compensating the importing country — unless the scheme works only one way!

Figure 15.6

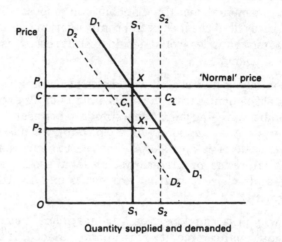

Quantity supplied and demanded

Income compensation schemes

The only way to overcome the induced instability of price compensation schemes is to formulate income compensation schemes which take account of both price and quantity changes. The practical difficulty is reaching agreement on a 'normal' level of income. With the trend rate of growth of output positive for most commodities, to settle for a fixed level of 'normal' income would be unjust. Each year's compensation could perhaps be based on deviations of actual export earnings from the moving average of a series of previous years. The IMF have a scheme in existence of the income-stabilisation type, which operates on these lines, called the Compensatory Finance Facility, which we discuss in chapter 16. The Stabex scheme operated by the EEC is another example.

Producer cartels

Impatience with the international community in the developing countries in formulating schemes to protect their balance of payments and terms of trade has led in recent years to the effective cartelisation of the production of certain raw materials by the developing countries themselves, especially where the number of producers is small and close relations are enjoyed by the producers in other respects. The feeling of the developing countries was well articulated at a meeting in Dakar in 1975 of over 100 developing countries where it was declared that the recovery and control of natural resources held the key to their economic freedom, and countries were urged to draw up a joint plan to protect the prices of their exported commodities. The classic example of cartelisation in recent years has been the action of the oil-producing countries of the Organisation for Petroleum Exporting Countries (OPEC) in raising the price of crude oil by 800 per cent since December 1973. The producers of bauxite have similarly joined together to raise prices. This trend may be expected to continue.

Developing countries are not only producers of raw materials, however, they are also consumers and what some countries gain with respect to the production and export of one commodity they may lose with respect to the import and consumption of another. Some developing countries, poor in all raw material production, may not benefit at all. It is not clear, except in the case of a few special commodities like oil, that cartelisation and monopoly pricing of the product will necessarily redistribute income from the developed to the developing countries taken as a whole. If this is so, bilateral commodity agreements between poor-country producers and rich-country users are probably preferable as a means of ensuring that all developing countries benefit from the general desire in the world economy to help poor, primary-producing countries.

Trade *vs* aid

'Trade not aid' has become a popular aphorism in developing countries in recent years. Let us now consider whether a unit of foreign exchange from exports is really worth more than a unit of foreign exchange from international assistance, or whether the slogan is more an understandable reaction to the debt-servicing problems arising from *past* borrowing (the benefits of which may have been forgotten) and to the political interference and leverage thay may accompany international assistance.

If the meaning of aid is taken literally (i.e. as a free transfer of resources), Johnson (1967) has shown than a unit of foreign exchange from exports can never be as valuable as a unit of foreign exchange from aid. The reason is that exports do not provide additional resources for investment directly, only indirectly by the opportunity provided to transform domestic resources into goods and services more cheaply than if the transformation had to be done domestically. Aid, on the other hand, both provides resources directly, and also indirectly by saving the excess cost of import substitution. The relative worth of exports compared to pure aid can therefore be expressed as:

$$\frac{cX}{(1+c)A} \tag{15.1}$$

where X is the value of exports, A is the value of pure aid, and c is the proportional excess cost of import substitution. The relative worth of exports will rise with the excess cost of import substitution, but it is clear that the worth of exports can never match the worth of an *equal* amount of pure aid ($X = A$) since $c < (1 + c)$. The fact that aid may be tied to higher-priced goods makes some difference to the argument but it can be shown that the excess cost of import substitution and the excess cost of tied goods would have to be relatively high for the worth of aid not to exceed the worth of trade. Let r be the ratio of the price of tied goods to the price of the same goods in the free market. The relative worth of exports may then be written as:

$$\frac{cX}{(1+c)A} \text{ x } r$$

(15.2)

Now exports will be worth more than aid if $cr > (1 + c)$. Different combinations of c and r could be thought of which satisfy this condition but both c and r would have to be quite high, e.g. $c = 2.0$ and $r = 1.5$.

The more important consideration, however, is that the term 'aid' in the slogan 'trade, not aid' should probably not be interpreted literally. The comparison that developing countries are making is not between trade and pure aid but either between trade and the **aid component** of an equal amount of foreign assistance, or simply between trade and an equal amount of foreign assistance. If these are the comparisons being made in practice, two interesting questions arise. First, under what circumstances will trade be more valuable? And second, which is the most appropriate comparison to make?

Consider first the comparison between exports and the aid component of an equal amount of foreign assistance. If this is the comparison that is being made by the developing countries, the Johnson formula can be modified by letting $A = Fg$, where A is the aid component of assistance, F is the nominal amount of foreign assistance, and g is the aid component as a proportion of nominal assistance (i.e. the grant element). Substituting Fg for A in equation (15.1) gives the relative worth of exports compared to the aid component of an equal amount of foreign assistance as:

$$\frac{cX}{(1+c)Fg}$$

(15.3)

or, if the aid is tied:

$$\frac{cX}{(1+c)Fg} \text{ x } r$$

(15.4)

From (15.3) the value of exports will exceed the value of the aid component of an *equal* amount of foreign assistance $(X = F)$ if $c > g(1 - c)$, and, from (15.4), if $cr > g(1 + c)$. The relative worth of exports is greater, the higher the excess cost of import substitution, the higher the excess cost of tied aid and the lower the grant element of assistance. It is still the case, however, that c and r would have to be quite high and g relatively low for the worth of exports to exceed the worth of the aid component of an equal amount of foreign assistance.

But even if a comparison of exports with the aid component of an equal amount of foreign assistance showed exports to be worth more, however, it is not clear that this is the correct comparison to make justifying the slogan 'trade, not aid'. Equations (15.3) and (15.4) assume that only the aid component of assistance saves the excess cost of import substitution. In fact, foreign borrowing *on any terms* saves the excess cost of import substitution. This being so, there are strong grounds for arguing that the comparison which should underly the slogan 'trade not aid' is a comparison of the worth of exports with the worth of foreign assistance itself of equal amount, which provides resources directly equal to Fg and indirectly equal to Fc. The relative worth of exports compared to foreign assistance can thus be expressed as:

$$\frac{cX}{Fg + Fc} = \frac{cX}{(g + c)F} \tag{15.5}$$

or, with tied assistance:

$$\frac{cX}{(g + c)F} \times r \tag{15.6}$$

The conditions for the worth of exports to exceed that of foreign assistance are clearly more stringent than for the worth of exports to exceed the worth of the aid component of an equal amount of foreign assistance. Now, ignoring the potential excess cost of tying, foreign assistance is always worth more than an equal value of exports as long as there is some grant element attached to the assistance (i.e. as long as $g > 0$).

The values of g, c and r give a pratical guide to any country of the relevance of the slogan 'trade, not aid', ignoring the secondary repercussions and the side-effects of the two resource flows.[9] The values of g, c and r for most developing countries are probably not such as to justify the slogan 'trade, not aid' on narrow economic grounds. As far as secondary repercussions are concerned, however, there is the question of the productivity of resources from abroad compared with those released by exports, and of the additional saving generated by the two means of resource augmentation. There is little evidence on the first point, but on the second it is sometimes claimed that foreign assistance discourages saving, while export earnings contribute positively to saving. There need be no dispute that some foreign assistance may be 'comsumed' but this is not the important consideration. The question is, which resource flow leads to the most investment? If 50 per cent of the foreign assistance is 'saved' and the propensity to save of the export sector is 50 per cent, the contribution of the two sources of foreign exchange to growth is exactly the same. There is no evidence to suggest that the propensity to 'save' out of foreign assistance is less than the propensity to 'save' out of exports. From the studies of Maizels and Lee reported earlier, the propensity to save out of exports would appear to be of the order of 0.6. On this basis, 40 per cent of foreign assistance would have to be 'consumed' for foreign assistance not to contribute as much to saving as exports. If anything, therefore, the economic secondary repercussions of exports and assistance favour assistance.

References

1. Prebisch (1950). See also his later work (1959). For an excellent evaluation of the Prebisch thesis, see Flanders (1964).

2. For an empirical investigation of the asymmetry hypothesis, see Thirlwall and Bergevin (1985). As it happens, the hypothesis does not seem to be supported in the years since the Second World War. See the section in this chapter on Recent Trends in the Terms of Trade for further discussion.

3. For one of the original theoretical exposistions, see Corden (1966).

4. Students might like to prove these propositions for themselves using the formula for the effective rate of protection.

5. See also the pioneer work of Lewis and Guisinger (1968) and the work of Balassa *et al*. (1971).

6. For an up-to-date discussion of the issues involved in this section, see Maizels (ed.) (1987).

7. For a comprehensive discussion of international commodity agreements and commodity problems in general see Maizels (1992).

8. For a good summary of the measures of instability and the empirical evidence of the effects of instability on the economies of developing countries, see Stein (1977).

9. For some illustrative calculations see Thirlwall (1976).

19. Import Substitution Revisited in a Darkening External Environment

H.W. Singer and Parvin Alizadeh

Summary

In the 15 to 20 years after the Second World War, import substitution (IS) was the dominant method of industrialisation, both in theory and in practice. In the subsequent fifteen years or so, say from 1965 to 1980, import substitution was heavily criticised and held responsible, particularly by the emergent neoclassical school, for many of the ills and distortions in developing countries. More recently, with the world recession, balance-of-payments crises, debt crises and rising protectionism in industrial countries, a definite reassessment of import substitution is clearly noticeable. The chapter argues that such a re-evaluation of import substitution should not be in the nature of a combination or synthesis of IS and EO — the export orientation (EO) heavily recommended and praised by the more recent critics of IS. The chapter argues that the Republic of Korea provides a good model of the right kind of synthesis, rather than the market-oriented 'neutrality' between IS and EO now preached by the neoclassicals.

The chapter argues that the main trouble with the IS strategy was not inherent in the strategy itself, but due to the way in which it was implemented. Recent empirical evidence has shown that since the onset of the first world recession of 1973, the countries which have relied on IS rather than EO have not done any worse, and for the most recent years the presumption must be that they have done better. The examination of this last proposition should be a high priority for research.

Import substitution and its critics

Development economists in the 1940s and 1950s put great emphasis on the necessity of a deliberate, intensive and guided effort to promote and encourage industrialisation in LDCs. A number of authors, including Rosenstein-Rodan, Nurkse, Prebisch, Hirschman and Dobb, while concerned with a variety of issues, argued that a radical transformation of backward economies with limited or no industrial base requires a deliberate and conscious industrial strategy because the market mechanism, notably in the context of LDCs, is an inadequate means of ensuring rapid industrial development.

The theoretical rationale for a deliberate industrial strategy, as discussed by those authors, rested on a number of grounds including infant industry, external economies and, broadly speaking, the dynamic benefits associated with industrialisation. The tautological use of 'advanced', 'developed' and 'industrial' countries indicated that industrialisation was not only the end-result but also the 'engine' of development.

H.W. Singer and Parvin Alizadeh: 'Import Substitution Revisited in a Darkening External Environment' from *POLICIES FOR DEVELOPMENT: ESSAYS IN HONOUR OF GAMANI COREA*, edited by S. Dell (Macmillan Press Ltd., 1988), pp. 60-86. © Sidney Dell 1988.

Another closely related argument favouring a deliberate industrialisation strategy rested upon the existing structural rigidity in the composition of LDCs' exports and its implication for growth in terms of trade. The Prebisch-Singer (PS) thesis (1949-50) of a secular decline in terms of trade for primary exporters implied that market forces can work to the secular disadvantage of the poorer countries (identified as exporters of primary commodities) and to the advantage of the more advanced industrial countries (identified as exporters of manufactures) in international trade and investment. It was argued that gains from international trade and specialisation are not equally distributed between the LDCs and advanced industrialised countries because of unfavourable demand, inferior market power and price conditions facing primary product producers while the opposite condition prevails in the case of exporters of manufactures.[1] 'Unequal exchange' and 'dependency' schools were the direct offshoots of the PS thesis.

This thesis argued that unregulated free markets work to the disadvantage of LDCs so that regulation or other intervention (including measures to reduce fluctuations in commodity prices, compensatory financing, or more generally a greatly expanded flow of soft aid to LDCs etc.) are needed to achieve a more equitable and sustainable international system. The failure to establish the ITO appeared to members of this school as a fatal gap in the Bretton Woods system, never filled. Moreover, the thesis by implication called for a deliberate industrialisation strategy as a means of altering the existing pattern of LDCs' specialisation within the international economy.

While the PS thesis was strenuously opposed by 'mainstream' economists it provided the intellectual mainspring for the foundation of UNCTAD in 1964 as well as a general conceptual framework which greatly influenced the 'development dialogue' between rich and poor countries (Maizels, 1984).[2]

Industrialisation in the context of this early literature implied import substitution. It was difficult in 1950 to visualise large exports of manufactured goods from LDCs when they lacked an industrial base and the age of the transnational corporations had only just dawned. Moreover, import substitution with the help of protective tariffs was the traditional and proved policy for infants (latecomers) in industrialisation. The 'infant industry' argument lent itself readily to generalisation into an 'infant economy' argument.

The critics of import-substituting industrialisation (ISI) often accuse development economists of this school and UNCTAD of a bias in favour of ISI and against export-oriented strategy. They also maintain that too much State intervention including high levels of protective duties relied upon to encourage ISI induces inefficiency and is thus an obstacle rather than an instrument for a viable industrial development in LDCs. On the other hand, it can be argued that the critics do not take sufficiently into consideration the impact of external pressures and obstacles on development efforts of LDCs, and that they presume that export-oriented strategy is a real possibility for all LDCs, disregarding the inherent fallacy of composition as well as internal technological and capital constraints in many LDCs.

As regards the first criticism of ISI 'bias', there are two answers to this:

1. In the 1940s and 1950s the productive structure of LDCs, generally speaking, was narrow and undiversified and hence it was difficult to foresee the growth of manufactured exports from these economies. As late as 1960, in the dawning days of UNCTAD, primary commodities constituted 79 per cent of the total exports of low-income countries and 89 per cent of those of middle-income countries (Singer, 1984a, p. 16). And even in 1980, these shares had only been reduced to 55 per cent and 63 per cent respectively. In fact, export substitution would have been equally favoured by the ISI advocates — their emphasis was on the S for *substitution*, rather than on the I for *imports*. The real message or 'bias' was on the last I for *industrialisation* — get out of primary commodities — but ISI seemed to be more realistic than ESI.

2. The critics of ISI, such as Ian Little *et al.* (1970), for the OECD, Bela Balassa *et al.* for the World Bank (Balassa, 1982) and Krueger and Bhagwati for the National Bureau of Economic Research (Bhagwati, 1978), all tended to disregard or underestimate the importance of a previous phase of IS as a necessary base for subsequent or even simultaneous export-led growth. This is confirmed by the actual experience of the two often-mentioned examples of successful exporters, the Republic of Korea and Taiwan Province of China. In both cases, an IS strategy was pursued in the 1950s; and even in the 1960s and 1970s, when substantial emphasis was laid on development of manufactured exports, a considerable degree of IS still took place in a number of industries (Park, 1981; Luedde-Neurath, 1984; Evans and Alizadeh, 1984). In the case of the Republic of Korea, it can be shown that IS and export promotion were carefully and consciously interlinked as alternating phases in shifting industrialisation between the different sectors. In the case of Brazil also, exports of manufactured goods were in those industries where large-scale IS had been successfully accomplished (Tyler, 1981; Chenery, 1980). This is not to underrate the importance of export-promotion policies which were introduced in these countries in the 1960s. Nevertheless, it is true that such export-promotion policies simply appeared as a way of exploiting the export potential which had been built up during the IS phase. The critics tend to argue that the shift from IS to export orientation was the result of enlightenment and of bad experience with IS. Yet the shift can equally be presented as a rational and natural sequential development in the progress of industrialisation (Singer, 1984a). (It can also be presented as due to a shift in the external environment in a more expansionist/optimistic direction at around 1960, as discussed in more detail in a subsequent section; this shift has been sharply reversed more recently.) Prior learning about the technology and product via production for the home market is usually considered a prerequisite for effective competition in world markets for manufactured goods; hence the emphasis by List, Hamilton and others on the 'transitional' or temporary nature of infant protection. Also IS was often needed to provide the necessary volume basis for competitive export production. Seen in this light, IS and export promotion are complementary rather than alternative strategies.

There is also a point of methodology here. If country A shows better growth and development when it moves from ISI to export oriented industrialisation (EOI) (and vice versa), the critics take this as evidence of the inferiority of ISO and the superiority of EOI. But another possible explanation is that the ISO phase is a necessary 'infrastructure investment' type of outlay which is needed to prepare the ground for the extra EOI 'push' — which then provides the 'pay-off' in terms of faster growth.

Turning to the second criticism of ISI, i.e. too much intervention and interference with the play of market forces and consequent departure from comparative cost principles, neoclassical critics of ISI have maintained that too much intervention not only has led to bureaucratic inefficiencies, corruption and delays but also that the imposition of a high level of protection duties for import-substituting industries has induced the establishment of high-cost inefficient industries; allowed overvaluation of domestic currency, and led to the neglect of agriculture and other sectors, etc.

The policy implications drawn from this analysis are that protective duties should be substantially reduced, the exchange rate should be devalued and the play of market forces should be encouraged. These policies are supposed to be a prerequisite for successful export oriented industrialisation. Of course EOI is not a crude *laissez-faire* strategy, but also requires appropriate government measures, incentives and subsidies to encourage exports, and to provide equal economic incentives to production for domestic and foreign markets (Kirkpatrick *et al.*, 1984; Krueger, 1983); also World Bank Report, 1984, 'Toward Sustained Development' (TDS Report). While the extent as well as the duration of government intervention, from this perspective, should possibly be reduced,[3] the main requirement is a change in its direction, and 'degrees' of interventionism are not easily measured or compared. But criticism of intervention and statism is not identical, although it may overlap, with criticism of ISI.

The fact that IS policies in certain instances have led to 'inefficiencies' and other undesirable side-effects should not be interpreted to imply that extensive State intervention is not of crucial importance for a rapid and viable industrial development. Excluding special cases of city States, like Hong Kong and Singapore, the industrial development of other newly industrialising countries (NICs) has been accompanied by a substantial degree of State intervention, far beyond what is often realised by the critics of ISI. But it must certainly be acknowledged that there are many other kinds of government intervention which may be more important and more constructive than 'distortion' (or correction) of market prices.

The high degree of intervention and 'statism', which has prevailed in Latin American NICs, including Brazil and Mexico, is well known. Moreover, the detailed study of economic policy in most NICs shows that industrial development has been accompanied by a high degree of centralised planning and government regulation, with strict import, banking, credit and foreign exchange controls (Kirkpatrick, Less and Nixson, 1984, p. 199; Luedde-Neurath, 1984; Park, 1981). The Republic of Korea 'is a country where a strong State overrides market forces without hesitation, with an effective tightly-planned economy, with strict controls, an essentially nationalised banking system, and a private sector organised in government-sponsored trade associations for easier control. It is as far removed from free market policies as it is possible to be'

(Singer, 1984b, p. 86). The government's overwhelming control over the banking sector provided the most important tool in influencing the direction and distribution of investible funds by varying the interest rate charged according to the field of investment, depending on the priorities attached to the different lines of economic activity.

In this respect it is worth remembering that in both the Republic of Korea and Taiwan Province of China, although import restrictions on average were substantially lowered since the early 1960s, most import-competing industries remained highly protected during the period of rapid growth of manufactured exports in the 1960s and 1970s. A statistical division of increases in domestic output as between import substitution, additional exports and 'indigenous increases' shows a continuing high share for the first category as compared with the second. Korean planners have also been consistently concerned to reduce the import content of exports. That is to say that ISI applied to exports. The high import content of exports, e.g. compared with Japan, also makes the net export performance, and the contribution of exports to the balance of payments, less impressive than the gross figures suggest. The legal tariff rates on textile fibres, fabrics and products, leather and leather products, rubber products, and wood and furniture products (which then constituted major Korean export commodities) were in the range of 50 per cent to 200 per cent throughout the period 1964-74 (Hong, 1977, p. 138). Also, quantitative restrictions on imports were quite substantial. In 1970, out of 1312 basic items, 524 were restricted and 73 were prohibited (Frank, *et al.*, 1975, p. 59).

Thus it is not surprising that Park, while summarising the relevance of the Republic of Korean experience concludes that 'one lesson is that the Korean experience hardly provides a model in which the functioning of a free trade regime, or operating close to such a regime, assure efficiency in resource allocation and reasonable growth as well' (Park, 1981, p. 115).

The Krueger/Balassa/Deepak Lak school, claiming 100 per cent virtues for outward orientation and 100 per cent damnation for import orientation, has a 'no-win' argument against its critics. If you point out that in fact countries like the Republic of Korea have had a good deal of import substitution, this is turned into an argument not in favour of emphasis on import substitution but on outward orientation. The argument runs as follows:

> apart from promoting exports, an outward-oriented policy contributes to efficient import substitution. In fact, it has been shown that during the 1973-78 period of external shocks, newly industrializing countries pursuing outward-oriented policies undertook more import substitution from [*sic*] their inward-oriented counterparts .... All in all, the advantages of outward orientation are to be found in the establishment of an efficient structure of production that entails exporting as well as import substitution (Balassa, 1985, p. 209).

Where does this leave us? The import substitution achieved by 'outward oriented' countries is declared to be 'efficient', and by implication the import substitution of other developing countries would be 'inefficient'. Hence the superiority of outward orientation is tautological and cannot be disputed. Any argument that the efficient countries showing a high rate of growth have in fact placed considerable emphasis on policies promoting import substitution and have, as Balassa admits, in fact had more import substitution than the so-called inward-oriented counties, is in this way nipped in the bud and in fact turned into an argument in favour of export promotion. The logical duplicity of this reasoning should be obvious. We have also argued that export promotion, as in the Korean case, has often implied complementary import substitution; but this argument is somewhat different from the one of Balassa and hopefully does not involve the same logical duplicity or tautologicality.

It may be added that Bela Balassa, in the paper quoted, also produces a second or parallel 'no-win' argument in favour of outward orientation. In criticising Mexican industrial policy, allegedly under the influence of the Cambridge Economic Policy Group and Dr Ajit Singh in particular, he finds that while industrial output was 43 per cent higher in 1979 than in 1970, 'productivity deteriorated' as indicated by an increase in industrial employment by 77 per cent (Balassa, 1975, p. 215). One should have thought that the fact that industrial employment increased so heavily could have been taken as evidence that the growth of industrial production was of a desirable labour-intensive character — of the kind alleged to be promoted by outward orientation and obstructed by inward orientation — and helped to reduce Mexican unemployment. But no: it is a sign of deteriorating efficiency. So the Cambridge group and Ajit Singh cannot win and take the credit for the increase in industrial employment! Is there a clearer example of having it both ways?

Argentina/Brazil versus the Republic of Korea

The inter-weaving of sequences of import substitution and export promotion pointed out for the Republic of Korea also applies to the two largest Latin American economies of Argentina and Brazil, even though the nature of the sequencing is rather different. The best source for this is a perceptive article by Simon Teitel and Francisco E. Thoumi on 'From import substitution to exports: the manufacturing exports experience of Argentina and Brazil' (Teitel and Thoumi, 1986, pp. 455-90). The authors, who are connected with the Inter-American Development Bank as well as academic institutions, find that the now conventional characterisation of the IS-dominated process of industrialisation in Latin America as inefficient is very questionable. They point out that the process of import substitution and development of domestic markets has served to develop technological capacity, economies of scale, linkages and infrastructure, which subsequently provided a useful basis for vigorous exports of manufactures. They state that

> IS policies followed by these countries do not seem to have resulted in permanent inefficiencies in many manufacturing industries. Rather, protection provided during the 1950s and 1960s to metalworking and metallurgical industries producing consumer durables, capital goods and transportation equipment has been later reduced, and efficiency has evolved leading — sometimes in spite of significant anti-export policy biases — to a substantial volume of exports in the 1970s (Teitel and Thoumi, 1986, pp. 485-6).

As they describe it, IS has been a preamble to the export stage, providing the learning required before reaching out for markets abroad.

Their final conclusion is to 'cast doubts on the wisdom of urging the larger and more industrialized countries of Latin America to follow, as in South-east Asia, an export-oriented strategy largely based on unskilled labour-intensive industries' (Teitel and Thoumi, 1986, p. 486). However, as we have argued in our own analysis, even in the economies of South-east Asia, at least as far as the Republic of Korea is concerned, there has been nothing like the conventionally alleged clear-cut export-oriented strategy.

Likewise in Taiwan Province of China, rapid growth of the industrial sector in general and of manufactured exports in particular during the 1960s and 1970s was not accompanied by the adoption of a free trade regime, or anything approaching it.[4] By the late 1970s, more than a quarter of imported items were still subject to quantitative restrictions and import control (Balassa, 1981, p. 415).

The purpose here is not to provide a blanket argument for any sort of State intervention, or to dismiss the fact that extensive State intervention in a number of instances has not been particularly successful in the development of a viable industrial base. Nevertheless, it is becoming increasingly clear that it is not the extent and the duration of State intervention which determines the success or failure of ISI or EOI. It is rather the economic-political situation the State faces both internally and externally, its political commitments and its administrative capacity which matter (Kirkpatrick, Lee and Nixson, 1984, p. 194). The State is not a *deus ex machina*, but neither is the international market. Which is the better guide, or rather which combination is best, depends on country-specific, or even sector-specific, conditions.

Effective and efficient implementation of any trade policy, whether IS or EO or a combination of both, depends on the organisational ability of the State as well as on the economic and political peculiarities of a given economy. This point has been well demonstrated by Datta-Chaudhuri in his comparative study of South Korea and the Philippines (Datta-Chaudhuri, 1981, pp. 47-79). The two countries are similar in terms of population size, and in the early 1960s they also had comparable levels of GDP per capita. Moreover, both countries, Datta-Chaudhuri argues, adopted more or less similar trade policies in the 1950s and 1960s, in the sense that in the early 1960s both countries shifted their trade policies to encourage manufactured exports. Nevertheless, the performance of the Korean economy in terms of overall growth, employment generation, rise in real wages, and particularly the expansion of manufactured exports, was far more spectacular than that of the Philippines in the 1960s and 1970s.

In explaining the differences between the two growth processes, Datta-Chaudhuri outlines certain factors which might have stronger explanatory power than trade policies, including the relationship between the State and the industrialist class, the administrative capability and political commitment of the State to formulate carefully and implement effectively an appropriate industrial strategy etc. In the case of the Republic of Korea, since the early 1960s the State devised a discretionary and selective regulatory system to guide the allocation of resources in the desired direction.[5] Also, export promotion policies were accompanied by a close collaboration between the State and a relatively well-developed industrialist class, so that the development priorities were defined in consonance with entrepreneurial interests. In the case of the Philippines, the dominant class with which the State collaborated was the agrarian hierarchy and the efficiency and planning capacity of government and administration were far inferior to that of the Republic of Korea.

Wanted: a new synthesis of ISI and EOI

The shift back in thinking 'towards favouring the domestic market', the 'avoidance of domestic inequalities', 'less emphasis on the market as sole allocator of resources', is particularly marked in Latin America which has suffered more in the recession and is more threatened by the debt crisis than Asia. All the above objections in quotation marks are taken from a publication by PREALC (the Latin American branch of the ILO World Employment Programme), which is typical of this recent shift in thinking ('Beyond the Crisis', PREALC, ILO, 1985). There is particular emphasis on the 'multiple distortions' of markets there which implies that concentration on the removal of one or two keys distortions (e.g. exchange rates or subsidies) may well increase rather than diminish overall distortions and the difficulties of reaching an optimum solution.

At the same time, there is also emphasis on avoiding the errors of the past. Any new domestically-oriented industrialisation strategy must pay more attention to monetary, price and balance of trade and payments implications than the old ISI did. It must also encourage exports more. In other words, it must be a synthesis of the old ISI and the more recent EOI, both of which have been proved to be flawed, at least in the case of Latin America; more a move forward to something new than a return to the old. In this sense, also, the debate between the proposals of ISI and EOI as exclusive alternatives is dangerously misleading. We need ISIEOI, a strategy which combines the best elements of both and utilises the complementarities of the two.

Paradoxically, both the old-style ISI and the recent attempted EOI resulted in an inefficient industrial structure, with insufficient vertical integration and horizontal linkages. The future synthesis must pay more attention to the structure and quality of industrialisation as distinct from its simple volume and simple industrialisation ratios. The purely quantitative Lima target (25 per cent of global industrial production for the LDCs) was also vulnerable in this respect. The PREALC report criticises the 'disarticulated structure' of industries resulting from ISI and the low weighting of the 'modern industries'.

In fact, an ISI which results in such a 'disarticulate structure' and absence of modern industries fails in the purpose of ISI, which was put forward as a natural escape out of primary commodities with their unfavourable price trends. The terms of trade of the 'old' industrial consumer products versus the 'new' and capital goods, may be no more favourable than those of primary commodities; hence old-style ISI often proved a dead-end way out of 'unequal exchange' (Singer, 1975). The watchword of the new synthesis must be 'Integrated Industrialisation'.

The PREALC study also rightly lists neglect of domestic food production leading to increased dependence on food imports (and food aid) as one of the weaknesses of old-style ISI. But here the advocates of EOI also find themselves in a dilemma. They advocate, like everybody else, greater emphasis on domestic food production and elimination of 'urban-bias' distortions. But if IS is right for food, why not for manufactures and specifically capital goods and 'modern' products? No really convincing answer has been given (or rather, the question has not been asked); and in the absence of an answer there must be a lingering suspicion of assignment of LDCs to be hewers of wood and drawers of water. The EOI tools of exchange devaluation and removal of food subsidies may serve to reduce 'urban bias', but more in the direction of increasing exports of food and agricultural products rather than food production for domestic consumption. The priority for domestic food production, although during the EO ascendancy labelled as removal of a distortion debited to ISI policies, is in fact a part of a return to a reformed IS. But undoubtedly the present dependency on food imports is also a consequence of unenlightened ISI. It is perhaps ironic that the removal of a consequence of ISI requires now a return to import substitution — but such complexities are part of the new synthesis.

Similarly, there is an irony in the relationship between a renewed emphasis on the domestic market and the basic needs strategy. Superficially, the two go well together. The poor are part of the domestic market; their needs are for the simple goods which — except for food — are usually home-produced, sometimes in the informal sector; their frustrated buying power potential, or lack of 'entitlements', represents a powerful opportunity for a new ISI, or at least inward-oriented push. Yet the emphasis on basic consumption goods may again lead to the 'disarticulate structures' with lack of vertical integration. So what is needed is a deepening of the basic needs concepts which encompasses the activities indirectly needed and related to basic needs. In other words, basic needs must be the orientation of the whole economy, a matter of macroeconomic management, rather than a selection criterion for specific commodities to be produced. When the domestic market is the engine of growth, and when incomes or entitlements are equally distributed, we can be philosophical as between sectoral and product priorities — by all means let the market decide. That must be the objective for the new enlightened ISI. In such an economy, the production of exports also serves the same purpose since the foreign exchange earned will be used for the better satisfaction of basic needs. So again the alleged cleavage of ISI 'or' EOI vanishes, and the desired synthesis emerges as blending both — ISIEOI.

The new industrial strategy must be less dualistic than either ISI or EOI, both of which have shown themselves capable of creating pockets of modernity, with more links abroad than domestically and many of the inputs imported, while leaving the poorer section to survive with an 'informal sector' capital-starved and discouraged. The new synthesis should blend the two technologies into an intermediate technology, or blend them purposefully together in both intra-firm and inter-firm linked structures. New technological advances have created opportunities in this direction, and their exploration in the framework of the new industrial strategies now widely groped for in Latin America and elsewhere opens up a big new agenda (Boon, 1983).

What is suggested here is not so much an industrialisation strategy which is 'neutral' as between IS and EO. This is the formulation favoured, among others, by the World

Bank (see, for example, the 1981 *World Development Report*). Rather, what is suggested is a systematic combination of IS and EO, with a different emphasis on IS and EO at different periods and for different sectors. In the nature of things in developing countries, the sequence from IS and EO will be more frequent than the reverse, both in time and for given sectors. But EO itself will also lead to new opportunities for IS to reduce the import content of exports and increase linkages from the export sector to the rest of the economy, preventing dualism and a disarticulated industrial structure.

In fact, certain successful exporters, including the Republic of Korea and Taiwan Province of China relied on high and non-uniform rates of effective protection, far above 20 to 30 per cent and sometimes as high as 100 per cent effective. Westphal (1981) in explaining the difference in industrial performance between these two and those developing countries that pursued more inward-looking policies argues that it is not so much the magnitude of protectionism but rather the selectivity of infant industry protection and attention to promotion of export growth which distinguishes the former cases from the latter.

He argues that promotion of fewer infant industries at a time can be more conducive to a rapid achievement of international competitiveness than a strategy of 'wholesale import substitution' which accompanies simultaneous protection of a large number of infant industries from the start. Greater selectivity permits scarce investment resources to be concentrated in one or a few sectors at a time; it also allows the concentration of scarce entrepreneurial resources and qualified technical personnel and thus avoids spreading the high-level manpower so thinly that no industry has adequate technical personnel. Greater selectivity 'also accompanies delaying the construction of initial plants until the market has grown to an appropriate size.' In other words, it is the quality of import substitution that counts, rather than its volume.

External environment and external pressures

The debate about ISI versus EOI is, in one sense, misplaced and hence partially senseless. Probably the best position in the light of available evidence is that neither ISI not EOI is the superior strategy in any overall and absolute sense, but rather depend for their relative advantages and disadvantages on assumptions about the external situation facing LDCs. The early advocates of ISI, consciously or unconsciously, made pessimistic assumptions about global growth and trade policies of industrial countries; such pessimistic assumptions were natural around 1950 when the more recent experience of the Great Depression of the 1930s was put together with the disruption and heavy setbacks caused by the Second World War. Similarly 20 years later, by 1970, it was equally natural for critics of ISI to project the favourable external environment of the 1950s and 1960s into the future. Perhaps both schools of thought were right on their own different assumptions. Given the recent much less favourable international outlook, it is as natural that ISI should have regained a great deal more respectability. Apart from explaining some of the fluctuating fortunes and fashions in ISI versus EOI, such a position would also indicate that the optimal industrial strategy in LDCs would be something that is flexible between ISI and EOI: switching emphasis towards ISI in times of global recession and towards EOI in time of global prosperity. It would also indicate that the choice between the two strategies is much more a matter of what is ultimately a *political* judgement about the state and future of the world economy, rather than a matter of firm *economic* analysis as it has usually been debated in the past.

Fortunately, we can confirm this approach as a result of a recent careful quantitative analysis (Kavoussi, 1985). Mr Kavoussi looked at the period 1967-77. Dividing it up into a period of favourable market conditions (1967-73) and unfavourable market conditions (1973-7), he found that when a sample of some fifty developing countries was divided by certain criteria into free trade — outward oriented, or trade restrictive — inward oriented, the correlation between export orientation and growth performance in the first favourable 1967-73 period showed superior performance by the export oriented countries; but in the less favourable 1973-7 period there was no evidence of any such correlation. In his own words:

> Free trade appears to enhance growth only when external demand is favourable. When foreign markets are slack, the association of the economy's growth with export-orientation tends to be quite weak. This result seems to imply that when free trade produces a moderate expansion of export earnings (when external demand is weak), the gains from openness are likely to be cancelled by its negative effects. On the other hand, when export-orientation leads to an exceptionally rapid expansion of export earnings (when external demand is strong), the benefits of openness clearly outweigh its costs.

He concludes:

> Different phases of the cycles of global economic activity require different commercial policies. While export-oriented policies can produce substantial gains during the phase of strong international demand, they may be self-defeating if followed by a large number of developing countries when world markets are depressed. (p. 391)

It is a pity that such an analysis is not available for, say, 1979-83 when the external situation was even less favourable than 1973-7. One can only surmise that for that period there may well be a definite finding that inward-oriented LDCs did better; the cases of India and China would seem to support such a conclusion. It is hoped that the results of such a more recent analysis will soon be available.

On Mr Kavoussi's findings that there is little difference in performance between inward and outward-oriented countries during unfavourable external periods, one may also surmise that in that case the ISI strategy may well appear to national decision-makers safer and more appealing on grounds other than growth rate arguments. ISI increases a country's national control over its own destiny and holds out the prospect that the growth could well be more stable from year to year, being less dependent on external conditions. On the other hand, one can also see that to an internationalist bureaucracy such as that of the IMF, EOI may be preferable even in the absence of a superior growth performance, since international integration is treated as a good thing in itself. This difference may well explain a good deal of the controversy between the IMF and many LDC governments on the question of the right way of adjusting to debt-induced balance-of-payments pressure.

Another reason why unfavourable external conditions have led to a revival of ISI strategy is the strong emphasis, recently fortified by the African drought and famine, on the need for developing countries to reverse the heavy shift from net food exports to net food imports during the post-war period. This near unanimous emphasis on higher priority for domestic food production and restoration of food security and food sufficiency in fact amounts to a recommendation of import substitution — of IS if not of ISI. Some of the sharpest critics of ISI are also among the keenest advocates of higher priority for domestic food production. There is nothing logically inconsistent in this position: one can stress the advantages of IS in agriculture and its disadvantages in industrialisation. However, it does throw a certain onus on the critics of ISI to explain what exactly are the differences between the two sectors which account for advocacy of such different strategies for them.

The critics of ISI also often overestimate the freedom of LDCs to choose their industrialisation strategy and underestimate the significance of external pressure in influencing the pattern and direction of resource allocation. Several problems which the industrialisation process of LDCs faces may be largely a result of the pressures exerted on LDCs by the imperfect markets of the advanced industrialised world (Bienefeld, 1985). Donors and foreign investors might represent interests that could conflict with the national interest of a developing country. Donors, whether international agencies or governments, might attach tying and other types of conditionality on utilisation of aid/loans; also inappropriate (e.g. too capital-intensive) design and selection of their projects might substantially contribute to inefficiency of investible resources. Similarly, foreign investors might press the recipient government to implement policies, including prolongation of a high level of protective duties, to ensure a high level of profit. In such conditions, debates on 'optimal industrialisation strategies' may be beside the point, and strategies of coping with such external pressures may be more relevant.

The importance of external pressure is particularly pronounced in the case of those LDCs with relatively weak economies, with limited financial resources, industrial base, infrastructure and technological expertise. Such economies may lack an adequate bargaining power *vis-à-vis* donors and foreign investors and at the same time may be highly dependent on international finance and expertise for the implementation of their development plans.

In a recent World Bank report on sub-Saharan Africa, which is concerned with the failure of IS strategy there, it is acknowledged that donors must take some responsibility for the current difficulties, including the inappropriate design and selection of their projects, and the lack of co-ordination among themselves, which all contributed to the low rates of return on investment (World Bank, 'Towards sustained Development', 1984). Nevertheless the report presumes that financial agencies and expertise are primarily neutral and it fails even to consider the possibility that such agencies might represent interests that could conflict with national interests (Bienefeld, 1985).

Furthermore the imperfect markets of the industrialised world can exert a considerable degree of pressure on development efforts of all LDCs including the NICs. The severe debt-servicing problems of LDCs (including those of NICs) due to high real rates of interest which originated among other things from monetary and fiscal policies in advanced industrialised countries since the mid-1970s, is a well-known example of an external obstacle to EOI, by reducing import capacity for investment in export industries, or indeed any kind of effective industrialisation. This creates settings in which the idea of a 'choice' between various industrialisation strategies may become quite unreal.

Export-oriented industrialisation and its prospects

The alternative industrial strategy which is proposed by the critics of ISI is an outward-looking strategy of EOI. There is no doubt that development and expansion of manufactured exports are of crucial importance for LDCs. Apart from the well-known 'vent for surplus' principle (i.e. the surplus part of domestic production, for which there is no domestic demand, can be exchanged for those goods and services required by the domestic economy, through exports), a country can overcome obstacles of a limited domestic market in those lines of industries which are highly susceptible to economies of scale. Also by competing in the world markets for manufactures, industries would be forced to attain a high standard of efficiency and product quality.

Nevertheless, the viability of EOI strategy for LDCs as a whole must remain subject to controversy notably in the international context of the coming decade. The question is not whether EOI is *desirable* but whether it is *possible*.

To begin with, it is a fallacy of composition to assume that what is possible for one or some of the LDCs or NICs can work for all, or the great majority, if all or most LDCs seek to pursue export-led growth at the same time. A recent analysis has indicated, on the basis of a simulation exercise, that if all LDCs in the mid-1970s had the same export intensity as the Republic of Korea, Taiwan Province of China, Hong Kong and Singapore, adjusting for differences in size and level of industrialisation, this would involve a more than 700 per cent increase in Third World manufactured exports (Cline, 1982). The analysis concludes that this would result in untenable market penetration into industrialised countries and protectionist backlash would be inevitable. Hence

> It is seriously misleading to hold up the East Asian 'Gang of Four' (i.e. Hong Kong, Taiwan Province of China, the Republic of Korea, and Singapore) as a model for development because that model almost certainly cannot be generalised without provoking protectionist response ruling out its implementation (Cline, 1982).

Even present market shares provoke protectionist response — is it conceivable to increase total trade in manufactures seven times over, to maintain present market shares? Access to the markets of OECD countries, which are the major markets for LDCs' manufactured products, is of considerable importance for the successful implementation of EOI strategy. Although there is scope for the expansion and promotion of South-South trade (to which we shall turn subsequently), entry into the markets of advanced industrialised countries will remain of crucial importance for some time. It is the continued likelihood of this market access by LDCs which requires careful assessment, notably in the coming decade.

With the drastic decline in the rate of global economic growth and global trade growth since the late 1970s the prospect for pursuing an EOI strategy in the coming decade clearly looks less promising for other LDCs which were not in 'the first wave' — even if we consider that the first wave is safely 'home'.

In contrast with the unprecedented expansion of global trade between 1950 to the mid-1970s, as the 1970s wore on the rate of global economic growth as well as the rate of growth of world trade declined. And trade seems highly sensitive to the rate of growth, with a multiplier effect (Singer, 1983b). The post-war expansion of global trade was greatly facilitated by a significant reduction in trade barriers administered by GATT. However, this situation has changed considerably since the late 1970s. In any case, the reduction in trade barriers was so considerable that it was almost by definition a 'once-for-all' rather than a continuing expansion factor.

Although there has been a general commitment to reduce tariff barriers, nevertheless 'non-tariff barriers' (NTBs) have served as the main form of protective measures in major OECD countries in recent years. Both GATT and UNCTAD have been compiling inventories of NTBs, recording both product-specific measures and general measures. Furthermore, as in the case of tariff measures, NTBs appear to be disproportionately directed at LDCs' exports, and increase as the degree of processing increases (UNCTAD, 1983). Moreover, protectionism appears to be particularly high in the labour-intensive sectors which constitute most of LDCs' manufactured exports, and are particularly important to them for employment and more equal income distribution, as emphasised by the critics of ISI.

If the economic problems now confronting the major industrial countries continue for some years, which seems a distinct possibility, the protective trade barriers are more likely to grow than decline.

In addition to protective measures, another factor which may adversely affect the export prospects of LDCs is radical technical change and diffusion of electronic-based automation technologies (Kaplinsky, 1984). With the development and diffusion of these two technologies, which are largely a phenomenon of the post-1970 period, the comparative advantage of LDCs in presently labour-intensive sectors may be considerably weakened. One of the impacts of automated technology is a general reduction in labour input which in turn undermines the advantage of low wage costs in LDCs.

South-South trade

At present, developing countries are highly dependent on developed countries, both for their export markets and for their imports, with trade among developing countries accounting for only a quarter of their total exports (and imports) (Adams, 1983). Nevertheless, with a growing tendency towards protectionism in the major developed countries, and also with lack of progress in North-South discussion on development of trade relations on the basis of a trading system more favourable to the South as part of a new international economic order, LDCs are now bound to look elsewhere and increasingly among themselves for markets if the growth of their trade is not to be stifled.

Intensified South-South trade can be either treated as outward-looking or EOI (from the viewpoint of the individual LDC) or as inward-looking or ISI (from the viewpoint of developed countries). That question is as insoluble — and as sensible — as debating whether a glass of water filled to the half-way mark should be described as 'half-full' or 'half-empty'. A lot will depend on whether South-South trade is developed to substitute for North-South trade (in which case it can reasonably be described as inward-looking or ISI) or to be additional or complementary (when it is reasonably considered as part of, or a stepping stone to, outward-looking EOI). As a general proposition, much of the expansion of South-South trade advocated by UNCTAD would be of the latter type and to the advantage of the North as well as the South (Singer, 1983a). But the main critics of ISI often include South-South as another manifestation of an inward-looking spirit and of a failure to accept integration into the world economy. Certainly, there is little enthusiasm for South-South among the proponents of EOI, while the proponents of ISI have seized upon the chance of adding the advantages of international trade to the case for self-reliance — as indicated by the phrase 'collective self-reliance'. So South-South has become more or less a part of ISI, by a process of self-selection, and is thus here included.

Developments during the 1970s suggest an emerging tendency towards the intensification of inter-developing countries' trade relative to their trade with developed countries. The share of developing countries' exports, excluding petroleum, going to other developing countries increased from 19.2 per cent in 1970 to 26.2 per cent in 1978. In particular, a number of developing countries including the East Asian 'Gang of Four', Brazil, Mexico, and a few other LDCs which have emerged as exporters of manufactures, have been able, to a growing extent, not only to penetrate the markets of OECD countries but also to capture an increasing share of markets in other developing countries.

Promotion of economic co-operation among developing countries (ECDC), including expansion of South-South trade, has been one of the main concerns of UNCTAD since the early 1970s, although there are a number of major obstacles for attainment of this objective. Some of these obstacles are posed by the present policies of developed countries and some by the policies of the developing countries themselves. Among the first type of obstacles are the tying of aid and the rules of origin in the generalised system of preference (GSP) and other preferential schemes (Singer, 1983a, p. 322). The endemic balance-of-payments problems which most LDCs face, and their dependence on international financial institutions, have provided through tied aid and other forms of restrictions pressures in favour of North-South trade and against LDC sources of supply.[6]

Among the second type of obstacles are the trade policies of developing countries themselves. For instance, those products which are the most promising for the expansion of South-South trade, including light consumer goods and semi-finished manufactures, are also those which are highly protected by tariff as well as 'non-tariff barriers' in developing countries. Moreover, consumer preferences are often biased against products of other developing countries, sometimes quite irrationally.

Of course important steps have been taken already by developing countries themselves as manifested by the initiation of a number of economic co-operation and integration schemes at the regional and similar levels, which include the great majority of the developing countries as members of one or other of such schemes. In most of these schemes the principal approach to trade co-operation has been the gradual liberalisation of trade barriers to 'intra-group' trade. Nevertheless the full potential for such co-operation among LDCs may take some time to be realised, and the landscape shows many disputes and lack of implementation, with lack of finance a main reason for failure to put sufficient steam behind ECDC.

Concluding remarks

The sluggish growth of the world economy and the rising trend towards protectionism, or what has been called the 'new protectionism', will adversely affect the export prospects of LDCs. It might be argued whether the same considerations do not also apply to protectionism on the part of LDCs. We cannot do better than reply to this in Gamani Corea's words:

> The answer has to be that there is no exact parallel between the two phenomena. The rationale for protectionism in developing countries has been well recognised in terms of the 'infant industry' argument — extended also to take into account the wider limitations in terms of infrastructure of a growing but weak economy. In the long term, such protectionism, which would still be temporary but of much longer duration, can be seen as contributing to growth and efficiency. The same cannot be said for the merits of protecting aging industries — except temporarily as a means of smoothing out the frictions that stand in the way of adaptation to change. Protectionism in the developing countries could of course be carried too far — to the detriment of growth and efficiency in these countries, and it is right to draw attention to this danger. But here the criticism is of the incorrect use of the instrument rather than of the instrument itself. From the international point of view there is another, even more important consideration. Protectionism imposed by the industrial countries can be directly restrictive to world trade by reducing the earning capacity of developing countries and hence their capacity to import. Protectionism imposed by the developing countries does not have quite the same effect since these countries tend in any case to spend all their export earnings, and more, on imports — mostly from the developed countries. The foreign exchange saved by restrictions on some types of goods are utilized for imports of other types. Hence protectionism has more of an impact on the pattern of imports than on their total.

> The entire question of market access and how to improve it is, of course, the central issue of the multilateral trade negotiations. It remains to be seen how far these negotiations will succeed in improving the access of developing countries to the markets of the industrialized countries. (1979, p. 119)

However, there is little likelihood that in the present international context multilateral trade negotiations will deal adequately and decisively with the problem of the new protectionism. Hence ISI will still have to play a significant role in the industrialisation process of LDCs, notably in the case of those developing countries which are in the very early stages of development.

The point made be Corea, that import substitution affects 'the pattern of imports more than the total' is of great importance. When thought through to its logical conclusion, it indicates that the identification of ISI with 'inward-looking' policies can be misleading. 'Inward-looking' policies are enforced upon the developing countries by the foreign exchange bottleneck, intensified in recent years by falling commodity prices, debts and by lower growth and protectionism in industrial countries. In other words, the critics of ISI would be well occupied in suggesting changes in the external environment as well as in the policies of developing countries. Some do, but others do not. EOI and the new international economic order should be natural allies. It is ironic that we find them so often on opposite sides of the fence.

One of the well-known difficulties with ISI is the difficult nature of transition from the early phase, the assembly or fabrication of consumer goods, to the production of intermediate inputs and capital goods, or expansion into export markets, or a combination of both. ISI is a highly sequential process, yet realisation of sequences beyond the easy or early phase has proved to be difficult in many instances (Kirkpatrick and Nixson, 1983, p.12). But EOI can also meet rising protectionist resistance increasing with successful penetration. A plague on both your houses?

The 'mainstream' economists have focused on protective trade regimes as the main underlying reason for the difficulties with ISI. They have argued that restrictive trade policies give rise to the establishment of high-cost industries which are not able to compete in the world market. Moreover, these industries cannot achieve vertical integration due to the limitation set by the small size of the domestic market in the case of intermediate inputs and capital goods which are highly susceptible to economies of scale.

However, one can equally argue that the difficult nature of transition beyond the first stage reflects an inappropriate choice of industry rather than an inescapable feature of protective trade regimes *per se*. In other words, the choice of the industry the State protects and promotes is of great importance so far as the future viability of any industrial strategy is concerned. There is no doubt that basic economic principles including size of the domestic market, the level of technological development of the country in question, resource endowment, etc., require careful consideration for an appropriate choice of industries. In other words, the difficulties arising from the transition of ISI to higher stages are not inevitable provided the industries which are protected and promoted are not 'white elephants', without export prospects or possibilities to grow into vertically integrated industries, and/or develop dynamic linkages.

In this respect, the knowledge and organisational and administrative abilities of the policy-makers to make and implement the right choices both in terms of industries as well as the package of policies are of considerable importance. Also, the political commitment of the State not to surrender to pressure groups, which for their own sectoral interest are in favour of a particular industry (regardless of its appropriateness for the national economy) is another important consideration. The hotly debated level and extent of State intervention is perhaps less important than the much less debated question of quality, consistency and administrative competence (as well as political support) which State intervention can enjoy, as well as the policy tools at its disposal.

Notes

1. The empirical (statistical) basis of the thesis has continued to be debated. But the recent authoritative study by Professor J. Spraos (1983) has reaffirmed a qualified version of the thesis, shifting from net barter Terms of Trade to the 'Employment Corrected Double Factoral Terms of Trade' (ECDFTT). Spraos gives the net barter Terms and Trade between primary products and manufactures since 1950. According to his data, based on United Nations statistics, this index of Terms of Trade deteriorated between 1950 and 1970 from 114 in 1950 to 85 in 1970, a deterioration of 25 per cent. Between 1970 and 1977 there was a further deterioration of 9 per cent in the net barter Terms of Trade between primary products and manufactures, excluding petroleum (Spraos, 1980), 'Statistical Debate', p. 123). However, if petroleum is included, obviously the picture changes dramatically. For the whole period 1900-1970, Spraos finds generally negative trends for the different series, but is doubtful about their statistical significance. However, Spraos agrees that a countercase for significant deterioration could be made (for further discussion on this, see also Singer, 1984c). Most recently, Spraos (1985) has conceded much of this in his response to Sapsford (1985) when Sapsford showed that when allowing for the once-for-all upward shift during the Second World War, the deterioration is valid for the whole period 1900-1970.

2. The original idea of the thesis was subsequently broadened away from concentrating on Terms of Trade, and ECLA under Prebisch's guidance, in the direction of a distinction between 'centre' and 'periphery' countries (laying foundations for 'dependency' theories), and by Singer in a 're-visit' in the direction of technological control (leading to the idea of inappropriate technologies in LDCs with harmful employment and income distribution effects and their exclusion from the most profitable dynamic new industries) (Singer, 1975).

3. The critics of ISI have more recently abandoned the extreme position developed since the late 1960s, which placed a large unqualified faith in the market's ability to rectify the problems of LDCs. For instance, compare Little *et al*. (1970) with more recent reviews of this subject including the World Bank Report on sub-Saharan Africa 1984. However, despite such recent shifts concerning the importance of State intervention, they still maintain that the basic problem in IS strategy was/is a failure to allow market forces to exert more influence over resource allocation. For an interesting discussion on this point, see Bienefeld (1985).

4. Balassa has himself pointed out that protection of a large magnitude in the forms of tariffs, as well as quantitative restrictions, prevailed in the 1960s and 1970s although there was tariff redundancy in most cases (Balassa, 1981, pp. 402-6; 415-416).

5. The government's overwhelming control of the banking sector provided the most important tool in influencing the direction and distribution of investible funds by varying the interest rate charged according to the field of investment.

6. For instance India, in negotiating a loan agreement with the World Bank in 1981 for upgrading the Indian railway system, faced a substantial degree of pressure from the World

Bank to import computer equipment from one of the major developed country suppliers. At the same time, the Indian Government felt that its own computer industry could supply the necessary equipment (cited in Adams, 1983, pp. 124-5). The World Bank in fact recognises the principle that domestic procurement should be encouraged by allowing a 15 per cent price preference to domestic suppliers before assessing the best-value offer for their projects. But one may question whether a 15 per cent preference is sufficient to allow for the dynamic comparative advantages, learning effects, employment and income effects, etc., of domestic procurement. Moreover, apparently the World Bank fails to extend the 15 per cent preference rule to other developing countries which could encourage South-South trade. (I am indebted to my colleague Adrian Wood for clarifying World Bank policy on procurement).

References

Adams, N. A. (1983) 'Trade Among Developing Countries: Trends, Patterns and Prospects', in B. Paulic *et al.* (eds), *The Challenges to South-South Co-operation* (Westmain Press) pp. 109-127.

Balassa, B. (1975) 'Reforming the System of Incentives in Developing Countries', *World Development*, vol. 3, pp. 215.

Balassa, B. (1978) 'Export Incentives and Export Performance in Developing Countries: A Comparative Analysis', *Weltwirtschaftliches Archiv*, vol. 114, pp. 24-61.

Balassa, B. (1981) *The Newly Industrializing Countries in the World's Economy* (New York: Pergamon Press, 1981).

Balassa, B. (1982) *Development Strategies in Semi-industrialized Economies* (Baltimore: Johns Hopkins University Press), for the World Bank.

Balassa, B. (1985) 'The Cambridge Groups and the Developing Countries', *World Economy*, vol. 8. (1985), no. 3, p. 209.

Beryman, J. (1974) 'Commercial Policy, Allocative and x-efficiency', *Quarterly Journal of Economics*, vol. LXXXVIII pp. 409-25.

Bhagwati, J. N. (1971) 'The Generalized Theory of Distortions and Welfare', in J. N. Bhagwati, R. W. Jones *et al.*, *Trade, Balance of Payments and Growth* (Amsterdam: North-Holland) pp. 69-90.

Bhagwati, J. N. (1978) 'Anatomy and consequences of exchange control regimes', *Foreign Trade Regimes and Economic Development*, vol. XI (Cambridge, Mass.: Ballinger, 1978), J. N. Bhagwati and A. O. Krueger (eds), for the National Bureau for Economic Research.

Bienefeld, M. (1985) 'The Lessons of Africa's Industrial "Failure"', *IDS Bulletin*, University of Sussex, vol. 16, no. 3.

Boon, Gerald K. (1983) 'Dualism and Technological Harmony for Balanced Development', *Industry and Development*, no. 9.

Chenery, H. B. (1980) 'Interaction between Industrialization and Exports?', *Proceedings of the American Economic Association, 1980*, World Bank Print Series, No. 150 (Washington, DC).

Cline, W. R. (1982) 'Can the East Asian Model of Development be Generalized?', *World Development*, vol. 10, no. 2, pp. 81-90.

Corea, G. (1979) *Need for Change: Towards the New International Economic Order*, Report to UNCTAD V — 1980 (Pergamon Press).

Datta-Chaudhuri, M. K. (1981) 'Industrialization and Foreign Trade: The Development Experience of South Korea and the Philippines', in E. Lee (ed.), *Export-led Industrialization and Development* (Geneva: International Labour Office).

Dobb, M. (1960) *An Essay on Economic Growth and Planning* (London: Routledge & Kegan Paul).

Donges, J. B. (1976) 'A Comparative Survey of Industrialization Policies in Fifteen Semi-industrial Countries', *Weltwirtschaftliches Archiv,* vol. 112.

Evans, D. and P. Alizadeh (1984) 'Trade, Industrialization and the Visible Hand', in R. Kaplinsky (ed.), *Third World Industrialization in the 1980s: Open Economies in a Closing World*.

Frank, C. R., K. S. Kim and L. Westphal (1975) *Foreign Trade Regimes and Economic Development* (Cambridge, Mass.: Ballinger).

Hirschman, A. O. (1958) *Strategy of Economic Development* (New Haven, Conn.: Yale University Press).

Hong, W. (1977) *Trade Distortions and Employment Growth in Korea* (Seoul: Korean Development Institute).

Kaplinsky, R. (1984) 'The International Context for Industrialization in the Coming Decade', in R. Kaplinsky (ed.) *Third World Industrialization in the 1980s: Open Economies in a Closing World* (Frank Cass) pp. 75-96.

Kavoussi, R. M. (1985) 'International Trade and Economic Development: The Recent Experience of Developing Countries', *The Journal of Developing Areas*, no. 19 (April) pp. 379-92.

Kirkpatrick, C. H. and F. J. Nixson (eds) (1983) *The Industrialization of Less Developed Countries* (Manchester University Press).

Kirkpatrick, C. H., N. Lee and F. J. Nixson (1984), *Industrial Structure and Policy in Less Developed Countries* (London: George Allen & Unwin, 1984).

Krueger, A. O. (1983) 'Trade Policies in Developing Countries', Institute for Economic Studies, University of Stockholm, Seminar Paper No. 249, ISS No. 347-8769.

Little, S., T. Scitovsky and M. Scott (1970) *Industry and Trade in Some Developing Countries* (London: Oxford University Press).

Luedde-Neurath, R. (1984) 'Import Controls and Export Oriented Development: A Re-examination of the South Korean Case, 1962-82', Institute of Development Studies (University of Sussex), mimeo.

Maizels, A. (1984) 'A Clash of Ideologies', *IDS Bulletin*, vol. 15 (University of Sussex) no. 3.

Park, Y. C. (1981) 'Export-led Development: the Korean Experience, 1960-78', *Export-led Industrialization and Development* (Geneva: ILO).

Rosenstein-Rodan P. N. (1970) 'The Theory of Big Push', *Leading Series in Economic Development*, G. Meier (ed.) (Oxford: Oxford University Press).

Sapsford, D. (1985) 'The Statistical Debate on the Net Barter Terms of Trade between Primary Commodities and Manufactures: Comment and some Additional Evidence', *Economic Journal*, vol. 95 pp. 781-8.

Singer, H. W. (1975) 'The Distribution of Gains Revisited', *The Strategy of International Development* (London: Macmillan, 1975).

Singer, H. W. (1977) and J. Ansari, *Rich and Poor Countries* (Baltimore: Johns Hopkins University Press).

Singer, H. W. (1979) Policy Implications of the Lima Target', *Industry and Development* (UNIDO, 1979), No. 3, Special issue for the Third General Conference of UNIDO.

Singer, H. W. (1983a) 'North-South and South-South: The North and the ECDC', *The Challenges of South-South Co-operation*, B. Paulic *et al.* (eds), pp. 317-29.

Singer, H. W. (1983b) 'North-South Multipliers', *World Development*, vol. 11, no. 5 pp. 452-4.

Singer, H. W. (1984a) 'Ideas and Policy: Sources of UNCTAD', *IDS Bulletin*, vol. 15, no. 3 (University of Sussex, 1984) p. 16.

Singer, H. W. (1984b) 'Industrialization: Where do we Stand? Where are we Going?', *Industry and Development*, no. 12 (Vienna: UNIDO) pp. 79-87.

Singer, H. W. (1984c) 'The Terms of Trade Controversy and the Evolution of Soft Financing', *Pioneers in Development*, G. M. Meier and D. Seers (eds), (Published for the World Bank by the Oxford University Press).

Spraos, J. (1980) 'The Statistical Debate on the Net Barter Terms of Trade between Primary Commodities and Manufactures', *Economic Journal*, vol. 90, pp. 107-128.

Spraos, J. (1983) *Inequalising Trade?* (Oxford: Clarendon Press).

Spraos, J. (1985) 'The Statistical Debate on the Net Barter Terms of Trade: a Response', *Economic Journal*, vol. 9, pp. 121-30.

Teitel, S. and F. Thoumi (1986) 'From Import Substitution to Exports: the Manufacturing Exports Experience of Argentina and Brazil', *Economic Development and Cultural Change*, vol. 34, no. 3.

UNCTAD (1983) 'Protectionism, Trade Relations and Structural Adjustment', in *Proceedings of the United Nations Conference on Trade and Development*, Sixth Session, Volume III, pp. 95-131, United Nations.

Tyler, W. G. (1981) 'Growth and Export Expansion in Developing Countries', *Journal of Development Economics*, vol. 9, pp. 121-30.

Westphal, L. E. (1981) 'Empirical Justification for Infant Industry Protection', World Bank Staff working paper, no. 445.

20. Export-led Development in East Asia: A Flawed Model

Walden Bello

The export-oriented newly industrialising countries (NICs) of East Asia, especially Korea and Taiwan, are often cited as development models for other Third World countries. This article argues that such models are flawed because the export markets depended upon are becoming more protectionist; agriculture in those countries is being wiped out, with implications for food security; the ecological costs of industrialisation have reached crisis proportions; the working class no longer accepts the legitimacy of the model and its associated repression of labour; and the lack of a sophisticated high-technology sector in these countries means that they have not avoided severe dependency on more advanced economies, especially Japan. Some lessons can be drawn from their experience, such as the usefulness of an actively interventionist state role in industry, but the general prescriptions of the export-oriented industrialisation (EOI) model are no longer valid.

For the last two decades, the NIC or newly industrialising country model of high-speed, export-oriented industrialisation has reigned as the orthodoxy in development economics. This intellectual hegemony coincided with a period when the so-called tiger economies of the Asia-Pacific region were registering 8-10 per cent growth rates which, for many observers, constituted the most convincing proof of the merits of the model.

Today, the growth rates remain respectable, but they have not been able to hide the serious flaws which have plunged the East Asian NICs into serious difficulties and undermined the strategy of export-oriented industrialisation.

The NIC model

What exactly the NIC model is must first be clarified. On the one hand, there is the notion, common among orthodox economists, that the essence of 'NICDOM' is achieving high growth rates through liberalisation and free trade. Structural adjustment programmes are, in fact, being sold to Third World countries on the promise that liberalisation and free trade will turn them into new Taiwans and Koreas. This is, however, a misreading of the NIC experience, since even at the height of their success in the mid-eighties, Korea and Taiwan — the NICs whose experience is most relevant to the Third World — had highly protected domestic markets, extremely restrictive foreign investment codes, and strongly interventionist states.[1]

The NIC model, it is now clear, involved a strong emphasis on export manufacturing grafted on to a protected domestic market, nurtured and guided by a powerful directive state that did not hesitate to use subsidies and deploy state resources behind NIC firms that were battling for shares in extremely competitive international markets. But at the centre of the NIC strategy was a draconian effort to achieve export competitiveness

Walden Bello: 'Export-led Development in East Asia: A Flawed Model'. *TRÓCAIRE DEVELOPMENT REVIEW* (1992), pp. 11-27. Reproduced with permission of the publishers.

by utilising repression to keep labour cheap. The crisis of the NIC model stems from the fact that the external and internal conditions of EOI — a liberal world trading order and cheap labour — no longer hold, at the same time that the costs of the strategy have caught up with the NICs in the form of a profound crisis in agriculture, massive environmental degradation, political instability, and deepening technological dependency on advanced industrial countries.

The demise of free trade

The most immediate threat is the spread of protectionism in the NICs' main markets. It is becoming increasingly clear that the NICs were the product of a unique and historically evanescent period when the US not only offered the world's largest and most dynamic market, but also served as the guardian of the post-war liberal world trading order.

From being the locomotive of East Asian growth, the US has, over the last five years, turned into an aggressively protectionist power. Indeed, a trade war against the NICs has been in progress since senior US Treasury official David Mulford issued what amounted to a declaration of hostilities in October 1987: 'Although the NICs may be regarded as tigers because they are strong, ferocious tigers, the analogy has a darker side. Tigers live in the jungle, and by the law of the jungle. They are a shrinking population'.[2]

The US protectionist offensive has been a multi-pronged effort.

- In January 1989, the US revoked the tariff-free entry of selected NIC imports under the Generalised System of Preferences (GSP). But even more damaging than this measure, which affected only about 10 per cent of NIC exports, were the quantitative restrictions of NIC exports that go by the euphemism of voluntary export restraints (VERs). Restrictive quotas placed on Korean textile imports had, in fact, already drastically reduced their rate of growth from 43 per cent per year in the 1970s to less than one per cent per year in the early 1980s. Though restrictions have also limited Korean steel to less than two per cent of total US steel imports.

- To make the NICs' exports more expensive and thus less appealing to American consumers, Washington, in bilateral trade negotiations with the two NICs, forced the appreciation of the New Taiwan dollar and the Korean won by 40 per cent and 30 per cent, respectively, between 1986 and 1989. Currency warfare has been extraordinarily effective in settling US external accounts with Korea. As a high executive of a leading Korean textile firm complained, 'We can absorb wage increases, but we can't take any more appreciation.'[3]

- Protectionist measures were coupled with an aggressive drive to abolish import restrictions and lower tariff barriers to US goods in the NIC markets. Threatened by the infamous Super 301 — legislation that required the US President to take retaliatory measures against those officially tagged as 'unfair traders' — Korea and Taiwan have been forced to liberalise trade restrictions on thousands of services and commodities, from foreign banking operations to cigarettes and beef.

- Washington and US corporations have teamed up to throttle unauthorised technology transfer to the NICs. While the US government has sought to place restrictive covenants on intellectual property rights in the General Agreement on Tariffs and Trade (GATT), US high-tech companies have initiated technological warfare against Korean and Taiwanese clone makers. IBM, Texas Instruments, and Intel now stand to make hundreds of millions of dollars in royalty payments from East Asian producers, who have no choice but to pay up, given their dependence on trouble-free entry into the US market.

The US techno-trade offensive has curbed further expansion of exports from Taiwan and Korea to the US market, and drastically turned Korea's trade surplus with the US of $9.5 billion in 1987 into a deficit of $335 million in 1991.

Faced with a US market that is becoming less hospitable, the NICs have been feverishly hunting for new markets, only to be dashed against the reality that there is really no substitute for the US as a locomotive of export led growth. Efforts to export to Western Europe have intensified, but so have anti-dumping moves against NIC producers, particularly the Koreans. NIC attempts to carve out a niche for their manufactured goods at the lower end of the Japanese market have met with the full force of Japanese protectionism. For instance, Korean knitwear manufactures have been successfully intimidated by Japanese bureaucrats and garment makers to limit their exports to Japan, or else.

The prospect of markets in China, the former Soviet Union and Eastern Europe has received a lot of hype in the NIC press, but recent developments have underlined the fact that these fragile post-socialist economies will generate no more than a fraction of the former US demand. The purchasing power of China's population remains extremely limited by poverty, while structural adjustment measures which close down inefficient factories, lay off surplus workers and radically reduce social subsidies have effectively eliminated Eastern Europe and the former Soviet Union as significant mass markets, at least in the short and medium term.

The immense difficulties of diversifying from the US market in an increasingly protectionist world are suggested by the following set of statistics. In 1988, Hyundai sold over 300,000 Excel subcompact cars in the US. In contrast, in the same year, it was able to sell only 20,097 in the European community and a minuscule 150 in neighbouring Japan.[4]

With the closing up of the US market, Korea's economic growth since 1990 has, in fact, been fuelled largely by domestic demand — the unintended result of the 60 per cent rise in real wages that Korean workers were able to gain from the waves of strikes they launched between 1987 and 1990. Yet the reigning doctrine in technocrat and business circles continues to be export-led growth. For not only do Korea's conglomerates refuse to admit that they have been saved from dire economic straits by labour's successful struggle for higher wages, but they also do not wish to grant any legitimacy to a Keynesian domestic demand-driven economic development strategy which could institutionalise ever-rising wages at the expense of profits.

Table 1: **Selected indicators of Korea's external trade**

	1989	1990	1991
Total exports (FOB $B)	62.4	65.0	71.5
Exports to US ($B)	19.7	18.5	17.0
US share of Korea's exports	32%	28%	24%
Total imports (CIF $B)	61.5	69.8	79.0
Trade balance US ($B)	.9	-4.8	-7.5
Trade balance with US ($B)	6.2	4.1	-.3*
Trade balance with Japan ($B)	-4.0	-6.0	-8.7*

Sources: Except where indicated, figures come from Office of the Pacific Basin, US
        Department of Commerce, July 1992
* Ministry of Finance, Republic of Korea, 1992

The ferocity of the American assault has stunned not only the NICs but also Third World countries which have adopted, at the advice of the World Bank and the International Monetary Fund, EOI programmes that are geared at also turning them into export machines that will service the US market. The more preceptive among them have begun to realise that the EOI prescription has become an ideology that no longer matches the reality of a world that is fast turning from free trade to a system of managed trade among emerging regional trading blocs.

These observers have also begun to notice that the internal costs of high-speed EOI, which were long papered over by dazzling growth rates, have begun to catch up with the NICs.

Table 2: **Selected indicators of Taiwan's external trade**

	1989	1990	1991
Total exports (FOB $B)	66.2	67.2	72.4
Total exports to US ($B)	11.3	11.4	13.1
US share of Taiwan's exports	17%	17%	18%
Total imports (CIF $B)	52.2	54.7	60.7
Trade balance ($B)	14.0	12.5	11.7
Trade balance with US ($B)	12.0	11.1	9.6
Trade balance with Japan ($B)	7.0	7.7	8.8

Source: Office of the Pacific Basin, US Department of Commerce, July 1992

Agriculture on the verge of extinction

Agriculture is facing extinction in both Taiwan and Korea, and this is directly related to the fact that since the mid-sixties, agriculture has been systematically subordinated to the development of export manufacturing. Not only was the sector deprived of investments, but it was deprived of both capital resources and people in order to build up the export platform, leaving it with less than 20 per cent of the population and consigning it to low productivity.

Was the subordination of agriculture intrinsic to the NIC phenomenon or simply an unfortunate by-product? The record appears to be in favour of the former: the technocrats in both Taiwan and Korea consciously squeezed agriculture to subsidise industry in order to make the latter export-competitive. Low grain price policies in Korea, says one expert in Korean agriculture, 'were adopted as a means of surplus extraction .... The state was, in effect, engaged in forming an export-oriented entrepreneurial class that was competitive in world markets. Keeping wage costs low facilitated this economic development strategy.'[5]

The subordination of agriculture to promote export industry was particularly central during the first, critical phase of EOI in the late sixties, when low grain price policies drove farm household income down, in the case of Korea, from rough parity with urban household income in 1965 to 67 per cent of the latter by 1970, and, in Taiwan's case, from 70 per cent to 60 per cent of urban income.[6] In Taiwan, low grain price policies were systematically employed not simply to provide cheap food for the labour force of export-oriented industries but to create that labour force itself. 'The government has intentionally held down the peasants' income,' admitted Lee Teng-Hui, a leading agricultural policy maker before he became President of Taiwan in 1988, 'so as to transfer these people — who originally engaged in agriculture — into industries.'[7]

Low grain price policies were phased out in the 1970s, but the pattern of sacrificing agricultural interests to export industry continued, this time via an implicit 'Faustian Bargain' with the NICs' biggest market, the US: Korea and Taiwan would absorb huge amounts of subsidised US agricultural surpluses in exchange for the US market being kept open to NIC manufactures. This policy has led to the extinction or near collapse of important agricultural sectors, like wheat, soybeans, and, most recently, tobacco. US pressure, which has increased in recent years, now threatens to visit extinction on the Korean beef industry, a development that it likely to bankrupt a great number of the almost 50 per cent of Korea's farmers who depend in varying degrees on raising cattle.[8]

Even rice farmers can no longer be assured that the government will be able to prevent the dumping of US rice surpluses, and it is this fear that has galvanised Korean farmers to organise against a continuation of a policy which they describe as making agriculture the 'sacrificial lamb' of industry. Against the neoclassical concept of efficiency which the technocrats are using to justify the shutting down of the Korean countryside, farmers are now constructing alliances with workers and middle class people around the concept of 'food security' as an element of national security. The struggle is not against food imports, as the western media have depicted it, but for a rational food import policy that would restrain the thrust of unmitigated free trade to drive the NICs' agriculture to extinction. For as the Taiwanese agricultural expert George Kuo eloquently put it, the agricultural question is not simply an issue of 'food price versus export economy but what form of balance [there should be] between food production, human value, economic growth, sustainable agriculture, and environmental integrity.'[9] As agriculture deteriorates and the number of family farms decreases, Kuo contends:

> the entire fabric of rural society is undermined. At the most personal and family level, foreclosure of a family farm is even more stressful than losing a job. At the next level, the rural community and cultural value of rural life are under siege. The loss of rural community means the loss of the rural patriarch to embrace the urban prodigal in the event of debacle in the industries. The rural crisis is affecting urban Taiwan as well. The destruction of the family farm system, whose values are inherent in the country's moral and ethical history, also affects the base on which urban centres are built. At the national level, the disappearance of food self reliance and indigenous commodities would be a great loss for a country with a strong tradition of culinary art. The decline of agriculture, whose values are especially critical in this humid, tropical milieu, also affects the natural ecosystems on which the whole nation is based.[10]

In both Korea and Taiwan, the campaign for a rational food import policy has met with some success, leading to the very real possibility that popular pressure will force the governments of both countries to reject any GATT covenant on agriculture, which could in turn lead to further US retaliation against NIC manufactured exports.

The ecological costs of EOI

Like agriculture, the environment has been traditionally sacrificed to the demands of export oriented manufacturing. From the very beginning of EOI in the mid-sixties, lax environmental regulation has matched low wages as an incentive for local and foreign investors in Taiwan and Korea. Official tolerance of pollution not only reduced costs for domestic exporters, making their products more competitive in the world market, but also attracted industries that were facing tighter environmental regulation in Japan in the 1970s and 1980s.

For many Korean and Taiwanese technocrats, in fact, some environmental destruction was regarded as the unavoidable price of economic growth. 'Some' however is a fairly elastic term. When processes of high-speed EOI telescope into a few decades transformations that took many more decades to unfold in earlier industrialising societies, then 'some' can be quite devastating.

In Taiwan, which has won the dubious accolade of being 'Asia's dirtiest spot', the lower reaches of virtually all of Taiwan's major rivers are now biologically dead, owing to a deadly combination of unregulated industrial and human waste dumping. Twenty per cent of farmland, the government itself admits, is now polluted by industrial waste water. As a result, 30 per cent of the rice grown on the island, claims Dr Edgar Lin, one of Taiwan's leading environmentalists, is contaminated beyond officially tolerated levels with heavy metals, including mercury, arsenic, and cadmium.[11]

It seems that in Korea these days, environmental skeletons from the past keep spilling out of the closet. Much of the country's tap water is not safe to drink owing to heavy metal content far above tolerable levels, and the country's two major rivers, the Han and the Nakdong, are said to be approaching biological death. Perhaps the most terrifying of environmental horror stories involved the Nakdong, which provides the water supply for the 10 million people who live in the Taegu-Pusan metropolitan complex, Korea's second most important industrial area. In April 1991, residents were informed by the government that the strange smell they had noticed in their tap water was caused by the surreptitious dumping of 325 tons of waste phenol, a highly toxic, cancer-causing chemical, by a subsidiary of Doosan, a Korean conglomerate. The dumping, they were informed, had been going on for over five months.[12]

Just like the agricultural question, the question of whether severe environmental damage is remediable or is inherent to export oriented development is now a matter of intense debate. What is clear is that, in both Taiwan and Korea, environmental laws are now in place. What is equally clear is that these laws go largely unenforced, except at times of great public indignation. As a Korean Ministry of Energy report conceded: 'The efficacy of [environmental] laws, especially in rural areas, is unknown ... since there is no information regarding actual practices, the level of adherence to these standards, or whether the appropriate expertise is available for determining if the pollutant concentrations require the rigorous procedures described by the law.'[13]

The problem, it appears, does not lie in the state's capacity for enforcement. The Korean government's record in strongarming industries to move along certain preferred policy paths is impressive. The Taiwanese state has also been an effective disciplinarian of private interests, that is, when it wants to. But despite massive public agitation for more effective environmental regulation, minimal and grudging enforcement of environmental laws continues to be the norm in both Taiwan and Korea. The main obstacle to effective environmental protection, it is clear, is the government business consensus that effective environmental regulation can only be achieved at the expense of reducing the competitiveness of NIC manufactures in the world market.[14]

Legitimacy crisis

The 7,000 strikes that Korean workers launched between 1987 and 1990 revealed to the world another crisis overtaking NIC-style export-oriented industrialisation: it may have delivered some degree of prosperity but it has not secured popular legitimacy.

This crisis is the direct result of a historical choice made early on by the state and business elites in Taiwan and Korea: to implement EOI, they opted to secure the compliance of labour via the shortcut of repression rather than through more complex democratic mechanisms. Perhaps this was inevitable since achieving success in export markets marked by cut throat competition meant having to drive down workers' wages below their market value. To do this one had either to prevent labour from organising, as in Taiwan and Korea, or disorganising an already organised work force, as in Singapore. Gary Rodan's observation on Singapore is just as relevant to Korea and Taiwan: '[I]t is hard to accept uncritically the notion of comparative advantage in labour costs as having any meaning in isolation from ... the state's role in helping define those costs.'[15]

In Taiwan, labour was controlled from top to bottom through the different levels of organisation of the ruling Kuomintang Party, which was structured along 'democratic centralist' lines. In Korea, the main impetus for the growth of the Korean Central Intelligence Agency (KCIA) was the need to monitor labour and abort any attempt at independent labour organising. Indeed, according to one Korean labour economist, the technocrats at the Economic Planning Board needed the KCIA to insulate 'the planning and implementation processes from any external political influences and controls, thereby minimising "distortions" and "irrationality".'[16]

The tremendous pressure that built up over two decades of tight authoritarian control finally forced decompression in both Taiwan and Korea in 1987. But when the new democratic politics arrived, it focused not on forging consensus on the strategy for economic growth but on a polarised struggle over the benefits of past growth. As the *Financial Times*, in its inimitable style, put it, 'the country's new-found democratic politics are putting wage push, labour unrest, and demands for welfare expenditure in the way of continued super-growth.'[17]

Militancy, not moderation, is the mainstream in Korean labour politics, a mood that was expressed by Lee So Sun, one of the most respected figures in the labour movement. Asked if labour's wage demands were not posing a problem for Korea's export competitiveness, she replied: 'The government says the economy is successful. But only a few benefit from the economy .... There is nothing in it for us.'[18] Such militant class consciousness hardly lends itself to institutionalising western-style collective bargaining processes or forging a labour-management consensus on a new economic strategy.

Authoritarianism in the NICs may have delivered stunning growth rates in the short term, but it also created 'two nations' within each society whose divergent social agendas now make it very difficult to forge consensus on policies for the next stage of development. Nowhere is this currently more evident than in Korea, where business and government elites cling ever more fervently to the doctrine of export-led growth despite the fact that the economy is now largely driven by domestic demand. Acknowledging the critical role of the domestic market in future growth, they fear, could lead to recognising the importance of income redistribution, which could in turn clear the path to a greater role for labour in the determination of economic policy.

The structural squeeze

From a strategic point of view, perhaps the most serious threat to the NICs is the 'structural squeeze', that is, a condition in which they have priced themselves out of the cheap labour market at the same time that they failed to develop the base for higher value-added, skill-intensive and technology-intensive production.

Pushed up by the rising cost of living and the drying up of labour reserves as well as by increasingly effective labour organising, the average wage in Taiwan and South Korea now stands at three times that in South east Asia and ten times that in China. In textiles, for instance, the average cost per operator hour stands at $3.56 in Taiwan, $2.87 in Korea, $0.68 in Thailand, and $0.40 in China.[19]

But as Lester Thurow says, 'high wages and high profits are not antithetical — they go together'.[20] There is, however, a big if — if firms make the requisite investments in research and development (R & D) and upgrading the skills of workers. Instead, many local entrepreneurs have followed the example of US and Japanese investors who are pulling up their stakes in Korea and Taiwan and relocating their operations to Thailand, Indonesia, China, and Malaysia. Indeed, a 'hollowing out' of manufacturing such as that which happened in the US now poses a very real threat to Korea and other NICs, except that in their case it would be a very premature development since, unlike the US, they still do not have a skill-intensive, high-technology sector to fall back on as they become increasingly non-competitive in labour-intensive manufacturing activities.

The responsibility for this crisis must be laid directly at the doorstep of the *chaebol* (Korean firms) and the Taiwanese firms. In the view of the government technocrats, despite the image of Korea as a roaring tiger in the 1980s, those years were actually a 'lost decade'. As one analyst sums up the now prevailing technocratic consensus:

> The worst part of the Chun [Doo-Hwan] era was the neglect of new investment in plants and equipment, introduction of new technologies, and development of new products — all attributes of a healthy export oriented economy. The trend was intensified by the presence of ample opportunities to make quicker returns by investing in property and service-related industries. Those industries, often condemned as economically unproductive and even socially unethical, flourished during the 1980s. Analysts argue that businesses, big and small, were busy sizing up such windfall opportunities, shifting the money they earned from manufacturing to the service sector.[21]

Taiwanese firms invested only a minuscule 0.44 per cent of sales revenue on R & D.[22] Where most of their profits went is indicated by the fact that nearly 20 per cent of Taiwan's publicly traded firms now earn more than 50 per cent of their pre-tax recurring profits from outside their principal operations — a sure sign of heavily playing the stock market.[23] Korean conglomerates, for their part, allocated only three per cent of their sales to R & D, compared to over 6 per cent in the case of Japanese firms.[24] Instead, the *chaebol* funnelled some $16 billion into the acquisition of real estate.[25]

Government technocrats are hardly in a position to criticise, however, since the state did not step into the breach in the R & D effort. In Taiwan, combined private and government expenditures in R & D came to only 0.99 per cent of GNP.[26] In Korea, where the state in the 1980s was constantly under pressure from the IMF to desist from an activist economic policy, government spending in R & D came to only 0.4 per cent of GNP, a level that was said to be even lower than that of Taiwan.[27] Indeed, total Korean R & D expenditures in 1988 came to only $3.43 billion — far short of the R & D budget of just one US company, IBM, which invested $5.9 billion in R & D.[28]

The consequences of starving the R & D sector are underlined by the following examples: Taiwan's famous 'computer industry' is actually a glorified description of the low-tech, labour-intensive mass cloning of easy-to-copy IBM models. As for Korea, its image of being a high tech producer is belied by a few sobering realities: the bestselling Hyundai Excel may be Korea's best-known export, but its body styling is Italian in origin, its engine is designed by the Japanese firm Mitsubishi and its transmission is both designed and manufactured by Mitsubishi. Korean television sets may be competing toe-to-toe with Japanese products in the US, but Japanese components account for 85 per cent of their value. Korea may be the world's fifth largest exporter of personal computers, but only the computer cabinet is actually made in the country.[29]

Korea is said to be a leader in semiconductor technology. But Samsung, which is said to be capable of mass producing the 16-megabit DRAM (dynamic random memory) chip, is more the exception than the rule. Most of the technological capabilities of other Korean electronics firms, in fact, come from the Japanese.

The fact of the matter is that Taiwan and Korea have not been able to graduate from being mainly assembly sites for foreign and specifically Japanese components. Indeed, nearly 30 years after initiating EOI, Taiwan and Korea are now even more dependent on technologically advanced Japan. This is revealed most dramatically by the two countries' $8 billion+ trade deficits with Japan, which cannot be alleviated through simple macro-economic manipulation of tariff and exchange rate policies owing to their structural character — that is, the trade statistics do not principally reflect normal trade movements but a fundamental technological dependency.

Japan, of course, has not hesitated to manipulate this dependency to keep Korea and Taiwan in line: despite Korean government demands for more liberal technology transfer, the Japanese government has prohibited the transfer for 200 ultra-modern high technologies to Korea until the year 1995, by which time the Japanese corporations will have exploited most of the market potential of these frontier technologies.

Instead of transferring state of the art high technology, Japan is using the transfer of second class technology to integrate Korean and Taiwanese firms as subordinate elements within an Asia Pacific wide division of labour designed by Japanese firms to enhance Japanese corporate profitability. The Japanese firm Hitachi, for instance, licensed its 1-megabit DRAM technology to the Korean firm Luck-Goldstar to acquire a subordinate firm that could specialise in turning out a product that was no longer state-of-the-art while it focused on developing a more profitable advanced product, the 4-megabit chip. As one analyst saw it:

> While one megabit DRAMS are currently the industry standard, Japanese producers are gearing up to produce chips that can hold four times as much information. Hitachi apparently can guarantee a stable source of one-megabit DRAMs through Goldstar, while concentrating on the more complicated and expensive four-megabit market.[30]

Practically all Taiwanese carmakers now have significant Japanese equity, and they have been reoriented into a division of labour which, in the words of one Japanese expert, 'is not an equal division of labour as seen in the European Community countries, but a vertical one within the automobile industry as a whole.'[31] In this 'inter-product division of labour', the Taiwanese firms will specialise in 'low price compact cars which have fewer parts and a higher percentage of labour in the entire process.[32] Perhaps unwittingly using historically loaded terms, the analyst concludes: 'China-Taiwan aims for coexistence and coprosperity with Japan by producing the items that are not economically suitable for Japan.'[33]

Was the structural squeeze unavoidable? The loss of the cheap-labour advantage to other Third World countries was probably inevitable, given the inexorable rise in living costs and the tightening of the labour market owing to the drying up of the pool of cheap rural labour in Taiwan and Korea. But the failure to move up to higher value-added, more skill-intensive production was probably not inherent to the model. In fact, the R & D debacle of the 1980s probably stemmed from a departure from one feature of the NIC model — from the weakening of the directive role of the state that marked the first two decades of EOI. Under pressure from the IMF, the US and liberalisers within the technocracy itself, the Korean state, for example, began to pull back from a more activist involvement in strategic economic planning, leaving much of this function to the *chaebol*. Increasingly free of technocratic oversight, the conglomerates promptly channelled their investments, not into risky R & D, but into speculative activities that promised quick, easy and high profits.

Conclusion

In sum, the NIC strategy of high-speed EOI is being unravelled by the conjunction of unfavourable external and internal conditions. The liberal world trading environment that allowed the NICs to flourish from the mid-sixties to the mid-eighties is fast disappearing while the long-suppressed internal costs of EOI have caught up with the NICs. This fatal coincidence of negative trends has left the ailing tigers stranded in the perilous zone between the developed and underdeveloped worlds, and it will take a new, bold set of economic policies to keep them from sliding back to the Third World in the 1990s.

The crisis of the NICs reminds one of the truth in the ancient saying that 'the owl of Minerva flies only at dusk'. Ideas congeal into doctrine only when the circumstances in the real world that they reflected have disappeared. Such is the cunning of history that the NIC model — be it the mistaken neoclassical liberal interpretation or the more accurate version of state led pursuit of export-oriented industrialisation — has become orthodoxy at the very moment that it has become obsolete. While there are certainly some features of the NIC strategy that might be usefully adopted by Third World countries, like the presence of an activist, directive state, the essence of the model — high speed economic growth achieved through export orientation and the subordination of agriculture, environment, and class relationships to the logic of EOI — is a questionable prescription for breaking out of underdevelopment under conditions prevailing in the last decade of the twentieth century.

Footnotes

1. See among other works, Alice Amsden, (1989), *Asia's Next Giant: South Korea and Late Industrialization*, New York, Oxford University Press; Robert Wade, (1991), *Governing the Market*, Princeton, Princeton University Press; Tony Mitchell, 'From LDC to NIC: the Republic of Korea: employment, industrialization and trade 1961-82', unpublished

    manuscript; and Walden Bello and Stephanie Rosenfeld, (1991), *Dragons in Distress: Asia's Miracle Economics in Crisis*, London, Penguin.

2. David Mulford, 'Remarks before the Asia-Pacific Capital Markets Conference', San Francisco, 17 November 1987.

3. Interview with Y. C. Park, senior manager, Tae Heung Ltd, by Walden Bello, Seoul, 23 May 1988.

4. Peter Montagnon, 'Wanted: a truly free market', *Financial Times*, 2 April 1990, sec. 3, p.v.

5. Larry Burmeister, (1988), *Research, Realpolitik and Development in Korea: The State and the Green Revolution*, Boulder, Westview Press, p. 68.

6. Song Byung-Nak, 'The Korean economy', unpublished manuscript, 1989, p. 244; Cheng Hsing-Yiu, 'Family farms, integrated rural development and multi-purpose cooperatives in Taiwan', *Economic Review*, Taipei, no. 222, November-December 1984, p. 14.

7. Quoted in Richard Kagan, 'The miracle of Taiwan', unpublished manuscript, Institute of Food and Development Policy, San Francisco, 1982, p. 37.

8. Mark Clifford, 'Cheap foreign beefs', *Far Eastern Economic Review*, 21 July 1988, p. 37.

9. George Kuo, 'Not by rice alone: hunger for justice in Taiwan', *Food Symposium 88 Newsletter*, Tokyo, 1988, p 88.

10. Ibid.

11. Neal Rudge, 'Edgar Lin', *Bang*, March 1988, p. 12.

12. 'Polluters considered criminals', *Youhap*, 25 March 1991, reproduced in *Foreign Broadcast Information Service: East Asia*, 26 March 1991, p. 32.

13. *Cooperative Energy Assessment*, Argonne, Illinois; Republic of Korea Ministry of Energy and US Department of Energy, September 1981, p. 127.

14. See, among other recent reports, *Environment and Development in Korea*, Seoul, Korea NGO Forum for UNCED, 1992.

15. Gary Rodan, 'Industrialization and the Singapore State in the context of the new international division of labor', in Richard Higgot and Richard Robinson, eds, *Southeast Asia: Essays in the Political Economy of Structural Change*, London, Routledge and Kegan Paul, 1985, p. 179.

16. Choi Jang Jip, 'Interest control and political control in South Korea: a study of labor unions in manufacturing industries, 1961-80', PhD dissertation, Department of Political Science, University of Chicago, August 1983, p. 339.

17. 'Sympathy of South Korea', *Financial Times*, 22 March 1990.

18. Personal interview with Lee So-Sun by Walden Bello, Seoul, 20 May 1988.

19. Werner International, 'Spinning and weaving labor cost comparisons', New York, Spring 1989.

20. Lester Thurow, (1992), *Head to Head*, New York, William Morrow, p. 273.

21. Kim Sam-O, 'A blip in the economy's growth prompts concern', *Business Korea*, February 1990, p. 30.

22. 'Competition worries Taiwan manufacturers', *Electronics Business*, 10 December 1986, p. 28.

23. Shigezaburo Kabe, 'Taiwan's Stock Market: a national pastime', *Japan Economic Journal*, 24 February 1990, p. 24.

24. Kim Ki Ung, 'The KIET analyses the present state of and future prospects of the automobile and home appliance markets', *Hanguk Kyongje Sinmun*, 14-15 July 1990.

25. See 'Presidential adviser Moon Hi Gab: aggressive, no-nonsense', *Business Korea*, November 1989, p. 28; 'Land tax reform: can the circle be broken?' *Business Korea*, November 1989, p. 28.

26. Liang Kuo-Shu and Liang Ching-Ing Hou, 'Trade strategy and industrial policy in Taiwan', in Thornton Bradshaw, *et al.*, eds, *America's New Competitors*, Cambridge, Ballinger, 1988, p. 65.

27. According to Yi Kyong Tae, industrial director of the Korea Institute of Economics and Technology; quoted in 'Small company technology discussed', *Kyongje Sinmun*, 24 November 1989, p. 17.

28. Suh Ki-Sun, 'Failure to restructure industry at root of economic woes', *Business Korea*, February 1991, p. 43.

29. Kang Duck Joong, 'Structural problems at root of illness', *Electronics Korea*, July 1990, p. 11.

30. Jacob Schlesinger, ' Hitachi joins Goldstar in plan for chip plant', *Asian Wall Street Journal*, 31 July 1989, p. 6.

31. Konomi Tomisawa, 'Development of and future outlook for an international division of labour in the automobile industries of Asian NICs', Briefing Paper for the First Policy Forum, International Vehicle Programs, 5 May 1987, p. 68.

32. Ibid.

33. Ibid. p. 34.

21. Agricultural Trade Liberalisation: Executive Summary

United Nations Conference on Trade and Development

This study analyses the possible effects, in the context of the liberalization of trade in agriculture, of policy changes by major agricultural trading nations (Australia, Canada, EEC, Japan and the United States) on the markets for selected agricultural products and attempts to assess the trade and welfare implications for developing countries. The analysis covers products accounting for the bulk of world agricultural trade, including the major traded tropical products. These are: cereals (wheat, maize, rice and sorghum), meat (beef and veal), sugar, oilseeds and oils (soya beans and soyabean oil, groundnuts and groundnut oil, palm oil and copra), coffee and coffee products, cocoa and cocoa products, tea, tobacco and cotton.

A series of models of agricultural markets in the five major agricultural trading countries (EEC being regarded as a single country for this purpose) is constructed in order to evaluate the production, consumption and trade effects of specific policy changes. For other countries, only net exports or imports are modelled. The basic theoretical framework is the commonly used partial equilibrium comparative static model based upon supply and demand elasticities. However, it is adapted to allow for the simulation of a broad array of distinct policy options. The world price is determined in a single world market in which import demand equals export supply. Import demand and export supply functions for each product are aggregated for all countries of the model to obtain world demand and supply functions. Once the equilibrium world price has been determined, it is passed back to the individual country equations to determine the change in national exports and imports.

The simulation results show the consequence of simultaneous changes in levels of agricultural support and tariffs and other border measures that prevailed in the five countries in the base period (1984-1986), assuming that policies in other countries are unchanged. The model is applied to four alternative scenarios of policy changes, corresponding to proposals under consideration in the Uruguay Round:[2]

- *Complete liberalization* — that is, the reduction of PSE and CSE levels[3] to zero and the elimination of all tariffs and quotas, as well as of internal taxes on tropical products. This scenario corresponds to the "zero option" proposal which has been put forward by the United States;

- *A reduction in producer price support by 20 per cent*, corresponding largely to the proposal of EEC, which envisages a reduction in the level of farm support for certain products without a fundamental change in the nature of market intervention;

United Nations Conference on Trade and Development: *AGRICULTURAL TRADE LIBERALISATION IN THE URUGUAY ROUND: IMPLICATIONS FOR DEVELOPING COUNTRIES* (New York: United Nations, 1990), UNCTAD ITP/48, pp. xii-xxiv.

- *Elimination of export subsidies*, corresponding to the minimum proposal of the Cairns Group;

- *An increase in imports of each product by 10 per cent* in each of the five markets. Where imports are limited by quota, it is assumed that quotas would be increased by 10 per cent. This scenario corresponds to the minimum access proposal supported by a variety of countries. For tropical products, it is also the scenario which is the most relevant to the argument that an expansion in demand for tropical products in OECD countries as a result of faster growth or through buffer stock purchases is what would bring the greatest benefit to developing countries.

The results given for individual countries and for each product should be interpreted with caution since they are necessarily approximate. While they indicate the direction and extent of change, it must be borne in mind that factors other than assistance to agriculture, such as technology, macro-economic developments in the different countries, assistance and support given to non-agricultural sectors, and population trends, are held constant. Also, there are likely to be other, *dynamic*, effects which are not captured — for example, changes in production, consumption and trade that result from the changes in world prices (including the interaction between the grain and livestock sectors). Finally, the response to the policy change assumed depends on the price elasticities and the form of assistance granted, and particularly on how agricultural support levels (in terms of their *ad valorem* equivalents) and effective domestic prices are measured. In this connexion, it should be noted that the data used for production, consumption, exports and imports of each product are average annual quantities in the period 1983-1985.

World price effects

Table 1 shows, for each of the four policy scenarios, the impact that can be expected on world prices of the various agricultural products. Among the grains, it is the world price of rice that increases the most when the policy change consists of reducing support to producers either by complete liberalization or by a 20 per cent reduction in the producer support price. However, if only export subsidies are eliminated (domestic support systems remaining in place) wheat has the biggest price increase, followed by beef and rice, while the increase in world sugar and maize prices would be only marginal.

For vegetable oils and tropical products, the price impact of complete liberalization and reduced domestic support is relatively small. This reflects the fact that border measures and internal taxes are the principal forms of market intervention for tropical products in the five countries. Prices rise when tariffs and internal taxes are eliminated because consumption increases in the five countries and generates an increase in world demand. It is noteworthy that the greatest rise in tropical product prices would occur under the assumption of an increase in imports of each of the five countries by 10 per cent, whether through quota increases or otherwise.[4]

Revenue and welfare effects

At the national level changes in world prices and in the balance between domestic supply and demand are reflected in changes in the value of production and net trade.

Table 1   **Estimated change in world prices of agricultural products (including tropical products) under alternative liberalization scenarios**
(Increase in per cent)

Product	SCENARIO			
	Complete liberalization	20 per cent reduction in producer support price	Export subsidy elimination	10 per cent increase in imports
Wheat	20.4	7.5	12.2	1.1
Maize	15.1	4.8	0.1	3.9
Rice	42.6	18.3	8.5	2.2
Sorghum	12.4	1.9	0.0	2.4
Soya beans	3.6	0.0	0.0	2.5
Soyabean oil	1.9	0.1	0.0	0.0
Beef and veal	12.5	13.0	11.1	1.6
Sugar	26.5	10.6	0.9	4.3
Cotton	0.1	0.9	0.0	9.1
Groundnut	0.1	1.5	0.0	5.1
Groundnut oil	2.8	0.6	9.0	3.9
Copra	0.0	0.0	0.0	10.1
Palm oil	0.4	0.0	0.0	1.6
Tea	2.9	0.5	0.0	8.3
Coffee:				
Green	4.4	0.4	0.0	29.9
Roasted	7.5	0.0	0.0	38.7
Extracts	7.8	1.4	0.0	1.3
Cocoa:				
Beans	0.1	0.0	0.0	19.7
Butter	2.8	0.5	0.0	9.1
Powder	5.2	0.8	0.0	4.2
Chocolate, n.e.s.	9.0	1.8	0.0	1.0
Tobacco:				
Leaves	2.6	0.3	0.0	12.3
Cigarettes	0.2	0.1	0.0	0.0
Cigars	3.2	0.8	0.0	0.1
N.e.s.	0.1	0.2	0.0	0.6

The net foreign exchange and welfare impacts[5] on developing countries of these changes in world prices are given in table 2 by region, and in table 3 for selected countries. The gains or losses are expressed in United States dollars, based on the 1985-1987 average world market price of each product.

Aggregation of the results for individual countries should be interpreted with caution since whereas arithmetically pluses and minuses offset each other, in reality the gains of one country cannot be used to offset the losses of another. The aggregate figures therefore provide only a rough indication of the extent of the net outcome at the regional level. It is necessary to look at the situation of individual countries to determine those that gain and those that lose and the extent of their gains or losses.

With this caveat in mind, the regional results reported in table 2 indicate that when the agricultural sector is completely liberalized, or the level of assistance is reduced by 20 per cent in the five major agricultural trading countries, the resulting increase in world prices would lead to a net loss of foreign exchange (i.e. a higher import bill) for the African region, but to net foreign exchange gains for Latin America and the Caribbean, and for the Asian and Pacific regions. The corresponding welfare changes would be positive for Latin America and the Caribbean, but negative for Africa, Asia and the Pacific. When only export subsidies are eliminated, the African region would again be a net loser both of foreign exchange and welfare, as would also Asian and Pacific countries. Latin America and the Caribbean, by contrast, would gain on both accounts. Only under the scenario of an exogenous increase of 10 per cent in the volume of imports in each of the five countries do all of the developing regions experience net gains in foreign exchange earnings, gains which are far larger than the corresponding gains — where they occur — under the alternative scenarios.

As regards tropical products in particular, the elimination of tariffs and internal taxes, and of domestic support where relevant, improves the net export earnings of all developing regions. The results indicate that an exogenous increase in the volume of imports of the five major agricultural trading countries yields by far the greatest gain in both foreign exchange and welfare for all developing regions.

Detailed results for individual developing countries, by region, for each product included in the study are reported in annex IV. Under the scenario of complete liberalization, the developing countries with the largest overall gains in major "temperature zone" agricultural producers are: Argentina (largely from cereals), Thailand (largely from rice, sugar and maize), Brazil (largely from sugar and meat), Myanmar (rice), Pakistan (rice), Uruguay (largely from meat and rice), Cuba (sugar) and Philippines (sugar). In certain cases, however, notably Colombia and India, although there is a net gain in foreign exchange earnings, there is a net decline in welfare. In general, African countries suffer losses both in foreign exchange and in welfare when agricultural assistance levels are reduced for these major agricultural products. Such losses stem mainly from the higher cost of imported cereals and from the reduced value of preferential sugar exports, most notable in the case of Mauritius.[6] Few developing countries (e.g. Argentina and Uruguay) are net gainers under the alternative scenario of confining liberalization to the elimination of support subsidies; gains are more widespread in all regions on the basis of a 10 per cent increase in import volumes.

As regards tropical products, Brazil gains most from complete liberalization (on account of coffee, cocoa and tobacco), followed by Colombia (coffee), Côte d'Ivoire (coffee and

Table 2: Estimated net foreign exchange and welfare impact on developing countries under different scenarios: summary by region
(Millions of 1985-1987 dollars)

I: Complete liberalization (PSE and CSE reduced to zero; and tariffs, quotas and internal taxes eliminated on tropical products)

Region	Selected agricultural products		Selected tropical products		All selected products	
	For. ex. earnings	Welfare change	For. ex. earnings	Welfare change	For. ex. earnings	Welfare change
Africa	-699	-953	219	143	-480	-810
Latin America & Caribbean	984	224	562	445	1546	669
Asia & Pacific	428	-483	141	77	569	-406
TOTAL	713	-1212	922	665	1635	-547

II: Reduction of producer price support (by 20 per cent)

Region	Selected agricultural products		Selected tropical products		All selected products	
	For. ex. earnings	Welfare change	For. ex. earnings	Welfare change	For. ex. earnings	Welfare change
Africa	-280	-402	32	21	-248	-381
Latin America & Caribbean	456	152	71	51	527	203
Asia & Pacific	145	-225	18	1	163	-224
TOTAL	321	-475	121	73	442	-402

III: Elimination of export subsidies

Region	Selected agricultural products		Selected tropical products		All selected products	
	For. ex. earnings	Welfare change	For. ex. earnings	Welfare change	For. ex. earnings	Welfare change
Africa	-256	-359	0	0	-256	-359
Latin America & Caribbean	262	37	0	0	262	37
Asia & Pacific	-89	-332	0	0	-89	-332
TOTAL	-83	-654	0	0	-83	-654

IV: Increase in imports by 10 per cent

Region	Selected agricultural products		Selected tropical products		All selected products	
	For. ex. earnings	Welfare change	For. ex. earnings	Welfare change	For. ex. earnings	Welfare change
Africa	-45	-67	1926	1337	1881	1270
Latin America & Caribbean	192	87	3446	2769	3638	2856
Asia & Pacific	19	-60	872	477	891	417
TOTAL	166	-40	6244	4583	6410	4543

cocoa), Indonesia (coffee and tea), Mexico (coffee) and India (tea and coffee). Other countries experiencing positive but relatively smaller gains include Uganda, Kenya, El Salvador, Costa Rica, Cameroon, Ecuador, Honduras (all due to coffee), Zimbabwe (tobacco), Sri Lanka (tea) and Malaysia (palm oil).

For the 25 agricultural products (including tropical products) covered in this study taken together, the major gainers in both foreign exchange and welfare terms under the complete liberalization scenario are, among the developing countries, Thailand, Argentina and Brazil. Notable gains are also made by, *inter alia*, Cuba, Myanmar, Colombia, Pakistan, India, Uruguay, and Philippines (see table 3). Among the developing countries, the major losers in both foreign exchange and welfare terms are Egypt, Republic of Korea, Algeria, Nigeria, Iraq, Islamic Republic of Iran, Saudi Arabia, Mexico, Mauritius and Morocco. Some countries gain in terms of foreign exchange earnings but suffer a net overall decline in welfare (e.g. Indonesia, United Republic of Tanzania, and Zaire). Gains are less widespread under the scenario of confining liberalization to the elimination of export subsidies, whereas they are most widespread in the event of a 10 per cent increase in the volume of imports of the selected products. Apart from this last scenario, the number of developing countries that are net losers consistently exceeds the number that are net gainers. In arithmetical terms, the sum of the country gains of foreign exchange earnings outweighs the sum of the country losses; however, the combined welfare improvement of the gainers is much smaller than the combined welfare decline of the losers.

Policy implications

A reduction or elimination of agricultural support and protection in the industrialized countries could have a dynamic impact on the development of agricultural production in developing countries and could provide the latter with an opportunity to expand foreign exchange earnings from their agricultural exports in the longer run. However, in the short-to-medium term, because of reduced production in developed countries and lags in expanding agricultural production in developing countries, world food prices can be expected to rise. While a rise in food prices could be beneficial in the long run, in the short run it would bring hardship to developing countries that are net importers of food, particularly to the poorer sections of the population. Higher prices would undoubtedly improve the profitability of the farming sector in some countries and reduce government expenditures on agricultural income support programmes in others. More remunerative prices in the long run could also contribute to making food production in food-deficit developing countries more attractive, provided that the benefits of the higher prices are passed on to the producers and are complemented by institutional and infrastructural improvements. In the short run, however, high food prices would continue to increase pressure on the balance of payments of many food-deficit countries, with serious consequences not only for their debt repayment capacity and their ability to maintain essential imports at adequate levels but also for the well-being of the poor, whose food intake is already inadequate.

The issue of gains and losses in multilateral trade negotiations is not new. However, for the developing countries which are net importers of agricultural products the extent of net gains or losses will depend upon the impact of trade liberalization in products of

Table 3: Major gainers and losers[a] in each country group (all selected products)
(Millions of dollars)

Country group/Country	Complete liberalization in producer support price		20 per cent reduction elimination		Export subsidy in imports		10 per cent increase	
	Revenue	Welfare	Revenue	Welfare	Revenue	Welfare	Revenue	Welfare[b]
POLICY COUNTRIES								
Australia	967	678	1037	348	1103	305	78	54
Canada	780	476	866	144	1051	231	-158	-53
EEC	-5141	1430	-2246	855	-2502	1301	-3912	-4
Japan	-2819	1345	-563	559	-208	198	-1135	-50
United States	4433	2829	294	869	704	6161	-769	-90
OTHER DEVELOPED MARKET ECONOMIES								
Austria	36	6	21	8	23	11	-40	-78
Finland	2	-12	5	0	4	0	-48	
New Zealand	104	59	107	66	91	57	43	
Norway	-16	-27	-2	-6	-2	-4	-44	
Sweden	32	2	19	7	23	12	-79	
Switzerland	3	-24	-2	-11	-4	-9	-55	
EASTERN EUROPE								
Czechoslovakia	14	-20	13	-5	-13	0	-43	-62
German Democratic Rep.	-10	-56	2	-20	1	-14	-58	-82
Poland	-44	-103	-17	-42	-27	-50	-40	-67
USSR	-42	-1049	-169	-436	-166	-402	-51	-210
CENTRAL AMERICA AND MEXICO								
El Salvador	24	17	3	1	-1	-2	176	141
Costa Rica	35	23	13	8	8	2	155	118
Guatemala	36	28	11	8	4	5	183	158
Honduras	23	16	10	7	6	3	94	72
Nicaragua	15	9	8	5	4	2	66	48
Mexico	-8	-76	-11	-32	-5	14	351	251
CARIBBEAN								
Cuba	128	68	47	22	-9	-20	68	45
Dominican Republic	43	26	15	10	1	-1	73	55
SOUTH AMERICA								
Argentina	679	438	259	171	228	149	118	66
Brazil	451	219	114	36	6	-48	1521	1175
Colombia	107	86	17	12	2	-3	597	546
Ecuador	10	3	0	-2	-2	-4	93	82
Peru	-9	-29	-6	-16	-9	-18	65	56
Uruguay	90	59	68	47	54	37	6	3
Venezuela	-31	-59	-12	-23	-9	-16	8	1

Table 3: (continued)   Major gainers and losers[a] in each country group (all selected products)
(Millions of dollars)

Country group/Country	Complete liberalization		20 per cent reduction in producer support price		Export subsidy elimination		10 per cent increase in imports	
	Revenue	Welfare	Revenue	Welfare	Revenue	Welfare	Revenue	Welfare[b]
SUB-SAHARAN AFRICA								
Cameroon	15	10	1	0	-1	2	165	131
Côte d' Ivoire	41	6	-5	-13	-8	-12	589	408
Ethiopia	3	1	-1	-2	-3	-4	62	61
Ghana	-4	-8	-3	-4	-2	-3	99	80
Kenya	27	13	2	0	-2	-2	194	117
Madagascar	-7	-16	-6	-8	-3	-4	62	48
Mauritius	-73	-80	-21	-24	-2	-3	78	57
Nigeria	-87	-119	-39	-54	-29	-39	252	152
Uganda	33	19	3	1	0	0	64	50
United Rep. of Tanzania	1	-4	-2	-3	-2	-2	-82	64
Zaire	3	-4	-2	-4	-3	-4		
Zimbabwe	24	16	8	5	2	1	83	65
NORTH AFRICA								
Algeria	-91	-118	-33	-43	-37	-48	-82	-93
Egypt	-172	-236	-69	-105	-87	-123	-16	-32
Morocco	-54	-68	-20	-25	-25	-32	-19	-24
WEST ASIA								
Iran (Islamic Rep. of)	-84	-167	-48	-81	-45	-68	-11	-19
Iraq	-85	-135	-44	-69	-41	-59	-13	-24
Saudi Arabia	-76	-107	-37	-50	-20	-31	-24	-31
SOUTH-EAST ASIA								
Bangladesh	-26	-52	-12	-22	-16	-26	3	4
India	96	21	37	9	1	-18	194	158
Indonesia	9	-61	-18	-41	-18	-34	381	266
Malaysia	-13	-69	-13	-33	-8	-18	858	31
Myanmar	109	75	44	31	20	14	6	4
Pakistan	99	88	41	18	16	44	18	
Philippines	61	20	21	4	-3	-11	52	33
Papua New Guinea	0	-5	-2	-5	-2	-3	66	53
Rep. of Korea	-96	-199	-44	-88	-27	-57	-37	-77
Thailand	688	478	267	188	100	70	87	58

[a] Countries for which welfare changes by more than $50 million under one of the four scenarios.

[b] Welfare calculations were not made for the policy countries under the scenario of a 10 per cent increase in imports, since this cannot be done without specifying how the increase in imports is to be brought about.

export interest to them. For many such countries, exports are concentrated notably on tropical products, sugar and certain natural resource-based products. For these products, with the exception of sugar, econometric studies do not indicate that trade liberalization would result in significantly higher world prices. Moreover, given the low elasticity of demand for these products, liberalization is not likely to lead to a substantial increase in world consumption. This suggests that for those countries whose exports consist predominantly of tropical products, gains from trade liberalization, at least in the short-to-medium term, could be much smaller than the losses incurred through higher expenditure on imports of other agricultural products. The finding of this study that many developing countries are likely to suffer net foreign exchange and welfare losses on account of higher world prices for basic foodstuffs as a result of agricultural reform is therefore a cause for concern. This suggests the need for accompanying measures, including trade and other measures, to "compensate" such countries and thus provide for them a balanced outcome of the Uruguay Round, supportive of their economic and social development.

Notes

2. For a review of proposals on agriculture under consideration in the Uruguay Round see, for example: Harmon Thomas, "Agriculture in the Uruguay Round: Interests and Issues", in UNCTAD, *Uruguay Round — Papers on Selected Issues* (UNCTAD/ITP/10), United Nations, New York, 1989.

3. The *producer subsidy equivalent* (PSE) for a product is a measure of the value of assistance in a given period (i.e. the value of transfers from domestic consumers and taxpayers) to producers resulting from a given set of agricultural policies; similarly, the *consumer subsidy equivalent* (CSE) is a measurement of the value of transfer from domestic consumers to producers.

4. The elimination of export subsidies scenario does not apply to tropical products, so that in this case there would be no significant effect on world prices.

5. The net foreign exchange impact refers to the change in net export earnings (positive) or in the net import bill (negative), as the case may be. The welfare impact is the sum of the *consumer surplus*, the *producer surplus* and the change in government tariff and tax revenue for each product. The *consumer surplus* is the change that would return the consumer to his initial standard of living following a given price change — estimated as the area under the (Marshallian) demand curve between the initial price and the new price. The *producer surplus* is the change in profits of the producer estimated by the area above the supply curve between the initial price and the new price.

6. See chapter III for further details on the losses of preferential sugar exports under alternative liberalization scenarios.

22. Aid: Concepts and State of the Discussion

Teresa Hayter

'AID' has never been an unconditional transfer of financial resources. Usually the conditions attached to aid[1] are clearly and directly intended to serve the interests of the governments providing it. For example aid must generally be used to buy goods and services from its provider. Aid from the United States must be carried in United States ships. Aid from the United States is not, under the Hickenlooper Amendment, available to countries which nationalize US-owned assets and fail to 'take appropriate steps' to rectify the situation within six months.[2] Aid from the World Bank is not, under an internal Policy Memorandum which has not been published, available to countries which nationalize foreign-owned assets without compensation, which fail to repay their debts or in which there are claims on behalf of foreign investors which the Bank considers should be settled. Aid is, in general, available to countries whose internal political arrangements, foreign policy alignments, treatment of foreign private investment, debt-servicing record, export policies, and so on, are considered desirable, potentially desirable, or at least acceptable, by the countries or institutions providing aid, and which do not appear to threaten their interests.

Some of the conditions attached to aid have also been justified in terms of the need to promote economic development in underdeveloped countries. Supporters of aid argue that promoting economic development in poor countries is in the long-term interests of the developed countries. Therefore they should try to ensure that development occurs.[3] The objective of development itself can be interpreted in different ways; some kinds of development in poorer countries are likely to benefit richer countries, or at least to be compatible with their interests; others are not, or so it is officially assumed. The subject of aid has been, and presumably will continue to be, peculiarly obfuscated by confusion about objectives. But even supposing an improvement in general standards of living were the only concern of the providers of aid, it could possibly still be argued that some effort should be made by developed countries to ensure that the resources they transferred did actually contribute to welfare in developing countries, and were not, for example, merely transferred to Swiss bank accounts, especially as aid competes with other claims on resources within industrialized countries.

This principle has sometimes been oddly applied. For example it has on occasion been used to justify the provision of aid in the form of loans rather than grants, on the grounds of the need to encourage financial discipline in developing countries.[4] Similarly with the practice of providing aid only for the direct foreign exchange costs of projects.[5] More credibly, the practice of tying aid to specific projects, whose choice and design must be negotiated and approved, has generally been regarded in developed countries as a means of ensuring a satisfactory use of resources, although it also, in the case of bilateral donors, provides a means of ensuring that aid promotes additional exports from

Teresa Hayter: 'Concepts and State of the Discussion' from *AID AS IMPERIALISM* (Penguin Books, 1971), pp. 15-24. Reproduced by permission of the author.

themselves, and enables them to choose visible projects, on which their label can be displayed.

More recently, increasing importance has been attached to the idea that developed countries, or international institutions, should use their power to withhold or increase aid as a means of influencing the *general* economic policies of developing countries in specific directions. It is with this idea, and its application, that this study is concerned.

The argument is that to regard aid merely as a transfer of resources not only does not ensure that it is not wasted, but fails to make full use of the opportunities of promoting 'satisfactory' economic policies that aid provides. Even insistence on choosing and financing particular projects, and perhaps on the adoption of other measures connected with the projects, will not adequately determine the use of the country's own resources. It will not prevent governments from financing other projects of which the donor may disapprove and in fact may enable them to do so, except in a few small countries with very low levels of savings; aid may thus, in practice, finance the marginal project.[6] Above all, the government's general economic policies probably have a much more significant effect than its choice of projects. Therefore aid, if used to influence these policies, can in theory act as a 'major catalyst' promoting development, or policies considered conducive to development or in other ways important. It is argued that donors, by attaching conditions to aid, should try to ensure that it does act in this way.

In so far as an attempt is made to use aid in this way, there are, broadly speaking, three possible alternatives. The agency administering aid can fail to agree with a government and decide that its policies are so unsatisfactory that it provides no aid, or stops or reduces existing aid.[7] It can agree with the government and merely provide aid to enable this government to carry out its policies, possibly suggesting modifications and improvements.[8] Or it can attempt to change the policies, usually in countries where it is considered that there are enough satisfactory elements for it to be worth supporting some policies against others and trying to 'improve' the government's total programme.[9] In the first two cases the decisions involved are mainly connected with the allocation of aid. In the last case, the aid agency or agencies attempt to work out their own solutions and policies for the country and to induce its government to adopt them. Of course the situations overlap. An important feature of the decisions on aid allocation is the effect they are expected to have on the policies adopted by other governments hoping to receive aid; in fact it is, for the moment, as will be seen, reasonably clear which kind of economic policies are likely to be approved, political and other things being equal, and which are not. But increasing importance is attached to the more positive action involved in the third case, in actually changing a government's policies.

Those who support policies of this variety usually claim that the choice of economic policies is a reasonably technical matter, on which sensible men can agree. They argue that it is possible for aid agencies, especially international agencies, to make objective decisions, free from political *arrière pensées;*[10] and that it is frequently easier for them to make such decisions and to press for them, than it is for national governments, which are distracted by internal political considerations. Their function is, according to this view, to provide the economic realism which otherwise might be lacking and to reinforce the position of those within the country who share this attribute.

It is sometimes also maintained that the promotion of 'better' economic policies can be achieved through discussion and 'dialogue' between governments and aid agencies, and through the close involvement of 'donors' in the choice of policies in the 'recipient' countries, but that the provision of aid should not be made conditional on the former agreeing with the latter.[11] But the idea of conditionality, or 'leverage' as it is called, is essential, and perhaps inherent, in the policies of the major financial agencies currently concerned with the general economic policies of developing countries. These are the World Bank, the International Monetary Fund (IMF), and the United States Agency for International Development (AID).[12]

These three institutions (which will be referred to as the 'international agencies') are now deeply involved in the business of setting 'general performance' conditions on the use of their resources. They are widely respected in developed countries on the basis of very little knowledge of, and even less published material on, the agencies' views on development and their methods of inducing developing countries to adopt them. There is, in Latin America in particular, considerable public debate on the policies of the IMF, and the debate has made some impact on the Fund. But much less is known of the opinions and activities of the World Bank. In particular there is little awareness of the fact that both the World Bank and the AID are promoting policies in Latin America similar to those of the IMF. Moreover little has been published on the actual operations of the three institutions in this field.[13] The negotiations for the adoption of their policies are conducted in much secrecy, and the subject is a sensitive one.

Similarly, although there are possibly more inhibitions outside these agencies, it is nevertheless quite widely assumed in developed countries that 'leverage', or the use of aid to influence the policies of developing countries in one way or another, is necessary and desirable; and in developing countries that it is inevitable. The idea of leverage, as such, has not been much discussed.[14] But there has been much discussion of the desirability of particular development polices and numerous changes of view and fashion. In addition, the relevance of economic theories evolved in industrialized countries to the current problems of developing countries and the ability of Western-trained economists to solve them have been questioned.[15]

This study was based on the view that, if the idea of leverage was to be generally accepted by the supporters of aid, it should be more carefully examined. As a contribution to the discussion, the study attempts to describe the activities of the World Bank, the IMF and the AID in Latin America.[16] Latin America is an area in which the issues emerge with particular force, for three main reasons: the relative complexity of the economies of Latin-American countries, the immediacy of their economic and financial problems and the particularly clear importance of political and social issues. The study is concerned solely with efforts to influence general economic policies and not, for example, with the World Bank's and the AID's project financing. From this, some conclusions emerged on the subject of leverage in general which differ considerably from, among other things, my own previous assumptions. These conclusions are set out in chapter 4. Chapter 2 describes the methods used by the IMF, the World Bank and the AID in influencing general economic policies in developing countries and the rationale for their involvement, and gives some indication of the policies they favour: it also describes briefly the role of the Inter-American Development Bank and the Inter-American Committee of the Alliance for Progress (CIAP), which are sometimes discussed in this connection, but whose influence is probably not as significant, and is certainly not as clearly perceived in Latin America, as that of the other three institutions. Chapter 3 describes the activities of the three major agencies, and their attitude towards policies, in the four countries I went to in the spring of 1967: Brazil, Chile, Colombia and Peru.

Because of the dearth of published material,[17] the study has had to rely mainly on unpublished, and unquotable, written material, and above all on a large number of interviews with officials of the World Bank, the AID, the IMF, the Inter-American Development Bank (IADB, or BID), the United Nations Economic Commission for Latin America (CEPAL, or ECLA), the Inter-American Committee of the Alliance for Progress (CIAP) and Latin-American governments, and with politicians, academics, journalists, businessmen and so on, mainly in Brazil, Chile, Colombia, Peru and Washington, but also in Britain and, recently, in Cuba. Where quotation marks are used in the text, this usually means that a comment or statement made in one of these interviews is being repeated verbatim; attribution is naturally impossible, but it can be taken that the sources quoted are official and/or reliable and/or representative.

Notes

1. The term 'aid' is currently used to describe transfers of resources from governments or official institutions to developing countries. It is used here, without inverted commas, because it is short, and in spite of its connotations.

2. 'Appropriate steps' can include 'speedy compensation' and 'arbitration'. See, for example, *Legislation on Foreign Relations, with Explanatory Notes*, printed for the use of the Committees on Foreign Relations and Foreign Affairs of the Senate and the House of Representatives, US Government Printing Office, Washington, 1965, p. 44.

3. For example the *Program Guidance Manual* of the United States Agency for International Development (AID) states: 'Aid as an instrument of foreign policy is best adapted to promoting economic development. Development is not an end in itself, but it is a critical element in US policy, for in most countries some progress in economic welfare is essential to the maintenance and the growth of free, non-communist, societies.' See also the UK White Paper, *Overseas Development: The Work of the New Ministry,* HMSO, August 1965, in which it is stated: 'But we must be clear about the political objectives which our aid programme can and cannot be expected to achieve. Aid is a means of promoting long-term economic development... Aid is not a means of winning the friendship of individual countries, though we are glad to offer aid to our friends. . . Nevertheless, we must recognize that poverty in a world of growing wealth causes discontent and unrest to which economic and social development is the only possible answer. We must therefore be ready to share our wealth and knowledge so as to help promote the progress and strengthen the stability of the developing countries by increasing the material well-being of their peoples .'

4. The effectiveness of this discipline depends on the continued acknowledgement by developing countries of their obligation to repay their debts. On the debt burden in developing countries, see p. 173.

5. This practice tends to result in the choice of excessively import-intensive projects. See Juliet Clifford, 'The Tying of Aid and the Problem of "Local Costs"'. *Journal of Development Studies*, January 1966.

6. Tying aid to projects, especially when only the direct foreign exchange cost of the project is financed, has other disadvantages, notably the possibility of making projects more capital-and import-intensive than they might otherwise be, and of distorting the pattern of imports so that existing capacity is not fully used.

7. The World Bank, the IMF and the US AID have, for example, reacted in this way in Cuba, in Brazil under Goulart, in Argentina under Illia, and in Haiti.

8. This was the case, for the World Bank, IMF and AID, in Brazil under President Castelo Branco and Dr Campos.

9. This was, broadly, the case in Chile in the first years of the Frei government, and has been so in many other countries.

10. See Irving S. Friedman, in his introductory speech at a seminar held by four World Bank officials for Brazilian economists and reproduced in a World Bank publication, *Some Aspects of the Economic Philosophy of the World Bank*, September 1968: 'First, what strikes me as very important is that both institutions (the World Bank and the IMF) are set up with specific purposes and defined objectives, which make clear that if the institutions are to operate properly they must make economic judgements in specific fields of international responsibility and that these economic judgements are to be based on objective economic analysis. It is clear from the origins of both these institutions, as well as the words of their Articles of Agreement, that they were not set up as political institutions. They were set up as technical institutions; and from the very first, great emphasis was given to the need for scientific, economic work as a basis for decision-making.' See also quotation p. 54.

11. See for example John White, *Pledged to Development*, ODI, 1967, especially pp. 180-86, in which it is suggested that the function of the providers of aid might be one of 'loyal opposition, whereby the donor 'does not seek to lay down the law' but to point out new issues and new choices. Also Andrzej Krassowski, *The Aid Relationship*, ODI, 1968, especially chapter 1, in which these themes are discussed and expanded, and the current practices of the United States AID are criticized on the grounds that they involve too great an attempt to 'control' recipients' policies.

12. The IMF is not usually regarded as an aid institution, and the rationale for its activities is rather different from those of the AID and the World Bank. But the activities themselves, in this field, are similar.

13. But see, for example, *Effective Aid*, ODI, 1966, *passim*; Andrzej Krassowski, op. cit., chapters 3-6; John White, op. cit., *passim*; *United States Foreign Aid in Action: A Case Study*, submitted by senator Ernest Gruening to the Subcommittee on Foreign Aid Expenditures of the Committee on Government Operations, United States Senate, Washington, 1966, especially pp. 102-14; various AID publications (see chapter 2, section on the AID); M. Hoffman, 'The Scaffolding of Aid', *Asian Review*, April 1968; David Gordon, 'The World Bank's Mission in Eastern Africa, *Finance and Development* (the Fund and Bank Review), No. 1, 1968; Richard Newton Gardner, *Sterling-Dollar Diplomacy*, Oxford, Clarendon Press, 1956; Raymond F. Mikesell, *Public International Lending for Development*, Random House, N.Y., 1966; Richard L. Maullin, 'The Colombia-IMF disagreement of November-December 1966: an interpretation of its place in Colombian politics', Memorandum RM-5314-RC, Rand Corporation, 1967; Marta Luisa Benavente, 'El Fondo Monetario Interanacional, mecanismo

de sus operaciones y posición de la República Argentina, *Revista Trimestral*, Banco Central de la República Argentina, July-September 1966; Neil H. Jacoby, *US Aid to Taiwan*, Praeger Series on International Economics and Development, 1966; Harry Magdoff, *The Age of Imperialism: The Economics of US Foreign Policy*, Monthly Review Press, 1969, chapter 4 on Aid and Trade; Edward S, Mason, *Foreign Aid and Foreign Policy,* New York, 1964, especially pp. 47-8; and forthcoming ODI study by Philip O'Brien, on the operations of US AID in Chile.

14. But see ODI publications cited in note 11. See also Manchester Conference on Teaching Economic Development, 1964, *The Teaching of Development Economics: Its Position in the Present State of Knowledge,* the proceedings, edited by Kurt Martin and John Knapp, Cass, 1967, especially paper by Dudley Seers, 'The Limitations of the Special Case'; *Towards a Strategy for Development Cooperation*, proceedings of a Conference on Asian Development, held by the Netherlands Economic Institute, Rotterdam University Press, 1967, *passim*; *Foreign Aid — A Critique and a Proposal*, Albert O. Hirschman and M. Bird, Essays in International Finance, No. 69, July 1968, Princeton University; and AID publications quoted in chapter 2 section on the AID, below.

15. See, for example, Manchester Conference on Teaching Economic Development, op. cit.: Gunnar Myrdal, *Asian Drama: An Inquiry into the Poverty of Nations*, 3 vols., Allen Lane The Penguin Press, 1968.

16. For the reasons for concentrating on these three institutions and somewhat neglecting the other institutions of the Inter-American system, see chapter 2.

17. cf. also the Gruening Report, cited in this chapter, note 13, which says on p. vii of its Preface: 'Publications by international organizations also were virtually useless. Filled with euphemisms in order not to offend anyone, they became so bland and obfuscated as to be virtually meaningless. Congressional hearings provided only a few tantalizing clues... Thus, the bits and pieces from published sources furnished only fragmentary insights.'

23.   Development Finance: Unmet Needs
The Brandt Commission

The developing countries obtain finance from a number of sources: government-to-government aid programmes and export credit agencies; international financial institutions, including the World Bank Group and Regional Development Banks, the IMF, the UN agencies and other multilateral funds; private investment, much of it by multinational corporations; and commercial banks. The creation and expansion of the system of financing development in recent decades amounts to a major change in international economic cooperation.

The Third World will have enormous financial requirements in the next few decades. We have surveyed the large unmet needs, particularly in the poorer countries, in food production, industrialization, development of energy and minerals, transport and communications, education and health. The developing countries' economic growth has slowed down from 6 per cent a year during 1967-72 to 5 per cent in the mid-1970s, and probably below that in the last three years. However great their own efforts, huge sums will be needed to enable the countries of the South to regain their momentum, to provide the jobs and incomes to overcome poverty, and to enable them to become more self-sufficient and to take a fuller part in the world's trading system.

The channels for aid

For the transfer of official funds there are two main channels: one flows directly between the countries concerned, and the other goes through the multilateral institutions. UN agencies receive their funds from donor governments. The World Bank gets some of its funds directly from governments, particularly those for its soft loans through the International Development Association (IDA) window; the rest of its money is borrowed on the world's capital markets, under guarantees provided by the subscriptions of the member governments. The Regional Development Banks have a similar structure.

A very big change has occurred in the composition of the total flows to the developing countries. In 1960, 60 per cent came from concessional aid or Official Development Assistance (ODA). By 1977, more than two-thirds was commercial, mainly from private bank loans, direct investment and export credits. The debt burdens of a number of countries have become extremely heavy. Both the amounts and types of available finance are now clearly inadequate. And the uncertainty of future flows threatens progress in development.

Most official assistance, whether bilateral or multilateral, covers the foreign exchange cost of specific investment projects: dams, power stations, railway and road systems, industrial projects, rural development schemes. Little is made available for 'programme lending', for national development programmes as a whole, which can support the entire

The Brandt Commission: 'Development Finance: Unmet Needs' from *NORTH-SOUTH: A PROGRAMME FOR SURVIVAL* (Pan Books, 1980), pp. 221-236. © The Independent Commission on International Development Issues.

set of projects and activities of a country in the face of low savings and fluctuating fiscal revenue and foreign exchange. The developing countries as well as many experts — including the Pearson Commission — have laid great stress on the need for this type of finance, which gives more flexibility and certainty to overall economic management. Similarly lacking is support for financing exports, particularly capital goods; and for economic integration between developing countries, through financing of payments arrangements. The issue of adequate finance for commodity price stabilization is still not fully settled; the refinancing of debts is handled in an *ad hoc* manner.

Growing debts

The better-off developing countries have been able to overcome a number of these problems with funds from commercial sources, mainly loans from banks and export credits. One of the most dramatic changes in recent years has been the increase in the loans of the international private market, which now account for nearly 40 per cent of the outstanding debt of developing countries, compared to only 17 per cent in 1970. Most of the private loans have gone to a few middle-income countries, helping them increase rapidly their investment, output and exports, giving these countries the freely usable foreign exchange which they need — not tied to individual projects, to orders from particular countries, or to any specific economic policy. But there are also drawbacks to these private loans as a method of financing. Their terms (though they improved in 1977 and 1978) have meant that the countries have to meet heavy debt-servicing burdens. In the three-year period 1979-81 the aggregate payments for servicing the debts of all developing countries excluding OPEC are estimated at $120 billion — on top of the sharply rising trade deficits. As we show below, the borrowing needs of these countries are likely to rise considerably further in the 1980s. As the loans fall due, they need to borrow more in order to repay and service them. The debtor economies and the entire international credit structure are now very vulnerable to any disruptions in the flows of capital, which can be caused by a greater demand for credit in the North, by a borrowing country being regarded as less creditworthy, by insufficient bank capital, or by the actions of regulatory authorities.

The heart of the debt problem is that a very large proportion of funds are lent on terms which are onerous for borrowers from the point of view of both the repayment capacity of the projects they finance and the time debtor countries need to correct structural imbalances in their external accounts. The debt servicing record of developing countries has been excellent on the whole and payments crises have been rare. But there are likely to be more difficulties with payments in the future. Already between 1974 and 1978 many more countries were in arrears on their current payments, or were renegotiating — or trying to renegotiate — their debts with private banks. These banks may be able to expand their credit still further; but the risks and constraints of the present unbalanced structure of debts will mean that developing countries must look for new sources of long-term finance. As we discuss in the next chapter, with trade deficits rising sharply and with the leading banks already highly exposed, there is great concern that the international banking system, which has played a crucial role in channelling OPEC and other surpluses to the deficit countries in the last five years, should be able to perform the same role in the future.

Relationships

It is not only the volume and kinds of finance which are inadequate: it is also the relationships between borrowers and lenders. The developing countries do not have an adequate share of responsibility for decision-making, control and management of the existing international financial and monetary institutions. The latter have made significant contributions to development through their lending and technical assistance. At the same time, they have been hesitant to engage in some of the activities of critical importance to developing countries, as we shall describe. Many countries also have misgivings about the involvement of some of these institutions in the determination of their domestic policies and priorities, which has in some cases gone beyond what could be justified by the need to protect current loans and guarantee their responsible use. Further, the major international financial institutions have not been able to secure universal membership. The USSR and most of the countries of Eastern Europe are not members, and the People's Republic of China has so far not taken its place in these institutions. The lack of universality, in addition to its political cost, deprives countries of the benefits of learning from each other's development experience and curtails the scope of international assistance.

Official aid: a disappointing record

The poorer and weaker countries have not been able to raise much money on commercial terms. For them, Official Development Assistance or aid is the principal source of funds. While the needs for concessional finance have been growing, the actual flows have faltered. It was a decade ago that the United Nations resolved on the objective of one per cent of the gross national product of developed countries for the net transfer of resources to developing countries, including private flows, and within it 0.7 per cent as a target for official development assistance. The ratio between these two figures reflected the relative flows at the time and the ODA target was largely a political goal. At the time this target was discussed, most of the industrialized countries accepted it, some with a time frame (e.g. Belgium, the Netherlands, Sweden) and others in principle (e.g. Federal Republic of Germany). But some others, most notably the United States, did not commit themselves to the target.

While the one-per-cent norm for overall net flows (including private investment and commercial lending) has been reached, the hopes aroused for the ODA target have been dashed. The average performance in this respect of the industrialized countries in the OECD was only 0.35 per cent of GNP in 1978. This is a deeply disappointing record. At the same time, we must point out that a number of individual countries, such as the Scandinavian countries and the Netherlands, have exceeded the target. It is very encouraging that the OPEC countries have, with their increased oil revenues in recent years, contributed nearly 3 per cent of their GNP. There effort is specially noteworthy because, in their case, aid does not result in export orders to the donors. On the other hand the United States contribution has fallen from 0.5 per cent in 1960 to 0.27 per cent. Japan at 0.23 per cent and the Federal Republic of Germany at 0.38 per cent also remain at low levels, although they had accepted the target in principle. Also disappointing is that the average performance of the Soviet Union and other CMEA countries, according to OECD estimates, has been only of the order of 0.04 per cent of their GNP.

Relative performance between different countries in meeting this target is a matter on which hard and fast comparisons may not be in order. Some donors have argued that while their aid performance has been low, their trade policies are liberal; some who have shown better performance also include expenditures on overseas commitments which in a proper reckoning should not qualify as aid; some donors allocate their aid as far as possible on need-based criteria; others concentrate theirs on countries with whom they have special historical, commercial or other ties. Assistance from the eastern countries has been available for public sector, industrial and resource sectors for which aid from other sources has been unavailable and they take goods in repayment of debt. These clarifications are important but they do not contradict the position that the industrialized countries as a whole, and the major ones among them, have failed to fulfil expectations and commitments.

This failure points to a marked lack of political will. We must face this issue squarely. In the annual aid reviews in the Development Assistance Committee (DAC), governments with poor aid performance often plead budgetary constraints and balance of payments difficulties, but it is clear that these are not insuperable obstacles. When GNP in industrial countries increases by 3 to 4 per cent a year, the allocation of one-fortieth to one thirtieth of the annual *increase* in GNP to foreign aid would close the gap between 0.3 and 0.7 per cent in only five years. The pressure on public funds is always intense, as our experience makes us well aware, but what the neglect of foreign aid expresses is ultimately the lack of political priority attached to it.

Why more aid is essential

We have been informed that in many countries the political climate is at present unfavourable to an increase in aid, with a range of serious domestic problems looming large. But this climate must be changed. Citizens of rich countries must be brought to understand that the problems of the world must be tackled too, and that a vigorous aid policy would in the end not be a burden but an investment in a healthier world economy as well as in a safer world community. International development issues must be given the attention at a high political level that their urgency entitles them to.

Public opinion in industrial countries has often been critical of aid. Some developing countries are highly inegalitarian, and there have been doubts whether aid was getting through to the poor. The mass media have given much publicity to cases of waste, corruption, and extravagance, and the resulting scepticism creates resistance to the aid-giving intentions of governments. There is no doubt that the use of aid can and should be made more effective. At the same time it would be wrong not to recognize that the overwhelming proportion of aid money is usefully spent on the purposes for which it is intended, and aid has already done much to diminish hardships in low-income countries and to help them provide a basis for progress in rural development, health and education. For the poorest countries, aid is essential to survival.

Fortunately there have recently been signs of a more favourable attitude to aid in some major countries as the importance of the Third World is slowly beginning to be more clearly perceived. Japan not long ago announced a doubling of its aid programme. The Federal Republic of Germany is increasing its aid. The French government is raising some parts of its multilateral assistance. A new and important source of aid in the 1970s has been the OPEC members which supplied about 20 per cent of all Official Development Assistance in 1978. This represents an average of 1.59 per cent of their GNP; but individual countries such as Saudi Arabia, Kuwait, the United Arab Emirates and Qatar have provided between 6 to 15 per cent of their GNP in past years, and between 4 and 5 per cent in 1978. Besides OPEC a number of other developing countries have in recent years provided assistance. So far most of this has taken the form of scholarships and the provision of technical assistance experts, but India, Yugoslavia and some Latin American countries are also extending financial assistance. The People's Republic of China although itself a developing country has also given significant aid to several other developing countries.

We argue below that an increase in total aid must remain a high priority for alleviating the worst deprivation in the developing world. The spreading practice of development aid makes us think the time has come to consider a universal system of contributions, based on present targets for the richest countries but also providing for contributions from all other countries, except the poorest, on a sliding scale related to income. This would be an expression of shared responsibility for international development. We return to this proposal later.

Gaps in financing development

As we have suggested, there are a variety of shortcomings in the network of development finance which taken together show the need for a number of fundamental changes. The overall flow of finance must increase, in the interests both of the Third World and the world economy. The poorest countries urgently need more concessional aid; the middle-income countries need loans on longer maturities. Types of finance which are currently difficult or impossible to obtain must become available in significant volumes. Loans for development need to be in more flexible forms and on a longer-term basis. Developing countries need better access, if necessary through intermediaries, to capital markets. And relations between borrowers and lenders must be improved. Multilateral institutions need to be restructured to enable the Third World to participate effectively in their management and control.

It is also urgent to fill the serious gaps in the existing financial flows to the developing world. We analyse these gaps from three perspectives: the needs of different groups of countries; sectors of activity; types of lending. The Commission has taken into account reliable estimates that have been made by international institutions. These requirements do not all add up to a total. There is a considerable area of overlap between needs related to country-groups and those identified in sectoral terms. Types of lending are a separate dimension. Our main purpose in this review of gaps is essentially to illustrate the nature, magnitude and high priority of unmet needs and to argue that a massive global effort is necessary to meet them. In the light of this analysis we go on to discuss, in the following chapter, which institutions and measures are most appropriate to meet the needs and fill the gaps.

Country needs

Least developed, low-income and lower middle-income countries

The low-income countries, which contain most of the world's poor people, have a very limited capacity, as we have seen, to participate in the world economy. They depend on exports of primary commodities; their agriculture is frequently threatened by drought; they have a thin margin between income and consumption; and their domestic savings are necessarily low. Looking into the future, the prospects for their food supplies are alarming. They need massive investments in irrigation and agriculture to avoid dangerous food deficits towards the end of the decade; and large outlays for improving health, nutrition and literacy.

The poverty belts of Asia and Africa need long-gestation projects for such purposes as water management, hydropower, transport, mining, afforestation, the prevention of soil erosion and desertification, and the elimination of diseases. These tasks alone will require extra finance of at least $4 billion a year over at least twenty years.

Whatever criteria are used, existing assistance to the poorer countries is inadequate, in both investment and recurrent spending. If present levels of assistance are merely continued, there cannot be much progress in meeting essential needs, and an annual growth in income per head of only one per cent in low-income Africa and only 2.8 per cent in low-income Asia would be possible. This, according to the World Bank's 1979 *World Development Report*, would actually widen the gap in living standards between the poor and the rich countries (from 1:40 in 1975 to 1:47 by 1990) even if the poor countries were to increase their savings sharply — an unacceptable situation. The aggregate needs of all the least developed countries for external capital are estimated by UNCTAD at $11 billion annually during the 1980s, and $21 billion during the 1980s, and $21 billion during the 1990s, to support a 6.5 per cent rate of GDP growth (3.5 per cent *per capita*). For the poorest countries the assistance should be highly concessional.

According to a study for the Overseas Development Council in Washington, countries with an income per head of below $520 (least developed, low-income and lower middle-income) will need annual aid in the 1980s in the range of $40-54 billion (in 1980 dollars), either for achieving a 3.5 to 4 per cent growth in *per capita* income, or for obtaining resources equal to half the costs of meeting essential human needs, the other half being borne by the countries themselves. If 1980 aid were no higher in real terms than in 1977, it would fall short of adequacy for such objectives by $21-35 billion. If this shortfall could be met in the early 1980s low-income and lower middle-income developing countries could tackle the worst forms of poverty, and they could finance industrial and agricultural projects, imports of raw materials, fertilizers, equipment and spare parts. Such assistance will have to be concessional but it need not be all in the form of grants, except for the least developed countries. Depending on circumstances, the transfers can be a blend of different types of finance — soft loans like those provided by IDA, bilateral long-term low-interest development loans, interest-subsidized market loans, export credits. Food aid may also play an important part. Developing countries will need project loans, which where appropriate can finance local currency costs; and also programme loans, to complement project lending and to meet maintenance needs.

Middle-income and higher-income countries

The middle-income and higher-income developing countries need development loans on terms and in forms which suit their stage of development. Their total borrowing requirements will be affected by the growth and openness of markets for their exports. They need improvement in the maturity structure of their debts. They need longer-term programme finance. Some lower middle-income countries will also need interest subsidization.

According to World Bank projections (which assume annual inflation of 7.2 per cent), borrowing by these countries from commercial banks and other private sources will be needed at a level of $155 billion in the year 1985 (in current dollars) compared to less than $40 billion annually in 1975-7. By 1990 it will be as much as $270 billion. Even this may turn out to be an under-estimate: the projected rate of growth of exports in the 1980s (6.3 per cent) may be too high in the light of the present prospects for the world economy, and oil prices have been assumed constant at their 1975 levels in real terms, although this assumption is already out of date. In any case, much more official lending is needed to reduce the pressure on the international credit structure and the associated risks; and to reduce the difficulties of the middle-income countries in servicing their debts. Their financing problems should also be tackled through other means, including better access to the bond markets of industrialized-countries. Their debt service ratio (the proportion of their exports absorbed by servicing debts), which in 1977 averaged 9.2 per cent and already exceeded 20 per cent for a few countries, is now projected almost to double from 1975-7 to 1990. If these countries are to receive adequate funds, at the right time and on terms that they can reasonably repay, there can be no substitute for a major expansion of public lending, mostly in the form of programme loans.

Sector needs

We now turn to the financial needs of the different sectors in the developing world, giving specific estimates for the capital needs in some sectors — agriculture, industry, energy and minerals — which also form part of the aggregate needs of countries which have been discussed above.

Food and agriculture

Rural development has already received much support, but the low-income food-importing countries need urgent assistance. The International Food Policy Research Institute (IFPRI) has estimated that, without more help, the gap between the production and consumption of cereals, which amounted to 37 million tons in 1975, may reach 120-145 million tons by 1990. Such huge shortages could cause mass starvation, besides seriously adding to world inflation. It is estimated that foreign aid to support half the capital spending, and 20 per cent of the recurring costs, for increasing agricultural production in low-income countries with food deficits should amount to $12 billion (1975 dollars) annually in the 1980s, calling for additional foreign aid of $8.5

billion (or $13 billion in 1980 dollars). Of this, 70 per cent would be for producing staple foods, and the balance for other agricultural spending. Some of the finance, particularly for financing recurring costs of imports of fertilizers and pesticides, should be in the form of programme loans on concessional terms.

Industry

To reach the Lima target for industrialization in the Third World would require an annual growth rate in manufacturing value added of 10-11 per cent: UNIDO has estimated that this would need a total annual investment of $40-60 billion between 1980 and 1990, and $120-140 billion between 1990 and 2000. Approximately 60 per cent of these sums would finance the imports of capital goods, technology and engineering services, including 10 per cent to finance training and technical assistance. If foreign financing is to meet fully the foreign exchange component of the projects, industry in the Third World would need $25-35 billion from abroad annually over the next decade. At present it obtains (as estimated by UNIDO) about $10 billion annually.

A large part of these extra funds will have to be borrowed from official agencies. Only some ten to fifteen developing countries in Latin America and South East Asia have received major direct investment by multinational corporations. Most countries in the past have financed industrial investment through export credits from the industrialized countries and by borrowing from the market; but the repayment terms have been short, and credit has frequently been very expensive. The poorer countries, as noted, have had only limited access to private funds. Most official aid has gone to such purposes as agriculture and infrastructure, and industry has not received adequate support. For a long time the multilateral development banks refused to finance government-owned industry altogether; they have recently made more finance available for industry, but still not enough to cover rising needs.

Energy and minerals

The need to finance exploration and development of energy and minerals is now increasingly recognized. The World Bank and Regional Development Banks are expanding or planning to expand in these fields, but there remain large gaps. For oil and gas alone the non-OPEC developing countries need additional annual capital of roughly $14 billion in the 1980s (at 1980 prices). This investment would need official multilateral loans of at least $3.3 billion a year, to finance two-thirds of the exploration costs and 20 per cent of the production costs. For coal, annual lending of $0.4-0.6 billion might support investment in exploration and production of $2-3 billion a year. The total extra finance required from multilateral sources of oil, gas and coal would thus be at least $4 billion per year: the balance would have to come from domestic sources and from the private capital market, supported through co-financing. Further large-scale finance is required to develop renewable sources of energy, particularly hydro-electric and solar.

For non-fuel minerals there are no precise estimates of investment needs, whether present or future; but the gap in external financing may be about $9 billion to enable the balance of the funds to be raised. Thus oil, gas, coal and minerals between them will need external finance of at least \$6.5 billion per annum, plus finance for renewable sources of energy which are so far unquantifiable, but still vital for the future.

These projects will be spread between different groups of countries — least developed, other low-income and middle-income — but many would be in the poorer countries which contain both minerals and large populations, and they will thus help to alleviate poverty. Financing exploration will generally need to be concessional, perhaps with grants for unsuccessful exploration; finance for investment will have to take into account the country's capacity to repay; market loans, interest-subsidized lending and official assistance will need to be appropriately blended.

Missing types of finance

For reasons which are partly historical, partly based on the self-interest of donors and partly due to an inadequate understanding of the role of external resources in helping development, most of the official finance which developing countries get is earmarked for the purchase of capital goods from outside. In the initial stages aid was no more than an extension of credits which industrialized countries were providing to promote the export of their capital goods, taking the shape of additions to such credits and the improvement of credit terms. The popularity of monumental projects, both in donor and recipient countries, further strengthened the trend. What was overlooked was that the shortage of domestic capital which creates the need for external resources is not identical with the gap in the capacity to pay for imported capital goods. The poorer developing countries need external finance to cover their local currency expenditure if they are to avoid inflationary pressures and balance of payments difficulties.

We now turn to the types of official finance which are lacking or difficult to obtain: programme loans, which provide long-term capital not specifically linked to projects and improve the structure of debt; export credits for capital goods; support of economic integration; finance for stabilizing commodity prices. They are the means of meeting some of the needs of countries and sectors which we have discussed. We discuss each type of finance below.

Programme lending

The most serious gap is in programme lending — that is, providing flexibly usable funds which are not tied to specific investment projects. Most bilateral and multilateral financing is available only for projects, as we have said; but project loans on their own are inefficient in facilitating an adequate transfer of resources. They are disbursed very slowly. In the experience of the World Bank, there is almost a ten-year cycle on average from the first identification of a project to its completion.

An exclusive reliance on project lending also produces certain important biases: firstly, it favours large projects over small, since lending agencies have minimum threshold size of operations, to keep down their administrative costs. Secondly, it favours new fixed investment, rather than using existing capacity more efficiently, since working capital (labour and raw materials) is not normally eligible for project finance. Thirdly, the specification of projects and the tying procedures of agencies may encourage capital-intensive processes, which may not suit the developing country. Fourthly, the industrialized countries and the lending agencies from time to time change their views on development priorities; this leads to changing preferences for the type of projects they want to finance, often irrespective of the developing countries' own priorities.

Project and programme lending are in fact complementary. Programme lending corrects some of the distortions which come from relying exclusively on project lending. Firstly, programme loans are disbursed quickly, normally over two or three years. When these loans finance imports which are sold on the domestic market, they generate local currency for the government. Thus they can help to finance the local costs of projects and accelerate their execution. Secondly, programme lending, by providing more flexible funds, can encourage self-reliance. A country may have its own industrial plants which may make it unnecessary to use scarce foreign funds on importing capital goods. Or a country may have a large excess industrial capacity from previous investments, which it cannot put into full production because it lacks foreign exchange; and this need cannot be met by project lending, which aims to create new capacity. In both cases, programme loans help to provide jobs and raise incomes throughout the economy. Thirdly, developing countries also need the long-term support of programme loans for undertaking changes which cannot be achieved through project lending alone — including building up their social infrastructure, administration and management, or diversifying economies which depend too heavily on a few commodities or minerals.

Expanded programme loans would help to lighten the debt burden especially if it involves the lengthening of maturities. Developing countries need foreign exchange to adjust to balance of payments difficulties which can arise from a variety of causes outside their control. These cannot be treated as projects; but if they are not adequately met, the whole development programme will be jeopardized. The distinction between temporary support for 'adjustment', which should normally be provided by the IMF, and longer-term borrowing is often blurred. In real life, a country's needs for short-, medium- and long-term external finance do not fall into tidy compartments; the line of demarcation is a shifting one. If finance for adjustment is available too little and too late, the only solution for a developing country is a quick correction, which curtails growth, lowers wages, reduces employment and worsens income distribution. It is particularly serious for the poorer and weaker countries who cannot borrow from commercial banks, and who need long-term programme lending. What is needed essentially is a bridge between the long-term project financing available from such institutions as the World Bank and the short term adjustment finance available from the IMF. Without this kind of bridge, in the form of long-term programme lending, developing countries have often slid back on their development programmes or have depended too heavily on commercial loans, jeopardizing their future capacity to borrow.

In highlighting these aspects of programme *vis-à-vis* project lending, we are not unaware that the industrialized countries of the North and the East have preferred to lend money to identifiable projects whose successful completion can be monitored and benefits from which can be clearly discerned. They have been apprehensive that general-purpose lending for balance of payments support might enable, if not encourage, diversion of foreign exchange to arms purchases, waste or misuse. They feel that the monitoring of the use of programme loans will raise very sensitive questions in borrower-creditor relationships, questions which both parties would prefer to avoid. The receiving countries, on the other hand, see the overwhelming emphasis on project loans as a constraint on their self-reliant development, and worse, as one more instance of lack of trust. We recognize this difference in perceptions but we believe that it should be possible to avoid this conflict. It should be feasible for programme lending to supplement and complement project lending, and for it to be related to well-conceived, clearly defined development programmes, the fulfilment of which can be monitored. In many developing countries, domestic public financing institutions such as industrial and agricultural development banks could be more extensively used as channels for external support to sectors and programmes. Later, we also deal with changes in international institutional structures that are necessary to build greater trust and confidence between borrowers and lenders.

Export finance

The developing countries need support for providing export credits, particularly for capital goods. The market for capital goods is highly competitive: not only in the price, quality, aftersale service and speed of delivery of the goods, but also in the availability and cost of export credit finance. A number of developing countries are now exporting capital goods and others are developing the potential to do so. To sell them, the exporters have to extend medium-term credit for which, being deficit countries, they need refinancing. Some developing countries in recent years have provided export credit finance, but further rapid growth of their capital goods exports would strain their institutions.

There have been many initiatives for refinancing schemes, but they have not been followed up. Only the Inter-American Development Bank can refinance export credits for capital goods, mainly within Latin America; and a new Latin American Export Credit Bank, with a modest equity participation of the International Finance Corporation, plans to refinance short-and-medium-term credit for non-traditional goods. One effect of giving broad support to export credit finance should be to stimulate trade among developing countries and their economic cooperation.

Economic integration

Developing countries need financial support to increase trade among themselves. Economic integration has long been a principal objective, intended to ensure closer cooperation and expansion of trade. But many integration schemes have achieved only slow progress, or have retrogressed. This has sometimes been due to political causes, but is also partly due to the balance of payments difficulties of the participants. Liberalizing trade under such schemes often creates payments deficits for one or more members *vis-à-vis* other partners. The difficulty can be overcome by expanding mutual credit through payments arrangements, but external assistance is needed when the partners, despite intra-group surpluses, have difficulty with overall payments and have individually little access to external finance. More generally, there is need for the periodic settlement of balances from intra-trade, and such payments will require outside finance. This can be provided by programme lending if it is on an adequate scale.

Commodity stabilization

In the chapter on commodities we have argued the case for more commodity agreements and for financing national stocks. Finance is urgently needed to stabilize the prices of primary products of developing countries, and to assure a price floor. Without this they cannot improve their external economic situation, and stable commodity export prices for the poor countries would also help to sustain their demand for manufactured goods and promote assured supplies of raw materials. This need has been recognized for a long time but no decisive action has been taken and unstable prices and earnings still dislocate the world economy. The weak economies which are heavily dependent on a few primary exports are especially vulnerable. This will entail larger capital support to the Common Fund in the course of time, or increased programme lending.

Relationships and institutions

We are not the first to have drawn attention to the missing elements in the structure of financing. Their common feature is that they involve difficult and sensitive policy issues in the economic and political relationships between North and South. Whether it is programme lending, or commodity stabilization, or promotion of developing countries exports, or finance to enable them to cooperate with each other more effectively — all of these, in their several ways, singly and together, are forms of finance which would enable the poor countries to become more self-reliant and independent participants in a more equitable exchange with the rich countries. Thus they all call for a new approach to decision-making.

These gaps have persisted, partly because the governments of the North have been reluctant to change their practices adequately; partly because the developing countries have not been able to influence critical decisions in international institutions. The quality of the relations between borrowers and creditors is vitally important to the character of financial institutions, and their ability to provide for the needs of their clients; the inequality between borrowers and lenders has made it harder to reach joint agreement and to generate mutual trust. Greater equality and participation by the developing countries can help to overcome these difficulties; it is with these ends in view that we make our proposals for reform.

24. What Do We Know About Aid's Macroeconomic Impact? An Overview of the Aid Effectiveness Debate

Howard White

Abstract: This paper reviews the academic literature on the macroeconomic impact of development aid, with a special emphasis on the question as to whether, as claimed by much of the empirical literature, aid does not increase growth. The inadequate theoretical foundation of models of aid's impact on savings, in particular their failure to consider economy-wide effects, make them a poor basis for conclusions about aid's impact. The combination of weak theory with poor econometric methodology makes it difficult to conclude anything about the relationship between aid and savings. The literature on the relationship between aid and growth suffers from similar problems. Country-level studies of aid's impact on a range of macroeconomic variables are required which may build on the relatively small existing literature in this area.

1. Introduction

We know surprisingly little about aid's macroeconomic impact. Though donors have become increasingly interested in the macroeconomic environment in which their aid is being used they appraise and evaluate their aid only at the *micro*economic level. They do not ask how the aid will directly affect the recipient macroeconomy. Academic work on aid might be expected to fill the gap, and this paper addresses the issue of what donor and recipient governments can learn from such work. A major empirical finding of the aid effectiveness literature is the absence of a relationship between aid and growth. This fairly well established result ought to be a great concern to aid practitioners, since their public pronouncements make it clear they believe aid *will* increase growth. The major issue in the analysis of aid's macroeconomic impact must be whether the assertion that aid does not improve growth performance is correct and, if so, what can be done about it.

This paper looks at these questions through a critical appraisal of the academic literature on the macroeconomic impact of development aid. It is argued in Section 2 that much of the theoretical literature provides only a very shaky foundation upon which to build empirical analysis. The critique of the two largest empirical literatures (on the relationships between aid and savings and aid and growth) in Section 3 indeed shows that they tell us very little about aid effectiveness. However, there is a more recent body of work, discussed in Section 4, that applies macroeconomic models to the analysis of aid impact and this offers promising avenues for further research. Section 5 concludes with a summary and proposed research agenda.

Howard White: 'What Do We Know About Aid's Macroeconomic Impact? An Overview of the Aid Effectiveness Debate', *JOURNAL OF INTERNATIONAL DEVELOPMENT* (1992), Vol. 4., No. 2, pp. 121-137.
© Howard White 1992. Reproduced by permission of John Wiley and Sons Ltd.

2. Theoretical models of aid's macroeconomic impact[1]

The Harrod-Domar equation and the dual gap model

Much theoretical and empirical analysis of aid remains wedded to the earliest model used to analyse aid impact: the Harrod-Domar model. This model embodies a 'bottleneck' approach in which capital shortage is the only constraint on growth, giving aid a central role in relieving that constraint. Aid may fill either the 'savings gap' (the difference between domestic savings and the level of investment needed to achieve the desired growth rate) or the trade gap (the excess value of import requirements over export earnings). *Ex post* the savings and trade gaps must be identical but this need not be so *ex ante*: foreign capital inflows must be sufficient to fill whichever is the larger if the target growth rate is to be achieved.

As shown by Chenery and Strout (1966), in the best-known exposition of this model, the impact of aid on income depends on the regime faced by the recipient economy. 'The marginal productivity of aid' is higher under a binding trade gap, since this creates redundant domestic resources which remain unused so long as the required imported complementary inputs are unavailable. Relaxation of the trade gap both contributes imported inputs *and* brings domestic resources into production, giving the larger impact. The actual value of the marginal productivity of aid in any country will depend on a range of economic parameters. One is the incremental output-capital ratio, but they also include the marginal propensities to save and import and the target growth rate.

The dual gap model provides a straightforward mechanism through which more aid automatically leads to higher growth. Many authors, including Chenery and Stout, have used the model to predict the levels of aid required to achieve target growth rates. Actual aid flows have now greatly exceeded those thought to be required to achieve self-sustaining growth (i.e. growth financed out of domestic savings and private foreign capital inflows). Yet the growth record of many recipients has fallen far short of the targets, few are self-sustaining and some have even experienced negative growth in the face of growing aid inflows. The dual gap model cannot explain these phenomena. We turn now to critiques of the model which seek to explain this failure.

The savings debate

The radical position in the savings debate, that aid displaces domestic savings, is most closely associated with Keith Griffin (1970) and Griffin and Enos (1970), who illustrated the argument with an inter-temporal budget constraint, reproduced as Figure 1. The without-aid budget constraint is CM and current consumption (C_t) out of total income (OC) is OQ. Savings are QC, which yield OE (equal to $(1 + r)$ QC, where r is the rate of return on investment) of future consumption (C_{t+1}). An aid inflow of CD shifts the budget constraint out to DP. The two gap model assumed that the new equilibrium would be at L, so that current consumption remains unchanged and future consumption increases to ON. However, if the marginal propensity to consume is between 0 and 1, the new equilibrium will lie between L and H at a point such as K. In this case current consumption has increased by QB and future consumption by EI (equal to $(1+r)$ GH). Therefore, total savings (domestic plus foreign) have increased (from QC to DB), but by less than the value of the aid inflow. Foreign savings (the aid inflow) have displaced domestic savings. These are now only BC, having fallen by QB; this is the extent to which the inflow is used to finance current consumption.

Several criticisms may be made of this argument which have unfortunately been overlooked in the subsequent rush to test the model. One is that it rests on a Harrod-Domar view of growth, so that consumption expenditures that improve nutrition, health and education make no contribution to increasing future income (Stewart, 1971). Furthermore, Griffin's argument ultimately rests on an accounting identity with little analysis of the economic mechanisms through which aid may displace savings. Exploring such mechanisms shows that there may be feedback effects that offset the direct impact of aid on savings. This argument may be considered either in growth models or a static macroeconomic framework.

The feedback from higher income to future higher savings was pointed to by advocates of the dual gap model as the mechanism by which aid enables countries to become self-sufficient. For example, Grinols and Bhagwati (1976) modelled how long it would take domestic savings to 'catch up' with what they would have been in the absence of aid, even allowing for a displacement effect, and find this to be a realistic possibility, though the time for it to occur varied greatly: from less than a year for Uruguay to more than 200 years for South Korea, with the average being around 40 years.

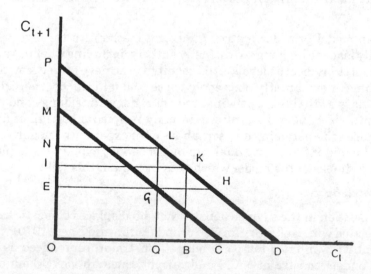

Figure 1   **Griffin's presentation of an aid inflow.**

Feedback effects should also be considered in a single-period static macroeconomic model though an aid multiplier. Eshag (1971) and Kennedy and Thirlwall (1971) both argued that aid inflows would increase output so that consumption may rise with no fall in savings. Griffin's analysis treats the aid inflow as being a one-for-one increment to national income; i.e. that the aid multiplier is unity. Elementary macroeconomics tells us that this is almost certainly not so. In Figure 1 the budget constraint should shift out not by A but by mA, where m is the value of the aid multiplier. Assuming that the aid multiplier is greater than unity then the value of domestic savings will clearly exceed BC. If the multiplier is sufficiently high domestic savings with an aid inflow can exceed QC (their value before the aid inflow) so that the relationship between aid and savings in the current period is positive. This flaw in Griffin's argument has serious implications when it comes to estimating the relationship between aid and savings, and remains a problem in the most recent development of the savings literature which explores the implications of an aid inflow for recipient fiscal policy.

The seminal contribution to this new literature is Heller (1975), and there have been subsequent theoretical elaborations by Gang and Khan (1976), Mosley *et al.* (1987) and White (1992a,b)

Heller analysed the effect of an aid inflow on fiscal behaviour by assuming the recipient government minimizes a loss function with taxes, borrowing and different forms of government expenditure in its argument. Mosley *et al.* embedded Heller's model in one of the whole economy in which, through a production function, changes in aid affect changes in output. The result highlights the relationship between aid and private investment as central to aid's macro-impact: showing aid to have an adverse net impact when there is a negative relationship between aid inflows and private investment, *and* public investment is not much more productive than private.[2]

Whilst the model offers useful insights as to how aid affects government expenditure, taxes, etc., it must be emphasized that these are only partial effects. As in the Harrod-Domar model, increases in aid only increase *future* output. This higher output in the future will mean higher income and taxes which may, in time, offset the displacement effect. Moreover, if a static macroeconomic framework were used, rather than a growth model, then aid can, through the aid multiplier, increase current income and a fall in taxes need not be observed even in the period of the aid inflow (White, 1992b).

These problems mean that the attempts by Mosley *et al.* to move beyond the aid-growth relationship to the determinants of aid effectiveness (1987 and their contribution in this issue) remain dogged by the weakness of the underlying theoretical perspective. As is now demonstrated, these theoretical shortcomings carry over to empirical analysis of aid effectiveness.

3. Empirical analyses of aid's macroeconomic impact

Introduction

Reviews of the empirical literature of how aid affects savings and growth are available elsewhere (Cassen *et al.*, 1986; Riddell, 1987; White, 1992b), and this paper restricts itself to a critique of such studies. Contributors to this debate may be divided into the 'atheists' who believe that such empirical analysis can tell us nothing of the value because of data problems and the large number of factors necessarily omitted from any analysis. Most studies are, however, conducted by 'believers' who place a lot of faith in their data and methodology. I remain agnostic. Whilst I believe that empirical analysis *can* yield useful insights I hope the following arguments will shake the faith of even the truest believer as to the usefulness of most existing studies.

There are many possible criticisms of the literature but, following on from the previous section, the main argument here is that the inadequate theoretical foundation of the literature makes it a poor basis for empirical estimation. This weak foundation would be exposed if the models were tested for mis-specification, but such procedures have been routinely ignored. This section examines first the aid-savings literature and then that on aid and growth. Problems of simultaneity and measurement are also discussed.

A *mis-specification test of the aid-savings relationship*

Griffin (1970) supported his argument that aid displaces savings by reporting a series of regressions (both cross-country and time series) of the savings rate on aid as a proportion of national income, finding coefficients of around -0.8. This amounts to no more than performing a simple correlation, and indeed Griffin has recently restated that there is 'an economically meaningful negative correlation between aid and savings and the correlation is strong and significant' (1990:26). The weakness of the theory behind this proposition was demonstrated above, but Griffin's estimated equation is wrong even by his own reckoning. In a rejoinder to his critics, Griffin (1971) stated his argument thus. Consumption is given by:

$$C = \alpha + \beta\,(Y + A) \tag{1}$$

where C is consumption, Y income and A aid. Since savings are given by:

$$S = Y - C \tag{2}$$

it follows that:

$$S/Y = (1 - \beta) - \alpha/Y - \beta A/Y \tag{3}$$

demonstrating the negative relationship between aid and savings. In a peculiar disregard for his own theory, Griffin 'suppresses' (i.e. ignores) the α/Y term to derive his estimated equation. Assuming equation (3) actually is the true model then his estimate of the coefficient on aid will be downward bias (i.e. more negative). This expectation was borne out by repeating Griffin's analysis with 1987 data for a cross-section of 66 developing countries.[3] The data were first used to regress gross domestic savings expressed as a percentage of GDP (S/Y) on aid as a proportion of GNP (A/Y) and a constant (figures in parentheses are standard errors):

$$S/Y = 19.14 - 0.87\,A/Y \qquad R^2 = 0.33 \tag{4}$$
$$(2.06) \quad (0.16) \qquad\qquad \text{RSS} = 10,358$$

The coefficient of -0.87, which is not very different from Griffin's results, is significant at the 1 per cent level, appearing to confirm the argument that aid will displace savings. However, re-estimation with the reciprocal of income on the right-hand side (as suggested by equation (3)) yields:

$$S/Y = 20.90 - 0.40 \, A/Y - 17375 \, (1/Y) \qquad R^2 = 0.57 \tag{5}$$
$$\quad (1.69) \quad (0.15) \qquad (2923) \qquad\qquad RSS = 6637$$

The magnitude of the negative relationship is halved. Therefore, even assuming Griffin's theoretical model is correct, the negative impact of aid on savings is much less than he claims.

Having started to examine the algebra of Griffin's analysis it is interesting to pursue the point that estimation of equation (4) (and equation (5)) holds income constant, whereas, as argued in Section 2, this is of course not the case. To capture the impact of aid on savings through changes in income it is necessary to complete the model, which may be done by adding the accounting identity.

$$Y = C + I \tag{6}$$

where I is investment. It is now possible to obtain reduced form expressions for the three endogenous variables. These are:

$$C = (\alpha + \beta I + \beta A)/(1 - \beta) \tag{7}$$

$$Y = (\alpha + I + \beta A)/(1 - \beta) \tag{8}$$

$$S = I \tag{9}$$

That is, the model has nothing to say about the behavioural determinants of savings; it collapses into an identity. It is therefore not surprising that the model in equation (5) is easily shown to be too simplistic by a mis-specification test comparing it to a more general model. This is now done, using the same data set as used to estimate equation (4). These results are *not* being presented as a correct model of developing country savings data. The use of cross-section data is, in itself, suspect. Omitted variables include demographic factors and possible dummy variables for oil exporters, disaster-struck countries etc.; it is extremely doubtful that all relevant determinants of savings could ever be included in cross-country analysis.

However, the regression of savings in a more general equation (equations of this form have been used during the third phase) gives:

$$S/Y = 11.33 - 0.29 \, (A/Y) + 0.00 \, (Y/P) + 0.38 \, (X/Y) - 0.01 \, (INFL) - 18064 \, (1/Y)$$
$$\quad (2.87) \quad (0.14) \qquad (0.00) \qquad (0.09) \qquad (0.01) \qquad\quad (2474)$$

$$R^2 = 0.71 \tag{10}$$
$$RSS = 4491$$

where Y/P is income per capita, X/Y the ratio of exports to GDP and INFL the annual rate of inflation.

The coefficients on aid and exports are both significant at the 1 per cent level. Of more interest, however, is the residual sum of squares (RSS) which is only 4491, compared to a RSS of 10,358 from the estimation of S/Y from equation (4). The implicit restrictions on the model tested in equation (10) contained in the simple aid-savings model may be tested through an F-test. The F-statistic is 19.56, compared to a critical value of 2.76, so that the restrictions may not be accepted as being valid (with 99.9 per cent confidence). That is, the simple aid-savings model is not an accurate representation of the data. Specification tests, such as the t-statistic, are valid only on the assumption that the specified model is correct: *since this assumption has been shown to be invalid, the 'significant' results reported by Griffin (and many similar studies) are meaningless.*

The model of equation (10) is static: it is preferable to have a more general model including lags. A regression using also 1986 values $((S/Y)_{-1}$, etc.) suggested that an equation in differences (e.g. $d(S/Y) = S/Y — (S/Y)_{-1})$ might be appropriate. This specification has intuitive theoretical appeal in that, whilst the use of cross-section data on levels is dubious, country-specific factors will drop out of the difference form of the model. Estimation of the model in differences gives:

$$d(S/Y) = — 0.09\ d(A/Y) — 0.00d\ (Y/P) + 0.54\ d\ (X/Y) — 11741\ d\ ((1/Y)$$
$$\quad\quad\quad (0.11) \quad\quad\quad (0.01) \quad\quad\quad (0.16) \quad\quad\quad (5194)$$

$$R^2 = 0.23 \quad\quad\quad\quad\quad\quad\quad\quad\quad\quad\quad\quad\quad\quad\quad\quad (11)$$
$$\text{RSS} = 1654$$

which, using an F-test, shows the model in differences to be a valid restriction of the unrestricted dynamic equation ($F = 0.64$). [4] In this new model the coefficient on aid is insignificant at the 10 per cent level. Changes in the share of exports in GDP appear to be a more important (and more robust) determinant of changes in the savings rate.

Whilst the above analysis demonstrates the invalidity of the simple aid-savings model it also shares many of its faults. The single-equation approach implies a rather simple causation running from aid to savings, the empirical equivalent of Griffin's theoretical analysis in which only the impact effect of aid is considered. No allowance is made for the possible effect that aid will have on savings by increasing income through a multiplier effect or its impact on other economic variables.

Savings will be determined by a host of factors, such as the degree of monetization of the economy, dependency ratios, the stage of development of financial intermediaries, etc. Cassen (1989) has pointed to the existence of a substantial literature on the determination of savings in developing countries that makes no mention of aid. Whilst this is so it is also true that aid affects the variables that are deemed to affect savings directly. Some of these factors are outside the scope of most macro-models, though in the short run some of these factors may be treated as constant (though they will *not* be constant across countries, which is why cross-section analysis cannot be expected to yield useful results). Unfortunately, data for developing countries are usually annual, so that any sufficiently large data set may extend beyond the short run. This is not a problem if these factors can be included on the right-hand side of the regression. But if (as may be hoped) aid has an impact on, say, infant mortality and thus dependency ratios, or on life expectancy, or on income distribution, this will cause indirect effects on savings that will be difficult to isolate.

It is possible to think of a number of economic channels through which aid will affect savings. The first is, as already mentioned, that if aid has any effect on the level of income at all then, unless the savings function is linear and passes through the origin, there will be a relationship between aid and the savings rate. Assume the savings function is linear with a negative vertical intercept (so MPS > APS and APS rises with income), and that the aid multiplier is greater than unity. An increase in aid leads to a drop in A/Y and an increase in S/Y; the negative relationship of the radicals will be observed but for quite different reasons. Further impacts on savings from aid may come from its impact on the interest rate, income distribution, exports and fiscal policy. This list is certainly not exhaustive; but, with the exception of the last point, the aid-savings literature has not examined any of these possibilities. By not considering the mechanisms by which aid may affect savings the literature has not advanced our understanding of the macroeconomics of aid.

The empirical literature on the last of these, i.e. recipient government response, is open to the same criticism as has been made above of the more general empirical literature on the aid-savings literature. As argued in the previous section, the effect on taxes, etc., predicted by Heller and those that have developed his model, is a *partial* effect. Once income changes are allowed for then aid may, say, increase taxes. The early contributions to this literature (Heller, 1975; Pillai, 1982; Holtham and Hazelwood, 1976: 190-200; and Cashel-Cordo, 1990) found that aid does indeed increase government expenditure by less than the value of the aid inflow and displace taxes (typically around 40 per cent of aid is used for purposes other than increasing developmental expenditure). Two more recent studies report contrary findings. Pack and Pack's (1990) study of Indonesia, and Gang and Khan's (1991) paper on aid to India, both argue that the marginal increase in government resources devoted to development in response to increased aid is greater than unity. They attribute this to donor requirements that recipients pay the local costs of projects. This may be so, but it may also reflect increased government resources resulting from the higher income caused by the aid inflow. A regression of government investment on aid and taxes, where taxes depend on income, which in turn depend on aid, is not allowing for this effect.[5] Without incorporating these concerns this new literature risks falling into the same inconclusive morass as the savings debate.

The conclusion of the above analysis must be that empirical work should be based on better-formulated macroeconomic models, that will probably require simultaneous estimation. It is also almost certainly the case that studies should be carried out on a country level rather than employing cross-section data. This latter point is now discussed in the context of the aid-growth literature.

Parameter instability in the estimation of the aid-growth relationship

The Harrod-Domar models are an imperfect characterization of the process of economic growth. Yet the econometric literature on aid and growth has done little to move beyond a single equation that is the empirical equivalent of the Harrod-Domar equation: many authors explicitly acknowledge their models as such (e.g. Voivodas, 1973; Mosley, 1980). Indeed, the literature for the most part does not even take on board the dual gap development of Chenery and Stout, since they demonstrated that the impact of aid would differ for each country according to whether that country faced a binding savings or foreign exchange constraint[6] and be dependent upon a range of parameters for the recipient (e.g. the marginal propensity to save or import). Chenery and Stouts's analysis shows that aid effectiveness will vary between countries, whereas subsequent work, by relying on cross-section studies, has assumed that it will be constant.

A more fundamental critique attacks the way in which the Harrod-Domar captures capital's impact on growth. There is a substantial literature that argues that health and education are not simply consumption goods but investment in human capital. Aid used in these sectors will not contribute to growth in the simple way contained in the Harrod-Domar model. The impact of aid will be different if it is used for building primary health clinics rather than for roads, extension services or an industrial line of credit. All these things should be expected to increase growth, but through different channels and certainly with different lag structures. Two points arise from this. First, single-equation regressions that try to include the impact of, say, labour force quality by including a variable such as literacy (e.g. Mosley *et al.*, 1987) will not capture aid's impact on growth through its impact on literacy. Second, by aggregating aid across sectors, cross-country analysis implicitly assumes either that the sectoral distribution of aid is the same in each country or does not matter. Neither is true.

The implications of the above argument are clear; *there is no theoretical foundation whatsoever for assuming that the impact of aid on growth is constant either across countries or across time*. It is not surprising that the few tests reported in the literature on the validity of pooling data across countries usually reject the procedure (e.g. Levy, 1988: Rana, 1987). To re-emphasize this point I present here tests of parameter constancy on panel data for 73 developing countries over the period 1970-88. GDP growth was regressed on domestic savings, exports, official transfers, long-term capital inflows (all expressed as a percentage of GDP) and a constant. Table 1 shows the results for the three regions (Africa, Asia and Latin America and the Caribbean) and those from pooling the data. If the parameters are the same in each of the regressions then the residual sum of squares from the pooled data will not be much different from the total of the residual sum of squares from each of the regional equations. Whether or not the difference that does exist is significant may be tested by means of an F-test. The F-statistic from this test is 6.21, compared to a critical value of less than 3, so that the null hypothesis that the parameters are the same between the three regions may be rejected with 99.9 per cent confidence. Pooling of the data is clearly an invalid procedure.

The invalidity of pooling has not been commonly remarked upon in the literature, partly as most studies fail to report either tests for this or statistics that would enable tests to be calculated. Most studies report little more than t-statistics (and sometimes not those). Given that the absence of significant coefficients is a major result of the literature it is especially surprising that no tests for heteroscedasticity are reported. Yet this is likely to be a problem in cross-section data, and one which results in inefficient estimates (i.e. a higher probability of invalidly rejecting a significant coefficient).

Table 1   **Test of parameter constancy for regression of growth on aid.**

Region	Savings	Exports	Official transfers	Long-term capital inflows	RSS
Africa	0.08 (0.02)	-0.02 (0.02)	0.15 (0.03)	0.08 (0.08)	26, 401
Asia	0.09 (0.03)	0.03 (0.01)	0.07 (0.07)	-0.17 (0.08)	3, 150
LAC	0.18 (0.03)	-0.09 (0.02)	0.08 (0.04)	-0.10 (0.11)	10, 290
All	0.11 (0.11)	-0.03 (0.01)	0.13 (0.02)	0.01 (0.05)	41, 717

Figures in parentheses are standard errors.

Source: Data from World Bank, *World Tables* and IMF, *International Finance Statistics*.

The problem of simultaneity I: are aid flows endogenous?

The simple equation used in much of the savings literature was shown to be mispecified, and it was also argued that direct estimation of how aid affects growth will omit much. Both of these relationships are likely to be part of a simultaneous system and so single-equation estimation will be subject to simultaneity bias. In fact, simultaneity bias may arise from two sources. In addition to that mentioned above, bias will arise if aid is endogenous as a result of the nature of the aid allocation process. Over (1975) demonstrated this bias by showing that, if donors allocate aid so as to fill the savings gap, two-stage least-squares estimation of the simple aid-savings equation yielded a positive relationship, compared to the negative relationship obtained by Griffin. However, there are a number of good reasons for discounting this bias as an important factor.

First, donors may conceivably allocate aid by income per capita but since income *level* is unrelated to *growth* of income there will be no simultaneity bias if it is aid's impact on growth that is being estimated. Accordingly, studies that have allowed for such simultaneity have found the effect to be minor. Second, studies have found aid allocation to be more strongly influenced by donor interests than by recipient need (e.g. Maizels and Nissanke, 1984; Gulhati and Nallari, 1988). Third, aid allocation mechanisms presumably affect commitments whereas it is disbursements that affect economic variables. There is very little relationship between commitments and disbursements (White, 1990: Chapter 6), thus making simultaneity bias from aid inflows an even more remote possibility.[7]

The results from Bowles' (1987) application of a test for Granger causality[8] to the relationship between savings and aid stand in apparent contradiction to the conclusion of the preceding paragraph. For a variable to be strongly exogenous it must not be Granger-caused by the dependent variable. If aid is Granger-caused by savings it is not strongly exogenous in the regression of savings on aid: the aid inflows are apparently related to an economic variable (in this case savings) and the use of OLS is inappropriate. Using time-series data for 20 countries over the period 1960-81, Bowles found that in half of the 20 cases examined there was no causality. In three cases changes in savings were shown to cause changes in aid, in five cases the converse (for one of these there was a positive relationship) and for two there was bi-directional causality. That is, in five cases out of 20, aid is not strongly exogenous. These findings may be reconciled with the argument that aid will not be endogenous in an economic model by resorting to Papanek's (1972, 1973) argument that there may be an exogenous variable causing changes in both aid and savings. Famine, for example, may both reduce savings and lead to higher aid. It would thus appear that savings were Granger-causing aid. Final resolution of this issue will require country-level analysis of cases in which aid appears to be endogenous.

The problem of simultaneity II: estimating macroeconomic models of aid's impact

If aid is exogenous then there will be no simultaneity bias. However, single-equation estimation remains inappropriate since the coefficient on aid will be a mongrel parameter. Estimation of the structural parameters requires that a full model be specified and estimated by one of the available techniques for structural equations (indirect least-squares, instrumental variables or two-stage least-squares).

This is a neglected area. Snyder (1990) sets out a simultaneous model of the relationship between aid and savings but estimates the model using OLS! Levy (1984) estimated the impact of aid on savings in a more fully specified economic model. He specified two savings functions, one for each of the public and private sectors, both including income on the right-hand side and the former also incorporating aid inflows. Savings fuel investment and thus, through a Cobb-Douglas production function, lead to higher income to allow feedback effects. He finds that aid still leads to a reduction in domestic savings as its negative impact on public savings is not fully offset by the positive impact on income. There are, however, problems in his analysis. The methodology is not reported, but it appears that OLS was used on each equation of the simultaneous system in turn. No account is taken of longer run considerations, when aid's increment to capital stock will remain but its negative impact on savings will have ceased.

The most substantial attempt to tackle the simultaneity problem is that by Gupta and Islam (1983), who include a range of demographic variables in their analysis. Their starting point is the problem of simultaneity between growth and savings, since growth depends on domestic savings and recent studies suggest savings are influenced by growth. To counter this problem they present a nine-equation system that includes many demographic variables. There are, however, few economic relationships in the model and it does not qualify as a macroeconomic model of aid impact. While this is an imperfect analysis it is one of the best to date, and its findings stand in contradiction to many of those in the rest of the literature. In particular, they find that the relationship between aid and savings is *positive* for the two lower-income groups. The impact of aid on growth is positive for the whole sample, though less for higher-income groups than lower ones (no *t*-statistics are reported so it is not possible to test the significance of these results).

The measurement and disaggregation of aid flows

There are many problems in working with developing country data, and aid is no exception to this. Griffin (1970) aggregated all capital inflows and identified these with the deficit on current account. This procedure was rightly criticized and subsequent work has disaggregated inflows, using DAC data for aid series. However, many problems of measurement still remain. First, which of disbursements (net or gross), transfers or commitments is the appropriate measure?[9] Second, should the figures be converted to their grant equivalents? Since it will be double-counting to use *net* figures and *grant* equivalent a choice between the two must be made. Third, what sort of adjustment should be made for tying (or at least formal tying, which is only a percentage of effective tying)? Further problems include the use of current or constant prices and choice of exchange rate. Since the value of the additional resources made available by the aid is presumably the variable of interest, the figures should be deflated by an import price index.

Even leaving all these questions aside, Riddell (1987: 108-112) points to a number of problems in DAC data, including definition (e.g. treatment of donor administrative costs) and data accuracy. In the face of all these problems Riddell suggests turning to recipient national accounts as an alternative source of data. For cross-country studies this would involve a massive research effort and raise many comparability problems. However, given the severe limitations of cross-country work it is advisable to restrict research to time-series analysis, so the suggestion is a practical one.

A problem only touched on by Riddell is the treatment of different types of aid. Aid is not only capital for projects, but consumption items (mainly food), technical assistance and programme support. The theory on which empirical estimates have been based tells us nothing about whether these different flows need to be handled differently. It is commonly held that consumption aid should be deducted before regressing aid on growth (e.g. Streeten, 1972: 189), but food aid is claimed to have productivity-increasing effects and can play a vital role in relaxing the foreign exchange constraint. Yet, as Lipton and Toye point out, 'these effects would not show up at all in the results of the kinds of econometric investigation of the aid-growth link which have been commonest' (1990:30). We are brought, once again, back to the need to develop better models of aid's macroeconomic impact.

4. Recent developments in the macroeconomics of aid

The above analysis may appear pessimistic, and the problems raised in analysing aid's impact perhaps insurmountable; but that is not the argument of this paper. It *is* being argued that we have at best an imperfect understanding of the determinants of growth and perhaps less still of how aid affects those determinants. We may learn more by trying to learn less. If it could be demonstrated that aid increases investment or imports (on each of which there are small literatures, e.g. Levy, 1987b; Moran 1989) then most economists would accept that these are channels through which aid contributes to higher growth. How aid does affect these variables will be the result of its impact on a range of macroeconomic variables such as the real exchange rate, prices (relative and level) and the real interest rate. These issues have been only little addressed but not completely ignored.

What I have elsewhere (White, 1990, 1992b) labelled the trade theory approach to aid impact has been concerned with aid's influence on the real exchange rate. This line of analysis can be traced back to the criticisms of dual gap theory by Joshi (1970) and Findlay (1973). It has re-emerged in the work of Michaely (1981) and van Wijnbergen (1985, 1986). The argument is that an aid inflow will cause an appreciation of the real exchange rate (that is the price of non-traded goods to that of traded goods). This view, which may also be found amongst theorists specializing on real exchange rate determination (e.g. Edwards, 1988), has been shown a theoretically robust result in a range of macroeconomic models with differing assumptions about the structure of the economy (White 1990). There is little empirical work in this area yet, but what there is is supportive of the thesis that aid will put pressure on the real exchange rate to appreciate. Taylor (1988) mentions that this may have occurred in Egypt and the Philippines. Van Wijnbergen (1985) examines a number of sub-Saharan countries using an econometric model of real exchange rate behaviour: aid inflows were found to exert a significant effect in the expected direction. White and Wignaraja (1991) estimated an equation for Sri Lanka in which transfers (aid flows and remittances) were a significant factor in the divergence between real and nominal exchange rates that emerged during the 1980s.

Also important is the resurgence of interest in the potential inflationary impact of counterpart funds, including useful modelling of financial aspects of this type of aid (Roemer, 1989). Whilst the review and empirical work by Barton and Hill (1991) concludes that counterpart funds do not have a net impact on inflation, this does not mean that there will not be an impact on *relative* prices. This literature, and that from the trade theory approach, indicate that there is still much to be learnt about the macroeconomics of aid, and offer insights into how this may be done.

5. Conclusions

Does aid increase growth? A survey of the academic literature can only leave us unsure about the answer to this question. The optimism of the dual gap model, and the Harrod-Domar equation on which it is based, is clearly misplaced simply because factors other than capital accumulation affect growth. Higher aid therefore cannot *ensure* higher growth. But this is not to say that growth with aid has not been higher than it would have been in its absence.

Those theories that suggest that aid will not play much role in increasing growth as it displaces savings fail to take account of ways in which aid may also increase savings, principally through increasing income in both current and future periods. The empirical work that supports the radical hypothesis also fails to allow for these effects. Moreover, the literatures on aid and savings and aid and growth ignore many other factors and pool data across countries in a way that appears quite invalid if tested.

Further work should be based on country-level studies and should employ more detailed macroeconomic models. These models should allow us to explore the impact of aid on a range of economic variables, such as the real exchange rate, investment and imports, and also allow us to distinguish between different forms of aid. Given our imperfect understanding of the determinants of growth, and our ignorance as to how aid affects many of these determinants, attempts to estimate how aid affects growth are attempts to run before we can walk (or maybe even stand). We can, however, try to analyse if aid increases, say, investment or imports (both of which may be expected to lead to higher growth), There are a very small number of contributions to each of these areas which may be built up on. No policy implications may be drawn from the literature on aid and growth because of its over-ambitious scope and ultimately inconclusive nature. Less ambitious studies are more likely to have implications that may be translated into donor policy. The small empirical literature on aid's impact on the RER supports the theoretical proposition that aid induces a RER appreciation. Lessons for macroeconomic management, similar to those for the managing of commodity booms, may be drawn from this.

This conclusion should *not* be interpreted as a call to throw readily available powerful econometrics packages at large computer databases. Better theoretical models are a priority, and they will help determine the required econometric methodology.

It was an exaggeration to say that the current empirical literature holds no lessons for donors. It does hold one very important lesson. More research on aid's macroeconomic impact is urgently required.

Acknowledgements

The author would like to thank the participants of the ESRC Development Economics Study Group Conference, Ganeshan Wignaraja, George Mavrotas and an anonymous reviewer, for comments and suggestions, and Maureen Smith for help in the preparation of this paper. The usual dislaimer applies. Parts of the paper are based on the author's D. Phil thesis, for which financial support was received from the ESRC.

Notes

1. This overview is necessarily brief. A more comprehensive version may be found in White (1992b).

2. These conditions are precisely the view of aid held by critics such as Bauer (e.g. 1984: Chapters 3 and 4).

3. The data were taken from the 1988 and 1989 *World Development Reports*.

4. It has been argued that the omission of a constant in this equation will bias the RSS (and hence the F-statistic). However, since the exclusion of the constant appears valid its omission has virtually no impact on the RSS (re-estimation of equation (11) with the constant included reduces the RSS by 0.6 per cent).

5. Gang and Khan's (1991) use of three-stage least-squares does not overcome this problem since they do not specify an equation through which aid can affect income in their model.

6. Weisskopf (1972) and Blomquist (1976) model the difference between regimes, and Voivodas (1973) mentions it but then fails to allow for it.

7. It might be argued that commitments matter as *expectations* as to the value of aid are important. But if there is no relationship between commitments and disbursements then

rational actors will not base their expectations of the latter on the former. The only paper to have modelled expected aid (Levy, 1987a) does so on the basis of past disbursements.

8. X is said to Granger cause Y if $\delta_i \neq 0$ for any i in the regression $Y_t = \Sigma\beta_i\, Y_{t-i} + \Sigma\delta_i\, X_{t-i} + u_t$.

9. Net disbursements deduct only repayments of capital; net transfers also deduct interest payments.

References

Bauer, P. T. (1984) *Reality and Rhetoric: Studies in the Economics of Development*, London: Weidenfeld & Nicolson.

Blomquist, A. G. (1976) 'Empirical evidence on the two gap hypothesis', *Journal of Development Economics* 3, pp. 181-193.

Bowles, P. (1987) 'Foreign aid and domestic savings in less developed countries: some tests for causality', *World Development*, 15, pp. 789-796.

Bruton, H. and Hill, C. (1990) 'The development impact of counterpart funds: a review of the literature', United States AID (Report PN-ABH-074), Washington, DC.

Cashel-Cordo, P. and Craig, S.G. (1990) 'The public sector impact of international resource transfers', *Journal of Development Economics*, 32, pp. 17-42.

Cassen, R. (1989) 'Aid and macroeconomic performance', Queen Elizabeth House, Oxford (word-processed).

Cassen, R. *et al* (1986) *Does Aid Work?* Oxford: Oxford University Press.

Chenery, H. and Strout, W. (1966) 'Foreign assistance and economic development', *American Economic Review*, 66 (September), pp. 679-733.

Edwards, S. (1988) 'Exchange rate misalignment in developing countries', *World Bank Occasional Paper No. 2*. Baltimiore: Johns Hopkins University Press.

Eshag, E. (1971) 'Comment', *Bulletin of the Oxford University Institute of Economics and Statistics*, 33 (May).

Findlay, R. (1973) *International Trade and Development Theory*. New York: Colombia University Press.

Gang, I. N. and Khan, H. (1986) 'Foreign aid and public expenditures in LDCs', *Atlantic Economic Journal*, 14 (September), pp. 56-58.

Gang, I. and Khan, H. (1991) 'Foreign aid, taxes and public investment', *Journal of Development Economics*, 34, pp. 355-369.

Griffin, K. (1970) 'Foreign capital, domestic savings and economic development', *Bulletin of the Oxford University Institute of Economics and Statistics*, 32 (May), pp. 99-112.

Griffin, K. (1971) 'Foreign capital: a reply to some critics', *Bulletin of the Oxford University Institute of Economics and Statistics*, 33 (May), pp. 156-161.

Griffin, K. (1990) 'Foreign aid after the Cold War', mimeo. Paris: OECD Development Centre.

Griffin, K. and Enos, J. (1970) 'Foreign assistance: objectives and consequences', *Economic Development and Cultural Change*, 18, pp. 313-327.

Grinols, E. and Bhagwati, J. (1976) 'Foreign capital, savings and dependence', *Review of Economics and Statistics*, 58, pp. 416-424.

Gulhati, R. and Nallari, R. (1988) 'Reform of foreign aid policies: the issue of inter-country allocation in Africa, *World Development*, 16 (October), 1167-84.

Gupta, K. L. and Islam, M. A. (1983) *Foreign Capital Savings and Growth: an international cross-section study*. Dordrecht, Holland: Reidel.

Heller, P. S. (1975) 'A model of public fiscal behaviour in developing countries: aid, investment and taxation', *American Economic Review*, 65 (June), pp. 429-445.

Holtham, G. and Hazlewood, A. (1976) *Aid and Inequality in Kenya*. London: ODI/Croom Helm.

Joshi, Y. (1970) 'Savings and foreign exchange constraints'. In Streeten, P. (ed.) *Unfashionable Economics*. London: Weidenfeld & Nicolson, pp. 111-133.

Kennedy, C. and Thirlwall, A. P. (1971) 'Comment'. *Bulletin of the Oxford University Institute of Economics and Statistics,* 33 (May).

Levy, V. (1984) 'The savings gap and the productivity of foreign aid to a devleoping economy: Egypt', *Journal of Developing Areas,* 19 (October), pp. 21-34.

Levy, V. (1987a) 'Anticipated development assistance, temproary relief aid, and consumption behaviour of low-income countries', *Economic Journal*, 97 (June), pp. 446-58.

Levy, V. (1987b) 'Does concessionary aid lead to higher investment rates in low income countries?', *Review of Economics and Statistics*, 69, pp. 152-156.

Levy, V. (1988) 'Aid and growth in sub-Sharan Africa: the recent experience', *European Economic Review,* 13, pp. 1777-1795.

Lipton, M. and Toye, J. (1990) *Does Aid Work in India? A country study of the impact of Official Development Assistance.* London: Routledge.

Maizels, A. and Nissanke, M. K. (1984) 'Motivations for aid to developing countries', *World Development* , 12 (September), pp. 879-900.

Michaely, M. (1981) 'Foreign aid, economic structure, and dependence', *Journal of Development Economics*, 9, pp. 313-330.

Moran C. (1989) 'Imports under a foreign exchange constraint', *World Bank Economic Review,* 3, pp. 279-295.

Mosley, P. (1980) 'Aid, savings and growth revisited', *Bulletin of the Oxford University Institute of Economics and Statistics*, 42 (May), pp. 79-95.

Mosley, P., Hudson, J. and Horrel, S. (1987) 'Aid, the public sector and the market in less developed countries', *Economic Journal*, 97 (September), pp. 616-641.

Over, A. M. (1975) 'An example of the simultaneous equations problem: a note on "Foreign assistance: objectives and consequences"', *Economic Development and Cultural Change*, 24 (July), pp. 751-56.

Pack, H. and Pack, J. R. (1990) 'Is foreign aid fungible? The case of Indonesia', *Economic Journal*, 100, pp. 188-194.

Papanek, G. (1972) 'The effects of aid and other resources transfers on savings and growth in less developed countries', *Economic Journal*, 82, (September), pp. 934-950.

Papanek, G. (1973) 'Aid, foreign private investment, savings and growth in less developed countries, *Journal of Political Economy*, 81, pp. 120-130.

Pillai, el. (1982) 'External economic dependence and fiscal policy imbalances in developing economies in developing countries: a case study of Jordan', *Journal of Development Studies*, 19 (October), pp. 5-18.

Rana, P. B. (1987) 'Foreign capital, exports, savings and growth in the Asian region', *Savings and Development*, 1, pp. 5-27.

Ravallion, M. and Abhijit, S. (1986) 'On some estimates of an Asian savings function', *Economic Letters*, 20, pp. 121-124.

Riddell, R. (1987) *Foreign Aid Reconsidered.* London: James Curry.

Roemer, M. (1989) 'Macroeconomics of counterpart funds revisited', *World Development*, 17 (June), pp. 795-808.

Snyder, D. (1990) 'Foreign aid and domestic savings: a spurious correlation?', *Economic Development and Cultural Change*, 38, pp. 175-181.

Stewart, F. (1971) 'Comment'. *Bulletin of the Oxford University Insitute of Economics and Statistics*, 33 (May), pp. 138-149.

Streeten, P. (1972) *The Frontiers of Development Studies*. London: Macmillan

Taylor, L. (1988) *Varieties of Stabilisation Experience*. Oxford: Clarendon Press.

Van Wijnbergen, S. (1985) 'Aid, export promotion and the real exchange rate: an African dilemma?', World Bank Country Policy Department Discussion Paper No. 1985-54.

Van Wijnbergen, S. (1986) 'Macroeconomic aspects of the effectiveness of foreign aid: the two gap model, home goods disequilibrium and real exchange rate misalignment', *Journal of International Economics*, 3, pp. 337-349.

Voivodas, C.S. (1973) 'Exports, foreign capital inflow and economic growth', *Journal of International Economics*, 2, pp. 25-38.

Weisskopf, T. (1972) 'Impact of foreign capital inflows on domestic savings in underdeveloped countries', *Journal of International Economics*, 2, pp. 25-38.

White, H. (1990) 'The macroeconomic impact of development aid'. Unpublished D. Phil. thesis, University of Oxford.

White, H. (1992a) 'Aid in the public sector and the market in less developed countries: a note', in *Economic Journal* (January).

White, H. (1972b) 'The macroeconomic impact of development aid: a critical survey', in *Journal of Development Studies* (January).

White, H. and Wignaraja, G. (1991) 'Real and nominal devaluation during trade liberalisation in Sri Lanka: a case of aid-induced Dutch disease', Centro Studi Luca d'Agliano/Queen Elizabeth House Development Studies Working Paper No. 38, Oxford (to be published in *World Development*).

25.　Aid, Capital Flows, and Development: A Synthesis
Uma Lele and Ijaz Nabi

External financing and development: the country experience

The authors of the case studies presented in this volume have tackled the complex questions concerning the role of external financing in development in the context of the long-term economic, political, social, and strategic objectives and policies of their respective countries. Their conclusions are summarized here.

Country economic performance. The rapid progress made by many developing countries until about 1980 is striking, given the poor conditions they inherited at independence and the adverse external shocks they have faced since then (such as border wars, famines, and a deterioration in external terms of trade). The African countries as a whole did less well than other developing countries, although there were a few notable exceptions such as Kenya. By and large, countries that performed well on a sustained basis also did well in agriculture and substantially reduced the proportion of their population living in poverty.

Of the countries studied in this book, Brazil, Thailand, Egypt, Mexico, Kenya, Colombia, and Pakistan (in that order) grew fastest, with GDP growth rates varying from 9 to 5 percent between 1965 and 1980 (see Table 1.1 in Chapter 1). [5] Sri Lanka and India followed with growth rates of 4 and 3.7 per cent respectively. Tanzania and Senegal experienced declines in per capita incomes. Pakistan and Egypt continued their strong growth rates even after the deterioration of the world economic situation in the early 1980s. Growth in Thailand, however, slowed somewhat from the high levels attained earlier, whereas growth in India and Sri Lanka improved. In contrast, growth rates fell sharply in Mexico, Brazil, and Tanzania, and somewhat less in Colombia and Kenya.

Growth was not always accompanied by a significant improvement in social indicators for the poor. Pakistan, for example, achieved strong growth rates and an impressive reduction in the incidence of poverty from 54 percent of the population in 1963 to 23 per cent in 1984, but other social indicators showed no improvement. In other cases, such as Tanzania, efforts to improve social indicators were thwarted by the collapse of production. Thailand, and to a lesser extent India and Kenya, achieved growth with improvement in equity. Sri Lanka and Pakistan provide interesting insights into the personal income and the social welfare components of the living standards puzzle, which we shall revisit later.

The macroeconomic effects of external capital. The macroeconomic effects of aid and commercial flows on recipients are subtle and manifest themselves with lags of varying length across sectors and countries. This makes it difficult to establish any

Uma Lele and Ijaz Nabi: Extracts from 'Aid, Capital Flows, and Development: A Synthesis' from *TRANSITIONS IN DEVELOPMENT: THE ROLE OF AID AND COMMERCIAL FLOWS*, edited by Uma Lele and Ijaz Nabi (International Center for Economic Growth, 1991), pp. 457-467, 470-474 and 513-515.

direct causality between aid and development, which may explain why econometric studies of aid's impact on domestic savings, investment, consumption, GDP growth, or poverty alleviation have been inconclusive (Cassen and Associates 1986). The relationship between aid and the recent macroeconomic adjustment efforts is even harder to establish using econometrics. A more useful approach, and the one taken in this volume, is to capture the macroeconomic effects of external assistance through detailed case studies.

A consistent theme emerging from the country studies is that domestic policies determine development outcomes, and as Gil Díaz puts it in the case of Mexico, policies are, in the final analysis, the sole responsibility of the domestic government. If the government is not committed to change, there can be no serious macroeconomic reform.

Moreover, donors often have competing political/strategic and development objectives that prevent them from taking a concerted stance to encourage painful macroeconomic adjustments. This is well illustrated in the cases of Tanzania, Sri Lanka, and Egypt. Collier and Bhalla show for Tanzania and Sri Lanka, respectively, that even though multilateral and bilateral aid in the 1970s was given for development reasons, donors did not agree on the merits of specific policies and thus weakened the overall macroeconomic effects of aid. Besides, when some donors withdrew, others stepped in, in the hope of persuading the country to adopt political stances favorable to them. The strong socialist leanings of the Sri Lankan and Egyptian governments during the first half of the 1970s, for example, attracted a large increase in aid from the communist bloc countries. In 1972, aid to Sri Lanka from these countries reached its highest-ever level of $85 million. Such competition could hardly encourage painful policy adjustments.

Even when aid objectives were clear, its economywide effects were subtle, as illustrated in the chapters by Lele and Agarwal on India and by Nabi and Hamid on Pakistan. Both countries experienced a steady decline in per capita incomes before independence. Since then India has had high domestic savings and investment rates, at nearly 22 percent of GDP in most years during the 1970s and 1980s. Pakistan's savings rate, in contrast, averaged only 13 per cent from 1961 to 1988, and its investment rate was well below 20 percent in most years. Yet, India's GDP growth rate was slower than that of Pakistan, which received larger (albeit highly unstable) aid flows and pursued a relatively more outward-oriented growth strategy. This shows that aid, even when not accompanied by improved domestic saving and investment, can result in high growth if recipients follow an outward-oriented strategy. Thus, econometric studies that seek to establish a relationship between aid and growth without accounting for inward or outward orientation of policies omit a crucial link.

Encouraging outward orientation is perhaps one of the more important roles that external financing has played. The advantages of outward orientation are many and are now well documented in the development literature: an outward orientation allows access to technology and markets, and forces domestic producers to become efficient by confronting them with completion. This raises productivity and contributes to growth. The policy instruments used to bring about outward orientation are the exchange rate and reform of tariff and nontariff barriers. The case studies in this volume are replete with episodes of donor-recipient dialogue on these instruments. What we learn is that there has been steady progress in this dialogue, although it is nearly always slow and often acrimonious.

Brazil, Mexico, Egypt, Tanzania, and Senegal all provide examples of the adverse macroeconomic effects of abundant but poorly deployed external capital. In the 1970s, the availability of large amounts of external capital led to wasteful expenditures on megaprojects and created a dependency syndrome. It contributed to the growth of public sector monopolies, increased expenditures on implicit and explicit subsidies, and resulted in a pervasive government presence in the economy. Overvalued exchange rates, which implied depressed prices of tradables relative to nontradable goods encouraged resources to flow into nontradable sectors. This led to the familiar Dutch disease and eventually to balance of payments difficulties.[6] Moreover, easy availability of external capital allowed these countries to increase wasteful public spending, creating rent-seeking vested interests that make it difficult to reform policies. The relationship between macroeconomic performance and external assistance in these countries is intricately linked to strategies for reducing debt, improving access to commercial capital markets, and resuming growth. We comment on these issues below.

Project and program aid. Until the late 1970s, official development assistance was given largely for individual projects. Program loans, precursors of the present-day structural adjustment loans, given by donors such as the World Bank and the United States, were for short-term balance of payments support. Such assistance was given infrequently and only when commercial credit was not forthcoming. The effects of development assistance before the 1980s are therefore best understood in terms of the contributions that donors made through project and program assistance. Several such contributions can be identified.

First, the case studies show that aid improved the efficiency of capital by instituting project evaluation and implementation procedures and techniques that helped recipients choose investment portfolios with relatively high returns to capital. Indeed, in some countries, donors made major contributions to the creation of technical capacity for project appraisal, implementation, and evaluation in key sectors — for example, transport and electricity in Colombia. The evidence, however, is mixed: the experience of a number of countries such as Kenya, Egypt, and Tanzania shows that even project aid could be wasted.

Second, by emphasizing the importance of agriculture in the economic transformation of countries and by focusing on the development of institutions, technology, and human resources, project and program aid helped accelerate the growth of entire sectors. An excellent example of this is the spectacular success of the Green Revolution in Asian agriculture, illustrated in the studies on India, Pakistan, Thailand, and Sri Lanka. The development of small-scale agriculture requires the government to play an active role in providing irrigation, roads, electricity, and education. Donors, who tend to operate through governments, can clearly help improve public sector capacity to carry out such investments.

Program aid also provided scarce foreign exchange for food imports during critical periods of shortage, as the experience of Asian countries shows. This assistance helped maintain consumption levels of the poor and checked inflation and wages — all crucial in providing the breathing room that policymakers needed to address the complex problems of increasing agricultural productivity and meeting the most basic foods needs. (Donors also supplied food aid, which is so controversial that we will visit it again to air the issues more fully.) Indeed, a primary factor behind the successes of Asian countries — in contrast to their African counterparts — has been their .ability to overcome the complex problems of developing agriculture.

Third, since projects were implemented as part of the overall economic strategy, such assistance provided opportunities to hold a policy dialogue at the broader sectoral and economywide level. This dialogue helped recipients formulate long-term strategies of development, improve the overall structure of incentives, and restore macroeconomic balance. In India, for example, the World Bank's 1964 Bell mission articulated the importance of appropriate exchange rate and trade regimes and helped set the course for agriculture. Although India had accumulated substantial stocks of foreign exchange and food by 1975, the World Bank's International Development Association (IDA) and the International Monetary Fund (IMF) did not discontinue assistance; instead, they helped reinitiate and sustain trade liberalization (after a disastrous first attempt in 1966). Similarly, the World Bank and US assistance played a crucial role in changing Thailand's investment policy in the late 1950s and early 1960s — public investments, including those assisted by donors, were confined to the provision of utilities and public services, while all other sectors were left open for private investment. Once the basic infrastructure had been developed, the policy dialogue between the Thai government and the World Bank/IMF helped maintain private sector growth as well as overall financial stability in the 1970s and 1980s.

More generally, the country studies make a strong case for well-designed project and food aid on a small but predictable basis to strengthen absorptive capacity of recipients by stressing education, training, and institution building in aid programs. In the 1960s, many Latin American countries, as well as others such as Egypt and Pakistan, received relatively small amounts of official assistance (mainly from the United States) and they used it effectively. US assistance focused on improvements in human and institutional capacity — especially analytical and policy-planning capabilities at the macroeconomic level and in agriculture. Under foreign assistance programs, policymakers and researchers staffing the new development institutions received training in the finest universities and research centers in the United States and other advanced donor countries.

Aid to Africa in the 1970s, however, placed insufficient emphasis on building the human and institutional capacity necessary for attaining sustainable growth, which may explain some of the policy disasters that followed. The example of Tanzania makes clear that even if aid is given on developmental grounds, ill-conceived assistance to small countries with poor policy environments and relatively little or no absorptive capacity is bound to be misused. Africa needs not only a continued emphasis on macroeconomic reform, but also smaller amounts of well-designed assistance that will increase absorptive capacity for the efficient use of larger amounts later.

Uses of food aid. Food aid is much maligned. It is alleged to create disincentives for domestic food production by reducing prices and to encourage dependency on food imports. Like overall financial aid, food aid *may* create disincentives, but it need not. Food aid to Asian countries in the 1960s helped maintain consumption levels among poor urban groups vulnerable to food shortages when balance of payments difficulties inhibited commercial grain imports. Also, counterpart funds generated by the difference between the cost of food aid imports and their market price allowed donors to influence agricultural policy and research, which helped to bring about technical change. Srinivasan argues that donors and governments ought to take a long-term view of the uses of food aid in the context of an overall agricultural development strategy. Lele and Agarwal have pointed out that in India the politics of food aid made it unpredictable and strengthened India's resolve to achieve food self-sufficiency and to adopt policies that facilitated the Green Revolution.

Although food aid in Africa has provided critical foreign exchange, government revenues, and food, it has not played as positive a role in agricultural development as it did in Asia. Srinivasan observes that this is partly because domestic policies are more distorted in the African countries. Moreover, at independence, research systems and human resources were better developed and irrigation potential was much stronger in Asia than in Africa, allowing for more rapid technical change. To transpose the successful Asian experience to the African countries will require the pursuit of macroeconomic and sectoral policies that do not discriminate against agriculture together with more efficient investments in agricultural support services and human capital. Policy reforms introduced in African countries since the early 1980s are creating an environment more conducive to productive uses of food aid (for example, by reconstructing decaying physical infrastructure such as feeder roads), although overall progress on these reforms has been slower than expected. As long as recipients do not use food aid to postpone necessary but difficult policy reforms and investments in agriculture, and as long as food aid is not made unpredictable by donors' political agendas, such assistance can make an important contribution to growth.

External capital and poverty alleviation. Perhaps the most important declared objective of donor aid programs is to reduce poverty in recipient countries. Poverty alleviation measures include not only direct welfare transfers but also investments in social amenities such as health, education, drinking water, and nutrition programs. These programs improve individual welfare and help to slow down population growth, which is an important contributor to the deepening of poverty in many parts of the developing world. In fact, by investing in social services, recipient countries also achieve their growth objectives: these services help upgrade the quality of human capital, which is essential for sound economic growth. In this sense growth and equity objectives do not conflict — they move in tandem, and the failure to address one ultimately inhibits the other.

To define the relationship between aid and poverty alleviation, we first summarize the country experiences and then outline the role aid can play in ameliorating poverty.

The growth pattern of countries suggests that, with some exceptions, growth was impressive until 1980 and then it slowed down, especially in the African and Latin

American countries. During their growth phases, most countries expanded employment and invested in education and health. However, in countries where income growth and public expenditures were unsustainable, as in Mexico, or where public expenditures were not backed by adequate growth, as in Tanzania, there were sharp reversals for the poor, in terms of both falling incomes and access to social services. As Collier has shown, in Tanzania, despite the rhetoric of participation, real rural living standards declined at an average annual rate of 2.5 percent and real urban income by 4.5 percent between 1969 and 1983. Per capita real private consumption fell by 43 percent between 1973 and 1984. Moreover, the government was unable to sustain its impressive investment in social sectors as the economy collapsed. In Mexico, stabilization and restructuring of the economy have halved the real wage, increased malnutrition, and forced sharp cutbacks in expenditures on health and education.

In contrast, the Asian countries have maintained their growth momentum and have continued to register declines in poverty. Between 1970 and 1985, mean per capita income in Thailand, Pakistan, Sri Lanka, and India increased by about 2 percent a year and the incidence of poverty fell by around 1.1 percent (World Bank 1990b). Within countries the record of poverty reduction and expansion of social services was quite different; this is best illustrated by comparing Pakistan and Sri Lanka. In Pakistan, despite the impressive reduction in poverty, there has been little improvement in social indicators of well-being. Between 1962 and 1984, the average annual income in Pakistan increased by 2.2 percent, of which the poor's share was 1.4 percent. There was also impressive growth of 6.9 percent a year in the agricultural real wage between 1980 and 1987. However, Pakistan's social indicators were dismal: in 1987 life expectancy was 55 years, infant mortality was 109 per thousand, and primary enrollment for boys was 55 percent and for girls an abysmal 32 percent. In Sri Lanka, however, social well-being was exceptional given its per capita income level: life expectancy was 70 years, infant mortality was 33 per thousand, and primary school enrollment for boys was 104 percent and for girls 102 percent. Sri Lanka's growth strategy, however, has reduced poverty (measured in income) less than Pakistan's has. In contrast to Pakistan, Sri Lanka's average income grew by 0.9 percent in the 1963-82 period, the poor's share in it was 0.5 percent, and the agricultural real wage actually fell 0.3 percent. Clearly, aid programs to Pakistan should stress more investment in the social sector to further increase efficiency of investment and growth and improve income opportunities for the poor, while in Sri Lanka the emphasis should be on greater employment-generating investment.

What is the donor record regarding the choice of strategies, programs, and projects to benefit the poor? The case studies show that much of the poverty alleviation content of aid programs was indirect, through investments in rural infrastructure that benefited the poor. Much more could have been done by directly addressing the poor. This situation is now being rectified. For example, in Pakistan, the World Bank has carried out extensive studies of the social sector, which have paved the way for substantial lending that will improve Pakistan's social indicators to complement its poverty-reducing growth strategy.

In addition to helping shape the long-term investment patterns, the donors can also encourage less costly (in terms of its effects on the poor) structural adjustment. In most countries, the poor are concentrated in agriculture: adjustment lending could thus encourage improvements in agricultural terms of trade following exchange rate realignments. To the extent that the poor do not benefit from price changes, nutrition programs could be put in place. Also, fiscal adjustment could be fine-tuned and closely supervised to minimize cuts in primary education and basic health programs that benefit the poor most. Indeed, given the massive fiscal adjustment needed in many countries, poverty reduction objectives may make it necessary to bring the issue of defense expenditure on the agenda in the dialogue between donors and recipients.

Finally, to adequately address poverty, it is crucial to have reliable and updated information about the poor, their sources of income, and their patterns of consumption. Gathering such information on a regular basis is costly in terms of both financial and human resources, and beyond the reach of many poor countries. An important donor contribution would be to help finance and carry out surveys for gathering such information. The multilateral agencies, such as the World Bank, could monitor poverty indexes on a regular basis as part of their overall economic reporting on their borrowers.

The instability of capital flows. Private and official capital flows to developing countries have been so unpredictable that virtually every author in this volume has emphasized the importance of increasing domestic resource mobilization to ensure greater stability in the rate of investment. Lele and Agarwal, Nabi and Hamid, and Handoussa, in their studies on India, Pakistan, and Egypt, respectively, show how political motives often dominated aid programs and resulted in considerable instability in flows. US food and financial aid (in real terms) declined sharply in the mid-1960s for geopolitical reasons, even when recipients were undergoing major economic reforms and continued assistance would have given them the necessary financial security to continue with industrial and trade liberalization. Sudden increases were just as disruptive as sharp cuts. Pakistan's accession to the Central Treaty Organization (CENTO) and the Southeast Asia Treaty Organization (SEATO) in 1955, for example, led to a large increase in US assistance for nearly a decade. US aid to Pakistan fell sharply after the 1971 civil war in East Pakistan, reaching an all-time low of $50 million in 1980-81. With the Soviet invasion of Afghanistan and Ayatollah Khomeini's seizure of power in Iran in 1979, however, total US aid commitments to Pakistan increased again, reaching nearly $1.7 billion for the period from 1982-87. This increase may have led Pakistan to postpone budget trimmings and domestic resource mobilization efforts and may therefore have contributed to its current fiscal difficulties.

Similarly, Egypt, at the crossroads of superpower interests, has had important strategic ties with the Soviet Union and the United States during different periods. Handoussa writes that from the mid-1950s to the mid 1970s, Egypt accounted for 20 percent of Soviet trade and aid flows and for 29 percent of its military sales. By the late 1970s, however, the United States had succeeded in neutralizing the Soviet influence. Egypt's diplomatic rapprochement with the West following the 1973 war with Israel and Anwar Sadat's attempts at economic liberalization in 1977 led to a massive increase in Western aid, with *net* inflows averaging $1.5 billion annually from 1978 to 1984. Egypt's experience shows that playing competing donors off one another helps to maintain overall aid volume.

Unfortunately, bilateral aid is usually tied to the condition that recipients buy the equipment and commodities, follow the technical advice, and use the shipping lanes of the donor. The technologies accompanying aid from such diverse donors are very different and can adversely affect the overall development strategy. The high cost of tied bilateral aid is recounted in several of the papers presented in this volume.

The discontinuity and unpredictability of aid has set back recipients' development strategies by cutting short their investment projects and adjustment policies (such as those to liberalize industrial and trade regimes) and preventing them from making the necessary long-term commitments to social services that could help alleviate poverty. In fact, large fluctuations in aid resources can result in irresponsible policies. For example, a government may go on an aid-financed spending binge to gain quick popularity. The programs, hastily thrown together, may be ill conceived and, in any case, my not be viable given local resources. When aid is withdrawn, countries are left with ill-designed programs that are politically difficult to close down. Many of the country studies presented in this volume contain such scenarios. In his chapter on Tanzania, Paul Collier argues that recipients should treat aid "booms" the same way they treat other commodity booms. Following the permanent-income hypothesis, they should recognize that both kinds of booms are short-term phenomena and are best used productively to increase long-term internal capacity for growth. This approach will usually involve donors working closely with governments to invest in infrastructure projects and in programs that improve the quality of the work force. These are important ingredients in creating an environment that enables the private sector eventually to play a leading role in development.

The instability in bilateral assistance has, to some extent, been checked by the more stable multilateral flows of the World Bank and other official multilateral agencies, as John Mellor and William Masters point out. Projects and programs left unfinanced because of bilateral withdrawal have often been completed with financing from multilateral institutions. At its best, the World Bank has also helped offset the small-country bias of bilateral aid by assisting large, poor countries. For example, India received substantial assistance from the World Bank's concessional window, the IDA, under Robert McNamara's leadership in the 1970s even though India's relations with the United States (the World Bank's major shareholder) has deteriorated in the wake of the 1971 war with Pakistan and US bilateral aid had declined to a trickle. The World Bank similarly expanded its lending to Thailand in the 1970s to compensate for declining US assistance following the Vietnam War, as Narongchai Akrasanee notes.

Commercial capital flows too have been volatile, and their instability has affected the Latin American countries the most. After lending indiscriminately to projects of questionable quality in the 1970s, private banks have been reluctant to lend new capital to Latin America since 1982. José Antonio Ocampo points out that despite relatively sound economic management, Colombia has suffered from inadequate access to private commercial finance because of this "Latin syndrome" of the private banks. Since the process of transition from official capital to private commercial flows has been temporarily arrested, if not reversed altogether, in countries such as Mexico, Brazil, and Colombia, official multilateral agencies like the IMF and the World Bank have become increasingly important — an issue explored more fully in our discussion of debt below.

Swings in policy advice and "fads." Over the past four decades, theories of development have undergone a substantial change as knowledge about complex development objectives and processes has grown. A fact frequently overlooked in discussions of aid effectiveness, but pointed out succinctly by the contributors to this volume, is that as the consensus on development theories shifted, donor advice itself underwent big swings — from import substitution in the 1960s and poverty alleviation in the 1970s, to policy reform and export orientation in the early 1980s, and back to poverty alleviation in the late 1980s, with the issues of women in development and the environment added on. Mellors and Masters contend that at times these swings degenerated into "fads."

These shifts in focus reflect several factors. In part, they reflect donor efforts to understand the development process. However, a three-to four year lag separates the establishment of a consensus on a policy theme among donors and its translation into projects and programs in recipient countries. Meanwhile, the intellectual consensus shifts to another policy theme. Aid rhetoric and practice therefore diverge, leading to the charge of aid faddism by recipients. For example, until the late 1970s, donors continued to promote development projects in recipient countries while the intellectual consensus was to focus on important domestic policy failures and developments in the international economic environment. In the 1980s, aid bureaucracies finally caught up with the intellectual debate and a wholesale shift toward structural adjustment and internal policy reform took place. But it appears to have gone too far: in the pursuit of policy-based lending, donors moved financial and human resources away from project assistance, impeding implementation of critical projects.

The policy swings also reflect the need of aid-dispensing institutions to appeal to aid lobbies that are effective in mustering resources from donor governments. For example, the recent doubling of the World Bank's capitalization reflects US congressional support for the bank's emphasis on private initiative, the free market, and environmental and women's issues. However, as has been argued in this book, if donors bear in mind that it is not the quantity of aid that matters but its quality, which includes stability and predictability in aid flows, there will be less need to appeal to the passing whims of the aid lobbies.

Aid dispensing organizations also contribute to the policy swings through a tendency to follow "top-down" policy initiatives that appear faddish. They could make better use of the considerable pool of technical and management talent they possess to prepare organization staff as well as recipients to incorporate new ideas into existing lending strategies. Flexibility in implementing new policies in different cultural settings is also essential.

The appearance of faddishness in donor policy erodes credibility among recipients and disrupts the development process — especially since recipients have to cope with their own vested interests built around the donor fads of the previous era. As knowledge of the development process improves over time, the challenge for donors is to maintain a stable policy focus within a consistent framework of assistance for projects and for macroeconomic reform. This strategy will help make donors' policy advice credible and will ensure more willingness by recipients to undertake reform in areas where past policy mistakes need correction.

* * * * * *

Some concluding lessons

The country experiences with aid and external financing presented in this book suggest some important lessons for recipients (developing countries), for donors (developed countries and international organizations), and for international private lenders and investors. We present these lessons in three groups:

Lessons for recipients.

1. *Aid is not the most important element in development, but it can play an important role in assisting governments committed to growth-oriented economic policies.* The most important factor is the existence of a long-term growth strategy with a consistent macroeconomic framework to ensure that fiscal and trade deficits remain manageable and the exchange rate gives the right pricing signals. In this setting, aid and other external financing can help fill short-term resource gaps. Also, limited amounts of well-designed assistance can help improve recipients' capacity to plan policies and to prepare and implement projects, and help develop the critical physical and social capital that is needed to accelerate the growth rate.

2. *In the long run, external capital is not a substitute for fiscal reform and domestic resource mobilization.* Persistent fiscal and trade deficits are unsustainable and are strong signals of fundamental instability in the economy. External capital eventually dries up and, in combination with capital flight, leads to debt problems and economic stagnation. External borrowing should therefore be used to complement policies for reducing deficits and increasing domestic resource mobilization.

3. *Political commitment is essential for responsible macroeconomic management and policy reform: aid can help cushion painful adjustments.* Given current economic problems in many developing countries, sound macroeconomic management and policy reform require painful adjustments in the trade regime and the financial market, the creation of a conducive legal and fiscal climate for private business, and a reduction in subsidies to trim public expenditures. These reforms are likely to hurt long-established interests and therefore require a strong political commitment. Aid and external financing can help by providing a temporary cushion to soften the adjustment process.

4. *External financing that promotes outward-oriented policies achieves more rapid growth in GDP and employment than support for inward-oriented policies.* An outwardly oriented growth strategy will improve balance of payments and provide resources to invest in technology for future growth. Although there are exceptions,

most aid recipients have been more outward oriented than other developing countries. Aid, therefore, has played an important role, complementary to countries' own industrial and trade policies, in shaping sustainable long-term growth strategies. Country experience suggests that, as part of this strategy, developing countries should increase trade among themselves while continuing to expand their share in the protected OECD markets.

5. *Countries that have done well in overall economic performance are those that succeeded in tackling the complex problems of developing agriculture, which employs the bulk of the population at early stages of development.* Agricultural growth was the major instrument for reducing the proportion of the population living in poverty and providing cheap food for workers. Much aid has gone into strengthening agricultural infrastructure, institutions and technological innovations, which have contributed to agricultural growth. This role of aid will continue to be important.

6. *Although food aid can create disincentives for domestic food production, a well-conceived food aid program can maintain consumption of poor and vulnerable groups while programs are implemented to increase domestic production.* Recurring droughts and foreign exchange shortages can be a major hurdle in early stages of development and can increase the vulnerability of the poor by increasing the price of food. Food aid can increase the internal supply of affordable food during periods when technological change in agriculture (with its long gestation lags) is occurring.

7. *The key to both growth and equity is investment in human capital.* Access to universal primary and secondary education, health care, and water, together with adequate transport and communications networks, is essential for broad-based participation of the poor in the growth process. By providing technical and financial assistance to these sectors, aid can make an important contribution toward brightening countries' growth prospects and improving equity.

8. Programs for women in development and the environment can benefit from external financial and technical assistance. Notwithstanding donors' passing whims, providing development opportunities to women (whose situation needs to be addressed in development programs) and managing the eco-environment should be important concerns of policymakers in developing countries. External financing can help initiate programs in these areas suitable to particular cultural and economic conditions. Donor agencies' technical know-how and their experience of what works and what does not can be quite valuable in designing such programs.

Lessons for official donors

1. In an unfavorable policy regime, charaterized by serious distortions, aid can harm a country by aggravating distortions and imbalances. By providing massive capital in periods of poor policy regimes, donors can exacerbate serious distortions and strengthen vested interests in inappropriate policies, making both trends difficult to reverse. Aid should be given only when countries are committed to sustainable growth-oriented policies.

2. *Supporting countries committed to policy reform will improve their future access to commercial capital markets, promote growth, and free up more resources for the less-developed countries.* As more countries realize their economic potential through policy reform, their access to commercial markets will improve, allowing donors to concentrate on those countries where acute poverty will require continued assistance.

3. *Aid programs are important in helping to create an environment that enables the private sector in recipient countries to play a leading role in development.* This objective requires donors to work closely with recipient governments to build infrastructure and improve the quality of the labor force. These, along with sound macroeconomic management, are the vital ingredients in an enabling environment.

4. *The success of aid depends on its stability and predictability. Donors should exercise constant vigilance to ensure that capital flows are stable.* Abruptly turning the aid taps on and off leads to perverse behavior by recipients, who may treat aid as a temporary windfall and go on a spending binge that can actually retard growth.

5. *Whatever the immediate motives for aid, the long-term development consequences must be kept in view.* Unfortunately too much aid is given for strategic and commercial objectives, and too little for long-term economic growth and development. Greater public accountability regarding uses of aid as well as more public awareness of aid-related issues in both donor and recipient countries will help in spelling out consistent objectives for giving aid.

6. *External financing can encourage the adoption of growth paths that alleviate poverty.* Through policy dialogues related to the provision of long-term financing and short-term adjustment lending, donors can encourage investment patterns and protect public expenditures that support the poor. Investing in human resources (education and health) in the long run and providing nutrition support to the poor in the short run will facilitate short-term adjustments and promote poverty-reducing growth.

7. *Humanitarian aid is necessary for the least-developed countries even if policies are distorted.* In the least-developed countries, which have substantial policy distortions, large concentrations of poor, and no commitment to reform, extensive aid programs may be suspended but donors must continue to provide humanitarian aid for ethical reasons, as well as to create a climate for future policy dialogue on reform.

8. *Donors should avoid rapid changes in focus and the stigma of fads.* New issues such as women in development and the environment should not be added on to programs hurriedly; such a move strengthens the perception that they are passing fads. These important issues should be incorporated into existing programs and projects gradually and should be tailored to suit local cultural and economic conditions. To encourage recipient participation, donors must first create a climate of cooperation through open discussion.

9. *Coordination among donors can result in better aid programs.* Aid coordination among donors has many advantages. It helps prevent a multiplicity of projects in any one sector and overburdening the recipients' nascent public service and administration, and it promotes consistency in policy dialogue. However, care should be taken that donor coordination is not seen by recipients as collusive behavior designed to dictate political or strategic agenda.

10. *Aid tying in bilateral programs can work against the development objective.* Bilateral aid tying is unpopular and can lead to suboptimal use of aid funds by promoting inefficient capital and technology transfer. It also strengthens self-serving aid lobbies in both donor and recipient countries.

11. *In the long run, sustainable capital and technology transfer from developed to developing countries is best done by promoting trade rather than aid.* Donors can strengthen this process and discourage aid dependency by reducing trade barriers against developing countries and by removing restrictions on the transfer of technology.

Lessons for international private lenders and investors

1. *Commercial banks need to develop more effective mechanisms for evaluating the longer-term macroeconomic, sectoral, and subsectoral effects of their loans and for monitoring their implementation.* Private capital has often been lent without adequate knowledge of the circumstances in which investments are made. Not surprisingly, past experience shows that large amounts of private capital have not necessarily been used more effectively than official assistance, as is usually believed, and may have caused serious Dutch-disease problems. Unless commercial banks invest in a better understanding of borrower circumstances, there is a real danger that a debt crisis may recur if lending resumes.

2. *Lessening the debt burden (through reduction or suspension) will help restore growth and recovery of debt in the long run.* Countries with a serious commitment to improve the investment climate have made a good case for debt restructuring to allow for growth. Without additional resources for investment, growth prospects will remain slim and the debt impasse will be perpetuated.

3. *Investors should sharpen their ability to assess risk in developing countries as a way to bridge the gap between the debtor countries' perception of their economic potential and that of investors.* It takes two to bridge this credibility gap. While developing countries must do all they can to restructure their economies to improve the investment climate, investors should improve their ability to read economic signals and respond quickly to opportunities. Multinational lending institutions that continually assess the economic prospects and performance of their borrowers can provide the information needed to build investor confidence.

* * * * * *

Notes

1. These include Argentina, Bolivia, Brazil, Chile, Colombia, Costa Rica, Ecuador, Jamaica, Mexico, Peru, Uruguay, Venezuela, Ivory Coast, Nigeria, Philippines, Morocco, and Yugoslavia. See World Bank (1988b).

2. Given India's population of 800 million, its ODA receipts (as well as those of China, not covered in this volume), in per capita terms and as a percentage of GNP, have been minuscule compared with those of the smaller African and Asian countries. India has received less than $2 per capita and 2 percent of GNP in most years, compared with $20-$50 per capita and 8-15 percent of GNP in Tanzania (with a population of 24 million), Senegal (7 million), and Sri Lanka (16 million).

3. Although the numbers presented here are estimates, the argument is, by and large, a valid one.

4. The US share of total bilateral and multilateral ODA declined from about one-half in the mid-1960s to less than a quarter by the end of the 1980s. The decline in the US share in total bilateral ODA from the OECD countries was even sharper — from nearly two-thirds during the 1960s to a quarter by the late 1970s. The US share rose again to about one-third by the mid-1980s, but mainly because the United States reduced its contributions to multilateral ODA while other donors increased their shares of multilateral ODA. In the aftermath of the Vietnam War and the subsequent changes in US strategic interests, the United States directed its smaller ODA share to only a handful of strategically important countries. In 1987, nearly 60 percent of total US economic and military assistance went to Israel, Egypt, Turkey, Pakistan and El Salvador.

5. In this chapter we have used the *World Development Report* data presented in Table 1.1, as well as information contained in the country studies (which is mostly derived from national sources) Because of problems of comparability between the two data sets, we have made selective use of both in order to present as consistent and accurate a picture as possible.

6. The so-called Dutch disease refers to the contraction or stagnation of traded goods in response to a favorable shock from either a resource discovery or an increase in the price of a commodity export (oil, for instance). This windfall causes a reallocation of productive factors, which initially move from other activities into the booming sector. Then, because of increased spending on nontraded goods, factors of production move from traded goods into the nontraded goods sectors.

References

Anand, Sudhir, and Ravi Kanbur. (1987) 'Price Policy and Basic Needs Provision: Intervention and Achievement in Sri Lanka.' Discussion Paper no. 74. Warwick: University of Warwick, Development Economics Research Center.

Cassen, Robert, and Associates. (1986) *Does Aid Work? Report to an Intergovernmental Task Force*. Oxford: Oxford University Press.

Cornia, G.A., R. Jolly, and F. Stewart, eds. (1987) *Adjustment with a Human Face*. Oxford: Clarendon Press.

Hancock, Graham. (1989) *The Lords of Poverty: The Power, Prestige, and Corruption of the International Aid Business*. New York: Atlantic Monthly Press.

Lele, Uma, ed. (1990) *Aid of African Agriculture: Lessons from Two Decades of Donor Experience*.Washington, D.C.: World Bank.

Lele, Uma, and Ellen Hanak, eds. Forthcoming.*The Politics of Agricultural Policy in Africa*. Washington, D.C.: World Bank.

Lewis, John. (1979) 'Reviving American Aid to India: Motivation, Scale, Uses, and Constraints.' In *India: A Rising Middle Power*, edited by John Mellor, 301-24. Boulder, Colo.: Westview Press.

Organization for Economic Cooperation and Development (OECD). (1985) *Twenty-five Years of Development Cooperation: A Review*. Paris.

World Bank. (1988a) *Adjustment Lending: An Evaluation of Ten Years of Experience*. Policy and Research Series no. 1. Country Economics Department. Washington, D.C.

— (1988b) *World Development Report 1988*. New York: Oxford University Press.

— (1989a) *Sub-Saharan Africa: From Crisis to Sustainable Growth*. Washington, D.C.

— (1989b) *World Development Report 1989*. New York: Oxford University Press.

— (1990a) *Women in Pakistan: A Social and Economic Strategy*. World Bank Country Study. Washington, D.C.

— (1990b) *World Development Report 1990*. New York: Oxford University Press.

26.   Foreign Private Investment
Jan S. Hogendorn

Investment from private sources abroad is an important alternative for LDCs that wish to invest more domestically than they are able to save. About $16 billion to $20 billion came in this form beginning in the mid-1980s. The amount has fallen because of the debt crisis.[32]

Such private investment O' may be portfolio, that is, the purchase by foreigners of stocks or bonds but not involving a controlling ownership. It may also be direct, meaning the creation or acquisition of capital assets that are owned fully or in amounts large enough to imply control. The dividing line between the two is not always very clear. Australia has a 25% minimum figure of equity ownership for the term direct investment to apply. France uses 20%; the United States, Germany, and Sweden use 10%. Great Britain and Japan make a value judgement and do not employ a fixed dividing line.

Portfolio investment

At the turn of the century private, nonbank portfolio investment was important, with investors in developed countries actively buying the shares and bonds of firms in the United States, Canada, Australia, New Zealand, Argentina, Chile, and others.[33] Britain was the chief source of the flows, investing 5% of its GNP abroad from 1870 to 1913. The funds, over one-quarter of all British saving, were used especially for railways and utilities (nearly two-thirds of the total) and for many types of heavy industry. There was also a vigorous government bond market involving the securities of national and regional governments. Both for private and government borrowing, the interest rates on the bonds were generally fixed and the maturities very long; 99-year bonds were not uncommon. After World War I, the United States emerged as the major source of long-term capital before the balance swung to borrowing by governments.

There had been some troubles in this market for a long time, with repudiations in Peru and Turkey in the 1870s and in Argentina and Brazil in the 1880s and 1890s. These did little harm, but the financial disasters of the 1930s were much more general. After Germany's default in 1932, many LDCs followed suit. In all of Latin America only Argentina continued to service its debt during the Great Depression. The result was severe restriction of this market, and for many years after World War II, private investors understandably considered portfolio investment in the LDCs a highly risky proposition. There are few recourses for a private holder of an LDC government bond if default occurs because the principle of sovereign risk permits a government to disallow suits against itself within its own borders. Neither were the LDCs very receptive to portfolio investment, which was discouraged with high taxation, foreign exchange restriction, and limits on the types of shares that could be held by foreigners.

From *ECONOMIC DEVELOPMENT*, 2nd Edition by Jan S. Hogendorn. Copyright © 1992 by HarperCollins Publishers Inc. Reprinted by permission.

As a result, such flows were only half a billion dollars or less annually in the 1960s and up to 1975, often as little as one-tenth the figure for direct investment. There was a revival from 1977 to 1979, mostly with bond issues in the Eurobond market and in the national markets of Switzerland and Japan. In 1978, bonds floated by a small number of highly reputable LDCs reached nearly 15% of the value of all international bond issues, involving a useful $5 billion. With the debt crisis of the early 1980s, however, this portfolio revival went into retreat to some 3.5% of all international bond issues in 1983 and 1984. (It should be remembered that the LDCs have *indirect* access to the bond markets through the bond-financed lending of the World Bank and the regional development banks.) The international bond market has continued in the doldrums, with bond sales by LDC governments in 1986 only $4.6 billion. Only 18 countries did all the borrowing, and of these just 8 in Asia and Europe issued 80% of the bonds. Currency uncertainty and high risk are the two main reasons for the slow growth of this capital market.

Direct investment: the multinationals

Private direct investment has in most years been much larger than portfolio investment as well as much more controversial because it involves the activities of the so-called multinationals. The common abbreviations for these are MNE for multinational enterprise, MNF for multinational firm, and MNC for multinational corporation.[34] Such enterprises usually have a home base with operations abroad. The UN and many scholars argue that the world *multinational* is thus not fully appropriate and prefer the term *transnational*.

There are about 10,000 such firms holding assets in more than one nation; about half have their home in Europe and a quarter in the United States. Over 60% have only one or two branches abroad, and only about 400 MNEs do much the greater part of all foreign investment. The United States is the biggest investor, with Britain second and Japan third. The top ten firms in 1986 by market value of shares, not including banks and utilities, were IBM, Exxon, GE, Toyota, GM, Royal Dutch, Daimler-Benz, DuPont, Philip Morris, Sears and British Petroleum. Their operations are imposingly large in scale: the foreign sales of affiliates of U.S. firms in the late 1970s were over five times larger than total U.S. exports at that time; foreign sales of manufactured goods by U.S. MNEs were as much as 20% of the domestic sales of these same firms; for every four workers employed in U.S. manufacturing, one was employed abroad by an affiliate of a U.S. firm.[35] The United Nations estimates that worldwide MNEs employ 65 million people, about 3% of the planetary labor force. U.S. MNEs employed 6.5 million people abroad in 1984, 32% of them in the LDCs.

Although three-fourths of this accumulated private direct investment has been in the developed world and only a quarter in the LDCs, its significance for development is large, and in the 1970s the LDC share was growing.* New multinational investment in these countries reached $19.7 billion in 1982, up from an average of $2.8 billion annually in the early 1970s.[36] The figure fell to only $9.9 billion in 1986. After some recovery to

---

* Before World War II, when many of today's LDCs were colonies, about two-thirds of all foreign direct investment was in these countries.

$14 billion in 1988, it sank back to $10 billion in 1989. In real terms, such investment would have to be more than doubled to reach its earlier peaks.

There is, interestingly, some multinational investment flowing from one LDC to another. Examples of moderately large investors are Brazil (active in the Middle East and West Africa), India (active in Indonesia and Malaysia), Hong Kong, Singapore, and South Korea. Brazil and Hong Kong are in the top 15 providers of multinational investment. LDC multinationals are said sometimes to provide more labor-intensive technologies and to be politically more acceptable than their developed-country brethren.[37]

The investment of MNEs in developing countries has most often followed the growth of new markets in these countries for goods where the firms' superior technology and popular brand names lend advantages over domestic firms. Rather commonly, they seek to establish operations inside the protectionist barriers of an LDC pursuing an "import substitution" strategy. Generally, they prefer investing where markets are relatively similar to those at home or where the combination of factor inputs is comparable to those the firm is already skilled at handling. MNEs have no special advantage in designing products or marketing goods in environments far different from those they face at home, nor in organizing and managing factors of production when the mix and qualities are far different from what they are used to. That is one important reason why such firms either avoid very poor countries or address themselves only to the middle-and upper-class markets in these countries familiar to them from their home operation.

Less frequently, though more in the news, MNEs have sought new sources of inputs. Examples include minerals and oil to offset declining reserves at home and to capture part of the rents on especially valuable deposits. Labor also can be an attraction, as when a multinational moves an operation overseas in search of cheaper wages, thereafter exporting the product back to the home market and elsewhere. As a company's multinational operations proliferate, the knowledge available to it about other markets increases, as does its confidence in that knowledge, which now comes at low cost. This is a reason why MNE reactions to changing economic conditions are both more rapid and tuned more finely than they were two decades ago.[38]

About a third of MNE investment has been in manufacturing, another third in oil, a tenth in mining, while the remainder, just under a quarter, is in the service sector, the most rapidly growing of them all. Taking the LDCs as a whole, it is commonly found that about 30% of their manufacturing output is produced by the multinationals. Sometimes it is much higher, for example, 63% in Singapore and 70% in Zambia. Often LDCs state that they do not welcome MNE operations in services, but such operations can be helpful to a country's export and general development effort if they increase efficiency, as for example when the telephone system works.

In general, the poorer the country, the smaller its domestic market, the lower its stock of skilled labor, the less committed it is to private enterprise, and the less stable its political-economic environment, the less private investment it receives. Most foreign direct investment is heavily concentrated in countries that have promoted export-led growth. Just five countries, Brazil, Mexico, Singapore, South Africa, and Malaysia, obtain the largest part of it. The least goes to sub-Saharan Africa, where the figure is falling and only about 10% of the total in the mid-1980s. Although the information is fragmentary and the range of data is wide, the share of exports accounted for by foreign majority-owned affiliates includes Hong Kong 10%, all of Latin America about 20%, Taiwan over 20%, South Korea over 15% to 31%, Mexico 25% to 34%, Brazil 43% to 51%, and Singapore 70% to 84%.[39] The amounts involved were once the largest form of private flow until the surge of private bank lending. As bank lending subsided during the 1980s debt crisis, direct investment again gained proportional ground.

Contrary to the early work on the subject, the most important benefits brought to the LDCs by the multinationals are not directly associated with the capital transfer itself. These benefits are wide in scope. The investment may make available, in larger quantity and better quality, goods and services formerly high in price so that consumers gain. The government may garner extra tax revenue form the expanded operations of foreign firms. Additional domestic investment may be stimulated because the new foreign operations open up profitable opportunities for supplying them with components or raw materials. The multinational may reduce production costs through its coordination of marketing and its ability in planning. MNEs may bring nonmarket, cost-reducing externalities to their hosts, including the technical knowledge that flows to the branches of MNEs, managerial ability, organizational competence, and the capacity to avoid the waste and inefficiency that might be present if the project were forced to depend on indigenous talent alone. These nonmarket advantages, especially the transfer of knowledge in all its forms, are now emphasized by most scholars as the key explanation why multinationals prefer to operate in an LDC themselves rather than licensing production to local firms. Some of these advantages will, of course, accrue as profit repatriated abroad by the MNE, but some will be reinvested or will be paid to local factors of production. Even when profit is repatriated, it must be kept in mind that no outflow will occur unless a profit is actually earned by the MNE, unlike debt where the outflow of interest and repayment of principal will occur in good times or bad. Thus countries hosting MNEs are less vulnerable to economic shocks than they would be if all capital were obtained from debt financing. Finally, MNEs can often export more easily from their host country because of their distribution and marketing networks. If they do wish to export some of their production from LDCs, they may become influential lobbyists for world free trade because tariffs and quotas in developed-country markets would other wise interfere with these plans. A country with little clout in the U.S. Congress or parliaments of the EC when it pushes for free trade may find it has puissant allies in its corps of multinationals.

Even the role of the multinationals in investment itself does not primarily involve the direct transfer of capital into an LDC. A large amount of capital is transferred by means of commercial bank loans to LDC subsidiaries of MNEs. To a significant degree, often more so than the direct and indirect capital transfers, MNEs also add to saving by building retained earnings, which may be reinvested in the operation. Much of this saving is still foreign, done by the corporate shareholders in the parent country, who receive lower dividends than they would have otherwise. (In the figures for foreign direct investment, these reinvested earnings are included. They generally make up about half the total.) To the degree that multinationals serve to raise local income, they also play a part in stimulating *domestic* saving.

MULTINATIONAL ACTIVITIES ARE SAID TO "FILL GAPS"

Economists sometimes speak of multinationals "filling gaps" in economic development. Their gap models usually emphasize the role of foreign companies in (1) bringing saving from abroad so that domestic investment can be larger than domestic saving; (2) generating foreign exchange receipts and thus filling a gap between the desired earnings of foreign exchange and what a country could otherwise acquire through exports, aid, and so forth in the absence of the multinationals; (3) alleviating the shortage of managerial and technical skills; and (4) mobilizing new government revenue through taxation of the multinational, thus filling a gap between the revenues a government wants to expend and what it can acquire through local taxation.

Benefits and costs of multinational operations

Ownership by foreign firms is much more visible both physically and politically than are bond holdings and bank loans. This makes the operations of multinationals a highly controversial topic, involving a wide variety of issues, some of which are only vaguely related to saving, investment, management, and technology. Yet a country cannot have these inflows without facing the other issues as well, so it is convenient to take them up here. LDCs have indeed gone through a long stage of learning how to deal with multinationals. The early "acceptance" school of thought gave way to "rejection" in many countries. Nowadays an "assertive pragmatism" marks policy in many LDCs, with total acceptance on the rise and rejection, although still found, sinking in importance.[40]

What positive and negative arguments can be made for the operations of these firms? Concerning their transfer of capital into a recipient LDC, the "normal" microeconomic argument in its favor is that foreign investment benefits both parties to the transaction. For the LDCs in particular, the rise in real income is greater than the profits earned by the investor and repatriated to the foreign country. The argument is presented in simple diagrammatic form in Figure 1.[41] A rich and capital-abundant country's marginal product of capital (MP of K) is shown by the downward-sloping line relating to origin O on the left side of the diagram; a poor and capital-short country's MP of K is drawn relating to origin O' on the right. Assume a large stock of capital (OK) in the rich country. If profits per unit (OA) are equal to the marginal product of capital ($KB = OA$), then total returns to domestic capital are $OABK$. Assume that the quantity of capital ($O'K$) in the poor country is small. Total returns to domestic capital in the poor country are thus $O'KCD$. Because the area under the MP curve is the return to all factors, then $O'KCJ$ is the total income earned, and this minus the return to capital is the return to other factors $O'KCJ - O'KCD = CJD$. This return will be wages if the model is limited to just the two factors, capital and labor.

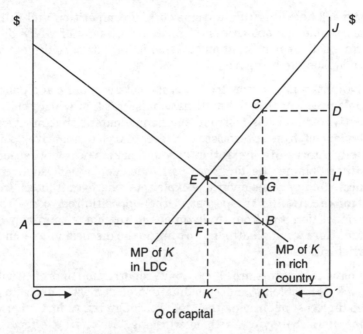

Figure 1   Advantages of MNE investment.

Now consider what happens if rich country owners of capital seek out the higher per unit returns in the LDC by making a transfer *KK'* of capital to the poor country, either by lending or direct investment (including reinvested earnings). Transferring that amount will equalize the return on capital in the two countries because the two MP curves cross there at *E*.

First, note the advantage to the rich country. Consider just the transferred capital *KK'*. Profits earned on that capital fall by *K'EGK*. There is a clear gain of *BEG*, thus providing the motive for the transfer from the investor's point of view. Indeed, the yield on U.S. investment in manufacturing in the LDCs has recently averaged about 19%, more than double the average yield in developed countries. The average risk on an individual investment in an LDC is higher, of course, but then the geographical diversification of the investments serves to spread it.[42]

Now consider the advantage to the poor country. It loses *K'EGK* either as interest on borrowing or profit repatriation on direct investment, but it gains *K'ECK* in greater total income, thus increasing its total income by *ECG*. The *world* is ahead by *BEG + ECG = ECB*.

Note the effects on income distribution. In the poor country, domestic capitalists find their returns reduced to *KGHO'*, but the real income of labor has risen to *EJH*, an increase of *ECDH*. Much of this rise is a transfer away from domestic capitalists to labor in the amount *GCDH*, but the rest *(ECG)* is a net addition to the incomes earned in the country receiving the capital.

The model portrayed here is within a framework of competition and full employment and ignores the possible monopolistic or oligopolistic behavior of MNEs discussed later. Yet it does make a salient point that on occasion is forgotten: Adding to capital where capital is scarce is likely to bring benefits.

Against these benefits must be weighed the costs, both economic and political. There is an active mythology concerning the multinationals, much of which, both pro and con, is politically motivated and has a strong emotional content that must be recognized. Hard-line defenders of free enterprise may see [nary] a negative, pointing to the overwhelming advantages of competition in free markets. The opposition, sometimes xenophobes with a "blame the foreigner" attitude, deplores foreign control over a country's resources and may see nefarious exploiters wherever it looks. Indeed, foreign firms *can* often make convenient scapegoats. Other opposition can come from local firms who fear the competition and from trade unions in the home country who claim that jobs are exported. Here we shall attempt to confine the discussion to economic analysis and forgo the rhetoric.

The major economic complaints are (1) excessive repatriation of profits with associated balance of payments problems and crowding out of domestic firms in local capital markets; (2) the high cost of enticing the MNEs through tax reduction or other means; (3) their monopolistic behavior, with overpricing, stultifying effects on domestic entrepreneurship and management that blunts local initiatives and displaces local firms, and political meddling that undermines sovereignty; (4) their overcharges for patents and technical knowledge through the use of an internal price system for transfers between branches of the same firm; (5) their marketing of inappropriate goods; and (6) their use of inappropriate technology. Next we expand on these accusations, weigh them, and allow the multinationals an opportunity for rebuttal.

Repatriation of profits. Repatriation of profits has been criticized as leading to lower levels of reinvestment in the country concerned, with attendant greater dependence on local capital markets and the crowding out of local borrowers. The repatriation involves foreign exchange, which has to be generated somehow. In an efficient economy with market-determined exchange rates and following the dictates of comparative advantage, this may not be a serious problem. Protectionism in the developed world plus artificial exchange rates in the LDCs defended by controls on currency movements may, however, mean that obtaining the necessary foreign exchange is not so easy.

A defender of the MNEs would argue that the fault lies with the controls and the protectionism rather than with the multinationals. If the MNE's investment is otherwise beneficial, then it makes much more sense to attack these problems directly. The defender would also point out that the sheer size of repatriated profits is not necessarily evidence of wrongdoing. All things being equal, one would expect profits to be higher where capital is in short supply, and indeed, predicted high returns should actually increase an LDC's leverage during the bargaining over entry by an MNE. A common measure of high profits — comparing repatriated earnings to new investment by a single MNE or by the multinationals as a group in a given year — is illegitimate, or so the defender would argue. Although this information is easily obtained from the balance of payments data, the comparison should instead be between repatriated earnings and the stock of capital accumulated from *previous* investment and on which the returns have been earned.

Another consideration is that the reinvested earnings of the multinational provides low-cost improvement for the balance of payments if the funds would otherwise have had to be borrowed abroad. In any case, these flows are not the only influence on the balance of payments; the positive increase in exports and decrease in imports caused by the MNE would also have to be considered.

As for the argument that crowding out of local investment will occur, MNEs and their supporters maintain that if the investment is otherwise beneficial, then it should be pursued. Any crowding out would be of investment with lower rates of return.

Cost of attracting multinationals. There is a cost to be considered whenever tax reductions, rebates, concessions, large investment allowances, low interest rates, cheap locations for factories, tariff protection, and public subsidies are granted to attract multinational companies to a particular LDC. For most MNEs, such breaks do not appear to provide the major lure.* More attractive are a large domestic market, cheap labor and raw materials, low inflation, steady growth, and market pricing. Unfortunately, many countries want to attract the investment of MNEs but are unable to offer these advantages. Thus a survey by the U.S. Commerce Department of U.S. branches of MNEs abroad showed 26% of them had been granted at least one incentive to invest. Of this group, 20% received tax breaks and 9% even got direct subsidies.[43] Given the intense competition among LDCs for MNE investment, it is conceivable that in the short run these costs could be larger than the economic benefits provided by the firms' operations, with resources shifted from more to less efficient uses. Consumers and taxpayers from a poor country would thus subsidize a firm from a rich one. Even though LDCs would learn from the experience, the dimension and longevity of the losses might be great. A code to harmonize these incentives among countries has been suggested but not adopted even though it probably makes good sense to reduce the availability of investment incentives. Some countries, Indonesia a prominent example, have done just that.

Monopolistic behavior. If there is price competition in world markets, we can define overpricing as

$$P_o = \frac{P_m - P_w}{P_w}$$

were P_m = the price charged by the MNE, P_w = the world price, and P_o = the percentage of overpricing.[44] There is no doubt that price discrimination of this sort is frequently found. It is, however, usually based on protection, as otherwise the differential could not be maintained. The defender of the MNEs would note that purely domestic firms (as opposed to multinationals) would also overprice if given the chance. In this sense, the LDC's own policies of protection lead to the exercise of market power. The

* A 1983 study by the Group of 30 found that tax breaks and investment subsidies were the primary attraction for only 13% of MNEs.

multinational might, of course, lobby to this end, especially when negotiating its initial entry to a country.

Worldwide monopoly overpricing is much rarer because an aspiring monopolist must face the potential competition from all countries, not just one. Some MNEs do appear to operate in a worldwide oligopolistic structure where they are able to utilize price discrimination based on product differentiation, proprietary technology, or some other secure asset. Different prices can be charged in different countries simply by ordering branch managers not to engage in unauthorized international trade. Even so, it is clear that the oligopolistic behavior of numerous industries in a national market (steel, autos, aircraft, ships, electronic goods) is very much less so when the firms face competition from other countries in LDC markets.

Still, the lessons of the past warn that LDC governments had better be vigilant and that, where it exists, uncontrolled behavior by a large and monopolistic MNE can be far from benevolent. Multinationals might attempt to bribe public officials for their benefit, Lockheed being a well-known example, or even conspire to overthrow governments, as with ITT's moves against Chilean president Allende in the 1970s. But the ITT case of 1973-1974 sparked worldwide protests and tightening up by both developed-country and LDC governments alike. A decade has brought greater experience and less naiveté; the ITT example now looks to be a low point rather than the trend. *(For another low point, see the box on the next page.)

Overcharging for patents and technical knowledge. The world trade in know-how is large — only $2.7 billion in 1965, but over $11 billion ten years later. Although most of this trade is within the developed world, the 10% or so between the developed countries and the LDCs can be a substantial percentage of the latter's export earnings and is more as a proportion of income than was spent by Europe, the United States, and Japan for imported technology during their periods of development. Over 11% of Mexico's export revenues, to take an example from a recent year, was paid out in royalties and fees for patents and technologies. Because the amounts involved are large, any potential for manipulation can be magnified in its effect.

Manipulation can arise because the payments often represent a transaction between a branch of a multinational firm in an LDC and another branch of the same firm somewhere abroad. Because the transaction is not on an open market, the real value is not easy to establish. The payment of whatever transfer price is chosen obviously boosts the year's profits for the branch doing the selling and reduces it in the branch doing the buying.† Often enough, the transfer price will be an honest one because it is in the MNE's interests to have an accurate profit yardstick to measure the success of its branches. A canny corporate treasurer can, however, try to achieve larger profits in countries with less stringent tax laws and lower profits where taxes are high through careful juggling of the transfer price. Many LDCs actually tax corporations at a lower

---

* Often enough the political pressures are the other way around, as in the attempts by Arab states to persuade the MNEs they host to embargo trade with Israel or moves by the United States to alter its firms' behavior in South Africa.

† The transfer pricing principle can also apply to the allocation of overhead expenditures within the firm.

rate than do developed countries, but the motive is still there if the shift avoids legal limits on profit repatriation, refutes charges by politicians and trade unions that high profits are being earned, or conceals these profits so as not to encourage competitors. Perhaps holdings of a weak currency can be minimized. Finally, if the government bases price controls on costs of production, then the transfer price can be used to raise costs and hence permitted higher prices. (The transfer price issue also arises in the shipment of goods between branches of a multinational firm or, for that matter between *any* indigenous firm and a foreign one. The price can be set with an eye on tariffs and other taxes. Overcharges for goods are usually more visible to the tax authorities by comparison with the question of a proper value for patents and technology.)

BE ON GUARD: THE STORY OF THE UNITED FRUIT COMPANY

It is salutary to trace the extraordinary life of the United Fruit Company to see why a country's public servants had best be on guard.[45] Central America was the fabled preserve of Unifruit, or *El Pulpo*, "the Octopus," as it was called. Close to a monopoly in the United States, its Norteamericano managers achieved virtually a monopsony in Central America from Panama to Guatemala, where at its peak it captured 92% of the business. Unifruit owned port facilities, the railways, and even the electric utilities in some capital cities. Its Great White Fleet of streamers, made economic by their lucrative mail contract, controlled the shipping trade of several countries. Unifruit often operated the communications system. It made unsecured personal "loans" to dictators, including among the known ones $1 million to Guatemala's Ubico, whereupon the company's taxes were sharply reduced, and $1.25 million to Lopez in Honduras. It held large tracts of unplanted land, at one point 95% of its total holdings of 3 million in Guatemala (42% of the country's arable land), apparently to reduce the potential for competition. Typically it paid tiny taxes and was almost exempt from import duties. It massaged its Washington connections to advantage. In the 1950s, Sullivan and Crowell, the law firm of Secretary of State John Foster Dulles, represented the company, and CIA director Allen Dulles was on the board of trustees. A propaganda film, *Why the Kremlin Hates Bananas*, showed El Pulpo fighting in the front lines of the Cold War.

Some would say this is what happens when MNEs are allowed to operate in a free market, but the point is different: A free market was *not* allowed to operate. Economic and political power were used by the company to eliminate competition, to keep taxes low, and to keep politicians pliable. In doing so, Unifruit found willing allies in the military or in the wealthy oligarchic hierarchy. The behavior was certainly not permanent, changing as its allies in government lost power. Consider that as early as the 1950s, Unifruit was being compelled by governments to share profits by means of taxation and abide by minimum wage laws, and it now pays wages far above the country averages and provides admittedly superior housing and education for its workers.

Its reputation for invincibility was lost with the great and successful 1954 strike of its workers in Honduras, the original banana republic. By the mid-1950s, its land holdings in Guatemala were only 1/12 the old figure, and a 30% profits tax had been levied by that country. Unifruit lost an antitrust suit in the United States in 1958, had to sell part of its operations to Del Monte, and found it the better part of valor to replace direct land ownership and direct management with local arrangements among producers. Competition developed; the now poorly managed company, renamed United Brands, was near bankruptcy in the early 1970s.* By 1981, the "dollar tax" on each bunch of bananas that had been a rallying cry for years in Costa Rica was actually being collected. The task of policing multinational behavior is far from hopeless, as the ease of the now-detentacled octopus shows. Further extensions to the argument that monopsonistic MNEs underpay for hastily extracted natural resources, usually process them not in the LDCs but in the developed countries, and pollute the environment of their host, are considered later in Chapters 12, 15, and 16.

From the early 1980s, national tax inspectors have tried to cope with the MNE transfer price problem using four primary methods. They try to apply a "comparable uncontrolled price," at which technology has been transferred after an arm's-length bargain. This is often hard to find. They attempt to calculate a "resale price," finding a price at which some technology left the group and applying that price when possible. They use "cost-plus," attempting to establish costs and then applying a markup. Finally, they fall back on negotiations with the MNE to see if the firm will accept a compromise solution. Large-scale simultaneous audits by two or more national tax authorities would help to cope with the problem and are in the offing.

Inappropriate goods. There has also been charges against some multinationals that they market inappropriate products in the LDCs. They cater to the demands of local elites, it is said, rather than to the needs of the common people. They transmit an undesirable home country ("Coca-Cola") culture, with their advertising leading demand.[46] They move the invisible hand rather than responding to it, according to their critics, whose evidence is thought provoking. These critics note the trend to bottled soft drinks instead of fruit drinks, detergents instead of soap. They cite dramatic cases such as a survey showing Samoans (in American Samoa) to be tremendously high per capita consumers of much advertised Pepto-Bismol in a society where no incidence of intestinal or digestive ailments had previously been visible.[47] They note sales of inflammable pyjamas and pesticides questionable from the point of view of safe use and environmental damage. Most vocally, perhaps, they point to the rapidly rising consumption of cigarettes exported by MNEs, freely advertised with no health warnings and frequently with higher levels of nicotine and tar content than in those marketed in the developed countries. Although the market for cigarettes is shrinking in the United States, smoking is sharply on the increase in the LDCs, at perhaps + 4% a year according to the World Bank. In a widely noted recent case from Taiwan, empty containers (five

* Its chief executive jumped to his death from his 44th-floor New York office in 1975.

packs of Winstons) were the entry ticket to a rock concert.[48] The MNE involvement with tobacco products is an "export of death and disease," charged former U.S. Surgeon General C. Everett Koop in 1990.[48]

For those who believe consumers are better off when free to choose, some of these points will not be persuasive (and it must be remembered that no charge of inappropriateness is made against a wide range of MNE production). Unsafe products would seem, however, to be another thing altogether. The Carter administration took the step of restricting the export of goods banned or limited in the United States, but the Reagan administration lifted the ban, and exports of these items are now running at over a billion dollars a year.* In December 1982, the UN General Assembly voted 146 to 1 with no abstentions to urge strict controls on the export of products that are banned in the exporting country. The negative vote was cast by the United States. Presently, informal talks are going forward in Geneva (at GATT, the General Agreement on Tariffs and Trade) on whether the export of items prohibited at home should be made illegal. For now it remains entirely legal.

Much attention was focused on Nestlé, the Swiss company that markets baby food on a worldwide basis, and other producers of infant formula. Many mothers switched from breast feeding to formula because of the billboard advertising promoting the bottle as the "modern way" and the distribution of free samples in hospitals. This along with the high birth rates in the LDCs brought greatly increased sales. Critics noted the inability of the formula to transmit natural immunity to disease, the malnutrition resulting from improper administration of the product, and the incidence of diarrhea caused by inadequate boiling of the water used. Nestlé replied that undernourished mothers may produce milk deficient in nutritive value and that the labels now stated that breast feeding is the superior method. But the criticism, including an international boycott, caused Nestlé to abandon consumer advertising and other promotional efforts.† A World Health Organization code of conduct on infant formula was eventually agreed upon.‡ It involved agreements with several producing multinationals to curtail or halt their direct advertising. Nestlé not only accepted the code but also set up an independent audit board chaired by former Secretary of State Ed Muskie to conduct an ongoing review of company practices, and in 1984 the consumer groups that had organized the boycott officially dropped it with the statement that the company had made "substantial progress" toward reform.

Other charges are aimed by the critics against the pharmaceutical multinationals, sometimes for the high prices of brand name drugs that could be purchased much more cheaply under the generic label and sometimes for allowing the unrestricted sale of drugs that require prescriptions in the United States or Europe. Drugs are big business in the LDCs, which spend 50% to 60% of their health care budgets on them as opposed

* See Charles O. Agege, "Dumping of Dangerous American Products Overseas: Should Congress Sit and Watch," *Journal of World Trade Law* 19, no. 4 (1985): 403-410. Foreign governments do, however, have to be notified under U.S. law that a banned product is being exported.

† The boycott began in 1977.

‡ In May, 1981. The code passed in the WHO by a vote of 118 to 1, with the United States casting the only negative vote.

to only 15% to 20% in developed countries. Doctors in LDCs often own their own pharmacies. Often countries purchase brand name drugs that on average are ten times higher in price than are generics. Lack of competition sometimes leads to big markups above the world price and much market segmentation. For example, streptomycin has been sold in Guinea at a price 12 times higher than in Egypt. In retaliation against this behavior, Bangladesh has banned 1700 drugs, India has used unpopular price controls, and Sri Lanka has a state marketing agency that buys pharmaceuticals at world prices, The UN has singled out Parke Davis' Chloramphenicol, which is severely restricted in the United States because it can cause blood disease problems but sold over the counter without prescription in many LDCs. Dipyrone, a painkiller that can cause fatal blood disease (the AMA says its "only justified use is as a last resort to reduce fever when safer measures have failed"), is severely limited in the United States but sold over the counter in some LDCs. In response to the problems of appropriateness and high cost, the World Health Organization has compiled a list of 220 drugs it considers most essential. For the LDCs, the WHO now undertakes large-scale buying of many of these at prices often only about half what the drugs had been costing.[49]

The United States bans the export of drugs not approved by the Food and Drug Administration (FAD), but U.S. firms want the ban repealed. It may seem reasonable to ban such exports, but there is another side to the issue. The World Health Organization has noted that the export ban may keep efficacious medicines for being used to fight diseases that do not occur in North America and may discourage the use of some cheap, although possibly more toxic, drugs because they have not been approved in the United States. The drug companies say regulation should be the responsibility of the importing nation. Critics point to the expense and technical barriers of having the LDCs do the testing. An economic office in the FAD to speed the obvious cases along may seem sensible, but there is no such thing.

Inappropriate technology. It is said that multinationals tend to favor capital-intensive production rather than the labor-intense production that is often more in line with LDC factor proportions. There are thus unfavorable repercussions for employment. Economists as opposed to politicians have tended to think that this last charge is especially important.

Controlling the multinationals

Controlling the conduct of foreign firms was much emphasized by LDCs in the 1960s and most of the 1970s. As countries weighed the costs and benefits discussed above, they frequently decided against allowing unfettered operation by the multinationals. Many steps were taken. Whole industries were declared off limits to the MNEs and reserved for local (often state-owned) enterprise. Controls took the form of maximum allowable ownership and profit repatriation. Both 100% foreign ownership and uncontrolled profit repatriation became much rarer than they had been . Of the affiliates of U.S. multinationals, only 44% of those established in the mid-1970s were wholly owned.* *Minority* participation became commonplace among European MNEs, 42% in the mid-1970s, and typical of Japanese operations, 74% in that time period.

* Previous experience was, however, very different, so that 83% of U.S. multinationals are still majority owned and 71% are wholly owned. See B. L. Barker, "A Profile of U.S. Multinational Companies in 1977," *Survey of Current Business* 61, no. 10 (1981): 38-57.

Strict rules on local participation in the investment and management of the firm became commonplace. Countries often required that any expansion of an enterprise be accomplished through domestic participation, and a steady rise in the proportion of local stockholding often was mandated by law. In some instances, joint ventures were mandated from the time a firm was first established, and foreign shareholders were under a legal obligation to sell out within a certain time period. Several South American countries (Bolivia, Colombia, Ecuador, Peru, and Venezuela) operated under a 15-to 20-year provision that outside ownership be reduced to a 49% maximum.

To counter the problem of inadequate training, quota targets akin to equal opportunity guidelines in the United States became widespread. Countries mandated a certain percentage of local managers at junior and senior levels, the target number growing larger as time passed. "Local content" requirements, prescribing the use of domestically produced inputs and similar in their economic effects to import quotas, also became common, as did export requirements for some of the MNEs' final output.† The permitted amount of local borrowing often was limited by law. In an attempt to meet the problem of the transfer price, many governments restricted royalties and fees to some fixed percentage of total sales in the country.

At the United Nations a move was made to adopt a code of conduct establishing behavioral rules for multinationals operating in LDCs. The proposed code was at one time bitterly opposed by the developed countries, but later they viewed it with more sympathy because the code would be voluntary and would not require ratification. Major areas of the voluntary code would include consumer and environmental protection, guidelines on transfer pricing, and government agreement not to discriminate against MNEs in return for a right to limit MNE entry into some specific areas. Still open are discussions on how much diplomatic protection a home country can provide an MNE and whether to allow "slate-cleaning" contract adjustments, that is, adjustments that can wipe out provisions too advantageous to an MNE as opposed to the permanent sanctity of contracts. The United States long ago announced that it would not support any code provisions that were compulsory, discriminated against foreign enterprise, and applied just to MNEs rather than to all firms, including government ones.

To some degree, multinationals did respond to these efforts at regulating them with new methods of organization and marketing. Direct control by expatriate managers is being replaced by participation in management, contract arrangements, and technology deals; in some LDCs equity-holding by foreigners was rapidly reduced. A trend set in toward what can be called the Japanese model; Japan in its development preferred to contract for capital and technology and provide Japanese managers rather than admitting the multinationals. The Germans used much the same tactics at an earlier time. It became popular to contract with MNEs for "build operate, and transfer" (BOT) plants or, in a slight variation, "build, own, operate and transfer" (BOOT) plants. In these schemes, an MNE builds a plant, runs it for perhaps ten years, then sells it to

† For example, Taiwan's export requirement was 5% to 10% of a new investment's output until the rule was changed in 1987. Its local content requirement was 50% on color TVs, 55% on VCRs, and 90% on motorcycles. Export requirements can have a "beggar-thy-neighbor" impact if a multinational reduces exports from country B in order to meet the new target imposed by country A. See Vernon, "Multinationals are Mushrooming," 44.

nationals of the country it is in. The idea has been used much by Turkey. It is said, reasonably, that the firm doing the building will do it well, knowing it will be the operator for a long period.

The turnabout in attitudes. A rather remarkable turnabout in attitudes took place, however, during the debt crisis. The realization spread that attracting direct investment is a competitive proposition. Numerous countries, particularly in Africa and the Caribbean, have failed to attract funds, controls or not, because their domestic markets are small and local natural resources are few. Unstable governments and changeable economic policies have proved even more discouraging to investors than have fixed rules on operations. Politicians recognized that the restrictions could result in cuts in investment, even sharp ones, and so could prove counterproductive. Further, the debt crisis led to more appreciation of direct investment in which no outflow occurs unless a profit is being made as compared with the debt on which interest and principal must be paid willy-nilly. More equity financing and less contractual lending would have been a help during the crisis and would prove highly advantageous if it were to deepen again. The foreign investor, not the LDC, would bear the risk of recessions, major shifts in the exchange rate, and so forth.

The countries with the toughest rules often found that they were experiencing the most serious depression in foreign capital inflows, inhibiting especially transfers of confidential technology. For example, Coca-Cola and IBM left India in the 1970s when the order was received to reduce their equity of 40%, and though the former may have been of little consequence for technology flows, the latter certainly was. Host governments also discovered several other perverse developments. Local stockholders sometimes preferred higher dividends to the reinvestment of retained earnings, and there was an increased incentive to engage in transfer pricing as a means to shift profits out to the LDC. The mandated local ownership was not even a sensible use of resources whenever the rate of return was below those in the scores of substitute uses for the local financial capital. Just because the MNE was there was no guarantee whatever that its returns would be the highest available. The countries that had gone the furthest — prohibiting foreign ownership (equity holdings) altogether — found the MNEs were extremely reluctant to reveal technology and management methods over which they wished to retain complete control.

The result has been rather more agreement on the advantages of MNEs, abetted by the rise in confidence among host governments and a lessening of the fear of domination by MNEs. Some countries once quite hostile to foreign investment, including Egypt, Jamaica, Korea, Mexico, Pakistan, the Philippines, and Turkey, have now adopted much more flexible and accommodative policies. In this group are countries that for years were among the most bitter foes of the MNEs. Most striking of all, the Andean nations with the stern regulations (Bolivia, Colombia, Ecuador, Peru, and Venezuela) in 1987 gutted their joint law that restricted foreign investment. Limits on repatriated profits, requirements for reinvestment, and limits on sectors where investment was permitted were unceremoniously dropped.* Less liberalization has affected the

* The only remaining part of the old law is that if a firm exports to other Andean countries, then it has to sell a majority holding to nationals within 30 years (37 years in Bolivia and Ecuador).

requirements on the use of domestic labor and managers. MNE reluctance to train employees if they, once trained, are likely to jump to a competing firm has caused some decline in the passage and enforcement of these laws.

The UN still supports adoption of a code of conduct, but in a major change in tone its most recent reports stress the advantages rather than the disadvantages of multinational investment. Debate over the code has taken a back seat to a new set of negotiations at Geneva undertaken as part of the Uruguay Round of trade talks due to conclude in 1990. (The Uruguay Round is being carried on within the GATT [General Agreement on Tariffs and Trade]. It is so named because it was first begun at Punta del Este, Uruguay, then moved to Geneva. It did not meet its deadline, and the negotiations resumed in 1991.) In these TRIM talks (trade-related investment measures), the United States and Japan have allied themselves in opposing many of the old investment regulations such as local equity requirements, remittance restrictions, local content, export requirements, technology transfer requirements, and so forth. India leads the group of LDCs still attempting to defend such requirements. The LDCs themselves are split, however, with some, particularly the most export-oriented countries, seeing the chance to trade off lower barriers to their exports against more liberalization of their investment measures.

The upshot for today's multinationals with branches in the LDCs is a curious combination of sometimes very strict regulations and performance requirements with sometimes very liberal investment incentives and a growing tendency to abolish both. For the host governments, controlling the multinationals is a contest that must be closely calculated. The aim, obviously, is to retain the benefits they bring while reducing their costs. Like a general, a gambler, or an oligopolist, an LDC government must weigh every decision concerning the MNEs in the light of what its rival will do. Will further regulation cut capital inflows substantially? Will access to the latest research and technological developments be curtailed? In short, will the economic penalties be worse than the benefits from any given regulation? The calculation is not an easy one where multinationals are free to move and where one of their chief complaints has always been the instability of the economic rules under which they must operate. If a prediction might be hazarded, MNEs will continue to threaten immediate withdrawal, they will constantly lecture the LDCs about overregulation and the large potential losses of valuable investment, and they will charge a risk premium. But in spite of their many threats to leave, they will continue to bring capital and know-how to the LDCs because, even with the regulations, it is profitable to do so.[50] On their part, host governments will more and more provide a welcoming environment because, whatever the problems encountered with a given multinational, the advantages they bring can be large.

Confiscation. Nationalization of MNE assets without adequate compensation, called confiscation or expropriation, is a side issue to this debate. From the point of view of a capital-hungry LDC, there is always the alternative of seizing assets. Yet doing so is likely to be devastating for future private capital inflows, not only by the affected firm but also by other foreign firms as well. U.S. aid must stop by law. Where wrangles over ownership and compensation are likely, commercial bank and World Bank loans will be less forthcoming. Foreign managers and technicians may depart. In technical terms, the present discounted value of the expropriated property would have to be balanced against the present discounted value of the reduced inflows and then weighed for political impact. The tactic always has a high degree of political and emotional content. The fear of nationalization may be an important matter even in a country with no history of such events, especially when politicians put their rhetoric into high gear. Fear, even when largely groundless, can quickly result in big cuts in private foreign investment. Hence it is important to maintain the business confidence of the relatively recent and small government insurance plans, the Overseas Private Investment Corporation (OPIC) in the United States, similar European and Japanese agencies, and the Multilateral Investment Guarantee Agency of the World Bank, which has already been discussed.

OPIC was founded in 1969; it was last extended by Congress in 1988 for three years. By 1987, it was insuring 144 projects, about 10% of U.S. investment in the LDCs. Studies show that 25% to 50% of OPIC-insured projects otherwise would not have been undertaken. Although there is plenty of private insurance available (pioneered by Lloyd's of London), premiums are frequently about five times higher than the rates charged by OPIC. Criticism of this otherwise sensible sounding idea has centered on the favoritism shown to relatively well-off LDCs and to large projects (83% of OPIC's newly insured commitments were to just 13 large projects valued at over $10 million each). Congress originally required OPIC to insure commitments only in low-income LDCs but lifted that requirement in 1981.* The AFL/CIO opposes OPIC on the grounds that it fails to promote growth abroad and causes the export of jobs from the United States.

Expropriation was at one time particularly pronounced among plantations, mines, oil companies, banks, utilities, and transportation facilities. Some compensation was frequently made, but the amount of the payment in the 1960s averaged only about 40% of book value. Since that time, however, there has been a massive retreat by the LDCs from outright expropriation, caused, so it appears, by self-interest. Some countries have passed laws prohibiting the tactic, a number have even put the prohibition into their constitutions, and there are currently about 200 treaties involving the protection of investment, some of them part of the U.S. Bilateral Investment Treaty (BIT) Program. In the 1960s, nearly three-fourths of the disputes involving U.S. firms abroad had to do with formal nationalization or expropriation. In the 1970s, this figure fell to less than a quarter, and the bulk of the controversies came to be over contract or management issues.* Many of the cases are now negotiated in the World Bank's International Center

---

* Such plans, however, usually insure less than 10% of total direct investment, far lower than the total amount of insurance written because more than one policy can be taken out to cover various types of risk. OPIC's policies are usually for 20 years, far longer than presently available private insurance, and they also usually cover "civil strife" See *WDR, 1985,* 131.

* Helleiner, *International Economic Disorder,* 169. The U.S. Bilateral Investment Treaty (BIT) program dates from 1981. It seeks to obtain agreements with LDCs guaranteeing certain rights and safeguards. A "model treaty" revised in 1984 is the basis for the negotiations and contains the following provisions: (1) equal treatment of nationals of the host country and foreigners, including the choice of manager who is wanted rather than one of the correct nationality; (2) unrestricted repatriation of profit and capital; (3) expropriation to be recompensed at fair market value; and (4) binding arbitration of disputes. The United States has discussed BIT treaties with 40 countries, with 8 ratified up to 1988. The reports of the U.S. ITC, *Operation of the Trade Agreements Program,* present annual updates of the BIT program.

for the Settlement of Investment Disputes (ICSID), which has 82 member countries. Nowadays very few LDCs use expropriation as a major tool; even in the period 1960 to 1977 when expropriation was more common, just seven nations — Algeria, Chile, Cuba, Ethiopia, Sri Lanka, Uganda, and Venezuela — accounted for nearly three-fourths (72.5%) of all reported seizures. Cuba and Uganda together were responsible for fully half of them.[51]

We have seen in this chapter that LDCs seek capital from abroad because they want to invest more than they are able to save at home. Generally, this makes good economic sense. Two of the most important ways in which capital can flow, however, are foreign aid and investment by multinational firms, and few areas of development economics are as politically loaded and involve such disputes and acrimony as do these two topics. For LDCs, what strategy to employ toward foreign capital is one of the most difficult questions to be faced; too often, the economic optimum and the political optimum will be far apart or even mutually exclusive. "Uneasy lies the head that wears a crown," said Shakespeare. Life is not much easier for those who have to design public policy on foreign capital flows.

Notes

32. See David Goldsbrough, "Foreign Private Investment in Developing Countries," IMF Occasional Paper No. 33 (1985), for a discussion.

33. For this section, I utilized *WDR, 1985,* (especially) 12-14.

34. For the pros and cons of multinationals, I benefitted from Khushi M. Khan, ed., *Multinationals of the South: New Actors in the International Economy* (New York, 1986): A.E. Safarian and Gilles Y. Bertin, *Multinationals, Governments and International Technology Transfer* (New York, 1987); Theordore H. Moran, ed., *Multinational Corporations: The Political Economy of Foreign Direct Investment* (Lexington, Mass., 1985); Thomas N. Gladwin and Ingo Walter, *Multinationals Under Fire* (New York, 1980); Jean-François Hennart, *A Theory of Multinational Enterprise* (Ann Arbor, Mich., 1982); Ian M. D. Little, *Economic Development: Theory, Policy, and International Relations* (New York, 1982), 182-189; V.N. Bala-subramanyam, *Multinational Enterprises in the Third World*, Thames Essay No 26 (London, 1980): C.F. Bergsten, T. Horst, and T. H. Moran, eds., *American Multinationals and American Interests* (Washington, D.C., 1978); Seymour E. Rubin and Gary C. Hufbauer, eds., *Emerging Standards of International Trade and Investment* (Totowa, N.J., 1984); and especially from the penetrating comments on this chapter by Wilson B. Brown of the University of Winnipeg. Two modern classics by Raymond Vernon are *Sovereignty at Bay* (New York, 1971) and *Storm Over the Multinationals* (Cambridge, Mass., 1974). *The Economist* publishes many articles on the activities of MNEs, which I utilized.

35. Peter B. Kenen, *The International Economy* (Englewood Cliffs, N. J., 1985), 157-158.

36. See IMF, *World Economic Outlook, 1990,* 170, for the later figures.

37. See Louis T. Wells, Jr., *Third World Multinationals: The Rise of Foreign Investment from Developing Countries* (Cambridge, Mass., 1983). A sceptical view of the supposed advantages in Sanjaya Lall et al., *The New Multinationals: The Spread of Third World Enterprises* (Chichester, 1984). Singapore has even invested in the United States in electronics and South Korea in semiconductors.

38. See Raymond Vernon, "Multinationals Are Mushrooming," *Challenge* 29, no. 2 (1986): 41-47.

39. The figures are for various years from studies by D. Nayyan and S. Lall (see Hubert Schmitz, "Industrialization Strategies in Less Developed Countries: Some Lessons of Historical Experience," *Journal of Development Studies* 21, no. 1 [1984]: 10-11) and from Magnus Blomström, Irving Kravis, and Robert Lipsey, "Multinational Firms and Manufactured Exports from Developing Countries," NBER Working Paper No. 2493 (1988). The exports have been much stimulated by the relatively new system of value-added tariffs now in use in both Europe and the United States and discussed in Chapter 14.

40. The terms are used by S.P. Schatz, "Assertive Pragmatism and the Multinational Enterprise," *World Development* 9, no. 1 (1981): 93-105.

41. Illustrating the MacDougall-Kemp model, from G. D. A. MacDougall, "The benefits and Costs of Private Investment from Abroad: A Theoretical Approach," *Economic Record* 36 (1960): 13-35; and M. C. Kemp, *The Pure Theory of International Trade* (Englewood Cliffs, N. J., 1964). The diagram is adapted from R. J. Ruffin, "International Factor Movements," in Ronald W. Jones and Peter B. Kenen, *Handbook of International Economics,* vol. 1 (Amsterdam, 1984), 255-256. See also Meier, *Leading Issues*, 4th ed., 323-324.

42. See *The Economist*, March 15, 1986, 67.

43. Reported in *The Economist*, December 12, 1981, 81.

44. I took the formula from the work of Subrata Ghatak.

45. See Walter Le Feber, *Inevitable Revolutions* (New York, 1983), for a discussion of the company.

46. John Kenneth Galbraith has been a leading exponent of this view, especially in *The New Industrial State* (Boston, 1967); and *The Affluent Society* (Boston, 1958).

47. See *The Economist*, June 6, 1981.

48. *Christian Science Monitor*, September 22, 1989.

49. All of these cases have been reported in *The Economist* in recent years.

50. This section and other analyses of MNEs in this chapter have been informed by Gerald K. Helleiner, *International Economic Disorder: Essays in North-South Relations* (Toronto, 1981). Some data are from his "Intrafirm Trade and the Developing Countries: An Assessment of the Data," *Journal of Development Economics* 6 (1979): 391-406. In this paragraph I utilized language by Carlos Diaz-Alejandro, "The Less Developed Countries and Transnational Enterprises," in Sven Grassman and Erik Lundberg, eds., *The World Economic Order: Past and Prospects* (New York, 1981), 251.

51. F. N. Burton and Hisashi Inoue, "Expropriations of Foreign-Owned Firms in Developing Countries," *Journal of World Trade Law* 18, no. 5 (1984): 396-414; and M. L. Williams, "The Extent and Significance of Nationalization of Foreign-Owned Assets in Developing Countries, 1956-1972," *Oxford Economic Papers* July, 1975, table V-1.

27.   Debt
The Argument: A Summary
Harold Lever and Christopher Huhne

We have made a labyrinth and have got lost in it. We must find our way again.

Denis Diderot

The flows of finance between the advanced and the developing worlds, which have in the past done so much to promote economic stability, employment and the progress of living standards, are now characterized by a perverse and dangerous anomaly. Until 1982 it was understood that there had to be, for a prolonged period, a one-way flow of resources from the advanced countries to the Third World to promote its development. The view went unchallenged in either official or private-sector circles and was supported by every school of economic thought, albeit for differing reasons. Since the debt crisis which broke in 1982, those flows have been reversed for each important group of countries in the Third World. IMF estimates imply that in 1985 there was a resource flow from the fifteen largest Third World borrowers to their more prosperous creditors worth $37 billion, or one quarter of their entire earnings from the sales of their exports of goods and services.[1]

This reverse or negative flow is a perversion of common sense and of sound economics. On a classical view, the developing countries should attract capital from the industrial world because they are able to increase output by more than rich countries for a given increase in investment. On an alternative view, the debtors need balance-of-payments finance because their domestic economies are capable of expanding more rapidly than they are able to increase their foreign exchange earnings and imports, due mainly to their reliance on export commodities whose demand grows less rapidly than world income. To our knowledge, no economist has yet advocated a large flow of resources from the poorer countries as a way of stimulating their economic progress.

Nor was this ever the intention of those who encouraged or undertook the original lending to the debtors, the interest payments on which are the main cause of the reverse transfer. It was always implicitly assumed that the financial markets would continue to refinance old debt and extend new credit so that the flow of resources to the developing world would continue, at least until some far-distant future in which the debtors would reach a level of development where it was feasible and desirable for them to export rather than import capital. This unplanned reverse flow of resources is made all the more extraordinary because it has been elevated into a necessary symptom of 'adjustment' by the official policy of the industrial countries, which are as unwilling today to take their proper responsibility for the healthy functioning of the world's

---

Harold Lever and Christopher Huhne: Extracts from *DEBT AND DANGER* (Penguin, 1987), pp. 11-16; 46-47; 61-63. Reprinted by permission of the Peters Fraser & Dunlop Group Ltd.

economy as they were after the first oil shock of 1973, which laid the foundations for this anomaly.

Yet such abdication of responsibility is singularly misplaced. The world's financial safety and economic health is balanced on a knife-edge. If defaults halt the reverse flows, many of the largest banks in the advanced countries will become insolvent. A crisis of the kind which we have thankfully not experienced since the Great Crash of 1929 would once again be a terrible reality. But if the Third World's debtors continue to generate the large trade surpluses required to make payment to the advanced countries, their economic development, already manifestly inadequate, will be hobbled for a generation. The effort to sustain the large trade surpluses required imposes enormous strains on the world's trading system, as industries in the advanced countries have to make way for Third World exports and resist the adjustment by means of ever more strident appeals for protectionism. Moreover, the very uncertainty of continued payments in these circumstances of rising political pressures in both debtor and creditor countries causes the banks themselves to slow down their lending, adding a further depressive influence to world trade.

The debtors can do no more to resolve their predicament. All the pressures on them are to expand their economies more rapidly, which would inevitably entail smaller rather than larger trading surpluses and would quite possibly result in creeping defaults on debt. The bankers cannot realistically lend more money to offset the interest payments coming back to them on the outstanding debt without a further loss of credibility. As it is, their outstanding lending to the Third World outstrips their own capital by a factor of two or more. Only the governments and monetary authorities of the advanced countries have the resources and the standing to reconcile the interests of both debtors and bankers — and to safeguard the world economy.

It is not, though, their unique financial power which alone casts the advanced-country governments in the natural role of managers of the debt crisis. They also bear a heavy responsibility for the events which led up to its occurrence. Until 1973 it was widely understood that commercial lending was not a safe or sure vehicle for development finance. Banks could neither impose conditions to ensure the fruitful use of the funds they lent, nor could they, when the need arose, postpone debt servicing and provide new funds without undermining the confidence of those who deposit money with them. After 1973 it was absolutely right for the advanced countries to seek to ensure that the developing world had the funds to continue to import the material they needed for development, despite the sharp rise in the price of oil. Without those funds, Third World imports would have collapsed and, with them, the jobs of millions in the advanced countries who sell to them. What was wrong was for the advanced-country governments to push the commercial banking systems of their countries into a role which should have been supported and regulated by the authorities whose public purposes it rightly fulfilled.

In the years after the first oil crisis of 1973-74 the banks took the unspent cash surpluses of the oil-rich countries and lent them to the oil-dependent Third World. Reinforced by the approval and encouragement of their governments, the banks happily developed the conviction that there was no risk in this lending to foreign governments. They came to believe that they had hit upon the most profitable area in banking history. Nowhere else could such huge sums be placed at an assured profit and with minimal administrative cost. The banks that lent in this field soon found that the profits from what they had convinced themselves was risk-free lending greatly exceeded those from the rest of their much more complicated and onerous activities.

In the years after 1974 the borrowing countries financed the trade deficits of their imports over their exports increasingly by borrowing from the banks. The borrowing was originally prompted by the need to cover the cartel's oil price rises. It was soon much extended to cover virtually any borrowing that the developing countries' governments saw fit to make. Indeed, countries like Mexico, Venezuela and Nigeria, which were beneficiaries of the oil price rises, were among the heaviest borrowers. There was no thought of servicing the debt by generating trade surpluses and reverse transfers. The service of interest and repayments was expected to be met, and was in fact met year after year, by new borrowing in addition to loans to cover current needs.

The happy-go-lucky assumption by governments and banks that the debts could be serviced indefinitely by new borrowing on the financial markets went virtually unchallenged. All the agreements with debtor countries for service of interest and capital were manifestly on terms which could not be met by the debtors' export earnings but only by new borrowing, as one of the present authors repeatedly warned both within the government between 1974 and 1979 and thereafter.

Yet uncritical self-congratulation over the advantages of these arrangements was the order of the day. The bankers liked them because apparently never were propriety and profit so happily conjoined. The borrowers liked them because they placed little restraint on the volume or the purposes of their borrowing. The Organization of Petroleum Exporting Countries (OPEC) liked them because they enlisted the banking system of the West in support of the ability of their poorest customers to meet the cartel's oil price rises. The aid lobby liked them because they provided a novel transfer of resources to the poorer countries on a scale greater than ever before. Santa Claus had appeared in the guise of sound commercial activity, and nobody wanted to shoot him. Western governments liked these arrangements because they appeared to support their belief that this lending was urgently needed in the world interest and could be dealt with indefinitely by unassisted bank intermediation rather than by recourse to public budgets.

The inexorable result, however, was the crisis of debt and growth which we suffer today. The period between borrowing and servicing of debt by a real flow of foreign currency back to the lender can be bridged by further commercial borrowing — but only as long as that real flow is a credible prospect. Nobody could claim that this prospect grew to match the ever-growing mountain of private debt, and this was bound to bring into question the credibility of most of the debtors and of the lending system itself. The build-up to crisis was inevitable. Prolonged recession and the move to higher real interest rates after 1979 speeded up the disintegration of confidence, but they were not its fundamental cause.

. . . The pyramid of debt has proved sustainable since the Mexican crisis of 1982 only because of extraordinary sacrifices on the part of the debtors and considerable effort by creditors and official institutions alike. But most of the factors which have encouraged a 'co-operative' handling of the debt crisis will be hard to sustain.

Reschedulings, whereby certain interest and principal repayments which come due are postponed when the banks put up some new lending partially to offset them, will become more and more difficult. As it is, the banks are increasing their outstanding loans to most of the debtors only under official duress. The structure of the banking market is such that each creditor has an individual interest in reducing its exposure to the debtor countries, though if all creditors followed their individual interest and reduced their exposure (and hence met even fewer of the interest and principal payments coming back to them), the debtor countries would be put in an impossible position very rapidly.

Even if such a crisis could be averted, the situation from the point of view of the debtors looks no happier. Negative transfers and their associated trade surpluses are enormous and growing, despite some new bank lending and funds from the IMF. They have been achieved largely by drastic cuts in imports engineered by a depression of demand, output and employment. The recent increases in exports from the debtor countries, which alleviate the import-cutting effects of the negative transfers, are nevertheless woefully dependent on the buoyancy of the American marketplace. That cannot be sustained as American growth slows down and the United States' trade deficit is reduced.

Moreover, several of the reasons why the debtors have so far been prepared to accept the enormous sacrifices demanded of them, rather than to default on their obligations in the face of domestic pressures, may also be waning. The threat of vanishing trade credit if a country defaults is less potent when foreign-exchange reserves are building up and barter trade is growing. They have also hoped that eventually Western governments will come to see the difficulty of their situation and intervene with debt relief. If that prospect is not kept alive, defaults could follow swiftly.

[In Chapter 3,] we turn to the origins of the crisis and look at the reasons why countries incurred debt. Money — and particularly foreign exchange — is 'fungible' in the sense that it is not always easy to track down its true end use because a loan can easily be transferred to purposes other than those for which it was contracted. Lending is thus general lending to the country concerned to maintain a higher level of imports than would otherwise be the case and in the hope that it will be able to repay. With these caveats, it is clear that the increased oil bill of the non-oil Third World countries was the main cause of the debt build-up from the debtor's point of view, though rising interest rates and mistaken exchange-rate policies also played a role.

* * * * * *

A further oil price rise and the rise in real interest rates were only part of the shock delivered to the debtors between 1978 and 1982. Once again, the effect of Western policy aimed at countering renewed inflation by depressing demand was to cause a sharp drop in the value of Third World exports. Even the upper-middle-income countries of Latin America remain strongly dependent on commodity exports. In Brazil soya beans, coffee and iron ore accounted for 83 per cent of merchandise exports in 1981-2.[9] In Argentina wheat, corn and beef provide one-third of exports. In Chile copper alone accounts for nearly half. As the industrial world went into recession, commodity prices fell by one-quarter between 1980 and 1982.[10] Rising oil prices, higher nominal and real interest rates, sluggish developed-country markets, a rise in the dollar in which most of the debt was denominated and falling export prices added up to a formidable shock, diminishing the sources of foreign exchange while increasing demand for it.

It is clear, however, that the attempt to compensate for external shocks to debtor economies was not the only use for foreign-currency finance and that some of the other explanations are decidedly less flattering to the Third World's policy-makers. Two classes of policy decision added unnecessarily to outstanding debt by the time of the 1982 crisis. (Alternatively, they can be seen as having reduced potential economic growth for the given increase in debt.) The first was the clear instances of political decisions to increase arms imports, which could not produce domestic investment, still less provide capacity which would increase the foreign-exchange earning power needed to service debt. The second were macro-economic policy errors which encouraged imports, discouraged exports and stimulated the build-up of private capital abroad by Third World residents.

* * * * * *

An unsupported and insufficiently regulated banking system was revealed, in the period 1979-82, to be an inherently unstable source of balance-of-payments funding for the developing world. When times were good, the banks thrust tempting loans on to favoured Third World governments, though they were in no position to ensure that sound economic policies would be pursued. When times turned bad, the banks were no longer prepared to fund mounting deficits.

The irony is that, with some clear exceptions, the private financing of Third World current-account deficits over the decade to 1982 was a considerable success story from the point of view of world growth and public policy. Neither the level of the debt nor its results need have caused alarm: the problem lay not so much in the amounts of money which were extended but in the nature of the lending. The debt, after all, did allow the non-oil developing countries to maintain far higher growth rates than they would otherwise have been able to do. Comparing the pre-1973 and post-1973 period, we know that industrial country growth slowed down markedly: the surprise is that the non-oil developing countries managed to compensate for this slow-down to a large degree in their main markets and the rise in the cost of their main imports by making up their import capacity with debt. Indeed, the average annual rate of growth of the non-oil Third World between 1973 and 1981 was 5.1 per cent, compared with 5.8 per cent in the period 1967-72.[15] In retrospect this was a quite remarkable performance. The industrial countries, by contrast, slowed down from an annual average growth of 4.4 per cent in 1967-72 to one of 2.8 per cent. If the developing world had slowed down still more, it would have cut its imports from the industrial countries and hence their growth. From the world's point of view, it was better for the lending to have taken place clumsily than not at all.

One cost, of course, was a rising debt burden for the debtors, though on conventional measures it looked far from unsustainable even at the end of the decade. The real value of total debt for the non-oil developing countries, expressed in constant 1975 dollars, rose from $169 billion in 1973 to $294.7 billion in 1979.[16] But even this rise went side by side with a substantial expansion in the Third World's foreign-currency earnings. The total debt to export ratio was 115.4 per cent in 1973 and rose to 130.2 per cent in 1978. But the following year it was back to 119.2 per cent, scarcely higher than at the beginning of the decade. The debt service to export ratio — the amount of interest payments and repayments of principal due in a year relative to exports — indicated a slightly graver problem: it rose from 15.9 per cent in 1973 to 19 per cent in 1979. If, however, the debt had been contracted at maturities longer than the typical eight-year loan, even this ratio could have been contained at more or less its level at the beginning of the decade. Clearly, the conventional debt ratios tell us little about the likelihood of crisis.

The truth is that neither conventional creditworthiness indicators nor the results of Third World policies suggest that the build-up of debt, at least to the end of the 1970s, was misplaced. What *was* unsustainable was the system and nature of that debt. The similarity of the conventional creditworthiness ratios at the beginning and the end of the period merely disguise a much more fundamental change in the structure of the outstanding debt.

The advanced countries had thrown a single vulnerable section of their economies, the banking system, into a task which it could not bear without official support. The key difference between the position of the Third World debtors in 1973 and at the end of the 1970s was that their debt was no longer largely official debt: it was commercial debt to the banks. Governments can afford to roll over interest and capital obligations as circumstances require. Banks cannot without embroiling themselves in a dynamic of increasing incredibility. The share of outstanding commercial debt in total loans rose from 11.6 per cent in 1973 to 37.5 per cent in 1982.[17] In the case of the richer debtors in Latin America the proportion rose from 23.8 per cent to 62 per cent. The debtors inevitably became vulnerable to the disintegration of market confidence. The sharp rise in bank debt would itself have eventually been enough to cause the lending to stop. External shocks such as the rise in interest rates merely accelerated the process. Unsupported private banks could never have provided enough time for the debtors to repay by generating export surpluses. There was no contemplation of this until the smooth, automatic new lending which had been expected failed to arrive.

The banks were simply unable to maintain their own confidence in the commercial nature of the loans they were making, with the result that the mechanism of the commercial banks' balance-of-payments financing became in 1982 the very opposite of what had been intended. The international credit market had been justified on the grounds that countries should have time to 'put their own houses in order', but it instead became a burden on developing countries already facing, in the commodity markets, a magnified impact of the industrial world's gathering recession. It acted to exacerbate the depressive forces in the world economy rather than to alleviate them. The unregulated international credit market had failed.

Notes

1. This figure is derived from IMF, *World Economic Outlook*, Washington D C, April 1985. See Chapter 2, Table 3.

9. Inter-American Development Bank, *Annual Report 1984*, Washington D C, 1985, Table 12, p. 126.

10. IMF, *International Financial Statistics Yearbook 1984*, All Commodities Index, p. 133.

15. See Kitchenman, 'Arms Transfers and the Indebtedness of Less Developed Countries'.

16. Rudiger Dornbusch. 'The Debt Problem and Options for Debt Relief' (mimeo), MIT, Boston, September 1984, Table 4, p. 7.

17. Carlos F. Diaz-Alejandro, 'Latin American Debt: I Don't Think We Are in Kansas Any More', *Brookings Papers on Economic Activity*, 2, 1984, Table I, p. 342. This paper gives a very useful table of real exchange rates in Latin America over time, on which we draw heavily in this passage.

28. The Effects of IMF Programs in the Third World: Debate and Evidence from Latin America

Manuel Pastor, Jr.

Summary. — *This article reviews the debate about the effects of IMF-sponsored stabilization programs in the Third World. After examining recent studies by Fund economists, results of a new study on a Latin American country set are presented. In this research, IMF programs are associated with insignificant changes in the current account, significant improvements in the overall balance of payments, increases in inflation, mixed effects on growth, and a strong and consistent pattern of reduction in labor share of income. The latter result is incorporated into a distribution-oriented critique of Fund policy.*

1. Introduction

Throughout the 1970s and 1980s, a debate has raged over the effects of the International Monetary Fund's (IMF) stabilization programs in the Third World. Many critics have offered a *growth-oriented critique*, contending that Fund supported stabilization programs have short-run recessionary impacts in the Third World setting and damage the prospects for long-run growth. Fund economists have challenged this view with cross-country studies of the actual effects of Fund programs that demonstrate mixed impacts on growth rates coupled with significant success in achieving the IMF's supposed goals: current account and balance of payments improvements and inflation rate reduction.

In this article, I will briefly review the debate, paying particular attention to the studies noted above. I argue against the growth-oriented critique and recast the criticism of the Fund in terms of class and income distribution. I then present my own overview of the effects of IMF programs in 18 Latin American countries in the period 1965-81. The major findings are that: (1) program countries did experience significant balance of payments improvement but this may be mostly due to increased capital inflow induced by the IMF's "seal of approval" and not significant current account improvement; (2) in contrast to official IMF goals, Fund programs in Latin America seem to be associated with accelerating inflation and not inflation rate reduction; (3) in contrast to the growth-oriented critique, Fund programs had mixed impacts on growth rates; and (4) Fund programs were most significantly and consistently associated with declines in wage share.

I close the article by suggesting that a class-analytic approach is consistent with these results. Moreover, awareness of the profound redistributive consequences of

Manuel Pastor, Jr: 'The Effects of IMF Programs in the Third World: Debate and Evidence from Latin America' from *WORLD DEVELOPMENT* (1987), Vol. 15, No. 2, pp. 249-262. © 1987 Pergamon Journals Ltd. Reproduced with permission of Elsevier Science Ltd.

Fund-sponsored programs may suggest some social limits to an IMF-directed resolution of the debt crisis of the 1980s.

2. The debate

In the post-World War II era, the IMF has served as an international "lender of last resort" (Moffit, 1983, p. 124) by providing short-term financial assistance to member countries with balance of payments deficits. Such assistance is generally "conditional" upon member countries agreeing to a stabilization program that the Fund considers appropriate for correcting the deficits. The programs are often quite detailed, specifying both general policy measures and certain quantitative targets for various macroeconomic variables. To promote compliance, credit is doled out in instalments as successive short-term quantitative targets are satisfactorily met.

What do Fund officials see as the goals of these programs? "For the Fund, the primary objective is balance of payments viability with weight given to a number of other goals, such as price stability..." (Eckaus, 1982, p. 774). Achieving these two objectives is frequently associated in the Fund perspective with a related goal of reducing government deficits and the consequent monetary emission. Another goal gaining prominence in the 1970s and 1980s has been "certifying" the ability to service external debt (Diaz-Alejandro, 1981; Gold, 1970, p. 39). In general, we can identify the major *official* macroeconomic goals of Fund programs as balance of payments amelioration and inflation rate reduction.

To this end, a typical program in Latin America embodies a variety of policies: devaluation, limits on banking credit and public borrowing, removal of price subsidies, reduction of tariffs and elimination of some import controls, encouragement of foreign investment, and, finally resistance to nominal wage increases (Diaz Alejandro, 1981; Lichtensztejn, 1983).

The specific impacts of Fund-supported stabilization programs have been debated at length. Fund economists argue that the overall intent of the sort of program outlined above is "to set the stage for sound and sustained rates of economic growth by improving the BOP (balance of payments) and bringing inflationary pressures under control" (Guitain, 1980, p. 25). Indeed , ". . . the full attainment of supply potential has always been the *ultimate* aim (of Fund policy)" (Guitain, 1981, p. 11). The main focus of the critics of the Fund has been that this is not true — that, instead, the Fund's goal and methods are fundamentally antithetical to economic growth and development in the Third World. This "growth-oriented critique" has been most associated with the so-called structuralist school.

(a) The structuralist critique

Structuralist economics is a broad term for those who take certain institutional specificities into account when discussing and modeling the economies of the "South." The usual "structural" characteristics considered include low productivity in agriculture, reliance on primary commodity exports (coupled with assumptions of an inelastic demand for and supply of these exports), and an underdeveloped system of financial intermediation. Formal models from this perspective have been offered by

Krugman and Taylor (1978), Taylor (1979 and 1981), Arida and Bacha (1984), and many others.

In the debate over Fund policy, the structuralists begin by suggesting that balance of payments problems in the Third World often arise from the characteristics of the development process itself. They argue that there is a "development deficit" associated with the importation of capital goods to provide an industrial base, a strategy usually associated with import-substitution industrialization (ISI). Such a deficit can ultimately be reduced only by a "new phase of import substitution" (*profundizacion* or "deepening") (Serra, 1979, p. 114; Hirschman, 1979; 1986) in which backward linkages would be established and the capital goods being imported for early ISI would be increasingly produced domestically. Moreover, it is argued that such deepening will not only eliminate balance of payments problems but reduce inflation by easing the cost-push pressures from structural bottlenecks (see Diamand, 1978). In the meantime, "to try to 'correct' the development deficit is to halt the development effort itself." Instead, the "efficiency" of the deficit should be measured by its contribution to growth (Abdalla, 1980, pp. 39-40).

Given this structural deficit, any of a series of *exogenous* changes — foreign debts coming due, a sudden plunge in primary commodity prices, a rise in the price of oil, a denial of aid — can easily and rapidly increase the existing payments deficits. Using this insight, structuralists argue that the deterioration in the current accounts of non oil-exporting developing countries (NDOCs) through the 1970s and 1980s was "due entirely to factors beyond their control" (Dell, 1982, p. 600; see also Dell and Lawrence, 1980 and most recently Cline, 1985).

This is in sharp contrast to the IMF view that payments problems, in both North and South, have been caused by "expansionary financial policies mainly associated with large budgetary deficits and/or from a complex of cost-push factors and expectations" (Dale, 1983, p. 4; also see Weisner, 1985).[1] For structuralists, the deficits are not primarily the result of countries "misbehaving" but are both endemic to the development process and aggravated mainly by external events. Given this, developing countries should not be "punished" for deficits with the monetary contraction and other measures embodied in Fund programs.

Moreover, structuralists argue, the sort of stabilization programs the Fund designs have perverse effects when implemented in the economies of the "South." In one important model, it is argued that "a deflationary impact from devaluation (a typical Fund policy) is more than a remote possibility; it is close to a presumption" (Krugman and Taylor, 1978, pp. 446-447). Typically, IMF programs produce:

> ... in the short run mainly in a drop in domestic output; this drop in turn acts to discourage investment, which reduces the economy's long-run capacity to earn foreign exchange... (Instead, IMF) economic policy should focus on removing supply bottlenecks and other structural rigidities, so that overall output capacity can be raised. In this way, excess demand would be reduced and resources generated for a balance of payments improvement ... (Crockett, 1981, p. 55)

Thus, in the structuralist perspective, the IMF — in both its refusal to provide long-run financing and its short-run stabilization policies — is seen as a recession-inducing growth-wrecking agent. In the relevant literature (see, for example, Dell, 1982; Diaz-Alejandro, 1981; Foxley, 1983; Bacha, 1983; Girvan, 1980; Krugman and Taylor, 1978; Taylor, 1979; 1981), this argument is developed using theoretical models and case studies of Fund interventions.

(b) The Fund responds

While some of the work cited above has also examined the distributional consequences of Fund programs, the IMF has until recently (see Sisson, 1986) primarily viewed its critics — both structuralist economists and Third World nations — as concerned with the growth issue. It has responded to this concern in two distinct ways. The first has involved changing some aspects of Fund operations to accommodate the critics. The structuralist notion of the development deficit led some to argue that the IMF should enlarge its resources and make payments financing available for long periods and with low conditionality (see Rweyemanu, 1980, pp. 85-91; Garvan, 1980, pp. 72-74; Dell, 1982, pp. 604-605). Through the 1970s, low conditionality facilities like the Oil Financing Facility and the Compensatory Financing Facility (both designed to deal with external shocks to a member country's terms of trade) were added or expanded. The Supplementary Financing Facility was developed in order to expand the credit available to member nations (Cutajar, 1980, p. 2). Finally, the Extended Fund Facility (EFF), with its two to three year programs, was created to allow longer adjustment periods and so avoid "unnecessary" output contraction.

Such policy changes did not come about merely because Fund economists are sensitive about the tarnishing of their image by academic critics. Rather, the new policies arose (1) to prevent an international financial collapse provoked by the increasing balance of payments deficits of developing countries, and (2) to overcome the Third World resistance to Fund advice and resources that led to the underutilization problem of the mid-to late-1970s.[2] Nonetheless, the Third World resistance, complaints about the inadequacies of the IMF, and calls for a new international monetary order were fueled by the growth-oriented critique.

This helps explain the second Fund response to its critics: a series of systematic cross-country studies of the effects of IMF-supported stabilization programs conducted by Fund economists and published in the IMF's *Staff Papers*. The two most important and general of the studies have been those by Donovan (1982) and Reichmann and Stillson (1978).[3] Unfortunately for the IMF's critics, both have demonstrated that the feared recessionary effects of IMF programs do systematically occur.

The Donavan Study examines the effects of IMF programs in the non-oil developing countries (NODCs) in the period 1971-80 by looking at the behavior of various variables (current account, balance of payments, inflation, growth, etc.) in the periods before and after the introduction of a program. He considers both one- and three-year periods and measures the variable performance both absolutely and relative to a series for all NDOCs. He concludes that:

> . . . in broad terms, program countries recorded significant reductions in their external deficits while they exhibited only marginal changes in their growth rates of real GDP and consumption — changes that were not significantly different from those experienced by non-oil developing countries in general (Donavan also demonstrates minor relative reductions in inflation). Thus, considering the group of program countries in the aggregate, the costs associated with the external adjustment effort appear to have been less severe than has sometimes been suggested by participants in the controversy on Fund conditionality. (Donovan, 1982, p. 197)

Earlier work by Reichmann and Stillson (1978) looked at the effects of IMF programs in both developed and developing countries in the period 1963-72. To determine the effects of the programs, Reichmann and Stillson compare the behavior of various variables for the eight quarters before and the eight quarters after the beginning of an IMF-supported program.[4] The significance of the change in pre- and post-IMF observations is determined by using a non-parametric procedure known as the Mann-Whitney U-test. Such a non-parametric procedure is necessary because of the expectation that the variance as well as the mean of the variable in question will change in response to a Fund program; this likely change in variance violates the homoskedasticity assumptions strictly required for a simple t-test of the means of the two periods. Further, since the Mann-Whitney procedure is essentially a test of the medians of the two periods, the significance levels obtained are not biased by the presence of outliers. For all these reasons, I rely on such non-parametric procedures in my own study below.

Testing the change in net foreign assets (a balance of payments measure), Reichmann and Stillson find some indication that Fund programs tend to improve balance of payments positions: of 75 cases examined, 18 cases showed statistically significant improvement (at the 90% confidence level), four cases showed a statistically significant worsening of their net foreign assets position, and 53 exhibited no significant change in either direction (Reichmann and Stillson, 1978, pp. 300-301). The record on inflation is less impressive: of the 19 cases where significant inflation (defined as an annual inflation rate in excess of 5.3%) occurred before the introduction of the IMF-supported program, seven showed a significant decrease in the inflation rate, six a significant increase, and 16 no significant change.

To perform the relevant quarterly tests on growth. Reichmann and Stillson examine the rate of change in either an industrial production index or an index of employment. For the 24 cases examined, two show a significant decline in growth, one a significant increase, and 21 no significant change. But this is not really an adequate refutation of the growth-oriented critique since much of this critique depends on the structural specificities of the LDCs and, as Reichmann and Stillson admit in a footnote:

> This group of programs (those where the above indices were available) is not representative of the programs considered in the other statistical tests, since 7 of the 24 cases in this group were from developed countries. For the less developed countries included in this test, the growth of industrial

production is not an adequate indication of the level of economic activity. (Reichmann and Stillson, 1978, p. 303.)

Turning toward a yearly GDP-based growth rate, Reichmann and Stillson find that, of 70 cases examined, growth rates increased in the post-program year in 33 countries, decreased in 28 countries, and "showed practically no change" in nine countries (Reichmann and Stillson, 1978, p. 303). Thus, despite the different country set and different methodology, their research reveals a pattern similar to that noted by Donovan: significant balance of payments improvements matched by unimportant changes in inflation and mixed effects on growth. The results of both studies are briefly summarized in Table 1.

The Fund, then, has fired back. In response to demands for change, it has altered certain policies. Moreover, a series of studies by IMF economists have evidenced an association of Fund programs with balance of payments improvement and, at the least, no negative inflationary consequences. Most important to the refutation of the IMF's critics, systematic cross-country analysis has revealed no generally negative impacts on growth. While the Fund does not promote growth, neither can it be termed a growth-wrecker.

Table 1   Results of studies by IMF economists*

Variables	Donavan	Reichmann & Stillson
Current account as % of GNP (current account ratio)	Absolute and relative reduction†	Not examined
Balance of payments measure	Absolute and relative improvement	Significant improvement in 24% of cases; significant worsening in only 5%
Inflation	Absolute increase but relative reduction	Mixed impacts
Growth rates	Mixed impact	Mixed impact
Growth rate of real consumption	Absolute and relative reduction in a slight majority of cases	Not examined

*The results presented here are described in the text and explained in detail in Donavan (1982) and Reichmann and Stillson (1978).

†As noted in the text, Donavan's *absolute* comparisons look at the performance of a variable before and after an IMF program; his *relative* comparisons contrast the change in a variable for countries with programs to the change in the same variable for a set of all non-oil developing countries.

(c) Another sort of critique

Marxist economists have also criticized the Fund, with most working within the dependency paradigm pioneered by Frank (1967) and others. In general, this Marxist-oriented dependency approach argues that the international capitalist system involves a drain of economic surplus from the Third World (periphery) to the First World (core). Such a "surplus drain" — through trade (unequal exchange), profit repatriation, and other devices — ensures that the economies of the periphery (Third World) ". . . remain underdeveloped for lack of access to their own surplus" (Frank, 1967, p. 9). Since the IMF is a major institution of international capitalism, it is not surprising that it is viewed as maintaining foreign domination and so frustrating growth and "autonomous development" in the Third World.

Cheryl Payer's *The Debt Trap* (1974) has been considered by many observers as the dominant application of this sort of analysis to the topic of IMF-Third World relations. Like the structuralists, she argues the short-run stabilization policies recommended in a typical Stand-by Arrangement have negative consequences for growth since they "open" the economy and thus effectively destroy any basis that may have been carefully laid for "autonomous" development along, say, ISI lines. In addition, the Fund's general encouragement of export production reinforces dependency by locking Third World economies into the vagaries of markets in the core. Moreover, she argues that the IMF leads peripheral economies into a so-called "debt trap." Since an agreement with the IMF can open the door to new official and private sources of credit, this allows Third World countries to survive balance of payments crises through either increasing indebtedness or "auctioning" of domestic assets to foreign investors. In the process, the nations become "aid junkies" — lurching from crisis to crisis with infusions of private and official credit. As a result, their economies fall increasingly under the control of multinational corporations, international banks, and core governments; the latter phenomenon maintains surplus drain and so prevents development.

Thus, in Payer's analysis, the IMF is seen as dampening growth potential and increasing dependency; in addition, its policies have helped create the debt problem it is now attempting to manage. Unfortunately for Payer and the dependency critique, the Fund's demonstration of mixed growth impacts may be used to argue as well against this approach as against the structuralist framework outlined earlier.

But has the Fund really refuted the *Marxist* criticism? I think not. While output growth is important for economists of any persuasion, the unique Marxist contribution to the development literature is its *focus* on the class character of different development processes. For Marxists, the question is not whether the Fund frustrates development *per se*, but whether it promotes a particular kind of development with benefits accruing to certain social groups. Payer's early work has indeed contributed to the Marxist understanding of the IMF by suggesting that the Fund's general promotion of an open economy and its specific policies allow the relatively stronger (or more "efficient") capitals of the core to dominate the relatively weaker capitals of the periphery. But this core-periphery (or intra-capitalist) dimension is only one aspect of Fund policy.[5]

By promoting an open economy and using conditionality to enforce balance of payments "discipline," the Fund also helps secure the domination of labor by capital in the various member countries' economies. This is because: (1) "an open economy generally serves the interests of the capitalists in resisting working-class demands for improved wages and social services" (Block, 1977, p. 7) and, (2) even though "the Fund holds that distributional considerations are none of its business" (Williamson 1983, p. 630), the specific policies of the IMF are designed to ensure that the burden of adjustment is placed onto non-elite classes. This is not merely because of the economic framework of the IMF but because securing the cooperation of local elites for the implementation of IMF programs involves sparing them the costs of adjustment.[6] As Williamson comments, "there must be a danger that the typical Fund mission will avoid suggesting cuts that impinge on the politically powerful" (Williamson, 1983, p. 63). As a result, the "austerity programs (of the Fund) favor the most powerful sectors of the (local) bourgeoisie as much as they favor imperialist powers" (Serulle and Boin, 1983, p. 128).[7]

Using this insight, we should expect Fund programs to be accompanied by a redistribution of power (and income) toward local ruling elites and away from working and popular classes. *Either* increasing or decreasing growth rates would be compatible with such a redistributive outcome; the actual movement of growth would depend on the relationship of income distribution to savings and consumption ratios, the relationship of savings to capital formation, and whether the economy is primarily demand-or supply-constrained in its growth prospects. The main point is this: the empirical demonstration of the Marxist thesis relies on showing a consistent negative "IMF effect" on some barometer of working class power and income. Below, I do exactly that.

3. The experience in Latin America

In this section, I report on my investigation of the effects of IMF programs in Latin America. I begin by explaining the construction and methodology of the study. Subsequently, I present the results. A more detailed description of variable construction, data sources, the country set, and the statistical methods is included in an appendix available from the author.

(a) Variables, domain, and method

The variables examined include balance of payments measures, inflation rates, growth rates and dependency measures, and, finally, indicators of labor's share of income; each variable is briefly defined as it is presented. The country set studied was limited to 18 Latin American countries. The data cover the time period 1965-81, longer than that of any published study.[8] The study examined two sets of program countries: (1) those engaged in stabilization programs under *any* Stand-by Arrangement or any EFF (which I call Type I), and (2) only those countries engaged in an upper credit SB or EFF (which I call Type II).[9] To shorten my presentation, I will focus on the results for the upper credit (Type II) set. There was a similar pattern of results when all programs were considered; where there are important differences or where the results for the Type I set are otherwise relevant, this is noted in the text or footnotes.

The methods employed here are modeled after the techniques used in the Fund-sponsored studies of Donavan (1982) and Reichmann and Stillson (1978). Like Donavan, yearly absolute and relative comparisons are made[10] Like Reichmann and Stillson, methods (both parametric and non-parametric) were used to attach statistical significance levels to the findings.

More specifically, absolute comparisons were made between the values of program country variables (or their rates of changes) in the year preceding the IMF program and in the year of the program.[11] The significance of the differences in pre-and post-program variables was determined through use of the paired sample t-test, the signs test, and the Wilcoxon ranked — sums tests. For clarity of presentation, only the results of the non-parametric signs tests are reported below. Of the cases where the assumptions required for the two parametric methods were met, most significance levels were similar to those obtained in the signs test; the exceptions are duly noted in the test or footnotes.

In Table 2, I report the one-tail significance levels of the signs tests for absolute comparisons. In Row 1, for example, I consider the current account as a percentage of GNP and test the simple alternative hypothesis, proposed by the IMF, that the level after an agreement exceeds the level before (post > pre); that is, that the current account deficit is reduced or a surplus is generated by an IMF-supported stabilization program. The significance level for this hypothesis is reported in the last column and will be discussed in the results section below.

Table 2   Absolute comparisons (upper credit programs)

Variable	Alternative Hypothesis	Significance Level
Current account as % of GNP (current account ratio)	[IMF] post > pre	(0.598)
Change in current account ratio	[IMF] post > pre	(0.344)
Overall BOP as % of GNP (BOP ratio)	[IMF] post > pre	(0.055)
Inflation rate (based on GDP deflator)	[IMF] post < pre	(0.990)
Change in inflation rate	[IMF] post < pre	(0.970)
Growth rate of GDP	[GOC] post < pre	(0.500)
Change in growth rate	[GOC] post < pre	(0.394)
Labor share of income	[MPJ] post < pre	(0.043)
Change in labor share	[MPJ] post < pre	(0.127)

*In all cases, the null hypothesis is that there was no change in the variable during the course of the IMF program (e.g., that post = pre); a low significance level indicates rejection of this null hypothesis in favor of the specified alternative.

Absolute comparison can be misleading, of course. To find, for example, that growth rates for the program countries decline is unimpressive if growth rates for the non-program countries are declining as rapidly or more rapidly in the same period of time. Thus, I broke the country set for each year into program and non-program groups to examine the *relative* performance of the program group. The significance of the difference between the two groups for each year was determined using both parametric (*t*-test) and non-parametric (Mann-Whitney) techniques. The significance levels reported below are based on the Mann-Whitney procedure; where the relevant assumptions were met, the parametric results followed a similar pattern.

The logic of the statistics summarizing these year-by year relative comparisons can best be appreciated by means of a graphical analogy. Consider the trend lines depicted in Figure 1. There, the dotted and solid lines represent the mean change in labor's share of income for *all* (Type I) program and non-program countries, respectively.[12] We can ask two sorts of questions about the relative performance of program countries: (1) do program countries *consistently* do worse — that is, is the dotted line usually beneath the solid line?; and (2) are the differences in the experience of program countries *dramatic* — that is, are the lines occasionally far apart (given the appropriate variance and degrees of freedom)?

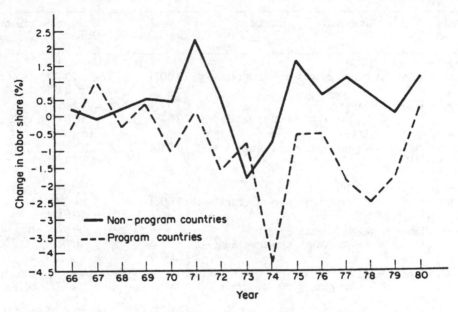

Figure 1. Mean change in labor share of income for program and non-program countries. The program country group consists of all countries in the set with IMF programs, either upper or lower credit.

In Table 3, these two points — the consistency of the result and the extent of difference in any year — are summarized in the following manner. To gauge consistency, a summary significance level for a specified simple alternative hypothesis is calculated for the yearly relative comparisons; this calculation relies on the use of a cumulative binomial probability as explained in the appendix. For example, in row 1 of Table 3, the difference between this year's current account ratio and last year's is tested against the alternative hypothesis, held by the IMF, that program countries fare relatively better (experiencing either a larger improvement in their current account ratios or a lesser worsening). In the table, this is indicated in column 2 by the statement "program > non-program (+)." Column 3 reports the overall significance of the test statistic in light of this hypothesis. In column 4, years are listed in which the differences between program and non-program countries were "significant."[13] The sign of the difference (positive if the program countries had the greater variable value; negative if not) is also noted.

Before proceeding to the results themselves, a few more methodological notes are in order. Note that significance and not confidence levels are reported; thus, a significance level of , say, 0.001, indicates that there is good reason to reject the null hypothesis in favor of the specified alternative. All significance levels are reported since as Donavan (1982) points out in criticizing Connors' (1979) study of Fund programs, it is "helpful to know how close the test statistics were to the 95% level" (Donavan, 1982, p. 182).

Table 3   Relative comparisons (upper credit programs)

Variable	Alternative Hypothesis	Overall Significance	Years of Significance Difference
Change in current account ratio	[IMF] program > non-program (+)	(0.402)	− + 1972 (**), 1973 (**), 1978 (**)
Change in BOP ratio	[IMF] program > non-program (+)	(0.038)	− + 1976 (**), 1978 (**)
Change in inflation rate (based on GDP deflator)	[IMF] program < non-program (—)	(0.850)	−1979 (*) + 1970 (*), 1974 (*), 1980 (*)
Change in growth rate	[GOC] program < non-program (—)	(0.697)	−1975 (**), 1980 (**), 1981 (**) + 1979 (**)
Change in labor share	[MPJ] program < non-program (—)	(0.001)	− 1971 (*), 1972 (*), 1978 (*) +
Growth rate of total real consumption	[MPJ] program < non-program (—)	(0.011)	−1966 (*), 1969 (*), 1967 (*), 1978 (*), 1980 (*) + 1973 (*), 1974 (*)

1) In each year, the null hypothesis is that the median of the variable for the program group is the same as the median for the non-program group; this hypothesis is tested using a Mann-Whitney rank test. An (**) by a "significant" year means that the difference between medians in that year ('+' if the program median is greater than the non-program median; '—' if it is less) was significant at a 10% *two-tail* level; (*) indicates significance at a 20% *two-tail* level.

2) In calculating overall significance, the null hypothesis is that the number of years in which the program median exceeds the non-program median is equal to the number of years in which the program median is exceeded by the non-program median; a low significance level indicates rejection of this null hypothesis in favor of the specified alternative.

Note further that except for the test statistics on the years of significant difference, all significance levels are one-tail. The justification for one-tails is rather simple: Each school of thought holds rather firm simple alternative hypotheses about the movements of various measures during an IMF-supported stabilization program. Moreover, one-tail tests are more powerful than two-tails in testing the simple alternative. They are, however, quite prone to the error of accepting the null hypothesis when, in fact, it should be rejected in favor of an absolutely opposing simple alternative. A significance level of, say, 0.990 is probably evidence of this latter situation.

(b) Results of the study

Balance of Payments. Two basic balance of payments measures were examined: (1) the current account ratio (the current account as a percentage of GNP)[14] and (2) the overall balance of payments as a percentage of GNP.[15] The yearly percentage change in the current account ratio — the difference between this year's value and last year's — was also examined.

The Fund argues that its programs lead to improvement in both sorts of measures. In the absolute comparisons, I represent this IMF position with the simple alternative hypothesis that current account ratios and the overall balance of payments improve concurrent with Fund programs. In the relative case, the IMF alternative hypothesis is that program countries experience more improvement (or less worsening) in these measures than non-program countries.

Looking at the absolute comparisons in Table 2, one finds no significant improvement in the current account ratios after an IMF program (as indicated by the 0.598 significance level); indeed, the results suggest that current account ratios worsened, albeit insignificantly. Did the worsening of the current account at least slow down? Looking at a measure for the change in the current account ratio one again finds results that are not significant at any reasonable level. However, turning to the overall balance of payments measure, we note an absolute improvement as indicated by the significance level of 0.055.

The relative comparisons described in Table 3 reveal that while there are a number of individual years in which the change in the current account ratio is larger (more positive) for program countries than for non-program countries, the overall significance level is very weak (at 0.402). In contrast, for the overall balance measure, the significance level is 0.038 and there are a few years in which the difference between program and non-program countries is significant .

What do these two sets of results indicate? One implication might be that the improvement in the overall balance of payments is coming not through the current account but rather through the capital account; at the least, it is the capital account improvement (perhaps in conjunction with current account improvement) which is essential to making the overall measure attain significance. Such capital account improvement might square with both the IMF's argument that Fund programs have a catalytic effect in attracting private funds (Killick, 1984, p. 230) and Payer's notion that the IMF's programs help to create a "debt trap." To investigate this and related issues, I examined absolute changes in various items in the balance of payments.

For the upper credit program countries, I found that the trade balance improved in only 49% of the cases; while this may be interpreted as lending credence to the structuralists' elasticity pessimism, it should be remembered that not all IMF programs recommend devaluation. On the other hand, the balance in other goods, services, and income *worsened* in 63% of the cases while the capital account *improved* in 65% of the cases.[16] Recall that this improved capital account *cannot* be occurring because of the IMF credit itself — official IMF assistance comes in "below the line" and so is not counted in the capital account.

Moreover, for the alternative hypothesis that capital account changes were larger (more positive) in dollar terms than changes in the balance of all goods, services, and income, the significance level was a strong 0.054 for the Type I countries but an anemic 0.315 for the upper credit group. This pattern of results is particularly interesting; the "stronger " significance when lower credit countries are included in the program set indicates that one reason for requesting Fund supervision of economic policy — even when balance of payments problems are not severe enough to require upper credit borrowing — might be to increase private capital inflows. Coupled with the evidence of general improvement in the capital account and overall balance, it seems that signing an IMF agreement amounted to a "seal of approval" that allowed program countries to obtain loans from private banks, attract foreign investors, and entice local capitalists to stay.[17]

Inflation. The Fund generally argues that its programs tend to reduce the rate of inflation or at least the rate at which it increases; in the absolute comparisons below, I consider this to be the Fund's alternative hypothesis. For relative comparisons, the Funds's alternative hypothesis is thought to be that the increase in inflation rates in program countries is less than the increase in non-program countries.[18]

For the IMF's alternative hypothesis that it lowers inflation rates, the results are abysmal. Indeed, the significance levels in Table 2 suggest that rather than being coincident with reductions in the inflation rate or with slowdowns in the rate of increase of the inflation rate, inflation rates increase and at a faster rate than they were rising before the introduction of the IMF-supported stabilization program.

Turning to the relative comparisons of Table 3, one finds a similar result: the overall significance level of 0.850 indicates that program countries may have been experiencing increases in their inflation rates larger than those experienced by countries without the "benefit" of Fund help and advice. A glance at the years of significant differences between program and non-program countries reinforces the notion of a lack of success in restraining inflation. In the years reported, there are more years of significantly greater inflation increases in program countries than years of significantly lower inflation increases. In Latin America at least, Fund programs probably tend to be coincident with an acceleration of inflation.

Why does inflation accelerate? I do not explore this here but refer the reader to a recent piece by Kirkpatrick and Onis (1985) that tackles this matter directly. Nonetheless, it is worth mentioning that in the face of the Fund's usual recommendation that the growth of nominal wages be restrained, inflation acceleration is consistent with the redistributive effects to be noted momentarily.

Growth. In examining growth, we consider the alternative hypothesis, "proposed" by the growth-oriented critique (GOC), that IMF programs dampen growth rates. A related hypothesis for the dependency framework is that the Fund promotes dependency (as measured, say, by exports and imports as a percentage of GNP). The IMF, of course, contends it has no such impact on growth and would see an increase in the dependency measure described above as evidence of increased international integration. Such integration, Fund economists would suggest, will ultimately promote growth and development.

Looking at the absolute comparisons of Table 2, one finds no evidence for the growth-dampening thesis. Significance levels for both the growth rate and the change in the growth rate (the difference between this year's growth rate and last year's) are 0.500 and 0.394, respectively. As the IMF has insisted, Fund programs have no consistent impact on growth.

How do program countries fare relative to non-program countries? In Table 3, we compare the change in growth rates in program countries relative to the change in those rates in non-program countries and find no evidence that the change in growth rates is relatively lower in program countries (i.e., either lower increases or greater decreases). While there are several years where the change in growth rates in program countries is significantly less (or more negative) than the change in non-program countries, there is at least one year in which the opposite is true. These results on growth are even more mixed if we examine all (including lower-credit) arrangements.

While not reported in the tables, a standard "dependency" measure does increase relatively;[19] however, since this seems to have few growth costs, this provides more evidence for the open economy prescriptions of the IMF than for the usual autarkic remedies of the dependency school. In short, this study reaffirms the Fund's rejection of the generalizability of the growth-oriented critique.

Labor Share. Finally, we turn to absolute and relative comparisons of labor's share of income (labor's share of the net domestic product; a discussion of its construction and theoretical appropriateness is in the appendix). As noted earlier, my simple alternative hypothesis (MPJ) is that there are reductions in labor's share of income during the course of Fund programs.[20]

Why would we expect evidence to reject the null hypothesis of no change in labor share in favor of this particular alternative? As argued before, the IMF's desire to secure the cooperation of local elites may lead them to design programs which place the burden of adjustment on workers and other "popular classes." In this vein, IMF programs have increasingly required nominal wage restraint at least for government employees (see Beveridge and Kelly, 1980, p. 240). Coupled with inflationary effects of devaluation and the removal of price controls and other consumer subsidies (which make up part of the "social wage"), workers will likely bear the brunt of adjustment.[21] If government deficit cutting hits basic social services (which would be likely in the case of an elite seeking to displace burdens), the "social wage" will decline further and the distributional consequences will be worse.

Turning to Table 1, we find that the alternative hypothesis that labor share is reduced obtains the strongest significance levels reported in *any* of the absolute comparisons (0.040). Further, it appears that this is not simply the result of a process that was already in place before the beginning of the program. Considering the relatively strong results (0.127) on the change in labor's share of income, one can conclude that even if labor share were declining at the beginning of a Fund program, that decline generally accelerates during the IMF program period. The results of parametric (*t*-test) absolute comparisons on these labor share measures are even stronger.

The results of relative comparisons also indicate strong evidence — an overall significance level of 0.001 — in favor of the author's alternative hypothesis that the program group experiences smaller increases or larger declines in labor share.[22] Further, there are three years in which the change in labor share of income is significantly lower in the program countries and none in which the reverse is true; moreover, the number of years of significantly lower changes in labor share in the program group increases to six in. the examination of all (including lower credit) arrangements. Indeed, for the upper credit programs, there is only one year (1967) in which the mean (or median) of the change in labor share in the program countries is even insignificantly greater than it is in the non-program countries.

This redistributive effect can also be confirmed by testing the rate of change of real total consumption, a measure Donavan (1982) uses; in addition, since this measure includes government consumption, it may also catch the reductions in social wage discussed above. The relative comparisons of Table 3 reveal that real consumption growth rates are lower in the program countries as indicated by an overall significance level of 0.011 and by the preponderance of years in which this measure was significantly lower in the program countries. Assuming that workers have a higher propensity to consume than elites and that cuts in government consumption fall most heavily on programs used by non-elite groups, this result squares with the earlier findings for labor share. In short, the single most consistent effect the IMF seems to have is the redistribution of income away from workers.

4. Conclusion

I have previously outlined the findings of the two IMF studies of the "effects" of Fund programs (Donavan, 1982; Reichmann and Stillson, 1978) — significant gains in reducing current account and balance of payment deficits, minor effects on the inflation rate (or its rate of increase), and few, if any, associated growth costs.

The profile that emerges from this study is somewhat different. For the time period and country set examined, we find: (1) insignificant improvement in current accounts accompanied by significant improvement in the overall balance of payments in general and the capital account in particular, (2) increases in both the inflation rate itself and its rate of increase, (3) mixed impacts on growth rates, and, (4) the strongest and most consistent effect of Fund programs: absolute and relative reductions in labor share of income.

Taken together, the results of this study provide ammunition for criticisms both of the Fund and of its traditional growth-oriented critics. For the Fund, it may be noted that rather than achieving their stated goals of inflation reduction and current account and long-term balance of payments equilibria, Fund programs — and the "seal of approval" they bestow — seem more effective at securing loans and other capital inflows for the program countries. This does not promote long-term balance of payments equilibrium for if the lending ever stopped (which it would in the early 1980s), balance of payments and debt crises would emerge. Thus, as Payer (1974) suggested earlier, the debt crisis the Fund now purports to manage is, in part, of its own making.

The growth-oriented critique of the Fund also stands challenged. First, the argument that the Third World's balance of payments deficits should be financed rather than corrected (due to the development deficit, etc.) seems actually to have been addressed by the capital inflow secured by the Fund's programs. More important, this study — like those of the Fund and other researchers — reveals no evidence that Fund programs consistently lower growth rates. A standard dependency measure does rise relatively; however, since there are no growth consequences to this increase in international integration, it may be difficult to argue that this is a negative result (unless one makes the argument for relative autarky on different grounds).

In contrast, a class analytic or *distribution-oriented* critique can provide a successful explanation of the two major findings: labor share reductions and capital flow increases. The labor share reduction is not surprising in light of the Fund's role of providing a structure for the dual domination of periphery by core *and* labor by capital. The macroeconomic prescriptions of Fund programs lower labor share and increase the surplus available to dominant classes, tilting the balance of power to those already in power. This is partly because, as argued previously, the cooperation of local elites can be obtained by sparing them the burdens of adjustment. This rise in surplus — given no general effects on growth rates — should lead to an increase in profitability sufficient to attract the private capital inflows demonstrated.[23] This inflow may allow a rosy picture of balance of payments improvement, but beneath it lies worsening income distribution, exacerbated social tension, and little or no improvement in the inflation, current account, and growth fundamentals.

In the current period of IMF "management" of the debt crisis, the growth-oriented critique so belittled by Fund economists has reemerged. It is true that in the last few years, IMF programs have been associated with output declines; determining whether these are relatively worse in program countries requires further empirical work. It is likely, however that the pattern of redistributive outcomes associated with Fund programs has continued.[24] It is these outcomes — and the social conflicts engendered by them — that impose social limits to debt management as "objective" as the standard full employment constraint.

After riots induced by IMF-recommended price increases left 60 dead, 200 wounded, and 4,300 arrested, the planning minister of the Dominican Republic rejected (temporarily) the IMF pact commenting that "It is not that we are unwilling to put our own house in order. It is that we want to keep our house and not let it go up in flames." Economic policymakers both inside and outside the Fund should recognize that the inequitable apportionment of adjustment burdens demonstrated in this article cannot persist without letting societies "go up in flames." The design of stabilization policies to replace the unfair and often ineffective Fund policies should be the object of new research.

Notes

*My thanks go to Samuel Bowles, Carmen Diana Deere, Karen Pfeiffer, and Gerald Epstein for their help in developing both the empirical and theoretical projects this work embodies. I would also like to thank Ann Helwege and two anonymous referees for suggesting ways to improve the analysis and reorganize the paper.

1. A recent IMF study (Khan and Knight, 1983) argues and demonstrates empirically that both external and internal factors led to NODC current account deterioration in the 1970s. In their view, however, since at least some of the external factors are unlikely to be reversed (particularly movements in the terms of trade), adjustment required and continues to require shifts in domestic demand policies. Thus, in this view, the fault still lies with the internal policies of the NODCs.

2. For example, in 1978, the repayments of non-oil developing countries to the IMF exceeded their borrowing (or "repurchases") by 700.8 million SDR. In 1979, borrowing exceeded repayment by only 154.0 million SDR (Cline and Weintraub, 1981, p. 6).

3. A similar pattern of results is noted in Connors (1979). Killick (1984) provides a good review of all the various studies and conducts some of his own tests as well.

4. These comparisons are also made for four quarters before and four quarters after; the pattern of results was similar although less significant.

5. A similar Marxist criticism of Payer is offered by Phillips (1983).

6. In different terms, this point has been acknowledged by two Fund economists who write that often: ". . .those with the most to lose from a program whose distributional objectives are egalitarian tend to be those with the most power. Moreover, if not provided for in the design of the program, these interests will tend to assert themselves" (Johnson and Salop, 1980, p. 21).

7. Melo and Robinson (1982) provide a model of the distributional impact of trade adjustment policies for three different archetype economies. For our purposes, what is most interesting is their findings that elites will either benefit or suffer less than other groups if they are able to maintain or create oligarchic (non-democratic) political regimes. The association of IMF-style policies with a turn to authoritarianism is discussed in Foxley (1983) and modeled more formally in Pastor (1987).

8. Killick's (1984) review of studies of IMF programs covers a similarly long period but his own empirical work only looks at the period 1974-79.

9. The distinction between lower and upper credit tranche Stand-bys for the whole time period of the study is not general public information. While IMF press releases and annual reports in recent years sometimes specify the nature of the credit tranches, this was not previously the practice. The information used here to distinguish SBs over the whole 1965-81 period for these particular countries was provided by the Public Relations Department of the Fund.

10. Such annual, rather than quarterly-based, comparisons are dictated by data limitations. While some of the series used below is available on a quarterly basis (specifically, *some* of the balance of payments variables from the International Financial Statistics series), critical

variables, such as growth rates and wage shares, are available only on an annual basis. For purposes of consistency, all the tests are for yearly changes.

11. The definition of what exactly constitutes a program period in both the absolute and relative comparisons more or less follows Donavan (1982). For clarification, see the available appendix. Comparisons were only for one-year periods since I believe that multiple-year comparisons hardly allow one to isolate the effects of the Fund programs.

12. The figure is constructed for all (Type I) program countries to avoid a discontinuity in 1976 (when there were no upper credit programs in the country set used to test labor share). In addition, to "smooth" this graph of means and give a more realistic idea of the difference between program and non-program groups, I eliminated one country from consideration that had both positive and negative outliers; the country is included in the statistical tests reported in the text since the non-parametric procedures are not as sensitive to outliers. If the tests reported are done with the country excluded, the results follow a similar pattern.

13. The significance levels employed in these yearly comparisons are both dictated by the small number of observations per year and consistent with those used by Reichmann and Stillson (1978); for them, a confidence level of 90% was sufficient to characterize a variable's movement as "significant".

14. Following Donavan (1982), the current account was defined as total savings minus total investment. Results for another more direct measure (the balance of goods, services, and income as a percentage of GNP) followed a similar pattern but with slightly weaker significance levels for the IMF's alternative hypotheses.

15. Donavan (1982) does not use GNP as a base because of the problem of choosing the appropriate exchange rate to convert the local currency-denominated GNP into a measure that can be compared with the dollar-denominated reserve changes measure (which both he and I use in calculating the overall balance of payments). My method of calculation avoids this exchange rate problem as explained in the appendix. Tests on a measure identical to Donavan's follow a similar pattern on the relative comparisons but were weaker on the absolute comparisons. I also tested a net foreign assets measure like that used in Reichmann and Stillson (1978). While the results were similar, the problem of choosing the appropriate exchange rate to convert this measure to dollars renders the tests theoretically suspect.

16. The capital account measure included net errors and omissions since the latter is usually made up of rapidly moving short-term capital. Leaving out net errors and omissions yields similar results.

17. This "seal of approval" effect is discussed in Williamson (1983, pp. 608-609). In 1983, the General Director of the IMF, Jacques de Larosiere, noted that each dollar of Fund credit led to four dollars in new commercial loans (Serulle and Boin, 1983, p.1). Such "parallel financing" became common practice in the 1970s and has become particularly important in the debt crisis of the 1980s.

18. In testing inflation, I examined inflation rates based on both the Consumer Price Index and the GDP deflator. I report only the results on the deflator-based rate since the results were fairly similar and because Donavan argues that ". . . the GDP deflator might for some purposes be a better indication of the underlying inflation rate (than the CPI)" (Donavan, 1982, p. 182). In addition, I considered both the inflation experience in all countries and, following Donavan, in a country set that excluded countries with rates above 35%. Again, similar results lead me to economize and present the results for the examination of *all* countries.

19. Let the alternative hypothesis be that dependency (as measured by DEP, exports plus imports as a percentage of GNP) rises during the course of Fund programs. In absolute comparisons, this alternative hypothesis obtains a significance level of only 0.198 for the upper credit programs. However, relative comparisons on the rate of change of the dependency measure (CHDEP) for upper credit arrangements obtains an overall significance level of 0.038 for the alternative hypothesis and there is a preponderance of years in which CHDEP is significantly larger in the program countries.

20. For reasons of data availability the country set is slightly different for the tests on labor share. This is discussed in the appendix.

21. See Feinberg (1982) for a more detailed discussion of the likely distributional impacts of IMF programs. Duncan (1985) provides an excellent study of the impacts of Fund-sponsored stabilization in Costa Rica in the early 1980s.

22. 1981 is not included in these relative comparisons because of the low number of observations on labor share for that year.

23. This is acknowledged by two Fund economists who argue that during a stabilization program, "real wage rates may have to fall and real profit rates increase so as to encourage increased foreign capital inflow and private domestic capital formation" (Johnson and Salop, 1980, p. 23).

24. Working along the lines of the class analytic perspective developed in this paper, Duncan (1985) analyzed the effects of Fund stablization in Costa Rica in the early 1980s. He, too, found that balance of payments improvement was mostly through the capital account. Most important, he argues that ". . . the findings of this study confirm the hypothesis that orthodox Fund stablization policies tend to redistribute real income to agro-exporters, particularly agri-business and larger landowners, at the expense of urban and most rural workers" (Duncan, 1985, p. 57).

References

Abdalla, Ismail-Sabri, (1980) 'The inadequacy and loss of legitimacy of the International Monetary Fund,' *Development Dialogue*, Vol. 2, pp. 25-53.

Arida, Persio, and Edmar Bacha, (1984) 'Balancao de Pagamentos: Uma Analise de Desequilibrio para Economias Semi-industrializadas,' *Pesquisa e Planejamento Economico*, Vol. 14, No. 1, pp. 1-58.

Bacha, Edmar L., (1983) 'Vicissitudes of recent stablization attempts in Brazil and the IMF Alternative,' in Williamson, pp. 323-340.

Beveridge, W. A. and Margaret R. Kelly, (1980) 'Fiscal content of financial programs supported by stand-by arrangements in the upper credit tranches, 1969-78,' IMF *Staff Papers*, Vol. 27, pp. 205-244.

Block, Fred L. (1977) *The Origins of International Economic Disorder: A Study of United States International Monetary Policy from World War II to the Present* (Berkeley and Los Angeles, California: University of California Press).

Cline, William R., (1983) 'Economic stabilization in developing countries: Theory and stylized facts,' in Williamson, pp. 175-208.

Cline, William R., (1983a) *International Debt and the Stability of the World Economy* (Washington, D. C.: Institute of International Economics).

Cline, William R., (1985) 'International debt: From crisis to recovery?' *American Economic Review,* Vol. 75, No. 2, pp. 185-190.

Cline, William R., and Sidney Weintraub (Eds.), (1981) *Economic Stablization in Developing Countries* (Washington, D.C.: The Brookings Institution.

Collier, David (Ed.), (1979) *The New Authoritarianism in Latin America* (Princeton, N. J.: Princeton University Press).

Connors, Thomas A., (1979) 'The Apparent Effects of Recent IMF Stabilization Programs,' *International Finance Discussion Papers*, No. 135, Board of Governors of the Federal Reserve System.

Crockett, Andrew, (1981) 'Stablization policies in developing countries: Some policy considerations,' IMF *Staff Papers*, Vol. 28, No. 1, pp. 54-79.

Cutajar, Michael Zammit, (1980) 'Background notes on the International Monetary Fund,' *Development Dialogue*, Vol, 2, pp. 95-112.

Dale, William B., (1983) 'Financing and adjustment of payments imbalances,' in Williamson, pp. 3-16.

Dell, Sidney, (1982) 'Stablization: The political economy of overkill,' *World Development*, Vol. 10, No. 8, pp. 597-612.

Dell, Sidney, and Roger Lawrence, (1980) 'The balance of payments adjustment process in developing countries' (New York: Pergamon Press).

Diaz-Alejandro, Carlos, (1981) 'Southern Cone stablization plans,' in Cline and Weintraub, pp. 119-147.

Diamand, Marcelo, (1978) 'Towards a change in the economic paradigm through the experience of developing countries,' *Journal of Development Economics*, Vol. 5, No. 1, pp. 19-53.

Donavan, Donal J., (1982) 'Macroeconomic performance and adjustment under Fund-supported programs: The experience of the Seventies,' IMF *Staff Papers*, Vol. 29, pp. 171-203.

Duncan, Cameron, (1985) 'IMF conditionality, fiscal policy, and the pauperization of labor in Costa Rica,' Paper presented at the American Economics Association meetings.

Eckaus, Richard S., (1982) 'Observations on the conditionality of international financial institutions,' *World Development*, Vol. 10, No. 9, pp. 767-780.

Feinberg, Richard E., (1982) 'The International Monetary Fund and basic needs: The impact of stand-by arrangements,' in Margaret E. Crahan (Ed.), *Human Rights and Basic Needs in the Americas* (Washington, D.C.: Georgetown University Press).

Foxley, Alejandro, (1983) *Latin American Experiments in Neoconservative Economics* (Berkeley and Los Angeles: University of California Press).

Frank, Andre Gunder, (1967) *Capitalism and Underdevelopment in Latin America: Historical Studies of Chile and Brazil* (New York: Monthly Review Press).

Girvan, Norman, (1980) 'Swallowing the IMF medicine in the Seventies,' *Development Dialogue,* Vol. 2, pp. 55-74.

Gold, Joseph, (1970) *The Stand-by Arrangements of the International Monetary Fund* (Washington, D.C.: International Monetary Fund).

Guitian, Manuel, (1980) 'Fund conditionality and the international adjustment process: The early period, 1950-70,' *Finance and Development*, Vol. 17, No. 4.

Guitain, Manuel, (1981) *Conditionality: Access to Fund Resources*, Pamphlet reprinted from *Finance and Development*, (Washington, D.C.: International Monetary Fund).

Hirschman, Albert, (1968) 'The political economy of import-substituting industrialization in Latin America,' *Quarterly Journal of Economics*, Vol. 82, No. 1, pp. 1-32.

Hirschman, Albert, (1979) 'The return to authoritarianism in Latin America and the search for its economic determinants,' in Collier, pp. 61-98.

Johnson, Omotunde, and Joanne Salop, (1980) 'Distributional aspects of stablization programs in developing countries,' IMF *Staff Papers*, Vol. 27, pp. 1-23.

Khan, Mohsin S., and Malcolm D. Knight, (1981) 'Stablization programs in developing countries: A formal framework,' IMF *Staff Papers*, Vol. 28 No. 1, pp. 1-53.

Khan, Moshin S., and Malcolm D. Knight, (1982) 'Some theoretical and empirical issues relating to economic stablization in developing countries,' *World Development*, Vol. 10, No. 9, pp. 709-730.

Khan, Mohsin S., and Malcolm D. Knight, (1983) 'Determinants of current account balances of non-oil developing countries in the 1970's: An empirical analysis,' IMF *Staff Papers*, Vol. 30, No. 4, pp. 819-842.

Killick, Tony, (1984) 'The impact of Fund stabilisation programmes,' in Tony Killick (Ed.), *The Quest for Economic Stabilisation* (New York: St. Martin's Press).

Kirkpatrick, Colin, and Ziya Onis, (1985) 'Industrialisation as a structural determinant of inflation performance in IMF stablisation programmes in less developed countries,' *Journal of Development Studies*, Vol. 21, No. 3, pp. 347-361.

Krugman, Paul, and Lance Taylor, (1978) 'Contractionary effects of devaluation,' *Journal of International Economics*, No. 8, pp. 445-456.

Lichtensztenj, Samuel, (1983) 'IMF-developing countries: Conditionality and strategy,' in Williamson, pp. 209-222.

Melo, Jaime de, and Sherman Robinson, (1982) 'Trade adjustment polcies and income distirbution in three archetype developing economies,' *Journal of Development Economics*, Vol. 10, No. 1, pp. 67-92.

Moffit, Michael, (1983) *The World's Money* (New York:Simon and Schuster).

Pastor, Manuel Jr., *The International Monetary Fund and Latin America: Economic Stablization and Class Conflict* (Boulder, Colorado: Westview Press, forthcoming 1987).

Payer, Cheryl, (1974) *The Debt Trap: The IMF and the Third World* (New York and London: Monthly Review Press).

Phillips, Ron, (1983) 'The role of the International Monetary Fund in the post-Bretton Woods era,' *Review of Radical Political Economics*, Vol. 15, No. 2).

Reichmann, Thomas M., and Richard T. Stillson, (1978) 'Experience with programs of balance of payments adjustment: Stand-by arrangements in the higher tranches, 1963-72,' IMF *Staff Papers*, Vol. 25, pp. 292-310.

Rweyemamu, Justinian F., (1980) 'Restructuring the international monetary system,' *Development Dialogue*, Vol. 2, pp. 75-91.

Serra, Jose, (1979) 'Three mistaken theses regarding the connection between industrialization and authoritarian regimes,' in Collier, pp. 99-163.

Serule, Jose, and Jacquelin Boin, (1983) *Fundo Monetario Internacional: Capital Financiero Crisis Mundial* (Santo Domingo: Ediciones Gramil).

Sisson, Charles A., (1986) 'Fund-supported programs and income distribution in LDC's,' *Finance and Development,* Vol. 23, No. 1, pp. 30-32.

Taylor, Lance, (1979) *Macro Models for Developing Countries* (New York: McGraw-Hill).

Taylor, Lance, (1981) 'IS/LM in the Tropics: Diagramatics of the new structuralist macro critique,' in Cline and Weintraub, pp. 464-503.

Wiesner, Eduardo, (1985) 'Latin American debt: Lessons and pending issues,' *American Economic Review*, Vol. 75, No. 2, pp. 1991-195.

Williamson, John (Ed.), (1983) *IMF Conditionality* (Washington, D.C.: Institute for International Economics, pp. 605-660.

Williamson, John, (1983) 'The lending policies of the International Monetary Fund,' in Williamson.

29. Structural Changes in the World Economy and New Policy Issues in Developing Countries

Lal Jayawardena

This paper highlights three key problems requiring resolution in the 1990s. The first is that of radically altering for the better the development experience of the developing countries during the 1980s which has been so disastrous as to elicit the description — the "lost" development decade. For the Third World as a whole, real growth which, according to the World Bank's most recent World Development Report, averaged 5.4 percent during 1973 to 1980 fell to 3.2 percent in the first half of the 1980s.

The growth of the low-income developing countries excluding the large land masses, India and China, fell to 3 percent, and in the case of low-income Africa to 0.7 percent from an already unacceptably low figure during the 1970s of 2 percent. The fall has been sharpest in the case of the debt-ridden middle-income group of developing countries — from 5.7 percent during 1973-80 to 1.6 percent during 1980-85. In per capita terms, these magnitudes translate at best into the stagnation of incomes and in many cases to actual declines. It is this dismal performance relieved only by the booming economies of the Pacific Rim which needs to be turned around in the 1990s.

The second problem is that of maintaining adequate growth in the developed economies while simultaneously correcting today's major payments imbalances between key developed countries. Clearly, the success with which this problem is tackled will crucially affect the outlook for the developing countries and the resolution of my first problem. This is particularly the case with the vast majority of developing countries which are commodity producers. While exports of the commodity-dependent countries at $118 billion are only one-quarter of the total exports of developing countries of $484 billion, the remaining three-quarters affect the fortunes of only a handful of developing countries — the four Pacific Rim tigers, together with Brazil, accounting for a little over $200 billion, mainly of manufactured exports, and a half a dozen or so petroleum exporters accounting for the remaining US$ 150 billion.

What most econometric studies of commodity markets have shown is that economic growth in OECD countries is one crucial determinant of commodity prices and, therefore, of the foreign exchange earnings of the overwhelming majority both of countries and of populations of the developing world. According to one recent study, an annual growth of 2.7 per cent in OECD industrial production is required "just to maintain the index of commodity prices at a stable level",[1] with slower growth being reflected in price declines. According to the UNCTAD secretariat, indeed, many of the commodities of export interest to developing countries require a much higher rate of growth just to maintain steady prices — threshold rates as high as 4.7 percent for aluminium, 4.4 percent for copper and 4.2 percent for rice.[2]

These orders of magnitude for OECD growth warranted by the needs of commodity price stability, contrast with the most optimistic medium-term growth scenarios projected for the industrial countries by the Bretton Woods institutions: — the 3 percent growth up to 1995 forecast by the World Bank in its most recent 1988 World Development Report, and the 2.9 percent to 1992 projected in the IMF's most recent World Economic Outlook. The World Bank's "base case" growth scenario is significantly worse — 2.3 percent up to 1995.

The best we can hope for on average is, therefore, rough commodity price stability at today's depressed price levels which are even lower, in real terms, than during the Great Depression of the 1930s, and represent a decline of almost 60 percent from the peak registered before the onset of the recession of the 1980s. What commodity producers obviously require are programmes of economic diversification to lessen their dependence on commodities and the task is not rendered easier by the stagnant price outlook. What is additionally needed is a combination of appropriate domestic polices and adequate external finance in support of the necessary structural adjustments. These are among the critical new policy issues that need to be tackled.

My third problem, therefore, is that of exploring what opportunities there might be in today's international situation to bring about a simultaneous assault on the two problems I have already identified. Specifically, I would like to examine how effectively the resolution of the developed country payments imbalance and growth problems can be married to finding a satisfactory solution during the 1990s for the problems of the developing countries.

1. Improving development performance

I shall begin with my first problem, that of improving upon the development performance of the developing countries in the 1980s. This issue has traditionally been approached in terms of a dichotomy between the need for policy reform in the country concerned and the need for an improvement in the external environment confronting that country. This has led to a somewhat unproductive polarization of views, with the developed countries pointing to success stories such as those of the Pacific Rim in justification of the priority attaching to domestic policy reform, and developing countries blaming it all on a forbidding external environment characterized by sluggish developed country growth, falling commodity prices and stagnant aid flows. Quite obviously, action has to proceed on both fronts, and there is an opportunity in the existence of today's substantial surpluses to improve significantly the import capacities of developing countries through recycling of surpluses, provided this goes hand in hand with domestic policy reform. Before developing this argument, however, it is nevertheless helpful to obtain a sense of the constraints imposed — and even opportunities provided — by the external environment as regards sound domestic policy formulation in various groups of countries.

The success stories

Let me begin with the success stories — a handful of Pacific Rim economies, namely, Republic of Korea, Taiwan, Hong Kong and Singapore. What is controversial about these countries are the factors making for success and how far they can be replicated elsewhere. While it is claimed on the one hand that their success is attributable to market forces, it is claimed on the other hand that the role of the state has been crucial.

What is worth recognizing, however, is that in these countries whatever support the state has extended to the development of entrepreneurship and to economic growth has received a massive boost in recent years from a key *external* opportunity — i.e. the expanding market represented by the U.S. current account payments deficit. This has been the principal origin of their surpluses estimated at $ 30 billion in 1987; and it is largely on the basis of the U.S. market that the aggregate exports of manufactures of the Asian NICs have been able to exceed those of France, Italy and the U.K. What is less certain is how far it was open to other developing countries to cash in on this same opportunity. Two considerations are relevant. There is the likelihood of any significant replication of the Pacific Rim model encountering protectionist obstacles. Second, the dynamo of growth in the Pacific Rim has been original equipment manufacturing (OEM) for a wide range of purchasers extending from retail chains to multinationals as these shifted production offshore to lower cost countries. It is a nice question whether the expansion in this market would have accommodated many other suppliers.

Primary commodity exporters

The next broad category of developing countries is the overwhelming majority who are dependent on primary commodity exports. There are some 130 countries involved with a total population of almost 1.8 billion. Although the average population of a country is 13 million, the countries range in size from small Pacific islands with under 10,000 people each to India with 760 million. The most severely affected sub-group here unquestionably is Sub-Saharan Africa, where the collapse of commodity prices since 1980 and the terms of trade loss have compounded difficulties caused by prolonged drought. Over 40 countries and 400 million people are involved.[3] By 1987, the purchasing power of exports from Sub-Saharan Africa had fallen to only 62 percent of the 1980 level, involving a cumulative loss over this period of $ 96 billion, or nearly $ 14 billion a year, on average. Of this loss, more than half ($ 58 billion cumulative, $ 8 billion annual average) reflected the contraction in export volume, while the rest represented the terms of trade loss.

Either magnitude is to be contrasted with the amount of offsetting finance theoretically available from the IMF even on the most stringent basis of conditionality. Total IMF quotas for Sub-Saharan Africa amount to SDR 3.6 billion, permitting access to Fund resources of up to twice that amount or SDR 7.2 billion (equivalent to $ 11 billion) if countries were all to make four tranche drawings on the IMF. In evident recognition of the scale of this problem and the need for concessional finance outside the general resources of the IMF, the managing director of the IMF launched new initiatives, most notably the Enhanced Structural Adjustment Facility approved in 1987. This was designed to add more than SDR 8 billion ($ 11 billion) to available resources for structural adjustment in Africa and other low income countries on a basis of three year macroeconomic and structural adjustment programmes to improve their balance of payments position and foster economic growth.

The annual changes in the purchasing power of exports from Sub-Saharan Africa can be seen more clearly in Fig. 1. The sharp rise in the terms of trade loss in 1986 and 1987 was due partly to the fall in petroleum prices, and partly to the fall in the exchange value of the U.S. dollar (which pushed up prices of imported manufacturers from Europe and Japan in terms of dollars).

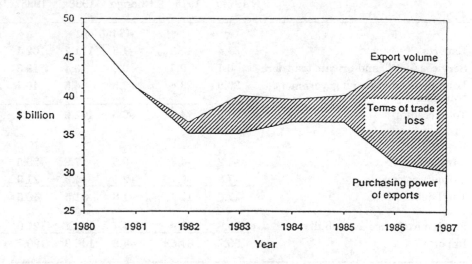

Source: WIDER estimates based upon data in UNCTAD *Handbook of International Trade and Development Statistics* (various issues).

Figure 1   Exports from Sub-Saharan Africa: 1980-1987

The decline in the purchasing power of exports was accompanied by a corresponding cut in import volume (1987 imports, for example, were some 30 percent below the 1980 level), and many countries in the region have been suffering from 'import strangulation'. For Sub-Saharan Africa as a whole, real per capita GDP declined, on average, by 3.5 percent a year from 1980 to 1986 (or from $ 575 per capita in 1980 to $ 465 in 1986, at 1980 prices). This represented a major set-back in economic welfare, including cuts in real wages, as well as in the provision of social services such as health care and education. Some rather limited data in the UNICEF study on "Adjustment with a Human Face" indicate the retrogression in child health in this region.

Also relevant to determining the influence today of external factors on domestic policy making is a comparison between the balance of payments experience of a wider group of commodity-dependent developing countries in the current recession with that in the previous (1974-75) recession. Export earnings of these countries fell off in 1975, but this fall was more than made good by an increase in capital inflows, including bank loans.

Moreover, amortisation on the foreign debt was also reduced in 1975, compared with 1974. The net result was an increase in foreign exchange availability of some $4 billion (7 percent) in spite of the fall in export earnings. This allowed expenditure on imports to rise (by almost $ 5 billion) in 1975 — See Table 1.

Table 1   Balance of payments of commodity-exporting developing countries:[a] 1974-75 and 1980-85

	Previous recession			Current recession		
	1974	1975	Change	1980	1985	Change
	($ billion)					
Exports	51.4	49.9	-1.5	111.7	102.1	-9.6
Services (net)[b]) and private transfers	0.1	0.6	+0.5	16.4	19.3	+2.9
Long-term capital and government transfers	20.3	23.8	+3.5	44.5	46.1	+1.6
Total credits	71.8	74.3	+2.5	172.6	167.5	-5.1
Debt service:						
Interest	-4.2	-4.7	-0.5	-17.2	-25.5	-8.3
Amortisation	-7.8	-5.7	+2.1	-14.3	-21.0	-6.7
Total debts	-12.0	-10.4	+1.6	-31.5	-46.5	-15.0
Foreign exchange availability	59.8	63.9	+4.1	141.1	121.0	-20.1
Imports	59.7	64.5	+4.8	146.9	129.2	-17.7

Source: UNCTAD *Handbook of international trade and development statistics* (various issues).
[a]) Excluding the least developed countries.
[b]) Excluding interest payments on foreign debt.

By contrast, in the 1980s, the fall in export earnings of this group of countries (almost $ 10 billion between 1980 and 1985) was compounded by a substantial increase in debt service payments (of $ 15 billion between these two years). Consequently, the amount available for purchasing imports declined, by some $ 20 billion (allowing for small increases in other credits).

Once again the comparison between the losses sustained by commodity dependent developing countries and their access to offsetting resources from the IMF is instructive. The IMF quotas of the countries covered amount to 16.4 billion SDRs or $ 22 billion. This means that access even to the equivalent of their IMF quotas on average — in effect through low conditionality first credit tranche drawings — would have barely sufficed to maintain imports at 1980 levels in 1985.

What this analysis shows is that the "import strangulation" of commodity producing countries in general is a principal factor affecting their growth outlook for the 1980s and for the future. This has implications not only for output and investment through the curtailment of import of intermediate and capital goods, but also, interestingly enough, for export performance and for this same reason. According to a recent study of 34 developing countries, a ten percent reduction in their import volume — the average annual decline registered for these countries during 1982 to 1988 — reduced export volume by 2 percent in the short run and by more than 5 percent in the longer run after the vicious circle of import reduction leading to export reduction leading in turn to further import reduction due to lower foreign exchange availability, had been completed.[4] Nevertheless, many of these countries have attempted to bite the bullet of domestic policy reform by entering into adjustment and stabilization programmes of the conventional kind, in an attempt to ease import strangulation, by obtaining access to the additional external resources that these programmes usually permit. The difficulty, however, with the system as it is, is that the balance between adjustment and financing appears to be unfairly struck from the stand-point of the adjusting countries.

When the Bretton Woods institutions were set up, the expectation was that adequate resources would be available in support of adjustment. What has happened instead is that IMF quotas in relation to world trade, have fallen significantly since the 1940s, affecting developing countries as well — from 16 percent to 4 percent. As we have seen, additional resources resulting from even the most draconian Fund programmes are fractional in relation to terms of trade losses especially for the poorest countries in Africa and also, in lesser degree, for other commodity dependent countries. Unless, therefore, the international system finds in the 1990s ways of redressing this situation, adjustment efforts are likely to involve impossibly far-reaching and almost certainly disruptive social and political costs on the apart of commodity dependent developing countries.

In the case of Sub-Saharan Africa, the acute economic and financial crisis has already called forth a significant response from the international community. Yet much more needs to be done. The report of the UN Advisory Group on Financial Flows for Africa (The Wass Report), published in 1988, after examining the situation in some detail, concluded that an additional amount of at least $ 5 billion annually, over and above what was now expected from established channels, is required for Sub-Saharan Africa, excluding Nigeria.[5] According to the report, additional financing is necessary despite previous inappropriate domestic polices to avoid "the adjustment policies being now put in place being put at risk".[6] How serious the situation is, is evident from the most recent IMF projection of the average debt service ratio for Sub-Saharan Africa for 1988-89 of 55 percent of export earnings, with the ratios for the sub-groups of market and official borrowers being still higher at 66 percent of export earnings.

The highly-indebted countries

A third group of developing countries consists of those traditionally classified as highly indebted. The classification straddles both commodity producers and some established NICs until their progress was arrested in the 1980s by the debt problem. The spectrum of countries in this group also shades from low income commodity dependant countries whose indebtedness is primarily to official creditors, to middle-income exporters of manufacturers whose debts are primarily to commercial banks and who were the beneficiaries or victims, depending on how you look at it, of the totally unconditional recycling extravaganza of the 1970s when OPEC surpluses were mediated by the private sector. The commodity producers are largely in Africa where of 44 countries identified by the IMF only four are classified as market borrowers with others relying on official sources. The middle-income countries are primarily in Latin America.

The tragedy of this latter middle-income group of debtor countries is that their present hardships signify a major lost opportunity for cooperative international action in the 1970s, something for which abdication is not too strong a word. There was a time in the early days of the oil crisis when it looked as if the international financial institutions might well have grasped the opportunity to recycle OPEC surpluses on the basis of an appropriate regime of long-range conditionality and deliberately seek to offset the deflationary implications of the sudden shift in world savings, while simultaneously re-directing them in support of needed structural change in the developing countries. Instead the early oil facility put speedily into place by a particularly far-sighted Fund Managing Director in 1973, was equally speedily abandoned and the commercial banks left to get on with the job of borrowing short and lending long, with little thought for the morrow to come. Investments, predictably, did not bear the expected fruit, debt servicing failed, and the whole structure of the international banking system placed in jeopardy. The Mexican crisis of 1982 marked the watershed.

Then began the truly Herculean effort at *ad hoc* adjustment on a country by country basis. The grim statistical harvest of that effort is now in and bears repetition. Countries with debt-servicing problems squeezed imports between 1983 and 1987, and ran significant trade surpluses of around $ 23 billion per year to repay banks. This meant cuts in investment by 8 percentage points, from 27 percent of GNP in the 1970s to 19 percent of GNP in 1983-1987, and of course reducing income levels. Even so, the trade surpluses were insufficient to meet interest obligations, so that countries were kept afloat by periodic packages involving the IMF which cobbled together official funds and stretched out maturities.

The principal effect of releasing budgetary resources to repay debt instead of meeting domestic needs was to erect insuperable obstacles to improved fiscal management in debtor countries which were driven to printing money to meet local expenses and risk explosive inflation. Fiscal policy proceeded on a stop go basis as financing packages fell apart almost as soon as they were put together with stipulated IMF credit ceilings being quickly exceeded. The market soon enough placed its discount both on the capacity of countries to manage their affairs in this fashion and to repay their debt in the current international environment and debt began to trade in secondary markets at fractions of their face value ranging from 20 to 50 percent.

We are now at the stage where the impossibility of official debt being repaid has been recognized. So far as commercial bank debt is concerned, the new element is that the course of debt management so far has enabled banks to restore their balance sheet positions from the critical levels of 1982. While total bank capital, of U.S. banks, for example, has increased significantly, their percentage exposure to developing countries has fallen substantially.

The stage is indeed now set for seizing once more the opportunity that was missed in the 1970s, namely that of providing financial flows under some form of multilateral stewardship if not management to developing countries under a regime of appropriate long-range conditionality. There is no lack of schemes to give effect to this concept. They all proceed on the central premise of the WIDER recycling plan[8] of passing down the discounts at which debt is trading today to debtor developing countries in exchange for long-range economic reform packages that will prove to be of an enduring character and will create a credible basis for the resumption of bank lending.

* * * * * *

2. Maintaining growth in the developed countries

I turn now to my second problem, that of maintaining adequate growth in the developed economies whilst simultaneously correcting today's major payments imbalance. It is now widely recognized that the United States cannot continue to run much further into debt without a crisis of confidence in the dollar, with the only corrective available to the U.S. — substantial rise in interest rates — in turn, bringing about a world wide recession. To the traditional 'failure of confidence' reason for precipitating a world wide recession must now be added the inflation risk reason, and this may well be the more immediate threat. This derives from the continuing investment boom in OECD countries. With U.S. unemployment declining to 5.2 percent — a level approaching its "natural" rate — the risk is now of overheating of the U.S. economy and of inflation, which if not checked early would, via tight monetary policy, also precipitate a major recession.

Just as much as there are recessionary risks in the failure on the part of the U.S. to act to correct its deficit, there are equivalent risks in uncoordinated action by the U.S. alone. Assuming that the desired correction is in the range often mentioned of $ 150 — $ 200 billion, this is equivalent to 8 to 10 percent of world exports, and a reduction in U.S. import demand of this order must obviously precipitate a major recession in world export markets unless offset by correspondingly expanded demand elsewhere. The conventional wisdom has it that the needed demand expansion should come from the surplus economies, Japan and Germany. If this were to happen, the recessionary impact of the correction in the US deficit would indeed be averted.

Yet, it makes little moral sense for countries which are already at high levels of consumption to be encouraged to consume and import more because this is the most immediate way in which persistent surpluses can be extinguished. It would make far better economic and moral sense to enable these countries to continue to run *moderate* surpluses and through deliberate policy action to recycle a substantial part of these surpluses in support of Third World development.

Three elements are needed by way of coordinated policy action. First, there is a current need for a phased deficit reduction strategy in the United States which does not throw the U.S. itself and the world into recession. Second, there is a need for some offsetting action in surplus economies if only to take up part of the initial slack resulting from U.S. deficit correction. Thirdly, there is the need for devising effective mechanisms to divert to developing countries the savings potential implicit in the difference between the full extent of the U.S. deficit reduction and the moderate expansion in surplus economies. This last element belongs, in fact, in the territory of my third problem, that of exploring the opportunities for combining balanced growth in developed economies with the development of the Third World in the 1990s.

In regard to the phasing out of the U.S. deficit, there has emerged a view[12] that this can be accomplished through a consumption recession in the U.S. which would not provoke a more general recession thanks to the current export boom and the strength of private investment. The consumption recession would result from a cut in the structural fiscal deficit through freezing nominal government expenditures particularly in defence, stretching out the inflation indexation of social security benefits, a rise in the gasoline tax — with a 25 cents per gallon increase raising tax revenues by $ 25 billion — and the introduction of a nation-wide consumption tax. Such a consumption recession will be deflationary on the rest of the world, and the question to ask is how deflationary this impact would be.

In Dr. Yoshitomi's lecture printed in this booklet, he reported the results of a simulation on the assumption that the U.S. budget deficit will decline as a result of consumption recession, by $ 15 billion each year from 1988 to 1992, compared with the present level of $ 150 billion, making, in other words, for a total reduction of $ 75 billion. On this simulation, the US external deficit would fall to $ 86 billion or 1.3 percent of GNP in 1992. While the growth rate of world trade would be reduced by no more than 0.5 percentage points from the assumed base line of 5 to 6 percent growth, the slowdown of real GNP would be marginal with a decline of 0.3 percentage points in the United States.

Several questions need to be asked about this strategy. First there is no successful precedent in the recent past for the U.S.'s present attempt to tackle a trade deficit on today's scale without sacrificing economic growth in a major way. Even the astonishingly rapid recovery of Japan's balance of payments after the second oil shock of 1979 -81, when it shifted resources equivalent to more than 4 percent of GNP into net exports, was accompanied by a slowdown in growth. In particular, a question arises as to whether the pace of adjustment for the United States, outlined by Dr. Yoshitomi, is too slow to provide the necessary assurances to the financial markets. *Per contra*, if the U.S. has for these reasons to adjust faster, then there is a real concern as to how far what was intended to be purely a transitional consumption recession is likely to become or merge into a major and more protracted recession. The answer is that we yet do not know exactly what the fall out would be. I can only say that WIDER has a major research project in hand being directed by Professor Jeffrey Sachs of Harvard University to examine the implications for the rest of the world of alternative scenarios for the correction of the U.S. deficit.

If the path of a consumption recession starting in the U.S. leads to a more generalized global recession, then there is a very clear risk that following the classic path of Keynesian adjustment, *world* income as a whole may fall, including Japan's, so that Japan's excess savings would just not be there to be lent to developing countries tomorrow. The question I am raising simply points to the difficulty of trying to fine tune the world economy in the face of today's uncertainties and the understandable caution of surplus countries.

Countries in surplus have been distinguished by having track records of extremely low inflation, and are understandably wary of embarking upon expansionary policies that might only serve to reignite inflation. Countries in surplus also have a concern about their levels of domestic public debt and about the scale of domestic expansion that can be undertaken without increasing domestic debt to uncomfortable levels. Countries in surplus also have legitimate concerns about the risks to steady economic growth involved in making too drastic a shift from a pattern of export-led growth to a pattern of domestic demand-led growth. It is essentially for these reasons that there are definite limits, viewed from the stand-point of stable growth in the world economy, to the degree to which domestic expansion in surplus economies can fully offset the deflationary impact of the desirable reduction in the U.S. deficit.

3. Recycling to counter debt and deflation

It is these considerations which lead me now to taking up my third problem, namely, that of marrying the resolution of the developed country payments imbalance and growth problems with finding a satisfactory solution during the 1990s for the problems of the developing countries. Recycling to developing countries of surpluses becomes then the obvious counter to the deflationary impact of a reduction in the U.S. deficit. Indeed, the most ambitious plan put forward for the Japanese surplus is that presented by WIDER. The WIDER plan calls for Japan to adopt over the medium-term a current account surplus target of U.S. $50 billion, equivalent to 2 percent of Japan's GNP, which happens incidentally also to be Japan's officially accepted current account target, instead of the $80 to $ 90 billion magnitude for her surplus which would be run without corrective domestic policies. The WIDER plan calls for the recycling through deliberate policy action of an amount of $ 25 billion annually, or half Japan's current account surplus target, so that over five years $ 125 billion would be recycled.

The WIDER plan also demonstrates that recycling to developing countries is on average about five times as effective in improving the U.S. trade balance than equivalent domestic expansion in Japan. According to estimates made by Professor Jeffrey Sachs for WIDER, while $ 25 billion recycling would improve the U.S. trade balance by $ 10 billion approximately, an equivalent domestic expansion programme in Japan would improve the U.S. trade balance by only U.S. $ 2 billion.

Similar evidence is available in the Overseas Development Council Agenda for 1988, "Growth, Exports and Jobs in a Changing World Economy". One result of the import compression enforced upon debtor developing countries to adjust has been the collapse of U.S. export markets — exports to developing countries dropping from U.S. $ 88 billion in 1980 to U.S. $ 77 billion in 1985. According to the ODC Agenda,[13] if U.S. exports to developing countries had grown in the first half of the 1980s at the same rate in the 1970s, they would have totalled about $ 150 billion in current dollars. This growth would have created 1.7 million jobs in the U.S. or nearly 21 percent of total official unemployment in 1986.

The question at issue is what alternative exists to a consumption based recession in the U.S. with all the attendant risks we have mentioned of its spreading into a general investment recession, in order to enable surpluses to be released for recycling to developing countries. One obvious alternative is whether the evolving world political situation does not permit the U.S. to grasp a range of opportunities for reducing its budget deficit which have been regarded as foreclosed up to now.

A paper by Sam Nakagama,[14] Chairman of Nakagama and Wallace Inc. of New York addressed the issue in an interesting way in June 1988 and deserves to be better known. Mr. Nakagama is a well-known Wall Street economic forecaster with an amazing track record of accuracy including the prediction of October 1987's stock market crash and his audience largely comprised his blue-riband clients. He talked of three magic magnitudes plaguing the U.S. economy, each of U.S. $ 150 billion. Two of these are readily recognisable — the U.S. current account deficits, respectively, in her balance of payments, and in her budget. The third, invisible up to now in public debate, Nakagama reckoned to be the cost of maintaining the U.S. defence commitment to Europe. He wondered whether in the current climate of glasnost, perestroika and detente and European insouciance about any threat from the East, reducing this commitment might not offer a relatively painless solution to the U.S. budget deficit conundrum. This struck me as being relevant radicalism — less far-reaching than most conventional disarmament nostrums, and within the realm of the possible for a new U.S. administration seeking a bold initiative. As I listened in the company of hard-bitten Wall Street bankers who had previously heard an appeal from a former U.S. Navy Secretary, for Japan to step up her defence role to the evident puzzlement of several Japanese present, I had a dream.

A phased reduction in the U.S. deficit through relaxing her commitment to Europe would free Japanese savings to flow to developing countries in ample and hitherto unprecedented volume. A debt reconstruction facility, setup on a Japanese initiative, would be allied to what I have described as self-reliant conditionality — i.e. reform packages that *countries* would design for *themselves* in consultation with the international financial institutions — or for that matter a Japanese Trust fund — for the first time in recent memory on a basis of sufficient finance. This would help defuse the tensions that currently exist between countries and the international financial institutions, which in large part stem from the use of conditionality to ration today's grossly inadequate volume of finance. Policy reform, accompanied by substantial programme lending and resulting dynamism in the Third World, would create both project development and private investment opportunities on a scale that could usher in for the developing countries during the 1990s, the kind of Golden Age that Europe enjoyed in the 50s and 60s in the wake of the Marshall Plan. Structural change in the U.S. economy and in Europe following detente, could reorient industrial capacities in the advanced economies in a manner that would meet the vast unmet needs of the Third World, and reduce if not eliminate today's substantial levels of European unemployment. In short, a virtuous circle could be set in motion by thinking what until recently has been the politically unthinkable.

In the cold light of day after Nakagama's presentation, I tried to do the homework needed to test out this intuition. The $ 150 billion magnitude for NATO mentioned by Nakagama turns out to be about half the nearly $ 300 billion appropriated for all U.S. defense expenditures in 1989, according to the report presented by the Secretary of Defence to the Congress on February 11, 1988.[15] Two categories within this $ 300 billion expenditure — for Procurement, and Research Development, Test and Evaluation — distinguished in the report, total around $ 120 billion and provide a rough measure of the weapons production capacity of the United States. Assuming that half this amount *pro rata* represents the capacity of the U.S. arms industry attributable to NATO related purposes, then the Nakagama proposal can be expected to release something like $ 60 billion of U.S. industrial capacity to meet the Third World's unmet needs.

The industrial capacity released by the Nakagama proposal for Third World use in the U.S. alone of $ 60 billion amounts precisely to half the combined surplus of Japan and West Germany expected for 1989, of $ 120 billion. Since even the most ambitious proposal so far made public for recycling the Japanese surplus — the WIDER plan — also envisages that no more than half her expected surplus should be recycled through deliberate policy action for Third World purposes, the proportions revealed by this piece of homework do not appear implausible.

The *Financial Times* said almost all, in its usual inimitable style, when commenting on July 7, 1988, on the 1988 World Development Report:

> "The report could surely have been more radical in its analysis of global macroeconomic adjustment, which repeats the conventional call for reduced current account surpluses in countries like Japan, Germany and Taiwan. For the World Bank, a more appropriate and innovative approach would be to welcome the surpluses, but complain about where they are going. What is needed is a call for developed countries to take a far more radical approach to the liquidation of developing country debt, for the U.S. to stop hogging the world's surplus capital and last but not least, for developing countries to undertake the fundamental reforms which will encourage renewed capital flows from the rich to the poorer countries of the world. If the world's premier development finance institution cannot articulate such a vision, how are the developing countries ever to escape the whirlwind?"

I am not presuming to say that it is only WIDER that has stepped in where the World Bank has feared to tread. Japan, too must be counted on the side of the angels in so far as, in addition to the proposals already made public, as well as the continuing rise in foreign aid, active thought is being given within the Government to more ambitious plans for recycling surplus savings to developing countries. But it would be idle to pretend that in the absence of coherently articulated views from outside of the major summit countries such recycling plans can attain their full potential. We have seen at the Toronto summit and more recently at the World Bank annual meetings of 1988, Japan's initiatives being either shelved or muted for a variety of no doubt understandable reasons. What the present situation cries out for is a *political* constituency outside the Summit group of five countries that could act as a pace-maker for change to which it would be open to Japan, for example, to respond. It could develop a platform that would point to the opportunities available through recycling surpluses for energizing world development. More ambitiously it could build up the momentum for rewriting the rule book governing international economic behaviour at a time when *ad hoc* mechanisms are still very much in vogue.

Notes

1. D. Hartman, 'Focus on Commodities', *Focus: World Outlook*, Data Resources, Inc., No.2, 1985.

2. *Revitalizing Development, Growth and International Trade*: UNCTAD secretariat report to UNCTAD VII, Geneva, 1987, page 109.

3. UNCTAD *Handbook of Trade and Development Statistics*, 1987 Supplement, Table 6.1.

4. Moshin Khan and Malcolm Knight, *Import Compression and Export Performance in Developing Countries,* Review of Economics and Statistics, May 1988.

5. United Nations, *Financing Africa's Recovery*, Report and Recommendations of the Advisory Group on Financial Flows to Africa, 1988.

6. *Ibid.* paragraph 49.

7. IMF Survey June 1988, page 189.

8. WIDER Study Group No. 2, *Mobilizing International Surpluses for World Development, A WIDER Plan for a Japanese Initiative*, May 1987.

12. *Op.Cit.* Masaru Yoshitomi.

13. *Growth, Exports and Jobs in a Changing World Economy: Agenda 1988*, Overseas Development Council, Washington, D.C., 1988, page 10.

14. Sam Nakagama, "Mathematics of a Falling Dollar: $ 150 Billion Budget Deficit, $ 150 Billion Trade Deficit, $ 150 Billion a year for NATO", Nakagama & Wallace Pacific Basin Seminar, New York, 29 June 1988.

15. I am grateful to Professor Emma Rothschild for her very valuable assistance in looking further into these magnitudes.

PROBLEMS OF
DEVELOPMENT

30.   Analytical Approaches to the Relationship of Population Growth and Development

Nancy Birdsall

This article reviews the principal analytical approaches to the study of the relationship between population growth and economic development used over the past two decades. The literature relating population to development is vast; no attempt is made here to summarize it. Where earlier reviews are useful, the reader is referred directly to them. The attempt is rather to describe major lines of research on the multiple relationships between population growth and economic development, with special attention to the implications for policy design of the various forms of analysis. The focus is on fertility, on mortality only as it relates to fertility, and not at all on population distribution.

Research in this field can be divided into two, clearly interrelated categories: research on the consequences of fertility and research on the determinants. From a policy perspective, the former might be said to generate interest in the need for a population policy and the latter to contribute to the optimal design of such a policy. Both consequences and determinants research can be further divided into two types: macro and micro...

This classification is useful as a basis for organization of our presentation of the analytical approaches, proceeding from macro- and micro-consequences of population growth and fertility to their macro- and micro-determinants. We begin by discussing the manner in which population growth was included in growth and development models up through the late 1950s and early 1960s; chronologically this type of work on the population-development relationship came first and has significantly influenced both the policies of bilateral and international donors and much of the research on population growth and development that has succeeded it. This work is in the "consequences" school — research and analysis that has focused on the consequences of rapid population growth for the economic development of nations. It can be further categorized as "macro" work, since it uses aggregated economic and demographic factors such as national birth and death rates, the dependency ratio, savings rates, and economy-wide production functions. We also briefly review macro-consequences studies that apply the principles developed in these analyses to particular country economies and/or to particular aspects of economies. In general, these studies conclude that in countries with high fertility rates, the net costs attached to meeting development objectives in such areas as education, health, and employment could be significantly reduced by increasing expenditures on explicit programs to reduce fertility, specifically family planning programs.

Nancy Birdsall: 'Analytical Approaches to the Relationship of Population Growth and Development' in *POPULATION AND DEVELOPMENT REVIEW* (March/June, 1977), 3, Nos. 1 and 2, pp. 63-74, 77-92. Reproduced by permission of The Population Council.

Second, we review a body of work on the consequences at the family level — the micro-consequences — of large numbers of children. Much of the relevant research in this area has been done by those in the medical and public health professions and by psychologists and nutritionists. The results of the work have not entered the mainstream of economists' thinking on population-development relationships, although the framework for studies of the loss in human capital exists. Nor has this research had an appreciable effect on policy-formulation.

Third, we consider the extensive and growing literature on the macro- and micro-determinants of fertility. This work has been most fruitful from a theoretical and empirical point of view at the micro-level, with economists analyzing the costs and benefits of children to the "household" or "family" and with sociologists implicitly concentrating more on the woman as the reproductive agent. In considering work on the determinants of fertility, special attention is given to variables that not only affect the parents' cost-benefit calculus regarding children but represent potential areas for policy intervention: reduction of infant mortality, female education and labor force participation, improved distribution of income, and implementation of family planning programs.

It would be logical to assume that research on the *consequences* of rapid population growth has pointed to the need for policies to cope with rapid growth and to slow down such growth; and that, in turn, governments have sought information on how to design effective policies, leading to further research on the *determinants* of growth. In fact, research on the subject has developed in a much more haphazard fashion, and government policies on population have not always evolved logically. Still, it is true that different types of research are more or less important for different countries, depending on their demographic situations, the priority given to population concern, and their general level of development. So this essay includes for each category of research some discussion of its contribution to policy, potential or realized, and of its peculiar relevance to certain countries.

Macro-consequences of population growth

The sustained economic growth of Western Europe and North America during the eighteenth and nineteenth centuries was accompanied by the first steady and sustained increase of population the world had ever known. Kuznets (1966, p. 20) has defined modern economic growth as a sustained increase in population attained without any lowering of per capita product, and some of the theorizing about the relationship between population and economic growth has sought a positive effect of the former on the latter. A growing population has been proffered as a net contributor to economic growth: (a) because of its stimulating effect on demand and its risk-reducing incentive to investment; (b) because it provides for constant improvement of the labor force with better-trained workers; and (c) because population pressure may encourage technological innovation, particularly in agriculture. Moreover, large population size permits economies of scale in production of large markets.

After World War II mortality rates declined dramatically and population growth accelerated in poor countries: if population growth had seemed to be directly related to economic progress in Europe and North America, it now seemed inversely related to the economic prospects of India, China, and Latin America. Population growth is no longer seen as an unequivocal benefit. The situation in the post-war developing world is, of course, different from that of industrializing Europe in a number of significant ways. Governments in the post-war epoch must be more responsive to education, health, and even income standards for their populations. Today's developing countries must achieve growth in the face of the competitive products of another, already-modernized group of countries. Most important, population in today's poor countries is growing at least twice as fast as it was in eighteenth century Europe, at rates of 2 and even 3 percent a year, in contrast to at most 1 percent. The resultant age composition of the developing countries, with as much as half the population in the young, nonproductive ages, is much less favorable to production and proportionately more burdensome with respect to consumption and social overhead investments.

Macro-economic models

These unprecedented rates of population growth, implying a doubling of populations every 20-30 years, renewed the attention of economists to the *rate* of population growth. The analytic models of Nelson (1956) and Leibenstein (1954) reintroduced population as an endogenous variable influenced by income. Their models are Malthusian: Increasing income leads to increasing population growth rates; and, as long as population growth exceeds income growth, per capita income falls, resulting in the low-level equilibrium trap.

A seminal contribution to the analysis of the consequences of population growth was the work of Coale and Hoover (1958). Constructing a mathematical model of the economy of India, Coale and Hoover made projections of per capita income for India under low, medium, and high (exogenous) fertility assumptions. They concluded that over a 30 year period, per capita income could be as much as 40 percent lower under the high compared to the low fertility assumption.

Over the years since publication of the Coale-Hoover model, many of the assumptions implicit in their analysis have been challenged. However, their study and the subsequent work on the macro-consequences of rapid population growth that it stimulated, are important in at least three respects: (1) this work reawakened economists and others to the demographic factor as a policy variable, whereas for some time population had been treated as a given in growth models: (2) it alerted those concerned with development to the importance of growth rates as well as absolute size of populations, making population an issue for Latin America and Africa as well as for the crowded countries of Asia; (3) it contributed significantly to the view, especially in the rich countries of the West, that, other things being equal, extremely rapid population growth rates exacerbate development problems in the world's poor countries.

Coale and Hoover's 1958 book generated an industry of economic-demographic simulations. By projecting into the future given population and cost trends, numerous studies have tried to assess the high costs to developing societies of supporting rapidly multiplying numbers of people. Most such studies project public-sector costs associated with provision of, for example, education, health, and job opportunities under alternative assumptions regarding population trends. Few introduce feedback from the changes in expenditures in particular areas or other assumed changes in the economy to changes in population trends. In this regard, the studies adopt the simplifying assumption made by Coale and Hoover that changes in mortality and fertility rates are exogenous to the model, although they can be affected by policies (such as government support for family planning) that are not incorporated into the model. Costs of social services can be projected into the future under alternative assumptions about mortality and fertility; the high cost of high fertility is then easily calculated. These studies for the most part are meant to be illustrative; authors maintain that they are not predicting the future, but illustrating what the future could entail given certain assumptions about rates of population growth.

Although projections of per capita income under different fertility assumptions vary substantially depending on the specific fertility assumptions in the models, they consistently indicate higher per capita income under low fertility assumptions than under high. For example, among seven projections examined, per capita income was 10-15 percent higher after 20 years and 25-40 percent higher after 30 years under low fertility assumptions than under high ones.

In addition to studies that project costs in such specific areas as education, health services, and absorption of labor into the modern sector, work on the macro-consequences of population growth for development includes descriptive essays on the consequences of rapid population growth for the balance of payments, the future supply of food, and the general availability of physical resources. . .

The principal findings with regard to *clarity* of the presumed effect of population increases on the indicator (i.e., directness of the effect regardless of the roles of other variables) and *strength* of the presumed effect, including lag time before the effect takes hold and the relative importance of population growth compared to other variables, can be summarized as follows:

Education. Rapid population growth has a strong, direct effect on future expenditures on education. High fertility now almost guarantees more children entering the school system five years hence; and while a number of factors including rising wages of teachers and rising enrollment rates may increase educational outlays, an absolute increase in the number of students has been shown to be the single most important factor in increasing educational expenditures. Expenditures can be held down by increasing the teacher-student ratio, decreasing the number of years students are enrolled, or decreasing enrollment ratios, but all these steps involve a decline in a country's per capita stock of human capital.

Health. Population growth similarly increases health costs: More people require more health services. High fertility rates have an immediate effect on costs of health services since obstetric and paediatric needs constitute a substantial proportion of total demand for health services. On the other hand, the contribution of rapid population growth *per se* to the problem of inadequate health care should not be overstated. Where health systems are urban oriented, are essentially curative rather than preventive, and do not serve the poor anyway, reforms in health care delivery (such as the much-discussed barefoot doctor system in China) might provide as much relief and improved health as an immediate reduction in demand due to lower rates of population growth. And in the long run, demand for health services may not be lower in populations experiencing low rather than high rates of fertility; low-fertility populations have historically enjoyed low mortality rates and have a larger proportion of older persons, placing special demands on health services. Unfortunately, the systematic attempts to demonstrate how lower population growth rates would reduce expenditures on health care... have not been matched by analyses of alternative ways to cut costs and maintain health services, so the true opportunity costs of rapid population growth to health care are unclear.

Labor absorption. Obviously, high fertility leads to rapid growth of the labor force — with a ten-to-fifteen-year lag between new births and new entrants to the labor force. Thirty-year projections for Sri Lanka, Chile, and Brazil indicate a doubling of the size of the labor force, even given "low" fertility, and an increase of as much as two-and-a-half times present size with "high" fertility. Furthermore, assuming a demographic transition to lower fertility rates in ten to fifteen years, labor force size then could be increased not only by the simple addition of today's current births at current rates of labor force participation, but an increase in the proportion of the population seeking work, as women with fewer births enter the work force at new, higher participation rates. On the other hand, rapid labor force growth leads to unemployment and poverty only under special assumptions: fixed capital-labor ratios in the modern sector combined with insufficient savings and investment and the inability of agriculture and the informal urban sector to absorb labor in socially productive activities. The deleterious effect of rapid population growth on the labor market could be mitigated if appropriate labor-intensive technologies were developed for production in the urban sector, if irrigation and other infrastructures permitting more labor-intensive use of land were created in agricultural areas, and if changes in product mix and general development strategy (such as the light-industry export-led growth of Korea and Taiwan) were available to all developing countries. Short of such adjustments, rapid rates of natural increase condemn a large portion of the labor force to low-productivity, low-wage jobs in agriculture or informal urban services.

Income distribution. High fertility among the poor in all countries, and in poor countries relative to rich, may exacerbate the problem of improving the distribution of income; however, there is little evidence on this relationship, and historically, improvements in income distribution have been more closely associated with other factors, economic, social, and political. The hypothesis that poverty associated with a skewed distribution of income also contributes to high fertility is discussed in more detail in the section on micro-consequences of high fertility below.

Food, resources, and environment. T.W. Schultz's (1971) appraisal of the consequences of population increase for food production is appropriately agnostic; he emphasises how many questions remain unanswered in this area. Long-range projections of the supply of and demand for food are plagued by such unknowns as income changes, changes in agricultural technology, the heterogeneity of agricultural conditions throughout the world and the political plausibility of redistribution. There is some evidence, however, that the rate of increase of population, if as rapid as in some areas today, increases the likelihood of "population overshoot," the outcome of which is "soil erosion in fields and overgrazed pastures to a degree that native plants cannot reestablish themselves after declining productivity results in abandonment" (Freeman, 1976, p. 41). Analysis of effects of population growth and development on the earth's carrying capacity requires collaboration of development analysts with geographers, ecologists, and others in the physical sciences; such effects, which will vary greatly by geographic location, are less well explored and understood than the effects of population growth on educational, health, and employment objectives. The indirect negative effects of technology that increases carrying capacity — such as the spread of river blindness and other waterborne diseases associated with the construction of dams for irrigation and power (Freeman, 1976) — are only recently being considered.

Cost-benefit analysis

Implicit in those studies that introduce various exogenously determined fertility trends is the assumption that governments can use some form of external intervention to direct fertility trends along the path chosen. In the 1960s this intervention was invariably seen to be the introduction or expansion of publicly subsidized family planning programs. A common approach of macro-consequences studies has been to compare the costs of a family planning program (which causes the lower fertility) to the projected savings realized in health or education costs. Usually the savings in the latter are shown to "pay" for the former in this form of analysis. Such comparisons necessitate a host of assumptions regarding costs of launching family planning programs, acceptor rates, and the relationship between acceptor rates and actual births averted, as well as assumptions about future costs in health, education, or other areas, and about the society's welfare function, which may value children per se in addition to per capita goods.

Among the earliest examples of this approach was the work of Enke (1966), who estimated the value of a "prevented birth" under specific assumptions. He used his estimate to compare the return from traditional development spending to the return from spending on family planning programs and concluded that spending on family planning was 100 to 500 times more effective than spending on other development projects. His micro-analysis thus capped the earlier macro-work; his result was widely disseminated and probably significantly influenced the policies of developed country donors regarding population. Enke's conclusion regarding family planning programs is now widely considered to be exaggerated. Enke's calculation was made before the real costs of providing family planning, and the difficulties of estimating such costs (discussed below) had been seriously considered. Estimation of the benefits of averted births is an even more problematical issue. Estimates of the cost of averting a birth through provision of family planning services range from $1 to $400, being extremely sensitive to, among other things, the selected discount rate. Estimates of the benefits of averted births range from $100 to $900.

The macro-economic models and cost-benefit analyses of the 1960s have come under increasing criticism in recent years, directed both at their underlying assumptions and at the uses to which they have been put. Summarized, their assumptions include:

1. That household savings and public savings are a decreasing function of the dependency burden (ratio of consumers to producers) in the household and in the nation as a whole.

2. That social overhead investment in, for example, education, health, and housing, contributes less to growth in the short run than investment in directly productive activities and tends to occur in greater proportions in societies with higher dependency ratios.

3. That there is little room for adjustment in the capital/labor ratio in modern manufacturing and agroindustrial production, and that capital/output ratios are constant or increasing, so that high-fertility countries are condemned to specialization in labor-intensive products (chiefly agriculture), which often suffer from poor and deteriorating terms of trade.

A limited amount of research has been conducted to test the assumption that the dependency burden adversely affects savings rates. Leff (1969), in a cross-section study using 1964 data from 74 developed and developing countries, examined the association between savings rates and both the young- and old-age components of the dependency burden. He concluded that the size of the dependency ratio has a significant effect on savings, not only for the countries considered as one group, but also within the two groups of developed and developing countries. But the correlation is apparently reduced if a few demographically atypical countries are excluded. And, of course, at the household level, a single characteristic — such as the propensity to plan — may cause certain families both to save more and to have fewer children. At the public level, governments willing and able to impose higher savings rates through taxation policies or imposition of a non-consumption-oriented industrial pattern, can and have done so, regardless of the dependency burden. Sources of savings in today's developing countries may be less the household sector and more the foreign, corporate, and small business sectors.

Still, short of major structural changes in developing economies, the assumptions regarding savings are probably sound; the possibility of major changes toward more labor-intensive technologies is at best a long-term one; and the political and ethical need to increase the expenditure on social overhead investments in proportion to population growth, irrespective of their impact on productivity, is obvious. As a result the work produced in the 1950s and 1960s on the macro-consequences of rapid population growth for development has not yet been effectively challenged, and has engendered a near-consensus on the excessive social costs of high fertility (with resultant rapid rates of population growth). It should be noted, however, that some critics of the macro-consequences work believe this to be a case in which correct conclusions are sustained by faulty logic and misleading use of modern analytic procedures.

Policy relevance of macro-consequences studies

Macro-consequences research, beginning with the contribution of Coale and Hoover, has alerted planners to the costs of rapid population growth. The types of analysis discussed in this section have had as a major objective persuasion: convincing governments that population matters. These studies have been most fruitful in those areas in which the relationship between rapid growth of the population and increases in public costs is obvious, and in those areas which are themselves major development concerns: education, health, and labor absorption. Resource and environment problems and inequitable income distribution have less often been linked to rapid population growth. Rapid population growth may not be an important factor in these areas; also the causal links between them and population growth are complex and difficult to analyze.

But countries differ. Creating employment in the cities in Africa is of more immediate concern than exploitation of land resources; the opposite may be true in Bangladesh. Keeping up with educational needs of an expanding population is of high priority in Brazil; in Sri Lanka raising per capita food production is more important. Work on the macro-consequences of population growth must be carried out on a country-specific basis — and, often, focusing on specific areas within the economy, as countries emphasize one or another development program.

Studies conducted in the 1960s normally included projections through the end of the century, with intermediate points in the 1970s, 1980s, and 1990s. Any future studies in this genre may be more effective if they analyze past trends in total costs and costs per capita of population served by health and education services, and compare those empirically derived costs to what might have been under a lower fertility regime. Similarly, expansion of the labor force, already a considerable problem in many countries in the 1970s might be related to fertility trends since World War II. The use of projections without proper analysis of past trends was sensible at a time when data on those aspects were scarce; but data scarcity has given way to data inundation for many countries. Admittedly, analysis of past tends is almost as thorny a methodological problem as the use of simulation models for projections, but it would inject greater reality into an approach that has to date been plagued by its resort to "illustrative" results.

On balance, it appears that macro-consequences research of the "other-things-being-equal" type is becoming less relevant for the developing world. Its major object is persuasion, and its major intended output is recognition by government planners of the need for population policy. Most of the population of the developing world now lives in countries that have national population policies to reduce fertility. Next steps for these countries include designing effective fertility-reducing programs based on research on the determinants of fertility. . .

Macro- and micro determinants of fertility

The basis for much of the policy directed at reduction of birth rates is the assumption that improved availability of family planning services leads naturally to fewer births. Research on the determinants of fertility (using both macro data, aggregated by country or by regions within a country, and micro data, collected from households or from individuals) has not disputed or refuted this assumption; it has sought to identify other factors besides availability of contraceptives that may influence fertility decisions.

A number of good reviews of the determinants of fertility, with citations to hundreds of studies, already exist. For research up to 1971, a Research Triangle Institute study, *Social and Economic Correlates of Family Fertility: A Survey of the Evidence,* is particularly useful. More recent reviews include Chapter 1, "Some determinants of fertility," in McGreevey and Birdsall (1974), Williams' (1976) essay, "Determinants of Fertility in Developing Countries." and Cochrane (1977). All of these summarize the literature by reviewing findings of the relation between fertility and a series of correlates or determinants of fertility: income, income distribution, education of men and women, female labor-force participation rates, age at marriage, own-family and community infant mortality, knowledge of modern contraceptives, use of contraceptives, availability of family planning services, and so on...

Here attention will be focused on (1) discussion of the macro-determinants approach, with reference to some recent studies that investigate the timing of the relation between fertility and socioeconomic development; (2) discussion of the theory and available data underlying the micro-determinants approach, with reference to several attempts at new types of analysis; and (3) discussion of some recent work on those variables that appear to have a critical effect on fertility and that are potential areas for public policy intervention.

Macro-determinants research

In the 1960s and 1970s, curiosity about the exact nature of the relationship between fertility and socioeconomic development has combined with the reduced cost and increased availability of computers to inspire a spate of cross-national studies. These studies use multivariate analysis, an approach that, with the quantitative reach and precision of the computer, permits the researcher to observe simultaneously relationships between a dependent variable and a number of independent variables. In these analyses, some measure of fertility is estimated as a function of some indicators of the degree of a nation's development: the literacy rate, proportion of labor in agriculture, per capita gross national product, the expectation of life at birth, primary and secondary school enrollment ratios, among others...

The traditional explanation of reduced fertility proposed by demographers is that with some lag, reduced fertility follows reduced mortality — the "demographic transition." Cross-national multivariate analyses seek other intervening factors that may have caused fertility to fall. Not surprisingly, certain indicators of advanced development are consistently correlated with low rates of fertility: high rates of literacy, high per capita consumption of energy, high rates of urbanization, low rates of infant mortality, high per capita income. But there are difficulties in the interpretation of such results.

The results of a cross-section analysis, which takes a picture of different countries at one point in time, do not necessarily mirror what has occurred within countries or what will occur over time. In fact, one multivariate analysis that estimated *trends* in fertility as a function of *trends* in several socioeconomic indicators within groups of countries indicated no particular relationship over time between changes in fertility and in the indicators (Janowitz, 1973). And several historical studies of the fertility decline in parts of eighteenth and nineteenth century Europe have led scholars to conclude that no particular indicator or set of indicators was related to changes in birth rates there.

A second difficulty with the macro-determinants approach is that it cannot elucidate the specific mechanisms through which changes in gross indicators over time, or differences in gross indicators across countries, influence the fertility behavior of individuals. Because higher levels of education and greater consumption of energy are associated with lower fertility, we cannot conclude that more classrooms and more lightbulbs will cause lower fertility, nor know, if they do cause lower fertility, exactly how. In this sense, it is actually a misnomer to use the term "determinants" in referring to these studies.

Two recent studies go beyond correlation of socioeconomic indicators with fertility rates, to identify how fertility change fits into the complex of other socioeconomic changes that development entails. Both studies pay special attention to the timing of fertility change, and its association with quantified differences in the other indicators.

In an analysis of the fertility-development relationship for countries of Latin America and the Caribbean, Oeschli and Kirk (1975) explicitly disavow the regression technique, which makes fertility a function of other variables, and construct instead a correspondence system, which is based on the premise that fertility and mortality are part of a holistic development process, the indicators of which cannot be disentangled into cause and effect relationships. The system describes quantitatively the relationships among ten indicators of development plus birth and death rates. From the ten indicators, the authors construct a development index, which can then be related to changes in birth and death rates. They find that countries above a certain level with respect to the development index have experienced rapid fertility decline — about .5 percent a year since 1962, their baseline year for measurement. The values for the Oeschli-Kirk socioeconomic indicators that correspond to the floor value of the development index above which countries experienced this marked fertility decline include: a literacy rate of 78 percent; an expectation of life at birth of 60 years; a primary school enrollment ratio of 65 percent; labor force in nonagricultural occupations of 52 percent; an urbanization rate of 40 percent; and a secondary school enrollment ratio of 22 percent.

These results are generally comparable with another study using 1950 and 1960 data from Latin American countries, in which Gregory and Campbell (1976) estimated the "modernization turning points" for several development indicators, that is, the levels below which improvements generate an increase in fertility, but above which improvements generate a decrease. Using different indicators from Oeschli and Kirk, they find that for changes in per capita income, the infant mortality rate, and the literacy rate, fertility begins to decrease only when the urbanization rate is at 69, 80, and 60 percent respectively. Both studies find the demographic transition occurring at levels of development that exceed those generally found throughout Africa and South Asia, though such levels have been reached in parts of Latin America and South-east Asia.

Micro-determinants research

Better understanding of how individual fertility decisions are affected by environmental changes (which the changes in the gross indictors imply) requires analysis of data collected directly from individuals, that is, micro-determinants research. This research uses census and survey data including information on characteristics of individuals — education, occupation, residence, desired or actual number of children, and so on.

Studies of individuals and households generally follow one of several conceptualizations of the fertility decision: the economic model, the psychological model, or the sociological model. The economic model explains changes in household fertility as a function of changes in the family's economic situation attendant upon socioeconomic development. The objective is to explain by one model both the dramatic growth of populations in developing countries and the equally dramatic large-scale control of fertility in the developed countries.

The "new home economics" of the family treats the child as both a produced (investment) and consumer good. Fertility is the result of rational economic choice within the household. Children, or more properly "child services," are consumed by the household; and because children are assumed to be noninferior goods, increased income increases the demand for them. Child services are also produced in the household, through inputs of parents' time and goods bought in the market, such as housing, formal education, and health services. Children may also be an investment, short-term if they work during their childhood, long-term if they support parents in old age.

If increased income increases the demand for child services, how do the new home economists explain the apparent fact that fewer children are "purchased" by high-income couples in high-income societies? There are two answers. First, though the income effect increases demand for children, the price or substitution effect reduces demand by increasing the price of children relative to other goods, inducing high-income couples to substitute other goods for children. The price effect operates chiefly through the increasing opportunity cost of the mother's time as women increase their educational attainment and employment opportunities. Second, with increasing income, parents opt for "higher quality" children rather than greater quantity, devoting more of their own time and income to children's health and education. Thus the use of the term "child services"; the demand for more child services can be satisfied with fewer but higher quality children.

Economic development increases the costs of children by increasing the value of parents' time and the costs of education, health, housing; at the same time it reduces the benefits of children, as they work less in the market and as institutional forms of old-age insurance substitute for support by children. By this approach the new home economics of the family explains the apparent link between economic growth and the so-called demographic transition.

This economic model thus concludes that for poor families in developing countries, children entail low net costs and, in the extreme case, may actually be a net benefit. (In the extreme case, parents would have as many children as they could and have a finite number of children only because of "supply" constraints: limited fecundity, high fetal and infant mortality.) Complementing the concept in the macro-consequences literature that high fertility entails a high net cost to poor societies, is an explanation in the micro-determinants literature that large family size entails low net costs or even a net benefit to individual poor families. This theoretical gap between the low private and high social costs of children in developing societies has been a principal justification for government policies to reduce fertility. (It has also been a source of some ambivalence in donor attitudes and local policymaker attitudes toward family planning programs, which some interpret as vaguely coercive; if poor families benefit from large numbers of children, why persuade them to limit their fertility?)

Two relatively new streams of research are relevant in this context. The first seeks to broaden the notion of the household as the unit of choice. The new home economics of the family assumes that the household has a common utility function with respect to children. Yet husband and wife are not always in accord regarding children; one analysis, which disaggregated the household decision-making process, found statistically significant differences in the demand for children between certain husbands and wives among Mexican-Americans. Furthermore, even if parents are in agreement in wanting many children, children themselves may prefer few siblings. Parents, who are merely this generation of decision-makers, may be better off with large families because they were able to exploit their children. When the children themselves grow up, the process is repeated.

A second recently evinced concern is to go beyond the household as the unit of choice, and to analyze fertility decisions within the context of the community in which individuals participate or of the clan or other unit that impinges on their behavior. McNicoll (1975) has called attention to the way communities can export the costs of their own rapid population growth through outmigration. Few existing studies address such questions as whether villages with different levels of services — schools, roads, health clinics, family planning services — or different cropping patterns, or different arrangements for the physical security of citizens, or different norms with respect to obtaining jobs for relatives have different patterns or levels of fertility. The apparent success of fertility reduction efforts in the People's Republic of China, where programs are grounded in community-level incentives, partly explains recent interest in examining the effect of community norms. Interest in community structure as well as the characteristics of households or individuals is the basis of recent suggestions that successful fertility-reduction programs be studied by anthropologists at the community level.

Some critical variables

Certain variables have emerged as consistently important in their relationship to fertility. A critical few describe characteristics of the socioeconomic environment that can be altered through public policy: infant mortality, female education and labor force participation, availability of family planning services, and, possibly, income distribution. The strength and direction of the effect on fertility of these policy variables is very different for countries at different stages of development and with different cultural environments.

Infant mortality and fertility. Almost all studies of the determinants of fertility indicate a positive effect of infant mortality on fertility, that is, countries with high rates of infant mortality on the whole have high rates of fertility. (Infant mortality is an important component of overall mortality, particularly in developing countries.) There is *no* country with high mortality and low fertility, taking high mortality as annual death rates above 15 per thousand and low fertility as annual birth rates below 30 per thousand.

What is the causal mechanism that links high fertility and high infant mortality? On the one hand, high infant mortality results in high fertility because parents who experience child loss early ultimately may more than replace lost children, and parents in high-mortality communities may insure themselves against future child loss by having more children than they would want. On the other hand, high fertility contributes to high infant (and child) mortality because close spacing of births and many births may deplete the mother's physical resources and reduce the family's per capita financial resources; a commonly noted phenomenon is the death of a child when, on the birth of a subsequent child, the mother ceases breastfeeding the older child.

The major point in the present context is that the relationship between infant mortality and fertility differs by country and by prevailing economic conditions within countries. For example, high fertility is most likely to contribute to high mortality among the poorest groups and is most likely to show up on a country basis in the poorest countries, as indeed it does in Africa. There kwashiokor is "the disease that kills the child whose mother carries another child in her womb"; it is often related to malnutrition exacerbated by early or sudden weaning.

There is some evidence that the extent to which parents replace lost children may vary with the level of socioeconomic development. Preston (1975, p. 192) suggests that populations at the highest and lowest levels of development exhibit the strongest replacement effects (Bangladesh, France, though by no means is replacement complete even for these), while countries in some intermediate stage exhibit weaker effects (Colombia, Taiwan). Heer and Wu (1975, p. 266) report that in Taiwan, women who suffer child loss are likely to have higher fertility than those who do not, but such women do not fully compensate for their loss; on average, for every child who dies, less than one additional child is born.

Opinion differs as to whether the poorest countries, even with a strong replacement effect, end up with more or fewer people as mortality falls. Studies that have dealt with the timing of the relationship, however, indicate that the response of lower fertility to lower mortality is maximized when the incidence of infant and child mortality is lagged two to four years. This tends to support the opinion that reduced infant mortality will in the long run reduce fertility enough so that the rate of natural increase will go down. This view would be strengthened if studies were better able to incorporate the indirect effect of reduced mortality: lower death probabilities induce parents to invest more in their children, which in turn leads them to lower their desired fertility. They replace a large quantity of children with fewer children of higher quality. In other words, lower mortality not only assists parents to achieve desired family size with fewer births; it may lead parents to reduce their desired family size.

Reduction of infant mortality is an important policy objective on its own merits. Because countries with high average levels of infant and child mortality also have higher levels of fertility, the policy objectives of reducing both mortality and fertility can be mutually reinforcing. (Countries with the highest rates are primarily in Africa and south Asia; most countries of Latin America now have much lower mortality and fertility rates.) Where political and cultural barriers to the advocacy of family planning and other fertility-reduction efforts exist, reducing infant mortality can be expected to lay the groundwork for later efforts concentrating on fertility.

Female education and labor force participation. Female education bears one of the strongest and most consistent negative relationships to fertility for a variety of reasons: through its effect on raising age of marriage; because it may improve the likelihood that a woman has knowledge of and can use modern contraceptives; and because it has some intangible effect on the woman's ability to plan, her interest in nonfamilial activities, and so on. No need to invoke fertility reduction to justify improving educational opportunities for women: better educated women will be more productive workers, better parents, and better-informed citizens; however, where male/female student ratios indicate that women suffer some schooling disadvantage, fertility effects provide additional justification for rectifying the imbalance. The fertility reducing effect of women's education holds true even for the highest levels of education; women who obtain secondary and higher education marry later, and increasing the age at marriage has a pronounced effect on a country's fertility rate (McGreevey and Birdsall, 1974, pp. 25-28).

But female labor-force participation appears to have an independent effect on fertility only for those women who work in high prestige, modern sector jobs. High rates of female labor-force participation, like virtually all other variables, are neither a necessary condition for fertility decline (consider Korea, Turkey) nor a sufficient condition for it (consider countries of West Africa). On the other hand, increasing opportunities for women to work in the modern labor force can accelerate a fertility decline; where women may desire more children than their husbands (as is possible in the Middle East and Pakistan, where custom deprives most women of opportunities in other endeavors), offering women some other avenue of activity than child rearing may reduce family size. Good earnings opportunities, like higher education, can increase the age of marriage for women. Similarly, in countries with high rates of urban migration, allocation of newly created urban jobs to women already residing in cities with working husbands could lower the expected employment rate of prospective new migrants, simultaneously reducing migration and increasing average family income within the cities. With two incomes per family rather than one, the tax and savings base in cities would be higher. (To what extent such benefits are offset by the admitted difficulty of creating jobs for even one member of each family has unfortunately not yet been the subject of any systematic study.)

From the point of view of policy, an important conclusion emerging from these analyses is the highly tentative nature of the effect of "status of women" on fertility. But "status of women" does not define an area where public intervention is possible; education and jobs for women do. Improving women's opportunities for education and for modern jobs, like reducing infant mortality, has its own justification; piggybacking its fertility-reducing benefit onto programs and projects geared to improving women's lives increases the measured benefits of such projects relative to their given costs.

Family planning services and fertility. Do family planning services reduce fertility more efficiently and more effectively than general development programs? The wide range of estimates of the cost of averting a birth (($1-$400) and its benefits ($100-$900) cited above illustrates the difficulty of answering such a question. Estimating the cost of averted births requires estimating the number of births averted because of a family planning program, itself a complicated task; some births might have been averted anyway if some couples are substituting publicly provided contraceptives for private efforts. And "costs per acceptor" is an unreliable measure since acceptors may make repeated visits in different areas, change contraceptives, and otherwise muddy the attendance statistics. Even where the existence of a family planning program is correlated over time with a decline in fertility, assurance that the program itself caused the decline requires the systematic elimination of such other possible causes as increases in income, changes in occupational structure, and increases in education. Few studies of the effect of programs have adequately controlled for the probable effect of these nonprogram changes on fertility.

Freedman and Berelson (1976) conclude tentatively regarding the effect of family planning programs on fertility: "If the fertility effect of family planning programs were always of overwhelming magnitude it would shine through; if it were always zero the question would not survive. In the middle-ground cases, while problems of data and measurement remain, we find plausible evidence that family planning programs made a difference that matters" (p. 19). Advocates of family planning programs argue that: many programs are still in their infancy and have been poorly run; they have absorbed tiny proportions of national budgets and of foreign aid expenditures; they provide many secondary benefits — improved health for mothers and infants, increased control by women over their own bodies, and greater control by families over their own future. Moreover, support of voluntary family planning programs is one of the few widely accepted direct interventions governments have made to reduce their rates of population growth; the immediate question is not whether support is warranted, but how much and in what form. What is the effectiveness of spending on family planning relative to other expenditures that also have both general development and fertility-reducing effects? Only investigations on a country basis can begin to answer such a question.

The current consensus on family planning programs is that their effects vary by country. Their effects will be more pronounced where they reinforce other factors that would tend to lead to a fertility decline. A series of studies in Taiwan, among the best studies from a methodological point of view, has indicated that the family planning program there has accelerated a fertility decline that was already under way. In a recent analysis Hermalin (1976, p. 11) concludes, using data from 1968 to 1972, that the family planning program in Taiwan had a negative impact on fertility, above and beyond other social, economic, and demographic factors. His result is consistent with Schultz's 1973 analysis showing a negative effect of the family planning program on birth rates, controlling for child mortality and parents' education (Table 4, pp. S259-261). Hermalin shows, moreover, that the rate of decline in fertility is different for rural and urban areas in different periods; in rural areas with initial high fertility, slow declines in the early years of the family planning program were followed by accelerating declines later. Rates of decline are presently lower in urban areas, which have already passed through a period of rapid change. These within-country differences indicate that within countries as across countries, estimates of the cost-effectiveness of a family planning program must take into account differential responses depending on development levels.

Income distribution and fertility. Will an improvement in the distribution of income within a country reduce its fertility rate? In an analysis of 1960 — 65 data on 64 countries. Repetto (1974) reports an elasticity of the general fertility rate with respect to the share of income received by the poorest 40 percent of households of -.36, compared to an elasticity of the general fertility rate with respect to increase in average per capita income of -.20.

Income distribution data are notoriously poor, and Repetto's result suffered in a subsequent estimation in which he omitted several East European countries (which have both low fertility and relatively equal income distributions); the income distribution variable was no longer statistically significant in explaining the fertility variable. Moreover, whether such cross-section results should be used to predict the pattern of a relationship over time is highly questionable.

Though statistically less sophisticated, simple cross-tabulations compiled by Kocher (1973) and Repetto (1974) are more appealing since they utilize time-series data. Repetto took countries (and a region) on which information for at least two points in time was available regarding income distribution and birth rates and grouped them according to changes in the two variables. He was able to show that fertility fell notably more in countries in which the income distribution apparently improved (Costa Rica, Sri Lanka, Taiwan) than in those in which it did not (Brazil, India, Puerto Rico). Kocher, in a similar exercise, found greater declines in crude birth rates for countries (and a region) with fairly equal income distributions (South Korea, Taiwan, West Malaysia) than for countries with less equal income distributions (Philippines, India, Thailand, Mexico, Brazil). His income distribution variable was unfortunately available for one point in time only.

To date no one has adequately distinguished between the *share* of income going to the poorest 40 percent and the average *level* of income of that group, nor has anyone drawn out whatever connection there may be between shares and levels. In fact most of the reasoning behind the apparent link between fertility and "income distribution" actually relies upon a simpler "incomes" sort of argument: once a certain level of economic and social well-being is achieved, fertility will begin to decline. Rich (1973) appeals to this logic in comparing fertility levels across countries with more and less equitable systems of health services and education. Kocher (1976, p. 85) explains his findings, for example, for Sri Lanka, in these terms.

There is thus no real indication that individuals' fertility behavior is affected by their relative income *per se*, over and above their absolute income; the income distribution fertility link found is more probably the result of a coincidence over the period since World War II between improvements in the level of absolute income of the poorest and increases in their relative share. In any event, insofar as "income distribution" is used to mean some nexus of programs, including income increases, to alleviate the poverty of the poorest, an inverse relationship to fertility seems to hold. Fertility-reducing effects can be added to the other benefits of raising income levels of the poorest groups.

Highlighted above are four areas of public policy intervention. All may contribute to reducing fertility at tolerable cost; all provide benefits in addition to fertility reduction. Careful design of policy in these areas can accelerate the fertility decline that general improvement in standards of living inaugurates.

Summary and conclusions

Research relating population and development demonstrates that extremely rapid population growth rates can exacerbate development problems. Early efforts to include population in growth models include the well known "trap" and low-level equilibrium concepts; although the assumptions of these and later more elaborated models are often questioned, even sceptics seldom question their basic premise that population growth has implications for capital accumulation, employment levels, income and its distribution, public expenditure on social services, and food availability.

Studies of the consequences of rapid growth of population for education, for health, for labor force absorption, and for progress in other problem areas complement the results of the more general models. These studies have been most useful in those areas in which the relationship between rapid growth of population and increases in public costs is obvious, and in those areas which are themselves major development concerns. Use of this approach must be on a country-specific basis, and often must focus on specific areas within the economy, as countries emphasize one or another program.

Research (mostly in developed countries to date) indicates that children from poor families that are also very large are more likely to suffer from malnutrition and less likely to reach any given level of education than are others in their age groups in the population. The consequences of large families for family welfare provide a rationale for provision of family planning in countries in which fertility reduction *per se* is not an official objective, and in those countries in which fertility reduction is an official objective, but receives little attention.

Within countries, moreover, research indicates that the burden of large families falls most heavily upon the poorest groups. Though data on income distribution are still poor, the weight of logic also suggests that the differential in fertility between the better-off groups and those less fortunate constitutes a drag on efforts to improve the share of income going to the poor.

However, careful analysis of the determinants of household fertility also indicates that high fertility rates are not an inexorable component of underdevelopment — there are policy interventions to reduce fertility that could be, and have been, effective at tolerable cost.

Availability of family planning services appears to have contributed to the speed of fertility decline in some areas. Still, there is considerable room for expansion and improvement of services, even in those countries, including India, Pakistan, Indonesia, the Philippines, and, recently, Mexico, where family planning is well established as a legitimate means to reduce aggregate fertility.

Nor is family planning the only feasible policy intervention. Reduction of infant mortality appears to be a natural prerequisite to reduction of fertility. Research on fertility determinants points to the critical role of female education in reducing fertility. Improvements in opportunities for women to work, under certain conditions, can hasten fertility decline. Any success in increasing incomes of the poorest groups is likely to have fertility-reducing benefits; this includes increasing availability of services in health and education to those groups. No one intervention can be expected to affect fertility in a simple downward direction: the relation between each variable and fertility is complex, as are the relations among these variables and their joint effect on fertility.

This article is based on work the author undertook as a consultant in the World Bank Population and Human Resources Division in collaboration with staff members Rashid Faruqee and Ricardo Moran. She wishes to acknowledge their comments and those of other Bank staff members, especially Timothy King, as well as the contribution of William P. McGreevey. The article does not necessarily represent the views of the World Bank.

References

Caole, Ansley J., and Edger M. Hoover, (1958) *Population Growth and Economic Development in Low-Income Countries*. Princeton: Princeton University Press.

Cochrane, Susan H. (1977) 'Education and Fertility: What do we really know?' Mimeo, World Bank.

Enke, Stephen, (1966) 'The economic aspects of slowing population growth.' *Economic Journal* 75.

Freedman, Ronald, and Bernard Berelson, (1976) 'The record of family planning programs.' *Studies in Family Planning* 7, no. 1 (January): 1-40.

Freeman, Peter, (1976) 'The environment and large scale water resources projects.' Prepared for International Institute for Environment and Development in preparation for United Nations Water Conference, March 1977.

Gregory, Paul, and John M. Campbell, Jr. (1976) 'Fertility and economic development.' In *Population, Public Policy and Economic Development*, ed. Michael C. Keeley, pp. 160-187. New York: Praeger.

Heer, David M. and Hsin-Ying Wu, (1975) 'The effect of infant and child mortality and preference for sons upon fertility and family behavior and attitudes in Taiwan.' pp. 253-379 in *Population and Development in Southeast Asia*, ed. John F. Kantner and Lee McCaffrey. Lexington, Mass.: D.C. Heath.

Hermalin, Albert I. (1976) 'Spatial analysis of family planning program effects in Taiwan.' Paper presented at Population Seminar, East-West Population Institute, Honolulu, June.

Janowitz, Barbara S. (1973) 'An econometric analysis of trends in fertility rates.' *Journal of Development Studies* (April): 413-425.

King, Timothy, et al. (1976) *Population Policies and Economic Development*. Baltimore: Johns Hopkins University Press.

Kocher, James E. (1973) *Rural Development, Income Distribution and Fertility Decline*. New York: The Population Council.

— (1976) *Socioeconomic Development and Fertility Change in Rural Africa*. Harvard Institute for International Development, Discussion Paper no 16.

Kuznets, Simon, (1966) *Modern Economic Growth*. New Haven: Yale University Press.

Leff, Nathaniel, (1969) 'Dependency rates and savings rates.' *American Economic Review* 59, no. 5 (December): 886-896.

Leibenstein, Harvey, (1954) *A Theory of Economic-Demographic Development*. Princeton: Princeton University Press.

McGreevey, Wiliam P. and Nancy Birdsall, (1974) *The Policy Relevance of Recent Research on Fertility*. Washington, D.C.: The Smithsonian Institution.

McNicoll, Geoffrey, (1975) 'Community-level population policy: An exploration.' *Population and Development Review* 1, no. 1 (September): 1-22.

Nelson, Richard, (1956) 'A theory of the low-level equilibrium trap in underdeveloped economies.' *American Economic Review* (December): 894-908.

Oeschli, Frank William, and Dudley Kirk, (1975) 'Modernization and the demographic transition in Latin America and the Caribbean.' *Economic Development and Cultural Change* 23, no. 3 (April): 391-420.

Preston, Samuel, (1975) 'Health programs and population growth.' *Population and Development Review* 1, no. 2 (December): 189-199.

Repetto, Robert, (1974) 'The interaction of fertility and size distribution of income.' Mimeo, Harvard University.

Research Triangle Institute, (1971) *Social and Economic Correlates of Family Fertility: A Survey of the Evidence*. Research Triangle Park, N.C.: Research Triangle Institute.

Rich, William, (1973) *Smaller Families Through Social and Economic Progress*. Washington, D.C.: Overseas Development Council.

Schultz. T. Paul, (1971) 'An economic perspective on population growth.' In *Rapid Population Growth*, vol. 2, pp. 148-174. Baltimore: Johns Hopkins University Press.

— (1973a) 'Explanation of birth rate changes over space and time: A study of Taiwan.' *Journal of Political Economy* 81, no. 2 (Part II): S238-S274.

— (1973b) 'A preliminary survey of economic analyses of fertility.' *American Economic Review* 53, no. 2 (May): 71-78.

Schultz, Theodore W. (1971) 'The food supply — Population growth quandary.' In *Rapid Population Growth*, vol. 2, pp. 245-272. Baltimore: Johns Hopkins University Press.

Williams, Anne D. (1976) 'Review and evaluation of the literature.' In *Population Public Policy and Economic Development*, ed. Michael Keeley, pp. 119-159. New York: Praeger.

31. Economic Consequences of Population Change in the Third World

Allen C. Kelley

I. Demographic change: past, present, and future

A. The past

To place current demographic trends in perspective, it is useful to review some features of the European "Demographic Transition," that 150-200 year period during which population growth rates rose from low to high and then returned to low rates again, but then on a considerably enlarged population base.

Beginning in the eighteenth century with low population growth rates of about 0.5 percent per year, the transition began with a gradual reduction in death rates, accompanied by persistently high birth rates. Although there was considerably country-specific variation in the patterns and levels of vital rates, the trends in Figure 1 are representative.[3] An important feature of most (but not all) of the individual country transitions was a delayed decline in the birth rate, often lagging mortality reduction by decades, which resulted in a period of rapid population growth of about 1.5 percent per year. This period was accompanied by sustained and substantial economic prosperity, urbanization, and structural transformation — all factors that eventually brought about reduced birth rates and low rates of natural population increase. Indeed, the transition was generally restricted to those countries that had entered into Modern Economic Growth.

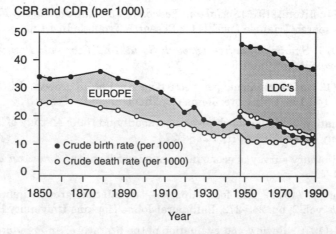

Figure 1. Crude Birth and Death Rates, 13 West European and 106 LDCs (Unweighted).

B. The present

For comparison and reference, Figure 1 shows vital rate trends since 1950 in the LDCs, whose demographic transition lags behind that of Europe by about 100 years. While the LDCs have similarities with the experience of Europe — an early reduction in mortality, followed by high, and then declining birth rates associated with a period of economic prosperity, urbanization, and structural change — there are also striking differences. In particular, LDC birth rates are on average considerably higher than those at the peak of the European transition. (Given data constraints, the earlier portion of the Demographic Transition in the Third World is not presented in Figure 1.) When combined with a particularly rapid decline in mortality rates, reaching low levels early in the transition, the result has been an exceptionally rapid pace of population change.

Table 1 documents the variation in the demographic experience by region. Given China's atypical demographic record and impact on the results, the Asian and total LDC aggregates have been computed with and without China. The text will refer to the series excluding China, unless otherwise noted.

Five rough generalizations are illustrated by this table.

The pace of population growth in the LDCs is exceptionally high. Currently expanding at an annual rate exceeding 2.25 percent (excluding China), this pace is well above that experienced in Europe during its period of rapid population growth. At this rate, the doubling time of the LDC population is 28 years. There is considerable variation by region, and even more by country. The current pace of population change is highest in Africa at about 3.0 percent, with individual countries, including such large ones as Nigeria and Kenya, growing at 3.5 and 4.2 percent, respectively. This region is followed by Latin America and South Asia with growth rates ranging between 2.0 and 2.2 percent, and East Asia at 1.9 percent. The slower pace of population change in Asia is shared by several countries, including Korea and Indonesia (1.7 percent). However, even these rates are high by historic standards. Regionally, the Demographic Transition is most advanced in East Asia, followed by Latin America and South Asia; it is least advanced in Africa.

Large reduction in death rates have contributed overwhelmingly to the increase in total population growth. The current death rate of 11/1000 has been cut in half since 1950-55, and by more than two-thirds (from around 37/1000) since 1937 (Samuel H. Preston 1980). This sizable reduction to a rate approaching that of industrial countries is largely responsible for the acceleration of total population growth in recent decades. The speed of this reduction has been four to five times as fast as that experienced in Europe in the nineteenth century (Kuznets 1980). But unlike Europe, where the decline can be attributed largely to gradual improvements in living standards and modernization, much of the mortality reduction in the LDCs has occurred without significant economic or institutional change. Instead, it has been related to a greatly enhanced capability to cope with infectious diseases, as well as improved communications and transportation which have brought about a wide diffusion of upgraded public health practices (Kuznets 1980).

497

Table 1

Measures of Demograpic Change, 1950-1990, by Region

Regions	Africa	Latin America	Asia[a]	Except China	LDCs	Except China	More Developed Countries[b]	World
Population in Millions								
1950	224	165	1,292	737	1,684	1,129	832	2,516
1985	555	405	2,697	1,637	3,663	2,603	1,174	4,837
Percent Annual Popul. Growth								
1950-55	2.12	2.73	1.96	2.04	2.04	2.13	1.28	1.79
1985-90	3.02	2.16	1.67	2.00	1.94	2.25	0.60	1.63
Crude Birth Rate per 1,000								
1950-55	48.3	42.5	44.2	44.6	44.4	44.7	22.7	37.3
1985-90	45.2	29.7	26.0	31.1	29.4	33.9	15.1	26.0
Total Fertility Rate								
1950-55	6.47	5.86	6.07	6.04	6.12	6.12	2.80	4.94
1985-90	6.22	3.73	3.26	4.03	3.69	4.33	1.97	3.28
Crude Death Rate per 1,000								
1950-55	27.1	15.4	24.8	24.6	24.2	23.8	10.1	19.6
1985-90	15.1	7.6	9.3	11.1	10.0	11.4	9.5	9.6
Life Expectancy at Birth								
1950-55	37.8	51.1	40.2	39.9	41.1	41.2	65.8	46.0
1985-90	51.3	65.7	62.0	57.1	59.1	54.9	74.0	61.1
Infant Mortality Rate/1,000								
1950-55	191	125	186	180	180	173	56	156
1985-90	101	56	68	92	79	98	14	71
Percent Urban Population								
1950-55	15.7	41.0	13.9	16.1	17.0	20.4	53.8	29.2
1985-90	29.7	68.9	24.9	27.7	31.2	35.5	71.5	41.0
Percent Dependency Under 15								
1950-55	42.4	40.5	36.7	39.1	37.9	40.0	27.8	34.5
1985-90	45.1	37.9	35.2	38.8	36.9	39.9	22.2	33.4
Over 65								
1950-55	3.6	3.3	4.3	3.7	3.9	3.6	7.6	5.1
1985-90	3.1	4.5	4.7	3.9	4.2	3.8	11.2	5.9

Source: United Nations (1986), medium variant projections.
[a] Asia excludes Japan.
[b] "More Developed Countries" include: North America, Japan, Europe, Australia-New Zealand and USSR.

While impressive, such progress requires qualification because the average crude death rate does not itself account for age-specific incidence of mortality which is better measured by life expectancy at birth. Here the record is slightly less dramatic but still notable, with life expectancy rising from 41.2 to 54.9 years since 1950-55 with much of this improvement due to a reduction of the infant mortality rate from 173/1000 to 98/1000.[4] Nevertheless, future improvements in life expectancy will be more difficult to achieve because mortality reductions must increasingly come from gains at older ages; they will also have less impact on future rates of population growth. For example, extending the life of women over 50 has little impact on future births, whereas reducing the mortality of children who will in turn raise a family contributes substantially to future population numbers.

Fertility rates, peaking in the mid-1960s, have begun to decline in most countries, although they remain high by historic standards and are still increasing or have not begun to decline in some countries. The average crude birth rate has declined from about 45/1000 to about 34/1000 since 1950. Even so, current rates are high by historic standards, roughly corresponding to those in many European countries during the peak of the Demographic Transition. Moreover, there is some indication that birth rate reductions in several Third World countries (e.g., Costa Rica, India, Korea, and Sri Lanka) may have stalled. Whether this is a temporary pause is an unanswered question (World Bank 1984, p.71).

There is considerable variation in fertility by region and country, with the crude birth rate ranging from around 25/1000 in East Asia to around 45/1000 in Africa; Latin America and South Asia are in between at 30/1000. The record of specific countries widens this spread, with crude birth rates in Nigeria and Kenya exceeding 50/1000 and Argentina and Chile approaching 20/1000. Most countries have shown some reduction in fertility rates in recent decades, but in some (mainly Africa) these changes have been small, and in a few, the rates are still rising.

High fertility has resulted in a relatively young age structure. The proportion of the LDC population under 15 is currently about 40.0 percent, almost twice that in the industrialized world. While the proportion of the elderly is small (3.8 percent), the share of the population of "working age" upon whom the young and elderly are dependent (1.3 workers per dependent) is still considerably smaller than that in the industrialized world (2 workers per dependent);[5] however, this situation is changing. On the one hand, declining birth rates are beginning to age the LDC populations, and a more economically favorable age structure will emerge in the future. Moreover, issues associated with accommodating an aging population are already beginning to emerge as a demographic concern for the twenty-first century. On the other hand, the present and upcoming decades will be dominated by the legacy of past rapid population growth, manifesting itself in a bulge of young people seeking jobs, forming households, bearing children, and raising a family.

Expansion in the share of the population in urban areas has been moderate, but the growth of very large cities has proceeded at a rapid pace. In analyzing urban trends, one must distinguish between the pace of urbanization (the share of the total population living in urban areas), and city growth. Consider each of these measures in turn.

Presently 35.5 percent of the LDC population lives in urban areas, up from 20.4 percent in 1950.[6] Latin America is the most urbanized region (68.9 percent). Even though the *absolute* size of urban populations has expanded notably in recent decades, this increase has occurred largely because urban growth has been taking place on an already sizable population base. The pace of structural transformation — changes in the urban *share*

— is broadly consistent with the historical experience of Europe at roughly comparable stages of development.[7] The primary explanation of urbanization trends is *not* the overall (rapid) rate of population growth but rather the course of underlying *economic* processes. Rural-to-urban migration, which has figured prominently in urbanization, has been primarily motivated by migrants responding to the economic opportunities of urban areas (Preston 1979; Allen C. Kelley and Jeffrey G. Williamson 1984; Williamson 1988).

It is the pace of city growth, especially the emergence of exceptionally large cities, that most distinguishes Third World urban trends.[8] This reflects the significantly faster rate of population growth in recent times. Indeed, international migration has accounted for a much smaller portion of Third World city growth than it did in Europe during its urban transition.

C. The future

In the year 2000, 20 of the 25 cities in the world with populations of over 10 million are projected to be in the LDCs. These include Mexico City and São Paulo, each having projected populations exceeding 25 million. Such large concentrations are without precedent and the economic implications of managing and providing public services for them are unknown.

Including China, LDC population growth peaked at 2.5 percent in 1965-70. This rate is expected to decline to 1.1 percent in 2025, when Third World population is projected to be 6.8 billion (United Nations 1986, medium variant). Thus, it is expected that over the 75-year period from 1950 to 2025, Third World population will have increased by 5.1 billion. While these numbers are large by any standard, it is notable that even in the year 2025, the majority of Third World countries will record population growth rates approximating those experienced in Europe at the peak of its Demographic Transition. The momentum of population change will be maintained throughout much of the twenty-first century, with projected world population stabilizing in about the year 2100 at about 10-11 billion.

How much confidence can be placed in these long-term projections? Paul Demeny (1984) aptly describes them as "speculative exercises rather than forecasts" (p. 108). They are fraught with uncertainty arising from difficulties in predicting fertility trends and the fact that forecasting errors cumulate over time.[9] This is illustrated by examining revisions in the UN projections compiled in 1974 which underestimated the pace of fertility decline in which the total fertility rate of 4.5 children in 1970-75 dropped to 3.5 children in 1980-85 (United Nations 1986, p. 33). The 1974 projections (medium variant) placed world population in the years 200 and 2100 at 6.4 and 12.3 billion, respectively; the revised UN estimates available in 1981 placed world population at 6.1 and 10.4 billion respectively (United Nations 1975; Rafael M. Salas 1982). While the projections differed by only .3 billion in the year 2000, this difference widened to 1.9 billion by the year 2100.[10] Clearly, the sensitivity of long-term projections to the highly uncertain course of fertility justifies caution in using such figures.[11]

How, then, can one select among the various projections for the year 2100? Tomas Frejka (1981b) offers guidelines concerning his own projections. He pretty much rules out his high projection of 13.4 billion (with replacement fertility in the years 2040-45) because it assumes a rate of fertility decline that is considerably lower than the one experienced in the past 10 or 15 years, and is similar to that experienced in Europe during the Demographic Transition.[12] He also rejects his low projection of 8.5 billion (with a replacement level in the years 2000-2005) because it assumes the total fertility rate (TFR) will continue to decline at the pace experienced in the last 10 to 15 years. This is improbable because conditions for sustained high fertility still prevail in most of Africa and in many countries of Asia. His median projection uses a replacement rate stabilizing in 2020-25 with a resulting population of 10.6 billion, a figure bracketed by the projections of the United Nations of 10.2 billion and the World Bank of 11.2 billion.

II. Analytical perspectives

A. Models of growth and development

1. The one-sector models. The aggregate production function represents the most widely used framework for identifying the impacts of population growth on the economy.

If the production function exhibits constant returns to scale, and if, for simplicity, we assume that labor is a constant proportion of population, then its productivity depends on the availability of complementary factors (e.g., land, resources, and human and physical capital) and on technology. An increase in population growth will reduce the growth of average productivity through diminishing returns — a "resource-shallowing" effect — if such a population increase does not also affect the growth of complementary factors and/or technology. If population growth diminishes the growth of the other factors and/or technology, labor productivity growth is reduced by even more; if it stimulates the growth of the other factors and/or technology (a "resource-augmenting" effect), labor productivity growth is increased or decreased, depending on the relative importance of the negative resource-diluting versus the positive resource-augmenting effects. (An empirical assessment of these effects is provided in Section V.)

In the standard growth model, where savings rates are exogenous to population growth, and where technical change is exogenous, an increase in population growth lowers the *level* but not the long-run *growth rate* of output per capita. This is because the capital-shallowing effect of an increase in population growth eventually drives down the long-run level of capital per worker enough so that it can be sustained by the (fixed) ratio of savings to output. As a result, increases in labor productivity are determined by changes in the rate of technological progress (Robert M. Solow 1956; Edmund S. Phelps 1968).[13] The impacts of increasing or decreasing returns to scale and changes in the rate of advance of technology can substantially alter these relationships.

Scale. If production is subject to increasing or decreasing returns to scale, population growth can itself directly increase or decrease the growth rate of output per capita. Negative scale effects would be unusual in the aggregate except possibly in countries that are already densely populated, and positive ones have been considered important to the growth of some presently developed countries. (A discussion of the nature and empirical relevance of scale effects is found in Sections IV and VI.)

Technology. Consider three alternative formulations of technical change. First, if technological advance takes place *independently* of factor supply growth, then the previous finding that population growth has a negative impact on the level of per capita income (and a neutral impact on long-run per capita growth) remains unaltered.

Second, if technical change is all or partially *embodied* in, say, new human or physical capital, a vintage specification is appropriate whereby new capital is relatively more productive than old (Solow 1960; Richard R. Nelson 1964). The average age of the capital stock, itself a determinant of labor productivity, is lowered (i.e., capital becomes more productive) when an increase in population growth causes total output and capital stock to expand more rapidly. Rapid population growth then quickens the pace at which new technology can be incorporated into production, and thereby has a positive impact on per capita output growth;[14] however, this impact takes place only during the transition between equilibrium age distributions of the capital stock. During such transitions the declining age of the capital stock acts as some offset to the decline in the stock of capital per worker.

Finally, population growth can directly affect the rate of technical change and/or its form (factor bias). [15] For example, Kenneth J. Arrow (1962) has hypothesized that learning-by-doing is quickened in an environment of rapid employment growth — a rate-of-change effect. Alternatively, relative price changes resulting from rapid population growth may stimulate the adoption of technologies more consistent with changing factor proportions, although the impact of this on total factor productivity is uncertain.

Saving. While the growth-theoretic literature assumes a constant saving rate that is unrelated to demography (for an exception, see James Tobin 1967), the economic-demographic literature considers several population-sensitive saving specifications. For example, in the life-cycle model, saving is influenced by the need to finance the maintenance of children (the child-dependency effect), and retirement. And in the income-distribution model, population growth can increase saving if the effect of a lower capital-labor ratio is to shift income toward recipients of nonlabor income, who are assumed to save more on average. (This effect reduces but does not erase the impact of population growth on capital dilution, and depends on the elasticity of capital-labor substitution.) It should be noted that in the age-specific formulations (like those with vintage capital above), the impact of aging in the very long run will be on the level as distinct from the rate of growth of income per capita. (An empirical assessment of the impact of population growth on saving is taken up in Section V.)

Summary of one-sector models. The long-run impact of population growth and size on per capita output growth in the one-sector models is theoretically ambiguous. Population growth and size have a negative impact through diminishing returns, diseconomies of scale, and perhaps savings; and it has a positive impact through induced technical change, economies of scale, and perhaps savings. In the short run, the net impact is more likely to be negative as result of resource-shallowing effects, which are immediate and take time to overcome; however, changing demographic age structures can stimulate or depress saving rates, depending on the saving model and its parameters. They can also stimulate or depress the rate of technical change, depending on the extent to which technology is embodied in capital and other factors. Having said this, we observe that most economists conclude that the negative resource-shallowing impacts of population growth dominate the countervailing induced feedbacks, even in the long run. As a result, unless scale effects associated with population are present and sufficient to offset substantially the adverse effects of resource shallowing, induced feedbacks take on the role of reducing, but not necessarily overturning, the negative impacts of population growth.

2. The dualistic models. Models of economic dualism fall into two categories: labor-surplus formulations where labor is paid more than its marginal product in some occupations, and neoclassical formulations where labor is paid its marginal product.

Labor-surplus model. The labor-surplus model highlights the transfer of labor from a relatively unproductive sector such as traditional agriculture to a more productive sector such as modern industry.[16] Population growth exerts a negative impact on development because labor fails to pay its way in the traditional sector, adds to the pool of unemployed or underemployed labor, and reduces the surplus needed to fuel modern-sector growth. The period of time when both sectors become "modern" — when all labor is paid its marginal product — is therefore postponed.

Neoclassical model. In the two-sector neoclassical model, labor receives its marginal product, and population growth exerts a smaller negative impact than in the labor-surplus paradigm (Dale W. Jorgenson 1961; Avinash K. Dixit 1973; Ryuzo Sato and Yoshio Niho 1971; Kelley, Williamson, and Russell J. Cheetham 1972). This negative impact is reduced somewhat in the Kelley, Williamson, and Cheetham (1972) formulation since population growth contributes to the overall rate of capital accumulation by increasing the economy-wide share of (nonlabor) income going to the relatively high savers. This specification is of methodological interest because it illustrates a role for feedbacks in modifying the first-order direct effects of population growth highlighted in most economic-demographic models.[17] This general-equilibrium perspective whereby initial impacts of population growth are dampened (but seldom overturned) by induced impacts explains in part the moderated and less pessimistic "revisionist" assessments of the consequences of population growth (see Footnote 2).

3. The multisector models. Given the problem of increasing analytical intractability as one moves beyond simple dualistic models, and the desire of government agencies to formulate population policies and provide quantitative assessments on the role of population, multisector simulation models have emerged as a major activity in economic-demographic research. Although the resulting literature is large, it has been reviewed by others so the present summary can be brief.[18]

Multisector models have primarily added complexity in the form of accounting detail. Population is broken down by age, sex, labor force participation, education, and location; production is divided into sectors, sometimes location-specific; factor inputs are disaggregated, usually highlighting demographic and skill attributes of the labor force; and demand is specified by commodity.

Three general observations are relevant to appraising the insights of these models into the impact of population. First, the analytical contributions have been modest. The models have been grounded almost entirely on the fundamental theoretical relationships highlighted in the one- and two-sector frameworks reviewed above. In fact, in most multisector models, the key qualitative predictions derive neither from the accounting detail nor from the empirical parameters, but follow directly from one or two analytical specifications. These typically emphasize areas in which population manifests a negative impact (e.g., diminishing returns) with limited or nonexistent countervailing influences. The numerical analysis serves mainly to illustrate the underlying analytic structures.[19]

Second, the empirical contributions of the multisector models have been limited. This is unfortunate because the raison d'être of such models is quantitative assessment; however, the paucity of Third World data required to accommodate the extensive demands for parameters and initial conditions has proved constraining. And given the size of the models, the use of sensitivity analysis to overcome data limitations has proven to be cumbersome and of limited generalizing value.

Third, a key purpose of such models — to account for the indirect effects of changes in economic and/or demographic structures — has seldom been fulfilled either analytically or empirically. While analytically a framework with considerable price endogeneity is required, the accounting detail of most models has resulted in data constraints that preclude a meaningful general-equilibrium specification.

4. The net impact of population in models of growth and development. It appears that neither formal growth theory nor the simulation models have provided a basis for making conclusive statements about the net impact of population on development although, as noted above, most economists conclude that the negative resource-shallowing impacts will dominate induced feedbacks and thus positive scale effects are required to overturn a net-negative impact assessment. Thus, as an alternative tack, it pays to return to basics: an empirical assessment of the key building blocks in the theoretical structures — for example, the impacts of population that derive from diminishing returns and scale, accumulation and saving, and technical change. We will return to these linkages below, but first we will apply the theoretical perspectives just reviewed to the evolution of population ideas over time.

B. *Overview of ideas and debates*

Few topics in economics have a longer tradition of controversy than the analysis of the impact of population on economic growth and development (for an early review, see Edward P. Hutchinson, 1967).

The debate rose to prominence in 1798 with the publication of *An Essay on the Principle of Population*, the famous pamphlet in which the Reverend Thomas Malthus argued that food production could not keep pace with population's natural proclivity to grow in an unchecked fashion. In the absence of prudential checks, the result would be starvation, vice, and misery, and a tendency for economies to stagnate at a subsistence level of income. In one of the most famous passages in all of economics, Malthus concluded:

> Population, when unchecked, increases in a geometrical ratio. Subsistence increases only in an arithmetical ratio. A slight acquaintance with numbers will show the immensity of the first power in comparison of the second. (1798, p. 14)

His pessimistic speculations caused the discipline of economics to be dubbed the "dismal science." This label and the Malthusian perspective on population have persisted to this day despite the fact that his predictions failed to materialize for the countries he studied.[20] Contrary to expectations, agricultural productivity rose steadily and population growth slowed in those countries that entered the process of Modern Economic Growth. Food surpluses, not food shortages, turned out to be agriculture's nemesis over time. The "Malthusian Devil" of recurrent famines resulting from the unyielding influence of diminishing returns was exorcised by an expansion of the land frontier, capital intensification of agriculture, and improvements in farming technology. In the industrializing countries, concern about the adverse consequences of rapid population growth subsided under the weight of these trends.[21]

Indeed, an about-face occurred in the 1930s when economists pinpointed *slow* population growth as one factor explaining the insufficient expansion of aggregate demand, and contributing to the prolongation of the Depression (John Maynard Keynes 1937; Alvin H. Hansen 1939; William B. Reddaway 1939). John R. Hicks (1939) provided one of the bolder assessments:

> One cannot repress the thought that perhaps the whole Industrial Revolution of the last two hundred years has been nothing else but a vast secular boom, largely induced by the unparalleled rise in population. (1939, p. 302n)

Apparently the negative "supply-side" effects of population emphasized by Malthus were being challenged by the positive "demand-side" effects stressed by Hansen and other "stagnationists." This challenge was short-lived.[22]

The 1960s and 1970s saw the pendulum of opinion swing decisively back to an emphasis on the negative supply-side impacts of population. This reorientation was spurred by several developments: the unprecedented rates of population growth in the Third World; the judgement that a deficiency of aggregate demand was not important in accounting for development trends in the LDCs; and the promotion and implementation of birth-control policies and programs by governmental agencies, notably the U.S. Agency for International Development, and the United Nations Fund for Population Activities. There was also a substantial broadening and strengthening of the intellectual foundations of the pessimistic evaluation of the impacts of population growth with the appearance of two quite separate strands of thinking.

The first strand not only revived the Malthusian notion of diminishing returns resulting from scarce farmland but also applied this framework to a host of renewable and nonrenewable resources. Representative of this literature were the studies by Jay Forrester (1971) in *World Dynamics* and Meadows et al. (1972) in *The Limits to Growth*, which predicted that the world had only about 100 years remaining before economies and/or biosystems collapsed. Central to this scenario were the adverse consequences of population growth pressing against the land, natural resources, energy, and the environment (see also Council on Environmental Quality and U.S. Department of State 1980). Even though economists severely criticized these studies for failing to model market- and politically induced feedbacks realistically, never since the early nineteenth century have Malthusian concerns exercised greater popularity (Simon and Kahn 1984).[23] Seldom have the consequences of a powerful economic idea — the law of diminishing returns — been applied more broadly and embraced with greater conviction.

The second strand of thinking related to an assessment of population's impact on the pace and composition of saving and investment. This emphasis coincided with the prominence attributed to capital in development models and the popularity of the neoclassical paradigm. The pioneering formulation was by Coale and Hoover (1958) in *Population Growth and Economic Development in Low Income Countries,* which identified three adverse effects of population growth:

Capital-Shallowing Effect. Rapid population growth lowers the ratio of capital to labor because there is nothing about population growth *per se* that increases the rate of saving.

Age-Dependency Effect. Rapid population growth results in high "youth-dependency," which increases requirements for household consumption at the expense of saving, and lowers the saving rate.

Investment-Diversion Effect. Rapid population growth shifts (mainly) government spending into areas such as health and education at the expense of more productive, growth-oriented investments.

These hypotheses had a strong impact on the analysis of economic-demographic relationships and even U.S. population policy. Indeed, political scientist and policy analyst Phyllis T. Piotrow (1973) observed that the Coale-Hoover thesis ". . . eventually provided the justification for birth control as a part of U.S. foreign policy" (1973, p. 15). Moreover, many of the early simulation models relied upon the Coale-Hoover ideas as the primary linkages between population growth and the economy (Barlow 1967; Enke 1971; William E. McFarland, James P. Bennett, and Richard A. Brown 1973; Frank T. Denton and Byron G. Spencer 1973, 1976; and Barlow and Davies 1974).

It is important to recognize that while these ideas, which stressed the adverse consequences of population growth, dominated academic writing and served as the intellectual foundations of the debates about the effects of population in the 1960s and 1970s, some scholars were offering a somewhat more guarded assessment.[24] A large body of empirical research was also accumulating during this period. Some economists cautioned that the *strength* of the conclusions concerning the negative consequences of population growth were not buttressed by the evidence (especially that relating to saving and investment). They added that some possible positive impacts (notably increasing returns to scale and induced technical change in agriculture, at least in some settings) were being overlooked or downplayed. But this literature attracted relatively little attention. (An examination of the conditions under which such scale and technological benefits of populations may be realized is taken up in Sections IV and VI.)

The 1980s saw the population-assessment pendulum swing again, this time toward the more eclectic, and somewhat less pessimistic revisionist interpretation adumbrated in the introduction to this article. Several developments contributed to this reorientation. The first was the accumulation of a large volume of empirical research that suggested (1) the possibility that population-induced technical change (largely in agriculture) could reduce or offset the effects of diminishing returns; (2) the capacity of individuals and firms to respond quite flexibly to resource scarcity and changing factor supplies; and (3) the apparent unimportance of some of the hypothesized Coale-Hoover effects. The second development was a changed political climate — a return to traditionalist views about the family, and challenges to government's family-planning policies, especially those relating to abortion — which was more conducive to an evaluation and airing of the accumulating research that roughly quantified a wide range of linkages between population and the economy.

The third event was the publication of Julian L. Simon's book, *The Ultimate Resource* (1981), which advanced the controversial conclusion that population growth in the long run could actually enhance the pace of economic growth in the Third World. While virtually alone in its optimism, Simon's book, written for a general audience,[25] generated heated debate. It was considered by some to represent a threat to by now well-established and intellectually grounded family-planning policies, and further stimulated empirical research on the consequences of population growth.

The timing of the present review may be opportune because the pendulum of scholarly opinion has swung toward a more centrist (or possibly a less pessimistic) position than at any other time in recent decades.[26] This environment facilitates a balanced review of a wide literature and affords an opportunity to point out some gaps in knowledge at a time when the research agendas are being formulated for the next round in the debate.

III. The evidence: a first pass

While several models predict a negative net impact of population growth on economic development, it is intriguing that the empirical evidence documenting this outcome is weak or nonexistent. The typical empirical study examines correlations between per capita output growth and population growth, sometimes measuring the sensitivity of the results to various data samplings over time and/or space (for example, Easterlin 1967; Kuznets 1967; Anthony Thirlwall 1972; John Isbister 1975; Tim Hazeldine and R. Scott Moreland 1977; Simon 1977; Mark Browing 1982). Figure 2 provides a representative set of results.

On the one hand, there has been a tendency to discount these reduced-form, bivariate correlations as simplistic and difficult to interpret. It is argued that causation is not revealed, and institutional variations among countries may mask the relationships. On the other hand, it has also been argued that few if any statistical associations establish causation; the cross-country results are consistent with the few studies using time-series data; a zero correlation in the face of strong (negative) priors merits attention; and the positive and negative effects of population growth may offset each other.

A more important difficulty in interpreting Figure 2 is the presence of simultaneous equation bias because population growth is influenced by income growth. This relationship is widely discussed in the historical literature on the Demographic Transition. Lee (1983) has discounted the importance of this reverse-causation bias by suggesting that as a first approximation, one would expect population growth to be more related to the level than to the rate of growth of income. His hypothesis seems quite reasonable with respect to explaining birth rate changes, and Preston (1980, 1986) finds that only 30 percent of the reductions in death rates over the period 1930 to 1970 are associated with improvements in income per capita and economic development, although these factors increased in importance in the 1970s. Preston observes that because mortality reductions have affected about equally the growth rates of the working and nonworking populations, whose impacts on income per capita growth are in opposite directions, a lack of correlation between income per capita and population growth in the aggregate is not surprising. At any rate, Lee's summary evaluation of this literature is instructive and provocative:

> . . . these cross-national studies have not provided what we might hope for: a rough and stylized depiction of the consequences of rapid population growth: unless, indeed, the absence of significant results is itself the result. (1983, p. 54)

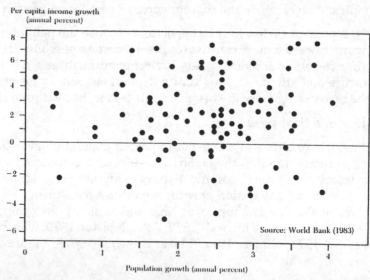

Figure 2. **Income per Capita Growth and Population Growth, Developing Countries, 1970-81.**

My own judgement, confirmed by the wide-ranging nature of the debate, is that these statistical correlations provide little prima facie information about the size or nature of the net impact of population growth on economic growth; however, they have attracted considerable notice and as such, merit attention. They have also encouraged empirical studies that attempt to isolate and measure population-development linkages, a literature to which I now turn.

IV. Economies of scale

An evaluation of scale effects of population size is complex because these effects originate from different sources and are exceptionally difficult to quantify. The narrowest point of reference focuses on *within-* firm variations in productivity when all factors of production change proportionally. It is usually acknowledged that with the exception of a few industries, most technical economies are exhausted by firms of moderate size (E.A.G. Robinson 1960). In a broader framework, scale economies emanate from indivisibilities in lumpy investments, including roads, communications, research and development, and markets. These economies can be quite important, especially in agriculture (Boserup 1981). In a still broader framework, scale economies derive from increased specialization and diversification *between* firms.[27] According to George J. Stigler (1961):

> The large economy can practice specialization in innumerable ways not open to the small (closed) economy. The labor force can specialize in more sharply defined functions... The business sector can have enterprises specializing in... repairing old machinery, in printing calendars... The transport system can be large enough to allow innumerable specialized forms of transport... (1961, p.61)

A critical qualification in Stigler's analysis is the assumption of a *closed* economy because many of the benefits of specialization in tradeables can be obtained through international trade. Moreover, even in a closed economy, market size is only partially and sometimes indirectly influenced by population size. For example, market size can be expanded by linking regional centers with improved transport, although the economic viability of investments in transport may itself be related to population size and density.[28] And some of the advantages of scale can be obtained by population concentrations as distinct from larger national populations.

Most analyses of scale economies have been directed to currently developed economies, where the positive effects of scale are often highlighted.[29] In a discussion of U.S. economic growth over the period 1869-1953, Moses Abramovitz notes:

> "the division of labor is limited by the extent of the market." If there is anything to the notion that when raw materials are plentiful, resources and output will be connected according to the law of increasing returns to scale, then the great expansion of total resources must have contributed substantially to the increase in productivity. (1956, p. 12)

And Denison (1962) offers a quantitative speculation:

> Economies of scale two or three times enough to offset the 'drag' of land should not strike economists as unreasonable. (1962, p. 175)

These studies, referring to a sparsely populated area with resource abundance, stressed that the ability to capture scale effects is related to the capability of utilizing scale-dependent modern technologies, and to the availability of capital and a favorable institutional environment. Such qualifications are critical to assessing the relevance of the historical experience of the developed countries to the third World where such preconditions are in general less favorable.

Have Third World nations benefited from scale effects of larger populations? The answer depends on the source of the effect. With respect to within-firm scale economies, the National Research Council (1986) concludes that the advantages of population size do not appear to be especially large in Third World manufacturing — or at least not as large as in the agricultural sector, because "localized" scale economies are more sensitive to the concentration than to the size of the population (J. Vernon Henderson 1987 and Jeffrey James 1987).[30]

Other reasons for discounting the importance of scale economies in the Third World have been advanced. First, economies in infrastructure are judged to be substantially exhausted in cities of moderate size. Second, as noted above, specialization through international trade provides a means of garnering some or many of the benefits of size. And third, scale effects are most prevalent in industries with relatively high capital/labor ratios and such industries are inappropriate to the factor proportions of developing countries. Having said this, it is important to recognize that inward-looking, import-substitution trade strategies are common in the Third World (Anne O. Krueger 1978, 1983). As a result, *given* these policies, an expanded national market and population are conducive to capturing economies of scale, albeit at some cost (Tibor Scitovsky 1960). This development, if it occurs, conveys benefits through reducing the adverse consequences of a harmful trade policy.[31]

It is in agriculture where the positive benefits of population size have been most discussed. Higher population densities can decrease per unit costs and increase the efficiency of transportation, irrigation, extension services, markets, and communications (Simon 1975; Glocer and Simon 1975; Boserup 1981).[32] These economies may be substantial where modern agricultural technologies require large infrastructural investments (Boserup 1981, ch. 16; Prabhu L. Pingali and Hans P. Binswanger 1984; Haymai and Ruttan 1985). Moreover, because the adaptation of new technologies may be specific to small agroclimatic areas, economies are realized by spreading research costs over larger outputs.[33]

The real issue, then, is not the existence of scale economies, but rather their quantitative importance over varying ranges of population sizes, as well as the conditions under which they may occur. On the one hand, while scale economies deriving from high population densities may have accounted for a portion of expanded agricultural output in recent decades, in several important Asian countries these densities were sufficiently high decades ago to justify the investments associated with the new technologies. In such cases, one must be cautious in attributing positive scale effects largely to increased population numbers. On the other hand, in some countries increased population numbers may well have made investments associated with the new technologies economically attractive. Unfortunately, empirical studies that provide quantitative precision to the interactions between population size and scale are unavailable.

Boserup (1981) appears less sanguine about the benefits of population size in the intermediate future because densities appropriate to modern technologies in Asia are three to four times the average for Africa and Latin America. She notes that:

> ... except for areas with much more than average density, establishment of efficient extension networks would require large and probably uneconomic investments in rural roads. (1981, p. 204).

(Of course, roads serve many important functions in rural production in addition to their interactions with extension activities.) Moreover, even in areas where densities are not limiting, it is frequently found that institutional conditions — such as land ownership patterns, poorly developed capital markets, and government policies — restrict the exploitation of technologies embodying positive scale effects. It is probably the differences between institutional conditions that most differentiate the putative favorable historical experience with scale effects in some developed countries with the apparently less favorable experience in many Third World nations.

Summary assessments of scale effects attributable to population size can only be impressionistic. I am inclined to attribute a qualified role to these effects in accounting for Third World development. First, the performance in Asian agriculture, the source of employment for the majority of the Third World labor force, has been impressive. "Green Revolution" technologies would not have conveyed the same advantages in sparsely settled regions; however, only a part of these scale-economy benefits can be attributed to larger population numbers. Second, the lower densities in many non-Asian countries reduce the potential for taking advantage of similar scale-dependent technologies in the intermediate future. (This situation will change in the long run when larger population sizes may convey some benefits.) Third, scale economies of the type Stigler describes, while never quantified, cannot but help to contribute positively to growth. While these division-of-labor/specialization effects may now be substantially exhausted in the larger and more densely populated Third World countries, in the future, as these countries continue to develop, additional advanced, scale-dependent technologies may be open to them; however, the benefits to the smaller and more sparsely populated countries may still lie in the future and take the form of minimizing the adverse consequence of inward-looking trade policies currently popular in the Third World

V. Saving and capital formation

In the postwar period the evaluation of the impacts of population growth on the pace and form of saving and capital formation has centered on capital shallowing, age dependency and investment diversion (Coale and Hoover 1958). [34] This section examines the theoretical basis of these linkages and their empirical importance in the Third World.

A. Capital shallowing

As noted in Section II, A, in the simple neoclassical model population growth exerts no impact on per capita output growth in the long run, although in the short to intermediate run (which may be decades) the impact through capital shallowing is negative, and in the long run, the level of per capita output is adversely affected.

While the quantitative importance of these impacts is difficult to assess, a rough approximation can be obtained by using the simple neoclassical growth model. For example, the National Research Council's (1986) illustrative calculation reveals an increase in the long-run level of per capita output of only 13 percent as a result of a reduction of population growth from 3 to 1 percent.[35] Several of the sources-of-growth studies also suggest a relatively modest role for capital, although the results are sensitive both to the measurement of capital and to the period of evaluation. Thus, while in Denison's (1974) calculations for the U.S. from 1948 to 1969, capital accounts for 20 percent of the growth in national income per person employed, the estimate by Barbara M. Fraumeni and Jorgenson (1981) places the figure at 42 percent. The higher estimate is based on the use of gross versus net weights, plus an adjustment for capital "quality" (especially the relative growth of short-lived capital in the U.S.).[36]

In general, although the capital-shallowing effects of population growth are unfavorable, their quantitative importance appears to be modest unless the output elasticity with respect to capital is considerably higher than that typically assumed in simple applications with growth-theoretic models, or estimated in many sources-of-growth studies, although there is considerable variance around these estimates; however the latter apply to developed countries, and capital may be more important in the Third World, thereby aggravating the capital-shallowing impacts of population growth.

B. Saving

1. Age-dependency formulation. The literature on population/saving rate linkages has focused almost exclusively on the household sector.[37] In its usual form, the age-dependency linkage (a narrow version of the life-cycle model) recognizes that an additional child has an incremental claim on household consumption, and asserts that this claim is a drain on household saving. Empirical representations of this thesis have typically specified an "adult equivalency" measure whereby each child's consumption is taken as a *fixed* proportion of an adult's. The problem with this formulation is that it is too narrow. Families may be so poor that they accumulate little or nothing; the options of financing additional children are therefore severely constrained — children must be financed out of household consumption. Moreover, the impact of children on the household can be quite complex because children may (1) substitute for other forms of consumption (which may adversely affect labor productivity), (2) contribute directly to household market and nonmarket income, (3) encourage parents to work more (or less), (4) stimulate the amassing (or reduction) of estates, and (5) encourage (or discourage) the accumulation of certain types of assets (e.g., education, or farm implements). The impact of expanded family size on household saving can therefore be negative, negligible, or positive; the issue is an empirical one. Unfortunately, there are few microeconomic studies that explore these relationships using data from developing countries.[38]

2. Life-cycle formulation. The life-cycle model broadens the analysis of household budgeting beyond the narrow age-dependency formulations, concerned with the costs of raising a family, to the need to save for retirement (Franco Modigliani and Richard Brumberg 1954; Modigliani and Albert K. Ando 1957; Tobin 1967; Arthur and McNicoll 1978).[39] At the aggregate level there are two separate effects of population growth on saving: a positive "rate-of-growth effect" resulting from a higher proportion of young workers (savers) to retirees (dissavers), and a negative "dependency effect" resulting from the need to support an increasing number of children . The net impact depends on which effect dominates, and this is an empirical matter about which there is little direct evidence.[40]

The relevance of the life-cycle formulation to the low-income setting has been challenged on the ground that credit markets may not be well equipped to facilitate the smoothing of consumption across time. However, such an institutional constraint may affect more the form of life-cycle planning than its relevance. In particular, resource transfers through the extended family may play a role in retirement planning (Laurence Kotlikoff and Avia Spivak 1981), and children may represent a form of "investment" for retirement. One should recognize, however, that while to the *household* children may represent an investment, in *society* they compete with other forms of retirement assets that could augment capital per worker. Children as pension assets are partially a consequence of financial-market failure, and as such may dampen per capita output growth.[41]

3. Distribution-of-income formulation. The impact of population growth on the distribution of income and thus on saving represents a potentially important linkage. Several development models have hypothesized, and empirical studies confirmed, that saving rates vary by level of income, and possibly by income source.[42] Because rapid population growth raises the level of population, *vis-à-vis* complementary factors, *ceteris paribus*, and thus the relative return to nonwage income (whose recipients may on average have higher overall income and correspondingly higher saving rates), it can also exert a positive impact on saving. (Of course, this effect must be qualified by the impact of population growth on the average level of income.)

4. Empirical analyses of economy-wide saving. Theory alone cannot predict even the direction of the impact of population growth on saving; the final arbiter must rest in the data. Indirect linkages of population growth with business and government saving complicate the analysis further, primarily because it is generally agreed that there is considerable substitution between forms of saving for the economy as a whole. This provides some justification for focusing on aggregate saving in the empirical analysis.[43]

Empirical studies typically use cross-country data to isolate age-dependency effects on economy-wide saving. The most popular model explains the domestic saving rate by (1) income per capita (in U.S. dollars using exchange rates for conversions), (2) growth of real income per capita (as one proxy for life-cycle influences), and (3) the dependency rate (the share of the dependent population — youth, aged, or both — to the total).

The pioneering study by Leff (1969), which found that youth, aged, and total dependency exerted a negative impact on saving, generated considerable debate centering largely on econometric and methodological issues (Nassau A. Adams 1971; Leff 1971, 1973, 1980; Arthur Goldberger 1973; Bilsborrow 1979, 1980). Numerous replications of the Leff model using alternative country samples, years, data definitions, data aggregations, and econometric procedures have generally failed to uncover notable dependency effects. Statistically significant results (positive or negative), when found, are often weak.[44] In short, the evidence does not support the hypothesis of a quantitatively important negative impact of population growth (through age-dependency effects) on saving.

This conclusion now widely held, merits qualification.[45] First, the empirical evidence is not particularly strong, resting as it does on international cross-country data. The results are sensitive to country selection, year of study, data aggregation, functional form, treatment of statistical issues such as heteroscedasticity, and official exchange-rate conversions.[46] Second, the financial saving variable omits in-kind saving/investments in agriculture which may be influenced by population pressures.[47] Third, if foreign capital inflows are responsive either to domestic interest rates or to demographic change, then an expanded model taking such impacts into account is required.

Finally, if the concept of saving is broadened to include the financing of investments in human as well as in physical capital, age-dependency impacts of rapid population growth may emerge. For example, Ram and Theordore W. Schultz (1979) have pointed out that a reduction in infant and child mortality rates increase the return on investing in human capital. Because expenditures on human capital bulk high in a broad measurement of asset accumulation, increased population growth, which in part results from mortality reduction, could increase total (but not necessarily per capita) savings/investments; however, Preston (1980) has used a series of hypothetical examples to illustrate the hypothesis that mortality reductions of the type experienced in the Third World exert a relatively small impact on the present value of human capital investments. At any rate, given the likely importance of children as a form of savings/investment in the Third World, additional evidence will be required to gauge the impacts of family size on the allocation of household accumulation of human and physical capital. At an economy-wide level, this analysis has taken the form of assessing the impact of population growth on the composition of investment.[48]

C. Composition of investment

In several economic-demographic models rapid population growth is assumed to shift (mainly governmental) spending away from growth-enhancing forms such as physical-capital investment, and toward allegedly less- or nonproductive forms such as schooling[49]. This "investment-diversion" hypothesis has been challenged by an accumulating empirical literature.

The most detailed study of government spending on schooling is by T. Paul Schultz (1987), who examines the experience of 89 countries over the period 1969-80. He presents a puzzle. On the one hand, Third World countries have not only kept pace in providing education services to increasing numbers of youths, but substantial human-capital deepening has taken place. Among the low-income countries in Schultz' sample, enrollment rates and average years of schooling completed per pupil have about doubled; and among the middle-income countries, these statistics rose significantly as well. On the other hand, this accomplishment was accompanied by a significant reduction in per pupil costs in the low-income countries, although in the middle-income countries, these costs increased. Surprisingly, demographic change appeared to be relatively unimportant in explaining enrollment rates, although Schultz emphasizes that expenditures per pupil are negatively related to enlarged school-age cohorts. Additionally, the relative size of the school-age population exerted no independent effect on the shares of GNP expended on education, causing Schultz to observe:

> This finding challenges the working assumption of Coale and Hoover (1958) that linked population growth to the share of income allocated by poor countries to "less productive" expenditures on education and social welfare programs. (1987, pp. 458-59)

Instead, increases in enrollment rates were financed by rising incomes per capita and, to an important extent (in the group of low-income countries), by a reduction in costs per pupil. These cost reductions were due partly to small increases in student-to-teacher ratios, but mainly to a relative decline in teachers' salaries, especially in cities. While a reduction in the quality of schooling probably occurred, the magnitude of this impact is qualified. Schultz speculates that the downward pressure on teachers' salaries may have been influenced by compensating amenities of urban areas that teachers valued, including the availability of part-time employment, by an expansion of the supply of teachers, and possibly by a deterioration in teacher quality.[50] Moreover, among middle-income countries, costs per pupil actually increased on average.

While these results are consistent with the findings of other studies, they should still be considered as preliminary (as Schultz cautions).[51] The various empirical studies are few in number and are based on international cross-country data subject to many of the difficulties discussed above (in Section V.B.4). Moreover, pupil outputs (e.g., achievement) are approximated by inputs (e.g., enrollments), and the data fail to account adequately for state and local, and especially private, spending on education. Finally, the explanation of changes in costs per pupil, and how these relate to the quality of education, requires additional elaboration.

Where does this leave us? Unfortunately with an inconclusive assessment which, in an area dominated by strong opinions, may itself represent an interesting finding. While the investment-diversion formulation has not been confirmed empirically, the challenge to this interpretation must still be considered as suggestive. Surely some investment diversion took place, but such a mechanism for financing schooling in response to population pressures has been neither the exclusive nor even the most important response. Governments, like households, face many alternatives in adjusting to demographic change.

The results showing substantial improvements in enrollment rates and average years completed per pupil also raise a fundamental issue concerning the impact of demographic change on capital formation. In particular, the classification of spending on items such as schooling as "unproductive" and spending on physical capital as "productive" is inappropriate because it downplays the value of literacy, numeracy, and other school-acquired skills as determinants of income growth. Both the relative and absolute returns to investing in human capital are likely to be modified by rapid population growth. For example, schooling is relatively labor intensive in production; moreover, the economy-wide average teacher salary is likely to be influenced by the rate of turnover of the teacher workforce. These types of impacts are seldom explored; however, the evidence presented above suggests that rapid population growth sets in motion forces that can modify the findings of simple models highlighting investment diversion.

* * * * * *

Acknowledgements

I am grateful for the assistance of Kathy Silvasi for word processing, editing, and preparing the references; for the research assistance of Michael Kelley and Carol Smith; and for the comments of Robert Bates, Nancy Birdsall, Martin Bronfenbrenner, Edwin Burmeister, Richard A. Easterlin, Anne O. Krueger, Stephen R. Lewis, Jr., Samuel H. Preston, T. Paul Schultz, T. N. Srinivasan, Jeffrey G. Williamson, and especially Moses Abromovitz.

Notes

2. The general-equilibrium perspective of the recent National Academy of Sciences report on population substantially explains its somewhat guarded assessment of the consequences of population change. The authors highlight "the key mediating role that human behavior and human institutions play in the relation between population growth and economic processes" (National Research Council, 1986, p. 4).

3. Following Kuznets (1966, pp. 52-53), this transition is represented as unweighed country averages, thereby emphasizing country-specific socioeconomic cultural factors important to explaining vital rate trends. Thirteen countries are included: Austria, Belgium, Denmark, Finland, France, Germany, Italy, Netherlands, Norway, Spain, Sweden, Switzerland, and the United Kingdom (England and Wales). Data from 1850-1950 are from H. J. Habakkuk and M. Postan (1965, pp. 68-69), and from 1950 to the present from United Nations (1986) (medium variant).

4. High infant mortality rates were experienced in Europe at the onset of the transition. Around 1800, these rates in Sweden and Germany were 250/1000 and 300/1000 respectively (World Bank 1984, p. 58). In Sweden, life expectancy for men in 1750 was only 34.2 years (World Resources Institute and International Institute for Environment and Development 1986, p. 16), a level exceeded by almost every Third World country today. The pace of infant mortality reduction in the LDCs has declined in recent years (Julie DaVanzo *et al.* 1985).

5. An adjustment in the usual definition of "working age" (15-65) to account for the relatively longer working span in the LDCs would narrow the dependency burden comparisons noted in the text.

6. A lower population boundary of 2,500-5,000 encompasses most country definitions of "urban areas" (United Nations 1980, pp. 121-24).

7. Early accounts by Bert Hoselitz (1957) emphasized "over urbanization" in the Third World, but recent analyses have documented a relatively conventional pattern. For example, the

urban share in the presently developed countries increased from 17.2 percent to 26.1 percent in the period 1875 to 1900, a change closely approximating the experience of the Third World from 1950 to 1975 (Preston 1979, p. 196).

8. While city growth between 1875 and 1900 in the presently developed countries increased by about 100 percent, the pace in the Third World during the period 1950-75 was 188 percent. "Cities" represent urban areas with populations exceeding 100,000 (United Nations 1980, p. 40).

9. Projections are made by modifying a base-year population by assumed mortality, fertility, and net migration. In terms of fertility, UN projections assume (1) a specific date (about the years 2005 and 2025 for medium- and high-variant projections, respectively) when the total fertility rate (TFR) is 2.0, (2) a linear decline in the TFR to that date, and (3) a replacement level of fertility thereafter. (The total fertility rate is the average number of children born to a group of women over their childbearing years if they experienced no mortality.) In terms of mortality, UN projections assume a quinquennial gain of 2.5 years in the expectation of life at birth until life expectancy reaches 62.5 years, followed by a slowdown in the gain thereafter. Adjustments are made for some developing countries (United Nations 1986, pp. 9-10). For a discussion of early projections, see Thomas Freika (1973, 1981a); for an explication of World Bank projections, see Demeny (1984).

10. Based on comparisons of past projections with subsequent experience, Nathan Keyfitz (1981) questions the usefulness of population forecasts that extend much beyond 20 years.

11. For example, the choice of dates when individual countries reach replacement fertility is based on the judgements of demographers, and descriptions of their procedures are vague. The United Nations (1986) fertility projections are based on "past and current fertility trends, ... placed within the social, economic, and political context of the country. Trends and anticipated changes in the socio-economic structure and cultural values of the society as well as policies and programs directed towards family planning are considered... " (p. 9-10). The World Bank (1984) projections "vary from country to country, depending on current fertility levels, recent trends, and family planning efforts" (p. 74).

12. Dudley Kirk's (1971) study of the Demographic Transition suggests that the pace of fertility decline is faster the higher the level from which it was initiated.

13. For a review of this growth-theoretic literature as it applies to population, see John Pitchford (1974) and McNicoll (1975).

14. Edward F. Denison (1964, 1967) places limited importance on embodiment in the U.S. and Western Europe; however, he notes that embodiment will be more important in situations where the capital stock is older, where its age distribution is distorted and where capital markets are not functioning well (because of, say, lack of competition or government regulations) — presumably conditions that are relatively prevalent in the Third World. P. J. Verdoorn (1949) identified a significant positive association between output and labor productivity growth, based on aggregate interwar data for 15 developed countries and on individual sector data for 4 countries. While the sources of this relationship have been subject to debate, Bryan L. Boulier (1984) demonstrates that, based on Verdoorn's formulation, it is not possible to distinguish between competing explanations: positive impacts of population growth through scale effects, embodied technical change, or labor-supply limitations.

15. These various models are surveyed and extended in Julian L. Simon (1986). See also Peter J. Lloyd (1969) and Gunter Steinmann and Simon (1980).

16. Theoretically, this model also admits "traditional" industrial and "modern" agricultural enterprises. The pioneering formulation by W. Arthur Lewis (1954) was subsequently formalized and elaborated by John C. H. Fei and Gustav Ranis (1964).

17. The nature and strength of this relationship depend critically on the elasticity of capital-labor substitution. In a simulation of the model parameterized to correspond to the experience of Meiji Japan, a tripling of the Japanese population growth rate over a 28-year period reduced aggregate output per capita, industrial output, and urban levels by 7.7, 3.7, and 4.4 percent, respectively (Kelley and Williamson 1974, p. 132-33).

18. The major review is by Warren C. Sanderson (1980), who evaluates Kelley, Williamson, and Cheetham (1972), Kelley and Williamson (1974), Food and Agricultural Organization (FOA) (1976), Simon (1976), and Irma Adelman and Sherman Robinson (1978). Arthur and McNicoll (1975) review Ansley J. Coale and Edgar M. Hoover (1958), Stephen Enke (1960), U.S. Census Bureau models as summarized in Joseph E. Quinn (1975), Purdue Development Model as summarized in T. Kelley White *et al.* (1975), and BACHUE as summarized in René Wéry, Gerry B. Rodgers and Michael J. D. Hopkins (1974). Simon and Herman Kahn (1984) review Council on Environmental Quality and U.S. Department of State (1980). Solow (1973) reviews Donella H. Meadows *et al.* (1972). Dennis A. Ahlburg (1987) reviews Robin Barlow and Gordon W. Davies (1974), Richard Anker and James C. Knowles (1983), Robert M. Schmidt (1983), and David Wheeler (1984). See also David E. Horlacher (1981) and Kelley (1974).

19. Referring to the TEMPO models that feature Cobb-Douglas production functions, Arthur and McNicoll (1975) observe: "This central assumption has the robust property that the derivative of per capita output with respect to labor is always negative. An increase in population can therefore never pay its way" (1975, p. 257). Referring to the BACHUE-2 ILO model, Arthur and McNicoll conclude: "Demographic effects on consumption would have to be extraordinarily large to run counter to the trivial theorem determining the fertility issue: slices of the economic pie (growing virtually independently of population) would get smaller the more people to divide it" (1975, p. 258). See also Rodgers, Wéry, and Hopkins (1976).

20. Although his earlier publications were more widely cited, Malthus' empirical assessments were modified in later writings (Coale 1978). Studies by economic historians have also confirmed the relevance of some Malthusian predictions on rents, wages, food prices, fertility, and mortality in England between the fourteenth and eighteenth centuries (Ronald D. Lee 1980b; World Bank 1984, p. 57).

21. A history and appraisal of Malthus' contributions are provided by Joseph J. Spengler (1945a, 1945b), Keyfitz (1972), and Coale (1978).

22. Stagnationist arguments have recently been applied to the current situation of slow population growth rates in the developed countries (Ben J. Wattenberg 1987).

23. Referring to the Forrester-Meadows model, Sollow (1973) points out that "... the characteristic conclusion... is very near the surface. The basic assumptions are that stocks ... are finite, that the world economy tends to consume the stock at an increasing rate, ... and that there are no built-in mechanisms by which approaching exhaustion tends to turn off consumption gradually and in advance. You hardly need a giant computer to tell you that a system with those behavior rules is going to bounce off its ceiling and collapse" (1973, p. 43).

24. Albert O. Hirschman (1958), Kuznets (1960, 1967), Ester Boserup (1965, 1981), Colin Clark (1967), Richard A. Easterlin (1967), Harvey Leibenstein (1971, 1976), Kelley (1974), Robert

H. Cassen (1976, 1978), Simon (1977), and Peter T. Bauer (1981) all pointed out potentially important positive as well as negative impacts of population growth.

25. The book was based on his extensive technical writings (e.g., Simon 1977).

26. This position is best represented by a recent report of the National Research Council (1986) which makes no quantative statements on the magnitude of population's net impact on development. The report (1) notes that the impact is likely negative in most cases, (2) highlights several positive impacts, and (3) provides some documentation suggesting the importance of market-induced feedbacks that have weakened the strength of previously hypothesized negative linkages between rapid population growth and the economy.

27. For an alternative classification, see Allyn A. Young (1928).

28. Donald R. Glover and Simon (1975) use cross-national data for 113 countries for 1968, and time-series data for 64 countries for the period 1957-68, to compute a strong elasticity of roads per area with respect to population density after controlling for per capita income. The results are invariant to level of development as measured by countries grouped by per capita income, and by type of road (paved or unpaved), although the estimated elasticities are higher for paved roads. Possible problems of interpretation arising from population moving to areas well served by roads are considered minimal given the relative unimportance of international migration. While data on roads are fraught with measurement problems, there appears to be no reason to believe that these errors are correlated with the population density variable.

29. In a cross-sectional study of manufacturing which controls for per capita income, Hollis B. Chenery (1960) estimates the partial elasticity of output with respect to population to be .20. See also Chenery and Moises Syrquin (1975).

30. Limited empirical evidence suggests that the rate of technical change in manufacturing (measured by industrial labor productivity growth) may be uninfluenced by population density and growth (James 1987).

31. This point is consistent with the World Bank (1984) report on population that observes "... countries such as India and China can seem to benefit from the sheer size of their domestic markets" (p. 79).

32. Robert E. Evenson (1984a) finds some negative effects.

33. Compare Evenson (1984b) and Binswanger and Pingali (1984) for contrasting views.

34. An early analysis of these relationships is found in Demeny (1965, 1967). See also Kelley (1973, 1988) and Jeffrey S. Hammer (1984).

35. The calculation assumes labor-augmenting technological progress at 2 percent annually, depreciation at 3 percent annually, and a constant-return-to-scale Cobb Douglas production function with a capital coefficient of .3 and a labor coefficient of .7. The economy takes 15 years to adjust halfway to the new steady-state capital/labor ratio. A variant with saving adjusting optimally (i.e., to maximize consumption) en route to steady state would mitigate the adverse effects of rapid population growth. See also Michael C. Keeley (1976) and Srinivasan (1988b).

36. If one considers a longer period from 1929 to 1969, Denison's calculations show a capital contribution to per capita income of 11 percent; however, this low figure, cited by the National Research Council (1986, p. 41) appears atypical because over the period 1929-48, the growth of capital per person employed was estimated to be negative.

37. Hypotheses relating to the impact of demographic factors on government saving are found in Nathanial H. Leff (1969), and on business saving in Richard E. Bilsborrow (1979, 1980).

38. One study using Kenyan data appears to show children as having a negligible impact on household saving when the induced impact of children on all sources of household income is taken into account (Kelley 1980). A study of U.S. nineteenth-century laborers in the iron, steel, glass, and textile industries suggests similar results (Kelley 1976a).

39. The life-cycle model has been extended and evaluated by Andrew Mason (1981, 1987) to take account of systematic impacts of children on household income; and by Lee (1980a) to account for differing family types and income-earnings profiles.

40. Frank D. Lewis (1983) concludes that about one quarter of the increase in nineteenth century U.S. saving was due to age-distributional changes. In another study using LDC data, Kelley (1973) combines estimates of differential savings impacts by cohort with information on changing cohort size associated with alternative population growth rates. Because in this study the dissaving impact of the aged cohort (through retirement) exceeds that of growth cohort (through child maintenance), a reduction in population growth that shifts the composition of the dependent population toward the aged reduces aggregate saving. These results must be qualified by the fact that some of the financing of youth dependency is done through nonmarket allocations within the family, and does not enter into national accounts that measure the impacts of age on saving.

41. The role of children as pension assets has been emphasized by Mead Cain (1983), Peter H. Lindert (1983), Jeffrey Nugent, K. Kan, and R. J. Walther (1983), and Srinivasan (1988a). In an interesting historical application, Williamson (1985) observes that nineteenth century English emigration increased the "default risk" of children as pension assets, which had a dampening impact on household fertility.

42. The W. Arthur Lewis (1954), Fei and Ranis (1964), and Kelley, Williamson, and Cheetham (1972) formulations represent examples. In practice, income-source distinctions can be blurred in the Third World setting, and particularly in peasant agriculture. Empirical studies of saving rates by income source include Kelley and Williamson (1968), Williamson (1968), and Surjit Bhalla (1978). Studies showing saving rates rising with income include Luis Landau (1971) and Bhalla (1980), and those linking increased income inequality with rapid population growth include Kuznets (1976, 1980) and C. R. Winegarden (1978). For a general survey of saving, see Raymond F. Mikesell and James E. Zinser (1973).

43. Studies of the interdependency of savings by source include Modigliani (1970), Paul David and John Scadding (1974), and Sateesh K. Singh (1975).

44. These results are reviewed by Jeffrey S. Hammer (1984). See Adams (1971), Kanhaya Gupta (1971, 1975), Singh (1975), Leff and Kazuo Sato (1975), Philip Musgrove (1978), Bilsborrow (1979, 1980), Rati Ram (1982), and Kelley (1988).

45. With respect to the age-dependency effect, the *World Development Report* concludes: "Recent empirical studies find only minor support for this view" (World Bank 1984, p. 82). Timothy King (1985) concurs: "In the litany of antinatalist argument, however, this one bears little weight. . . most modern theories suggest that the proportion of children in the population is not very important" (1985, p. 4). Hammer's review of the literature (1984) concludes: "While there is much evidence to indicate that these two aspects of development [population and saving] are intertwined in many ways, no simple generalizations are justified" (1984, p. 3). See also McNicoll (1984), Kelley (1985), National Research Council (1986), and Nancy Birdsall (1988).

46. Robert Summers and Alan Heston (1984) discuss the difficulties in using official exchange rates in making comparisons of income across countries. Investment, and thus saving which is computed as a residual, may also be poorly measured by internal price deflators. (Gross domestic saving is computed as the difference between gross capital formation and current account deficits.) The real value of investment is understated because producer durables are relatively expensive in the price structure of the typical low-income country. According to Irving B. Kravis (1986), this measurement bias implies that "developing countries spend a relatively large part of their incomes on producer durables, but do not get as much as appears for what they spend" (p15).

47. Based on a sample of 48 countries for 1965, Simon (1975) finds that cross-country variations in the proportion of cultivated land that is irrigated is strongly related to population density, after controlling for the level of per capita income. Possible problems of interpretation arising from population moving to irrigated areas are considered minimal given the unimportance of international migration.

48. Studies using U.S. data suggest that saving is influenced more by the timing of children than by their age and/or number (Thomas. J. Espenshade 1975; James Smith and Michael Ward 1980), and that the relationship in family size may be nonlinear and, in particular, that a negative impact on saving is found mainly for smaller families (W. Eizenga 1961)

49. In most models, spending on education is classified as consumption (Coale and Hoover 1958; McFarland, Bennett, and Brown 1973; Rodgers, Hopkins, and Wéry 1978; Anker and Knowles 1983). The *World Development Report 1984* presents a variant of the investment-diversion hypothesis, speculating that the schooling requirements of an expanding population (capital widening) diverts resources from quality improvements (capital deepening) in education (World Bank 1984, p. 85). See also Gavin W. Jones (1971, 1975, 1976).

50. Such a reduction in relative teacher salary rates may also be due to the rapid infusion of less-expensive and experienced teachers. Manuel Zymelman (1982, 1985) found this impact to be important in 15 developing countries in the 1970s.

51. Three additional studies downplay the importance of population pressures in explaining shifts in the composition of spending on education. In a study of 40 LDCs for 1970, Simon and Adam M. Pilarski (1979) provide results suggesting that the proportion of school-age children in the population, as well as the fertility rate, had no independent effect on primary enrollment rates or expenditures per child, although secondary enrollment rates were adversely affected. In a cross-country study of 1977 government expenditure patterns, Alan A Tait and Peter S Heller (1982) uncovered no statistically significant impacts of youth dependency on the composition of government spending (excepting defense, but including education). In a cross-country study of 1961-63 data, Kelley's (1976b) findings suggest that aggregate government spending shares are relatively insensitive to youth dependency rate. See also Bilsborrow (1978), Hiroshi Miyashita et al. (1982), and T J Meeks (1982).

References

Abramovitz, Moses. (1956) 'Resource and Output Trends in the United States Since 1870,' *Amer. Econ. Rev.*, May, 46(2), pp. 5-23.

Adams, Nassau A. (1971) 'Dependency Rates and Savings Rates: Comment,' *Amer. Econ. Rev.*, June, 61(3), pt. l, pp 472-75.

Adelman, Irma and Robinson, Sherman. (1978) *Income distribution policy in developing countries: A case study of Korea.* Stanford, CA: Stanford U. Press.

Ahlburg, Dennis A. (1987) 'The Impact of Population Growth on Economic Growth in Developing Nations: The Evidence from Macroeconomic-Demographic Models,' in D. Gale Johnson and Ronald D. Lee, pp. 479-521.

Alexandratos, Nikos. (1986) 'Population Carrying Capacities of African Lands: a Re-Assessment,' Mimeo. Paper presented at the Seminar on Economic Consequences of Population Trends in Africa, International Union for the Scientific Study of Population. Nairobi, Kenya, Dec.

Anker, Richard and Knowles, James C. (1983) *Population growth, employment, and economic-demographic interactions in Kenya.* NY: St. Martin's.

Arrow, Kenneth J. (1962) 'The Economic Implications of Learning by Doing,' *Rev. Econ. Stud.,* June, *29*(3), pp. 155-73.

Arthur W. Brian and McNicoll, Geoffrey. (1975) 'Large-Scale Simulation Models in Population and Development: What Use to Planners?' *Population Devel. Rec.,* Dec. *1*(2), pp. 251-65.

— (1978) 'An Analytical Survey of Population and Development in Bangladesh,' *Population Devel. Rec.,* Mar. *4*(1), pp. 23-80.

Bale, Malcolm D. and Duncan, Ronald C. (1983) 'Food Prospects in the Developing Countries: A Qualified Optimistic View,' *Amer. Econ. Rev.,* May, *73*(2), pp. 244-48.

Bale, Malcom D. and Lutz, Ernst. (1981) 'Price Distortions in Agriculture and Their Effects: An International Comparison,' *Amer. J. Agr. Econ.,* Feb. *63*(1), pp. 8-22.

Barlow, Robin. (1967) 'The Economic Effects of Malaria Eradication,' *Amer. Econ. Rev.,* May, *57*(2), pp. 130-57.

Barlow, Robin and Davies, Gordon W. (1974) 'Policy Analysis with a Disaggregated Economic-Demographic Model,' *J. Public Econ.,* Feb. *3*(1), pp. 43-70.

Barnum, Howard N. and Sabot, Richard H. (1977) 'Education, Employment Probabilities and Rural-Urban Migration in Tanzania,' *Oxford Bull. Econ. Statist.,* May, *39*(2), pp. 109-26.

Bates, Robert H. (1983) *Essays on the political economy of rural Africa.* Cambridge: Cambridge U. Press.

— (1986) *Markets and states in tropical Africa: The political basis of agricultural policies.* Berkeley, CA: U. of California Press.

Bauer, Peter T. (1981) 'The Population Explosion: Myths and Realities,' in *Equality, the Third World and economic delusion.* Cambridge, MA: Harvard U. Press, ch. 3, pp. 42-65.

Bhalla, Surjit S. (1978) 'The Role of Sources of Income and Investment Opportunities in Rural Savings,' *J. Devel. Econ.,* Sept. *5*(3), pp. 259-81.

— (1980) 'The Measurement of Permanent Income and Its Application to Savings Behavior,' *J. Polit. Econ.,* Aug. *88*(4), pp. 722-44.

Bilsborrow, Richard E. (1978) 'The Relationship Between Population Growth and the Expansion of Education Systems in Developing Countries, 1950-1970," *Pakistan Devel. Rev.,* Summer, *17*(2), pp. 212-32.

— (1979) 'Age Distribution and Savings Rates in Less Developed Countries,' *Econ. Develop. Cult. Change,* Oct. *28*(1), pp. 23-44.

— (1980) 'Dependency Rates and Aggregate Savings Rates Revisited: Corrections, Further Analyses, and Recommendations for the Future,' in *Research in population economics,* Vol. 2. Eds.: Julian Simon and Julie Davanzo. Greenwich: JAI Press, pp. 183-204.

Binswanger, Hans P. and Pingali, Prabhu L. (1984) 'The Evolution of Farming Systems and Agricultural Technology in Sub-Saharan Africa.' World Bank Discussion Paper ARU-23. Washington, DC: World Bank.

Birdsall, Nancy. (1988) 'Economic Approaches to Population Growth and Development,' in *Handbook of development economics*. Eds.: Hollis B. Chenery and T. N. Srinivasan. Amsterdam: Elsevier Science Pub..

Boserup, Ester. (1965) *The conditions of agricultural growth*. Chicago: Aldine.

— (1981) *Population and technological change*. Chicago: U. of Chicago Press.

Boulier, Bryan L. (1984) 'What Lies Behind Verdoorn's Law?' *Oxford Econ. Pap.*, June, *36*(2), pp. 259-67.

Breman, H. and De Wit C. T. (1983) 'Rangeland Productivity and Exploitation in the Sahel,' *Science,* Sept. 30, No. 221, pp. 1341-47.

Brown Lester R. (1981) 'World Population Growth, Soil Erosion, and Food Security,' *Science,* Nov. 27, No. 214, pp. 995-1002.

Brown Lester *et al.* (1985) *State of the world 1985*. A Worldwatch Institute Report on Progress Toward a Sustainable Society. NY: Norton.

Browning, Mark. (1982) 'An Econometric Investigation of the Relationship Between Population Growth and Income Growth in Developing Countries.' PhD dissertation. U of Michigan.

Cain, Mead. (1983) 'Fertility as an Adjustment to Risk,' *Population Devel. Reo.,* Dec. *9*(4), pp. 688-702.

Cassen, Robert H. (1976) 'Population and Development: A Survey,' *World Devel.,* Oct.-Nov. *4*(10/11), pp. 785-830.

— (1978) *India: Population, economy and society,* NY: Holmes & Meier.

Chenery, Hollis B. (1960) 'Patterns of Industrial Growth' *Amer. Econ. Rev.,* Sept. *50*(4), pp. 624-54.

Chenery, Hollis B. and Syrquin, Moises. (1975) *Patterns of development, 1950-1970*. NY: Oxford.

Clark, Cloin. (1967) *Population growth and land use*. NY: St. Martin's.

Coale, Ansley J (1978) 'T. R Malthus and the Population Trends in His Day and Ours,' Ninth Encyclopaedia Britannica Lecture. Edinburgh: U of Edinburgh.

Coale, Ansley J. and Hoover, Edgar M. (1958) *Population growth and economic development in low-income countries*. Princeton, NJ: Princeton U. Press.

Council on Environmental Quality and U.S. Dept. of State. (1980) *The Global 2000 report to the president*. Washington, DC: U.S. GPO.

Crosson, Pierre R. (1982) 'Agricultural Land,' in *Current issues in natural resources policy*. Eds.: Paul R. Portney and Ruth B. Hass. Washington, DC: Resources for the Future, pp. 253-82.

— (1983) 'Soil Erosion in Developing Countries: Amounts, Consequences, and Policies.' Working Paper No. 21. Center for Resource Policy Studies, School of Natural Resources, U. of Wisconsin, Madison.

— (1984) 'National Costs of Erosion Effects on Productivity.' Unpublished. Washington, DC: Resources for the Future.

Daly, Herman E. (1986) 'Review of *Population Growth and Economic Development: Policy Questions,*' *Population Devel. Rev.,* Sept. *12*(3), pp. 582-85.

Darity, William A., Jr. (1980) 'The Boserup Theory of Agricultural Growth: A Model for Anthropological Economies,' *J. Devel. Econ.,* June, 7(2), pp. 137-57.

Dasgupta, Partha. (1987) 'The Ethical Foundations of Population Policy,' in D. Gale Johnson and Ronald D. Lee, pp. 631-60.

DaVanzo, Julie *et al.* (1985) 'Quantitative Studies of Mortality Decline in the Developing World.' World Bank Staff Working Paper No. 683. Washington, DC: World Bank.

David, Paul and Scadding, John. (1974) 'Private Savings: Ultrarationality, Aggregation, and 'Denison's Law,' ' *J. Polit. Econ.,* Mar.-Apr. *82*(2), pt. 2, pp. 225-50.

Demeny, Paul. (1965) 'Investment Allocation and Population Growth,' *Demography, 2,* pp. 203-32.

— (1965) 'Demographic Aspects of Saving, Investment, Employment and Productivity.' World Population Conference, NY: UN, 1967.

— (1984) 'A Perspective on Long-Term. Population Growth.' *Population Devel. Rev.,* Mar. *10*(1). pp. 103-26.

— (1986) 'Population and the Invisible Hand,' *Demography.* Nov. *23*(4), pp. 473-87.

Denison, Edward F. (1962) *The sources of growth in the United States.* NY: Committee for Economic Development.

— (1964) 'The Unimportance of the Embodied Question,' *Amer. Econ. Rev.,* Mar. *54*(2), pt. 1, pp. 90-94.

— (1967) *Why growth rates differ: Postwar experience in nine Western countries.* Washington, DC: Brookings Inst.

— (1974) *Accounting for United States economic growth,* 1929-1969. Washington, DC: Brookings Inst.

Denton, Frank T. and Spencer, Byron G. (1973) 'A Simulation Analysis of the Effects of Population Change on a Neoclassical Economy,' *J. Polit. Econ.,* Mar./Apr. *81*(2), pt. 1, pp. 356-75.

— (1976) 'Household and Population Effects on Aggregate Consumption,' *Rev. Econ. Statist.,* Feb. *58*(1), pp. 86-95.

Dixit, Avinash K. (1973) 'Models of Dual Economies,' in *Models of economic growth.* Eds.: Janies A. Mirrlees and N. H. Stern. NY: Wiley, pp. 325-52.

Dudal, R. *et al.* (1982) 'Land Resources for the World's Food Production,' in *Managing soil resources to meet the challenges to mankind.* International Congress of Soil Science. New Delhi, India, pp. 1-26.

Easterlin, Richard A. (1967) 'Effects of Population Growth on the Economic Development of Developing Countries,' *Ann. Amer. Acad. Polit. Soc. Sci.,* Jan. 369, pp. 98-108.

_____ ed. (1980) *Population and economic change in developing countries.* Chicago and London: U. of Chicago Press for the National Bureau of Economic Research.

Easterlin, Richard A.; Pollak, Robert A. and Wachter, Michael L. (1980) 'Toward a More General Economic Model of Fertility Determination: Endogenous Preferences and Natural Fertility,' in Richard A. Easterlin, pp. 81-149.

Eicher, Carl. K. (1984) 'Facing Up to Africa's Food Crisis,' in *Agricultural development in the Third World*. Eds.: Carl K. Eicher and John M. Staatz. Baltimore: Johns Hopkins U. Press, pp. 452-79.

Eizenga, W. (1961) *Demographic factors and savings*. Amsterdam: North Holland.

Enke, Stephen. (1960) 'The Gains to India from Population Control: Some Money Measures and Incentive Schemes.' *Rev. Econ. Statist.*, May, *17*(2), pp. 175-81.

— (1971) *Description of the economic-demographic model*. Santa Barbara CA: General Electric Co., Tempo Center for Advanced Studies.

Espenshade, Thomas J. (1975) 'The Impact of Children on Household Saving: Age Effects Versus Family Size,' *Population Stud.*, Mar. *29*(1), pp. 123-25.

Evenson, Robert E. (1984a) 'Benefits and Obstacles in Developing Appropriate Agricultural Technology.' in *Agricultural development in the Third World*. Eds.: Carl K. Eicher and John M. Staatz. Baltimore: Johns Hopkins U. Press, pp. 348-61.

— (1984b) 'Population Growth, Infrastructural Development, Technology and Welfare in Rural North India.' Paper prepared for the International Union for the Scientific Study of Population Seminar on Population, Food and Rural Development. New Delhi, India.

Fei, John C. H. and Ranis, Gustav. (1964) *Development of the labor surplus economy: Theory and policy*. Homewood, IL: Richard D. Irwin.

Food and Agricultural Organization (FAO). (1976) 'A Systems Simulation Approach to Integrated Population and Economic Planning with Special Emphasis on Agricultural Development and Employment: An Experimental Study of Pakistan.' PA 4/1 INT/ 73/PO2, Working Paper Series 11. Rome: FAO.

— (1981) *Agriculture: Toward 2000*. Rome: FAO.

— (1983) 'Land, Food, and Population.' FAO Conference, Session 22, Rome, Nov. 5.

Forrester, Jay W. (1971) *World dynamics*. Cambridge, MA: Wright-Allen.

Fraumeni, Barbara M. and Jorgenson, Dale W. (1986) 'The Role of Capital in US Economic Growth, 1948-1979,' in *Measurement issues and behavior of productivity variables*. Ed.: Ali Dogramaci. Boston: Kluwer Nijhoff Pub. pp. 161-244.

Frejka, Tomas (1973). *The future of population growth: Alternative paths to equilibrium*. NY: Wiley.

— (1981a) 'World Population Projections: A Concise History,' NY: Population Council, Mar.

— (1981b) 'Long-Term Prospects for World Population Growth,' *Population Devel. Rev.*, Sept., *7*(3), pp. 489-511.

Ghatak, Subrata and Ingersent, Ken. (1984) *Agriculture and economic development*. Baltimore: Johns Hopkins U. Press.

Glover, Donald R. and Simon, Julian L. (1975) 'The Effect of Population Density on Infrastructure: The Case of Road Building,' *Econ. Develop. Cult. Change*, Apr., *23*(3), pp. 453-68.

Goldberger, Arthur S. (1973) 'Dependeney Rates and Savings Rates: Further Comment,' *Amer. Econ. Rev;.*, Mar., *63*(1), pp. 232-33.

Gourou, Pierre. (1980) *The tropical world: lts social and economic conditions and Its future status*. 5th ed. NY: Longman.

Greenwood, Michael J. (1969) 'The Determinants of Labor Migration in Egypt,' *J. Reg. Sci.*, Aug., *9*(2), pp 283-90.

— (1971) 'A Regression Analysis of Migration to Urban Areas of a Less-Developed Country: The Case of India,' *J. Reg. Sci.*, Aug. 1971, *11*(2), pp. 253-62.

— (1978) 'An Econometric Model of Internal Migration and Regional Economic Growth in Mexico,' *J. Reg. Sci.*, Apr., *18*(1), pp. 17-32.

Gupta, Kanhaya L. (1971) 'Dependeney Rates and Savings Rates: Comment,' *Amer. Econ. Rev.*, June, *61*(1), pt. 1, pp. 469-71.

— (1975) 'Foreign Capital Inflows, Dependeney Burden, and Savings Rate in Developing Countries: A Simultaneous Equation Model,' *Kyklos*, *28*(2), pp. 358-74.

Habakkuk, H. J. and Postan, M. (1965) eds. *The Cambridge economic history of Europe,* Vol. 6, pt. 1. Cambridge: Cambridge U. Press.

Hammer, Jeffrey S. (1985) 'Population Growth and Savings in Developing Countries: A Survey.' World Bank Staff Working Paper, No. 687. Washington, DC.

Hansen, Alvin H. (1939) 'Economic Progress and Declining Population Growth,' *Amer. Econ. Rev.*, Mar. *29*(1), pt. 1, pp. 1-15.

Hayami, Yujiro and Kikuchi, Masao. (1981) *Asian village economy at the crossroads: An economic approach to institutional change.* Baltimore: Johns Hopkins U. Press, and Tokyo: U. of Tokyo Press.

Hayami, Yujiro and Ruttan, Vernon W. (1984) 'The Green Revolution: Inducement and Distribution,' *Pakistan Devel. Rev.*, Spring, *23*(1), pp. 38-63.

— (1985) *Agricultural development: An international perspective.* Baltimore: Johns Hopkins U. Press.

— (1987) 'Population Growth and Agricultural Productivity, in D. Gale Johnson and Ronald D. Lee, pp. 57-101.

Hazeldine, Tim and Moreland, R. Scott. (1977) 'Population and Economic Growth: A World Cross-Section Study,' *Rev. Econ. Statist.*, Aug. *59*(3), pp. 253-63.

Henderson, J. Vernon. (1987) 'Industrialization and Urbanization: International Experience,' in D. Gale Johnson and Ronald D. Lee, pp. 189-224.

Hicks, John R. (1939) *Value and capital.* Oxford: Clarendon.

Higgins, G. M. *et al.* (1982) *Potential population supporting capacities of lands in the developing world.* Technical Report FPA/INT/513 of Project Land Resources for Population of the Future. Rome: FAO.

Hirschman, Albert O. (1958) *The strategy of economic development.* New Haven, CT: Yale U. Press.

Horlacher, David E., ed. (1981) *Population and development modelling.* NY: UN.

Hoselitz, Bert F. (1957) 'Urbanization and Economic Growth in Asia,' *Econ. Develop. Cult. Change*, Oct. *6*(1), pp. 42-54.

Hutchinson, Edward P. (1967) *The population debate: The development of conflicting theories up to 1900.* Boston: Houghton Mifflin.

Isbister, John. (1975) 'Population Growth and the Productivity of Capital in the Third World' in *Population growth and economic development in the Third World*. Vol. 2. Ed.: Leon Tabah. Dolhain, Belgium: Ordina Editions, pp. 619-48.

James, Jeffrey. (1987) 'Population and Technical Change in the Manufacturing Sector of Developing Countries,' in D. Gale Johnson and Ronald D. Lee, pp. 225-56.

Johnson, D. Gale. (1974) 'Population, Food, and Economic Adjustment,' *Amer. Statist.*, Aug. *28*(3), pp. 89-93.

— (1984) 'World Food and Agriculture' in *The resourceful earth: A response to global 2000*. Eds.: Julian Simon and Herman Kahn. NY: Basil Blackwell, pp. 67-112.

— (1985) 'World Commodity Market Situation and Outlook,' in *U.S. agricultural policy: The 1985 farm legislation*. Ed.: Bruce L. Gardner. Washington, DC: American Enterprise Inst., pp. 19-50.

Johnson, D. Gale and Lee, Ronald D. eds. (1987) *Population growth and economic development: Issues and evidence*. Madison: U. of Wisconsin Press.

Jones, Gavin W. (1971) 'Effect of Population Change on the Attainment of Educational Goals in the Developing Countries,' in *Rapid population growth: Consequences and policy implications*. Ed.: National Academy of Sciences. Baltimore: Johns Hopkins U. Press for the National Academy of Sciences, pp. 315-67.

— (1975) *Population growth and education planning in developing nations*. NY: Wiley.

— (1976) 'The Influence of Demographic Variables on Development via Their Impact on Education,' in *Economic factors in population growth*. Ed: Ansley J. Coale NY: Halstead/Wiley, pp. 553-80.

Jorgenson, Dale W. (1961) 'The Development of a Dual Economy,' *Econ. J.*, June, *71*(282), pp. 309-34.

Jorgenson, Dale W. and Griliches, Zvi. (1967) 'The Explanation of Productivity Change,' *Rev. Econ. Stud.*. July, *34*(3), pp. 249-83.

Keeley, Michael C. (1976) 'A Neoclassical Analysis of Economic-Demographic Simulation Models,' in *Population, public policy and economic development*. Ed.: Michael C. Keeley. NY: Praeger, pp. 25-45.

Kelley, Allen C. (1973) 'Population Growth, the Dependency Rate, and the Pace of Economic Development,' *Population Stud.*, Nov. *27*(3), pp. 405-14.

— (1974) 'The Role of Population in Models of Economic Growth,' *Amer. Econ. Rev.*, May, *64*(2), pp. 39-41.

— (1976a) 'Savings, Demographic Change and Economic Development,' *Econ. Develop. Cult. Change*, July, *24*(4), pp. 683-93.

— (1976b) 'Demographic Change and the Size of the Government Sector,' *Southern Econ. J.*, Oct. *43*(2), pp. 1056-66.

— (1980) 'Interactions of Economic and Demographic Household Behavior,' in Richard A. Easterlin, pp. 403-48, 461-70.

— (1985) 'The Population Debate: A Status Report and Revisionist Interpretation,' *Population Trends and Public Policy*, Feb. No. 7, pp. 12-23.

— (1988) 'Population Pressures, Saving, and Investment in the Third World: Some Puzzles,' *Econ. Develop. Cult. Change,* Apr. *36*(3), pp. 449-64.

Kelley, Allen C. and Williamson, Jeffrey G. (1968) 'Household Savings Behavior in the Developing Economies: The Indonesian Case,' *Econ. Develop. Cult. Change,* Apr. *16*(3), pp. 385-403.

— (1974) *Lessons from Japanese development: An analytical economic history.* Chicago: U. of Chicago Press.

— (1984) *What drives Third World city growth? A dynamic general equilibrium approach.* Princeton: Princeton U. Press.

Kelley, Allen C.; Williamson, Jeffrey G. and Cheetham, Russell J. (1972) *Dualistic economic development: Theory and history.* Chicago: U of Chicago Press.

Keyfitz, Nathan. (1972) 'Population Theory and Doctrine: A Historical Survey,' in *Readings in population.* Ed.: William Petersen. NY: Macmillan, pp. 41-69.

— (1981) 'The Limits of Population Forecasting,' *Population Devel. Rev.,* Dec. 7(4), pp. 579-93.

Keynes, John M. (1937) 'Some Economic Consequences of a Declining Population,' *Eugenics Review,* Apr. *29*(1), pp. 13-17.

Khan, A. R. (1984) 'Population Growth and Access to Land: An Asian Perspective.' Paper prepared for the International Union for the Scientific Study of Population Seminar on Population, Food, and Rural Development, New Delhi, India.

Kincher, J. W. *et al.* (1985) 'Carrying Capacity, Population Growth and Sustainable Development.' in *Rapid population growth and human carrying capacity.* Eds.: Dennis J. Mahar *et al.* World Bank Statf Working Paper No. 690, Population and Development Series No. 15. Washington, DC: The World Bank.

King, Timothy. (1985) 'Population and Development: Back to First Principles,' in *Population Trends and Public Policy,* Feb. No. 7, pp. 2-11.

Kirk, Dudley. (1971) 'A New Demographic Transition?' in *Rapid population growth: Consequences and policy implications.* Ed.: National Academy of Sciences. Baltimore: Johns Hopkins U. Press for the National Academy of Sciences, pp. 123-47.

Kotlikoff, Laurence J. and Spivak, Avia. (1981) 'The Family as an Incomplete Annuities Market,' *J. Polit. Econ.,* Apr. *89*(2), pp. 372-91.

Kravis, Irving B. (1986) 'The Three Faces of the International Comparison Project,' *The World Bank Research Observer,* Jan. *1*(1), pp. 3-26.

Krueger, Anne O. (1978) 'Alternative Trade Strategies and Employment in LDCs,' *Amer. Econ. Rev.,* May, *68*(2), pp. 270-74.

— (1982) 'Analyzing Disequilibrium Exchange-Rate Systems in Developing Countries,' *World Devel.,* Dec. *10*(12), pp. 1059-68.

— (1983) *Trade and employment in developing countries. 3: Synthesis and conclusions.* Chicago: U. Of Chicago Press.

Kuznets, Simon. (1960) 'Population Change and Aggregate Output,' in *Demographic and economic change in developed countries.* A Conference of the Universities-National Bureau Committee for Economic Research. Princeton: Princeton U. Press, pp. 324-40.

— (1966) *Modern economic growth: Rate, structure and spread.* New Haven: Yale U. Press.

— (1967) 'Population and Economic Growth,' *Proceedings of the Amer. Philosophical Soc.*, June 22, *111*(3), pp. 170-93.

— (1976) 'Demographic Aspects of the Size Distribution of Income: An Exploratory Essay,' *Econ. Develop. Cult. Change*, Oct. *25*(1), pp. 1-94.

— (1980) 'Recent Population Trends in Less Developed Countries and Implications for Internal Income Inequality,' in Richard A. Easterlin, pp. 471-511, 515.

Landau, Luis. (1971) 'Saving Functions for Latin America,' in *Studies in development planning*. Eds.: Hollis B. Chenery *et al.* Cambridge, MA: Harvard U. Press, pp. 299-321.

Lee, Ronald D. (1980a) 'Age Structure, Intergenerational Transfers and Economic Growth: An Overview,' *Revue Econ.*, Nov. *31*, pp. 1129-56.

— (1980b) 'A Historical Perspective on Economic Aspects of the Population Explosion: The Case of Pre-Industrial England,' in Richard A. Easterlin, pp. 517-57, 563-66.

— (1983) 'Economic Consequences of Population Size, Structure and Growth,' *IUSSP Newsletter*, Jan.-Apr. No. 17, pp. 43-59.

— (1984) 'Malthus and Boserup: A Dynamic Synthesis.' Paper presented at the conference 'Forward from Malthus,' Cambridge, England, Sept.

Leff, Nathaniel H. (1969) 'Dependency Rates and Savings Rates,' *Amer. Econ. Rev.*, Dec. *59*(5), pp. 886-96.

— (1971) 'Dependency Rates and Savings Rates: Reply,' *Amer. Econ. Rev.*, June, *61*(3), pt. 1, pp. 476-80.

— (1973) 'Dependency Rates and Savings Rates: Reply,' *Amer. Econ. Rev.*, Mar. *63*(1), pp. 234.

— (1980) 'Dependency Rates and Savings Rates: A New Look,' in *Research in Population Economics*, Vol. 2. Eds.: Julian Simon and Julie Davanzo. Greenwich: JAI Press, pp. 205-14.

Leff, Nathaniel H. and Sato, Kazuo. (1975) 'A Simultaneous-Equations Model of Savings in Developing Countries,' Dec. 1975, *J. Polit. Econ.*, Dec. *83*(6), pp. 1217-28.

Leibenstein, Harvey. (1971) 'The Impact of Population Growth on Economic Welfare—Nontraditional Elements.' in *Rapid population growth: Consequences and policy implications*. Ed.: National Academy of Sciences. Baltimore: Johns Hopkins U. Press for the National Academy of Sciences, pp. 175-98.

— (1976) 'Population Growth and Savings,' in *Population growth and economic development in the Third World*, Vol. 2. Ed: Leon Tabah. Dolhain, Belgium: Ordina Editions, pp. 593-618.

Lele, Uma L. and Mayers, L. R. (1980) 'Growth and Structural Change in East Africa: Domestic Policies, Agricultural Performance and World Bank Assistance, 1963-1986.' Research Report No. 1, Managing Agricultural Development in Africa. Washington, DC: World Bank.

Lewis, Frank D. (1983) 'Fertility and Savings in the United States: 1830-1900,' *J. Polit. Econ.*, Oct. *91*(5), pp. 825-40.

Lewis, W. Arthur. (1954) 'Economic Development with Unlimited Supplies of Labour,' *Manchester Sch. Econ. Soc. Stud.*, May, *22*(2), pp. 139-91.

Lindert, Peter H. (1983) 'The Changing Economic Costs and Benefits of Having Children,' in *Determinants of fertility in developing countries*. Vol. 1: *Supply and demand for children*. Eds.: Rodolfo A. Bulatao and Ronald D. Lee. NY: Academic, pp. 494-516.

Linn, Johannes F. (1983) *Cities in the developing world.* NY: Oxford U. Press.

Lloyd, Peter J. (1969) 'A Growth Model with Population as an Endogenous Variable,' *Population Stud.,* Nov. *23*(3), pp. 463-78.

Malthus, Thomas R. (1798) *An essay on the principle of population, as it affects the future improvement of society. With remarks on the speculations of Mr. Godwin, M. Condorcet, and other writers.* London: J. Johnson.

Mason, Andrew. (1981) 'An Extension of the Life Cycle Model and Its Application to Population Growth and Aggregate Saving.' East-West Population Institute Working Papers 4, Honolulu. Jan.

— (1987) 'National Saving Rates and Population Growth: A New Model and New Evidence,' in D. Gale Johnson and Ronald D. Lee, pp. 523-60.

Mazumdar, Dipak. (1983) 'The Rural-Urban Wage Gap Migration and the Working of Urban Labor Market: An Interpretation Based on a Study of the Workers of Bombay City,' *Indian Econ. Rev.,* July-Dec. *18*(2), pp. 169-98.

— (1985) 'Rural-Urban Migration in Developing Countries.' Paper prepared for the Conference on Population Growth, Urbanization, and Urban Policies in the Asia-Pacific Region. Honolulu: East-West Center.

McClelland, Peter D. (1975) *Causal explanation and model building in history, economics, and the new economic history.* Ithaca: Cornell U. Press.

McFarland, William E.; Bennett, James P. and Brown, Richard A. (1973) *Description of the Tempo II Budget Allocation and Human Resources Model.* Santa Barbara, CA: General Electric Co., Tempo Center for Advanced Studies.

McNamara, Robert S. (1973) *One hundred countries, two billion people: The dimensions of development.* NY: Praeger Press.

McNicoll, Geoffrey. (1975) 'Economic-Demographic Models,' in *Population growth and economic development in the Third World,* Vol. 2. Ed.: Leon Tabah. Dolhain, Belgium: Ordina Editions, pp. 649-76.

— (1984) 'Consequences of Rapid Population Growth: An Overview and Assessment,' *Population Devel. Rev.,* June, *10*(2), pp. 177-240.

Meadows, Donella H. *et al.* (1972) *The limits to growth: A report for the Club of Rome's Project on the Predicament of Mankind.* NY: Universe Books.

Meeks, T. J. (1982) 'The Effect of Population Growth upon the Quantity of Education Children Receive: A Comment,' *Rec. Econ. Statist.,* May, *64*(2), pp. 348-52.

Mellor, John W. and Johnston, Bruce F. (1984) 'The World Food Equation: Interrelations Among Development, Employment, and Food Consumption,' *J. Econ. Lit.,* June, *22*(2), pp. 531-74.

Mikesell, Raymond F. and Zinser, James E. (1973) 'The Nature of the Savings Function in Developing Countries: A Survey of the Theoretical and Empirical Literature,' *J. Econ. Lit.,* Mar. *11*(1), pp. 1-26.

Miyashita, Hiroshi *et al.* (1982) 'The Effect of Population Growth upon the Quantity of Education Children Receive: A Reply,' *Rev. Econ. Statist.,* May, *64*(2), pp. 352-55.

Modigliani, Franco. (1970) 'The Life Cycle Hypothesis of Saving and Intercountry Differences in the Saving Ratio,' in *Induction, growth and trade: Essays in honour of Sir Roy Harrod.* Eds.: W. A. Eltis, M. FG. Scott, and J. N. Wolfe. London: Clarendon Press, pp. 197-225.

Modigliani, Franco and Ando, Albert K. (1957) 'Tests of the Life Cycle Hypothesis of Saving: Comments and Suggestions,' *Bull. Oxford Univ. Inst. Econ. Statist.*, May, *19*(2), pp. 99-124.

Modigliani, Franco and Brumberg, Richard. (1954) 'Utility Analysis and the Consumption Function: An Interpretation of Cross Section Data,' in *Post-Keynesian economics.* Ed.: Kenneth K. Kurihara. New Brunswick, NJ: Rutgers U. Press, pp. 388-436.

Mohan, Rakesh. (1984) 'The Effect of Population Growth, the Pattern of Demand and of Technology on the Process of Urbanization,' *J. Urban Econ.*, Mar. 15(2), pp. 125-56.

Musgrove, Philip. (1978) 'Determinants of Urban Household Consumption in Latin America: A Summary of Evidence from the ECIEL Surveys,' *Econ. Develop. Cult. Change*, Apr. *26*(3), pp. 441-65.

National Academy of Sciences. (1971) *Rapid population growth: Consequences and policy implications.* 2 vols. Baltimore: Johns Hopkins U. Press for the National Academy of Sciences.

National Research Council. (1986) *Population growth and economic development: Policy questions.* Working Group on Population Growth and Economic Development, Committee on Population, Commission on Behavioral and Social Sciences and Education. Washington, DC: National Academy Press.

Nelson, Richard R. (1964) 'Aggregate Production Functions and Medium-Range Growth Projections,' *Amer. Econ. Rev.*, Sept. *54*(5), pp. 575-606.

Nerlove, Marc; Razin, Assaf and Sadka, Efraim. (1987) *Household and economy: Welfare economics of endogenous fertility.* NY: Academic.

Ng, Yew-Kwang. (1986) 'On the Welfare Economics of Population Control,' *Population Devel. Rev.*, June, *12*(2), pp. 247-66.

North, Douglass C. and Thomas, Robert P. (1973) *The rise of the Western world: A new economic history.* Cambridge, England: Cambridge U. Press.

Nugent, Jeffrey; Kan, K. and Walther, R. J. (1983) 'The Effects of Old-Age Pensions on Household Structure, Marriage, Fertility and Resource Allocation in Rural Areas of Developing Countries.' Mimeo. U. of Southern California.

Parikh, Kirit S. and Rabar, Frans, eds. (1981) *Food for all in a sustainable world.* Laxenburg, Austria: International Institute for Applied Systems Analysis.

Phelps, Edmund S. (1968) 'Population Increase,' *Can. J. Econ.*, Aug. *1*(3), pp. 497-518.

Pingali, Prabhu L. and Binswanger, Hans P. (1984) 'Population Density and Farming Systems: The Changing Focus of Innovations and Technical Change.' Paper prepared for the IUSSP Seminar on Population, Food and Rural Development. New Delhi, India.

— (1986) 'Population Density, Market Access and Farmer-Generated Technical Change in Sub-Saharan Africa.' Mimeo. Paper presented at the Seminar on the Consequences of Population Trends in Africa. International Union for the Scientific Study of Population, Nairobi, Kenya, Dec.

— (1987) 'Population Density and Agricultural Intensification: A Study of the Evolution of Technologies in Tropical Agriculture,' in D. Gale Johnson and Ronald D. Lee, pp. 27-56.

Piotrow, Phyllis T. (1973) *World population crisis: The United States response.* NY: Praeger.

Pitchford, John D. (1974) *Population in economic growth.* NY: American Elsevier.

Poleman, Thomas. (1982) 'World Hunger: Extent, Causes and Cures.' Paper prepared for Conference on the Role of Markets in the World Economy, Minneapolis, MN, Oct. 14-16.

Preston, Samuel H. (1979) 'Urban Growth in Developing Countries: A Demographic Reappraisal,' *Population Devel. Rev.,* June, 5(2), pp. 195-215.

— (1980) 'Causes and Consequences of Mortality Declines in Less Developed Countries During the Twentieth Century,' in Richard A. Easterlin, pp. 289-360.

— (1986) 'Mortality and Development Revisited,' in *UN Population Bulletin* No. 18. NY: UN, pp. 34-40.

Pryor, Frederic L. and Maurer, Stephen B. (1982) 'On Induced Economic Change in Precapitalist Societies,' *J. Devel. Econ.,* June, 10(3). pp. 325-53.

Quinn, Joseph E. (1975) 'The Use of the LRPM and PDM Models for Structural Analysis and Development Planning.' Mimeo. Washington, DC: U.S. Dept. Of Commerce, Bureau of the Census.

Ram, Rati. (1982) 'Dependency Rates and Aggregate Savings: A New International Cross-Section Study,' *Amer. Econ. Rev.,* June, 72(3), pp. 537-44.

Ram, Rati and Schultz, Theodore W. (1979) 'Life Span, Health, Savings and Productivity,' *Econ. Develop. Cult. Change,* Apr. 27(3), pp 399-421.

Reddaway, William B. (1939) *The economics of a declining population.* London: Allen & Unwin.

Rempel, Henry. (1981) *Rural-urban labor migration and urban unemployment in Kenya.* Laxenburg, Austria: International Institute for Applied Systems Analysis.

Revelle, Roger. (1975) 'Will the Earth's Land and Water Resources Be Sufficient for Future Populations?' in *The population debate: Dimensions and perspectives.* Papers of the World Population Conference, Bucharest, 1974. ST/ESA/SER.A/57. Population Studies, No. 57. Vol. II, Part 5. NY: UN, pp. 3-14.

Robinson, E. A. G., ed. (1960) *Economic consequences of the size of nations.* NY: St. Martin's.

Robinson, Warren and Schujter, Wayne. (1984) 'Agricultural Development and Demographic Change: A Generalization of the Boserup Model,' *Econ. Develop. Cult. Change,* Jan. 32(2), pp. 355-66.

Rodgers, Gerry B.; Wéry, Réne and Hopkins, Michael J. D. (1976) 'The Myth of the Cavern Revisited: Are Large-Scale Behavioral Models Useful?' *Population Devel. Rev.,* Sept./Dec. 2(3-4), pp. 395-409.

Rodgers, Gerry; Hopkins, Mike and Wéry, Réne. (1978) *Population, employment and inequality: BACHUE—Philippines: An application of economic-demographic modelling to development planning.* West Mead, England: Saxon House for the International Labor Organizatio.

Rosensweig, Mark R. (1988) 'Labor Markets in Low-Income Countries: Distortions, Mobility and Migration,' in *Handbook of development economics.* Eds.: Hollis B. Chenery and T. N. Srinivasan. Amsterdam: Elsevier Science Pub.

Rosenzweig, Mark R.; Binswanger, Hans P. and McIntyre, John. (1984) 'From Land-Abundance to Land-Scarcity: The Effects of Population Growth on Production Relations in Agrarian Economies.' Paper prepared for the International Union for the Scientific Study of Population Conference on Population, Food, and Rural Development. New Delhi.

Ruttan, Vernon W. and Hayami, Yujiro. (1984) 'Towards a Theory of Induced Institutional Innovation,' *J. Devel. Stud.*, July, *20*(4), pp. 203-23.

Salas, Rafael M. (1982) 'State of the World Population' *Populi*, *9*(2) pp. 3-12.

Sanderson, Warren C. (1980) *Economic-demographic simulation models: A review of their usefulness for policy analysis*. Laxenburg, Austria: International Inst. for Applied Systems Analysis.

Sato, Ryuzo and Niho, Yoshio. (1971) 'Population Growth and the Development of a Dual Economy,' *Oxford Econ. Pap.*, Nov. *23*(3), pp. 418-36.

Schmidt, Robert M. (1983) 'Incorporating Demography into General Equilibrium Modeling,' in *Modeling growing economies in equilibrium and disequilibrium*. Eds.: Allen C. Kelley, Warren C. Sanderson, and Jeffrey G. Williamson. Durham: Duke U. Press, pp. 317-37.

Schultz, T. Paul. (1987) 'School Expenditures and Enrollments, 1960-1980: The Effects of Income, Prices and Population Growth, in D. Gale Johnson and Ronald D. Lee, pp. 413-76.

Schultz, Theodore W., ed. (1974) *Economics of the family: Marriage, children, and human capital*. Chicago and London: National Bureau of Economic Research.

Scitovsky, Tibor. (1960) 'International Trade and Economic Integration as a Means of Overcoming the Disadvantages of a Small Nation,' in *Economic consequences of the size of nations*. Ed.: E. A. G. Robinson. NY: St. Martin's, pp. 282-90.

Sen, Amartya K. (1981) *Poverty and famines: An essay on entitlement and deprivation*. Oxford: Clarendon.

Shah, M. M. *et al.* (1984) *People, land and food production: Potentials in the developing world*. Laxenburg, Austria: International Institute for Applied Systems Analysis.

Simon, Julian L. (1975) 'The Positive Effect of Population Growth on Agricultural Saving in Irrigation Systems,' *Rev. Econ. Statist.*, Feb. *57*(1), pp. 71-79.

— (1976) 'Population Growth May Be Good for LDCs in the Long Run: A Richer Simulation Model' *Econ. Develop. Cult. Change*, Jan. *24*(2) pp. 309-37.

— (1977) *The economics of population growth*. Princeton: Princeton U. Press.

— (1981) *The ultimate resource*. Princeton: Princeton U. Press.

— (1986) *Theory of population and economic growth* NY: Basil Blackwell.

Simon, Julian L. and Kahn, Herman eds. (1984) *The resourceful earth: A response to global 2000*. NY: Basil Blackwell.

Simon, Julian L. and Pilarski, Adam M. (1979) 'The Effect of Population Growth upon the quantity of Education Children Receive,' *Rev. Econ. Statist.*, Nov. *61*(4), pp. 572-84.

Simon, Julian L. and Steinmann, Gunter. (1981) 'Population Growth and Phelps' Technical Progress Model: Interpretation and Generalization,' in *Research in population economics*, Vol. 3. Eds.: Julian L. Simon and Peter Lindert. Greenwich: JAI Press, pp. 239-54

Singh, Sateesh K. (1975) *Development economics: Some findings*. Lexington, MA: Lexington Books.

Smith, James and Ward, Michael. (1980) 'Asset Accumulation and Family Size,' *Demography*, Aug. *17*(3) pp. 243-60.

Solow, Robert M. (1956) 'A Contribution to the Theory of Economic Growth,' *Quart. J. Econ.*, Feb. *70*(1), pp. 65-94.

— (1960) 'Investment and Technical Progress' in *Mathematical methods in the social sciences, 1959, proceedings of the First Stanford Symposium.* Eds.: Kenneth J. Arrow, Samuel Karlin, and Patrick Suppes. Stanford, CA: Stanford U. Press, pp. 89-104.

— (1973) 'Is the End of the World at Hand?' *Challenge,* Mar.-Apr. *16*(1), pp. 39-50.

Spengler, Joseph J. (1945a) 'Malthus's Total Population Theory: A Restatement and Reappraisal,' *Can. J. Econ. and Political Science,* Feb. *11*(1), pp. 83-110.

— (1945b) 'Malthus's Total Population Theory: A Restatement and Reappraisal,' *Can. J. Econ. and Political Science,* May, *11*(2), pp. 234-64.

Srinivasan, T. N. (1982) 'Hunger: Defining It, Estimating Its Global Incidence, and Alleviating It.' Paper prepared for Conference on the Role of Markets in the World Food Economy, Minneapolis MN, Oct. 14-16.

— (1987) 'Population and Food,' in D. Gale Johnson and Ronald D. Lee. Madison: U. of Wisconsin Press, pp. 3-26.

— (1988a) 'Fertility, and Old-Age Security in an Overlapping Generations Model,' *J. Quantitative Econ.,* Jan.

— (1988b) 'Population Growth and Economic Development,' *J. Policy Modeling,* Spring, *10*(1).

Steinmann, Gunter and Simon, Julian L. (1980) 'Phelps' Technical Progress Model Generalized,' *Economics Letters, 5*(2), pp. 177-82.

Stigler, George J. (1961) 'Economic Problems in Measuring Changes in Productivity,' in *Studies in income and wealth,* Vol. 25. Conference on Income and Wealth. Princeton: Princeton U. Press, pp. 47-77.

Stryker, J. Dirck. (1976) 'Population Density, Agricultural Technique, and Land Utilization in a Village Economy,' *Amer. Econ. Rev.,* June, *66*(3), pp. 347-58.

Summers, Robert and Heston, Alan. (1984) 'Improved International Comparisons of Real Product and Its Composition: 1950-1980,' *Rev. Income Wealth,* June, *30*(2), pp. 207-62.

Tait, Alan A. and Heller, Peter S. (1982) *International comparisons of government expenditure.* International Monetary Fund Occasional Paper No. 10. Washington, DC: IMF, Apr.

Thirlwall, Anthony. (1972) 'A Cross-Section Study of Population Growth and the Growth of Output and Per-Capita Income in a Production Function Framework,' *Manchester School Econ. Soc. Stud.,* Dec. *40*(4), pp. 339-56.

Tobin, James. (1967) 'Life Cycle Saving and Balanced Growth,' in *Ten economic studies in the tradition of Irving Fisher.* Eds.: William Fellner et al. NY: Wiley, pp. 231-56.

Todaro, Michael P. and Stilkind, J. (1981) *City bias and rural neglect: The dilemma of urban development.* NY: The Population Council.

United Nations. (1975) 'Recent Population Trends and Future Prospects: Report of the Secretary-General,' in *The population debate: Dimensions and perspectives.* Papers of the World Population Conference, Bucharest, 1974. ST/ESA/SER.A/57, Population Studies, No. 57. NY: UN, Vol. 1, pp. 344.

United Nations, Dept. of International Economic and Social Affairs. (1980) *Patterns of urban and rural population growth.* Population Studies, No. 68. NY: UN.

— (1986) *World population prospects: Estimates and projections as assessed in 1984.* Population Studies, No. 98. NY: UN.

Verdoorn, P. J. (1949) 'Fattori che regoleno lo sviluppo della produttivitá del lavaro,' *L'Industria, 1,* pp. 3-10.

Wall, Wendy L. (1987) 'World's Grain Output Surges as Nations Seek Food Self-Sufficiency,' *Wall Street Journal,* 6 Apr. pp. 1, 10.

Wattenberg, Ben J. (1987) *The birth dearth.* NY: Pharos Books.

Wéry, Réne; Rodgers, Gerry B. and Hopkins, Michael J. D. (1974) 'BACHUE-2: Version-1, a Population and Employment Model for the Philippines,' WEP 2-21/WP. 5, Population and Employment Project, Geneva: International Labour Office, July.

Wheeler, David. (1984) 'Female Education, Family Planning, Income, and Population: A Long-Run Econometric Simulation Model.' Mimeo. Boston U.

White, T. Kelley *et al.* (1975) 'The PDM: A Systems Approach to Modeling Demographic-Economic Interaction in Agricultural Development.' *Station Bulletin,* Agricultural Experiment Station, Purdue U.

Williamson, Jeffrey G. (1968) 'Personal Saving in Developing Nations: An Intertemporal Cross-Section from Asia,' *Econ. Rev.,* June, *44*(106), pp. 194-210.

— (1985) 'City Immigration, Selectivity Bias and Human Capital Transfers During the British Industrial Revolution.' HIER Paper 1171, Harvard U., July.

— (1988) 'Migration and Urbanization in the Third World,' in *Handbook of development economics.* Eds.: Hollis B. Chenery and T. N. Srinivasan. Amsterdam: Elsiever Science Pub. B. V.

Winegarden, C. R. (1978) 'A Simultaneous-Equations Model of Population Growth and Income Distribution,' *Appl. Econ.,* Dec. *10*(4), pp. 319-30.

World Bank. (1982) *World development report 1982.* Washington, DC: World Bank.

— (1983) *World tables,* 3rd ed., Vols. I & II. Baltimore: Johns Hopkins U. Press.

— (1984) *World development report.* Washington, DC: World Bank.

— (1986) *World development report.* NY: Oxford U. Press.

World Resources Institute and International Institute for Environment and Development. (1986) *World Resources 1986.* NY: Basic Books.

Yap, Lorene Y. L. (1977) 'The Attraction of Cities: A Review of the Migration Literature,' *J. Devel. Econ.,* Sept. *4*(3), pp. 239-64.

Young, Allyn A. (1928) 'Increasing Returns and Economic Progress,' *Econ. J.,* Dec. *38*(152), pp. 527-42.

Zymelman, Manuel. (1982) 'Educational Expenditures in the 1970's.' Mimeo. Washington, DC: World Bank, Education Dept..

— (1985) 'Educational Budgets and Quality of Instruction: Are They Unequivocally Related?' Mimeo. Washington, DC: World Bank, Education Dept.

32.   Investment in Human Capital
Theodore W. Schultz

Although it is obvious that people acquire useful skills and knowledge, it is not obvious that these skills and knowledge are a form of capital, that this capital is in substantial part a product of deliberate investment, that it has grown in Western societies at a much faster rate than conventional (nonhuman) capital, and that its growth may well be the most distinctive feature of the economic system. It has been widely observed that increases in national output have been large compared with the increases of land, man-hours, and physical reproducible capital. Investment in human capital is probably the major explanation for this difference.

Much of what we call consumption constitutes investment in human capital. Direct expenditures on education, health, and internal migration to take advantage of better job opportunities are clear examples. Earnings foregone by mature students attending school and by workers acquiring on-the-job training are equally clear examples. Yet nowhere do these enter into our national accounts. The use of leisure time to improve skills and knowledge is widespread and it too is unrecorded. In these and similar ways the *quality* of human effort can be greatly improved and its productivity enhanced. I shall contend that such investment in human capital accounts for most of the impressive rise in the real earnings per worker.

I shall comment, first, on the reasons why economists have shied away from the explicit analysis of investment in human capital, and then, on the capacity of such investment to explain many a puzzle about economic growth. Mainly, however, I shall concentrate on the scope and substance of human capital and its formation. In closing I shall consider some social and policy implications.

I. Shying away from investment in man

Economists have long known that people are an important part of the wealth of nations. Measured by what labor contributes to output, the productive capacity of human beings is now vastly larger than all other forms of wealth taken together. What economists have not stressed is the simple truth that people invest in themselves and that these investments are very large. Although economists are seldom timid in entering on abstract analysis and are often proud of being impractical, they have not been bold in coming to grips with this form of investment. Whenever they come even close, they proceed gingerly as if they were stepping into deep water. No doubt there are reasons for being wary. Deep-seated moral and philosophical issues are ever present. Free men are first and foremost the end to be served by economic endeavor; they are not property or marketable assets. And not least, it has been all too convenient in marginal productivity analysis to treat labor as if it were a unique bundle of innate abilities that are wholly free of capital.

The mere thought of investment in human beings is offensive to some among us.[1] Our values and beliefs inhibit us from looking upon human beings as capital goods, except in slavery and this we abhor. We are not unaffected by the long struggle to rid society of indentured service and to evolve political and legal institutions to keep men free from bondage. These are achievements that we prize highly. Hence, to treat human beings as wealth that can be augmented by investment runs counter to deeply held values. It seems to reduce man once again to a mere material component, to something akin to property. And for man to look upon himself as a capital good, even if it did not impair his freedom, may seem to debase him. No less a person than J. S. Mill at one time instituted that the people of a country should not be looked upon as wealth because wealth existed only for the sake of people [15]. But surely Mill was wrong; there is nothing in the concept of human wealth contrary to his idea that it exists only for the advantage of people. By investing in themselves, people can enlarge the range of choice available to them. It is one way free men can enhance their welfare.

Among the few who have looked upon human beings as capital, there are three distinguished names. The philosopher-economist Adam Smith boldly included all of the acquired and useful abilities of all of the inhabitants of a country as a part of capital. So did H. von Thünen, who then went on to argue that the concept of capital applied to man did not degrade him or impair his freedom and dignity, but on the contrary that the failure to apply the concept was especially pernicious in wars; ". . .for here . . . one will sacrifice in a battle a hundred human beings in the prime of their lives without a thought in order to save one gun." The reason is that, ". . . the purchase of a cannon causes an outlay of public funds, whereas human beings are to be had for nothing by means of a mere conscription decree"[20]. Irving Fisher also clearly and cogently presented an all-inclusive concept of capital[6]. Yet the main stream of thought has held that it is neither appropriate nor practical to apply the concept of capital to human beings. Marshall[11], whose great prestige goes far to explain why this view was accepted, held that while human beings are incontestably capital from an abstract and mathematical point of view, it would be out of touch with the market place to treat them as capital in practical analyses. Investment in human beings has accordingly seldom been incorporated in the formal core of economics, even though many economists, including Marshall, have seen its relevance at one point or another in what they have written.

The failure to treat human resources explicitly as a form of capital, as a produced means of production, as the product of investment, has fostered the retention of the classical notion of labor as a capacity to do manual work requiring little knowledge and skill, a capacity with which, according to this notion, laborers are endowed about equally. This notion of labor was wrong in the classical period and it is patently wrong now. Counting individuals who can and want to work and treating such a count as a measure of the quantity of an economic factor is no more meaningful than it would be to count the number of all manner of machines to determine their economic importance either as a stock of capital or as a flow of productive services.

Laborers have become capitalists not from a diffusion of the ownership of corporation stocks, as folklore would have it, but from the acquisition of knowledge and skill that have economic value[9]. This knowledge and skill are in great part the product of investment and, combined with other human investment, predominantly account for the productive superiority of the technically advanced countries. To omit them in studying economic growth is like trying to explain Soviet ideology without Marx.

II. Economic growth from human capital

Many paradoxes and puzzles about our dynamic, growing economy can be resolved once human investment is taken into account. Let me begin by sketching some that are minor though not trivial.

When farm people take nonfarm jobs they earn substantially less than industrial workers of the same race, age, and sex. Similarly non-white urban males earn much less than white males even after allowance is made for the effects of differences in unemployment, age, city size and region[21]. Because these differentials in earnings correspond closely to corresponding differentials in education, they strongly suggest that the one is a consequence of the other. Negroes who operate farms, whether as tenants or as owners, earn much less than whites on comparable farms.[2] Fortunately, crops and livestock are not vulnerable to the blight of discrimination. The large differences in earnings seem rather to reflect mainly the differences in health and education. Workers in the south on the average earn appreciably less than in the North or West and they also have on the average less education. Most migratory farm workers earn very little indeed by comparison with other workers. Many of them have virtually no schooling, are in poor health, are unskilled, and have little ability to do useful work. To urge that the differences in the amount of human investment may explain these differences in earnings seems elementary. Of more recent vintage are observations showing younger workers at a competitive advantage; for example, young men entering the labor force are said to have an advantage over unemployed older workers in obtaining satisfactory jobs. Most of these young people possess twelve years of school, most of the older workers six years or less. The observed advantage of these younger workers may therefore result not from inflexibilities in social security or in retirement programs, or from sociological preference of employers, but from real differences in productivity connected with one form of human investment, i.e., education. And yet another example, the curve relating income to age tends to be steeper for skilled than for unskilled persons. Investment in on-the-job training seems a likely explanation, as I shall note later.

Economic growth requires much internal migration of workers to adjust to changing job opportunities[10]. Young men and women move more readily than older workers. Surely this makes economic sense when one recognizes that the costs of such migration are a form of human investment. Young people have more years ahead of them than older workers during which they can realize on such an investment. Hence it takes less of a wage differential to make it economically advantageous for them to move, or, to put it differently, young people can expect a higher return on their investment in migration than older people. This differential may explain selective migration without requiring an appeal to sociological differences between young and old people.

The examples so far given are for investment in human beings that yield a return over a long period. This is true equally of investment in education, training, and migration of young people. Not all investments in human beings are of this kind; some are more nearly akin to current inputs as for example expenditures on food and shelter in some countries where work is mainly the application of brute human force, calling for energy and stamina, and where the intake of food is far from enough to do a full day's work. On the "hungry" steppes and in the teeming valleys of Asia, millions of adult males have so meager a diet that they cannot do more than a few hours of hard work. To call them underemployed does not seem pertinent[3]. Under such circumstances it is certainly meaningful to treat food partly as consumption and partly as a current "producer good," as some Indian economists have done. Let us not forget that Western economists during the early decades of industrialization and even in the time of Marshall and Pigou often connected additional food for workers with increases in labor productivity.

Let me now pass on to three major perplexing questions closely connected with the riddle of economic growth. First, consider the long-period behavior of the capital-income ratio. We were taught that a country which amassed more reproducible capital relative to its land and labor would employ such capital in greater "depth" because of its growing abundance and cheapness. But apparently this is not what happens. On the contrary, the estimates now available show that less of such capital tends to be employed relative to income as economic growth proceeds. Are we to infer that the ratio of capital to income has no relevance in explaining either poverty or opulence? Or that a rise of this ratio is not a prerequisite to economic growth? These questions raise fundamental issues bearing on motives and preferences for holding wealth as well as on the motives for particular investments and the stock of capital thereby accumulated. For my purpose all that needs to be said is that these estimates of capital-income ratios refer to only a part of all capital. They exclude in particular, and most unfortunately, any human capital. Yet human capital has surely been increasing at a rate substantially greater than reproducible (nonhuman) capital. We cannot, therefore, infer from these estimates that the stock of *all* capital has been decreasing relative to income. On the contrary, if we accept the not implausible assumption that the motives and references of people, the technical opportunities open to them, and the uncertainty associated with economic growth during particular periods were leading people to maintain roughly a constant ratio between *all* capital and income, the decline in the estimated capital-income ratio[3] is simply a signal that human capital has been increasing relatively not only to conventional capital but also to income.

The bumper crop of estimates that show national income increasing faster than national resources raises a second and not unrelated puzzle. The income of the United States has been increasing at a much higher rate than the combined amount of land, man-hours worked and the stock of reproducible capital used to produce the income. Moreover, the discrepancy between the two rates has become larger from one business cycle to the next during recent decades[5]. To call this discrepancy a measure of "resource productivity" gives a name to our ignorance but does not dispel it. If we accept these estimates, the connections between national resources and national income have become loose and tenuous over time. Unless this discrepancy can be resolved, received theory of production applied to inputs and outputs as currently measured is a toy and not a tool for studying economic growth.

Two sets of forces probably account for the discrepancy, if we neglect entirely the index number and aggregation problems that bedevil all estimates of such global aggregates as total output and total input. One is returns to scale; the second, the large improvements on the quality of inputs that have occurred but have been omitted from the input estimates. Our economy has undoubtedly been experiencing increasing returns to scale at some points offset by decreasing returns at others. If we can succeed in identifying and measuring the net gains, they may turn out to have been substantial. The improvements in the quality of inputs that have not been adequately allowed for are no doubt partly in material (nonhuman) capital. My own conception, however, is that both this defect and the omission of economies of scale are minor sources of discrepancy between the rates of growth of inputs and outputs compared to the improvements in human capacity that have been omitted.

A small step takes us from these two puzzles raised by existing estimates to a third which brings us to the heart of the matter, namely the essentially unexplained large increase in real earnings of workers. Can this be a windfall? Or a quasirent pending the adjustment in the supply of labor? Or, a pure rent reflecting the fixed amount of labor? It seems far more reasonable that it represents rather a return to the investment that has been made in human beings. The observed growth in productivity per unit of labor is simply a consequence of holding the unit of labor constant over time although in fact this unit of labor has been increasing as a result of a steadily growing amount of human capital per worker. As I read our record, the human capital component has become very large as a consequence of human investment.

Another aspect of the same basic question, which admits of the same resolution, is the rapid postwar recovery of countries that had suffered severe destruction of plant and equipment during the war. The toll from bombing was all too visible in the factories laid flat, the railroad yards, bridges, and harbors wrecked, and the cities in ruin. Structures, equipment and inventories were all heaps of rubble. Not so visible, yet large, was the toll from the wartime depletion of the physical plant that escaped destruction by bombs. Economists were called upon to assess the implications of these wartime losses for recovery. In retrospect, it is clear that they overestimated the prospective retarding effects of these losses. Having had a small hand in this effort, I have had a special reason for looking back and wondering why the judgements that we formed soon after the war proved to be so far from the mark. The explanation that now is clear is that we gave altogether too much weight to nonhuman capital in making these assessments. We fell into this error, I am convinced, because we did not have a concept of *all* capital and, therefore, failed to take account of human capital and the important part that it plays in production in a modern economy.

Let me close this section with a comment on poor countries, for which there are virtually no solid estimates. I have been impressed by repeatedly expressed judgments, especially by those who have a responsibility in making capital available to poor countries, about the low rate at which these countries can absorb additional capital. New capital from outside can be put to good use, it is said, only when it is added "slowly and gradually."

But this experience is at variance with the widely held impression that countries are poor fundamentally because they are starved for capital and that additional capital is truly the key to their more rapid economic growth. The reconciliation is again, I believe, to be found in emphasis on particular forms of capital. The new capital available to these countries from outside as a rule goes into the formation of structures, equipment and sometimes also into inventories. But it is generally not available for additional investment in man. Consequently, human capabilities do not stay abreast of physical capital, and they do become limiting factors in economic growth. It should come as no surprise, therefore, that the absorption rate of capital to augment only particular nonhuman resources is necessarily low. The Horvat[8] formulation of the optimum rate of investment which treats knowledge and skill as a critical investment variable in determining the rate of economic growth is both relevant and important.

III. Scope and substance of these investments

What are human investments? Can they be distinguished from consumption? Is it at all feasible to identify and measure them? What do they contribute to income? Granted that they seem amorphous compared to brick and mortar, and hard to get at compared to the investment accounts of corporations, they assuredly are not a fragment; they are rather like the contents of Pandora's box, full of difficulties and hope.

Human resources obviously have both quantitative and qualitative dimensions. The number of people, the proportion who enter upon useful work, and hours worked are essentially quantitative characteristics. To make my task tolerably manageable, I shall neglect these and consider only such quality components as skill, knowledge, and similar attributes that affect particular human capabilities to do productive work. In so far as expenditures to enhance such capabilities also increase the value productivity of human effort (labor), they will yield a positive rate of return.[4]

How can we estimate the magnitude of human investment? The practice followed in connection with physical capital goods is to estimate the magnitude of capital formation by expenditures made to produce the capital goods. This practice would suffice also for the formation of human capital. However, for human capital there is an additional problem that is less pressing for physical capital goods: how to distinguish between expenditures for consumption and for investment. This distinction bristles with both conceptual and practical difficulties. We can think of three classes of expenditures: expenditures that satisfy consumer preferences and in no way enhance the capabilities under discussion — these represent pure consumption; expenditures that enhance capabilities and do not satisfy any preferences underlying consumption — these represent pure investment; and expenditures that have both effects. Most relevant activities clearly are in the third class, partly consumption and partly investment, which is why the task of identifying each component is so formidable and why the measurement of capital formation by expenditures is less useful for human investment than for investment in physical goods. In principle there is an alternative method for estimating human investment, namely by its yield rather than by its cost. While any capability produced by human investment becomes a part of the human agent and hence cannot be sold; it is nevertheless "in touch with the market place" by affecting the wages and salaries the human agent can earn. The resulting increase in earnings is the yield on the investment.[5]

Despite the difficulty of exact measurement at this stage of our understanding of human investment, many insights can be gained by examining some of the more important activities that improve human capabilities. I shall concentrate on five major categories: (1) health facilities and services, broadly conceived to include all expenditures that affect the life expectancy, strength and stamina, and the vigour and vitality of a people; (2) on-the-job training, including old-style apprenticeship organized by firms; (3) formally organized education at the elementary, secondary, and higher levels; (4) study programs for adults that are not organized by firms, including extension programs notably in agriculture; (5) migration of individuals and families to adjust to changing job opportunities. Except for education, not much is known about these activities that is germane here. I shall refrain from commenting on study programs for adults, although in agriculture the extension services of the several states play an important role in transmitting new knowledge and in developing skills of farmers[17]. Nor shall I elaborate further on internal migration related to economic growth.

Health activities have both quantity and quality implications. Such speculations as economists have engaged in about the effects of improvements in health,[6] has been predominantly in connection with population growth, which is to say with quantity. But surely health measures also enhance the quality of human resources. So also may additional food and better shelter, especially in underdeveloped countries.

The change in the role of food as people become richer sheds light on one of the conceptual problems already referred to. I have pointed out that extra food in some poor countries has the attribute of a "producer good." This attribute of food, however, diminishes as the consumption of food rises, and there comes a point at which any further increase in food becomes pure consumption.[7] Clothing, housing and perhaps medical services may be similar.

My comment about on-the-job training will consist of conjecture on the amount of such training, a note on the decline of apprenticeship, and then a useful economic theorem on who bears the costs of such training. Surprisingly little is known about on-the-job training in modern industry. About all that can be said is that the expansion of education has not eliminated it. It seems likely, however, that some of the training formerly undertaken by firms has been discontinued and other training programs have been instituted to adjust both to the rise in the education of workers and to changes in the demands for new skills. The amount invested annually in such training can only be a guess. H. F. Clark places it near to equal to the amount spent on formal education.[8] Even if it were only one-half as large, it would represent currently an annual gross investment of about $15 billion. Elsewhere, too, it is thought to be important. For example, some observers have been impressed by the amount of such training under way in plants in the Soviet Union.[9] Meanwhile, apprenticeship has all but disappeared, partly because it is now inefficient and partly because schools now perform many of its functions. Its disappearance has been hastened no doubt by the difficulty of enforcing apprenticeship agreements. Legally they have come to smack of indentured service. The underlying economic factors and behavior are clear enough. The apprentice is prepared to serve during the initial period when his productivity is less than the cost of his keep and of his training. Later, however, unless he is legally restrained, he will seek other employment when his productivity begins to exceed the cost of keep and training, which is the period during which a master would expect to recoup on his earlier outlay.

To study on-the-job training Gary Becker[1] advances the theorem that in competitive markets employees pay all the costs of their training and none of these costs are ultimately borne by the firm. Becker points out several implications. The notion that expenditures on training by a firm generate external economies for other firms is not consistent with this theorem. The theorem also indicates one force favoring the transfer from on-the-job training to attending school. Since on-the-job training reduces the net earnings of workers at the beginning and raises them later on, this theorem also provides an explanation for the "steeper slope of the curve relating income to age," for skilled than unskilled workers, referred to earlier.[10] What all this adds up to is that the stage is set to undertake meaningful economic studies of on-the-job training.

Happily we reach firmer ground in regard to education. Investment in education has risen at a rapid rate and by itself may well account for a substantial part of the otherwise unexplained rise in earnings. I shall do no more than summarize some preliminary results about the total costs of education including income foregone by students, the apparent relation of these costs to consumer income and to alternative investments, the rise of the stock of education in the labor force, returns to education, and the contribution that the increase in the stock of education may have made to earnings and to national income.

It is not difficult to estimate the conventional costs of education consisting of the costs of the services of teachers, librarians, administrators, of maintaining and operating the educational plant, and interest on the capital embodied in the educational plant. It is far more difficult to estimate another component of total cost, the income foregone by students. Yet this component should be included and it is far from negligible. In the United States, for example, well over half of the costs of higher education consists of income foregone by students. As early as 1900, this income foregone accounted for about one-fourth of the total costs of elementary, secondary and higher education. By 1956, it represented over two-fifths of all costs. The rising significance of foregone income has been a major factor in the marked upward trend in the total real costs of education which, measured in current prices, increased from $400 million in 1900 to $28.7 billion in 1956[18]. The percentage rise in educational costs was about three and a half times as large as in consumer income, which would imply a high income elasticity of the demand for education, if education were regarded as pure consumption.[11] Educational costs also rose about three and a half times as rapidly as did the gross formation of physical capital in dollars. If we were to treat education as pure investment this result would suggest that the returns to education were relatively more attractive than those to nonhuman capital.[12]

Much schooling is acquired by persons who are not treated as income earners in most economic analysis, particularly, of course, women. To analyze the effect of growth in schooling on earnings, it is therefore necessary to distinguish between the stock of education in the population and the amount in the labor force. Years of school completed are far from satisfactory as a measure because of the marked increases that have taken place in the number of days of school attendance of enrolled students and because much more of the education of workers consists of high school and higher education than formerly. My preliminary estimates suggest that the stock of education in the labor force rose about eight and a half times between 1900 and 1956, whereas the stock of reproducible capital rose four and a half times, both in 1956 prices. These estimates are, of course, subject to many qualifications.[13] Nevertheless, both the magnitude and the rate of increase on this form of human capital have been such that they could be an important key to the riddle of economic growth.[14]

The exciting work under way is on the return to education. In spite of the flood of high school and college graduates, the return has not become trivial. Even the lower limits of the estimates show that the return to such education has been in the neighborhood of the return to nonhuman capital. This is what most of these estimates show when they treat as costs all of the public and private expenditures on education and also the income foregone while attending school, and when they treat all of these costs as investment, allocating none to consumption.[15] But surely a part of these costs are consumption in the sense that education creates a form of consumer capital[16] which has the attribute of improving the taste and the quality of consumption of students throughout the rest of their lives. If one were to allocate a substantial fraction of the total costs of this education to consumption, say one-half, this would, of course, double the observed rate of return to what would then become the investment component in education that enhances the productivity of man.

Fortunately, the problem of allocating the costs of education in the labor force between consumption and investment does not arise to plague us when we turn to the contribution that education makes to earnings and to national income because a change in allocation only alters the rate of return, not the total return. I noted at the outset that the unexplained increases in U.S. national income have been especially large in recent decades. On one set of assumptions, the unexplained part amounts to nearly three-fifths of the total increase between 1929 and 1956.[17] How much of this unexplained increase in income represents a return to education in the labor force? A lower limit suggests that about three-tenths of it, and an upper limit does not rule out that more than one-half of it came from this source.[18] These estimates also imply that between 36 and 70 percent of the hitherto unexplained rise in the earnings of labor is explained by returns to the additional education of workers.

IV. A concluding note on policy

One proceeds at his own peril in discussing social implications and policy. The conventional hedge is to camouflage one's values and to wear the mantle of academic innocence. Let me proceed unprotected!

1. Our tax laws everywhere discriminate against human capital. Although the stock of such capital has become large and even though it is obvious that human capital, like other forms of reproducible capital, depreciates, becomes obsolete, and entails maintenance, our tax laws are all but blind on these matters.

2. Human capital deteriorates when it is idle because unemployment impairs the skills that workers have acquired. Losses in earnings can be cushioned by appropriate payments but these do not keep idleness from taking its toll from human capital.

3. There are many hindrances to the free choice of professions. Racial discrimination and religious discrimination are still widespread. Professional associations and governmental bodies also hinder entry; for example, into medicine. Such purposeful interference keeps the investment in this form of human capital substantially below its optimum [7].

4. It is indeed elementary to stress the greater imperfections of the capital market in providing funds for investment in human beings than for investment in physical goods. Much could be done to reduce these imperfections by reforms in tax and banking laws and by changes in banking practices. Long-term private and public loans to students are warranted.

5. Internal migration, notably the movement of farm people into industry, made necessary by the dynamics of our economic progress, requires substantial investments. In general, families in which the husbands and wives are already in the late thirties cannot afford to make these investments because the remaining payoff period for them is too short. Yet society would gain if more of them would pull stakes and move because, in addition to the increase in productivity currently, the children of these families would be better located for employment when they were ready to enter the labor market. The case for making some to these investments on public account is by no means weak. Our farm programs have failed miserably these many years in not coming to grips with the costs and returns form off-farm migration.

6. The low earnings of particular people have long been a matter of public concern. Policy all too frequently concentrates only on the effects, ignoring the causes. No small part of the low earnings of many Negroes, Puerto Ricans, Mexican nationals, indigenous migratory farm workers, poor farm people and some of our older workers, reflects the failure to have invested in their health and education. Past mistakes are, of course, bygones, but for the sake of the next generation we can ill afford to continue making the same mistakes over again.

7. Is there a substantial underinvestment in human beings other than in these depressed groups?[2] This is an important question for economists. The evidence at hand is fragmentary. Nor will the answer be easily won. There undoubtedly have been overinvestments in some skills, for example, too many locomotive firemen and engineers, too many people trained to be farmers, and too many agricultural economists! Our schools are not free of loafers and some students lack the necessary talents. Nevertheless, underinvestment in knowledge and skill, relative to the amounts invested in nonhuman capital would appear to be the rule and not the exception for a number of reasons. The strong and increasing demands for this knowledge and skill in laborers are of fairly recent origin and it takes time to respond to them. In responding to these demands, we are heavily dependent upon

cultural and political processes, and these are slow and the lags are long compared to the behavior of markets serving the formation of nonhuman capital. Where the capital market does serve human investments, it is subject to more imperfections than in financing physical capital. I have already stressed the fact that our tax laws discriminate in favor of nonhuman capital. Then, too, many individuals face serious uncertainty in assessing their innate talents when it comes to investing in themselves, especially through higher education. Nor is it easy either for public decisions or private behavior to untangle and properly assess the consumption and the investment components. The fact that the return to high school and to higher education has been about as large as the return to conventional forms of capital when all of the costs of such education including income foregone by students are allocated to the investment component, creates a strong presumption that there has been underinvestment since, surely, much education is cultural and in that sense it is consumption. It is no wonder, in view of these circumstances, that there should be substantial underinvestment in human beings, even though we take pride, and properly so, in the support that we have given to education and to other activities that contribute to such investments.

8. Should the returns from public investment in human capital accrue to the individuals in whom it is made?[19] The policy issues implicit in this question run deep and they are full of perplexities pertaining both to resource allocation and to welfare. Physical capital that is formed by public investment is not transferred as a rule to particular individuals as a gift. It would greatly simplify the allocation process if public investment in human capital were placed on the same footing. What then is the logical basis for treating public investment in human capital differently? Presumably it turns on ideas about welfare. A strong welfare goal of our community is to reduce the unequal distribution of personal income among individuals and families. Our community has relied heavily on progressive income and inheritance taxation. Given public revenue from these sources, it may well be true that public investment in human capital, notably that entering into general education, is an effective and efficient set of expenditures for attaining this goal. Let me stress, however, that the state of knowledge about these issues is woefully meager.

9. My last policy comment is on assistance to underdeveloped countries to help them achieve economic growth. Here, even more than in domestic affairs, investment in human beings is likely to be underrated and neglected. It is inherent in the intellectual climate in which leaders and spokesmen of many of these countries find themselves. Our export of growth doctrines has contributed. These typically assign the stellar role to the formation of nonhuman capital, and take as an obvious fact the superabundance of human resources. Steel mills are the real symbol of industrialization. After all, the early industrialization of England did not depend on investments in the labor force. New funds and agencies are being authorized to transfer capital for physical goods to these countries. The World Bank and our Export-Import bank have already had much experience. Then, too, measures have been taken to pave the way for the investment of more private (nonhuman) capital abroad. This one-sided effort is under way in spite of the fact that the knowledge

and skills required to take on and use efficiently the superior techniques of production, the most valuable resource that we could make available to them, is in very short supply in these underdeveloped countries. Some growth of course can be had from the increase in more conventional capital even though the labor that is available is lacking both in skill and knowledge. But the rate of growth will be seriously limited. It simply is not possible to have the fruits of a modern agriculture and the abundance of modern industry without making large investments in human beings.

Truly, the most distinctive feature of our economic system is the growth in human capital. Without it there would be only hard, manual work and poverty except for those who have income from property. There is an early morning scene in Faulkner's *Intruder in the Dust*, of a poor, solitary cultivator at work in a field. Let me paraphrase that line, "The man without skills and knowledge leaning terrifically against nothing."

* Presidential Address delivered at the Seventy-Third Annual Meeting of the American Economic Association, Saint Louis, December 28, 1960. The author is indebted to his colleagues Milton Friedman, for his very helpful suggestions to gain clarity and cogency, and Harry G. Johnson for pointing out a number of ambiguities.

Notes

1. This paragraph draws on the introduction to my Teller Lecture [16].

2. Based on unpublished preliminary results obtained by Joseph Willett in his Ph.D. research at the University of Chicago.

3. I leave aside here the difficulties inherent in identifying and measuring both the nonhuman capital and the income entering into estimates of this ratio. There are index number and aggregation problems aplenty, and not all improvements in the quality of this capital have been accounted for, as I shall note later.

4. Even so, our *observed* return can be either negative, zero or positive because our observations are drawn from a world where there is uncertainty and imperfect knowledge and where there are windfall gains and losses and mistakes aplenty.

5. In principle, the value of the investment can be determined by discounting the additional future earnings it yields just as the value of a physical capital good can be determined by discounting its income stream.

6. Health economics is in its infancy; there are two medical journals with "economics" in their titles, two bureaus for economic research in private associations (one in the American Medical and the other in the American Dental Association), and not a few studies and papers by outside scholars. Selma Mushkin's survey is very useful with its pertinent economic insights, though she may have underestimated somewhat the influence of the economic behavior of people in striving for health [14].

7. For instance, the income elasticity of the demand for food continues to be positive even after the point is reached where additional food no longer has the attribute of a "producer good."

8. Based on comments made by Harold F. Clark at the Merrill Center for Economics, summer 1959; also, see [4].

9. Based on observations made by a team of U.S. economists of which I was a member, see *Saturday Rev.,* Jan. 21, 1961.

10. Becker has also noted still another implication arising out of the fact that the income and capital investment aspects of on-the-job training are tied together, which gives rise to "permanent" and "transitory" income effects that may have substantial explanatory value.

11. Had other things stayed constant this suggests an income elasticity of 3.5. Among the things that did change, the prices of educational services rose relative to other consumer prices, perhaps offset in part by improvements in the quality of educational services.

12. This of course assumes among other things that the relationship between gross and net have not changed or have changed in the same proportion. Estimates are from my essay, "Education and Economic Growth" [19].

13. From [19, Sec. 4]. These estimates of the stock of education are tentative and incomplete. They are incomplete in that they do not take into account fully the increases in the average life of this form of human capital arising out of the fact that relatively more of this education is held by younger people in the labor force than was true in earlier years; and, they are incomplete because no adjustment has been made for the improvements in education over time, increasing the quality of a year of school in ways other than those related to changes in the proportions represented by elementary, high school and higher education. Even so the stock of this form of human capital rose 8.5 times between 1900 and 1956 while the stock of reproducible nonhuman capital increased only 4.5 times, both in constant 1956 prices.

14. In value terms this stock of education was only 22 per cent as large as the stock of reproducible physical capital in 1900, whereas in 1956 it already had become 42 per cent as large.

15. Several comments are called for here. (1) The return to high school education appears to have declined substantially between the late 'thirties and early 'fifties and since then has leveled off, perhaps even risen somewhat, indicating a rate of return toward the end of the 'fifties about as high as that to higher education.(2) The return to college education seems to have risen somewhat since the late 'thirties in spite of the rapid influx of college-trained individuals into the labor force.(3) Becker's estimates based on the difference in income between high school and college graduates based on urban males adjusted for ability, race, unemployment and mortality show a return of 9 percent to total college costs including both earnings foregone and conventional college costs, public and private and with none of these costs allocated to consumption (see his paper given at the American Economic Association meeting, December 1959 [2]). (4) The returns to this education in the case of nonwhite urban males, of rural males, and of females in the labor force may have been somewhat lower (see Becker [2]). (5) My own estimates, admittedly less complete than those of Becker and thus subject to additional qualifications, based mainly on lifetime income estimates of Herman P. Miller [12], lead to a return of about 11 per cent to both high school and college education as of 1958. See [19, Sec. 5].

Whether the consumption component in education will ultimately dominate, in the sense that the investment component in education will diminish as these expenditures increase and a point will be reached where additional expenditures for education will be pure consumption (a zero return on however small a part one might treat as an investment), is an interesting speculation. This may come to pass, as it has in the case of food and shelter, but that eventuality appears very remote presently in view of the prevailing investment value of education and the new demands for knowledge and skill inherent in the nature of our technical and economic progress.

16 The returns on this consumer capital will not appear in the wages and salaries that people earn.

17. Real income doubled, rising from $150 to $302 billion in 1956 prices. Eighty-nine billions of the increase in real income is taken to be unexplained, or about 59 per cent of the total increase. The stock of education in the labor force rose by $355 billion of which $69 billion is here allocated to the growth in the labor force to keep the per-worker stock of education constant, and $286 billion represents the increase in the level of this stock. See [19, Sec 6] for an elaboration of the method and the relevant estimates.

18. In per cent, the lower estimate came out to 29 per cent and the upper estimate to 56 per cent.

19. I am indebted to Milton Friedman for bringing this issue to the fore in his comments on an early draft of this paper. See preface of [7] and also Jacob Mincer's pioneering paper [13].

References

1. G. S. Becker, (1960) preliminary draft of study undertaken for Nat. Bur. Econ. Research. New York.

2. —, (1960) "Underinvestment, in College Education?," *Proc., Am. Econ. Rev.*, May, *50,* 346-54.

3. P. R. Brahmanand and C. N. Vakil, (1956) *Planning for an Expanding Economy.* Bombay .

4. H. F. Clark, (1959) 'Potentialities of Educational Establishments Outside the Conventional Structure of Higher Education,' *Financing Higher Education, 1960-70,* D. M. Keezer, ed. New York.

5. Solomon Frabricant, (1959) *Basic Facts on Productivity Change,* Nat. Bur. Econ. Research, Occas. Paper 63. New York, Table 5.

6. Irving Fisher, (1906) *The Nature of Capital and Income.* New York.

7. Milton Friedman and Simon Kuznets, (1945) *Income from Independent Professional Practice,* Nat. Bur. Econ. Research. New York.

8. B. Horvat, (1958) 'The Optimum Rate of Investment,' *Econ Jour.,* Dec, 68, 747-67.

9. H. G. Johnson, (1960) 'The Political Economy of Opulence,' *Can. Jour. Econ. and Pol. Sci.,* Nov, 26, 552-64.

10. Simon Kuznets, (1952) *Income and Wealth in the United States.* Cambridge, England. Sec. IV, Distribution by Industrial Origin.

11. Alfred Marshall, (1930) *Principles of Economics,* 8th ed. London. App. E, pp. 787-88.

12. H. P. Miller (1960) 'Annual and Lifetime Income in Relation to Education: 1939-1959,' *Am. Econ.* Rev., Dec, 50, 962-86.

13. Jacob Mincer, (1958) 'Investment in Human Capital and Personal Income Distribution,' *Jour. Pol. Econ.,* Aug, 66, 281-302.

14. S. J. Mushkin, (1958) 'Toward a Definition of Health Economics,' *Public Health Reports,* U.S. Dept. of Health, Educ. and Welfare, Sept, 73, 785-93.

15. J. S. Nicholson, (1909) 'The Living Capital of the United Kingdom,' *Econ. Jour.,* Mar. 1891, 1, 95; see J. S. Mill, *Principles of Political Economy,* ed. W. J. Ashley, London, p. 8.

16. T. W. Schultz, (1959) 'Investment in Man: an Economist's View,' *Soc. Serv. Rev.,* June, 33, 109-17.

17. ———— , (1956) 'Agriculture and the Application of Knowledge,' *A Look to the Future,* W. K. Kellogg Foundation, Battle Creek, 54-78.

18. ———— , (1960) 'Capital Formation by Education,' *Jour. Pol. Econ.,* Dec, 68, Tables 3 through 7.

19. ————, (1961) 'Education and Economic Growth,' *Social Forces Influencing American Education,* H. G. Richey, ed. Chicago.

20. H. Von Thünen, (1875) *Der isolierte Staat,* 3rd ed., Vol. 2, Pt. 2, transl. by B. F. Hoselitz, reproduced by the Comp. Educ. Center, Univ. Chicago, pp. 140-52.

21. Morton Zeman, (1955) *A Quantitative Analysis of White-Nonwhite Income Differentials in the United States.* Unpublished doctoral dissertation, Univ. Chicago.

33. Returns to Education: An Updated International Comparison

George Psacharopoulos

One of the first questions that was asked following on from what Mary Jean Bowman (1966) described as the human capital revolution in economic thought, was: what is the profitability of investing in the new form of capital? Hesitantly, at first, but more eagerly thereafter, researchers around the world started estimating the social or private returns associated with educational and other human-capital-related expenditures for diverse population subgroups, from special samples, using a variety of assumptions and methodologies ranging from back of envelope calculations to extremely sophisticated econometric techniques.

The year 1973 was a landmark in the 'rate of return' literature — as it came to be known thereafter — because of the publication of the first systematic comparative study in this respect, (Psacharopoulos, 1973). A total of 53 rate of return case-studies were reviewed covering 32 countries.

This paper is an attempt to update the earlier rate of return evidence by considering studies that have been conducted in the seventies. The result of this update is the addition of 13 new country cases and a revision of most of the figures in the old country set.

However, I go beyond the compilation of the comparable figures and discuss a series of controversial arguments that have been associated with the rate of return literature of the 1970s. Also, I try to give an interpretation of the summary findings following the expanded data set.

Trends in the rate of return literature

Putting aside what is claimed to be the first empirical cost-benefit analysis of education by a Soviet economist (Strumilin, 1929) the real rate of return estimation activity started in the late fifties (see, e.g. Becker, 1960), T.W. Schultz's (1961) presidential address to the American Economic Association and the publication of Becker's (1964) NBER book gave a further boost to the subject, especially as a topic of PhD dissertations in US universities. The estimation procedure used during this first wave of rate of return literature was of the 'elaborate type', as described in the next section.

The second wave of the 'rate of return' literature starts somewhere in the early 1970s and is established with the publication of Mincer's (1974) NBER book. The estimation technique now becomes increasingly of the 'earnings function' type, as described in the next section. This technique is still going strong today and tends to be the dominant rate of return estimation procedure.

George Psacharopoulos: 'Returns to Education: An Updated International Comparison', *COMPARATIVE EDUCATION* (1981), Vol. 17, No. 3, pp. 321-341. Reproduced by permission of Carfax Publishing Company, PO Box 25, Abingdon, Oxon, CX14 3UE.

It is also interesting to note that the alternative to the rate of return cost-benefit measure, the 'net present value', has lost ground in the recent literature, mainly because if does not have a readily intelligible interpretation.

Rate of return estimation procedures

For the purpose of this paper it is sufficient to distinguish three main methods for estimating the rate of return to investment in education: the elaborate method, the earnings function method and the short-cut method.

(a) *The elaborate method*

This follows from the exact algebraic definition of the rate of return, which is the discount rate that equates a stream of benefits to a stream of costs at a given point in time. For example, consider the estimation of the private rate of return to investment in higher education in Fig. 1. If Y stands for labour earnings, and h and s subscripts for higher and secondary education, respectively, the rate of return (r) in this case is found by solving the following equation for r.

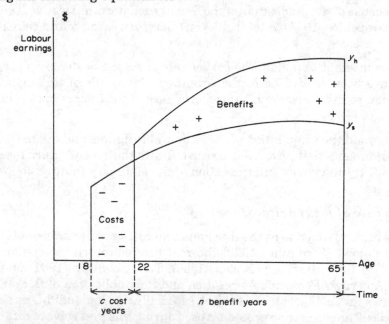

Fig. 1   A rate of return estimation according to the elaborate method.

discounted benefits to age 22 = cumulated costs at age 22.

(+ + + area) = (- - - area)

$$\sum_{t=1}^{n} (Y_h - Y_s)_t (1+r)^{-t} = \sum_{t=1}^{c} (Y_s)_t (1+r)^{t} .$$

(1)

This high power equation is usually solved by an iterative computer programme that starts from an arbitrary value of r and keeps modifying it by small increments in the right direction until the left-hand side is equal to the right-hand side.

Note that in the above *private* rate of return calculation the only cost of the 'education project' under evaluation is the opportunity cost of staying on in school beyond the age of 18 instead of working in the labour market. This opportunity cost is measured by the earnings of labour with secondary school qualifications.

Should the estimation of a *social* rate of return be desired, one can simply add the resource cost of an university place in the right-hand side of equation (1) and repeat the calculation. Of course earnings in this case should be before tax, whereas in the private rate of return calculation earnings should be after tax. But contrary to popular belief, the post-versus pre-tax treatment of earnings does *not* make a big difference in a rate of return calculation. It is the addition of the *direct cost* of schooling that mainly accounts for the fact that a social rate of return is lower relative to a private rate of return.

This way of estimating the profitability of investment in education requires in the first place detailed data on age-earnings profiles by educational level. This information is rare in most countries. Even if this information were available, the problem of small number cells arises. Namely, the plotted actual age-earnings profiles exhibit a saw-tooth pattern making the rate of return estimation very sensitive, especially regarding the initial years after graduation which carry a high weight in the discounting.

It is for this reason smoothing-out procedures have been used, the rate of return being estimated in three steps: in step one a regression of the type:

$$Y_i = a + b \cdot \text{AGE}_i + c \cdot \text{AGE}_i^2 \tag{2}$$

is fitted within subgroups of workers with the same educational level for the purpose of summarising the data.

In step 2 an idealised age-earnings profile is constructed by predicting the value of Y for given ages and educational levels, using the estimated function (2).

In step 3 the predicted values of earnings are inserted in formula (1), in order to compute the rate of return.

(b) *The earnings function method*

Equation (2) in the above smoothing out procedure should not be confused with what is known as the earnings function method of estimating the rate of return. This is a regression of the basic form

$$\ln Y_i = a + b \cdot S_i + c \cdot \text{EX}_i + d \cdot \text{EX}_i^2 \tag{3}$$

where S is the number of years of schooling of the individual *(i)* and EX his years of labour market experience. Equation (2) is an *ad hoc* fitting regression. Equation (3) is based on human capital theory where $b=r$, i.e. the estimated regression coefficient *(b)* is interpreted as the *average private* rate of return to one extra year of schooling.

An illustrative proof of this proposition (that is essentially due to Mincer, 1974) is that

$$b = \frac{\delta \ln Y}{\delta S} = r,$$

(4)

i.e. the rate of return is nothing else than the relative change in earnings ($\delta \ln Y$) following a given change in schooling (δS).

There exist two ways one can add an educational level dimension to this 'average' rate of return concept. The first way is to add an $e.S^2$ term in equation (3), where e is the estimated coefficient on years-of-schooling-squared. In this case, differentiation with respect to S yields

$$r = B + 2eS.$$

(5)

By substituting different values of S in the right-hand side of equation (5), one can arrive at a regression-derived rate of return structure corresponding, say, to primary education ($S = 6$), secondary education ($S = 12$) and higher education ($S=16$).

The second way is to specify different educational levels in the earnings function by means of a series of dummy variables, say PRIM, SEC and HIGH, having a value of 1 if the individual belongs to the particular educational level and 0 otherwise:

$$\ln Y = a + b . \text{PRIM} + c . \text{SEC} + d . \text{HIGH} + e . \text{EX} + f . \text{EX}^2.$$

(6)

In this case, the rate of return to the different levels of education are derived from the estimated coefficients b,c and d in the above function as follows:

$$r\text{(primary vs illiterates)} = \frac{b}{S_p}$$

$$r\text{(secondary vs primary)} = \frac{c-b}{S_s - S_p} \qquad r = \frac{d-c}{S_h - S_s}$$

where S stands for the number of years of schooling of the subscripted educational level (p=primary, s= secondary and h= higher).

The rationale of this procedure is that effectively one computes the rate of return by means of the following formula that is educational-level-specific.

$$r_k = \frac{\ln Y_k - \ln Y_{k-\Delta S}}{\Delta S}$$

(7)

Here k is the higher educational level in the comparison and ΔS the difference in years of schooling between k and the control group.

The advantage of estimating the rate of return by the dummy variable method rather than the years-of-schooling-squared method is that a great deal of sensitivity is added; i.e. the actual rate of return structure might not be as smooth as that suggested by formula (5).

However, the problem with the earnings function approach in general is that the rates of return are estimated on the basis of the following implicit assumptions:

(i) the age-earnings profiles are either flat or equidistant between adjacent educational levels throughout their range;

(ii) the age-earnings profiles last for ever (to infinity); and

(iii) the only cost of schooling is the foregone earnings of the individual (see Fig. 2).

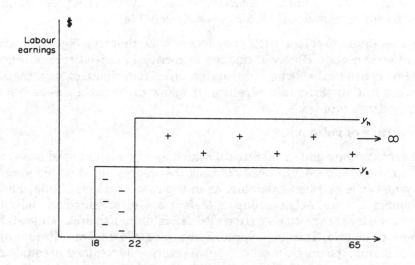

Fig. 2.   The rate of return estimation procedure implicit in the short-cut method.

These assumptions are not as damaging or unrealistic as they seem and they have been sufficiently defended (and debated) in the earnings function literature (see, e.g. Blinder, 1976). For example, the fact that age-earnings profiles are assumed to last for ever makes little difference to the discounted present value and hence the estimated rate of return.

The main problems with this method, however, are first one cannot readily incorporate cost data in order to estimate social rates of return, and secondly this method understates the returns to primary education. The reason for the downward bias on the return to primary education is that *the estimation formula automatically assigns foregone earnings to primary school children.* This is just not true in most country settings and one should have this understatement in mind when interpreting the results.

(c) *The short-cut method*

This amounts to doing in an explicit way what the earnings function method is doing implicitly, i.e. the returns to education are estimated on the basis of the simple formula

$$r_k = \frac{\overline{Y}_{k} - \overline{Y}_{k-\Delta S}}{S \cdot (\overline{Y}_{k-\Delta S})} \tag{8}$$

where $\overline{Y}$ refers to mean earnings of employees with the subscripted education level. Formulae (7) and (8) are very similar, the difference lying in the mathematical approximation $\ln(1+x) \approx x$ which is good for values of x of the order of the rate of return to education. The great advantage of this formula is that one can use already tabulated information on the earnings of workers by educational level in order to estimate the private rate of return. Also, it is rather easy to add the resource cost of schooling in the denominator in order to estimate the social returns. Hence, it is of great value in cases where information on individual earnings is not available.

Of course the main problem with this formula is that the age (or experience) standardisation is absent. However, this can be rectified in case the mean earnings by educational level are available for large age groups. Then choice of, say, the 35-45 age group for computation of the rate of return somehow prevents biases associated with the early experience profiles.

An updated rate of return set

Table 1 presents private and social rates of return by educational level in 44 countries. This is an update of table 4.1 in my 1973 book. Estimates based on old surveys were replaced by newer ones when available, as in the case of Kenya, India, Philippines, Brazil, Colombia, Greece, Belgium, Japan, Malaysia, United Kingdom and the United States. New country observations were added referring to Ethiopia, Malawi, Morocco, Sierra Leone, Indonesia, Taiwan, Cyprus, Spain, Yugoslavia, Iran, France and Italy. And, faute de mieux, the previous set of rates of return was retained in countries where no newer estimates were available.

As in the previous compilation, an attempt was made to include rates of return as comparable as possible between countries. Thus, where the relevant information was available in the original study, the reported rates are:

Marginal, in the sense that they refer to investment at the margin between the educational levels considered (e.g. primary graduation vs illiterates, secondary general vs primary and higher education vs secondary general).

Unadjusted, for economic growth, ability differences and unemployment. (The rationale for this choice is explained in a later section of this paper.)

Elaborate-method derived in most cases (except in the cases of Colombia, Cyprus, and the United Kingdom where the regression method was used, and Malawi, Indonesia and Italy where the short-cut method was used).

Rate of return patterns

Nobody can claim that the combination of diverse assumptions, estimation procedures, sample data and years of reference would have ever resulted to an absolutely comparable rate of return set to the last decimal point. But Table 1 contains some strong features that cannot be due to comparability biases. The rate of return patterns in this table are fully compatible, validate and reinforce the conclusions reached on the basis of the 1973 international comparison. It is easier to discover the underlying patterns by averaging within country groups, as shown in Table II.

Pattern No. 1   The returns to primary education (whether social or private) are the highest among all educational levels.

Pattern No. 2   The private returns are in excess of social returns, especially at the university level.

Pattern No. 3   All rates of return to investment in education are well above the 10% common yardstick of the opportunity cost of capital.

Pattern No. 4   The returns to education in developing countries are higher relative to the corresponding returns in more advanced countries.

The above four propositions not only make economic sense, but also have important policy implications to be elaborated in the last section of this paper.

Table I   **Returns to education by level and country type (%)**

Country	Survey year	Private			Social		
		Prim.	Sec.	Higher	Prim.	Sec.	Higher
Africa							
Ethiopia	1972	35.0	22.8	27.4	20.3	18.7	9.7
Ghana	1967	24.5	17.0	37.0	18.0	13.0	16.5
Kenya*	1971	28.0	33.0	31.0	21.7	19.2	8.8
Malawi	1978					15.1	
Morocco	1970				50.5	10.0	13.0
Nigeria	1966	30.0	14.0	34.0	23.0	12.8	17.0
Rhodesia	1960				12.4		
Sierra Leone	1971				20.0	22.0	9.5
Uganda	1965				66.0	28.6	12.0
Asia							
India	1965	17.3	18.8	16.2	13.4	15.5	10.3
Indonesia	1977	25.5	15.6				
South Korea	1967				12.0	9.0	5.0
Malaysia	1978		32.6	34.5			
Philippines	1971	9.0	6.5	9.5	7.0	6.5	8.5
Singapore	1966		20.0	25.4	6.6	17.6	14.1
Taiwan	1972	50.0	12.7	15.8	27.0	12.3	17.7
Thailand	1970	56.0	14.5	14.0	30.5	13.0	11.0
Latin America							
Brazil	1970		24.7	13.9		23.5	13.1
Chile	1959				24.0	16.9	12.2
Colombia	1973	15.1	15.4	20.7			

Table I   (cont)   Returns to education by level and country type (%)

Country	Survey year	Private			Social		
		Prim.	Sec.	Higher	Prim.	Sec.	Higher
Mexico	1963	32.0	23.0	29.0	25.0	17.0	23.0
Venezuela	1957		18.0	27.0	82.0	17.0	23.0
Intermediate							
Cyprus	1975	15.0	11.2	14.8			
Greece	1977	20.0	6.0	5.5	16.5	5.5	4.5
Spain	1971	31.6	10.2	15.5	17.2	8.6	12.8
Turkey	1968		24.0	26.0			8.5
Yugoslavia	1969	7.6	15.3	2.6	9.3	15.4	2.8
Israel	1958	27.0	6.9	8.0	16.5	6.9	6.6
Iran	1976		21.2	18.5	15.2	17.6	13.6
Puerto Rico	1959		38.6	41.1	21.9	27.3	21.9
Advanced							
Australia	1969		14.0	13.9			
Belgium	1960		21.2	8.7		17.1	6.7
Canada	1961		16.3	19.7		11.7	14.0
Denmark	1964		10.0				7.8
France	1970		13.8	16.7		10.1	10.9
Germany	1964			4.6			
Italy	1969		17.3	18.3			
Japan	1973		5.9	8.1		4.6	6.4
Netherlands	1965		8.5	10.4		5.2	5.5
New Zealand	1966		20.0	14.7		19.4	13.2
Norway	1966		7.4	7.7		7.2	7.5
Sweden	1967			10.3		10.5	9.2
United Kingdom†	1972		11.7	9.6		3.6	8.2
United States	1969		18.8	15.4		10.9	10.9

Source:
Ethiopia   from Hoerr (1974, table 3).
Kenya   private rates, from Fields (1975, table II).
Malawi   preliminary estimate based on Heyneman (1980a).
Morocco   from Psacharopoulos (1976, p. 136).
Sierra Leone   from Ketkar (1974, table 5).
India   from Pandit (1976) as reported by Heyneman (1980b, p. 146).
Indonesia   from Hallak & Psacharopoulos (1979, p. 13).
Malaysia   from Lee (1980).
Philippines   from ILO (1974, p. 635).
Singapore   from Clark & Fong (1970).
Taiwan   from Gannicott (1972).
Brazil   from Jallade (1977, table 4).

Table I (cont)   Sources

Colombia	regression-derived from Fields & Schultz (1977, table 8A, col. (4)).
Cyprus	from Demetriades & Psacharopoulos (1979, table 9).
Greece	from Psacharopoulos & Kazamias (1978, table 19.1).
Spain	from Quintas & Sanmartin (1978, table 1).
Turkey	from Krueger (1972, table 4).
Yugoslavia	from Thomas (1976, table 3).
Iran	from Pourhosseini (1979).
Puerto Rico	from Carnoy (1972).
Australia	from Blandy & Goldsworthy (1973, p. 9).
Belgium	from Meulders (1974, table II).
France	from Eicher & Lévy-Garboua (1979, chapter 5).
Italy	based on income data from Bank of Italy (1972, table 10).
Japan	from Umetani (1977, pp. 113-114).
United Kingdom	private rates from Psacharopoulos & Layard (1979, table IX).
USA	from Carnoy & Marenbach (1975).

Ghana, Nigeria, Uganda, South Korea, Thailand, Chile, Mexico, Venezuela, Israel, Canada, Denmark, Germany, Netherlands, New Zealand, Norway, Sweden and the United Kingdom (social returns only) from Psacharopoulos (1973, p. 62).

Notes
* Social rates refer to 1968.   † Social rates refer to 1966.

Table II   The returns to education by region and country type (%)

		Private			Social		
Region or country type	N	Prim.	Sec.	High.	Prim.	Sec.	High.
Africa	(9)	29	22	32	29	17	12
Asia	(8)	32	17	19	16	12	11
Latin America	(5)	24	20	23	44	17	18
LDC average	(22)	29	19	24	27	16	13
Intermediate	(8)	20	17	17	16	14	10
Advanced	(14)	(a)	14	12	(a)	10	9

Source: Table I.
(a) Not computable because of lack of a control group of illiterates.
N = Number of countries in each group.
Prim. = primary educational level.
Sec. = secondary educational level.
High. = higher educational level.

Evidence from earnings functions

Table III presents another compilation of rates of return, this time derived exclusively from earnings functions. In most cases, the reported coefficient is the partial derivative of the logarithm of earnings with respect to years of schooling, years of labour market experience or age, being held constant. As noted earlier, the resulting rate of return is private and does not refer to any particular educational level. In poor countries, however, it must refer to the typical year of primary education as the mode of years of schooling distribution corresponds to this level. It is in this sense that the rates of return reported in Table III are underestimates of the true profitability of education at the lower educational level as they incorporate the implicit assumption of foregone earnings at an early age.

Table IV provides a summary of earnings-functions derived rates of return by country type. Again the same overall pattern is observed, namely the returns decline with the level of economic development.

On qualifications and controversies

The 'rate of return' subject is still highly controversial in the literature, although it is now more widely accepted than, say, 15 years ago. Let us give a brief summary of the major objections raised against the usefulness of rates of return as a tool for the formulation of educational policy, along with the answer of the proponents of this concept.

Data quality

This is a problem common in all empirical work and the rate of return estimation makes no exception to it. In the above international comparison. I would put greatest faith in the estimates referring to the United States and the United Kingdom, since I know these numbers come from official census statistics using rigorous sampling techniques covering the population as a whole. At the same time I would put least faith in the rate of return estimates for Yugoslavia, the information coming from a short article where the reporting of the exact sampling procedures, response errors etc. cannot be described in detail. This does not mean, however, that one has to dismiss such estimates as unreliable. The criterion here is that the particular author and/or journal referee/or PhD thesis committee felt the quality of the work was suitable for 'publication' (in the wider sense of the term).

In some country cases I had a choice between alternative estimates from several authors using different estimation procedures or sample bases. The rates of return I retained in such cases were from the study that in my opinion was the best in terms of comparability to the rest.

Table III   **The percent increment in earnings associated with one extra year of schooling**

Country	Year	$\dfrac{\delta \ln Y}{\delta S}$	Source
Africa			
Ethiopia	1972	8.0	Hoerr (1974)
Kenya	1970	16.4	Johnson (1972)
Morocco	1970	15.8	Psacharopoulos (1977a)
Asia			
Malaysia	1978	22.8	Lee (1980)
Singapore	1974	8.0	Fong (1976)
S. Vietnam	1964	16.8	Stroup & Hargrove (1969)
Thailand	1971	10.4	Chiswick (1976)
Taiwan	1972	6.0	Cannicott (1972)
Latin America			
Brazil	1970	19.2	Psacharopoulos (1980a)
Colombia	1973	20.5	Fields & Schultz (1977)
Mexico	1963	15.0	Carnoy (1967)
Intermediate			
Cyprus	1975	12.5	Demetriades & Psacharopoulos (1979)
Greece	1977	5.9	Psacharopoulos & Kazamias (1978)
Iran	1976	10.7	Scully (1979)
Advanced			
Canada	1971	5.2	Gunderson (1979)
France	1964	10.9	Riboud (1975)
Japan	1970	7.3	Kuratani (1973)
Sweden	1974	6.7	Gustafsson (1977)
United Kingdom	1975	7.8	Psacharopoulos (1980b)
United States	1973	8.2	Young & Jamison (1975)

Table IV   The returns to education irrespective of educational level, country group averages

Region or country type	*N*	Rate of return (%)
Africa	(3)	13.4
Asia	(5)	12.8
Latin America	(3)	18.2
LDC average	(11)	14.4
Intermediate	(3)	9.7
Advanced	(6)	7.7

Source: Table III.

Note: rate of return is private, estimated by an earnings function and refers to the average year of schooling.

The social productivity of education

This is the most often cited objection to rate of return estimations; namely, one cannot approximate the true social productivity of education by working with the earnings of employees by level of educational attainment. This common-sense objection has recently been weakened because of an accumulation of studies on the effect of education on farmers' productivity (see, e.g. Jamison & Lau, 1978). If more education (mostly at the basic level) contributes (other things being equal) to extra rice production, this extra rice is an ultimate demonstration of the social productivity of education.

At the higher levels of education where the production of, say, university graduates, cannot be measured in such tangible terms, objections here have been raised to the use of earnings as a proxy for productivity. These objections take specific labels and the major ones are known in the literature as 'screening or certification', 'bumping or job competition' and 'labour market segmentation'. All these are very sensible, common-sense hypotheses and have appealed to many analysts and politicians alike. However, these hypotheses are found wanting when put to the test.

Screening or certification [1]

What this theory says is that schools produce just diplomas or sheepskins helping the holder to get a privately well paid job, although the *social* payoff of the human investment he has undertaken might be minimal [2]. However, there exists one major objection to this view: when one makes the distinction between 'initial' and 'persistent' screening, it is very hard to find evidence corroborating the latter, namely that employers keep paying wages above the worker's productivity *after* they have the employee under their observation for some time [3]. Initial screening certainly exists, i.e. employers may hire someone on the basis of his expected productivity given his educational qualifications. But there is nothing wrong with it as, after all, it has an informational social value (see Psacharopoulos, 1980c).

Differential ability

Embedded in the screening argument is the ability factor: because those who have more education than others allegedly also have a higher level of ability, wage differentials are not solely due to learning, a great part of them being due to differential ability. This highly intuitive argument combined with some aggregate, cross-tabulation evidence by Becker (1964) and Denison (1967) resulted in the enthronement of this myth. However, micro-data plus scrutinisation of what 'ability' really means resulted in the highly counter-intuitive findings that ability differentials do not account for much of the variation in earnings (see Psacharopoulos 1975 and Griliches, 1979).

The job competition or bumping model

This is another highly intuitive notion, i.e. workers compete for jobs rather than wages, and those with more educational qualifications bump out from the labour queue the less qualified and get the job [1]. That is certainly true, but this view fails to show why such bumping should be socially wrong. If the more qualified perform better in the job they are in, this is socially healthy. There exists plenty of micro-evidence that the latter is likely to be the case as the more qualified earn more relatively to the less qualified even after one standardises for occupation.

Is there a dual labour market?

Another attack comes from the so-called dual or segmented labour market hypothesis (Gordon, 1972). According to it, education helps workers belonging to the 'primary segment' of the market (i.e. those in good jobs), but not those in the 'secondary segment' (i.e. those with inferior jobs). For several reasons the dual labour market fashion that started in the early 1970s has already faded away, although it is still echoed in some quarters (for a critique see Cain, 1976). In the first place, testing it is extremely difficult because the hypothesis has never been stated in a rigorous manner. Secondly, the separation of the upper from the lower segment is a major problem on its own. Where should one draw the dividing line between the two allegedly separate labour markets? Also, empirical attempts to test whatever bits and pieces of the theory are testable have failed to reject the orthodox functioning of labour markets (see Psacharopoulos, 1978 and McNabb & Psacharopoulos, 1981).

On social class

Another commonly held belief is that education serves the maintenance of the status quo from generation to generation (Bowles, 1972). Although this might be true to a large extent, it does not constitute a challenge to the use of earnings as a proxy for productivity. For two interesting recent results show that, first, family background (or social class) has only an indirect effect on earnings and this is via education. The direct effect of social background on earnings is rather weak. Also, it is those who acquire more education that are socially more upwardly mobile (Psacharopoulos, 1977b and Psacharopoulos & Tinbergen, 1978).

The role of the public sector

In some instances, rates of return have been estimated on the basis of public sector earnings. Since the public sector is the major employer of educated labour in developing countries, its non-profit maximising behaviour has been used as an argument against the use of earnings in rate of return computations. However, recent evidence from Brazil and Malaysia on public-private sector comparisons indicates that the contrary is likely to be the case. Namely, public sector based rate of return calculations are likely to underestimate the true returns to education, as judged from private sector employment (see Psacharopoulos, 1980d).

Graduate unemployment

One widespread view is that education produces unemployed graduates. This is a more serious challenge relative to the ones mentioned above, as it denies even the private benefits accruing to the individual investor. However, this argument is put in the right perspective when a distinction is made between the *incidence* and the *duration* of unemployment. Unemployment is high among young people; but in the majority of cases it lasts for a few months at the most. (For detailed evidence on the incidence and duration of unemployment as related to education in developing countries, see Psacharopoulos, 1980d.) Hence, one might consider the lack of employment immediately after graduation to be the reflection of a 'job search' process. And certainly it would be a mistake to reduce a whole age-earnings profile by the average rate of unemployment that mainly refers to young people.

Some policy implications

To the extent that the figures presented above, represent valid indicators of the true relative rate of return structure by level of education and country type, they have at least the following specific policy implications:

Policy implication no. 1

A look at Fig. 3 leaves no doubt that top priority should be given to primary education as a form of human resource investment.

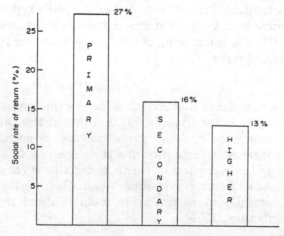

Fig. 3. **The social returns to investment in education by school level in LDCs.**
Source: as in Table I.
Note: LDCs refer to 22 African, Asian and Latin American countries.

Policy implication no. 2

Secondary and higher education are also socially profitable investments and therefore should be pursued alongside with primary education in a programme of balanced human resource development.

Policy implication no. 3

The large discrepancy between the private and social returns to investment in higher education (24 vs 13%, respectively) suggests there exists room for private finance at the university level. A shift of part of the cost burden from the state to the individual and his family is not likely to lead to a disincentive of investing in higher education given the present high private profitability margin.

Policy implication no. 4

As a country develops and/or the capacity of its educational system expands, the returns to education are definitely falling, although not to a large extent. Therefore, the fear of a drastic fall of the returns to education following educational expansion is unfounded.

Since this fear is a commonly held belief among educational planning practitioners, the following sub-section elaborates this point.

Educational expansion and rates of return

The evidence needed to investigate this topic is time-series rates of return, a luxury available in only a couple of countries. But even if one had a complete historical time trend of rates of return, this is no guarantee that their structure will be valid in the future beyond the available range of observations. Therefore, in making predictions in this respect one must also rely on a theory of some sort.

The international comparison presented earlier provides the basis for a cross-sectional reconstruction of time series by comparing the returns to education at different levels of economic development. From Table II one gets the following world wide picture:

Country type	Social returns to investment in education (%)		
	Primary	Secondary	Higher
LDC	27	16	13
Intermediate	16	14	10
Advanced	na	10	9

Namely, the returns do fall as a country passes from one stage of development to the next, which occurs *pari passu* with educational expansion. However, the decline of the returns is minimal when one considers the big educational expansion steps implied between rows in the above tabulation.

Also, the international comparison of earnings functions yields the following picture regarding the returns to the typical year of schooling by country type:

Country type	Rate of return
LDC	14
Intermediate	10
Advanced	8

Namely, the same conclusion is supported regarding the gradual fall of the overall rate of return associated with economic development (read, educational expansion).

Moving beyond these extremely aggregate figures, we can concentrate on what has happened within single countries where time-series evidence is available on the returns to education. One cannot be very choosey in this respect, so here is the picture of what has happened in one DC and one LDC.

The United States

Rate of return estimates for this country exist for every census year since 1939 and for every single year since 1970. Table V gives a summary picture of the evolution of the rate of return over nearly 40 years. The returns to education have been falling, although to a limited extent. The rate of return to secondary education fluctuates since 1959 at above the 10% level. The rate of return to higher education has been virtually constant at the 11% level between 1939 and 1969, in spite of the tremendous college expansion that occurred during the 1960's. Thereafter, it seems to be dropping, although there exists great controversy in the literature on the validity and interpretation of this decline [5].

Table V   Time series returns to education in the United States (%)

Year	Secondary	Higher
1939	18.2	10.7
1949	14.2	10.6
1959	10.1	11.3
1969	10.7	10.9
1970	11.3	8.8
1971	12.5	8.0
1972	11.3	7.8
1973	12.0	5.5
1974	14.8	4.8
1975	12.8	5.3
1976	11.0	5.3

Source: 1939-69 social rates from Carnoy & Marenbach (1975, table 2).
        1970-76 private rates from Psacharopoulos, (1980e, table 4).

The apparent 'puzzle' of the stability of the returns to education in the presence of educational expansion has been explained in terms of supply and demand terms, namely the demand for educated labour keeps pace with a rapidly increasing supply, the end result being a near constant rate of return (see, e.g. Welch, 1970). Or, to put it in Tinbergen's (1975) terms, this phenomenon can be explained in terms of a 'race' between education (supply curve shifting to the right) and technology (demand curve shifting to the right), as shown in Fig. 4.

Colombia

As shown in Table VI the structure of the Colombian labour force has shown a dramatic improvement within a decade, the proportion of university graduates doubling between 1964 and 1974. The question is what happened to the rate of return during this period?

As expected, the rates of return have in fact fallen (Table VII) although investment in education at all levels remains a highly profitable activity.

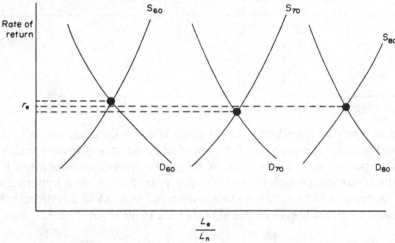

Fig. 4. A hypothetical 'race' between education and technology resulting in a more or less constant rate of return to education over time. S = supply curve; D = demand curve; L = labour; r = rate of return. Subscripts: e = educated; n = non-educate; 60, 70, 80 = year.

Table VI   The changing educational structure of the Colombian labour force (%)

Educational level	1964	1974
Illiterates	5.0	3.5
Primary school	57.3	45.4
Secondary school	29.5	34.8
Higher education	8.2	16.3

Source: Bourgignon (1980, table 1).

Table VII   The returns to education in Colombia by educational level

Educational level	1963-66	1974
Primary	53.1	36.0
Secondary	31.7	21.9
Higher	29.2	18.5

Source: based on Bourgignon (1980, table 5). Rates are private calculated by the short-cut method.

Additional evidence from earnings functions analysis corroborates this result:

Year	Rate of return
1963-66	19.8
1965	17.3
1971	16.7
1974	15.1

Source: Bourgignon (1980, table 4).

An earlier analysis by Dougherty (1971) using 1963-66 data has actually simulated the behaviour of the rate of return as a function of educational expansion in Colombia. Fig. 5 shows the expected path of the rate of return to secondary education if enrolments followed the historical growth rate of 10% per year (path A) or a hypothetical 15% rate (path B). As expected, the returns to education fall but not so drastically that this type of investment becomes socially unprofitable in a 16-year interval.

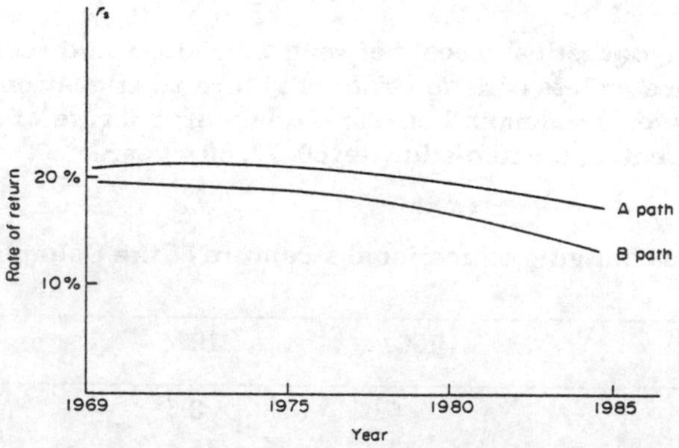

Fig. 5.   An actual simulation of the social rate of return to secondary education in Colombia as a function of enrolments. Note: figure is approximate, r_s = rate of return to secondary education; A path = based on the assumption of a 10% per year historical expansion of enrolments; B path = based on a hypothetical 15% per year growth of enrolments.

This earlier analysis has also demonstrated using Colombian data the importance of the 'elasticity of substitution' between different types of educated labour in affecting the future structure of rates of return [6]. This concept measures the degree of easiness or flexibility that exists in a given economy to accommodate different labour skill mixes in production without affecting the relative labour rewards. The higher the value of the elasticity of substitution, the longer a present rate of return measure will remain valid in the future following educational expansion.

Table VIII **Estimates of the elasticity of substitution between highly trained and other labour (absolute values)**

Nature of study	Elasticity estimate	Author
Cross-section, 22 countries	1	OECD (1971)
Cross-section, 22 US States	3.3-9.0	Dougherty (1972)
Cross-section, 12 countries	4.8	Bowles (1969)
Cross-section, 18 countries	2.2	Psacharopoulos & Hinchliffe (1972)
Time series, USA 1956-68	3.8	Dresch (1976)
Cross-section, 22 countries	0.6-3.5	Fallon & Layard (1975)
Time series, USA 1929-68	4.9-6.1	Bernt & Christensen (1974)
Time series, USA	2.3	Freeman (1971)
Time series, USA 1900-63	1.5	Ullman (1972)

Source: As compiled from original sources by Tinbergen & Psacharopoulos (1980).

There exists an immense literature on empirical estimates of elasticities of substitution between different types of labour in a variety of country settings. As shown in Table VIII this elasticity is on the high side, i.e. well above the value of unity. This evidence supports a theory on the basis of which one can confidently plan for educational expansion without affecting the rate of return to the point of such investment becoming socially unprofitable. At least this is what might be expected in the medium term in LDCs where the returns to the lower levels of schooling are of such magnitude that the possibility of over-investing in education is extremely remote.

Acknowledgement

This paper is based on part II of a background document prepared for the 1980 World Development Report. (See T. King, Ed., *Education and Income*, World Bank Staff Working Paper No. 402, July 1980). The views expressed here are those of the author and should not be attributed to the World Bank.

Notes

1. This sub-section partly draws from Psacharopoulos (1980b) to which the reader is referred to for further elaboration of points.

2. For a formal analysis of the screening hypothesis see Arrow (1973). For empirical tests see Layard & Psacharpoulos (1974).

3. For a theoretical distinction and an empirical test between the 'weak' versus the 'strong' version of the screening hypothesis, see Psacharopoulos (1979).

4. For the main variant of this model see Thurow & Lucas (1972).

5. See Freeman (1976), Smith & Welch (1978) and the exchange in the Winter 1980 issue of the *Journal of Human Resources*.

6. See also Dougherty (1972).

References

Arrow, K. (1973) 'Higher education as a filter', *Journal of Public Economics,* July.

Bank of Italy (1972) *Quindicinale di Note e Commenti.* Anno VII, N. 162-63, 15 May.

Becker, G. (1960) 'Underinvestment in college education?', *American Economic Review*, May.

Becker, G. (1964) *Human Capital,* 1st edn (NBER).

Brent, E.R. & Christensen, L.R. (1974) 'Testing for the existence of a consistent aggregate index of labour inputs,' *American Economic Review,* p. 391.

Blandy, R. & Goldsworthy, T. (1973) 'Private returns to education in South Australia'. *Working Paper No. 3* (Institute of Labour Studies. The Flinders University of South Australia).

Blinder. A.S. (1976) 'On dogmatism in human capital theory'. *Journal of Human Resources,* Winter.

Bowles, S. (1969) *Planning Educational Systems for Economic Growth* (Harvard University Press).

Bowles, S. (1972) 'Schooling and inequality from generation to generation', *Journal of Political Economy,* May-June Supplement.

Bowman, M.J. (1966) 'The human investment revolution in economic thought'. *Sociology of Education* Vol. 39, No. 2.

Bourgignon, F. (1980) 'The role of education in the urban labour market during the process of development: the case of Colombia', paper presented at the *6th World Congress of the International Economic Association*, Mexico City, August.

Cain, G. (1976) 'The challenge of segmented labour market theories to orthodox theory: a survey', *Journal of Comic Literature,* December.

Carnoy, M. (1967) 'Earnings and schooling in Mexico', *Economic Development and Cultural Change*, July.

Carnoy, M. (1972) 'The rate of return to schooling and the increase in human resources in Puerto Rico', *Comparative Education Review*, February.

Carnoy, M. & Marenbach, D. (1975) 'The return to schooling in the United States', 1939-69, *Journal of Human Resources,* Summer.

Chiswick. C. (1976) 'On estimating earnings functions for LDCs'. *Journal of Development Economics,* pp. 67-78.

Clark, D. H. & Fong, P.E. (1970) 'Returns to schooling and training in Singapore', *Malayan Economic Review,* October.

Demetriades, E. & Psacharopoulos, G. (1979) 'Education and pay structure in Cyprus', *International Labour Review,* January-February.

Denison, E.G. (1967) *Why Growth Rates Differ?* (The Brookings Institution).

Dougherty, C.R.S. (1971) 'Optimal allocation of investment in education', in: Chenery, H. B. (Ed.) *Studies in Development Planning* (Harvard University Press).

Dougherty, C.R.S. (1972) 'Estimates of Labour Aggregation Functions', *Journal of Political Economy*, November.

Dresch, S.P. (1976) 'Demography, Technology and higher education', *Journal of Political Economy.*

Eicher J.C. & Levey-Garboua, L. (1979) *Economique de l'Education* (Paris, Economica).

Fallon P. & Layard, R. (1975) 'Capital-skill complementarity, income distribution and output accounting', *Journal of Political Economy.*

Fields, G.S. (1975) 'Higher education and income distribution in a less developed country', *Oxford Economic Papers,* July.

Fields G. S. & Schultz, T. P. (1977) 'Sources of income variation in Colombia: Personal and regional effects', *Paper No. 272* (Economic Growth Centre, Yale University).

Fong, P.E. (1976) 'Education, earnings and occupational mobility in Singapore' (ILO, World Employment Programme). *Paper WEP 2-18/WP 13.*

Freeman, R. (1971) 'The Market for College Trained Manpower' (Harvard University Press).

Freeman, R. (1976) *The Overeducated American* (London, Academic Press).

Gannicott, K. (1972) *Rates of return to education in Taiwan, Republic of China* (Planning Unit, Ministry of Education, Mimeo).

Gordon. D. (1972) *Theories of Poverty and Unemployment* (Lexington).

Griliches, Z. (1979) 'Sibling models and data in economics: beginnings of survey', *Journal of Political Economy,* October, Supplement.

Gunderson M. (1979) 'Earnings differentials between the public and private sectors', *Canadian Journal of Economics.* May.

Gustafsson, S. (1977) 'Rates of depreciation of human capital due to nonuse', *Working Paper No. 14.* (The Industrial Institute for Economic and Social Research).

Hallak, J. & Psacharpoulos, G. (1979) 'The role of education in labour recruitment and promotion practices in Indonesia'. *HEP Working Paper.*

Heyneman, S. (1980a) *The Status of Human Capital in Malawi,* March draft (World Bank, Education Department).

Heyneman, S. (1980b) 'Investment in Indian education: uneconomic?' *World Development*, pp. 145-163.

Hoerr, D. (1974) 'Educational returns and educational reform in Ethiopia'. *Easter Africa Economic Review,* December.

ILO (1974) *Sharing in Development: a Programme of Employment, Equity and Growth for the Philippines.*

Jallade, J. P. (1977) 'Basic education and income inequality in Brazil: the long term view', *Staff Working Paper No. 268* (World Bank).

Jamison D. & Lau, L. (1978) *Farmer education and farm efficiency*, (World Bank, mimeo).

Johnson, G. E. (1972) 'The determination of individual hourly earnings in urban Kenya'. *Paper No. 22* (Center for Research on Economic Development, University of Michigan).

Ketkar, S. L. (1974) 'Benefit-cost analysis, manpower training and the Sierra Leone educational system, no affiliation'.

Kreuger, A.O. (1972) R'ates of return to Turkish higher education', *Journal of Human Resources*, Fall.

Kuratani, M. (1973) 'A theory of training, earnings and employment: an application to Japan', *unpublished PhD dissertation*. Columbia University.

Layard R. & Psacharopoulos, G. (1974) 'The screening hypothesis and the returns to education', *Journal of Political Economy*.

Lee, K. H. (1980) 'Education earnings and occupational status in Malaysia 1978', *unpublished PhD dissertation,* London School of Economics.

McNabb R. & Psacharopoulos, G. (1981) 'Further evidence on the relevance of the labour market hypothesis for the UK', *Journal of Human Resources,* Summer.

Meulders, D. (1974) 'Coûts et avantages sociaux des dépenses d'enseignement: Un example belge', *Cahiers Economiques de Bruxells*, No. 2.

Mincer, J. (1974) *Schooling, Experience and Earnings* (NBER).

OECD (1971) *Occupational and Educational Structures of the Labour Force and Economic Development* (Paris OECD).

Pandit, H.N. (1976) 'Investment in Indian education: size, sources and effectiveness', *IIEP Occasional Paper No. 43.*

Pourhosseini M. (1979) 'The social and private rate of return to investment in education in Iran'. NEP Research Paper No. 89 (University of Birmingham).

Psacharpoulos, G. (1973) *Returns to Education: an International Comparison* (Jossey-Bass, Elsevier).

Psacharpoulos, G. (1976) 'Earnings determinants in a mixed labour market, in Van Ruckeghem', W. (ed). *Employment Problems and Policies in Developing Countries: the case of Morocco* (Rotterdam University Press).

Psacharopoulos, G. (1975) *Earnings and Education in OECD Countries,* (Paris, OECD).

Psacharopoulos, G. (1977a) 'Schooling, experience and earnings: the case of an LDC', *Journal of Development Economics,* pp. 39-48.

Psacharopoulos, G. (1977b) 'Family background, education and achievement', *British Journal of Sociology,* September.

Psacharopoulos, G. (1978) 'Labour market duality and income distribution: the case of the U.K.', in Krelle, W. & Shorrocks, A. (eds), *Personal Income Distribution* (Amsterdam, North-Holland).

Psacharopoulos, G. (1979) 'On the weak versus the strong version of the screening hypothesis', *Economic Letters*.

Psacharopoulos, G. (1980a) *Unpublished Estimates using the 1970 Brazilian 1 percent Census Tape* (London School of Economics).

Psacharopoulos, G. (1980b) 'Educational planning and the labour market', *European Journal of Education*, 15, pp. 201-220.

Psacharopoulos, G. (1980c) 'Qualifications and employment at IDS', Sussex, *IDS Bulletin.*

Psacharopoulos, G. (1980d) *Higher Education in Developing Countries: a Cost-Benefit Analysis* (World Bank, Education Department.)

Psacharopoulos, G. (1980e) 'Spending on education in an era of economic stress', *Journal of Educational Finance.*

Psacharopoulos, G. & Hinchliffe, K. (1972) 'Further evidence on the elasticity of substitution among different types of educated labour', *Journal of Political Economy.*

Psacharopoulos, G. & Kazamias, A. (1978) *Report of the Post-Secondary Education Study Team,* (Greek Ministry of Education, in Greek).

Psacharopoulos, G. & Layard, R. (1979) 'Human capital and earnings: British evidence and a critique', *Review of Economic Studies,* July.

Psacharopoulos, G. & Tinbergen, J. (1978) 'On the explanation of schooling occupation and earnings: some alternative path analyses', *De Economist,* Vol. 126, No. 4.

Quintas, J. R. & Sanmartin, J. (1978) 'Aspectos economicos de la education', *Informaçion Comerical Española,* May.

Riboud, M (1975) 'An analysis of the income distribution in France', paper presented at the *Workshop on the Economics of Education,* London School of Economics.

Schultz, T. W. (1961) 'Investment in human capital', *American Economic Review,* March.

Scully, G. W. (1979) *Economic development, income and wealth inequality,* Southern Methodist University (mimeo).

Smith, J. P. & Welch. F. (1978) 'The overeducated American?' A review article, *paper P-6253.* The Rand Corporation.

Stroup, R. H. & Hargrove, M. M. (1969) 'Earnings and education in rural South Vietnam', *Journal of Human Resources,* Spring.

Strumlin, S. G. (1929) 'The economic significance of national education'. *The Planned Economy,* reprinted in UNESCO, *Readings in the Economics of Education,* 1968.

Thurow, L. & Lucas, R. (1972) *The American Distribution of Income: A Structural Problem* (Joint Economic Committee, U.S. Congress).

Tinbergen, J. (1975) *Income Distribution: Analysis and Policies* (Amsterdam, North-Holland).

Tinbergen, J. & Psacharopoulos, G. (1980) *Long Range Educational Perspectives in OECD Countries,* mimeo (Paris, OECD).

Thomas, H. (1976) 'Labour markets and educational planning in Yugoslavia', *Economic Analysis and Workers' Management,* Vol. 10, No. 1-2.

Ullman, C. (1972) 'The growth of professional occupations in the American labour force', 1900-1963, *unpublished PhD dissertation.* Columbia University.

Umetani, S. (1977) 'The college labour market and the rate of return to higher education in Postwar Japan', 1954-1973, *unpublished PhD dissertation,* University of Wisconsin-Madison.

Welch, F. (1970) 'Education in production', *Journal of Political Economy.*

Young, K. H. & Jamison D. (1975) 'The effects of schooling and literacy on earnings', paper presented at the *3rd World Congress of the Econometric Society,* Toronto.

34. Returns to Education: A Further International Update and Implications

George Psacharopoulos

Abstract

This paper updates evidence on the returns of investment in education by adding estimates for new countries and refining existing estimates to bring the total number of country cases to over 60. The new cross-country evidence confirms and reinforces earlier patterns, namely, that returns are highest for primary education, the general curricula, the education of women, and countries with the lowest per capita income. The findings have important implications for directing future investment in education which, for efficiency and equity purposes, should concentrate on these priority areas.

Estimates of the profitability of investment in human capital have proliferated since the field was established in the early 1960s. Such estimates have been used to illuminate a number of key development issues, like the explanation of past economic growth rates (Schultz [74]), the optimality of resource allocation within education and between education and other sectors (Dougherty and Psacharopoulos [17]), the determinants of income distribution (Chiswick and Mincer [13]), and the behavior of students and their families as investors and consumers of education (Freeman [21]).

One of the earliest questions following the human capital revolution in economic thought was: If education is a form of capital, what is the rate of return to it? This led to a related question: How does the profitability of investment in education compare to investment in physical capital? Such comparisons, it was thought, would serve as ex ante signals to guide resource allocation between two forms of capital in developmental planning. They have also been used ex post to explain a great part of the "residual" that puzzled scholars examining economic growth in the 1950s.

Other questions follow. What priority should be given to primary versus university education? Allocative decisions have to be made within education, and rates of return have been used as guides to such decisions. Furthermore, a given level of education can offer various types of curricula — for example, secondary general versus secondary technical — and estimates of the profitability of investment by type of schooling can illuminate decisions on where the relative emphasis should lie.

If human capital investment is like any other type of investment, diminishing returns should apply to it. Hence, another major issue in the early days was whether and by how much the yield on human capital investment would decline following the expansion of education. When the human investment revolution began, there was no time-series estimates of the rate of return.

George Psacharopoulos: 'Returns to Education: A Further International Update and Implications' from *THE JOURNAL OF HUMAN RESOURCES* (April, 1985) Vol. XX, No. 4, pp. 583-597. © 1985 by the Regents of the University of Wisconsin System.

The contrast between the social and private rate of return could highlight the extent of public subsidization of education. The size of the private returns could also explain the individual demand for certain types of schooling. And since the private rate of return is the price one receives on his or her human resource endowments, it could further explain personal income distribution.

For all the above reasons researchers in the United States, and later around the world, began estimating the returns of investment in education. The first rate of return to education collection appeared in the Summer 1967 issue of the *Journal of Human Resources* and covered only four countries-Mexico, Italy, the United States, and Great Britain. Three years later Hansen [28] produced another review covering 14 countries as background for an OECD conference on education. My 1973 book [56] attempted to derive rate-of-return patterns based on evidence from 32 countries. Seven years later I updated and expanded the rate-of-return estimates, covering 45 countries, as a background to the World Bank's *World Development Report* that dealt with human resources (Psacharopoulos [57]). Since that collection, further estimates have been published for additional countries or for more recent years in countries for which evidence on the returns to education already existed. As a result of the literature growth in this field, my "Rate of Return — New Estimates" file has become overly thick and unmanageable. Perhaps the time has come for another stock-taking exercise to determine if the earlier documented rate-of-return patterns have been maintained, or whether new ones are emerging. The enlarged and updated data set on which this paper is based covers 61 countries.

The evidence

The rate-of-return evidence has been organized into a set of master tables that appear in the Appendix. The tables correspond roughly to issues to be discussed in this paper. When several rate-of-return estimates were available for a given country, year, or level of education, I have selected for inclusion in the master tables the one that in my judgment would be most comparable to the rest. This was not an easy task since many authors of the original studies do not always state explicitly the nature of the sample used (for example, urban, rural, national) or the methodology according to which the estimates are made (especially what adjustments have been made on the benefits sides). Although correspondence with several authors has resulted in a more comparable set of figures, methodological and sample-reference differences remain. Hence, the reader should be cautious in attaching importance to one (or even two) percentage point differences in the returns across countries and years. Of course, greater reliance should be placed on within-country estimates (for example, by level of education or by gender) that are based on a common sample and methodology.

Most of the lengthy reference list is "marginal" in the sense that the reader can refer to Psacharopoulos [56, 58] to trace the original source of previously reviewed estimates. The reader is also referred to these earlier publications for details on the theoretical and methodological aspects of rate-of-return estimations.

Table 1 is a summary of the master table that provides estimates of average private and social returns by level of education for countries grouped by their level of economic development.[1]

The table confirms the earlier well-documented declining rate of return pattern by level of education. Primary education is the most profitable educational investment opportunity, followed by secondary education. This decline is the result of the interaction between the low cost of primary education (relative to other levels) and the substantial productivity differential between primary school graduates and those who are illiterate. The productivity of primary school graduates is not only proxied by their earnings, but has also been confirmed by studies using differences in physical output as an educational outcome.[2]

Table 1   Average returns to education by country type and level (percent).

Region/ Country Type	Social			Private		
	Primary	Secondary	Higher	Primary	Secondary	Higher
Africa	26	17	13	45	26	32
Asia	27	15	13	31	15	18
Latin America	26	18	16	32	23	23
Intermediate	13	10	8	17	13	13
Advanced	NA	11	9	NA	12	12

Source: Based on Appendix Table A-1, latest year available.

Note: NA = not available because of lack of a control group of illiterates.

Table 2   Index of public subsidization of education by level and region.

Region/Country Type	Educational Level		
	Primary	Secondary	Higher
Africa	92	51	157
Asia	58	13	9
Latin American	104	47	50
Intermediate	51	6	7
Advanced	NA	21	44

Source: Based on Appendix Table A-1, strictly comparable rates.

Notes: The subsidization index for a given level of education is defined as the percent by which the private rate of return exceeds the social rate. NA = not available.

The declining rate-of-return pattern is also observed across levels of per capita income. For example, the returns to any level of education are highest in Africa and lowest in the advanced industrial countries. This is explained by the relative scarcity of human-to-physical capital within each group of countries.

In all countries and levels of schooling, private returns exceed social returns because education is publicly subsidized. However, the private-public distortions are greatest in the poorest group of countries and in the higher levels of education (Table 2). Figure 1 illustrates this phenomenon for Africa. Whereas the social rates of return following a declining pattern by ascending level of education, the private rates are not only higher than social rates, but they increase after the secondary level.

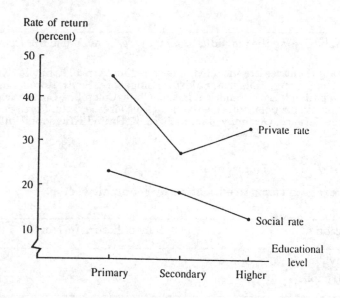

Figure 1   Differences between the private and social returns to education in Africa.
Source: Based on Appendix Table A-1, strictly comparable rates.

Table 3 gives means of the regression coefficient on years of schooling in a semi-log (Mincer-type) earnings function in which log earnings is a function of years of schooling, years of experience, and years of experience squared. The figures are interpreted as private returns to the typical year of education (that is, undifferentiated by level). Again, the declining pattern of the returns across country type is largely maintained.

Rate-of-return estimates in recent years have been refined in the sense that they are increasingly based on the earnings of those employed in the competitive sector of the economy where the benefits of education better reflect the worker's productivity. Table 4 shows that in studies where the returns have been differentiated by economic sector, the returns in the competitive setting exceed those in the noncompetitive sector by three percentage points. This means that previous estimates based on the earnings of workers in all sectors have in fact *under*estimated the returns to education. The inclusion of public-sector earnings in particular, because of the equalization policy of pay scales, flattens mean earnings differentials and, hence, depresses the returns of education.

Table 3   **Mincer-type returns to education by country type.**

Region/Country Type	Coefficient on Years of Schooling (percent)
Africa	13
Asia	11
Latin America	14
Intermediate	8
Advanced	9

Source: Master table listing the individual country rates is available from the author on request.

Note: The following countries are included in each region: Africa: Ethiopia, Kenya, Morocco, Tanzania; Asia: Hong Kong, Malaysia, Pakistan, Singapore, South Korea, South Vietnam, Sri Lanka, Taiwan, Thailand; Latin America: Brazil, Chile, Colombia, Costa Rica, El Salvador, Guatemala, Mexico, Venezuela; Intermediate: Cyprus, Greece, Iran, Portugal; Advanced: Australia, Canada, France, Germany, Japan, Sweden, United KIngdom, United States.

Table 4   **Average returns to education by economic sector.**

Sector Specification	Rate of Return (percent)
Competitive, private	13
Noncompetitive, public	10

Source: Master table listing individual countries is available from the author on request.

Note: The countries included in this table are Brazil, Colombia, Greece, Guatemala, Japan, Malaysia, Pakistan, Portugal, United Kingdom, Tanzania, and Venezuela.

For a variety of reasons, women in all countries earn on average substantially less than men. Because the rate of return is a relative concept, it should not be surprising if the profitability of investment in women's education is greater than that of men. This is, indeed, the case, as shown in Table 5, where in developing countries the Mincer-type average rate of return for women exceeds that for men by four percentage points. This rate-of-return differential in favor of women may be an underestimate because the rate of return to investment in women's education, as commonly calculated, does not take into account the increased probability of more educated women participating in the labor force. For example, Mohan [47] reports that in Colombia in 1984 the labor force participation rate of working-age women aged over 15 ranged from 31 percent for those who had no schooling to 53 percent for those with a university education.

Table 5   Average returns to education by gender (percent).

Country Group	Educational Level	Men	Women
All countries	Primary	19	17
	Secondary	16	21
	Higher	15	14
Developing countries	Overall	11	15

Source: Based on Appendix Table A-2.

It is commonly thought that introducing a vocational element in the secondary school curriculum, especially in developing countries, is conducive to economic development. But, as shown in Table 6, the returns to investment in traditional academic (general) curricula are greater on average than the returns to investment in specialized subjects. Again, this is due to the higher unit cost of producing technical graduates and the fact that graduates from both streams are absorbed equally well by the labor market.

Table 6   Average returns to alternative secondary school curricula.

Curriculum Type	Rate of Return (percent)
General, academic	16
Vocational, technical	12

Source: Master table listing individual countries is available from the author on request.

Note: Countries included in this table are Colombia, Cyprus, France, Indonesia, Liberia, Taiwan, and Tanzania.

The same pattern observed regarding the type of secondary school curriculum also applies to higher education programs. The high-cost specialities like agronomy exhibit low returns, whereas humanities and the social sciences exhibit high returns (Table 7).

Table 7   Average returns for selected university programs.

Program	Rate of Return (percent)
Economics	13
Law	12
Social sciences	11
Medicine	12
Engineering	12
Sciences, math, physics	8
Agriculture	8

Source: Based on Appendix Table A-3.

Rate-of-return estimates over time within countries are rare. What is even rarer are estimates based on the same sampling frame and methodology from year to year. In the country where the highest quality time series data exist, the United States, the returns have shown a remarkable stability over a 30-year period. For example, the social returns to higher education fluctuated around the 10-11 percent mark between 1939 and 1969 (Appendix Table A-1). In Japan, the corresponding returns fell from 6.4 to 5.7 percent in a seven-year period. In Great Britain, the returns remained virtually constant between 1971 and 1978. In Colombia, the returns to education (Mincer-type estimation) declined from 17.6 to 14.4 percent between 1973 and 1978, while in the same five-year period the percentage with higher education in the labor force has more than doubled (from 6 percent in 1973 to 13 percent in 1978, based on Mohan [48], pp. 40, 43).

This relative stability of average returns over time has been explained by the fact that the demand for educated manpower has kept increasing along with the supply of education (a phenomenon Jan Tinbergen has lucidly described as the race between technology and education [80]).

Table 8 presents comparisons of average returns to physical and human capital in two time periods. Given the roughness of the data, the evidence suggests that in advanced countries the gap has narrowed somewhat between the returns to physical and human investment, and the convergence indicates that a 10 percent return may be indicative of some equilibrium. In developing countries, however, there is a clear advantage of human versus physical capital investments. Of course, this advantage diminished from the 1960s to the 1970s, following the relatively greater investment in developing countries.

Table 8   **Returns to human and physical capital by type of country (percent).**

Type of country	1960s			1970s		
	Human		Physical	Human		Physical
Developing	20	>	15	15	>	13
Advanced	8	<	10	9	<	11

Source: 1960s from Psacharopoulos [56], Table 5.3; 1970s from Psacharopoulos [64], Table 8.

Note: Developing countries included in the table are Mexico, Colombia, Venezuela, Chile, Brazil, India, Philippines, Ghana, Kenya, Uganda, and Nigeria. Advanced countries are United States, United Kingdom, Canada, Netherlands, and Belgium.

Implications

These rate-of-return patterns have several implications for the shaping of educational policy, especially in developing countries.

Underinvestment exists at all levels of education, especially in Africa. This proposition is supported by evidence that the social returns to education in the region are well above any plausible social discount rate used in project evaluation.

Primary schooling remains the number-one priority for investment. This is evidenced by the fact that the social rate of return to primary education exceeds by several percentage points the returns to secondary and higher education.

The degree of public subsidization of higher education is such that there is considerable margin for reducing subsidy levels. This stems from the calculations that a reduction of public subsidies to higher education would drive down the private rate closer to the social rate, still leaving an attractive return to private investment. The savings from the reduction of university subsidies could be used to expand primary education.

Reducing public subsidies to higher education and reallocating them to primary education would have additional benefits that can be viewed as equitable. To a great extent, universities are attended by those who can afford to pay, whereas the less well-off portion of the population would now find educational opportunities more open and accessible.

Expanding the provision of school places to cover women is not only equitable but socially efficient as well. Although counter-intuitive, this proposition is based on the evidence that the rate of return to women's education is at least as attractive as the rate of return on investment for men.

Within the secondary or university level, the general curricula or programs offer as good investment opportunities as the more vocational pursuits. This is because the higher unit costs of vocational/technical education depress the social rate of return to this type of schooling.

Judging from past trends and the degree of underinvestment in education in developing countries, the fears that further educational expansion would lead to unemployed graduates or would lower social rates of return are unfounded. This proposition is based on time series evidence which shows that rates of return have not changed much as educational investment increases.

The traditionally estimated returns on the basis of observed earnings may underestimate the true social profitability of education. The flatness of civil service pay scales depresses the size of earnings differentials on which early rate-of-return estimates were based.

Finally, it should be mentioned that the conclusions presented here are based on estimates of the returns to education that follow the accepted methodology over the past 25 years. But when one adds the series of qualifications (such as externalities and nonmarket effects) recently enumerated by Haveman and Wolfe [29], then all of the above implications are strengthened.

* I am grateful to all those who over the years have kept me informed on their work, and especially those who by correspondence provided clarifications so that the figures appearing here are more

comparable. The views expressed are those of the author and should not be attributed to the World Bank. [Manuscript received February 1985, accepted April 1985.]

Notes

1. All figures in the text tables are simple arithmetic averages of the corresponding rates in the master table.

2. See D. Jamison and L. Lau, *Farmer Education and Farm Efficiency* (Baltimore: Johns Hopkins University Press, 1982).

References

Many of these citations are not referenced in the text but are included for the benefit of other researchers.

1. A. D. Adamson and J. M. Reid. (1980) 'The Rate of Return to Post-Compulsory Education During the 1970's: An Empirical Study for Great Britain.' United Kingdom, Department of Education and Science, Mimeo.

2. Lascelles Anderson. (1980) 'Rates of Return to Human Capital: A Test Using El Salvador Data.' *American Economic Review* 70 (May): 138-41.

3. A. Armand. (1976) 'The Rate of Return to Education in Iran.' Ph.D. dissertation. University of Maryland.

4. J. Armitage and R. Sabot. (1984) 'Efficiency and Equity Implications of Subsidies of Secondary Education in Kenya.' In *Modern Tax Theory for Developing Countries*, eds. D. Newbery and N. Stern. Washington: Development Research Department, The World Bank, Mimeo.

5. Moo-Ki Bai. (1977) *Education, Workers' Behavior and Earnings: A Case Study of Manufacturing Workers in Korea*. Seoul: Institute of Economic Research, Seoul National University, August. (Also in *Seoul National University Economic Review* (December): 1-69.)

6. M. Baldares-Carazo. (1980) 'The Distribution of Income and Wages in Costa Rica.' Ph.D. thesis, University of Birmingham.

7. A. Berhanu. (1982) 'Modeling Manpower in Development Planning: Methodological and Empirical Problems with Sudanese Illustrations.' Ph.D. dissertation, University of Pennsylvania.

8. M. Boissiere, J. B. Knight, and R. Sabot. (1984) 'Earnings, Ability and Cognitive Skills.' Washington: Development Research Department, The World Bank, (April). Mimeo.

9. Botswana Ministry of Finance and Development Planning. (1984) 'Botswana: Education and Human Resource Sector Assessment.' USAID, (June). Mimeo.

10. F. Bourgignon. (1980) 'The Role of Education in the Urban Labor-Market During the Process of Development: The Case of Colombia.' Paper presented at the 6th World Congress, International Economic Association, Mexico City, (August).

11. Martin Carnoy. (1972) 'The Rate of Return of Schooling and the Increase in Human Resources in Puerto Rico.' *Comparative Education Review* 16 (February): 68-86.

12. Barry R. Chiswick and P. W. Miller. (1984) 'Immigrant Generation and Income in Australia.' Department of Economics, University of Western Ontario, Mimeo.

13. Barry R. Chiswick and Jacob Mincer.. (1972) 'Time Series Changes in Personal Income Inequality in the United States from 1939, with Projections to 1985.' *Journal of Political Economy* 80. (May-June): S34-71.

14. Carmel U. Chiswick. (1977) 'On Estimating Earnings Functions for LDCs.' *Journal of Development Economics* 4. (March): 67-78.

15. W. Clement. (1984) *Kinkimmenverteilung und Qualifikation: Empirische Ergebnisse aus dem osterreichischen Mikrozensus 1981*. Signum-Verlag.

16. W. Clement, M. Tessaring, and C. Weisshuhn. (1983) *Ausbildung und Einkommen in der Bundesrepublik Deutschland*. Beitrab 80. Nurnberg: Institut fur Arbeitsmarkt- und Berufsforschung der Bundesanstalt.

17. Christopher Dougherty and George Psacharopoulos. (1977) 'Measuring the Cost of Misallocation of Investment in Education.' *Journal of Human Resources* 12. (Fall): 446-59.

18. J. Ducci and K. Terrell. (1980) 'Earnings and Occupational Attainment in a Developing Country.' Department of Economics, Cornell University. Paper presented at the Econometric Society Meetings, (September).

19. A. Dumlao and A. Arcelo. (1979) 'Financing Private Education.' *FAPE Review* 16. (July-October).

20. A. C. Edwards. (1983) 'Wage Indexation, Real Wages and Unemployment.' Washington: Development Research Department, The World Bank, Mimeo.

21. Richard B. Freeman. (1976) *The Overeducated American*. New York: Academic Press.

22. A. Gabregiorgis. (1979) 'Rate of Return on Secondary Education in the Bahamas.' Ph.D. thesis, Department of Educational Administration, University of Alberta.

23. K. Gannicott. (1984) 'Male and Female Earnings in a Developing Economy: The Case of Taiwan.' Department of Economics, University of New South Wales. Mimeo.

24. N. Gebre-ab. (1983) 'Cost-Benefit Analysis of Education in Lesotho.' Lesotho Ministry of Education, (November).

25. S. E. Guisinger, J. W. Henderson, and G. W. Scully. (1984) 'Earnings, Rates of Return to Education and the Earnings Distribution in Pakistan.' *Economics of Education Review*. (December).

26. E. Gutkind. (1984) 'Earnings Functions and Returns to Education in Sri Lanka.' Geneva: International Labor Office. Mimeo.

27. K. A. Hamdani. (1977) 'Education and the Income Differentials: An Estimation for Rawalpindi City.' *Pakistan Development Review* 16. (Summer): 144-64.

28. W. Lee Hansen. (1970) 'Patterns of Rates of Returns in Education: Some International Comparisons.' In *Conference on Policies for Educational Growth*. Paris: OECD. Mimeo, DAS/EID/70.3.

29. Robert H. Haveman and Barbara L. Wolfe. (1984) 'Schooling and Economic Well-Being: The Role of Nonmarket Effects.' *Journal of Human Resources* 19. (Summer): 377-407.

30. J. W. Henderson. (1983) 'Earnings Functions for the Self-Employed.' *Journal of Development Economics* 13. (August-October): 97-102.

31. J. W. Henderson and G. W. Scully. (1984) 'The Impact of the Elasticity of Substitution on Rates of Return to Education.' Waco, TX: Baylor University. Mimeo.

32. W. J. House and O. Stylianou. (1981) 'Population, Employment Planning and Labor Force Mobility in Cyprus: An Interim Report.' Nicosia: Department of Statistics and Research, Ministry of Finance,. (1982)

33. Fan-Sing Hung. (1982) 'Private and Social Rates of Return on Investment in Education in Hong Kong.' Master's thesis, School of Education, Chinese University of Hong Kong.

34. J-P. Jarousse. (1984) 'La Rentabilite des Etudes en France entre 1970 et 1977.' Paris: CREDOC. Mimeo.

35. Chang Yong Jeong. (1974) 'Rates of Return on Investment in Education: The Case of Korea.' KDI Working Paper No. 7048, (September).

36. Hwai-I Juang. (1972) 'Rates of Return to Investment in Education in Taiwan and Their Policy Implications: A Cost-Benefit Analysis of the Academic High School and the Vocational High School.' D. Ed. thesis, Teachers College, Columbia University.

37. J. B. Knight and R. Sabot. (1981) 'The Returns to Education: Increasing with Experience or Decreasing with Expansion.' *Oxford Bulletin of Economics and Statistics* 43. (February): 51-71.

38. Kwok-Chuen Kwok. 'An Analysis of the Earnings Structure in Hong Kong.' M. Phil. thesis, Graduate School, Chinese University of Hong Kong, 19??.

39. Yong Woo Lee. (1984) 'Human Capital and Wage Determination in South Korea.' Kyungbook National University.

40. L. Levy-Garboua and A. Mingat. (1979) 'Les Taux de Rendement de l'Education.' Ch. 5 in *Economique de l'Education*, eds. J-C. Eicher and L. Levy-Garboua. Paris: Economica.

41. Liberia Ministry of Planning and Economic Affairs. (1983) 'Liberia: Education and Training Sector Assessment.' Joint Committee for the Government of Liberia/USAID Education, Training and Human Resources Assessment, (December) Mimeo.

42. Pak-Wai Liu and Yeu-Chim Wong. (1984) 'Human Capital, Occupation and Earnings.' Department of Economics, Chinese University of Hong Kong.

43. D. Mazumdar. (1981) *The Urban Labor Market and Income Distribution: A Study of Malaysia*. Oxford: Oxford University Press.

44. P.W. Miller. (1982) 'The Rate of Return to Education: The Evidence from the 1976 Census.' *Australian Economic Review*. (3rd quarter).

45. A. Mingat and J-P Jarousse. (1985) 'Analyse Economique et Fondements Sociaux des Disparites de Salaires en France.' Paris: CREDOC. Mimeo.

46. A. Mingat, J-P. Tan, and M. Hoque. (1984) 'Recovering the Cost of Public Higher Education in LDCs: To What Extent Are Loan Schemes an Efficient Instrument?' Washington: Education Department, The World Bank. Mimeo.

47. R. Mohan. (1984) 'Labor Force Participation in a Developing Metropolis, Does Sex Matter?' Paper presented at the Latin American Econometric Society Meeting, Bogota. Washington: Development Research Department, The World Bank, (July) Mimeo.

48. — (1981) *The Determinants of Labor Earnings in Developing Metropoli: Estimates from Bogota and Cali, Colombia*. Staff Working Paper No. 498. Washington: The World Bank.

49. R. M. Morgan, ed. (1971) *System Analysis for Educational Change: The Republic of Korea*. Tallahassee: Florida State University.

50. K. Okachi. (1980) 'An Analysis of Economic Returns to Educational Investment: Its Role in Determining the Significance of Educational Planning in Japan.' Ph.D. dissertation, Florida State University.

51. — (1983) 'An Analysis of Economic Returns to Japan's Higher Education and Its Application to Educational Finance.' *Journal of Education Finance* 9. (Fall).

52. Funkoo Park. (1976) 'Return to Education in Korea.' *Journal of Economic Development* 1, No. 1.

53. Funkoo Park and Seil Park. (1984) *Wage Structure in Korea*, Korea Development Institute.

54. Seil Park. (1980) 'Wages in Korea: Determination of the Wage Levels and the Wage Structure in a Dualistic Labor Market.' Ph.D. dissertation, Cornell University.

55. M. Pourhosseini. (1980) 'Investment in Human Capital and Educational Planning in Iran.' Ph.D. thesis, Department of Economics, University of Birmingham.

56. George Psacharopoulos. (1973) *Returns to Education: An International Comparison*. San Francisco: Elsevier-Jossey Bass.

57. — (1980) *Higher Education in Developing Countries: A Cost-Benefit Analysis*. Staff Working Paper No. 440. Washington: The World Bank.

58. — (1981a) 'Returns to Education: An Updated International Comparison.' In *Education and Income*, ed. T. King. Staff Working Paper No. 402. Washington: The World Bank, 1980. Reprinted in *Comparative Education* 17: 321-41.

59. — (1981b) 'Education and the Structure of Earnings in Portugal.' *De Economist* 129: 532-45.

60. — (1982a) 'Indonesia: Manpower Considerations in the Energy Sector.' Washington: Education Department, The World Bank, (May) Mimeo.

61. — (1982b) 'Peru: Assessing Priorities for Investment in Education and Training.' Washington: Education Department, The World Bank. Mimeo.

62. — (1982c) 'Upper Volta: Is It Worth Spending on Education in a 'High-Cost' Country?' Washington: Education Department, The World Bank. Mimeo.

63. — (1982d) 'Earnings and Education in Greece, 1960-1977.' *European Economic Review* 17: 333-47.

64. — (1982e) 'The Economics of Higher Education in Developing Countries.' *Comparative Education Review* 26. (June): 139-59.

65. — (1983a) 'Sex Discrimination in the Greek Labor Market.' *Modern Greek Studies* 1. (October): 339-58.

66. — (1983b) 'Education and Private Versus Public Sector Pay.' *Labour and Society* 8. (April-June): 123-34.

67. George Psacharopoulos and W. Loxley. (1985) *Diversified Secondary Education and Development: Evidence from Colombia and Tanzania*. Baltimore: Johns Hopkins University Press.

68. George Psacharopoulos and A. Zabalza. (1984) 'The Effect of Diversified Schools on Employment Status and Earnings in Colombia.' *Economics of Education Review* 3, No. 3.

69. J. R. Quintas. (1983) *Economia y Educacion*. Piramide.

70. M. Riboud. (1978) *Accumulation du Capital Humain*. Paris: Economica.

71. E. Rodriguez. (1981) *Rentabilidad y crecimiento de la Educacion Superior en Colombia*. Facultad de Estudios Interdisciplinarios, Pontificia Universidad Javeriana.

72. P. N. Savvides. 'Work Experience and Earnings Differentials: The Case of Cyprus.' M. A. thesis, Department of Economics, Southern Illinois University, 19??.

73. T. P. Schultz. (1979) 'Conventional Income Equations for Rural and Urban Workers by Current Residence and Birthplace: Colombia 1973.' Yale University, (April) Mimeo.

74. T. W. Schultz. (1961) 'Education and Economic Growth.' In *Social Forces Influencing American Education*. Chicago: National Society for the Study of Education.

75. K. Sethasathien. (1977) 'Thailand: Using Cost-Benefit Analysis to derive the Rates of Return in Different Levels of Education.' Ph.D. dissertation, College of Education, Florida State University.

76. Somalia Ministry of National Planning. (1984) 'Somalia: Education and Human Resources Sector Assessment.' USAID, (January) Mimeo.

77. F. Steier. (1985) 'Educational Policies in Venezuela: An Appraisal.' Ph.D. dissertation, Columbia University, in progress.

78. D. A. Sumner. (1981) 'Wage Functions and Occupational Selection in a Rural Less Developed Country Setting.' *Review of Economics and Statistics* 63. (November): 513-19.

79. J. B. C. Tilak. (1980) 'Inequality in Returns to Education.' Ph.D. dissertation, Delhi School of Economics.

80. J. Tinbergen. (1975) *Income Distribution: Analysis and Policies*. Amsterdam: North-Holland.

81. G. Weisshuhn and W. Clement. (1982) 'Analyse de qualifikations spezifischen Verdienstrelationen in der Bundesrepublik Deutschland auf der Basis der Bescheftigtenstatistik 1974/1977.' *Mitteilungen aus der Arbeitmarkt und Berufsforschung* 1: 36-49.

35.   The Diploma Disease Revisited
Ronald Dore

I suppose, if narcissism could overcome boredom, I ought to sit down and read through *The Diploma Disease* [1976] to make sure, but I do not **think** there are many passages which I would blush to read because I now think I got them badly wrong. I am not aware of having undergone any major intellectual conversion since I wrote the book, but I **have** learned things that would make me want to alter some of the things I said, and to put some things differently. I ended the preface by saying that many of the 'conclusions' which I presented in that book were in fact hypotheses which the research of IDS colleagues would doubtless throw some light on. Indeed it has.

Before I explain how, perhaps I should begin by summarising what the book originally tried to say. Briefly, the 'message' was as follows:

> the 'bureaucratisation of economic life' in all modern societies is making selection for jobs/careers by educational attainment more and more universal. From this fact flows a variety of consequences diagrammed in the chart below:

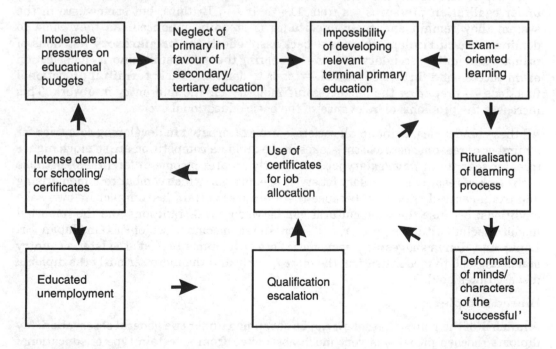

Ronald Dore: 'The Diploma Disease Revisited', The Institute of Development Studies *BULLETIN* (1980), Vol. II, No. 2, pp. 55-61.

First, the level of qualification required for any particular job tends to rise over time, because of overproduction of job-seekers (educated unemployment) and competition between professional bodies and employing organisations to 'tap the pool of talent' at the highest possible point. So there is more and more schooling (over and above the generally desirable extension to basic education) for reasons which have nothing to do with the actual knowledge acquisition necessary for **doing** jobs. Nor does it have much to do with personal development and self-fulfilment, or learning for its own sake, since a lot of the schooling is 'reluctant schooling' — the ritual acquisition of qualifications necessary to **get** jobs. (The triad of alternative education purposes — a) learning for self-fulfilment, for personal development, for 'its own sake', etc; b) learning to **do** jobs; and c) learning to **get** jobs — plays an important role in the book.)

All this reluctant schooling is very expensive to society. And it may well produce people at the highest levels who — because of the reluctant and ritual nature of their prolonged schooling — have attitudes towards work, and towards self-advancement by competitive conformity to external (rather than internalised) authorities, which are far from likely to transform them into productive, innovative, public spirited managers and administrators. It also has 'incapacitating' consequences at lower levels because, as graduating final certificates become more and more important for life changes so, too, do selection exams within the educational system. The crucial selection exams which track people and determine what sort of final diplomas they can get may be postponed under egalitarian pressures (as from 11+ to 16+ in Britain), but somewhere in the system they remain and their importance is steadily enhanced. As they come to dominate the curriculum, there is a 'backwash' effect: the **preparatory** functions of primary and junior secondary schools — preparing the 'successful' minority for selection exam success and further education — tends to dominate their **terminal** educational functions — preparing the 'unsuccessful' majority for life and entry into work. This increases the problems of 'relevance' of the basic educational cycle.

All these tendencies, found in all societies, are exacerbated in developing countries for a number of reasons: because the stakes in the diploma competition are so much higher (greater scarcity of wage/salary jobs and vastly greater income differentials); because of the lack of resources necessary for styles of education which combat rote-memorising and exam-centred ritualism; because there are less certain learning-for-its-own-sake traditions; because the wide cultural gap between rural traditions and the imported modern sector culture is greater, and so on. In fact a comparison of Britain, Japan, Sri Lanka and Kenya suggested a systematic 'late development effect': the later a country starts its push to modernisation, the more quickly and the more seriously the diploma disease takes hold.

Biased sample?

A number of the points that follow can be subsumed under one general observation. My diploma disease model was very much abstracted from a certain type of educational system. The British and the British-legacy systems of Sri Lanka, Kenya and Tanzania were my chief examples, together with those of Japan and China. Those systems have in common the following features:

— a high proportion of higher education in general arts and science rather than in professional subjects;

— quite strict rationing by ability, rather than by the purse, for higher education opportunity;

— a system of national examinations with universal standards to use for that ability selection;

— well developed systems of career bureaucracy (at least in government, and to varying degrees in the private sector) and a tradition of the 'generalist' administrator.

The inclusion in our study of Mexico which does **not** share these features was therefore highly instructive.

Vocational and general schooling

In the first place, the case of Mexico showed — particularly the comparative labour market studies with Sri Lanka — that my discussion of the use of certificates in the job market did not distinguish clearly enough between vocational qualifications and certificates of competence in general education subjects. A diagram will help to clarify the matter. It oversimplifies somewhat; sometimes there is a two-stage selection process, at junior and at senior secondary level, instead of the single link between 'basic' and 'further' education pictured here, but the simplified scheme will suite our purposes.

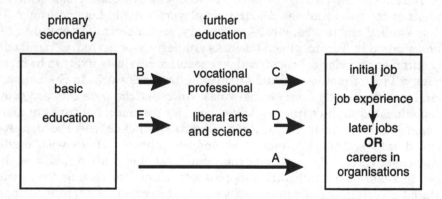

Implicit in the diploma disease model is the assumption that employers use educational certificates primarily as 'screening' devices — as measures of general ability (intelligence and powers of application) which indicate a person's likely 'trainability' over a whole range of skills, rather than as indicators of the cognitive and other skills which he has acquired as 'human capital' through his schooling. Clearly, this is more likely to be true at links A and D in the diagram, when people come into the job market with certificates of competence in general education subjects — basic literacy and numeracy, history and geography or a university training in arts or science — than when they come with clearly career-relevant qualifications in engineering or accountancy or nursing or pharmacy at link C. At C, employers are much more likely to be interested in acquired human capital, in **what** a person has studied and how much he knows than in measures of his general 'trainability'.

Whether the **bulk** of certificate-using recruitment goes through link C, or through links A or D, is therefore very likely in any given society to colour general perceptions of the meaning of certificates as signals. In that regard, there is a striking difference between Mexico and Sri Lanka. Mexican education is much more vocationally oriented at all levels than the Sri Lanka system. The latter is much more influenced by the aristocratic emphasis on 'for its own sake' education (humanities and 'pure' science, plus social science as bastard latter-day humanities rather than as disciplines-for-use) which was derived from the British model. At the junior secondary level in Mexico, only a little over 50 per cent of students were taking general courses in 1973, many of the remainder being enrolled in those of the 8,000 private institutions in Mexico offering training in all kinds of occupations — technical and commercial — that accept primary school graduates. At the senior secondary level there are a variety of technical institutions, most notably the vocational school which also prepares students for entrance to the National Polytechnic. In the National University, the country's largest, in 1974 fewer than 10 per cent of the students took courses in general arts and humanities. In Sri Lanka, on the other hand, although the very brightest students are creamed off into the two prestige faculties of engineering and medicine, the bulk of students at the tertiary level (some 86 per cent in 1967) are taking general arts or science degrees, and at the secondary level vocational training is practically nonexistent.

These differences are clearly reflected in the institutional rules which govern recruitment in the two countries. Mexican employers seem to take note only of what a person has studied and to what level — secondary, senior secondary or university — he or she has studied it. Technical and business studies are preferred. General education is rarely sufficient for clerical posts, and, at executive levels, is likely to be interpreted as showing a lack of motivation and orientation towards work. In Sri Lanka, on the other hand, one frequently comes across rules which discriminate between people who have been educated to the **same** level favouring, for instance, honours graduates over general degree holders, science specialists over arts specialists (only the highest scorers are allowed into science streams in secondary schools), those with credits and distinctions over those with passes (at the same level of education), those with passes or credits in notoriously 'difficult' as opposed to 'easy' subjects, or those who have accumulated a certain set of subject passes in fewer rather than more sittings of the examination — all rules which, not being concerned with the substantive content of what has been learned, only make sense if the certificates are being used as some measure of 'general ability'.

This is a point of striking importance for the academic debate between the proponents of 'human capital theory' and the advocates of 'screening theory' which has enlivened discussion of the economics of education in recent years. I did make the point in my book that these debates are too often conducted — given the mixture of evidence (for example, a study in the US, regression analysis in France and a survey in Guatemala) — as if they were debates about **the** role of **the** school system in **the** economy — as if the whole world were the same. Even so, I had not realised that the effects of variations in institutional practices could be as striking as they proved to be between Mexico and Sri Lanka. In the one case, assumptions of 'human capital' operated obviously. In the second, screening theory offered a better explanation of what happened.

Standardised national examinations

The other major difference between the two countries lies in the fact Sri Lanka has, and Mexico does not have, a national system of examinations. There are levels of achievement: 'Ordinary' and 'Advanced' school leaving certificates, and ordinary, honours and masters university degrees. There are also gradations within each level: pass, credit, distinction. The levels and gradations are supposedly standardised across schools and universities. For employers, then, they provide stable reference points for the reliable measurement of abilities. In Mexico, graduating examinations (and in primary schools grade-promotion examinations) are all internal to the school so that grades achieved have little universal meaning: no employer can be sure that a 60 per cent mark from one school is worse or even better than a 70 per cent mark from another. At best, he can make the assumption that someone who has passed all the promotion and leaving examinations to get into a university is likely to have an average or above-average mix or ability and persistence. Competitive entrance examinations for the 'best' universities — and for the 'best' high schools which prepare for them — are only just beginning, and the competition is not yet very intense; hence there is no ability-ranking significance generally attached to the university or high school attended as happens in other societies (where those who 'make it' into Tokyo University or Oxbridge or the Grandes Ecoles must, it is thought, be bright to do so). Rationing of higher-education opportunity is chiefly by the purse (or, because there is a good deal of part-time study-while-you-work, by strength of determination).

This difference is, of course, intimately related to the human capital/screening difference. One reason why Mexican employers do not use educational certificates as proxy measures of relative 'trainability', while Sri Lanka employers do, is that the Sri Lankan, but not the Mexican, certificates represent a currency of known value; the information they signal is more precise.

The extent to which national examination systems do provide overall ability-ratings, and the segments of the ability range for which they do so, vary from country to country. Britain, for example, provides some kind of age-sixteen grading for the whole age group, marks off the 15 per cent or so who get the two A levels necessary to enter a university, and within them, the small proportion who get into Oxbridge (competitively rather than on the old boy network, though there is no certain means of telling), those who get firsts, etc. The Japanese system only provides a rough division at the lower end of the range between the lowest 10 per cent or so who do not enter high school, the 40 per cent or so who cannot get into a public or 'good private' academic high school and are relegated to the vocational and 'spillover private' high schools, and the 15 per cent or so who go no further than high school. But above the level, it provides a highly refined ranking of the top 35 per cent who go to the universities. For the universities themselves are openly ranked by the difficulty of the competitive examination that each sets to select its students. France has a similar ranking (based on the assumption that everyone would get into the Grandes Ecoles if they could) for a tiny minority at the top of the ability spectrum. And so on. Whether, and over what range of jobs, certificates are used for ability screening, depends very much on how far the certificating system lends itself to being so used. (To another kind of screening, social class screening, we will return in a moment).

Bureaucracy

Part of my failure to give enough weight to the difference between vocational qualifications and general-education selection was a failure to put enough stress on the 'bureaucratisation of economic life' as a precondition for the latter. I did recognise it implicitly when I argued that one of the reasons why late-developing countries get a worse bout of the diploma disease is that a higher proportion of their modern sector employment is in highly bureaucratised organisations. Nevertheless, it has more importance in the genesis of certificate selection in **industrial societies** than I gave it. The chart below suggests a rather crude outline scheme. That I have in mind in suggesting a transition from the middle capitalist to the bureaucratic (either Japanese capitalist or Russian socialist) type of system, is this. It was not an accident that in Britain it was the East India Company and the civil service which, whether willingly or not, pioneered the practice of using general education attainments to select recruits. They were the most bureaucratic organisations in contemporary society in the sense that a) their operations were rule-bound and prescribed by a range of regulations designed to check favouritism, and b) they took people not just for jobs but for **careers**, and hence were interested in the lifelong development potential of a man, not in his specific ability to do a particular job over the next six months. They alone were Stage 5 organisations in my scheme, whereas outside them, most of the rest of the population was in Stage 4 — preparing for apprenticeship and institutional training to earn their living in fluid markets — directly selling services or goods (carpenters, doctors, masons, barbers) or selling their labour to employers interested in filling certain job functions for relatively short periods.

Gradually, however, Stage 5 organisations have increased in importance: not only the vast educational, social service, medical bureaucracies in the public sector, but also the ICIs, the Shells in the private sector, organise systematic 'talent searches' for the recruitment of the young for 'careers'. It is this which makes 'general ability', 'trainability' a central concern of a steadily increasing proportion of hirings. Again it was the Mexican and Sri Lanka comparison which highlighted the importance of the link between the organisation of work and the use of diplomas. Sri Lanka — or rather Sri Lanka's modern sector — is firmly in bureaucratic Stage 5, particularly since state corporations are responsible for such a large proportion of manufacturing. The Sri Lanka study estimated that nearly a half of all non-agricultural wage and salary employment in Sri Lanka was accounted for by the public sector or 'permanent employees' in the medium-to-large private modern sector (in which the old merchant houses, much imbued with old East India Company bureaucratic traditions, played a large role).

In Mexico, by contrast, not even the central administration is properly bureaucratised. With every sexennial change of President, the whole civil service is turned upside-down. Careers are far from secure. So too in the private sector; labour markets remain extremely fluid and the mobility of labour is brisk. Fewer hirings are therefore seen as career hirings; immediate job capabilities rather than long-term potentialities and trainability are a more dominant concern.

	type of society	mechanisms of occupational selection	form of occupational training	how individuals gain incomes
1	Feudal/tribal 'natural economies'	inheritance	informal family training	family subsistence loosely reciprocal exchange
2	Proto-industrial	inheritance plus sending to apprenticeship	Some general education: apprenticeship training as extension of family training	sale of goods and labour services in the market
3	Early capitalist	ditto	formal vocational training to supplement apprenticeship	sale of goods and labour services in the market
4	Middle capitalist	ditto, plus acquiring pre-apprenticeship qualifications	formal institutional training **before** career entry, plus work experience	sale of goods and labour services in the market
5	Bureaucratic (late capitalist and socialist)	certificated levels of general education	pre-career vocational training for technical, in-career training plus work experience for administrative careers	by entry into work organisations for careers

Class

I did mention at one stage, in discussing the determinants of the diploma disease, that it tended to be worse in the 'classless' societies of Africa — where everyone was in the race for success — than in class societies where aspirations and perceptions of mobility possibilities were likely to be lower for the subordinated lower orders. But having mentioned it, I promptly forgot about it.

Again the comparison between Mexico and Sri Lanka or Ghana shows that one must not forget about it. Mexico **is** a society with historically deeply rooted class divisions. I shall never forget my astonishment when (in 1976, not several decades ago) the Mayoress of a little town in Guanajuato produced her draft for a publicity brochure describing the town: 'San Jose', it said, 'has two classes, the middle class and the humble class. The middle class has three meals a day and the humble class two . . . . As for the relations between the classes, it seems to be one largely of indifference, since the humble class shows little sign of wishing to better itself'. By contrast, even in Sri Lanka, which was traditionally a caste society, one would be hard pressed to find such matter-of-fact acceptance of class differences in a public document.

These differences do have considerable consequences for the extent to which the village school becomes predominantly defined as the place where one gets the exit visas from the village, and the extent to which the so-called primary leaving certificate exam is seen **only** as a competitive secondary entrance exam. They affect the extent to which those who leave the school system with such a certificate are thought of, not as carrying with them some celebration of their accomplishment, but as being 'drop-outs' — with all the backwash effects of examination-orientation, the problems of 'relevance' etc, which naturally result from these conceptions of the purpose of schooling.

In Ghana, Kwasi Boakye found these features present to a high degree. The present generation of leaders started in the village and the present generation of village children see no reason why they should not follow in their footsteps to become leaders. Where everyone is in the race, the 'updraught' in the system is strong. Not so in Mexico. Nigel Brooke's villagers, and especially those of Tarascan Indian culture, often men and women who still bore the bruises of unpleasant experiences in trying to make their way in the city, were not prone to see much prospect, in their class society, for the advancement of their children by means of certificates. They did want their children to read and write and to be able to stand up to officials. But there was little competitive pursuit of academic success, little backwash from mobility aspirations.

The other aspect of the class society syndrome was the discovery, in the Mexican labour market survey, of a different form of screening from the ones discussed above — not ability screening, nor attitude screening ('if a man opted for business studies it shows he's got the right motivation'), but class screening. The correlation between class status and university attendance has until recently been sufficiently close for employers to be able to assume that graduates have a much higher probability of being congenial and loyal, of 'fitting in', of having a good presence, a good way with customers, etc. One or two employers deplored the 'democratisation' of the university which reduced the certainty that graduates would have such qualities.

The China cure

Brooke found that, although there was little diploma disease backwash from selection examinations spoiling the change of 'good and relevant' village primary education, there were plenty of other factors which ensured that village children had poor quality education, of little relevance to their future lives, and giving them little beyond the basic skills of literacy and numeracy. That, of course, is a finding highly relevant to my argument about 'delinking' the school from occupational selection. I suggested that, unless recruitment patterns were altered so that the schools were relieved of the difficult balancing job of trying to combine the function of educating children with the function of sorting and labelling them, improving the quality of education would be an impossible task. I specified this as a necessary condition. I was at least careful not to claim that it would be sufficient.

The great question when I wrote, of course, was how far the Chinese attempt to 'delink' would succeed in making education more generally effective as a preparation for life as it has to be lived in China. I was favourably, if in some respects sceptically, disposed, though perhaps the most blush-making sentence in the book is the one in which I say that the Chinese system seems to have changed so fundamentally that it is likely to stay changed! I was sceptical — and Jonathan Unger had already fed me a great deal of information on the problems of Chinese education in the period 1970-74 — on two grounds: first that the absence of the objective achievement test standard **was** leading to selection by favouritism; secondly that there were enormous functional difficulties in systems of selection which refused to recognise differences in human talent and developed skills, which recruited people for engineering courses on the basis of their devotion to approved political ideals without checking whether they could add two and two to make four.

Unger's work, and subsequent discoveries since the 'mess in education' has been exposed as not the least of the Gang of Four's crimes, show that there were, indeed, **very** serious problems. Favouritism was apparently rampant at both the crucial points: first when children were allocated on graduation to their initial work units (the favoured to the town factories, the disfavoured to the country) and secondly, when they applied — as they could after two years — for admission to a tertiary institution. Attempts to enforce standards either at the point of entry to, or within, higher education institutions were very much liable to be denounced as capitalist-roaders' plots.

There appear to have been two other problems. First, the teachers were demoralised. Liberated as they were from examination pressures, they did not know what to do with their freedom. A large proportion of them having had the humiliating experience of being denounced — and perhaps physically maltreated — by one or other faction during the Cultural Revolution, were in no mood to risk an initiative. It was safer to concentrate loyally on encouraging the memorisation of Mao's thoughts.

Secondly, it seems that higher education institutions never were (with few exceptions) transformed into in-service, career-development institutions. The small number of exceptions included engineering departments which took technicians from factories, upgraded their skills, and sent them back to their factories. But the vast majority remained what they had been before: institutions for **pre-career** qualification. The Normal Colleges in Shanghai and Peking, for instance, did not take, say, experienced primary teachers and upgrade them into school principals or senior secondary teachers. They continued to be places where youths at the start of their career could get a ticket of entry to a middle class occupation and so escape from traditional sector work in the communes. The reforms only meant that one had to wait out two years of hard labour on the farm before one could apply for entry; secondly, that entry was supposed to depend on 'redness' (but often depended on favouritism), and thirdly, that you did not need actually to know anything to graduate, provided that you could make vociferous and sincere political speeches. At least that is how the reforms are described nowadays in China, though doubtless with a touch of exaggeration.

Presumably it had to be like that. To have revamped the higher education system entirely on the lines of the engineering departments just mentioned — making all tertiary education a means of furthering the education and training of people in careers they had already started — would have condemned the millions of young urban secondary leavers 'sent down' to the country, to staying in the country all their lives. The change to apply for a university after two years and so get back on track for an urban professional occupation — the mere existence of that chance — was perhaps necessary to reconcile them to the vast sending down operation.

At any rate, the China chapter is one in the book which I suppose I should certainly rewrite if I had the chance. Not many people have asked me with *schaden freudelich* glee: 'so what price your modest proposals now, when even China has admitted its error?' But I suppose what I would want to say would be an implicit answer to that question. The fact that the 1970-76 Chinese system collapsed with few regrets is not proof of the unviability of a real 'delinking' effort on the lines I proposed in the book, viz:

— genuinely revamping higher education on recurrent, in-service lines;

— developing criteria which take account of the range of clearly relevant differences in human achievement and potential in selecting people for initial career experience and for subsequent upgrading;

— eliminating, or at least vastly reducing, the importance of selection in the processes of schooling and education; and finally,

— engaging creative teachers in the development of a new, workable pedagogy which might get children learning either from interest or from a conviction of the substantive worth of what they are learning.

Is it really impossible to create schools without the goal of the bread-and-butter, certificate-seeking, lifelessly instrumental motive for learning which, I persist in believing, is steadily eroding the quality of schooling throughout the world?

36.   Gender Matters in Development
Ruth Pearson

In recent years there has been an increasing awareness that as development has proceeded, or not proceeded, in Third World countries, the impact on men and women has been different. In fact, there is substantial evidence that women have consistently lost out in the process.

Some of the inequalities between men and women had their basis in colonial rule. Although social relations between men and women, as between other groups, were by no means egalitarian in many pre-colonial settings, there is no doubt that colonial capture and the introduction of exploitative labour regimes led to a marked deterioration in the social and economic status of women relative to that of men. The development of a world economy, and the spread of wage labour in both agricultural and industrial production, assumed very different roles for women and men in the economy, sometimes excluding women from wage employment while relying on their unpaid work on family farms or on low-paid work within the informal sector. Even since the Second World War, when national governments and multilateral and bilateral aid agencies have initiated development programmes and projects, there is overwhelming evidence that such assistance has generally bypassed women or sometimes made women worse off. Such was the concern of development professionals that 1975 was declared International Women's Year, followed by the Decade for the Advancement of Women 1976-85. But even after these initiatives there is considerable concern about the lack of understanding of gender relations and the fact that development policies and projects are still in the main gender blind if not actually biased against women.

Q   Why has development affected women and men differently? Are women too weak and powerless to take advantage of the challenges and opportunities that development offers? Is it tradition or backwardness that keeps women in a secondary position in Third World societies?

Q   Do planners and policy makers discriminate against women because they make mistaken assumptions about women's roles and involvement in production and reproduction? Or, more fundamentally, is the whole process of development, both as historical social change, and in terms of development policies and projects, deeply rooted in the unequal relations between men and women so that it is necessary totally to rethink the objectives and strategies of development?

This chapter will help address these questions by presenting a framework for thinking about gender relations. First, some basic analytical concepts are introduced to help in understanding the social processes that give rise to the disadvantaged position of women. Then I examine some ways in which women are subordinated. These concepts

Ruth Pearson: 'Gender Matters in Development'. Reprinted from *POVERTY AND DEVELOPMENT IN THE 1990s*, edited by Tim Allen and Alan Thomas (Oxford University Press in association with The Open University, 1992). © Open University 1992. Reprinted by permission of Oxford University Press.

are then used to look at some development initiatives and examine how they have affected men and women differently. Finally, I review some attempts to make women's issues and interests more central in the development field, and argue that the effects of more recent economic policies indicate that there is still a long way to go.

But — be warned — the conclusion of this chapter is that we can't think in terms of analysing development and then looking at its effect on women. On the contrary, whether it is recognized or not, development process or policy inevitably affects and is affected by the relations between the genders in any society. All policies, however technical or neutral they may appear to be, will have gendered implications. One task is to understand how different aspects of social and economic organization are already based on a system of gender relations and thus to clarify how assumptions about the roles of men and women form the backdrop against which policies are formulated, even if these assumptions remain unspoken and unacknowledged.

Conceptualizing gender and understanding gender relations

'Gender' rather than 'sex' is the key concept here because we are concerned with the social roles and interactions of men and women rather than their biological characteristics. Gender relations are social relations, referring to the ways in which the social categories of men and women, male and female, relate over the whole range of social organization, not just to interactions between individual men and women in the sphere of personal relationships, or in terms of biological reproduction. In all aspects of social activity, including access to resources for production, rewards or remuneration for work, distribution of consumption, income or goods, exercise of authority and power, and participation in cultural and religious activity, gender is important in establishing people's behaviour and the outcome of any social interaction.

As well as interactions between individual men and women, gender relations describe the social meaning of male and female, and thus what is considered appropriate behaviour or activity for men and women. What is considered as male or female work, or male or female attributes, behaviour or characteristics, varies considerably between different societies and different historical periods. But it is also important to realize that notions of gender identity, and thus what is fitting for men and women to do or be, have a strong ideological content. For example, in Britain, with nearly 50% of women of working age in the labour force, Patrick Jenkin, Minister of State for social services claimed in 1979: 'Quite frankly, I don't think mothers have the same right to work as fathers do. If the Good Lord had intended us to have equal rights to go out to work he wouldn't have created men and women. *These are biological facts*' (emphasis added). In rural sectors of the Third World both men and women often report that women don't do any agricultural work, or that they are just involved as family helpers, or carry out only domestic work. In fact, many of their waking hours are spent in activities such as weeding and harvesting, or collecting animal fodder or fuel wood, which have a direct effect on the productivity of agriculture whether the output is used for self-provisioning or processed and sold on the market.

Because notions of gender roles and activities have such a strong ideological content, policy often reflects normative or prescriptive versions of female and male roles rather than activities actually practised by women and men. But, as will become clear later, it is essential to understand the precise nature of what women and men actually do, and their real contribution to production and reproduction, if development policy is to cease being biased against women.

Using women as an analytical category

Although most people accept that women and men have different social positions, it is of course true that other social divisions such as class, race, ethnicity and age will also affect people's life chances. However, in common with much feminist literature, this chapter 'starts from the premise that all women share a common experience of oppression and subordination' (Young, 1988, p. 4).

It is possible to gain some notion of women's common interests, even though the forms of women's oppression and subordination vary widely, both historically and across or within specific societies.

For example, all women are potentially vulnerable to violence from men. Many women in Britain avoid travelling or walking alone at night. However, if a woman is rich enough she can avoid some of the constraints this places on her life by driving her own car, or using expensive forms of transport such as taxis. But her vulnerability to male violence stems from the fact that she is a woman, not from her economic circumstances. Her economic power may be deployed to mitigate the constraints and threats that male violence imposes on her as a woman, but it cannot abolish them.

Other situations can look different. In January 1991 rich women in Riyadh sought to challenge the very strict code of conduct that gender relations in contemporary Saudi Arabia imposed on them. They organized a drive-in to the centre of the city, dismissed their chauffeurs and drove their expensive cars themselves. The authorities retaliated by dismissing many of them from their employment in the University. Again, in this situation the constraints on their action stemmed directly from their gender, which was the basis of the social and political control on their autonomy. Being rich gave them big cars and chauffeurs, but it could not allow them the freedom to drive.

Many examples given in this chapter detail the work burden of poor women in the Third World, which systematically exceeds that of men in the same households (and therefore, the same class position). Without focusing on the social relations which produce and perpetuate this situation, it is impossible to go beyond a mere description of the conditions of women in different situations. But if we are concerned to devise policy initiatives and promote social changes which will improve the material and social condition of women, we need to understand how profound and pervasive the structures of women's subordination really are.

Table 15.1   Wages of females as a percentage of wages of males.

	1977	1986
Developing countries		
Cyprus	49.6	56.1
El Salvador	80.8	81.5[a]
Hong Kong	—	77.9
Kenya	55.6	75.6[a]
South Korea	44.7	48.5
Singapore	—	63.4[a]
Sri Lanka	—	75.5
Developed countries		
Czechoslovakia	67.4	67.9
France	75.8	79.5
West Germany	72.3	72.9
Greece	68.8	76.9
Japan	46.0	42.5
New Zealand	73.3	71.8
Sweden	87.4	90.4
United Kingdom	70.8	67.9

Source: UN (1989) *Report on the World Social Situation*, United Nations, Geneva, p. 13.
[a] Based on 1985.

Table 15.2   Percentage of women in parliament.

Region	Lower chamber of bicameral assembly		Upper chamber of bicameral assembly	
	1975	Latest year	1975	Latest year
Africa	4.1	6.3	—	4.9
Asia	13.2	12.8	6.9	6.9
Latin America and Caribbean	3.4	10.6	4.2	6.5
North America	3.6	7.0	2.9	7.4
Oceania	1.9	4.9	9.4	22.4
Europe	13.2	17.6	6.4	8.2
Soviet Union	32.1	34.5	30.5	31.1

Source: UN (1989) *Report on the World Social Situation*, United Nations, Geneva, p. 13.

How gender makes a difference

One way of measuring how people's gender makes a difference to their share of the benefits of society is to examine macro-level indicators which are differentiated by sex. Tables 2.6 and 3.3 gave literacy rates, educational enrolments and activity rates. Tables 15.1 and 15.2 show some further differences (wage rates and political participation) for selected countries and regions. On all the indicators shown, it is clear that women have an unequal share in some of the 'benefits of development'. Although national average figures hide an enormous amount of variation — by class, occupation and so on, they cannot hide the importance of gender in determining people's access to resources or opportunities.

Competing concepts: subordination or patriarchy

We can go further than talking about *inequality* with respect to gender relations: we can say that men are dominant and women are **subordinated**.

Subordination of women: A phrase used to describe the generalized situation whereby men as a group have more social and economic power than women, including power over women. As a result, women come off worse in most measurable indices of the outcome of social and economic processes. In short, the way the two genders relate to each other is that the male gender is dominant and the female gender is subordinate.

Another term which is often used to describe the unequal relations between men and women is *patriarchy*. This was originally an anthropological term which described the kind of social systems in which authority is vested in the male head of the household (the patriarch) and other male elders within the kinship group. Older men were entitled to exercise socially sanctioned authority over other members of the household or kinship group, both women and younger men.

Some writers prefer to use the term patriarchy to describe the general situation of male dominance over women, in order to develop an analysis of the structures of patriarchy within specific societies (Walby, 1990). However, the form this relationship of domination/subordination takes differs strikingly between different societies and is constantly undergoing change and negotiation. I therefore prefer to use the term *subordination* as it has no connection with any specific system of social organization and does not rest on the basis of a specific structure of male authority over women (Pearson *et al.*, 1984).

Subordination of women

Although the subordination of women is universal, this does not mean that gender relations are the same in every society. In every case, the social meaning of being female or male will be the result of the history of that society, influenced by the nature of the local economy that evolved over time, religious beliefs and political systems. It is necessary to analyse each situation separately in order to understand the precise nature of gender relations, the different factors which influence them, and how gender relations themselves have an impact on social and economic development. It would be a mistake, for example, to pick out one independent variable such as religion and assume that the gender ideologies and related gender roles implied by that religion have a uniform, or even a determining, impact on the specific relationship between men and women. Box 15.1 gives an example.

Structures of subordination

How and where are women subordinated? The mechanisms of distribution of resources and exercise of power between women and men vary widely, but one can expect to find structures of subordination in areas of life such as property relations, divisions of labour, in law and the state, and in how households are organized. Although I look at these areas separately, there are links between them which will become apparent (for example, between state policy and property relations, or sexual divisions of labour and household organization).

Box 15.1 Gender and 'culture' in the Middle East

That women's legal status and social positions are worse in Muslim countries than anywhere else is a common view. The prescribed role of women in Islamic theology and law is often argued to be a major determinant of women's status. Women are viewed as wives and mothers, and gender segregation is customary if not always legally required. Economic provision is the responsibility of men, and women must marry and reproduce to earn status. Men but not women have the unilateral right of divorce; a women can work and travel only with the written permission of her male guardian; family honour and good reputation, or the negative consequence of shame, rest most heavily on the conduct of women. Muslim societies are characterized by higher than average fertility, higher than average mortality, and rapid rates of population growth. Age at marriage affects fertility. An average of 34% of all brides in Muslim countries in recent years have been under 20 years of age, and the average level of childbearing is 6 children per women. The Moroccan sociologist Fatima Mernissi has explained this in terms of Islamic fear of *fitna*: social and moral disturbance caused by single unmarried women. Early marriage and childbearing, therefore, may be regarded as a form of social control.

The Muslim countries of the Middle East and South Asia also have a distinct gender disparity in literacy and education, and in Bangladesh low rates of women in the labour force. High fertility, low literacy and low labour force participation are linked to the low status of women, which in turn is often attributed to the prevalence of Islamic law and norms in these societies. It is said that because of the continuing importance of values such as family honour and modesty, women's participation in non-agricultural or paid labour carries with it a social stigma, and gainful employment is not perceived as part of their role.

Box 15.1 Gender and 'culture' in the Middle East   (continued)

However, these conceptions are too facile. In the first instance, the view of women as wife and mother is present in other religious and symbolic systems. The Orthodox Jewish law of personal status bears many similarities to the fundamentals of Islamic law, especially with respect to marriage and divorce. Secondly, the demographic patterns mentioned above are not unique to Muslim countries; high fertility rates are found in sub-Saharan African countries today, and were common in Western countries at the first stage of the demographic transition. Thirdly, high maternal mortality and an inverse sex ratio exist in non-Muslim areas as well. [The sex ratio measures the number of women to men in the population. Normally the ratios have a higher number of women to men, reflecting greater vulnerability of male infants, adult males and women's longer life expectancy. In a few countries the normal ratio is reversed.] In north India and rural China, female infanticide has been documented. In the most patriarchal regions of West and South Asia (including India) there are marked gender disparities in delivery of health care and access to food, resulting in an excessive mortality rate for women. Thus, women's disadvantaged position in the Middle East cannot be attributed solely to Islam. Religious and cultural specificities do shape gender systems, but they are not the most significant determinants and are themselves subject to change.

There is also considerable variation in gender codes in Muslim countries, as measured by differences in women's legal status, educational levels, fertility trends, and employment patterns. For example, sex segregation in public is the norm and the law in Saudi Arabia, but not so in Syria, Iraq or Morocco. Following the Iranian Revolution, the new authorities prohibited abortion and contraception, and lowered the age of consent to 13 for girls. But in Tunisia contraceptive use is widespread and the average age of marriage is 24. Women's employment levels are dissimilar in such countries as Turkey, Saudi Arabia, Iran, South Yemen and Algeria. Changes and variations across the region and within a society are linked to state economic and legal policies. It is important not to regard 'culture' as a constant; it is variable, and the extent of its impact depends on other factors, notably on the depth and scope of development, on state policy, and on class and social structure.

(Extracted and adapted from Moghadam, 1991, pp. 4-5)

Property relations: ownership and access to land

Systems of land tenure and inheritance vary widely. In most cases women have use rights rather than outright ownership rights to land. Where full rights to ownership exist in traditional legal codes, a woman's share is not usually equal to a man's. And even where traditionally women are entitled to inherit land, new laws often reduce women's rights to succession. For example, the Colombian land reform law confined land redistribution to married males over 18, and deprived women of rights they had in the pre-reform system (Whitehead, 1985, p. 53).

Even where women have customary use rights to land, these are rarely exercised in their own right, but only through kin relationships with individual men — brothers, fathers, other male relatives or, most commonly, husbands. In many African systems which prescribe the payment of bridewealth to the husband's family, women very often can only farm residual land after the rest of the kin group have had the allocation, even though, as wives, they are required to work on their husband's land. Without direct ownership or right to farm land, a woman has little say in the allocation of the income of crops. Since, as we detail below, men and women have different responsibilities within a household, lack of access to land can mean not just dependence on the head of the household, but real difficulties in meeting her own and her children's needs for food and clothing.

Even in quite different systems where property is combined in marriage, which is common in many Asian societies, a women rarely receives direct proceeds from the land, but depends on her husband to support her and her children. Although property relations are determined at the level of social and legal institutions, women's subordination in the realm has important consequences reaching into the allocation of resources, income and product within the household (Whitehead, 1985, pp. 55-6).

The sexual division of labour

Another important aspect of women's subordination is the allocation of different tasks and responsibilities to men and women. Strictly this should be called the 'gender division of labour'; however, although it refers to social, not biological, categories, the tern *sexual division of labour* is generally used. One division often made is that between productive work and domestic labour. Women are generally regarded as responsible for the latter, although men may also play a role (Table 15.3). However, it does remain true that women carry out the bulk of what has been called reproductive work — including biological, generational and daily reproduction. In Britain in 1988, 72% of women claimed total responsibility for domestic work; and in Cuba, where by law, men are supposed to share domestic tasks, 82% of women in Havana and 96% of the women in the countryside have sole responsibility for domestic chores (Momsen, 1991).

In many Third World societies, in the urban informal sector and in the rural economy, it is extremely difficult in practice to distinguish between domestic labour and productive work. Many apparently domestic tasks are part of maintaining production. But allocation of time to different activities including so-called domestic labour in rural production systems does vary to a certain extent according to the seasonal and other demands of production. Table 15.4 gives a seasonal breakdown of time spent on different tasks by men and women. The sexual division of labour within both agricultural and household tasks is fairly rigid. During peak times, women's time allocated to domestic work is reduced — though only by 13%. Men's domestic tasks are usually of a different nature (house maintenance, fencing, preparation of land for gardens, etc). In this example, women have much longer work time overall and consequently less time for leisure or sleep in both peak and slack seasons.

Table 15.3   Gender divisions of time use in Nepal.

	Time input into village and domestic work(%)	
	Men	*Women*
Cooking and serving	10	90
Cleaning	5	95
Maintenance	7	93
Laundry	10	90
Shopping	54	46
Other domestic	22	78
Childcare	16	84
Animal husbandry	55	45
Family farm enterprise	45	55
Gathering and hunting	60	40
Fuel gathering	34	66
House construction	72	28
Food processing	13	87
Water collection	8	92
Outside earning activity	69	31
Local market economy	43	57

Source: adapted from Joss, S. (1990). Table 15.3 first appeared in *Your Husband is your God*, GADU Pack 12, published by Oxfam UK and Ireland, 274 Banbury Road, Oxford, OX2 7DZ.

The sexual division of labour therefore operates not just between domestic and productive work but within each category of work as well. Also, what is considered to be a male or female occupation varies considerably between different societies, and in some cases between different groups and classes within the same society. A number of activities which are 'male' in one place (petty trade in North India, for example) are predominantly female tasks in others, such as Jamaica or Nigeria. On the other hand, the vast majority of domestic servants are women in South American cities, whereas in Lagos they are men; most typists in Jamaica are women, but not so in Madras.

The sexual division of labour may be modified to respond to changes in economic circumstances which alter the supply of men or women to carry out 'male' or 'female' tasks. For example, when the plough was introduced earlier this century in Zimbabwe, women were displaced from tasks associated with the preparation of ground for farming. However, in recent years, with large-scale male out-migration from rural areas, women have largely taken over ploughing and land preparation. In the northern province of neighbouring Zambia, the response to male out-migration has been different. Women have responded by hiring in casual labour to carry out traditional male tasks such as tree cutting and ploughing.

Table 15.4   Gender divisions of time use (hours per month) in the dry zone of Sri Lanka.

	Peak season		Slack season	
	Male	Female	Male	Female
Agricultural production	298	299	245	235
Household tasks	90	199	60	220
Fetching water and firewood	30	50	30	60
Social and religious duties	8	12	15	15
Total work hours	426	560	350	530
Leisure/sleep	294	160	370	190

Source: Momsen, J. (1991) *Women and Development in the Third World*, Routledge, London, table 4.3.

Gender roles have their own dynamic, evolving and adapting over many generations, exhibiting considerable resistance to changes in economic circumstances, or even to market forces. Often strategies which avoid changing the sexual division of labour are pursued, as in the Zambian case. Another example occurred when many women, often mothers of young children, migrated from Sri Lanka and other South Asian countries to the high-income Gulf states during the 1980s to work as domestic servants. Most often their childcare and domestic work at home devolved on other female family members, rather than on the fathers or male kin. This persistence of a strict sexual division of labour in domestic work is common all over the world (possibly more so than in household production) and should warn us not to assume too readily that gender relations can be modified or changed in response to change in the demand for or availability of male or female labour.

Sexual divisions of labour are neither constant in any particular society nor paralleled between different societies. But in every society there are clear demarcations which define what is appropriate, or possible, for women and men in that society — demarcations which may be transgressed by individuals without necessarily challenging the principle of allocation of tasks according to gender. Box 15.2 gives an example of how sexual divisions of labour are established in childhood and are carried through into adult life.

Box 15.2 Your husband is your God

Rural women are the backbone of Nepal's subsistence economy. Their work starts in the early morning and goes on throughout the day with little time for rest. Their endless toil is taken for granted. Their major role is to be a wife and a mother carrying out most of the domestic tasks in the household. No one questions the

---

Box 15.2 Your husband is your God   (continued)

division of roles. In the research conducted by Tribhuvan University Centre for Economic Development and Administration into the 'Status of Women in Nepal', it was calculated that on average women work 10.81 hours each day compared with men's 7.51 hours. Also, 86% of all domestic activities, 64% of the village work and 62% of the agricultural activities are done by women.

The disadvantaged life of a woman starts at birth when everyone is disappointed that the baby is not a boy. Girls cost a lot to marry (i.e. in dowry) and although by the age of 7 years they are contributing to the household income, they are considered a burden. In rural Nepal relatively few girls go to school, although numbers are increasing in primary schools. Education is now seen as a plus for a better marriage. Any difficulty at home and the girl is the one to take time off lessons, particularly if it is to look after younger siblings. But she is lucky to go to school at all; most girls have to stay at home helping their mothers in the fields and with the never-ending domestic chores. It is the family's dependence on girls' labour that keeps them out of school. Female literacy rate is 18%, whereas the male rate is 52%.

In comparison, everyone makes a fuss of the boys. They are important and soon learn that they can order their sisters around to serve them. They wash first, they eat first and never have to clear up afterwards. Their early life is one of playing games with other boys in the village. Sometimes they might have to look after cattle but many jobs like cooking, cleaning, laundry, food processing and water collection are never theirs. A boy's education at school is important.

When girls start menustrating they are hidden away in a dark room for 9 days. The second month it is less time and from then onwards the young woman knows that each month she is unclean for 4 days. She must not enter the kitchen, touch anyone else's food but her own and must eat and sleep separately. At the end of the 4 days she must wash all the clothes she has worn as well as the bedclothes. If it were not for the feeling of being ostracized, she could enjoy her days 'off'.

Legal marriage has a very high position in society. If the parents have arranged the marriage they will do everything to protect it. In marriage it is the Nepali woman who has to adapt — in fact, one of a bride's virtues is the ability to adjust to her new home. She is the one who moves house, she is the one in a new family coping with a mother-in-law whom she must please to make her life bearable. She has a lot of work to do in the home, up at 4 a.m. to start preparing *dal bhat* (main meal eaten morning and evening) for the whole family and finishing her day about 8 p.m. Then she has to get to know a total stranger, who is now her husband. Having previously been very inhibited about showing any part of her body, she is now thrown into living with a man.

In modern families there is a terrible dilemma that mothers face. If they have learnt some independence with the agreement of their husband, it would seem right to

Box 15.2 Your husband is your God   (continued)

teach their daughters the same. But this could 'jeopardize' their chances of a 'good' marriage, so the cultural traditions keep the status quo. It is often thought that a woman with 'too much' education might fail to make a 'good' wife as she could well not be used to housework and might even consider herself above it. But times are changing, particularly in the urban areas, like Kathmandu; families allow love marriages and allow sons' families to live separately from the extended family home much more often. Also, work can necessitate living away from home. In contrast, in rural areas parents often marry their children off before they are 14 years old.

Under Nepali law men and women are equal. Women do not inherit property or land: only sons benefit. The one exception is an unmarried woman over 35 years of age, since she has the rights to some of her father's land. But unmarried women are rare. Divorce is exceptional and there is a small percentage of separations. Widows are considered unlucky since, for some reason, they must have caused their husband's death. Men are able to remarry, whereas women cannot, and, although illegal, some have two wives. If the wife fails to produce a male child it is considered very inauspicious and the husband is within his rights to find another wife.

The women undertake 62% of all subsistence agricultural activities. The backbreaking weeding, irrigation, harvesting, muck spreading of crops is done by women. Men take a major role in land preparation, terrace upkeep, crop protection and spreading of chemical fertilizer. If there is anything needing technology or 'modern' understanding men insist it is their responsibility. So if any new development is brought to the village it is assumed that it will be taught and discussed with the men. The 'Status of Women in Nepal' did find that women's high input into agriculture production is not reflected by a commensurate level of participation in farm management decisions, although often choice was made according to tradition, e.g. crop choice, seed selection.

Outside the immediate household men dominate any economic activity. Of all earnings outside the home, 69% is earned by men, and they make most of the decisions on how the money is spent. Wives are consulted from time to time regarding household durables and clothing. Transactions concerning land or animals or major household loans are primarily decided by men. This outside earning capacity, meeting others in market places, bargaining and selling, etc. contributes to men gaining confidence to dominate decision-making. A number of men in Nepal, particularly in the far west, migrate into India for work. Since the extended family prevails, women are still subject to decisions made by men other than their husbands, in the family. Women do have a voice in how the house is run, particularly as they get older; also by giving guidance to their daughters and daughters-in-law.

(Extracted from Joss, 1990, pp. 1-3). Box 15.2 first appeared in *Your Husband is your God*, GADU Pack 12, published by Oxfam UK and Ireland, 274 Banbury Road, Oxford, OX2 7DZ.

The state, law and gender relations

The state influences how women are viewed in society in various ways: through legislation, in how public institutions are staffed and run, and through social policies. These mechanisms can affect whether women are seen as autonomous individuals or as dependents of men. In some countries, women's civil rights (in divorce, custody of children, ownership of property, autonomy in matters of employment, financial contracts) are discriminatory. Entitlement to benefits such as health insurance, pensions and welfare payments are often linked to women's relationship with men, rather than granted in their own right. In many countries the police and law courts treat physical and sexual assaults of women within the family quite differently from other forms of assault.

The state also appoints public officials in the judiciary, the civil service, industrial planning and regulatory boards, etc. Where such appointments are not adequately shared between men and women it reinforces the notion that primarily it is men who have the authority and competence to represent the whole population in serious matters. While many discriminatory laws have been repealed, particularly in the socialist Third World countries, in many places the extensive powers and practices of the state continue to legitimate unequal rights and unequal treatment of men and women.

Gender relations within households

In developing countries, most households are the site of many different kinds of activity: residence and consumption, subsistence and market production, distribution of resources and output, socialization of children, care of the elderly, and so on. These activities may take place in a single unit or in several connected ones. Different members of households may have different rights (over property, labour and income) and obligations (particular productive tasks, food provision, domestic work, etc.), often depending on age and marital status, as well as sexual divisions of labour.

Development policies are often directed to an idealized model of households where production, income and consumption are shared: they are seen to have convergent interests in which all members contribute according to their ability and share the benefits according to their needs. However, empirical studies have shown that far from being a unit in which all resources and benefits are pooled equitably, the use of resources and labour, and the distribution of income and output, have constantly to be negotiated, and intra-household relations are often conflictive (Dwyer & Bruce, 1988). In different households systems, men and women have different responsibilities in terms of work in domestic or other activities, obligations to provide food and other resources (water and cooking fuel), and cash income or meet family needs such as school fees, clothing, agricultural inputs, etc. In some households, far from a pooling situation, women trade grain they have grown themselves for cash to buy clothing and other necessities. In others, women's labour in family farms and enterprises give them no direct rights to cash, no 'owned resources' to exchange for cash, and little influence in deciding how household income is to be allocated between competing demands. In each of these cases, intra-household relations can be seen as a form of *co-operative conflict* (Sen, 1987):

although household members may depend on each other in terms of labour and output, there is considerable negotiation and conflict about how such inputs and benefits should be distributed.

As well as these intra-household divisions, the distribution of inputs and benefits can also systematically disadvantage women. For many households, especially those on the margins of subsistence, women contribute a major proportion of their labour time, and their total income, to the needs to the household, particularly to their children. In contrast, men tend to have considerable autonomy over how they spend their income:

> "A general finding is that women's income is almost exclusively used to meet collective household needs, whereas men tend to retain a considerable portion of their income for personal spending. A key source of male bargaining power within the household is determining what proportion of their income to pass on to other household members. Rather than personal spending money for male adults being residual after other household needs have been met, it is often a priority and the amount allocated to household expenditure is residually determined by the difference between male income and personal spending. The good husband is the one who strictly limits his personal spending, but his prerogative to enjoy such spending remains."

(Elson, 1991, pp. 3-4)

Box 15.3 is an illustration of how household divisions are linked to access to land, sexual divisions of labour and changes brought by commoditization.

Using gender to analyse development

In the previous sections I have mapped out some basic concepts necessary to analyse the changing social relations of gender. I have stressed that the precise nature of gender relations differs according to specific historical contexts. We will now see how these concepts can be applied by analysing briefly two examples of change in developing countries.

Box 15.3 The impact of cash cropping in Ghana in the 1920s

In the earlier period, peasant households largely concentrated in food-crop production. The principal food crop then was yam, although vegetables were also grown. Both men and women cultivated the same plot. The men generally cleared the land on their own, but the women shared the work of weeding, planting and harvesting. However, when cocoa cultivation became profitable, a new sexual division of labour emerged. Men took over the production of the cash crop and women were left to produce the food crops for subsistence. Land that earlier had been cultivated jointly by both sexes was gradually taken over by the men to cultivate cocoa, and the women were left with small, infertile plots. Men now devoted their

---

Box 15.3 The impact of cash cropping in Ghana in the 1920s (continued)

labour almost exclusively to cocoa and stopped helping with the food crops. The money from the sale of cocoa did not contribute to the family's subsistence: rather it was used for larger investments either in the cocoa crop, in house-building, and occasionally on the children's education. Often the money was also spent by the men on their own clothes and on drink.

Where women managed to produce a surplus for sale, the cash they obtained could not be spent by them but was controlled by the male heads of households and used for the family's subsistence needs. In the absence of help from the men, the women found it increasingly necessary to shift out of yam and vegetable cultivation into the cultivation of less labour-intensive crops such as maize and cassava. These crops, however, had a higher starch content than yam and were less nutritious.

The desire to have control over some cash income, as well as the takeover by men of land previously used for food crops, caused the women to try and establish separate farms. Women's access to independent plots, however, was severely constrained by a number of factors. An important one was the increased privatization of communal land, and the confining of inheritance rights of this land to men. Hence, where previously women had the same rights to communal property as men, even though the social structure was patrilineal, now they had to ask permission from male relatives for the use of the latter's fallow land. With an intensification in the competition for land this became increasingly difficult. Another problem related to the fact that women had no direct access to labour other than their own or that of their children, and hired labour was difficult to get (quite apart from problems of payment); hence they were constrained in the type of land they could cultivate. For example, they could not use forest land, which would need manual clearing, even though such land was usually the most fertile; rather they had to opt for a less fertile plot, but one that was locationally accessible and that they could prepare on their own or plough with a hired tractor (hiring a tractor was cheaper than hiring labour).

The difficulties of access to land and labour as well as to extension services and credit meant that survival became a battle for many women and their children. In short, the introduction of cash cropping in Ghana may be seen to have (a) significantly increased women's work burden; (b) led to a fall in the nutritional standard of their diets because it necessitated a shift from yam to cassava and, for some, even a fall in their absolute levels of consumption; and (c) brought no gain in terms of their cash, since the scale of their independent activities was usually so small as to make it very difficult to produce enough even for subsistence needs.

(Agarwal, 1985a, pp. 106-7)

Women and the Green Revolution

The 'Green Revolution' is regarded as an important example of successful development. A technological package based on new seeds, but with biochemical, mechanical and institutional aspects (i.e. new forms of credit and training) has been responsible for substantial increases in production of wheat and rice, particularly in Asia.

The Green Revolution started in the mid-1960s and continues today. It is probably the first systematic attempt to increase worldwide food production. Agricultural production is increased in three ways: average yields are increased, the area devoted to agriculture is extended, and the number of crops grown in a year is increased.

The major technical elements are:

1. Mechanization — the introduction of tractors, and other machinery for harvesting and irrigation etc. These may be used to extend the cropped area; often machines are used to replace labour.

2. Biochemical innovations — such as new seed varieties and new inputs such as fertilizers, pesticides and weed killers. These can all increase crop yields.

Most assessments of the impact of the Green Revolution in India recognize that as well as increasing overall productivity, it has also increased socio-economic stratification. This has resulted in worsening of income distribution between rich farmers on the one hand and poor farmers on the other, many of whom have joined the ranks of landless labourers.

The economist, Bina Agarwal (1985a), has used gender to analyse this particular development process within the three major rural groups or classes in India, identified as:

1. agricultural labour households (which have no land or insufficient land for household subsistence);

2. small cultivator households (which have sufficient land to provide for household needs using family labour);

3. large cultivator households (which have sufficient land and other resources to farm using hired, i.e. paid, labour, and which do not use the women of the household for field work).

For women in the landless or land-short households the impact of Green Revolution technology was complex. The numbers of households in this group increased (including a large number of female headed households) and there was a rise in the number of women who had to hire themselves out as casual wage workers because many families were living on lower material resources than before the changes. Women had to increase their time and energy devoted to agricultural work for wages as well as maintain their subsistence production and domestic labour to ensure their household's survival. Women were squeezed between conflicting demands — the need to earn income, and the need to increase time devoted to domestic activities.

While there was a rise in the total amount of hired labour required by larger farm households, the increase in employment has not been gender neutral. The new technology package requires additional labour for tasks such as transplanting and weeding (normally women's work) but it is not clear that this has kept pace with the increase in the numbers of women seeking such work. Other activities, particularly harvesting, threshing and grain-processing, have been subject to substantial mechanization, reducing the employment opportunities for poor women. The widespread adoption of grain processing mills has vastly reduced women's employment in dehusking of rice, for example (Agarwal, 1985).

The Green Revolution has at best had a mixed impact on the employment opportunities and incomes of poor women. Statistics show increases in days worked and in wage rates, but the latter have been offset by price increases (Agarwal, 1985, p. 97). Even where women's incomes have improved, it is not clear that they experience the benefits: women in landless and land-short households continue to suffer chronic deficits in food intake, both in absolute terms and in relation to men.

Women working as casual wage labour also face health hazards from standing in water containing fertilizers and pesticides to do weeding and transplanting. There are reports of women field workers suffering intestinal and parasitical infections, leech bites, skin complaints, rheumatic joints, arthritis and gynaecological infections (Agarwal, 1985, p. 329).

Women from small cultivator households are in a different position. Although in general they are not required to work outside family farms for wages, their work within the family holdings has intensified. New seed varieties shorten the gestation period and make possible two harvests a year. Since most of women's agricultural tasks are not mechanized, their work burden has increased. In addition, they still carry the burden of domestic work. They are of course subject to the same health hazards described above.

Total household incomes of this group have in general increased, but decisions on the spending of this income remain biased against women. For instance, substantial shares of the extra income have been spent on tractors which save male labour time — but few households in this group have invested in home-grinding mills which would reduce women's domestic work burden in food processing.

The impact on women from large cultivator households is more closely linked to the considerable rise in household incomes. Although male bias in intra-household distribution remains, women have generally shared in the new prosperity. But even prosperity has implications for women. With increasing wealth, women are withdrawn from field production (a common way of demonstrating prosperity), but this does not necessarily signal an increase in women's autonomy. First, there may be an increase in domestic labour as women are responsible for preparing food for the increased numbers of hired labourers, and for other farm management tasks. Secondly, women's ability to bargain over allocation of household income may be further constrained. Withdrawal from field work can often lead to total seclusion and an increase in women's dependence on men.

The effect of the Green Revolution therefore cannot be measured just in terms of increased production or rises in aggregate household incomes. Consideration should also be given to the increases in women's workloads and to the fact that women often fail to receive an equitable share in the extra income earned, even though their labour is often central to achieving higher levels of productivity. Increased demand for casual waged work for women from the poorest households has not necessarily increased household income where, as has often been the case, real wage levels have declined. Since women are in danger of losing out (of working harder, for less reward, with added health risks), this policy for improvement in agricultural productivity cannot be considered an unqualified success.

Development projects: the dangers of gender blindness

Many development initiatives have been introduced in areas of the Third World in the form of large-scale projects financed by external aid and organized by technical experts. One well-known example was the attempt in the 1970s to introduce irrigated rice production in an area in The Gambia where, traditionally, men had farmed groundnuts as a cash crop (with the aid of family labour) and women had cultivated rice for household consumption on unirrigated wetlands. The irrigation project was unsuccessful largely because the planners failed to understand the specific dynamics of gender relations within the local household-based farming system (Dey, 1982; Carney, 1988).

> "The lack of success stemmed in part from [a] 'male dominant', 'domestic sharing' model of the household which shaped the project. An initial assumption was that the men were the rice growers with full control over the necessary resources. Incentive packages included cheap credits, inputs and assured markets offered to male farmers. But it was women who traditionally grew rice for household consumption and exchange, within [a] kind of complex set of rights and obligations... The scheme proposed to develop irrigated rice production on common lands to which women had secured use rights. Backed by project officials, men established exclusive rights to these common lands, pushing the women out to inferior scattered plots to continue cultivating traditional rice varieties. All access to inputs, labour, and finance was mediated through husbands, and women became notably reluctant to participate in their planned role as family labour. For what work the women did do on the irrigated rice fields husbands had to pay their wives ... the disappointingly low levels of improved rice production arose substantially from these misunderstandings."

> (Whitehead, 1990, pp. 63-64)

As well as assumptions about the structure and operation of households, the planners took other things for granted. First they assumed that women were 'free' labour — that their labour would not have to be recompensed in any way, and thus involved no resource cost. Secondly, they assumed that women's labour had no existing productive use and therefore was available for intensive application to irrigated rice production. In fact, women were busy with their own rice lands in the rainy season, during which men did not have access to their labour and, therefore, did not grow a further rice crop as planners had expected. Men only grew rice in the dry season when their women were free to work for them (for wages) and when they themselves earned higher wages elsewhere. In addition, ignoring that women were farmers in their own right, planners neither took advantage of women's expertise in swamp land rice nor helped women to improve their own output.

The Gambian example illustrates two further points. Women are not necessarily the passive victims of circumstances with no possibility of resisting. By refusing to make their labour available at no cost and to the convenience of the male farmers involved in irrigated rice production, the Gambian women demonstrated their determination to defend their existing gender position as separate producers, albeit with various obligations as well as rights within the household. The example demonstrates that in households where men and women hold separate purses with no pooling of cash income, and have responsibility for different items of household expenditure and food production, as well as different access to resources for production, it cannot be assumed that increasing household production and incomes will of necessity improve the living standards of all members.

Putting gender on the development agenda

The concern with the effects of development on women goes back some 10-20 years. The UN's Decade for the Advancement of Women (1976-85), which was preceded by the International Women's Year in 1975, was the culmination of successful pressure by women activists and academics (Pielta & Vickers, 1991). The argument was that development policies, co-ordinated by the leading multinational agencies, such as the World Bank, UNIDO and FAO, as well as many bilateral development agencies and NGOs, had ignored the needs of poor women in Third World countries.

It was not just in economic terms that the marginalization of women needed to be addressed. There was concern that women were being 'left out' in four critical areas: political rights; legal rights; access to education and training; and their working lives (Boyd, 1988).

'Women in Development' policies

The new emphasis led many agencies and experts to commit themselves to Women in Development policies in order to enable women both to enjoy the fruits of development, and to make an appropriate and necessary contribution to the development process. Many development agencies financed projects aimed at helping poor women, particularly setting up income-generating projects ranging from poultry and fishing co-operatives to handicrafts and school uniform sewing, with various inputs of credit, technical expertise and training provided. Of course, women's labour was unpaid, since the income depended on the sale of the project's output.

A parallel development was the establishment of Ministries for Women's Affairs or Women's Bureaux, particularly in Commonwealth countries. These were charged with negotiating and co-ordinating the activities of the various international agencies keen to finance projects for women. These agencies also helped to raise the profile of women's issues, and divert some aid resources to targeted women's groups. Unsurprisingly, they were chronically understaffed and under-resourced and most have found it extremely difficult to meet their broad range of objectives (Gordon, 1985).

A major criticism of the Women in Development approach is that its basic assumptions are flawed: it starts from the premise that women have been excluded from development. But as our previous discussion has clearly illustrated, women's time, energy, work and skills are involved in every aspect of the development process; it is the inequality of gender relations and the continuing subordination of women that ensure that women's contribution is not matched by recognition and remuneration in social, political and economic terms.

The shortcomings of the Women in Development approach, which focuses on women rather than on gender relations, is illustrated by research which has assessed various projects aimed at improving the situation of poor women (Buvinic, 1986). Most projects focused on one aspect of women's problems (often lack of access to cash income) without considering the implications of such initiatives. For example, income-generating projects do not take into consideration how women's time budgets are already overstretched. Furthermore, many projects were staffed by unpaid leaders, with little commercial or technical expertise available, rather than professional salaried workers. Many projects are based on what are assumed to be women's traditional skills (embroidery, handicrafts etc.), though in many cases the women have no direct experience of these activities. Few have identified any attainable market and as a result are continually dependent on further aid for survival.

Increasing visibility of women?

One clear advance from the UN Decade has been an enhanced understanding of the nature and variety of women's work in the Third World. This has been accompanied by an increasing recognition that conventional methods of collecting statistics consistently underestimate the extent of women's work (Waring, 1989). But even a more comprehensive recording of women's paid work would not represent the real extent to which all economies rely on women, both in productive activities and in the range of reproductive activities discussed above.

> "Women often contribute to family earnings in a number of ways, making it important that all income-earning activities be reported. For example, a women may help on the family farm or in a family enterprise. During the off-season she may take in laundry, produce handicrafts, brew beer for sale, or work on someone else's farm. Especially if she is poor, she may scrape together a living by engaging in several such activities. Unless there is an inquiry into time use or a sequence of questions on multiple jobs, secondary occupations may well be omitted... Unpaid family work on farms and in small non-farm enterprises is an important part of women's work in developing countries ... A special effort is often necessary to make certain that it will not be overlooked."

> (Mueller, 1983, pp. 276-7)

In spite of the increase in research and awareness of the specific circumstances of women, there was still no evidence at the beginning of the 1990s that the implications of taking gender seriously are understood or acted upon at the level of macro-economic planning.

Structural adjustment policies: lessons from the past

The 1980s saw widespread implementation of structural adjustment policies, which were intended to transform Third World economies into efficient and competitive producers for international markets.

What have we learned about the nature of gender relations that might be relevant to the analysis of those market-oriented policies? It should be clear that economies do not only work through market relations. Given the complexity of gender relations within smallholder households, the invisibility of women's work both in the rural and urban sectors, and the multiple and complex roles women actually perform, market-only policies such as structural adjustment are likely to have specific, and probably negative, effects on women.

For example, women agricultural producers may grow marketable crops, but their energies are often directed to producing food for household consumption. If prices are allowed to rise as an incentive to increasing marketed production, women will often be in a situation where they are under pressure from husbands and other male kin to work harder in order to produce more cash crops at the expense of household food. Women also often find that their workload is increased because new crops and technology intensify the need for weeding and other female agricultural tasks. Even so, they will not necessarily be compensated by payment for their labour or increased cash income from the sale of the new crops. Furthermore, there is no certainty that cash earned will be used to purchase food to compensate for the reduction of their own provisioning, or that the money earned will be sufficient to purchase equivalent food products on the open market.

These problems are borne out by a nutritional study carried out in Zambia in 1988, after an adjustment programme had been in place. It was found that 'in the predominantly maize growing areas it is the children of the farmers growing maize for sale who are most likely to suffer from nutritional stress' (Feldman, 1989, p. 17). In this case, it was also suspected that the extra burden of work imposed on women by producing for the market gave them less time for children, infant feeding and food preparation. Thus, as well as underestimating the centrality of women's work in agricultural production, policies based on market models also ignore women's domestic or reproductive roles. Not only is time taken away from non-market production, it can also squeeze the time required to carry out essential domestic tasks. Women will always attempt to stretch themselves in order to meet their multiple obligations, with the result that their total work burden is increased, but their ability to ensure the well-being of their families is jeopardized, to say nothing of their own health and welfare.

Raising prices as an incentive to increase agricultural production for sale, plus the reduction of state control of food markets has meant sharply rising prices for consumers. Together with increased costs of housing, water, school fees and medicines, households can only survive by acquiring several incomes. Women especially have been forced to find alternative income sources, mainly in the informal sector of the economy. A recent survey in Dar Es Salaam showed that women of all classes were doing extra work for cash (Feldman, 1989, p. 25). Young girls contributed by selling cooked food before and after school. In addition, 58% of households reported that they had reduced the number of meals taken from three to two.

The other plank of structural adjustment policies — that of reducing government spending — has had specific and direct effects on women, who, as teachers, health workers and public sector office workers, have often taken the brunt of cuts in public sector employment. Many women have had to turn to the informal sector for work. Cuts in public services such as health and education have also taken their toll on the poor. In some places, health budgets have been reduced by 50% or more, and a lack of foreign exchange has led to shortage of medical supplies within state-run hospitals and health centres. In Tanzania, mortality of children under 5 has increased since 1980 from 193 per thousand to 309 in 1987. In Zambia there has been a sharp increase in childhood malnutrition, and a decline in the child immunization programmes. The uptake of antenatal care has also fallen off. In countries such as Jamaica, where the government has introduced charges for previously free public health care, many women, who face declining incomes and increased prices for basic needs, have simply been unable to afford medical attention for themselves or their children (Antrobus, 1988).

Reduction in other areas of state expenditure also affects women in ways which are less obvious. Housing, sanitation, clean water programmes, rural road projects — all these have been the victims as governments seek to reduce 'unnecessary' or 'unproductive' expenditure. But all these services affect the ability of women to manage their conflicting roles. Without rural roads, women are unable to travel to urban centres for health care, for education, or to market their own crops. Without sanitation and clean water, women use much time and energy fetching water from insanitary and distant points; intestinal and other diseases afflict children and adults alike, adding care of the sick to women's already overburdened tasks.

In some countries, governments have also introduced or increased school fees as a means of raising revenues. This has contributed to the marked fall-off of enrolment of girls in schools, for several reasons. Additional expenditure cannot be justified where household incomes are falling. The possibility of women obtaining a job where literacy is necessary is slight. Girls have been withdrawn from school in order to care for younger children as women have increasingly had to take up income-generating work. The girls themselves are also required to contribute to household income either by assisting relatives, or working as domestic servants (Pittin, 1990).

Adjustment policies which favour deregulation of the market are premised on ideas about 'getting the prices right' — that is, eliminating what are seen to be distortions in the market. But within a conceptualization of the economy which ignores any analysis of gender, women's time and energy have no price: they become further stretched. As earnings of other members of the household decline, women extend the range of income-generating activities, seeking new sources of cash and investing their time and resources in new activities — hence the increase within the urban economy of activities such as vegetable growing, petty trading, beer brewing, poultry keeping and tailoring. Common strategies to reduce household expenditure initially focus on purchasing cheaper commodities, either by seeking cheaper sources of supply or by purchasing more basic goods which require home processing — both of which involve time and work undertaken by women. As the crisis deepens, items of expenditure are eliminated. As the total amount of goods and services the household can afford to buy falls, the share of women and girls of these shrinking resources also tends to decline. For example, it is common for male family members' food consumption to be protected as food intake of women and young girls is sacrificed.

A more market-oriented economy will not have negative consequences for all women in Third World economies. Increased market-based economic relations tend to cause increased stratification in the economy, with some groups doing better and being in a position to accumulate, as was the case in the Green Revolution. Inevitably, groups who have weaker claims on resources lose out. For many women in both rural and urban Third World communities, adjustment has meant increasing workloads and falling living standards as they have struggled, often unsuccessfully, to maintain their standard of living and to ensure the basic survival of their households.

A challenge for the 1990s

The 1990s will present enormous challenges to all those who are concerned with development. However, all development issues require analysis from the perspective of gender relations if they are to be successful and serve the needs for women as well as men. There is some evidence that the World Bank is drawing back from its 1980s policy agenda and prioritizing areas of social investment which are crucial to women's survival. But other key issues such as environmental conservation, political stabilization and democracy all need to be subjected to a similar scrutiny. Efforts to halt soil degradation will not succeed if they rely on (unlimited and unrewarded)applications of women's scarce time and energy resources; democracy will be meaningless unless women are represented and have full access to political office and power. The whole of the development agenda will need to be reformulated if the message that gender matters is to be taken seriously.

Summary

1. Gender relations are social relations, not biological or natural.

2. Like all other social relations, gender relations will be affected by, and will affect, how societies and economies change over time.

3. Therefore, gender *matters* — in development analysis as in any other sphere of social analysis and policies. Without understanding gender relations policies can go wrong.

4. The key to redressing the inequality of gender relations and the mis-match between women's contributions to society and their rewards goes much further than directing aid programmes to women.

5. The importance of analysing gender applies at all levels of development policy — planning, implementation and evaluation.

37.   MV Research and the Poor
Michael Lipton with Richard Longhurst

We now draw together a few conclusions, and suggest implications for international and national agricultural research planners seeking to help the poor. We have tried to avoid hectoring criticisms of MV [Miracle Variety] researchers. The above numbers tell us much about their achievements. The persistence of mass poverty in some LDCs — either despite adopting MVs, or whilst neglecting them — should be blamed on socio-economic structures and resultant policy biases, rather than on the features of MVs themselves.

Indeed, if social scientists had in 1950 designed a blueprint for pro-poor agricultural innovation, they would have wanted something very like the MVs: labour-intensive, risk-reducing, and productive of cheaper, coarser varieties of food staples. (Even better might have been a wider range of MVs, concentrating on less-favoured 'rainparched' areas, and on casava and millet. But natural scientists could reasonably retort that, given the genetic potentials, such emphases could not in the 1960s have produced enough extra food to avoid disaster.)

However, it is not quite good enough — although it is *fair* enough — to blame socio-political distortions for the inadequate 'translation' of MVs' large spread into gains for the poor. MVs are an evolutionary technique, not one that requires (or stems from) a transformation of the structure of rural power. An evolutionary technique — especially if used first by richer, less risk-averse farmers, with better access to information and inputs — tends, when introduced into an entrenched power structure, to be used so as to benefit the powerful. Even labour-saving and 'consumption-cheapening' MVs may not, in highly stratified societies, bring gains mainly to poor people.

Planners of agricultural research cannot fine-tune its results to each recipient village. They should, however, allow for the general features of the societies into which research results are introduced. Moreover, those features are changing. Increasingly, the near-landless, not 'small farmers', comprise most of the poor.

Our understanding of how MV impacts work themselves out, too, is changing. We have learned that the employment gains per hectare, created by MVs, fall off as better-off farmers seek labour-replacing ways to weed and thresh. We have also learned that price restraint (due to extra MV-based food supply), while helpful to poor food buyers in the short run, is soon reflected in wage restraints as the supply of labour increases.

Finally, our scientific understanding — both of poverty and of MVs' impact on it — is changing too. Social scientists now see most threats to poor people's food access, whether from population growth or from technical change, as operating to reduce entitlements to food, whatever the impact on its availability. Natural scientists now realise that the

Michael Lipton with Richard Longhurst: Extracts from 'MV Research and the Poor', pp. 400-425, from *NEW SEEDS AND POOR PEOPLE* (Unwin Hyman, 1989). Reproduced by permission of Routledge.

best MVs — apparently helping the poor (who are least able to bear risks) by strongly resisting crop pests and diseases — can endanger the poor by their very success. A successful variety tends to replace other crops and varieties, thereby reducing diversity in the field, stimulating new pathotypes, and thus creating new risks, against which the poorest are the most defenceless.

How can national and international research centres improve the effect of agro-biological discoveries on the world's poor? At first glance, the scope is severely limited by national policy. In most poor countries, political pressures and preferences induce most parts of the State apparatus to discriminate against rural people (including farmers), except to the extent that such people provide food, savings, skills, or export products to the articulate urban élites. If very few resources flow to rural infrastructure, to locating and (where economic) managing groundwater, or to the health or education of farm families; if farm price policy is used mainly to extract surpluses for urban use; or if agricultural research itself receives scanty or fluctuating current funding — then how can such research do much, for poor people or anybody else?

While research success cannot overcome policy failure (or policy vacuum), it can improve agricultural policy. For example, it was not lectures on price policy that persuaded the Indian Government to offer farmers more attractive wheat prices in 1965-70; it was evidence that MVs would enable many farmers to respond to such price incentives with markedly increased outputs. Another example is that of Sri Lanka, where the repeated successes of plant breeders ever since the late 1950s in developing robust intermediate and modern rice varieties, suitable for widespread use, was partly cause and partly effect of the major involvement of leading rice researchers with agricultural policy decisions on many matters, from trade through land tenure to agricultural extension. If researchers show that they can deliver the goods, politicians become readier to listen to them on the agricultural policy issues that so greatly affect the impact of research.

So the scope of agricultural researchers for improving their impact on policy, and in particular on poor people, is quite large. In seeking to redesign their research to use that scope, they need to respond to seven main issues, identified in this book.

- The setting of pro-poor research priorities requires clear, published, formal decision rules. Such rules would encourage LDC and IARC researchers, managers and funders to be objective in face of pressures and fashions, scientific and political. Carefully selected rules can encourage, not reduce, nonconformist and interdisciplinary challenges to current research paradigms.

- Such priorities are needed, in part, to select — in the light of new scientific prospects and risks — ways to consolidate, extend and redirect past improvements in the efficiency of food plants in handling water, nutrients, light and pests.

- But 'efficiency' needs environmentally careful definition. The poor will suffer most if nutrients and water are used efficiently now in ways that prove unsustainable later; or if plants, efficient now, lose diversity and stimulate virulent new pests later.

- The weak impact of MVs in some circumstances — regions, crops, agroclimates, administrative regimes — endangers more poor people, and requires new actions from IARCs and national crop researchers.

- MV researchers need to identify more precisely the groups, in each environment, most needing help ('small farmers', large poor farming households, urban workers, or rural landless; men, women, or children). Large and growing proportions of the poorest depend on income from rural labour, and are threatened as their increasing population reduces their bargaining power and hence food *entitlements*. Yet the IARC system was designed to increase food *availability*, seen as threatened for small-farm and urban populations as they increased.

- MV research has produced extra food and income which have saved many lives. Yet its approach to human nutrition requires a more appropriate research menu. Today's menu is too optimistic that — even without specific decisions on policy priorities or research directions — MV research will reduce the prices of poor people's food (relative to their incomes). Also, protein requires much less emphasis from researchers; the energy needs and absorption of vulnerable groups, much more.

- MV research, in both natural and social sciences, now concentrates too heavily on farmers, including 'small farmers', in areas where MVs have spread. To remedy this, IARCs (and several national research centres in LDCs) will require to develop new approaches in natural and social sciences; greater readiness to analyse the interactions of MVs with total systems (of power, of ecology, of economic transactions); and more awareness of history.

* * * * * *

Earlier we sketched how the choice between research into one or other region — or into one or other crop, varietal type, or characteristic — could formally take account of five things: a scientific estimate of (i) the probability, extent and timing of 'success'; a sociological estimate of (ii) the likely rate of adoption by various types of farmers; and socio-economic evaluations of (iii) the size of gains from adoption, (iv) the impact on real income of main income-groups of farmers, rural labourers, and townspeople, (v) the downside risks around the above four components. Such an explicit system of choices — while merely making more open and rational what is done already — will be opposed by those who now claim to make these choices by 'common sense'. Partly, these are people defending their freedoms or preferences. They also include, however, research directors and planners who fear that formal criteria may discourage nonconformist researchers.

We have stressed that agricultural research needs more mavericks, more people who question the paradigms. The past successes of IARCs with irrigated rice and wheat encourage people who want 'more of the same' research. Yet many things — BT, the shift to Africa, the need for field diversity, the need to improve crops grown in environments generally more diverse than rice and wheat, new knowledge on population, the effects of MVs on 'backward' regions — may require shifts of the classical paradigm, that of transfer of one robust technology (and MV group) to many places. The complex problem of developing MVs and farming methods that absorb labour, yet do not stimulate poor people to produce even larger populations of potential workers, will not readily yield to conformist research. Nor will the need for research more responsive to the farming (and labouring!) systems and experiments of the rural poor themselves.

However, formal and quantitative published criteria for research funding will *help* the nonconformists. They can argue their case — say, for weed research, or for Leontief-type models, or for understanding agricultural progress in eleventh-century China — in the light of its expected returns: faster success in varietal innovation, more or faster adoption, more GNP gains from adoption, or a larger share of those gains for the poor. Today, a research nonconformist must often struggle against the undeclared criteria of a superior. These, while partly sensible, can also partly reflect the accidents of a research director's personal experience, the pressures of powerful political interests and scientific establishments, or on occasion even family or sectional concerns.

How could formal criteria, in choosing among research strategies, help directly? One example is the emphasis, in much African research, on farm practices or MVs that save labour where it is now scarce, at least seasonally. Formal research pre-assessment would compel intending researchers to estimate the pace of likely research success and adoption — and to assess whether, when the innovation comes onstream, the growing workforce would have made the labour-saving innovation inappropriate. If hand-weeding were judged inadequate, researchers in such circumstances would be guided, by this quantitative pre-assessment, to seek MVs that diminished the main weed threat (or re-timed their growth, so that weeding requirements missed the peak times of labour demand) — rather than to test herbicides, or to seek MVs compatible with them.

Formalising the choice, among plant breeding goals or strategies, will not remove the need for judgement. Is the breeder to aim at productivity, robustness and sustainability in respect of food plants, of plant populations, or of dietary energy for the poor? At neglected regions containing mainly poor farmers, or at advanced regions whose surplus feeds mainly poor workers? Should varieties be conserved *in situ* or *ex situ*? The answers are not obvious, nor universal. But the five-component, formalised choice procedure at least helps to get the answering procedures clearer, and more open.

It also, we admit, makes research administration harder. If the decision procedure means confronting a scientific establishment — e.g. one that wants research into high-lysine maize, when the probable gains to undernourished people are small — the normal processes of compromise, by which the world works, may suffer. Researchers' worries about their place in their sub-disciplines — which is already sometimes endangered by engagement in the not-quite-pure, multidisciplinary, at times a bit political, atmosphere of an applied food-crop research centre — are sharpened by management procedures that may well induce research less publishable in learned journals, especially if the most respected journals (and the best promotion prospects) are founded in outstanding work within the established paradigms of a single discipline. New incentives and career structures are needed, to insert young and able researchers happily into the more 'target-orientated' forms of research suggested here.

* * * * * *

Our second conclusion is that those emphases in research (both in IARCs and nationally) which have led to past successes with MVs need to be protected, and modified, in the light of experience and of new scientific approaches. For example, MVs make better *use of plant nutrients* than older varieties; but researchers need to ask what MVs and practices would encourage (i) more use of organic nutrient sources (as complements, not substitutes, for commercial fertilizers), and (ii) 'substitution of labour for fertilizer' by better timing, placing or combining of nutrient sources. Both the need to create productive employment, and the secular (albeit interrupted) rise in feedstock prices, render this important. The effects of MV-fertilizer options on outputs and employment in subsequent seasons and years, too, needs review. So does the right balance of research among biotechnology, other routes to nitrogen fixation, and nitrogen supplementation. Answers will vary by crop and agro-climate, and the question urgently demands the sort of formal decision procedures advocated above. Poor farmers' special need to avoid costly inputs and higher risks — and even poorer labourers' need for innovations that do not destroy employment — will be critically affected by these nutrient-related research choices.

Management of *light response*, mostly by breeding for photoperiod-insensitivity, is another area of successful MV research. However, it is increasingly recognised that farmers need plants that are insensitive to photoperiod at some seasons but not at others; especially for poor farmers, this is due to the risks of delayed access to fertilizer, and to the need to avoid harvesting when crops must be stored wet. MV research is only beginning to respond to these complex needs.

Resistance to moisture stress in some MVs, such as IR-20 rice, is greater than in the competing varieties they displace. However, maize MVS have displaced more robust (although lower-yielding) sorghums and millets, with special risks to the poor. MS is a complex matter; the effects on different crops, even varieties, depend critically — and differently — on when water is short. More work is needed to link agricultural researchers to irrigation researchers; accepting the new International Institute for the Management of Irrigation into the IARC system would be a good start. Much more response by formal researchers to farmers' own methods of water risk management is also required. The approach of formal research to MS, even with the help of BT, is limited by the fact that a food plant's response to MS partly depends on its surroundings — terrain, soil structure, and organisms (including other food plants, weeds, worms, etc.); most of this interaction is not heritable. Even the heritable part of a plant's MS response is polygenic and therefore hard to understand or manipulate. Such complexity is likely to be summarised in rules of thumb: in the wisdom of experience. Hence, in handling MS, agricultural researchers need to give close attention to farmers' and irrigators' perceptions and practices — and to the possibility that, in many cases of alleged MS, it is in fact nitrogen shortage that does the damage.

Despite earlier allegations that MV researchers neglected *pest control* in their search for higher yields, it is, increasingly, robustness in face of pests that gives new MVs their extra attractiveness. But, from the standpoint of the poor, is it the right sort of robustness, in face of the right sort of pests? More knowledge is needed about the scale of losses caused by different sorts of pests, and about whether the victims of such losses (workers and consumers as well as farmers) are poor and vulnerable. However, the quantity — and sometimes, compared to research into other pests, the specifity — of work on MVs' interaction with 'unfashionable' pests (weeds, rats and birds) is plainly far too low, relative to their economic importance. Herbicides play a huge role in weed research, yet are costly for poor farmers, and may displace poorer weeding labourers. Bird-resistant varieties — though carefully selected by farmers, as with the awned rice varieties of West Africa — remain largely unresearched, as does rat resistance.

As for the triumphs of pest research in MV selection, they have indeed greatly reduced losses to many insects, fungi, and bacterial and viral diseases. However, this very success carries new dangers, especially to the poor. Such dangers imply new research strategies — as may the MV scientists' great successes in developing plants for improved nutrient management. New definitions of 'efficiency', for plant populations and for single plants, may be required.

* * * * * *

Successful breeding, for yield and vertical resistance, has led to the expansion of MV rices and wheats which — despite the diverse origins of many a variety — are bred for extreme purity, drive out less successful varieties, and produce large areas with very little genetic diversity. These MVs challenge pests to develop virulent new pathotypes or die. Thus safe, successful single varieties in the short run often mean less diverse, riskier plant populations in the long run. The 'efficiency formula' needs to allow for such risks. That apart, what more can MV researchers do about them?

The shift from vertical to horizontal resistance — and sometimes to tolerance — is widely agreed, verbally, to be desirable. Yet many researchers clearly doubt whether it is feasible: for their practice is mainly to seek new, better vertical resistance, to keep one step ahead of the pathotype. In large part, this is a scientific judgement that outsiders, such as ourselves, should respect, even if we question it. We do, however, note that the benefits of success in such research last no longer than the resistance itself, while the risks if vertical resistance breaks down are borne wholly by farmers and consumers and are severest for the poorest. Poor farmers, for example, cannot often afford emergency prices for back-up chemical pest control.

Crop diversity, within and among seasons and fields, is as important as varietal diversity in securing plant populations against dangers of eventual new pathotypes. This is a very important addition to the case for shifting MV research towards neglected, less successful crops, which are driven out of many areas by the very success of wheat, rice and maize MVs. The need for crop diversity as insurance also argues for more attention by researchers to mixed-cropping systems than an attempt to maximise *expected* GNP gains — even if weighted to emphasise gains to the poorest most — would indicate. Diversity further requires to be preserved by well administered, fully catalogued, and (at least) duplicated seed libraries, whether *ex situ, in situ,* or both.

Diversity, for long-run pest protection, is one of the two main 'environmental' issues facing MV researchers. The other is the need to avoid creating varietal sources of, or incentives to, soil exhaustion. Given the degree of sustainable robustness, MVs need to be selected for better nutrient conversion efficiency always; for better partitioning efficiency sometimes (provided the crop parts 'selected against' are not vital to the poorest); but for better extraction efficiency only rarely, and then consciously and overtly. Experiments need to distinguish — as they seldom now do — between extra food yields due to four sources: each of the three above types of improved plant efficiency, and extra intakes of nutrients. Experiments should also assess the impact of the higher-yield package in later seasons, and upon mixed crops, on the affected area.

* * * * * *

As MVs spread to more regions, crops and seasons, the threats to diversity and sustainability may become more worrying. Right now, however, this is for most poor countries a less immediate problem than the fact that large numbers of growers rely upon regions, crops, and agroclimates where MVs have made little impact. Such growers can well lose, as extra output from MVs elsewhere depresses their product prices. (The very poorest — landless labourers — may on balance gain from the process, but in most 'MV-unaffected' areas, even in Asia, most poor people are still farmers, not labourers, most of the time.)

There is a true 'regional dilemma': research on food crops in promising, advanced, well-watered areas omits many of the poorest *producers;* research on neglected areas may do less to raise food output, and hence may not help the poorest food *consumers.* However, the expertise and past success of researchers into MV lead regions, crops, and topics gives these specialists status and power, so that the possibly diminishing returns to their efforts tend to be overlooked, as do the threats to diversity (e.g. among North Indian wheats) and the limited gains to the poorest. The lower prestige of forms of research that have in the past been less tightly organised conceptually, and also less successful — work on mixed crops, on upland areas, or on weeds — is also self-confirming; it leads to missed opportunities for big gains by assigning more resources, and more of the ablest and least conformist researchers, to such matters. The proportion of IARC efforts devoted to 'neglected' crops and agroclimates almost certainly needs to increase further, in view of these built-in biases to 'self-confirm' earlier, successful lines of enquiry.

However, the problem of 'neglected areas' need to be better defined. It is not simply a question of assigning cash to semi-arid uplands, humid valleys, etc. Researchers need to explore the reasons — unusually good water management, or good infrastructure for input delivery [Ahmed and Hossain, 1987]? — for 'spots of success' with MVs in otherwise unsuccessful areas. Also, these areas need to be classified better, so as to allow for (i) areas that can diversify into crops abandoned in MV lead areas; (ii) areas that can take up 'second-generation MV crops', such as the improved finger-millets; (iii) areas where MVs do raise output, but too slowly to offset the cost-price squeeze; and (iv) areas where poverty can be reduced through migration to nearby MV lead areas — leading to remittances, smoother flows of income, and more land-per-person for family members who remain.

Distinct research guidelines for each type of area are needed, because poor farmers are, in each area, differently affected by MVs elsewhere. Such guidelines become increasingly important as MVs of maize, sorghum and perhaps cassava spread in Africa.

Many areas (perhaps some entire countries) in Africa will remain untouched by any MVs in the early 1990s. Yet poverty will in most countries still mean for the most part, small-farm poverty, with few poor households mainly dependent upon hired work, and with non-farm incomes still largely dependent on farm outputs (e.g. via processing, or the manufacture of hoes or harnesses).

Most MV crops and regions have so far been linked to growing urban demand — for wheat, rice, even hybrid maize, from better-watered areas near big cities. As this changes, so should research priorities. In particular, attention to 'remote' areas or crops implies an new approach to farmers who produce mainly for 'subsistence'. Most researchers, agricultural or economic, assume that they can do little for such farmers, and can help poor farmers and their employees only with 'commercial' production. 'Near-subsistence' farmers are allegedly more or less outside the cash economy, and have little or no money to buy even highly cost-effective new inputs — seeds, fertilizer, tools, micro-irrigation. Yet we know that, even in remote places, 'near-subsistence' farmers typically spend a quarter of their time, and earn a third of their income, in non-farm occupations [Chuta and Liedholm, 1979]. These tasks bring in resources which can be used to buy farm inputs, if this is judged safe and profitable. Then, even food deficit farmers will use cash to buy MV seeds and fertilizers — rather than to buy food so as to make up for low levels of production from TVs.

This new perception of near-subsistence farming as a major client for MVs is a necessary part of any research shift to 'neglected' crops and areas. 'Neglected' crops are usually consumed by (or very near) the producers, partly because the high weight/value ratio precludes distant transport. 'Neglected' areas usually have costly and bad transport, partly because populations are dispersed over large areas of bad land (with few urban agglomerations, for want of rural food surpluses). So the shift to such crops and areas involves analysis of the timings, transport and delivery, and credit systems appropriate to local near-subsistence. Maize and sorghum research into composites rather than hybrids, for example, might be indicated, especially to reach the poorest farmers.

The basic reappraisal of 'near-subsistence' farming implies a new view of rural infrastructure. Often, this should be seen as a route to diversity and exchange *within* a region — not to national economic integration via long-distance trade *among* specialised regions. In particular, poor people's crops often have high weight/value ratios, or (like cassava) short shelf-life. MVs of such crops, in remote areas, can form the basis of dynamic modernisation only as tools for *intra*-regional trade, probably involving a nearby small town as 'growth pole' [Perroux, 1962].

Such a shift to neglected crops and areas, as a tool for poverty reduction through MVs, will also need specific changes in agricultural research priorities. Two examples suffice. (i) Upland crops (not only rice) — as compared with classic MV rice and wheat areas — require research to cope with denser, different, and differently timed weeds. (ii) Sorghum and millet are much likelier to be grown in mixed stands than wheat and rice; the need to shift research towards such mixtures is well understood at ICRISAT, but meets severe resistance in practice among single-crop specialists in national research systems.

* * * * * *

It is notable that research into the impact of MVs upon nutrition largely neglects areas and crops *not* affected by MVs. Yet such areas and crops represent the best prospect for overcoming the 'entitlements problem': that — even where MVs raise food supply — not much extra demand builds up in the hands of the hungry, so that the extra output raises stocks (or cuts imports) but does little for nutrition. If extra MV-based food is mainly eaten by its hungry growers and their children — or else is paid to hire extra farmworkers, who eat it — the entitlements problem does not arise: extra MV food goes straight into better nutrition. If MV research is to perform better in alleviating poverty, a shift to 'near subsistence' crops and regions is strongly indicated, especially if power-structures will otherwise steer benefits even of labour-using and food-producing research to the better-off. (This is not a defence of restrictions upon trade in food: if local 'near-subsistence' is to be made less uncomfortable, it should be through production rather than protection.)

* * * * * *

In the process leading to the establishment of the IARCs, the entitlements problem was largely disregarded. The poor were seen as (i) 'small farmers' in areas where MVs could be widely spread, who would gain (as yields rose) much more than enough to offset the cost-price squeeze; and (ii) food consumers, mainly urban, who would gain as MVs restrained food prices. These perceptions of 'who are the poor' since the early 1960s, have changed dramatically. Yet the consequential changes in MV research priorities are, at best, just beginning.

Even among farmers in MV areas, it is those with low household income (from all sources) per consumer-unit who face serious poverty. This at-risk group overlaps rather badly with 'small farmers', i.e. those with few acres (of whatever quality) per household. Both agricultural scientists and socio-economists need to look more closely at the effect of MV options upon the capacity of poor farm households — i.e., for the most part, those with many members, high child/adult ratios, and limited income sources — to earn income, from non-MV and non-farm activities as well as from the MVs. Timing of labour requirements of MVs, to avoid clashes with options for casual unskilled wage-employment, could be crucial here.

However, neither agricultural nor socio-economic researchers need spend much more research time on offtake of, or benefit from, MVs among poorer farm households in MV lead areas. The facts are well known. Such households adopt MVs, and gain thereby. However, unless helped (by well understood methods, both agro-technical and socio-economic), they adopt later and gain less than the better-off, risk-taking innovators.

More important, poverty — and MVs' impact upon it — is not a problem mainly for farm households in MV lead areas, but for farm households outside them — and in most areas for households that depend for income mostly on labour. Already, these include most poor rural households in Bangladesh, Eastern India, Java, Mexico, North-East Brazil, and parts of the Philippines, Kenya and Rwanda. By 1995, rural labour poverty will be more prevalent than small-farm poverty in most of Asia and Latin America, and in large parts of Africa. Research planning decisions, taken now, will if successful, lead to widespread innovations in 1995-2005. Yet these decisions, where they emphasise poverty, still look almost entirely at the impact of MV options upon 'small farmers', not upon rural labourers. *The main needed shift in poverty-oriented MV research priorities is to move the focus from 'small farmers' to rural labourers.*

The impact of MVs on demand for labour, while still clearly favourable, has been deteriorating sharply. Around 1965-70, if a hectare of land was shifted to MVs and thereby doubled its yield, demand for labour would rise by about 40 per cent. Today the rise would be about 10-15 per cent: still a gain, but only 3 to 6 years' worth of workforce increase. Yet this is a favourable instance, even for MVs, the most promising of labour-using innovations.

Part of this setback has been due to aid-supported research into ways to accompany MVs with labour-displacing innovations: herbicides, threshers, direct planting methods. Partly, it is due to failure to screen MVs for possible perverse effects on employment, e.g. of post-harvest labour. Some MV-linked research, e.g. into methods of fertilizer placement, has special prospects for improving employment, but does not appear to receive higher priority on such grounds. Commercial research is bound to respond to the bulk of effective demand by Western consumers and producers — and to some extent by big farmers in LDCs — to save labour-costs: it is therefore of crucial importance that publicly financed research, in IARCs and nationally, redress the balance. Given the expected rates of return, research directors should favour MVs, crops, regions, and characteristics where research outcomes will raise the demand for hired, unskilled labour — or reduce its supply, by generating innovations that make it more profitable or safer for deficit farmers to redirect family labour for the job markets to their own farms. The 5-15 year time-lag of research, together with steady growth in rural workforces, means that such labour-using priorities are usually correct even where, as in much of rural Africa, 'labour scarcity' is the theme of *today's* complaints and pressures (anyway mainly from not-so-poor employers).

Three problems arise. Should not MV research seek to moderate the peak-season demand for labour? Can it ensure that small, poor farmers and urban consumers not lose from a shift in research priorities towards labour-intensity? What will impede such a shift from inducing parents to opt for more children — tomorrow's workers?

Machines such as tractors, or inputs such as weedicides, can in principle merely add their forces to peak-season labour, thereby raising output, and hence jobs in other seasons. In practice, however, such equipment and inputs (i) seldom raise output, (ii) once acquired, are also used to displace workers in slack seasons. Alternative ways of spreading the labour peak, such as MVs with different maturity patterns — or of dealing with it, e.g. by developing complementary farming systems (and migratory patterns) for nearby regions — should almost always be preferred to subsidised imports, or research, to displace even 'peak-season' labour.

Although maximum welfare for poor *farmers*, as an aim, requires different research priorities from maximum welfare for poor *labourers*, there is seldom violent conflict. Farms with less land-per person are likely to support poorer households and to make more use of labour. Steering resources to such farms thus helps not only 'small farmers' but also labourers, since such resources will be used with more extra labour — either from hired labourers, or from family workers who thus compete less than before against hired labourers for wage-work — than if they were assigned to larger farmers.

Could poor urban *consumers* be harmed by a switch to labour-oriented priorities in MV research? Food staples for consumers, like work for labourers, should be increased by small-farm emphasis. Smaller farms usually produce more food and more employment per hectare — and work new inputs, including MVs, more labour-intensively also. The three anti-poverty aims — that poor groups should obtain more food, more work, and more small-farm income — may however, together constrain policy options quite seriously. If poor *farmers* are to gain from MVs, the productivity of farm labour must usually rise. It must rise faster than the demand for food; otherwise, poor *consumers* could lose, from rising food prices or growing import dependence. But it must rise more slowly than output per hectare; otherwise, once the expansion of arable farmland slows to a trickle, poor *workers* lose as farm employment falls off.

Of course, this does not mean that all MV linked innovations always have to walk this tightrope! Some LDCs have enough foreign exchange for extra food imports *and* development imports; some have very few poor farm labourers, or can absorb almost all extra workers outside farming; some have spare land. Most have none of these advantages; but even then it is only farm growth as a whole — not every single MV innovation — that needs to have just the right critical impact on growth of labour productivity, large enough to relieve poor consumers, not so large as to 'unemploy' poor workers. All the same, the existence of the 'tightrope' underlines the critical importance of planning MV developments as a whole. Competitive, imported, and private-sector research — all on balance desirable — complicate, and sometimes invalidate, both predictions and requirements for an innovation's effect on labour markets. However, at very least, an 'onus of proof' rests upon any proposed innovation in food farming that raises labour productivity more than yield, or less than the demand for food. If alternative innovations can be sought that have a good chance of successfully 'walking the tightrope', there is an *a priori* case for this.

Another important way out for MV research, seeking innovations that absorb labourers yet enrich small farmers, is to make use of the double meaning of 'labour productivity'. More food output *per worker*, obtained by innovations that substantially raise demand for person-hours, could be consistent with only a tiny rise, or even a fall, in food output *per hour*. Such innovations could help food output-per-worker to grow faster than food demand (thus assisting poor food consumers), while keeping the growth of food output-per-hour below the growth of yields (thus providing more employment per hectare, assisting poor workers). To achieve this, MV researchers will need to know how different MVs, timings, and cropping patterns fit into 'farm labour household systems' — not just farming systems.

Thus it is possible for MV research, if carefully planned, to serve poor farmers and consumers, while shifting the priority — as it must — to providing livelihoods for the labourers who by 1995 will form a growing majority of the world's poor. But would not such a shift of priority encourage poor parents to produce more children, in the hope that such children will soon bring back labour incomes? Policymakers should not ignore this risk. There is evidence, however, that widespread distribution of income gains, awareness of the spread of health benefits, and female education — separately or jointly — bring about fertility transition much faster than was once believed. Thus a more labour-oriented MV research programme, preferably but not necessarily linked with improved planning for health and educational provision could well help transition.

* * * * * *

The original thrust of MV research might suggest that these concerns about labourers are misplaced. Labourers, even if partly paid in kind, usually buy much more food than they sell. If MVs raise food supply and bring prices down, surely labourers must gain, as net buyers of food?

Unfortunately, this does not work well. (i) In many countries, domestic food prices are determined largely by world prices, not by domestic food supply. (ii) Even if workers gain from food price restraint, there is an offsetting loss, because such restraint reduces the employer's incentive to hire them. (iii) As workers move into each MV area — and as population and workforce increase — their competition means that, within a year or two of the shift to MVs, employers can hire labourers at much the same real wage as before; food-price restraint (via MVs) permits money-wage restraint, and again the poor gain little.

There *has* been some price effect — and, in the lead areas, a small real wage effect — from MVs. Food supply has become more local (with lower transport cost), more smoothly available, and more concentrated on inexpensive (coarse) forms of rice and wheat, standing at a price discount. The risks attached to income from food production, and to availability of food, have (on sensible definitions of risk) been reduced. Nevertheless, the incidence and severity of 'food poverty' — income-per-person too low to afford enough food — and of frank undernutrition have, even in some leading MV regions, declined little if at all.

The menu of MV-linked nutrition research may have made matters worse. It has diverted resources — from increasing, cheapening and stabilising sources of dietary energy, towards building in nutritional goals of secondary importance or less. The search of MVs rich in protein, or in specific amino-acids — while it was wisely aborted at ICRISAT — continues elsewhere, despite evidence that success would have scanty or no nutritional benefits, even if, as is not the case, it were clearly obtainable, heritable, and costless in terms of yield and robustness. The search for aesthetic or cooking qualities, unless clearly time-saving for poor working women, is likely to be harmful to the nutrition of poor people.

Of nutritional goals of current MV research, only improved absorption — via breastmilk and via weaning foods — properly addresses primary needs among persons at risk. Even there, attention to low cost and to seasonal availability should replace some of the current concern for 'energy density', which could become as dubious a slogan as the 'protein gap' used to be. Low-cost, ample, labour-intensive, robust calories, with some attention to the special needs of vulnerable groups (especially infants and weanlings), remain the best main focus for MV research. That focus is blurred by superficial add-ons, requiring breeders to incorporate this or that nutrient or characteristic because rats die if they eat only a cereal lacking it.

Nutritionists do, however, have major (and largely undischarged) functions in food crop breeding institutions. They should investigate the main nutritional deficiencies in actual human diets, especially of poor infants, based on each main staple. They should establish, with breeders and economists, the prospects, costs and benefits of developing MVs that correct those deficiencies (and compare those costs and benefits with other approaches, e.g. fortification). Also nutritionists should help to set MV research into the context of 'agriculture-health linkages'; infants' capacity to absorb different foods in infections, and measures to limit those infections alongside measures to improve access to food, may — given real incomes — largely determine the nutritional effectiveness for a household of an MV innovation. Finally, nutritionists should investigate the health-nutrition impact of labour requirements and income sources, especially for pregnant and lactating women, associated with alternative MV innovations.

* * * * * *

Many of these specific suggestions would require agricultural researchers to communicate across disciplines, or to engage new specialists. Even within a discipline, the type of economist or agronomist who analyses how MVs affect labour is often different from the type who looks mainly at 'small farmers'. The experience of IARCs with anthropologists has not been uniformly happy. In national crop research centres, posts for economists are often either unfilled, or occupied by persons without the seniority, esteem , colleagues, or career structures to communicate effectively with crop scientists.

How, then, is the need to place MVs into total contexts to be met, given the discipline-centred nature of careers in crop science and the effort (and strain) already involved in the unusually high degree of interdisciplinary task-orientation that characterises many IARCs and such leading national institutions as the Indian Agricultural Research Institute? These total contexts — 'systems', in the unpleasant jargon now current — are required for most of the anti-poverty work that we have outlined, from the analysis of MVs' effects on non-MV regions, though the appraisal of MV-related options relatively unlikely to be filtered to the well-off through local structures of power, to the general equilibrium approaches of sections 6, b to 6, f.

Four issues, raised in Ch. 7, c-j, increase the urgency of a new direction in the IARCs *Population pressure* requires them to incorporate demographic skills; to examine the impact of MV options upon poor people's nutritional entitlements, especially in large households; to use, but change, their farming systems research capacity for this purpose; and to reinterpret the whole IARC brief, which was written in the early 1960s to embody a now outdated view of the relations between population, food and poverty. *The shift to Africa* requires that IARCs develop clear views of their proper relationships to water research, to national research systems, and probably to 'slow and clean' versions of farming/labouring systems research. As just shown, the reduction of *labour poverty* increasingly requires quite new research priorities.

Finally, and tugging the other way, *biotechnology* requires that the public sector's 'traditional plant breeders' widen and deepen their disciplinary knowledge. At present, public-sector research into poor people's food plants in LDCs is of the 'fifth order of smalls' for BT research. Today's BT research (tissue culture development), however, is inherently pro-poor unless non-competitively privatised. The risks and hopes for poor people from tomorrow's BT research are enormous. Herbicide bonding, for instance, could harm them — yet, in the long run, BT could well greatly increase the comparative advantage of tropical and sub-tropical labour-intensive farmers in producing food staples. If the hopes are to be realised and the fears dispersed, LDCs need access to the highest quality of independent scientific BT research, closely linked to traditional plant breeding skills. Only Brazil, China, India and Mexico — and perhaps Indonesia and Pakistan — could conceivably achieve this on their own. Other LDCs, and the tropics as a whole, certainly need international support. Yet IARCs' own comparative advantage does not clearly lie in BT, nor indeed in basic science.

It would be dishonest to present a pat solution to this dilemma. Disciplinary deepening is needed by agricultural researchers seeking to serve the poor of the LDCs in face of a huge, still vague set of hopes and threats from BT. Interdisciplinary and contextual work, also incorporating new subjects from history to demography, is needed if agricultural researchers are to transcend more of their past, agroeconomistic, partial-equilibrium oversimplifications.

It is no solution to cry for more of everything. African countries need help to set up small, simple, indigenised research systems, with a few clear priorities. Within any research system, including that of the IARCs, communication across disciplines — or within a discipline, if its scope is allowed to become increasingly deep or complex — suffers from very rapidly rising marginal cost.

We shall not, however, close this book with a hedge. The IARCs have shown great comparative advantage in the poverty-oriented and applied linkage of 'traditional' plant breeding to other sciences, biological and socio-economic. They can afford *poverty-orientation* better than many otherwise excellent national crop research centres, which are pressed to meet the needs of powerful groups: urban labour and capital élites; big farmers in MV lead areas who supply them with food and exportables. IARCs are also better able to encourage *applied* and *interdisciplinary* work, because their high quality and past achievement reduce the reluctance of young researchers to risk deviations from the purer and more single-discipline approaches that usually advance a career in 'normal science'.

A twin, massive, and inherently interdisciplinary challenge is posed to the IARCs' technology-transfer paradigm: by the success of MVs without major poverty alleviation in much of South Asia; and by the very limited spread of MVs to the main crops and agroclimates of Africa. To meet that challenge will require more interdisciplinary work (often jointly with farmers and labourers), and more risk-taking with new disciplines — demography, hydrology, history — and new paradigms. Probably, only the IARCs can do these things on the requisite scale, and with the requisite capacity to concentrate on poor people rather than pure science.

IARCs have been right to move into BT, and also right to do so cautiously and cheaply. The main role here is to know, say and do just enough to pre-identify and avert specific major risks (and to identify, and to seize upon, specific major potential gains) from BT to the poorest, by main crops, regions, and types of poverty group. IARCs should, in our view, not undertake major basic, or applied BT research. It would divert them from their main tasks and their main comparative advantages. The first is in traditional plant breeding (and its allied agricultural and socio-economic sciences) orientated towards: yield and robustness in smallholder conditions; preserving and increasing diversity; avoiding soil or water mining; and embracing the newly enhanced needs for labour-intensity, and for a spread to new regions, crops and farming/labouring systems. The second is in applied interdisciplinary work to identify which MVs and associated farm practices can best home in on major poverty groups — given that, as we now know, an innovations's capacity to cut risks, raise output of cheap food, and employ labour need not *suffice* to enable poor farmers, workers and consumers to gain from that innovation, because such gain must be 'sucked through the filter' of a power-structure that favours the strong.

Except with unusually dramatic innovations, IARCs can reliably and substantially raise farm output — let alone help the poor — only in countries with functioning national research systems, able to screen and adapt exotic germ plasm for local conditions, and to deal with new pathotypes in time. Yet some African and a few Asian governments, under financial pressure, have repeatedly slashed research funds — not only preventing proper research, but not seldom forcing the research station to use its fields to grow food for its unpaid workers! More frequently, domestic agricultural research in LDCs make a real contribution, but is overburdened, overdiffused, and neglectful of main food crops, especially those consumed mainly in rural areas. In very few countries is BT work a sensible goal for national agricultural research systems.

This raises (at least) two main problems for the future of poverty-reducing research into MVs. First, can or should LDCs other than Brazil, China, India and Mexico — and perhaps Pakistan and Indonesia — divert, or muster, cash or researchers to provide, at least, early information on specific major 'hopes and fears' for poor people from BT for their main crops? Neither national centres nor IARCs are obviously suitable. UNIDO's new institute has few funds, and is apparently not concentrating on food crops. Perhaps some LDCs could use aid funds to purchase BT information from private and public sources; but problems of what to buy and of how to interpret it, apply it, and integrate it into national research and extension — will remain. A low-cost solution, that does not divert IARC or national personnel or cash from their prime tasks, is urgently needed.

An even bigger problem is how to develop effective, poverty-reducing agricultural research in countries now deficient in this. ISNAR, one of the IARCs, is the 'Institute for the Support of National Agricultural Research', and had developed — and helped governments to implement — recommendations in many LDCs. In few cases, however, has ISNAR found explicit commitment in national agricultural research to poverty alleviation; in Kenya it found that planning priorities for this were unreflected in research priorities [Lipton, 1985].

Such a situation is perhaps defensible. Some 'standard economists' might say: produce efficiently first, then redistribute to the poor. Even the radical economist Joan Robinson upbraided Sri Lanka for its welfarism, for seeking 'to eat the fruit before it has planted the tree'. Yet all this, in the context of research priorities, is abstraction of the wrong sort. Focusing national research upon poor people's crops, regions or techniques is one of the few hopeful ways to achieve lasting gains, without dependency, for poor rural people in most LDCs. Such a focus — involving more use of labour, and more research attention to long-neglected crops and areas — is not normally in conflict with growth.

In such countries as Kenya, Botswana or the Ivory Coast — which have a considerable infrastructure for national research, though one in need of concentration on fewer key issues — donors could reasonably ask that their aid be used, among other things, to help steer that research more firmly towards poverty reduction. A much more serious problem is posed by the many countries, in Africa probably a majority, whose governments have not shown much commitment towards research into main food crops. Why should they? Dispersed smallholders, with little or no experience of gains from such research, seldom press for it effectively. Money and experts are scarce. Governments, lacking even approximate knowledge of areas and outputs under main food crops, cannot assign research wisely among crops or regions; for main export crops, far more is usually known (and past results are known to have helped to finance governments and to pay off debts). Finally, most research takes 5 to 15 years from inception to widespread adoption; many governments are hard pressed to survive financially, even sometimes physically, in the next 5 or 15 *months*.

How is a constituency for national-level food-crop research to be built up under such circumstances? It is tempting to say: pick winners; don't complicate the issue by seeking poverty-orientation. The temptation should be resisted. *Socially*, experience in many countries shows that 'winners', having obtained a pattern of research to help them get further ahead, gain strength to prevent this pattern from shifting to help the poor afterwards. *Economically*, 'winners' tend to supply the extra food so capital-intensively as to create very little extra demand for it; for example, Botswana's grain needs could be supplied in most years by irrigating big areas of maize for a handful of tractor/combine farms along the Limpopo River, but almost all the incomes would go to rich farmers, input suppliers, etc. who would not demand much of the extra grain (and who do not require it nutritionally). *Politically*, a broad base of support for agricultural research requires that many farmers, or many consumers, expect gains; a few growers of food staples, even if each is big, are unlikely to have lasting power in countries as dominated by urban interests (and food imports) as most of those that currently lack basic agricultural research systems. *Internationally*, a counterweight to the excellent but 'biased' research embodied in imported machinery, inputs, and techniques needs to be constructed. Hence, even in countries starved of national food-crop research, it is mistaken to delay poverty-orientation until such research is well developed.

* * * * * *

MV research in and for LDCs is, in part, a prisoner of its own success. This naturally leads practitioners and funders to ask for 'more of the same'. Yet change is urgently required: by diminishing returns to 'the same', by radical changes in our understanding of poverty, and by the exposure of big gaps in MVs' impact upon it. Luckily, some of the necessary changes can build upon the proven comparative advantages of the IARCs. Others can be developed only through successful national agricultural research systems. Many LDCs have, or are constructing, such systems. Even for LDCs that are not, however, broad constituencies for poverty-reducing MV research have to be developed, alongside that for research itself. For poverty-orientated, MV-based food agriculture is the only chance to provide the growing poor populations of Asia and Africa with livelihoods during the many decades before their widespread industrialisation.

38. Africa's Agricultural Crisis: An Overview
Michael F. Lofchie

An increasing number of African countries cannot feed themselves. In many, domestic food production is inadequate to supply even the minimal needs of growing populations, and earnings from exports are insufficient to permit enough food imports to make up the difference. As a result, starving children have become a universal symbol of deepening economic deterioration. As television documentaries portray a human tragedy of unutterable anguish, World Bank reports provide cold statistical confirmation of the underlying phenomenon, an agricultural breakdown that is now continent-wide and has taken on ever-deepening proportions. Many African countries have suffered a precipitous decline in per capita food production since the 1970s, and as a result, Africa now imports approximately 10 million tons of grain per year, an amount roughly equivalent to the needs of its entire urban population.[1] With a population growth rate of approximately 3.5 percent per year (the highest in the developing world), Africa has been able to manage an increase in food production of only about 1.5 percent per year. In 1980, per capita food production was only about four-fifths of its 1970 level. Africa is the only one of the world's developing areas to have suffered such a decline and skyrocketing food imports during the past five years; this suggests that the problem of agrarian failure may be worsening.

It is impossible to calculate the extent of chronic malnutrition and hunger-related deaths with any precision because there are no continent-wide surveys: most estimates are based on rough calculations within individual countries. But the World Bank estimates that by the end of 1984 as much as 20 percent of the total population of sub-Saharan Africa was receiving less than the minimum amount of food necessary to sustain health. If correct, this would mean that the total number of severely hungry or malnourished persons may now have reached 100 million.[2]

Because export-oriented agriculture has also been subject to stagnating production, Africa does not produce a sufficient volume of agricultural exports to finance the purchase of minimal food requirements. The gross figures for export agriculture are at least as alarming as those for the food sector. By the end of the 1970s, Africa's marketed volumes of key agricultural exports were no higher than they had been some 20 years earlier. This resulted in a sharp drop in the continent's share of the world market for such vital commodities as coffee, tea, cotton, bananas, and oilseeds. Today, it appears extremely unlikely that Africa will be able to recapture its former share of the agricultural world market. There is no indication whatsoever of a significant reversal in production trends. As a result, food aid, once considered a short-term response to momentary episodic events such as drought or political turbulence, has not taken on permanent status as the long-term moral imperative of the world's donor nations.

Michael F. Lofchie: 'Africa's Agricultural Crisis: An Overview' from *AFRICA'S AGRARIAN CRISIS: THE ROOTS OF FAMINE*, edited by Michael F. Lofchie *et al* (Lynne Rienner Publishers, Inc., 1986), pp. 3-18. Reproduced by permission of the editor.

Human starvation on an appalling scale is only the most visible and dramatic outcome of agrarian decline. Africa has also become a continent of convulsive social and political turbulence that functions as both cause and effect of the agricultural breakdown. As a measure of its extreme instability, Africa, though it has only about 10 percent of the world's total population, now accounts for at least 25 percent of its refugee population. Approximately 2.5 million Africans are refugees, and this figure would be even higher if refugees remaining within their own countries were included.

There is a very real sense in which the human toll of agrarian breakdown extends to the entire population of most African countries. African governments, hard-pressed to find currency to sustain food imports, have often been compelled to cut back drastically on public services. The usual result of these cutbacks has been a drastic deterioration in the quality and availability of these services. In some countries, the educational and medical systems are so deprived of vital inputs that they function in name only.

In the political sphere, such endemic phenomena as corruption and repression also appear to be a direct outgrowth of economic decline. Political leaders, intent on maintaining their status and material perquisites in a context of diminishing overall resources, have used any means available to do so. Corruption in Africa also has its structural roots in the financial predicament of middle and upper class elites whose real incomes have been severely eroded by the inflationary process that has accompanied agrarian stagnation. This is most apparent in African societies such as Ghana, Tanzania, and Uganda, where the processes of economic decline are most advanced. In these countries, a civil servant's monthly salary is often inadequate even to finance a family's food requirements, let alone its other expenses, and corruption becomes the only alternative to white collar destitution. But these countries are simply the most extreme examples of economic trends that are, in fact, continent-wide. Political instability is compounded by the fact that corruption and repression inevitably give rise to a larger process of social and political demoralization.

To this degree, Africa's agrarian collapse is at the basis of a widespread breakdown of political legitimacy and a loss of social trust. Governments that cannot provide an adequate supply of reasonably priced foodstuffs to their urban populations have experienced sharp increases in public opposition, manifested most dramatically in the high incidence of food riots in many capital cities. Political demonstrations triggered by food scarcity have occurred, for example, in Cairo, Tunis, Monrovia, Lusaka, Khartoum, and Nairobi. The collapse of at least two of these governments, Liberia and Sudan, was rooted partially in sudden price increases for food staples. The collapse of the imperial government of Ethiopia in 1974 also grew from an agricultural crisis: the regime of Emperor Haile Selassie lost both domestic and international credibility because it could not resolve the problem of food scarcity in drought-stricken regions. Although the widespread loss of public trust in African governments is the outcome of a complex assortment of political and economic factors, none has as direct a bearing on popular attitudes toward government as the effectiveness of national political leaders in managing their countrys' food systems.

The deterioration of the agricultural sector has had reverberations that extend to other important economic spheres such as industry and commerce. Africa's industrial sector was built largely on the principle of import substitution and is thus almost wholly dependent upon the foreign exchange earned by agricultural exports to finance the import of raw materials, capital goods, and energy supplies. As agricultural export earnings have sunk, so has the availability of these essential industrial items. In countries that are most seriously affected, the industrial sector is now operating at approximately 25 percent capacity or less, and, given the numerous other pressures on foreign exchange reserves, it appears that the rate of capacity utilization in industry will only drop further in the foreseeable future. This creates a rapid increase in urban unemployment. In addition, the rapid proliferation of squatter settlements and peri-urban slums has been abetted by the massive influx of rural dwellers who are no longer able to sustain livelihood in the countryside.

As a result, Africa's cities are increasingly unable to provide economic opportunity for an economically displaced peasantry. With the decline of industrial activity, the rate of urban unemployment has shot upward, and unemployment rates of 40 percent or more are by no means uncommon. Even countries not so economically distressed, already confront a situation in which the number of school-leavers annually far exceeds the number of new job opportunities. In those countries where agricultural decline is more acute, annual job creation in the modern sector is a negative number. Such economic opportunities as are now available seem almost wholly confined to the informal sector where they provide barely enough income to sustain survival. Thus, the inexorable decline of Africa's agricultural base has also produced a steady widening of the gap between the poor and the well-to-do. Under these conditions, it is difficult to foresee any future other than a continued high incidence of military coups and other forms of political instability coupled with more serious manifestations of urban discontent such as food riots, political demonstrations, and anomic violence.

There is little basis for optimism that these trends can be reversed. Major economic indicators point in the direction of a further worsening of the present situation. During the past decade or so, Africa has become one of the world's major debtor regions, a status that, in itself, seriously complicates the process of economic recovery because of the burden of debt repayment. As late as 1974, the annual cost of debt repayment for the low-income countries of independent sub-Saharan Africa was less than $500 million. By 1984, that figure had climbed to almost $1.4 billion and was rising steadily. During this period, the average debt service ratio (debt repayments as a percentage of foreign exchange earnings form exports and services) for this group of countries increased from approximately 7 percent to more than 30 percent, and this figure will grow higher as borrowing from the International Monetary Fund (IMF) expands.[3] In the more serious cases, the debt service ratio is substantially higher, and for Sudan, Africa's most extreme example of debt problems, annual debt service actually exceeds total foreign exchange earnings.[4] Though unique, the predicament of Sudan may actually portend the future since other African countries have already had to reschedule their debt, and many have fallen far behind in their payments on foreign trade accounts.

A large proportion of Africa's foreign exchange earnings are now allotted to non-productive economic purposes. Debt-servicing is high among these but others include the cost of imported food and consumer goods, and energy supplies for nonindustrial or nonagricultural purposes (e.g., gasoline for private automobiles). There is almost no prospect whatsoever that foreign capital inflows will compensate for Africa's inability to invest in itself. For although foreign aid has continued to flow to Africa in generous amounts, it is clear that the continent's economic decline has had a chilling effect on foreign private investment which, outside the Republic of South Africa, has diminished drastically during the past five years. Africa may now have become a net exporter of capital. If the expatriation of capital by political elites interested in securing their personal resources abroad is added to other categories of capital outflow, the total could well exceed the net amount of capital entering the continent.

Contending explanations

Africa's economic decline has given rise to a burgeoning academic and professional literature that seeks to establish the causes and potential remedies for this decline. Much of this literature ranges along an intellectual continuum that can roughly be described as externalist-internalist in character. Such broad categorization inevitably involves an unfortunate element of oversimplification, since no serious author falls unambiguously into a single analytic position, and the particular mix of causal factors may vary considerably from one country to the next. It does provide, however, a useful point of departure for establishing the enormous range of analytic opinion that currently exists. Broadly speaking, externalists are inclined to place primary emphasis on causal factors outside Africa and, therefore, beyond the jurisdiction of its political systems, while internalists place greater emphasis on the policy failures of African governments.

External factors

Among externalists, there is a tendency to assign primary responsibility for the crisis to salient features of the international economic system including the declining terms of trade for primary agricultural exporters. There is a general consensus among observers of Africa's present economic crisis that the continent has suffered badly because of adverse changes in the international terms of trade and that its current parlous state can be traced in large measure to the fact that the costs of the goods African countries need to import have risen far more rapidly than the price of exported commodities. The most recent research on Africa's terms of trade shows an especially sharp downward trend beginning in 1979. It assesses this decline in the following stark terms:

> Between 1980 and 1982, prices of nonoil primary commodities declined by
> 27 percent in current dollar terms. The loss of income due to deterioration
> in the terms of trade was 1.2 percent of GDP for sub-Saharan Africa;
> middle-income oil importers suffered the biggest loss (3 percent of GDP)...
> and low income countries a loss of 2.4 percent of GDP.[5]

This trend helps account for the critical scarcity of foreign exchange currently experienced by the overwhelming majority of African states.

For some countries, the potential benefits of increased production have been completely eroded by decreasing prices for their products. Sudan, for example, was able to increase cotton production by about 50 percent in 1981 and 1982, but, due to a sharp drop in the world market price for this product, its foreign exchange position continued to deteriorate badly. World Bank economists now anticipate a continued fall in the terms of trade throughout the 1980s with price levels for Africa's key exports at least 15-25 percent lower than those that prevailed in the 1960s.[6] Price declines of this magnitude make it extremely difficult for governments to implement policy reforms, such as price increases, to improve production. An increase in domestic producer prices could result easily in enormous budget deficits if the world market price of that particular commodity were to drop further. Externalists believe that the critics of African governments generally fail to distinguish between poor pricing policies and the depressed price levels of primary agricultural commodities on world markets. They argue, as well, that the drop in foreign exchange reserves resulting from falling prices has constrained the implementation of infrastructural improvements intended to facilitate increased exports.

The scarcity of foreign exchange is compounded by another salient feature of the international economic system; namely, the markedly low demand elasticities for Africa's key agricultural commodities. World demand for such critically important agricultural exports as coffee and cocoa has been virtually static for the past decade or more and is generally expected to remain so for the remainder of this century. The World Bank's study of anticipated demand for Africa's principal agricultural exports over the next decade presents a particularly gloomy picture, suggesting that world consumption of the majority of these products will increase by only about 3 percent or less for the foreseeable future.[7] For such critical commodities as coffee, tea, and cocoa, overproduction combined with sluggish demand growth could well result in a further downward trend of commodity prices, thus accentuating the already severe foreign exchange constraint. Of all Africa's agricultural exports, only palm oil is expected to benefit from a growth in international demand approaching 5 percent per year. Ironically, due to the collapse of Nigerian palm oil production, most of this increase in demand will probably be satisfied by non-African producers.

These trends would appear to rule out almost entirely the feasibility of a development process based on the strategy of export-led growth. As agricultural exporters, African countries do not have the option of stimulating world demand for their products by cutting prices. In sharp contrast to world demand for industrial goods or manufactured consumer products, world consumption of Africa's most important agricultural commodities rises very sluggishly in response to falling prices. This means that African countries as a whole cannot compensate for low price levels by increasing the volume of agricultural goods they market. Although any given agricultural exporter could potentially expand its market share by lowering prices, its increased volume of exports would necessarily occur at the expense of other countries dealing in the same commodity. Export-led growth is not a development strategy available to African nations in general; it is a competitive market tactic available to individual producers.

Recent adverse trends in the international terms of trade gives every indication of being long-term in character. The downward pressure on price levels for African agricultural goods has been further reinforced by the introduction of a number of synthetic products that substitute cheaply for natural items and, thereby, compete with them in the international marketplace, synthetic rubber for natural, soft drinks for coffee and tea, artificial chocolate for cocoa, non-caloric sweeteners for natural sugar, dacron and polyester fabric for cotton, etc. The impact of multinational corporations on Africa's agricultural trade is also a topic much deserving of further exploration. It seems clear that the companies that buy and sell agricultural commodities in world markets are in a far stronger position to take advantage of the potential profitability of these products than the producer countries, and that their interest in profit maximization is also a significant factor exerting downward pressure on producer prices.[8]

The economic future of African countries will be a direct function of their earnings from agricultural exports. As small nations with limited internal markets, they have almost no prospect of developing diversified and internally self-sufficient economic systems. The harsh reality of today's international economic system is such that there is almost no prospect whatsoever that their foreign earnings from agricultural exports will increase appreciably. Instead, there is far greater likelihood that the majority of countries will be compelled by circumstances beyond their control to make do with lower and lower levels of export revenues.

African countries have also been buffeted by a host of other external shocks. These include, for example, the precipitous increase since 1973 in the price of petroleum, an escalation that has drastically increased the cost of agricultural production since so many agricultural inputs are petroleum derivatives. A rapidly growing tendency toward administered protectionism by the world's advanced industrial societies also has been harmful. This policy discourages incipient efforts toward industrialization based on export-processing.[9] Adding to the list of external factors that have suppressed African economic growth is the overvaluation of the U.S. dollar, which has created innumerable economic difficulties. It has severely compounded the difficulty of debt repayment, for example, since international loans are typically denominated in U.S. dollars and has contributed indirectly to the steep increases in petroleum costs since trade in this commodity is also conducted in U.S. dollars. Overvaluation has also increased the cost of a host of critically important consumer goods such as educational and medical supplies as well as vital agricultural and industrial inputs.

This inventory of adverse international circumstances could be compounded still further by taking into account the effects of the current global recession and high interest rates on hard currencies. Economic recession in industrial nations, for example, has contributed directly to sluggish demand for Africa's agricultural exports. High interest rates have not driven up production costs but put still further pressure on foreign exchange reserves by adding to the cost of loan repayments. The major point, however, seems well established and not in need of additional argument. Taken together, these external factors add up to a strong case that African countries have had to confront a deeply inhospitable international environment, one that would have created critical economic difficulties even under the best internal management conditions.

Internal factors

Authors who emphasize the internal sources of agricultural decay are inclined to attach greater importance to the economic policies pursued since independence by African states. Chief among these is the continent-wide tendency to control and suppress agricultural producer prices. Writing elsewhere, as well as in chapter 3 of this volume, Robert Bates has made this policy central to his analysis of Africa's agricultural crisis. In his classic study, *Markets and States in Tropical Africa*, for example, Bates notes that "the producers of cash crops for export. . . have been subject to a pricing policy that reduces the prices they receive to a level well below world market prices."[10] John C. de Wilde has commented as well on the extent to which African farmers have been burdened by governmental interventions in agricultural markets.

> The prices that farmers receive for their produce or that they pay for necessary production inputs and consumer goods have been significantly affected, not only by direct and deliberate price fixing but also indirectly by the cost and efficiency of parastatal organizations charged with the promotion of production,. . . by direct and indirect taxation of farm income, by differential exchange rates and by the maintenance of unrealistically high foreign exchange rates. Increasingly, too, the inflation engendered by government deficits. . .has impaired the ability to maintain adequate farm prices in real terms and caused serious delays in paying farmers for their products.[11]

Africa's agricultural crisis is continent-wide, but it occurs within individual countries and takes place on a country-by-country basis. Within any given African country, faltering agricultural production can be explained in large part by government policies that significantly reduce the incentives to agricultural producers.

The policy of price suppression is rooted in a variety of objectives including the desire to maintain a low-cost food supply for the cities and the belief that agricultural exports should generate an economic surplus adequate to finance the development of an industrial sector and the growth of important public services. It now seems clear that this policy has had effects that are precisely the opposite from those intended. It has become a major factor in accounting for the stagnation of Africa's agricultural exports. The disincentive posed by low food prices has severely constrained the available supplies of marketed food staples. Indeed, suppression of agricultural producer prices may well be the single most important factor in accounting of the sharp decline of Africa's share of world trade in agricultural commodities relative to other developing areas and for the skyrocketing increase of food imports.

A second major policy with adverse effects on agricultural productivity has been the ubiquitous tendency toward currency overvaluation.[12] The effects of this policy have been more severe in Africa's anglophone countries whose currencies are not tied directly to that of a major European power, but it occurs even in the francophone nations whose currency is tied officially and directly to the French franc. Currency overvaluation operates as a hidden tax on the financial return to the producers of export goods and thus has precisely the same effect on agricultural exports as the suppression of producer prices. It also depresses the availability of marketed food stapes for local consumption. By artificially cheapening the cost of importing foods, it sets up an unfair competition with domestic food producers. The broad impact of currency overvaluation is to subsidize the cost of living of urban consumers at the expense of rural dwellers.

The widespread use of parastatal corporations also has had a substantial and deleterious effect on Africa's agricultural sector. Africa's parastatals are characterized almost everywhere by destructive levels of corruption, inefficiency, and mismanagement. In some cases, the expenses of the parastatal corporations are actually higher than their returns from crop sales, leaving no margin whatsoever with which to pay the producers. The result has been a consistent and growing tendency toward nonpayment, late payment, or partial payment of farmers, a major disincentive in and of itself to the production of marketed agricultural surpluses. In a number of African countries, agricultural parastatals also are given responsibility for the implementation of key agricultural services such as the provision of fertilizers and pesticides, and here, too, the record of parastatal performance is, with rare exceptions, a uniformly poor one.

A poor choice of development strategies has also contributed to the present crisis. Some observers feel that the decision to pursue a policy of industrialization through import substitution, for example, may be held at least partially accountable for the continent's deteriorating agricultural performance. This policy has sapped away capital and other resources that might otherwise have gone into financing needed agricultural improvements. Michael Roemer, for example, has criticized import-substitution strategies in Africa because "they focus development efforts on industrialization although it is agriculture that remains the base of the economy and that employs the great majority of workers."[13] One of the factors that has undermined Africa's position in world agricultural trade has been its inability to respond flexibly to changing market conditions, by introducing new, high demand crops or more productive varieties of old ones. This rigidity seems rooted largely in the scarcity of capital for agricultural investment, and this scarcity is fundamentally the product of an industrial policy that is not oriented toward the generation of its own sources of foreign exchange.

Industrialization by import substitution has also required high levels of tariff protection for the new industries, and this, in turn, has meant that Africa's farmers have been confronted with extremely high prices for consumer goods and for the agricultural imports manufactured in the new industries.[14] Moreover, in many cases Africa's new industries have been marked by inefficient management, and this has sometimes resulted in severe scarcities of essential agricultural inputs. Urban industries also affect agricultural performance by competing in the same labor markets; by bidding up the wage levels, they can contribute to a labor bottleneck in the countryside.

The donor impact

In the broad dialogue between externalists and internalists, the impact of donor policies often is omitted, for the donor community operates in the interstices between the international economic system and the agricultural policies of host governments. The omission is regrettable since the international donor community is a vitally important actor in Africa's economic affairs, and donor policies often have an extremely significant effect on the process of African development. This is nowhere more conspicuous than in the rural sector where the influence of donor agencies is sometimes so strong that it can have a determinative effect on agricultural trends. It is clear that certain policies pursued by members of the donor community have played an important part in worsening Africa's agricultural crisis.

Tempting as it has been to some to conceptualize the international dimension of development in Manichean terms that define the key actors in relation to good and evil, this viewpoint adds little to an understanding of the complexity of the African rural sector. Although it might be morally comforting to believe that the process of agricultural decline could be arrested by removing the villains from the scene, this view has little basis in political reality. In the real world of African development, the rural policies of donor-actors are generally well-intentioned, and no small part of Africa's current tragedy lies in the fact that well-intentioned policies may generate unexpectedly negative effects. The discovery of workable solutions to Africa's agricultural crisis involves far more than a change of heart on the part of the donor agencies.

The rural policies of Africa's international donor community can be viewed usefully in historical terms. They arise as a response to the problem of development as it is construed at a particular moment. The projects that are set in place by donor-actors then quickly become in integral part of the rural landscape which is then transformed because of their presence. This injects an almost dialectical quality into the process of rural development. Thus, as donor policies trigger a process of rural transformation, the problem of rural development is altered and takes on a new configuration. The new set of conditions then calls for a different set of policies and programs. It may be useful to illustrate this highly abstract formulation by referring specifically to donor policies in postindependence Africa. This would help to place the question of donor policy in broader perspective and, thereby, illuminate the ever-changing nature of the interaction over time between donor agencies and the African milieu in which they operate. More specifically, it may help to show how donor policies that are intended to help promote rural development can become part of the problem of the agricultural sector.

Although Africa's agricultural crisis has reached epochal proportions only during the last dozen or so years, its initial symptoms were clearly visible in the decade immediately following independence. Africa had become a net food importer as early as the 1960s, but, at that time, the problem was not identified as one of major structural weaknesses in the agricultural sector. Not only were Africa's key agricultural exports still enjoying a robust performance in the wake of the post-Korean War commodities boom, but the volume of food imports was relatively low and did not pose a serious financial burden. Since grain prices on world markets were both cheap and stable, and since it was increasingly possible to obtain food assistance on concessional terms, the need for food imports appeared to be an easily manageable problem, one well within the financial capacity of the countries concerned. Even though the volume of food imports had doubled by the end of the decade, the most intensely debated questions about development did not focus on agriculture at all but rather on the best means of achieving urban industrial growth.

From the standpoint of international donors interested in rural development, the critical problem was how to improve the productivity of the food-producing sector so that food imports would not continue to be a drain on financial reserves needed for industrialization. The principal constraint on this improvement as identified by these agencies was the absence of agronomic or technological development among peasant food-producers. In the economic argot of the era, food production was a "backward" sector. It is not at all difficult to understand why development experts adopted this point of view. Africa's colonial governments had generally pursued a set of agricultural policies that were designed to promote the production of exportable crops, and that often did so at the expense of the food-producing regions. In many instances, export agriculture was assigned the best quality arable land, often on highly favorable terms, and was generously subsidized with physical infrastructure, extension services, and marketing assistance. Colonial governments also employed a variety of tax, trade, and labor policies to maximize the growth of the export sector.

Food production, by contrast, had generally been neglected during the colonial era. In contrast with export agriculture, for example, the food-producing areas had been systematically deprived of vital inputs such as extension services or improved infrastructural facilities. Food staples were generally produced on small-scale peasant farms that had changed little, if at all, during colonialism. The dominant technology was the hand-held hoe, and even animal-drawn cultivation was relatively rare. Land tenure was typically communal in character, and this, too, was used by colonial administrations to constrain development since land that was held in this fashion was considered unacceptable as collateral for loans to finance farm improvements. Indeed, the very same policies that had contributed to the prosperity of the export farms were often the source of backwardness among food-producing farmers. Producer prices for staple foods, for example, were set often at unrealistically low levels so that peasant food-growers would have to make their labor available in the export sector. As a result of these policies, the most conspicuous feature of African agriculture when independence occurred was the glaring discrepancy between the modernity of export agriculture and the almost completely undeveloped state of the food-growing regions.

The challenge of rural development, as perceived by innumerable professional experts and academic observers, was to complete the diffusion of modern agricultural practices throughout the countryside so that food production could keep pace with rising national needs. The policy chosen to achieve this goal was the creation of large-scale farms that could demonstrate scientific agriculture and the beneficial cost/benefit equations associated with advanced agricultural practices. This strategy for rural development has generally been called the "project approach," and its hallmark characteristic is intensive research in such areas as new methods of husbandry, the development of new high yielding seed varieties, and the most economic methods of implementing these improvements at the level of the individual producer. [15] The operative idea underlying this strategy was that once peasant farmers had been made aware of the benefits to be derived from agricultural innovation, their traditional resistance to change would be overcome, and sweeping improvements in the process of food production would take place.

The project approach did achieve a few dramatic successes.[16] But as a general policy, it not only failed by a wide margin to attain the ambitious goals its proponents had claimed, it may even have contributed measurably to a worsening of economic conditions in the countryside. It is clear, for example, that the project approach rested on a highly questionable assumption about the nature of the African peasantry; namely that peasant cultural conservatism was the principal obstacle to agrarian innovation. Today, observers of the African rural scene are virtually unanimous in their conviction that African peasants are not bound by cultural constraints; that they respond with alacrity to economic opportunity; and that when financial incentives are present, their production for the marketplace increases accordingly.

The project approach failed to diffuse improved agricultural methods for reasons that had little, if anything, to do with peasant cultural proclivities for traditional agricultural methods. Basically, it did not address inherited systems of producer pricing that left the vast majority of farm families with only the most meager cash incomes. As a result of these pricing systems, Africa's peasant farmers were simply in no position to take advantage of higher cost agricultural methods. The only real beneficiaries were governmental elites who were in a position to invest in large-scale farms and to take advantage of the opportunities for patronage and corruption that the projects made available.

The project strategy not only failed to diffuse new methods of production to the food-producing areas, it may even have contributed to the problem of declining per capita food production. Food crops grown on heavily subsidized demonstration farms sometimes competed on the market with those grown by peasant producers, and this probably contributed to low price levels that drove marginal producers off the land. In addition, the demonstration projects were so expensive to maintain that, once donor support was withdrawn, African governments were almost invariably forced to abandon them, though not before some had expended invaluable personnel and financial resources in vain efforts to maintain donor goodwill by keeping the projects alive. By the early 1970s, the African countryside was littered with the debris of failed agricultural projects. The costs of this policy, in financial and human terms, have never been fully calculated. But Africa's donor community in the aggregate must certainly have spent hundreds of millions of dollars on projects that had little realistic prospect of success and in so doing, diverted comparable amounts of scarce local resources into failed ventures.

Large-scale, capital-intensive projects are also vulnerable to criticism on ecological grounds. There is serious concern about the environmental impact of temperate zone agricultural technologies when these are transferred to tropical regions. Systems of cultivation which require that large areas of land be cleared of their original cover of forest and perennial grasses and which replace indigenous farming systems that involved mixed cropping and long fallow periods are highly destructive of tropical ecosystems. The annual harvesting of large areas of land leaves the harvested acreage exposed to the elements during the off-season and, thereby, contributes directly to the degradation of the soil base, making it progressively less suitable for agricultural purposes. This point was put most succinctly by Erik Eckholm in his study of global environmental problems:

> [In the tropical regions] the soil is less a nutrient source than a mechanical support for plant life which constitutes an almost closed cycle of growth and decay. When the land is stripped of its dense cover, the soil temperature soars under the intense equatorial sun, hastening biological activity and the deterioration of remaining organic matter. Torrential downpours, sometimes bringing six to eight inches of rain in a single day, wash away the thin topsoil and leach the scant nutrients it holds downward, beyond the reach of crop roots.[17]

This description of the human origins of desertification has direct relevance to vast regions of western Africa, where, it is now estimated, the Sahara Desert may be moving southward as a rate of several miles per year. Indications of the same problem can also be identified in eastern and southern Africa where such processes as soil erosion, nutrient-leaching, and laterization can be traced to the introduction of environmentally inappropriate cropping systems. There is also reason to believe that drought itself partly originates in changing patterns of human land use, particularly in areas where new forms of agricultural production have involved the massive stripping away of the earth's green cover.

Despite its shortcomings, the project approach has remained extremely popular with the donor community, and even today it remains a cornerstone of donor strategy for developing the African countryside. The donor nations' reluctance to abandon the project orientation may be explained partially by the fact that it retains a certain amount of popularity among African governments that welcome the vast inpouring of resources it makes available and the opportunities for patronage it creates at the local level. The donors' preference for large projects may also reflect the bureaucratic character of some of the donor agencies. Like other large-scale governmental bureaucracies, the donor organizations are often committed by their budget cycles to the expenditure of very large sums of money within very short periods of time, and they therefore frequently find it administratively impractical to fund numerous small-scale projects. There is clearly a continuing belief among many donor experts that the principal reason for the failure of the project strategy lies not in its intrinsic unsuitability, but, rather, in the cultural an educational inadequacy of the African peasantry.

It is clear that a decade of post-1974 famine development efforts based on the project model have done little, if anything, to prepare West Africa's agricultural systems for the effects of a period of climatic irregularity. Neither the innumerable large-scale projects that have been set in place nor the extensive programs of agricultural training and extension services that were developed to go along with them provided any cushioning whatsoever in the region's food producing capacity. As a result, when drought occurred, only massive programs of grain relief were able to limit the extent of human starvation. The famine of the 1980s is a watershed in the history of western approaches to African agricultural development. It has provided dramatic and incontrovertible evidence of the failure of the project approach. Indeed, if any single event could be said to have initiated a rethinking of the process of agrarian improvement and the possible contribution of western donors to that process, that event must surely be this famine. It also has altered substantially the present policy environment as it affects the African rural sector.

Conclusion: the policy environment in the 1980s

The single most influential example of the new research has been the World Bank report entitled *Accelerated Development in Sub-Saharan Africa: An Agenda for Action,* sometimes referred to as the "Berg Report" after its principal author, Professor Elliot Berg. This report represents a fundamental shift away from the project approach that dominated donor approaches to rural development throughout the 1960s and 1970s. It explicitly rejects the notion that improved agricultural productivity can be achieved through the diffusion of practices and techniques developed on large-scale, capital-intensive government farms. Whereas the project orientation was undergirded by a set of attitudes toward the African peasantry that bordered on the contemptuous, the Berg Report sees the African smallholder class in deeply admiring terms as the essential basis for any workable strategy of agricultural recovery. It states, for example, that "all the evidence points to the fact that smallholders are outstanding managers of their own resources — their land and capital, fertilizer and water."[18] The Report is unqualified in its insistence that African farmers already possess the requisite knowledge and agronomic skills to achieve both greater food output and a larger volume of agricultural production for export.

The most important feature of the Berg Report, however, is its unremitting antistatist position. Whereas the project orientation was based on the premise that African governments would have to play a major role in the dissemination of innovative agricultural practices, as well as in providing the proper climate for overall economic growth, the Berg Report is fundamentally committed to the proposition that the free market provides the most efficient stimulus to economic progress. Its analysis of the root causes of Africa's agricultural decline is decidedly internalist in character and its key arguments are strikingly similar, in many essential respects, to those of Robert Bates, noted above. The core argument, in a nutshell, is that African governments have pursued a set of policies that, taken cumulatively represent a systematic bias against the agricultural sector. The effect of these policies has been to lower drastically the incentives for agricultural producers, and, thereby, to contribute directly to stagnating agricultural production, both of domestic food items and of export crops. The solution to Africa's agricultural conundrum is to constrain the role of the state as much as possible and to allow the free market to allocate resources and to set agricultural prices.

The importance of the Berg Report lies not so much in its content as in its impact on Africa's donor community. Its intellectual influence has been astonishing and now extends far beyond the World Bank to encompass a very large proportion of the national and international donor organizations that operate within African countries. Within the brief space of a few years, nearly all of Africa's major donors have sought ways to introduce approaches to rural development that combine the project orientation with the forces of the free market and the potential for greater productivity of the individual peasant farmer. A large number of donor governments and agencies now insist that African governments shift their own policies to allow greater scope for market forces as a condition of further assistance.

The donor community's heightened reliance on the market mechanism is nowhere clearer than in the conditionality practised by the International Monetary Fund (IMF): it tends to insist that policy reforms of the sort advocated by Berg be implemented as a condition of financial assistance. Supporters of the IMF defend its conditionality on the basis that it is not a development organization but, rather, a lending institution whose principal interest is economic stablization. Its role as a provider of capital to low-income African countries has today become so great, however, that this distinction is difficult, if not impossible, to sustain. The policy reforms it attaches to its loans have a vital and direct bearing on the patterns of development that are occurring in a number of African countries.

One example of the IMF's impact is treated in detail in the final section of this volume, in Biswapriya Sanyal's essay "Rural Development and Economic Stabilization: Can They Be Attained Simultaneously?" There would be little value, therefore, in an extended recitation of Sanyal's findings. Suffice it to say here that the free market reforms insisted upon by the IMF did not generally produce the results intended; the evidence tends to show that the socioeconomic changes that took place were adverse to increased productivity on the part of smallholder farmers. IMF conditionality did not promote an increase of national investment in agriculture but, rather, led to a continuation of past investment policies that had concentrated the nation's capital in the mining industry. Nor did implementation of IMF reforms shift the internal terms of trade back toward the countryside and against the urban areas. Indeed, Sanyal's evidence shows unmistakably that the more distant smallholders were in substantially poorer circumstances after the implementation of the economic reforms than they had been previously. Although it might be premature to reach broad conclusions on the basis of a single case study, Sanyal's essay suggests strongly that the free market approach of African rural development merits more intensive scrutiny before its unbridled imposition on the African countryside.

In medical circles, there is an aphorism to the effect that a doctor who is not absolutely certain that the available cures will improve the patient ought to refrain from prescribing any treatment whatsoever. This advice, however sound in doctor-patient relations, does not seem at all realistic when applied to the interactions between donor and recipient nations in Africa. For twenty-five years, western and African nations have been mutually involved in a variety of aid relationships. These relationships seem destined to continue in one form or another for the foreseeable future. On the basis of past performance, however, there is little evidence to suggest that these relationships hold any significant promise of helping the continent to solve its agrarian crisis or the all-pervasive human starvation that this crisis entails. If future aid programs contribute as little to solving Africa's agricultural crisis as those that have been in place since independence, then the prognosis for Africa's human future is so unspeakably dim that it may be appropriate after all to consider the wisdom of the medical metaphor.

Notes

1. The figures here are taken from the World Bank report, *Toward Sustained Development in Sub-Saharan Africa: A Joint Program of Action* (Washington, D.C.: World Bank, 1984). See esp. pp. 1-3, 9-14, and 21-22.

2. Ibid., p. 9.

3. *Coping With External Debt in the 1980's* (Washington, D. C.: World Bank, 1985), pp. 6-7.

4. *Toward Sustained Development,* p. 13.

5. Ibid., pp. 11-12.

6. *Sub-Saharan Africa: Progress Report on Development Prospects and Programs* (Washington, D.C.: World Bank, 1983), pp. 3-4.

7. *Coping with External Debt,* p. 8.

8. For a full account of this issue, see Barbara Dinham and Colin Hines, *Agribusiness in Africa* (London: Earth Resources Research Ltd., 1983). Also, Mohamed S. Halfani and Jonathan Barker, "Agribusiness and Agrarian Change," in Jonathan Barker, ed., *The Politics of Agriculture in Tropical Africa* (Beverly Hills: Sage, 1984), chapter 3.

9. For a full account, see *The Political Structure of the New Protectionism* (Washington, D.C.: World Bank Staff Working Paper No. 471, 1981).

10. Robert Bates, *Markets and States in Tropical Africa* (Berkeley and Los Angeles: University of California, 1981), p.28.

11. John C. de Wilde, *Agriculture, Marketing and Pricing in Sub-Saharan Africa* (Los Angeles: African Studies Center and Crossroads Press, 1984), p. 118.

12. For an excellent survey of the relationship between currency exchange rates and performance of the agricultural sector in Africa, see Delphin G. Rwegasira, "Exchange Rates and the Management of the External Sector," *The Journal of Modern African Studies,* vol. 22 (September 1984), pp. 451-467.

13. Michael Roemer, "Economic Development in Africa: Performance Since Independence, and a Strategy for the Future," in *Daedalus* (Spring 1982), p. 132.

14. For an excellent discussion of the burden of industrial policy on Africa's agricultural sector, see chapter 4 in Bates, *Markets and States,* pp. 62-77.

15. For a discussion of the project strategy, see de Wilde, *Agriculture, Marketing and Pricing,* pp. 1-3.

16. The most widely cited of these is the case of the hybrid maize in Kenya that during the late 1960s and early 1970s was widely adopted by peasant farmers and resulted in a production increase of between 50 and 100 per cent, enough to keep pace with that country's population increase for approximately a decade.

17. Erik P. Eckholm, *Losing Ground; Environmental Stress and World Food Prospects* (New York: Norton, 1976) p. 137. See also Antoon de Vos, *Africa: The Devastated Continent* (The Hague: Dr. W. Junk, 1975).

18. World Bank, *Accelerated Development in Sub-Saharan Africa: An Agenda for Action* (Washington D.C.: IBRD, 1981), p. 35.

39. Food vs. Cash Crops in Africa
Andrew Storey

This article by Andrew Storey of the Economic and Social Research Institute compares the 'competition argument' that export crops crowd out food crop production with the 'complementarity' claim that there is a place for both kinds of production in the food policy of thirty-three sub-Saharan African countries. Empirical results indicate that export and food crop production can be complementary and can help to raise consumption levels provided adequate foreign exchange and agricultural services are directed towards food production.

Introduction

No one questions today the need to give greater priority in Africa to agricultural production, but there is considerable debate about the appropriate production strategy between advocates of food self-sufficiency, on the one hand, and of export promotion, on the other. This debate was heightened by the publication of the World Bank Berg Report *Accelerating Development in Sub-Saharan Africa* in 1981. This report recommended an expansion of peasant exports, but was criticised by those who argued that food self-sufficiency should be the continent's first priority. Critics fear that the production of agricultural exports will increasingly be controlled by an expanded agribusiness, and thus lead to an increase in rural poverty and hunger through competition between food and export crops for scarce capital, land and other inputs, and through a growing consolidation of land ownership and control which would decrease the access of small farmers to the land and create a larger rural proletariat.

Two of these concerns are considered in this article. Section I examines the criticism that export crop production 'crowds out' the production of basic food staples. This will be referred to as the competition argument, to be contrasted with the complementarity argument, put forward by the proponents of export crop production, notably the World Bank. The complementarity advocates claim that export crop production need not affect food production levels negatively and that, in fact, the two forms of production are most likely to expand or decline at the same time in any one country.

There is also a sense in which those recommending export crop promotion regard the complementarity versus competition debate as a side-issue. They argue that if export crop production is undertaken on the basis of comparative advantage there is no problem even if it does displace domestic food production. This is because the foreign exchange earned should finance food imports capable of raising, or at least maintaining, domestic food consumption levels. Section II looks at the relationship between export crop production and food consumption in Africa.

We should define what is meant by export crop and food crop. African export crops are those for which over 50% of production is exported in over 50% of the countries surveyed.

Andrew Storey: 'Food vs. Cash Crops in Africa' in *TRÓCAIRE DEVELOPMENT REVIEW* (1986), pp. 44-57.

Six crops are thus identified from FAO production data — cotton, coffee, cocoa, tea, sisal and tobacco. Food crops consist of cereals, pulses, roots and tubers. The comparisons below are based on aggregated trends for both types of crops.

I. Export food production and food crop production

The arguments outlined

The competition argument seems intuitively plausible: countries with limited resources of land, labour and capital can only allocate those resources to a limited number of activities. If priority is accorded to export crop production then food production seems certain to suffer as a result. Land devoted to the production of coffee cannot be used to grow food staples.

There are, however, a number of factors which could allow production of export crops and food crops to be complementary. Let us take the example of small farmers engaged in subsistence food production who introduce a new export crop. Bearing in mind that agricultural production is a combination of land area and crop yield, food production can be prevented from declining if:

(a) there is an increase in the total land area under cultivation;
or (b) food crop yields rise sufficiently to compensate for the land area given over to the export crop.

How important each of these effects is in a practice will depend on the resource constraints faced by the farmers. If land is in short supply then (a) is unlikely to operate. But there could, for example, be significant seasonal underemployment of labour in the area and this reserve could be called upon to help generate more intensive food production from a reduced food-producing area some of whose land is devoted to the new export crop.

At a formal level at least four factors could be expected to foster complementarities in production at a microeconomic level (World Bank, 1985).

1. Extension, input supply, and marketing services built up around the export sector could simultaneously be used for the benefit of food producers.

2. Fertiliser residues remaining from a commercial lead crop could directly benefit later food production.

3. Farmers specialising in export crop production may themselves develop a food deficit, thus creating a market for local food crop producers which would likely be more secure and stable than distant urban markets.

4. The additional income earned through export crop production could allow producers to adopt productivity-improving inputs which could boost staple crop production even when labour is diverted. (This argument can be broadened to apply at the macroeconomic level — the foreign exchange necessary to sustain and increase food crop production may first have to be earned by agricultural production for export.)

On an *a priori* basis one would not expect the land use constraints which might cause at least some degree of crop competition to arise in the generally land-extensive environment of Africa. Nevertheless Lappe and Collins (1982) cite examples of such competition at work. In Kenya the development of a new variety of cotton meant that food crops could be no longer planted in the same field as the cotton crop — the new cotton was insufficiently hardy to adapt to these conditions. Similarly in Burkina Faso farmers were obliged by the government to plant a certain acreage of cotton and had to find a supplementary crop which could be planted later but still fitted into the short planting season — traditional food crops of sorghum and millet could not meet this schedule which forced the farmers to turn to the low-nutrition cassava crop. Similar substitution of cassava for other food crops is apparently taking place in Tanzania, in this case because cassava is relatively less labour-intensive than other food crops and labour is increasingly needed for seasonal tobacco production. For Kenya and Tanzania as a whole Lappe and Collins point to evidence collected by World Bank rural economist Uma Lele (1973) of substantial substitution effects between food and export crops (tea, cotton and tobacco) (Lappe and Collins, 1982, pp. 160-1).

The advocates of the complementarity argument respond by claiming that institutional factors are creating a degree of competition where none might necessarily have existed. Lappe and Collins themselves point out that much of the problem in Tanzania lies with the government's failure to transfer the agricultural extension techniques and incentive systems developed for the cash crop sector to the food crop sector. Thus the potential for complementary increases in production (along the lines of factor 1 above) is being neglected. This insight is borne out by Odegaard (1985) who shows that the great bulk of modern farming inputs — chemical fertilisers, pesticides, hybrid seeds, etc. — were made available only to the cash crop sector (e.g. tobacco) in Tanzania's post-colonial period. Research and developmental funding for food production has been disproportionately allocated to large-scale farmers while the peasant sector has largely been neglected. Odegaard suggests that the more widespread provision of modern inputs to the food-producing sector could improve productivity sufficiently to allow land to be freed for cash crop production without any negative effect on food production levels (Odegaard, 1985, ch. 6).

In a later work, Lele (1975) also suggests that it is often policy failure which prevents export cropping from being associated with positive rather than negative effects on food production. Her evidence is also drawn from Tanzania, and in particular, from tobacco-growing schemes in Uranbo and Tumbi. From 1964 onwards these schemes provided additional services to food production, including credit to help smallholders purchase seed and fertiliser for paddy and maize production. The results were dramatic increases in food grain production and off-farm sales (Lele, p. 29).

Previous research

The problem in assessing these conflicts is to know how extensive they are and whether they are inevitable. Much of the criticism of export cropping is based on anecdotal evidence. Arguments of this kind are seriously weakened if counter-examples can be cited. As far as the increase in cotton production in Burkina Faso is concerned one could equally well point out that those areas which do not engage in significant export crop production tend to be food deficit regions or are at best self-sufficient in food, while the cotton-producing areas continue to market substantial quantities of cereals (World

Bank, 1985, p. 4). Between 1960 and 1983 cotton production did increase 32-fold for Burkina Faso as a whole but millet and sorghum production levels actually remained unchanged (George, 1984, pp. 72-3). This may be evidence of misplaced government priorities but it certainly lends no support to the competition argument. The same trends are identifiable in Mali yet both these countries are resource-poor, countries where one might most expect a trade-off between the two types of production to arise (World Bank, 1985, p. 4).

A more comprehensive examination of the trends in food and export crop production is clearly called for. Von Braun and Kennedy (1985) examine 78 less developed countries (LDCs) over the period 1968-82, looking both at their levels of food and cash crop production and at the proportions of land areas devoted to each. Their findings suggest that the majority of countries which managed to expand their *per capita* production of basic food staples simultaneously increased, rather than reduced, their share of land area devoted to cash crops. The opposite combination tends to hold for most low-income African countries: per capita food production levels stagnated or declined at the same time as the allocation of land shares to cash crops declined or remained constant.

This means that complementarity was being sustained by yield increases in food production at the same time as land was actually being switched away from such production. Most countries which cut back on land allocations to the cash crop sector ended up with production declines in both food **and** cash crop sectors.

> "If there is a general message . . . it is probably that an appropriate agricultural policy permits joint growth in both the cash crop sector and the staple food crop sector, and that failure in agricultural policy affects both subsectors alike." (Von Braun and Kennedy, 1985, p. 32).

Another study looked at the food and non-food[2] production performances of 38 African countries over two periods: 1960-70 and 1970-82 (World Bank, 1985). Its main findings were that:

- in 25 countries (66%) *both* the rate of growth of food production and of non-food production fell in 1970-82 compared to 1960-70;

- in 6 countries (16%) the rates of growth in *both* types of production for 1970-82 registered an increase over the earlier period;

- in 5 countries (13%) the rate of growth in non-food production declined while that of food production increased;

- in 2 countries (5%) it was the rate of growth in food production which declined while that of non-food production accelerated.

Thus only 18% of the sample countries suggest the existence of a possible trade-off along the lines predicted by the competition argument. Interestingly none of the resource-poor Sahelian countries register a trade-off between the two types of production, while those which do show food production growth accelerating at the same time as non-food production growth slows down appear to have few resource constraints regarding land (e.g. Liberia, Central African Republic) or labour (e.g. Ivory Coast). This evidence also seems to cast doubt on the inevitability of a food crop — cash crop conflict. The study concludes: "The general point is that the benefits of a changing, dynamic agriculture are not restricted to a single crop or set of crops. When change accelerates, the productivity of the whole farming system also increases." (p. 5)

While these studies contrast food production performance with cash crop or non-food production performance they do not specifically address the issue of *export* cropping and its effect on staple food production. There is considerable overlap between the 'cash', 'non-food' and 'export' categories but it is nonetheless desirable to investigate the relationship between food and export crops for precisely defined sectors. This is done for 33 sub-Saharan African countries over the period 1963-81 in the following sections.

The relationship between export crop production and food crop production in Africa 1981

Graph 1 plots the 1981 *per capita* levels of food crop and export crop production in each of the 33 countries. (See below for a guide to the country numbering system). This graph is divided into four quadrants based on the average per capita levels for both types of production for the continent as a whole to allow comparisons across countries:

- 6 countries (18%) had above-average levels of both export and food crop production: Cameroon, Central African Republic, Ivory Coast, Madagascar, Malawi, and Zimbabwe;

- 14 countries (42% did relatively badly in both forms of production: Angola, Congo, Ethiopia, Guinea, Lesotho, Liberia, Mauritania, Mozambique, Senegal, Sierra Leone, Somalia, Uganda, Zaire, and Zambia;

- 5 countries (15%) had an above-average level of export crop production but performed relatively poorly in terms of food production: Chad, Ghana, Mali, Sudan, and Tanzania;

- 8 countries (24%) performed well in food production and poorly in export crop production: Benin, Burundi, Kenya, Niger, Nigeria, Rwanda, Togo and Upper Volta.[3]

Graph 1   Levels of Food Crop and Export Crop Production, 1981

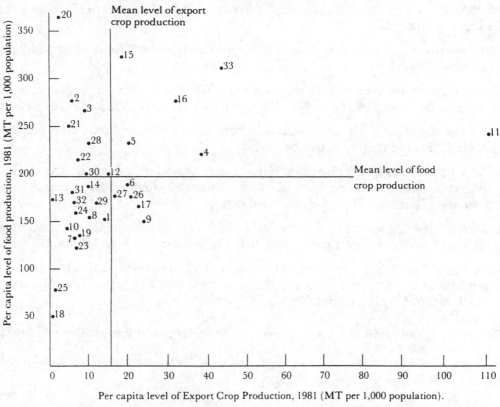

Per capita level of Export Crop Production, 1981 (MT per 1,000 population).

Guide to country numbering system, used in graphs

1 Angola	12 Kenya	23 Senegal
2 Benin	13 Lesotho	24 Sierra Leone
3 Burundi	14 Liberia	25 Somalia
4 Cameroon	15 Madagascar	26 Sudan
5 Central African Republic	16 Malawi	27 Tanzania
6 Chad	17 Mali	28 Togo
7 Congo	18 Mauritania	29 Uganda
8 Ethiopia	19 Mozambique	30 Upper Volta
9 Ghana	20 Niger	31 Zaire
10 Guinea	21 Nigeria	32 Zambia
11 Ivory Coast	22 Rwanda	33 Zimbabwe

The export crop and food crop sectors thus tend to register similar performances, for better or worse, in 60% of the countries. These results are not, however, particularly conclusive as a sizeable minority of countries (33%) do suggest the existence of a trade-off between the two types of production. On the other hand there is no evidence that those countries with relatively high levels of export crop production achieved those levels at the *expense* of their food-producing sectors; in fact the 4 top export crop producers — Ivory Coast, Zimbabwe, Cameroon, and Malawi - were all above-average food crop producers.

The relationship between export crop production and food crop production in Africa 1963-81

Graph 2 shows the percentage changes in per capita levels of export crop and food crop production between 1963 and 1981. A country-by-country breakdown reads as follows:

- 3 countries (9%) achieved increases in both export crop and food crop production: Malawi, Rwanda, and Zimbabwe;

- 14 countries (42%) registered declines in both types of production: Angola, Benin, Burundi, Central African Republic, Chad, Ethiopia, Ghana, Mozambique, Nigeria, Somalia, Tanzania, Togo, Uganda, and Zaire;

- 3 countries (9%) increased their levels of food crop production but experienced declining levels of export crop production: Cameroon, Niger, and Sudan;

- 10 countries (30%) increased export crop levels but saw their food production performance deteriorate: Congo, Guinea, Ivory Coast, Kenya, Liberia, Madagascar, Mali, Sierra Leone, Burkina Faso, and Zambia.[4]

Graph 2   Changes in Per Capita Levels of Food Crop and Export Crop Production, 1963-81 (%)

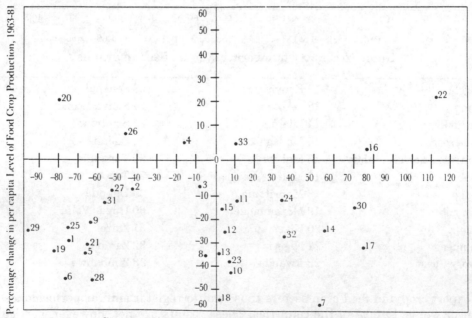

Percentage change in per capita Export Crop Production, 1963-81

The most striking fact to emerge from these figures is that 72% of countries registered declines in their food crop production levels over the period examined. Of these 24 countries, 14 experienced declining export crop production over the same period, which would indicate a tendency towards poor performance in both rather than improvement in one at the expense of the other. Six countries did improve their levels of food production, and these were equally divided between those which did so in association with increases or decreases in export crop production levels.

The figures are once again inconclusive. Advocates of the competition argument will point to the fact that 10 countries increased their export crop production levels but did not enjoy the food production increases the complementarity argument anticipated. This evidence therefore offers ammunition to both sides of the debate.

To sum up on the relationship between export crop production and food crop production: writers such as Lappe and Collins have identified ways by which competition could arise between the production of food crops and export crops, and have cited examples of such competition in practice. One can, however, equally identify ways in which the two forms of production may be complementary, and blame many of the various forms of competition on a failure of policy to exploit this complementary potential.

Although previous studies tend to support the complementarity argument, the examination of sub-Saharan Africa carried out for this study suggests a weaker level of association between the two forms of production though it remains generally positive. There is insufficient evidence to warrant a strong conclusion in favour of one or other argument, but the competition argument of an inevitable conflict between export crops and food production has the least empirical support.

II. Export crop production and food consumption

We noted earlier that for advocates of an export-oriented agricultural strategy for Africa it is the relationship between export crop production and food consumption which is the bottom line. We now turn to examine the evidence on the relationship between export crop production and domestic food consumption. The opponents of export crop promotion anticipate such effects to be negative owing to the alleged negative impact on food production levels (see Section 1), the supposedly limited and uncertain foreign exchange earning capacity of LDC export crops, the claim that those who receive most of the foreign exchange benefits — TNCs and domestic elites — use them for purposes other than food imports, e.g. military expenditures and western-style consumer goods.

If these arguments are valid then one would expect increased export crop production to be associated with declining levels of per capita calorie supply, and those countries with the largest export crop sectors to be worst off nutritionally. As mentioned at the outset, the advocates of export crop production claim that such production undertaken on the basis of comparative advantage will generate sufficient foreign exchange to pay for food imports which will stabilise or boost domestic food consumption levels, i.e. there would be a positive relationship between export crop production and per capita calorie supply. Some argue that this applies regardless of the effect on domestic food production but, crucially, it does depend on the foreign exchange earned being used on food imports. These arguments are examined for the sample of African countries, firstly by comparing levels of export crop production and per captia calorie supply in 1981, and secondly by comparing trends in those two variables for the period 1963-81.

The relationship between export crop production and per capita calorie intake, 1981

Graph 3 plots the level of *per capita* export crop production and food consumption (calorie supply) for the 33 African countries studied. Vertical and horizontal lines are also drawn through the mean levels of each so that countries with above or below average performances can be identified.

Graph 3   Levels of Export Crop Production and Food Consumption, 1981

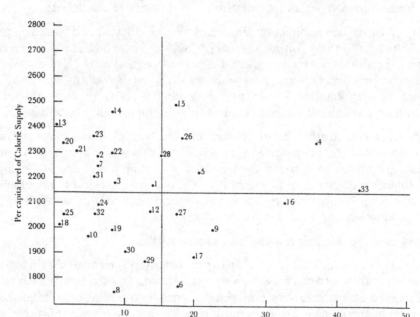

Per capita level of Export Crop Production, 1981 (MT per 1,000 population).

The following results emerge:

- 6 countries (18%) had above-average performances in both export crop production and food consumption: Cameroon, Central African Republic, Ivory Coast, Madagascar, Sudan, and Zimbabwe;

- 10 countries (30%) had below-average performances in both export crop production and food consumption: Ethiopia, Guinea, Kenya, Mauritania, Mozambique, Sierra Leone, Somalia, Uganda, Burkina Faso, and Zambia;

- 6 countries (18%) performed well in export crop production but relatively poorly in terms of food consumption: Chad, Ghana, Malawi, Mali, Tanzania, and Togo;

- 11 countries (33%) registered above-average levels of food consumption along with below-average concentrations on export crop production: Angola, Benin, Burundi, Congo, Lesotho, Liberia, Niger, Nigeria, Rwanda, Senegal, and Zaire.

This pattern would seem to indicate little if any correlation between the two variables, although there is a slightly positive statistical association. This positive result may be partially attributable to the fact that three of the countries which combined good performances in export crop production and food consumption were also those which had the *highest* per capita levels of export food crop production — Ivory Coast, Zimbabwe, and Cameroon — i.e. those countries which did best in export crop production suffered no negative nutritional effects.

What of those six countries which showed poor levels of food consumption despite (or because of?) good export crop production levels? In Togo and Malawi per capita *food* production performance was also above the African average so export crop production does not appear to have led to poor nutrition levels through its damaging displacement of food production. Chad, Ghana, Mali and Tanzania seem to offer greater support to the anti-export crop approach, especially Ghana which is a significant export crop producer. Of course third factors may be in operation here, e.g. Mali and Chad are known to have extremely poor infrastructures which could be held responsible for unnecessary resource competition and/or poor food supply to the country.

Advocates of food self-sufficiency might also draw support from the eleven countries which showed relatively good food consumption levels but below-average export crop production levels. However, six of these countries also exhibited poor performances in food production so that the anticipated benefits of a lower concentration on export crop production do not appear to have been realised. Benin, Burundi, Niger, Nigeria, and Rwanda do not exhibit higher than average levels of food production and consumption, in association with relatively low levels of export crop production. Nigeria at least is a special case owing to its high foreign exchange earnings from oil and mineral resources but countries such as Niger have poor natural resource bases, so that their relatively high levels of food consumptions can only be explained by their success in domestic food production.

No discernible pattern is evident in the ten countries which did badly in both food consumption and export crop production except, not surprisingly, that all but two also performed poorly in food production. One of the exceptions on this front is Kenya which would generally be regarded as a 'success story' in the context of African agriculture. Its inclusion in this quadrant at all probably indicates the dangers of drawing any strong conclusions from a study focused on a single year.

The apparent inconclusiveness of these findings should not be a particular source of surprise as country-specific features make the drawing of general conclusions a hazardous exercise. On the whole, though, there *is* a positive correlation between food consumption levels and export crop production for the period 1979-81 so that the balance of the evidence *need not* lower the nutritional status of the population.

The relationship between export crop production and per capita calorie intake, 1963-81

Graph 4 plots the percentage changes in *per capita* export crop production and food consumption over an 18-year period for the 33 African countries studied. The most immediately striking feature of the graph is its apparent lack of any specific pattern, an observation confirmed by a very slight statistical association. The following is a breakdown at the level of individual countries:

- 9 countries (27%) combined increases in export crop production with increases in food consumption: Congo, Guinea, Ivory Coast, Liberia, Madagascar, Malawi, Rwanda, Sierra Leone, and Zambia;
- 6 countries (18%) registered decreases in both export crop production and food consumption: Chad, Ethiopia, Ghana, Mozambique, Togo, and Uganda;
- 4 countries (12%) improved their export crop performance but experienced deteriorating nutrition levels: Kenya, Mali, Burkina Faso, and Zimbabwe;
- 11 countries (33%) improved food consumption levels at the same time as their levels of export crop production declined: Angola, Benin, Burundi, Cameroon, Central African Republic, Niger, Nigeria, Somalia, Sudan, Tanzania, and Zaire.[5]

Graph 4 Changes in levels of export crop production and food consumption, 1963-81

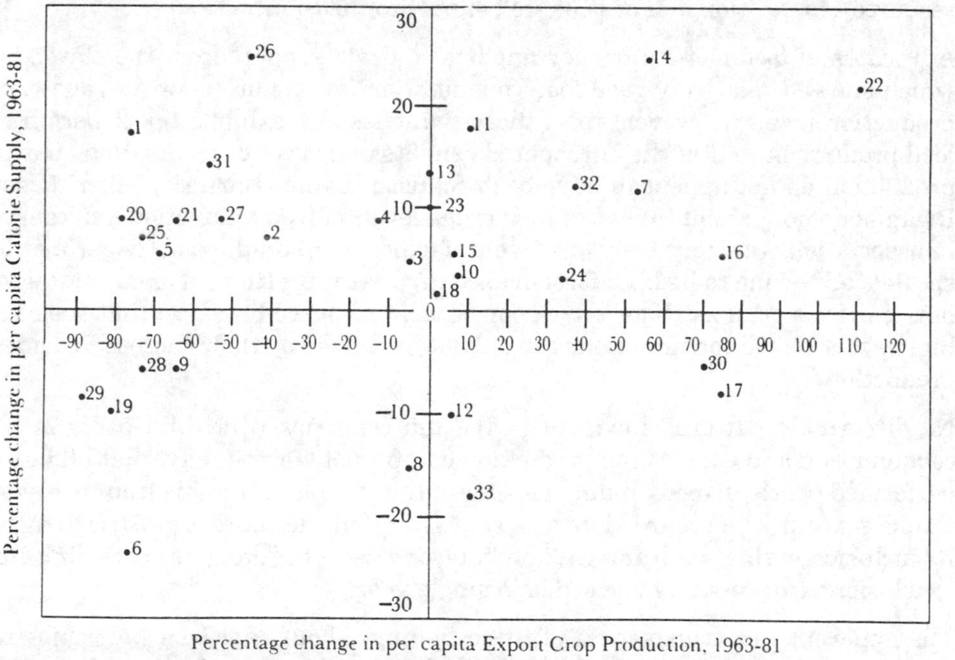
Percentage change in per capita Calorie Supply, 1963-81
Percentage change in per capita Export Crop Production, 1963-81

Some interesting inferences can be drawn from the distribution of observations. The most notable is that of the thirteen countries which increased export crop production, only four experienced negative nutritional effects. Of the nine which did not, only two — Malawi and Rwanda — increased their levels of food production, which implies that their increased food supply was derived from other sources (presumably food imports). This implies that increasing export crop production, even when it is associated with declining food crop production, does not necessarily lower levels of nutrition.

Of the eleven countries which improved their food consumption levels as their export crop sectors declined, only two — Cameroon and Sudan — did so by improving their food production levels. The consumption improvements in the other countries can only be explained by some other factor, again presumably food imports, which may have been made all the more difficult to pay for by declining agricultural production for export. The suggestion that one can improve the level of national nutrition through a diversion of resources away from the export-producing sector and towards the food-producing sector is not supported by this evidence.

To recap on the relationship between export crop production and per capita calorie intake: there was a positive association between levels of export crop production and levels of per capita calorie supply for thirty-three sub-Saharan countries in 1981. Observations of the trends in these variables between 1964 and 1981 also suggests that a positive (though weak) relationship exists. A breakdown of these results does not appear to yield any significant regional or other pattern. Two particular observations are worthy of emphasis:

- the 3 countries which had the highest per capita levels of export crop production in 1981 also enjoyed above-average levels of food consumption;

- 9 of the 13 countries which increased their levels of export crop production between 1963 and 1981 also enjoyed improvements in food consumption levels.

These observations lend support to the claim that expanding export crop production can boost national levels of food consumption, and has done so in the past. However, the potential of export crop production to bring about this result is dependent on the appropriate utilisation of foreign exchange earnings.

Conclusion: policy implications

The empirical results offer at least partial support to the proponents of export crop production — export crop and food crop production can be complementary, and expanding export crop production can be associated with improved levels of food consumption. However, the achievement of these results remains dependent upon the implementation of at least two specific policies:

- the transfer of services, such as extension, input supply, research and development, and non-discriminatory pricing, traditionally concentrated on the export-producing sector to the food-producing sector, along the lines of the Tanzanian tobacco schemes referred to above;

- the use, where necessary, of the foreign exchange earned by export crops for the purchase of appropriate food supplies for the domestic population.

Failure to meet either or both of these conditions may result in declining levels of both domestic food production and consumption as resources are increasingly devoted to export crop production. Those concerned with food consumption levels in Africa should devote more attention to the fulfilment of these conditions than to the advocacy of perhaps undesirable levels of food self-sufficiency.

Finally, it must be emphasised that national-level analysis such as this may say little about the welfare of the poorest sections of society, frequently the rural majority. The effect of export crop production on these groups depends upon factors such as changes in land ownership and control, and the generation of employment in rural areas. Such distributional implications of agricultural production strategies merit a separate discussion in themselves.

Acknowledgement

The assistance of the Department of Foreign Affairs in partially funding the research on which this article is based is gratefully acknowledged.

Notes

1. In order to determine aggregate trends in food and export crop production an appropriate weighting system is required — we cannot, for example, add together a ton of tobacco and a ton of coffee. The weighting system employed is based on the differing primary objectives of export and food crop production, to earn foreign exchange and to feed the domestic population respectively. Export crops are thus assigned a weight according to their foreign exchange-earning capacity over the period of time examined (average export unit values, 1963-1980), while food crops are weighted according to their relative calorific content (roots and tubers accorded one-third the weight of cereals and pulses).

2. The 'cash crop' and 'non-food' categories used by the Von Braun and Kennedy and World Bank studies respectively do not perfectly correspond to the export crop category under examination. However, there tends to be a considerable overlap between categories of this sort.

3. Two countries (7%) had exactly average levels of food crop production and below-average levels of export crop production.

4. Three countries (9%) showed no significant export crop production changes over the period while their food production performance deteriorated.

5. Three countries (9%) showed no significant change in export crop production levels while improving their food consumption levels.

40. Industrialization
Amiya Kumar Bagchi

Industrialization is a process. The following are essential characteristics of an unambiguous industrialization process. First, the proportion of the national (or territorial) income derived from manufacturing activities and from secondary industry in general goes up, except perhaps for cyclical interruptions. Secondly, the proportion of the working population engaged in manufacturing and secondary industry in general also shows a rising trend. While these two ratios are increasing the income per head of the population also goes up, except again for temporary interruptions (Datta, 1952; Kuznets, 1966, 1971; Sutcliffe, 1971). There are cases in which the per capita income goes up, income derived from secondary industry per head of the population also goes up, but there may be little growth either in the proportion of income derived from the secondary sector or in the ratio of the working force engaged in that sector. Such cases, except when they are observed for a highly developed country, not only make the unambiguous labelling of the process of development as industrialization difficult; they also pose questions regarding the sustainability of the process that has been observed.

Other characteristics are also often associated with industrialization or a more general process of what Kuznets has called 'modern economic growth' (Kuznets, 1966, ch. 1). These include a narrowing and ultimate closing of the gap between productivity per head in the secondary sector and in the primary sector (that is, agriculture, forestry and fishing), continual changes in the methods of production, the fashioning of new products, rise in the proportion of population living in towns, changes in the relative ratios of expenditures on capital formulation and consumption and so on.

Most of these associated characteristics were derived from the experience of Great Britain, or more narrowly, England and Wales, which was the first country to industrialize. That experience has remained unique in many ways. But since England was the original centre of diffusion of the economic and technical changes associated with the industrialization process, it is important to understand what happened in that country.

At least since the days of Karl Marx, England has been known as the first country in which feudalism broke down, and capitalism brought the economy under its sway (Dobb, 1946). This meant that all means of production came to be owned by a small group of property-owners called capitalists, and the rest of the working people became free wage-workers who earned their livelihood by selling their labour power to the capitalists (Dobb, 1946). It has been claimed that while serfdom broke down all over western Europe, England was the only country where a group of landlords managed to concentrate most of the land in their hands and prevent the consolidation of a free peasantry which could be used by an absolutist state to defeat the rise of capitalist

A.K. Bagchi: 'Industrialization' from THE NEW PALGRAVE: A DICTIONARY OF ECONOMICS, edited by John Eatwell, Murray Milgate and Peter Newman. (Macmillan, 1989), pp. 160-173. © The Macmillan Press Limited 1987.

agriculture (Moore, 1967, ch. 1; Brenner, 1976). It has been further claimed that economic individualism which has been taken as the hallmark of the motivation of an entrepreneur in capitalist society, goes back in England to the 12th-13th centuries, so that capitalism went through a long process of birth in the first industrializing nation (Macfarlane, 1978, chs 5-7). By the time of the first industrial revolution, England was a society in which the abiding interest of the rulers was to make money from agriculture, trade and industry, and in which the rulers were prepared rationally to order the affairs of the state so as to enable the entrepreneurs to conquer foreign countries and markets, by the force of arms if need be and had the financial and military might to carry out those plans. England had also become the leader in trade and finance among the countries of western Europe, after the decline of Amsterdam (Braudel, 1984).

The English industrial revolution is traditionally associated with the rise of machine-based industry powered by steam (Marx, 1887, chs XIV and XV; Mantoux, 1928). Certainly the classic age of British dominance of world industry, which is roughly the period from the end of the Napoleonic wars up to 1870, was characterized by the conquest of production methods by machines with moving parts of iron and steel, powered by steam, and operated by scores or even hundreds of operatives concentrated in single factories. However, what is becoming apparent is that for practically the whole of the eighteenth century, traditional techniques and materials (such as wood), and traditional sources of power such as muscles of men, women and children, animals, and water and wind, were responsible for growth and spread of factory industry (Musson, 1972; Von Tunzelmann, 1978; Crafts, 1985).

The experience of England lends credence to the postulation of a stage of 'industrialization before industrialization' or 'proto-industrialization' (Mendels, 1972). This has been defined as 'the development of rural regions in which a large part of the population lived entirely or to a considerable extent from industrial mass production for inter-regional and international markets' (Kriedte, Medick and Schlumbohm, 1981, p. 6). The growth of industry in England was spearheaded by an explosion in the development of cotton spinning; and the cotton mills which utilized the new spinning machines sought out suitable sources of water power and labour — mostly in the rural areas or small towns. Steam engines were an element in the industrial revolution, but they did not come into their own as the major prime movers in manufacturing industry until perhaps the second quarter of the nineteenth century.

In England, cotton textiles were a relatively new industry; and they grew at first by redressing the balance of labour power needed in traditional spinning methods, so that no major displacement of labour took place within the system of proto-industrialization, in the 18th century. But machine spinning stimulated handloom production, and handloom weavers were pauperized even in England when powerlooms displaced handlooms (Bythell, 1969). In other countries, were traditional handicrafts were displaced by the new machine-made fabrics, and because of political or internal social factors they were not replaced, or not replaced quickly enough, by any considerable growth of machine industry, pauperization and de-industrialization were widespread and in some cases they became endemic phenomena (Bagchi, 1976; Kriedte, 1981). So Ricardo's worries about the possible employment — displacing effects of machinery were justified after all (Ricardo, 1821, ch. 31; see also Hicks, 1969). But in Britain, continued growth of external trade and the coming of the railway age helped in overcompensating the labour-displacing effects. Not all countries had the same advantages.

The proto-industrialized order was succeeded in England by the system of machine manufacture perhaps because the former faced its severest crisis there: social relations there had already been transformed in a fully capitalist mould by the time smallscale manufacture reached its fullest development. Developments in science, technology and statecraft almost certainly helped resolve the crisis in favour of a higher stage of industrial development.

The fact that England had a decisive lead in the use of machine manufacture and steam power, and had formal or informal colonies where she could ignore barriers erected by the USA or Continental European countries made her the supreme industrial nation of the world for almost three-quarters of a century (cf. Robinson, 1954).

Once the revolution in textiles and steam power had been pioneered in England it could, however, be diffused to other countries, provided the latter possessed suitable political and social conditions. It is on the basis of the timing, speed and social mechanism of diffusion of the industrial revolution that we can distinguish three clusters of countries which have gone through an unambiguous process of industrialization. The first is the cluster of countries on both sides of the North Atlantic seaboard and overseas colonies with populations of predominantly European origin; the second consists of Japan and the four islands of industrialization in the Far East, viz., South Korea, Taiwan, Hong Kong and Singapore, and the third is the cluster of socialist countries led by the Soviet Union. The rest of the world are still struggling, with only varying degrees of success, to get a sustained process of industrialization going (Bagchi, 1982).

The English industrial revolution was, to start with, very much a matter of textiles; it was only in the 19th century that it affected other industries, especially iron and steel and mechanical engineering in general, on a large scale. The uniqueness of England, with all the advantages of a first start (Robinson, 1954) allowed her to expand her markets overseas in an almost unrestrained manner until the USA and other western European countries expanded their home production, not only of textiles, but also of other manufactures, often behind walls of protection against the English manufactures. The west European industrialization was helped very much by the nearness of England: from Britain flowed information about the new inventions, machines, men and capital, although there was for a time an attempt to restrict the exports of new machinery from England (Landes, 1965). Capital flows from England and to a lesser extent from France, were particularly important in supporting the movement of European populations to the USA, Canada, Australia, South Africa, New Zealand and Argentina (Kuznets, 1971; Bagchi, 1972; Edelstein, 1982).

Yet despite more active support by politically independent governments, the spread of industrialization to western Europe took a surprisingly long time to get going (Lewis, 1978, chs. 7 and 8; Crafts, 1985, ch. 3). One set of reasons had to do with political, social and structural factors. The French needed a major revolution before the bourgeoisie could take possession of the state apparatus. Even then, the entrenchment of peasant agriculture in the countryside probably delayed the full conversion of the primary sector to capitalist relations. In other countries, even the 1848 revolution did not complete the process of capitalist take-over. Associated with these lags went the fact that by English standards, too high a proportion of population continued to depend on agriculture and a large gap between agricultural and industrial productivity continued to persist down to the eve of World War I. Such political and social lags, of course, even more impeded the process of industrialization in the countries of central, southern and eastern Europe down to the period between the two world wars. We will have to pay separate attention to the case where the logjam in the process of industrialization was only broken with the Bolshevik Revolution, with most other countries of eastern Europe following after World War II (Berend and Ranki, 1982).

As the process of industrialization spread, the supply of importable technologies and the financial requirements for implementing such technologies both increased. According to one estimate, gross domestic investment as a proportion of GDP in Great Britain increased from around 4 per cent in 1700 to 5.7 per cent in 1760, 7.9 per cent in 1801 and 11.7 per cent in 1831 (Crafts, 1983), and remained between 10 and 12 per cent between 1831 and 1860 (Feinstein, 1978, p. 91). By contrast in countries such as Germany, Sweden or Denmark the rate of investment in their phase of industrialization (after 1860) often reached 15 per cent and more of GDP. In the USA the social preconditions for industrialization were much more favourable than in most European countries, and the export of capital from Europe considerably aided her industrialization process until she in turn became a creditor nation around the turn of the 19th century.

The latecomers among the western European countries, and Japan on the other side of the world, used state intervention on a much wider scale and much more purposively than Britain did. This intervention did not take the same form in all countries: in a country such as Germany, financing of industry was far more widely supported by the state and by new instruments of finance created for the purpose than, say, in Italy. It is doubtful whether a general pattern of successful state intervention to overcome economic backwardness can be discerned from the historical experience as has sometimes been claimed (Gershenkron, 1962). What can be asserted is that state intervention in industry was much more likely to succeed in countries where capitalist relations had advanced far then where intervention from the top was used as a substitute for social change which might upset the balance of class forces among the rulers (cf. Berend and Ranki, 1982).

The example of Russia is especially instructive in showing the limits of state action in a society where capitalist relations had taken root only to an imperfect degree. In Russia serfdom had been consciously introduced in the 17th century, and the system bore particularly heavily on regions producing grain which was a major export of eastern European lands. The so-called village communes (*obshina*) produced both agricultural products and handicrafts. Beginning around the 1830s modern machinery was employed in the processing of beet sugar and in the spinning of cotton yarn. Even after the abolition of serfdom in 1861, handicrafts remained predominant (Crisp, 1978), but later on, the system of domestic production and production by handicrafts became more and more integrated into the system of capitalist production (Lenin, 1898). It was only in the 1880s that large-scale industry employing modern machines experienced an accelerated growth in Russia (Lyaschenko, 1949; Crisp, 1978).

The development of modern industry and capitalism in general in Russia gave rise to a vigorous debate which still has contemporary relevance in many countries of the third world. Some of the Russian Populists (*Narodniks*) contended that the development of capitalist industry was impossible in a backward country such as Russia. They argued that modern machine-based industry destroys handicrafts and small peasant agriculture, the incomes of people dependent on them consequently shrink, and thus modern industry faces a severe — indeed insurmountable — realization problem. Countering this argument, Lenin pointed out that capitalism created its own markets by converting goods produced within a household or barter economy into tradeable commodities and by continually generating new methods of production. The latter in their turn create demands for new equipment and materials (Lenin, 1897, 1899). Lenin did not deny that capitalism needed foreign markets. But at that stage he attributed the need not to the impossibility of realizing the surplus value but to intercapitalist competition and the continuous drive of capital towards expansion. In the process of discussing the analytical issues involved Lenin enunciated a law of development of capital, namely that 'constant capital grows faster than variable capital, that is to say, an ever larger share of newly-formed capital is turned into that department of the social economy which produces means of production' (Lenin, 1897, pp. 155-6).

While markets expanded in Russia with state support for development of railways and war-related industries, the process of industrialization before the Revolution of 1917 remained ridden with numerous contradictions. Before the Stolypin reforms (which were initiated after the abortive revolution of 1905) the spread of individual ownership in agriculture was held up by numerous restrictions on peasant mobility and on the transferability of land. Even after the Stolypin reforms (or reaction) landlords' social and economic power continued to limit the development of capitalism in agriculture (see e.g., Lenin 1912). A substantial proportion of growth in the industrial capital stock was financed by foreign banks and foreign entrepreneurs (McKay, 1970). Large-scale industry was regionally and sectorally concentrated (Portal, 1965) and the proportion of the working force engaged in industry (including construction) was only 9 per cent in 1913; it was only after the Bolshevik Revolution and the implementation of the two Five Year Plans that there was a decisive change in the occupational structure. The proportion of the working force engaged in industry and construction climbed to 23 per cent in 1940 and 21 per cent in 1979; correspondingly the proportion engaged in agriculture and forestry declined from 75 per cent in 1913 to 54 per cent in 1940 and 21 per cent in 1979 (Sarkisyants, 1977, p. 180; see also Kuznets, 1966, p. 107).

In Japan, the course and the pattern of industrialization differed considerably from the sequence witnessed in western Europe and the USA, and also from that followed in socialist countries. Under Tokugawa rule, Japan was characterized by what has been called 'centralized feudalism' (Ohkawa, 1978, p. 140) with the *shogun* exercising supreme power through the *daimyos* and a rigid hierarchy going down to the village level. But the increasing use of money for the payment of taxes, countrywide transactions in money required to support the *daimyos'* and their retainers' expenditures in their travels to the capital and back, and the increasing indebtedness of many *daimyos* to merchants enhanced the power of the latter. The merchants' ambitions, the peasants' discontent and the frustrations of many of the feudal lords in the face of the increasing threat posed by the military and technological advance of the Western powers ultimately led to the end of the shogunate and the restoration of the Meiji emperor. The fierce nationalism bred among the nobility under the isolation enforced on the country earlier by the shogunate led them to define their objectives in the image of the activities of the Western imperialist powers (Beasley, 1963; Norman, 1943; Smith, 1961).

While abolishing many of the privileges of the warrior class the new Japanese rulers held on to the rigid rules of hierarchal control descending from the emperor through the nobility and the higher ranks of merchants to the village headmen, and down to the peasants working in the fields. The rigid subjugation of family members, especially of women, to the patriarch and the use of communal ties to enforce authoritarian rule continued unabated, and was adapted to the requirements of modern industry (Morishima, 1982). A high level of land taxes imposed on the peasantry financed much of the economic growth in Japan which accelerated from the 1880s. Young women, more or less bonded to the factories by their fathers or other family heads provided cheap labour. The first steps in the industrialization process were taken under the guidance of the state which built or financed shipyards, telegraph lines, railways and armament works (Lockwood, 1968). The actual pace-setter in the industrialization process, in Japan as in Britain, was textiles, and for a long time, handicraft methods continued to be used alongside of machine methods in producing Japan's industrial goods. Silk, indemnities from foreign conquest, and exports of cotton yarn and cotton goods allowed Japan to do without much foreign investment in her drive towards industrialization. As in Britain, so in Japan, external markets and imperial conquest played an important role in the rise of modern industry (Lockwood, 1968).

Japan's industrial growth was already impressive in its diversity and sophistication during the interwar years. But it is since World War II that her growth has surpassed earlier historical standards (Ohkawa, 1978; Armstrong, Glyn and Harrions, 1984). The reserve army of labour in agriculture was finally exhausted there under the dual impact of land reforms imposed by the American occupation authorities and rates of industrial growth that often exceeded 15 per cent per year. Accompanying the Japanese growth was domination of trade and industry by a handful of giant conglomerates, the *zaibatsu*, giant firms and general trading corporations or *soga sochas*, acting in close collaboration with the Ministry of International Trade and Industry, and the subjugation of the labour movement to company objectives. It is these characteristics combined with a systematic exclusion of foreign capital from practically all fields that led observers to use the phrase 'Japan Inc.' to characterize the Japanese system of management. Japan eventually surpassed all capitalist countries except the USA in the value of her industrial production and in her technological advance.

While the countries on the two sides of the north Atlantic seaboard were industrializing and Japan was slowly emerging as a challenger to the industrial and political supremacy of the Western powers in the Far East, the majority of the people living in Asia, Africa and Latin America hardly experienced any positive process of industrialization. The movement of neither capital nor labour favoured such a process in China, India, Egypt, Peru, Brazil or Mexico, even in the exceptional days of massive British investments overseas that enriched the USA, Australia or Canada with men or materials (Edelstein, 1982; Davis and Huttenback, 1985). Only a small fraction of foreign investment made by Britain and France went to the non-white dependent colonies, or formally independent, but effectively dependent countries peopled by non-white populations. These investments went generally into plantations, mines, railways rather than manufacturing industries. While the British dominions such as Canada or Australia pursued their economic policies largely independently of metropolitan control and protected their nascent industries, India, Egypt or even China and Turkey were forced to pursue *laissez faire* policies under the pressure of the metropolitan powers. The small flows of foreign investment into the colonies were swamped in the case of India, West Indies or even Brazil by the outflow of capital to the metropolitan countries (and thence to the colonies of settlement) as political tribute, and profit on external trade, foreign exchange transactions or plantation and railway enterprises (Bagchi, 1982, chs 3 and 4).

Policies of free trade or state intervention in favour of metropolitan trade and industry generally led to a decline in handicrafts and domestic industry on a large scale in such countries as India, China and Turkey. This erosion of proto-industrial output and employment was only very inadequately compensated by the rise of modern industry. Colonial rule also led in many cases to the strengthening of ties of bondage of various kinds in the rural areas. When migration occurred on a large scale from these countries, it was often organized by the merchants from the metropolitan countries, and the migrants often entered into a semiservile condition in the plantations of Assam (India), Trinidad, Guyana, or mines of South Africa. The effective control of modern plantation and mining enterprises and many areas of trade, especially wholesale internal and external trade by merchants from metropolitan countries, policies of free trade and processes of de-industrialization retarded the development of an indigenous mercantile community in most of the dependent colonies and often delayed the onset of any process of industrialization until the 1950s.

In many Latin American countries industrialization was quickened in the 1930s as a result of import restriction policies forced on the governments by the deep depression, especially in primary commodity exports, and attendant balance of payments crises. Following on from this experience, many of them adopted industrialization as a strategy of development and the basic objective of planning. The Prebisch-Singer thesis of a secular decline in terms of trade of primary products provided the rationale for such a strategy in Latin America (Prebisch, 1950; Singer, 1950; Spraos, 1982). Elsewhere, the success of the Soviet experiment provided an inspiration for planning.

However, after some initial successes, in most countries of the third world, the process of industrialization was caught up in multiple contradictions. In few countries were there land reforms conferring the right of ownership and control on the cultivating peasantry. This failure rendered the supply of food grains and other farm products inelastic and enabled the entrenched landlords and traders to speculate in these commodities. As a result, any stepping up of investment through governmental efforts soon met inflation barriers and balance of payments crises. The latter were aggravated by a tendency to import newer and newer consumer goods for the upper and the middle classes, by an inability to bargain from a position of strength with the suppliers of technology, and by the oversell practised by many of the aid-givers wanting to tie the loans or grants to purchases of goods from the donor country. In many Latin American countries, threats of social revolution were met by imposition of authoritarian regimes, generally with US connivance or assistance. The case of Chile where a popular government under the presidentship of Salvador Allende was replaced by a brutal military dictatorship is perhaps the most glaring example of this tendency, but Argentina, Brazil and Uruguay all fitted the same pattern. The primary commodities boom in the early 1970s, rise in oil prices in 1973-4 and 1978-9, along with attraction provided to transnational corporations by explicit polices of wage repression and labour regimentation, boosted the rate of industrial growth in countries as widely dispersed as Brazil and Iran. However, in most of these countries, including some oil-exporters such as Mexico and Nigeria, astronomically large external debts and debt servicing charges put a stop to most development efforts by the early 1980s.

A few economies in east Asia, more specifically the two enclaves of Hong Kong and Singapore, and the medium-sized economies of South Korea and Taiwan went through a process of successful industrialization. In South Korea and Taiwan, radical land reforms, partly brought about through the defeat of the Japanese in 1945 who had been major land-holders in these two provinces, and partly imposed by the US authorities fearing a Communist revolution in emulation of the People's Republic of China, enormously speeded up the movement of trading capital into industry, increased the elasticity of supply of farm products and widened the market for basic consumer and producer goods. Chinese overseas capital had for a long time dominated trade and money-lending in many countries of east and south-east Asia. Communist take-over of mainland China drove out a sizeable section of big mercantile capital. The newly migrating and old Chinese overseas capital then turned to industrial investment in many of these countries. Increased US military activities in the region, attempted economic blockade of Communist China by the Western capitalist countries and the large expenditures attending US military aggression in Vietnam provided multiple opportunities to the traders and industrialists in the region for capital accumulation and expansion. Many Japanese, American and western European transnational corporations found Singapore, Hong Kong, Taiwan and South Korea useful as export platforms since these four economies provided the attraction of low wages, a disciplined (and regimented) labour force and privileged access to US, EEC and Japanese markets.

However, despite the fact that many Asian economies have continued to experience positive growth in a period of global recession, it cannot be said yet that the east Asian experience is catching or easily diffusible. Most of Africa is experiencing negative growth, and large clusters of population are caught there in the clutches of famine. Most Latin American economies are yet to get out of the debt trap. The only other countries which are still experiencing a positive process of industrialization to a greater or lesser extent are the socialist countries which have embraced some variant of Marxism as their guiding ideology. The share of industry in GNP rose steeply in most of these countries and often exceeded 40 per cent. The high rate of economic growth in these countries was financed by the confiscation of rent incomes from land, by the channelling of all surpluses into investment and by allowing only a moderate rise in real wages until an acceptable level of GNP was reached (cf. Ellman, 1975; Lippit, 1974). One feature that has distinguished socialist industrialization is that usually the share of services in GNP and employment has been lower than in most non-socialist economies. In a country such as China, the abnormally low share of services has been seen as a defect associated with the phase of extensive growth.

Most of the socialist countries are also now grappling with problems of lower productivity growth. Effective decentralization of planning processes, increased responsiveness to changes in relative scarcity and signalling of such changes through changes in relative prices and provision of adequate incentives to managers and workers have been generally seen as the answer to these problems. Increased imports of technology from the OECD countries and their effective absorption are also seen as part of the answer, but the successful pursuit of such strategies is intertwined with the issue of economic reforms on the one hand and geopolitical manoeuvring between the two blocks on the other.

One problem that will continue to bedevil industrialization strategies in most large third world countries for a long time is the very high ratio of the working population engaged in agriculture to the total working force. Even in a country such as China, which has experienced a trend rate of industrial growth of more than 10 per cent over the years since the Communist revolution in 1949, and where the share of industry in national income went up to 42.2 per cent in 1982, agriculture and forestry continued to employ 71.6 per cent of the labour force in the same year (China, 1983, pp. 24, 121). It is only some medium-sized economies with a high rate of industrial growth such as South Korea and Taiwan that have experienced any major shift in the population balance towards industrial employment.

The experience of the structural changes within the east Asian group of capitalist economies shows that under favourable circumstances, it is possible for the less industrialized economies to grow at high rates if there is a sustained shedding off of the lower-productivity sectors by the more advanced regions and the grafting of the shedded output on to the structures of the less developed economies (Yamazawa, Taniguchi and Hirata, 1983). The process is very similar to that observed in western Europe in the early part of the 19th century, except that the role of migration of population to countries outside the region (such as the USA in the case of western Europe) in easing population pressure has been minimal. But the roles of direct investment by Japanese and other OECD firms and of privileged access to extra-regional markets have been more significant than in the case of western Europe. (It could, of course, be argued that western European countries had a privileged access to markets in their dependent colonies.)

The general developments in the advanced capitalist bloc of countries (within which Japan occupies a unique position because of her maintenance of moderate to high rates of growth and near full employment and her large trade surpluses with most other countries), however, preclude the replication of the east Asian pattern in the rest of the third world. Most of them are afflicted by high rates of unemployment — exceeding levels witnessed since the end of the 1930s. Some countries such as the UK experienced an absolute decline in manufacturing (Singh, 1977). These developments aggravated protectionism in these countries, thus creating barriers against the expansion of exports from the third world countries, while the OECD group of countries continued to constitute the biggest market for manufactured goods in the world. Developments in microelectronic technology posed major threats to the further expansion of labour-intensive textile products and clothing exports from the third world to the OECD countries (UNCTAD, 1981). More generally, the spread of microelectronic technologies embracing whole branches of manufacture are threatening to remove many assembly operations which the OECD-based transnational corporations had earlier found it profitable to subcontract to the favoured export enclaves including the east Asian group of nearly industrializing countries (Kaplinksky, 1984).

Within the OECD group, the USA has become the biggest magnet for capital flows from all over the world. The high interest rate and large budget deficits maintained by the US government have forced most other OECD governments to pursue deflationary policies within their borders. There is little sign as yet that such trends will be reversed. The Japanese, who have run up large trade surpluses (exceeding US $40 billion) with the USA have proceeded to invest most of their export surplus in the US. Thus the diffusion that is borne on the backs of foreign investment within the order of capitalism has been severely hampered by these developments

The only alternative that is left for most third world countries is to rely on building industries on the basis of domestic resources and domestic markets. But the guidelines laid down by the International Monetary Fund seeking to impose severely deflationary policies on most countries applying for its assistance in meeting their debt problems, the power exerted by OECD-based transnational corporations in effectively restricting the flow of technology, and the internal social structures in most of these countries blocking the spread of literacy and accrual of purchasing power to common people are likely to hamper the feeble efforts at industrialization on a self-reliant basis. The other path of industrialization, building on growing exports and expanding international investment flows, would appear also to be beset with dangerous pitfalls for most of the poor countries of the world. Thus the spread of industrialization in the near term to the poorer countries is likely to be very slow compared with the speed witnessed between, say, 1950 and 1978. At the other end of the spectrum, in countries such as the USA and UK, services and finance have gained tremendously at the expense of manufacturing industry, and it is through the use of financial instruments as much as advanced technology in manufacturing (including armaments production) and services that the USA dominates the economies of most of the capitalist countries. But as Japan continues to forge ahead even in frontier technologies such as the mass production of semiconductor chips for use in the most advanced microelectronic processes (cf. Gregory, 1985), a change in the balance within the capitalist order is very likely. In the meanwhile continued growth in the socialist world will also affect the global balance in manufacturing and economic power.

Bibliography

Armstrong, P., Glyn, A. and Harrison, J. (1984). *Capitalism since World War II: The Making and Breaking of the Great Boom.* London: Fontana.

Bagchi, A.K. (1972) 'Some international foundations of capitalist growth and underdevelopment'. *Economic and Political Weekly* 7 (31-33), Special Number, August, 1559-70.

Bagchi, A.K. (1976) 'De-industrialization in India in the nineteenth century: some theoretical implications'. *Journal of Development Studies* 12 (2), January, 135-64.

Bagchi, A K. (1982) *The Political Economy of Underdevelopment.* Cambridge and New York: Cambridge University Press.

Bairoch, P. (1975) *Economic development of the Third World since 1900.* London: Methuen.

Beasley, W. G. (1963) *The Modern History of Japan.* New York: Praeger.

Berend, I. T. and Ranki, G. (1982) *The European Periphery and Industrialization 1780-1914.* Cambridge: Cambridge University Press.

Blackaby, F. (ed.) (1979) *De-industrialization.* London: Heinemann.

Braudel, F. (1984) *The Perspective of the World: Civilization & Capitalism, 15th-18th Century.* London: Collins; New York: Harper & Row.

Brenner, R. (1976) 'Agrarian class structure and economic development in pre-industrial Europe'. *Past and Present* 70, February, 30-75.

Bythell, D. (1969) *The Handloom Weavers: A Study in the English Cotton Industry during the Industrial Revolution,* Cambridge: Cambridge University Press.

China. (1983) *Statistical Yearbook of China 1983.* Hong Kong: State Statistical Bureau PRC and Economic Information Agency.

Crafts, N.F.R. (1983) 'British economic growth, 1700-1831: A review of the evidence'. *Economic History Review* 36(2), May, 177-99.

Crafts, N.F.R. (1985) *British Economic Growth during the Industrial Revolution.* Oxford: Clarendon Press.

Crisp, O. (1978) 'Labour and industrialization in Russia'. In Mathias and Postan (1978).

Datta, B. (1952) *The Economics of Industrialization.* Calcutta: World Press.

Davis, L. and Huttenback, R.A. (1985) 'The export of British finance, 1865-1914'. *Journal of Imperial and Commonwealth History* 13(3), May, 28-76.

Dobb, M. (1946) *Studies in the Development of Capitalism,* London: Routledge & Kegan Paul; New York: International Publishers, 1947.

Edelstein, M. (1982) *Overseas Investment in the Age of High Imperialism; The United Kingdom 1850-1914.* London: Methuen.

Ellman, M. (1975) 'Did the agricultural surplus provide the resources for the increase in investment in the USSR during the first five year plan?' *Economic Journal* 85, December, 844-63.

Feinstein, C.H. (1978) 'Capital formation in Great Britain'. In Mathias and Postan (1978).

Gershenkron, A. (1962) *Economic Backwardness in Historical Perspective.* Cambridge, Mass.: Harvard University Press.

Gregory, G. (1985) 'Chip shop of the world'. *New Scientist,* 15 August, 28-31.

Habakkuk, H.J. and Postan, M. (eds) (1965) *The Cambridge Economic History of Europe.* Vol. VI: *The Industrial Revolution and After*, Pts 1 and 2, Cambridge: Cambridge University Press.

Hicks, J. (1969) *A Theory of Economic History,* Oxford: Clarendon Press.

Hilton, R. (ed.) (1976) *The Transition from Feudalism to Capitalism.* London: New Left Books.

Kaplinsky, R. (1984) 'The international context for industrialization in the coming decade'. *Journal of Development Studies* 21 (1), October, 75-96.

Kriedte, P. (1981) 'The origins, the agrarian context, and the conditions in the world market'. In Kriedte, Medick and Schlumbohm (1981).

Kreidte, P., Medick, H and Schlumbohm. J. (1981) *Industrialization before Industrialisation: Rural Industry before the Genesis of Capitalism.* Cambridge and New York: Cambridge University Press.

Kuznets, S. (1966) *Modern Economic Growth: Rate, Structure and Spread.* New Haven: Yale University Press.

Kuznets, S. (1971) *Economic Growth of Nations: Total Output and Production Structure.* Cambridge, Mass.: Harvard University Press.

Landes, D. (1965) 'Technological change and development in Western Europe 1750-1914'. In Habakkuk and Postan (1965).

Lenin, V.I. (1897) 'A characterisation of economic romanticism' (Sismondi,and our native Sismondists). Trans. from Russian in Lenin, *Collected Works,* Vol. 2, Moscow: Foreign Languages Publishing House, 1963.

Lenin, V.I. (1898) 'The handicraft census of 1894-95 in Perm Gubernia and general problems of handicraft industry'. Trans. from Russian in Lenin, *Collected Works*, Vol. 2, Moscow: Foreign Languages Publishing House, 1963.

Lenin, V.I. (1899) *The Development of Capitalism in Russia.* Text of the 2nd edn of 1908, trans. from Russian in Lenin, *Collected Works*, Vol. 3, Moscow: Progress Publishers, 1964.

Lenin, V.I. (1912) 'The last valve. Trans. from Russian in Lenin', *Collected Works*, Vol. 18. Moscow: Progress Publishers, 1968.

Lewis, W.A. (1978) *Growth and Fluctuations 1870-1913.* London: Allen & Unwin.

Lippit, V.D. (1974) 'Land reform and economic development in China'. *Chinese Economic Studies* 7 (4), Summer, 3-181.

Lockwood, W.W. (1968) *The Economic Development of Japan.* Princeton: Princeton University Press.

Lyashenko, P.T. (1949) *History of the National Economy of Russia to the 1917 Revolution.* London and New York: Macmillan.

Macfarlane, A. (1978) *The Origins of English Individualism.* Oxford: Basil Blackwell.

McKay, J.P. (1970) *Pioneers for Profit: Foreign Entrepreneurship and Russian Industrialization.* Chicago: University of Chicago Press.

Mantoux, P. (1928) *The Industrial Revolution in the Eighteenth Century.* London: Jonathan Cape.

Marx, K. (1867 -94) *Das Kapital.* Trans. by S. Moore and E Aveling as *Capital: A Critical Analysis of Capitalist Production,* Vol. 1. Reprinted, Moscow: Foreign Languages Publishing House, n.d.

Mathias, P. and Postan, M. M. (eds) (1978) *The Cambridge Economic History of Europe.* Vol. VII, *The Industrial Economies: Capital, Labour and Enterprise,* Pts 1 and 2, Cambridge and New York: Cambridge University Press.

Mendels, F. (1972) 'Proto-industrialization: the first phase of the industrialization process'. *Journal of Economic History* 32 (1), March, 241-61.

Moore, B. Jr., (1967) *Social Origins of Dictatorship and Democracy: Land and Peasant in the Making of the Modern World.* London: Allen Lane

Morishima, M. (1982) *Why has Japan 'succeeded'?* Cambridge: Cambridge University Press.

Musson, A.E. (ed.) (1972) *Science, Technology and Economic Growth in the Eighteenth Century.* London: Methuen.

Norman, E.H. (1943) *Soldier and Peasant in Japan.* New York: Institute of Pacific Relations.

Ohkawa, K. (1978) 'Capital formulation in Japan'. In Mathias and Postan (1978).

Portal, R. (1965) 'The industrialization of Russia'. In Habakkuk and Postan (1965), Pt 2.

Presbisch, R. (1950) *The Economic Development of Latin America and its Principal Problems.* United Nations, New York: Reprinted in *Economic Bulletin for Latin America* 7 (1), February 1962, 1-22.

Ricardo, D. (1821) *On the Principles of Political Economy and Taxation.* 3rd edn, reprinted in *The Works and Correspondence of David Ricardo,* Vol. I, ed. P. Sraffa with the collaboration of M. H. Dobb, Cambridge: Cambridge University Press, 1951; New York: Cambridge University Press.

Robinson, E.A.G. (1954) 'The changing structure of the British economy'. *Economic Journal* 64, September, 443-61.

Sarkisyants, G.S. (ed) (1977) *Soviet Economy: Results and Prospects.* Moscow: Progress Publishers.

Singer, H. (1950) 'The distribution of gains between investing and borrowing countries'. *American Economic Review* 40, May, 473 -85.

Singh, A. (1977) 'UK industry and the world economy: a case of de-industrialisation?' *Cambridge Journal of Economics* 1(2), June, 113-36.

Smith. T. C. (1961) 'Japan's aristocratic revolution'. *Yale Review* 50 (3), Spring, 370-83.

Spraos, J. (1982) 'Deteriorating terms of trade and beyond'. *Trade and Development, An UNCTAD Review,* No. 4, Paris: UNCTAD.

Sutcliffe, R.B. (1971) *Industry and Underdevelopment,* London: Addison-Wesley.

UNCTAD. (1981) *Fibres and Textiles: Dimensions of Corporate Marketing Structure.* Geneva: United Nations.

Von Tunzelmann, G.N. (1978) *Steam Power and British Industrialization to 1860.* Oxford: Clarendon Press.

Yamazawa, I., Taniguchi, K. and Hirata, A. (1983) 'Trade and industrial adjustment in Pacific Asian countries'. *Developing Economies* 21 (4), December, 281-312.

41.   Privatisation and Regulation in LDCs: The Issues

Ron Ayres

1. Introduction

Privatisation programmes, involving the selling of state enterprises to the private sector, are being implemented in developing countries as diverse as China and Mexico and advanced countries like the UK have virtually completed the process. This paper outlines what appear to be the main economic and political goals of privatisation and then goes on to assess to what extent they can be achieved through public asset sales.

2. The goals of privatisation

The current debate within LDCs suggests that there are three broad goals of privatisation:

1. To achieve gains in economic efficiency by liberalising markets and increasing incentives.

2. To raise revenue for the government and facilitate an improvement in public finance.

3. To design procedures for privatisation that ensure that asset sales are transparent and result in a fair outcome. This inevitably raises questions about the meaning of fairness and has important implications about how to privatise.

The first two goals are part of the broader aim of managing external debt and eliminating inflation so that economic growth can be revived. Such pragmatic considerations rather than a clear ideological position have meant that support for and opposition to privatisation within LDCs is often based on calculations of individual gains or losses. Thus consumers are concerned that the removal of subsidies and price rises will affect them adversely. The trade unions and public sector salariat are generally antagonistic since privatisation creates considerable uncertainty about business and employment prospects. Managers of businesses that prospered under ISI and are mainly committed to supplying the domestic market are hostile to privatisation whereas managers of export oriented firms are generally in favour.

In the short term there may also be a conflict between macroeconomic and microeconomic policies. Macroeconomic policy in many LDCs is driven by stabilisation goals set after negotiations with the IMF and this is likely to remain broadly contractionary for some time. But in the context of stagnating macroeconomic activity it will be difficult for privatisation or other microeconomic supply-side policies to kick-start a weak economy into renewed growth. Ultimately, it is hoped that privatisation will increase efficiency and generate economic growth but unless or until this occurs someone has to pay for the economic reforms. Under the circumstances there is considerable uncertainty in the case of LDCs whether there will be sufficient support to complete the rolling back of the state. Nevertheless, as will be made clear later, there will continue to be important functions for government — new forms of regulation, macroeconomic stability and necessary public investments — even if privatisation does proceed.

Before considering to what extent the privatisation goals can be achieved it will be helpful to outline the theoretical framework that will be used to analyse the relative economic performance of public and private enterprises.

3. Privatisation: incentives and performance

There is a strong belief in the importance of markets for economic efficiency. An extreme market view, as represented by the neo-Austrian School, would limit the public sector to providing the administrative and legal framework within which markets can operate effectively (Hayek, 1944). The core of the arguments against public ownership are based on the theories of property rights and public choice (Buchanan, 1986). Under private enterprise property rights lie with the owners (shareholders) who are assumed, therefore, to have an interest in increasing the net worth of the enterprise. When this is reinforced by competition and the bankruptcy threat it is further assumed that it ensures both technical and allocative efficiency. On the other hand, under public enterprise ownership is non-transferable and it is assumed that managers have no concern for net worth. Ministers who might take a collective view are more concerned with short-run political issues or narrow vested interests. Therefore, monitoring of public enterprises is performed inadequately and there is likely to be political interference with adverse effects on staffing levels, investment and overall efficiency.

There are problems with both theories. There are numerous examples of efficient and responsive public enterprise around the world, particularly where they operate under competitive conditions. Although the threat of bankruptcy is virtually non-existent and there is still the possibility of government interference, it is likely that public enterprises facing product market competition will achieve high levels of both technical and allocative efficiency.

On the other hand, the monitoring of large private enterprises may be inadequate where there are monopoly elements and/or a separation of ownership and control. In the absence of product market competition private firms are more likely to suffer from technical inefficiency (X-inefficiency) although this may be partially offset by the bankruptcy and take-over threats. It is important, therefore, to consider how effective the take-over threat associated with the market for corporate control is likely to be in LDCs.

Although stock markets are not new in many LDCs, and some of the oldest exchanges (e.g. Sao Paulo, Brazil) have a record going back over ten years, there are reasons for doubting the effectiveness of the market for corporate control as a mechanism for disciplining large companies. Brazil now has over 600 companies quoted on its stock markets, more than three times the number in Mexico, yet by OECD levels the markets are relatively small and underdeveloped. But more significantly LDC stock markets can be highly volatile, for two reasons. Firstly, political and economic uncertainty is a source of turbulence which can sap investor confidence and inhibit the demand for securities. The uncertainty at the root of this volatility will remain as long as governments fail to achieve monetary and fiscal discipline. Secondly, the influence of speculative capital and the lack of transparency in many share dealings means that share markets are vulnerable to manipulation and as a result are often illiquid. This problem needs to be addressed and the stock market authorities within each country may need to liberalise trading rules within a tighter legal and regulatory framework which enforces stricter reporting requirements and provides more reliable performance indicators. In the absence of these reforms it is unlikely that quoted companies will be monitored adequately so that the market for corporate control will be ineffective and the threat of takeover therefore nullified.

This is given some support by US and UK empirical evidence on the effect of dispersed shareholdings (Grossman and Hart, 1980), the effect of takeovers (Singh, 1971) and managements comparative profit performance. There is also considerable evidence from the UK that the threat of takeover may lead to short-termism with long-term investments sacrificed in favour of quick gains with adverse effects on economic welfare.

The discussion so far implies that there are two parameters to consider when analysing privatisation: ownership and market structure. Privatisation by definition involves a movement along the horizontal axis (see Figure 1) but anything less than a complete ownership transfer may indicate a weakening of the bankruptcy incentive and the possibility of continuing political interference. Moreover, our analysis has indicated that the effects of a change in ownership will also depend on the market structure. This is not a new idea. The Harvard School stresses the importance of markets but using the structure-conduct-performance analysis the emphasis is on the virtues of competition. The conversion of a public monopoly into a private monopoly is likely to bring few, if any, benefits and may conceivably have negative effects. Although privatisation eliminates government interference, the takeover and bankruptcy incentives may do little to increase the efficiency of the private monopolist. Indeed, the concentration of market power that occurs under private monopoly may result in higher prices and lead to both technical and allocative inefficiency. As Swann (1988, p. 298) rightly observes, public monopoly may be superior to private monopoly "although where the balance ultimately lies is an empirical matter which depends on the strength of these conflicting influences".

The discussion so far indicates that privatisation without any change in market structure (a horizontal movement in terms of Figure 1) may not create any benefits in the case of a monopoly enterprise but should improve the efficiency of competitive firms. In the latter case it is the combined effects of the market for corporate control, if applicable, the bankruptcy incentive and the absence of political interference which result in efficiency gains. But it would appear that the greatest potential gains in efficiency will be achieved when there is a downward shift from left to right in terms of Figure 1, i.e. privatisation with increasing competition.

Figure 1   Privatisation and market structure

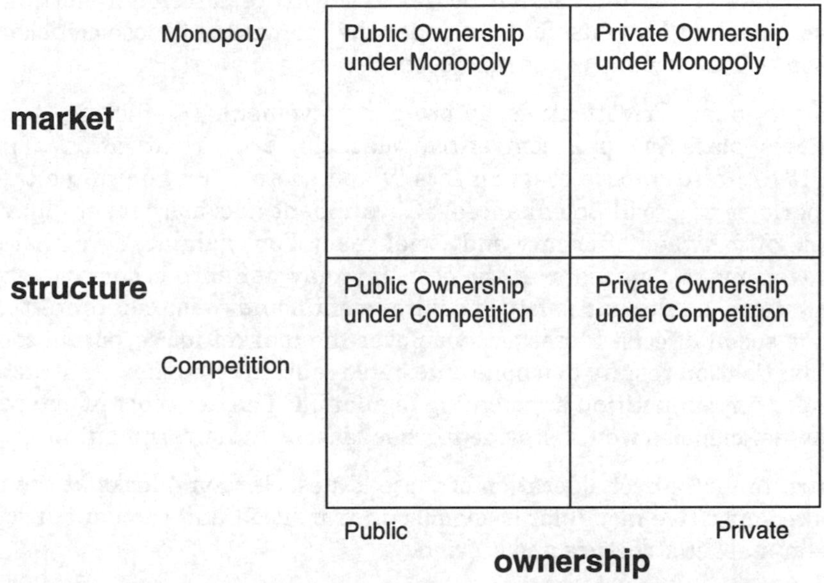

	Monopoly	Public Ownership under Monopoly	Private Ownership under Monopoly

Layout described by figure:

market

Monopoly	Public Ownership under Monopoly	Private Ownership under Monopoly
Competition	Public Ownership under Competition	Private Ownership under Competition

structure

Public   Private

ownership

Nevertheless, the real world is more complex than the simple static model assumes and under different assumptions it becomes clear that privatisation into a competitive market may be neither necessary nor sufficient for the achievement of economic efficiency for a number of reasons.

Firstly, where there is a natural monopoly, privatisation will create a dominant firm. The Chicago School (Stigler, 1971) point out that concentration in production may be preferable where there are significant economies of scale or a natural monopoly. Moreover, recent analysis of contestable markets (Baumol, 1982) suggests that concentration does not matter as long as the market is contestable. The danger is, however, that in the absence of contestability large firms are able to abuse their market power (this might also occur if there is collusion) and competition augmenting regulation may need to be introduced. This is considered further in sections 5 and 6.

Secondly, piecemeal privatisation under conditions where subsidies and government regulations are widespread elsewhere in the economy may nullify the potential benefits of competition. This implies that privatisation needs to be accompanied by deregulation.

Thirdly, it is important to bear in mind that privatisation which results in a competitive product market may conflict with a broader view of public interest. For instance, where externalities exist or there are information deficiencies the profit criterion is too narrow and leads to a misallocation of resources. Or, where merit goods like health and education will only be provided if they are profitable and the consumer is willing and able to pay the market price. Not everyone will be able or willing to buy and this can be socially divisive.

Finally, for developing countries and economies in transition there are further reasons for being sceptical about the economic advantages of liberalisation, free trade and a complete roll back of the state. Dirigisme was based on the perceived defects of the open competitive model and it is useful to consider the relevance of those criticisms for the current debate. This is done in the next section.

To summarize so far. Privatisation can bring improvements in efficiency, particularly when it takes place in open competitive markets, but privatisation alone is not sufficient. It can also impose costs on society and there is no guarantee that overall economic performance will be enhanced.[1] Government decision-makers may be faced with a trade-off between efficiency and social goals. For example, deregulation which removes government controls over the economy may enhance economic performance but when it affects health and safety or environmental and consumer protection it often has negative social effects. Moreover, whenever the market for corporate control fails or when privatisation results in a non-contestable concentrated market structure there may be a need for competition augmenting regulation. The existence of externalities or information deficiencies would provide further reasons for government intervention.

We now turn to further consideration of these issues. Section 4 looks at the relevance of the open competitive model for economies in transition and section 5 discusses the link between market structure and efficiency.

4. The competitive model

While the logic of the open economy competitive model may be unassailable there are serious grounds for questioning the assumptions and the relevance of the model (Felix, 1992). It is a static equilibrium model which pays little attention to the dynamics of change and can offer little insight into policy priorities and the sequencing of reforms. This is a focal issue in the current debates about privatisation in Eastern Europe. There can be no guarantee that the route to an open, free market system will be smooth or successful and the recent belated recognition that the transitional paths and final outcomes will be affected by the initial conditions provides further grounds for questioning the unqualified acceptance of the competitive model.

The open economy competitive model is also selective in its openness. It stresses the importance of the domestic mobility of labour for allocative efficiency while at the same time it assumes that labour is immobile at the international level. The reasons would appear to be obvious and relate to the economic, social and political problems of accommodating mass international migration in the developed countries. Moreover, the attempt to resurrect the free trade case (in the absence of international mobility) through the factor price equalization theorem is based on such restrictive assumptions as to make it irrelevant.

Price formation is also a problem for the open economy model. Asymmetries of information and bargaining power mean that prices are manipulated and may not provide the 'right' signals to economic agents. The developing countries have long recognised the means by which the developed countries have abused their market power to charge monopoly prices and earn economic rents. The LDCs have responded in a number of ways. Sometimes, for example, it has been through price-fixing and/or commodity agreements. In the case of foreign owned enterprises they were often taxed heavily, their activities regulated or, as a final solution, they were nationalised. There is no reason to believe that such controls will be any less necessary in the 1990s.

Another issue relates to the effects of opening up capital and financial markets. There is no conclusive evidence to indicate that privatisation increases aggregate savings or 'crowds in' private investment. LDC governments have often been forced to intervene in financial markets to lower the cost and increase the supply of credit. Opening up financial markets to foreign competition will not necessarily reduce the cost of borrowing to domestic firms because of the risk premium that is typically charged. Moreover, offering concessions to financial institutions in return for low interest rates conflicts with equity considerations, so the reasons for maintaining state banks often remain.

A final reason for questioning the relevance of the open economy model for LDCs relates to the bias in the generation and control of new technology. It is likely that most LDCs will be dependent on expensive imported technology for some time and there are obvious reasons why their governments should try to negotiate the best terms possible. However, in the longer term, dependence on imported technology not only means continuing to pay technological rents but it also limits the ability of domestic firms to respond in the most flexible optimising way to changed market conditions. Such considerations mean that the justification for a state directed and co-ordinated research and development strategy is now widely recognised as is the case for protecting new ventures. Economies in transition are often at an early point on the learning curve ready to achieve higher levels of productive efficiency while learning-by-doing stimulates technological innovation (Felix, *op. cit*. p. 44). It is not clear that an open, competitive economy will necessarily provide the ideal conditions to promote such developments.

While the success of the East Asian economies is open to different interpretations one cannot assume that government interventions to influence the allocation of resources through industrial, trade and credit allocation policies was unimportant. Equally, there seems little doubt about the positive contribution of research and development and investment in human capital to the development effort although why such government intervention has been so successful in South East Asia remains unclear (Summers and Thomas, 1993).

We now turn to the link between market structure and economic efficiency.

5. Market structure and efficiency

Whether privatisation is necessary for achieving economic efficiency (both productive and allocative) may be open to debate but there can be no question that it is not a sufficient condition. Ultimately the case for privatisation is about satisfying consumer wants in the most efficient way. But this implies that consumers of final goods or services (and buyers of intermediate products or inputs) must have a choice. There are three important ways that consumer (buyer) choice can be restricted after privatisation:

1.   The market is dominated by a single monopoly firm.

2.   There are several firms in the market but there is collusion amongst them.

3.   There is competition-restricting regulation.

The profit motive and the bankruptcy incentive under the pressure of competition are essential ingredients for achieving economic efficiency, yet each of the above structural features limits the degree of competition in markets. Moreover, they invariably create distortions in the allocation of resources and may prevent new firms offering wider choice and improved services from entering the market. Where there are natural monopolies they need to be regulated. In the absence of natural monopoly a policy of privatisation and economic reform which aims to eliminate inefficiency must promote cost reductions, innovation and flexibility through competition. Let us consider these issues further.

As we have seen, the conversion of a public monopoly to a private monopoly cannot guarantee efficiency and almost all recent contributions to the debate indicate that wherever possible the authorities should aim to create competitive markets. Yet there are instances when a single supplier is deemed to be superior. The most obvious case is where there is a natural monopoly. It is assumed that gas, electricity, water and telecommunications are industries where elements of natural monopoly exist. In such situations it does not make economic sense to duplicate or multiply the productive activity or the transmission network. Another reason is the belief that large firms are often more efficient and more powerful and therefore better able to compete in global markets. Moreover, breaking up state enterprises may come into conflict with the goal of maximising public receipts from asset sales. However, the danger is that the monopoly firm may abuse its market power and there will be little incentive to invest in new technology. In such circumstances competition augmenting regulation becomes necessary but the failure to carry through any restructuring can make the job of regulation very difficult.

Let us illustrate this last point. Where the newly privatised monopoly is also a vertically integrated firm it is more difficult to regulate its activities. Such a firm may be able to manipulate its costs through strategic behaviour. Thus a monopolist can use its position to favour its own input or equipment businesses and this raises the possibility of transferring profit from regulated to unregulated activities. Regulatory agencies need to be aware of these transfer pricing strategies as they also need to monitor quality levels, but access to relevant information is asymmetrical and preventing abuse of monopoly power may be difficult. This is discussed further in section 7.

If the overall goal is competition and efficiency, then upstream and downstream sectors of activity may also need to be regulated. The aim must be to create competition and contestable markets in both the input and equipment supply sectors and at the point of sale or distribution, including the retail and wholesale sectors, whenever it is feasible. It is important to ensure that privatisation and the elimination of state subsidies does not end up generating a new income transfer mechanism. Vertically integrated firms may be able to restrict competition at a certain stage and create an effective barrier to entry. Cross-subsidisation, predatory pricing or the imposition of discriminatory conditions on independent firms denies access to those wishing to compete and may result in monopoly profits for the vertically integrated firm. The implication is that even where a single monopoly is regarded as desirable at a certain stage of production the privatizing agency needs to consider whether and to what extent the firm should also be vertically integrated. Where there is no economic or technological justification for vertical integration privatisation should be used to disintegrate state enterprises and ensure there is effective competition at each stage of production.

Even where privatisation leads to the creation of several firms in an industry there is no guarantee that this will create competition or that the outcome will be significantly different from monopoly. If left to themselves most businessmen would probably prefer not to compete. One of the dangers of oligopoly is that firms will have an incentive to collude. Informal collusion will be difficult to control and the best policy may be a combination of anti-collusion legislation and effective anti-competitive regulating agencies. Nevertheless, the impact of such measures will depend partly on the powers of the agencies and the severity of the penalties imposed on those who violate the law.

In cases where a nationalised industry consists of a holding company with a number of subsidiary firms it is important for the privatising agency to ensure that the holding company is disbanded when the state assets are sold. The failure to do this can leave the holding company in a position to coordinate the policies of the subsidiary firms, thereby limiting competition and permitting monopoly profits at the expense of the consumer.

A similar danger arises when competition-restricting regulation is allowed to survive in the post-privatisation period. This is particularly important in LDCs that have a history of state directed development. Years of dirigisme may have left in place a plethora of regulations imposed by state and regional governments and other public bodies. Economic regulation was often introduced as part of an ISI policy and in many cases it was designed to protect domestic 'infant' industry for strategic reasons or as part of a plan for structural reform. The result was that prices and outputs were often controlled, subsidies were introduced and entry and exit restrictions were put in place. In an environment where competition is lacking market signals will be distorted, inefficiency will be widespread and protected markets will allow economic agents to earn economic rents.

If the regulation of certain activities continues after privatisation, not only may the potential benefits of competition be denied but it is possible that economic rents may be redistributed to upstream or downstream operations where regulation remains in force. To prevent this, apart from instances of market failure or where there is a case for social regulation (see below), price subsidies, cross-subsidisation, quota restrictions, licensing arrangements and other distortions need to be eliminated at every stage of production. In general prices need to be unregulated and firms should be free to add or subtract capacity and introduce new products. New sources of production should be able to come forward at all stages of operations if it is profitable to do so. It is only when firms are required to function in deregulated markets where import and export activities have been opened up that the full potential benefits of competition will materialise.

The exceptions to complete deregulation, even in industries which are subject to competition, occur when there is market failure. External effects like environmental degradation or cases of information deficiency often mean that 'social' regulation is necessary. Hence most counties have some degree of regulation of the environment and it is increasingly common to find consumer protection and health and safety legislation.

Given the complexities of market structures and the existence of information asymmetries the job of promoting competition will never be easy. Nevertheless, it is still important to have a comprehensive competition-augmenting regulatory structure with appropriate public bodies that have effective legal powers. At the same time it is just as necessary to remove the existing competition restricting-regulation which thwarts attempts to achieve economic efficiency. We consider each of these issues in turn, beginning with the need for deregulation.

6. Deregulation

Government regulation of economic activity in many LDCs grew rapidly from the 1930s. Dirigisme, with its emphasis on import-substituting industrialisation and the creation of large numbers of public enterprises resulted in a vast array of regulations relating to prices, subsidies, quantities and entry from both domestic and foreign sources. In the 1970s and 1980s regulation came under increasing attack throughout the world from neo-classical/liberal economists who were concerned with its distorting effects as well as the failure of direct state intervention (Shackleton, 1986; Allen, 1984; Kay and Vickers, 1988; Stigler, 1971). However it was not until the early 1980s that deregulation got on to the political agenda in many LDCs.

Many of the early attempts at deregulation have concentrated on simplifying some of the bureaucratic arrangements and procedures in order to speed up decision-making and improve overall efficiency. Yet the fact that debureaucratization has remained on the agenda of many LDCs in the last decade gives some indication of the immensity of the task and the limited progress that has been made so far. Moreover, the continuing concern with simplifying the bureaucracy must be seen as part of a broader failure on the part of many LDCs to reform the whole of public administration. We shall return to this issue later.

In many LDCs regulation which had been intended to nurture infant industries has often instead aided established public enterprises which are protected from competition from new entrants by entry limiting regulations and price controls. As a result the development and introduction of new technologies and products has often been retarded. In other cases cross-subsidisation within state regulated industries and fiscal or financial incentives have impeded allocative efficiency and ossified an inefficient structure of production with perverse transfers of income from one sectoral activity to another. Moreover, public enterprises are frequently overstaffed and the supply of labour highly regulated.

There are many examples of progress in deregulation throughout the Third World. Yet the apparent success of deregulation also provides examples of how private enterprise seeks alternative ways of restricting competition. The deregulation of the Brazilian steel industry is a case in point. As regulation has been removed there are signs that it has been replaced by price-fixing and other forms of collusive practices. This provides a clear indication that governments need to introduce regulation against anti-competitive behaviour at the same time as deregulation is pursued.

Furthermore, in the face of a comprehensive system of regulation of industry the extent to which competition augmenting domestic deregulation has been pursued and achieved so far in most LDCs is insignificant but it also gives rise for concern. As was made clear previously, the danger of partial deregulation is that scarcity rents will not be eliminated but merely transferred to other property rights owners. Despite some headway the extent of deregulation in many LDCs is disappointing and much remains to be done.

There are also dangers in piecemeal deregulation. Greater competition in the provision of a particular service and the removal of labour market restrictions will not be sufficient to improve efficiency and lower costs if monopoly elements remain elsewhere. As was made clear earlier both upstream and downstream activities also have to be deregulated, including ancillary services between suppliers and consumers, if rents and monopoly profits are to be eliminated.

Yet in many LDCs there seems to be no clear general position on the significance of comprehensive deregulation for competition enhancement. The distribution of power and responsibility between central, state and regional government can also give rise to conflicting objectives. Politicians generally want to hold on to their areas of control and influence since it can be traded off against political support. In such cases it is not surprising that they often oppose deregulation when it threatens their own leverage. Part of the explanation for the incomplete deregulation of the services sector is that many LDC governments are reluctant to give up their control over them. The survival of many small state banks and the reluctance of those in power to deregulate radio and television services can be explained in the same way. Government procurement is another major source of economic rent in LDCs yet there have been few attempts to cut costs by opening it up to competitive tender.

Foreign investment also remains highly regulated in many sectors of activity despite the possibility of creating a regulatory framework that could prevent abuse of market power. Nevertheless, there has been significant progress in many LDCs in the elimination of import restrictions and the reduction of tariffs but how far this has stimulated foreign competition and eliminated distortions is difficult to gauge because of the continued existence of non-tariff barriers. Luxury import restrictions, national content requirements, right of establishment restrictions and national treatment of foreign firms are some of the non-tariff barriers that have persisted in LDCs. The administrative allocation of export quotas in cases of voluntary export restrictions 'imposed' by developed countries is another instance where deregulation would remove distortions and eliminate economic rents. Whether the lack of progress in these many instances is due to inertia or the lobbying of sectional interests the result is the same. Market distortions, restricted competition and widespread economic rents are indicators of the failure to achieve productive and allocative efficiency.

7. Regulation

Privatisation inevitably results in some degree of market concentration and there is always the danger of collusion. Moreover, when public utilities (e.g. telecommunications and electricity) are privatised the issue of market domination becomes even more urgent as natural monopoly problems arise.

Under such circumstances the control of monopoly and restrictive practices becomes a central issue in LDCs and experience elsewhere indicates the need for two distinct regulatory structures or arrangements: firstly, anti-monopoly legislation with a strong anti-cartel or anti-trust agency equivalent to the UK's Monopolies and Mergers Commission; secondly, an industry regulator with powers to introduce competition augmenting regulation when domestic or import competition is weak. A few LDCs have made progress with the first but, so far, there has been little headway with the second type of regulation.

Brazil, whose record goes back to 1962 when the Administrative Council for Economic Defence (CADE) was established, is one of the few LDCs to have introduced anti-trust regulation. CADE dealt with anti-competitive complaints by firms against other firms but its volume of work was relatively small and like many other anti-trust agencies, it was largely ineffective for a number of reasons (Farina, 1990). It was never entirely free of government interference and its decisions had to be confirmed before the courts. CADE had no authority to force through a restructuring of an industry and its power to penalise was limited to the relatively small fines imposed by the law courts.

The Brazilian experience indicates the importance of both a strong anti-trust agency and a political will to use the regulatory mechanism if competition, efficiency and equity are to be taken seriously. Nevertheless, even if the anti-trust agencies are functioning effectively there are inherent difficulties of dealing with the abuse of market power. Predatory pricing and entry deterring activities are not easily detected and the dividing line between predatory pricing and aggressive, but wholly legitimate, competitive behaviour is difficult to define and apply. In some cases the resources necessary to detect anti-competitive practices may be prohibitive and beyond the scope of the anti-trust agencies. There is another major problem with anti-trust agencies and that is they are required to react after the event and the process of correcting the abuse can be long and protracted. It is for these reasons that a second regulatory arrangement may be required to augment competition.

Some lessons have been learnt from the American experience of regulation. In the US the principle of 'cost of service' regulation is often applied. This means the regulators set maximum allowable prices based on the observed costs of the firm, whether or not the costs observed represent an efficient allocation of resources. The allowable price includes an element for a 'fair' or 'reasonable' rate of return. One of the problems is that this procedure provides little incentive for cost efficiency or cost reducing innovations, since prices would be reduced to give the same 'fair' rate of return as previously. Indeed, it may encourage firms to over-invest in capital equipment as allowable prices will be adjusted upwards to accommodate higher observed costs.

The underlying problem is the regulator's lack of information about the economic opportunities for innovation but the cost of service regulation also has the disadvantage that it takes the incentives away. One way of attempting to overcome the disincentive effect of cost of service regulation has been to introduce a regulatory lag. This means that reviews of prices are spaced out and in between reviews any reductions in cost due to increased internal efficiency will be reflected in higher profits. Even in this case, however, there is a potential loss, that is a trade-off between internal efficiency and allocative efficiency since prices may not reflect costs of production.

New economic thinking on the form of regulation emphasises structural considerations, that is the need to promote entry and competition rather than detailed regulation of conduct. In the UK conduct regulation is confined to a restricted set of rules, most notably relating to price. Under the RPI -X formula[2] price rises are controlled while at the same time permitting profits from lower costs. With a positive X real prices must fall overtime and firms have an incentive to minimise costs rather than engage in unnecessary investment. The formula is not perfect for, as was mentioned previously, firms can manipulate their output mix and quality levels and through transfer pricing relocate profit from regulated to unregulated activities. These problems are known by the regulators who often acquire special knowledge of the industry concerned and are able to counter anti-competitive behaviour. Nevertheless, regulation is made easier whenever the industry is competitive since this provides the regulator with several sources of information on costs and efficiency.

In establishing a new regulatory framework LDC governments will need to avoid regulatory failure and as a first step it will be important to create regulators that are independent. The experience of anti-trust agencies is that they are not immune to capture by government and as a consequence they have not always been able to act in the 'public interest'. This danger will remain as long as LDC governments maintain a heavy hands-on approach to the economy. Some liberalisation has taken place but the residue of dirigisme continue to permeate all levels of government in many LDCs. Government reform which opens up political decisions to public scrutiny, simplifies and clarifies ministerial structures and responsibilities and establishes a scrupulous civil service is an essential first step towards competent corruption-free government. It is equally important that regulators remain independent of the industries they oversee. Nevertheless, given the importance of market structure, competitive markets, unfettered by quotas and price controls, with free entry may be the best way of guaranteeing efficiency.

We now turn to the second goal of privatisation — boosting public finances.

8. Improving public finances

This has been a major aim of all countries pursuing privatisation. The perceived benefit is that new sources of revenue can be used in three ways. Firstly, to pay off part of the public debt; secondly, to remove some of the constraints on current expenditure; or thirdly, to reduce levels of taxation. These are not equivalent as we will argue but there is another issue to consider — the conditions under which the fiscal position will improve.

The sale of public assets does not always lead to improved public finances. If the earnings stream is the same both before and after privatisation the government merely exchanges or receives the present value of the future earnings stream.[3] In other words the net worth of the government remains unchanged. By using the proceeds to pay off public debt there is a saving in interest payments which is equivalent to the earnings stream that was sold off. There is a zero net effect on public finances.

Gains to the public purse, on the other hand, are possible when privatisation leads to an increase in net worth. For example, loss-making public enterprises may become profitable after privatisation. This then raises the question as to why this improvement takes place? If it is due to increased productive and/or allocative efficiency then public finances will show a clear net gain. If, however, net worth increases because the newly privatised enterprise is able to exploit its market power then there may be a trade-off between improved public finances and higher prices to consumers. In this case there is a distributional effect and consumers end up being 'taxed' more heavily.

The central issues for LDCs focus on how the revenues should be used and what forms of private financial assets are acceptable as legal tender for the sales. The decision to accept a wide range of non-cash private financial assets, including public sector debt, for conversion to equity is likely to be a distinctive feature of LDC privatisation programmes. Given the market value of major public enterprises the current flow of domestic savings are unlikely to be large enough to absorb the stock of state assets. There is a stock-flow constraint (Bolton and Roland, 1992). Governments, therefore, have no choice but to allow both cash and non-cash purchases of shares by means of debt conversions. The controversy surrounding debt-equity conversions relates to the types of public debt accepted and their valuation.

In Brazil most of the public debt conversions were for medium to long term securities and this has been criticised because of the lost opportunity to swap highly liquid short term bonds for equity. The criticism collapses into a variant of the argument in favour of cash payments but it misses the central point. If the main goal is to improve the fiscal position it is better for the government to restrict debt conversions to the highest interest bearing securities. In so far as short-term bills or bonds yield the highest interest rates then they should have been the preferred debt for conversion. Other goals (e.g. equity) might lead to a different solution as we will argue presently.

The Brazilian government having decided to accept public debt in exchange for equities further agreed to convert them at face value despite the fact that they were being traded in secondary markets at highly discounted prices. Whatever the underlying reasons for this decision, and one cannot rule out interest group or political pressure, it is difficult to support on grounds of equity but it was also misguided on two other counts. Firstly, it ran counter to the stated aim of maximising the contribution to public finances. Secondly, it resulted in unanticipated wealth transfers to speculators in the secondary markets.

An important issue facing LDCs is whether public assets sales should be open to foreign investors and, if so, the level of participation permitted. There is also the related issue of whether debt equity swaps are acceptable (this is discussed in section 9 below) and, if so, what is the required discount rate on foreign debt conversions? On the latter the rate of discount operating in the secondary markets may provide a useful marker but this issue may need to be settled as part of any wider debt renegotiations that are taking place.

LDCs also have to decide whether foreign participation should be limited to 49 per cent of voting shares. The 49 per cent rule, designed to maintain domestic control of industry, misses an essential point. Foreign ownership of domestic based companies does not threaten sovereignty if they operate in competitive markets. Indeed, just like import competition, overseas ownership can be an important factor in improving efficiency in an industry. Nevertheless, when public utilities like telecommunications and electricity come to be privatised the 49 per cent rule may make more sense because of the natural monopoly element. But even in such cases the foreign domination fear recedes if the industry is competitively structured with unrestricted entry and regulation is competition augmenting.

The question of how the revenues from public assets sales should be used has also led to confusion and there has been a notable absence of a clear and consistent approach to the fiscal deficit. While deficits can be financed in several ways[4] there is overwhelming evidence that large deficits damage economic performance (Easterly, 1993). Inflation, high interest rates or financial repression leading to negative effects on investment and loss of international competitiveness and growing external deficits are some of the adverse effects that can occur. Fiscal adjustment is not sufficient even though it may be a necessary step towards improved long-run economic performance.[5] Nevertheless, while an economy is being restructured it is important for the government to consider the priority areas of expenditure. Equity considerations might lead to the promotion of a social reform programme but the track record of many LDC governments suggests that serving the poor is likely to be ranked low on the agenda.

The greatest danger is that revenue raising activities will be ignored and the sales receipts will be used either to finance current expenditure or reduce the need to raise taxation. Receipts from public assets sales may temporarily ease the public sector borrowing requirement, but they are merely providing the authorities with time to implement fiscal adjustment measures and achieve a fundamental reform of both the public sector and the wider economy.[6] Failure to recognise this will simply delay the day of reckoning and the size of the problem may grow considerably in the meantime.

9. Equity and incentives

There is widespread distrust of the system of government in many LDCs. Under these circumstances it is very important that the process of disposing of public assets should be seen to be fair and equitable and, to avoid suspicion of corruption, open to public scrutiny. We also wish to consider the effects of the disposal of assets on incentives and the allocation of resources.

With respect to the disposal of state assets, there are two inter-related criteria to consider — equity and incentives. There are no easy answers to these issues and the forms that privatisation programmes are taking throughout the world indicates considerable diversity between countries depending on their priorities and country-specific factors. Nevertheless, there are two broad alternatives for disposing of public assets. They can be sold or distributed free. There is the related question of how?

Free distribution has been argued for by Blanchard *et al.*, (1991) in their study of Eastern Europe. It has the advantage that it appeals to fairness and it can generate considerable popular support in favour of privatisation and market reforms. Moreover, everyone becomes a shareholder and therefore has in interest in improving the efficiency of the economy. All citizens can be given a share in collectively owned assets. Give away (or should they be called 'return back') schemes also appear to have the edge if quick mass privatisation programmes are favoured.

There is considerable uncertainty as to how these incentives might operate but the major disadvantage to free shares is the impact it would have on public receipts. For LDCs with large budgetary deficits privatisation is seen as a way to improve the fiscal position and achieve macroeconomic stability. This is regarded as a prerequisite for a revival of economic prospects.

Free share schemes also have the potential disadvantage that they may leave the incumbent management in place. This might be an important factor where there is an inefficient management team unless procedures can be set up to monitor and replace management whenever necessary.

Most privatisations throughout the world so far have involved the sale of public assets. However, given the stock-flow constraint in the typical LDC both cash and non-cash sales are necessary. This opens up the possibility that governments could allow wealth-constrained individuals to participate by lending to them on the basis of the future revenues generated by the privatised enterprise. In this case there would be no cash receipt nor would public debt be cancelled but instead the government would acquire a claim on future cash flows produced by the assets. An alternative would be for the government to maintain a golden share of the equity in privatised enterprises, although this may create other problems as is mentioned below.

There is widespread agreement that if public assets are to be sold they should be auctioned off in exchange for cash and non-cash bids. The advantages of auctions are that they may achieve a better matching between firms and management teams, they overcome the valuation problem and very importantly they also allow the government to write-off public enterprise debt without adversely affecting revenue from sales.

Nevertheless, there is a risk that the newly privatised firm will be heavily geared and that debt obligations under conditions of great uncertainty will be dangerous. Debt can be an incentive to greater efficiency and cost reductions but it can threaten the future of the enterprise in case of default. The Chilean experience in 1982-83 when it was necessary to re-nationalize some privatisations is a vivid reminder of the potential dangers. The alternative of partial equity sales may be the preferred solution although to give the government some degree of protection it is likely that a proportion of the non-cash bids will have to be in the form of debt.

It is also important to consider the effect of non-cash bids, in the form of government lending to individuals, on the incentives of privatised firms. On the one hand, it means that the new owners have not necessarily achieved their position because of an ability to pay but a willingness to buy. Assuming there are no frivolous bids, or they can be discouraged, such non-cash acquisitions indicate a belief that the company can be run efficiently. On the other hand, it is not clear what effect government debt, or partial equity holding, will have on the operation of the business. If the prevailing view is that the state is there to bail out unprofitable firms there may be little incentive to strive for efficiency. Under such circumstances it would be a pretence to suggest that complete privatisation has taken place.

The case of debt-equity swaps raises different concerns. Investors may be merely taking the opportunity to convert what is perceived as "bad" public debt into private sector equity without any real interest in the company they buy into. Alternatively, another firm in the industry may use its public sector debt to acquire a competitor which will give the new enlarged company a dominant share of the market. Such an outcome can rarely be justified and is likely to transgress both efficiency and equity criteria.

In the case of large privatisations where individual non-cash shareholdings are permitted the problem of separation of ownership and control is likely to emerge. Under these circumstances efficient money and capital markets are essential both to monitor firms' performance and to achieve an efficient allocation of resources. In this case, even if the initial distribution of shares meets the equity criterion, and there are few grounds for believing that governments will want to insist on equity, it is likely that private banks or other financial institutions will sooner or later be dominant shareholders. There are clearly dangers in this although the experience of Germany suggests that this system of supervising and monitoring can produce positive economic results.

10. Summary and conclusions

Privatisation in most LDCs is part of a wider public policy response to poor public enterprise performance, high levels of inflation and unsustainable public sector deficits. Given the relative newness of privatisation insufficient time has elapsed to pass judgement on the performance of privatised enterprises although because of unfavourable conjunctural factors the economic benefits may turn out to be limited, at least in the short run.

A major goal of public assets sales is to improve efficiency but whether privatisation is the important element is unclear. Privatisation is unlikely to succeed if it merely involves the conversion of quasi-public monopolies into private oligopolies with all the attendant dangers of collusion, predatory pricing and barriers to entry. A simple assumed relationship between ownership and performance has to be treated with caution. An alternative hypothesis is that the level of competition in markets, improvements in management and changes in employment contracts are more important for increasing efficiency.

This implies that there will continue to be an important role for government after privatisation, but it is not clear that LDC governments recognise the full significance of this. In addition to intervention to correct for externalities and public goods it is necessary for governments to both foster competition and provide support for domestic industry. It is now widely recognised that privatisation needs to be accompanied by effective regulation of anti-competitive practices, new forms of competition augmenting regulation and deregulation. The latter is particularly important in LDCs with a long history of dirigisme which has left a plethora of controls and subsidies. Many of them need to be removed if competition is to be enhanced and resource allocation improved. Incomplete deregulation and ineffective anti-competitive regulation will not eliminate economic rents but merely transfer them to another activity.

The relation between government and the open market is particularly important for economies in transition. The experience of the South East Asian economies indicates that governments have a vital role in designing development policies to support domestic enterprises. Governments are in a unique position to coordinate economic development and investments in a physical infrastructure, and education along with appropriate backing for research and development can make a significant contribution to successful economic transformation.

But structural reforms invariably result in lost jobs and a changing, more unequal distribution of income with adverse effects on economic welfare. Deregulation too can have detrimental effects if it results in the removal of regulations controlling health and safety, poverty and the environment. These may be too high a price to pay in the absence of a comprehensive social programme and new forms of regulation, in which case the process of privatisation may be delayed or abandoned. LDCs need to give due consideration to equity in other ways too. The regulations governing privatisation and the institutions created to carry through the programme must be open to scrutiny in order to dispel any doubt on the fairness and transparency of the process. Moveover, privatisation could be used to promote widespread share ownership although evidence so far accumulated indicates that in the long-run it is likely that shareholdings will be concentrated in the hands of a relatively small number of large financial institutions.

Finally, the impact of privatisation on public finances has been negligible to date in all but a few LDCs. There are serious doubts whether the form of debt-equity swaps and the way that the revenues may be used are consistent with the need to achieve fiscal adjustment, economic reform and equity. The danger is that privatisation will be used as another way of allocating the cost of structural adjustment and economic reform to those least able to resist.

Notes

1. There are serious grounds for believing that the economic benefits of privatisation will be limited at this juncture. The reasons are (Felix, 1992):

    - the failure of macroeconomic stabilization programmes

    - the difficulties of trying to restructure productive capacity after a decade of public and private underinvestment

    - The continuing global debt deflation cycle.

2. The pricing policy was based on one of the following formulas:

    RPI — X

    RPI — X + y

RPI + k

Where RPI = Retail Price Index (rate of inflation)

X = the required efficiency gains, which can be varied

y = automatic price adjustment applied to electricity firms to allow for cost rises beyond their control

k = the annual increase in prices above the rate of inflation that was allowed to the water companies in order to bring the quality of piped drinking water up to EC standards.

3. This would not be the case if the government took the decision to sell public assets at a discount in which case there would be a transfer of net worth from society to the acquiring owners.

4. There are three ways of financing the fiscal deficit:

   - money financing via the Central Bank

   - domestic borrowing

   - external borrowing.

5. Eliminating a large public sector borrowing requirement is rarely painless and in the short-run there is likely to be a trade-off between jobs and fiscal adjustment.

6. As a first step towards fiscal adjustment it is essential that the fiscal accounts are accurate and transparent. It is also important to give priority to the simplification and rationalisation of taxation.

References

Allen, F. (1984) 'Reputation and Product Quality', *Rand Journal of Economics*.

Baumol, W. J., Panzer, J. and R. Willig. (1982) *Contestable Markets and the Theory of Industry Structure*, New York: Harcourt Brace and Jovanovich.

Blanchard, O., Dornbusch, R., Krugman, P., Layard, R., and L. Summers. (1991) *Reform in Eastern Europe*, Cambridge, MA: MIT Press.

Bolton, P. and G. Roland. (1992) 'Privatisation in Central and Eastern Europe', *Economic Policy*.

Buchanan, J. M. (1986) *Liberty, Market and State*, Brighton, Harvester.

Easterly, W. and K. Schmidt-Hebbel. (1993) 'Fiscal Deficits and Macroeconomic Performance in Developing Countries', *Research Observer*, V ol. 8, No. 2, The World Bank.

Farina, E. (1990) *Politica Antitruste: A Experiencia Brasileira*, Sao Paulo: mimeo. (Quoted by Abreu and Werneck, op. cit.)

Felix, D. (1992) 'Privatizing and rolling back the Latin American State', *CEPAL Review*, No. 46, April.

Grossman, S. and O. D. Hart. (1980) 'Take-over bids, the free-rider problem and the Theory of Corporation', *Bell Journal of Economics*.

Hayek, F. A. (1944) *The Road to Serfdom*, London, Routledge and Kegan Paul.

Kay, J. A. and J. Vickers. (1988) 'Regulatory Reform in Britain', *Economic Policy*, March.

Stigler, G. (1971) 'The Theory of Economic Regulation', *Bell Journal of Economics*, Vol. 1.

Summers, L. H., and V. Thomas. (1993) 'Recent Lessons of Development', *The World Bank Research Observer*, Vol. 8, No. 2, July.

Singh, A. (1971) *Take-overs*, University of Cambridge Department of Applied Economics, Monograph 19, Cambridge, Cambridge UP.

Swann, D. (1988) *The Retreat of the State*, London, Harvester Wheatsheaf.